SEVENTH EDITION

SERVICE-ORIENTED COMPUTING AND SYSTEM INTEGRATION

SOFTWARE, IOT, BIG DATA, AND AI AS SERVICES

YINONG CHEN

ARIZONA STATE UNIVERSITY

Cover image and all interior photos courtesy of Yinong Chen.

www.kendallhunt.com
Send all inquiries to:
4050 Westmark Drive
Dubuque, IA 52004-1840

Copyright © 2008, 2010, 2011, 2014, 2015, 2018, 2020 by Kendall Hunt Publishing Company

PAK ISBN: 978-1-7924-3088-6
Text alone ISBN: 978-1-7924-3089-3

All rights reserved. No part of this publication may be reproduced, stored in a retrieval system, or transmitted, in any form or by any means, electronic, mechanical, photocopying, recording, or otherwise, without the prior written permission of the copyright owner.

Published in the United States of America

Table of Contents

Preface

Service-Oriented Computing (SOC), web software development, cloud computing, big data processing, and artificial intelligence represent the modern software engineering theories, practices, and technologies, which have reshaped the world in all aspects. The amount of the data is not the key. The relationship among all data and the meaning behind the data are the key. Efficiently finding the connections of all related data and using these connections to make intelligent decisions become possible after the maturity of these cutting-edge theories, practices, and technologies. The goals of the book are to introduce and exercise these cutting-edge theories, practices, and technologies through lectures and assignments based on the lectures.

The text takes a comprehensive and coherent approach to studying the latest service-oriented architecture, distributed computing paradigm, and distributed software development and system integration technologies. The goal is to learn the concepts, principles, methods, development frameworks, and their applications. The methodology is learning by developing examples. In the service development part, we assume that students have good knowledge in object-oriented computing, such as C++, C#, Java, or Python. Students learn to build services through class definition, interface specification, the association between class methods and service operations, service deployment, and service hosting. In the system integration part, we assume that students have a basic understanding of software architecture through a general software engineering course. We take an architecture-driven approach to help students create the working solution step-by-step from their architecture design. The first step is to design the architecture, which includes the major components and the interconnection. The next step is to define the interfaces among the components using the standard data types. Finally, the behavior of each component is linked to remote services or local objects. The elaborated architecture is automatically translated into the executable.

The text consists of 12 chapters and 3 appendices. They are organized into three parts. Each part can be taught as a separate course, even though they are intrinsically related to the central goals and objectives of the book.

Part I: Distributed Service-Oriented Software Development and Web Data Management

Chapter 1	Introduction to Distributed Service-Oriented Computing
Chapter 2	Distributed Computing with Multithreading
Chapter 3	Essentials in Service-Oriented Software Development
Chapter 4	XML and Web Data Formats
Chapter 5	Web Application and State Management
Chapter 6	Dependability of Service-Oriented Software

Part II: Advanced Service-Oriented Computing and System Integration

Chapter 7	Advanced Services and Architecture-Driven Application Development
Chapter 8	Enterprise Software Development and Integration
Chapter 9	IoT, Robotics, and Device Integration via Visual Programming
Chapter 10	Interfacing Service-Oriented Software with Databases
Chapter 11	Big Data Processing and Cloud Computing

Chapter 12	Artificial Intelligence and Machine Learning

Part III: Appendices: Tutorials on Service-Oriented System Development

Appendix A	Web Application Development
Appendix B	Visual IoT/Robotics Programming Language Environment
Appendix C	ASU Repository of Services and Applications

Part I includes the first six chapters, which can be used for a distributed computing, service-oriented computing, or web software development course at the junior, senior or graduate level of universities. This part emphasizes the computing paradigm, data representation, state management, and programming languages based SOC software development. It introduces fundamental concepts and principles, in addition to technologies and tools, which are not being taught in traditional software engineering courses.

Chapter 1 gives an overview and explains fundamental concepts of distributed software architecture, design patterns, distributed computing, service-oriented architecture, and enterprise software architecture. The connections and distinctions between object orientation and service orientation are discussed in detail.

Chapter 2 studies parallel computing in multithreading. It discusses threading, synchronization, coordination, event-driven programming, and performance of parallel computing under multicore computers.

Chapter 3 introduces the essential concepts and techniques in service-oriented architecture, particularly the three-party model of service-oriented software development: Service providers, service brokers, and service consumers. Service interfaces, service communication protocols, and service hosting are keys for supporting this new computing paradigm.

Chapter 4 discusses XML and related technologies, which are used almost everywhere in service-oriented software development. XML is used for representing data, interface, standards, protocols, and even the execution process definition. This chapter studies not only XML representations, but also XML processing and transforming.

Chapter 5 is a longer chapter and comprises application logic, data and state management, and presentation design. It involves application building based on architecture design using existing services and components, stateful web application development using different state management techniques, including view state, session state, application state, file management, and web caching. At the presentation layer, it discusses dynamic graphics generation, animation, and phone app development.

Chapter 6 deals with the dependability issues in web-based applications, including access control through Forms security, encryption and decryption applications, and Secure Sockets Layer in web communication. The chapter also discusses the reliability issues in web application design and particularly in web communication.

Part II includes the next six chapters. These chapters are built on the basic concepts and principles discussed in Part I, yet they do not rely on the details of the first six chapters. This part emphasizes software and system composition and integration using existing services and components. It is based on an architecture-driven approach, workflow, higher-level data management, and message-based integration. The material is good for an advanced software engineering, software integration, or system integration course at the senior or graduate level of universities.

Chapter 7 starts with reviewing service-oriented computing and service development covered in Part I. Then the chapter moves on to discuss more advanced service development that supports self-hosting and asynchronous communications. It also presents more detail in RESTful service development that has been briefly discussed in Part I, as well microservices. Finally, the chapter moves on to advanced web application development in HTML5, MVC, and .Net Core architecture development.

Chapter 8 starts with workflow-based software development and Workflow Foundation that supports architecture-driven software development. It uses examples and case studies to demonstrate software development by drawing the flowchart consisting of blocks of services and local components, adding inputs/outputs to the blocks, and then compiling the flowchart into executables. The chapter further discusses flowchart-based and architecture-driven software development by using other process languages and development environments. It first discusses BPEL (Business Process Execution Language) and BPEL-based development environments. Then the discussion is extended into message-based software integration and Enterprise Service Bus tools for integrating web contents.

Chapter 9 extends web-based computing to Internet of Things (IoT) and Robot as a Service (RaaS). As an example, robotics applications are studied in detail, using the service-oriented Visual IoT/Robotics Programming Language Environment (VIPLE) developed at Arizona State University. Full programming examples in VIPLE and hardware platform supported are discussed.

Chapter 10 covers service-oriented database management, which focuses on the interface between service-oriented software and relational databases, XML databases, and LINQ (Language Integrated Query), and using LINQ to access object, relational, and XML databases.

Chapter 11 studies the cutting-edge topics in big data and cloud computing. It discusses major issues in big data, including big data infrastructure, big data management, big data analytics, and big data applications. Hadoop and VIPLE are used for illustrating automated data splitting and parallel computing. The relationship between big data and cloud computing is discussed. Finally, the chapter presents cloud computing and its main layers: Software as a Service, Platform as a Service, and Infrastructure as a Service. As examples, cloud platforms from Amazon Web Services, Google, IBM, Microsoft, and Oracle are discussed.

Chapter 12 presents the latest artificial intelligence, machine learning, and ontology theories and technologies. The latest generation of artificial intelligence is based on big data analysis and processing. This chapter presents its development, main concepts, and examples of developing machine-learning programs. Ontology is presented as a part of knowledge representation for big data processing and artificial intelligence applications.

Part III consists of three appendices that supplement and support the main contents on web application development and IoT/robotics application development.

Appendices A and B contain tutorial-based materials that provide stepwise instructions, without missing pieces, to build working applications from scratch. These tutorials and exercises can help students to learn concepts by examples. This part, in conjunction with parts of Chapter 3 and Chapter 9, can also be used for a freshman level course to introduce computing concepts through basic web application development and robotics programming.

Appendix C is the entrance to ASU Repository of Services and Applications. It lists and explains some of the deployed examples and URLs of SOAP services, RESTful services, web applications, and other resources used in this text. Free services found on the Internet come and go without any guarantee on quality of service. The repository provides a stable resource for teaching from this book without worrying about the availability and performance of the free services found on the Internet. ASU Repository of Services and Applications is open to the public and can be accessed at:

http://neptune.fulton.ad.asu.edu/WSRepository/

Updates are carried out throughout the book, and major revisions have focused on several chapters in this edition. The programming examples using the early editions of Visual Studio programming environment are updated to Visual Studio 2019 edition. The links to external services have been checked and updated where applicable.

In this edition, Chapter 7 is significantly extended. Microservices are included, and the advanced web application architecture is extended to HTML5 and Core MVC architecture. Workflow-based application development and Workflow Foundation are moved from Chapter 7 to Chapter 8, forming a stronger composition and integration-oriented enterprise application development chapter.

Major revisions are made in Chapter 9. The latest VIPLE version is incorporated, and new functions and examples are added. For example, CodeActivity–Python and TORCS autonomous driving simulation are included in this edition.

In Chapter 10, a section on installing a database and using SQL Server Management Studio to create local SQL database projects are added.

Major revisions and extensions are done to Chapter 11, resulting in its splitting into two chapters in this edition. The new Chapter 11 keeps big data processing and cloud computing contents, while the new Chapter 12 focuses on artificial intelligence, machine learning, and ontology. VIPLE simulation is used for illustrating automated parallel computing principles in big data processing. New case studies, on a guide dog project and on flight data collection, training, and flight path recognition are added to Chapter 12.

The book embraces extensive contents. It can be used in multiple courses. At Arizona State University, we use the book as the text for two major required courses. The first course is CSE445/598 (Distributed Software Development), where the CSE445 session is for juniors and seniors, while the CSE598 session is for graduate students. The course started in Fall 2006, and first edition of the book was developed for this course in 2008. The first six chapters in Part I of this text are used for this course.

A second course CSE446/598 (Software Integration and Engineering) was piloted in 2010 and 2011, and the course became a regular course in 2012. The six chapters in Part II of this text is used for this course.

Both CSE445 and CSE446 are required courses of the Software Engineering Concentration in the Computer Science program at Arizona State University.

The following table illustrates the lectures of CSE445/598 and CSE446/598. Each lecture is 75-min long and counts as 1.5 lecture hours. Each course is completed in about 44 lecture hours.

The first course focuses on distributed software development, including multithreading programming, event-driven programming, Web data representation, service development, and application building using programming languages as the composition language. Both C# and Java are used in the development. The course objectives and outcomes of ASU CSE445/598 are as follows:

1. To develop an understanding of the software engineering of programs using concurrency and synchronization.
    - The student can identify the application, advantages and disadvantages of concurrency, threads, and synchronization.
    - The student can apply design principles for concurrency and synchronization.
    - The student can design and write programs demonstrating the use of concurrency, threads, and synchronization.
2. To develop an understanding of the development of distributed software.
    - The student can recognize alternative distributed computing paradigms and technologies.
    - The student can identify the phases and deliverables of the software life cycle in the development of distributed software.
    - The student can create the required deliverables in the development of distributed software in each phase of a software life cycle.

- The student understands the security and reliability attributes of distributed applications.

3. To develop an ability to design and publish services as building blocks of service-oriented applications.
    - The student understands the role of service publication and service directories
    - The student can identify available services in service registries.
    - The student can design services in a programming language and publish services for the public to use.
4. To build skills in using a current technology for developing distributed systems and applications.
    - The student can develop distributed programs using the current technology and standards.
    - The student can use the current framework to develop programs and web applications using graphical user interfaces, remote services, and workflow.

CSE445/598 Lecture by Lecture Contents	CSE446/598 Lecture by Lecture Contents
L01 - 1. Intro to Computing	Unit 1-1 Introduction
L02 - 1. Intro to Distributed Architecture	Unit 1-2 Self Hosting Service
L03 - 1. Intro to SOC Concepts	Unit 1-3 Advanced WCF Service
L04 - 1. Intro to SOC Development	Unit 1-4 RESTful Concepts
L05 - 2. Multithreading concepts	Unit 1-5 RESTful Services
L06 - 2. Multithreading in Java	Unit 1-6 Advanced Web App Architecture
L07 - 2. Multithreading in C Sharp	Unit 2-1 Enterprise Architecture and Process
L08 - 2. Event-driven programming	Unit 2-2 Workflow 1 Concepts
L09 - 2. Threading-Multicore Performance	Unit 2-3 Workflow 2 Case Studies
L10 - 3. SOC Service Development	Unit 2-4 BPEL 1 Process
L11 - 3. SOC Hosting and Brokerage	Unit 2-5 BPEL 2 Case Study
L12 - 3. SOC Service and App in Java	Unit 2-6 BPEL 3 Frameworks
L13 - 3. SOC App Development in C#	Unit 2-7 Message-Based Integration
L14 - 4. XML basics	Unit 2-8 WebCaching-Recommend
L15 - 4. XML processing	Unit 3-1 Device Integration
L16 - 4. XML Schema	Unit 3-2 VIPLE Programming
L17 - 4. XML Transformation	Unit 3-3 VIPLE FSM and Maze
L18 - 4. Other Web Data and Standards	Unit 4-1 ADO
L19 - 5. Web Application Structure	Unit 4-2 LINQ to Object
L20 - 5. Web Application Controls	Unit 4-3 Lambda and LINQ to SQL
L21 - 5. Config-Global-DLL-Cookies	Unit 4-4 LINQ to XML
L22 - 5. Session and File System	Unit 4-5 XML Database
L23 - 6. Security-Reliability Concepts	Unit 5-1 Big Data Concepts and Domains
L24 - 6. Forms Security	Unit 5-2 Big Data Processing
L25 - 6. Data Encryption-Hash-Reliable Msg	Unit 5-3 AI and Machine Learning
L26 - 6. Error Control and SSL	Unit 5-4 Ontology
L27 - 5. Dynamic Graphics - Animation	Unit 5-5 Cloud Computing
L28 - 5. MVC Summary and Outlook	Unit 5-6 Cloud Computing Case Studies

The second course focuses on software and system integration using workflow languages and cutting-edge topics in software and system development. The course objectives and outcomes of ASU CSE446/598 are as follows:

1. To understand software architecture and software process.
    - Students understand the requirement and specification process in problem solving.
    - Students understand software life cycle and process management
    - Students can identify advantages and disadvantages of software architectures and their trade-offs in different applications.
2. To understand and apply composition approach in software development.
    - Students can apply software architecture to guide software development in the problem-solving process.
    - Students understand interface requirement of software services.
    - Students can compose software based on interfaces of services and components.
    - Students can develop software system using different composition methods and tools.
3. To understand and apply data and information integration in software development.
    - Students can compose software systems using different data resources in different data formats.
    - Students can integrate application logic with different databases.
    - Students can apply the entire software life cycle to develop working software systems.

We recommend teaching the two courses in a sequence. However, the two courses can be taught independently without making one to be the prerequisite of the other. In this case, the basic concepts and principles from Part I, including those from a part of Chapter 1 and the first section of Chapter 4, should be reviewed or be assigned as reading materials for preparing the course using Part II. It is also sensible to choose a few topics from Part I and Part II to teach one course from the book. For example, Chapters 1, 3, 5, and 8 can form a good service-oriented computing course. Chapter 9 and Appendix B can be used for a computational thinking-based robotics course for students who do not have much programming language background.

We like to thank my colleagues at Arizona State University in preparing this book and related courses. Prof. Wei-Tek Tsai has taught CSE445/598. He was a coauthor of the book's first five editions. Dr. Janaka Balasooriya has been teaching CSE445/598 for several semesters and has constantly provided feedback and suggestions for improving the contents of the course and the book. Prof. Yann-Hang Lee contributed to the course contents related to IoT and robotics development. Prof. Hessam Sarjoughian and Prof. Stephen Yau contributed to the development of CSE445/598 and CSE446/598 courses. Many of our sponsors, colleagues, cooperators, and students have been involved in this project, including Prof. Xiaoying Bai of Tsinghua University, Prof. Farokh Bastani of University of Texas at Dallas, Dr. J. Y. Chung of IBM, Prof. Zhongshi He of Chongqing University, Prof. Mei Hong of Beijing Institute of Technology, Prof. Yingxu Lai of Beijing University of Technology, Prof. Yinsheng Li of Fudan University, Prof. Zhongtao Li of University of Jinan, Prof. K. J. Lin of University of California at Irvine, Mr. John Oliver of Intel, Dr. Raymond Paul of DoD OSD NII, Profs. Qian Wang and Yongkang Xing of Chongqing University, Profs. Ruzhi Xu and Zhizheng Zhou of Qilu University of Technology, and Prof. I-Ling Yen of University of Texas at Dallas. They contributed to our understanding of the materials. We also acknowledge the generous support from Intel, the US Department of Education, the US Department of Defense, and the National Science Foundation. Without their support, this book would not be possible. We also thank the teaching assistants and research assistants at Arizona State University, including Calvin Cheng, Gennaro De Luca, Jay Elston, Qian Huang, Adam Lew, Wu Li, Gavin Liu, Mengxue Liu, Sami Mian, Xin Sun, Jingjing Xu, Xinyu Zhou, Thomas Zelpha, and Peide Zhong. Gennaro De Luca is the main developer of the VIPLE environment. They implemented and validated many of the examples and assignments used in the book. Finally, we would like to thank our families for their support and understanding of taking on such a project while carrying out a full research and teaching load at the university.

Note for Instructors

All the assignments and projects have been classroom-tested at Arizona State University for many years. Furthermore, all the code presented in this book has been developed and tested. Contact the authors if you are interested in obtaining more materials in this book. Instructor-only resources, such as complete presentation slides, assignments, and tests, can be obtained by directly contacting the authors at yinong@asu.edu.

Yinong Chen

April 2020

Part I
Distributed Service-Oriented Software Development and Web Data Management

Chapter 1
Introduction to Distributed Service-Oriented Computing

This chapter introduces computer architecture, different computing paradigms, and particularly, the distributed computing paradigm and Service-Oriented Computing (SOC) paradigm.

1.1 Computer Architecture and Computing Paradigms

Software architectures and distributed software development are related to the computer system architectures on which the software is executed. This section introduces the computer architectures and various computing paradigms.

1.1.1 Computer Architecture

The computer architecture for a single-processor computer often refers to the processor architecture, which is the interface between software and hardware or the instruction architecture of the processor (Patterson 2004). For a computer with multi-processors, the architecture often refers to the instruction and data streams. *Flynn's Taxonomy* (Flynn 1972) categorized computer architecture into four types:

1. Single Instruction stream and Single Data stream (SISD), which refers to the simple processor systems;
2. Single Instruction stream and Multiple Data streams (SIMD); for example, the vector or array computers;
3. Multiple Instruction streams and Single Data stream (MISD); for example, fault-tolerant computer systems that perform redundant computing on the same data stream and voting on the results;
4. Multiple Instruction streams and Multiple Data streams (MIMD), which refers to the systems consisting standalone computer systems with their own memory and control, ALU, and I/O units.

The MIMD systems are often considered distributed systems, which have different areas of concerns, as shown in Figure 1.1. Distributed computing is about the principles, methods, and techniques of expressing computation in a parallel and/or distributed manner. Distributed software architecture concerns organization and interfacing among the software components. Network architecture studies the topology and connectivity of network nodes. Network communication deals with the layers of protocols that allow the nodes to communicate with each other and understand the data formats of each other. Some studies use operating systems to differentiate distributed systems and networks. Distributed systems have coherent operating systems, while a set of network nodes has independent operating systems.

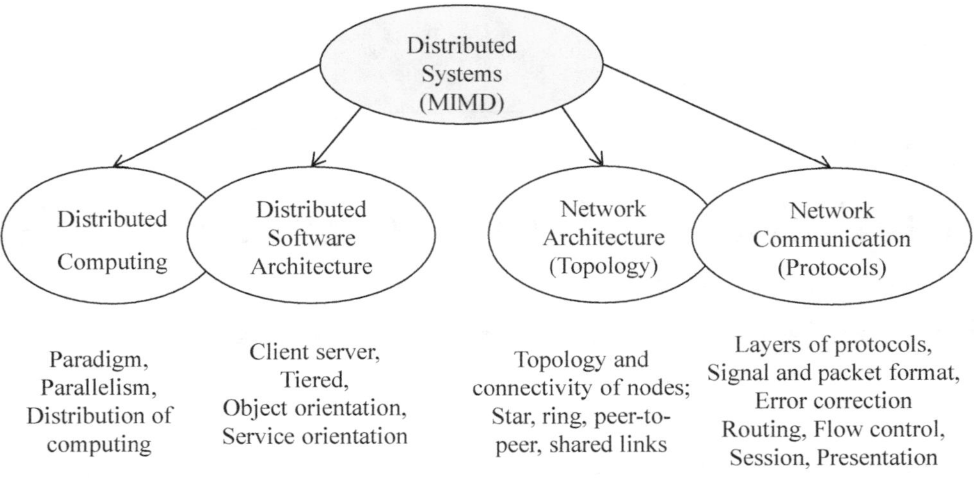

Figure 1.1. Distributed systems and networks

1.1.2 Software Architecture

The software architecture of a program or computing system is the structure, which comprises software components, the externally visible properties of those components, and the relationships between them (Bass 2003). The design of software architecture does not mean to develop the operational software. Instead, it can be considered a conceptual model of the software, which is one of the development steps enabling a software engineer to:

- analyze the effectiveness of the design in meeting its stated requirements;
- consider architectural alternatives at a stage when making design changes is still relatively easy;
- define the interfaces between the components;
- reduce the risks associated with the construction of the software.

It is important to design software architecture before designing the algorithm and implementing the software, because software architecture enables the communication between all parties (stakeholders) interested in the development of a computer-based system. The service-oriented architecture (SOA), which is a main topic of the book, explicitly involves three parties—service providers, service brokers, and service requesters—in the software architecture design, while each party conducts its algorithmic design and coding independently.

The software architecture highlights early design decisions that will have a profound impact on all software engineering work that follows and on the ultimate success of the system as an operational entity.

1.1.3 Computing Paradigms

Numerous programming languages have been developed in history, but only several thousands of them are actually in use. Compared to natural languages that were developed and evolved independently, programming languages are far more similar to each other. They are similar to each other because of the following reasons. They share the same mathematical foundation (e.g., Boolean algebra, logic). They provide similar functionality (e.g., arithmetic, logic operations, and text processing). They are based on the same kind of hardware and instruction sets. They have common design goals: to find languages that make it simple for humans to use and efficient for hardware to execute. The designers of programming languages share their design experiences.

Some programming languages, however, are more similar to each other, although some other programming languages are more different from each other. Based on their similarities or the paradigms, programming languages can be divided into different classes. In programming language's definition, **paradigm** is a set of basic principles, concepts, and methods of how computation or algorithm is expressed. The major paradigms include imperative, OO, functional, logic, distributed, and SOC.

The **imperative**, also called the **procedural**, computing paradigm expresses computation by fully specified and fully controlled manipulation of named data in a step-wise fashion. In other words, data or values are initially stored in variables (memory locations), taken out of (read from) memory, manipulated in ALU (arithmetic logic unit), and then stored back in the same or different variables (memory locations). Finally, the values of variables are sent to the I/O devices as output. The foundation of imperative languages is the **stored program concept**-based computer hardware organization and architecture (von Neumann machine) (see for example http://en.wikipedia.org/wiki/Von_Neumann_machine). Typical imperative programming languages include all assembly languages and earlier high-level languages like FORTRAN, Algol, Ada, Pascal, and C.

The **object-oriented** computing paradigm is the same as the imperative paradigm, except that related variables and operations on variables are organized into classes of **objects**. The access privileges of variables and methods (operations) in objects can be defined to reduce (simplify) the interaction among objects. Objects are considered the main building blocks of programs, which support the language features like inheritance, class hierarchy, and polymorphism. Typical OO programming languages include Smalltalk, C++, Java, and C#.

The **functional**, also called the **applicative**, computing paradigm expresses computation in terms of mathematical functions. Since we have been expressing computation in mathematical functions in many of the mathematical courses, functional programming is supposed to be easy to understand and simple to use. However, since functional programming is rather different from imperative or OO programming, and because most programmers first get used to writing programs in imperative or OO paradigm, it becomes difficult to switch to functional programming. The main difference is that there is no concept of memory locations in functional programming languages. Each function will take a number of values as input (parameters) and produce a single return value (output of the function). The return value cannot be stored for later use. It must be used either as the final output or used immediately as the parameter value of another function. Functional programming is about defining functions and organizing the return values of one or more functions as the parameters of another function. Functional programming languages are mainly based on the lambda-calculus. Typical functional programming languages include ML, SML, and Lisp/Scheme.

The **logic**, also called the **declarative**, computing paradigm expresses computation in terms of logic predicates. A logic program is a set of facts, rules, and questions. The execution process of a logic program is to compare a question to each fact and rule in the given fact and rulebase. If the question finds a match, then we receive a yes-answer to the question. Otherwise, we receive a no-answer to the question. Logic programming is about finding facts, defining rules based on the facts, and writing questions to express the problems we wish to solve. Prolog is the only significant logic programming language.

All these computing paradigms support both "programming-in-the-small" and "programming- in-the-large." The former emphasizes the development of program components or modules using basic programming constructs such as sequential, conditional branching, and looping constructs. The latter emphasizes developing large applications. Large applications often require more people and effort, and they are used in critical applications such as banking, e-business, embedded systems, and e-government.

Another important paradigm is **component-based computing**. This paradigm emphasizes composing large applications based on preprogrammed components or modules. Components or modules are often precompiled program units, and they are linked into the application prior to the execution. Conceptually, component-based computing is not new. OO computing is widely considered component-based computing, where each class or object is a component. A namespace (a group of classes) can also be considered a component. However, both of these views are tightly coupled with the specific definition of a "class." Component-based computing can have a broader meaning, which allows any unit or module to be considered a component, and thus, can be considered a distinct paradigm different from OO computing. A component can be as small as an object and can be as large as an application, and a component is often well encapsulated. Thus, for some, SOC is really component-based computing, as services can be components. In their minds, SOC is essentially component-based computing but each component is specified using open standards.

Distributed computing involves computation executed on more than one logical or physical processor or computer. These units cooperate and communicate with each other to complete an integral application. The computation units can be functions (methods) in the component, components, or application programs. The main issues to be addressed in the distributed computing paradigms are concurrency, concurrent computing, resource sharing, synchronization, messaging, and communication among distributed units. Different levels of distribution lead to different variations. **Multithreading** is a common distributed computing technique that allows different functions in the same software to be executed concurrently. If the distributed units are at the object level, this is **distributed OO computing**. Some well-known distributed OO computing frameworks are CORBA (Common Object Request Broker Architecture) developed by OMG (Object Management Group) and Distributed Component Object Model (DCOM) developed Microsoft.

Service-oriented computing (SOC) is another distributed computing paradigm. SOC differs from distributed OO computing in several ways:

- SOC emphasizes distributed services (with possibly service data) rather than distributed objects;
- SOC explicitly separates development duties and software into service provision, service brokerage, and application building through service consumption;
- SOC supports reusable services in (public or private) repositories for matching, discovery, and (remote or local) access;
- In SOC, services communicate through open standards and protocols that are platform independent and vendor independent.

Figure 1.2 summarizes the features of different computing paradigms.

It is worthwhile noting that many languages belong to multiple computing paradigms; for example, C++ is an OO programming language. However, C++ also includes almost every feature of C. Thus, C++ is also an imperative programming language, and we can use C++ to write C programs.

Java is more an OO language, that is, the design of the language puts more emphasis on the object orientation. However, it still includes many imperative features; for example, Java's primitive type variables use value semantics and do not obtain memory from the language heap.

Lisp contains many nonfunctional features. Lisp and Scheme are functional programming languages, but they also contain many nonfunctional features such as sequential processing when input and output are involved.

Prolog is a logic programming language, but its arithmetic operations use the imperative approach.

In summary, these computing paradigms often overlap with each other; for example, OO computing languages are often imperative programming languages, and SOC languages such as C# and Java are OO programming languages. Thus, a single programming language can be used to write programs in different computing paradigms. See (Chen 2006) for an introduction to these computing paradigms using C, C++, Scheme, and Prolog.

1.2 Distributed Computing and Distributed Software Architecture

In distributed computing, computation is distributed over multiple computing units (processors or computers), rather than confined to a single computing unit. Virtually all large computing systems now are distributed, as the multi-core processor design is introduced.

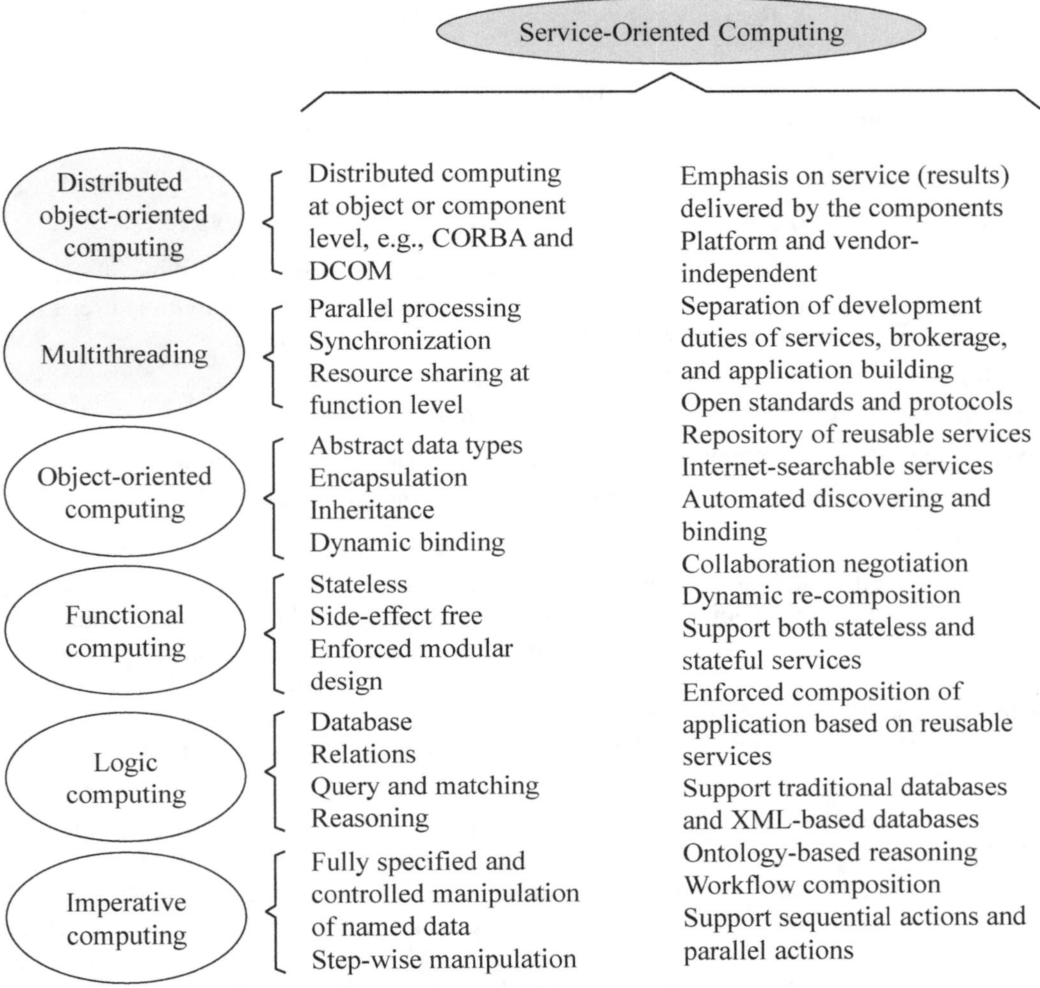

Figure 1.2. Features of different computing paradigms.

1.2.1 Distributed Computing

Software architecture describes the system structure and functionality allocation over a number of logical or physical computing units. Having the right architecture for an application is essential to achieve the desired quality of service.

Distributed computing often has to deal with multiple dimensions of challenges, including complexity, communication and connectivity, security and reliability, manageability, and unpredictability and nondeterministic behaviors. These challenges are well expressed in the following eight **fallacies of distributed computing**, proposed by Sun Microsystems fellows (http://en.wikipedia.org/wiki/Fallacies_of_Distributed_Computing):

1. The network is reliable.
2. Latency is zero.

3. Bandwidth is infinite.
4. The network is secure.
5. Topology does not change.
6. There is one administrator.
7. Transport cost is zero.
8. The network is homogeneous

The first four fallacies, called the fallacies of networked computing, were proposed by Bill Joy and Tom Lyon in 1991. Peter Deutsch added the next three, which are often referred to as Deutsch's seven fallacies. James Gosling added the eighth fallacy in 1997.

1.2.2 N-Tier Architecture

Similar to the OSI seven-layer network architecture, **distributed software architecture** often has a layered structure, in which components are organized in layers and refers to N-Tier Architecture; for example, complex business software can be organized in the following five-tier model:

1. **Presentation tier**: The layout of the Graphical User Interface (GUI);
2. **Implementation of the presentation tier**: Program the GUI in certain programming language;
3. **Business logic tier**: Implementation of the business objects, rules, and policies;
4. **Data access tier**: Interfaces from the business logic to the databases;
5. **Data tier**: Databases.

The tiered design is well suited for distributed computing, with one tier or a number of adjacent tiers residing on one node of the distributed system. Another advantage is the flexibility in maintaining the system; the tiers can be modified relatively independently; for example, if tier 2, the implementation of the presentation, needs to be changed, none of the other tiers needs to be changed from the logic point of view. The user can still use the same interfaces and the business logic can remain unchanged. From the programming point of view, the tier above may need to be changed if different user interfaces are offered at the modified tier.

Two-tier architecture and three-tier architecture are the most widely used distributed architecture. In the **two-tier architecture**, also known as **client-server architecture**, the application is modeled as a set of services that are provided by servers and a set of clients that use these services. Clients know of servers, but servers do not need to know of clients. Both clients and servers are logical processes, which can reside on the same computer or on different computers. Figure 1.3 shows an example of the client-server architecture. The servers can form a federation, which allows them to back each other up to provide dependable services to their clients. The federation is often transparent to the clients. Data services provided by databases are important to most business applications, and the databases are part of the server in this architecture.

The client-server architecture can be further classified into **thin-client** and **fat-client** architectures. In the thin-client architecture, all of the application processing and data management are carried out on the server. The client is simply responsible for running the presentation software.

In the fat-client architecture, the software on the client implements the application logic and the interactions with the system user. The server is responsible for data management (database) only.

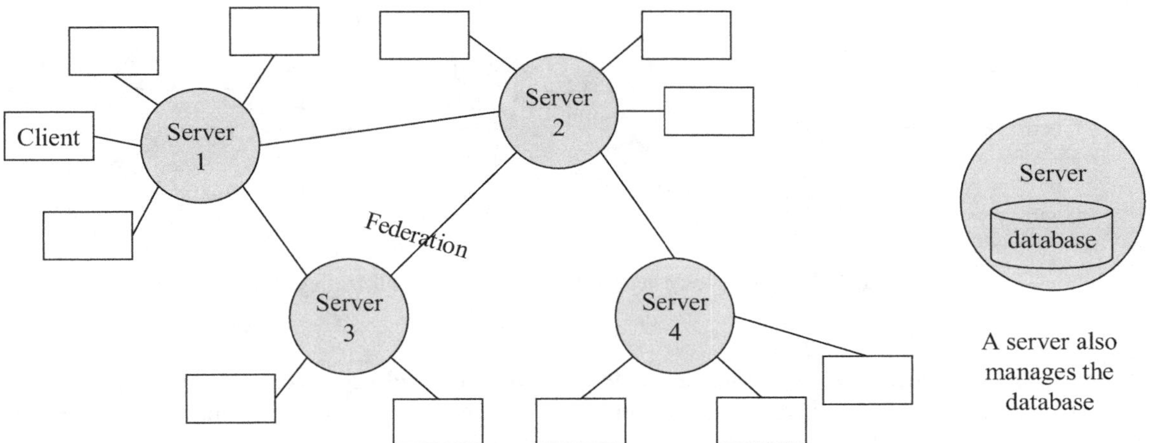

Figure 1.3. Client-server architecture, with the federation among the servers.

The further development of the federation of client-server architecture is the **virtualization**, which allows multiple servers to be seen as a single virtual server, as well as a single server to be seen as multiple virtual servers. Each virtual server can be used in a similar way as a physical server. To further improve resource-sharing efficiency, a virtual server can host multiple tenants, each of which can share the environment and resources in the environment. Virtualization and **multitenancy** are the key technologies of implementing cloud computing.

Three-tier architecture consists of three layers as shown in Figure 1.4. Each layer is executed on a separate processor. It is a more balanced approach, which allows for better performance than a thin-client approach and is simpler to manage than a fat-client approach. Three-tier architecture is a more scalable architecture—as demands increase, extra servers can be added.

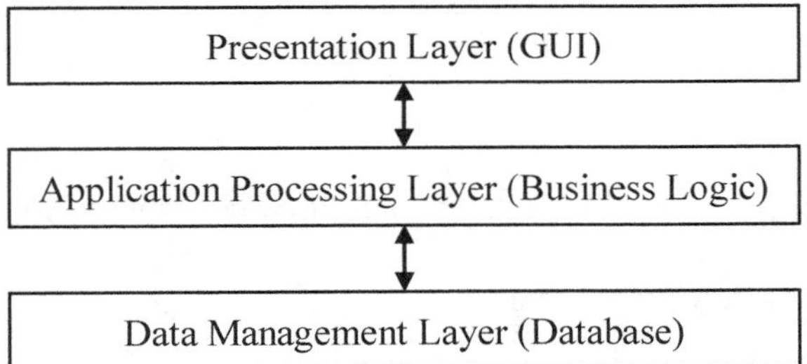

Figure 1.4. Three-tier architecture.

Figure 1.5 shows an example of a three-tier Internet banking system, where the clients can include GUI of ATM (Automated Teller Machine), POP (Point of Purchase), and web access to the user account. The application-processing layer can reside in the bank's IT center, responsible for processing all the requests. The data, such as account information and balance, are stored in a different server managing the databases.

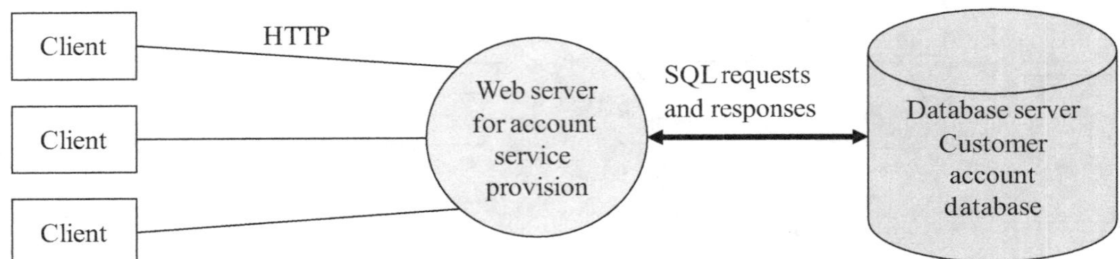

Figure 1.5. Example of a three-tier Internet banking system

The service-oriented architecture can be implemented as **four-tier architecture**, as shown in Figure 1.6(a), which consists of a presentation layer, application layer, service repository layer, and data management. However, service-oriented architecture does not have to be tied to this architecture, where only adjacent tiers can communicate with each other. Figure 1.6(b) and (c) show two possible variations of implementing the SOA.

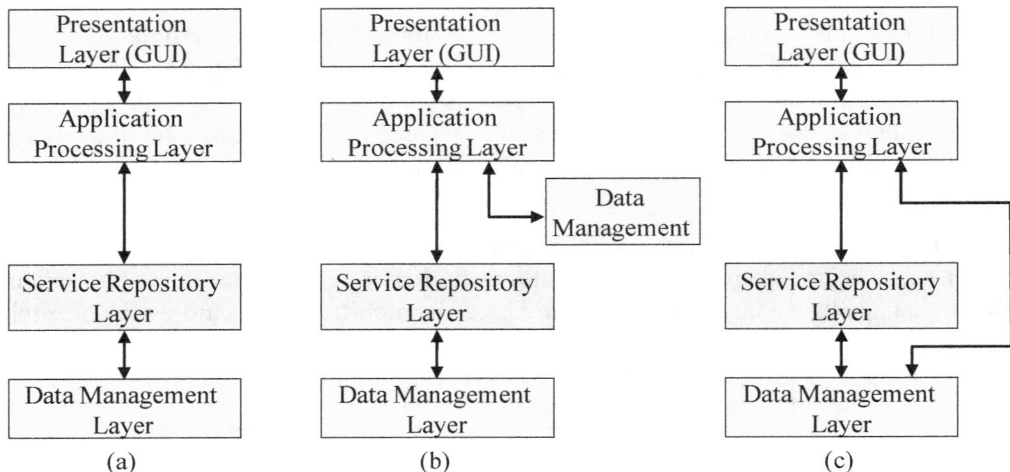

Figure 1.6. Four-tier architecture and its variations

1.2.3 Distributed Object Architecture

Different from the N-tier architecture, where the clients and servers are explicitly differentiated, the distributed object architecture makes no explicit distinction between clients and servers. Each distributable entity is an object that provides service to other objects and receives services from other objects.

Distributed object architecture is more generic in implementing different applications. However, it is more complex to design and to manage than the tiered architecture, because it allows the system designer to delay decisions on where and how services should be provided. In other words, it is an open system architecture that allows new resources to be added to the system as required. The system built on distributed object architecture is flexible and scalable. It is possible (e.g., written in the same language) to reconfigure the system dynamically with objects migrating across the network as required. As a logical model, distributed object architecture allows developers to structure and organize the system. In this case, developers can focus more on provision of the application functionality in terms of services and combinations of services.

The two major implementations of the distributed object architecture are CORBA (Common Object Request Broker Architecture) developed by OMG (Object Management Group) and Distributed Component Object Model (DCOM) developed by Microsoft.

In CORBA, object communication is through a middleware system called an Object Request Broker (ORB), also called software bus, as shown in Figure 1.7.

CORBA objects are comparable, in principle, to objects in C++, C#, and Java. The objects have a separate interface definition that is expressed using a common language IDL (Interface Definition Language), which is similar to C++. The interfaces of an object can be written in any language. A program translator can be used to translate the interface code; for example, in C++ and Java, into IDL code, and thus the objects written in different programming languages can communicate with each other. The ORB handles object communication through the stubs written in IDL. A service provider will make its service ports known as the IDL stubs. If a service requester calls a stub, the call will be translated to a call to the function of the service provider.

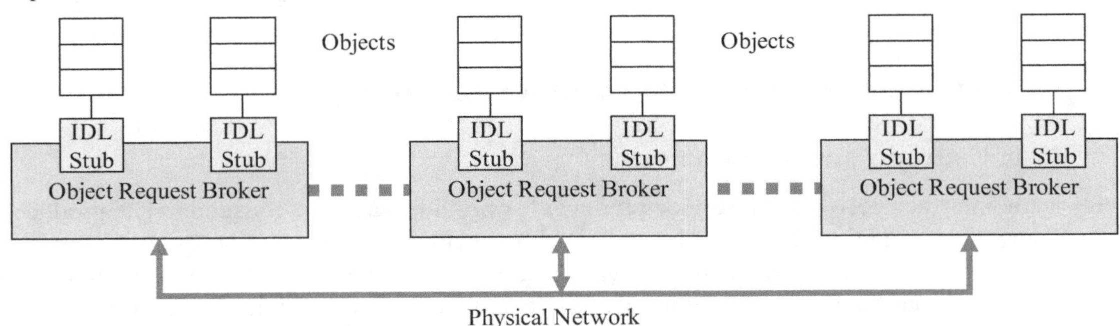

Figure 1.7. CORBA architecture

Another platform that supports distributed object architecture is the Java Enterprise Edition (Java EE). Java Message Service (JMS) is the software bus to connect the Java objects. Java Remote Method Invocation (Java RMI) over Internet Inter-Orb Protocol (RMI-IIOP) provides an IDL interface to communicate with CORBA. Java RMI over IIOP was jointly developed by Sun and IBM. Java EE objects can also communicate with Microsoft platforms. Java Native Interface (JNI) can be used to communicate with C++ and C# programs.

DCOM (Distributed Component Object Model) is Microsoft's distributed software development framework before Visual Studio .Net. DCOM allows software components to distribute across several networked computers to communicate with each other. Initially, the distributed software development framework was called OLE (Object Linking and Embedding), a distributed object system. The framework evolved for several generations. It was extended into "Network OLE" and then to COM (Component Object Model) in 1993, which provides the communication capacity among objects. In Windows 2000, significant extensions were made to COM and it was renamed COM+, before it evolved into DCOM. All technologies in DCOM were integrated into or replaced by Visual Studio .NET, which is an all-in-one OO, distributed, and service-oriented software development environment.

Distributed object architecture is a predecessor of SOC. It has many characteristics of SOC. The significant improvements and achievements made in SOC include:

- All major computer companies have agreed on the SOC standards, protocols, and interfaces for creating interoperable services, which are platform and language independent. In the case of distributed object architecture, CORBA and DCOM have similar functionality and goals; however, the systems developed in the two environments are not interoperable, and DCOM is platform dependent.
- SOC has explicitly separated the duties of development: The service providers develop services, the service requesters build the application using existing services, and service brokers publish the services and facilitate the matching and discovery of services. In distributed object architecture,

there is no explicit separation of duties, and there are no external mechanisms for service publication and discovery.

- The web service implementation of SOC makes use of the pervasive Internet infrastructure to deliver the services, while allowing using local area networks to build private SOC applications using the same technologies and standards.

Multithreading is the basic distributed computing model, which allows the parallel computing units to be specified by the programmer at the function and class levels, which are executed as independent operating processes and are running on the same processor or on different processors, depending on the operating system's scheduling and dispatching. Communication, resource sharing, and synchronizations among the threads are managed by the programmer. Chapter 2 will cover multithreading in detail.

1.3 Service-Oriented Architecture and Computing

1.3.1 Basic Concepts and Terminologies

A **service** is the interface between the service producer (or provider) and the consumer. The producer (also called provider) of a computing service is the person who develops the computer program (or the computer that runs or hosts the program) for others to use, while a service consumer is a person or a computer program that uses a service. From the producer's point of view, a service is a function module that is well-defined, self-contained, and does not depend on the context or state of other functions. These services can be newly developed modules or just modules wrapped around existing legacy programs to give them new interfaces.

From the application builder or service consumer's point of view, a service is a unit of work done by a service provider to achieve desired results. Different from an application, a **service** normally does not have the human user's interface. Instead, it provides Application Programming Interface (API) so that the service can be called (invoked) by an application or another service. For human users to use a service, a user interface needs to be added. A service with a user interface is an **application**.

The discovery of services by service consumers can be facilitated by service brokers. A service broker allows a service producer to publish their service definitions and interfaces, and at the same time allows a service consumer to search its database to discover the desired services.

An important feature of SOC is to divide the software development into three parties (stakeholders): service requesters or consumers, providers, and brokers. This three-party structure adds significant flexibility to the software system structure and supports a new approach of software development: composition.

Service-Oriented Architecture (SOA) is a distributed software architecture, which considers a software system consisting of a collection of loosely coupled services that communicate with each other through standard interfaces, such as WSDL (Web Services Description Language) interface and via standard message-exchanging protocols such as SOAP (Simple Object Access Protocol). These services are autonomous and platform independent. They can reside on different computers and make use of each other's services to achieve their own desired goals and end results. Software in SOA should be developed and maintained by three independent parties, service requester (application builders), service brokers, and service providers. Service providers develop services and publish them in service brokers, while the service requesters discover the services via service brokers using the available services to compose their applications. As the same services can be published by many service providers, the service requesters can dynamically discover new services and bind them into their applications at runtime, as better services are discovered.

Service-Oriented Computing (SOC) refers to the computing paradigm that is based on the SOA conceptual model. SOC includes the concepts, principles, and methods that represent computing in three parallel processes: service development, service publication, and application composition using services that have been developed. The essential difference between SOA and SOC is that SOA is a conceptual model that does not concern the algorithmic design and implementation to create operational software, while SOC involves a large part of the software development life cycle from requirement, problem definition, conceptual modeling, specification, architecture design, composition, service discovery, service implementation, and testing, to evaluation. As a result, SOA is more of a concern to the application builders (service requesters), while SOC is of concerned to all three parties of the SOC software development.

Service-Oriented Development (SOD) refers to the entire software development cycle based on SOA concepts and SOC paradigm, including requirement, problem definition, conceptual modeling, specification, architecture design, composition, service discovery, service implementation, testing, evaluation, deployment, and maintenance, which will lead to operational software.

In the literature, SOA is often extended to include the meaning of the SOC, and thus, SOA and SOC are used interchangeably, particularly when the specific differences between SOA and SOC are not the concern of the discussion. On the other hand, SOC is often extended to include the meaning of SOD, particularly when the specific differences between SOC and SOD are not the concern of the discussion. Thus, in this book, we will use SOC for SOA and SOD as well, to simplify the use of terminology, if the differences among them are not the concern of the discussion.

Figure 1.8 illustrates the relationship between SOA, SOC, and SOD. The dotted circle shows the coverage of this book.

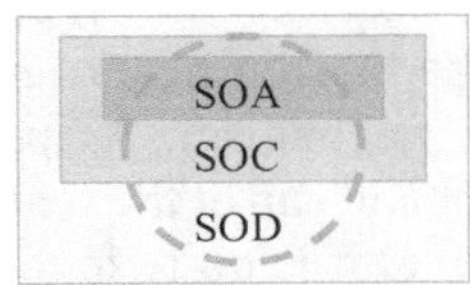

Figure 1.8. SOA, SOC, and SOD

We use "Distributed Service-Oriented Software Development" as the title of the book to contrast the widely used Distributed Object-Oriented Software Development approach, and to emphasize the fact that service-oriented software development is distributed in nature. Not only is the software under development distributed in different computers in different locations, but also the development process is distributed in the sense that the application builders, service brokers, and service providers are developers working independently in different locations, but following the same interfaces and standards. Furthermore, Chapter 2 discusses distributed computing in general and how SOA, SOC, and SOD fit into the framework of general distributed computing.

Web services (WS) are services accessible over the web. Web services-based computing is a specific implementation of SOC. It is perhaps the most widely known SOC example; however, other SOC implementations are also possible. Web services support SOC, and have a set of enabling technologies including WSDL, SOAP, and XML. XML is the standard for data representation; SOAP enables remote invocation of services across network and platforms. WSDL is used to describe the interfaces of services. UDDI (Universal Description Discovery and Integration) and ebXML (electronic business eXtensible Markup Language) are used to publish web services, which enable publishing, searching, and discovery, manually and programmatically. More standards and protocols are being included in the WS technology set every day. Web services have several technical aspects:

- Services are functional building blocks. Multiple services can form a composite service, and the composite service becomes a new building block. However, the code of a web service does not need to be imported and integrated into the application. Instead, a service runs at the service provider's site and is loosely coupled with the application using messages. Thus, the service does not have to been written in the same programming language and does not have to be developed or running on the same platform.

- Services are software modules that can be identified by URL (Uniform Resource Locator) and whose interfaces and bindings are capable of being defined, described, and discovered as XML artifacts.
- Web services are often described by WSDL, accessed by the protocol SOAP over HTTP. With an added human interface, a single service or a composite service can form a web application. Web services are normally accessed by computer programs, whereas web applications are accessed by human users using a web browser.

Composition is a key concept in SOC, which uses available services to compose a composite service or an application. Two composition methods are proposed and realized: Orchestration and Choreography. In **orchestration**, a central process, which can be a service itself, takes control over the involved services and coordinates the execution of different operations. The involved services communicate with the central process only. Orchestration is useful for private business process. BPEL (Business Process Execution Language) is the major composition language that supports orchestration. In **choreography**, there is no central coordinator. Each service involved can communicate with any partners; choreography is useful for public business process and allows dynamic composition. WS-CDL (Web Services Choreography Description Language) is a composition language that supports choreography.

Service-Oriented Infrastructure (SOI): This term can have two meanings. The first meaning refers to the hardware and software support for SOC, as SOC involves many new kinds of operations not commonly used in traditional computing such as publishing, discovery, policy-based governance, orchestration, and choreography; for example, if the number of services is huge, the search algorithm needs to be efficient, with a good caching mechanism. Otherwise, a significant amount of time will be spent on discovery. Another example is the policy governance mechanism. As policies need to be enforced at runtime, the enforcement mechanism needs to be efficient and run at the real time as the application is running. As some of the SOC operations can be quite expensive, it is quite logical that some of these operations should be executed by hardware or supported by hardware to save cost and time. This is particularly true if the SOC system needs to be used in mission-critical real-time systems.

Another meaning of SOI is that a hardware system can be organized in a service-oriented manner like a software system. An example of this kind of SOI is now being developed by Intel in their SOI group. The principal idea is to treat computing components, memory components, and networking components as virtual services. Essentially, they are treating these hardware components as services like software services, and they control these hardware services like software services in a service-oriented manner. Intel calls this PaaS (Platform-as-a-Service) so to compare the SaaS (Software-as-a-Service) concept. In this way, a hardware system can be composed and recomposed like a software system and managed like an SOC system. Another interesting implication is that once a hardware system is organized in an SOI manner, hardware is constructed as recomposable services, which allow hardware components to be replaced or upgraded without stopping the operation of the system. This means that current fault-tolerant computing techniques can be seamlessly integrated into the architecture design. This will be a research topic for the future.

Web 2.0 is the proposed next generation of web or Internet. The core concepts include users as *active* contributors (rather than just passive observers), peer collaboration, collective intelligence, moving the computing platform from desktop to the web, user-centric computing, and service orientation. One well-known example is Wikipedia, where millions of users participate in writing an online encyclopedia. This approach has been particularly successful as Wikipedia has become a popular way for people to learn. Note that the Wikipedia Company had only 280 employees in 2017, yet it has produced millions of pages of knowledge, and almost all the knowledge is contributed by users. This is an excellent example how massive collaboration can create something that is of great value. This book has many citations to Wikipedia, which proves that the materials in the Wikipedia are indeed useful, particularly for the rapidly developing disciplines. The approach of conducting business using Web 2.0 is now called Wikinomics (http://en.wikipedia.org/wiki/Wikinomics). Numerous organizations are now trying to duplicate this approach in creating something of great value.

Semantic Web. Semantic Web is defined by W3C, which provides a vision for the future of the web. The Semantic Web provides a common framework that allows data to be shared and reused across application, enterprise, and community boundaries. The idea is to give information explicit meaning, to make it possible for web services to automatically process and integrate information available on the web. Semantic Web is now also called Web 3.0 (http://en.wikipedia.org/wiki/Web_3), as the name Web 2.0 has been used.

Ontology. The word "ontology" comes from philosophy, where it means a systematic explanation of being. In computer science, ontology is defined to be the formal specification of the terms and objects in a domain and the relationships among them. One of the principal relationships is classification. Often an ontology system defines a vocabulary of terms (words), their meanings (semantics), their interconnections (e.g., synonym and antonym), and rules of inference (reasoning), which is used in the semantic web projects as the main means of implementation.

Service-Oriented Databases (SODB). As SOC became popular, the database technologies also become relevant. SOC applications use XML-based data and message, which have tree-structures, whereas traditional databases consist of tables of rows and columns. There are several approaches to address the mismatch between data structures.

The first approach is to use traditional databases and an adapter to convert the XML-based data and message to and from data of tables in the traditional databases. This is the current business practice in this area.

The second approach is to encode data in the XML format and store the XML files as database. The main challenge is to design and implement efficient XML-based query language to retrieve data from, and store data into, the XML database. The XQuery language has been defined by W3C to serve this purpose.

The third approach is to encapsulate the existing database management systems such as relational database systems as service and develop related services so that an SOA application can talk to the database system. Those related services are called **information services**.

Ontology can also serve as a database for SOC applications. In fact, an XML database can be viewed as a simplified ontology system.

1.3.2 Service-Oriented Computing

In traditional software development paradigms, the developer takes the requirements, converts them into specification, and then translates the specification into an executable file that meets the requirements. Several approaches are available to translate the specification into an operational system, including the waterfall model, incremental development, object-oriented computing (OOC), and component-based computing. Each approach has its own engineering processes and techniques.

SOC is a new paradigm that evolves from the OOC and component-based computing by splitting the developers into three independent but collaborative parties: the **application builders** (also called **service requesters**), the **service brokers** (or **publishers**), and the **service developers** (or **providers**). The responsibility of the service developers is to develop software services with standard interfaces. The service brokers publish or market the available services. The application builders find the available services through service brokers and use the services to develop new applications. The application development is done via discovery and composition rather than traditional design and coding. In other words, the application development is a collaborative effort from the three parties.

Services are platform-independent and loosely coupled so that services developed by different providers can be used in a composite service. Many standards have been developed to ensure the interoperability among services. However, the competition is fierce. Only the best services can survive because, for a given known service requirement; for example, password encryption and "add-to-cart" services, many providers can implement and publish the same service for application builders to use in their applications.

In SOC, individual services are developed independently based on standard interfaces. They are submitted to service brokers. The application builders or service requesters search, find, bind, test, verify, and execute services in their applications dynamically at runtime. Such a service-oriented architecture gives the application builders the maximum flexibility to choose the best service brokers and the best services. Figure 1.9 shows a typical service-oriented architecture, its components, and the process of registering and requesting a service. The components and steps shown in the diagram are explained as follows:

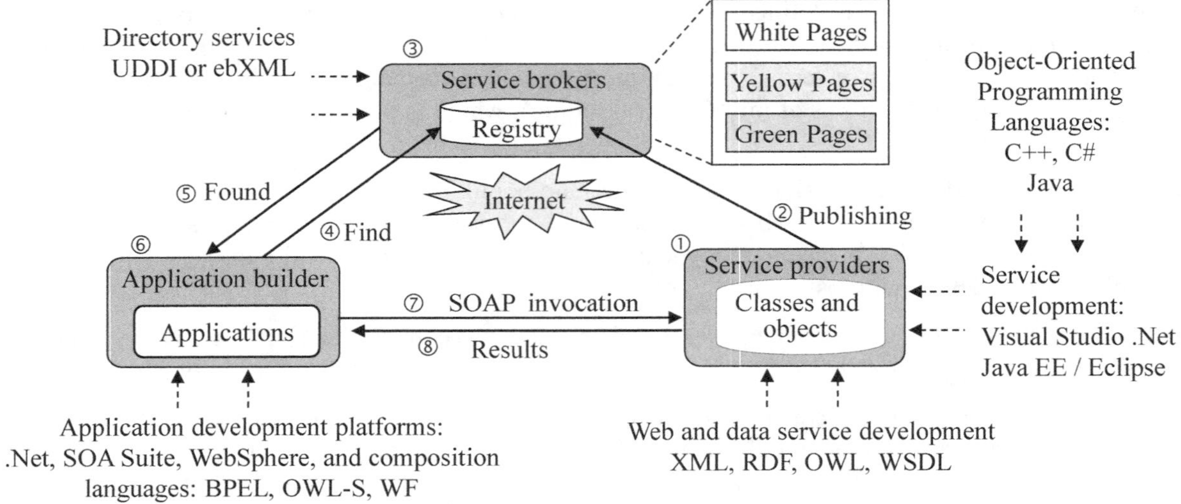

Figure 1.9. A typical service-oriented architecture

1. The services providers develop software components, corresponding to classes and objects in OOC to provide different services using programming languages, such as C++, C#, and Java, and service-oriented software development environment, such as .Net, J2EE, and the Eclipse.
2. The service providers register the services to a service broker and the services are published in the registry.
3. Current service brokers use UDDI or ebXML standards that provide a set of standard service interfaces for registering and publishing web services. For UDDI, the information needed for registering a service includes: (1) White Pages information: Service provider's name, identification; for example, the DUNS number, and contact information; (2) Yellow Pages information (business category): industry type, product type, service type, and geographical location; and (3) Green Pages information: technical detail on how other web services can access (invocate) the services, such as APIs (Application Programming Interfaces). UDDI's White and Yellow Pages are an analogy to the telephone White and Yellow pages. The UDDI standard supports directory only, whereas ebXML supports both directory and repository.
4. An application builder looks up, through the Internet, the broker's service registry, seeking desired services and instructions on how to use the services. The ontology and standard taxonomy in the service broker can help automatic matching between the requested and registered services.
5. Once the service broker finds a service in its registry, it returns the service's details (service provider's binding address and parameters for calling the service) to the application builder.
6. The application builder uses the available services to compose the required application. This is higher level programming using service modules to construct larger applications. In this way, the application builders do not have to know low-level programming. With the help of an application development platform, the application code can be automatically generated based on the constituent services. The

current application development platforms include .Net, J2EE, SOA Suite, and WebSphere from IBM, which can support high-level composition of applications using existing services.

7. The code of services found through a broker resides in a remote site, normally in the service provider's site, or in the service broker if service repository is offered by the broker. SOAP invocation can be used to access the services remotely.
8. The service in the service provider's site directly communicates with the application and delivers service results.

1.3.3 Object-Oriented Computing versus Service-Oriented Computing

SOC is different from Object-Oriented Computing (OOC) in many ways, even though SOC evolves from OOC and they may look similar. In the past, some mistakenly thought that OOC is not much different from procedural computing, because traditional procedural languages already have the concept of data abstraction such as structure, which is similar to class, and procedures, which is similar to methods. Even though OOC may look similar to traditional computing, the fact that designers think in terms of classes and objects fundamentally change their way of thinking. As a result, many new concepts and methods emerge in OOC, such as design patterns, inheritance, dynamic binding, polymorphism, design hierarchy, and UML (Unified Modeling Language).

Similarly, SOC is different from OOC, because now designers will think in terms of services, workflows, service publishing, discovery, application composition using reusable services, and policy governance. These concepts are indeed different from OOC.

Furthermore, services can be available on the web or in a private repository, and an application can use runtime search to discover new services and bind the service into the application. The application builder may not need to buy and install the **service component** (the software that provides the service); instead, the application can access the service component remotely and pay for the service used. Software upgrade will become easier. Once the service components are upgraded, the new services will be immediately available to the applications, saving significant cost of uninstalling and reinstalling software on client computers. Software will be charged based on the extent of use. Thus, users will not have to pay for unnecessary software. In other words, SOC provides a new model of software application: instead of buy-install-and-use, SOC provides a new model of pay as you go.

The SOC also has a significant impact on the system structure, dependability attributes, and mechanisms, such as system reliability, security, system reconfiguration, and recomposition. These mechanisms will be drastically different from OOC; for example, instead of static composition (with dynamic creation of objects and dynamic binding) in OOC, SOC allows dynamic composition in real time and at runtime using services just discovered, and with knowledge of the service interface only. Because new services will be discovered at runtime, SOC also needs a runtime ranking and selection mechanism based on runtime interoperability evaluation, testing, and other criteria. In case of system failures or requirement changes, the SOC also needs a distributed reconfiguration and recomposition strategies. Such strategies will be rather different for OOC.

In OOC, it is necessary to develop the code manually, even though some forms of dynamic binding can be used. The current OOC dynamic binding mechanism allows polymorphism, that is, methods that belong to a family of classes can replace each other at runtime. Yet SOC allows an unrelated service to replace an existing service as long as the new service has the same WSDL specification.

In SOC, a faulty service can be easily replaced by another standby service by a DCS (Dynamic Composition Service). The DCS is also a service that can be monitored and replaced. The key is that each service is independent of other services, and thus, replacement is natural. Only the affected services will be shut down. This approach allows the mission-critical application to proceed with minimum interruption.

Although SOC shares certain concepts and technologies with OOC, such as component design and component reuse, the innovation in SOC is significant. Figure 1.10 contrasts the main technologies and the development methodologies between the two paradigms.

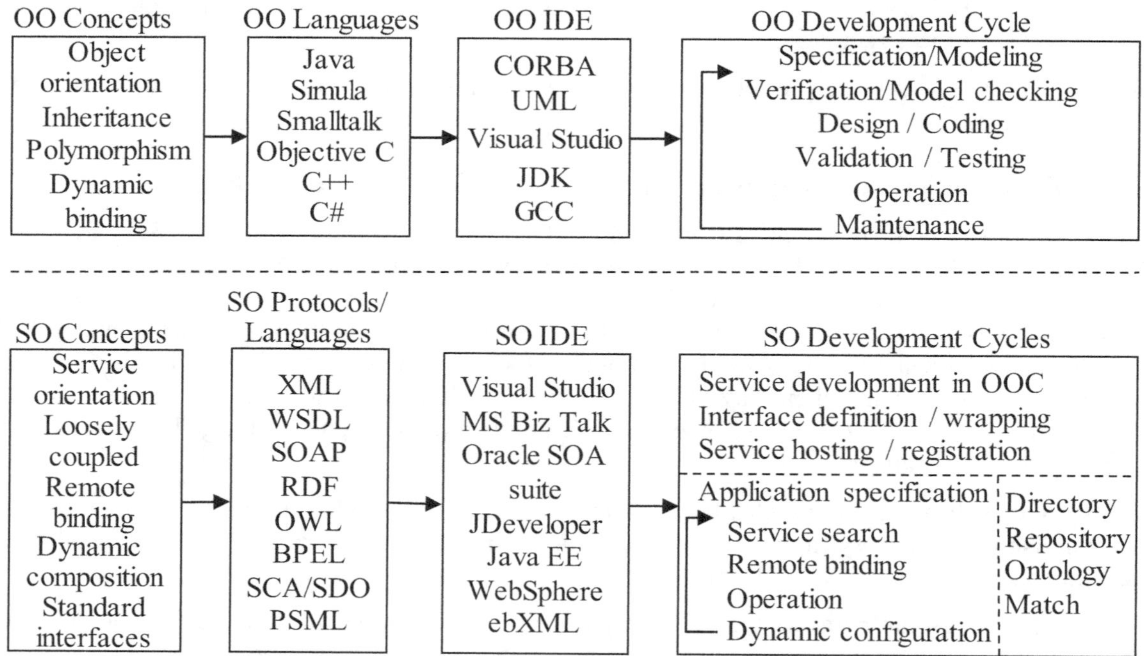

Figure 1.10. OOC and SOC concepts and technologies

Table 1.1 shows a more in-depth comparison between OOC paradigm and SOC paradigm in terms of major features in the software development process.

1.3.4 Service-Oriented System Engineering

Service-Oriented System Engineering (SOSE) is a combination of system engineering, software engineering, and service-oriented computing. It suggests developing service-oriented software and hardware under system engineering principles, including requirement, modeling, specification, verification, design, implementation, testing (validation), operation, and maintenance. Current research and practice on SOC are largely focused on functionality and protocols of SOC software. As SOC moves into mission-critical applications, as well as the entire computing and communication infrastructure moves to SOC, SOSE issues need to be addressed.

Table 1.2 lists typical SOSE techniques in each development phase. Many of the techniques are collaborative; for example, test cases may be contributed in a collaborative manner by all three parties. The service provider can provide sample unit test cases for the service broker and service requestors to reuse. The service broker can provide its own test cases via a specification-based test case generation tool, and the broker may even make the tool available for all the parties. The application builder can examine the sample test cases by the service broker, apply the test case generation tool provided by the service broker, and even contribute its own application test cases.

Even though we mainly use software to illustrate SOSE, the same can be applied to hardware and networks. Major computer companies are developing SOI and SON (Service-Oriented Networks) to support SOC applications at this time. They will need to develop the related SOSE techniques.

While the basic engineering principles remain the same, the way they are applied will be different in the SOC paradigm. Specifically, most engineering tasks will be done on the fly at runtime in a collaborative manner. Because systems will be composed at runtime using existing services, many engineering tasks need to be performed without complete information and with significant information available just in time before application. In this way, SOSE in some way may be drastically different from traditional engineering where engineers have complete information about the system requirements and thorough analyses can be performed even before system design is started.

Table 1.1. Object-oriented computing versus service-oriented computing

Features	Object-Oriented Computing	Service-Oriented Computing
Methodology	Many methodologies are available to develop OO programs.	In addition, SOC involve service discovery, architecture, application composition, and software monitoring.
Cooperation among developers	Development is by a single team responsible for entire life cycle. Cooperation is among software engineers working on requirement, designers, coding, and QoS.	Development is delegated to three independent parties: application builder, service provider, and service broker. Cooperation is among these three parties.
Abstraction	Abstract data type (class) and encapsulation of data and methods within a program.	Abstraction is at the service (including workflows) and architecture levels.
Code reuse	Inheritance allows code reuse within one application or within one platform. OO design patterns and application frameworks can be used to promote software reusability.	Services can be shared to promote reusability. Service brokers with ontology information enable systematic sharing of services.
Dynamic binding	Associating names to variables and methods at runtime.	Can dynamically allocate remote service required through the service directory.
Re-composition	Often it is necessary to determine and import the components at design time.	Can remove remote services and find and add newly available services through the service directory.
Component communication and interface	Importation of component code and integration at compilation time. Often this is platform and language dependent.	Remote invocation without importing the code. Platform and language independent. Open standard protocols ensure interoperability from different vendors.
System maintenance	Users need to maintain and/or upgrade their hardware and software regularly.	Hosting software needs to be maintained by provider, but services may be maintained by third parties.
Reliability	Software reliability can be obtained via testing and reliability modeling. Fault-tolerant software can be designed with redundant components.	Application reliability depends on the reliability of application, of services used, and of their execution environments. Software reliability can be obtained with collaboration and contributions from all parties. Fault-tolerant software can be designed with redundant services.

Table 1.2. Different SOSE techniques

Development phase	SOSE techniques
Collaborative specification and modeling	Service specification languages, model-driving architecture, ontology engineering, and policy specification.
Collaborative verification	Dynamic completeness and consistency checking, dynamic model checking, and dynamic simulation.
Collaborative design	Ontology engineering, dynamic reconfiguration, dynamic composition and recomposition, dynamic dependability (reliability, security, vulnerability, safety) design
Collaborative implementation	Automatic system composition and code generation
Collaborative validation	Dynamic specification-based test generation, group testing, remote testing, monitoring, and dynamic policy enforcement
Collaborative run-time evaluation	Dynamic data collection and profiling, data mining, reasoning, dependability (reliability, security, vulnerability, etc.) evaluation
Collaborative operation and maintenance	Dynamic reconfiguration and recomposition, dynamic reverification and revalidation

SOC is a new paradigm for computing and thus, new engineering techniques need to be developed to make SOC software and hardware dependable, reliable, safe, and secure. SOSE techniques are different from traditional system engineering techniques even though the basic engineering principles such as mathematics remain the same. Due to the dynamic features such as runtime composition and recomposition, new applications may not be evaluated by traditional system engineering because many components may be dynamically discovered and composed, and their source code may not be available. Thus, dynamic runtime system engineering techniques need to be applied.

1.4 Service-Oriented Software Development and Applications

1.4.1 Traditional Software Development Processes

Software development processes define the steps of development that lead to high-quality software. Several processes have been proposed and applied, including waterfall, iterative, object-oriented, and component-based development processes. Object-oriented and component-based software development processes are similar; Figure 1.11 shows a possible process. Both development processes require decomposition of the system to be developed into components, to develop the code of the components first, and then to use the components to build the applications. The object-oriented development process is a more specific approach than the component-based approach, which is defined by a set of specific features, such as encapsulation, inheritance, polymorphism, and dynamic binding. Generally speaking, object-oriented development is certainly component-based. However, component-based development may or may not be object-oriented.

1.4.2 Service-Oriented Software Development

Traditional computing paradigms affect mainly the design (algorithms) and implementation (programming) phases in the software development process. SOC affects the entire software development process as well as the cycle of the software. To better understand the impacts, let us first examine the unique features of SOC software:

- Self-contained and self-describing: Services are published through service brokers, and the published services contain sufficient information for other services to discover, match, bind, and invoke remotely and at runtime.
- Reconfigurable and recomposable: A newly discovered service can be composed into an existing service in two different ways: reconfiguration and recomposition.
- Reconfiguration: An existing service can be replaced by a new service satisfying the same function specification. Reconfiguration is performed when a service is faulty or becomes unavailable.
- Recomposition: In a SOC system, the user could change the specification of a service at runtime theoretically, result in a recomposition, during which, new services could be included in a composite service and existing services could be excluded.
- Dynamic verification: The dynamically modified specification must be dynamically verified to assure the required properties of the specification.
- Dynamic validation: The dynamically reconfigured or recomposed service must be dynamically validated (tested) to assure that it meets the specification.
- Dynamic evaluation: The dynamic reconfiguration and recomposition may lead to structural change of a service, and the attributes (reliability, security, safety, and performance) must be dynamically evaluated.

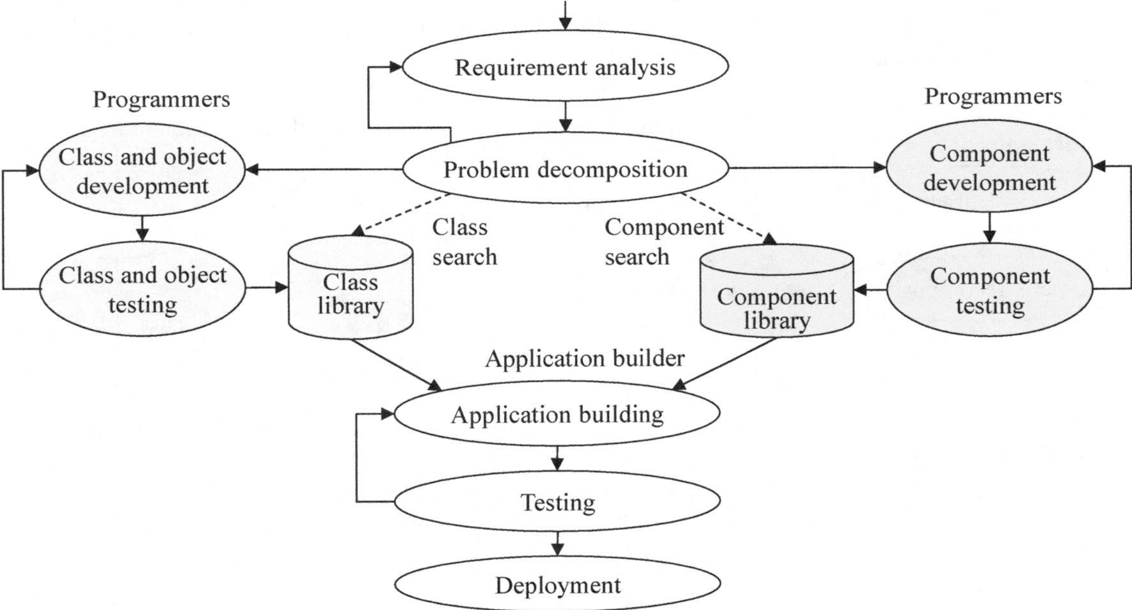

Figure 1.11. Object-oriented and component-based software development processes

In traditional software development process, the entire process is often managed by the same organization of developers. The new service-oriented software development is divided into three parallel processes: service development, service publishing to the service brokers, and application building (composition).

The services are of two kinds: atomic and composite. An atomic service is an object with standard interface. Thus, the development of atomic services is not much different from that of the object-oriented software development. The main difference is that an object normally needs to be integrated into the application written in the same programming language, whereas an atomic service can reside on a remote computer and can be invoked by applications written in different programming languages. Thus, the interface of an atomic service must be designed following certain predefined standards. The interface must contain the description of the functions of the service and the technical detail of invoking the service, so that the service can be discovered and can be properly invoked by other programs. WSDL (Web Services Description Language) is a major language used to describe the interfaces of services and SOAP (Simple Object Access Protocol) is used to transport messages between services. An atomic service can either be developed from scratch or be a wrapped service from an existing software component.

The development of composite services is different from that of the traditional software development process. Although traditional software development allows the construction of larger components from smaller components, the construction is static and manual. The construction of composite service can be static and manual. However, it can also be dynamic and automatic, that is, a service can be composed at runtime when a required service does not exist and needs to be composed from the existing services. Existing services include those services that are published through service brokers. Once a service is composed, the composite service can be published as a new service for future service or application composition. An SOC application is a little different from a composite service. The former has a GUI for human users to access, while the latter has programmatic interfaces exclusively for computer programs (applications or services) to access.

The development processes in OOC and in SOC are elaborated in Figure 1.12. Typically, an OOC application is developed by the same team in the same language (as shown on the left part of the figure), whereas an SOC application is created by using predeveloped services developed from independent service providers. To find the required services, the application builder looks up the service directories and repositories. If a service cannot be found, the application can publish the requirement or develop the service in-house. Service providers can develop services based on their own requirement analysis or look up the requirement published in the directories.

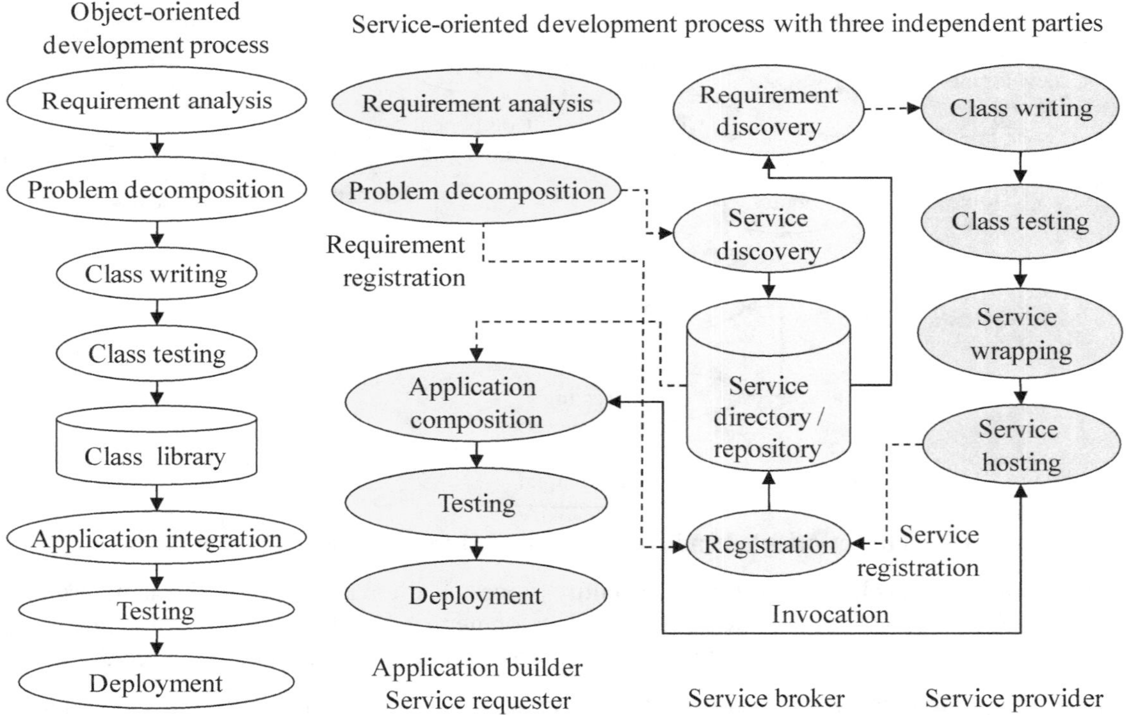

Figure 1.12. Object-oriented versus service-oriented software development process

Like traditional software development, the SOC software development process starts with the requirement analysis and definition. Figure 1.13 shows the steps of a typical requirement definition. At the end of the requirement, the system to be developed will be more formally modeled and specified in a modeling and specification language.

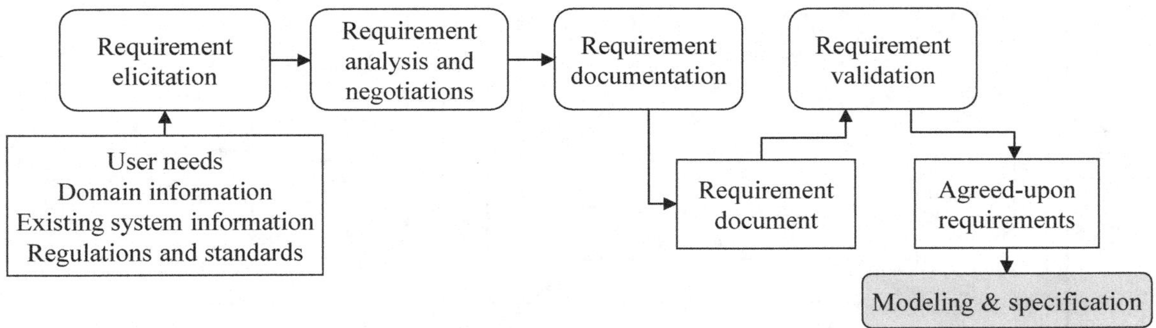

Figure 1.13. Requirement development process

The rest of the application-building process is significantly different from the traditional software development. Application builders use the existing services published by service brokers to build an application. In this process, the application builder can focus on its business logic, instead of programming tasks. If the existing services cannot meet an application's functional requirement, the application builder can construct a composite service to meet the requirement. Figure 1.14 outlines the steps of the software composition process from the application builder's perspective.

In Figure 1.14, we separate the data and ontology specification from the functional specification. In SOC, to facilitate the dynamic composition and recomposition, it is recommended to separate data such as policies, rules, and configuration parameters from the functional specification. Storing these data in an ontology or a configuration file allows them to be modified and to take effect at runtime without stopping the program. Policy-based computing is a good example of such separation.

The functional specification and data/ontology specification are verified using traditional verification techniques, such as model checking. Test cases can be generated from the specifications based on either the functionality or process flow in the specification.

Once the workflow is verified, the remote services need to be discovered or developed separately if no existing services are available. Once all services are bound into the workflow, the workflow becomes executable in the given environment, such as a simulation environment. The application will be tested in the simulation environment before being deployed into the field environment or a more realistic environment in which execution data can be collected for various analyses. If semantic information, such as policies, is stored in the ontology, the execution can be validated by the ontology or the policies. Based on the validation and evaluation, the system can be reconfigured by binding to different services at runtime. The requirement can be revised too. In this case, the system needs to be stopped to be manually revised of the models and specifications.

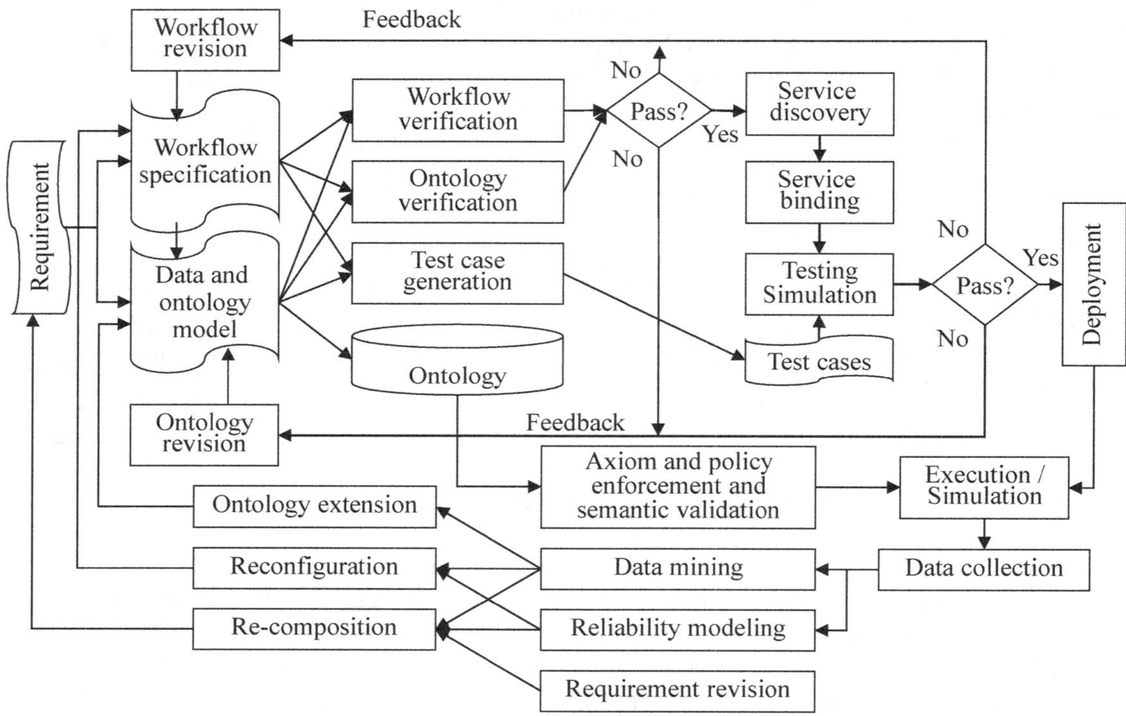

Figure 1.14. Service-oriented application development process

1.4.3 Applications of Service-Oriented Computing

As a general-purpose computing paradigm, SOC can be applied in any domains where OOC can be applied. Especially, OOC can be considered as a part of SOC. Every OOC application can be theoretically considered as an SOC application. However, in many situations, SOC provides unique advantages.

Electronic business has been the stronghold of SOC, where many services are dynamic and have to be remote and over the Internet; for example, a travel agency has to remotely invoke the services offered from the airliners, hotels, and car rentals. It is not doable to import the code of the services into the local server of the travel agency. Similarly, building an online bookstore requires access to the services from multiple parties, including banks, publishers, and freighters. The other emerging application areas include banking, health care, and e-government, where the services from different divisions are loosely coupled to provide collaborative services to their customers.

Robotics and embedded computing are traditional application fields where control programs are an integral part of the device. The introduction of SOC into this field makes it more flexible in accomplishing the mission of a robot or an embedded system. Instead of preloading the entire control program to the system, parts of the programs are implemented as remote services. The modification of the remote services can change the behavior and the course of the application without interrupting its execution. This feature is particularly attractive because the robot or the embedded system may have been in a location that is not physically reachable.

Many manufacturing processes today are controlled by computers. The introduction of SOC software in the processes makes the modification of the process much easier and more efficient.

Figure 1.15 shows a part of the SOC research and application projects at Arizona State University. The development of SOC software and hardware is the core of the research and applications. Concepts, principles, models, techniques, methods, tools, and frameworks have been developed to support the applications in a number of areas, including e-business, industrial process control, command and control, embedded systems, robotics, bio/medical information system, and ontology-based education systems. Most the research and practice have been incorporated into the cloud-computing environment.

Many of the topics will be covered in this book, not only at the conceptual level, but also at the development and implementation levels.

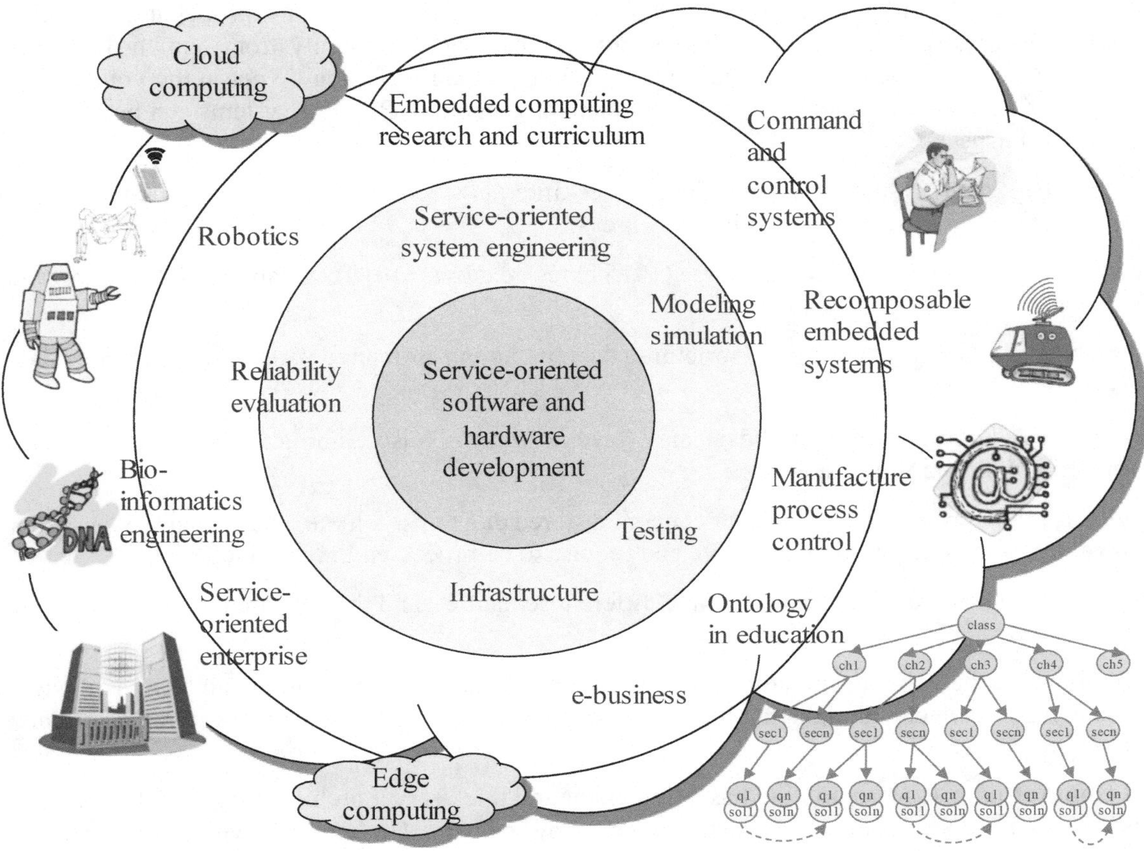

Figure 1.15. SOC research and applications at Arizona State University

1.4.4 Web Application Composition

A traditional desktop application has a unique entry point, the main method. It can be compiled into a standalone executable file. Although an application can consist of many executable and data files, a project file exists that organizes them into a well-defined application domain.

A **web application** consists of a collection of web pages, each of which is associated with executable and data files. We can enter a web application from different pages, even though the designer has an "entry" page in mind. Web applications typically follow the event-driven computing model to deal with user interaction and data communication. However, a web application is considered an application in the same sense as a desktop application, if it has an application domain consisting of a coherent mission to accomplish and common resources in the web environment. The web application domain can be distributed, with remote web services and data as its functional and data units. Each web page in a web application is an active object. The pages communicate with each other in a loosely coupled manner. Shared memory and synchronous and asynchronous callbacks can be supported.

Web applications are rapidly expanding, as service-oriented computing and related technologies progress, such as Web 2.0, Web 3.0, and cloud computing. For almost every desktop application, one can find a web version, or will find a web version soon. Cloud computing, enabling program and data accesses anywhere and anytime, is the latest driving force to move computing from desktop applications to web-based applications.

Big data is the term for a collection of data sets so large and complex that it becomes difficult to process using on-hand database management tools or traditional data processing applications (http://en.wikipedia.org/wiki/Big_data). The sources of big data are mainly from human through social networking and from devices in IoT. The challenges in big data processing lie not in the volume, but also in the types of data and the velocity of new data that are generated. Big data systems can be characterized by a number of aspects.

- Value: Big data is the next big thing after Internet (communication) and Cloud Computing (computation). It has been applied in many areas.
- Volume: A moving target from petabyte (1015 bytes), exabyte (1018), zettabyte (1021). The volume is increasing rapidly.
- Variability in data structures: poly-structured data, including structured data, semi- structured data, and unstructured data.
- Veracity: A large portion of the data may have no sense. Noise elimination and fault tolerance are required in bid data processing.
- Velocity: In many situations, the data cannot be stored due to its volume, and in many other situations, the values of the data are time sensitive and require to be processed in real time.
- Variety: Data from different sources have different semantics, and the data are integrated into different applications.
- Volatile: Due the volume, velocity, and veracity, not all data need to be stored, and data will have to be permanently deleted, and big data processing systems are required to selectively store and organize the data to maximize its value.

Cloud Computing. Cloud computing has a thin client and thick server architecture. The client could be as thin as a special purpose computer that runs a web browser only. The server is typically a virtual server, called cloud, which could consist of many physical servers that could be owned by different organizations. Computing is done by services in the cloud, and data are stored in the file systems or data centers in the cloud too. Cloud computing emphasizes a number of key concepts:

- Software-as-a-Service (SaaS): Software that performs various tasks are not installed on the client machines. They are installed in the cloud as services. SaaS emphasizes that not only components of applications, such as web services, but also the entire web applications, should be considered to be services.
- Platform-as-a-Service (PaaS): Software development environments such as Eclipse for Java-based software development and Visual Studio for C# are not installed on the client machine. They are installed in the cloud and developers use them remotely.
- Infrastructure-as-a-Service (IaaS): The infrastructure supporting computing and information management is not in the client, including computing resources, storage, communication bandwidth, and databases.
- Data centers, which store data as services to be used by other services.

For all the cloud resources, the cost model is pay-as-you-go. No need to purchase or to own the infrastructure, hardware, software, the programming environments, and the data. There are many cloud providers today, including Amazon Elastic Compute Cloud (Amazon EC2), Google's App Engine, and Microsoft's Azure, Oracle Exalogic Elastic Cloud, and Saleforce.com.

Cloud computing is being extended to include many features, such as Device as a Service (DaaS), Robot as a Service (RaaS), Test as a Service (TaaS), and X as a Service (XaaS), where X can represent different resources. Cloud computing is often used to process big data systems.

1.5 Enterprise Software Development

Enterprise software or enterprise application software (EAS) is typically composed of multiple components that need to communicate with each other through data exchanges. Electronic business, or e-business, is a typical EAS system. The enterprise software is more than all the systems within a business unit; rather it is the collection of all systems across multiple units or even multiple corporations; for example, a supply chain system for a major retail store, such as Wal-Mart or Target, is example of an enterprise system. Another enterprise system example is the US DoD (Department of Defense) system that controls and commands a major DoD function. The system for an army unit in a given location is not an enterprise system, but a part of an enterprise system. Thus, an enterprise system may consist of hundreds of systems residing in multiple states or nations. Service-oriented computing is widely used to develop enterprise software.

A **Service-Oriented Enterprise** (SOE), proposed by Intel researchers and standardized by OASIS, is a stack of technologies that implement and expose the business processes through an SOA system. SOE provides a framework for managing the business processes across an SOA landscape. At its core, the SOE is a system structure that supports core enterprise computing. A SOE is a system that supports the enterprise-wide operations.

As an enterprise-wide system, the traditional elements of SOA, that is, searching, discovery, interfacing, and service invocation, are not the focus of SOE, even though they are the common elements shared by the participating systems. These elements describe how to construct services and how to use services. They do not describe how sets of services support enterprise business processes or how atomic services function within an enterprise.

The central challenge facing the SOE is to design service-oriented business processes within an enterprise in such a way that the process is visible and manageable end-to-end. As the number of services available within the enterprise increases, the execution pattern becomes increasingly difficult to define and to track. An SOE is still a relatively young research area within SOC, which itself is a young discipline at this time.

Figure 1.16 shows an example of the layers in an SOE with composite e-business applications and web services as its foundation. The top layer of SOE is the configurable business logic. The next layer is the ebSOA (SOA for electronic business), which is a standard for service broker, including both registration and repository. The next layer is the Service-Oriented Management (SOM), which implements the nonfunctional features such as fault-tolerant computing, reliability, security, and policies. Service-Oriented Infrastructure (SOI) provides virtual services that represent the services that can be provided by hardware components; for example, Intel is developing this layer to map its hardware layer resources, including computing resources, memory resources, networking resources, devices, sensors, and actuators, to the service-oriented architecture. The bottom layer comprises the hardware devices that perform the required tasks.

The development of enterprise software and e-business systems evolve with the supporting technologies. On the other hand, their requirements have been the driven force of the technology advancement. Figure 1.17 shows the interaction and development of e-business and supporting technologies. **Enterprise**

Application Integration (EAI) is a milestone in e-business development. It is an integration framework composed of a collection of technologies and services. It is a middleware to enable integration of systems and applications across the enterprise; for example: a supply chain management application (for managing inventory and shipping) and a customer relationship management application for managing current and potential customers. The requirements for EAI include (https://en.wikipedia.org/wiki/Enterprise_application_integration):

- Data (information) Integrity: Ensuring that information in multiple systems is kept consistent.
- Vendor independence: If one of the business applications is replaced with a different vendor's application, the business rules do not have to be reimplemented.
- Common Facade: An EAI system could be a cluster of different applications. However, it can provide a single consistent access interface to these applications and shielding users from having to learn to interact with different software packages.

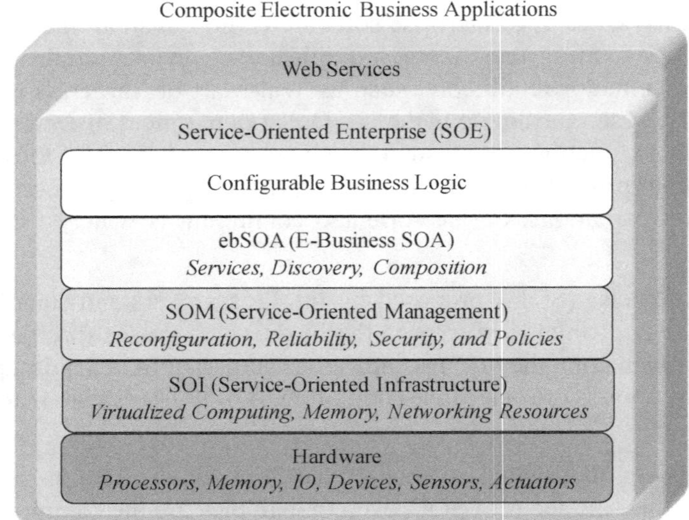

Figure 1.16. SOE framework

EAI is a complex process and management of EAI has to follow an engineering process. Enterprise Architecture Framework (EAF) is designed for dealing with such architecture integration. EAF is an organizing mechanism for managing the development and maintenance of architecture descriptions. It provides a structure for organizing resources and describing related activities. Federal Enterprise Architecture Framework (FEAF) is standard developed by the Chief Information Officers Council of the United States (https://en.wikipedia.org/wiki/NIST_Enterprise_Architecture_Model). The purposes of the framework are to organize federal information and promote federal interoperability; promote information sharing among Federal organizations; help Federal organizations developing their architectures; help Federal organizations quickly developing their IT investment processes; serve customer needs better, faster, and more cost effectively; and provide potential for Federal and Agency reduced costs. There are eight key components in the framework. They are the architecture drivers for business and design stimuli; the current architecture or the as is enterprise architecture; the target architecture: the to-be-built enterprise architecture; the strategic direction providing the overall guidelines to the development from current architecture to the target architecture; the transitional processes providing the concrete support to the migration from the current to the target architecture; the architectural segments of the existing enterprises within the total federal enterprise; the architectural models (business and design models) that describe the segments of the enterprise; and all the standards—all standards, some of which may be mandatory, guidelines, and best practices. These components define how the enterprise integration should be conducted and managed.

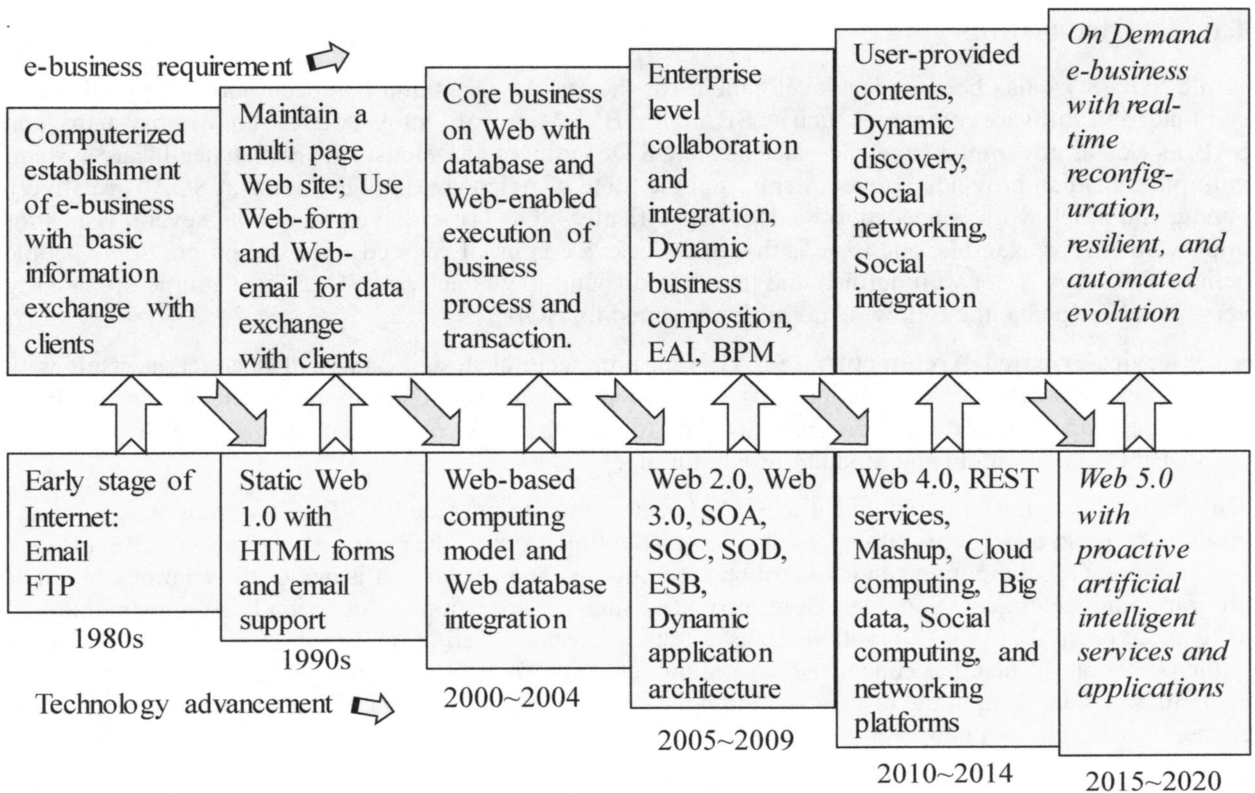

Figure 1.17. Interaction between business requirements and technologies

Business Process Management (BPM) is the next milestone in e-business development. It is a management approach that focuses on aligning all aspects of an organization with what the clients want and need. BPM allows organizations to abstract business process from technology infrastructure, and it goes beyond automating business processes or solving business problems using software. Instead, BPM enables business to respond to changing consumer, market, and regulatory demands faster than competitors—creating competitive advantage. The BPM life cycle consists of:

- Design: Process design encompasses both the identification of existing processes and the design of to-be processes.
- Modeling: takes the theoretical design and introduces combinations of variables or parameters;
- Execution: develop an application that executes the required steps of the process;
- Monitoring: tracking processes and statistics on the performance of one or more processes;
- Optimization: retrieving information from modeling or monitoring phase; identifying the potential or actual bottlenecks and the potential opportunities for cost savings or other improvements; and then, applying those enhancements in the design of the process.

The latest **business requirements** include:

- Business intelligence applications (for finding patterns from existing data from operations)
- Dynamic Business Composition requirement deals with changing environment and changing partners; reconfiguring business without stopping operations; and manual reconfiguration
- On Demand Business with Artificial Intelligence requirement deals with proactive discovery; responsive reconfiguration in real time; resilient around the world and around the clock; automated reconfiguration

1.6 Discussions

While SOC/SOA has been under development for the last 10 years and has been adopted by all major computer and software companies such as BEA, HP, IBM, Microsoft, Intel, Oracle, Sun Microsystems, and SAP, as well as government agencies such as the US Department of Defense, the British healthcare system, multiple Canadian provincial governments, and the State of Arizona. Many believe that SOA is relatively young, and much work is needed to be done. Specifically, SOA critics have pointed out several issues for improvement; for example, one issue is that SOA lacks a commonly agreed-upon definition. Some people believe that SOA is not well defined and thus it is difficult to characterize SOA; for example, in an early version at Wikipedia, the following definition is stated for SOA:

> "**Service-oriented Architecture (SOA)** is an architectural design pattern that concerns itself with defining loosely-coupled relationships between producers and consumers. While it has no direct relationship with software, programming, or technology, it is often confused with an evolution of distributed computing and modular programming."

This definition is not good enough for SOA, because this description also fits OO computing. An OO program can also be loosely coupled. In fact, loose coupling is one of the principal attributes of OO software. Furthermore, OO computing can be distributed computing, and certainly it is one of the common modular programming techniques. Some key SOA attributes, such as separation of definition from implementation, have also been used in OO software, as a class interface definition has been separated from its implementation. In fact, the concept of separating definition from implementation has been attempted for over 30 years in computing history, including data abstraction and procedural abstraction. Thus, this concept is certainly not new or unique.

Some SOA definitions are based the common SOA protocols used; for example, if a software program uses XML, WSDL, OWL, BPEL and/or other protocol or standards, then it is an SOA software. This definition is still not good enough, because these SOA protocols are constantly being updated and revised. It is even possible that later versions of these protocols will have little resemblance to previous versions, as the SOA history certainly can testify that several SOA protocols have been completely replaced by newer protocols. Specifically, BPEL has replaced several SOA composition languages before.

Some SOA authors also use SOA properties as definitions. However, this is not good enough either, specifically because some often-touted SOA properties are actually not available at this time; for example, dynamic composition is often an important characteristic of SOA. However, this feature is not available in a practical SOA environment yet. In other words, it is still a research topic. Most of the SOA tools today actually use *static* composition, that is, selecting services at the design time rather than at runtime dynamically. Thus, defining SOA by dynamic composition is not appropriate at this time. Furthermore, as SOA progresses, other SOA characteristics will emerge, and defining SOA by current SOA properties will prove to be too restrictive.

Some define SOA software as a collection of services. However, this definition is too loose. If so, what is the definition of a service? Does a service have a state? Is a service passive, autonomous, thin, or fat? Some people say that a service should be a *fat* service, that is, a service that has many supporting facilities and tools and can be even more autonomous like a software agent. This definition looks interesting and makes a software service more intelligent and probably more useful than a traditional "passive" service. However, this definition actually makes the current SOA infrastructure almost invalid, as it does not support "intelligent" services yet. The current SOA infrastructure does not support those common SOA operations such as composition, deployment, governance, modeling, and interoperability. Unless a new SOA infrastructure framework is developed, it is difficult to support those autonomous services using the current SOA infrastructure.

We prefer the definition from OASIS. According to the SOA reference model specification, SOA is a paradigm for organizing and utilizing distributed capabilities that may be under the control of different ownership domains. It provides a uniform means to offer, discover, interact with, and use capabilities to produce desired effects consistent with measurable preconditions and expectations. The SOA reference model specification bases its definition of SOA on the concept of "needs and capabilities," where SOA provides a mechanism for matching the needs of service consumers with capabilities provided by service providers.

OASIS also has a definition of service: A mechanism to enable access to one or more capabilities, where the access is provided using a prescribed interface and is exercised consistent with constraints and policies as specified by the service description. Moreover, a service has service description, visibility, interaction, real-world effect, execution context, and contract and policy. However, this definition is too loose, because it can fit a passive or thin service, as well as a fat and intelligent service.

Using these definitions, the SOA approach essentially allows a person to publish software components following some standards and allows others to discover and reuse. Note carefully that the above definition does not say that only software services can be published and discovered. In fact, numerous things such as workflows, collaboration templates, application templates, data, data schema, policies, test scripts, and user interfaces can be published, discovered, and reused by others, as listed in Table 1.3.

Table 1.3. SOA publishable items

Reusable artifacts	Description
Methods (or services)	Basic building blocks in SOA and allows software development by composition.
Workflows	Specify the execution sequence of a workflow with possibly multiple services. They allow rapid SOA application development.
Application templates	Specify entire applications with their workflows and services. They allow rapid SOA application development.
Data, data schema, and data provenance	Data and associated data schema such as messages produced during SOA execution can be published and discovered.
Policies	Policies are used to enforce SOA execution and can be published for reuse.
Test scripts	Consumers, producers, and brokers can publish test scripts to be used in verification by other parties.
Interfaces	GUI design can be used and linked at runtime to facilitate dynamic SOA application with changeable interfaces.

Thus, potentially, SOA can publish and reuse not only software services, but also other software artifacts such as workflow, policies, and data. Let us attempt a working definition of SOA:

> An SOA is an approach for software construction, verification, validation, maintenance, and evolution that involves specification, implementation, and publication of software artifacts such as services, workflows, collaboration patterns, and application templates following certain open interoperability standards. This approach develops software by composition with reusable software artifacts.

This working definition excludes an agent to be a service, but allows centralized and distributed SOA, as well as code, to be mobile. This definition allows various web service protocols to be used as a part of open interoperability standards, but it does not mention any specific protocols. In this way, all kinds of protocols, including future protocols, can be included as a part of SOA. Thus, various open interoperability standards for service specification (such as WSDL), workflow language (such as BPEL), and collaboration specifications (such as CPP/CPA) can be used. At the same time, these standards can be updated or even replaced in future, while the working definition does not need to be updated. Of course, the working definition of SOA can be updated and be changed from time to time, as we understand SOA more in the future.

Many outstanding books and papers that cover SOA are now available. Most of them are more suitable for working professionals. The standard organizations OASIS and W3C have developed most SOA-related standards and reference models. Furthermore, as SOA has started mainly from the computer industry, instead of from academia, one should search and navigate the SOA websites from the major industry players, the most notable ones including BEA, HP, IBM, Microsoft, Oracle, SAP, and Sun Microsystems. Readers can also find a large amount of SOA materials at DoD sites and DoD conference proceedings, as DoD is one of the earliest adopters of SOA. Many DoD engineers and contractors have worked on SOA, and they have gained significant experience. Due to the relative youth of SOA, many concepts and ideas are expressed in white papers or web blogs.

Many universities around the world (mainly in Asia, Australia, North America, and Europe) also offer SOA courses. However, as SOA is a wide area, different topics are actually covered in them. Most of these classes have offered their materials on the web, and readers can search their websites for information.

US federal government agencies, including the Department of Defense (DoD), have been actively promoting cloud computing and service-oriented computing (SOC). The Federal CIO (Chief Information Officer) Vivek Kundra made the following comments (Kundra 2009):

- "I'm all about the cloud computing notion. I look at my lifestyle, and I want access to information wherever I am. I am killing projects that don't investigate software as a service first."
- "The cloud will do for government what the Internet did in the '90s. We're interested in consumer technology for the enterprise. It's a fundamental change to the way our government operates by moving to the cloud. Rather than owning the infrastructure, we can save millions."
- "It's definitely not hype…Any technology leader who thinks it's hype is coming at it from the same place where technology leaders said the Internet is hype."
- The federal CIO office also noted the significant productivity gain by using this new approach, "In a traditional IT procurement environment, it would have taken us about 6 months to upgrade USA.gov to better meet the needs of our citizens. However, in the cloud environment we are now able to do upgrades in one day."

In February 2011, Vivek Kundra released his "Federal Cloud Computing Strategy." In the report, he stated that an estimated $20 billion of the Federal Government's $80 billion in IT spending could be used for migration to cloud computing solutions (https://www.dhs.gov/sites/default/files/publications/ digital-strategy/federal-cloud-computing-strategy.pdf).

Another important event is the network-based operating system (OS) by Google—Chrome OS—and it is a radical departure from the conventional desktop-based OS, because it does not install any software on the desktop computer, that is, all applications must be software services from the web. In other words, Chrome OS forces all of its users to adopt SOC. This shows the commitment of Google to cloud computing and SOC.

Name: ____________________

Date: ____________________

1.7 Exercises and Projects

1. Multiple choice questions. Choose one answer in each question only. Choose the best answer if multiple answers are acceptable.

1.1 Which of the following are fallacies of distributed systems?

(A) Latency is zero.
(B) Bandwidth is infinite.
(C) The network is secure.
(D) Topology does not change.
(E) All of them are fallacies.

1.2 Generally speaking, a service is an interface between the

(A) service provider and the service broker.
(B) service requester and the service broker.
(C) Yellow Pages and the Green Pages.
(D) producer and the consumer.

1.3 Which architecture is always a tiered architecture?

(A) Client-server architecture
(B) CORBA
(C) Service-oriented architecture
(D) DCOM

1.4 Which concept is least related to coding?

(A) Service-oriented architecture
(B) Service-oriented computing
(C) Service-oriented software development
(D) Object-oriented programming

1.5 Which entity does not belong to the three-party model of SOC software development?

(A) Service provider
(B) Service broker
(C) Application builder
(D) End user of software

1.6 What is the most significant difference between the Distributed Object Architecture (DOA) (e.g., CORBA and DCOM) and the Service-Oriented Architecture (SOA)?

(A) SOA software has better modularity.
(B) SOA software does not require code-level integration among the services.
(C) DOA software has better reusability.
(D) DOA software better supports cross-language integration.

1.7 Which concept is least related to the application composition?

(A) BPEL
(B) Choreography
(C) Orchestration
(D) Code integration

1.8 XML is

(A) an object-oriented programming language.
(B) a service-oriented programming language.
(C) a database programming language.
(D) a standard for data representation.

1.9 Which protocol enables remote invocation of services across network and platforms?

(A) XML (B) SOAP (C) WSDL (D) UDDI

1.10 Which of the following is/are the proposed features of Web 2.0?

(A) Software as operational services.

(B) Users are treated as codevelopers.

(C) Use loosely coupled and easy-to-use services to compose applications.

(D) Use services and data from multiple external sources to create new services and applications.

(E) All of the above.

1.11 The main idea of cloud computing is to shift computing from

(A) web to desktop. (B) service orientation to object orientation.

(C) desktop to web. (D) Web 2.0 to Web 3.0.

1.12 What of the followings is not a key concept in cloud computing?

(A) Infrastructure as a service (B) Platform as a service

(C) Programming language as a service (D) Software as a service

2. What are SOA, SOC, SOD, SOE, SOI, and SOSE? Briefly state their definitions based on your understanding.

3. What are the main differences between requirement analyses in the OOC paradigm and those in the SOC paradigm?

4. What are the major benefits of separating an application builder from the service providers?

5. What are the main techniques in SOSE (service-oriented system engineering)? For each technique, write one or two sentences to describe its purpose.

6. Compare and contrast the traditional software development process and the service-oriented software development process. For each step of the development, write a paragraph to describe the purposes, responsibilities, and functions of the step.

7. What is a service registry? What is a service repository? What are their differences?

8. An electronic travel agency needs to be developed. What is your responsibility if you are:

8.1 A service provider?

8.2 A service broker?

8.3 An application builder?

9. You plan to invent a unique online game:

9.1 Describe what you must do as an application builder and what you can expect the service providers to do for you.

9.2 Describe your invention idea and list everything you must do as an application builder.

9.3 List everything that you can possibly find through service brokers.

10. List a few application areas where you believe SOC is a better fit than OOC. State your reasons and justifications.

11. What are the impacts of the SOC paradigm to the IT market and to computer science graduates?

12. Search on the Internet to find the major tools that support the Mashup-based application development.

13. Search on the Internet to find the major tools that enable the development and deployment of cloud computing applications.

14. This is an open problem. Search on the Internet to find a web service testing tool. Download their reports and white papers, and write a half-page summary about the tool.

Project

A Service-Oriented Computing Workshop

As SOC is a young discipline, students will learn a great deal by doing their own research on SOC. One way to facilitate the research is to organize a workshop within the class. Specifically, each student needs to submit a paper to the workshop organized by the instructor and the teaching assistants. A sample call for papers is given below.

"CALL FOR PAPERS"

Workshop on Introducing Service-Oriented Computing (WISOC)

Scope – Workshop on Introducing Service-Oriented Computing (WISOC) serves as an initial meeting for participants of distributed service-oriented software development course at Arizona State University to exchange results and visions on all aspects of Service-Oriented Computing (SOC), Service-Oriented Architecture (SOA), and Service-Oriented System Engineering (SOSE). Starting with this new paradigm and their realization in Web Services (WS), WISOC covers all areas related to architecture, semantics, language, protocols, dependability, reliability, security, discovery, composition, publishing, testing and evaluation, interoperability, business process, as well as the deployment and experience of real service-oriented systems.

Topics of Interests – WISOC invites state-of-the-art survey submissions on all topics related to service-oriented computing, including (but not limited) to the following:

- Service Orientation Concepts and Definitions
- Service Modeling and Specification
- Service Requirements Engineering
- Service Semantics and Ontology
- Services and Business Processes
- Services, Components, and Agents
- Design Patterns and Service-Oriented Design Patterns

- Service-Oriented Development Processes and Methods
- Service Publishing, Discovery, and Invocation
- Service Composition, Interoperability, Coordination, Orchestration, and Chaining
- Service Reputation and Trust
- Intelligent Selection, Service Brokering, and Service Level Agreement and Negotiation
- Services and Legacy Systems
- Service-Oriented Enterprise Architecture
- Service-Oriented System Implementation and Deployment
- Service-Oriented Verification, Testing, and Evaluation
- Service QoS, Dependability, Reliability, and Performance
- Service Policy Management
- State Management
- Service-Oriented Database and Service-Oriented Information Management
- Service Privacy, Confidentiality, and Security
- Service Oriented Real-Time and Embedded Systems
- Service-Oriented Robotics Computing
- Service on Peer-to-Peer Network
- Service-Oriented Embedded Systems
- Service on Grid Network
- Web 2.0 and Web 3.0
- Linked Data
- Cloud Computing, Software as a Service, Platform as a Service, and Infrastructure as a Service
- Enterprise application software

This project consists of the following activities. The total number of points each student can obtain is 100. Ten percent of the papers will receive 10 bonus points as the best paper award.

1. The paper: 80 points

The points will be awarded based on the instructor's evaluation, as well as the peer evaluation, according to the following evaluation criteria, with 10 points for each criterion:

1) The paper is relevant to one of the focus areas given in the call for papers.
2) The paper has well-defined questions to address, and the materials are coherent and consistent.
3) The paper clearly presents the ideas and is easy to read.
4) The paper is technically sound and correct.
5) The paper is interesting and informative, which makes the reviewers feel it is useful to read.
6) The abstract and the summary, which summarize the paper well at the beginning and at the end, are concise.
7) The paper effectively uses diagrams and/or tables to present the ideas.
8) The paper closely follows the IEEE conference paper format and the given guidelines in the call for papers.
9) If the paper is a team project, the workload must be divided equally among the team members. It must be made clear which sections are written by (are the responsibility of) which member. The reviewers may give different scores to different team members based on the sections and the paragraph each member responsible for.
10) Peer Evaluation: 10 points
11) Each student will act as a reviewer and will review three papers and submit three review reports. The quality of the review reports will be evaluated by the instructor. Up to 10 points will be awarded.
12) Improvement of the paper based on the review reports: 10 points.

13) The authors of each paper must improve the paper based on the comments in the review reports. The changes made must be shown in "Track Changes" in MS Word. You can turn on the track changes in the Tool menu. Resubmit the paper after the revision. The instructor and the teaching assistants will determine if the improved paper addresses the comments given by the reviewers. A camera-ready copy must be submitted, and the papers will be published in an electronic form.
14) Previous workshop proceedings are available at the website: http://www.public.asu.edu/~ychen10/teaching/cse445/index.html

Typical Components of Technical Papers/Reports

Title

Author(s)

Abstract

Summary of important issues and results, assuming the readers have not read the full report.

Introduction

This section may cover background information, related work, the purposes of this writing this paper, outline of the paper, and so forth.

The Main Sections

They may contain several or all of the following components:

- **Overview**, including the architecture of the system;
- **Model development**: explore a few models—model refinements, include graphic, equations, and so forth;
- **Procedure** (the steps are you going to use to complete this design, assumptions);
- **Design of experiment, simulation, implementation**;
- **Discussion of results**: the numerical and graphic results, and from models, upper and lower limits.

Summary/Conclusions

Summary of the work and the important results, assuming the readers have read the full report.

Acknowledgments

Who have helped the authors in preparing the research and on what issues?

References

List the all the references that you have based your work on, related to, referred to, and so on. Each reference you have listed must be cited in the paper. List the references in IEEE proceedings reference format.

Appendices (if any)

For example, Excel spreadsheet, diagrams, and extra explanations.

Other issues: Include page numbers, cite the references the content is based on, related to, and referred to. Follow the required format.

Review Form

Workshop on Service-Oriented Computing (WSOC)

Paper ID:

Paper Title:

1. Numerical Evaluation

Scale: (0–2) Strongly disagree, (3-–4)Weakly disagree, (5–6) Marginal, (7–8) Weakly agree, (9–10) Strongly agree

Evaluation questions:

1) The paper is relevant to one of the focus areas given in the call for papers (0–10).
2) The paper has well defined questions to address, and the materials are coherent and consistent (0–10).
3) The paper clearly presents the ideas and is easy to read (0–10).
4) The paper is technically sound and correct (0–10).
5) The paper is interesting and informative, which makes the reviewers feel it is useful to read (0–10).
6) The abstract and the summary, which summarize the paper well at the beginning and at the end, are concise (0–10).
7) The paper effectively uses diagrams and/or tables to present the ideas (0–10).
8) The paper closely follows the IEEE conference paper format and the given guidelines in the call for papers (0–10).

2. Detailed Comments

Please supply detailed comments to support each of your scores. You may also indicate any errors you have found. The length of the comments must be between 15 and 30 lines.

Chapter 2
Distributed Computing with Multithreading

From this chapter, we will not only study the concepts, but also implement the concepts using real programming language examples. We believe the implementation of a concept in a piece of code can best explain the concept and its context. We assume the readers are familiar with the object-oriented (OO) computing concepts and have used one of the OO programming languages such as C++, Java, or C# in writing OO programs. However, we start the chapter with a brief introduction to C# and .Net in order to prepare the readers who have not used C#. Then, the chapter moves to the general issues in multitasking and multithreading, including parallel processing, synchronization, deadlock, and order of executions, which form the foundation of a distributed computing paradigm. To better understand the concepts discussed, we will use Java and C# to develop multithreading programs. Finally, we discuss the exception and event-driven programming approach in distributed computing. The concepts and techniques are widely used in distributed service-oriented computing.

This chapter is not tightly related to the remaining chapters in the book, because most problems and techniques studied in this chapter have been embedded into the service-oriented development environment, and thus the application builders are freed from solving many of these problems. If a service provider uses server software, such as IIS, most of the problems are also embedded in the server software. However, if a service provider wants to write their own hosting services, the concepts studied in this chapter are important. If a reader is concerned with service-oriented software development using advanced tools and infrastructure, they can skip this chapter. However, the event-driven programming style and call back mechanism discussed in this chapter is important for developing asynchronous distributed services and applications.

2.1 Introduction to C# and .Net

We will briefly introduce C# in this section. If you are familiar with C#, you can skip this section. Java and C# are both OO programming languages, and they are the two major languages that are used to write multithreading programs, as well as create SOC services. Each thread in Java is created from an object. A thread in C# can be created either from an object or from a function (method) within an object. In a service-oriented application, the constituent services are defined by Java or C# objects, which are wrapped with open standard interfaces to become services.

C# inherits most of its syntax from the C/C++ family of languages and supports most features that Java supports. It is a strongly typed language with automatic garbage collection. C# is supported by a large set of functions coming from the .Net Framework Class Libraries, which allow the developers of both OO and service-oriented software to reuse these functions. Assuming the readers have taken a full programming class in C++ or Java, this section introduces a subset of C# that will be used in the book.

2.1.1 Getting Started with C# and .Net

Microsoft Visual Studio .Net is a programming environment that supports multiple programming languages and multiple programming paradigms. As shown in Figure 2.1, in the first compilation step, a high-level language program is compiled to a low-level language called **intermediate language** (IL). The IL is similar in appearance to an assembly language. Programs in IL language are managed and executed by the **common**

language runtime (CLR). Similar to Java's bytecode, the purpose of IL is to make the CLR independent of the high-level programming languages.

Unlike the Java environment, the .Net Framework is language agnostic. Although C# is considered its flagship, the .Net Framework is not designed for a specific language. Developers are open to use the common Framework Class Libraries (FCL) and functionality of the environment, while coding their high-level application in the language of their choice. CLR is based on a generic type system, which makes it possible to support many different programming languages. Based on the type system, nearly any programming language, say X, can be easily integrated into the system. All one needs to do is to write a compiler that translates the programs of the X language into IL. The execution of IL programs is done by a just-in-time (JIT) compiler and the CLR. The JIT compiler uses a strategy of compile-when-used, and it dynamically allocates blocks of memory for internal data structures when each method is first called. In other words, JIT compilation lies between the complete compilation and statement-by-statement interpretation.

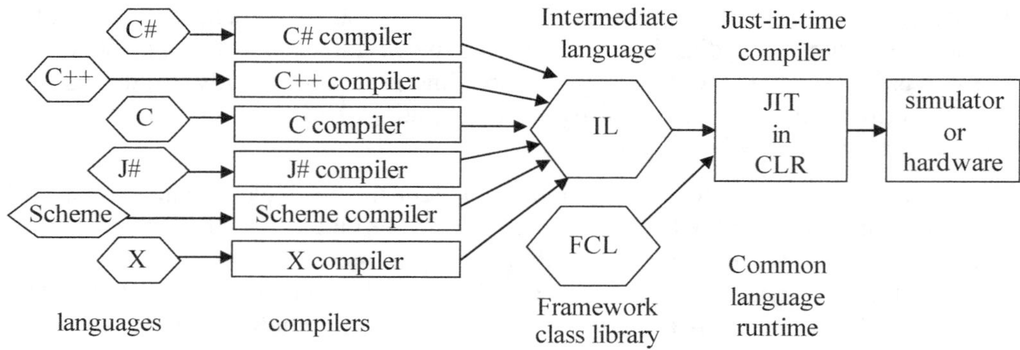

Figure 2.1. Microsoft's Visual Studio .Net programming environment

Now let us get started writing our first C# program that prints the string "Hello, World!"

```
using System;
public class MyFirstClass {
   public static void Main() {
      Console.WriteLine("Hello, World!");
   }
}
```

To execute this C# program on Visual Studio .Net, you can follow the following simple steps:

1. Start .Net from Windows "Start" menu.
2. Choose .Net menu "File - New - Project..." A "New Project" dialog box will pop up, in which you can choose different languages, including C/C++, J# (Java), and C#.
3. Once you have selected C# in the box on the left-hand side, you can further choose a template to facilitate the application you want to develop; for example:
    a. Choose "Console Application" to start a text and command line-based programming template.
    b. Choose "Windows Application" to start a forms-based application template, which allows you to define graphic user interfaces.
4. At the bottom of the same dialog box, you can choose a Name for your project, choose a Location (directory) where you want to save your project, and choose a Solution Name. You can put multiple projects in the same Solution.

A project template with appropriate libraries (depending on the template that you select) will be created. If you have selected C#, you can type your C# program in the file with the extension .cs that is created when you start a new project.

2.1.2 Comparison between C++ and C#

Compared to C++, the features of C# are much more similar to that of Java. Table 2.1 compares and contrasts the main features between C++ and C#. As can be seen, C# moves toward automatic management like Java, while trying to keep the C++ features where possible.

Table 2.1. Comparing and contrasting C++ and C# [*Java*] features

Feature	C++	C# [*Java*]
Main()	Global function outside any class	Public static function in a class
Use of library functions	Both header files (#include directives) and the **using** directive can be used	Header files may not be used. The **using** [**import**] directive is used to reference types/classes in other namespaces.
Preprocessor directives	Preprocessor directives and macros are allowed. A macro is an enforced inline function.	Preprocessor directives are allowed, but cannot create macros. Directives can be used for conditional compilation.
Global and static variables or functions	Both global and static variables and functions are allowed. Both acquire memory from static memory, but have different scope.	Global variables and functions are not allowed. They must be contained within a type declaration (such as class or struct). Static variables and functions are allowed.
Multiple inheritance	Multiple inheritance is allowed. Must use virtual classes to resolve the overlapped members.	A class can inherit implementation from one base class only. However, a class or an interface can implement multiple interfaces.
Override	Declaring override functions does not require the **override** keyword.	Declaring override methods requires the **override** keyword.
Garbage and destructor	No automatic garbage collector. Destructors are called automatically, but a programmer can call destructors.	There is an automatic garbage collector. Programmer cannot call the destructors.
Word length	Machine dependent. Minimum length guaranteed; for example, int type can be 16 bits and above.	Machine independent. Int type is always 32 bits. Integer types can also be written as Int16, Int32, and Int64.
Array declaration	The brackets "[]" appear following the array variable; for example, `int myArray[] = {1,2,7};` `int myArray = new int[8];`	The brackets "[]" appear following the array type; for example, `int[] myArray = new int[100];`
String	An array of characters with a terminator. Have to use library functions to compare strings.	A string type is defined. One can use `==` and `!=` to compare two string objects.
Pointer	Allowed	Pointers are allowed only in unsafe mode, e.g., `unsafe { swap(&x, &y); }`

Table 2.1. Comparing and contrasting C++ and C# [*Java*] features (continued)

Feature	C++	C# [*Java*]
switch statement	Support fall through from one case label to another. Use **break** to exit.	Does not support fall through from one case label to another.
foreach statement	Not supported	Used to iterate through arrays and collections.

Tables 2.2 and 2.3 list the data types supported in C/C++ and C#, respectively. Some of the data types in C/C++ are machine-dependent, and thus, the language standard specifies the guaranteed minimum ranges only; for example, the integer type int can take 16, 32, or 64 bits, depending on the computer architecture on which the language is implemented.

Table 2.2. Data types in C/C++

Type	Minimum bits	Minimum range
`bool` (C++ only)	1 (8)	`true/false`
`char`	8	from -127 to 127
`signed char`	8	from -127 to 127
`unsigned char`	8	from 0 to 255
`wchar_t` (C++ only)	16	from 0 to 65 535
`int`	16	from -32 768 to 32 768
`signed int`	16	same as `int`
`unsigned int`	16	from 0 to 65 535
`short int`	16	from -32 768 to 32 768
`signed short int`	16	same as `short int`
`unsigned short int`	16	same as `unsigned int`
`long int`	32	±2 147 483 647
`signed long int`	32	same as `long int`
`unsigned long int`	32	from 0 to 4 294 967 295
`float`	32	6 decimal digits of precision
`double`	64	10 decimal digits of precision

On the other hand, C# is running on a layer of virtual machine, the .Net framework. The size of all data types is machine independent. The type int is always 32 bits. To be more explicit, one can use Int32, instead. Particularly, a decimal type is included, which uses a small number of bits for the exponent part, while it uses many more bits for the fraction part of the floating-point number, resulting in a high precision type of numbers. Decimal type is often used in monetary types of computation.

2.1.3 Namespaces and the "using" Directive

A namespace is used to group a set of classes, and a "using namespace" is also used to quote the classes in the namespace as library functions to be used in a program. The following code segment shows the very basic code template for a C# program.

```
using <namespace>       // using existing namespace as library
namespace myNamespace1 // define my own namespace
class myclass1 {
   public static void Main() {
```

```
    ...
    }
class myclass2 {
    public double PiValue() {
    ...
    }
}
```

Header files in C/C++ do not exist in C#. Instead, namespaces are used to reference groups of libraries and classes. The first line of the code shows this application. Programmers can define their own namespaces, as shown in the second line of the code above, to group multiple classes together. One can define multiple namespaces in the same program to prevent naming conflicts; for example:

```
namespace VirtualStore {
    namespace Customer {
        //define customer classes
        class ShoppingCartOrder( ) { ... }
    }
    namespace Admin {
        //define administration classes
        class ReportGenerator( ) { ... }
    }
}
```

Table 2.3. Data types in C#

Data type	Description	bits	Data range	Example
`byte`	Short integer of 8 bits	8	0 thru 255 (2^8-1)	`byte b = 123;`
`int` `Int32`	Integer of 32 bits	32	-2^{31} thru 2^{31} -1	`int x;` `Int32 y = 200;`
`long` `Int64`	Integer of 64 bits	64	-2^{63} thru 2^{63} -1	`long x = 300;` `Int64 y;`
`float`	Real number, floating-point number	32	$\pm 3.4 * 10^{38}$ 7-decimal precision	`float z = 3.4;` `z = z + 5.1`
`double`	Double precision real number	64	$\pm 1.7 * 10^{308}$ 16-decimal precision	`double d = 3.000000001;`
`decimal`	Smaller data range, but much higher precision	128	$\pm 7.9 * 10^{28}$ 28-decimal precision	`decimal z = 3.0000004m;`
`char`	One Unicode character	16	0 thru 2^{16} -1	`char ch = 'A';`
`String`	Sequence of Unicode characters	16 each	Length determined when it is initialized using `new()`.	`string str = "Hello World";`
`bool`	Boolean	8	true or false	`bool flag;` `flag = true;`

A string in C# is an object, and a string variable is a reference to the object. We can use `""` to represent an empty string. This representation will require creating an object that does not contain any character. It is not efficient. For example, instead of using `string str = "";` we can use `string str = string.Empty;` which is more efficient, as the object is not created for an empty string. On the other hand, `string str = null;` is different. It means that the string variable (reference) is not pointed to any string. For example, if `str` is `""`, `str.length` is 0. However, if `str` is null, `str.length` will return an error.

The “using” directive tells the compiler where to find definitions for namespace class’s member methods that are used in the program as library functions; for example, using VirtualStore.

Furthermore, .Net Framework’s GUI functionality, the forms, can be accessed by using a directive that includes a namespace:

```
using System.Windows.Forms;
...
private Button Button1; // class Button is defined in System.Windows.Forms;
```

An alternative to using directives, as shown above, is to fully qualify each single reference in the program like this:

```
private System.Windows.Forms.Button Button1;
```

2.1.4 Class and Object in C#

Like Java, all C# programs require a unique program entry point, or Main method, implemented as a member method within a class. This differs from C++, where Main is a function that must be located outside any class. In C# programs, Main’s location is determined by the compiler, and it does not matter which class defines the Main. Main is required to be defined as static and may optionally receive arguments or return a value. An optional public access modifier notifies the C# compiler that anyone can call this member method. The required static keyword means that Main is called without requiring an object instantiation. Obviously, Main is the first method to be executed, and no other method can instantiate the Main.

A class is a user-defined type, a structural design, and a blueprint of functionality for variables (objects) of that type. A class consists of a list of members. Each member can be a data member (also called a variable) or a member function (also called a method). A special member function is called a constructor, which has the same name as the class name. A constructor is used to initialize the data members in the class and to pass values into the class, if the values will be used by multiple member functions. Other member functions are used to manipulate data members and to provide reusable functions for other classes to call.

The instances created from a class are called objects from the class. As an analogy, a class can be considered a cookie cutter, while the objects are cookies cut from the cutter. An object is accessed by named reference after the object is linked to the reference. Instantiating a class with the new function creates an instance or an object with information about member methods and other members allocated on the heap. For all OO languages, an object created by new function, including all its members defined inside a class, such as variables, constants, and methods, obtain the memory from the heap.

In C#, accessing static members of a class is accomplished, like Java, using class name and the “.” dot operator.

```
<className>.<memberName>
Console.WriteLine("Hello World!");
```

where memberName is a method call or a variable name, respectively.

Accessing the members of a reference object is also accomplished as it is in Java, with the “.” dot operator. In C++, the pointer operator “->” is used if the reference is a pointer.

```
<referenceName>.<memberName>
time.printStandard( );
```

where memberName is a method call or a variable name, respectively.

C++ offers a second way to define objects, not as reference types on the heap, but as local types on the stack. This is done by simply instantiating without the new function. In C#, the new keyword is the only way to create an object instance.

The class syntax can be described using the following syntax diagram, where the item in square brackets is optional.

```
[attributes][modifiers] class <className> [: baseClassName]
{
   [class-body]
}[;]
```

Attributes can be thought of as inline notes and declarative statements that the programmer can attach to a class, members, parameters, or other code elements. Through a library called **reflection**, this extra information can be retrieved and used by other code at run time. Attributes provide a generic means of associating information with declarations, a powerful tool in numerous scenarios.

The access **modifiers** public, protected, and private have equivalent semantic in C# and C++. Both C# and C++ will default to private if no access modifier is explicitly defined.

Other possible method modifiers include sealed, override, and virtual, as well as the class modifier abstract that deals with class inheritance functionality and scope.

In C++, programmers have the choice of defining class members inside the class declaration, or outside the class declaration with use of the scope-resolution operator. In C#, programmers must define all class members inside the curly brackets of that class. The simple idea of grouping related objects inside the same class is designed to create more modular bundles of code.

A key feature of OO programming is to decompose the application into multiple classes. One of the classes will contain the Main() method, while other classes will contain reusable members and methods.

Let us consider a program that helps a person to prepare for travel, including the computation of the amount of US dollars and local currency needed and local temperature converted into Fahrenheit. The program is decomposed into four classes, as shown in Figure 2.2.

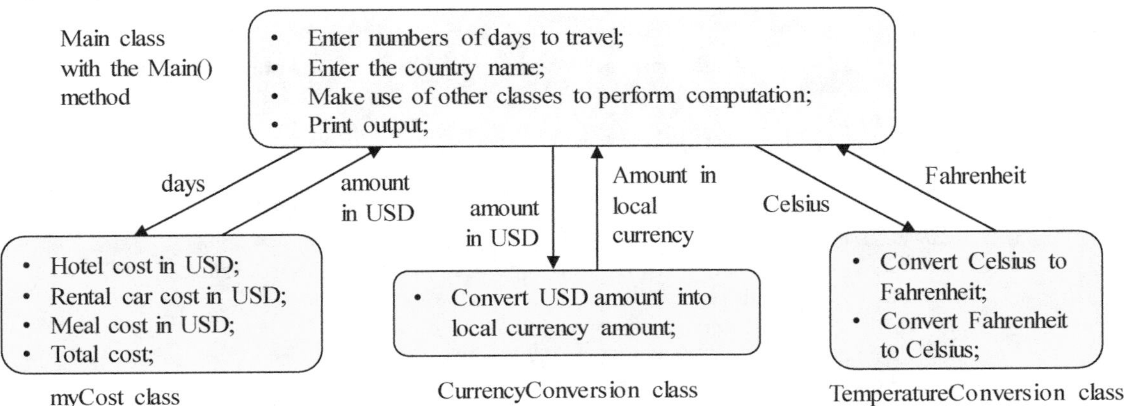

Figure 2.2. Problem decomposition into multiple classes

The sample code implementing the travel preparation is given as follows. A constructor with a parameter is given in the class myCost. Since the parameter is used by multiple member functions in the class, it is more productive to pass the parameter through the constructor. The parameter value will be passed to the object when the object is instantiated by the new function. On the other hand, we do not have to have a constructor for the other two classes: CurrencyConversion and TemperatureConversion. In these classes, the parameters are used by one member function only, and thus, we can pass the parameters directly to the member functions, instead of creating data members to hold the parameter values.

```
using System;
class TravelPreparation {   // Main Class
```

```
    static void Main(string[] args) {    // The main method
        Console.WriteLine("Please enter the number of days you will travel");
        String str = Console.ReadLine();     // read a string of characters
        Int32 daysToStay= Convert.ToInt32(str);          // Convert string to integer
        myCost usdObject = new myCost(daysToStay);   // Create an object
        int usdCash = usdObject.total(); // Call a method in the object
        Console.WriteLine("Please enter the country name you will travel to");
        String country = Console.ReadLine();
        CurrencyConversion exchange = new CurrencyConversion();
        Double AmountLocal = exchange.usdToLocalCurrency(country, usdCash);
        Console.WriteLine("The amount of local currency is: " + AmountLocal);
        Console.WriteLine("Please enter the temperature in Celsius");
        str = Console.ReadLine();
        Int32 celsius = Convert.ToInt32(str);
        TemperatureConversion c2f = new TemperatureConversion();
        Int32 fahrenheit = c2f.getFahrenheit(celsius);
        Console.WriteLine("Local temperature in Fahrenheit is: " + fahrenheit);
    }
}
class myCost {
    private Int32 days;            // Data member
    public myCost(Int32 daysToStay) { // Parameter passed into the class
        days = daysToStay;             // through the constructor, which is
    }                                  // used to initialize the data member
    private Int32 hotel() {
        return 100 * days;         // Parameter value used in all methods
    }
    private Int32 rentalCar() {
        return 30 * days;          // Parameter value used in all methods
    }
    private Int32 meals() {
        return 20 * days;   // Parameter value used in all methods
    }
    public Int32 total() {
        return hotel() + rentalCar() + meals();
    }
}
class CurrencyConversion  {
    public Double usdToLocalCurrency(String country, Int32 usdAmount)  {
        switch(country)  {
            case "Japan": return usdAmount * 117;
            case "EU": return usdAmount * 0.71;
            case "Hong Kong": return usdAmount * 7.7;
            case "UK": return usdAmount * 0.49;
            case "South Africa": return usdAmount * 6.8;
            default: return -1;
        }
    }
}
class TemperatureConversion {
    public Int32 getFahrenheit(Int32 c) {
        Double f = c * 9 / 5 + 32; return Convert.ToInt32(f);
    }
    public Int32 getCelsius(Int32 f) {
        Double c = (f - 32) * 5 / 9; return Convert.ToInt32(c);
    }
}
```

The classes used in this program are synthetic. When service-oriented computing is studied in the later chapters, we will show that we can access remote objects over the Internet, called web services, which provide real-time services, such as obtaining the temperatures of given locations, and actual currency exchange rates.

2.1.5 Parameters: Passing by Reference with ref & out

In C#, parameter passing by reference, or giving the receiving method access to permanently change the value in the caller, is done with the **ref** keyword, as seen in the example below:

```
using System;
class Point {
   public Point(int x) {
        this.x = x;
   }
   public void GetPoint(ref int x) {
        x = this.x;            // this.x refers to the class member
   }
   int x;
}
class Test {
   public static void Main() {
        Point myPoint = new Point(10);
        int x = 0;
        myPoint.GetPoint(ref x);       //x = 10
   }
}
```

C# offers a second way to pass parameters by reference, with the **out** keyword. The out keyword makes it possible to pass an uninitialized parameter by reference.

```
using System;
class Point {
   public Point(int x) {
        this.x = x;
   }
   public void GetPoint(out int x) {
        x = this.x;
   }
   int x;
}
class Test {
   public static void Main() {
        Point myPoint = new Point(10);
        int x;
        myPoint.GetPoint(out x);          //x = 10
   }
}
```

2.1.6 Base Class and Base Calling Class Constructor

C# takes after the C++ model for defining a parent class in the class header. Classes may inherit from one base class at most. The C# syntax for defining a base class and for calling the base class constructor might look like this:

```
class CalculatorStack: stack {
```

```
    public CalculatorStack(int n) :stack(n) {
    ... // other code here
    }
}
```

2.1.7 Constructor, Destructor, and Garbage Collection

Like C++, if the programmer does not define a constructor, C# creates a default constructor for each class. This ensures that the member variables of the class are set to appropriate default values, rather than pointing to random garbage. Multiple constructors can be overloaded for a class. Constructor header syntax includes the public modifier and the class name with zero or more parameters. Constructors are called automatically when the class object is instantiated, and they do not return a value.

In general, destructors release a reference an object holds to other objects. In C++, the programmer is responsible for implementing a class destructor to de-allocate heap memory after the object is no longer referenced. Without manual cleanup, memory leaks may ultimately crash the system. C# avoids this potential problem with automatic object cleanup and tracking of all memory allocation by the .Net Garbage Collector (GC). The GC is nondeterministic. It does not take up processor time by running constantly. It only runs when heap memory is low. There are some cases when the C# programmer wants to release resources manually; for example, when working with non-object resources such as a database connection or window handle. To ensure deterministic finalization, the Object.Finalize method can be overridden. C# does not have a delete function. Other than that small difference, overriding the Object.Finalize method has the same syntax and effect as using a C++ destructor, as shown in the code below.

```
public class DestructorExample{
    public DestructorExample( ){
        Console.WriteLine('Woohoo, object instantiated!');
    }
    ~DestructorExample( ){
        Console.WriteLine('Wow, destructor called!');
    }
}
```

2.1.8 Pointers in C#

C# supports the following pointer operations, which will appear familiar to C++ programmers:

& The address-of operator returns the memory address of the variable.

* The primary pointer operator is used in two scenarios:

1. to declare a pointer variable;
2. to dereference or access the value in the memory location the pointer points to.

-> The member access operator first gets the object the pointer points to, and then accesses a given member of that object. * can accomplish the same operation. These expressions equally access a member x of an object pointed to by pointer p: `(*p).x; p->x;`

Semantics for C/C++ pointers, as well as syntax for referencing and dereferencing their values, are upheld in C#. The main difference in C# is that any code using pointers needs to be marked as unsafe. The **unsafe** keyword is used as a modifier in the declarations of unsafe methods, and to mark blocks of code that call unsafe methods. Code written in the unsafe context is not explicitly unsafe—it simply allows the programmer to work with raw memory and sidestep compiler type checking. Unsafe code should not be confused with unmanaged code; the objects in unsafe code are still managed by the runtime and GC.

Pointers in C# can point to either value types (basic data types) or reference types. However, you can only retrieve the address of a value type. Another thing to note is, if you are working with the Visual Studio .Net, the code needs to be compiled with the unsafe compiler option.

This example illustrates pointers in C#:

```
public class MyPointerTest {
   unsafe public static void Swap( int *xVal, int *yVal) {
        int temp = *xVal;
        *xVal = *yVal;
        *yVal = temp;
   }
public static void Main(string[] args) {
   int x = 5;
   int y = 6;
   Console.WriteLine("Original Value: x = {0}, y = {1}", x, y);
   unsafe {
        Swap(&x, &y);
   }
        Console.WriteLine("New Value: x = {0}, y = {1}", x, y);
   }
}
```

The console outputs are:

```
Original Value: x = 5, y = 6
New Value: x = 6, y = 5
```

2.1.9 C# Unified Type System

C# uses a **unified type system** that makes the value of every data type an object. Reference types (complex types) and value types share the same roots through the base class System.Object. Value types have a minimum set of abilities inherited through this hierarchy. The following are all valid C# code examples:

```
5.ToString( )                  //Retrieves the name of an object
b.Equals( ) == c.Equals( )     //Compares two object references at runtime
w.GetHashCode( )               //Gets the hash code for an object
4.GetType( )                   //Gets the type of an object
```

Because all types inherit from objects, it is possible to use the dot (.) operator on value types without first wrapping the value inside of a separate wrapper class. This solves some of the inefficient code that OO programmers must write in C++ (and in Java) to wrap value types before using them like reference types.

In C++, if you want to create a method with a parameter that accepts any type, you have to write a wrapper class with overloaded constructors for each value type you want to support; for example:

```
class AllTypes {
public:
   AllTypes(int w);
   AllTypes(double x);
   AllTypes(char y);
   AllTypes(short z);
   //a constructor must be overloaded for each desired type
   //retrieving a value from this class would require overloaded functions
};
class CTypesExample {
   public Example(AllTypes& myType) {
   }
};
```

In C#, whenever a value type is used where an object type is required, the compiler will automatically box the value type into a heap-allocated wrapper. **Boxing** is the compiler process that converts a value type to a reference type. **Unboxing** is explicitly casting the reference type back to a value type.

Boxing and unboxing example 1

```
int v = 55;
Console.WriteLine ("Value is: {v}", v);
// Console.WriteLine accepts objects / references only.
// The compiler wraps value types automatically.
int v2 = (int) v;                              //Unboxing needs casting
```

Boxing and unboxing example 2:

```
int v = 55;
object x = v;      //explicitly box int value type v into reference type x
Console.WriteLine ("Value is: {0}", x); // Console.WriteLine accepts objects
```

Boxing a variable in fact generates a different variable. If you modified the original variable, it would not modify the boxed variable, as shown in the following code example:

```
class testBox {
   static void Main(string[] args) {
         int val = 55;
         object box = val;    //box int value val into reference type
         val = val * 2;             // modify the original variable
         Console.WriteLine ("val value is: {0}", val); // val = 55
         int va2 = (int)box; // unbox the object and put into va2
         Console.WriteLine("va2 value is: {0}", va2);  // va2 - 110
         // A different value will be printed
         // int va3 = box.val;     is INCORRECT: val is NOT a member of box
   }
}
```

A unified type system makes cross-language interoperability possible. Other benefits of the type system include guaranteed type safety, a security enhancement where each type in the system is tracked by the runtime. The overall effect is a safer and more robust code, with mainstream functionality creating a conceptually simpler programming model.

2.2 Memory Management and Garbage Collection

When a program is started, the operating system will allocate a segment of memory to the program. The memory allocated to a program is managed by the programming language environment (runtime system) and it is divided into three areas: **static**, **stack,** and **heap** areas, as shown in Figure 2.3.
The programmers can choose from which area to obtain memory by declaring their variables in different ways. In both C# and Java:

- All **static** variables obtain memory from the static memory. In other words, if we want to have memory from the static area for any variable, we can add the qualifier static before the variable declaration; for example, “static int s;” will declare a static integer variable. In C++, global variables are allowed, and all global variables (variables declared outside any functions) also obtain memory from static memory, whether the qualifier static is used or not.
- All non-static class variables will obtain memory dynamically from the heap when an object is created through the new() function.
- All non-static local variables within a method obtain memory from the stack. This stack is also called **program runtime stack** to differentiate from other possible stacks used in the computer system.

Now the question is, what difference will it make to a programmer by using these different memory areas? This question will be answered in the following subsections.

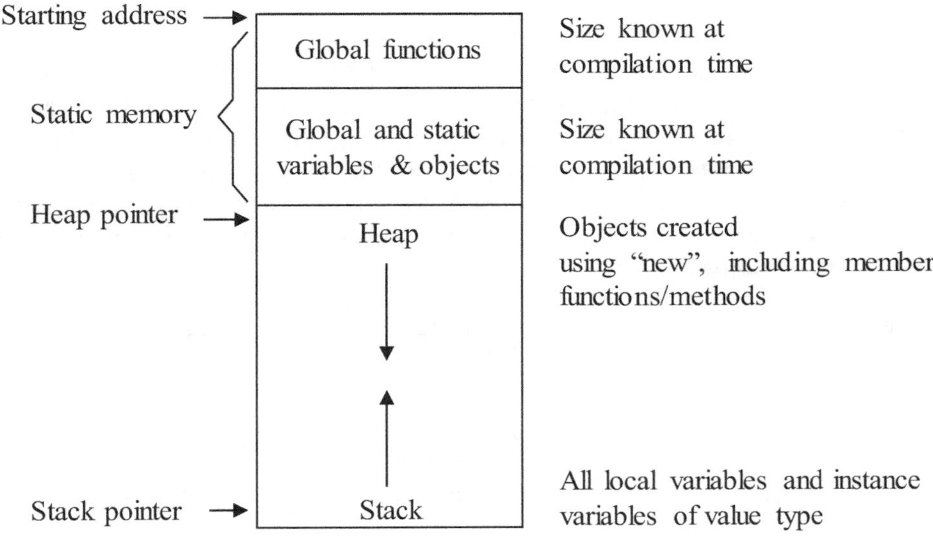

Figure 2.3. Partition of the memory allocated to a program

2.2.1 Static Variables and Static Methods

Consider a static variable of a class. Memory is allocated to the variable statically, that is, during the compilation stage (before the program is executed). There is one copy of the memory only for each static variable, no matter how many objects are created from the class. Changes made to a static variable in one object will change the variable's value in other objects. A static variable will go out of scope only if the program is terminated.

Why do we need a static local variable? We need static variables to hold the values that can be shared among different objects; for example, we can define a static variable "counter" to count how many times a resource has been accessed by different objects. The following function shows an example in which a static variable is used to count how many users have successfully logged into an area where access is restricted.

```
void login() {
   static int counter = 0;  // will be initialized only once
   readId_pwd( );
   if (verified( ))
        counter++;          // count the # of users logged in
}
```

One can declare a **static method**. A static method can be called without creating an object that contains the method, while a non-static method can be called only after an object is created. A static method is called by className.methodName, while a non-static method is called by referenceName.methodName.

2.2.2 Runtime Stack for Local Variables

Local variables are variables declared within a method. When the control enters a method, a block of memory (called a **stack frame**) is created on the stack. All non-static local variables obtain memory from the stack frame. When the control leaves the method, all these local variables are freed, and the contents of these variables are no longer valid (no longer accessible).

The stack memory allocation is illustrated in the example in Figure 2.4. As shown in the left part of Figure 2.4, the program consists of two methods. The Main method has one local variable i. The method bar has two local variables j and k. Please note that the formal parameter of a method is a local variable to the method.

The state (0) shows the initial state of the stack before the Main method is executed. When the control enters the Main method, the local variable i obtains the memory on the top of the stack, as shown in stack state (1). The value of i is initialized to 0 and then incremented to 1. Then i is passed as the actual parameter to the method bar. When the control enters the method bar, the two local variables j and k obtain memory on the top of the stack, as shown in state (2). The value of i is passed to the formal parameter j. Please note that j and i have different memory locations. j has a copy of i's value. When j is modified in the method bar, the modification has no impact on variable i.

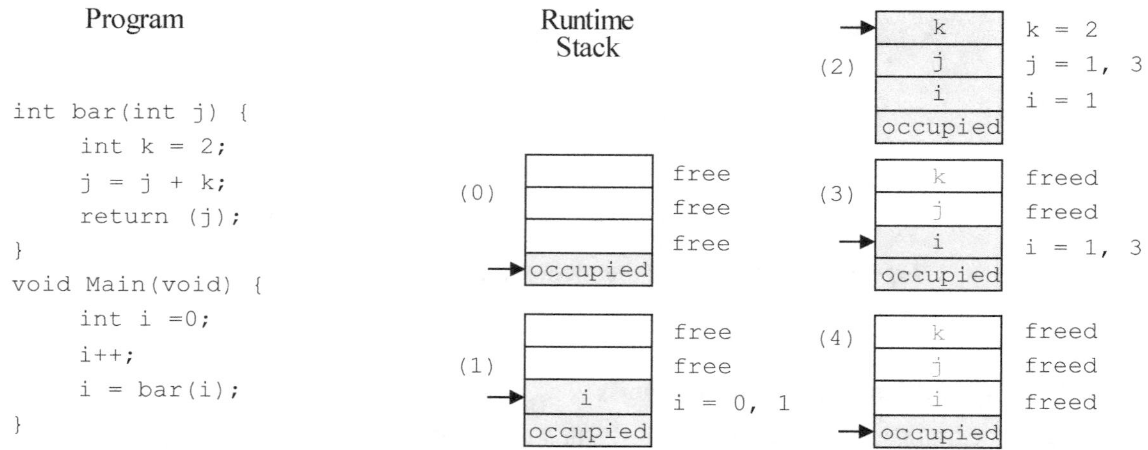

Figure 2.4. A simple program and its runtime stack

When the control exits method bar, variables j and k go out of scope. The stack pointer returns to its original position before it entered the method. The memory used for variables j and k is thus freed, as shown in stack state (3). Therefore, we cannot access j and k outside the method. Finally, when the control exits the Main method, variable i is also freed and stack pointer returns to its position before it entered the Main method, as shown in state (4) in Figure 2.4.

Since local variables are automatically garbage-collected by the runtime stack when they go out of scope, there is no need for programmers to explicitly return the memory to the system.

Having understood the stack used to allocate memory for local variables, we can easily understand how recursive methods are implemented. In fact, no special mechanism is needed. The stack that handles all local variables handles the variables in recursive methods, too.

Let us examine the following recursive method fac(n). There are two local variables in the method: the formal parameter n and a temporary variable fac that holds the return value from (n-1)th iteration. Figure 2.5 shows the runtime stack before and during the execution of the recursive method fac(3).

```
using System;
namespace myNamespace1 {
    class stackExample {
        static void Main(string[] args) {
            int i = 3, j;
            j = fac(i);
            Console.WriteLine("j = {0}", j);
```

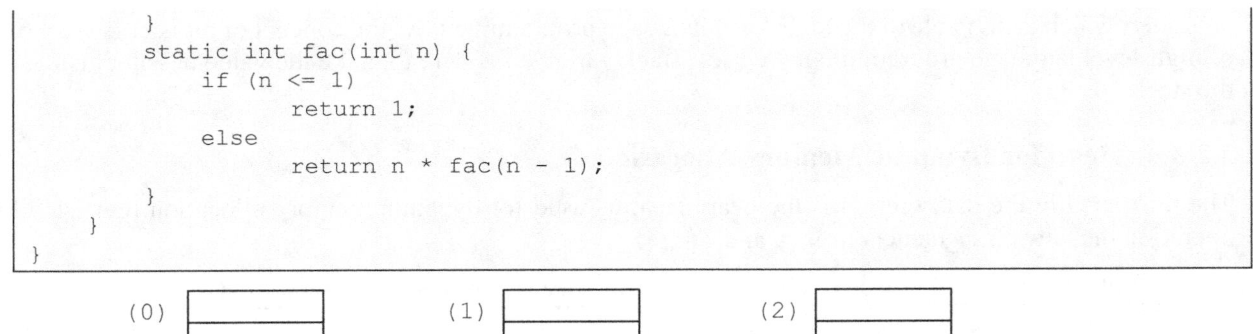

```
    }
    static int fac(int n) {
        if (n <= 1)
                return 1;
        else
                return n * fac(n - 1);
    }
  }
}
```

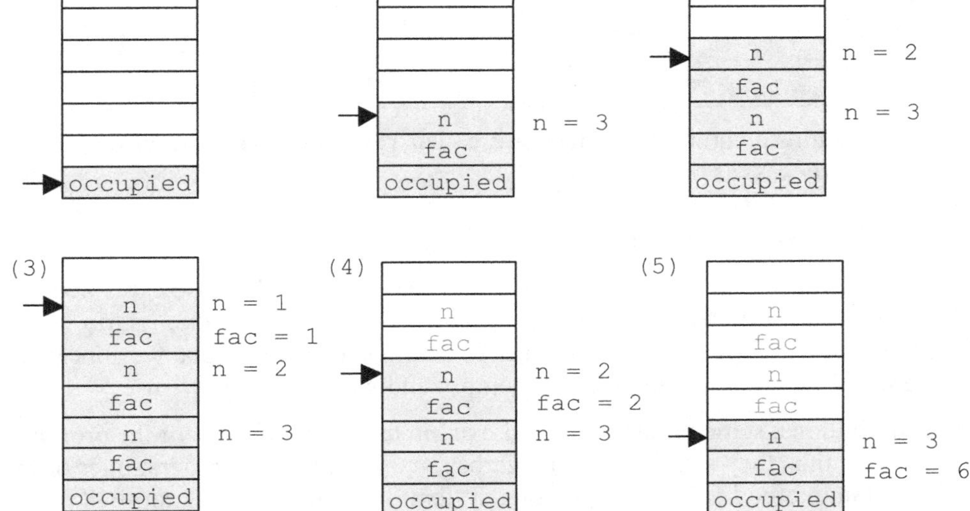

Figure 2.5. The runtime stack of a recursive program

State (0) is the state before the method fac(3) is called. When the control enters the method fac(n) for the first time, the two local variables n and fac obtain memory on the stack, as shown in state (1). Formal parameter n is initialized to the actual parameter 3, but variable fac is not given a value yet. Within the first iteration, fac(n-1) is called and the method is reentered. Again, the two local variables obtain memory from the stack. Now, n is initialized to the actual parameter value 2 and fac is not given a value, as shown in state (2) in Figure 2.5. The variables n and fac in the second iteration are different from n and fac in the first iteration, although they happen to have the same names. Since they have different scopes, they are considered different variables.

Within the second iteration, fac(n-1) is called again. In this iteration, n is initialized to 1 and the condition (n <= 1) is true. Now the method fac(1) is actually completed. It was not complete before. Now a value is returned to fac in this iteration, as shown in state (3). The return of iteration 3 completes the method call fac(1) in iteration 2 and the return value fac = 1 is passed into iteration 2. The operation n*fac(1) then will produce a value 2, as shown in state (4). The return value 2 will, in turn, be passed to iteration 1 and produces a value 6, as shown in state (5) in Figure 2.5. When the final iteration is completed, the fac(n) method exits and the stack pointer will return to its original state(0).

If you compare the recursive method call here and the ordinary method call in the previous example, you can see that the processes of variable allocation on the stack are handled exactly in the same way.

In fact, at the assembly language (or machine code) level, the variable fac used to hold the return value is not on the stack. Instead, a register is used. A register can be considered a global variable used by the compiler, which is invisible to the high-level language programmers. As the concept of register is not a part of high-level language programming, we use a stack variable fac here to make the value passing visible on the stack.

2.2.3 Heap for Dynamic Memory Allocation

The third area in the data section is the heap. Heap is used for dynamic memory allocation requested by operation the new class_name() in Java and C#.

For example, the following piece of code acquires memory for an object of Invoice class.

```
class Invoice { // define a class
   float price;
   int phone;
};
Invoice p = new Invoice();
```

The data types that acquire memory from heap are called **reference types** because their variables take memory addresses (references) as their values.

2.2.4 Scope and Garbage Collection

So far, we explained when we should use static, stack, and heap memory. We also explained how we acquire memory from static, stack, and heap areas. The last question we need to answer is, do we need to worry about garbage collection? In other words, do we need to de-allocate memory that we allocated? The answer to the question depends on where we acquire the memory and what language we use.

According to the definitions, static variables should exist in the entire lifetime of the program (even when they are invisible), and thus they should never be garbage-collected by the programmer or by the runtime system. When the Main method exits, the operating system that starts the program will reclaim the entire memory segment allocated to the program. Thus, if a variable or method is static, we do not need to worry about collecting its memory.

If a variable obtains its memory from the stack, the memory will be de-allocated automatically by the system. As we explained before, when the control enters a method, local variables or objects obtain memory from the stack. When the control exits the method, the stack pointer moves back to the original position when it entered the method, that is, the memory allocated to the local variables is returned to the stack. This memory de-allocation is managed by the scope rule of the language: the scope of a variable starts from the declaration and ends at the end of the block. When a variable goes out of scope, the memory allocated to the variable returns to the system.

However, if variables or objects acquire their memory from the heap, it is much more complex. Java uses a complex automatic garbage collector to de-allocate the unused memory. C# uses an automatic garbage collector for the managed code. For the unmanaged code, manual (explicit) de-allocation of heap memory is required. In C++, all heap memory requires manual garbage collection.

Table 2.4 summarizes the memory allocation, de-allocation mechanisms, and the applications of static, stack, and heap memory.

Table 2.4. Summary of memory management

Memory	Allocation	De-allocation	Application
Static	Class variables or local variables with static prefix	De-allocated by the system when the main function exits	Unique copy in global or local context
Stack	Local variables declared in a method	De-allocated by the system when the method exits	Temporary variable used in a method
Heap	Use new operator	Use automatic or manual garbage-collection	Variables that should never go out of scope unless deleted or garbage-collected

2.3 General Issues in Multitasking and Multithreading

This section discusses the general issues in multitasking and multithreading, including parallel processing, synchronization, deadlock, and order of executions. These topics are the foundation of distributed computing paradigm.

2.3.1 Basic Requirements

Multitasking in operating systems (OS) and multithreading in application programs are similar, providing the ability to execute different parts of a code simultaneously, while maintaining the correct results of computation.

In the OS case, the parts of code executed in parallel are called **processes** or **tasks** and are often semantically independent of each other (but can be related). OS performs process scheduling and resource (processors, memory, peripherals, and so on) allocation. OS system calls allow users to create, manage, and synchronize processes. In the case of the application program, the parts of code executed in parallel are called **threads**. More often, they are semantically dependent (but can be independent).

In both cases, software developers must carefully design the OS/application in such a way that all the processes/threads can run at the same time without interfering with each other, and produce the same result in a finite amount of time no matter in what order they are executed.

We differentiate a program from a process and a function (method) from a thread. A program or a function (method) is a piece of code written by a programmer, which is static, while a process or thread consists of an executing program/function, its current values, state information, and the resources used for supporting its execution, which include the dynamic factors when it is executed. In other words, a process or thread is a dynamic entity, which exists only when a program or a method is being executed.

To execute multiple processes/threads truly in parallel, multiple processors must exist. If only one processor exists in the system, multiple processes/threads appear to execute simultaneously, but actually execute sequentially in time-sharing mode.

From the same piece of code, multiple processes/threads can be created. The code and data contained within different processes/threads are, by default, separated: each has its own copy of executable code, its own stack for local variables, and its own data area for objects and other data elements.

Typically, a distributed OS can consist of multiple instances or replicas on different computers, each of which can manage multiple processes. Again, each process can be a multithreading program consisting of multiple threads, as shown in Figure 2.6.

2.3.2 Critical Operations and Synchronization

Processes/threads can have shared resources or objects. Accesses to the shared resources are called **critical operations** and need to be carefully managed and synchronized to prevent; for example, simultaneous read and write, which can cause incorrect and nondeterministic behaviors. A simple way of synchronization is to lock a resource before accessing it. Figure 2.7 shows a scenario in which two travel agencies see the same seat in a flight, and a double booking is made due to the lack of synchronization. A simple solution to this problem is to lock the object (seat) before reserving it so that other agents cannot access the object while being locked. Although a simple lock can prevent the shared resources being accessed simultaneously, it also eliminates the possibility of parallel processing. A more thoughtful implementation is not to lock the parallel read operations, while locking the parallel read-write and write-write combinations.

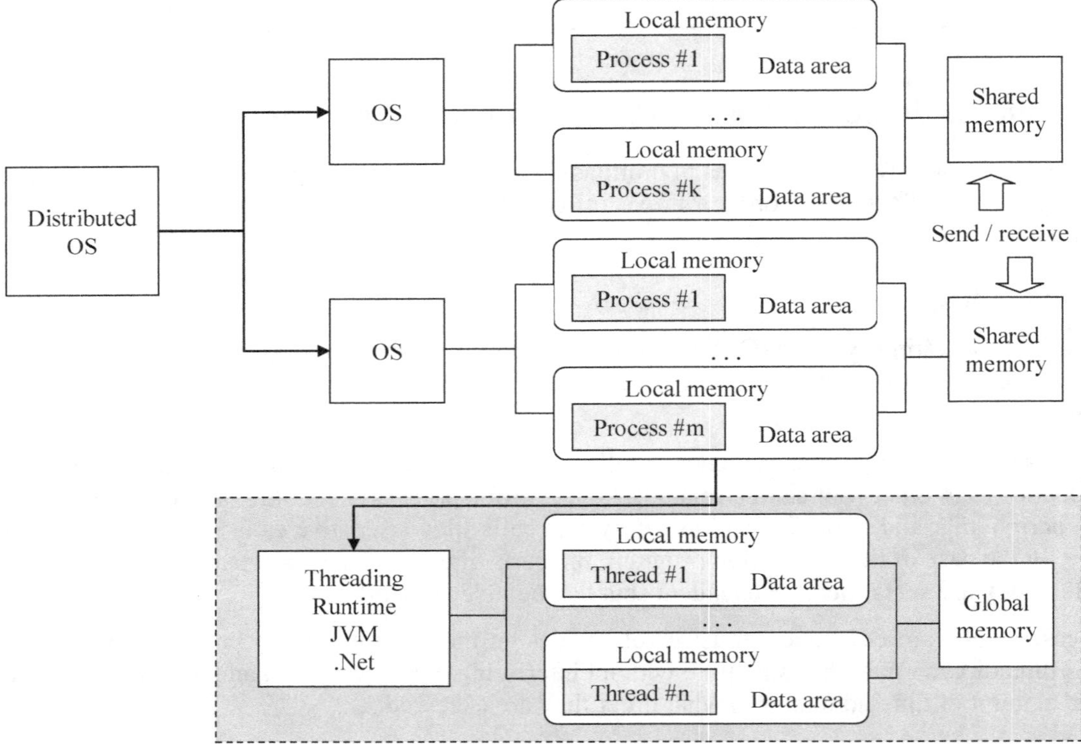

Figure 2.6. Multitasking and multithreading

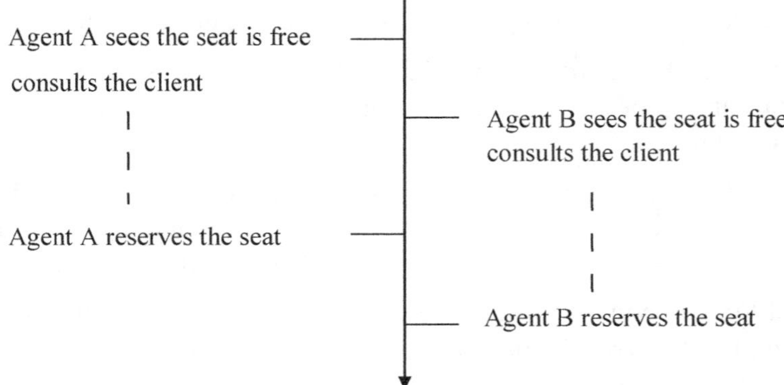

Figure 2.7. Lack of synchronization resulting in double booking

Figure 2.8 shows a more complex example where a Producer and two Consumer threads share the same buffer of multiple cells. The Producer continuously puts the items into the buffer until the buffer is full, while the Consumers continuously take items from the buffer until the buffer is empty. How can we write a program to simulate the problem that allows the Producer and the Consumers to write and read the buffer in parallel without causing a synchronization problem?

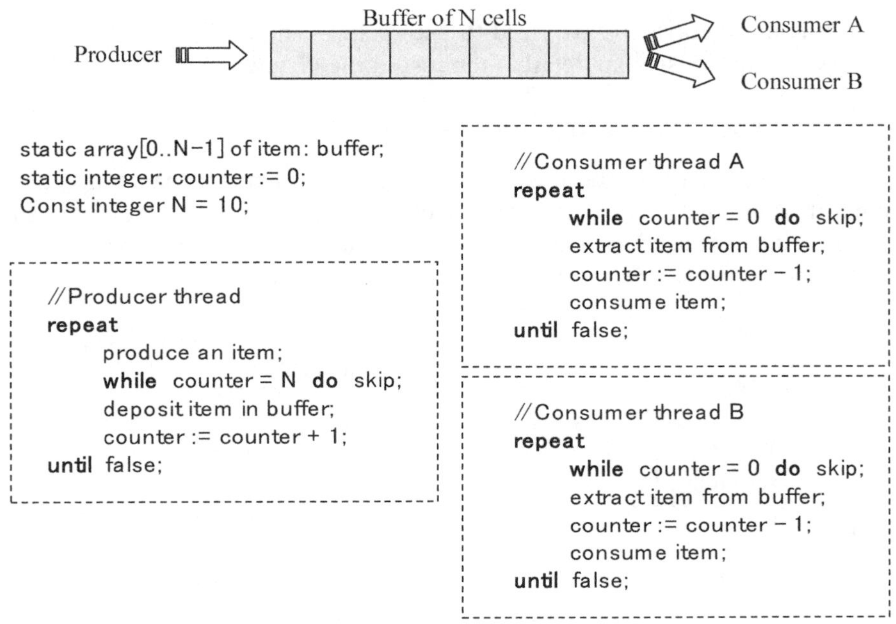

Figure 2.8. An attempt to solve the Producer and Consumer problem.

We can use three threads to simulate the Producer and the Consumers and use a global (or static) array of items (e.g., integers) to simulate the buffer of N cells, as shown in Figure 2.8. The pseudocode shows a possible solution to the problem.

Does the pseudocode correctly solve the problem? The code uses a shared variable counter to make sure that the Producer cannot deposit items into the Buffer if the Buffer is full (counter = N), and the Consumers cannot take items from the Buffer if the Buffer is empty (counter = 0). This is in fact the logic of the Producer–Consumer problem, and it does not solve the synchronization problem that could occur in a distributed computing system. Let us examine the following scenario:

1. The counter value is 5, and the Producer thread is executing the statement "counter = count + 1;" It obtains the value of counter and adds one to the counter to make it 6.
2. Before the new value 6 is written back into the variable counter, the Producer thread is interrupted for one of the following reasons: quantum (time slice) value expired, a higher priority process arrives and OS assigns the processor to the newly arrived process, or an exception occurs and the processor has to handle the exception.
3. A Consumer thread is assigned the processor, and it decreases the counter value from 5 to 4.
4. The Producer thread regains the processor and it starts from the point where it is interrupted – It writes the value 6 into the counter – An incorrect value is given to the counter.

Let us consider another scenario:

1. The counter value is 1 and the Consumer A thread extracts the only item from the buffer.
2. Before Consumer A performs "counter = counter -1;" the thread is interrupted, and Consumer B thread obtains the processor. It still sees the counter value is 1 and thus, it extracts an item from the buffer that does not exist. In fact, the buffer is an array and the value will be read twice, which is a logic error.

To implement multithreading correctly, we need to use proper synchronization mechanisms provided by the language, which will be discussed in detail in the rest of the chapter.

2.3.3 Deadlock and Deadlock Resolving

Another major issue in distributed computing is the deadlock problem. A deadlock is a situation wherein two or more competing operations are waiting for the other to finish, and thus neither ever does. A typical situation is: two or more threads need more than one resource to proceed, and each holds one resource while waiting for other threads to release the resources, as shown in Figure 2.9.

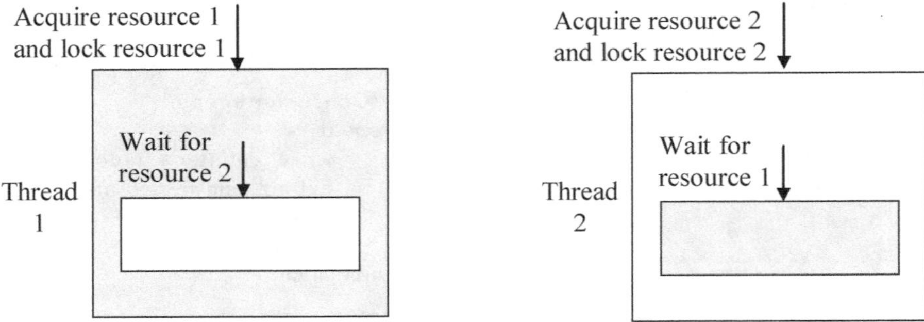

Figure 2.9. A scenario of deadlock

A classic problem of deadlock is the **Dining Philosophers Problem**: Five philosophers are thinking and eating. They share a round table with five bowls and five chopsticks. Thinking is independent. When eating, they share the chopsticks with their two neighbors, with the restriction that a philosopher may pick up only one chopstick at a time, as shown in Figure 2.10.

Three techniques can be used to resolve the deadlock problems:

1. **Deadlock prevention**: use an algorithm that can guarantee that no deadlock can occur.
2. **Deadlock avoidance**: use an algorithm that will anticipate that a deadlock is likely to occur and therefore refuse a resource request.
3. **Deadlock detection and recovery**: use an algorithm to detect the occurrence of a deadlock and force the threads to release the resources that are on hold while waiting.

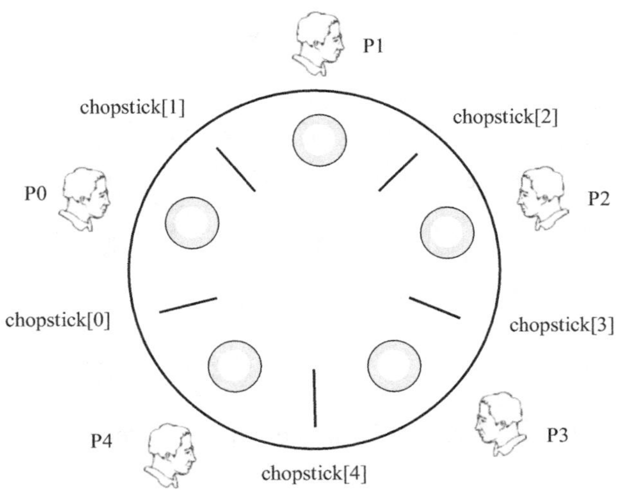

Figure 2.10. Dining Philosophers Problem

Deadlock is not the only problem. Livelock and starvation are two related problems that can occur.

Livelock is a condition that occurs when two or more threads continually change their state in response to the changes of other threads. The result is that none of the threads will obtain the resources to complete its task; for example, two threads try to acquire a lock at the same time, sleep for the same amount of time if the lock is on, then wake up and try to acquire the lock again at the same time. An analogy is when two persons meet in a hallway. Each tries to step aside to let the other person through, but they end up swaying from side to side, getting in each other's way as they try to get out of the way. Different from deadlock, where the resources are held, the resources in the livelock are still free. To avoid livelock, different waiting times should be used; for example, Ethernet uses the CSMA/CD protocol with binary exponential backoff to avoid livelock:

- Before sending, a node on Ethernet listens to the bus and sends if the bus is free;
- If a collision occurs, it waits for a random time:
  - by the 1st collision, wait 0 or 1 slot of time;
  - by 2nd collision, wait 0, 1, 2, or 3 slots;
  - by 3rd collision, wait 0, 1, 2, 3, 4, 5, 6, or 7 slots;
  - by 4th collision, wait 0, 1, 2, 3, ..., or 15 slots;
  - ...
  - by nth collision, wait 0, 1, 2, 3, ..., or 2^{n-1} slots.

Starvation: A thread is theoretically able to gain access to the shared resource (lock), but practically unable to gain regular access and is unable to make progress. This is more likely to occur, when the threads are given priorities, and there are too many threads with high priority. The threads with low priority may starve. One of the solutions is to change the priority of threads dynamically. The longer a thread waits, the higher the priority of the thread will become.

2.3.4 Order of Execution

Threads can represent different action takers, and we may put different requirements, such as order of execution, on the threads. Synchronization prevents multiple threads from accessing the same resource simultaneously, but it does not care which thread accesses the resource first or in what particular order; for example, we can define an order to let the Producer fill the entire Buffer before allowing the Consumers to take items from the Buffer. We can also make the two Consumers take turns taking the items from the Buffer.

Consider another example. We want to write a multithreading program to simulate the matches of table tennis. We need to define the order of the execution; for example, A1-B2-A2-B1-A1-...-B1, as shown in Figure 2.11.

Coordinating the execution order of the threads needs a different mechanism and we will further discuss this topic in a later section and with programming examples.

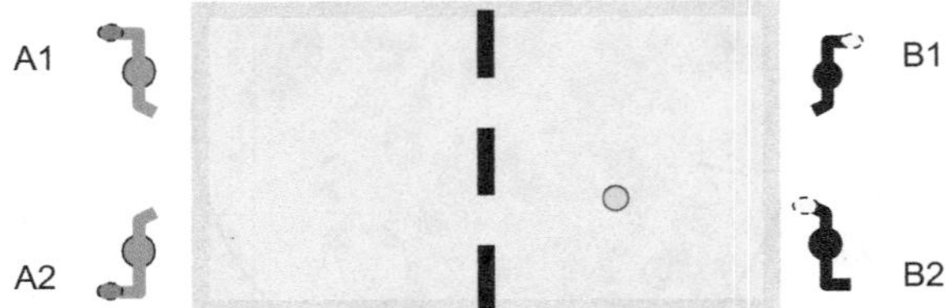

Figure 2.11. Defining the order of execution

2.3.5 Operating System Support for Multitasking and Multithreading

Most operating systems support multitasking programming; for example, in Unix, several system calls are provided for users to start parallel processes.

```
int fork( );
```

is a Unix system call for starting a new process. When fork() is executed in a process, it creates a new (child) process, which is basically a copy of its parent process: The same program code, including the fork() statement, status, user-data, and system-data segments, will be copied. The only difference is that the two processes (parent and child) will receive different return values from the system call fork().

The child receives a 0 return value, whereas the parent receives the process-ID of the child. If the parent receives "-1" value, an error has occurred in creating a child process. fork() has no arguments, the caller could not have done anything wrong. The only cause of an error is resource exhaustion (e.g., out of memory). In the exception handling, the parent process may want to wait a while (with a sleep call) and try later again.

Another Unix system that usually works with fork() in tandem is the exec(parameters). Usually, the child process executes an exec(parameters) system call after the return of fork(), whereas the parent either waits for the child to terminate or goes off to do something else. Figure 2.12 shows a typical use of fork() and exec(parameters).

The exec(parameters) system call reinitializes the child process from the given program and data files in the parameters. The steps of the creation and reinitialization of the new process are marked on the lower part of the diagram in Figure 2.12.

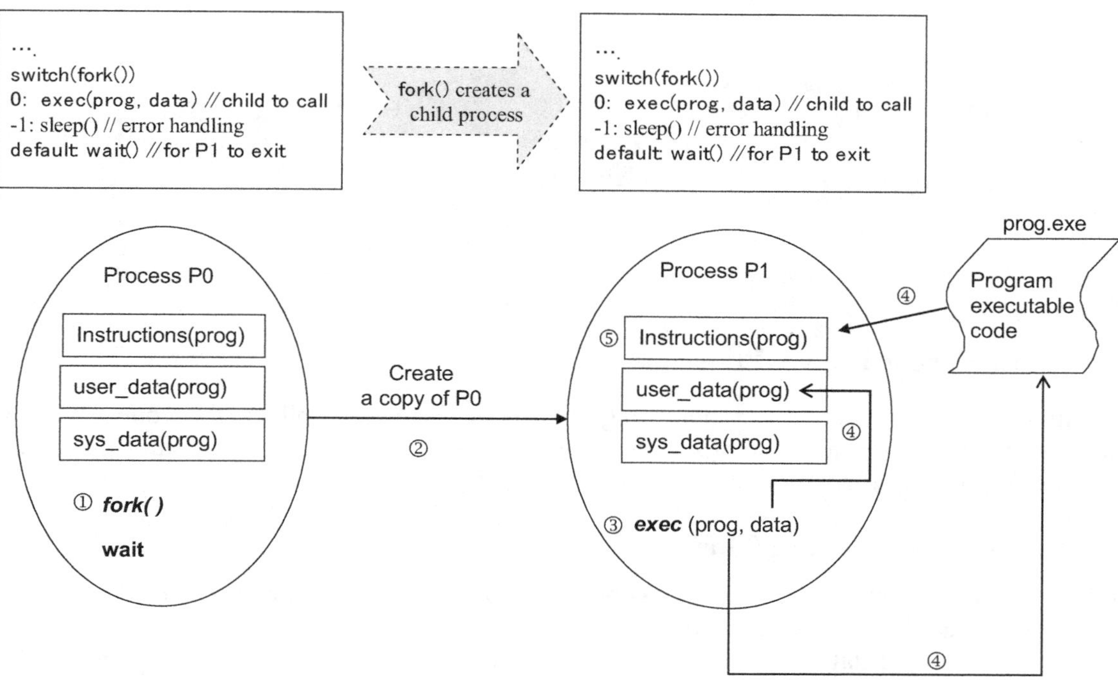

Figure 2.12. A typical application of system calls fork() and exec()

Different versions of the system call are used to facilitate different parameter formats. Below are C specifications of two versions of the system call:

```
// Version 1: list all parameters
int execl(path, arg0, arg1, ..., argn, null )
   char *path;       // path (location) of program file
   char *arg0;       // first argument (program file)
   char *arg1;       // second argument
   . . .
   char *argn;       // last argument
   char *null;       // null indicates end of arguments
// Version 2: Use a file name and an array as the parameters
int execvp(file, argv )
   char *file;       //program file name
   char *argv[ ];    // pointer to the array of arguments
```

The following C program shows a simplified design of a command line interpreter (CLI), which waits for a command to be entered, and starts the program associated with the command as a child process of itself:

```
#include <fcntl.h> // Command Line Interpreter
static void main (int argc, char *argv[ ]) {
   while (TRUE) { // read, execute a command and wait for termination
        read_command(argv);
        // read command name in argv[0] and data in argv[1] ... argv[argc-1]
        switch(fork()) {
           case -1:
              printf("Cannot create new process \n");
              break;
           case 0:
              execvp (argv[0], argv);
              // The execvp function should never return. If it returns
              printf("Cannot execute \n"); // an error must have occurred
```

```
            break;
        default:     // CLI process itself will come to this case
            if (wait(NULL) == -1)
            printf("Cannot execute wait system call \n");
            // Parent process receives the PID of child process
            // and then waits for the termination of child
        }
    }
}
```

2.4 Multithreading in Java

This section discusses creating and managing threads in Java, as well as the communication and synchronization among threads. The programs shown in this section can be executed using J# and .Net, Eclipse, or other Java programming environments.

2.4.1 Creating and Starting Threads

The Java programming environment supports multithreading program through a Thread class, which is defined in the Standard Java libraries, with the methods: start, run, wait, sleep, notify, notifyAll, and so on. Figure 2.13 illustrates the state transitions controlled by these methods, as well as by the events and system functions such as dispatch, quantum expiration, block by accessing a locked object, unblock after an object is unlocked, and completion.

Java provides two ways to create a new thread: Extending the Thread class and implanting the Runnable interface.

- Extending the Thread class:
    - Inherit the Thread class;
    - Override the run() method;
    - Create a thread with new MyThread(...);
    - Start the thread by calling the start() method;
- Implanting the Runnable interface:
    - Implement the Runnable interface;
    - Override the run() method.;
    - Create a thread with new Thread(runnable);
    - Start the thread by calling the start() method.

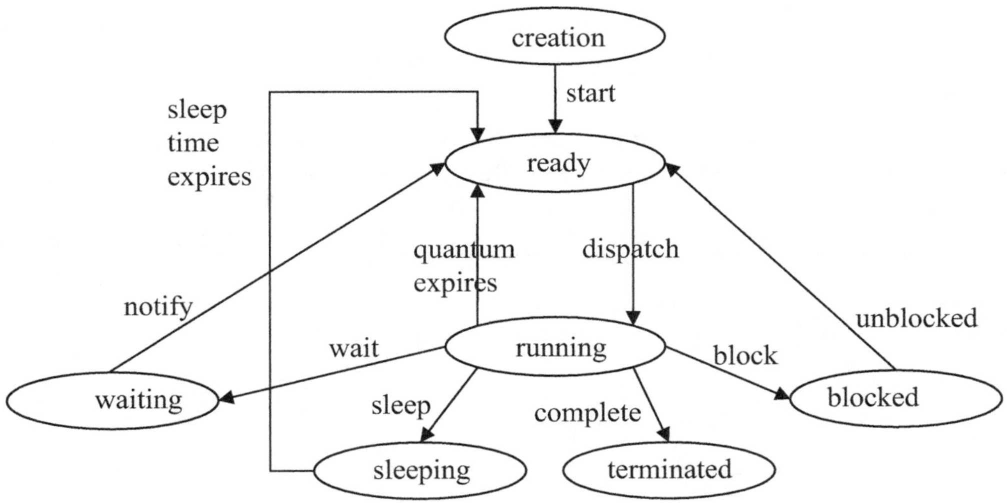

Figure 2.13. State transition diagram of Java threads

Using the first method, for each thread that you want to create, you define a class that extends the Thread class. A run() method must be defined in this class as the entry point of the thread, just like the Main() method serves as the entry point of a program. You can define multiple classes, each with a run() method, but you can only define one class with the Main() method. The following program shows an example in which two Thread classes and one Main class are defined. In the Main class, each Thread class is used to create two threads. A thread is created just like an object is created. A thread starts to execute when the start() method in the Thread class is called. The process of creating and starting a thread is similar to that of creating and starting a process in OS, as discussed in the previous section.

```
class myThread1 extends Thread {
   // other members
   public void run() {
        // do something in this thread
   }
}
class myThread2 extends Thread {
   // other members
   public void run() {
        // do something else in this thread
   }
}
public class TestMyThreads {      // main class
   public static void main ( String args[] ) {
        myThread1 threadA = new myThread1();  // creating a thread
        myThread1 threadB = new myThread1();
        myThread2 threadC = new myThread2();
        myThread2 threadD = new myThread2();
        threadA.start();                          // starting a thread
        threadB.start();
        threadC.start();
        threadD.start();
   }
}
```

Extending the Thread class has a limitation in creating threads. Since Java does not support multiple inheritance, that is, Java class can extend one class only, you cannot extend the Thread class if your class has already extended a class.

In this case, you can declare a class that implements the Runnable interface. Then in this class, you write a run() method to implement the functionality of your thread. An instance of the class can then be allocated, passed as an argument when creating the thread and being started. The following program shows an example in which both extending the Thread class and implementing the Runnable interface are illustrated.

```
class myThread1 extends Thread { // Using extends Thread
   int myID;
   myThread1(int id) {              // constructor
        myID = id;
   }
   public void run() {
        for (int i = 1; i < 5; i++) {
              int second = (int)(Math.random() * 500);
              try {
                   Thread.sleep(second);
              }
              catch (InterruptedException e) { }
              System.out.println("myThread1-id" + myID + ": " + i);
        }
   }
} //end class myThread1
class myThread2 implements Runnable { // Using implements Runnable
   int myID;
   myThread2(int id) {
        myID = id;
   }
   public void run() {
        for (int j = 1; j < 5; j++) {
              try {
                   Thread.sleep((int)(Math.random() * 500));
              }
              catch (InterruptedException e) { }
              System.out.println("myThread2-id" + myID + ": " + j*j);
        }
   }
} //end class myThread2
public class testMyThreads {
   public static void main(String[] args) {
        Thread t1 = new myThread1(1);                   // extends Thread
        Thread t2 = new Thread(new myThread1(2));       // implements Runnable
        Thread t3 = new Thread(new myThread2(3));       // implements Runnable
        Thread t4 = new Thread(new myThread2(4));       // implements Runnable
        t1.start();
        t2.start();
        t3.start();
        t4.start();
   }
} //end testMyThreads
```

From the two examples above, one can see that multiple instances of a thread can be created and started. This is a common application of threading; for example, you can define a Producer thread and a Consumer thread. Then, you can create a Producer–Consumer problem with multiple Producers and Consumers. Creating multiple threads from a single Thread class is called **spawning** a thread.

You can set a priority to a thread, which is a number between 1 and 10. Three constants (macros) are also defined in the Thread class: MIN_PRIORITY, NORM_PRIORITY, and MAX_PRIORITY, corresponding to the priority levels 1, 5, and 10, respectively. By default (without setting the priority), a thread will have the NORM_PRIORITY. If all threads have the same priority, they will be served in the first-in-first-out manner in the waiting, blocked, and ready queues. However, if threads are given different priorities, the threads with higher priorities will be placed before the threads with lower priorities, regardless of their arrival time.

Where highlighted, the following piece of code shows setting different priorities to the four threads before starting them. During the execution of the thread, the priority level is read and printed.

```
class myThread1 extends Thread {          // Using extends Thread
   int myID;
   myThread1(int id) {                    // constructor
      myID = id;
   }
   public void run() {
      for (int i = 1; i < 5; i++){
            int second = (int)(Math.random() * 500);
            try { Thread.sleep(second); }
            catch (InterruptedException e) { }
            System.out.print("myThread1-id " + myID + ": " + i);
            System.out.println(" my priority is " + getPriority());
      }
   }
} //end class myThread1
class myThread2 extends Thread {    // Using extends Thread
   int myID;
   myThread2(int id){
      myID = id;
   }
   public void run() {
      for (int j = 1; j < 5; j++) {
            try {
                  Thread.sleep((int)(Math.random() * 500));
            }
            catch (InterruptedException e) { }
            System.out.print("myThread2-id " + myID + ": " + j);
            System.out.println("my priority is " + getPriority());
      }
   }
} //end class myThread2
public class testMyThreadsPriority
{
   public static void main(String[] args) {
      Thread t2 = new myThread1(12);
      Thread t1 = new myThread1(11);
      Thread t3 = new myThread2(21);
      Thread t4 = new myThread2(22);
      t1.setPriority(Thread.MIN_PRIORITY);
      t2.setPriority(3);
      t3.setPriority(Thread.NORM_PRIORITY);
      t4.setPriority(Thread.MAX_PRIORITY);
      t1.start(); t2.start();
      t3.start(); t4.start();
   }
} //end testMyThreadsPriority
```

2.4.2 Thread Synchronization

In Java multithreading programming, you can lock an object before entering (accessing) the object and unlock the object before exiting the object. As shown in Figure 2.14, each object created on heap, which is the part of memory for dynamic memory allocation through the new() function, has an additional management bit in the header part of the object for storing the state if the object is locked. When a synchronized method/statement accesses any object, the runtime checks if the lock is on/off. If the lock is on (true), the thread trying to access the object is blocked and the thread enters into the "blocked" state in Figure 2.13. If the lock is off (false), and the accessing method/statement is a critical operation marked "synchronized," the lock is turned on and then the thread can access the object. The lock is turned off when the synchronized method or block exits.

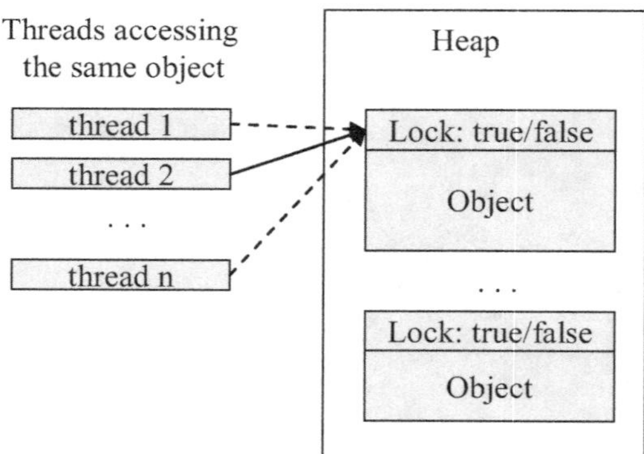

Figure 2.14. Objects on heap are lockable

This mechanism is called **intrinsic lock** or **monitor**, and is used to prevent multiple threads from accessing the same (shared) object simultaneously.

Synchronization is semantically difficult to understand. Many problems, such as deadlock, starvation, and incorrect access to the shared resource, can occur. The following sections use examples to demonstrate these problems.

2.4.3 Synchronized Method

There are two ways to gain synchronization in Java: synchronized method and synchronized statement. Below are two examples of using them.

Synchronized method:

```
class MyClass {
   synchronized void myMethod() {
         statements
   }
}
```

Synchronized statement:

```
synchronized(exp) {
   statements
}
```

For example:

```
synchronized(RandomCharacters.this) {
   // do something
   RandomCharacters.this.wait();
}
```

You can set a priority to a thread, which is a number between 1 and 10. Three constants (macros) are also defined in the Thread class: MIN_PRIORITY, NORM_PRIORITY, and MAX_PRIORITY, corresponding to the priority levels 1, 5, and 10, respectively. By default (without setting the priority), a thread will have the NORM_PRIORITY. If all threads have the same priority, they will be served in the first-in-first-out manner in the waiting, blocked, and ready queues. However, if threads are given different priorities, the threads with higher priorities will be placed before the threads with lower priorities, regardless of their arrival time.

The structure of the program is shown in Figure 2.15, in which we define four classes: a Main class that creates and starts the threads; a class that defines the code of the Producer thread; and a class that defines the code of the Consumer thread. Finally, we use a class to define the buffer that will be shared between the Producer and Consumer threads.

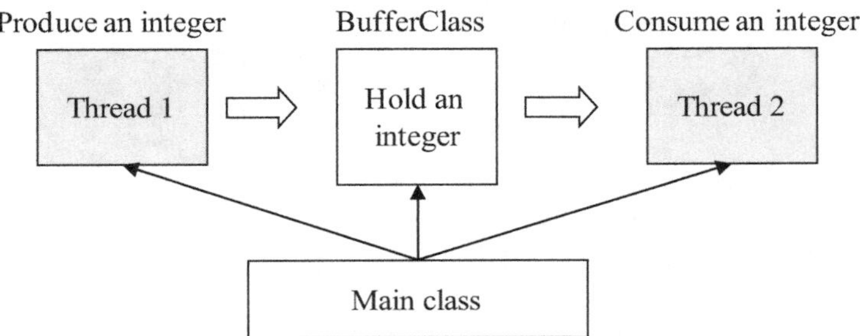

Figure 2.15. Structure of the Producer–Consumer program

```
class BufferClass {
   private int bufferCell = -1;           // buffer for an integer
   private boolean writeable = true;  // flag
   public void setBuffer(int val) {
         while (writeable) {
               bufferCell = val;
               writeable = false;
         } // end while
   }
   public int getBuffer() {
         while (!writeable) {
               writeable = true;
         }
         return bufferCell;
   }
}
class ProduceInteger extends Thread {
   private BufferClass pBuffer;
   public ProduceInteger(BufferClass h) { pBuffer = h; }
   public void run() {
         for (int count = 0; count < 10; count++) {
               try {
                     Thread.sleep((int)(Math.random() * 3000));
               }
               catch (InterruptedException e) {
                     System.err.println(e.toString());
               }
               pBuffer.setBuffer(count);   // put integer
               System.out.println("Producer sets bufferCell " + count);
         }
```

```
    }
}
class ConsumeInteger extends Thread {
   private BufferClass cBuffer;
   public ConsumeInteger(BufferClass h) { cBuffer = h; }
   public void run() {
        int val;
        for (int count = 0; count < 10; count++) {
              try {
                     Thread.sleep((int)(Math.random() * 3000));
              }
              catch (InterruptedException e) {
                     System.err.println(e.toString());
              }
              val = cBuffer.getBuffer();
              System.out.println("\tConsumer retrieved " + val);
        }
    }
}
public class ProducerConsumer
{
    public static void main(String args[])
    {
        BufferClass h = new BufferClass();
        ProduceInteger p = new ProduceInteger(h);
        ConsumeInteger c = new ConsumeInteger(h);
        p.start();
        c.start();
    }
}
```

In this program, the Producer generates a sequence of numbers 0, 1, 2, ..., 9 and deposits the numbers into the buffer. Since the buffer has one cell only, the Producer has to wait for the Consumer to remove the number before depositing another number. As a result, the Producer and Consumer must alternatively access the buffer in order for all numbers generated by the Producer to be correctly received by the Consumer. However, when the program is executed, the following output is generated:

```
Producer sets bufferCell 0
Producer sets bufferCell 1
Producer sets bufferCell 2
   Consumer retrieved 0
Producer sets bufferCell 3
   Consumer retrieved 3
Producer sets bufferCell 4
   Consumer retrieved 4
Producer sets bufferCell 5
   Consumer retrieved 5
Producer sets bufferCell 6
Producer sets bufferCell 7
   Consumer retrieved 6
   Consumer retrieved 6
Producer sets bufferCell 8
Producer sets bufferCell 9
   Consumer retrieved 8
   Consumer retrieved 8
   Consumer retrieved 8
   Consumer retrieved 8
```

As can be seen from the output, the Producer and the Consumer are out of synchronization, resulting in incorrect receiving of the numbers from the Consumer's side; for example, after the Producer generated and deposited the first number 0, the Consumer retrieved the number 0. Nevertheless, before the Consumer thread printed the retrieved number, the Producer thread regained the processor and deposited the number 1 and 2. Of course, number 2 overwrote number 1. Then, the Consumer regained the processor and printed the retrieved number 0. Again, the Producer thread obtained the processor and deposited number 3 into the buffer, which overwrote the number 2. Then, Consumer thread obtained the processor and retrieved the number 3. Thus, consumer missed numbers 1 and 2.

Note that, in the Producer and Consumer threads, a random function is used to generate a random amount of sleep time. The output is thus nondeterministic, which means multiple executions of the same program can generate different output sequences. In fact, distributed computing is nondeterministic by its nature. Even if the random function is not used, the different sequences can still be generated, due to; for example, the workload at the time the program is executed.

To solve the problem, we need to use the monitor mechanism to protect the buffer from being accessed while another thread is in the middle of the manipulation. The redesigned Buffer class is given in the code below. The rest of the program will remain unchanged.

```
class BufferClass {
    private int bufferCell = -1;  // buffer for an integer
    private boolean writeable = true;       // flag
    public synchronized void setBuffer( int val ) {
        while ( !writeable ) {
             try {
                  wait();   //voluntarily enter the waiting state
             }
             catch ( InterruptedException e ) {
                  System.err.println("Exception: " + e.toString() );
             }
        } // end while
        bufferCell = val;
        writeable = false;
        notify();
    }
    public synchronized int getBuffer() {
        while (writeable) {
             try {
                  wait();   //voluntarily enter the waiting state
             }
             catch (InterruptedException e) {
                  System.err.println("Exception: " + e.toString());
             }
        }
        writeable = true;
        notify();
        return bufferCell;
    }
}
```

In this synchronized buffer program, we also used the functions wait() and notify(). The former forces the calling thread into the waiting state, while the latter moves the first thread in the waiting state queue into the ready state, as shown in state transition diagram in Figure 2.13. Once this revision is made, the program can correctly complete the Producer–Consumer process. The output of the revised program is as follows:

```
Producer sets bufferCell 0
  Consumer retrieved 0
Producer sets bufferCell 1
```

```
   Consumer retrieved 1
Producer sets bufferCell 2
   Consumer retrieved 2
Producer sets bufferCell 3
   Consumer retrieved 3
Producer sets bufferCell 4
   Consumer retrieved 4
Producer sets bufferCell 5
Producer sets bufferCell 6
   Consumer retrieved 5
   Consumer retrieved 6
Producer sets bufferCell 7
   Consumer retrieved 7
Producer sets bufferCell 8
   Consumer retrieved 8
   Consumer retrieved 9
Producer sets bufferCell 9
```

It looks like the highlighted lines are out of order. However, a closer look reveals that the "out of order" is for the printing statement only, because the thread is interrupted just before printing. The Consumer received all the 10 numbers in the correct order.

The Thread class offers a number of other methods for the programs to manage their threads. In the following program, the Thread.activeCount() method is used to check the number of threads alive and to make the Main thread not to exit until all child threads have terminated.

```
public class main {
   public static void main(String[ ] args) {
         int originalThreadCount = Thread.activeCount();
         System.out.println("thread count=" + originalThreadCount);
         for (int j = 0; j < 1; j++) {
                Thread producer = new Thread(new ProducerThread(j));
                Thread consumer = new Thread(new ConsumerThread(j));
                producer.start();
                consumer.start();
                System.out.println("main thread count=" + Thread.activeCount());
         }
         while (Thread.activeCount() > originalThreadCount) {
                System.out.println("The count = " + Thread.activeCount() );
                Thread.sleep(300);
         }
   }
} //end myMainClass
```

Another method that can be used to wait for other threads to terminate is the join(). Assume p is the reference to a Thread object, p.join() will cause the current thread (caller thread) to pause execution until p's thread terminates.

2.4.4 Synchronized Statements

The synchronized method is syntactically simple to use. However, it may not be the most efficient way to manage synchronization. A method can have many statements. If a synchronized method accesses multiple objects, all objects will be locked. It may cause unnecessary blocking and reduce the capability of parallel computing. Since all objects accessed will be locked in a synchronized method, we do not need to specify the object that needs to be locked.

On the other hand, the synchronized statement allows fine-grained management by limiting the critical operations to the statements involved, and locking only the object that needs to be locked.

Assume we have a class userClass with two members, counterProducer, and counterConsumer, which keep track of the number of Producers and Consumers in the system, respectively. When a Producer or a Consumer joins, it updates the counterProducer or counterConsumer. Obviously, the updates of the counters must be synchronized, because multiple Producers and/or Consumers can join at the same time and update the counters at the same time. However, there is no reason to prevent counterProducer and counterConsumer from being updated at the same time. Using synchronized statements can prevent each counter from being updated at the same time by two threads but will allow the updates of the two independent counters to interleave, as shown in the following segment of code.

```
public class userClass {
   private int counterProducer = 0; private int counterConsumer = 0;
   private Object lock1 = new Object();
   private Object lock2 = new Object();
   public void inc1() {
        synchronized (lock1) { counterProducer++; }
   }
   public void inc2() {
        synchronized (lock2) { counterConsumer++; }
   }
   public static void main() { // do something
   }
}
```

Another application of the synchronized statement is in the case when you do not have access to the source code of the class and thus you cannot modify the class by adding the "synchronized" keyword to the method. In this case, you can add the "synchronized" keyword to the statement that calls the method.

2.5 Multithreading in C#

Microsoft Visual Studio .Net is a programming environment that supports multiple programming languages and multiple programming paradigms. Section 2.1 discussed the basis of creating OO programs, and this section presents multithreading in C# and .Net.

Different from Java, C# threads do not have to be defined as separate classes. They can be any methods within a class. Furthermore, C# provides more mechanisms to control and manage the threads. This section will introduce most of the mechanisms and show examples of using these mechanisms.

2.5.1 Thread Classes and Properties

The .Net Framework Class Library (FCL) defines a number of threading classes, as members of System.Threading namespace, as shown in Table 2.5. All these classes will be discussed in the following subsections.

Table 2.5. FCL threading classes

Classes/Functions	Description
Thread	Methods: Start(), Suspend(); Resume(); Interrupt(); Join(); Sleep(); Abort();
Monitor	Prevents more than one thread from accessing a resource rsc at the same time; for example, Monitor.Enter(rsc); Monitor.Exit(rsc); Monitor.Wait(rsc); Monitor.Pulse(rsc); Monitor.PulseAll(rsc);
Conditional Locks	Checks if the lock is available, and can program the thread to wait for locks or do something else, and can come back to check the lock later
ReaderWriterLock	Enables multiple threads to read a resource simultaneously, but prevent overlapping reads-writes, and overlapping writes-writes
Mutex	Prevents more than one thread or more than one application process from accessing a resource at the same time
AutoResetEvent	Blocks a thread until another thread sets the event
ManualResetEvent	Blocks one or more threads until another thread sets the event

Table 2.6 lists the properties of threads whether they are readable, writable, or static. A static property can be accessed using the class name and without instantiating an object first. A nonstatic property requires the creation of an object and using the reference name to the object to access the property. These properties allow threads to be better controlled and managed.

Table 2.6. Properties of the Thread class

Property	Description	Get	Set	Static
CurrentPrincipal	The thread principal (identity) assigned to the calling thread	√	√	√
CurrentThread	Returns a thread reference, representing the calling thread	√		√
IsAlive	A thread is alive, if it is started and not yet terminated	√		
IsBackground	Background or foreground (default)	√	√	
Name	The thread's human readable name	√	√	
Priority	Highest, AboveNormal, Normal (default), BelowNormal, Lowest		√	
ThreadState	The thread's current state	√		

2.5.2 Monitor

Similar to the Java monitor section, we first consider the Producer–Consumer problem without using the monitor. The structure of the program is shown in Figure 2.16, where the bufferCell and writeable are static variables that are shared by the two Producer threads and two Consumer threads. The Producer thread 0 will generate 10 numbers 0, 1, 2, ..., 9, and the Producer thread 1 will generate 10 numbers 100, 101, 102, ..., 109. These 20 numbers will be received by the two Consumer threads in random order.

The C# program is given as follows. It consists of three classes: ProducerThread, ConsumerThread, and myMainClass. In the ProducerThread, the Producer waits for the bufferCell to be writeable, writes the item into the shared bufferCell, and sets the writeable to be false. In the ConsumerThread, the consumer waits for the bufferCell to be readable (not writeable), reads the item, and then sets the writeable to be true.

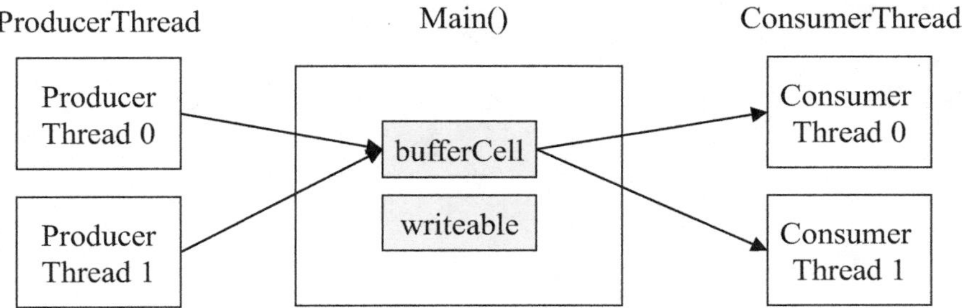

Figure 2.16. Structure of the Producer–Consumer of the C# program

```
using System;
using System.Threading;
class ProducerThread {
    System.Random RandNum = new System.Random();
    int myId;
    public ProducerThread(int id) {
        myId = id;
    }
    public void runProducer(){
        int baseVal = myId * 100;
        for (int i = baseVal; i < baseVal + 10; i++) {
            while (!myMainClass.writeable) {
                Thread.Sleep(RandNum.Next(1, 100));
            }
                if (myMainClass.writeable) {
                  Console.WriteLine("Producer" + myId + " generates Item= " + i);
                  myMainClass.bufferCell = i;
                  myMainClass.writeable = false;
                }
            }
        }
   } //end class ProducerThread

class ConsumerThread {
    int myId, myItem;
    System.Random RandNum = new System.Random();
    public ConsumerThread(int id) {
        myId = id;
    }

    public void runConsumer(){
        for (int i = 0; i < 10; i++) {
            Thread.Sleep(RandNum.Next(1, 2000));
            while (myMainClass.writeable) {
                Thread.Sleep(RandNum.Next(1, 100));
            }
            if (!myMainClass.writeable) {
                myItem = myMainClass.bufferCell;
                Console.WriteLine(" Consumer"+myId+" receives Item="+myItem);
                myMainClass.writeable = true;
            }
        }
    }
    public void consumer() {
```

```
        int myItems = myMainClass.bufferCell;
        if (myItems <= 0)      // buffer empty
            Thread.Sleep(RandNum.Next(1, 2000));
        Console.WriteLine("     Consumer" + myId + " bufferCell=" +
myMainClass.bufferCell);
        myItems--;
        myMainClass.bufferCell = myItems;
    }
} //end class ConsumerThread

public class myMainClass {
    public static int bufferCell = 0;       // static variable for sharing
    public static bool writeable = true;
    public static void Main() {
        ProducerThread p0 = new ProducerThread(0);
        ConsumerThread c0 = new ConsumerThread(0);
        ProducerThread p1 = new ProducerThread(1);
        ConsumerThread c1 = new ConsumerThread(1);
        Thread producer0 = new Thread(new ThreadStart(p0.runProducer));
        Thread consumer0 = new Thread(new ThreadStart(c0.runConsumer));
        Thread producer1 = new Thread(new ThreadStart(p1.runProducer));
        Thread consumer1 = new Thread(new ThreadStart(c1.runConsumer));
        producer0.Start(); // First producers will be started
        consumer0.Start(); // First consumers will be started
        producer1.Start(); // Second producers will be started
        consumer1.Start(); // Second consumers will be started
        producer0.Join();  // Main waits for child threads to complete
        consumer0.Join();
        producer1.Join();
        consumer1.Join();
        Console.WriteLine("main thread completed");
    }
} //end myMainClass
```

Note, you can define a parameterized constructor to take parameters when creating an object, so that the thread can take input from the parent thread. However, your thread function, in this example, the runConsumer and runProducer, cannot take parameters.

The output of the program is as follows: As highlighted, the item 100 generated by Producer 1 and the item 8 generated by Producer 0 were never received by any of the Consumers.

```
Producer0 generates Item= 0
    Consumer0 receives Item=0
Producer0 generates Item= 1
    Consumer1 receives Item=1
Producer0 generates Item= 2
    Consumer1 receives Item=2
Producer0 generates Item= 3
    Consumer0 receives Item=3
Producer0 generates Item= 4
    Consumer1 receives Item=4
Producer0 generates Item= 5
    Consumer0 receives Item=5
Producer0 generates Item= 6
Producer1 generates Item= 100
    Consumer1 receives Item=6
Producer0 generates Item= 7
    Consumer0 receives Item=7
Producer1 generates Item= 101
```

```
    Consumer1 receives Item=101
Producer0 generates Item= 8
Producer1 generates Item= 102
    Consumer0 receives Item=102
Producer0 generates Item= 9
    Consumer1 receives Item=9
Producer1 generates Item= 103
    Consumer0 receives Item=103
Producer1 generates Item= 104
    Consumer1 receives Item=104
Producer1 generates Item= 105
    Consumer1 receives Item=105
Producer1 generates Item= 106
    Consumer0 receives Item=106
Producer1 generates Item= 107
    Consumer1 receives Item=107
Producer1 generates Item= 108
    Consumer0 receives Item=108
Producer1 generates Item= 109
Consumer0 receives Item=109
main thread completed
```

The problem occurs when the Producer is interrupted after it writes the item into the bufferCell and before its sets the writeable to false, resulting in data that are overwritten by other data.

To solve the problem, we wrap the bufferCell into a class so that the object of the class can be protected by a monitor.

The structure of a C# monitor is similar to the synchronized statement in Java:

```
Monitor.Enter(bufferCell); // Lock the object to be protected
try {
   // access the object referenced by bufferCell;
}
finally {
   Monitor.Exit(bufferCell);     // Unlock the object referenced by bufferCell
}
```

In this piece of code:

- Monitor.Enter(bufferCell) locks the object referenced by bufferCell: A monitored object cannot be accessed by more than one thread;
- Monitor.Exit(bufferCell) cancels the lock;
- Putting Monitor.Exit(bufferCell) in the finally block ensures that it will be executed even if an exception occurs. Always put the unlock operation in the finally block to eliminate the risk of orphaning a lock and causing other threads to hang indefinitely!

Figure 2.17 illustrates the lock put on by Monitor.Enter and canceled by Monitor.Exit.

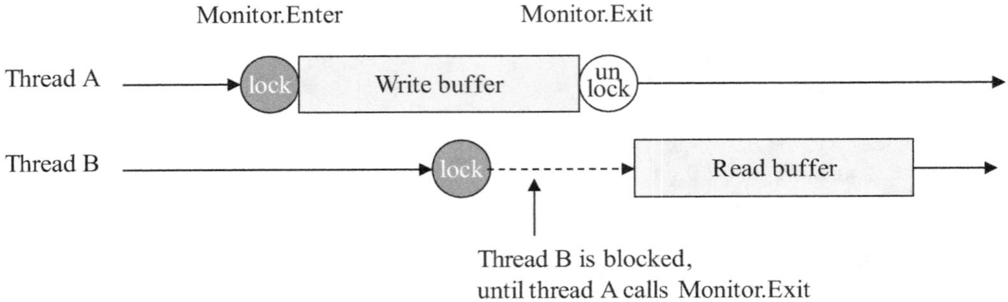

Figure 2.17. Locking and unlocking an object

The structure of the new program is shown in Figure 2.18, which is similar to the structure in Figure 2.15.

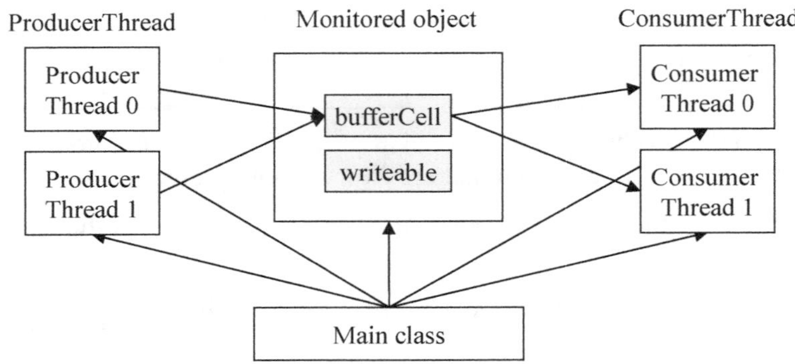

Figure 2.18. Structure of the Producer–Consumer program with monitored object

The program that implements the monitored access to the buffer is given below:

```
using System;
using System.Threading;
public class BufferClass {
   private int bufferCell = -1;          // buffer for an integer
   private bool writeable = true;           // flag
   public void setBuffer( int val ) {
        while ( !writeable ) {
             try {
                  Monitor.Wait(this);  //voluntarily enter the waiting state
             }
             catch { Console.WriteLine("error"); }
        } // end while
        bufferCell = val;
        writeable = false;
         Monitor.PulseAll(this);
   }
   public int getBuffer() {
        while (writeable) {
             try {
                   Monitor.Wait(this);//voluntarily enter the waiting state
             }
             catch { Console.WriteLine("error"); }
```

```
        } // end while
        writeable = true;
        Monitor.PulseAll(this);
        return bufferCell;
    }
}
class ProducerThread {
    System.Random RandNum = new System.Random();
    int myId;
    public ProducerThread(int id) { myId = id; }
    public void runProducer() {
        int baseVal = myId * 100;
        for (int i = baseVal; i < baseVal + 10; i++) {
            Thread.Sleep(RandNum.Next(1, 2000));
            Monitor.Enter(myMainClass.bufferCellRef);
            try {
                myMainClass.bufferCellRef.setBuffer(i);
                Console.WriteLine("Producer"+myId+" generates Item= "+i);
            }
            finally { Monitor.Exit(myMainClass.bufferCellRef); }
        }
    }
} //end class ProducerThread
class ConsumerThread {
    int myId, myItem;
    System.Random RandNum = new System.Random();
    public ConsumerThread(int id) { myId = id; }
    public void runConsumer() {
        for (int i = 0; i < 10; i++) {
            Thread.Sleep(RandNum.Next(1, 2000));
            Monitor.Enter(myMainClass.bufferCellRef);
            try {
                myItem = myMainClass.bufferCellRef.getBuffer();
                Console.WriteLine("  Consumer" + myId + " receives Item=" + myItem);
            }
            finally { Monitor.Exit(myMainClass.bufferCellRef); }
        }
    }
} //end class ConsumerThread
public class myMainClass {
    public static BufferClass bufferCellRef = new BufferClass();
    // static object for sharing
    public static void Main() {
        ProducerThread p0 = new ProducerThread(0);
        ConsumerThread c0 = new ConsumerThread(0);
        ProducerThread p1 = new ProducerThread(1);
        ConsumerThread c1 = new ConsumerThread(1);
        Thread producer0 = new Thread(new ThreadStart(p0.runProducer));
        Thread consumer0 = new Thread(new ThreadStart(c0.runConsumer));
        Thread producer1 = new Thread(new ThreadStart(p1.runProducer));
        Thread consumer1 = new Thread(new ThreadStart(c1.runConsumer));
        producer0.Start(); // First producers will be started
        consumer0.Start(); // First consumers will be started
        producer1.Start(); // Second producers will be started
        consumer1.Start(); // Second consumers will be started
        producer0.Join();  // Main waits for child threads to complete
        consumer0.Join(); producer1.Join(); consumer1.Join();
```

```
        Console.WriteLine("main thread completed");
    }
} //end myMainClass
```

The output of the program is:

```
Producer0 generates Item= 0
    Consumer1 receives Item=0
Producer1 generates Item= 100
    Consumer0 receives Item=100
Producer1 generates Item= 101
    Consumer1 receives Item=101
Producer0 generates Item= 1
    Consumer0 receives Item=1
Producer1 generates Item= 102
    Consumer1 receives Item=102
Producer0 generates Item= 2
    Consumer0 receives Item=2
Producer1 generates Item= 103
    Consumer1 receives Item=103
Producer0 generates Item= 3
    Consumer0 receives Item=3
Producer1 generates Item= 104
    Consumer1 receives Item=104
Producer0 generates Item= 4
    Consumer0 receives Item=4
Producer1 generates Item= 105
    Consumer1 receives Item=105
Producer0 generates Item= 5
    Consumer0 receives Item=5
Producer0 generates Item= 6
    Consumer0 receives Item=6
Producer1 generates Item= 106
    Consumer1 receives Item=106
Producer1 generates Item= 107
    Consumer1 receives Item=107
Producer0 generates Item= 7
    Consumer0 receives Item=7
Producer1 generates Item= 108
    Consumer1 receives Item=108
Producer0 generates Item= 8
    Consumer0 receives Item=8
Producer1 generates Item= 109
    Consumer1 receives Item=109
Producer0 generates Item= 9
    Consumer0 receives Item=9
main thread completed
```

As can be seen from the outputs, all numbers generated by the Producers are received by the Consumers.

- Can a deadlock occur when this program is being executed? There are four threads that access the shared resources. There are two shared variables: bufferCell and writeable. In the code above, both variables are in the same object of the Buffer class. Thus, they are considered one resource and are locked at the same time. No deadlock can occur if there is one shared resource only. However, if we put the two variables into two different objects and the threads can lock them one after the other, then deadlocks become possible.
- When a thread executes Monitor.Enter(object) and the object is locked, the thread will be put into the blocked state. If the programmer does not want the thread to be blocked, they can conditionally acquire a lock using Monitor.TryEnter(object), which does not block the thread;

- It acquires the lock and returns true, if the lock is available;
- It returns false, if the lock is not available.

For example, one can use the following code:

```
if (Monitor.TryEnter(this)) {
   // access bufferCell;
} else {
   // do something else and try the lock later again
}
```

A simpler way to lock the critical operations is to use C# lock keyword:

```
lock(this) {
        // access bufferCell;
}  // guarantee the finally section is included
```

This piece of code is functionally equivalent to the following piece of code:

```
Monitor.Enter(bufferCell);  // Lock the object to be protected
try {
   // access bufferCell;
}
finally {
   Monitor.Exit(this);  // Unlock the object
}
```

In Java, several thread methods, wait(), notify(), notifyAll(), are used to coordinate the access of shared resources, as discussed in the previous section. C# Monitor class has equivalent methods that perform the same functions. They are Monitor.Wait(), Monitor.Pulse(), and Monitor.PulseAll(). The following piece of code shows an example of using these methods to solve the Producer–Consumer program.

```
static void Producer() {
   string[ ]  str = new string[ ] {"item1", "item2", "item3"};
   lock(queue)  {
        foreach (string item in str) {
              quene.Enqueue (item);
              Monitor.Pulse(queue);    // notify an available item
              Monitor.Wait(queue);
              Thread.Sleep(500);
        }
   }
}
static void Consumer() {
   lock(queue)   {
        while (true) {
              if (queue.Count > 0) {
                   while (queue.Count > 0) {
                        string item = (string) queue.Dequeue();
                        ConsoleWriteLine(item);
                   } // endwhile
                   Monitor.Pulse(queue);  // space available
              } // endif
              Monitor.Wait(queue)
        } // endwhile
   } // endlock
}
```

Figure 2.19 shows how the monitor/lock is implemented. Before entering an object referenced by "buffer," the runtime checks if the lock is on/off.

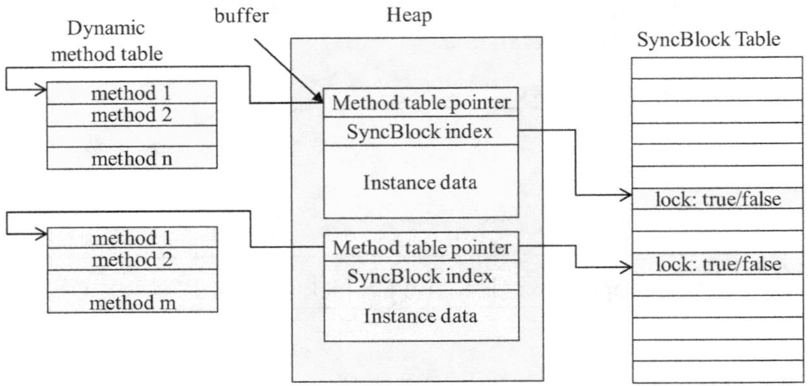

Figure 2.19. Implementation of monitor/lock on object

- If the lock is on (true), the thread issuing the Monitor.Enter is blocked. The locks of the objects on the heap memory (memory allocated using new() operation), are stored in a separate table called SyncBlock table.
- If the lock is off (false), the thread issuing the Monitor.Enter turns on the lock to prevent other threads from entering while accessing the object referenced by the buffer.
- Please note that the monitor methods take a reference variable (object) as the parameter and protect the object pointed to by the reference. Syntactically, one can use a value type variable as the parameter and reply on the automatic boxing function to wrap a value type variable into a reference type variable. However, a semantic error may occur. Figure 2.20 shows an example where an integer variable is passed to Monitor.Enter() and Monitor.Exit() methods. In this example, the compiler is obligated to issue a boxing operation for each use of value type variable `va` in the place of a reference type, resulting in two different objects created for lock and unlock operations, respectively, instead of applying the two operations on the same object to lock and unlock the object.

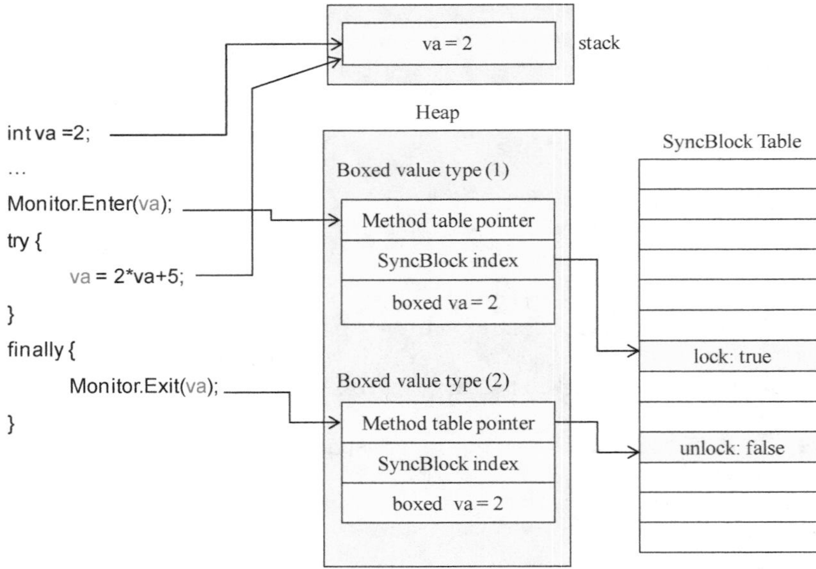

Figure 2.20. Passing a value type variable to the monitor methods can cause a semantic error

We need to manually box the variable, so that the compiler does not create two boxed variables, as shown in the code below:

```
int va =2;
object box= va;    // The compiler will perform boxing here
Monitor.Enter(box);
try {
   va = 2*va+5;
}
finally { Monitor.Exit(box); }
```

However, the code above has another problem. The variable `va` is not synchronized by the monitor, because `va` is still a different variable on stack. The following code addresses this issue by manipulating the boxed value, instead of the instance value on stack.

```
class testBox {
   static void Main(string[ ] args) {
        int va = 2;
        object box = va; // manual boxing here
        Monitor.Enter(box);
        Try {
               box = 2 * (int)box + 5;
        }
        Finally { Monitor.Exit(box); }
   }
}
```

2.5.3 Reader and Writer Locks

Reader and writer locks have the same functions as the monitor to prevent simultaneous access to the shared resources, which can cause problems. However, reader and writer locks are thoughtful: they do not allow overlap between read and write, or between write and write operations, but allow simultaneous reads, which leads to better performance without causing data integrity problems. The .Net FCL class that supports the reader and writer locks is ReaderWriterLock.

The following sorting example illustrates how to use this class and the methods in the class to protect the critical operations. The program structure is shown in Figure 2.21. In the Main method, a shared array of integers, called buffer[ ], is declared. A sorter thread is used to initialize the array with random numbers, and then, the SortArray method is used to sort the array. In the meanwhile, multiple independent adder threads read the buffer and compute the sum, called checksum. Without using a synchronization mechanism, the checksums from the adder threads will be completely messed up. If a monitor is used, the multiple adder threads will not be able to read the array simultaneously, resulting in lower performance.

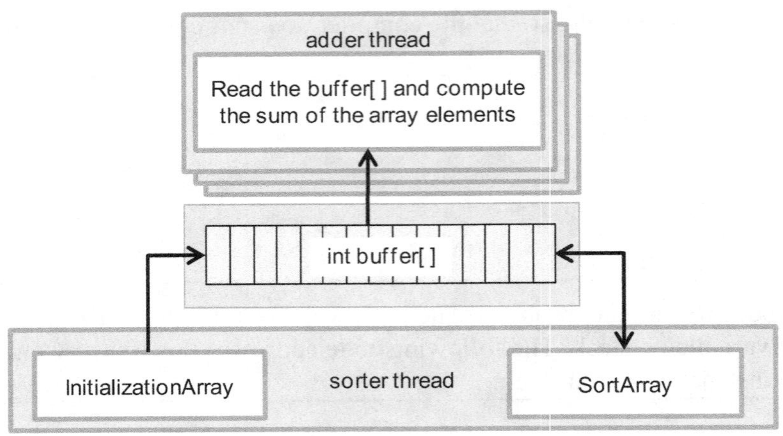

Figure 2.21. Structure of the example

The program below uses ReaderWriterLock() class to allow reader threads to overlap their execution, while blocking the overlap between read–write and write–write.

```
using System;
using System.Threading;
class ArraySorter {
    const int size = 10;
    static Random randv = new Random();
    static int correctSum = 0;
    static int[] buffer = new int[size];
    static Thread wref;
    static ReaderWriterLock rwl = new ReaderWriterLock(); // lib class
    static void Main() {
        wref = new Thread(new ThreadStart(sorter));
        wref.Start();              // Start one sorter thread
        Thread[] readers = new Thread[5]; // Start five reader threads
        for (int i = 0; i < 5; i++) {
            readers[i] = new Thread(new ThreadStart(adder));
            readers[i].Name = (i + 1).ToString();
            readers[i].Start();
        } // end for
    } // end Main()
    static void adder() {
        for (int i = 0; wref.IsAlive; i++) { // Loop until the sorter thread ends
            int sum = 0;
            rwl.AcquireReaderLock(Timeout.Infinite);
            try {
                for (int k = 0; k < size; k++) // Sum values in the buffer
                  sum += buffer[k];
               if (sum != ArraySorter.correctSum) { // Report an error if the sum is
incorrect
                  string message = String.Format("Thread {0} " +
                  "reports corrupted sum {1} against {2} on iteration {3}",
Thread.CurrentThread.Name, sum,
                  ArraySorter.correctSum, i + 1);
                  Console.WriteLine(message);
                  wref.Abort();
                  return;
               }
```

```
            }
            finally { rwl.ReleaseReaderLock(); }
            Console.WriteLine("Thread {0} has sum = {1}",
                                    Thread.CurrentThread.Name, sum);
        } // end for
    } // end adder
    static void sorter() {
        DateTime start = DateTime.Now;
        // Loop for up to 5 seconds
        while ((DateTime.Now - start).Seconds < 5) {
            InitializeArray();
            SortArray();
        }
    }
    static void InitializeArray(){// Initialize array w. random numbers
        rwl.AcquireWriterLock(Timeout.Infinite); // or use a number
        try {
            for (int i = 0; i < size; i++)
                buffer[i] = (int)randv.Next(0, 20);
            ArraySorter.correctSum = 0;
            for (int i = 0; i < size; i++) {
                Console.Write("{0} ", buffer[i]);
                ArraySorter.correctSum += buffer[i];
            }
        }
        finally { rwl.ReleaseWriterLock(); }
        Console.WriteLine();
        Console.WriteLine("Correct sum of array values is: " + correctSum);
    }
    static void SortArray() { // Using insertion sort algorithm
        int j, k;
        for (j = 1; j < size; j++) {
            int key = buffer[j];
            for (k = 0; key > buffer[k] && (k < j); k++) ;
            // shift the list elements if the element's position is found
            if (k < j) {
                rwl.AcquireWriterLock(300); // timeout in 300 millisecs
                try {
                    insert(j, k);
                    for (int i = 0; i < size; i++)
                        Console.Write("{0} ", buffer[i]);
                    Console.WriteLine();
                }
                finally { rwl.ReleaseWriterLock(); }
            }
        }
    } // end Sorter
    static void insert(int j, int k) {
        // insert current element into right position
        int temp = buffer[j];
        while (j > k) {
            buffer[j] = buffer[j - 1];
            j--;
        }
        buffer[k] = temp;
    }
}
```

The following printout shows a part of the outputs when the program is executed.

```
Correct sum of array values is: 129
4 15 17 18 8 15 1 17 17 17
4 8 15 17 18 15 1 17 17 17
4 8 15 15 17 18 1 17 17 17
Thread 2 has sum = 129
Thread 2 has sum = 129
1 4 8 15 15 17 18 17 17 17
Thread 2 has sum = 129
1 4 8 15 15 17 17 18 17 17
Thread 4 has sum = 129
1 4 8 15 15 17 17 17 18 17
Thread 5 has sum = 129
Thread 4 has sum = 129
Thread 1 has sum = 129
Thread 3 has sum = 129
Thread 2 has sum = 129
1 4 8 15 15 17 17 17 17 18
Thread 2 has sum = 129
3 10 8 11 7 16 1 13 5 8 Thread 5 has sum = 82
Thread 5 has sum = 82
Thread 2 has sum = 82
The correct sum of the array values is: 82
3 8 10 11 7 16 1 13 5 8
3 7 8 10 11 16 1 13 5 8
1 3 7 8 10 11 16 13 5 8
1 3 7 8 10 11 13 16 5 8
1 3 5 7 8 10 11 13 16 8
1 3 5 7 8 8 10 11 13 16
Thread 5 has sum = 82
```

As can be seen from the outputs, the printout from different threads is completely mixed up, but the computation from the reader threads and sorting from the writer thread are all correct.

In the program above, one can replace the Reader/Writer locks and the releases with Monitor.Enter and Monitor.Exit. The program will behave the same way except for the difference in execution speed. However, if the locks are removed, the program will corrupt the data and generate incorrect results. The following sample output shows a part of the situation after the Reader/Writer locks and releases are removed.

```
1 5 11 15 15 17 18 12 19 6
1 5 11 12 15 15 17 18 19 6
1 5 6 11 12 15 15 17 18 19
9 Thread 1 has sum = 119
Thread 1 reports a corrupted sum 78 against 0 on iteration 215
Thread 5 reports a corrupted sum 78 against 0 on iteration 144
Thread 4 has sum = 119
Thread 3 has sum = 119
Thread 2 has sum = 119
```

Carefully compare and contrast the ReaderWriterLock class and the Monitor class, more differences can be identified:

- ReaderWriterLock class allows reader-reader to overlap, while monitor class blocks any kinds of overlaps, as has been explained above.
- We need to instantiate an object of ReaderWriterLock class before using the methods of the class, as can be seen in the code:

  ```
  static ReaderWriterLock rwl = new ReaderWriterLock();
  ```

However, we do not need to instantiate an object of Monitor class before using its methods. They are static methods.

- ReaderWriterLock class's lock acquiring methods have a parameter for timeout, specifying how long to wait before being blocked, as can be seen from the following statements:

  ```
  rwl.AcquireReaderLock(Timeout.Infinite); // wait forever without being blocked
  rwl.AcquireWriterLock(300); // wait for up to 300 millisec before being blocked
  ```

  Monitor.Enter will let the thread be blocked immediately and Monitor.TryEnter gives up immediately without being blocked, if the object to be accessed is locked;

- Monitor class methods use a parameter, e.g., Monitor.Enter(buffer), to define what object to lock, while ReaderWriterLock class's lock acquiring methods do not specify what object to lock. Thus, it locks all objects quoted by the method. This is same as Java's synchronized method.

Can Reader/Writer locks perform better in all cases than Monitor locks? The answer is no. The Reader/Writer locks are more complex to implement and take a longer time to check the different conditions, as they have to differentiate the read request and write requests. The implementation has to deal with two queues: a read queue and a write queue. It then raises the question of the priority between the read and write requests. Read requests typically take a shorter time than write requests, and particularly, multiple readers can read at the same time. Thus, giving reader threads a higher priority and allowing them to finish their jobs in a batch processing mode can significantly increase the throughput of the entire system. As the result, the writer threads may starve if there are many readers. Therefore, the developers need to know the profile of usage, or the percentage of read and write requests, and to implement an adequate policy and priority between the reader and writer threads.

Another difference between the sorting example and the Producer–Consumer example discussed above is that of the object used to create the threads.

In the Producer–Consumer example, the Producer thread and the Consumer thread are instantiated from two different classes. The shared buffer object is also from a different class. On the other hand, in the sorting example, there is one class only. The adder thread and the sorter thread are instantiated from two methods in the same class. These two threads can share the class members without using parameter passing.

2.5.4 Mutexes

Mutexes are another mechanism to prevent simultaneous access to shared resources. This mechanism has the following distinct features:

- Mutexes have the power to synchronize both threads and processes belonging to different applications in the operating system, whereas monitors and locks do not!
- If a thread can acquire a mutex and terminate the thread without having to free the mutex, the operating system can detect the orphan situation and automatically free it;
- Mutexes are orders of magnitude slower than the inner-application synchronization mechanisms. Do not use them unless you want to synchronize processes among different applications.

The following piece of code shows the syntax of using Mutexes. The name of a Mutex is used to establish the link between the processes: if two processes create a Mutex using the same name, the two processes will share the Mutex.

```
Mutex myMutex = new Mutex("named_shared_mutexes");
...
myMutex.WaitOne(); // build-in method
Try {  // objects here will be mutually exclusive
   ...
```

```
}
finally {
   myMutex.ReleaseMutex();
}
```

2.5.5 Semaphore

A **semaphore** is a flag used in operating system and multithreading programming environment to prevent more processes/threads (P) than permitted from accessing a pool of resources (R) at the same time, that is, the relation $P \leq R$ must be maintained at all times.

A semaphore is usually implemented by a non-negative integer $s \geq 0$, which can be modified by certain operations only, such as Unix system calls wait(s) and signal(s):

```
wait(s):        if s > 0 then s := s - 1 else
                wait until s > 0, then s := s - 1;
signal(s):      s := s + 1;
```

The Windows operating system allows semaphores to have names. A named semaphore is system wide. In other words, once a named semaphore is created, it is visible to all threads in all processes. Like Mutexes, named semaphore can be used to synchronize the activities among operating system processes as well as among threads.

Caution: Because named semaphores are system-wide, another process that uses the same name can access your semaphore unexpectedly. Malicious code executing on the same computer could use this as the basis of a denial-of-service attack.

In .Net FCL, a Semaphore class is defined to control the access to a pool of resources. The following piece of code creates a semaphore with an initial value i and a maximum value m.

```
i = 0;
m = 5;
s = new Semaphore(i, m);     // create a semaphore
s.Release(5);           // Set the semaphore value to 5
s.WaitOne();            // acquire resource
s.Release();            // release a resource
```

Threads decrement the semaphore by calling the WaitOne() method and increment the semaphore by calling the Release() method. When the count is zero, subsequent requests block until other threads release the semaphore. When all threads have released the semaphore, the count is at the max value specified when the semaphore was created. When the count is at its max value, a release call will throw an exception!

A semaphore is a flag for observation. It does not directly prevent a thread from accessing the resource. If enforcement is needed, you must use a lock on the resource, which prevents the resource from being accessed. As an analogy, you can consider a parking garage application. You can use a semaphore to display how many parking slots are available. However, even if the semaphore shows 0 slots available, one can still drive into the garage and hunt for a free slot. To prevent the situation, you must have another mechanism, such as using a gate. Once the semaphore is 0, the gate will not open. The gate is not a part of the semaphore. It is more like a lock. Another example is the lavatory system in a passenger plane that can display how many lavatories are available and can lock individual lavatories. When the semaphore value is greater than 0, one can walk to the lavatories, but still needs to check which one is not locked.

2.5.6 Coordination Event

Monitors, Reader/Writer Locks, and Mutexes are used to guard shared resources from being accessed simultaneously. The threads compete for resources, but it does not matter which thread wins the resource. In some cases, order could be defined; for example, if there is no item to consume, the Consumer has to wait for the Producer.

On the other hand, coordination events are specifically designed to coordinate the order of executions among the threads—also called thread triggers. The focus is not on the resources to share; for example, a Producer wants to fill the buffer before allowing the Consumer to read the buffer. This requirement cannot be done using monitors/locks.

Windows supports two types of coordination events: auto-reset events and manual-reset events. The .Net class library wraps these operating kernel objects into language classes to offer AutoResetEvent and ManualResetEvent.

Both of the two event classes contain methods: Set: set an event; Reset: reset an event; and WaitOne: blocked until the event becomes set. If called on an event that is set, it runs immediately without waiting.

If an AutoResetEvent Class event is used in a program, event.reset is automatically called before event.WaitOne method is called; WaitOne will always be blocked and activated by a later event.set; and it only triggers one thread at a time. If a ManualResetEvent Class event is used, event.reset needs to be called before each event.WaitOne call, and it triggers all threads waiting for the event.

We can use the analogy of doubles matches in tennis and in table tennis to compare and contrast monitor/lock and coordination events.

As shown in Figure 2.22, the order of the shots among the two players on the same side is defined. They cannot compete to strike the ball. They must strike the ball alternatively. This rule can be implemented using the coordination mechanism.

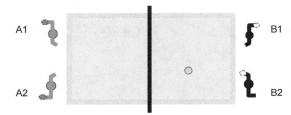

Figure 2.22. A double match in table tennis

In the case of tennis, the two players on the same side can compete to strike the ball. One player is allowed to return the ball multiple times without giving the other player a turn, as long as the two players do not strike the ball at the same time. This rule can be implemented using the monitor/lock mechanism.

The following segment of code (incomplete) shows the components needed in implementing a doubles tennis game.

```
class TableTennis {
    Random rand;
    Object aLock, bLock;
    AutoResetEvent A1event, A2event, B1event, B2event;
    int turn, rate, Apoints, Bpoints, totalServes;
    bool serve, gamePlay, aSwung, bSwung;
    public TableTennis() {
        aLock = new Object();
        bLock = new Object();
        A1event = new AutoResetEvent(false);
        A2event = new AutoResetEvent(false);
        B1event = new AutoResetEvent(false);
        B2event = new AutoResetEvent(false);
        Thread A1 = new Thread(playerA1);
        Thread A2 = new Thread(playerA2);
        Thread B1 = new Thread(playerB1);
        Thread B2 = new Thread(playerB2);
        A1.Start();
        A2.Start();
        B1.Start();
        B2.Start();
    }
    public bool shot(int rate)  { ... }
    public void notifyNextServer(){
```

```
        switch (turn) {
            case 0: A1event.Set(); break;
            case 1: B1event.Set(); break;
            case 2: A2event.Set(); break;
            case 3: B2event.Set(); break;
        }
    }
    public void aSwing(string str){
        if (!aSwung && gamePlay){
            aSwung = true;
            //if I got to the ball first
            if (shot(rate)){
                Console.Write(str + " - in ");
                //wake up other side
                B1event.Set();
                B2event.Set();
            }
            else {
                Console.Write(str + " - out \n");
                Bpoints++;
                Console.WriteLine("Side B1B2 wins. Score = ({0}, {1})",
                    Apoints, Bpoints);
                //check if that was the winning point
                if (!gameDone()){
                    serve = true;
                    notifyNextServer();
                }
            }
        }
        else
            aSwung = false;
    }
    public void aServe(string str) {
        if (shot(rate)) {
            Console.Write(str + " - in ");
            //wake up other side
            B1event.Set();
            B2event.Set();
        }
        else {
            Console.Write(str + " - out \n");
            Bpoints++;
            Console.WriteLine("Side B1B2 wins. Score = ({0}, {1})",
                Apoints, Bpoints);
            //check if that was the winning point
            if (!gameDone()){
                serve = true;
                notifyNextServer();
            }
        }
    }
    public void playerA1(){
        //while game in play
        do {
            A1event.WaitOne();        //wait on my event
            if (serve && turn == 0){ //if it is my turn to serve
                serve = false;        //then serve
```

```
                turn = 1;
                totalServes++;
                aServe("A1");
            } else
            lock(aLock) {                      //if I got to the ball first
                aSwing("A1");
            }
        } while (gamePlay);
    }
  }
}
```

In the following section, we will further discuss the more general form of events, user-defined events, and event-driven programming.

2.6 Event-Driven Programming

Event-driven programming is a programming style in which the flow of the program is determined by events such as user actions, sensor outputs to the program, or message arrivals from other programs. These events can occur at the times that are unknown to the program. Event-driven programming requires a parallel computing mechanism to listen and process events without interrupting the currently executing processes and without having to waiting for the processes to complete. A parallel thread is created to handle each event.

Exception handling can be considered to be a special case of event handling, where the events are the abnormal situations that occur during computation. Although the mechanisms used for handling exceptions and events look different, the underlying principles are the same. Exception handling uses a pair of operations: throw and catch, where the throw is an event, while the catch is an event handler. The main difference is that a process throwing an exception will be stopped, waiting for the exception being processed, while an event handler normally does not force any other process to stop. This section starts with discussing exception handling.

2.6.1 Exception Handling

An **exception** is a forced deviation caused by a known yet unknown event, which represents a situation abnormal from the normal execution sequence of the program. It is known because we have to define the types of exceptions that can be handled. However, it is unknown when an exception will occur.

There are **internal exceptions** and **external exceptions**. An internal exception is caused by a message to the CPU seeking attention from a source within the CPU itself; for example, when an operation performs a division by 0, which causes an overflow, or it executes an illegal (undefined) operation, which cannot be executed.

An external exception is caused by a message to the CPU seeking attention from a source outside the CPU; for example, bus error and device busy, and so on. Memory-related exceptions, such as out-of-memory and memory access violation, can be considered to be internal or external in different systems, because memory used to be outside CPU. However, memory is built as a part of the processor in the latest computer architecture. External exceptions are also called **interrupts**. Events such as mouse click, tasks competition, and sensory inputs are similar to the interrupts. However, they are not considered to be abnormal situations, and thus they are not considered exceptions. However, they can be considered to be interrupts. The division line is often not clear. We will discuss the events and event-driven programming in the next subsection.

Exceptions are difficult to handle and are normally handled at all levels of a computer system. At hardware level, when an exception occurs, the hardware will identify the exception source, compute the exception handler's entry address, and load the address into the program counter of the CPU. Thus, CPU starts to execute the exception handler's code. A very limited number of exceptions can be handled at the hardware level; for example, the Motorola 68000 processor can handle up to 256 exceptions and interrupts. At operating system level, more exceptions can be handled. For each exception, a simple exception handler will be provided. At the program language level, most program languages provide exception handling mechanisms. At the user program level, a programmer can write application-specific exception handlers to handle various semantics-related exceptions. Only the programmers know the semantics of their programs.

At each level, exception handling can make use of the exception handlers below and can add extra exception handlers.

If an exception is not caught by an exception handler at the current level, there are two possibilities. The exception may be caught by a lower level of exception handler and an error message will normally be shown. The programmer can either terminate the program or enter the debugging state to see what instruction or operation caused the exception. If the exception is not caught by any exception handler at any level, the program will normally crash or freeze.

Exceptions in C# provide a structured, uniform, and type-safe way of handling both system-level and application-level error conditions. System.Exception is the root class for all external and internal exceptions. According to the language specification, the class has a few common properties that all exceptions share:

- Message is a read-only property of type string that contains a human-readable description of the reason for the exception.
- InnerException is a read-only property of type Exception. If its value is non-null, it refers to the exception that caused the current exception, that is, the current exception was raised in a catch block handling the InnerException. Otherwise, its value is null, indicating that this exception was not caused by another exception. The number of exception objects chained together in this manner can be arbitrary.

The external exceptions are directly defined in System.Exception, which includes System.IOException and System.WebException. The internal exceptions are subdivided into two types: System.ApplicationException, which includes exceptions generated by executing a user program, and System.SystemException, which includes exceptions generated by the common language runtime.

At the application layer, the programmers can define the application-level exception classes, by extending one of the language-level exception classes, making the System.Exception root class for all exceptions in C#. The syntax of user-defined exception structure, which is similar to that of C++ and Java, is given in BNF notations as follows:

```
<exception-structure> ::= try <code-block> <handler-list>
<handler-list> ::= <catch-clause-list> |
                   <catch-clause-list> finally <code-block>
<catch-clause-list> ::= <empty> | <catch-clause> |
                        <catch-clause-list> <catch-clause>
<catch-clause> ::= catch (<except-declaration>) <code-block>
<except-declaration> ::=   <type-name> | <type-name> <identifier>
<throw-statement> ::= throw | throw <expression>
```

The following code shows an example of the syntax structure of the BNF notation, where the code in each clause is not given. Concrete examples will be given later.

```
Try {
   // Statements that perform required operations.
   // These operations may cause exceptions; for example,
   // they request memory dynamically, and memory may not be available, or
   // they open a disk file and the file may not exist or may not be open.
   // "throw" statements may be used to call a particular handler.
```

```
}
catch(Type1 e1) { // variable e1 is optional
   // Exception handler handling Type1 exceptions. If a Type1 exception
   // occurs, this handler will be called automatically.
}
catch(TypeN eN)    { // variable eN is optional
   // Exception handler handling Type1 exceptions. If a TypeN exception
   // occurs, this handler will be called automatically
}
Finally {
   //The finally block will always be executed, no matter whether an exception
   //has occurred or not, no matter whether an exception has been caught or not.
}
```

The code block following the try keyword is the code that is a part of the code required by the semantics of the program. However, an exception condition may occur in this part of the code; for example, if there is a division operation on a variable whose value could be zero, or a memory request is made, which may or may not receive the required memory.

The handler list may consist of zero, one, or multiple handlers (catch clauses), with or without a final handler. Each of these catch clauses handle a different type of exception. Each catch clause starts with the keyword catch and is followed by declaring an exception reference and a block of code. The reference will be used to receive the "return" object of a throw statement in the try statement. The code block in the catch statement will handle the exception in a specific way; for example, print an error message contained in the object of the exception reference.

The throw statement is similar to a return statement. It is normally used in the try statement to exit (return from) the block and possibly to pass an object to an exception reference. Multiple throw statements can be used. If the types (exception classes) of the return objects are different, different exception handlers (multiple catch statements) must be used. We can also consider that catch is a function and throw statement is a function call to the catch function. Since there can be multiple catch statements, catch is an overloaded function with different parameter types. The object in the throw statement will be parameter-passed to the catch function.

When an exception occurs, the system searches for the nearest catch clause that can handle the exception, as determined by the runtime type of the exception. First, the current method is searched for a lexically enclosing try statement, and the associated catch clauses of the try statement are considered in order. If that fails, the method that called the current method is searched for a lexically enclosing try statement that encloses the point of the call to the current method. This search continues until a catch clause is found that can handle the current exception, by naming an exception class that is of the same class, or a base class, of the run-time type of the exception being thrown. A catch clause that does not name an exception class can handle any exception.

Once a matching catch clause is found, the system prepares to transfer control to the first statement of the catch clause. Before execution of the catch clause begins, the system first executes, in order, any finally clauses that were associated with try statements more nested than the one that caught the exception

Let's first see a small example that handles the divided-by-zero internal exception:

```
using System;
class ExceptionDemo1 {
    public static void Main() {
        Int32 x = 2, y = 2, z = 5;
        Try {
            z = (x + y) / (x - y);
            Console.WriteLine("What is the value of z?");
        }
```

```
        catch (DivideByZeroException) { // no variable
            Console.WriteLine("A divide-by-zero exception has occurred.");
        }
        finally {
            Console.WriteLine("The finally block is always executed.");
        };
        Console.WriteLine("The original value of z = {0}", z);
    }
}
```

This program does not have a varaiable name in the catch clause. The exception handler is matched by the type of the exception defined in the system. The output of the program is shown as follows:

```
A divide-by-zero exception has occurred.
The finally block is always executed.
The original value of z = 5.
```

The following code shows a more complex example, where two user-defined exception classes, rangeException and heapException, are defined, and two throw statements are used in the try-block to pass parameter values into the catch clauses.

```
using System;
class rangeException : Exception {
    private Int32 r;
    public rangeException(Int32 i) { // constructor
        r = i; ;
        Console.WriteLine("User defined exception called with parameter value: {0}",
i);
    }
    public Int32 getRange() { return r; }
}
class heapException : Exception {
    private string msg;
    public heapException(string str) {
        msg = str;
        Console.WriteLine("User defined exception called: {0}", str);
    }
    public string getMsg() { return msg; }
}
class ExceptionDemo2 {
    public static void Main() {
        Int32[] queue;
        Console.WriteLine("Enter queue-size >= 10:");
        String str = Console.ReadLine(); // read a string of characters
        Int32 n = Convert.ToInt32(str);  // Convert string to integer
        try {
            if (n < 10)
                throw new rangeException(n); // throw exception
            queue = new Int32[n];        // Create an array of integers
            if (queue == null)
                throw new heapException("heap request failed");
        }
        catch (rangeException range) {
            Console.WriteLine("range exception occurred: input = {0}",
range.getRange());
        }
        catch (heapException h) {
            Console.WriteLine("Heap exception: {0}", h.getMsg());
        }
```

```
    }
}
```

The output of the program, when 5 is entered, is shown below:

```
Enter queue-size >= 10:
5
User defined exception called with parameter value: 5
range exception occurred: input = 5
```

2.6.2 Event-Driven Programming Concepts and Mechanisms

Exception handling deals with the abnormal situations that occur during computation. The same idea can be applied to handle special interesting situations that occur at the time unknown to the program.

Event-driven programming or **event-based programming** is a programming style in which the flow of the program is determined by user actions (mouse clicks, key presses), sensor outputs to the program, or messages' arrival from other programs. Event-driven programming can also be defined as a software architecture technique, in which the execution flow is clearly divided into two sections: the first is the event selection or the event detection section, and the second is the event-handling section. Typically, the application is running in a loop, checking for the arrival of an event.

Before we start to discuss the programming detail, we discuss differences of the two different programming styles: the control flow-driven approach and the event-driven approach. The control flow-driven approach is based on the assumption that the system has one processor only, which can do one thing at any time. Thus, programming is about defining the sequence (order) of tasks that need to be done by the processor sequentially. On the other hand, event-driven approach does not assume that there is one processor only. In fact, you can assume that the number of processors is unlimited. If an event occurs, the event handler will be triggered and executed immediately, without having to wait for the availability of the processor. If multiple events occur, all the event handlers will be triggered and executed simultaneously. If the real system has one processor only, the event handlers will be executed sequentially. However, the programmer does not define the order which handler will be executed first. Instead, they compete for the resource. The program should give correct result, no matter which event handler wins.

This execution style changes the way we write our programs. As an example of the control flow-driven approach, we consider a possible daily routine of a medical professor, who runs between the office and other locations outside the office to perform the duties, as shown in Figure 2.23.

This is a fully scheduled program that has a balanced consideration to handle all the duties that the professor needs to handle. There are several problems in this approach.

- Students or patients do not need the presence of the professor at the time the professor is scheduled to see them, resulting in a waste of the professor's time;
- Students or patients, particularly the ICU (Intensive Care Unit) patients, need access to the professor at unscheduled times, but the professor is not available.
- The professor's time in the office is split into small pieces, which makes it hard for them to concentrate on the work that requires a large piece of time, such as research.

In traditional procedural programming, a method (procedure) is a named block of code that can be called and reused by other programs. A method is identified by the name, parameter list, and return type. When programming, a method is coded as a component in the program and is part of the control flow, which is similar to the approach shown in Figure 2.23.

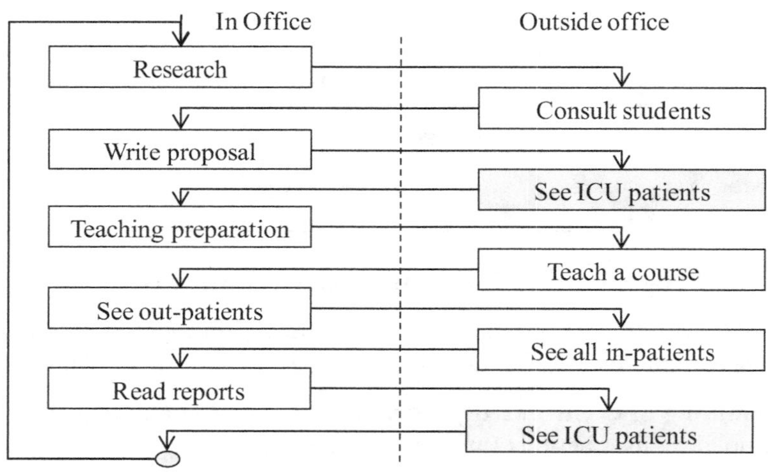

Figure 2.23. Fully scheduled routine of a medical professor

The control flow-driven approach can be demonstrated in the computing model in Figure 2.24. In this model, there is a unique entry point for the program. The input data can be given at different points in time. However, the input data will be processed when the control flow returns to the point. The input handlers are methods that are called after the input statements. This approach corresponds to the polling model for input processing in hardware design.

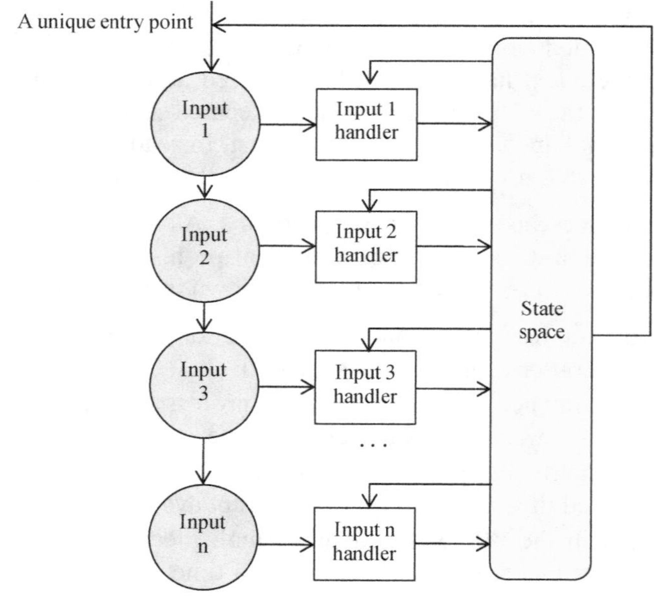

Figure 2.24. Flow-driven model with inputs at different points

A better solution is to use the event-driven approach, as shown in Figure 2.25. In this approach, mechanisms called event board and alert board are provided. The event board will allow less urgent requests to be recorded. The professor can check (poll) the event board regularly; for example, twice a day. On the other hand, the alert board is for more urgent requests, which will send an alert to the professor once an urgent request has arrived.

Different from procedural programming, in event-driven programs, methods can be written as event handlers that are not in the control flow. The programmer does not know when the handlers will be called, as shown in Figure 2.26.

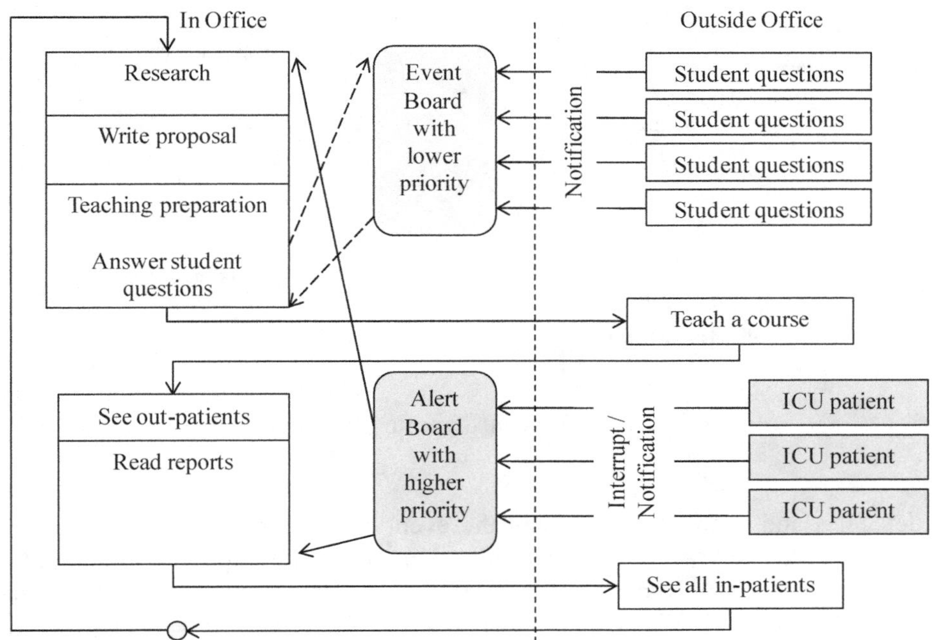

Figure 2.25. Routine of a medical professor in event-driven approach

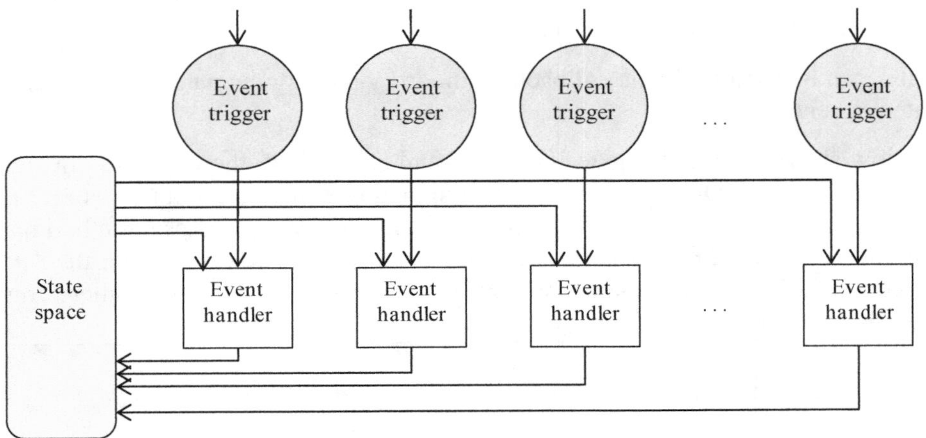

Figure 2.26. Event-driven model with multiple entry points

The event-driven approach allows the developer to "subscribe" to particular actions carried out by the user, as shown in Figure 2.27. Therefore, instead of expecting everything, the developers can choose what they want to be notified of and react to that action.

In C#, an event is a notification that a certain interesting "event" has occurred. Each event contains information about the specific event; for example, a mouse click on a GUI would say which button was clicked and where on the form it was clicked. Then, the program can call a specific method to perform a certain computation.

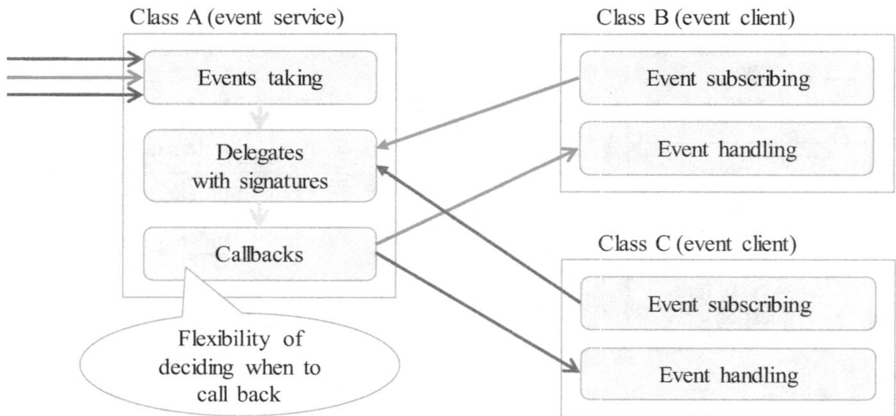

Figure 2.27. Event-handling mechanism

C# combines delegates and events to implement the event-driven programming. A delegate declaration defines a reference type that can be used to encapsulate a method with a specific signature (return type and parameter types of the method). A delegate can be used like a class to create an instance, which encapsulates a static or an instance method. A delegate is similar to a function pointer in C++. However, delegates are type-safe and no implicit type-casting will be performed.

Delegates have the following properties:

- Delegates allow a method name to be passed as a parameter, and thus allow the same method call to be associated with different methods.
- Delegates can be used to define callback methods by passing the name of the event handler to the delegate reference.

The program below shows how a delegate is defined and used. First, the keyword "delegate" is used to define the reference name MyDelegate. The method signature contains a double return value and an int type parameter. Then, a wrapper method CallDelegate is defined, which takes a method name mName as the formal parameter. When the CallDelegate method is called in the Main method, the actual parameters (method names) DelegatePiValue and DelegateEValue are passed to the formal parameter, resulting in them being called, respectively.

```
using System;
delegate double MyDelegate(int i);    // Declare a delegate
class Program {
    public static void Main() {
        // Call the delegate as static methods
        CallDelegate(new MyDelegate(DelegatePiValue));
        CallDelegate(new MyDelegate(DelegateEValue));
        // call the delegates as instance methods
        MyDelegate d1 = new MyDelegate(DelegatePiValue);
        d1(10);
        MyDelegate d2 = new MyDelegate(DelegateEValue);
        d2(20);
    }
    public static void CallDelegate(MyDelegate mName) {
        mName(100);
```

```
    }
    public static double DelegatePiValue(int i) {
        double p = i + System.Math.PI;
        System.Console.WriteLine("Handler Pi: {0}", p);
        return p;
    }
    public static double DelegateEValue(int i){
        double e = i + System.Math.E;
        System.Console.WriteLine("Handler E called: {0}", e);
        return e;
    }
}
```

After we have understood the delegate, we can define events and associate an event with a delegate. The event keyword allows us to specify a delegate that will be called upon the occurrence of an event in our code. The delegate can have one or more associated methods that will be called when the code indicates that the event has occurred. An event in one program can be made available to other programs that target the .NET Framework common language runtime. The following steps can be followed in order to create and use C# events:

1. Create a new or identify a predefined delegate. When we define the event, we must make sure that there is a delegate to use with the event keyword. If the event is predefined, the handler of the event need only know the name of the delegate.
2. Create an event class, which contains following members:
   - An event created from the delegate.
   - A method (optional) that verifies that an instance of the delegate declared with the event keyword exists. Otherwise, this logic must be placed in the code that triggers the event.
   - Methods that call the event. These methods can be overrides of some base class methods.
3. Define one or more classes that connect methods to the event. Each of these classes will include:
   - Association of one or more methods with the event in the base class using the += (add) and -= (remove) operators.
   - The definition of the methods that will be associated with the event.
4. Use the event:
   - Create an object of the class that contains the event declaration.
   - Create an object of the class that contains the event definition, using the constructor that you defined.

The following code shows an example of combining delegate and event to handle events using different event handlers.

```
using System;
public delegate void MyDelegate();    // delegate declaration
public interface EventInterface {
    event MyDelegate MyEvent;         // Define an event
    void EventEmitter();              // to be implemented in EventClass
}
public class EventClass : EventInterface {    // implement the interface
    public event MyDelegate  MyEvent;         // Define an event
    public void EventEmitter() {
        if (MyEvent != null)
            MyEvent();                        // emit an event
    }
```

```
}
public class MainClass {
    static private void TouchSensor(){    // Event handler touch sensor
        Console.WriteLine("Touched");
    }
    static private void MotionSensor(){  // Event handler motion sensor
        Console.WriteLine("Motion Detected");
    }
    static public void Main(){
        EventInterface i = new EventClass();
        i.MyEvent += new MyDelegate(TouchSensor);    // Add an event method
        i.EventEmitter();                            // Emit an event
        i.MyEvent -= new MyDelegate(TouchSensor);    // Remove the method
        i.MyEvent += new MyDelegate(MotionSensor);   // Add an event method
        i.EventEmitter();                             // Emit an event
    }
}
```

As we discussed in the previous section, there are two different programming styles: the control flow-driven approach and the event-driven approach. The event-driven approach assumes that the number of processors is unlimited. If an event occurs, the event handler will be triggered and executed immediately. Thus, event-driven approach can be used for starting parallel computing threads. You can follow the examples above to write your own class to start a new thread using event-driven approach. You can also use the library functions created for this purpose.

In .Net Framework Library, a class BackgroundWorker is provided to start an operation in a separate thread. It is particularly useful if you need to run a time-consuming operation that may prevent your main program from progressing or make your GUI seem to freeze; for example, downloading a file, access a database, or calling a web service. The class offers a way of performing asynchronous communication. An example is given in MSDN library that demonstrates the use of the BackgroundWorker class:

http://msdn.microsoft.com/en-us/library/vstudio/system.componentmodel.backgroundworker

2.6.3 Case Study: An Electronic Commerce Application in Event-Driven Approach

A chicken farm sets the chicken price based on its constraints and business model. The chicken farm can change the price at any time. It publishes the chicken price in an electronic board whenever the price changes. This is similar to the prices published by a gas station or the stock of a company.

There are multiple retailers that buy the chickens from the farm. They can check the price at any time and make their decision to buy at the time that can maximize the profit. Checking the price will take some effort from the retailer, and thus the retailers will not check the price too often. The problem is that they can miss a price cut if they do not check the price all the time. The farm then implements a mechanism called a "Price Cut" event. The retailers can subscribe to the event. Whenever the chicken price goes down, the subscribers will receive a notification.

In this example, we will focus on implementing an event-driven model that facilitates the e-commerce application. We will not discuss the business models that can maximize the profit of the farm or the retailers.

We define three classes called ChickenFarm, Retailers, and myApplication, respectively, as shown in the upper part of Figure 2.28. The lower part of the diagram shows the threads started from ChickenFarm and Retailers classes.

The application works as follows. The Main method in the myApplication class starts one ChickenFarm thread and N Retailers threads. It registers the chickenOnSale() method (event handler) in all the Retailers threads to the priceCut event in the ChickenFarm thread. The priceCut event is defined as a delegate that can call all the subscribed event handlers when the event occurs.

The C# program below implements a simplified version of the e-commerce application. We use a random number generator to generate the chicken prices between 5 and 10 every 500 milliseconds, and 50 iterations will be executed. Whenever a smaller number is generated, a price cut event will be emitted. Three retailer threads are created, and each thread will check the price every 1,000 milliseconds. As you can see in this example, the price changes every 500 milliseconds, while the retailers check the price every 1,000 milliseconds. Without the event notification, the retailers will miss price cuts. Why does a retailer need to check the price if there is a notification system? If the price keeps increasing and the retailer runs out of chickens, the retailer will still need to check the chicken price and buy chickens.

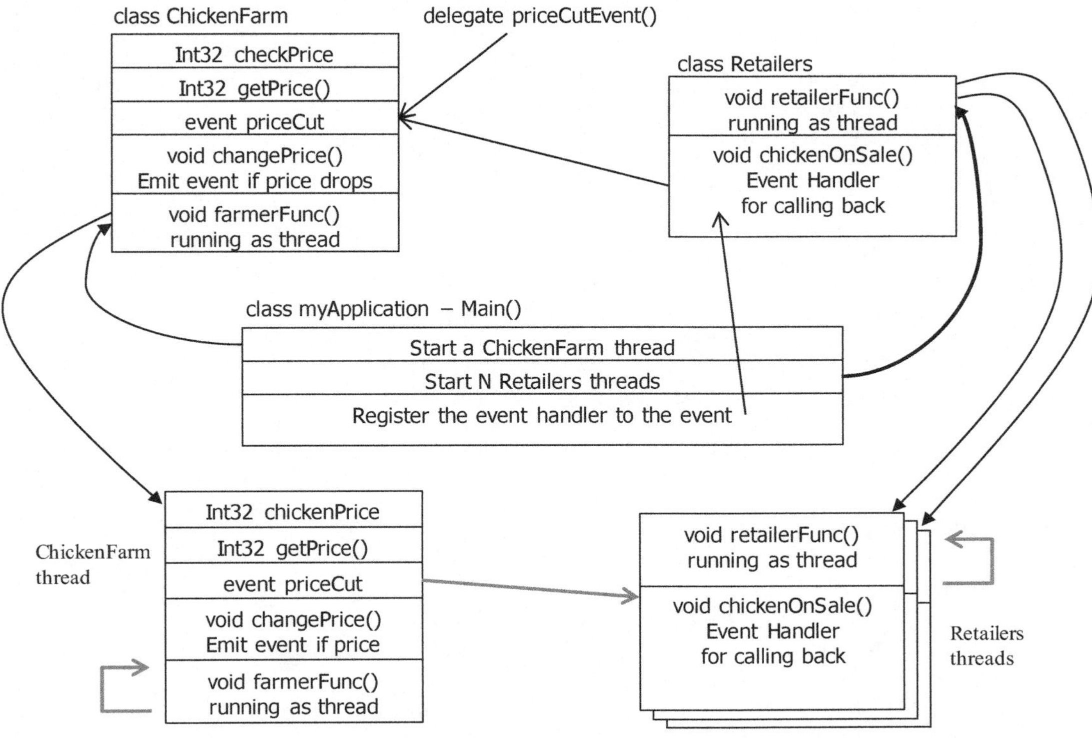

Figure 2.28. Class diagram and the threads started

You can test the program by creating a console application in Visual Studio and copy-paste the following program into the application.

```
using System;
using System.Threading;
namespace eCommerce {
    public delegate void priceCutEvent(Int32 pr); // Define a delegate
    public class ChickenFarm {
        static Random rng = new Random(); // To generate random numbers
        public static event priceCutEvent priceCut; // Link event to delegate
        private static Int32 chickenPrice = 10;
        public Int32 getPrice() { return chickenPrice; }
        public static void changePrice(Int32 price) {
            if (price < chickenPrice) { // a price cut
                if (priceCut != null)   // there is at least a subscriber
                    priceCut(price);    // emit event to subscribers
            }
            chickenPrice = price;
```

```
        }
        public void farmerFunc() {
            for (Int32 i = 0; i < 50; i++) {
                Thread.Sleep(500);
                // Take the order from the queue of the orders;
                // Decide the price based on the orders
                Int32 p = rng.Next(5, 10);
                // Console.WriteLine("New Price is {0}", p);
                ChickenFarm.changePrice(p);
            }
        }
    }
    public class Retailer {
        public void retailerFunc() {    //for starting thread
            ChickenFarm chicken = new ChickenFarm();
            for (Int32 i = 0; i < 10; i++) {
                Thread.Sleep(1000);
                Int32 p = chicken.getPrice();
                Console.WriteLine("Store{0} has everyday low price: ${1} each",
Thread.CurrentThread.Name, p); // Thread.CurrentThread.Name prints thread name
            }
        }
        public void chickenOnSale(Int32 p) {  // Event handler
           // order chickens from chicken farm - send order into queue
            Console.WriteLine("Console.WriteLine("Thread {0}: chickens are on sale:
as low as ${1} each", Thread.CurrentThread.Name, p); // It prints thread name
        }
    }
    public class myApplication {
        static void Main(string[] args) {
            ChickenFarm chicken = new ChickenFarm();
            Thread farmer = new Thread(new ThreadStart(chicken.farmerFunc));
            farmer.Start();         // Start one farmer thread
            farmer.Name = "farmer";
            Retailer chickenstore = new Retailer();
            ChickenFarm.priceCut += new priceCutEvent(chickenstore.chickenOnSale);
            Thread[] retailers = new Thread[3];
            for (int i = 0; i < 3; i++) { // N =  3 here
                // Start N retailer threads
                retailers[i] = new Thread(new
ThreadStart(chickenstore.retailerFunc));
                retailers[i].Name = (i + 1).ToString();
                retailers[i].Start();
            }
        }
    }
}
```

In the foregoing code, an event handler "chickenOnSale" is a special piece of code. It resides in the retailers, but the caller is the chickenFarmer. The question is, where is the event handler "chickenOnSale" being executed, in the chickenFarmer or in the retailers? The answer is in the chickenFarmer. The output of the code is as follows, when the code is executed.

```
Thread farmer: chickens are on sale: as low as $5 each
Store3 has everyday low price: $5 each
Store2 has everyday low price: $5 each
Store1 has everyday low price: $5 each
Store1 has everyday low price: $8 each
```

```
Store2 has everyday low price: $8 each
Store3 has everyday low price: $8 each
Store3 has everyday low price: $9 each
Store1 has everyday low price: $9 each
Store2 has everyday low price: $9 each
Thread farmer: chickens are on sale: as low as $6 each
Store2 has everyday low price: $6 each
Store1 has everyday low price: $6 each
Store3 has everyday low price: $6 each
Thread farmer: chickens are on sale: as low as $8 each
Store2 has everyday low price: $8 each
Store1 has everyday low price: $8 each
Store3 has everyday low price: $8 each
Thread farmer: chickens are on sale: as low as $7 each
Thread farmer: chickens are on sale: as low as $5 each
Store2 has everyday low price: $5 each
Store3 has everyday low price: $5 each
Store1 has everyday low price: $5 each
Thread farmer: chickens are on sale: as low as $6 each
Store3 has everyday low price: $6 each
Store2 has everyday low price: $6 each
Store1 has everyday low price: $6 each
Thread farmer: chickens are on sale: as low as $5 each
Store1 has everyday low price: $6 each
Store2 has everyday low price: $6 each
Store3 has everyday low price: $6 each
Store2 has everyday low price: $8 each
Store1 has everyday low price: $8 each
Store3 has everyday low price: $8 each
Thread farmer: chickens are on sale: as low as $7 each
Thread farmer: chickens are on sale: as low as $6 each
Store1 has everyday low price: $6 each
Store3 has everyday low price: $6 each
Store2 has everyday low price: $6 each
Thread farmer: chickens are on sale: as low as $5 each
Thread farmer: chickens are on sale: as low as $6 each
Thread farmer: chickens are on sale: as low as $5 each
Thread farmer: chickens are on sale: as low as $6 each
Thread farmer: chickens are on sale: as low as $5 each
Thread farmer: chickens are on sale: as low as $5 each
Thread farmer: chickens are on sale: as low as $6 each
Thread farmer: chickens are on sale: as low as $5 each
Thread farmer: chickens are on sale: as low as $6 each
Thread farmer: chickens are on sale: as low as $7 each
Thread farmer: chickens are on sale: as low as $5 each
Thread farmer: chickens are on sale: as low as $6 each
Press any key to continue . . .
```

Event-driving programming assumes that you have unlimited number of workers to do the jobs. Whenever a job is doable, one worker will do it. You do not know who will do it. What is important is that the job is done. The developer must write the code in such a way that the correct result will be generated no matter which worker does the job and when is the job done. This is the theory. In practice, the workers are limited. The language environment normally uses a predetermined worker to do certain job. In C#, it is done by the worker that runs the event emitter or the caller thread, that is, the same worker executing the chickenFarmer thread. The worker process will create a new unnamed thread to execute the event handler. Of course, it also depends on the configuration of the program: you can configure your program to run in perCall mode, perSession mode, or Singleton mode. A new worker process will be started for each call to the event handler if perCall mode is selected. We will further discuss the concurrency and state sharing issues in Chapter 7 in Part II of this book.

We can extend the example above to a more general situation as shown in Figure 2.29, which puts many of the concepts and mechanisms discussed in this chapter together, including multithreading, deadlock, synchronized buffers, semaphore, and event-driven programming.

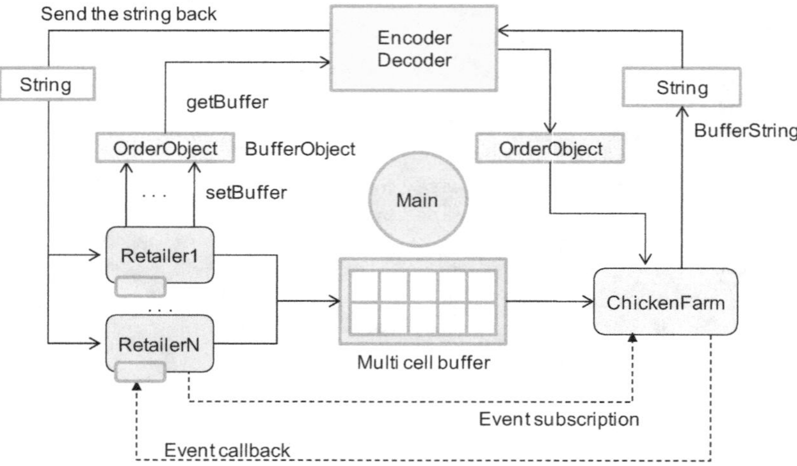

Figure 2.29. Extended chicken farm example

Below is an operation scenario of the e-commerce system:

(1) A retailer generates an OrderObject and sends the order to the Encoder/Decoder for encryption.
(2) In order to transfer an OrderObject to the Encoder/Decoder, we define a BufferObject, which contains an OrderObject as data, plus a few methods such as get and set methods.
(3) Once the Encoder/Decoder receives the OrderObject, it converts the object into a string, and then encrypts the string.
(4) The Encoder/Decoder sends the encrypted string back to the retailer.
(5) The retailer sends the encrypted string to the ChickenFarmer through a queue. The farmer sends the encrypted string to the Encoder/Decoder for decryption through the BufferString. The buffer is similar to the BufferObject. BufferObject contains an object as data, while BufferString contains a string as data.
(6) The decrypted order is then sent back to the chicken farm.

The components of the diagram are explained as follows:

1. **BufferObject** class: The BufferObject class contains data of the OrderObject, which has at least the following private data members and public methods:

- senderId: the identity of the sender, you can use thread name or thread id;
- cardNo: a long integer that represents a credit card number;
- amount: an integer that represents the number of chickens to order;
- setID and getID: methods allow the users to write and read senderId member;
- setCardNo and getCardNo: methods allow the users to write and read cardNo member;
- setAmt and getAmt: methods allow the users to write and read Amount member.

You can define OrderObject to be a class containing the data members listed above. In this way, the BufferObject class will contain one data member of OrderObject class, and two methods: getOrderObject() and setOrderObject(). If you directly define the BufferObject to contain the data members listed above without an OrderObject class, you will need to define a get- and a set-method for each data member.

The methods getOrderObject() and setOrderObject() must be synchronized/monitored, as multiple retailers share the buffer and the encoder/decoder thread can read the buffer at the same time.

An alternative implementation of this Buffer class is to have one data member, one set-method, and one get-method. Then, one can create three objects to transfer the three pieces of data: senderID, cardNo, and amount of the OrderObject, respectively.

2. **BufferString** class for string: The class is similar to the BufferOrder, except containing a string as data, instead of containing OrderObject as data.

3. **Encoder/Decoder** is a class and will be instantiated as a service thread or two service threads that offer two service operations: encoding and decoding. One can implement different functions here; for example, encryption and decryption for security purpose, or format transformation for interoperability purpose.

4. **Retailer1** through **RetailerN**, each is a thread instantiated from the same class or a method in the class; for example, N = 5. In each retailer thread, a loop is used to generate m (e.g., m = 10) orders. Each order is an OrderObject class object. The object is sent to the encoder/decoder threads for encoding. The encoded string is sent back to the retailer. Different ways are possible; for example, one can define a one-cell buffer with a getID method. A retailer reads the string if the ID matches. Then, the string is sent to the chicken farm thread through a multicell buffer. A semaphore can be used to manage the cells. Each retailer thread will print a list of human-friendly output (orders placed).

5. **Event** and **Handler**: The ChickenFarm class will define a price-cut event and emit an event if there is a price-cut: it calls the retailers if a price-cut occurs. Each retailer will define an event handler for the chicken farm to call back when a price-cut event occurs. More examples of event-driven programs such as web services GUI programming, XML validation, and robotics programming will be discussed in later chapters.

6. **MultiCellBuffer** class: This class has n data cells. The number n of cells is smaller than the number of retailers N. A setOneCell and a getOneCell methods can be defined to write and to read the data. A semaphore of value n can be used to manage the cells.

7. **Main**: The Main thread will perform necessary preparation, create the Buffer classes, instantiate the objects, create threads, and start threads.

A **deadlock** can occur in such a complex multithreading program if the threads and shared resources are not properly planned and designed; for example, if one creates three objects to transfer the three pieces of data: senderID, cardNo, and amount, respectively, and different retailers can hold (lock) an object while waiting for the second object, or holding two objects and waiting for the third object, a deadlock can occur. Figure 2.30 shows a design where deadlock can occur.

That a deadlock can occur does not mean a deadlock will occur every time. It also depends on timing. This situation actually makes things worse, as you may not detect the deadlock possibility during the test phase.

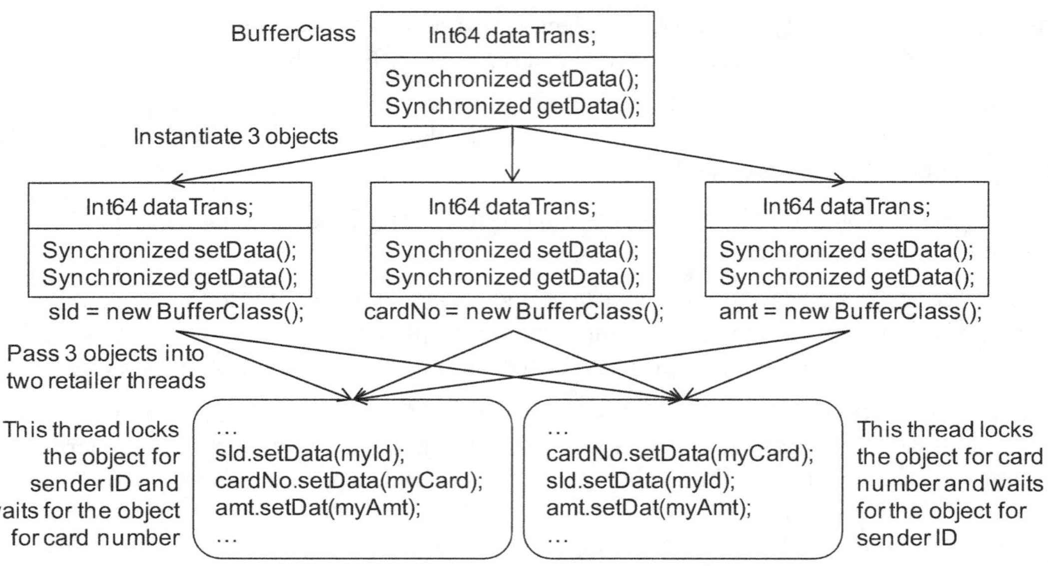

Figure 2.30. A design of the Buffer class where a deadlock can occur

2.7 Multithreading Performance

In this section, we first define the parameters we use to measure the performance. We use Amdahl's Law to caluate the speedup and the overhead. We then present the experiments that measure the parameters.

2.7.1 Amdahl's Law

The performance of multithreading programming can be measured in two parameters: speedup and efficiency. The speedup measures how much faster is the parallel execution than the serial execution:

$$\text{Speedup} = \frac{\text{SerialExecTime}}{\text{ParallelExecTime}}$$

Assume that the number of processor used to execute the multithreading program *P* is *N* and the speedup is *S*(*P*), the efficiency is then

$$\text{Efficiency} = \frac{S(P)}{N}$$

The performance of multithreading programming is determined by a number factors: the portion of computing that is being executed in parallel on multiple processors, the number of processors that execute the parallel threads, and the overhead to create and manage the threads. Assume that fraction or portion of the program that can be executed in parallel is *f*, and this fraction is executed in N processors. The overall performance can be calculated using Amdahl's Law: overhead

$$\text{Speedup} = \frac{\text{SerialExecTime}}{\text{ParallelExecTime}} = \frac{\text{SerialExecTime}}{\frac{f * SerialExecTime}{N} + (1 - f) * SerialExecTime + \text{Overhead}}$$

$$= \frac{1}{\frac{f}{N} + (1 - f) + \text{Overhead}}$$

where, the Overhead is the time needed to create and manage the threads.

We can measure the Overhead by running the multithreading program using one processor only of the multiprocessor computer. In this case, $f = 0$ and the Speedup = 1 / (1 + Overhead), resulting in Speedup < 1. Then, we can measure the Overhead by:

$$\text{Overhead} = \frac{1}{Speedup} - 1$$

How do we find the value of f in the formula? We can count the instructions of the code and determine the fraction by examining which code are executed in parallel and which are executed in serial. We can also detemine f by experiment. We run the multithreading program on N processors and measure value of Speedup. Then, we calculate f by transforming the formula above into

$$f = \frac{\frac{1}{Speedup} - \text{Overhead} - 1}{\frac{1}{N} - 1}$$

2.7.2 Multithreading Experiments

The problem we choose for the multithreading experiments is the Collatz conjecture proposed by Collatz in 1937. The problem is well known as a counterexample of program termination. In proving the total correctness of a program, we need to prove the partial correctness and termination:

- Partial correctness: For every valid input, the program gives correct output. Different methods exist for proving the partial correctness: induction, symbolic execution, and so on.
- Termination: For every valid input, the program terminates in finite steps (or time). The best practice of ensuring that a program terminates is to define a loop variable that decreases strictly.

The Collatz's conjecture shows how difficult it is to show the program can terminate if the loop variable does not decrease strictly.

Take any natural number n. If n is even, divide it by 2 to obtain n/2. If n is odd, multiply it by 3 and add 1 to obtain 3n + 1. Repeat the process until the result is 1. The problem is also known as Half Or Triple Plus One (HOTPO). Collatz's conjecture is that no matter what number you start with, you will always reach 1 and the program always terminates.

No one is able to prove that the algorithm described in the Collatz conjecture will terminate or find counterexample showing that the algorithm does not terminate. Many people have been using computer programs to try to validate or find a counterexample.

In this experiment, we will write a multithreading program to try to find a counterexample. We use a 32-core computer in the Intel Manycore Testing Lab (MTL) to run the program and try to outperform many efforts that people started running years ago. Can our program be 32 times faster than those programs running on a single-core computer?

In the experiment, we will have the program being executed in 1, 4, 8, 16, and 32 threads on the 32-core machine, so that we can explore these questions:

- What would happen if we make use of more cores by increasing the number of parallel threads?
- Can the execution time, speedup, and efficiency improve proportionally to the number of cores?
- What are the overheads by increasing the number of threads?

For a given number P, we will validate all the numbers between 1 and P will terminate. In the first attempt, we simply partition the numbers into N parts for the N-thread implementation, with the first set of P/N numbers for the first thread, and the second set of P/N nnumbers for the second thread, and so on. We measure the total execution time, the speedup against the single-thread implementation, and the efficiency in each of the configurations. Table 2.7 shows the data measured and calculated. Figure 2.31 illustrates the numbers in diagrams.

Table 2.7. Execution times, speedups, and efficiencies of attempt 1

Input size	1 thread	4 Threads	8 threads	16 threads	32 threads	Speedup 4/1	Speedup 8/1	Speedup 16/1	Speedup 32/1	Efficiency 4/1	Efficiency 8/1	Efficiency 16/1	Efficiency 32/1
16000	46	16	18	37	85	2.88	2.56	1.24	0.54	72%	32%	8%	4%
32000	52	17	27	52	76	3.06	1.93	1.00	0.68	76%	24%	6%	5%
48000	64	23	27	40	88	2.78	2.37	1.60	0.73	70%	30%	10%	4%
64000	88	28	30	57	94	3.14	2.93	1.54	0.94	79%	37%	10%	5%
80000	105	34	32	57	91	3.09	3.28	1.84	1.15	77%	41%	12%	5%
96000	129	40	34	49	101	3.23	3.79	2.63	1.28	81%	47%	16%	5%
112000	151	46	47	62	107	3.28	3.21	2.44	1.41	82%	40%	15%	5%
128000	175	53	46	66	108	3.30	3.80	2.65	1.62	83%	48%	17%	5%
144000	204	62	47	79	113	3.29	4.34	2.58	1.81	82%	54%	16%	5%
160000	228	66	49	63	119	3.45	4.65	3.62	1.92	86%	58%	23%	5%
Average						**3.15**	**3.29**	**2.12**	**1.21**	**79%**	**41%**	**13%**	**5%**

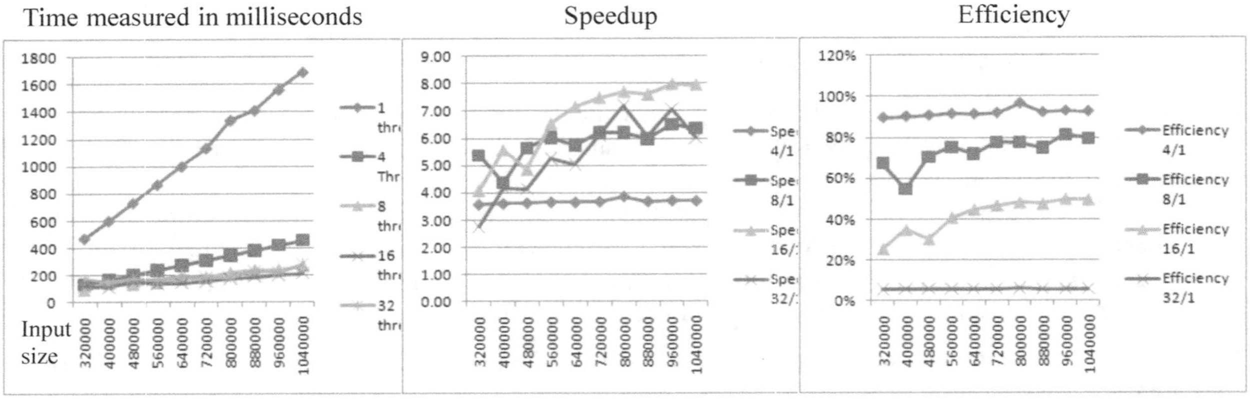

Figure 2.31. Illustration of execution times, speedups, and efficiencies in attempt 1

From the table and the figure, we observe:

- The 4-thread program's average speedup is 3.15 and the efficiency 79%. This the best performance we have in this set of experiments.
- The 8-thread program's average speedup is 3.29 and the efficiency 41%. The 8-thread performance is the highest (3.29–41%), but the efficiency is 41% only.
- The 16-thread program's performance is even worse. The average speedup is 2.12 and the efficiency 13%.
- The 32-thread program's performance is the worst. The average speedup is 1.21 and the efficiency 5%.

What is wrong with the implementation? Why do more threads make both speedups and efficiencies worse? A carefully done examination identified that the simple partition of the inputs numbers is to blame: The first thread processes all the small numbers, while the last thread processes all the large number. The larger numbers need more time to process, resulting in the last thread taking much longer to finish. The slowest thread counts for the overall performance.

To address this problem, we mix small numbers and large numbers in each subset, so that each thread will take about the same amount of time to finish. We use modulo N operation to group all the numbers with the same residue into the same subset, where N is the number of threads. We store the grouped numbers in an array. Thus, we have N arrays (0.. N-1) to store the numbers to be validated. The number with residue r goes into array r. Table 2.8 shows the data measured and calculated in the second attempt.

Table 2.8. Execution times, speedups, and efficiencies of attempt 2

Input size	1 thread	4 Threads	8 threads	16 threads	32 threads	Speedup 4/1	Speedup 8/1	Speedup 16/1	Speedup 32/1	Efficiency 4/1	Efficiency 8/1	Efficiency 16/1	Efficiency 32/1
10000	64	6	8	23	45	10.60	8.48	2.78	1.42	265%	106%	17%	16.6%
210000	327	75	40	34	68	4.38	8.19	9.63	4.79	109%	102%	60%	6.8%
410000	691	145	73	51	89	4.77	9.43	13.59	7.79	119%	118%	85%	7.5%
610000	978	223	137	68	101	4.39	7.14	14.29	9.68	110%	89%	89%	6.9%
810000	1357	302	167	96	110	4.49	8.13	14.08	12.29	112%	102%	88%	7.0%
1010000	1694	382	212	114	126	4.43	8.00	14.92	13.45	111%	100%	93%	6.9%
1210000	2051	465	224	132	135	4.41	9.14	15.54	15.22	110%	114%	97%	6.9%
1410000	2418	549	263	225	143	4.40	9.18	10.77	16.89	110%	115%	67%	6.9%
1610000	2845	633	301	176	198	4.49	9.46	16.17	14.38	112%	118%	101%	7.0%
1810000	3159	717	346	198	168	4.41	9.13	15.98	18.78	110%	114%	100%	6.9%
Average						**5.08**	**8.63**	**12.77**	**11.47**	**127%**	**108%**	**80%**	**8%**

From the table, we observe:

- The 4-thread program's average speedup is 5.08 and the efficiency is 127%. This performance is too good to be true, as the efficiency is over 100%.
- The 8-thread program's average speedup is 8.63 and the efficiency 108%. This performance is also too good to be true.
- The 16-thread program's average speedup is 12.77 and the efficiency 80%. This performance is very good if it is true.
- The 32-thread program's average speedup is 11.47 and the efficiency 8%. We see the significant drops in the efficiency.

What is wrong with the implementation? How can the efficiency go beyond 100%? A careful examination identified that the single thread is unfairly implemented: the single thread program uses a single large array, while the multithreading implementations use one smaller array for each thread. The memory management of the system must have been placed in a large array far from the processor, resulting in slower data access. The data structure's impact dominates in the single thread implementation.

To address this problem, we use T arrays in in both single thread and T-thread implementations, where T = 4, 8, 16, and 32, as shown in Figure 2.32.

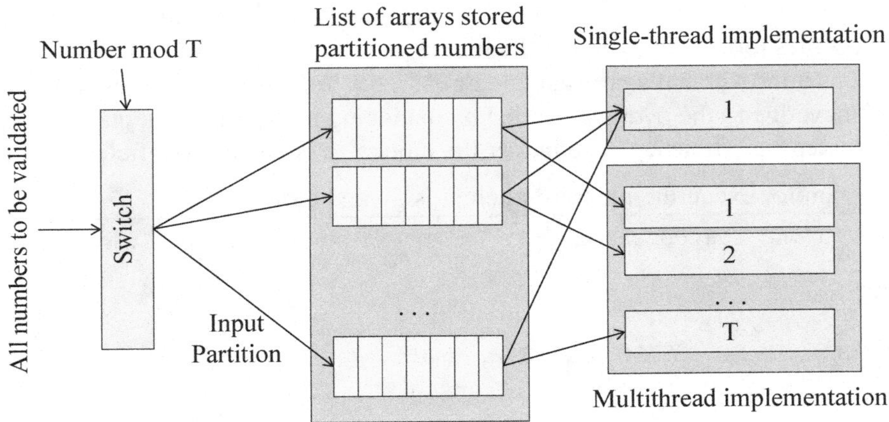

Figure 2.32. Illustration of execution times, speedups, and efficiencies

Table 2.9 shows the data measured and calculated in the third atempt. Figure 2.33 illustrates the numbers in diagrams.

Table 2.9. Execution times, speedups, and efficiencies of attempt 3

Input size	1 thread	4 Threads	8 threads	16 threads	32 threads	Speedup 4/1	Speedup 8/1	Speedup 16/1	Speedup 32/1	Efficiency 4/1	Efficiency 8/1	Efficiency 16/1	Efficiency 32/1
50000	95.8	46.3	44.7	60.3	110.4	2.07	2.14	1.59	0.87	52%	27%	10%	3.2%
550000	879.4	263.2	166.6	166.6	214.9	3.34	5.28	5.28	4.09	84%	66%	33%	5.2%
1050000	1748.5	497.1	297.5	250.9	328.9	3.52	5.88	6.97	5.32	88%	73%	44%	5.5%
1550000	2658.1	738.1	439.4	325.6	349.1	3.60	6.05	8.16	7.61	90%	76%	51%	5.6%
2050000	3589.4	1119.7	625.1	436.5	380.3	3.21	5.74	8.22	9.44	80%	72%	51%	5.0%
2550000	4534.7	1430.1	845.2	583	436.5	3.17	5.37	7.78	10.39	79%	67%	49%	5.0%
3050000	5497.1	1685.9	1037	735.9	463	3.26	5.30	7.47	11.87	82%	66%	47%	5.1%
3550000	6468.9	1954.5	1150.8	839	512.6	3.31	5.62	7.71	12.62	83%	70%	48%	5.2%
4050000	7443.9	2208.7	1261.6	931.1	594.1	3.37	5.90	7.99	12.53	84%	74%	50%	5.3%
4550000	8434.8	2397.4	1428.6	988.6	625.3	3.52	5.90	8.53	13.49	88%	74%	53%	5.5%
Average						**3.24**	**5.32**	**6.97**	**8.82**	**81%**	**66%**	**44%**	**5%**

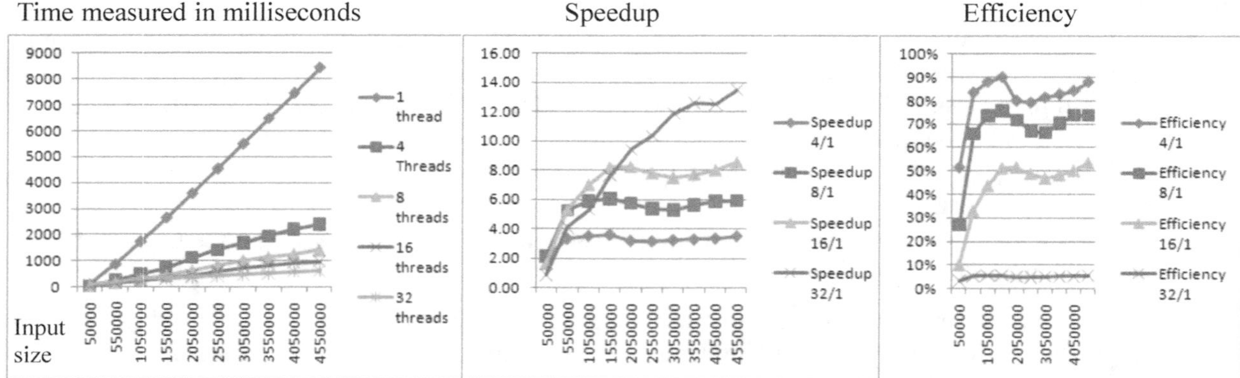

Figure 2.33. Illustration of execution times, speedups, and efficiencies in attempt 3

From the table and the figure, we observe sensive results:

- For the measured execution time, increasing threads makes use of more cores, and thus reduces the execution time. The overhead can exceed the time saved by parallel execution once the thread number becomes too big. The bigger the input size is, the more time is saved.
- For speedup (improvement against single thread), the trend is similar to execution.
- For efficiency, due to the overhead added by managing multithreading, the more the threads are used, the lower the efficiency. The bigger the input size is, the more efficient will be.

The complete program for executing the third attempt is given below:

```
using System; using System.Threading; using System.Collections.Generic;
namespace Collatz {
   class HOTPO {
      List<Int64> vs;
      public HOTPO(List<Int64> validationSet)   {
         vs = validationSet;
      }
      public void hotpoFunc(){//Collatz conjecture: Half Or Triple Plus One
      foreach(Int64 e in vs) {
         Int64 n = e;
            while (n > 1)   {
               if (n % 2 == 0)  // if n is even
                  n = n / 2;       // Integer division
               else
            n = 3 * n + 1;
```

```
} }   }  }
class Program  {
   static void Main(string[ ] args)  {
   Int64 repeatNo = 10;
   for (Int64 k = 0; k <= 5; k++) { // threadnum = 1, 2, 4, 8, 16, 32
      Int64 threadnum = (Int64)System.Math.Pow(2, k);
      for (Int64 r = 1; r <= 100; r = r + 10)  {
         float totalTime = 0;
         Int64 t = r * 50000; // define the step length of iteration
         Console.Write("The program validate HOTPO function for numbers ");
         Console.WriteLine("from 1 To " + t);
         try  {
            HOTPO[] h = new HOTPO[32];
            List<Int64>[] vSetList = new List<Int64>[32];
            for (Int64 i = 1; i <= t; i++) {
               if (vSetList[i % 32] == null)
                  vSetList[i % 32] = new List<Int64>();
               vSetList[i % 32].Add(i);
            }
            Thread[] ht = new Thread[32]; // create 32 thread object
            for (int i = 0; i < repeatNo; i++) {
               DateTime startMT = DateTime.Now;
               for (Int64 b = 0; b < threadnum; b++) {
                  for (Int64 count = 0; count < (Int64)System.Math.Pow(2, k);
count++){
                     Int64 cc = 0;
                     for (Int64 m = 0; m < 32; m++) {
                     Int64 c = b % threadnum;
                     Int64 d = m % threadnum;
                     if (c == d) {
                        if (h[c] == null)
                           if (c != m)
                              vSetList[c].AddRange(vSetList[m].ToArray());
                     } cc = c;
                  } h[cc] = new HOTPO(vSetList[cc]);
               }
            }
            for (int g = 0; g < threadnum; g++)
               ht[g] = new Thread(new ThreadStart(h[g].hotpoFunc));
            for (int g = 0; g < threadnum; g++)
               ht[g].Start();
            bool itag = true;
            while (itag)  {
               itag = false;
               for (int g = 0; g < threadnum; g++)
                  if (ht[g].IsAlive)
                  itag = true;
            };
            float manyThreadTime = (DateTime.Now - startMT).Seconds;
               if (manyThreadTime < 0)
                  Console.WriteLine(i + ": Error");
               if (manyThreadTime != 0) {
                  manyThreadTime = manyThreadTime * 1000 + (DateTime.Now -
startMT).Milliseconds;
               } else
               manyThreadTime = (DateTime.Now - startMT).Milliseconds;
                  totalTime = totalTime + manyThreadTime;
```

```
                Console.WriteLine(i + ": Time consumed by " + threadnum + " threads
in milliseconds is " + manyThreadTime);
            }
        }
        finally  { }
        Console.WriteLine("Average time consumed by " + threadnum + " threads in
milliseconds is " + totalTime / repeatNo); ;
        }
    } Console.ReadLine();
  }
}
```

2.8 Discussions

In this chapter, general distributed computing issues, particularly multitasking and multithreading, are discussed. Resource sharing and mutual exclusion in critical operations are the main problems that are addressed in this chapter. Java and C# multithreading mechanisms are studied in detail and are used to describle problems and their solutions. Event-driven programming is discussed at the end of the chapter, which is a major technique in distributed computing and is widely used in service-oriented computing in conjunction with other distributed computing techniques.

Synchronization is a critial issue in distributed computing. It is easy to make mistakes, and it is hard to detect them because of the nondeterministic nature. Incorrect design and implementation could cause not only deadlock and livelock, but also catastrophic consequences.

Therac-25 is a computer-controlled radiation-therapy machine for cancer treatment. It was first released in 1983. Between 1985 and 1986, there were multiple fatal accidents in Canada, France, and the United States, caused by radiation overdoses. The problem was traced to the synchronization mechanism among parallel threads (http://en.wikipedia.org/wiki/Therac-25). For certain operations, the execution sequence will be correct if the operator is fast. However, if the operator takes longer than the expected time to complete the operations, the patients will be overdosed.

In service-oriented computing, large parts of the synchronization and mutual exclusion have been managed by the hosting software, and the application builders are freed from worrying about such detailed arithmetic and programming issues. However, if you are designing hosting software, you will have a complex task to manage a large number of parallel threads and their syncronizations. Furthermore, if you are designing mission critical systems, you are also responsible for understanding and knowing the reliability of any systems that you use in your system. You must test and evaluate the entire system as a whole.

Name: ______________________

Date: ______________________

2.9 Exercises and Projects

1. Multiple choice questions. Choose one answer in each question only. Choose the best answer if multiple answers are acceptable.

1.1 A thread

(A) is a synonym for a method.

(B) is an antonym for a method.

(C) exists after the corresponding code is compiled.

(D) exists when the corresponding code is running.

1.2 Two threads need two resources each to proceed, and each holds one resource while waiting for the other to release the resource. This situation is called

(A) deadlock.

(B) livelock.

(C) starvation.

(D) the dining philosophers problem.

1.3 What technique can be used to make sure that parallel withdrawals cannot exceed the given limit of a bank account?

(A) Add a random delay before writing back the account balance.

(B) Implement a lock mechanism to prevent simultaneous access.

(C) Make sure a single withdrawal does not exceed half of the limit.

(D) Anyone of the above will work.

1.4 Compare and contrast livelock and deadlock.

(A) Livelock is a synonym of deadlock.

(B) Livelock is a deadlock-resolving technique.

(C) In the case of deadlock, the resources are held. In the case of livelock, the resources are still free.

(D) In the case of livelock, the resources are held. In the case of deadlock, the resources are still free.

1.5 In the state transition diagram of Java multithreading environment, a thread can enter the "running" state directly from the

(A) "blocked" state.

(B) "sleep" state.

(C) "ready" state.

(D) "waiting" state.

(E) All states above.

1.6 How many threads can be created (started) from a user-defined Thread class?

(A) None

(B) One exactly

(C) Two exactly

(D) Many

1.7 The monitor class's methods (Monitor.Enter and Monitor.Exit) in C# can be used to synchronize

(A) the entire method only, similar to the synchronized method in Java.

(B) the entire class with multiple methods.

(C) a single statement, similar to the synchronized statement in Java.

(D) All statements above are correct.

1.8 The lock(...) method in C# does not need to use try finally exception handling, because

(A) exception handling is implied.

(B) an exception can never happen if the lock(...) method is used.

(C) the lock(...) method is used for read-only.

(D) the lock(...) method is used for write-only.

1.9 What method in C# can ensure that the calling thread will not be blocked, even if the object to be accessed is locked by another thread?

(A) Monitor.Enter(...);

(B) Monitor.TryEnter(...);

(C) lock(...);

(D) ReaderWriterLock(...);

(E) None of the above

1.10 What method in the C# is used to move one thread from the "wait" state to the "ready" state?

(A) Monitor.Wait(...);

(B) Monitor.Notify(...);

(C) Monitor.Wake(...);

(D) Monitor.Pulse(...);

(E) All of the above

1.11 What method in C# can be set to wait for a locked object for a specified amount of time?

(A) Monitor.Enter(...);

(B) Monitor.TryEnter(...);

(C) lock(...);

(D) ReaderWriterLock(...);

(E) None of the above

1.12 How can a value type (instance type) of variable be synchronized in Monitor.Enter and Monitor.Exit methods?

(A) The automatic boxing and unboxing functions will handle the problem correctly.

(B) Manual boxing is required before using the variable as the Monitor methods.

(C) There is no way in which a value type of variable can be synchronized.

(D) ReaderWriterLock has to be used, instead of Monitor methods.

1.13 Can Reader/Writer locks perform better in all cases, in terms of execution time of the threads, than Monitor locks?

(A) Yes. Reader/Writer locks do not make unnecessary locking, and they are simpler in their implementations than the Monitor locks.

(B) No. Although Reader/Writer locks do not make unnecessary locking, it takes longer to execute the Reader/Writer locks.

1.14 What is the major difference between the Monitor class and the Mutex class?

(A) Mutex allows reader–reader threads to overlap.

(B) Mutex allows conditional entering of an object.

(C) Mutex can be used to synchronize the processes between different applications.
(D) Mutex methods are faster than Monitor methods.

1.15 A semaphore is a flag that can be used to
(A) prevent more processes (or threads) than permitted from accessing a pool of resources.
(B) prevent any two processes (or threads) from accessing a shared resource simultaneously.
(C) replace Mutex, because Mutex is not efficient in execution time.
(D) coordinate the order of executions among the threads.

1.16 Coordination events in C# are used to
(A) prevent more processes (or threads) than permitted from accessing a pool of resources.
(B) prevent any two processes (or threads) from accessing a shared resource simultaneously.
(C) replace Mutex, because Mutex is not efficient in execution time.
(D) coordinate the order of executions among the threads.

1.17 Event-driven programming is a programming paradigm that
(A) allows interactions between the computer program and the user or the environment.
(B) uses large modules to build an application program.
(C) supports loosely coupled communications between the modules of the program.
(D) does not allow the interruption between two indivisible instructions.

1.18 A C# delegate
(A) allows a method name to be passed as a parameter.
(B) allows the same method call to be associated with different methods.
(D) encapsulates a method with a specific signature.
(D) All of the above.

1.19 What statement is true about an event handler residing in a class?
(A) An event handler is a part of the control flow in its residing class.
(B) An event handler is a part of the control flow in calling class.
(C) An event handler does not belong to the control flow of any class.
(D) All of the above.

1.20 What is the main difference between a multicell buffer and queue?
(A) They handle different types of data.
(B) They differ in the way the cells are accessed.
(C) They differ in the architecture style they are used in.
(D) All of the above.

2. What are the differences between a program/method and process/thread?

3. Compare and contrast a multiprocess (multitask) operating system and a multithreading programming environment.

4. What are critical operations? What methods can be used to protect critical operations?

5. What is a deadlock? What strategies can be used to resolve deadlock problems?

6. Modify the algorithm for the dining philosophers problem, so that no deadlock can occur.

7. Explain the differences between Java's Thread methods sleep and wait. Explain the differences between the Thread methods wait and suspend.

8. What Unix system calls can be used to create and start a child process? Draw diagrams to illustrate how Java Virtual Machine (JVM) creates and starts Java threads.

9. Compare and contrast Thread classes in Java and C#. What methods are comparable (equivalence)? What methods are unique in each language?

10. Compare and contrast the processes of creating and starting threads in Java and C#.

11. Explain how Monitor is implemented. Explain why the Monitor.Enter/Monitor.Exit cannot take value type variable with automatically boxing and unboxing?

12. Why are C# Reader/Writer locks more efficient than Monitor locks?

13. Can a thread be interrupted (moved from running state to the ready state), when the thread is executing a section of code protected by the lock operation? Explain your answer.

14. Explain how shared objects are protected by the synchronization/monitor mechanisms.

15. What are events? What are the major differences between events and locks? What are the differences between AutoResetEvent and ManualResetEvent?

16. What are the major differences between exception handling and event-driven programming?

17. What are major differences between control flow-based programming and event-driven programming?

18. What is the difference between a delegate and a class?

19. What is the difference between a delegate and a method?

20. Use delegates and events to define your own exception handling mechanisms.

21. Based on following code, write a working Command Line Interpreter.

```
include <fcntl.h> // Command Line Interpreter
static void main (int argc, char *argv[])  {
    while (TRUE) {  // read, execute a command and wait for termination
        read_command(argv);
        // read command name in argv[0] and data in argv[1] ... argv[argc-1]
        switch(fork()) {
        case -1:   printf("Cannot create new process \n");
                   return;
        case 0:    execvp (argv[0], argv);            // It should never return
                   printf("Cannot execute \n"); // It returns only by error
                   exit (1);
        default:   if (wait(NULL) == -1)
```

```
                    printf("Cannot execute wait system call \n");
                    // Parent process receives the PID of child process
                    // and then waits for the termination of child
          }
     }
}
```

22. Given the following Java code:

```
class BufferClass {
     private int bufferCell = -1;  // buffer for an integer
     private boolean writeable = true;     // flag
     public synchronized void setBuffer(int val) {
          while (!writeable) {
               try {
                    wait();  //voluntarily enter the waiting state
               }
               catch (InterruptedException e) {
                    System.err.println("Exception: " + e.toString());
               }
          } // end while
          bufferCell = val;
          writeable = false;
          notify();
     }
     public synchronized int getBuffer() {
          while (writeable) {
               try {
                    wait();  //voluntarily enter the waiting state
               }
               catch (InterruptedException e) {
                    System.err.println("Exception: " + e.toString());
               }
          }
          writeable = true;
          notify();
          return bufferCell;
     }
}
class ProduceInteger extends Thread {
     private BufferClass pBuffer;
     public ProduceInteger(BufferClass h) { pBuffer = h; }
     public void run() {
          for (int count = 0; count < 10; count++) {
               try {
                    Thread.sleep((int)(Math.random() * 3000));
               }
               catch (InterruptedException e) {
                    System.err.println(e.toString());
               }
               pBuffer.setBuffer(count);  // put integer
               System.out.println("Producer sets bufferCell " + count);
          }
     }
}
class ConsumeInteger extends Thread {
     private BufferClass cBuffer;
     public ConsumeInteger(BufferClass h) { cBuffer = h; }
```

```
    public void run() {
        int val;
        for (int count = 0; count < 10; count++) {
            try {
                Thread.sleep((int)(Math.random() * 3000));
            }
            catch (InterruptedException e) {
                System.err.println(e.toString());
            }
            val = cBuffer.getBuffer();
            System.out.println("\tConsumer retrieved " + val);
        }
    }
}
public class ProducerConsumer {
    public static void main(String args[]) {
        BufferClass h = new BufferClass();
        ProduceInteger p = new ProduceInteger(h);
        ConsumeInteger c = new ConsumeInteger(h);
        p.start();
        c.start();
    }
}
```

22.1 Compile and execute the program in a Java environment such as Eclipse.

22.2 Write the program using the Runnable interface instead of the Thread class to create and start the threads.

22.3 Write the Main class, creating and starting n threads from each Thread classes.

22.4 Add code to the Main class to make sure that the Main thread does not terminate before the child threads.

23. Given the following C# code:

```
using System;
using System.Threading;
class SummationApp {
    static Random rng = new Random();
    static byte[] buffer = new byte[100];
    static Thread writer;
    static void Main() {
        for (int i = 0; i < 100; i++)    // Initialize the buffer
            buffer[i] = (byte)(i + 1);
        writer = new Thread(new ThreadStart(WriterFunc));
        writer.Start();                             // Start one writer thread
        Thread[] readers = new Thread[10];
        for (int i = 0; i < 5; i++) {    // Start 5 reader threads
            readers[i] = new Thread(new ThreadStart(ReaderFunc));
            readers[i].Name = (i + 1).ToString();
            readers[i].Start();
        }
    }
static void ReaderFunc() {
      for (int i = 0; writer.IsAlive; i++){         //Loop until the writer ends
        int sum = 0;
        for (int k = 0; k < 100; k++) // Sum the values in the buffer
            sum += buffer[k];
```

```
            if (sum != 5050) {          // Report an error if the sum is incorrect
                string message = String.Format("Thread {0} " +
                         "reports a corrupted read on iteration {1}",
                Thread.CurrentThread.Name, i + 1);
                Console.WriteLine(message);
                writer.Abort();
                return;
            }
        }
}
static void WriterFunc() {
        DateTime start = DateTime.Now;
        // Loop for up to 10 seconds
        while ((DateTime.Now - start).Seconds < 10) {
            int j = rng.Next(0, 100);
            int k = rng.Next(0, 100);
            Swap(ref buffer[j], ref buffer[k]);
        }
    }
    static void Swap(ref byte a, ref byte b) {
        byte tmp = a;
        a = b;
        b = tmp;
    }
}
```

23.1 Execute the program in .Net C# programming environment.

23.2 Explain what problems have occurred.

23.3 Use Monitor to solve the problems.

23.4 Use lock to solve the problems.

23.5 Use conditional Monitor methods to solve the problems.

23.6 Use Reader/Writer locks to solve the problems.

24. Give the following piece of code:

```
int a = 2;
…
Monitor.Enter(a);
try { a = 2*a+5; }
finally { Monitor.Exit(a); }
```

24.1 What is the problem with this piece of code?

24.2 Draw the memory (heap) map showing the problem of the code.

24.3 How can the problem be removed?

25. Given the code below, answer the following questions:

```
using System;
using System.Threading;
public class SemaphoreExample {
    private static Semaphore _pool;
    private static int padding = 0;
    public static void Main() {
        _pool = new Semaphore(0, 3);
```

```
        for (int i = 1; i <= 5; i++) {  // create a semaphore of 3
            Thread t = new Thread(new ParameterizedThreadStart(Worker));
            t.Start(i); // i is passed to the constructor of Worker()
        }
        Thread.Sleep(500);
        Console.WriteLine("Main thread calls Release(3).");
        _pool.Release(3);
        Console.WriteLine("Main thread exits.");
    }
    private static void Worker(object num) {
        // Each worker thread begins by requesting the semaphore.
        Console.WriteLine("Thread {0} starts " + "& waits for semaphore", num);
        _pool.WaitOne();
        padding = padding + 100;
        Console.WriteLine("Thread {0} enters the semaphore.", num);
        Thread.Sleep(1000 + padding);
        Console.WriteLine("Thread {0} releases the semaphore.", num);
        _pool.Release();
    }
}
```

25.1 Explain what this program does.

25.2 How many child threads are created in the Main thread?

25.3 What line of code initializes the semaphore?

25.4 What line of code sets the semaphore to its maximum value?

25.5 What line of code decrements the semaphore?

25.6 What line of code increments the semaphore?

26. Sleeping barber problem: A hypothetical barbershop has one barber, one barber chair, and a number of chairs for waiting customers. When there are no customers, the barber sits in the barber chair and sleeps. As soon as a customer arrives, he either awakens the barber or, if the barber is cutting someone else's hair, sits down in one of the vacant chairs. If all of the chairs are occupied, the newly arrived customer simply leaves. Assume all the actors (barber and customers) are implemented as parallel threads, communication and resource sharing must be considered carefully, otherwise multithreading/inter-process communication problems of starvation and deadlock may occur; for example, the barber could end up waiting on a customer and a customer waiting on the barber, resulting in deadlock. Alternatively, customers may not decide to approach the barber in an orderly manner, leading to process starvation as some customers never get the chance for a haircut even though they have been waiting. The following algorithm uses three semaphores to solve the problem.

```
// Semaphore Customers
// Semaphore Barber
// Semaphore accessSeats (mutex)
// int NumberOfFreeSeats
// The Barber (Thread):
 while(true) // runs in an infinite loop {
    Customers.p()
    // tries to acquire a customer - if none is available he goes to sleep
    accessSeats.p()
    // he has been awakened -> wants to modify the no. of available seats
    NumberOfFreeSeats++       // one chair gets free
    Barber.v()                // the barber is ready to cut
    accessSeats.v() // we don't need the lock on the chairs anymore
 }                            // here the barber is cutting hair
```

```
// The Customer (Thread):
 while (notCut) // as long as the customer is not cut {
     accessSeats.p() // tries to get access to the chairs
     if NumberOfFreeSeats>0 // if there are any free seats
           NumberOfFreeSeats -- // sitting down on a chair
           Customers.v() // notify the barber, who's waiting a customer
           accessSeats.v() // don't need to lock the chairs anymore
           Barber.p() // now it's this customer's turn, but wait if barber is
busy
           notCut = false
     else // there are no free seats, tough luck
           accessSeats.v() // but don't forget to release the lock on the seats
 }
```

(1) Use Java or C# to implement the single sleeping barber problem and test if the given algorithm and the semaphores correctly handle the multithreading communication.

(2) Extend the single sleeping barber problem to a multiple sleeping barber problem: define the necessary semaphores and give the algorithm.

(3) Implement the multiple sleeping barber problem in Java or in C#.

27. Assume that you use an NXT Mindstorms robot with a touch sensor and an ultrasonic range sensor to build an automatic toilet flusher. You write the following pseudocode as the control program.

```
While (true) {
     if touch sensor value == 1
            Trigger the motor;
     else
     if sonar distance < 3 feet {
           while sonar distance < 5 { }
           Trigger the motor;
     }
}
```

(1) What is wrong with the program?

(2) How can you use the flow control-driven approach to address the problem?

(3) How can you use the event-driven approach to address the problem?

Project 1

Write a Java or C# multithreading program to simulate a table tennis doubles match, as shown in Figure 2.22. In this question, you must use both monitors and events.

Assume the match will follow these **simplified** rules:

(1) There are four players. A1 and A2 form a team, and B1 and B2 form another team. A1 will serve first (start the ball), then B1, A2, and finally B2 will serve. Each player will serve six balls in each turn.

(2) The players do not change their positions.

(3) During the play, the players on two sides must serve the ball alternatively (use events to define the order) and the two players in a team can compete for serving the ball (use monitor to synchronize them).

(4) A random function called shot(rate) will be called by each player at his/her turn to simulate the play. It returns "in" at the given probability rate and returns "out" at the probability 1 – rate; for example, if rate = 85%, the probability to serve the ball "in" bound is 85% and "out" bound is 15%.

(5) If a shot is "in" bounds, one of the players on the other side must return the ball by calling the shot function.

(6) If a shot is "out" of bounds, the opposite side of players will win one point, and a new serve of ball must be started.

(7) The match is over when each player has served six balls and the side with most points wins the match. The match is a tie if both sides have the same number of points.

Implement each player as a thread. Use the .Net AutoResetEvent class events to define the order of the execution of the threads on different sides and use Monitor to synchronize the players in the same side. The program must print the sequences of shots played by each player and the result of each shot and maintain the points of each side. A possible scenario of printout is:

```
A1 - in -  B2 - in - A2 - in - B2 - in - A2 - in - B1 - out
---- The side A1A2 wins one point. Score = (3, 5)
     ...
B1 - in - A2 - out ---- The side B1B2 wins one point. Score = (8, 12)
     ...
Final score = (9, 24). The team B1B2 wins.
```

Project 2

The purpose of this project is to exercise the concepts of multithreading, thread communication, synchronization, and event-driven programming. It is not the purpose of this assignment to create a realistic application. We will create more realistic applications in the subsequent assignments. Implement an extended chicken farm example given in Figure 2.29. Consider the following alternative implementations:

(1) Assume that the encoder/decoder class will convert the order object into a SOAP message in a string and convert the SOAP string back into the order object.

(2) Assume that the encoder/decoder class will further encrypt/decrypt the SOAP string; for example, using cipher encryption, which adds a number to the ASCII code of each character.

(3) Implement a first-in-first-out queue, instead of the multiCellBuffer.

(4) Study the deadlock situation given in Figure 2.30 and discuss the ways of preventing, avoiding, detecting, and recovery of the deadlocks.

Chapter 3
Essentials in Service-Oriented Software Development

While it is possible to grip the main concepts and techniques of SOC without actually developing SOC software, it will make a tremendous difference if we do so, even if we create synthetic services and applications only. This chapter will focus on using tools to develop SOC software, without touching the underlying languages, protocols, and standards, so that software engineers and project managers who are responsible for programming-in-the-large can understand this chapter. The purpose of this chapter is to give readers a deep understanding of concepts and techniques through limited coding. If you are an experienced programmer, you can apply the concepts, techniques, and resources to create real-world applications immediately after this chapter.

This chapter puts the main concepts, techniques, and tools together to show step-by-step how to create web services, publish services, and compose SOC applications. The chapter is organized as follows: Section 3.1 gives an overview of different SOC software development environments; Section 3.2 studies how to create a set of platform-independent web services with standard interfaces. The section also discusses different services hosting mechanisms and how to use the Internet Information Services (IIS) to host the services; Section 3.3 explores the service publishing and discovery services in public UDDI, ebXML, and ad hoc service directories and repositories; Section 3.4 discusses application building using our own services and using the services discovered in the public service directories. Both synthetic and real-world applications will be studied; finally, in Section 3.5, we explain how to use Java and Eclipse development environment to create web services.

3.1 Service-Oriented Software Development Environments

Service-oriented software development is different from object-oriented software development in the way that it offers standard interfaces to programming, communication, publishing, integration, and deployment. The development environments play an important role in relieving developers from creating these syntax-intensive interfaces, so that they can focus on the business model and the application logic of the software.

3.1.1 Overview

A number of service-oriented software development environments are available for creating web services, service directories, and client applications using existing services. Table 3.1 lists some such development environments, their features, and the primary languages used in these environments. The upper eight environments in the table are from Microsoft, while the other environments are from Java and BPEL communities, including IBM, Oracle, and Sun Microsystems. From the table, we can see that some environments support service development only; some environments support application development only; and some environments support both. Among the features, platform-independent and platform-dependent are related to service development only. Platform-independent web services are the major building blocks of SOC applications and are supported by most service development environments.

Platform-dependent services are sensible where the application is limited to one platform, such as .Net or JEE. In such cases, developing platform-dependent services, without the translation between different interfaces, would be more efficient. .Net remoting is specifically designed for such purposes. JEE could be used to develop standard web services, as well as Java-specific components such as JavaBeans.

Table 3.1. Service-oriented software development environments

SOC Software Development Environment	Service Development		Service Development Application Development		Application Development		
	Platform-independent service	Platform-dependent service	Distributed transaction	WS-* specification	Desktop	Web	Primary language
ASP .Net	X				X	X	C# / VB
.Net Remoting		X					C#
Enterprise Services: BizTalk			X				XLang / BPEL
WSE: WS Enhancement	X			X			C# / VB
WCF	X	X	X	X			C# / VB
Workflow Foundation			X	X	X	X	C# / VB
Presentation Foundation			X	X	X		C# / VB
Silverlight			X	X		X	C# / VB
Eclipse / Axis / Tomcat	X		X	X	X	X	Java
JEE: Java Enterprise Edition	X	X	X	X	X	X	Java
JDeveloper / Oracle SOA Suite			X	X	X	X	BPEL
ActiveBPEL / Tomcat			X	X	X	X	BPEL
WebSphere			X	X	X	X	BPEL

Distributed transaction and WS-* specification are related to both service and application development. Distributed transaction ensures that a transaction between two business partners, such as a balance transfer from one account to another account, can be successfully completed, or no change is made if the transaction is unsuccessful. Rollback is often used to recover from a failure during the transaction. WS-* specification includes a number of dependability standards, such as WS-Security and WS-ReliableMessaging.

The features supported by these environments are evolving, and new features are added to the environments. Thus, Table 3.1 may not precisely characterize all the features supported by the environments.

ASP .Net was the main platform in Visual Studio for platform-independent web service development, as well as for the desktop application and web application development. ASP .Net service development is no longer the primary platform since Visual Studio 2010 and .Net Framework 4. However, ASP .Net is still used as a primary application development platform.

Released with .Net 2008, WCF (Windows Communication Foundation) is Microsoft's all-inclusive service development environment that supports all features. Platform-independent services, platform-independent services, Enterprise Services in BizTalk, and Web Services Enhancement (WSE) are now a part of WCF.

In the rest of the chapter, we will use WCF to develop platform-independent web services (as a service provider), discuss the service brokers that support service publishing and discovery, and study ASP .Net-based application building using platform-independent web services. Finally, Java-based web services development environments are discussed briefly.

The BPEL-based SOC software development and its development environments will be studied in in Chapter 8.

3.1.2 Windows Communication Foundation

Windows Communication Foundation (WCF) extends ASP .Net to better support service-oriented software development, particular in reliability and security. WCF is a part of WinFx, which is a programming environment in Windows Vista, Windows 7, and Windows Servers after 2008. As shown in Figure 3.1, WinFx consists of three packages:

- WCF: Communications Foundation (code name Indigo), which is the
    - next generation of distributed communications API and infrastructures
    - integrated development environments for web services with advanced features;
- WPF: Presentation Foundation (code name Avalon) and Silverlight, which are the platforms for building Windows applications, web applications, and Smart Client applications that integrate graphical applications, GUI, media, and documents;
    - WPF is used for desktop application. The XML-based markup language, XAML (Extensible Application Markup Language) is used to define the GUI;
    - Silverlight is used for web applications and mobile applications with extensive graphical and media GUI. Silverlight library is a subset of the WPF library.
- WF: Workflow Foundation (also see Chapter 8), which
    - is the programming model, engine, and tools for building workflow enabled applications on Windows;
    - is a declarative language that can be used to define BPEL-like executable business processes;
    - XAML is used for declaring the structure of a workflow. However, the workflow may also be expressed in code using a .NET language (like C# and VB).

WinFx is the next generation of Microsoft's computing environment. The main difference with its predecessor, Visual Studio, is that the new environment is more geared toward supporting distributed service-oriented software development. WinFx separates workflow composition from service development. The WF composition language is exclusive used for workflow composition, while WCF is used for service development as well as workflow composition in traditional programming languages like C# and VB. Although one can still develop native applications directly based on Win 32 architecture, all managed applications are based on .Net Framework.

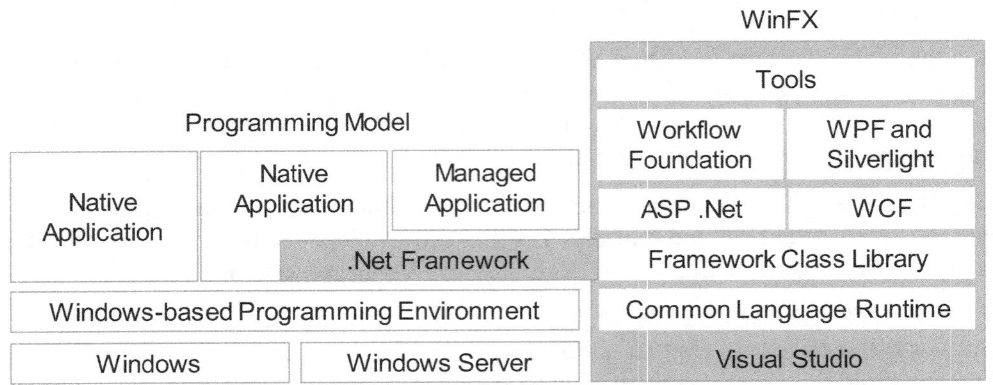

Figure 3.1. Windows and .Net-based programming model

As can be seen in Table 3.1, WCF offers all the features available in the other service development environments, including Platform-independent service (ASP .Net); Platform-dependent service (.Net remoting); Distributed transactions (Enterprise services such as BizTalk); and WS-* specification (WSE). The new WCF features also include RESTful service and data service development environments.

In Chapter 6, we will discuss distributed transactions, WS-Security, and WS-ReliableMessaging. In Chapter 7, we will learn platform-dependent service (.Net remoting services), and RESTful services in WCF. In this chapter, we will focus on the development of platform-independent services (interoperable services).

3.1.3 Service Interface: Address, Binding, and Contract

WCF offers multiple sets of interfaces to accommodate platform-dependent and platform-independent communications. The reason that platform-dependent services are useful is that many applications are based on a single platform. In this case, the reduced complexity in interface can make the platform-dependent communication more efficient. Platform-independent communication also has two major standards: (1) use WSDL and SOAP to define the interfaces among the services and their communications, including the port, port type, data type, message type, operation definition, and message format; (2) Use HTTP for all communications among RESTful services. We will present the platform- independent definition of the interfaces in the WCF endpoints. A WCF endpoint is defined by three entities known as ABC:

Addressing: It defines the network address where the invocation message should be sent to; for example, http://www.webservicex.net/uszip.svc or http://localhost:49187/Service.svc.

The address format consists of a base address and optional URI parts, and the base address consists of [transport]://[domain][:optional port], where the transport is usually http and the optional port is used if the service is running on the developer's server.

Binding: It specifies the channel to connect the endpoints between the client and the service, or between two services. The channel has two layers:

- The lower layer is the transport protocol. WCF supports TCP, Named Pipes, HTTP, HTTPS, MSMQ, and Custom protocols;

- The upper layer is the binding policy, such as basicHttpBinding and wsHttpBinding. wsHttpBinding provides the common WS-* specification, including WS-Security, WS-Reliability, and WS-Transaction functions.

Contract: There are different types of contracts: A service contract defines an interface to be implemented as a class. An operation defines the operation that an endpoint exposes and the message format that the operation requires. The operation contract maps to a method of a class that implements an endpoint. A data contract defines what data types are passed to and from a service operation, which is the signature of the parameters passed in and the return value of the method.

If the contract is based on SOAP and WSDL, it defines the standard web services, which is platform-independent (also see Chapter 5). If the contract is based on HTTP verbs, the service is RESTful, which will be discussed later in this chapter and further studied in Chapter 7.

Figure 3.2 shows the message exchange between the endpoints of service client and the services. The two parties can communicate, as long as their ABCs match.

A WCF process can be hosted by a server such as IIS and can be self-hosted by a Windows host process, which removes the dependent on an IIS server.

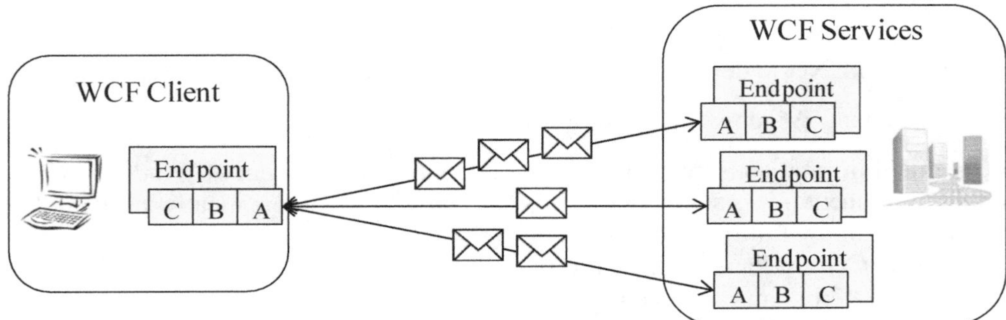

Figure 3.2. WCF client and server communication

In the next section, we will show examples that define endpoints and access the services through the endpoints. We will also discuss hosting of services using a server and using self-hosting. We will also discuss the development of RESTful services that do not need endpoints.

3.2 Service Provider: Creating and Hosting Services

Web services are platform independent. However, the service software that actually performs the computation (job) must be written in a specific programming language. In other words, a web service is an interface that converts the service call (remote invocation) represented in the standard service description language (e.g., WSDL) into the function call represented in the programming language (e.g., C# or Java), in which the service software is written, as shown in Figure 3.3.

In principle, we can manually wrap any function with a standard WSDL interface, which will be discussed in Section 3.5. This chapter will use tools to generate the WSDL interface file in XML automatically. This is analogous to writing a web page. You can either directly use the html language to write a web page or use a web authoring tool.

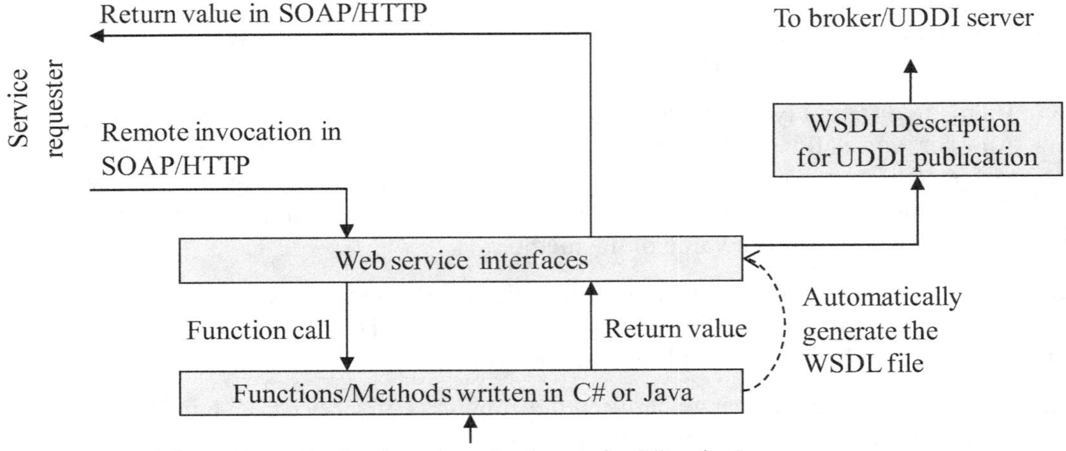

Figure 3.3. Translating a service invocation to a function call

We will first use C# and .Net to develop web services. The system and tools required include:

- Operating system. Windows or Windows Server.
- IIS (Internet Information Services), which is an optional component of Windows XP. You need to add this component if it is not installed. In Vista and 7, IIS is automatically installed; however, you need to turn it on by following the steps:
  - Open Control Panel, select "Programs;"
  - Select "Programs and Features;"
  - On the left-side menu, select "Turn Windows features on or off;"
  - Turn on IIS.

  Once IIS is installed, you should see a file directory named inetpub. A subdirectory in inetpub is called wwwroot, which will be a small server on your computer to host the web services that you will create. You can also create a virtual directory in wwwroot directory and link the virtual directory to the physical directory where you have your executable code of your web services.
- The latest Visual Studio .Net Professional Edition. You can also use the .Net C# Express Edition, which is free for download at the Microsoft download site http://msdn.microsoft.com/vstudio/express/

3.2.1 Getting Started with Developing WCF Services

When we develop web projects in Visual Studio, we need a web server to host and to run the services and applications. We can choose different web servers, including the built-in Visual Studio IIS (Internet Information Services) Express, and the IIS in Windows server.

In order for us to focus on the process of creating services and hosting services, we start with creating a simple service. The service defines three operations: return Hello World, return the PI value, and compute the absolute value. The client will create a proxy to the service and use the proxy to access the operations in the service.

WCF offers different ways for developing different services. The easiest way to get started with WCF service development is to use the given WCF template in Visual studio and use the IIS Express server to host the service in the following steps.

Step 1: Start Windows Communication Foundation Project

Start Visual Studio 2019 and choose "Create a new project". You can search "WCF" and then choose "WCF Service Application" template, as shown in Figure 3.4.

Figure 3.4. Creating a new project and choose WCF Service Application template

If you do not find this template, you need to start Visual Studio Installer. Run Visual Studio Installer and modify your Visual Studio adding components. When you add new components, you will not see Windows Communication Foundation in the Workloads tag. You need to click the "Individual components" tag and add Windows Communication Foundation, as shown in Figure 3.5.

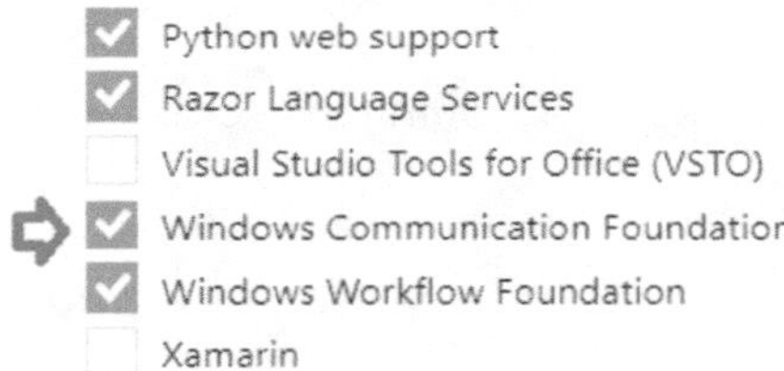

Figure 3.5. Install Windows Communication Foundation through individual components

You may also add Windows Workflow Foundation in your Visual Studio, which will be used in Chapter 7 of the text.

After you have installed the WCF component, you can create a new WCF project. Note, do not choose "ASP .Net Web Application" or "ASP .Net Core Web Application", which are different packages.

Then click the "Next" button. A new window will be open. Name your project "WcfService1" and choose a location on your C drive. Note, do not use the default location within Visual Studio folder, which can cause a permission problem later.

A solution will be created with one project, as shown in Figure 3.6. Under the project, you will see two C# files named IService1.cs and Service1.svc.cs in the solution stack. Open each of the two files, and you can see a code template.

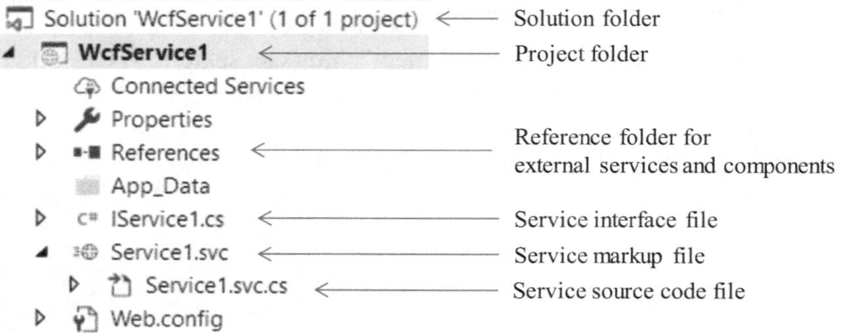

Figure 3.6. WCF project stack for a WCF service

Step 2: Define your service interface IService1.cs

Open the IService1.cs. A template with a pair of sample interfaces are given:

```
namespace WcfService1
{
    [ServiceContract]
    public interface IService1
    {
        [OperationContract]
        string GetData(int value);

        [OperationContract]
        CompositeType GetDataUsingDataContract(CompositeType composite);

        // TODO: Add your service operations here
    }

    // Use a data contract as illustrated in the sample below to add composite types
to service operations.
    [DataContract]
    public class CompositeType
    {
        bool boolValue = true;
        string stringValue = "Hello ";

        [DataMember]
        public bool BoolValue
        {
            get { return boolValue; }
            set { boolValue = value; }
        }

        [DataMember]
        public string StringValue
        {
            get { return stringValue; }
            set { stringValue = value; }
        }
    }
}
```

You can modify the IService1.cs template to include your interface into the service:

```
namespace WcfService1 {
  [ServiceContract]
  public interface IService {
      // Add the following interface code into the template
      [OperationContract]
      string Hello();
      [OperationContract]
      double PiValue();
      [OperationContract]
      int absValue(int intVal);
  }
}
```

As can be seen in the code, you are defining an interface for three simple operations: return a string, return the Pi value, and get the absolute value of the given input.

Step 3: Implementation of the Service.svc.cs

Now, we will implement the interface defined in the step above. Open the file Service.svc.cs. Replace the code given in the template by the following code.

```
namespace WcfService1 {
    public class Service1 : IService1 {
       // Add the following implementation code into the template
       public string Hello() {
           return "Hello World";
       }
       public double PiValue() {
           double pi = System.Math.PI;
           return (pi);
       }
       public int absValue(int x) {
           if (x >= 0) return (x);
           else return (-x);
       }
    }
}
```

In the steps above, we showed developing a web service from scratch by defining the interfaces (contracts) and the functionalities that implement the interfaces.

You can also create a new WSDL web service using existing library functions or APIs as its implementation. In this case, we just need to define the web service interface for the implementation. There are many different APIs with different types of interfaces, For example, ASU repository has random string service for generating a strong password, which return a string for a given length.

The API is in RESTful service format:

http://neptune.fulton.ad.asu.edu/WSRepository/Services/RandomString/Service.svc/GetRandomString/X,

where X is the length in integer. For example, if the length is 8, the full query is

http://neptune.fulton.ad.asu.edu/WSRepository/Services/RandomString/Service.svc/GetRandomString/8

Now, we will develop a WSDL service based on the RESTful API call. We define service contract IService.cs as follows:

```
[ServiceContract]
public interface IService {
  [OperationContract]
   string getRandom(int length);
```

```
}
```

The implementation of the interface is given in the Service.cs file below:

```
using System;           // include URI class
using System.Net;       // include WebClient class
using System.Xml.Linq;  // include XElement class
public class Service : IService {
   public string getRandom(int len) {
         string baseURL =
"http://neptune.fulton.ad.asu.edu/WSRepository/Services/RandomString/Service.svc/Get
RandomString/";
        string fullURL = baseURL + Convert.ToSingle(len);
        Uri ServivrUri = new Uri(fullURL); // convert string to Uri type
        WebClient proxy = new WebClient(); // Creating a proxy
        byte[] abc = proxy.DownloadData(ServivrUri); // byte[] type
        string str = System.Text.UTF8Encoding.UTF8.GetString(abc);//convert to
string
        XElement xmlroot = XElement.Parse(str);
        string txtContent = ((XElement)(xmlroot)).Value;
        return txtContent;
   }
}
```

In the service code above, we combine the base address and the length (input) into the full URL of the remote RESTful service. We then use Uri class to convert the URL in string format into Uri type. The WebClient class creates a proxy object, which uses the service URL to invoke the service. The remote service returns the data in a byte[] array, and we convert the array into a string as the return type of the service. The returned value is in XML, for example:

<string xmlns="http://schemas.microsoft.com/2003/10/Serialization/">**8Gw{Z=9y**</string>

We then use XElement class to parse the XML string and extract the value. XML processing will be further discussed in Chapter 4 and Chapter 10. As XElement class is a part of LINQ (Language Integrated Query), it will be discussed in full detail in Chapter 10. As the result, the service will return the string: "**8Gw{Z=9y**".

The WCF random string service is deployed in ASU Services and Applications Repository at:

http://neptune.fulton.ad.asu.edu/WSRepository/Services/RandomStringSVC/Service.svc

3.2.2 Testing Web Services in WCF Test Client

In the service project discussed in the previous section, we can build and then right-click file Service.svc and choose "View in Browser," a service page will be generated as shown in Figure 3.7. Unlike ASP .Net service (with .asmx extension), no test page will be generated for WCF services in the web view. Click the link: http://localhost:55621/Service1.svc?wsdl, we will see the WSDL file generated for the service.

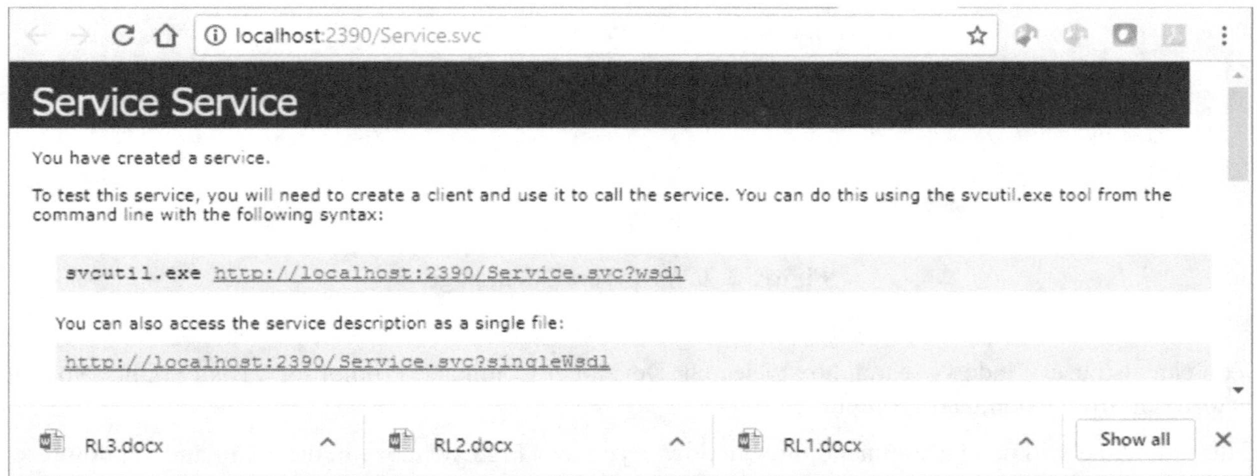

Figure 3.7. WCF service hosted on .Net Development server

WCF services can be tested using the building WCF Test Client. For the BasicThree service, select the file Service1.svc and then use menu command: Debug → Start without Debugging, the WCF Test Client will be open, as shown in Figure 3.8. Double click each operation, you can enter the input, invoke the operation, and see the return value.

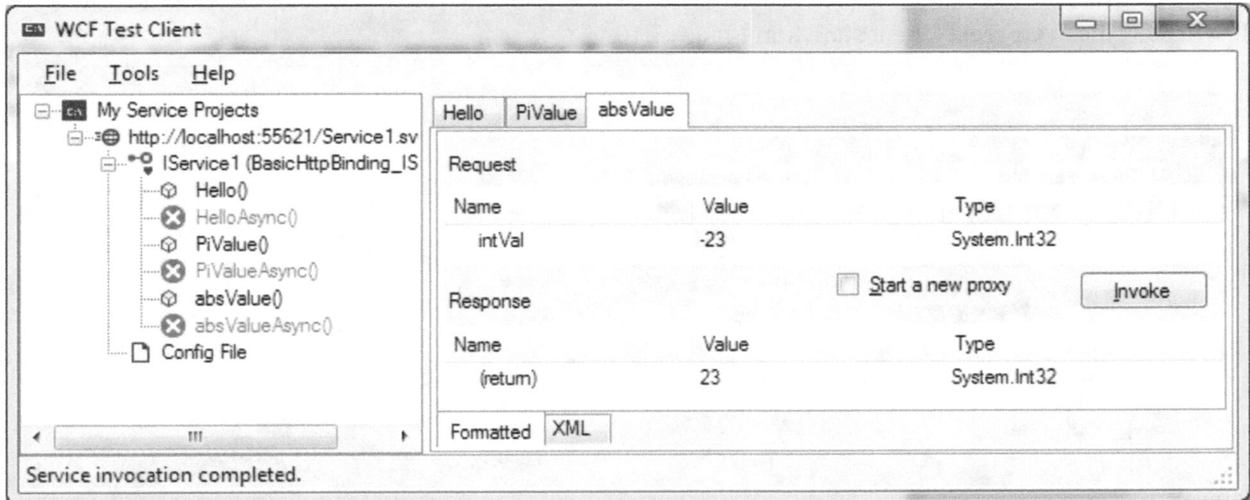

Figure 3.8. WCF Test Client page

WCF Test Client can also be open outside Visual Studio application and be used to test any services found in the public repository before you add the service into your application. In the Start menu of your PC, choose WcfTestClient, as shown in Figure 3.9.

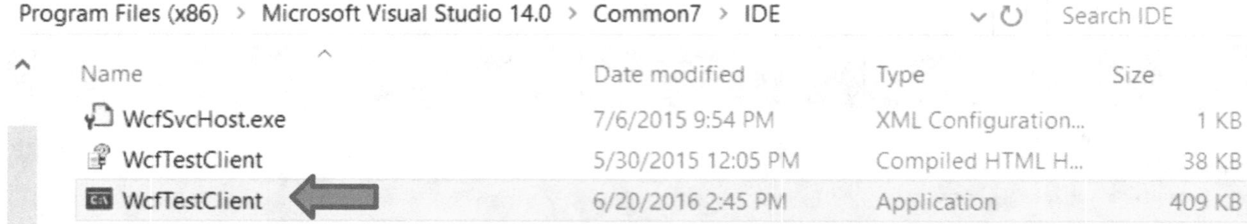

Figure 3.9. WCF Test Client page

You can also use Windows search box to search: Developer Command Prompt for Visual Studio. Note, it is different from Command Prompt CMD.

This command will open a command line window. Type: wcfTestClient.exe in the command window.

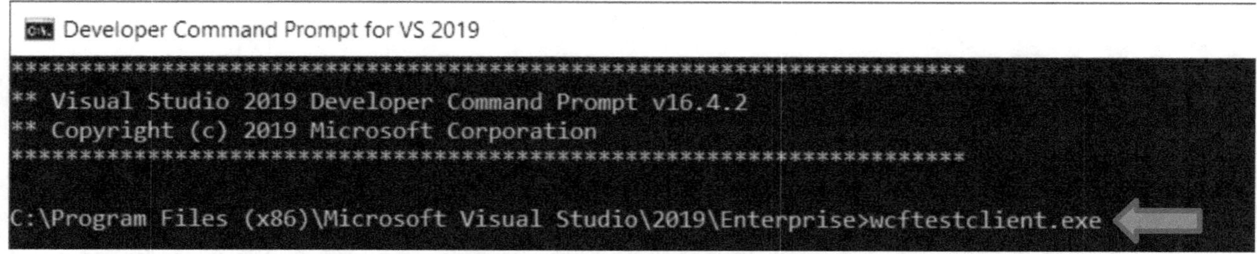

It will start the WCF Test Client shown in Figure 3.10

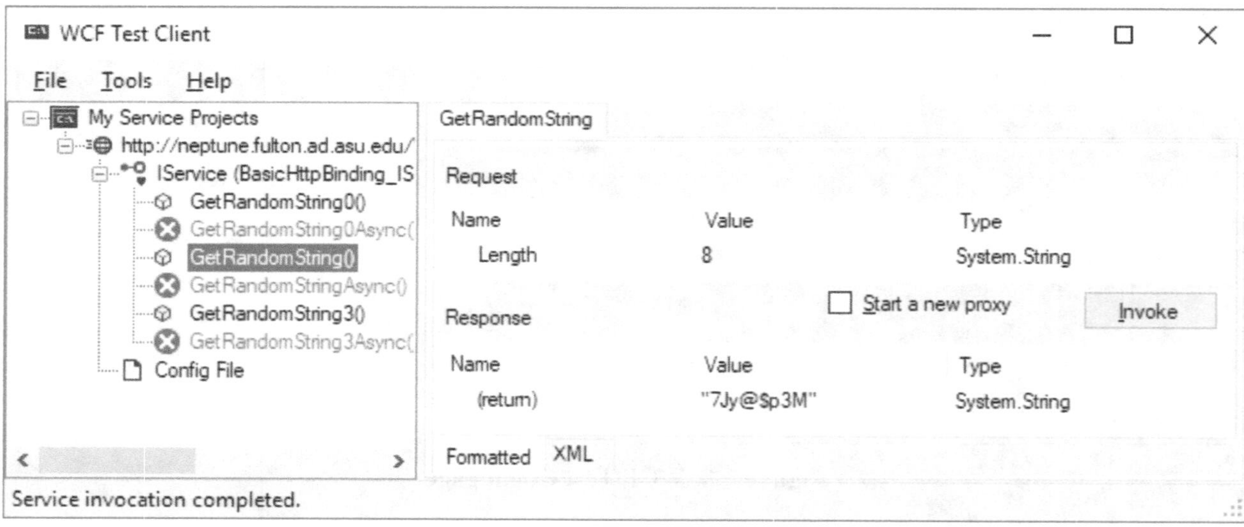

Figure 3.10. Using WCF Test Client to test the encryption service in ASU Service Repository

You can use this Test Client to test any WCF services. For example, to test this service: http://neptune.fulton.ad.asu.edu/WSRepository/Services/RandomStringSVC/Service.svc, you use the File menu of the Test Client and choose Add Service. Paste the service address into the textbox:

Add Service ×

Please enter the endpoint address:

OK

Cancel

http://neptune.fulton.ad.asu.edu/WSRepository/Services/RandomStringSVC/Service.svc

Then, the WCF Test Client will load this service. You can choose a service operation and provide input and then click "Invoke" to test the service.

An independent client test tool is also available in ASU Service and Application Repository:

http://neptune.fulton.ad.asu.edu/WSRepository/services/wsTesterTryIt/

3.2.3 Writing a Console Application to Consume a WCF Service

After testing the service using the WCF Test Client, we can start to consume the service in different applications (clients). Visual Studio offers many different client templates, including Console App (.Net Framework), Windows Forms Application (Section 3.6.2), and Website Application (Section 3.6.3).

To make it simple, we will develop a simple Console App to test the service in this section.

(1) In the Solution Explorer, right-click the current solution, select Add, and then choose Add New Project. In the Add New Project dialog box, select C# and Windows Classic Desktop, choose the Console App template, and name it TestWcfServiceConsoleApp. Click OK to move to the next step. Figure 3.11 shows the Solution after the Console App project is added into the same solution.

(2) Start the service: Right click the Service1.svc in WcfService1 project and choose View in browser. Copy the service URL in the browser and keep the browser window open before moving into the next step.

(3) Add the WCF service: Right-click the TestWcfServiceConsoleApp project and choose "Add Service Reference..." Paste the service URL http://localhost:55621/Service1.svc?wsdl from the previous step into the textbox, as shown in Figure 3.12, and then click the Go button. Note that WCF services use Add Service Reference, while ASP .Net Services use Add Web Reference.

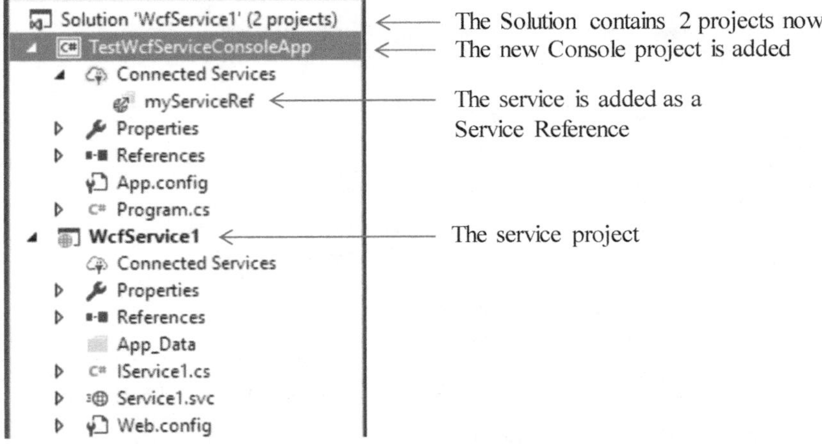

Figure 3.11. A Console project is added into the Solution

Figure 3.12 shows the dialog window of the Add Service Reference, where the operations of the service are displayed. We name the proxy to the service "myServiceRef" and type the name under Namespace.

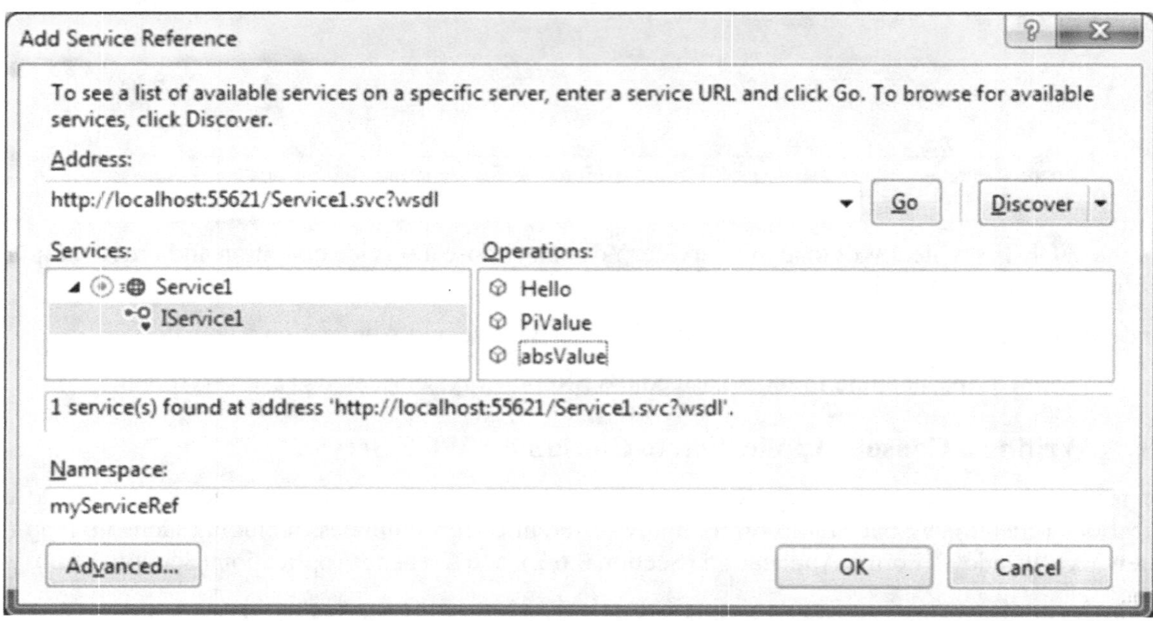

Figure 3.12. Add the WCF service as a reference in the client

Open the file Program.cs in the TestWcfServiceConsoleApp project. Add the following code into the template.

```
namespace TestWcfServiceConsoleApp {
    class Program {
        static void Main(string[] args) {
            //(1) Create a proxy to the WCF service.
            myServiceRef.Service1Client myPxy = new myServiceRef.Service1Client();
            // (2) Call the service operations through the proxy
            string str = myPxy.Hello();
            double pi = myPxy.PiValue();  // call PiValue operation
            Int32 test1 = 27;    // Create test input 1
            Int32 test2 = -132; // Create test input 2
            Int32 result1 = myPxy.absValue(test1); // call operation
            Int32 result2 = myPxy.absValue(test2); // call operation
            Console.WriteLine("Hello returns {0}", str);
            Console.WriteLine("PI value = {0}", pi);
            Console.WriteLine("Absolute values of {0} is {1} and of {2} is {3}",
test1, result1, test2, result2);
            // (3) Close the proxy, the channel to the service
            myPxy.Close();
        }
    }
}
```

In the code above, we use myServiceRef.Service1Client to access the remote service.

Note that, in order to test the client, you must have the service started first to make the object an active object! You can start the service by right-clicking the file **Service.svc** and choose "Browser with."

Then, right-click the console **client** project and choose: Set as StartUp Project, so that it can start when you start the execution. Then, you can use the Debug menu and choose Start without Debugging. The results are shown in the console window.

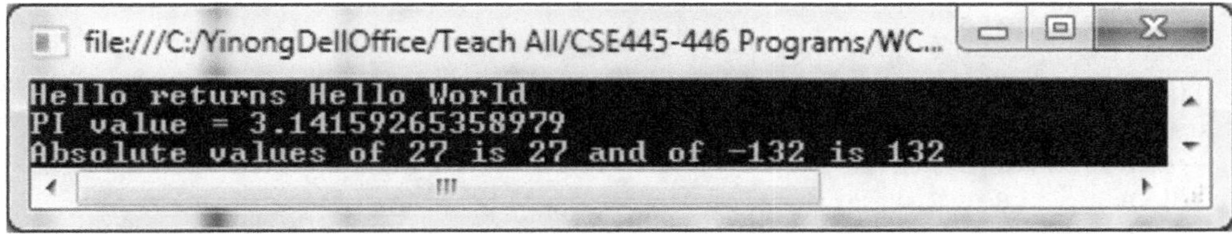

From the development process above, we can see WCF development environment enforces the explicit separation of interface (contracts) and the implementation of the interface, which gives the service a better structure and is easier to re-implement a service without changing its contracts. Furthermore, WCF development environment offers many functional and nonfunctional features that can better meet the requirement of different applications. In the next section, we will go through more complex processes of creating and hosting WCF services.

3.2.4 File Service and Data Management

Any large computing and information system will require data storage and data management. Before we discuss more complex service-oriented data management in Chapter 4 (XML files) and Chapter 10 (database), we present a simple text file service here, so that you can start to implement your services and applications with basic data management capacities.

The text file service offers two operations, as defined in the interface file, IService.cs, below:

```
[ServiceContract]
public interface IService {
   [OperationContract]
   void PutStringToFile(string fileName, string value);
   [OperationContract]
   string GetStringFromFile(string fileName);
}
```

The implementation of the interface is given in the following Service.cs file:

```
using System;
using System.Web;
using System.IO;
public class Service : IService {
     public void PutStringToFile(string fileName, string value) {
          string fLocation = Path.Combine(HttpRuntime.AppDomainAppPath, @"App_Data");
// From server root to current
          fLocation = Path.Combine(fLocation, fileName);
                                              // From current to App_Data
          if (File.Exists(fLocation)) {
              File.Delete(fLocation);
          }
          using (StreamWriter sw = File.CreateText(fLocation)) {
              sw.WriteLine(value);
          }
     }
     public string GetStringFromFile(string fileName) {
```

```
        string fLocation = Path.Combine(HttpRuntime.AppDomainAppPath, @"App_Data");
// From server root to current
        fLocation = Path.Combine(fLocation, fileName);
                                          // From current to App_Data
        if (!File.Exists(fLocation)) {
            return "File not exist";
        }
        using (StreamReader sr = File.OpenText(fLocation)) {
            string s = "";
            s = sr.ReadLine();
            return s;
        }
    }
}
```

A key difference between this code and a code running on a local computer is that the path from the root to the file location is not known to the service developers. We have to call a system function to find the path. The function: HttpRuntime.AppDomainAppPath returns the path from the server root to the current directory. Then, we use Path.Combine(HttpRuntime.AppDomainAppPath, @App_Data); to extend the path to the App_Data folder. This text file service is deployed at the site:

http://neptune.fulton.ad.asu.edu/WSRepository/Services/FileService/Service.svc?wsdl

and a test page (TryIt page) is developed to test the service at:

http://neptune.fulton.ad.asu.edu/wsrepository/Services/FileServiceTryIt/

3.2.5 Hosting Your Web Services as a Service Provider

There are different ways to host your services and to allow remote accesses to the services that you have created in the Windows environment: .Net Development Server, IIS Express, IIS on Windows or on Windows Server, and self-hosting. IIS are services running on most web servers. It can be installed on Windows OS, which makes a portion of the file system a server. IIS are running all the time, listening to the requests and handling queuing of requests. IIS redirect requests from remote clients, who want to activate services on the server, to the right services hosted under IIS. IIS manage resources sharing among services on IIS. IIS can authenticate remote callers and safeguard data on the server with a Secure Sockets Layer (SSL).

- IIS Express is a built-in local host in Visual Studio, which allows you to test and to access your web services on the same computer without having to have Internet connection and without installing IIS. The examples discussed in the previous sections are running on the local host. If you use the web address on local host as the service address in the application program running in the same solution, you can access the services in the application after the service is first started. Accessing web services in an application program will be discussed in the next section.

- IIS on Web Server: If you are developing the services on a server with IIS, such as the Windows Server, the full web address will be created in the test Window when you run your service or open the service in a web browser.

- IIS on Windows: IIS can make any folder (directory) on your computer a server. Beside the folder [C:\inetpub\wwwroot\], you can create a virtual directory (alias) in IIS and link it to a physical directory anywhere in your file system. Once your services are in the wwwroot directory or in an IIS virtual directory, you can replace the portion "localhost" in the web address created on IIS Server with the IP address of your computer to obtain the full web address of your services; for example, if your computer's IP address is [149.169.177.107], the full web address of your services is: http://149.169.177.107/WCFService/Service.svc

- Self-hosting. You can also write your own hosting service to host the web services that you develop. We will discuss self-hosting in Chapter 7.

If you are using a Windows computer, IIS has been installed. But you may need to turn it on by following these steps: Open "Control Panel;" Choose "Programs" and then "Programs and Features;" Click "Turn Windows features on or off" in the task list on the left-hand side of the window; and enable the Web Management tools.

After you have installed or turned on IIS, you will see the directory [C:\inetpub\wwwroot\]. To test if your IIS works properly, you can copy the folder "myService" into [C:\inetpub\wwwroot\], and then copy the http://localhost/WCFService/Service.svc into a web browser to access the service. Note the difference between the addresses of a .Net development server and IIS: the IIS address does not contain the number after the "localhost."

Next, we will study how we can create a virtual directory to make a physical directory of your choice with a web server.

To better organize your files and programs, you do not have to deploy all your services directly into the directory [C:\inetpub\wwwroot\]. Instead, you can create a virtual directory in IIS following the steps below:

1. Locate / decide where your service (created by Visual Studio) is. Assume the "physical" directory that contains your services is [C:\WCFService].
2. Use the IIS configuration manager in the Control Panel to create a virtual directory (Alias) named; for example, "myIisService" and link it to "myService" in the following sub steps:
    1) Open the "Control Panel" of your computer
    2) Open "Administrative Tools."
    3) Open Internet Information Services (IIS).
    4) Right-click on the "Default Web Site," choose "New," and choose "Virtual Directory…"
    5) You will be asked to name the virtual directory. You can name it MyIisServce.
    6) You will be asked to link the virtual directory to what physical directory. You can browse to the directory [C:\WCFService].
    7) After completing the steps above, you will see myIisService in the IIS Default Website. Right-click myIisService, and choose "Convert to Application." This step will register your service to the IIS Web Administration Service (WAS), which lists the service into the IIS service directory.
    8) You may also choose the permissions that you give to the clients of your website. At least, you will give them the read permission. To enable the scripts embedded in many web pages, you may also allow the clients to run scripts on your site. Security issues will be discussed in a later chapter.
3. Now, everything in the directory [C:\WCFService] will be visible on the Internet. If you want to change the settings and properties of your virtual direction, right click on "MyIisService" and Choose "Properties"

Please note that, if your computer is behind a firewall, you need to ask the firewall administrator to open the http port for external access.

After you have created a Virtual Directory and registered (converted to application), you can access your service at the address: http://localhost/MyIisServce/service.svc. Change "localhost" to your computer's IP address, which will allow the service to be accessed by other computers over the Internet. You can also publish a service in an existing virtual directory by following these steps:

1. After you have successfully built a web service project, instead of choosing to execute the project, you can choose, in the .Net menu command, "Publish Web Site."
2. Then a dialog window will be open. You can choose a virtual directory in your computer to host the services; for example, you can choose the location: C:\Inetpub\wwwroot\MyIisServce that you have created.
3. Once the website is published, a web page with the address http://localhost/MyIisServce/Service.svc will be open.
4. Replacing the word "localhost" by the IP address of the local machine, you have the URL of the web services; for example, http://149.169.177.107/MyIisServce/service.svc will be the URL of the services.

If you want to deploy the application to the Azure cloud computing environment, you can host the application in Azure's AppFabric application server extensions.

A server normally has different restrictions and limitations from your localhost. If you receive an error when accessing the services that you have deployed in an IIS server, you can check the HTTP status code and error message code at: http://support.microsoft.com/kb/943891/en-us; for example: 400 – Bad request. The request could not be understood by the server due to malformed syntax. If you are calling a RESTful service, it means that your request syntax, most likely, the way you express the variables in URI, is incorrect. You must follow the UriTemplate that you defined in the operation attributes to make the request.

An error code can have sub code; for example, 404 is an error "Not Found." If it gives subcode, it may have different meanings; for example: 404.13 – Content length too large, 404.14 – Request URL too long, and 404.15 – Query string too long. Some of the limitations, such as input and output sizes, can be defined in the service or application configuration. You can change the value to bigger value; for example:

<requestLimits maxAllowedContentLength="1000000" />

3.2.6 Source Code Deployment and Precompiled Code Deployment

There are two different ways of deploying a project into a web server. Source code deployment and precompiled code deployment. To deploy source code, you can simply copy the project root folder containing the App_Code folder, App_Data, and service files, application files, and Web.config file into the IIS server. The root folder must be converted into an application, by performing "Convert to Application" operation in IIS, as we discussed in the previous section. The deployed source files will be compiled when the code is to be executed for the first time. The compiled code will be saved for future re-execution. This compilation process is called just-in-time (JIT) compilation. The advance of JIT is that you can replace any file in the deployed folder without a full redeployment. The modified source code will be recompiled next time when it is to be executed.

Note, if the root folder has been converted to application, when you redeploy, you should redeploy the contents of the root folder. Do not replace the root folder. It requires the administrator to perform the convert to application again if it is replaced.

Source code deployment will have a cold start when the code to be executed is not compiled. To avoid the cold start, one can precompiled the code and deploy the compiled code. Another advantage is deploying precompiled code is to have the protection of proprietary code, as the source code is not deployed into the server.

To create the precompiled code, you can use the built-in mechanisms in Visual Studio in the following steps.

1. Create a new folder in a selected location on your local file system. For example: C:\PublishAppsOnC.

2. Start the web application or web service that you want to publish. Choose Visual Studio menu command Build → Publish Web App.
3. Click on Custom and enter a New Custom Profile. Choose a name for your services.
4. It will ask you to give a Profile name. We call it AppsOnDesktop.
5. In the "Publish Web" window, where "Connections" tag is selected, choose Publish methods → File System, and choose Target location → C:\PublishAppsOnC, as shown in Figure 3.13.
6. Select the "Settings" tag, expand the "File Publish Options." Make sure that you check "Precompile during publishing, as shown in Figure 3.14. You could click the option "Configure" to choose if you want to allow the precompiled code to be partially updated.
7. Click Publish button. The web application will be published into folder C:\PublishAppsOnC.

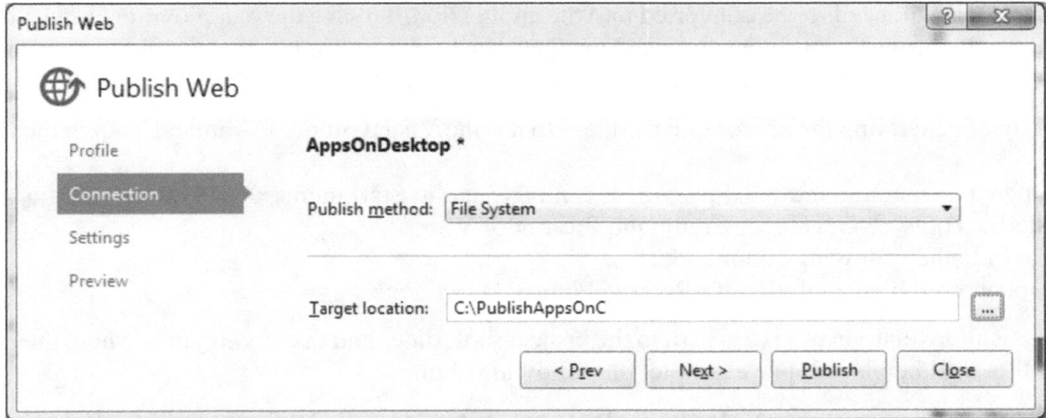

Figure 3.13. Publish a web application on local file system

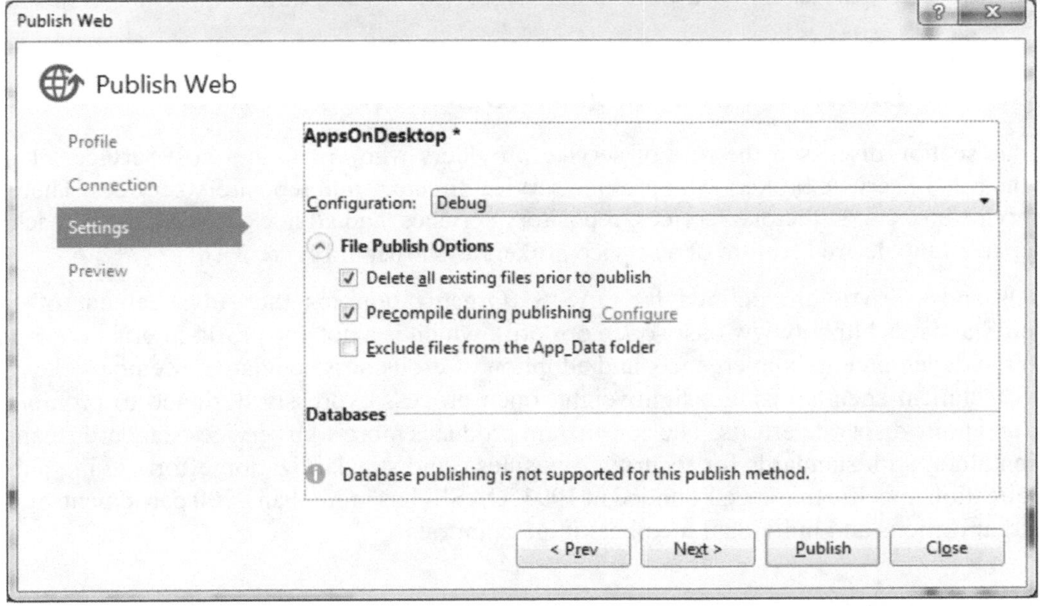

Figure 3.14. Select precompile during publishing option

The screenshots in Figure 3.15 shows the files of source code and precompiled code of a web service MyService and Compiled, respectively.

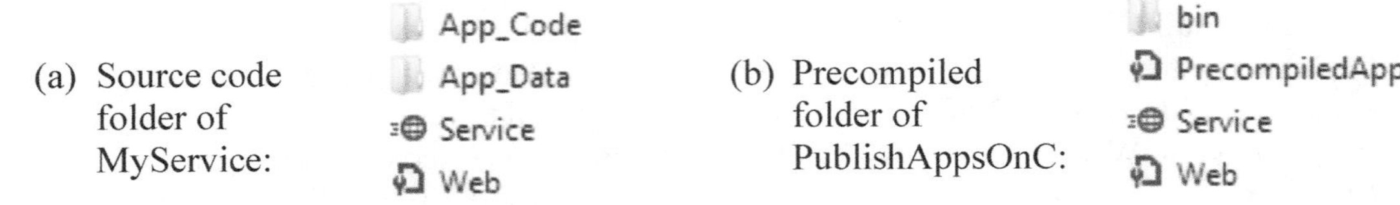

Figure 3.15. The file folder (a) with source code and (b) without source code

To deploy the precompiled project, copy the root folder PublishAppsOnC into the IIS server. The folder PublishAppsOnC still needs to be converted into the application. To save the redeployment time, you should never replace the project root folder PublishAppsOnC. Instead, you simply replace the files in the project root folder, and thus you do not need to perform the "Convert to Application" operation.

Another way of generating the precompiled code is to use the Visual Studio Command Tool in the following steps.

1. Open a .Net command window, which can be found in Start menu → MS Visual Studio → Visual Studio Tools → Developer Command Prompt of VS.
2. Execute the following command:
   aspnet_compiler -p physicalOrRelativePath -v / targetPath

where, physicalOrRelativePath is the path to the project root folder and the targetPath is where the generated compiled files will be placed. For example, the following command:

```
C:\Program Files\Microsoft Visual Studio 11.0>aspnet_compiler -p C:\MyService -v / C:\ PublishAppsOnC
```

will compile the root folder called MyService in C-drive and generate a new folder in C-drive called PublishAppsOnC, where, the first part C:\Program Files\Microsoft Visual Studio 11.0> is the command prompt and the second part aspnet_compiler -p C:\ MyService -v / C:\ PublishAppsOnC is the command.

3.3 Service Brokers: Publishing and Discovering Services

The previous section discussed the role of service providers who create and host services. This section discusses the role of service brokers who provide service directory and repository services. There are three kinds of service brokers: Directory services, repository services, and ad hoc service listings, each of which contains a part of the desired feature of a service broker, as shown in Figure 3.16.

Both UDDI and ebXML are defined by OASIS (Organization for the Advancement of Structured Information Standards https://www.oasis-open.org/org), which is a not-for-profit, international consortium devoted to the development, convergence, and adoption of e-business standards. Members themselves set the OASIS technical agenda, using a lightweight, open process expressly designed to promote industry consensus and unite disparate efforts. The consortium produces more web services standards than any other organization along with standards for security, e-business, and standardization efforts in the public sector and for application-specific markets. Founded in 1993, OASIS has more than 5000 participants representing over 600 organizations and individual members in 65 countries.

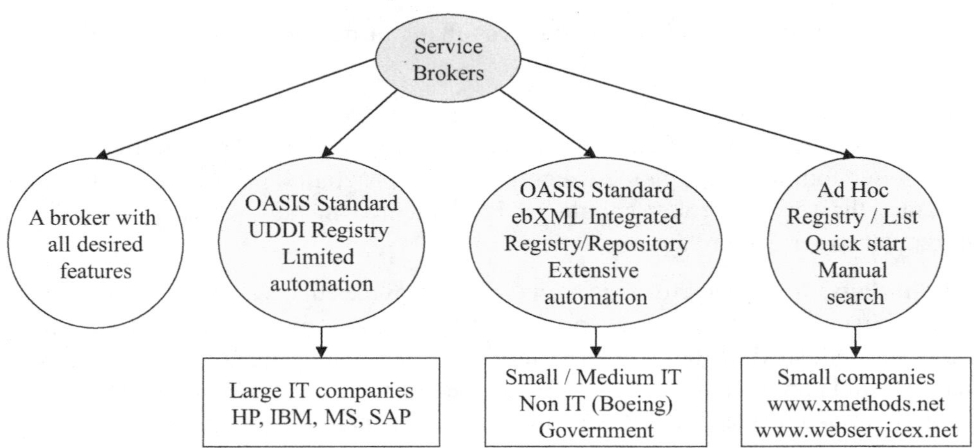

Figure 3.16. Different kinds of service brokers

In the framework of this course, a directory and a repository of web services and web applications are created and listed in Appendix C of the book and are available online at http://neptune.fulton.ad.asu.edu/WSRepository/. The services and applications in the repository are discussed and applied throughout the book as examples.

In the following subsections, we will discuss the general requirements of a service broker and elaborate on three existing types of service brokers.

3.3.1 An Ideal Service Broker with All Desired Features

This section discusses the features that a service broker should possess, in order to better support the development of SOA software.

Service registry: This is a fundamental function of a service broker, which allows service providers to register the catalog, description, contact information, and access point (such as the URL) of their services and allows service requesters to find the services they want based on the partial information they have.

Service repository: Host the executables of services. The hosting server must have super computing power and high-speed Internet connection, in order to facilitate a high volume of accesses.

Service specification and requirement: If a service requester cannot find a service, they can publish the specification or requirement, so that the service providers can develop the service that meets the specification or requirement. The service requirement can be written in the natural language, while the service specifications can be written in a specification or in the interface definition languages such as WSDL.

Application templates: Not only services, but also applications consisting of multiple services and Graphic User Interfaces (GUI) can be shared in SOC paradigm. Application templates specify the application workflow, participating service description, service acceptance criteria, and application integration criteria. An application builder can adopt an application template as the starting point to develop the application.

GUI templates: GUI is often the key to the success of a software product. Publication of GUI templates can facilitate the application builders to create user-friendly and efficient GUI by using existing GUI designs.

Collaboration protocols and templates: Collaboration protocols and templates define what languages should be used to define the collaboration and how services communicate with each other. The publication of collaboration protocols and templates regulate how service providers define the application, GUI templates, and service interfaces. They also reduce the development cycle because collaboration protocols and templates provide reusable collaboration patterns that can be adopted in the application and service development.

Policies: Policy-based computing suggests separating data from computing. Data items that reflect changeable policies are stored in configuration files or a policy database. The modification of policies can be done at runtime without interrupting the execution of the program. Policies can be published for reuse. On the other hand, the service broker should be implemented in policy-based computing to meet the dynamic requirement to service brokers.

Database and ontology: A service broker is a server that provides different kinds of services to its clients. Database support is essential to store and to manage a large amount of data and services. However, a traditional database is not sufficient to support a service broker that needs not only to retrieve data but also to discover services and application templates. Automated service and application template discovery is an important requirement of a service broker. An ontology with semantic attributes and reasoning capacity can extend the power of a traditional database to better support the automated service discovery.

Integrated testing and evaluation tools: Testing and evaluation, including test case generation, oracle (correct output for given input), verification, validation, reliability evaluation, and security evaluation, are crucial and difficult steps in software development. The service broker can offer tools that can help the application builders to test a service before binding the service into the application.

Quality of service: It is desired that the service broker can keep track of the performance and dependability data of the services, including the response time, throughput, reliability, and security, as well as the cost effectiveness.

Ideally, the service broker is implemented in SOA and thus can be dynamically extended and recomposed. Figure 3.17 shows the concept of a community service broker, which allows the publication of not only the specifications, policies, services, and data, but also the models and tools (system services) of the broker, such as the reliability evaluation tool, test generation tool, and ranking tools. In this way, the tools used in the broker system can be evaluated and eliminated if they are outperformed by other tools.

Based on the features of a service broker, a typical SOA software development process can be illustrated in Figure 3.18. The service providers can query the service brokers to learn what applications, GUIs, and services are demanded, and thus they develop and publish the application templates, GUIs, and services to meet the demand. The service providers can use the test tools in the service broker to test the services, and they can choose to host the services in the broker or on their own server. The service requesters or application builders can simply publish their requirements. They may query the service broker to find certain templates as the basis of developing their requirements, application templates, and GUIs. Once they finalize their application and GUI template, they can start to query the required services to fill up the components needed in the templates.

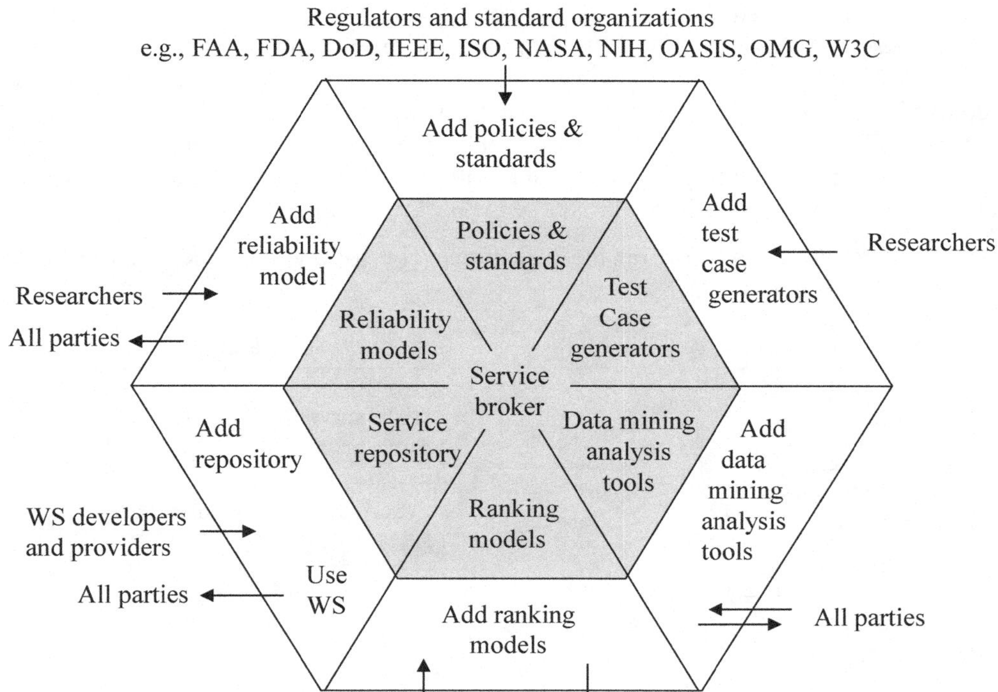

Figure 3.17. An expendable and recomposable service broker

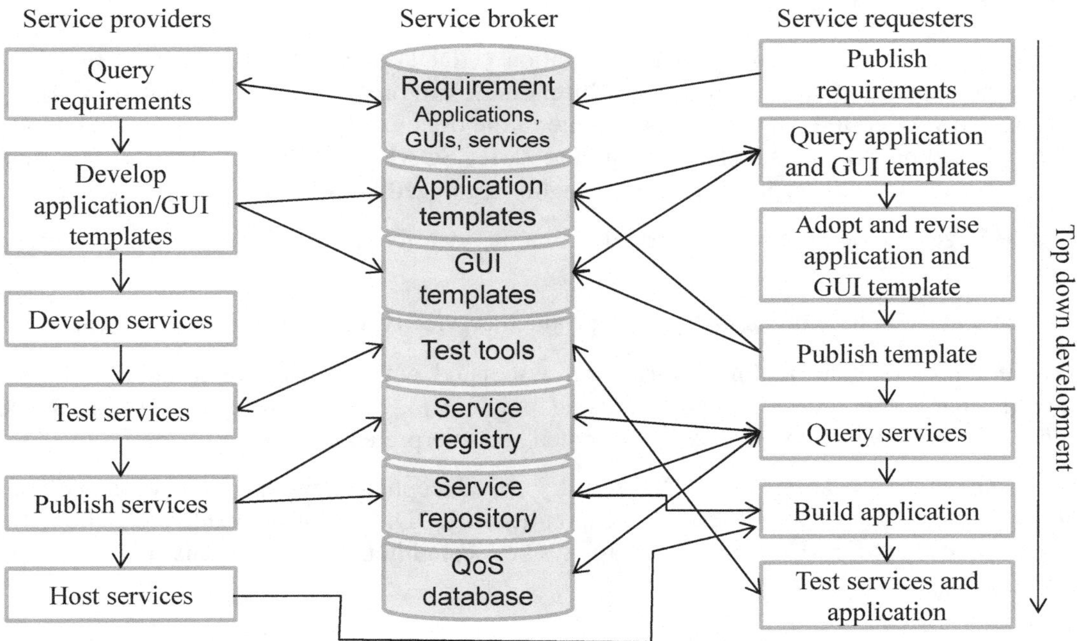

Figure 3.18. Software development process around a service broker

Application builders (service requesters) use a service broker to discover services of interest. They may remotely invoke these services once the APIs (Application Programming interfaces) of the services are discovered. Figure 3.19 shows a typical process of a service requester's searching for a service. The functional request is wrapped in a SOAP package, further wrapped into an HTTP package, and then sent to the service broker. The service broker unpacks the HTTP and SOAP wrappers to obtain the functional request. Typically, it uses an ontology with semantic attributes to match the request to the best suitable service that meets the request. The service broker sends back the API to the service requester.

Current service brokers do not support all these features. The following subsections elaborate the three existing kinds of service brokers.

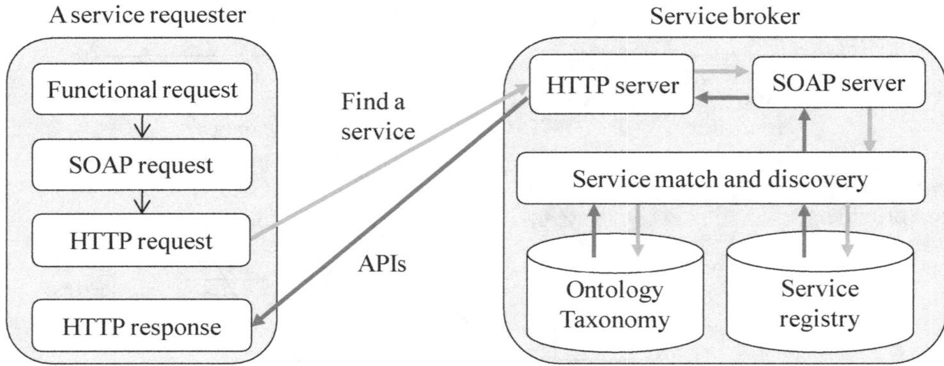

Figure 3.19. A service requester searches for a service

3.3.2 UDDI Service Registry

The Universal Description, Discovery, and Integration (UDDI) is an OASIS standard that is used to represent, to model, and to publish web services (http://uddi.xml.org). UDDI was initiated by IBM, Ariba, and Microsoft. Now, over 300 companies participate in the organization, including HP, Intel, Novell, and SAP. UDDI is based on existing standards, including XML, SOAP, and WSDL. UDDI's main function is a service registry, and its registry information is roughly organized in three groups:

- **White Pages** include the service provider's name, identity (e.g., the DUNS number), and contact information.
- **Yellow Pages** include the industry type, product, service type, and geographical location.
- **Green Pages** include binding information associated with services, references to the technical models that those services implement, and pointers to various file and URL-based discovery mechanisms. The information can be searched and interpreted by programs.

At the data organization level, data in a UDDI registry are conceptually divided into five data models, also called data structures, each of which represents an entity in UDDI. Every such entity is assigned its own Universally Unique Identifier (UUID) and can always be located in the context of that UDDI registry with these identifiers:

1. businessEntity;
2. businessService;
3. bindingTemplate;
4. tModel;
5. publisherAssertion.

The first two entries refer to the white pages and yellow pages, respectively, while the green pages are related to entries 3 and 4. However, the analogy between the telephone books and UDDI entries is more at the conceptual level. At the technical level, they are rather different.

We elaborate on each of the items by their members and their XML Schema definition. XML Schema (XMLS) is language used to define the syntax of other languages and data structures. Although XMLS will be formally further discussed in the next chapter, these definitions given here are intuitively understandable.

1. businessEntity

This data structure contains information about the company itself (service provider), including the following items of information:

- Universally Unique Identifiers (UUIDs) of the company, which are assigned when the company registers at the UDDI registry;
- Company web address
- Contact information;
- Industry categories;
- A list of services provided.

The XMLS definition of businessEntity is as follows:

```
<element name="businessEntity" type="uddi:businessEntity" />
<complexType name="businessEntity">
   <attribute name="businessKey" type="uddi:businessKey" use="required" />
   <attribute name="operator" type="string" use="optional" />
   <attribute name="authorizedName" type="string" use="optional" />
   <sequence>
        <element ref="uddi:discoveryURLs" minOccurs="0" />
              <element ref="uddi:name" maxOccurs="unbounded" />
              <element ref="uddi:description" minOccurs="0" maxOccurs="unbounded" />
              <element ref="uddi:contacts" minOccurs="0" />
              <element ref="uddi:businessServices" minOccurs="0" />
              <element ref="uddi:identifierBag" minOccurs="0" />
              <element ref="uddi:categoryBag" minOccurs="0" />
   </sequence>
</complexType>
```

An example of the instance of the data entry, based on the aforesaid structure definition, is given as follows:

```
<businessEntity
        businessKey="uuid:B1D2A3B4-E445-4F32-75BA-67D123451C39"
        operator=" http://www.public.asu.edu/~ychen10/teaching/cse445/"
        authorizedName="Course Instructor">
   <name>ASU CSE 445-598</name>
   <description> We provide sample services for SOC education </description>
   <contacts>
        <contact useType="general information">
              <description>Email</description>
              <personName> Course Instructor</personName>
              <phone>(480) 965 2769</phone>
              <email>cse445598instructor@asu.edu</email>
        </contact>
        <contact useType=" assignments and projects ">
              <description>Email</description>
              <personName> Teaching Assistant</personName>
              <email>cse445598TA@asu.edu</email>
```

```
        </contact>
    </contacts>
    <businessServices>
        SOC Education, SOC software development, and SOC research
    </businessServices>
    <identifierBag>
        <keyedReference tModelKey="uddi:02016094-9c03-47e9-a52b-1dec2d0c1454"
            name="D-U-N-S" value=" 913360445 " />
    </identifierBag>
    <categoryBag>
        <keyedReference tModelKey="UUID:C0B9FE13-179F-413D-8A5B-5004DB8E5BB2"
            name="NAICS" value="246359" />
    </categoryBag>
</businessEntity>
```

2. businessService:

The businessService data model represents an individual web service provided and published by the service provider. Universally Unique Identifiers (UUIDs) are used in the businessKey and serviceKey attributes of the entry. Every business entity and business service is uniquely identified in all UDDI registries through the UUID assigned by the registry when the information is first entered. A reference is given to the bindingTemplates, which holds the technical service description information related to a given business service. The XMLS definition of this data structure and an example (instance) are shown as follows:

```
<element name="businessService" type="uddi:businessService" />
<complexType name="businessService">
    <attribute name="serviceKey" type="uddi:serviceKey" use="required" />
    <attribute name="businessKey" type="uddi:businessKey" use="optional" />
    <sequence>
            <element ref="uddi:name" minOccurs="0" maxOccurs="unbounded" />
            <element ref="uddi:description" minOccurs="0" maxOccurs="unbounded" />
            <element ref="uddi:bindingTemplates" minOccurs="0" />
            <element ref="uddi:categoryBag" minOccurs="0" />
    </sequence>
</complexType>
```

Example:

```
<businessService serviceKey="uuid:C0B9FE13-179F-413D-8A5B-5004DB8E5BB2"
businessKey="uuid:01F83FCE-54AC-4C39-B274-C4A390B8EE8C">
    <name>Array2String</name>
    <description>
        Convert an array of floats into a string, and a string back into an array of
floats
    </description>
    <bindingTemplate> ... </bindingTemplate>
    <categoryBag> … </categoryBag>
</businessService >
```

3. bindingTemplate

Binding templates are the technical descriptions of the web services represented by the businessService data structure. The same web service may have multiple binding templates. Each binding template represents the actual implementation of the web service; for example, one can implement the same service specification in different languages (Java and C#) to better support the applications using different languages. Although web services are supposed to be completely language independent, if language-specific data structures are used in the web services, the proxy created in the application may not be understood by the language of the application program. Another motivation for using multiple binding templates is to allow the service to be bound to a different set of protocols or a different URL address for flexibility and reliability reasons; for example, besides SOAP binding, one can also use MIME binding (MIME: Multipurpose Internet Mail Extension).

```
<element name="bindingTemplate" type="uddi:bindingTemplate" />
<complexType name="bindingTemplate">
   <attribute name="serviceKey" type="uddi:serviceKey" use="optional" />
   <attribute name="bindingKey" type="uddi:bindingKey" use="required" />
   <sequence>
             <element ref="uddi:description" minOccurs="0" maxOccurs="unbounded" />
             <choice>
                  <element ref="uddi:accessPoint" />
                  <element ref="uddi:hostingRedirector" />
             </choice>
             <element ref="uddi:tModelInstanceDetails" />
   </sequence>
</complexType>
```

Example:

```
<bindingTemplate serviceKey="uuid:c1acf26d-9672-4404-9d70-39b756e62ab4"
bindingKey="uuid:67153d5b-3659-afb4-8510-adda2c034649">
   <description>SOAP Binding</description>
   <accessPoint URLType="http">
        http://neptune.fulton.ad.asu.edu/WSRepository/Array2String/Service.asmx
   </accessPoint>
   <tModelInstanceDetails>
        <tModelInstanceInfo tModelKey="uddi:02016094-9c03-47e9-a52b-1dec2d0c1454">
             <instanceDetails>
                  <overviewDoc>
                       <description>
                            references the WSDL service definition
                       </description>
                       <overviewURL>
        http://neptune.fulton.ad.asu.edu/WSRepository/Array2String/Service.asmx?wsdl
                       </overviewURL>
                  </overviewDoc>
             </instanceDetails>
        </tModelInstanceInfo>
   </tModelInstanceDetails>
</bindingTemplate>
```

4. tModel

A tModel is a technical way (specification) of describing the type of any business, service, template structures, and so on, stored within the UDDI registry. Any abstract concept can be registered within UDDI as a tModel. Each business registered with UDDI categorizes all of its services according to a defined list of service types (tModels). When registering, one can choose to belong to an existing tModel type, and thus, must be compliant with the existing specification, or define a new tModel; for example, if one defines a new WSDL interface, one can define a tModel that represents that interface within UDDI. Then, one can specify that a given web service implements that interface specification by associating the tModel with one of that business service's binding templates. The XMLS definition of this entry and an example are given as follows:

```
<element name="tModel" type="uddi:tModel" />
<complexType name="tModel">
```

```
   <attribute name="tModelKey" type="uddi:tModelKey" use="required" />
   <attribute name="operator" type="string" use="optional" />
   <attribute name="authorizedName" type="string" use="optional" />
   <sequence>
            <element ref="uddi:name" />
            <element ref="uddi:description" minOccurs="0" maxOccurs="unbounded" />
            <element ref="uddi:overviewDoc" minOccurs="0" />
            <element ref="uddi:identifierBag" minOccurs="0" />
            <element ref="uddi:categoryBag" minOccurs="0" />
   </sequence>
</complexType>
```

Example:

```
<tModel tModelKey="uddi:02016094-9c03-47e9-a52b-1dec2d0c1454"
      operator="http://www.public.asu.edu/~ychen10/teaching/cse445"
      authorizedName="Course Instructor">
   <name>Array2String Port Type</name>
   <description>
      An interface for general float array to string conversion
   </description>
   <overviewDoc>
      <overviewURL>
            http://149.169.177.107/Array2String/service.d.wsdl
      </overviewURL>
   </overviewDoc>
</tModel>
```

5. publisherAssertion

For large corporations and enterprises, a single business entry cannot sufficiently represent the businesses of these corporations. UDDI allows multiple business entries to be published, representing individual departments or subsidiaries. The data model publisherAssertion helps them to make their relationships visible in their UDDI registrations. To eliminate the possibility that one publisher falsely claims a relationship with another, both publishers have to publish exactly the same information, in order for the relationship to become visible.

The publisherAssertion structure consists of the three elements: fromKey (the first businessKey), toKey (the second businessKey), and keyedReference, which designates the asserted relationship type in terms of a (keyName keyValue) pair within a tModel, uniquely referenced by a tModelKey. The XMLS definition of this data structure is given as follows:

```
<element name="publisherAssertion" type="uddi:publisherAssertion" />
<complexType name="publisherAssertion">
   <sequence>
            <element ref="uddi:fromKey" />
            <element ref="uddi:toKey" />
            <element ref="uddi:keyedReference" />
   </sequence>
</complexType>
```

UDDI data entries can be created and accessed through UDDI APIs offered to the service providers and application builders. The following API operations are supported for such purposes.

```
Inquiry Operations:
  Find
      find_business
      find_service
      find_binding
      find_tModel
```

```
   Get details
        get_businessDetail
        get_serviceDetail
        get_bindingDetail
        get_tModelDetail
        get_registeredInfo
Publishing Operations:

   Save
        save_business
        save_service
        save_binding
        save_tModel
   Delete
        delete_business
        delete_service
        delete_binding
        delete_tModel
        get_registeredInfo
Security operations:
   get_authToken
   discard_authToken
```

Take find_business as an example, which searches for businesses that match the specified criteria. The syntax of this API is defined as follows:

```
<find_business generic="2.0" [maxRows="nn"] xmlns="urn:uddi-org:api_v2">
        [<findQualifiers/>]
        [<name/> [<name/>] ... ]
        [<discoveryURLs/>]
        [<identifierBag/>]
        [<categoryBag/>]
        [<tModelBag/>]
   </find_business>
```

The parameters of the API are explained as follows:

- *maxRows:* Optional attribute to specify the maximum number of rows to be returned.
- *findQualifiers:* Optional element to override the default search functionality; for example, the find qualifier exactNameMatch will match exact business names.
- *name:* The full or partial name of the business. UDDI 2.0 enables you to specify up to five business names.
- *discoveryURLs:* Optional element to search by discovery URLs.
- *identifierBag:* Optional element to search by identifier.
- *categoryBag:* Optional element to search by category; for example, you can search by NAICS codes.
- *tModelBag:* Optional element to search by tModel records.

Currently, large computer corporations, such as IBM, Microsoft, and SAP, are running publicly accessible UDDI services, as well as providing UDDI server software that allows users to implement their own UDDI services for Intranet and Internet uses. UDDI is a standard component of Windows server A standard installation of the server will have the Microsoft Enterprise UDDI component installed, which allows the server to register service providers and services from the registered providers. A UDDI component can be installed in the IBM WebSphere SOA development environment to provide service registry services.

Figure 3.20 shows the architecture of the Microsoft Enterprise UDDI component. It provides both human and programming interfaces for manual and automatic registration and search of the registry.

The UDDI request manager receives the incoming requests from the ASP.NET pages or the web service interfaces and invokes the appropriate services in the UDDI class library.

The UDDI class library encapsulates different types of functions into standard web services, including services offered by MSDE and SQL databases.

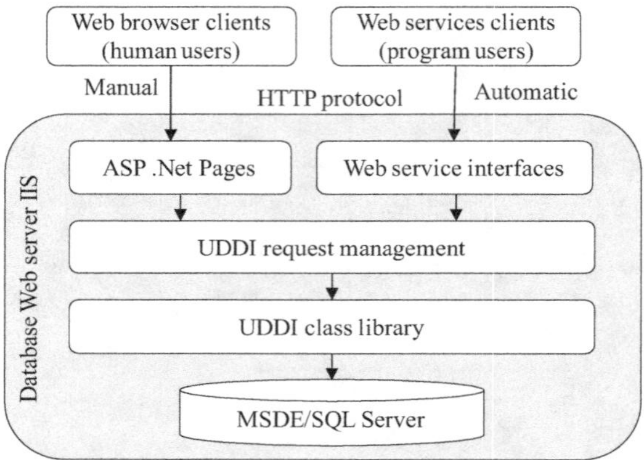

Figure 3.20. The architecture of the Microsoft UDDI services

As a human user, one can manually use the following steps to register as service provider, register the services, and search for services.

As a program user, you can access the Enterprise UDDI services in C# in .Net programming environment. At the beginning of your C# program, you can import the built-in UDDI namespaces/libraries, which give the necessary classes and functions to access the UDDI services:

```
using Microsoft.Uddi;
using Microsoft.Uddi.Services;
using Microsoft.Uddi.TModels;
```

Then, you can use the following classes and member functions of the classes to access the services:

```
UddiConnection conn =
   new UddiConnection("http://localhost/uddi/inquire.asmx");          // 1st
FindService fs = new FindService(txtName.Text);                      // 2nd
ServiceList servList = fs.Send(conn);     // 3rd
foreach (ServiceInfo servInfo in servList.ServiceInfos) {            // 4th
   MessageBox.Show("Service: " + servInfo.Names[0].Text
                                   + "" + servInfo.ServiceKey);
}
```

The first statement creates an instance of the UddiConnection, using the address of the Enterprise UDDI Services as the parameter for the constructor. This statement establishes a connection to the UDDI that is to be accessed.

The second statement creates an object of class "FindService" to find a required business. The search keys are passed into the object by the text file "txtName.Text."

The third statement invokes the Send method (member function) of the FindService object, passing in the the previously created UddiConnection object as the argument. The Send method returns the list of available services in the form of a ServiceList object.

The fourth statement, which is a for-loop, display the service name and unique identifying key for each service found in the loop.

Accessing UDDI entities is conceptually and syntactically similar to the database operations. Chapter 7 of the book will discuss in more detail the interface between program and database and database accesses and manipulations.

3.3.3 ebXML Service Registry and Repository

ebXML (Electronic Business using eXtensible Markup Language) is a modular suite of specifications/standards that enables enterprises of any size and in any geographical location to conduct business over the Internet. Using ebXML, companies now have a standard method to exchange business messages, conduct trading relationships, communicate data in common terms, and define and register business processes (http://ebxml.org/). From the service broker's point of view, it defines more features than that of UDDI. The most significant difference is that ebXML offers service repository in additional to service registry. Since the large computing companies such as Microsoft, IBM, and Oracles, have resources to host their own services, they prefer the UDDI. On the other hand, ebXML is preferred by medium and small IT companies, the companies whose core business is not was in IT, and governmental organizations. ebXML was started in 1999 as an initiative of OASIS and the United Nations/ECE agency CEFACT. The original project envisioned and delivered five layers of substantive data specifications, including XML standards for:

- **ebXML Business Process Specification Schema**, or ebBP (ebXML Business Process Specification Schema), which defines a standard language to configure systems for business collaboration execution between partners. A business process definition, or an ebBP definition, describes interoperable business processes that allow partners to achieve business goals: support process design/description, enable collaboration monitoring and validation, and guide execution. The ebBP specifies the Business Transaction(s), choreography for using those in Business Collaborations (BC), and BC themselves. Business Signals are exchanged for technical state alignment between parties. Core capabilities include:
    - Standard and extensible business transaction patterns.
    - State alignment.
    - Business collaboration for two or more parties.
    - Composition for visibility and relationships: allowing third-party visibility in a business transaction, when that process definition exists elsewhere.
    - Enabling use of hybrid, ebXML, or web services.
    - Complex support for party/role definitions.
    - Improving linking constructs and transitions for process lifecycle.
    - Using semantic information to specialize processes and documents.
- **Core Components**: The ebXML Core Components Technical Specification (CCTS) presents a methodology for developing semantic building blocks to represent the general business data types in use. This enables reusable and commonly understandable data, using CC and Business Information Entities (BIEs). Developed in the United Nations Centre for Trade Facilitation and E-Business (UN/CEFACT), CC provide:
    - Common modeling concept for objects/data.
    - Naming convention for definition of the generic semantic meaning in Dictionary Entry Names.
    - Fixed set of reusable data types for consistent business value representation.
- **Collaboration Protocol Profiles and Agreements** (CPPA), which provide a conduit between technical capabilities and partner expectations for business collaborations. The Profile contains technical capabilities of a business partner. It outlines the capabilities and preferences of protocol

features and properties for specific roles in component services and activities used in processes. It enables monitoring of sessions and verification of delivery channel features used in collaborative processes. The second set (Agreement) contains data to configure shared aspects of business collaboration protocols. The CPP/CPA v2.1 includes:
    - Extension framework for alternative messaging, business process, and capabilities such as for ebBP.
    - Expanded transport capabilities for message exchange patterns.
    - Increased composability of multiple exposed services.
    - Improved Party identification.

- **Message Service**, which defines a communications-protocol neutral method for exchanging eBusiness messages. It defines messaging functions, protocol and envelope intended to operate over SOAP (SOAP v1.1 and SOAP with Attachments). Binding to lower transport layers relies on standard SOAP bindings; ebMS complements them where required.

- **Registry and Repository**: In v3.0, the ebXML Registry and Repository provide services for registering, locating, and accessing information resources in a distributed (or federated) secure environment. Current v3.0 features include:
    - Registry federation support.
    - Replicated content/metadata.
    - Security enhancements: XACML, SAML.
    - Extensible service interfaces and protocols.
    - Definition of new service request and response types.
    - HTTP binding to ebXML Registry Services interfaces.
    - Uses a REST-style architecture.
    - Content management (validation and catalogue management).
    - Query enhancements.

ebXML targets to provide a migration path of technologies for Small-Medium Enterprises (SME) and government organization to an integrated e-business platform. The heterogeneous nature of e-business transactions requires a flexible infrastructure/framework that supports simple service calls and complex document exchange. For e-business, the key integration patterns realize SOA benefits in a pragmatic iterative manner.
A number of case studies are presented at http://www.oasis-open.org/casestudies/ and http://www ebxml.org/, where ebXML is used as the key platform for service provision, message and document exchange, and ontology-based data services, including:

- The UK's National Programme for Information Technology, which is the world's largest civil IT project. A central component of the system is the National Health Service (NHS), which will link healthcare professionals to improve sharing of patients' records with those health professionals involved in the care of the patient across the NHS. It will allow patients to look at their own health records from home using a protected link into the NHS. Healthcare records, appointment details, prescription information, and up-to-date research into illnesses and treatment will eventually be accessible to patients and health professionals whenever they need it to make health or care decisions. The Care Records Service in NHS is the Transactional Messaging Service (TMS) Spine that uses the ebXML Messaging Service.

- Norway's National Insurance Administration (NIA) communications infrastructure, which is used to connect to its business partners with an architecture based on open standards, including the ebXML Messaging OASIS Standard, ISO 15000-2.

- T-Mobile, which operates an ebXML-based B2B gateway, which implements the ebXML Message Service and the ebXML Collaboration Protocol Profile and Agreement.

- The Centers for Disease Control and Prevention (CDC), an agency of the US Department of Health and Human Services, operates the Public Health Information Network Messaging System (PHINMS), with state and local health agencies, clinical facilities, and medical labs across the United States. PHINMS makes use of ebXML Messaging Service and Collaboration Protocol Agreement specifications to provide a secure and reliable messaging system. The system is platform-independent and loosely coupled among its subsystems that produce outgoing messages or consume incoming messages.
- The Government of Ontario, Canada, which has created an ebXML-based e-government that integrates business, citizen, and employee services. Now in its second phase, a project called XML in Ontario (XiO) is being implemented, which evolves the architectural design and prototype of the key technologies of ebXML implemented in phase 1, while continuing to monitor changes in standards, tools, and user trends. The XiO team is concentrating on ebXML Registry and Repository. During this project phase, they reviewed tool sets, worked with ministry teams to set up a process to use common schemas and tool sets, and worked with other government entities to further the use of standards and technology.

3.3.4 Ad Hoc Registry Lists

Less formally, many organizations offer a simple list of services or a manually organized service registry. Users can instantly register a new service and manually search a service by browsing through the list. Some of the useful service lists include:

- ASU Services and Application Repository (http://neptune.fulton.ad.asu.edu/WSRepository/repository/).
- National Digital Forecast Database (NDFD) with SOAP and RESTful web services: http://graphical.weather.gov/xml/
- National Geophysical Data Center Web Services with online map services: http://www.ngdc.noaa.gov/dmsp/maps.html
- Geo Names Web Services: https://www.geonames.org/export/ws-overview.html
- U.S. Government Open Data: https://www.data.gov/
- NASA API link to the documentation that explains how and where to find the solar / wind / many other types of data: https://power.larc.nasa.gov/docs/v1/#introduction
- Microsoft Web services and API: https://msdn.microsoft.com/en-us/library/
- Programmable Web (https://www.programmableweb.com/apis/directory/).
- Web service X (http://www.webservicex.net/).
- Flight Booking Service: http://ws.51book.com:8000/ltips/services/

3.4 SOAP and HTTP

SOAP (Simple Object Access Protocol) can be generally used for exchanging structured information in a distributed environment. In web services, it is frequently used for remote invocation of services across network and platforms. SOAP is fundamentally a stateless and one-way message exchange protocol. However, more complex interaction patterns and interfaces (e.g., request/response and request/multiple responses) can be created by combining such one-way exchanges with features provided by an underlying protocol such as HTTP.

3.4.1 SOAP Format

Like any communication protocol, a SOAP message consists of wrapper information and payload, as shown in Figure 3.21. The envelope identifies the starting and ending of a SOAP message. The header contains a collection of zero or more SOAP header blocks, each of which might be targeted at any SOAP receiver within the SOAP message path. The body contains a collection of zero or more *element information items* targeted at an ultimate SOAP receiver in the SOAP message path.

<soap:Envelope>	<soap:header> . . . </soap:header>	<soap:body> . . . </soap:body>	<soap:Envelope>

Figure 3.21. SOAP message format

A SOAP message is an XML document, as shown in the following example, which represents a travel reservation request. In this message, there are two header blocks in this message: `<m:reservation>` and `<n:passenger>`. There are two body blocks: `<p:itinerary>` and `<q:lodging>`.

```
<?xml version='1.0' ?>
<soap:Envelope xmlns:env="http://www.w3.org/2003/05/soap-envelope">
 <soap:Header>
  <m:reservation xmlns:m="http://travelcompany.example.org/reservation"
          soap:role="http://www.w3.org/2003/05/soap-envelope/role/next"
           soap:mustUnderstand="true">
   <m:reference>uuid:093a2da1-q345-739r-ba5d-pqff98fe8j7d</m:reference>
   <m:dateAndTime>2001-11-29T13:20:00.000-05:00</m:dateAndTime>
  </m:reservation>
  <n:passenger xmlns:n="http://mycompany.example.com/employees"
          soap:role="http://www.w3.org/2003/05/soap-envelope/role/next"
           soap:mustUnderstand="true">
   <n:name>Åke Jógvan Øyvind</n:name>
  </n:passenger>
 </soap:Header>
 <soap:Body>
  <p:itinerary
    xmlns:p="http://travelcompany.example.org/reservation/travel">
   <p:departure>
     <p:departing>New York</p:departing>
          <p:arriving>Phoenix</p:arriving>
          <p:departureDate>2006-11-24</p:departureDate>
          <p:departureTime>late afternoon</p:departureTime>
          <p:seatPreference>aisle</p:seatPreference>
   </p:departure>
   <p:return>
     <p:departing>Phoenix</p:departing>
          <p:arriving>New York</p:arriving>
          <p:departureDate>2006-11-30</p:departureDate>
          <p:departureTime>early-morning</p:departureTime>
          <p:seatPreference>window</p:seatPreference>
   </p:return>
  </p:itinerary>
  <q:lodging
   xmlns:q="http://travelcompany.example.org/reservation/hotels">
   <q:preference>none</q:preference>
  </q:lodging>
 </soap:Body>
</soap:Envelope>
```

3.4.2 HTTP

HTTP (Hypertext Transfer Protocol) is an application-level protocol for distributed, collaborative, and hypermedia information systems (https://tools.ietf.org/html/rfc2616).

HTTP is the most widely used protocol to access the resources on the Internet. An HTTP client identifies the server via a URI or URL, connects to it using the underlying protocols; for example, TCP/IP issues an HTTP request message, and receives an HTTP response message over the same TCP/IP connection. HTTP messages are always two ways: a request from the client to the server and a response from the server to the client. The format is HTTP-message = Request-Line | Status-Line, where,

- Request-Line = **Method** SP Request-URI SP HTTP-Version CRLF,
- Response: Status-Line = HTTP-Version SP Status-Code SP Reason-Phrase CRLF, where, SP: Space and CRLF: end of line mark

The HTTP **Method** indicates the operation to be performed on the resource identified by the Request-URI. The method is case-sensitive and can take the following values:

- GET: For retrieving the information (entity) identified by Request-URI. If the Request-URI refers to a data-producing process (method), the produced data shall be returned in the response.
- HEAD: the method is identical to GET, except that the server do not return a message-body in the response. It is used to obtain meta-information about the entity implied by the request without transferring the entity-body itself. Head thus can be used for one-way call.
- PUT: For creating and modifying/replacing resource. It requests the enclosed entity to be stored under the supplied Request-URI.
    - If the Request-URI refers to an already existing resource, the enclosed entity SHOULD be considered to be a modified version of the one residing on the origin server.
    - If the Request-URI does not point to an existing resource, and that URI is capable of being defined as a new resource by the requesting user agent, the origin server can create the resource with that URI.
    - If a new resource is created, the origin server must inform the user agent via the 201 (Created) response.
- POST: For requesting the server to accept the (data) entity enclosed in the request as a new subordinate of the resource identified by the Request-URI in the Request-Line. It is used for
    - Annotation of existing resources;
    - Posting a message to a bulletin board, newsgroup, mailing list, or similar group of articles;
    - Providing a block of data, such as the result of submitting a form, to a data-handling process;
    - Extending a database through an append operation.

POST and PUT have some similarity but are used in different situations: POST is used for appending and PUT is used for replacing or creating.

- DELETE: For requesting that the origin server deletes the resource identified by the Request-URI.
    - The client cannot be guaranteed that the operation has been carried out, even if the status code returned from the origin server indicates that the action is successful. The reason for returning success response is not to block the client for too long.
    - However, the server SHOULD NOT indicate success unless, at the time the response is given, it intends to delete the resource or move it to an inaccessible location.
- TRACE: For invoking a remote, application-layer loop-back of the request message.
- CONNECT: For use with a proxy that can dynamically switch to being a tunnel (e.g., SSL tunneling)

A few frequently used HTTP response codes are: 200 (OK), 201 (Created), 202 (Accepted), 204 (No Content), 301 (Moved Permanently), and 501 (Not Implemented).

HTTP is used with SOAP for the communication between clients and web services. In Chapter 7, we will discuss RESTful services that directly use HTTP, without using SOAP, for the communication between the clients and services.

3.4.3 SOAP over HTTP

As a higher-level protocol, SOAP messages are carried by a lower-level protocol. In principle, it can be carried by different protocols. However, it is often bound to HTTP, just like TCP (Transmission Control Protocol) is normally bound to IP (Internet Protocol).

SOAP is a one-way message exchange protocol, and it relies on HTTP to relate the return message to the requesting message. HTTP implicitly correlates the SOAP request message with its response message. Therefore, an application using this binding can choose to infer a correlation between a SOAP message sent in the body of an HTTP request message and a SOAP message returned in the HTTP response. The HTTP binding makes use of the SOAP Web Method feature to allow applications to choose the so-called Web Method – restricting it to one of GET or POST – to use over the HTTP message exchange. As a result, it makes use of two message exchange patterns that offer applications two ways of exchanging SOAP messages via HTTP:

- The use of the HTTP POST method for conveying SOAP messages in the bodies of HTTP request and response messages;
- The use of the GET method in an HTTP request to return a SOAP message in the body of an HTTP response.

The first usage pattern is the HTTP-specific instantiation of a binding feature called the SOAP *request-response message exchange* pattern, while the second uses a feature called the SOAP *response message exchange* pattern.

The purpose of providing these two types of usages is to accommodate the two interactions well established on the web:

- The first type of interaction allows for the use of data within the body of an HTTP POST to create or modify the state of a resource identified by the URI to which the HTTP request is destined.
- The second type of interaction pattern offers the ability to use an HTTP GET request to obtain a representation of a resource without altering its state in any way.

In the first case, the SOAP-specific aspect of concern is that the body of the HTTP POST request is a SOAP message. The message will be processed using the SOAP processing model as a part of the application-specific processing required to conform to the POST semantics. In the second case, the typical usage that is foreseen is the case where the representation of the resource being requested is returned not as an HTML, but as a SOAP message.

The following code pieces show two examples of SOAP over HTTP, one with an HTTP response and the other without an HTTP response.

HTTP Request

```
GET/StockQuoteService
Host: www.ibm.com HTTP/1.1
Accept: application/soap+xml
Accept-Charset: utf-8
Content-Type: application/soap+xml
Content-Length: nnnn
<soap:Envelope>
<soap:Body>
<abc:GetStockQuote>
<abc:symbol>IBM</abc:symbol>
</abc:GetStockQuote>
</soap:Body>
</soap:Envelope>
```

HTTP Response

```
HTTP/1.1 200 OK
Content-Type: application/soap+xml;
charset="utf-8"
Content-Length: nnnn
<soap:Envelope>
<soap:Body>
<abc:GetStockQuoteResponse>
<abc:value>85.00</abc:value>
</abc:GetStockQuoteResponse>
</soap:Body>
</soap:Envelope>
```

HTTP Request	*HTTP Response*

`HEAD/DataService HTTP/1.1`
`Host: www.ibm.com`
`Accept: *;q=0`
`Content-Type: application/soap+xml;`
`charset="utf-8"`
`Content-Length: nn`
`<soap:Envelope>`
`<soap:Body>`
`<cds:INSERT>`
`<abc:SomeDataToInsert />`
`</cds:INSERT>`
`</soap:Body>`
`</soap:Envelope>`
	`HTTP Response`
	`HTTP/1.1 204 No Content`

Note that, in the second message, the web method in the SOAP body is INSERT. Why do we not use the HTTP method PUT, instead, we used HEAD? The reason is that the detail of the operation (INSERT) is given in the SOAP message. It does not matter which HTTP method is used. Normally, we simply use GET. We use HEAD here to create a non-blocking (loosely coupled, asynchronous) one-way communication. When we discuss RESTful services in Chapter 7, we will explicitly choose the HTTP method to perform the required services, as SOAP layer has been removed from the protocol stack.

3.5 WSDL: Web Services Description Language

WSDL (Web Services Description Language) is a language that can be used to describe web services in the common XML syntax. WSDL describes four critical aspects of web services:

- Functionality of the services;
- Data types for parameter values and return type of the function (service) calls;
- Binding information about the transport protocol to be used, usually SOAP;
- Address information for locating the specified service.

In other words, WSDL represents a contract between the service requester and the service provider. This is similar to the method (member function) interfaces of classes in object-oriented languages, where the users can use the interfaces to the functions defined in the classes. The crucial difference here is that WSDL is platform and language independent, and is used primarily (although not exclusively) to facilitate SOAP calls.

Using WSDL, a client can locate a web service and invoke any of its publicly available functions. With WSDL-aware tools, you can also automate this process, enabling applications to easily integrate new services with little or no manual coding. Therefore, WSDL is important in the web service architecture, because it provides a common language for describing services and a platform for automatically integrating those services into applications.

Potentially, this feature can allow applications to perform automated reconfiguration and recomposition. Reconfiguration changes/replaces a constituent web service in the application with a web service of the same functionality, but of, say, better performance and reliability. Recomposition changes the structure and the functionality of the application.

3.5.1 Elements of WSDL Documents

A WSDL document defines one or more **services**, and each service is a collection of network endpoints called **ports**. The definition is abstract because the ports and messages are separated from their implementation detail regarding network deployment or data format bindings. This allows the reuse of definitions of **messages**, which are abstract descriptions of the data being exchanged, and **port types**, which are abstract collections of **operations**. The concrete protocol and data format specifications for a particular port type constitute a reusable **binding**. A port is defined by associating a network address with a reusable binding. A service is defined by a collection of ports. Hence, a WSDL document uses the following elements in the definition of network services:

- The element **definitions** is the root element that defines the name of the web service, declares namespaces used in the document, and contains all the service elements described here.
- The element **service** is a collection of related endpoints. It defines the address for invoking the specified service. Most commonly, this includes a URL for invoking the SOAP service.
- The element **port** is a single endpoint defined as a combination of a binding and a network address.
- The element **binding** is a concrete protocol and data format specification for a particular port type. The element describes the detail of how the service will be remotely accessed. WSDL includes built-in extensions for defining SOAP services.
- The element **portType** can combine multiple message elements to form a complete one-way or round-trip operation; for example, a portType can combine one request and one response message into a single request/response operation, most commonly used in SOAP/HTTP services.
- The element **message** is an abstract, typed definition of the data being communicated. It can be a one-way message request or a one-way message response. This element defines the name of the message and contains zero or more message parts, which can refer to message parameters or message return values.
- The element **operation** is an abstract description of an action supported by the service.
- The element **types** is a container for data types using a certain type system (such as DTD and XSD). It describes all the data types used between the client and the server. WSDL is not tied exclusively to a specific typing system, but by default it uses the W3C XML Schema definition (XSD). If the service uses XSD built-in simple types only, such as strings and integers, the types element is not required.

Figure 3.22 shows the structure of the elements, where each WSDL file defines a namespace of services. Each service can contain multiple endpoints, and each endpoint is defined by a method that takes the input message, performs the operation, and delivers the output message. As the <service> element is not the root element, a WSDL file can have multiple <service> elements and thus can define more than one service. In this case, a WSDL file corresponds to a namespace of classes.

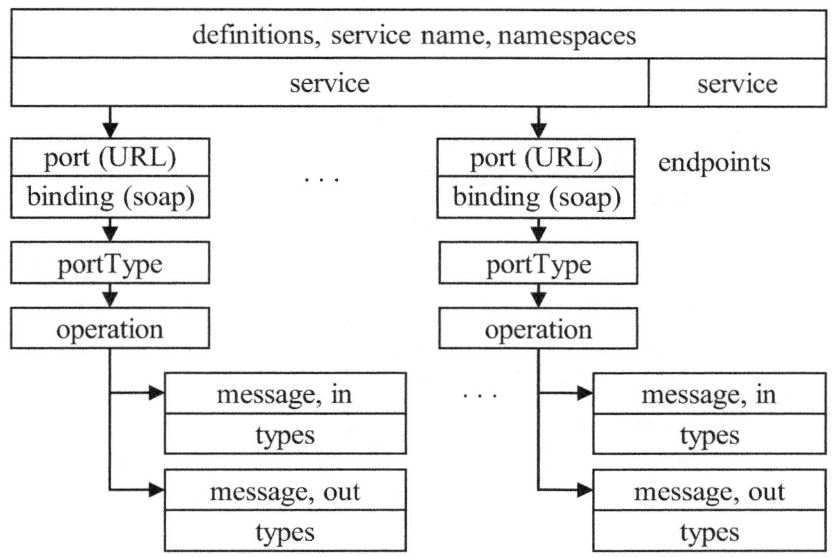

Figure 3.22. Elements of a WSDL file

3.5.2 WSDL Document Example

WSDL files are represented in XML. The following example shows the WSDL definition of a simple service providing stock quotes. The service supports a single operation called GetLastTradePrice, which is deployed using the SOAP 1.1 protocol over HTTP. The request takes a ticker symbol of type string and returns the price as a float number [Christensen et al. 2001].

```
<?xml version="1.0"?>
<definitions name="StockQuote" targetNamespace="http://example.com/stockquote.wsdl"
        xmlns:tns="http://example.com/stockquote.wsdl"
        xmlns:xsd1="http://example.com/stockquote.xsd"
        xmlns:soap="http://schemas.xmlsoap.org/wsdl/soap/"
        xmlns="http://schemas.xmlsoap.org/wsdl/">
  <types>
      <schema targetNamespace="http://example.com/stockquote.xsd"
          xmlns="http://www.w3.org/2000/10/XMLSchema">
         <element name="TradePriceRequest">
            <complexType>
               <all>
                  <element name="tickerSymbol" type="string"/>
               </all>
            </complexType>
         </element>
         <element name="TradePrice">
            <complexType>
               <all>
                  <element name="price" type="float"/>
               </all>
            </complexType>
         </element>
      </schema>
  </types>
  <message name="GetLastTradePriceInput">
      <part name="body" element="xsd1:TradePriceRequest"/>
```

```
    </message>
    <message name="GetLastTradePriceOutput">
        <part name="body" element="xsd1:TradePrice"/>
    </message>
    <portType name="StockQuotePortType">
        <operation name="GetLastTradePrice">
            <input message="tns:GetLastTradePriceInput"/>
            <output message="tns:GetLastTradePriceOutput"/>
        </operation>
    </portType>
    <binding name="StockQuoteSoapBinding" type="tns:StockQuotePortType">
        <soap:binding style="document" transport=
                "http://schemas.xmlsoap.org/soap/http"/>
        <operation name="GetLastTradePrice">
           <soap:operation soapAction=
                "http://example.com/GetLastTradePrice"/>
           <input>
               <soap:body use="literal"/>
           </input>
           <output>
               <soap:body use="literal"/>
           </output>
        </operation>
    </binding>
    <service name="StockQuoteService">
        <documentation>My first service</documentation>
        <port name="StockQuotePort" binding="tns:StockQuoteBinding">
           <soap:address location="http://example.com/stockquote"/>
        </port>
    </service>
</definitions>
```

The first line of the document identifies that the document uses XML syntax. The second line starts the definition of the WSDL document, followed by the namespace listing. The `types` element then defines the data types used in the document, which is followed by two pieces of messages. The `portType` combines two messages into a round-trip message. The `binding` element specifies that the `service` will be accessed using SOAP protocol. Finally, the service element contains one `port` element that defines the address for invoking the specified service.

A stock simulator service in WCF SVC Service is implemented and deployed at:

http://neptune.fulton.ad.asu.edu/WSRepository/Services/Stockquote/Service.svc

To test this service, you can use the TryIt application page deployed at:

http://neptune.fulton.ad.asu.edu/WSRepository/Services/Stockquote/

A RESTful service is also implemented and deployed at:

http://neptune.fulton.ad.asu.edu/WSRepository/Services/StockquoteRest/Service.svc/getStockquote?symbol=IBM

The service returns a JSON value. To test different stock prices, you can replace the stock symbol value *IBM* using a common stock symbol, such as, AAPL, ABB, AIG, AMZN, AXP, BA, BABA, BAC, BIDU, BOC, CIT, COST, CVX, FDX, FIT, GOOG, GPS, HD, HPQ, IBM, INTC, JPM, K12, KR, LULU, LZB, MSFT, NYT, TMUS, TXN, ULTA, WFC, WMT, XOM, XRX, and so on.

3.6 Service Requesters: Building Applications Using Services

In Section 3.2, we studied in detail how to create and host individual services. In Section 3.3, we discussed the service registries and repositories where publicly available services can be found. This section discusses building SOC applications using existing services. We will focus on using the C# and .Net platform to do so in this section. In a later chapter, we will use BPEL process and Workflow Foundation for composing SOC applications.

The main idea of using remote services for application building is to create a proxy of the remote services in the application and to access the functions in services through the proxies.

3.6.1 Connecting Endpoint and Proxy

A web service is seen from outside to be a collection of endpoints. An **endpoint** is a service interface (method name and parameters) exposed to outside, so that a client can access the operation (method) of the service. An endpoint includes the address (entry point), operation name, return value type, and parameters and their types, and so on.

Remote accesses among web applications and services are implemented using SOAP and the concepts of endpoint and proxy. A **proxy** consists of a set of **endpoint references**, which is often defined to be a virtual object, an object with abstract methods in terms of the object-oriented computing. The proxy creates a channel from a service client to a (remote) service, so the remote service can be accessed as though the service is a local object. A client accesses the operations of a service by calling the abstract methods in the proxy, as shown in Figure 3.23.

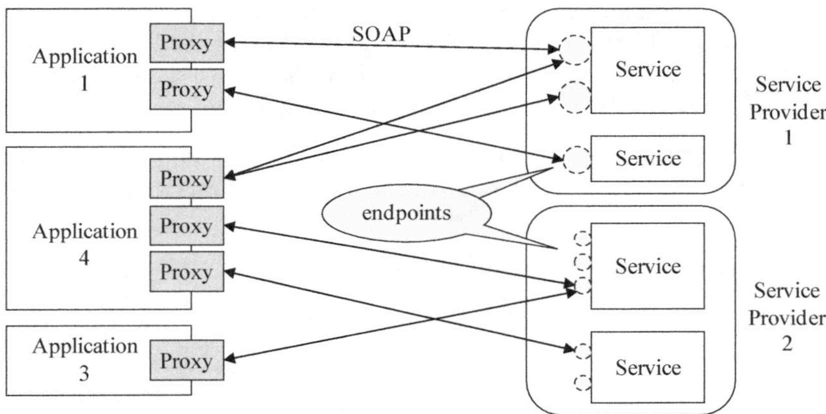

Figure 3.23. Proxies and endpoints

Figure 3.24 shows an example of the three-party model consisting of service client, service provider, and service broker (registry), where the service provider registers the service by making a SOAP request to register the service. A service client looks up the service using a SOAP request, which will result in the discovery of the endpoints of the required service. The client creates a proxy or references to the endpoints, which binds the client to the remote web methods represented by the endpoints. During the execution of the client, the remote endpoints are accessed, and results are delivered to the client.

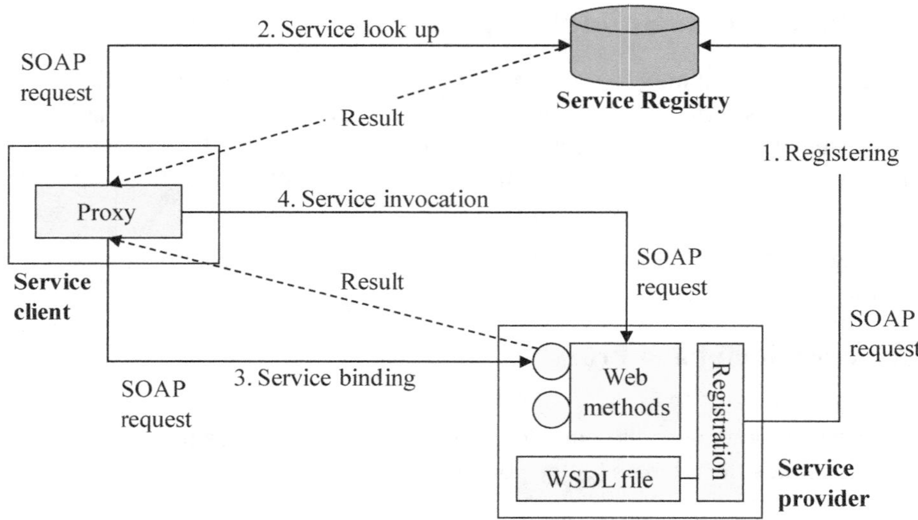

Figure 3.24. Three-party model represented in proxy and endpoints

3.6.2 Creating a Windows Forms Application in ASP.Net

In Section 3.2.3, we created a console application to consume a WCF service. In this section, we will create an application with a graphic user interface. We will use the Windows Forms Application template to create a local application that runs on a PC. However, the Windows Forms Application will access the WCF services. We will need the Internet to run the application from the PC. In the next section, we will present an example that consumes a WCF service (.svc file) in a website application.

Note that Visual Studio supports many different templates for different purposes. The following link lists and explains different templates: https://msdn.microsoft.com/en-us/library/ee377605(v=vs.110).aspx. We will not be able to cover the templates.

We can create a Windows Forms Application in following steps:

1. If you have already created a service project and want to add this new project into the same solution, you can right-click the solution (not the project) folder. Choose Add → New Project... Alternatively, if you want to start a new solution, in the "File" menu of Visual Studio, choose New → Project...
2. Choose C# as the project type and "Windows Forms Application" as the template. Enter a name for the project; for example, WindowsFormsApplication1 and a location. You will create a new solution for the project. You can also add the project in an existing solution. For example, if you can add a WCF Web service project into the same solution. Then a solution with two projects, the service project and WindowsFormsApplication1, with a stack of other folders and files will be created.
3. Once the project is created, a form called Form1.cs will be generated for creating the Graphical User Interface (GUI). Before we design the GUI, we first link the remote service into the project.
4. To add remote web services into the application (creating proxies of services), in the Solution Explorer, right-click the "References" folder in the project stack, and then choose "Add Service Reference," which is used for accessing .svc services developed in Windows Communication Foundation.

5. A dialog window will open. You can add a service that you want to use in the application. There are two possibilities here: Use a service in a public service repository or use a service that you developed on your localhost.

   a. Use a public service. We will use the basic service developed in ASU Service and Application Repository at:

      http://neptune.fulton.ad.asu.edu/WSRepository/Services/BasicThreeSvc/Service.svc

   b. Use a localhost service. We use the WCF service we developed in Section 3.2.1: http://localhost:55621/Service1.svc?wsdl. In order to make the localhost service available, you must start the service by right-clicking the service file Service1.svc and choose "View in Browser," as shown in Figure 3.25.

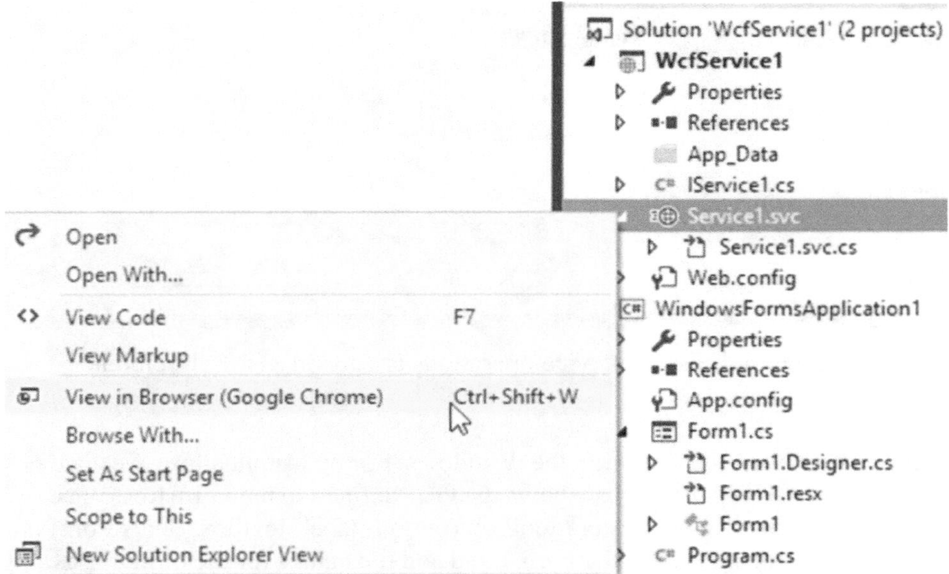

Figure 3.25. Start a service by viewing the service in a web browser

   Find the URL for your service in the web browser. In this example, the URL is http://localhost:55621/Service1.svc?wsdl.

6. Now, while keeping the service running, copy and paste the service URL into the URL textbox of the Window in Figure 3.26 and click on "Go." The three services will be found and linked into the application. You can choose a name for the proxy class created. In the example, we choose "myFirstServices." Click on the button "Add Reference:" the services in the proxy "myFirstServices" will be added into the application.

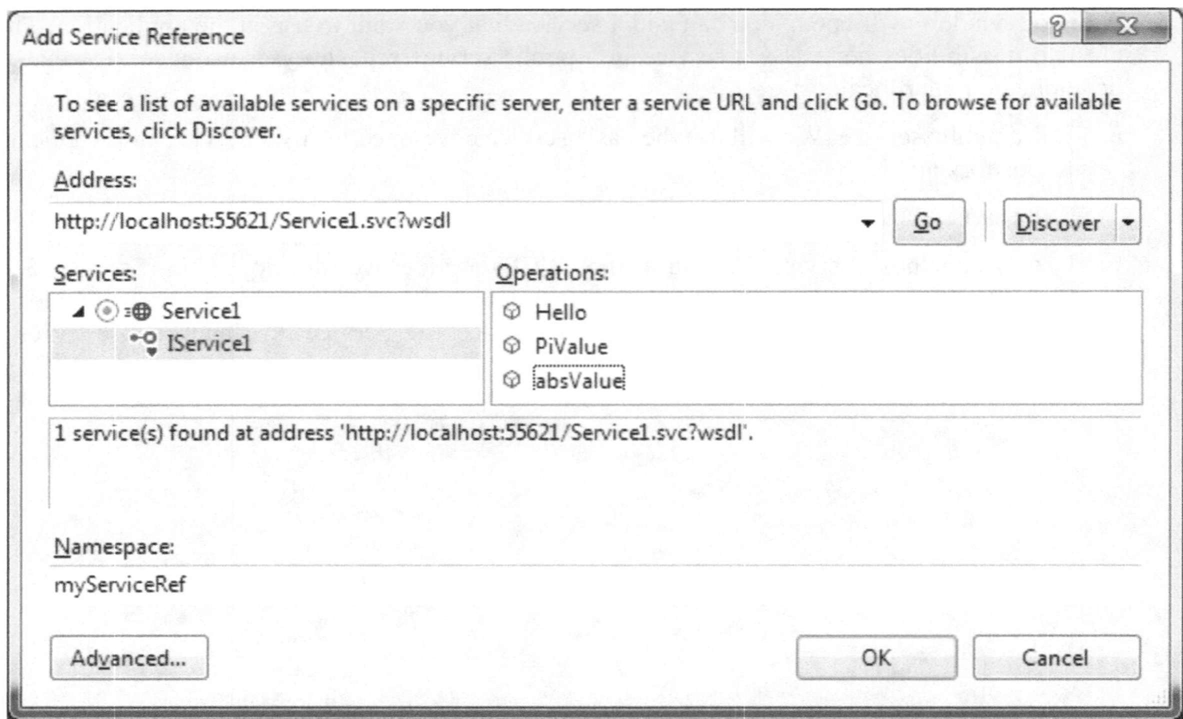

Figure 3.26. Existing service operations are added as a web reference

After linking the remote web service into the Windows Forms Application, we can now design the Graphical User Interface (GUI). Figure 3.27 shows the GUI defined in the Form1.cs. We can drag and drop the GUI controls (components) in the system toolbox (button, label, textbox, and so on.) on the left-hand side of the diagram into the blank area of the Form1 and add the names for them. In this example, we added four buttons and named them, respectively:

1. Invoke String Service: This button will be linked to the web service function HelloWorld() and the returned string will be displayed in the Label area named "Print String Value Here."
2. Get Pi Value: This button will be linked to the web service function PiValue() that returns the pi value and the returned value will be displaced in the Label area named "Print Pi Value Here."
3. Get Absolute Value: This button will be linked to the web service function abs() that returns the absolute value. The returned value will be displaced in the Label area named "Print Return Value Here."
4. Add Pi and Abs Value: This button will be linked to the web service functions that composed of PiValue() plus abs(). The sum will be displaced in the Label area named "Print Result Here."

Each function above can be considered an independent application. The first three applications use one web operation each, while the fourth application uses two web operations.

While adding the GUI controls (button, label, textbox) into the form, the default names are button1, button2, label1, label2, textbox1, textbox2, and so on. To make the code more readable, we have renamed buttons to btnString, btnPi, btnAbs, and btnPiAbs. We have renamed the labels to lblString, lblPi, lblAbs, and lblPiAbs. We leave textbox1 and textbox2 unchanged. Note that renaming is done in the Property list, and it must be done before we click the button and add the code for the button.

Once the graphic interface is designed, the code that draws the graphic items such as buttons, labels, and textboxes are automatically generated from the library functions, so that we can focus on the part of the code that performs the functions we want to perform. In the code below, we have highlighted the part of the code we added into the template in boldface text.

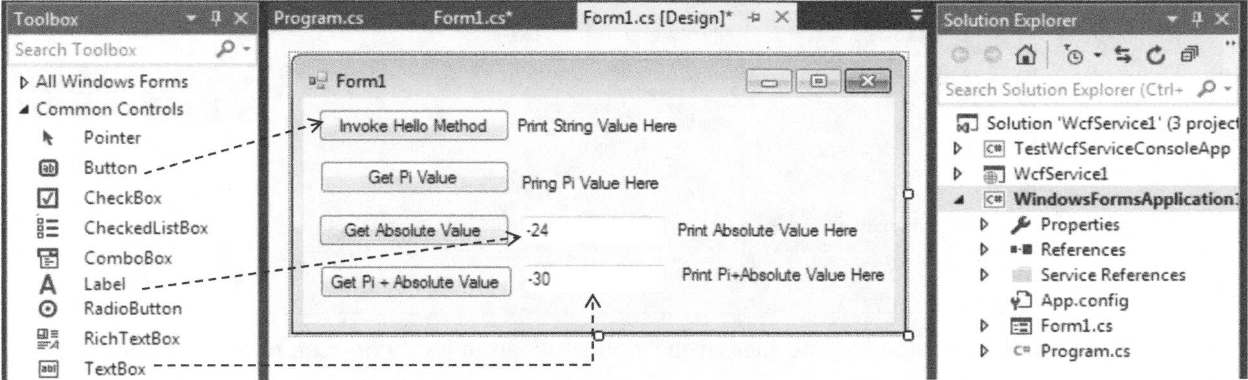

Figure 3.27. Using the toolbox to design the GUI

To add your code, double-click each button in the form. After each click, a method template (an empty method) will be created. All you need to do is to add code in the template to perform the task the button is supposed to perform. The C# code below shows the completed code after all the buttons are programmed. Note that you must add the code button by button. You cannot copy the code all together. In this way, the link between the button and the code will not be created.

```
namespace WindowsFormsApplication1 {
    public partial class Form1 : Form {
        public Form1() { InitializeComponent(); }
        private void button1_Click(object sender, EventArgs e) {
            myServiceRef.Service1Client myPxy = new myServiceRef.Service1Client();
            this.label1.Text = myPxy.Hello();
        }
        private void button2_Click(object sender, EventArgs e) {
            myServiceRef.Service1Client myPxy = new myServiceRef.Service1Client();
            this.label2.Text = myPxy.PiValue().ToString();
        }
        private void button3_Click(object sender, EventArgs e) {
            myServiceRef.Service1Client myPxy = new myServiceRef.Service1Client();
            int number = Convert.ToInt32(this.textBox1.Text);
            int result = myPxy.absValue(number);
            this.label3.Text = result.ToString();
        }
        private void button4_Click(object sender, EventArgs e) {
            myServiceRef.Service1Client myPxy = new myServiceRef.Service1Client();
            int number = Convert.ToInt32(this.textBox2.Text);
            double result = myPxy.absValue(number) + myPxy.PiValue();
            this.label4.Text = result.ToString();
        }
    }
}
```

A part of the code is generated when we double-click the buttons. The code that we add is highlighted. Four functions are added behind the four buttons, respectively.

Compile and execute the program, the application GUI will be generated. Click on the buttons, with proper input values if required, and the results are displayed in the label areas, as shown in Figure 3.28.

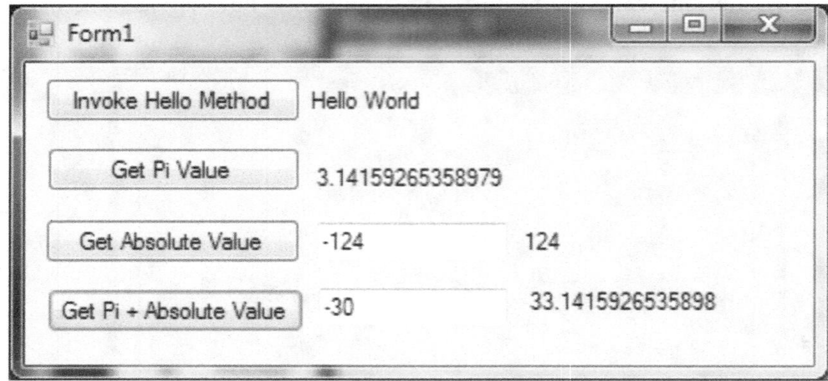

Figure 3.28. Graphic user interface of the web application based on remote web services

In the code above, a remote service "Service1()" is used as class to instantiate an object and the methods in the object are used to perform the required function:

```
myServiceRef.Service1Client myPxy = new myServiceRef.Service1Client();
```

However, the object linked to the reference hw is a "virtual object" or a proxy, which does not contain the code for the methods. It creates a channel to each method in the remote service, as shown in Figure 3.29.

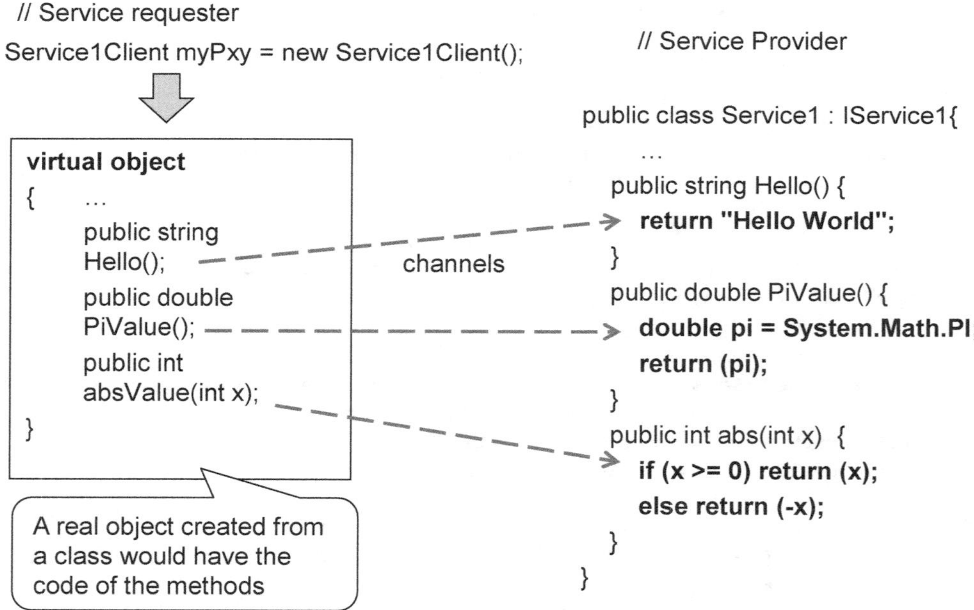

Figure 3.29. Proxy in application accessing the remote services

Please note that, since this application is a Windows Forms application, it does not need to be deployed to a web server; for example, if we develop a game based on web services, the game can be a Windows Forms Application. In this case, the application can be downloaded to a Windows computer to play. However, the computer must have Internet access while playing the game because the game will contact the web services at runtime. On the other hand, website applications must be deployed to a web server. If we develop a game as a website application, one can play the game in a web browser without downloading. In the next example, we will go through the development of a website application.

3.6.3 Developing a Website Application to Consume WCF Services

ASP .Net can be used for developing services as well as service clients. WCF is designed for developing services only. WCF services can be consumed by different clients, including console application, ASP .Net applications, Workflow Foundation applications, Windows Presentation Foundation applications, and Silverlight applications.

Before you read this section, you may want to read the tutorials in Appendix A and follow the tutorials to create a few simple applications.

Similar to creating a Windows Forms application that runs on a Windows machine as discussed in the previous section, you can create a website application template as follows:

1. In the "File" menu of Visual Studio, choose New → Project…
2. Choose "ASP .Net Web Forms Application" as the template.
3. In the Solution Explorer, a file named Default.aspx will be created, which is the platform for drawing the web GUI. This form is equivalent to the Form1.cs in the Windows Forms Application template.

A web application will be deployed to a web server, and the users will access the web application through a web browser, just like accessing many business sites on the web. A website project can be composed of several types of files, including:

1. ASPX files containing web forms for interface design;
2. ASCX files containing user controls;
3. Web.config files containing application and system configuration settings;
4. A Global.asax file containing global application elements;
5. DLL (dynamic link library) files containing custom types employed by the application.

The ASPX files will be discussed in this section and the other files will discussed in Chapters 5 and 6, when we study the advanced features, such as stateful services, security, and reliability of web-based applications.

Similar to the previous section, we can use the simple WCF service developed in section 3.2.1 to develop a simple application. To show a different example, we will develop an ASP website application that consumes the encryption and decryption service developed in Chapter 6, section 6.3.1. The encryption and decryption service has been deployed into the ASU service repository at: http://neptune.fulton.ad.asu.edu/WSRepository/Services/EncryptionWcf/Service.svc. You do not need to know the implementation detail. You can simply bind the service into your application. If you have followed the steps in Section 6.3.1 to develop the encryption and decryption service, you can also use the service on local host in the following steps. If you are using the deployed service, you can create a new website and jump to Step 3 listed below.

Step 1. Add an ASP .Net Website into the WCF Service Solution

(1) Right-click the Solution EncryptionWcf. Select Add → New → Website …

(2) Select ASP .Net website and name the Website "TestClient."

Step 2. Start Service by Viewing Service in Browser

If a service is not deployed and is in the same solution as the service client, we must have the service running before we can add the service reference the service. Right click file service.svc and choose View in Browser. A web page will open showing the service is running, as shown Figure 3.30. Click the file Service.svc, it will show you the WSDL address: http://localhost:61372/EncryptionWcf/Service.svc?wsdl

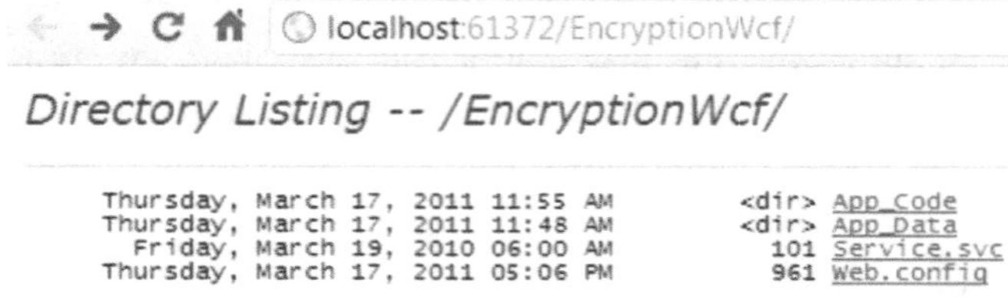

Figure 3.30. The service is running in local host

Step 3. Add Service Reference

Now, we can add the service address into our service test client. Right-click the website project "TestClient" folder and choose "Add Service Reference…" Note that WCF services use Add Service Reference, while ASP .Net Services use Add Web Reference.

Type the service's WSDL address "http://localhost:61372/EncryptionWcf/Service.svc?wsdl" into the Add Service Reference dialog window, as shown in Figure 3.31. We name the proxy to the namespace "AspProxyToWcf."

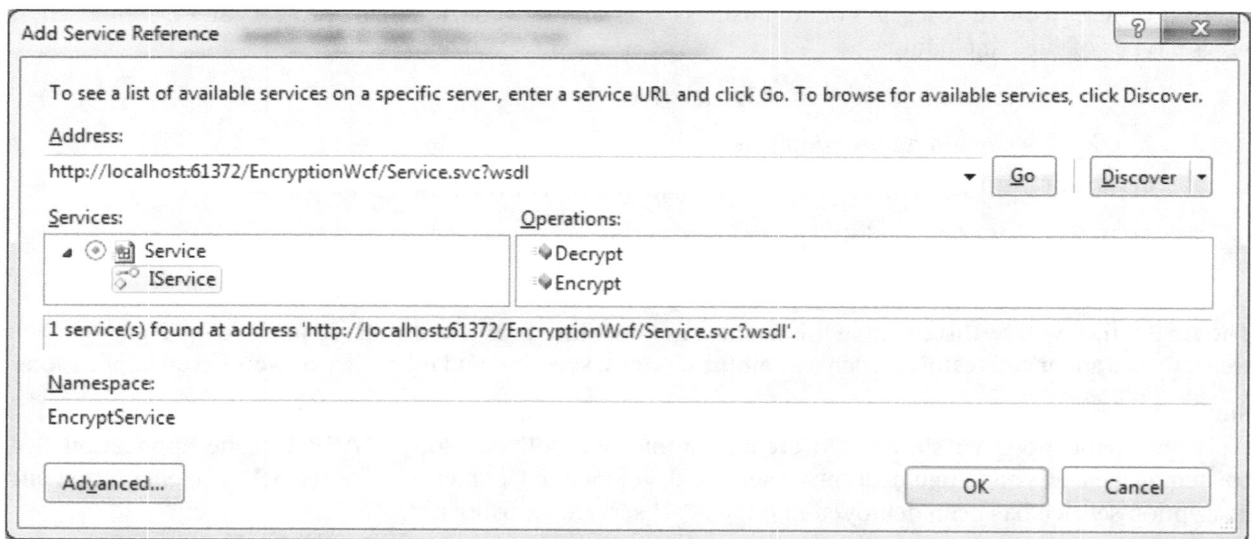

Figure 3.31. Add service reference to ASP .Net website

Alternatively, as the encryption service has been deployed in web server, we could use the deployed service address, instead of the local hosted service address. The WSDL address of the deployed service is at: http://neptune.fulton.ad.asu.edu/WSRepository/Services/EncryptionWcf/Service.svc?wsdl

Step 4. Design GUI to Access WCF Service

Open the Default.aspx page. Create a GUI (in Source View) as shown below:

```
<%@ Page Title="Home Page" Language="C#" MasterPageFile="~/Site.master"
AutoEventWireup="true"
```

```
    CodeFile="Default.aspx.cs" Inherits="_Default" %>
<asp:Content ID="HeaderContent" runat="server" ContentPlaceHolderID="HeadContent">
</asp:Content>
<asp:Content ID="BodyContent" runat="server"
                                    ContentPlaceHolderID="MainContent">
    <h2>ASP .Net Test Client</h2>
        <p>Please enter a string for encryption:
        <asp:TextBox ID="txtInput" runat="server" Width="200px">a secrete
word?</asp:TextBox>
     <asp:Button ID="btnSubmit" runat="server" onclick="btnSubmit_Click"
            Text="Submit" /></p>
        <p>The encrypted string looks like this:
        <asp:Label ID="lblEncrypted" runat="server"></asp:Label></p>
        <p>Check if the decrypted string is correct --&gt; 
        <asp:Label ID="lblDecrypted" runat="server"></asp:Label></p>
</asp:Content>
```

The design view of the Default.aspx page is shown in Figure 3.32.

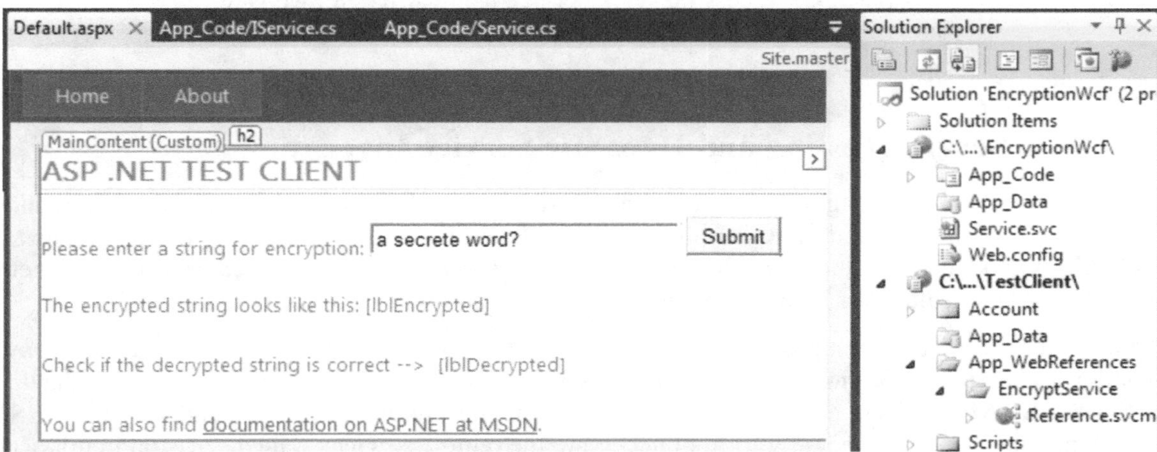

Figure 3.32. Design view of the Default.aspx page

Step 5. Write Client Code to Consume WCF Service

The C# code behind the submit button in the Default.aspx page is given below:

```
using System;
public partial class _Default : System.Web.UI.Page {
    protected void btnSubmit_Click(object sender, EventArgs e){
        EncryptService.ServiceClient myClient = new
                                    EncryptService.ServiceClient();
        try{lblEncrypted.Text = myClient.Encrypt(txtInput.Text);}
        catch (Exception ec){lblEncrypted.Text = ec.Message.ToString();}
        try{lblDecrypted.Text = myClient.Decrypt(lblEncrypted.Text);}
        catch (Exception dc){lblDecrypted.Text = dc.Message.ToString();}
        }
}
```

Step 6. Test the ASP .Net Client

If you have multiple websites in a solution, you can choose one website as the start page. In our example, we choose the test client as the start page: Right-click the Default.asp page and choose “Set As Start Page.” We can use View in Browser to start the services. Figure 3.33 shows the test client in execution.

You can also test the application that calls the .asmx encryption/decryption service at:

http://neptune.fulton.ad.asu.edu/WSRepository/Services/EncryptionTryIt/Sender.aspx

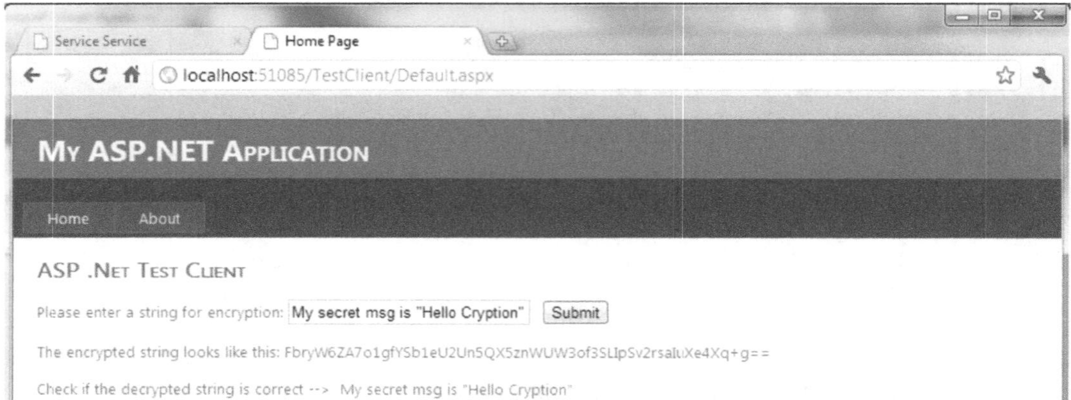
Service Service
Home Page
localhost:51085/TestClient/Default.aspx
MY ASP.NET APPLICATION
Home
About
ASP .NET TEST CLIENT
Please enter a string for encryption:
My secret msg is "Hello Cryption"
Submit
The encrypted string looks like this: FbryW6ZA7o1gfYSb1eU2Un5QX5znWUW3of3SLIpSv2rsaluXe4Xq+g==
Check if the decrypted string is correct --> My secret msg is "Hello Cryption"

Figure 3.33. Accessing WCF service using ASP .Net website

3.7 Web Service Testing and Dynamic Service Invocation

In object-oriented programming, dynamic binding allows a method call to be bound to the initial address of a method at run time, instead of at compilation time. Dynamic binding allows polymorphic calls to the child class's method that redefines the parent's method. To allow the child class to redefine a parent method, the method must be declared as a virtual method.

In service-oriented programming, dynamic binding to another service corresponds to dynamic proxying, which allows a service invocation to be bound to the service address (URL) at run time, instead of at design time. For the SOAP services, both static proxies and dynamic proxies can be created. For the RESTful service, dynamic proxies are the only form of accessing the remote services. The discussion in this section mainly refers to SOAP services.

Why do we need dynamic proxy? Dynamic proxying has many potential applications, such as in web service testing and dynamic business applications that can discover new services at run time.

Software testing is a major part of software development. Web service testing is even more important, as the software developers are relying more on the software components that can be developed by unknown parties.

You can always add a service into your client application and test the service, as we discussed in the previous section. The problem is, if it does not work, you may not be sure if it is because the service does not work, or it is because your application code or the part of the invocation code does not work. It would be more convenient and more efficient if we have a testing tool that can test a web service based on the WSDL file of the service.

To test a remote web service based on the URL of its WSDL and without statically binding the service into the application, we need to perform a number of tasks. We will discuss these tasks in the following subsections. Visual Studio provides a Test Client to test a web service before binding the service into the application. The way to implement the test client is to dynamically create a proxy based on the service URL. We will explain the use of dynamic proxy by developing our own test client.

3.7.1 Get Web Content from URL

To test a remote web service based on the URL, we need to fetch the content of the WSDL. We can use the Web2String service in ASU Service Repository to perform this task. The service address is

http://neptune.fulton.ad.asu.edu/wsRepository/Services/Web2StringSVC/Service.svc

This service will download the webpage at the given URL and return the text in the page as a string. The operation offered by this service is: string GetWebContent(string url).

A test client page of the service is available at:

http://neptune.fulton.ad.asu.edu/wsRepository/Services/Web2StringSVC/tryit.aspx

This service reads the content of any web page. It can be used in many other applications for analyzing any web page based on its URL; for example, using this service, one can write a service to perform the following tasks:

- Analyze the web page at a given URL and return the 10 most-frequently occurred words in the web page.
- Analyze a string of words and filter out the function words (stop words) such as "a," "an," "in," "on," "the," "is," "are," "am," as well as the element tag names and attribute names quoted in angle brackets < … >, if the string represents an XML page or HTML source page.
- Analyze a string of words and replace the inflected or derived words to their stem or root word; for example, "information," "informed," "informs," and "informative" will be replaced by the term word "inform." This service can help find useful keywords or index words in information processing and retrieval.
- Analyze a web page and return all WSDL addresses in that web page in an array of strings. The WSDL address can have these formats: xxx.wsdl (e.g. developed Java), or ?wsdl (e.g., .php?wsdl, .svc?wsdl and .asmx?wsdl).

3.7.2 Analyze WSDL Document

Once we have fetched the WSDL content in a string, we can extract the operations (methods), the parameters required, and the return value of each operation. We can use a simple string processing program to extract the data we need. However, this approach is complex and error-prone. A better approach is to use the XML processing library classes to be discussed in Chapter 4 of this book. The most appropriate way of extracting the required data is to use the reflection.

Reflection provides objects (of type Type) that encapsulate assemblies, modules and types. One can use reflection to dynamically create an instance of a type, bind the type to an existing object, or get the type from an existing object, and invoke its methods or access its fields and properties. More detail of reflection can be found in MSDN library at http://msdn.microsoft.com/en-us/library/ms173183(v=vs.100).aspx.

Below is an example of using Reflection.MethodInfo class to discover the attributes of a method and provides access to method metadata.

```
List<object> test = new List<object>();
for (int i = 0; i < parameters.Length; i++)  {
          test.Add(insertTestType(parameters[i], param[i].ToString()));
}
MethodInfo mInfo = wsdlClass.GetType().GetMethod(op[opName]);
object result = mInfo.Invoke(wsdlClass, test.ToArray());
```

The code below shows using reflection to extract the operation names in a WSDL file.

```
public string[] findOperations(string wsdl) {
   string text = " ";
```

```
    string[] methods;
    object wsvcClass = createServiceInstance(wsdl);
    MethodInfo[] mi = wsvcClass.GetType().GetMethods();
    foreach (MethodInfo temp in mi) {  //Find the end of normal methods
         if (temp.Name == "get_ChannelFactory") {
              break;
         }
         text += temp.Name + ' ';
    }
    text = text.Trim();
    methods = text.Split(' ');          //Split methods into separate strings
    return methods;
}
```

3.7.3 Test Web Service through Dynamic Proxy

Once we have extracted the operation name, parameters, and the return value of each operation, we can create a dynamic proxy. As an example, the code below shows creating a service instance using the DynamicProxyFactory class.

```
public object createServiceInstance(string wsdl) {
    object wsvcClass = null;
    if (wsvcClass == null) {
         DynamicProxyFactory factory = new DynamicProxyFactory(wsdl);
         foreach (ServiceEndpoint endpoint in factory.Endpoints) {
              DynamicProxy proxy = factory.CreateProxy(endpoint);
              wsvcClass = proxy.ObjectInstance;
         }
    }
    return wsvcClass;
}
```

Dynamic proxy can also be used for creating dynamic web applications that can dynamically discover web services and dynamically bind the web services into the applications.

Another way of accessing WSDL service dynamically is through a tool such as Fiddler. Fiddler is an HTTP debugging proxy server application written by Eric Lawrence (Wikipedia.org/, Fiddle Software). Based on Fiddle software, van Lisdonk gives an example on how to call a SOAP web service in without using the dynamic proxy class or Add Service Reference operation:

https://www.roelvanlisdonk.nl/2011/01/28/how-to-call-a-soap-web-service-in-net-4-0-c-without-using-the-wsdl-or-proxy-classes/

3.7.4 Test Web Service Using Independent Tools

Web services can be tested using the built-in tools of the development environments. For example, Visual Studio has a built-in tool to test WCF service. There are also independent service testing tools available. For example, SOAPUI (https://www.soapui.org/) offers testing tools to test WSDL/SOAP services. The tools can also test RESTful services, but they are less convenient than as a WSDL/SOAP service test capacity.

Chrome browser has a plugin called Postman (https://chrome.google.com/webstore/detail/postman/fhbjgbiflinjbdggehcddcbncdddomop?hl=en) for convenient RESTful service testing.

3.7.5 Dynamic Web Services and Web Applications

A typical web application can consist two types of services. The required services are those that are an integral part of the application, and the alternative services are those that are not essential, but desired. Take a travel agent as an example. The required services can include user authentication, authorization, accounting, performance optimization, banking, airline, hotel, and rental services. Some of the services are unique and no alternatives are allowed, such as the authentication, authorization, and accounting services. Some of the services allow alternatives, such as the banking, airline, hotel, and rental services.

For the alternative services, dynamic discovery, addition, and subtraction are often required by the business logic. If new airlines, new hotels, and new car rentals become available, the travel agent system should be able to discover and include the services without modifying the system. One of the solutions of implementing the dynamic business is to store the services addresses (URLs) into an editable file. The system can read and write the file at run time. Based on the service URL, dynamic proxy can be created to access the service.

3.8 Java-Based Web Service Development

While Microsoft provides a number of development environments for C# and .Net-based SOC software development, Sun Microsystems largely leaves the development of the Java-based SOC software to the community projects and third-party products, resulting in a diverse range of products from different companies, including J# in ASP.Net, AJAX, Java EE, Eclipse, Tomcat, JDeveloper, Oracle SOA suite, and WebSphere. This section discusses some of the Java-based SOC software development environments.

3.8.1 Web Application Building Using AJAX Programming

AJAX (Asynchronous JavaScript and XML) programming is widely used in Java web service development environment. It is a technology to build dynamic web pages on the client side (as an application builder) by embedding JavaScript code into the HTML page. Data is read from the server or sent to the server by JavaScript and HTTP requests. Request and data processing can be implemented at the client and server sides.

A feature of AJAX is to make the user interfaces of web applications more responsive and interactive by updating only part of the dynamic page at a time, instead of reloading the entire web page; for example, while you are filling out a web form, you want to check the updated stock price. If partial updating is not implemented behind the page, a complete reload will reset (clear) the form that has been filled out. Figure 3.34 illustrates the process of updating a dynamic web page programmed in AJAX.

1. In Figure 3.34, the item marked ① in the user interface contains dynamic content that is time-sensitive and requires regular reloading, whereas the other items are static and do not require reloading frequently. The item can be programmed to send out updating requests at certain intervals.
2. The request in JavaScript call is sent to the service in the application logic or workflow that processes the XMLHttpRequest.
3. The HttpRequest is sent to server-side service to process the request.
4. The request is translated into a data request in the language of the database.
5. The database retrieves the request data and sends it back to the request processing service. The data is translated into XML format if the database is not an XML database.
6. The XML-formatted data is sent back to the client side XMLHttpRequest processing service.

7. The XMLHttpRequest processing service uses JavaScript callback to update the item in the user interface.

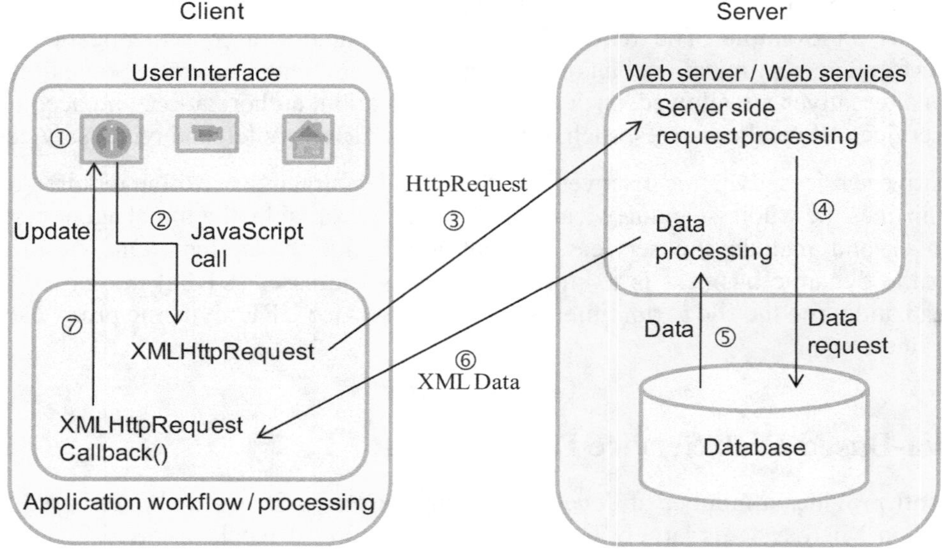

Figure 3.34. Process of updating a dynamic web page

This process allows a part of the web page to be updated dynamically. The XMLHttpRequest object is used to exchange data asynchronously between the client and the web server. The following code segment shows how the XMLHttpRequest is made in JavaScript in different web browsers (Source: http://developer.mozilla.org/en/docs/AJAX:Getting_Started).

```
<script type="text/javascript" language="javascript">
  function makeRequest(url) {
      var httpRequest;
      if (window.XMLHttpRequest) { // Mozilla, Safari, ...
            httpRequest = new XMLHttpRequest();
            if (httpRequest.overrideMimeType) {
                 httpRequest.overrideMimeType('text/xml');
            }
      }
      else if (window.ActiveXObject) { // IE
            try {
                 httpRequest = new ActiveXObject("Msxml2.XMLHTTP");
            } catch (e) {
            try {
                 httpRequest = new ActiveXObject("Microsoft.XMLHTTP");
            } catch (e) {}
      }
  }
  httpRequest.onreadystatechange = function() { alertContents(httpRequest); };
      httpRequest.open('GET', url, true);
      httpRequest.send(null);
   }
   function alertContents(httpRequest) {
  if (httpRequest.readyState == 4) {
      if (httpRequest.status == 200) {
            alert(httpRequest.responseText);
```

```
        } else alert('There was a problem with the request.');
    }
}
</script>
<span
    style="cursor: pointer; text-decoration:
            underline"onclick="makeRequest('test.html')">
        Make a request
</span>
```

AJAX programming can be done on different programming environments. Most Java development environments can be used. Numerous development environments have been developed, with specific tools and AJAX libraries to facilitate AJAX programming.

DWR (Direct Web Remoting) http://getahead.org/dwr/ allows using Java functions as if they are part of the browser, from HTML code. A JavaScript part is used to update the page and another to get data with servlets. This technique generates in real time Java code from JavaScript code, sends it to the server, and runs it.

GWT (Google Web Toolkit) is an open-source Java-based development framework that makes writing AJAX applications, such as Google Maps and Gmail, easy for developers (http://www.gwtproject.org/). The toolkit helps reduce the requirement of dealing with the incompatibilities between web browsers and the lack of modularity in JavaScript. Using GWT, one can implement the entire client-side application logic in Java, and the GWT compiler converts the Java classes to browser-compliant JavaScript and HTML.

ASP .Net AJAX (previously called Microsoft Atlas) is a free framework for creating AJAX interactive and personalized web pages (http://ajax.asp.net/). It takes advantage of both ASP .Net and AJAX; for example, you can take an existing application and add additional client-side behaviors to it using AJAX. ASP .Net AJAX Video Tutorials are available at: http://www.asp.net/. A detailed example of AJAX programming is given in the appendix of this book.

3.8.2 Java-Based Web Service Development and Hosting

There are different frameworks for developing Java-based web services. Java EE (Enterprise Edition) is a comprehensive development environment on the Sun Java System Application Server. In Chapter 8, we will discuss the Oracle SOA Suite, which is a comparable environment to the Java EE. In this section, we will discuss two environments that can be installed on the Windows operating system.

For both environments, we need to use Apache Tomcat to host the service, which can be downloaded from: https://tomcat.apache.org/download-60.cgi. Extract the files and place in a directory. When you configure your Java IDE later, simply point it to this extracted directory. To support your Java service development, you need create a user account that has the administrative privilege. To do so, in the Tomcat files under /.../tomcat6/conf/tomcat-users.xml, add a user; for example,

```
<user username="superAdmin" password=Admin123" roles="manager-gui,admin-gui,manager-
script,admin"/>
```

Java Web Service Development Using NetBeans

Download Netbeans 7.4 SE from: https://netbeans.org/. Make sure the .sh script is an executable and then run it by executing, e.g.:

sudo ./netbeans-7.4-javase.linux.sh --javahome /usr/lib/java/jdk1.7.0_55

If you receive a Proxy Error in the following process, click the Try Again, as it may not connect in the first time. If the problem is persistent, you may need to restart NetBeans.

Once your NetBeans are correctly installed and configured, you can start to write a Java service in the following steps:

- Open Netbeans, Tools->Plugins->Settings.
- Select Netbeans Distribution.
- Select the Available Plugins tab and press Reload Catalog.
- Select SOAP web services and install it. There is a RESTful service plugin available as well if you want to develop RESTful service.
- Restart when finished.
- You might need to run NetBeans as sudo to allow it run Tomcat.

A full tutorial on creating a web service can be found from the official Netbeans site:

https://netbeans.org/kb/docs/websvc/jax-ws.html

Java Web Service Development Using Apache Tomcat and Axis

To get started, you need to install two pieces of software. First, the Tomcat apache Windows Server software at http://tomcat.apache.org/download-60.cgi, which will host the Java services to be developed. Choose the file Windows Server Installer, under the version 6.0.14, or the latest version. A setup wizard will guide you to complete the installation process. You will be asked to choose an HTTP connection port. You can choose default port 8080. Once the installation process is complete, you will have a folder under the path: Apache Software Foundation/Tomcat6.0/webapps.

Then, you need to install the Axis software package. The installation guide is at http://ws.apache.org/axis/java/install.html. After you have read the guide, you can download the package at http://axis.apache.org/axis/java/releases.html, and choose the latest edition; for example, axis-bin1_4.zip. Unzip the file, and you will have a folder called axis-1.4. You need locate a folder named axis following the path axis-1.4/webapps/axis. Move the folder axis into the location: Apache Software Foundation/Tomcat6.0/webapps. The axis package will interpret the Java class hosted in the folder; for example, if we can define a simple java class named a.jws:

```
public class a {
   public int add(int i1, int i2) {
        return (i1+i2);
   }
}
```

We place the file a.jws in the folder Apache Software Foundation/Tomcat6.0/webapps/axis/. A service will be created from the Java class, and the service can be accessed at URL: http://localhost:8080/axis/a.jws

Java Web Service Development Using Eclipse Web Tools Platform (WPT)

Based on the reference https://www.eclipse.org/webtools/, the platform will allow you to develop the full SOA solutions with:

- The Web Services Explorer for publishing, discovering, and invoking web services;
- The Web Service wizard for creating new web services bottom-up from Java or top-down from WSDL;
- The Web Service Client (application) wizard for creating web service client proxies and sample JSP clients from WSDL.

Once the installation is completed, you can use the three functions (of the SOA three-party model) in the platforms.

(1) Services directory exploration:

1. Launch the Eclipse WTP workbench;
2. From the main menu bar, select Run -> Launch the Web Services Explorer;
3. Enter the URL of a service directory; for example, http://xmethods.net; then, you will be to discover, view, and test a web service in the Web Services Explorer.

(2) Build a web service bottom-up from Java

1. Start the Eclipse WTP workbench.
2. Open Window -> Preferences -> Server -> Installed Runtimes to create a Tomcat installed runtime for service hosting.
3. Open File -> New -> Other... -> Web -> Dynamic Web Project to create a new web project named Converter.
4. Enter Converter into the Name field.
5. Choose a web version of 2.3.
6. Choose a Target server of Apache Tomcat v4.1.
7. Deselect Add module to an EAR project.

(3) Building a Web Service Client (Application)

An application can be developed in the following steps.

1. Import the wtp/Converter.java class into Converter/JavaSource (be sure to preserve the package).
2. Select the file.
3. Open File -> New -> Other... -> Web Services -> Web Service. The step-by-step wizard will help you to create a new web service.

Once the Finish button is clicked, methods in GUI will occur, which allow the methods (services) in a remote class to be accessed.

3.9 Discussions

This chapter first introduced different service-oriented software developments. Then, the chapter used ASP .Net and WCF as platforms to develop service-oriented software, including services, service brokers, and service clients. As a service provider, one can use object-oriented programming language such as C# and Java to develop classes and objects. Then, the classes can be published as services and registered with the service brokers. The major service broker standards, UDDI and ebXML, and their registries are discussed. As application builders, the service requesters can use services running locally, or services running remotely, to compose their applications. Finally, Java-based service-oriented software development is briefly discussed.

Current service brokers are largely directory and hosting services. The brokers are not responsible for the dependability of the services they list. It is mainly the responsibility of the service providers. It has been proposed to develop trustworthy service brokers, where the broker and the service provider collaboratively test and maintain the dependability of the services listed in the broker, so that even small service providers can gain credibility for the provision of their services. Amazon is a service provider. However, it is also a service broker that allows other vendors to sell items through Amazon. Amazon as well as other independent organizations will rank the credibility of the vendors, so that the buyer can obtain a certain degree of trust in the unknown vendors.

Services are building blocks of service-oriented software. There are many services available in public service directories and repositories. However, most of the services are not free. Those that are free may not be maintained properly and may not be reliable. For the education purposes, we have developed a public services and applications repository, which offers free and reliable services. The services include ASP .Net services in .asmx format, WCF services in .svc format, workflow services in .xaml format, and RESTful services accessed through URI.

A part of the services are listed at the end of the book in the Appendix C. Each service has a try-it page that provides a simple application of the service. Among the services, a test service is offered, that allows you to test a service before linking the service into your application.

Services are important in service-oriented computing paradigm. However, the purpose of service-oriented computing is to develop applications more cost-efficiently, more rapidly, and more reliably. Chapter 5 will focus on developing applications using existing services. State management is the focus of the chapter. Chapter 6 will extend the application to security and reliability management. After the study of Chapters 5 and 6, you will be in the position to develop the web applications with most of features that you have seen in the existing web applications.

Part II of the text will move a step further toward creating cost-efficient and reliable web applications in a short development cycle. The focuses of Part II are software integration using integration tools and higher level of languages, including the flowchart-based workflow languages, including Workflow Foundation, BPEL (Business Process Execution Language), and VPL (Visual Programming Language). These languages support the idea of architecture-driven development. They start from drawing the architecture diagram, configure the diagrams, and then compile the diagrams into executable code.

Service-oriented computing and web application development lead to the development of Cloud Computing concepts and environments.

Name: ______________________

Date: ______________________

3.10 Exercises and Projects

1. Multiple choice questions. Choose one answer in each question only. Choose the best answer if multiple answers are acceptable.

1.1 What entity does not belong to the WCF endpoint?

(A) Address (B) Binding (C) Client (D) Contract

1.2 What operation is designed for adding a WCF service into an ASP .Net client?

(A) Add Reference... (B) Add Service Reference...

(C) Add Web Reference... (D) Add WCF Reference...

1.3 What features does Windows Communication Foundation support?

(A) Platform-independent communication.

(B) WSDL and RESTful service development.

(C) WS-Security and WS-ReliableMessaging.

(D) All of the above

1.4 The WSDL file of a WCF (Windows Communication Foundation) service, compared to a standard WSDL file, contains

(A) exactly the same types of the elements.

(B) few types of the elements.

(C) more types of the elements.

(D) completely different types of the elements.

1.5 What clients can be used for consuming (accessing) a WCF service?

(A) Console Application (B) ASP .Net Website

(C) Workflow Foundation Application (D) All of the above

1.6 What web services hosting server does not support external access?

(A) .Net Development Server/IIS Express (B) IIS

(C) Web server (D) None of them support external access

1.7 What is the basic feature that all service brokers should have?

(A) Service registry (B) Service repository

(C) Service requirement and specification (D) Application Templates

(E) All of the above

1.8 What are the desired features of a service broker from an SOC point of view?

(A) Service registry (B) Service repository

(C) Service requirement and specification (D) Application Templates

(E) All of the above

1.9 Why does a service broker need an ontology, instead of a traditional database?

(A) Ontology allows more data to be stored.

(B) Ontology allows faster data retrieval.

(C) Ontology can better facilitate service match and discovery.

(D) Ontology can better store executables while databases can better store data.

1.10 Where is the tModel located in UDDI?

(A) It is a part of the White Pages in UDDI.

(B) It is a part of the Yellow Pages in UDDI.

(C) It is a part of the Green Pages in UDDI.

(D) It is a part of all the three Pages in UDDI.

1.11 How many binding templates can a web service have in UDDI?

(A) One exactly.

(B) Two exactly.

(C) Three exactly.

(D) It can have multiple binding templates.

1.12 A service endpoint in service-oriented architecture is

(A) a synonym of the server broker.

(B) a synonym of the service requester.

(C) the interface of a service that is exposed to outside.

(D) a virtual object in the service requester that creates a channel to a (remote) service.

1.13 A service proxy in service-oriented architecture is

(A) a synonym of the server broker.

(B) a synonym of the service requester.

(C) the interface of a service that is exposed to outside.

(D) a virtual object in the service requester that creates a channel to a (remote) service.

1.14 What should not be contained in a service proxy?

(A) Method name of the remote method.

(B) Code of the remote method.

(C) Parameter list of the remote method.

(D) Return type of the remote method.

1.15 Which of the following components in a Java SOC development environment is responsible for converting a Java object into a web service?

(A) Java programming language itself.

(B) Eclipse programming environment.

(C) Axis2.

(D) Tomcat.

1.16 Which of the following components in a Java SOC development environment is responsible for hosting the execution of a web service?

(A) Java programming language itself.

(B) Eclipse programming environment.

(C) Axis2.

(D) Tomcat.

2. List and discuss the existing SOC software development environments and their features.

3. What is a proxy? What are the differences between a proxy and the service that it represents? How can a proxy be created?

4. Describe the roles of SOAP in SOC software development.

5. Does SOAP support two-way communication? If not, how is the response message being correlated to the sender?

6. What information is included in the header, and what information is included in the body in the SOAP protocol?

7. Describe the roles of WSDL in SOC software development.

8. What critical aspects of web services are described in WSDL? What aspects are not described in WSDL? How are these elements organized?

9. What is a service endpoint? What information should an endpoint contain?

10. What kinds of host services are available for hosting your web services in the development process?

11. What is IIS? What is the role of IIS in web services-based applications?

12. What is a virtual directory? Why do we need a virtual directory? What is the process of creating a virtual directory?

13. What are desired features that an ideal service broker should offer? What features do current service brokers (UDDI, ebXML, and ad hoc registry list) offer?

14. What data models (data structures) does a UDDI registry implement? Explain the purpose of each data model.

15. What information must be provided in order to register as a service provider in UDDI? What information must be provided in order to register a new service?

16. What operations (APIs) does a UDDI registry offer?

17. Discover and explore the (free) web services available online; for example, from Amazon, Google, Microsoft, Xmethods.net, and use the services to build a meaningful application, such as an online bookstore, a search engine in your web page, or a map service.

18. Develop and host the web services that offer the array to string and string to array services. The following C# sample code gives an implementation of the method.

```
// convert an array of floats into a string
public String Array2String(float[ ] array)  {
        String result = "";
        for (int i = 0; i < array.Length; i++) {
             result += array[i].ToString() + " "; // separated by spaces
        }
        return result;
}
```

```
// convert the string back into an array of floats
public float[] String2Array(String in_str)  {
        // The following statement converts a string into an array of strings
        string[] elements = in_str.Split(' ');
        float[] result = new float[elements.Length - 1];
        for(int i = 0; i < elements.Length-1; i++)
            result[i] = float.Parse(elements[i]);
        return result;
}
```

19. Discover the available map services from; for example,
    – http://msdn.microsoft.com/en-us/library/cc966738.aspx
    – http://code.google.com/
    – http://neptune.fulton.ad.asu.edu/WsRepository/repository.html
    to develop a web application that allows the users to get the driving direction to your location from any given location.

Project

The purpose of this project is to exercise service provision, service discovery, remote binding, and application composition using your own services and external public services. Some of the services to be developed can be synthetic; for example, banking service, while others can be realistic; for example, encryption and product catalog. However, you should make your services and overall application as realistic as possible.

In this project, each team of three or four should develop a requirement document, a service directory, the architecture of the web application, and a set of services.

1 Requirement Document

Describe the service-oriented computing system that your team plans to develop: What does the system do? Draw a diagram showing the overall system design, its layers, components, and the connections among the components. A sample diagram is given in Figure 3.35. Your team must come up with your own system. You do not need to implement the system described in this requirement. The implementation should be done after Chapter 5. See the project assignment at the end of Chapter 5.

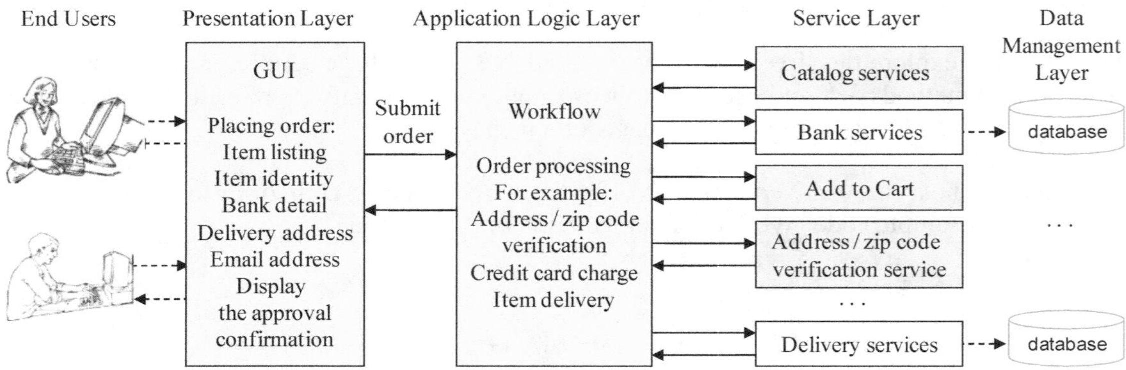

Figure 3.35. A four-tier service-oriented computing system

2 Service Directory

Service Directory: The team must create a directory (table) of all the services developed by the team members. You can use either an html page or an ASPX website for the directory. The directory must provide a test page for each service developed. Table 3.2 shows an example of the service directory.

Table 3.2. An example of the service directory to be develop in this project.

This page is deployed at: http://webstrarX.fulton.asu.edu/index.html				
This project is developed by: Put your team name here.				
Provider name	Service name, with input and output types	TryIt link	Service description	Actual resources used to implement the service
Member 1 name	Encryption and decryption: Input: String Output: String	TryIt	Cipher encryption and decryption	Use library class and local component to implement the service
Member 1 name	SolarPower Inputs: zip code and size Output: integer	TryIt	Output annual KW number for a given panel size at a given zip code location	Retrieve information from national database at: http://graphical.weather.gov/xml/
Member 1 name	findStore Input: zipcode Output: list of string	TryIt	Use an existing online service or API to find the locations of a given store name	Use the service from Yelp site at: http://www.yelp.com/
Member 2 name	…		…	…
Member 2 name	textToPhone inputs: string Account, string Password, string Receiver, string Subject, string Body Output: Boolean	TryIt	Send a text to a cell phone and return if the message is sent successfully	Use google gmail account and carrier services: phone_number@tmomail.net phone_number@messaging.sprintpcs.co m phone_number@vtext.com phone_number@txt.att.net
…	…		…	…

3 Service Development

This is an individual task. Each team member must develop at least five services (or operations) individually. The difficulty of each service (operation) will be rated by the instructor and teaching assistants into one of the three levels:

(1) Easy: The method (operation) in this service can be done using less than 20 lines of code; for example, Fahrenheit and Celsius temperature conversion.

(2) Moderate: There are algorithmic issues to address, and the code for each method will be at least 50 lines; for example, encryption/decryption service, sorting, and equation system solving. If a service operation can be done in less than 50 lines, but you use more than 50 lines, it will be counted as an easy service.

(3) Challenging: Services that will use states, such as creating a simulated (synthetic) banking service that allows users to sign up, to create an account, to deposit funds, to spend funds, and so on; or services that make use of available services or APIs provided by other providers, such as Google's

APIs (not in WSDL standard) and Amazon's services. The data received from other services should be processed (value-added) before presenting to the users.

4 Deployment of Services

Create an IIS server in your Windows or use a web server to deploy your services and service directory. Write a user manual with full details of testing your directory and each service in the directory.

Chapter 4
XML and Web Data Formats

XML is used to represent almost all languages, protocols, and data structures in service-oriented computing and development, including SOAP, WSDL, UDDI, ebXML, BPEL, OWL, return values from service invocation, and so on. Even the internal files used in .Net are in XML; for example, the configuration file Web.config, which stores application settings, user data, and security options and XHTML, which is used for the pages generated from accessing ASPX pages. XHTML is a stricter version of HTML based on XML standard. DataSet in ADO .Net database management also uses XML to represent collection of data tables, which serve as the data unit between C# programs and databases.

This chapter introduces XML language and related technologies, including XML processing, document type definition, schema, validation, and transformation, as shown in Figure 4.1. The XML-based database and query language XQL will be discussed in Chapter 10. The rest of the book will also be strongly related to XML and its applications, including the web services Description Language and the composition languages in Chapter 5 and the ontology languages in Chapter 7.

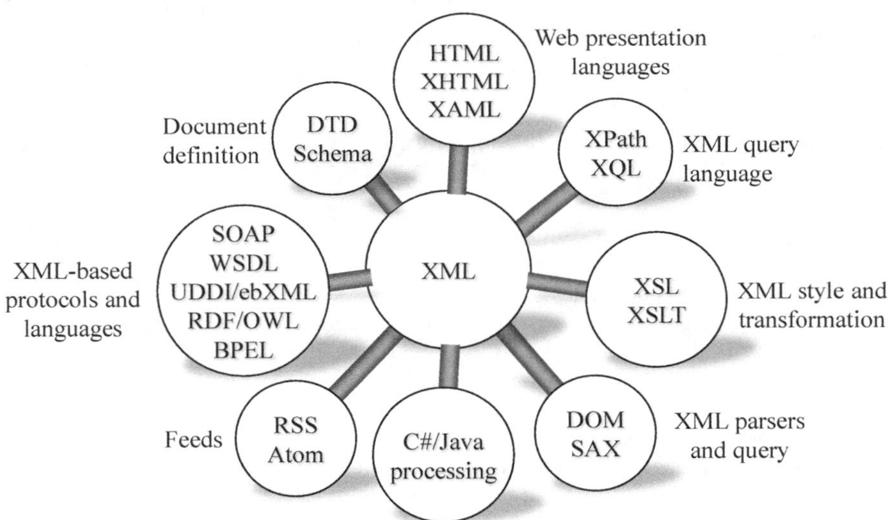

Figure 4.1. XML and related technologies

4.1 XML Fundamentals

XML (extensible markup language) is a universal metalanguage used to define other web services standards, protocols, interfaces, documents, and data. XML is of plain text and self-describing. It uses original markup tags surrounding sentences, statements, paragraphs, and even complete documents. The tags provide additional information about the data they envelop. It uses elements and attributes to provide both a logical structure and a physical structure to the document. XML contains metadata, that is, data about data. It is a metalanguage: a language used to define other languages.

4.1.1 XML versus HTML

Before we discuss XML, let us look at the HTML (Hypertext Markup Language), which is the standard formatting language for writing web pages. It uses different tags to define different formats of the text and graphs shown in web pages; for example:

```
<html>
<h3>IEEE International Workshop on Object-Oriented Real-Time Dependable Systems,
Sedona</h3>
<li>IEEE Computer Society Press, 2005, <b>ISBN</b> 0 7695 2347 1</i><br>
<li>Object-oriented computing</li>
<li>Real-time computing</li>
<li>Dependable computing</li>
</html>
```

This piece of HTML code is to be displayed on the web page as follows:

IEEE International Workshop on Object-Oriented Real-Time Dependable Systems, Sedona

IEEE Computer Society Press, 2005, ***ISBN*** *0 7695 2347 1*

- Object-oriented computing
- Real-time computing
- Dependable computing

The format is controlled by the tags. The tag pair <h3> </h3> specifies that the text quoted is of level 3 header format. The tag pair <li></li> specifies that the text quoted is a list item. The tag pair <b></b> specifies that the text quoted is in boldface. The tag pair <i></i> specifies that the text quoted is in italic. The single tag <br> introduces a newline.

If we use XML to describe the same information, it can look like this:

```
<?xml version="1.0">
<proceedings>
   <title>IEEE International Workshop on Object-Oriented Real-Time Dependable
Systems</title>
   <location>Sedona</location>
   <publisher>IEEE Computer Society Press</publisher>
   <year>2005</year>
   <ISBN>0 7695 2347 1</ISBN>
   <keyword>Object-oriented computing</keyword>
   <keyword>Real-time computing</keyword>
   <keyword>Dependable computing</keyword>
</proceedings>
```

The similarities between an HTML code and XML are obvious: they both use tags to define the data elements; both define attributes; both can use nested tags; and both are designed for both machine and human readers. The differences are less obvious but more significant, as listed in Table 4.1.

Table 4.1. Differences between HTML and XML languages

Features	HTML	XML
Purpose of tags	Format data for display.	Define attributes on data that can be interpreted by users.
Syntax of tags	Tags may be left open; for example, .	All tags must be in pairs.
Semantics of tags	Tags are predefined with given formatting meaning. Tags are limited.	The user can choose any tags and the meanings can be defined separately. Assigning meanings to a set of tags defines a vocabulary and thus a new language.
Semantics of data	It is difficult for a machine to understand; for example, is Sedona a part of the title?	Once the tags are defined, it is easy for machine to understand. Sedona is a location, not a part of the title.

4.1.2 XML Syntax

An XML document starts with a prolog consisting of a declaration and an optional reference to external documents, followed by the root element, which can consist of child elements:

```
<?xml version="1.0" encoding="UTF-8">
<instructor course="Service-Oriented Computing">
   <name>
        <first>John</first>
        <last>Doe</last>
   </name>
</instructor>
```

The first line declares that the document follows XML version 1.0 and uses encoding method UTF-8. The remaining lines contain data, called "elements," stored in the XML file. Each element contains contents quoted by a pair of tags (start and end tags). Tag names are not predefined and can be chosen freely except for a few restrictions. A tag must start with a letter, an underscore, or a colon. It may not start with the reserved word xml (case insensitive).

In BNF-like notation, an element can be defined as follows:

```
Element ::= EmptyElement | <StartTag> Content <EndTag>
EmptyElement ::= <StartTag><EndTag> | <StartTag/>
StartTag ::= TagName | TagName Attributes
EndTag ::= /TagName
Attributes ::= Attribute | Attribute | Attributes
Attribute ::= name = 'CDATA string' | name = "CDATA string"
Elements ::= Element | Element Elements
Content ::= PCDATA string | Elements
```

An empty element <StartTag><EndTag> can be represented with a single tag of the form <StartTag />. The question is, why do we need an empty element? The reason is that an empty element can still have attributes; for example:

<photo image ="myPhoto.jpeg" />

which is a shorthand notation of:

<photo image ="myPhoto.jpeg"> </photo>

CDATA and PCDATA in the definition will be explained shortly. The example below shows an XML document with sub-elements and attributes.

```
<instructor course="Service-Oriented Computing" officeHours="4">
    <title>Professor</title>
    <name>
        <first>John</first>
        <last>Doe</last>
    </name>
</instructor>
```

There is no fixed rule on what information should be stored as a child element or as an attribute. However, normally,

- **Elements** are used to define data that are integral to the document.
- **Attributes** are used to define out-of-band data, which give "additional" information

An XML document must be written following certain syntax rules and conventions:

- The document must conform to XML specification at: www.w3.org/TR/REC-xml
- There is a unique root element. All other elements are children or descendants of the root element.
- Each element is quoted between an open and a closing tag.
- Nested tags are allowed, but tags may not overlap; for example, the following is not allowed: <**title**>Professor<name>Doe</**title**></name>
- The tags should be self-describing and depict the true meaning of the data embedded in them.
- Element and tag names must meet certain restrictions.
- Attribute values must always be in quotes. Both single and double quotes are valid. Double quotes are most common though.
- Attributes are always contained within the start tag of an element:

  <course level = "Sophomore" required = "true">

  Service-Oriented Computing

  </course>
- Multiple attributes within an element are allowed, but the attributes must have unique names, that is, the same attribute name can appear once only within an element.
- Attributes are more difficult to manipulate by program code than elements.

An XML document can be represented in a rooted tree, as shown in Figure 4.2, where the oval nodes are start-tag names, the parallelograms are attributes, and the rectangles are element content.

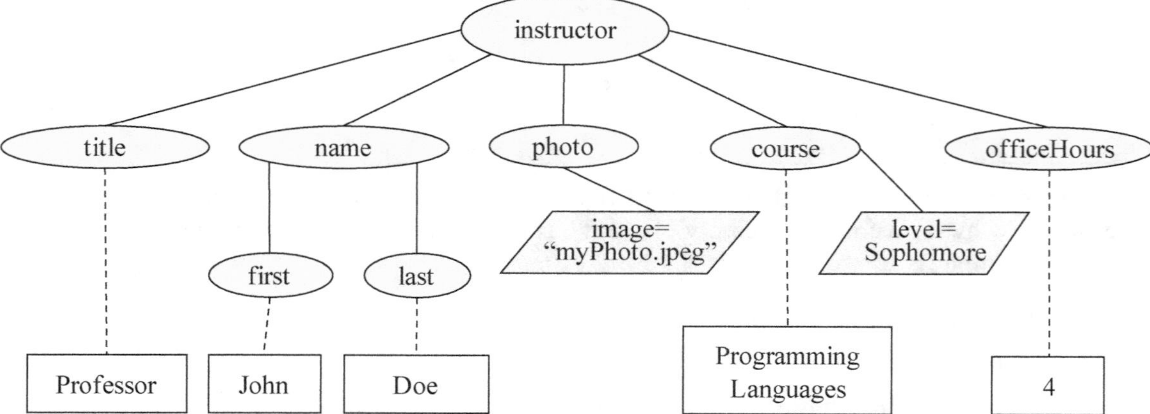

Figure 4.2. Representing an XML document in a rooted tree

XML documents use two types of data, CDATA (Character Data) and PCDATA (Parsed Character Data), to handle the appearances of reserved characters. Five characters are reserved for markup purpose. The parsers need to differentiate them from content characters.

Character	*Entity name*	*Meaning*
<	lt	less than
>	gt	greater than
&	amp	ampersand
'	apos	apostrophe; for example, computer's keyboard
"	quot	quotation

Different methods are allowed in XML to differentiate them:

- Use **Entity Reference** for these characters
  For example, to represent $0 < x < 100$, we can use:
  <Range> 0 < x < 100</Range>
- Use **Character Reference** (ASCII code) for these characters

  For example,

  <Range> < x < 100</Range>

However, an XML document may become hard to write and read, if many reserved characters are used; for example, if we want to encode the following piece program in an XML document:

```
<myCode>
   function AND(a, b) {
        if (a == "true" && b == "true") then
              { return "true" }
        else
        { return "false" }
   }
</myCode>
```

the reference method of the code looks as follows, which makes the program hardly readable:

```
<myCode>
   function AND(a, b) {
        if (a == &quot;true&quot; &amp;&amp; b == &quot;true&quot;) then
              { return &quot;true&quot; }
        else
        { return &quot;false&quot; }
   }
</myCode>
```

To address this problem, a different approach can be used. XML parsers differentiate two types of textual data:

- CDATA – Data that appears between a pair of special tags "<![CDATA[" and "]]>"
- PCDATA – Any data that are not in CDATA tags.

Using CDATA tags for text with many markup characters makes the text more readable:

```
<myCode>
   <![CDATA[
        function AND(a, b) {
              if (a == "true" && b == "true") then
```

```
                { return "true" }
            else
            { return "false" }
        }
    ]]>
</myCode>
```

XML parsers will ignore (not do syntax checking) CDATA but parse PCDATA – that is, interpret it as markup language. The practical implication is that data between the tags "<![CDATA[" and "]]>" do not have to conform to the syntax of XML. Outside the tags "<![CDATA[" and "]]>," they must conform to the syntax of XML.

Whitespaces may or may not have a meaning in an XML document. XML defines four characters to be **whitespace**. The names and Unicode values are: tab (#x9), newline (#xA), carriage return (#dX), and space (#x20). In XML definition or processing, two options can be defined: default and preserve. By default, multiple whitespaces will be collapsed (normalized). If preserve is specified, additional spaces will not be removed.

One can add comments in an XML document. Any text quoted between <!-- and --> will be considered comments and will not be parsed.

4.1.3 XML Namespaces

Namespaces are a mechanism for qualifying (scoping) element and attribute names, identifying the source where the name is defined, and avoiding naming collisions. We can use the namespace prefixes (scope resolution operator in C++) to qualify, as shown in the following example:

```
<?xml version="1.0"?>
<cse:Courses
   xmlns:cse="http://neptune.fulton.ad.asu.edu/WSRepository/xml/Course.xsd"
   xmlns:asu="http://neptune.fulton.ad.asu.edu/WSRepository/xml/rooms.xsd">
   <cse:Course>
        <cse:Name>Distributed Software Development</cse:Name>
        <cse:Code >CSE445</cse:Code>
        <cse:Level>Senior</cse:Level>
        <asu:Room asu:Image="layout210.jpeg" >BYAC210</asu:Room>
        <cse:Cap>40</cse:Cap>
   </cse:Course>
   <cse:Course>
        <cse:Name>Introduction to Programming Languages</cse:Name>
        <cse:Code >CSE240</cse:Code>
        <cse:Level>Sophomore</cse:Level>
        <asu:Room asu:Image="layout110.jpeg">BYAC110</asu:Room>
        <cse:Cap>82</cse:Cap>
   </cse:Course>
</cse:Courses>
```

Note, an element's attributes are not automatically scoped to a namespace. In the following example, the Image attribute does not belong to a namespace:

```
<asu:Room Image="layout110.jpeg"></asu:Room>
```

However, you can explicitly use a namespace prefix to qualify an attribute to namespace:

```
<asu:Room asu:Image="layout110.jpeg"></asu:Room>
```

Namespaces will be further discussed in the section on XML schema, where namespaces can be defined as a schema file.

4.2 XML Data Processing

Once we understand how data are represented in an XML document, we can start to process (read from and write into) XML documents.

There are two main types of parsers for extracting data from XML:

- DOM: Document Object Model, defined by W3C at www.w3.org/TR/DOM-level-2-core, it reads the entire document into the memory for random access. It is a problem if the XML document is large, which may take the entire memory. MSXML is a free package that supports both DOM as well as SAX type processing.
- SAX: Simple (Stream) API for XML, defined by the Java community (not by W3C) at www.saxproject.org, is an event-based API, which reads the document in a stream.
- XPath: Path-oriented data extraction.

XML parsers are integrated into .Net. The .Net Framework Class Library (FCL) defines a namespace System.Xml, with a variety of classes for reading and writing XML documents. The XmlDocument class is similar to MSXML. If you want to use a stream-based approach (SAX), you can use XmlTextReader or the schema-aware XmlvalidatingReader, instead. A complementary class named XmlTextWriter allows you to create XML documents.

In the remainder of this section, we will use the following XML example to illustrate how an XML file is processed. The file is stored at the location:

http://neptune.fulton.ad.asu.edu/WSRepository/xml/Courses.xml

```
<!-- File name: Courses.xml -->
<?xml version="1.0" encoding="UTF-8"?>
<Courses>
   <Course>
        <Name Short="Intro to PL">
              Introduction to Programming Languages
        </Name>
        <Code>CSE240</Code>
        <Level>Sophomore</Level>
        <Room>BYAC110</Room>
        <Cap>82</Cap>
   </Course>
   <Course>
        <Name Short="Distr Soft Dev">
              Distributed Software Development
        </Name>
        <Code>CSE445</Code>
        <Level>Senior</Level>
        <Room>BYAC210</Room>
        <Cap>40</Cap>
   </Course>
</Courses>
```

Figure 4.3 illustrates a part of the XML file in a rooted tree. Note that different shapes of the nodes represent different types of nodes.

4.2.1 DOM: Document Object Model

XmlDocument class and related classes provide a set of methods to manipulate the XML documents in DOM. It represents a document as a rooted tree of nodes. Each node is an instance of XmlNode class, which exposes methods and properties for navigating XML trees, reading, and writing node content, adding and removing nodes, and so on. XmlNode class is the base class in the .Net implementation of the DOM.

XmlDocument derives (inherits) from *XmlNode* and adds methods and properties of its own supporting the loading and saving of documents, the creation of new nodes, and other operations.

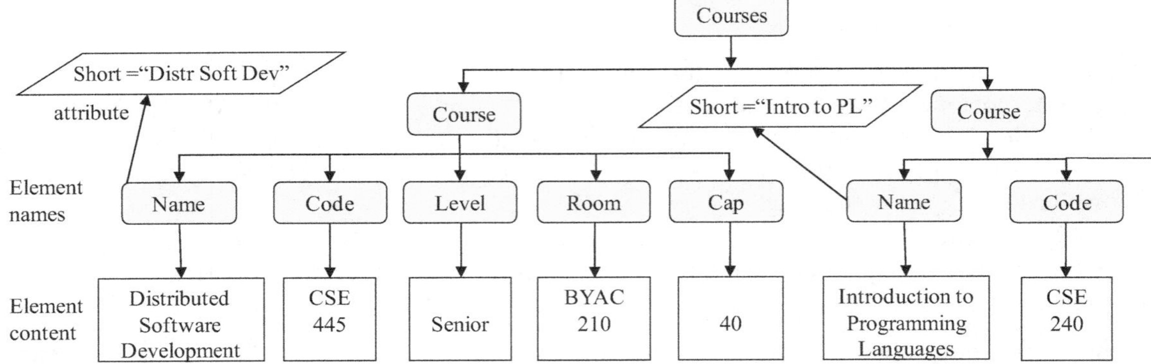

Figure 4.3. Representing an XML document in a rooted tree

The following statements create an XmlDocument object and initialize it with the contents of the XML document Courses.xml:

```
XmlDocument xref = new XmlDocument ();    //create an object
xref.Load ("Courses.xml"); // call Load method to instantiate the object
```

The method Load parses the file "Courses.xml" and builds an in-memory tree representation. It throws an XmlException if the document is not well formed. In other words, the method is doing the validation while reading. The XML document can be given in URL. The following web-embedded code creates an XmlDocument object and initializes it using the Courses.xml from the given URL.

```
<%@ Page language=C# debug="true" %>
<%@ Import Namespace="System.Xml" %>
<SCRIPT runat="server">
void Page_Load(Object Sender, EventArgs e)
{
   XmlDocument xref = new XmlDocument();
   xref.Load("http://neptune.fulton.ad.asu.edu/WSRepository/xml/Courses.xml");
   Console.WriteLine(xref.FirstChild.Name);
}
</SCRIPT>
```

Once an XML document is read into the memory in the form of an object, it can be manipulated in a programming language. The following C# code shows an example of manipulating an XML tree. It prints the tree elements recursively. Note, in Visual Studio, if your program does not recognize a class you are trying to access by showing a red underline, for example XmlDocument class, you can right-click the red underlined class and select "Quick Actions and Refactorings". It will suggest namespaces, for example, System.Xml, to import as long as it's already added into your project. Otherwise, you need to Add Reference… and add the library class into your project. If Visual Studio does not suggest anything to you, you can search for the class name on Google from Microsoft documents to find the instruction to add the class. Then you'll be able to do the Quick Actions again to find/import the namespace from that assembly.

```
using System;
using System.Xml; // The namespace is required for XML classes used in the program
class XMLDocApp {
    public static void Main() {
        XmlDocument xref = new XmlDocument();
        xref.Load("Courses.xml"); // or its URL
        preorderTraverse(xref.DocumentElement);
```

```
    }
    static void preorderTraverse(XmlNode node) { // recursive method
        Console.WriteLine("Type={0}\tName={1}\tValue={2}",
                    node.NodeType, node.Name, node.Value);
        if (node.HasChildNodes) {
            XmlNodeList children = node.ChildNodes;
            foreach (XmlNode child in children)
                preorderTraverse(child); // recursive call
        }
    }
}
```

The code parses the XML tree in preorder, that is, it prints the root element first and then prints the child element sequentially, as shown in the following printout of the code:

```
Type=Element    Name=Courses    Value=
Type=Element    Name=Course     Value=
Type=Element    Name=Name       Value=
Type=Text       Name=#text      Value=Introduction to Programming Languages
Type=Element    Name=Code       Value=
Type=Text       Name=#text      Value=CSE240
Type=Element    Name=Level      Value=
Type=Text       Name=#text      Value=Sophomore
Type=Element    Name=Room       Value=
Type=Text       Name=#text      Value=BYAC110
Type=Element    Name=Cap        Value=
Type=Text       Name=#text      Value=82
Type=Element    Name=Course     Value=
Type=Element    Name=Name       Value=
Type=Text       Name=#text      Value=Distributed Software Development
Type=Element    Name=Code       Value=
Type=Text       Name=#text      Value=CSE445
Type=Element    Name=Level      Value=
Type=Text       Name=#text      Value=Senior
Type=Element    Name=Room       Value=
Type=Text       Name=#text      Value=BYAC210
Type=Element    Name=Cap        Value=
Type=Text       Name=#text      Value=40
```

As can be seen in the printout, the library functions treat the content of an element as a text node and the value of the element content as the value of the text node. There are many other classes and methods in the .Net Framework Class Library (FCL) and they can be found in .Net online documents.

The following pseudocode illustrates the three common orders of traversing a tree: preorder, in-order, and post-order.

```
preorderTraverse(p)      Pre-Order Tree Traversing Algorithms
if p ≠ 0 then
   print(p->data);
   for each child node
        preorderTraverse(p->nextChild);

inorderTraverse(p) // In-Order Tree Traversing for binary tree only
if p ≠ 0 then
   inorderTraverse(p->left);
   print(p->data);
   inorderTraverse(p->right);

postorderTraverse(p     // Post-Order Tree Traversing Algorithms
```

```
if p ≠ 0 then
    for each child node
        postorderTraverse(p->nextChild); print(p->data);
```

4.2.2 SAX: Simple API for XML

DOM allows you to load the entire XML document into the memory and to access (read and modify) the elements in the tree forward, backward, and sideways. However, if you simply want to read XML contents and are less interested in the structure, you can use the SAX model and use the XmlTextReader class in .Net FCL.

XmlTextReader, which, like XmlDocument, belongs to the System.Xml namespace, provides a forward-only and read-only API to XML documents. It is stream-based, like reading a text file using standard file operations. It is more memory-efficient than XmlDocument, because it does not read the entire document into memory at once. It is simpler and easier than XmlDocument to read through a document, searching for particular elements, attributes, or other content items.

The basic idea is to create an XmlTextReader object from a file, a URL, or other data source. Then call XmlTextReader.Read() repeatedly until you find the content you are looking for. Each call to Read() advances an imaginary cursor to the next node in the document (normally, in preorder traversing). The operation stops if it reaches the end of the file (EOF).

XmlTextReader properties, such as NodeType, Name, Value, and AttributeCount expose information about the current node, and its methods, such as GetAttribute, MoveToFirstAttribute, and MoveToNextAttribute, and allow users to access the attributes, if any, attached to the current node.

The following program has all the functions of the one in the previous program that uses XMLDocument class. In addition, this program will handle the exception and print the attributes embedded in the XML file.

```
using System;
using System.Xml;
class XMLSAXApp {
    public static void Main() {
        XmlTextReader reader = null;
        try {
            reader = new XmlTextReader(
            "http://neptune.fulton.ad.asu.edu/WSRepository/xml/Courses.xml");
            reader.WhitespaceHandling = WhitespaceHandling.None;
             while (reader.Read()) {
                    Console.WriteLine ("Type={0}\tName={1}\tValue={2}",
                     reader.NodeType, reader.Name, reader.Value);
                    if (reader.AttributeCount > 0) { // print attributes
                        while (reader.MoveToNextAttribute())
                         Console.WriteLine("Type={0}\tName={1}\tValue={2}",
                          reader.NodeType, reader.Name, reader.Value);
                  }
            }
        }
        finally {
           if (reader != null) reader.Close();
        }
    }
}
```

The output of the program is given below:

```
Type=XmlDeclaration    Name=xml  Value=version="1.0" encoding="utf-8"
Type=Attribute  Name=version    Value=1.0
Type=Attribute  Name=encoding   Value=utf-8
```

```
Type=Element     Name=Courses     Value=
Type=Element     Name=Course      Value=
Type=Element     Name=Name        Value=
Type=Attribute   Name=Short       Value=Intro to PL
Type=Text        Name=    Value= Introduction to Programming Languages
Type=EndElement Name=Name         Value=
Type=Element     Name=Code        Value=
Type=Text        Name=    Value=CSE240
Type=EndElement Name=Code         Value=
Type=Element     Name=Level       Value=
Type=Text        Name=    Value=Sophomore
Type=EndElement Name=Level        Value=
Type=Element     Name=Room        Value=
Type=Text        Name=    Value=BYAC110
Type=EndElement Name=Room         Value=
Type=Element     Name=Cap         Value=
Type=Text        Name=    Value=82
Type=EndElement Name=Cap          Value=
Type=EndElement Name=Course       Value=
Type=Element     Name=Course      Value=
Type=Element     Name=Name        Value=
Type=Attribute   Name=Short       Value=Distr Soft Dev
Type=Text        Name=    Value=Distributed Software Development
Type=EndElement Name=Name         Value=
Type=Element     Name=Code        Value=
Type=Text        Name=    Value=CSE445
Type=EndElement Name=Code         Value=
Type=Element     Name=Level       Value=
Type=Text        Name=    Value=Senior
Type=EndElement Name=Level        Value=
Type=Element     Name=Room        Value=
Type=Text        Name=    Value=BYAC210
Type=EndElement Name=Room         Value=
Type=Element     Name=Cap         Value=
Type=Text        Name=    Value=40
Type=EndElement Name=Cap          Value=
Type=EndElement Name=Course       Value=
Type=EndElement Name=Courses      Value=
Press any key to continue . . .
```

4.2.3 XML Text Writer

XmlDocument class is used to read an XML document. It can be used to modify an existing XML document once read into the memory using tree operations. However, it cannot be used to generate a new XML document from scratch. The .Net Framework Class Library includes a writer class XmlTextWriter, which includes a number of write methods to create elements, attributes, comments, and so on. The segment of the C# code below shows commonly used write methods in XmlTextWriter class.

```
writer = new XmlTextWriter ("Courses.xml", System.Text.Encoding.Unicode);
writer.Formatting = Formatting.Indented;
writer.WriteStartDocument();
writer.WriteStartElement("Courses");
writer.WriteStartElement("Course");
writer.WriteElementString("Name", "SOC");
writer.WriteElementString("Code", "CSE445");
writer.WriteElementString("Level", "Senior");
writer.WriteStartElement("Room");
writer.WriteAttributeString("Image", "layout210.jpeg"); // add attribute
```

```
writer.WriteString("BYAC210");
writer.WriteEndElement();
writer.WriteElementString("Cap", "40");
writer.WriteEndElement();
writer.WriteEndElement();
writer.WriteEndDocument();
```

As the result, the code above will generate the following XML document:

```
<?xml version="1.0" encoding "utf-16"?>
<Courses>
  <Course>
       <Name>SOC</Name>
       <Code>CSE445</Code>
       <Level>Senior</Level>
       <Room Image="layout210.jpeg">BYAC210</Room>
       <Cap>40</Cap>
  </Course>
</Courses>
```

XmlTextWriter class can be used in combination with XmlDocument class to write the modified XML tree back into the XML file in the following steps:

- Load an XML file into memory as a tree:
  - XmlDocument xd = new XmlDocument();
  - xd.Load("Courses.xml");
- Modify the tree, by performing the tree data structure operations, such as
  - insertion(), deletion(), balancing(), traversing()
- Write the tree back using
  - XmlTextWriter writer = new XmlTextWriter(Courses.xml);
  - writer.Formatting = Formatting.Indented;
  - xd.WriteContentTo(writer);

The method WriteContentTo(writer) is not a part of XmlDocument standard, but a Visual Studio extension to the standard, which may not be available in other XmlDocument classes.

4.2.4 XML Processing in Java

While C# and its applications are mainly supported by Microsoft, Java applications are supported by a community and thus, different programming environments and packages are available for Java-based XML processing. This section will introduce a few of them:

- JAXP: Java API for XML Processing provides a common (vendor-independent) interface for creating and using the standard SAX, DOM, and XSLT APIs .
- JAXB: Java Architecture for XML Binding defines a mechanism for creating Java objects as XML (marshalling: use in other applications), and for creating Java objects from such structures (unmarshalling: use those objects in your own application).
- JDOM: Java DOM creates a tree of objects from an XML document.
- JAX-RPC: API for XML-based Remote Process Calls provides a mechanism for publishing available services in an external registry, and for consulting the registry to find those services.

Let us discuss the JAXP in more detail. It consists of the following packages:

- javax.xml.parsers: provide common interfaces for different vendors' SAX and DOM parsers.
- org.w3c.dom: defines a DOM class, as well as classes for all of the components of a DOM.
- org.xml.sax: defines the basic SAX APIs.
- javax.xml.transform: defines the XSLT APIs that let you transform XML into other forms; for example, the HTML.

In the javax.xml.parsers package (http://java.sun.com/j2se/1.5.0/docs/api/), a set of classes are defined including:

- SAXParserFactory: defines a factory API that enables applications to configure and obtain a SAX-based parser to parse XML documents.
- SAXParser: defines the API that wraps an XMLReader implementation class.
- DocumentBuilderFactory: defines a factory API that enables applications to obtain a parser that produces DOM object trees from XML documents.
- DocumentBuilder: defines the API to obtain DOM Document instances from an XML document.

The package provides four major classes for processing of XML documents. It uses the SAXParserFactory class to create an instance (object) with a number of interfaces or parsing methods without the implementations. Written in event-driven programming, the SAXParser class wraps the SAXReader class, which carries on the conversation with the SAX event handlers. Each event handler implements an interface in the SAXParserFactory object. A set of DefaultHandlers for ContentHandler, ErrorHandler, DTDHandler, and EntityResolver are implemented, so that the user can use these handlers if they do not implement their own. Figure 4.4 illustrates the concept.

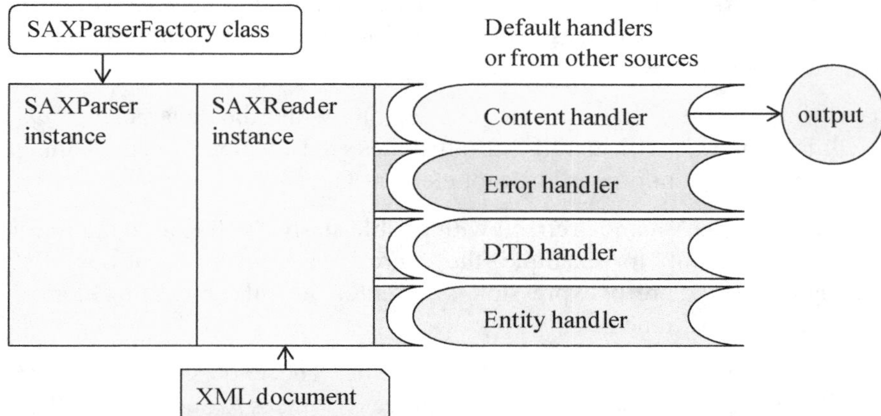

Figure 4.4. Classes and event handlers implementing the interfaces

The sample code below shows how these classes and handlers are used in a Java program.

```
import java.io.FileReader;
import org.xml.sax.XMLReader;
import org.xml.sax.InputSource;
import org.xml.sax.helpers.XMLReaderFactory;
import org.xml.sax.helpers.DefaultHandler;
public class MySAXApp extends DefaultHandler  {
  public MySAXApp () { super(); }    // constructor
  public static void main (String args[]) throws Exception {
       XMLReader xr = XMLReaderFactory.createXMLReader();
       MySAXApp handler = new MySAXApp();
       xr.setContentHandler(handler);
       xr.setErrorHandler(handler);
       // Parse each file provided via the command line input
       for (int i = 0; i < args.length; i++) { // get number of file names
             FileReader r = new FileReader(args[i]);  // Open file reader object
             xr.parse(new InputSource(r));       // parse the file opened
} }    }
```

4.3 XPath

XPath stands for XML Path Language. It is a language for accessing parts of an XML document in a way that a file system accesses its files using the path name and the file name.

In a file system, a path \Courses\CSE445\Assignments\assignment1.doc identifies the file "assignment1.doc" that is in the Assignments subdirectory of the directory's CSE445, which is a subdirectory of the directory Courses.

In XPath, an XML document is viewed as a rooted tree. A path is called an XPath expression. An expression will return an object that can be one of the following types:

- A set of nodes (empty node possible);
- A string;
- A Boolean value (true or false);
- A number, including both integers and floating-point numbers.

One can use the full path starting from the root to the node (element) to be selected, or use a local path to define an expression; for example, /Courses/Course identifies all elements (nodes) named Course that are children of the root element Courses.

To identify an attribute, one can use an expression with the character "@," for example, /Courses/Course/@Image, which will identify all attributes (not elements) named Image that belong to Course elements that in turn are children of the root element Courses.

XPath supports pathless search. A name prefixed with double slash // will lead to the runtime searching for the name in the entire document; for example, the expression //Course identifies all Course elements anywhere in the document. The // prefix expression is extremely useful for locating elements in a document regardless of where they are positioned.

XPath also supports wildcards widely used in file systems. The expression /Courses/* will select all elements that are children elements named Courses, whereas /Courses /Course/@* will select all attributes belonging to Course.

One can apply a filter operator [ ] to select one or more nodes that meet the given criteria. The filter operator can be applied to attributes and to elements; for example, the expression /Courses/Course[Cap>40] returns those Courses whose Cap value is greater than 40, whereas /Courses/Course[Level='Senior'] returns all Senior level courses. When the expression returns a set of nodes with the same name, you have a collection returned; for example, the expression //Course returns two Course nodes in the given example. You can apply the filter operator as index operator and specify which item from the collection you want to select. Please note that the index starts at one, instead of zero. The expression //Course[2] returns the second Course node. The order of the selected nodes is the same order as in the XML document. You can combine the index operator with other operators; for example, //Course[2]/Cap, which selects the Cap in the second course. The arithmetic operators available include:

```
= (equal operator)                      Example: //Course[. = 'Senior']
!= (unequal operator)              Example: //Name[@Short != 'Intro to PL']
<= (less than/equal operator)      Example: //Course [Cap<=40]
< (less than operator)             Example: //Course [Cap<50]
>= (greater than/equal operator)        Example: //Course [Cap>=40]
> (greater operator)                    Example: //Course [Cap>60]
```

One can also apply the logic operators "and," "or," and "not" to connect multiple expressions to create compound expressions; for example:

```
//Course[Level = 'Senior' and Cap < 50]
//Course[Room='BYAC110' or Cap >= 80 or Code != 'CSE445']
//Course[not(Room='BYAC210')]
```

Similar to the DOS file system, one can use a dot to represent the current directory, and use two dots ."." to represent the parent directory in XPath.

XPath language and its application are fully described in the XPath specification found at http://www.w3.org/TR/xpath. Only major features are presented in this section.

XPath is also integrated in different programming environments. In .Net, System.Xml.XPath namespace contains a set of classes for supporting XPath operations in C# applications. These classes can be used in the following steps to create the query object, perform the queries, and store the data returned from the query.

1. XPathDocument class creates a wrapped XPath document from an XML document. The class contains a variety of constructors for instantiating an XPathDocument from a stream, a URL, a file, a TextReader, or an XmlReader. The following statement creates an XPathDocument object and initializes it with the content found in the Courses xml:

   ```
   XPathDocument dx = new XPathDocument("Courses.xml");
   ```

2. XPathNavigator class provides a mechanism for performing XPath queries. The following statement creates an XPathNavigator object from the XPathDocument created in step 1:

   ```
   XPathNavigator nav = dx.CreateNavigator();
   ```

3. XPathNodeIterator class represents the node set generated by XPath query and lets the users iterate over them. XPathNodeIterator contains several methods for executing XPath queries:
   - Evaluate method executes any XPath expression. It returns a generic Object that can be a string, a float, a bool, or an XPathNodeIterator (node set), depending on the expression and the type of data stored in the XML document.
   - Select method works exclusively with the expressions that return a node set, and it selects specific node from the node set. The following statements use Select to create a node set representing all nodes that match the expression //Course, and then print the count (number of) nodes in the set.

     ```
     XPathNodeIterator iterator = nav.Select ("//Course");
     Console.WriteLine("Select finds {0}, nodes", iterator.Count);
     ```

There are series of properties and methods in the XPathNavigator class that allow users to access the data returned; for example, Current property represents the current node, while a number of Move methods can be called to move current position in any direction: up, down, and sideways. The following program uses some of the classes and methods.

```
using System;
using System.Xml.XPath;
class MyApp {
    static void Main() {
        XPathDocument xdoc = new XPathDocument
("http://neptune.fulton.ad.asu.edu/WSRepository/xml/Courses.xml");
        XPathNavigator xpdoc = xdoc.CreateNavigator();
        XPathNodeIterator xset = xpdoc.Select("/Courses/Course");
        while (xset.MoveNext()) {
            XPathNodeIterator xnode = xset.Current.Select("Name");
            xnode.MoveNext();
            string shortName = xnode.Current.GetAttribute("Short", "");
            string courseName = xnode.Current.Value;
            xnode = xset.Current.Select("Code");
```

```
            xnode.MoveNext();
            string courseCode = xnode.Current.Value;
            xnode = xset.Current.Select("Cap");
            xnode.MoveNext();
            double courseCap = xnode.Current.ValueAsDouble;
            Console.WriteLine("Name={0}\nShort Name={1}\nCode={2}\n Cap={3}\n",
courseName, shortName, courseCode, courseCap);
        }
    }
}
```

The output of the program is:

```
Name=Introduction to Programming Languages
Short Name=Intro to PL
Code=CSE240
Cap=82

Name=Distributed Software Development
Short Name=Distr Soft Dev
Code=CSE445
Cap=40
```

4.4 XML Type Definition Languages

Why do we need type definition languages for XML? XML is a metalanguage used for defining XML-based languages. Each type or schema definition defines a new XML-based language, including vocabulary, syntax, and semantics (rules). As we have seen, a piece of information can be encoded in an XML document in different ways and any tags (vocabulary) can be used. When the information is transferred from the source to its destination, the receiver (or receiving program) needs to know how the document is structured, what tags are allowed, whether the format is indeed compliant with the XML standard, and whether the data in the XML file are valid data; for example, consider the following two pieces of XML data. It is obvious that the piece of data on the upper part does not meet the convention of representing time. Less obviously, what about the piece of data at the lower part? Is it acceptable?

```
<time>
   <hour>15</hour>
   <minute>72</minute>
   <second>-5</second>
</time>

<time>
   <hour>15</hour>
   <minute>20</minute>
   <second>5</second>
</time>
```

It is acceptable if Military Time is used, but not acceptable if standard time is used. Document type and schema definition languages allow the XML document authors to define the syntax and semantics (business rules) of their documents, which can be validated by the receivers of the documents, as shown in Figure 4.5. The XML file created based on the type and schema definition file is an instance of the type definition.

There are two methods to define the tags and structure of a user-defined XML file: Document Type DTD and XML. XML Document Type Definition and XML Schema.

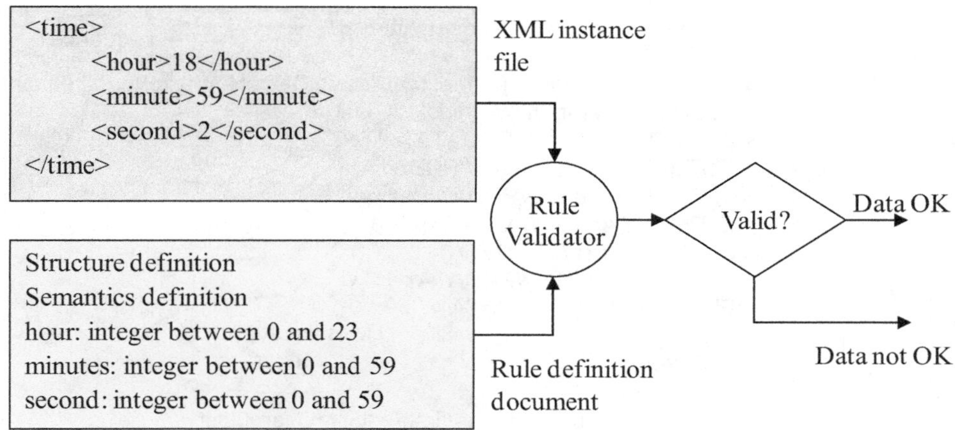

Figure 4.5. Validating an XML instance file against its definition document

4.4.1 XML Document Type Definition (DTD)

A DTD (Document Type Definition) file holds information about the structure and the syntax of an XML document. A DTD file can be defined in a separate file (external DTD) or within the XML document itself (internal DTD). An external DTD stored on the Internet can be shared by multiple XML documents.

A DTD document consists of a root element and a sequence of document type declarations, each of which is called an element:

```
<!DOCTYPE root-element
[
   doctype-declarations
]>
```

Each element is defined in the syntax:

```
<!ELEMENT element-name content-model>
```

which associates a content model with all elements in the XML document of the given name.

The content-model can be one of the following:

- EMPTY: no content is allowed;
- ANY: any content is allowed;
- PCDATA (parsed character data) and their combinations of certain operators.

The allowed combination operators include:

- | (choice); for example (a | b | c);
- , (sequence); for example (a, b, c);
- ? (optional); for example a?;
- * (zero or more); for example b*;
- + (one or more); for example c+.

For the XML document defining the instructor, the DTD file is shown in Figure 4.6.

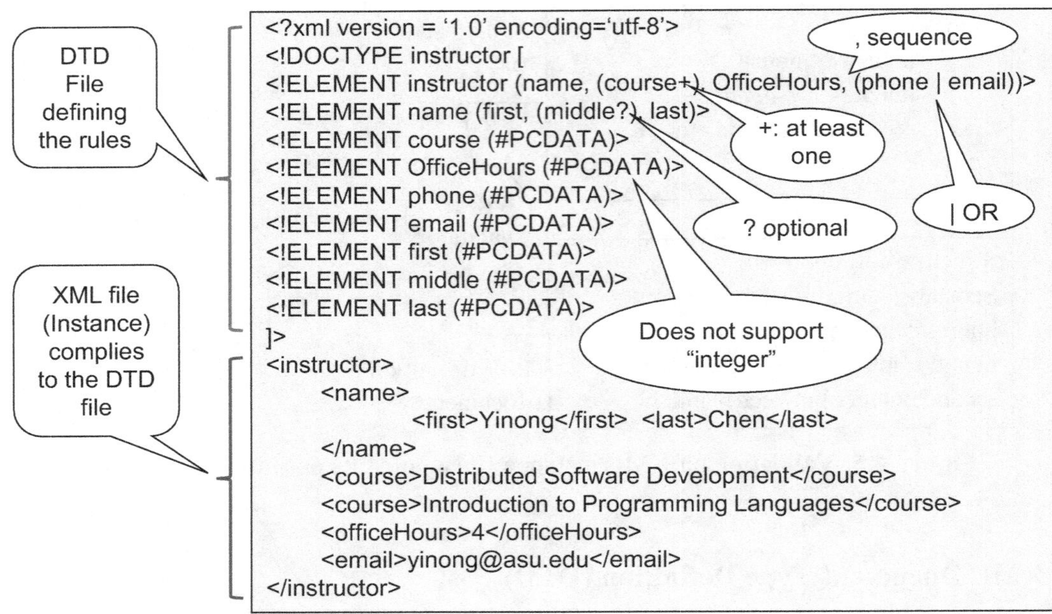

Figure 4.6. An XML file with an internal DTD definition

The DTD file can be separated and stored in a given URL site. The instance file can refer the DTD file via a reference, as shown in the code below.

For the XML document defining the instructor with attributes, the DTD file looks like:

```
<?xml version = '1.0' encoding='utf-8'>
<!DOCTYPE instructor SYSTEM
"http://neptune.fulton.ad.asu.edu/WSRepository/xml/instructor.dtd">
<instructor>
   <name>
        <first>Yinong</first> <last>Chen</last>
   </name>
   <course>Distributed Software Development</course>
   <officeHours>4</officeHours>
   <phone>480-965 8300</phone>
</instructor>
```

DTD defines a list of attributes in a given element in the following syntax:

```
<!ELEMENT course (#PCDATA)>
<!ATTLIST course  level     CDATA     #REQUIRED
                  text      CDATA     #IMPLIED
                  camp      CDATA     "Tempe"
>
```

In the definition, #REQUIRED means that this attribute must be provided, while #IMPLIED means that this attribute is optional and no default will be provided if the attribute is not provided. The campus attribute is given a default attribute "Tempe," which will be used if the instance document does not provide a value for the attribute. The following example shows an instance of the definition above:

```
<course level = "senior"
        text = "Service-Oriented Architecture & Computing"
        camp = "West">
   Distributed Software Development
</course>
```

The course elements must be of PCDATA typ201e, while the attributes can be either PCDATA or CDATA, because attribute values will be quoted and any quoted text will not be parsed.

4.4.2 XML Schema

XML Schema is a more powerful alternative to DTD that defines the structure (grammar) and types of an XML document. The advantages of the schema over DTD include:

- DTD is not XML-based and requires separate tools to process DTD documents, whereas XML Schema is XML-based. The same tools can be used to process XML documents as well as XML Schema documents.
- XML Schema is extendable and reusable. One can easily add new types, restricting existing types, and combine existing schemas.
- DTD is limited to string type. Similar to a typical programming language, XML schema support basic types, including integer, float, and string, and can define other complex types.

An XML schema namespace includes elements and data types that can be used to construct schemas, including: schema, element, complexType, sequence, Boolean, integer, and string.

XML schema has 44 built-in types, including 19 simple (primitive) and 25 derived complex types. The user can define further types of simple and complex types.

In an XML document, a schema is introduced as an element with an opening tag <schema> with a number of optional attributes; for example, referring to the source and version:

```
<schema xmlns ="http://www.w3.org/2000/10/XMLSchema" version "1.0">
```

The declaration refers the schema to the XML Schema defined at W3C's website. The prefix xsd denotes the namespace (domain) of the schema. Compared to DTD, XML Schema provides much more powerful types from simple to complex. Similar to a programming language, one can define structure type; for example, we can define a personnelType type as follows:

```
<complexType name = "personnelType">
  <sequence>
      <element name="firstname" type="string"/>
      <element name="lastname" type="string"/>
      <element name="id" type="integer"/>
  </sequence>
  <attribute name="salary" type "Float" use="required"/>
</complexType>
```

The following example shows the definition of two complex types "Bookstore" and "Book," and two simple types "First" and "Last."

```
<?xml version="1.0" encoding="UTF-8" ?>
<xsd:schema xmlns:xsd="http://www.w3.org/2001/XMLSchema"
   xmlns="http://neptune.fulton.ad.asu.edu/WsRepository/xml"
   targetNamespace="http://neptune.fulton.ad.asu.edu/WsRepository/xml"
   elementFormDefault="qualified" attributeFormDefault="unqualified">
  <xsd:element name="Book">
      <xsd:complexType>
         <xsd:sequence>
            <xsd:element name="Title" type="xsd:string" minOccurs="1"
maxOccurs="1"/>
            <xsd:element name="Author" type="xsd:string" minOccurs="1"
maxOccurs="unbounded"/>
            <xsd:element name="Year" type="xsd:string" minOccurs="0"
maxOccurs="1"/>
            <xsd:element name="ISBN" type="xsd:string" minOccurs="0"
maxOccurs="1"/>
```

```
            </xsd:sequence>
         </xsd:complexType>
    <xsd:element name="Bookstore">
         <xsd:complexType>
            <xsd:sequence>
               <xsd:element name="Book" minOccurs="1" maxOccurs="unbounded"/>
            </xsd:sequence>
         </xsd:complexType>
    </xsd:element>
     </xsd:element>
     <xsd:element name="First" type="xsd:string"/>
     <xsd:element name="Last" type="xsd:string"/>
</xsd:schema>
```

In addition to using constraints "`minOccurs`" and "`maxOccurs`" that define the number of appearances of the element allowed, XML schema offers three operators to define optional members of a complex type:

- sequence: the members must appear in the given order;
- choice: only one of the list members allowed;
- all: all members must appear (unless minOccurs="0"), but can be in any order.

The following example shows the use of these operators:

```
<?xml version="1.0" encoding="UTF-8"?>
<Bookstore
   xmlns ="http://neptune.fulton.ad.asu.edu/WsRepository/xml"
   xmlns:xsi="http://www.w3.org/2001/XMLSchema-instance"
   xsi:schemaLocation="http://neptune.fulton.ad.asu.edu/WsRepository/xml
Bookstore.xsd">
<xsd:element name="Book">
   <xsd:complexType>
        <xsd:sequence>
              <xsd:element name="Title" type="xsd:string" />
                   <xsd:element name="Author" type="xsd:string" />
                   <xsd:element name="Year" type="xsd:string" />
              <xsd:choice>
                   <xsd:element name="ISBN-10" type="xsd:string" />
                   <xsd:element name="ISBN-13" type="xsd:string" />
              </xsd:choice>
        </xsd:sequence>
   </xsd:complexType>
</xsd:element name="Book">
```

Similar to the inheritance property in object-oriented programming languages, inheritance can be used in XML schema to define new types based on existing types. A type can be extended without redefining the elements and attributes in an existing type; for example, we can define a researchType based on the personnelType as follows:

```
<complexType name = "researchType">
   <extension base = "personnelType">
        <sequence>
              <element name="researchInterests" type="string"/>
        </sequence>
        <attribute name="rank" type "string"/ use="optional">
   </extension>
</complexType>
```

In this extended type, one element and one attribute are added to the base type. The extended definition is equivalent to the following definition:

```
<complexType name = "researchType">
   <sequence>
        <element name="firstname" type="string"/>
        <element name="lastname" type="string"/>
        <element name="id" type="integer"/>
        <element name="researchInterests" type="string"/>
   </sequence>
   <attribute name="salary" type "Float" use="required">
   <attribute name="rank" type "string"/ use="optional">
</complexType>
```

Using extension is a much better way of defining types:

- It is more compact.
- It is easier to maintain; for example, if the base type is modified, the extended type is automatically updated.
- It associates all related types in a hierarchical tree, where the direct base type is the parent type of the extended type.

4.4.3 Namespace

An XML document can use more than one DTD and more than one schema, which are defined by different providers. Obviously, the same names could be used in these DTD and schemas for different things. Namespace is used to limit the scope of the name, and thus, it eliminates the conflict. For example, it is perfectly all right for a British university's schema buSchema at http://www.bu.ac.uk to use the term faculty for an academic unit, and for a US university's schema asuSchema at http://www.asu.edu to use the term faculty for an academic member. To differentiate the meanings of these two terms, we can define a namespace for each of the documents. In the following piece of code, two namespaces, bu and asu, are defined and used.

```
<?xml version="1.0" encoding="UTF-8"?>
xmlns:bu="http://www.bu.ac.uk/buSchema"
xmlns:asu="http://www.bu.ac.uk/asuSchema"
</personnel>
   <bu:faculty bu:name="Engineering" type="xsd:string" />
   <asu:faculty asu:name="Joe Miller" type="xsd:string" />
</personnel>
```

A namespace is declared as an attribute of an element. It binds a prefix name (qualifier) to a schema definition, and then uses that prefix wherever required. Namespaces are often declared at the root element. Then the scope of the declared namespaces applies to the entire document. However, namespaces can be declared at any element in an XML document. Their scope applies to the entire element only. A namespace can be overridden. An inner namespace declaration with the same prefix name (qualifier) will override the outer namespace. As an example, Figure 4.7 shows the namespaces defined for the bookstore XML scheme as well as the attributes in the namespace definition.

It is painful to repeatedly qualify each element you wish to use from a namespace, if they appear frequently. In this case, you can declare a default namespace. Once you have defined a default namespace, all elements within the scope that are not explicitly qualified will be qualified implicitly, that is, to be considered to be from the default namespace. Please note that, at any point in time, there can be one default namespace only.

We define the name of a namespace using the syntax of "xmlns myNamespace = ..." How do we declare a default namespace? We use the same syntax without "myNamespace." In the aforesaid example, the default namespace is defined by:

xmlns = "http://neptune.fulton.ad.asu.edu/WSRepository/xml/bookstore"

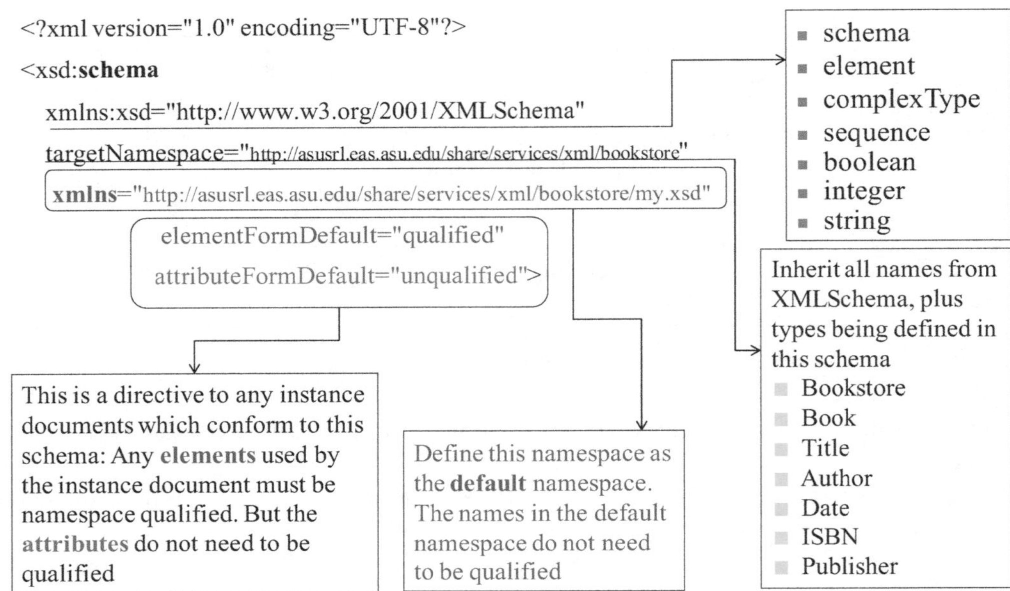
<?xml version="1.0" encoding="UTF-8"?>
<xsd:**schema**
xmlns:xsd="http://www.w3.org/2001/XMLSchema"
targetNamespace="http://asusrl.eas.asu.edu/share/services/xml/bookstore"
xmlns="http://asusrl.eas.asu.edu/share/services/xml/bookstore/my.xsd"
elementFormDefault="qualified"
attributeFormDefault="unqualified">
schema
element
complexType
sequence
boolean
integer
string
Inherit all names from XMLSchema, plus types being defined in this schema
Bookstore
Book
Title
Author
Date
ISBN
Publisher
This is a directive to any instance documents which conform to this schema: Any **elements** used by the instance document must be namespace qualified. But the **attributes** do not need to be qualified
Define this namespace as the **default** namespace. The names in the default namespace do not need to be qualified

Figure 4.7. An XML file with an internal DTD definition

Prefixed namespace and the default namespace do not apply to attributes within the element. To apply a namespace to an attribute, the attribute must be explicitly qualified. In the example below, the attribute "edition" has no namespace, whereas the attribute "cover" is associated with the namespace bs.

```
<Book  xmlns = "http://neptune.fulton.ad.asu.edu/WSRepository/xml">
  <Title bs: cover = "paper back" > Programming Languages </Title>
  <Author>Yinong Chen</Author>
  <Author>W.T. Tsai</Author>
  <Year edition = "2" >2006</Year>
  <ISBN>0-7575-2974-7</ISBN>
</Book>
```

We can also define a target namespace, which can include the namespaces that you use into the namespace that defines the target namespace. In the example in Figure 4.7,

targetNamespace = "http://neptune.fulton.ad.asu.edu/WSRepository/xml/bookstore"

will include the vocabularies defined in the following two namespaces:

http://www.w3.org/2001/XMLSchema

http://neptune.fulton.ad.asu.edu/WSRepository/xml/bookstore

The purpose of defining a schema is to use the schema to define XML instances. Using the bookstore schema defined above, we can define an instance (XML) as follows:

```
<?xml version="1.0"?>
<Bookstore xmlns ="http://neptune.fulton.ad.asu.edu/WSRepository/xml"
          xmlns bs =
"http://neptune.fulton.ad.asu.edu/WSRepository/xml/bookstore.xsd"
          xmlns:xsi="http://www.w3.org/2001/XMLSchema-instance"
xsi:schemaLocation="http://neptune.fulton.ad.asu.edu/WSRepository/xml/bookstore.xsd"
>
  <Book>
       <Title bs: cover = paperback >
             Introduction to Programming Languages
```

```
        </Title>
        <Author>Yinong Chen</Author>
        <Author>W.T. Tsai</Author>
              <Year edition = "2" > 2006</Year>
              <ISBN>0-7575-2974-7</ISBN>
        <Size>A4</Size>
   </Book>
   <Book>
        <Title>Distributed Service-Oriented Software Development</Title>
        <Author>Yinong Chen</Author>
        <Author>W.T. Tsai</Author>
              <Year>2008</Year>
              <ISBN>978-0-7575-5273-1</ISBN>
        <Size>A4</Size>
   </Book>
</Bookstore>
```

Please note that the prefixed namespace and the default namespace do not apply to attributes within the element. To apply a namespace to an attribute, the attribute must be explicitly qualified. In the foregoing example, the attribute "edition" has no namespace, whereas the attribute "cover" is associated with the namespace bs. As the attributes are often considered supplementary information, they do not have to be checked by the XML validator. In the namespace definition in Figure 4.7, the clause below:

```
elementFormDefault="qualified" attributeFormDefault="unqualified">
```

states that all elements must be qualified, whereas the attributes do not need to be qualified.

Summarizing the namespace section, we start with the W3C standard definition of XML schema XML Schema Namespace http://www.w3.org/2001/XMLSchema and use it to define our own schema of bookstore. We define a target namespace that includes the vocabularies from both schemas. Using all the combined vocabulary, we can define XML documents (instances) that are in compliance with the bookstore schema.

4.4.4 XML Validation

Each XML file needs to be validated against its type definition files in DTD or XML Schema to see if it complies with the syntax definition. Further, the user-defined DTD and schema type files must conform to its standard as defined by W3C. Figure 4.8 shows the two levels of validation.

The class XMLReader and its .Create(... ...) method in .Net framework can be used to perform the validation. It supports both DTD and XSD type files. Figure 4.9 illustrates how the class and method are used.

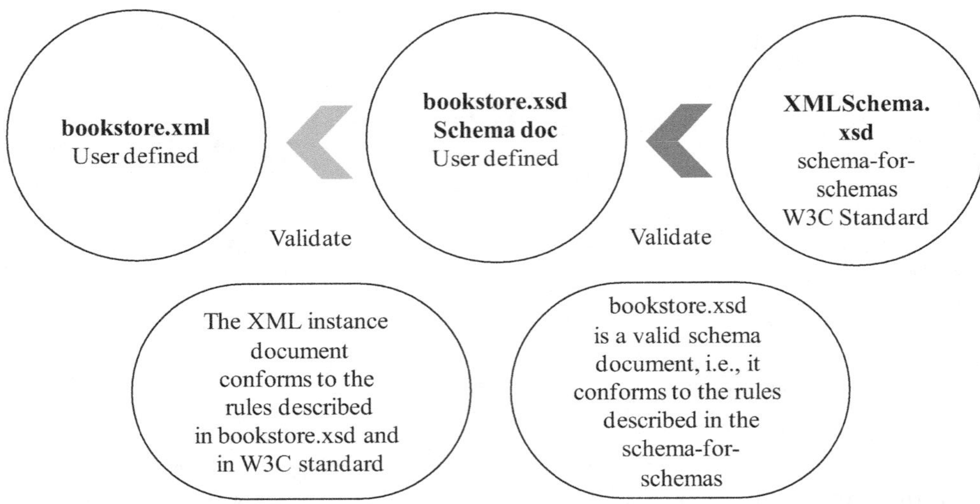

Figure 4.8. Validation of XML document and its type definition files

Figure 4.9. The process of validating an XML document

It first uses XmlSchemaSet class to define the settings necessary. It then uses XmlReader.Create() to create a reader that associates the XML file to be validated and the settings. The C# program shows an example of how an XML file can be validated.

```
using System; using System.Xml;
using System.Xml.Schema; using System.IO;
public class Sample {
    public static void Main(){
        // Create the XmlSchemaSet class.
        XmlSchemaSet sc = new XmlSchemaSet();
        // Add the schema to the collection before performing validation
        sc.Add(null,
"http://neptune.fulton.ad.asu.edu/WSRepository/xml/Courses.xsd");
        // Set the validation settings.
        XmlReaderSettings settings = new XmlReaderSettings();
        settings.ValidationType = ValidationType.Schema;
        settings.Schemas = sc;
        settings.ValidationEventHandler += new
ValidationEventHandler(ValidationCallBack);
        // Create the XmlReader object.
        XmlReader reader =
XmlReader.Create("http://neptune.fulton.ad.asu.edu/WSRepository/xml/Courses.xml",
settings);
        // Parse the file.
        while (reader.Read()) ; // will call event handler if invalid
```

```
        Console.WriteLine("The XML file is valid for the given xsd file");
    }
    // Display any validation errors.
    private static void ValidationCallBack(object sender, ValidationEventArgs e) {
        Console.WriteLine("Validation Error: {0}", e.Message);
    }
}
```

The XML file Courses.xml contains no errors. The program should print "The XML file is valid for the given xsd file." If we test another file, CoursesWithErrors.xml, error messages will be printed for each error found in the file.

Note, for the validation program to work properly, you must define the namespaces correctly, as discussed in the previous section. For example, some XML editors will put a default namespace in the XML file, such as: xmlns="http://tempuri.org/XMLSchema.xsd".

This namespace should be replaced by xmlns= "http://www.w3.org/2001/XMLSchema", or use a named namespace: xsd:schema xmlns:xsd="http://www.w3.org/2001/XMLSchema".

4.5 Extensible Stylesheet Language

HTML is a language with format but without structure. It is a typesetting language, and it is not extensible. On the other hand, XML is language with structure but without format. It defines elements using predefined and self-defined tags. XSL (Extensible Stylesheet Language) is a set of language technologies for defining XML document transformation and presentation. It includes:

- XSL Transformations (XSLT), which transfers an XML document into another XML document with different structure, and presents XML data in a better readable format in a web page, such as a table.
- XSL Formatting Objects (XSL-FO) is a markup language for XML document formatting, which is most used to generate PDF and special formats.

Figure 4.10 shows a scenario where transformation is needed. An XML document presented in the given tree structure can be transformed into an XML document with a different structure using XSLT. An XML document can also be transformed into a format that is better for humans to read; for example, a table.

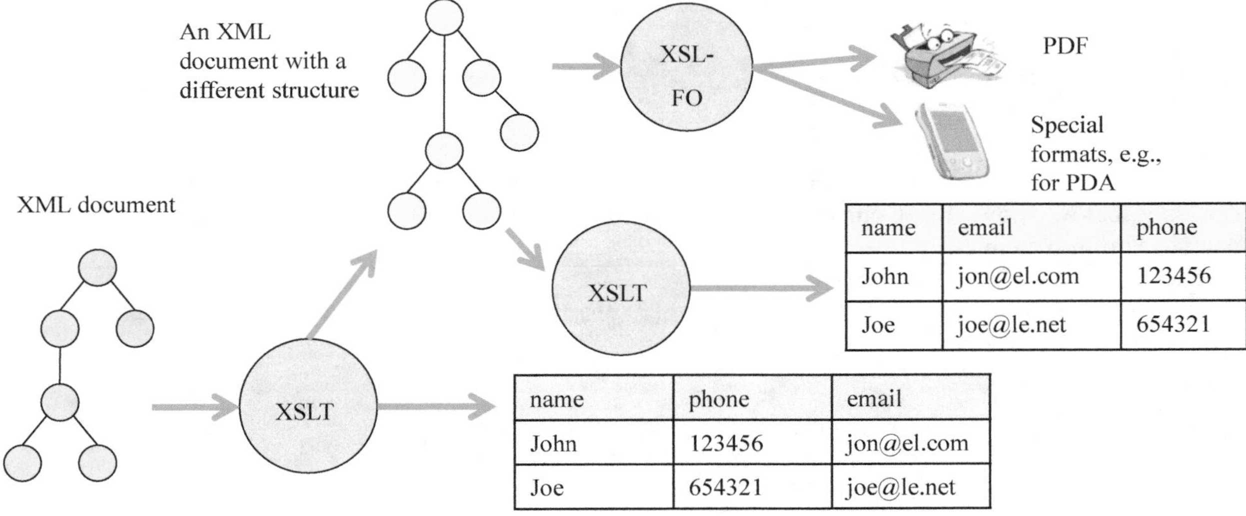

Figure 4.10. XML transformation

XSLT is in fact a declarative (functional) programming language with constructs such as if-then-else and foreach loop. XSLT is a language of Turing-complete in theory, but its expressiveness is limited in practice. It is mainly used for transforming one XML structure to another and for creating formatted output by adding HTML format to XML structure.

For a given XML document, say, Courses.xml, we need to create an XSL file, Courses.xsl, to define how to transform Courses.xml, as shown in Figure 4.11.

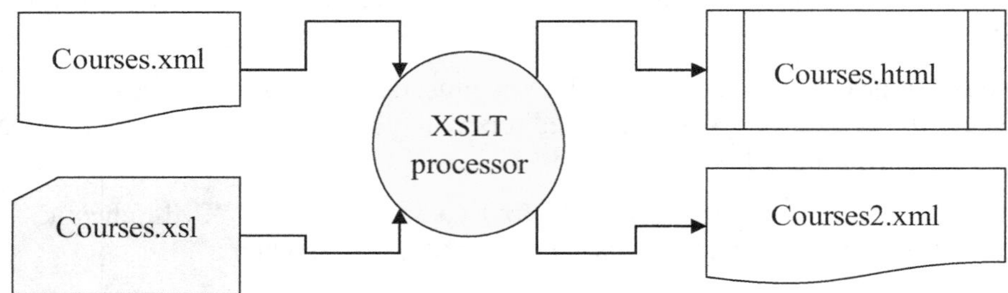

Figure 4.11. Use XSL file to define the translation schema

The code below shows the Courses.xml, with an additional line (at line 2) of code to indicate where the XSL file is located.

```
<?xml version="1.0"?>
<?xml-stylesheet type="text/xsl" href="Courses.xsl"?>
<Courses>
  <Course>
      <Name>Introduction to Programming Languages</Name>
      <Code>CSE240</Code>
      <Level>Sophomore</Level>
      <Room>BYAC110</Room>
      <Cap>82</Cap>
  </Course>
  <Course>
      <Name>Distributed Software Development</Name>
      <Code>CSE445</Code>
      <Level>Senior</Level>
      <Room>BYAC210</Room>
      <Cap>40</Cap>
  </Course>
</Courses>
```

The code below shows the Courses.xsl, which instructs how to translate the two elements of data in Courses.xml into a table.

```
<?xml version="1.0"?>
<xsl:stylesheet xmlns:xsl="http://www.w3.org/1999/XSL/Transform" version="1.0">
  <xsl:template match="/">
      <html>  <body>
            <h1>My Courses</h1>
            <table border="1">
                  <tr bgcolor="yellow">
                        <td><b>Name </b></td>
                        <td><b>Code</b></td>
                        <td><b>Level</b></td>
                        <td><b>Room</b></td>
```

```
                        <td><b>Cap</b></td>
                    </tr>
                    <xsl:for-each select="Courses/Course">
                        <xsl:sort select="Name" />
                        <tr style="font-size: 10pt; font-family: verdana">
                            <td><xsl:value-of select="Name"/></td>
                            <td><xsl:value-of select="Code"/></td>
                            <td><xsl:value-of select="Level"/></td>
                            <td><xsl:value-of select="Room"/></td>
                            <td><xsl:value-of select="Cap"/></td>
                        </tr>
                    </xsl:for-each>
                </table>
        </body> </html>
    </xsl:template>
</xsl:stylesheet>
```

If we put the XML document above into a website; for example,

http://neptune.fulton.ad.asu.edu/WSRepository/xml/Courses.xml

without defining the XSL file, we will see the XML document in XML format, as shown in the left window of Figure 4.12.

If we add the style file:

http://neptune.fulton.ad.asu.edu/WSRepository/xml/Courses.xsl

and add the following line of code into the Courses.xml:

```
<?xml-stylesheet type="text/xsl" href="Courses.xsl"?>
```

then we will see the formatted output as shown in right window in Figure 4.12.

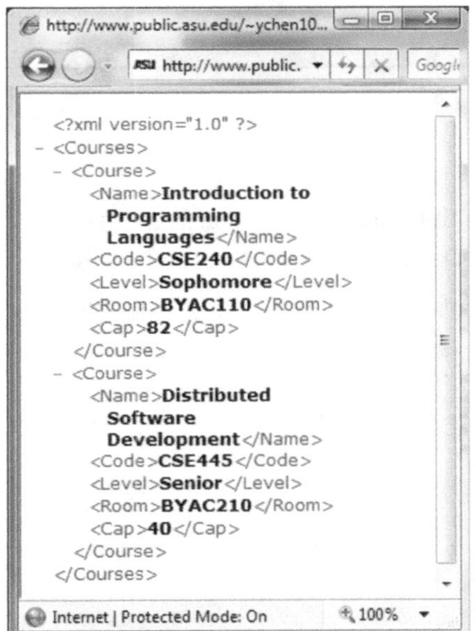

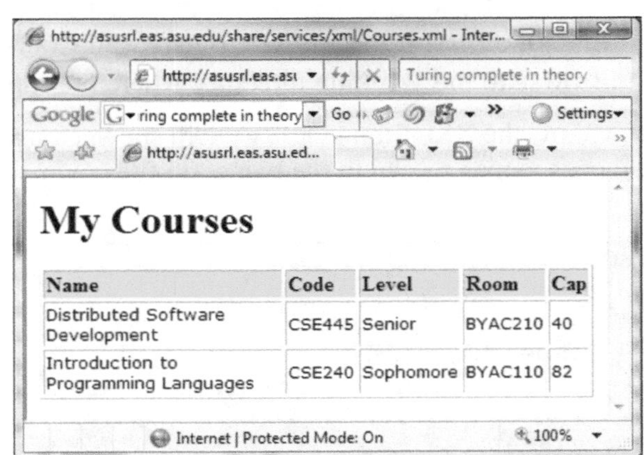

Figure 4.12. Displaying an XML document without and with style information

There are two potential problems with the client-side conversion approach of using a web browser:

- We need to modify the XML document to reference the xsl file;

- It is browser-dependent. Not all browsers and not all versions of browsers have an embedded XSLT processor. In some web pages, you read a note to indicate what browser or browser version is required to view the web page.

To ensure that your page can be displayed properly for all browsers, you need to program the conversion on your server side by writing an .aspx file using a program to do the conversion. .Net FCL provides a number of classes and methods to perform the translation. As an example, we will use the XSLCompiledTransform class to show the transformation code.

The following code takes two files (an XML file and an XSL file) in args[0] and args[1] as the command line input, and it will output the .html file to display the XML file.

```
using System;
using System.Xml.XPath;
using System.Xml.Xsl;
class MyXSLTApp {
    static void Main(string[] args) {
        if (args.Length < 2) {
            Console.WriteLine("Error: Files required not found");
            return;
        }
        try {
            XPathDocument doc = new XPathDocument(args[0]);
            XslCompiledTransform xslt = new XslCompiledTransform();
            xslt.Load(args[1]);
            xslt.Transform(doc, null, Console.Out);
        }
        catch (Exception ex) {
            Console.WriteLine(ex.Message);
        }
        string x = Console.ReadLine();
    }
}
```

To set up the command line input in .Net:

- Choose Visual Studio menu Project → Properties...;
- Click on Debugging tag → Command Arguments;
- Enter the files; for example, Courses.xml Courses.xsl, as the command line arguments;
- Browse to the Working directory where the files Courses.xml and Courses.xsl are located.

To better show the XSLT language, we will show a longer example of the XML and XSL files Fallacies.xml and Fallacies.xsl, as shown in the two code files.

```
<?xml version="1.0"?>
<Fallacies>
  <Fallacy>
    <Number>1</Number>
    <Text>The network is reliable.</Text>
    <Author>Bill Joy and Tom Lyon</Author>
  </Fallacy>
  <Fallacy>
    <Number>2</Number>
    <Text>Latency is zero.</Text>
    <Author>Bill Joy and Tom Lyon</Author>
  </Fallacy>
  <Fallacy>
    <Number>3</Number>
```

```
    <Text>Bandwidth is infinite.</Text>
    <Author>Bill Joy and Tom Lyon</Author>
  </Fallacy>
  <Fallacy>
    <Number>4</Number>
    <Text>The network is secure.</Text>
    <Author>Bill Joy and Tom Lyon</Author>
  </Fallacy>
  <Fallacy>
<Number>5</Number>
    <Text>Topology does not change.</Text>
    <Author>Peter Deutsch</Author>
  </Fallacy>
  <Fallacy>
    <Number>6</Number>
    <Text>There is one administrator.</Text>
    <Author>Peter Deutsch</Author>
  </Fallacy>
  <Fallacy>
    <Number>7</Number>
    <Text>Transport cost is zero.</Text>
    <Author>Peter Deutsch</Author>
  </Fallacy>
  <Fallacy>
    <Number>8</Number>
    <Text>The network is homogeneous.</Text>
    <Author>James Gosling</Author>
  </Fallacy>
</Fallacies>
```

The following XSL file defines how the Fallacies.xml should be displayed.

```
<?xml version="1.0"?>
<xsl:stylesheet xmlns:xsl="http://www.w3.org/1999/XSL/Transform" version="1.0">
  <xsl:template match="/">
    <html> <body>
        <h1 style="background-color: blue; color: white; font-size: 18pt; text-
align: center">
          Eight Fallacies in Distributed Computing
        </h1>
        <table border="1">
          <tr style="font-size: 12pt; font-family: verdana; font-weight: bold">
            <td style="text-align: center">Number</td>
            <td style="text-align: center">Fallacy</td>
            <td style="text-align: center">Author</td>
          </tr>
          <xsl:for-each select="Fallacies/Fallacy">
            <xsl:sort select="Number" />
            <tr style="font-size: 12pt; font-family: verdana">
              <td><i><xsl:value-of select="Number"/></i></td>
              <td><xsl:value-of select="Text"/></td>
              <td><xsl:value-of select="Author"/></td>
            </tr>
          </xsl:for-each>
        </table>
      </body> </html>
  </xsl:template>
```

```
</xsl:stylesheet>
```

Since the Fallacies.xml file contains multiple parallel data, the XSL uses a foreach loop to repeat the format.

4.6 Other Web Data Formats

XML is universal and standard for representing data on web. However, there are so many different types of data and resources on the web, which may be better represented in other formats and using other technologies. In the REST architecture to be discussed in Chapter 7, multiple data formats can be used to present the output of RESTful service invocation. Table 4.2 lists a few widely used web data formats that can be used in different situations.

Table 4.2. Web data formats for representing data and resources

Web formats	Description
XML	The premier format for defining data, protocol, and languages
HTML	The traditional format for representing web data and format
XHTML	Extended HTML 4.01 to conform with the XML format
RSS	RSS (Really Simple Syndication) for feed readers and web blogs
Atom	Atom extends RSS, and it is also used for representing feeds for feed readers and blog publishing. It has been used in wider context, including the REST architecture.
POX	Plain-Old-XML is used for representing SOAP data, which does not need the header information for complex processing.
JSON	JavaScript Object Notation is efficient for representing data processed or to be processed by a program, such as JavaScript.
Protocol buffers	Google's web data structure for search engine.
BigTable	Google's data structure for large database management.

4.6.1 XHTML

XHTML (eXtensible HTML) is a format defined to address the irregularity issues in HTML. It adds the DTD of XML into HTML to make HTML extensible and in XML format. XHTML allows three different ways to add a DTD file to define the tags and types in HTML:

1. Strict DTD: Enforce the structure by restricting to those tags defined in the DTD;
2. Transitional DTD: Allow all the depreciated features/tags to be migrated into the new page;
3. Frameset DTD: Same as Transitional DTD, but replaces the <body> with the <frame>, which allows developers to share the frames in multiple pages.

XHTML is extended from HTML 4.01. XHTML is used as the ASP .Net web page markup language. The pages generated from the ASPX page and sent to the client browsers are in XHTML format. For every GUI page (.APSX page) designed using the toolbox items, an XHTML page will be generated. Figure 4.13 shows a web application GUI design. In this GUI design, four buttons and three labels are defined using the items in the toolbox.

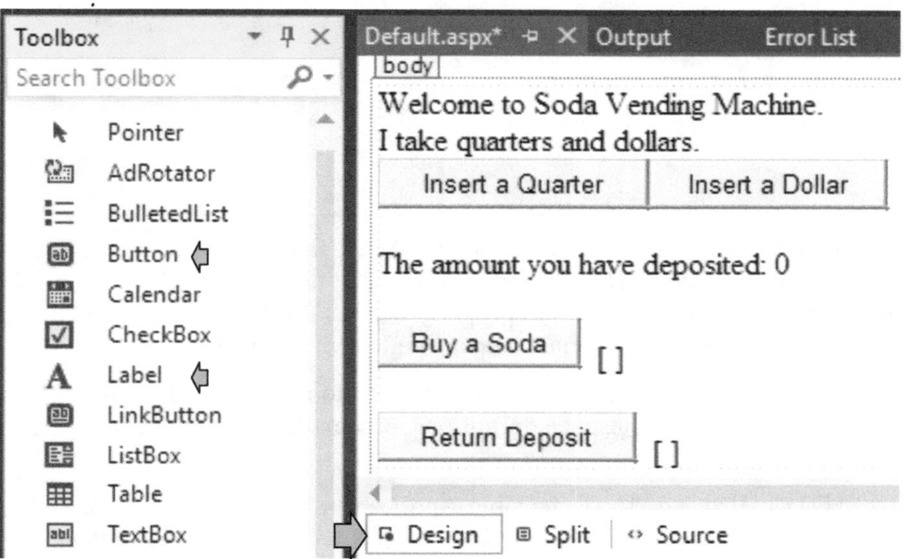

Figure 4.13. Website GUI design in the "Design" view

If we switch from the "Design" view to the "Source" view, the XHTML code below will be displayed. As can be seen, each of the buttons and labels is an element in the XHTML document. The document also contains other HTML elements that represent other data items in the GUI design. In fact, you can design and modify your web page interface either using the Design view interface in graphic format or using the source view interface in XHTML.

```
<%@ Page Language="C#" AutoEventWireup="true"  CodeFile="Default.aspx.cs"
Inherits="_Default" %>

<!DOCTYPE html PUBLIC "-//W3C//DTD XHTML 1.0 Transitional//EN"
"http://www.w3.org/TR/xhtml1/DTD/xhtml1-transitional.dtd">

<html xmlns="http://www.w3.org/1999/xhtml">
<head runat="server">
    <title>Vending Machine</title>
</head>
<body>
    <form id="form1" runat="server">
    <div>
        Welcome to Soda Vending Machine. <br />
        I take quarters and dollars.<br />
    </div>
    <asp:Button ID="Button1" runat="server" onclick="Button1_Click"
        Text="Insert a Quarter" />
    <asp:Button ID="Button2" runat="server" onclick="Button2_Click"
        Text="Insert a Dollar" />
    <p>
        The amount you have deposited:
        <asp:Label ID="lblAmount" runat="server" Text="0"></asp:Label>
    </p>
    <asp:Button ID="btnSoda" runat="server" onclick="Button3_Click"
        Text="Buy a Soda" />
    <asp:Label ID="lblSoda" runat="server" Text="[  ]"></asp:Label> <br />
    <br />
```

```
    <asp:Button ID="btnRtn" runat="server" onclick="Button4_Click"
        Text="Return Deposit" />
    <asp:Label ID="lblRtn" runat="server" Text="[          ]"></asp:Label>
    <br />
    </form>
</body>
</html>
```

The difference between XHTML and HTML is small. If you are familiar with HTML, you can write XHML code in the same way that you write HTML code, except you need to make sure that XHTML elements meet XML standard: all XHTML elements are properly nested; must always have a closing tag; and must be in lowercase. All XHTML documents must have a single root element.

As XHTML documents are XML documents, all the rules and tools discussed in this section can be applied to XHTML documents, including namespace definitions, processing of special characters, readers, writers, and XSL transformation.

An alternative to XHTL, called XAML (Extensible Application Markup Language), has been designed as a part of the Windows Presentation Foundation (WPF) and Silverlight to markup the GUI applications. It plays the same role as the XHTML does in ASP .Net GUI design, as we discussed above.

4.6.2 RSS

A **feed** is a data structure that contains a list of items (called entries). Each item is described by a few attributes, including the hyperlink and other information of the item, such as title and author. RSS is a language used to describe syndicated feed data. A number of RSS versions exist. An early version of RSS, **RSS** 1.0, stands for **RDF Site Summary**, which is defined using RDF (Resource Description Framework). RDF is an ontology language widely used in Semantic Web authoring. RSS 1.0 makes the syndicated feeds to become part of the Semantic Web. RDF and Semantic Web will be further discussed in Chapter 11 of the book.

RSS 2.0 stands for **Really Simple Syndication**, which is an XML-based format with a given schema that allows the syndication of collections of different data, including hyperlinks, metadata, and other types of data, such as text, date, addresses, and images. RSS 2.0 has been widely used for representing input and output data in a variety of web applications, including newsreader, web blogging, and RESTful services.

As an XML document, RSS 2.0 is fully defined by an XML schema. The basic elements (incomplete) of the XML schema are given below:

```
<xs:schema xmlns:xs="http://www.w3.org/2001/XMLSchema"
          elementFormDefault="unqualified" version="2.0.2.16">
  <xs:element name="rss">
    <xs:complexType>
      <xs:sequence>
        <xs:element name="channel" type="RssChannel"/>
      </xs:sequence>
      <xs:attribute name="version" type="xs:decimal" use="required" fixed="2.0"/>
    </xs:complexType>
  </xs:element>
  <xs:complexType name="RssItem">
    <xs:sequence>
      <xs:choice maxOccurs="unbounded">
        <xs:element name="title" type="xs:string" minOccurs="0">
        </xs:element>
        <xs:element name="description" type="xs:string" minOccurs="0">
        </xs:element>
        <xs:element name="link" type="xs:anyURI" minOccurs="0">
        </xs:element>
```

```
        <xs:element name="author" type="EmailAddress" minOccurs="0">
        </xs:element>
        <xs:element name="category" type="Category" minOccurs="0">
        </xs:element>
        <xs:element name="pubDate" type="Rfc822FormatDate" minOccurs="0">
        </xs:element>
        <xs:element name="source" type="Source" minOccurs="0">
        </xs:element>
      </xs:choice>
    </xs:sequence>
  </xs:complexType>
  <xs:complexType name="RssChannel">
    <xs:sequence>
      <xs:choice maxOccurs="unbounded">
        <xs:element name="title" type="xs:string">
        </xs:element>
        <xs:element name="link" type="xs:anyURI">
        </xs:element>
        <xs:element name="description" type="xs:string">
        <xs:element name="copyright" type="xs:string" minOccurs="0">
        <xs:element name="webMaster" type="EmailAddress" minOccurs="0">
        <xs:element name="pubDate" type="Rfc822FormatDate" minOccurs="0">
        <xs:element name="image" type="Image" minOccurs="0">
      </xs:choice>
      <xs:element name="item" type="RssItem" minOccurs="1" maxOccurs="unbounded">
      </xs:element>
    </xs:sequence>
    <xs:anyAttribute namespace="##any"/>
  </xs:complexType>
  <!-- other elements are omitted. For more details see
  http://www.rss-specification.com/rss-2.0-specification.htm
  and http://www.thearchitect.co.uk/schemas/rss-2_0.xsd
  -->
</xs:schema>
```

The part of the schema defines a few key elements, including two complex types of structures:

- rss: root element. The root element consists of one or more RssChannel-type child elements.
- RssChannel: a complex type defined by a number of optional string-type elements and one or more RssItem elements. The optional string-type elements include title, link, description, copyright, webmaster, pubDate, and image.
- RssItem: a complex type defined by a number of optional string-type elements, including title, description, link, author, category, pubDate, and source.

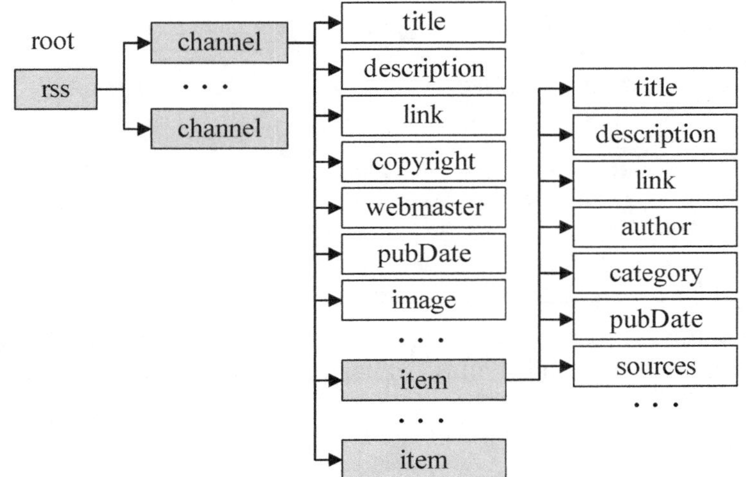

Figure 4.14. Tree view of the RSS structure

Figure 4.14 shows the tree view of the RSS elements, where the shaded elements are containers with sub-elements.

An instance document that complies with the aforesaid RSS schema follows:

```
<?xml version="1.0"?>
<rss version="2.0">
  <channel>
    <title>Computer Science Books</title>
    <link>http://mylibrary.asu.edu/</link>
     <description>
        This example will be further discussed in RESTful service design
        in Chapter 7 of the book.
     </description>
    <item>
       <title>Operating Systems</title>
       <link>http://mylibrary.asu.edu/authors/{author=Aaron}</link>
       <description>Operating system design and analysis</description>
       <author>aaronauthor@asu.edu</author>
    </item>
    <item>
       <title>Compilers</title>
       <link> http://mylibrary.asu.edu/years/{year=1999}</link>
    </item>
    <item>
       <title>Algorithm Analysis and Design</title>
       <author>zetaauthor@asu.edu</author>
    </item>
  </channel>
  <channel>
    <title>My Books</title>
    <link>http://mylibrary.asu.edu/</link>
    <item>
       <title>Programming Languages</title>
       <link>
http://www.kendallhunt.com/index.cfm?PID=219&AUT=&ISB=0757503675&DIS=0&GRA=0&DES=&MT
C=exact&BOOL=AND&KEY=&PPS=25&SRT=rank&CMD=detail&SRH=&PRD=1231
       </link>
       <description>
          Introduce different programming paradigms and program techniques
       </description>
       <author>yinong.chen@asu.edu</author>
    </item>
    <item>
       <title>Service-Oriented Computing and Web Data Management</title>
       <link>http://www.public.asu.edu/~ychen10/book/socwdm.html</link>
    </item>
  </channel>
</rss>
```

An online RSS and Atom (next section) validator that checks the instance document against its XML schema can be found at https://validator.w3.org/feed/.

4.6.3 Atom

RSS 2.0 widely used for representing feed data for its simplicity. On the other hand, it is a really simple syndication, which does not have many features that today's feed data desires to have. Furthermore, there are frequent reports with the interoperability problems with different readers and protocols. **Atom** is a more recent language designed to describe feed data with more features and with improved structure. Figure 4.15 gives the tree view of the Atom elements and attributes in XML syntax. The official specification is defined at (http://www.ietf.org/rfc/rfc4287.txt). The root element of an Atom document is <feed>, and thus, an Atom document is also called an **Atom feed** document. Atom specification allows each <entry> element to be an independent document called Atom entry document.

An instance document that complies with the RSS schema above is given below.

If we compare and contrast Figure 4.14 and Figure 4.15, we can see that RSS and Atom contain similar information. The key differences include:

- RSS has one additional layer of elements called <channel>. An RSS document allows multiple channel elements, with each channel element equivalent to an Atom feed document.
- Most of the noncontainer elements of RSS are of string types, while Atom's noncontainer elements allow more flexibility in associating with different types of data; for example, the <content> element can contain language-specific data structure.
- Atom has introduced many automated features such as autoupdate that automatically adds timestamp when a feed is changed; autodiscovery for clients who know the URI of a web page to find the location of that page's associated Atom feed automatically; and a "self" pointer, with which a newsreader can auto-subscribe given only the content of the feed, based on web-standard dispatching techniques.

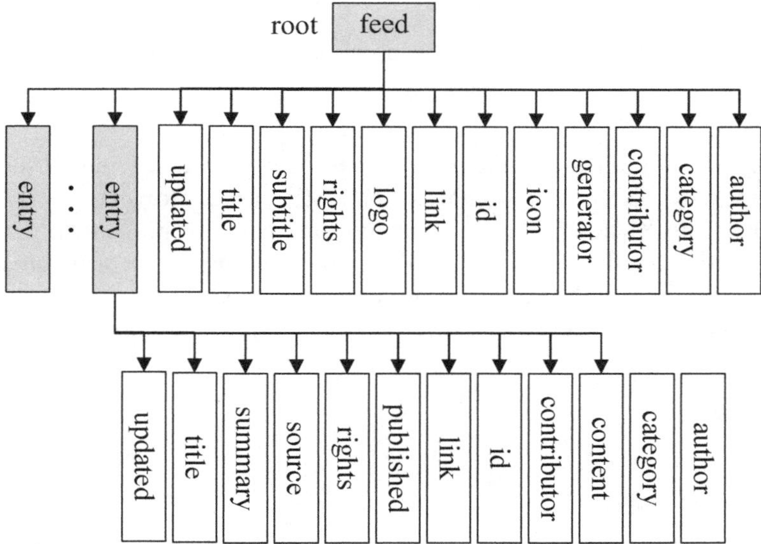

Figure 4.15. Tree view of the Atom feed structure

An example of the Atom feed document follows:

```
<?xml version="1.0" encoding="utf-8"?>
<feed xmlns="http://www.w3.org/2005/Atom">

  <title> Computer Science Books </title>
  <link href=" http://mylibrary.asu.edu/"/>
  <updated>2010-05-15T14:31:05Z</updated>
  <author>
    <name>Aaron Smith</name>
  </author>
  <id>urn:uuid:123456bf-a321-327b-4567-0014431a67e3</id>
  <entry>
```

```
    <title>Operating Systems</title>
    <subtitle type="html">Unix and Windows explored</subtitle>
    <id>urn:uuid: 345678ac-123d-b2467-9a71-000ab345e9f0</id>
    <author>
      <name> Aaron Smith</name>
      <uri>
         href="http://mylibrary.asu.edu/authors/{author=Aaron Smith}/
      </uri>
      <email> aaronauthor@asu.edu </email>
    </author>
    <contributor>
      <name>Ann Miller</name>
    </contributor>
    <updated>2010-04-18T08:24:19Z</updated>
    <summary>A new way of teaching operating systems</summary>
  </entry>
  <entry>
    ...
  </entry>
</feed>
```

RSS and Atom data can be processed using .Net FCL library functions. MSDN listed different ways of processing these data, as discussed in the reference:

https://msdn.microsoft.com/en-us/library/cc296253(v=vs.95).aspx

4.6.4 JSON

JSON (JavaScript Object Notation) is another data representation format widely used in web services and web applications [http://www.json.org/]. JSON is not XML-based. However, it is of text format and is language independent. Like XML, JSON data structures are easy for humans to read and write and easy for machines to parse and generate. JSON is based on programming object structures, and it is convenient for developers who are familiar with programming languages, such as C, C++, C#, Java, and JavaScript. Figure 4.16 shows the definitions of the key data structures in syntax graphs.

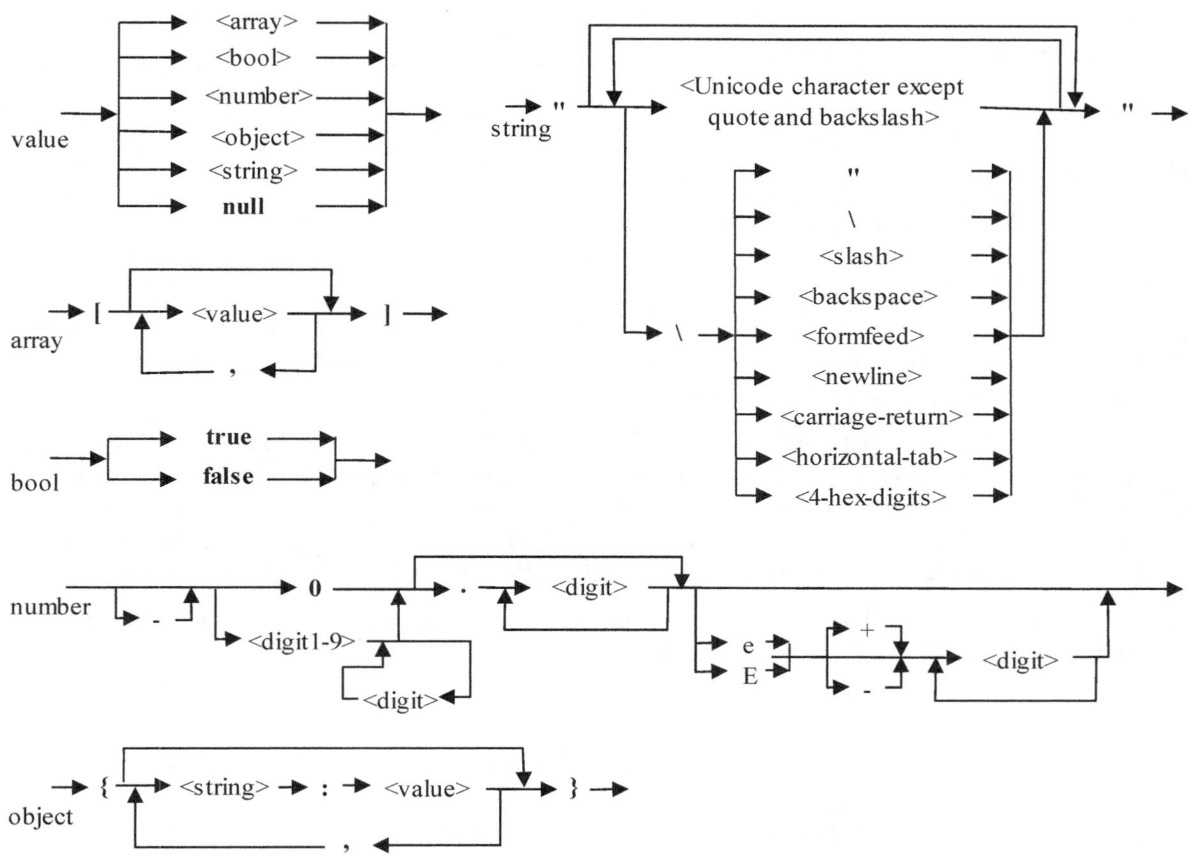

Figure 4.16. JSON data structure definitions

JSON values have three primary data types: number, string, and boolean; two collection types: array and objects; and null value.

A string is a sequence of zero or more Unicode characters, wrapped in double quotes. It is similar to the strings used in most programming langauges. Special characters in a string must be prefixed as a backslash character. JSON does not have a different character type. It is represented as a single character string.

An array is an ordered list values, separated by comma, where the values can be of any types and their combinations. For example, a list of strings ["John Doe," "Marry," "Smith"], a list of arrays (an array of arrays) [[1, 2, 3, 4], [2, 3, 4, 5], [5, 2, 3, 5]], and a list of mixed types of values [{"John Doe" :25}, {"Marry":30}, "Smith," 20, true].

An object is an unordered set of string:value pairs; for example:

{"name" : "John Doe", "age" : 25, "married" : true, "University" : "ASU", "Graduated" : false, "Courses" : {"CSE240" : 200,"CSE310" : 300,"CSE446" : 400, "GPA" : 3.75}}

JSON data can be easily processed using library .Net FCL library functions. MSDN listed different classes for loading and processing JSON data in similar ways as we discussed in XML sections, as discussed in the reference:

https://msdn.microsoft.com/en-us/library/cc197957(v=vs.95).aspx

The following code use JsonArray class to load data from a responseStream, and then use these LINQ library to query and process JsonArray.

```
JsonArray users = (JsonArray)JsonArray.Load(responseStream);
var members =from member in users
       where member["IsMember"]
       select member;
foreach (JsonObject member in members) {
   string name = member["Name"];
   int age = member["Age"];
   // Do something...
}
```

LINQ (Language Integrated Query) is a query language for data objects, database, and XML files, and it is discussed in full detail in Chapter 10 of the book.

There are independent tools that help create JSON-based applications. For example, the tool at the website http://json2csharp.com/ can create C# classes based on the JSON data model you paste in. Another website, https://jsonlint.com/, among other functions, can help you validate your JSON objects. We will use the following Microsoft document as an example to install the JSON processing tool Newtonsoft.Json NuGet package: https://docs.microsoft.com/en-us/nuget/quickstart/install-and-use-a-package-in-visual-studio

To add NuGet packages into Visual Studio, right-click project name and choose Manage NuGet Package, as shown in Figure 4.17.

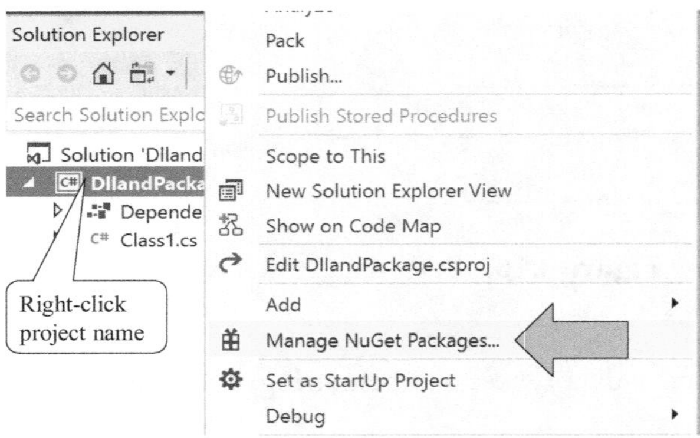

Figure 4.17. Add NuGet packages into Visual Studio

Then, choose the package that you want to install. We will install Newtonsoft.Json NuGet package, as shown in Figure 4.18.

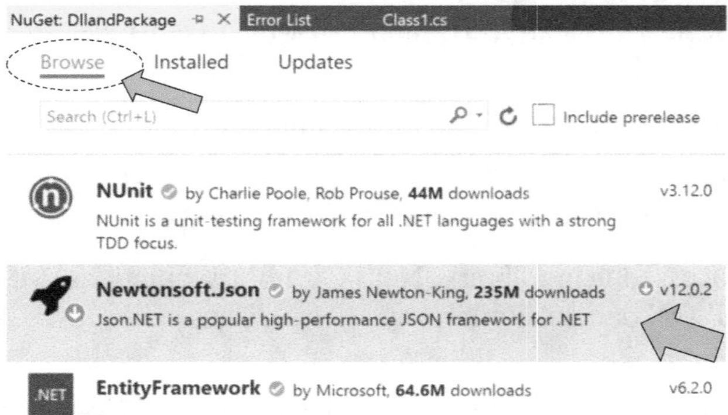

Figure 4.18. Add Newtonsoft.Json NuGet package into Visual Studio

Next, in Visual Studio Tools menu, choose NuGet Package Manger and choose Package Manger Console, as shown in Figure 4.19

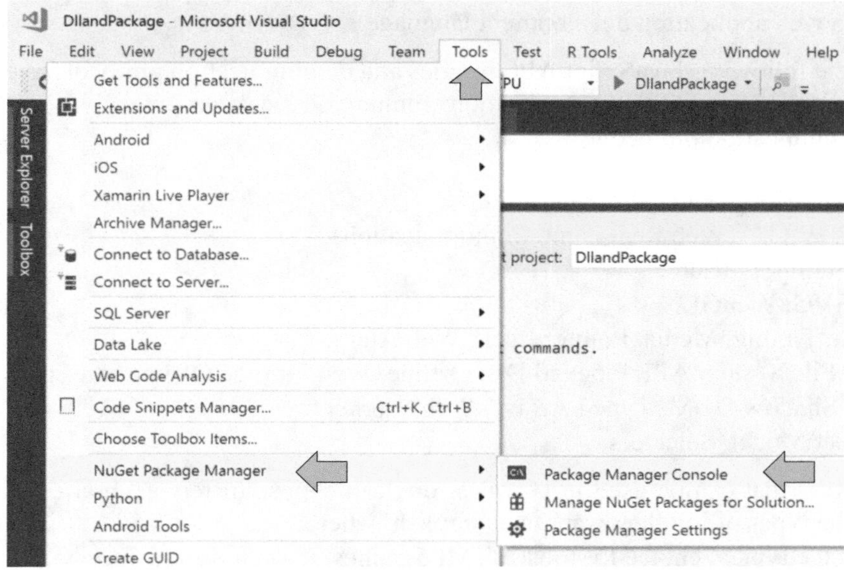

Figure 4.19. Open Package Manager Console

The console window will open as shown in Figure 4.20. From the drop-down list, select the project that you want to use the package. Enter the command: Install-Package Newtonsoft.Json

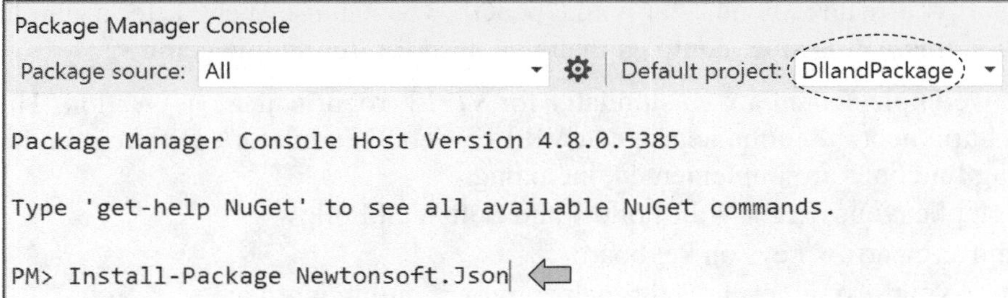

Figure 4.20. Package Manager Console

The package is now installed and you can use the functions in Newtonsoft.Json. You can follow the document at https://docs.microsoft.com/en-us/nuget/quickstart/install-and-use-a-package-in-visual-studio to use the JSON processing functions through the reference using Newtonsoft.Json.

4.6.5 HTML5

A brief development time of HTML and related technologies is listed as follows:

- 1991 HTML
- 1994 HTML2
- 1996 CSS1 + JavaScript
- 1997 HTML4
- 1998 CSS2
- 2000 XHTML, HTML comply to XML format
- 2005 AJAX, Asynchronous JavaScript And XML
- 2008 XAML = XHTML + CSS + AJAX + Silverlight, where animation can be programmed.

- 2009 HTML5= HTML + CSS + JavaScript / JQuery, where animation can be programmed.

Like XHTML, HTML5 is an HTML with a document type definition. By including JavaScript API calls, HTML5 become a web application development language.

HTML5 can use the following JavaScript API libraries and communication protocols to communicate with the other web applications and with the applications running on local computer:

- Web communication protocols:
    - Web Sockets
    - Messaging, and
    - WebRTC (Web Real-Time Communication)
- Drag and Drop, Fullscreen
- Canvas, SVG, WebGL
- Animation Timing, Media, Pointer Lock, Web Audio
- File API, File System API, Indexed DB, Offline, Web Storage Offline and Storage
- Browser, Shadow DOM, Typed Arrays, Web Workers
- CSS Object Model, Selectors

For the graphic APIs that can be used in HTML5, one can choose different libraries based on their skill background and the types of job they want to acomplish, where:

- Canvas is the typical choice for most HTML5 games. It's simple and speedy, particularly for games with many objects.
- SVG: While canvas provides simplicity and speed, SVG provides flexibility. For example: Each graphic object is part of the DOM tree for flexible access, and each graphic object in the game can have one or more associated event handlers for process.
- WebGL: If you're already familiar with OpenGL, you can use WebGL for a simple 2D game. If you're not, this API is more complex than you need for this simple game.

As an example, we implemented a web simulator for VIPLE robot's maze navivation. The simulator can be accessed at: http://neptune.fulton.ad.asu.edu/VIPLE/Web2DSimulator/. Different animation functions and programming functions are implemented, including:

- Sample applications: Right Wall Follow and Left Wall Follow
- Robot move by arrow keys on keyboard
- Implement your own algorithms through an programming interface

Figure 4.21 shows the Web 2D simulator implemented in HTML5. To test the simulator using a built-in program, simply click the button "Left Wall Follow" or "Right Wall Follow". You can also implement your own algorithm.

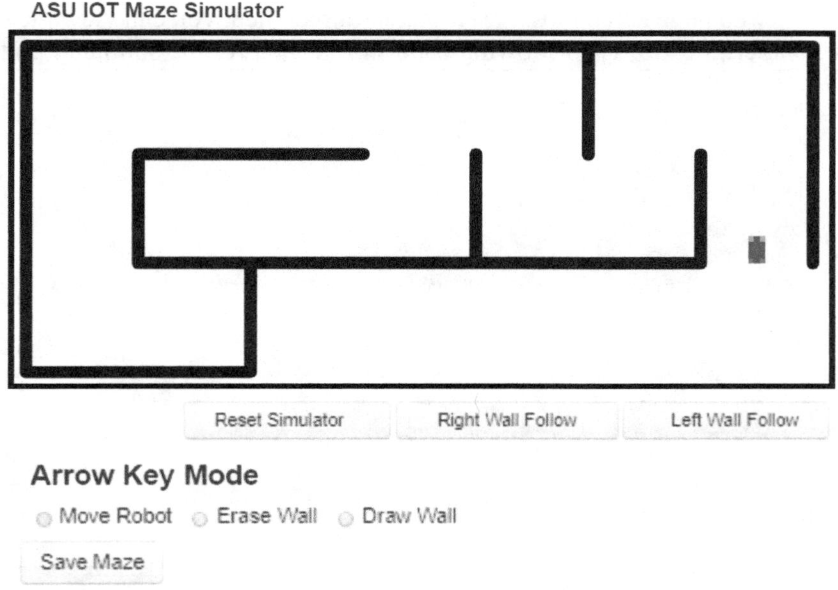

Figure 4.21. Web simulator implemented in HTML5: built-in tools

Figure 4.22 shows the programming tool on the web simulator page. A two-distance algorithm is shown in the figure. The algorithm instruct the robot to move forward until the distance is less than 30 pixels. Then, it tests the distance on the left and right sides. The robot turns to the side with longer distance. You can test your code by clicking the Run button. You can also implement "Left Wall Follow" or "Right Wall Follow" algorithms.

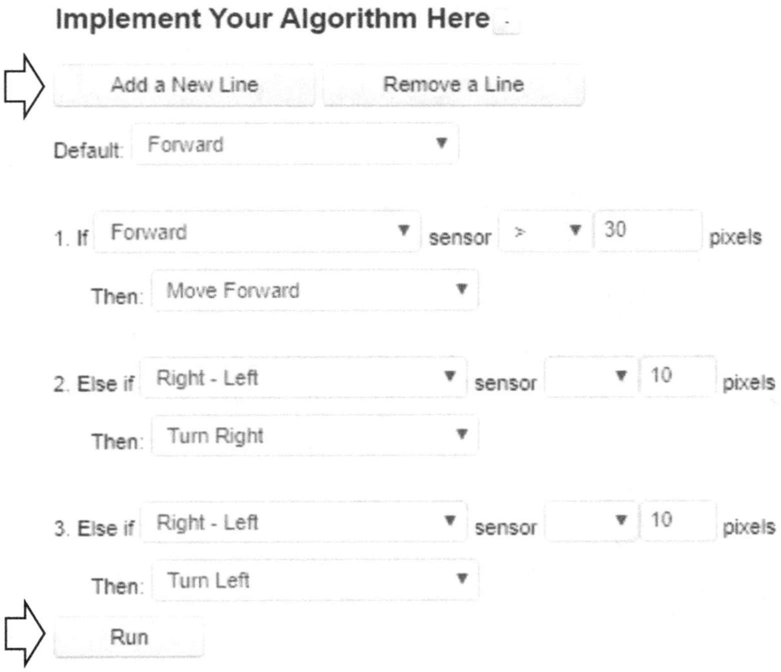

Implement Your Algorithm Here

Add a New Line | Remove a Line

Default: Forward

1. If Forward sensor > 30 pixels
   Then: Move Forward

2. Else if Right - Left sensor 10 pixels
   Then: Turn Right

3. Else if Right - Left sensor 10 pixels
   Then: Turn Left

Run

Figure 4.22. Web simulator implemented in HTML5: programming part

You can right-click the web page and choose View Page Source, then, you can view the entire source code in HTML5 and its JavaScript code. The following code shows a part of the simulator code.

```
<!DOCTYPE html>
<html lang="en">
<head>
    <meta charset="utf-8">
    <link rel="icon" type="image/png" sizes="32x32" href="favicon.png">
    <title>Robot Maze Simulator</title>
    <!-- Bootstrap Core CSS -->
    <link href="css/bootstrap.min.css" rel="stylesheet">
    <!-- Custom CSS -->
    <link href="css/modern-business.css" rel="stylesheet">
    <!-- Custom Fonts -->
    <link href="font-awesome/css/font-awesome.min.css" type="text/css">
    <!-- HTML5 Shim and Respond.js IE8 support of HTML5 elements -->
    <!-- WARNING: Respond.js doesn't work if you view the page via file:// -->
        <script
src="https://oss.maxcdn.com/libs/html5shiv/3.7.0/html5shiv.js"></script>
        <script
src="https://oss.maxcdn.com/libs/respond.js/1.4.2/respond.min.js"></script>
    <![endif]-->
    <script type="text/javascript">
        function zoom() {
            document.body.style.zoom = "75%"
        }
    </script>
    <style>
        p { text-indent: 25px; }
    </style>
</head>
<body onload="zoom()">
    <!-- Header Carousel -->
    <!-- Page Content -->
    <div class="container">
        <!-- Marketing Icons Section -->
        <div class="row">
            <div class="col-lg-12">
                <h1 class="page-header" style="padding-left: 40px; 40px;">
                    ASU IOT Maze Simulator
                </h1>
                <!-- BEGIN MAZE CODE -->
                <div style="padding-left: 40px; padding-right: 40px;
position:relative; width:1450px; height:700px;">
                    <canvas id="mazecanvas" style="z-index: 0; position: absolute;
left:0px; top:0px; border: 10px solid black" width="1450" height="640">Can't load
the simulator, because your browser doesn't support HTML5.</canvas>
                    <canvas id="robot" style="z-index: 1; position: absolute; left:
0px; top: 0px;" width="1450" height="640"></canvas>
                </div>
                    function reset() {
                        currRectX = 1315;
                        currRectY = 380;
                        mazeWidth = 1450;
                        mazeHeight = 640;
                        rHeight = 50;
                        rWidth = 30;
                        rTemp = 0;
```

```
                //mazeImg = new Image();
                //mazeImg.src = "mazebold.jpg"
                leftWheelPower = 0;
                rightWheelPower = 0;
                heading = 0;
                accuLeft = 0;
                accuRight = 0;
                newX = currRectX;
                newY = currRectY;
                // cancel turning animation
                clearInterval(rotationInterval);
                var resetSpaceStatus = readPixelDataForReset();
                if(resetSpaceStatus == "whiteSquare") {
                  // reset angle
                  angle = 0;
                  // draw AFTER angle
                  drawRectangleToRobotCanvas();
                }
                // Remove distance readings
                while (document.getElementById("testing").hasChildNodes()) {

               document.getElementById("testing").removeChild(document.
                    getElementById("testing").lastChild);
                }
                if (isConnectedWS) {
                    closeWSConnection();
                }
                //End auto movement
                var highestTimeoutId = setTimeout(";");
                while (highestTimeoutId--) {
                    clearTimeout(highestTimeoutId);
                }
                    document.getElementById("driveRadio").checked = true;
                    setDriveMode();
            }
```

The simulator can also be used with ASU VIPLE (Visual IoT/Robotics Programming Language Environment) to implement more complex algorithms, The topic will be further discussed in Chapter 9.

4.6.6 Google Protocol Buffers and BigTable

Google uses a different data representation in its search engine. The amount of data is huge and encoding and decoding times are critical. Even a small addition can be amplified into large delay at the end. Google uses a data structure called **protocol buffers**, which is not XML-based. Google claims that, compared to XML and XML schema, protocol buffers are simpler and faster: 3 to 10 times smaller in presenting the same information and 20 to 100 times faster in processing; and protocol buffers generate data structures that are similar to object-oriented classes and thus are easier to use programmatically. As protocol buffers do not comply with the XML standard, they are less flexible and adaptable. The following example shows representing data in protocol buffers:

```
message Person {
   required string name = 1;
   required int32 id = 2;
   optional string email = 3;
   enum PhoneType {
        WORK = 0;
        HOME = 1;
```

```
        MOBILE = 2;
    }
    message PhoneNumber {
        required string number = 1;
        optional PhoneType type = 2 [default = WORK];
    }
    repeated PhoneNumber phone = 4;
}
```

The presentation of the same information above can be represented in XML as follows:

```
<element name = Person>
   <complexType>
     <sequence>
        <element name = "Id" type="integer" minOccurs="1" maxOccurs="1"/>
        <element name = "Name" type="string" minOccurs="1" maxOccurs="1"/>
        <element name = "Email" type="string" minOccurs="0" maxOccurs="1"/>
        <element name = "Phone" type="string" minOccurs="1" maxOccurs="1"/>
     </sequence>
   </complexType>
</element>
<element name = "Phone" >
   <simpleType>
     <restriction base = "string" >
        <enumeration value = "Work" type=minOccurs="1" maxOccurs="1"/>
        <enumeration value = "Home" minOccurs="0" maxOccurs="1"/>
        <enumeration value = "Mobile" minOccurs="0" maxOccurs="1"/>
     </restriction>
   </simpleType></element >
```

Google's database for the search engine, BigTable, also uses a unique design. The BigTable is a fast and extremely large-scale database management system. It is a compressed, high-performance, and proprietary database system built on Google File System (GFS). It departs from the convention of relational database, with a fixed number of columns. The database is "a sparse, distributed multi-dimensional sorted map." The idea is similar to the B+ Tree that allows for efficient insertion, retrieval, and removal of nodes. It is a tree. It represents sorted data in a way that allows for efficient insertion, retrieval, and removal of records, each of which is identified by a key. It is a dynamic, multilevel index, with maximum and minimum bounds on the number of keys in each index node.

In a B+ tree, in contrast to a B- tree, all records are stored at the lowest level of the tree. Only keys are stored in interior blocks. The presorted data index helps to search and retrieve information quickly from the large file system. More details about Google Cloud Platform, Google BigTable, and Google File System can be found in Chapter 11.

4.7 Discussions

XML and related technologies are used to represent data as well as languages and protocols used in service-oriented software development. This chapter discussed major technologies related to XML definition, type definition, processing, validation, and transformation. XML and related technologies are so important in web services and web applications that web services are also called XML services. Other frequently used web data formats include RSS, Atom, and JSON.

There are many other XML extensions and applications that are not discussed in this chapter. HTML5 is the latest HTML version, which is the successor to HTML4 and XHTL. One of the significant extensions in HTML5 is the ability to markup multimedia, graphical contents, and animation. It is considered a competing technology with the current Adobe Flash and Microsoft Silverlight.

In Chapter 7, we will discuss applications of XML, RSS, and JSON in connection with REST architecture and RESTful services. We will also discuss the XAML (Extensible Application Markup Language), which takes the place of XHTML used as the markup language in ASP .Net. XMAL is used as the markup language in Windows Communications Foundation, Workflow Foundation, Windows Presentation Foundation, and Silverlight. In Chapter 8, we will study the XML-based languages and protocols, including BPEL and OWL-S. Even in the robotics applications discussed in Chapter 9, XML plays an important role in representing the data and the manifests that interfacing the services with the concrete devices connected to robot hardware. In Chapter 10, we will discuss the XML-based database and their query languages. In Chapter 11, we will present ontology languages RDF, RDFS, and OWL. All of them are defined in XML and XML schema.

Name: ______________________

Date: ______________________

4.8 Exercises and Projects

1. Multiple choice questions. Choose one answer in each question only. Choose the best answer if multiple answers are acceptable.

1.1 What is required for a well-formed XML document?

(A) There is a unique root element.

(B) Each element is quoted between an open and a closing tag.

(C) There are no overlapped tags.

(D) All of the above.

1.2 An XML document can be best illustrated by a

(A) complete graph. (B) binary tree.

(C) rooted tree. (D) star structure.

1.3 Where can an attribute be placed in an XML document?

(A) Between any pair of elements.

(B) Inside the opening tag of an element.

(C) Inside the closing tag of an element.

(D) Before the first element or after the last element.

1.4 What are CDATA and PCDATA in an XML document?

(A) CDATA contains nonprintable characters only, while PCDATA contains printable characters only.

(B) PCDATA contains nonprintable characters only, while CDATA contains printable characters only.

(C) CDATA contains digits only, while PCDATA contains letters only.

(D) CDATA will not be checked for syntax errors by XML parsers, while PCDATA will be checked for syntax errors.

1.5 What XML processing model reads the entire XML document into the memory?

(A) DOM (Document Object Model) (B) SAX (Simple API for XML)

(C) XMLTextReader (D) XMLTextWriter

1.6 What .Net class contains the method to obtain the root element of an XML document?

(A) XmlDocument class (B) XmlNode class

(C) XmlTextReader class (D) XmlTextWriter Class

1.7 What .Net class contains the method called WriteElementString?

(A) XmlDocument class (B) XmlNode class

(C) XmlTextReader class (D) XmlTextWriter class

1.8 A Document Type Definition file

(A) follows XML syntax.

(B) is used to define the structure of an XML file.

(C) is used to define the structure of an XML schema file.

(D) extends the C# XmlDocument class.

1.9 What does the following line of code in a DTD file mean?

```
<!ELEMENT instructor (name, course+, officeHours*, phone | email)>
```

(A) The XML instance file must have an element <course>

(B) The XML instance file must have an element <officeHours>

(C) The XML instance file must have an element <phone>

(D) All of the above

1.10 Why do we need to invent XML Schema after DTD has been invented?

(A) DTD cannot be used to validate the syntax of XML files.

(B) A DTD file must be embedded in the XML file and cannot be placed externally.

(C) DTD cannot define child elements.

(D) DTD does not follow XML syntax.

1.11 What is the purpose of defining a default namespace in an XML file?

(A) To introduce a new element that has not been defined in other namespaces.

(B) To reduce the number of namespace qualifiers prefixed to the element names.

(C) To define a new type instantly.

(D) To override an existing namespace.

1.12 What data format is not typically supported by RESTful services?

(A) Atom (B) JSON (C) SOAP (D) XML

1.13 What type of file does the following piece of code most likely belong to?

```
<Book>
        <Title>Introduction to Programming Languages</Title>
        <Author>Yinong Chen</Author>
        <Year>2006</Year>
        <ISBN>0-7575-2974-7</ISBN>
</Book>
```

(A) Document Type Definition file (B) XML Schema file

(C) XML instance file (D) XML namespace file

1.14 An attribute within an element

(A) is always implicitly qualified by the namespace-qualifier of the element.

(B) is implicitly qualified by the default namespace only.

(C) is never implicitly qualified by the qualifier of the element.

(D) (A) and (B).

1.15 The Extensible Stylesheet Language Transformations (XSLT) can be used to transform an XML file to

(A) an HTML file, but not to another XML file.

(B) another XML file, but the tree structure cannot be changed.

(C) another XML file, with the same or a different structure.

(D) None of the above.

1.16 Where are RSS and Atom feeds currently used?

(A) Input and output of VIPLE applications

(B) Input and output of RESTful services

(C) Input and output of BPEL services

(D) Input and output of assembly language programs

1.17 What is not a new feature implemented in Atom?

(A) Three-level tree structure.

(B) Allow autoupdate.

(C) Allow autodiscovery.

(D) Copyright information.

2. What is XML? What are XML elements and attributes?

3. How are the special markup characters presented in XML files? What are CDATA and PCDATA? What are their differences? What is the difference between entity reference and CDATA?

4. What is an XML namespace? Why is it useful? How is a namespace defined?

5. What are DOM, SAX, and XPath models? List their strengths and weaknesses. What .Net FCL classes and methods exist for reading and writing XML files?

6. Compare and contrast XML DTD and XML XSD. What .Net FCL classes and methods exist for validating XML files?

7. Compare and contrast HTML, XML, XSD, and XSL. Why is XSLT useful? What .Net FCL classes and methods exist for transforming XML files into HTML files?

8. Compare and contrast RSS and Atom feeds. What are their similarities and differences? Where are they being used?

9. Define an XML schema for the database for storing contact information, consisting of name, phone, e-mail, and address. Based on the schema, write a C# program in Windows application to create an XML database of contact information. You can make use of the available XML classes in .Net FCL.

   a. Define a graphic interface that allows users to (1) enter the contact information; (2) search the database by name; (3) list all entries and sort them by name; and (4) delete an entry.

   b. Write an addEntry method that adds a new set of contact information.

   c. Write a deleteEntry method that deletes an entry for the given name and (phone number or e-mail).

d. Write a searchName method to search the database and display the contact information if the entry is found.

e. Write a listAll method to display all the contact information stored in the database. The information must be sorted by name.

f. Write a saveFile method to save the XML tree into disk as an XML file. This method should be called before the quitting the application.

g. Write a validateSchema method that validates an XML file against the given XML schema.

h. Write a loadFile method to load an XML file into memory as an XML tree. Before loading the XML, the validateSchema method must be called to make sure that the file to be loaded complies with the given XML schema.

10. Use a subset (at least 10 courses) of the university's courses offered to create a course web page.

    a. Define a structure (tree) that well depicts the relations among the courses. Write the Courses.xsd file that defines the schema based on the structure tree.

    b. Create an XML file Courses.xml for storing course information, and enter the selected course information into the Courses.xml file.

    c. Write a C# program in Windows application that takes the Courses.xml and Courses.xsd as input, validates the correctness of the XML files against the Courses.xsd, and prints (traverses) the tree in preorder.

    d. Write the Courses.xsl file that defines the HTML style for web display. You can make your own design to display the page in the best readable way.

    e. Write an .aspx file with embedded C# program to convert the Courses.xml, using Courses.xsd as the style sheet, into an HTML page.

    f. Write a Windows or a web application that allows a user to add a new course into the Courses.xml file and delete a course from the Courses.xml file.

Project

The diagram in Figure 4.23 shows the structure of the XML file and an instance under this structure. Note that different shapes of boxes have different meanings.

1 Write the Courses.xsd file that defines the XML schema specified in the structure shown in the diagram. You can use any tool to edit the file.

2. Create an XML file Courses.xml for storing course information. Use the latest university class schedule to find at least five (5) CSE courses, and enter the course information into the Courses.xml file. You can use any tool to edit the file.

3. Write the Courses.xsl file that defines the HTML style for displaying the courses in Courses.xml in a formatted table. You can use any tool to edit the file.

4. Write C# web services that take the URL of an XML (.xml) file, the URL of the corresponding XMLS (.xsd) file, and the URL of the XSL file as inputs, respectively. The web services will perform two functions (web methods):

(1) Validate the XML file against the corresponding XMLS (XSD) file and return "No Error" or error message.

(2) Generate the HTML file based on the XML and XSL files. The generated HTML file must be stored in a text file or in a .htm (or .html) file.

5 Create a Windows application with a GUI, which allows entering the three URLs, and with two buttons, which activate the validation of the XML file against the schema file and generate the HTML file, respectively. The application must use the web services created in the previous step to perform the required processing, and display the return message in the GUI.

6 Testing: Place the three files Courses.xml, Courses.xsd, and Courses.xsl, into a website and use them to test your program. For this question, you must submit (1) a screenshot of the GUI with the output of the XML validation displayed in the GUI, and (2) The Courses.htm file (or Courses.html) file generated. After testing, make sure you remove these files from the website. Make sure the students in the same class will not see your assignment before the submission due date. When the teaching assistant grades the assignment, they will place the files in a different location.

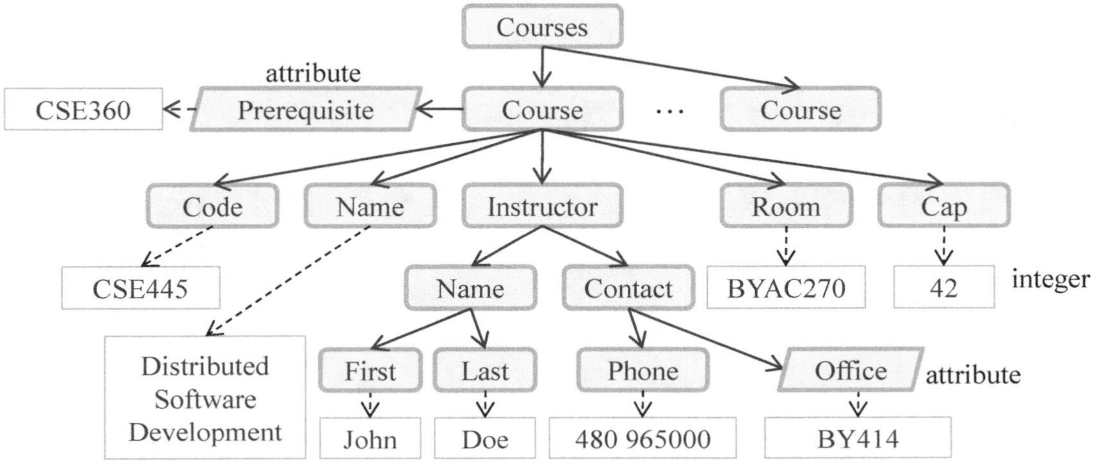

Figure 4.23. Tree representation of an XML file

Chapter 5
Web Application and State Management

A traditional desktop application has a unique entry point and the entire application is typically compiled into a standalone executable file. An application can consist of many classes and files, and a project file is used to organize them into a well-defined application domain. On the other hand, a web application can consist of multiple web pages and other files. One can enter a web application from any page, even a home or default page, which suggests the most logical entry point to start with. Web applications are often event-driven to better accommodate their interactive nature. As web services and HTTP protocol are stateless, state management in web applications is a critical issue and completely different techniques have to be applied in contrast to those used in object-oriented software development.

This chapter will focus on building web applications using existing web services available on the Internet as well as local components created within the application domain. We start with the execution models of web-based applications.

5.1 Models of Web Applications

Web applications refer to the web pages with computing capacities. In the first generation of the web, HTML was the only language supported by the browsers, while later browsers supported many more languages, including many scripting languages and other methods of computing. The increasing capacities of web technologies led to different web application models.

5.1.1 Pure HTML-Based Web Application

Pure HTML web page does not support computing. However, it provides a number of methods and forms, such as GET, POST, PUT, HEAD, and DELETE, for sending data to and receiving data from the server. For example, the following code allows a user to enter data and operation and send the data to the server for computing.

```
<html>
   <body>
      <form>
            <input type="text" name="operand1" VALUE="number" />
            <input type="text" name="operation" VALUE="operation" />
            <input type="text" name="operand2" VALUE="number" />
            <input type="submit" value=" = " />
      </form>
   </body>
</html>
```

On the server side, a process can be instantiated when a request comes from the website to process the data and send the result back to the page. Typically, a programmer must come up with their own way of collecting sufficient information and performing extensive string processing to the extra data and interpreting the data before performing the computation. With the advancement of web computing technologies, fewer people are still using this way to develop web applications.

5.1.2 Client-Side Scripting

The addition of the capacity executing script languages in web browsers is a major milestone of moving desktop-based computing to web-based computing. JavaScript is one of earliest and most widely used script languages.

Developed by Brendan Eich of Netscape, under the name Mocha and later renamed LiveScript, the first generation of JavaScript was introduced in December 1995 with the release of Netscape browser 2.0B3. Not long after the release of LiveScript, the popular scripting language took the new name "JavaScript" in a co-marketing deal between Netscape and Sun Microsystems. "JavaScript" is now a trademark of Sun Microsystems. The code below shows an example of an HTML page with a <script> element that contains a JavaScript function.

```
<html>
   <body>
        <script type="text/JavaScript">
              function add2Nos() {
                   document.sum.z.value = parseInt(document.sum.x.value) +
                   parseInt(document.sum.y.value)
              }
        </script>
        <form name="sum">
              <input type="text" name="x" size=5 maxlength="5">
              +
              <input type="text" name="y" size="5" maxlength="5">
              <input type="button" value =" = " name="Submit"
                   onClick="add2Nos()">
              <input type="text" name="z" size="5" maxlength="5">
        </form>
   </body>
</html>
```

As can be seen, the script program is embedded in the HTML code and is loaded into the client's web browser. The script is executed within the browser. This technique is called **client-side scripting**. In this example, the web page takes two numbers from the input form and performs addition in the page by calling the JavaScript function. No data communication with the server is needed.

As the popularity of scripting languages increases, more and more scripting languages are developed, and their interpreters embedded in the web browsers. Many traditional programming languages are also updated to provide scripting capacity. Due to the limitation of the browser size, many of the script languages are not supported by the browsers; instead, they can be used in the server side only, where the server practically has to support any scripting and traditional programming languages. The scripting languages can also be categorized according to their functions and usages into the following groups:

- Job control languages and shells, including IBM JCL, Unix Script, and AppleScript;
- GUI/ Visual programming languages, including Graphic BPEL supported by Oracle SOA Suite, Microsoft VPL, ASU VIPLE, and National Instrument LabView;
- Application-specific languages, including QuickC, Emacs List, and Parallax C for robotics programming;
- Extension/embeddable languages, including SpiderMonkey embedded in Yahoo Widget Engine, Adobe Flash (ActionScript), and Silverlight, TCL, Perl, and Python;
- Web client-side scripting, including AJAX, CSS, XSLT, JavaScript, ECMAScript, and VBScript;
- Dynamic and server-side Scripting languages, including Java, PHP, C#, and Ruby on Rails.

Figure 5.1 illustrates some of the programming languages and the approximated positions of these languages in the domains of traditional programming languages and scripting languages. Note that a browser typically supports a few scripts languages only, whereas many more languages can be used as the server-side scripting languages.

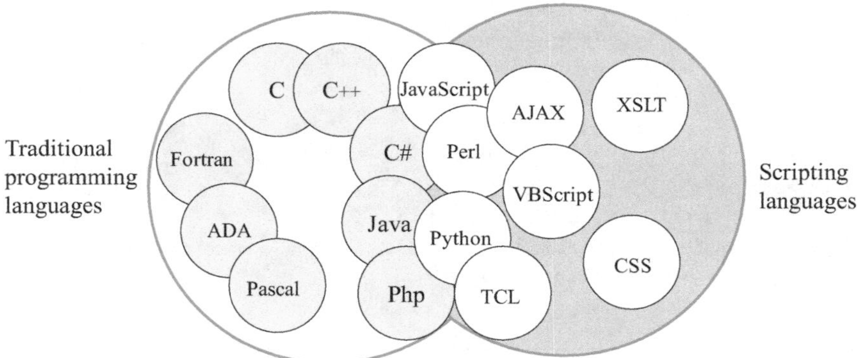

Figure 5.1. Traditional and scripting languages

The main benefit of client-side scripting is that computing is done in the client browser, which reduces the overhead of sending data back and forth between the client and the server. However, there are several major drawbacks, including:

- Script code is interpreted. Interpretation normally is slower than executing compiled code.
- Script code is not reusable. One cannot call the script function from a different web page.
- Script code does not support modularity and is not extensible. Individual functions can be defined, but they do not take advantage of late binding and inheritance.
- The capacity of a web browser is limited in computing speed, memory size, and accessing to other resources. Script code is normally used for simple calculations only.
- Security and proprietary issues: Allowing the code running in the browser presents a security hazard to the client machine. On the other hand, script code is visible via the "View Source" feature of the browser, which provides a hint to the hackers to attack the server if security related code is in the script. Generally speaking, proprietary algorithms should never be implemented in client scripting. Chapter 6 will discuss more detail on security issues.

With the advancement of browser technologies, library availability, and framework support, developing complex client-side applications is becoming feasible. HTML5 largely uses client side for developing complex and dynamic applications.

5.1.3 Server-Side Scripting and Code-Behind Page Computing

To address issues in client-side scripting, server-side scripting and code-behind page computing can be used. Server-side scripting looks similar to client-side scripting, except it avoids many of the problems that client-side scripting has. The following code shows an example of server-side scripting, where a C# function is included in the HTML file.

```
<%@ Page Language="C#" AutoEventWireup="true" CodeFile="Default.aspx.cs"
Inherits="_Default" %>
<!DOCTYPE html PUBLIC "-//W3C//DTD XHTML 1.0 Transitional//EN"
"http://www.w3.org/TR/xhtml1/DTD/xhtml1-transitional.dtd">
<html xmlns= "http://www.w3.org/1999/xhtml">
<head runat= "server">
   <title>ServerScripting</title>
</head>
```

```
<body>
  <form id="Form1" runat="Server">
        <asp:TextBox ID= "op1" Runat="server" />
        +
        <asp:TextBox ID= "op2" Runat="server" />
        <asp:Button ID="Button1" Text= "=" OnClick ="add" Runat= "server" />
        <asp:Label ID= "result" Runat="server" />
  </form>
</body>
</html>
<script language= "C#" runat="server">
    void add(Object sender, EventArgs e) {
        Int32 a = Convert.ToInt32(op1.Text);
        Int32 b = Convert.ToInt32(op2.Text);
        result.Text = Convert.ToString(a + b);
  }
</script>
```

However, server-side scripting still shares some of the problems that client-side scripting has, including the reusability, modularity, and extensibility.

The more widely used solution to these problems is using server-side computing with the code-behind pages. Separating code from its user interfaces also supports the tiered architecture concept of separating presentation from application logic. The example discussed in Section 5.1 applies the concept of server-side computing with the code-behind pages. This chapter will mainly discuss server-side computing techniques.

Server-side computing models also suffer their own problems. In certain applications, the frequent communications with large amount of data between client and server can present a problem for server-side computing models. AJAX is a useful technique that can significantly reduce the communication if only a small part of the page is changed frequently. However, if large amounts of data are dynamically changing, AJAX cannot help; for example, dynamic graphics generation and frequent modifications of images and animations on the server side can cause a large amount of data transfer from the server to the client. Such problems cannot be addressed by using AJAX. Out-of-browser computing is a solution to such problems.

5.1.4 Client-Side Out-of-Browser Computing

The idea of **out-of-browser computing** is to download a self-contained program and data unit on the client's local disk along with a web page. The web page will be the access point of the application, which will call the functions in the attachment and have the computations completed in the local machine without transferring a large amount of data with the server back and forth. Similar to client-side scripting, this approach is not appropriate for applications where security and proprietary algorithms are involved, as the client has the code in the local disk. Client can decline the execution of the script code in the browser or decline to download the attachment containing the out-of-browser code and data. Adobe Flash and Microsoft Silverlight use this approach.

The sandbox solution is used in Silverlight to prevent any Silverlight application to access the native applications in the local operating system. The only possibility of allowing a Silverlight application to communicate with a native application in the local operating system is through public APIs or services. The sandbox is a security mechanism widely used in shared environments, such as cloud computing environments, for separating running programs.

Table 5.1 summarizes the four different web-based computing models. Note that, except the pure HTML with server support, all the web computing models listed in the table are current and are widely used. These techniques are often combined.

In the remainder of the chapter, we will focus our discussion on the server-side code-behind page computing model, as it is the general and more advanced web computing model.

Table 5.1. Web-based computing models and their features

Web computing model	Pure HTML with server support	Client-side scripting	Server-side scripting	Server-side code- behind page	Out-of-browser computing
Size of problem to be processed	Small	Small	Small	Small and large	Small and large
Computing site	Server side	Client side	Server side	Server side	Client side
Execution model	Compiled	Interpreted	Interpreted or compiled	Compiled	Compiled
Data transfer overhead	High	Low	High	High	Low
Code reusability and extensibility	Low	Low	Low	High	High
Security and proprietary	High	Low	High	High	Low
Client-server architecture	Thin client	Thin and thick client	Thin client	Thin client	Thick client

5.2 Web Application Structure and Architecture

An ASP.Net website application is defined by all the files in the application's directory and its sub-directories. Some of the directories and files are generated by the system, whereas other directories and files are created by developers. All the files, even the system-generated files, can be edited by the developers.

5.2.1 Components of Web Applications

An ASP.Net website application normally consists of the following types of files and components. Some files are required, and others are optional.

- **ASPX files**: Each ASPX file is a web form, creating a GUI page for the users to interact with the program. When an ASPX website application is created, a Default.aspx is created. At least one ASPX file is required, and more can be added by the developer. A Default.aspx page is generated when a new website is created.
- **ASCX files**: Each ASCX file creates a custom control built from an HTML page with server-side script or code behind the page. A user control does not create an entire page; instead, it adds a (user-controlled) reusable item into one or more ASPX pages.
- **Web.config file** contains configuration settings that can be used for mode definition, access control, and parameterizing the applications behaviors.
- **Global.asax global application class** contains event handlers to respond to global events, such as application starting and a new session starting. This file will be placed in the root directory of the application if created.
- **DLL (Dynamic Link Library)**: It contains common library functions in the Windows environment, which have the same format as the .exe files. They can be called at any time by another program

that is running in the computer; for example, the program that allows another program to communicate with a specific device, such as a printer and keyboard, is often packaged as a DLL program. DLL files that support specific device operations are known as **device drivers**.

- **C# files** or .cs files are event handlers behind the other pages that handle the events such as user input (mouse click), program callback, and exception.
- **XHTML pages** are markup pages for the ASPX pages. An XHTML page can be generated from the ASPX design page or created by developers. On the other hand, the ASPX page can be generated from the XHTML page. XHTML pages can contain C# code as script.

The root directory of the application typically contains the Default.aspx, the Global.asax file, a Web.config file, and any other top-level ASPX and ASCX files. An ASP.Net website application can also create a number of subdirectories to sort the files generated in the application. Typically, these directories include:

- **Bin**: contains executable code and DLL files;
- **App_Code**: contains source code of programs, such as the C# programs;
- **App_Data**: store XML files and database files;
- **App_WebReferences**: store references to web services that are added to the application.

The simplest web application has one file only, which is an ASPX file that provides a GUI for user to use. Limited computing capacity can be built in an ASPX file. For a more complex application, multiple files are needed, and they can be organized in a tree of files, as shown in Figure 5.2.

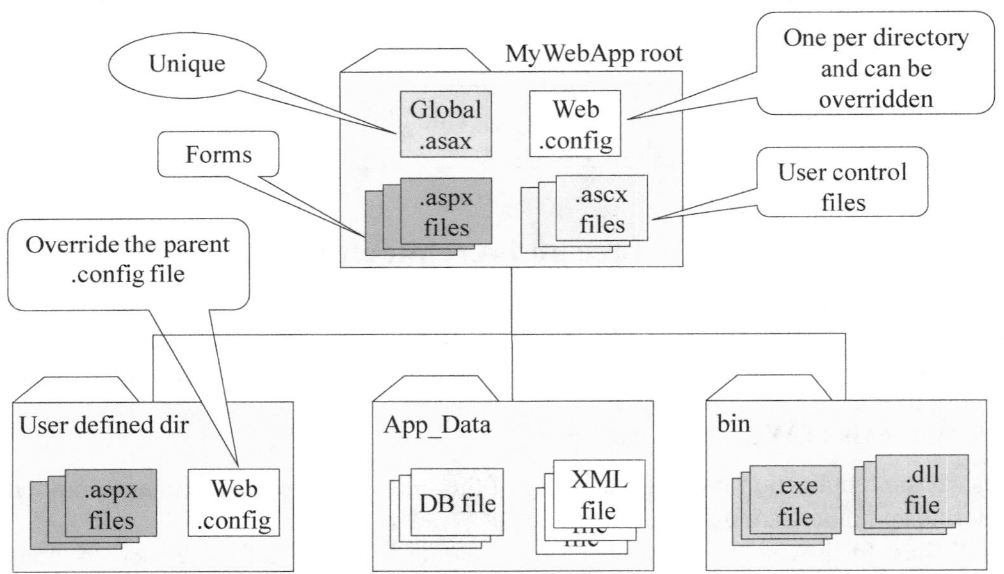

Figure 5.2. Organization of an ASP .Net website application

If a global file is defined, it must be in the root directory, and only one global file can be defined for any application. Any number of ASPX files, ASCX files, and DLL files can be defined in any directory. One Web.config file can be defined in each directory. As a Web.config file is the file that can be used for security, we will focus on this file.

ASP .Net can create the software that allows XCOPY installation, that is, the software can be installed by simply drag and dropping the software folder into a location of the user's choice and be uninstalled by deleting the folder. The mechanism supporting the XCOPY is to keep the Web.config file in the directory where the application software is located, instead of putting the file in the Windows system registry. Another purpose of Web.config file is to parameterize an application's behavior, and to allow the behavior to be modified without changing and recompiling the source code. It is essentially a form of policy-based computing. Policy-based computing is a common SOA feature; however, it is still an active research area, and thus this book will not cover it in detail.

Each subdirectory in web application can contain a web configuration file, all named Web.config. The settings in a Web.config file apply to the directory in which it is located, and all its subdirectories. A Web.config file in a directory takes precedence over (overrides) the settings that are specified in its parent directory. A user can also create subdirectories and use them to hold the subpages of the application. Figure 5.2 shows an example of the files and their organization in the application domain.

The Web.config files are protected by IIS, so that clients cannot view them in their web browsers. Attempts of accessing the file will receive an access denied error message.

A Web.config file is in XML format and is stored as a simple text file. One can use any standard text editor or XML parser to create and to edit Web.config files. A Web.config file consists of two segments of data, as shown in the skeleton of the file:

```
<configuration>
   <appSettings>
        <!- application setting values go here -->
   </appSettings>
   <system.web>
         <!- ASP.Net configuration settings go here -->
   <system.web>
<configuration>
```

The `<appSettings>` element in the Web.config file hold the application specific values; for example, the connection strings needed by an application to access a database, which allows the developer to parameterize the application. In the following code, the connection string to an SQL database is hard-coded into the C# program:

```
SqlDataAdapter adapter = new SqlDataAdapter ("select * from name where year = 2008,
"server=myServer; database=myDatabase; Integrated Security=SSPI; User
ID=myID;Password=MyPassWord");
DataSet refDataSet = new DataSet ();
adapter.Fill(refDataSet);
```

It will force the C# code to be modified and recompiled if; for example, the password is changed. A better way is to define the connection string in the `<appSettings>`, so that the code does not need to be modified if a different database needs to be used. The following portion of the Web.config file puts the server specific into the `<appSettings>` element:

```
<configuration>
   <appSettings>
        <add  key= "MyConnectionString"
              value= "server=myServer; database=myDatabase;
              Integrated Security=SSPI; User ID=myID;Password=MyPassWord"/>
   </appSettings>
</configuration>
```

Then, the C# code uses path ConfigurationSettings.appSettings and a parameter (key) MyConnectionString to access the connection string stored in the Web.config file, as defined in MSDN library.

```
String refString = ConfigurationSettings.appSettings[MyConnectionString];
SqlDataAdapter adapter = new SqlDataAdapter("select * from name where year = 2008",
refString);
DataSet refDataSet = new DataSet();
adapter.Fill (refDataSet);
```

5.2.2 Server Controls

An ASPX page's Graphical User Interface (GUI) can be built using a set of server controls listed in the toolbox. A server control is an object instantiated from a control class defined in .Net Class Library. These controls form components in the ASPX page. A control can take input and emit an event upon an input, and thus, we can write an event handler behind a control to process the input in an event-driven manner. The controls in graphic design view are also represented into the XHTML format, which can be sent to the client browser for being displayed as a web page. ASP .Net offers three kinds of server controls: Web controls, html controls, and, in addition, users can define their own classes to create user controls.

HTML controls are objects that generate equivalent HTML components on server side, so that all html functions can be handled in an ASPX application. Handlers can be linked behind the controls through an event, and thus, the input control or data can be processed immediately;

Web controls provide additional components that do not exist in traditional html pages. These components are often more powerful than the HTML controls.

User controls: HTML controls and web controls are provided through the classes in .Net Class Library. If you need a control that is not found in the library, you can create a custom control (object). The user control is defined through a separate ASCX page with server-side scripting or code behind the page support. As the user control is saved as a separate XHTML file, it can be modified without modifying the ASPX page that the user control is associated to. A user control can be shared by multiple ASPX pages.

Both ASPX page and ASCX page have two different views: the (graphic) design view and the (XHTL) source view. One can develop the page in both views. Figure 5.3 shows the design view of an ASPX page. The web application consists of two ASPX pages Sender.aspx and Receiver.aspx. The application uses a web service Encryptor to perform encryption and decryption.

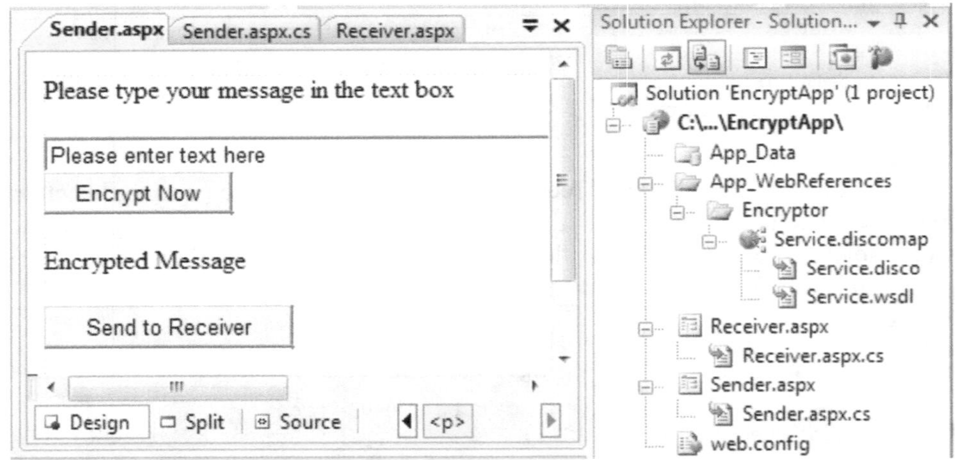

Figure 5.3. Design view of an ASPX application

If you type a plain text message in the textbox and click the "Encrypt Now" button, the encrypted message will be displayed; for example, if you type a word "Alice," the encrypted message would look like: "04C55C9CA8D0DCA6F7113F2292363467BEAC2FA8." Then, if you click the button "Send to Receiver," the encrypted message is sent to the receiver page. The receiver page should open automatically. If it does not open by itself, you can go back to your application, select the "Receiver.aspx" page, and then run (Start without Debugging) the application. The Receiver page will be open now and you will be able to see the encrypted message. Click the button "Decrypt Now," and you will see the original message "My password is SuperMan1."

The source view of the ASPX page is shown in the following example:

```
<%@ Page Language="C#" Debug = "True" AutoEventWireup="true"
CodeFile="Sender.aspx.cs" Inherits="_Default" %>
<!DOCTYPE html PUBLIC "-//W3C//DTD XHTML 1.0 Transitional//EN"
"http://www.w3.org/TR/xhtml1/DTD/xhtml1-transitional.dtd">

<html xmlns="http://www.w3.org/1999/xhtml">
<head runat="server">
    <title>Encryption Sender</title>
</head>
<body>
    <form id="form1" runat="server">
    <p>Please type your message in the text box</p>
    <div>
        <asp:TextBox ID="txtInput" runat="server" Width="616px">Please enter text
here</asp:TextBox>
    </div>
    <asp:Button ID="btnEncrypt" runat="server" onclick="btnEncrypt_Click"
        Text="Encrypt Now" />
    <br />
    <asp:Label ID="lblEncryptedMessage" runat="server" Text="Encrypted
Message"></asp:Label>
    <br />
    <asp:Button ID="btnSend" runat="server" onclick="btnSend_Click"
        Text="Send to Receiver" />
    <br />
    </form>
</body>
</html>
```

The source view in XHTM contains two HTML controls: <head runat="server"> and <form runat="server">. Any HTML element with an attribute runat="server" is an HTML control.

The source view in XHTM contains two Web controls: <asp:Button runat="server"> and <asp:Label runat="server">. Any element with the qualifier asp and the attribute runat="server" is Web control. For the definitions of XML and XHTML, please refer to Chapter 4.

To make this example a working example, we need to add the Encryptor service as a Web Reference into the application. The address of the service is:

http://neptune.fulton.ad.asu.edu/WSRepository/Services/Encryption/Service.asmx

The C# code behind the Sender.aspx page is given as follows:

```
public partial class _Default : System.Web.UI.Page {
    protected void Page_Load(object sender, EventArgs e){ }
    protected void btnEncrypt_Click(object sender, EventArgs e){
        // import remote Web service to do the difficult part of the work
        Encryptor.Service prxyEncrypt = new Encryptor.Service();
        // Take the message from the text box
        string msg1 = txtInput.Text;
        // Call the Encryption method in the Web service
        string msgEncrypted = prxyEncrypt.Encrypt(msg1);
        // Display encrypted message at the position of the label
        lblEncryptedMessage.Text = msgEncrypted;
        // Save the encoded message into a "Session Variable", so that
        // the Receiver.aspx page can retrieve the message
        Session["msgEncoded"] = (object)msgEncrypted;
    }
```

```
    protected void btnSend_Click(object sender, EventArgs e) {
        Response.Redirect("Receiver.aspx");
    }
}
```

There is second ASPX page in the application, the Receiver.aspx. The XHTML source page of the page is given as follows:

```
<%@ Page Language="C#" AutoEventWireup="true" CodeFile="Receiver.aspx.cs"
Inherits="Receiver" %>
<!DOCTYPE html PUBLIC "-//W3C//DTD XHTML 1.0 Transitional//EN"
"http://www.w3.org/TR/xhtml1/DTD/xhtml1-transitional.dtd">

<html xmlns="http://www.w3.org/1999/xhtml">
<head runat="server">
    <title>Encryption Receiver</title>
</head>
<body>
    <form id="form1" runat="server">
    <div>
        The message received</div>
    <asp:Label ID="lblMessageReceived" runat="server"></asp:Label>
    <br />
    <br />
    <asp:Button ID="btnDecrypt" runat="server" onclick="btnDecrypt_Click"
        Text="Decrypt Now" />
    <br />
    <asp:Label ID="lblMessageDecrypted" runat="server" Text="Decrypted
Message"></asp:Label>
    </form>
</body>
</html>
```

The C# code behind the Receiver.aspx page is given as follows:

```
public partial class Receiver : System.Web.UI.Page {
    protected void Page_Load(object sender, EventArgs e){
        lblMessageReceived.Text = (string)Session["msgEncoded"];
    }
    protected void btnDecrypt_Click(object sender, EventArgs e) {
        // import remote Web service to do the difficult part of the work
        Encryptor.Service prxyDecrypt = new Encryptor.Service();
        // Take the message from the session variable using the same index string
        string msg1 = (string)Session["msgEncoded"];
        // Check if the session variable contains any data.
        if (Session.Count==0) {
            // (Session.Count==0) means no data is stored by the sender
            lblMessageDecrypted.Text = "No Message to Display";
        }
        else {
            // Call the Decryption method in the Web service
            string decrypted = prxyDecrypt.Decrypt(msg1);
            // Display the decrypted message at the label
            lblMessageDecrypted.Text = decrypted;
        }
    }
}
```

By assembling the GUI design pages and C# pages, we have a working application.

This is another example of HTML controls and web controls. A list of frequently used HTML controls is given as follows:

```
<button runat= "server">                    HtmlButton
<input type="button" runat="server">        HtmlInputButton
<input type="reset" runat="server">         HtmlInputButton
<input type="submit" runat="server">        HtmlInputButton
<input type="checkbox" runat="server">      HtmlInputcheckBox
<input type="file" runat="server">          HtmlInputFile
<input type="hidden" runat="server">        HtmlInputHidden
<input type= "image" runat="server">        HtmlInputImage
<input type="radio" runat="server">         HtmlInputRadioButton
<input type="password" runat="server">      HtmlInputText
<input type="text" runat="server">          HtmlInputText
<a runat= "server">                         HtmlAnchor
<form runat= "server">                      HtmlForm
<select runat="server">                     HtmlSelect
<table runat= "server">                     HtmlTable
<td runat="server">                         HtmlTableCell
<th runat="server">                         HtmlTableCell
<tr runat="server”>                         HtmlTableRow
<textarea runat="server">                   HtmlTextArea
<img runat="server">                        HtmlImage
```

There are many Web controls implemented in the .NET Framework Class Library (FCL), including the following groups of controls:

- **Button controls**, which create various types of buttons in an ASPX page, as we have used in the example above.
- **Calendar control**, which add an interactive calendar to an ASPX page.
- **Data-bound controls**, which use data binding to display information obtained from databases and other data sources.
- **List controls**, which display a list of items.
- **Simple controls**, which wrap a simple HTML control into web controls.

5.2.3 User Controls

Server controls are the basic building blocks of ASPX pages. We can combine these controls into large GUI components within an ASPX page. However, these combinations are not reusable in other pages. If a combination will be used in multiple ASPX pages; for example, a login window that consists of two textboxes, one checkbox, and one button, we can define this combination as a user control, so that we add this control into different pages.

How are user controls different from other components? A User Control consists of a GUI file (.ascx) and a code behind file (.ascx.cs). They are different from all other existing components in ASP .Net programming environment.

- Compared with an ASPX form or page:
  A user control does not create a "form" or a separate GUI page, and an ASPX page cannot be directly accessed from a browser. Instead, it adds a user-controlled GUI (a patch) into an ASPX page;
- Compared with a server control:
  A server control does not have a separate GUI and code files. They are parts within an .aspx file and an .aspx.cs file.

- Compared with a DLL function:
  A user control is not precompiled, and the just-in-time compilation model can apply. Furthermore, a DLL function does not create GUI.

To demonstrate the use of the **user control**, we will add a user control as a new feature to the sender and the receiver pages in the encryption/decryption example. The user control will display the date and time. We will first add it to the sender page under the "Send to Receiver" button. The user control can be created in the following steps:

1. Choose Visual Studio menu command Website → Add New Item…
2. Select Web User Control in the pop-up window.
3. Name the new item SenderDateTime.ascx, and click Add. The user control item will appear in the Solution Explorer of the application, as shown in Figure 5.4.
4. Double-click the file name SenderDateTime.ascx to open the file. The "Source" view will appear. Add two labels, lblDateMsg and lblDate, into the page, as shown in the following example. The contents of these two labels will be generated by the C# code behind the page, and the contents will be displayed in an ASPX page that registers the user control.

```
<%@ Control Language="C#" AutoEventWireup="true" CodeFile="SenderDateTime.ascx.cs"
Inherits="SenderDateTime" %>

<asp:Label ID="lblDateMsg" runat="server" Text="The date and time are "></asp:Label>
<asp:Label ID="lblDate" runat="server" Text=""></asp:Label>
```

5. Click the "Design" tag to switch the design view to see the labels in the graphic view.
6. Double click the blank area in the page to open the C# code page and add the following C# code in this page.

```
public partial class SenderDateTime : System.Web.UI.UserControl {
    protected void Page_Load(object sender, EventArgs e){
        String date = DateTime.Now.ToLongDateString();
        String time = DateTime.Now.ToLongTimeString();
        this.lblDate.Text = date + ", " + time;
    }
}
```

Now, we have the user control created. Next, we need to link the user control into the ASPX pages where we need the content of the user control. To link to Sender.aspx page, open its XHTML Source view and register the user control by adding the following line of code below the first line of the code:

```
<%@ Register TagPrefix = "myControl" TagName="SenderDateTime"
             src="SenderDateTime.ascx" %>
```

Then, place the following line of code in the place where you want to display the date and time in the Sender.aspx page:

```
<myControl:SenderDateTime ID="SenderDateTime" runat = "server" />
```

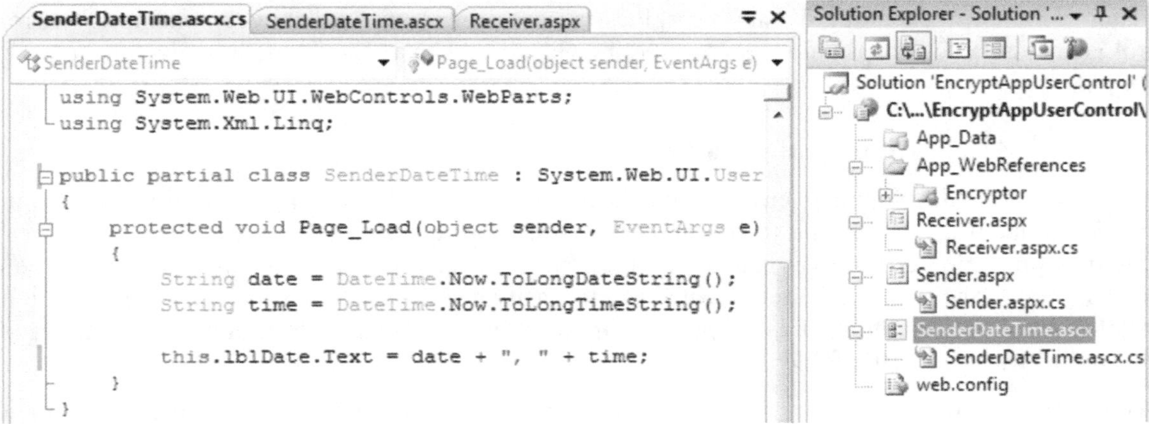

Figure 5.4. User control added to the solution

The complete XHTML code of the Sender.aspx page with the addition of the user control is given as follows, where the additional code is highlighted in boldface.

```
<%@ Page Language="C#" Debug = "True" AutoEventWireup="true"
CodeFile="Sender.aspx.cs" Inherits="_Default" %>
<%@ Register TagPrefix = "myControl" TagName="SenderDateTime"
             src="SenderDateTime.ascx" %>

<!DOCTYPE html PUBLIC "-//W3C//DTD XHTML 1.0 Transitional//EN"
"http://www.w3.org/TR/xhtml1/DTD/xhtml1-transitional.dtd">
<html xmlns="http://www.w3.org/1999/xhtml">
<head runat="server">
    <title>Encryption Sender</title>
</head>
<body>
    <form id="form1" runat="server">
    <p> Please type your message in the text box</p>
    <div>
        <asp:TextBox ID="txtInput" runat="server" Width="616px">
             Please enter text here</asp:TextBox>
    </div>
    <asp:Button ID="btnEncrypt" runat="server" onclick="btnEncrypt_Click"
        Text="Encrypt Now" />
    <p />
    <asp:Label ID="lblEncryptedMessage" runat="server" Text="Encrypted
Message"></asp:Label>
    <p />
    <asp:Button ID="btnSend" runat="server" onclick="btnSend_Click"
        Text="Send to Receiver" />
    <p />
    <myControl:SenderDateTime ID="SenderDateTime" runat = "server" />
    </form>
</body>
</html>
```

The purpose of the foregoing simple example is to illustrate the creation and inclusion of a user control into an ASPX page. Obviously, such a function can be easily implemented using a Web control "Label" and have the C# code directly behind the Sender.aspx page. The major benefit of user control is its reusability. The same user control can be shared by multiple ASPX pages, whereas the server control and the code behind are bound to a single ASPX page and cannot be shared. In the example just discussed, you can add the same user control to the Receiver.aspx page.

In a later section on generating dynamic graphics in user control, we will show an example, where user control is necessary to encapsulate the streamed image and to display the image in a given location in the ASPX page.

5.2.4 Web Application Configuration

The Visual Studio development environment keeps all files, including the configuration file, in the application domain under a single (root) directory. If the configuration file is put in the system registry outside the application domain, an installation program is necessary to put the configuration in the right place. As a result, the .Net application created can be easily installed and uninstalled. The application can be installed by simply dragging and dropping the application folder to anywhere in the file system and can be uninstalled by deleting the folder.

The configuration file, Web.config, of the ASP .Net application is an XML text file, which is automatically created when the application is created. You can use any standard text editor or XML parser to read and write the configuration file. The file is never locked, and it can be edited when the application is running. ASP.NET detects changes to configuration files and automatically applies new configuration settings to web resources affected by the changes. The server does not have to be rebooted for the changes to take effect. Hierarchical configuration settings are automatically recalculated and re-cached whenever a configuration file in the hierarchy is changed. Multiple configuration files, all named Web.config, can appear in multiple directories on an ASP.NET web application server. Each Web.config file applies configuration settings to its own directory and all child directories below it. Configuration files in child directories can supply configuration information in addition to that inherited from parent directories, and the child directory configuration settings can override or modify settings defined in parent directories. ASP.NET protects configuration files from outside access by configuring Internet Information Services (IIS) to prevent direct browser access to configuration files. HTTP access error 403 (forbidden) is returned to any browser attempting to request a configuration file directly.

The file that follows is the Web.config of the encryption example just discussed.

```
<?xml version="1.0"?>
<!-- Note: As an alternative to hand editing this file you can use the
     Web admin tool to configure settings for your application. Use the
     Website->Asp.Net Configuration option in Visual Studio. A full list
     of settings and comments can be found in machine.config.comments
     usually located in \Windows\Microsoft.Net\Framework\v2.x\Config
-->
<configuration>
  <configSections>
      <sectionGroup> . . . </sectionGroup>
  </configSections>
  <appSettings>
  <add key="Encryptor.Service" value=
"http://neptune.fulton.ad.asu.edu/WSRepository/Services/Encryption/Service.asmx"/>
  </appSettings>
  <system.web>
      <!-- Set compilation debug="true" to insert debugging
           symbols into the compiled page. Because this
           affects performance, set this value to true only
           during development.
      -->
      <compilation debug="true">
           <assemblies> . . . </assemblies>
      </compilation>
      <!-- The <authentication> section enables configuration
           of the security authentication mode used by
```

```
            ASP.NET to identify an incoming user.
        -->
        <authentication mode="Windows"/>
        <!-- The <customErrors> section enables configuration
            of what to do if/when an unhandled error occurs
            during the execution of a request. Specifically,
            it enables developers to configure html error pages
            to be displayed in place of an error stack trace.
        <customErrors mode="RemoteOnly" defaultRedirect="GenericErrorPage.htm">
            <error statusCode="403" redirect="NoAccess.htm" />
            <error statusCode="404" redirect="FileNotFound.htm" />
        </customErrors>
        -->
        <pages>
            <controls> . . . </controls>
        </pages>
        <httpHandlers> . . . </httpHandlers>
        <httpModules> . . . </httpModules>
    </system.web>
    <system.codedom>
        <compilers> . . . </compilers>
    </system.codedom>
    <!-- The system.webServer section is required for running ASP.NET AJAX
        under Internet Information Services 7.0.  It is not necessary
        for previous version of IIS.
    -->
    <system.webServer>
        <validation validateIntegratedModeConfiguration="false"/>
        <handlers>
            <remove name="WebServiceHandlerFactory-Integrated"/>
            <remove name="ScriptHandlerFactory"/>
            <remove name="ScriptHandlerFactoryAppServices"/>
            <remove name="ScriptResource"/>
            <add name="ScriptHandlerFactory" verb="*" path="*.asmx" />
            <add name="ScriptHandlerFactoryAppServices" verb="*" />
            <add name="ScriptResource" preCondition="integratedMode" />
        </handlers>
    </system.webServer>
    <runtime>
        <assemblyBinding xmlns="urn:schemas-microsoft-com:asm.v1">
            <dependentAssembly> . . . </dependentAssembly>
        </assemblyBinding>
    </runtime>
</configuration>
```

Let us take a closer look at the Web.config file. The file is an XML file consisting of many elements. The root element is <configuration>. The level-one child elements are the main sections of the configuration file.

- Section <configSections>: contains the section declaration for each section to appear in this configuration file. This is similar to variable declaration in a program. We need to declare all the variables to be used in the program at the beginning of the program.
- Section <appSettings>: holds the application specific values (strings) that can be read during execution.
- Section <system.web>: holds configuration settings used by the system—ASP.NET
- Section <system.codedom>: holds configuration settings used by the compiler for each of the language used in the application.

- Section <system.webserver>: holds configuration settings used by the web server that hosts the web service or web application
- Section <runtime>: holds configuration settings used by the Runtime system related to binding, assembling, and identification.

The ASP.NET configuration system is extensible. You can define new configuration sections, write program code to read a specific section, and use the data to make decisions. Thus, Web.config file can be used to support the policy-based computing.

We will use an example to demonstrate how we can read, write, and delete elements in AppSettings section in Web.config file. Figure 5.5 shows the GUI design of the example, which allows a user to choose variable name (key) and variable value (key value) and save the key and value, read and display the key and value pairs, and delete the stored key value pairs.

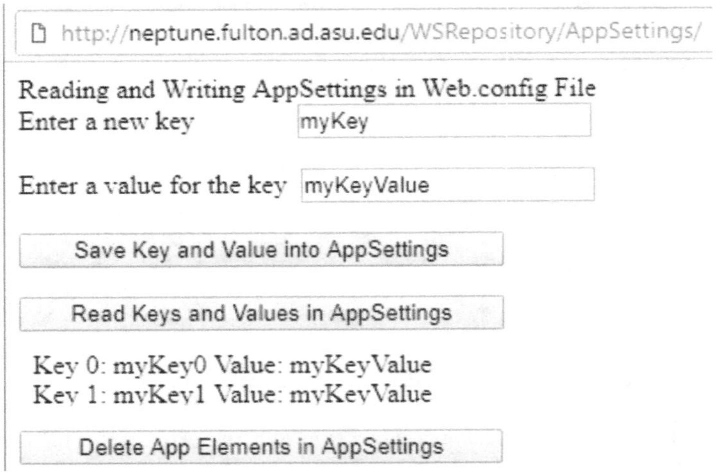

http://neptune.fulton.ad.asu.edu/WSRepository/AppSettings/

Reading and Writing AppSettings in Web.config File

Enter a new key myKey

Enter a value for the key myKeyValue

Save Key and Value into AppSettings

Read Keys and Values in AppSettings

Key 0: myKey0 Value: myKeyValue
Key 1: myKey1 Value: myKeyValue

Delete App Elements in AppSettings

Figure 5.5. GUI accessing AppSettings in Web.config file

The event handlers behind the buttons in the GUI are shown as follows. In the first two handlers, we used the methods in the library classes, such as Configuration, WebConfigurationManager, OpenWebConfiguration, and System.Configuration.ConfigurationManager.AppSettings. In the third handler, we simply consider that the Web.Config as an XML file and use XmlDocument class and methods to read and write the Web.Config file.

```
using System;
using System.Xml;
protected void btnSave_Click(object sender, EventArgs e) {
   System.Configuration.Configuration config =
        System.Web.Configuration.WebConfigurationManager.
                    OpenWebConfiguration("~/"); // Open Web.config file
   // Create a new element into appSettings.
   int index =
              System.Configuration.ConfigurationManager.AppSettings.Count;
   string newKey = txtKey.Text + index.ToString();
   string newValue = txtValue.Text;
   // Modify the appSettings in Web.config file.
   config.AppSettings.Settings.Add(newKey, newValue);
   // Save the changes into the Web.config file.
   config.Save(System.Configuration.ConfigurationSaveMode.Modified);
}
protected void btnRead_Click(object sender, EventArgs e) {
```

```
    System.Collections.Specialized.NameValueCollection myKeys =
            System.Web.Configuration.WebConfigurationManager.AppSettings;
    lblDisplay.Text = "";
    for (int i = 0; i < myKeys.Count; i++) {
        string appEntry = String.Format("Key {0}: {1} Value: {2} <br/>",
                i, myKeys.GetKey(i), myKeys[i]);
        lblDisplay.Text += appEntry;
    }
}
protected void btnDelete_Click(object sender, EventArgs e) {
    XmlDocument myCF = new XmlDocument();
    myCF.Load(AppDomain.CurrentDomain.SetupInformation.ConfigurationFile);
    foreach (XmlElement appElement in myCF.DocumentElement) {
        if (appElement.Name.Equals("appSettings")) {
            appElement.RemoveAll();
            lblDisplay.Text = "All AppSettings elements are removed";
        }
    }
     myCF.Save(AppDomain.CurrentDomain.SetupInformation.ConfigurationFile);
     }
```

We discussed earlier about using a text file to store data to provide a message service. We can also use AppSettingsfield. The following code shows the interface definition of such a service.

```
 [ServiceContract] // The interface definition IService.cs
public interface IService {
    [OperationContract]
    void SetData(string myData);
    [OperationContract]
    void SetCode(string code);
}
```

The service offers two operations. SetData writes data into AppSetting using a key. GetData retrieves the data using the same key. The implementation of the service code is given as follows:

```
public class Service : IService {
    public void SetData(string myData) {
        System.Configuration.Configuration config =
        System.Web.Configuration.WebConfigurationManager.
        OpenWebConfiguration("~/"); // Open Web.config file
        config.AppSettings.Settings.Remove("DataKey");
        config.AppSettings.Settings.Add("DataKey", myData);
        config.Save(System.Configuration.ConfigurationSaveMode.Modified);
    }
    public string GetData() {
        System.Collections.Specialized.NameValueCollection myKeys =
            System.Web.Configuration.WebConfigurationManager.AppSettings;
        string myData = myKeys["DataKey"];
        return string.Format("{0}", myData);
    }
}
```

If you prefer, you can also edit the Web.config file using the ASP.Net Website Administration Tool, instead of directly using a text tool to edit the XML elements. In ASP .Net menu, select Website → ASP .Net Configuration. You can define and edit all the sections that concern you.

We will further discuss the sections and subsections of the Web.config file in the sections and chapters when they are used; for example, we will discuss the <authentication> and <authorization> elements when we discuss the development of security mechanisms.

5.2.5 Global Application Class

ASP .Net offers a global application class Global.asax consisting of a collection of event handlers in response to global events. Global variable can be used through the application state in the form of Application["index"], which offers an array of objects to store the global information. To add the global application class into your application, right-click the application folder and select "Add New Item..." and then select the "Global Application Class." The Global.asax will be added to the root directory of the application. Open the file, the template with the event handler's interfaces included. The following code shows an example of the global application class with a few simple event handlers added.

```
<%@ Application Language="C#" %>
<script runat="server">
    void Application_Start(object sender, EventArgs e) {
        // Code that runs on application startup
       Application["SessionCounter"] = 0;
    }
    void Application_End(object sender, EventArgs e) {
        //  Code that runs on application shutdown
        Response.Write("<hr />The Website was last visited on " +
DateTime.Now.ToString());
    }
    void Application_Error(object sender, EventArgs e) {
        // Code that runs when an unhandled error occurs
    }
    void Session_Start(object sender, EventArgs e) {
        // Code that runs when a new session is started
        Int32 count = (Int32)Application["SessionCounter"];
        count++;
        Application["SessionCounter"] = count;
    }
    void Session_End(object sender, EventArgs e) {
        // Code that runs when a session ends.
        // Note: The Session_End event is raised only when the session state
        // mode is set to InProc in the Web.config file. If session mode is
        // set to StateServer or SQLServer, the event is not raised.
        Int32 count = (Int32)Application["SessionCounter"];
        count--;
        Application["SessionCounter"] = count;
    }
</script>
```

A web application can be accessed by many users at the same time. Each access will open a new session. The purpose of these event handlers is to keep track of how many sessions are currently opened.

In the Application_Start() event handler, we initialize the application state variable Application["SessionCounter"] to 0. This event handler will be called automatically when the application is started.

In the Session_Start() event handler, we increment the state variable Application["SessionCounter"]. This event handler will be called automatically when a new session is started.

In the Session_End() event handler, we decrement the state variable Application["SessionCounter"]. This event handler will be called automatically when a session is terminated.

In this implementation, the counter will be reset to zero if the application is restarted. If we also want to keep track of the total number of sessions ever opened, we can use another application state variable, say, Application["TotalSessions"]. We save the value of this variable to a disk file in the Application_End()

event handler, and retrieve the value in the Application_Start() event handler. More about application state and saving application data to the server's file system will be discussed in a later section in this chapter.

5.2.6 Dynamic Link Library and Package

ASP .Net offers multiple ways of code reuse. We have discussed creating a service or a user control class to share the code in multiple applications or multiple pages of an application. Creating a DLL (Dynamic Link Library) class is the traditional way of code-sharing through a library class.

To create a DLL class, choose Visual Studio menu "File → New → Project..." to start a new project. Then, in the Visual Studio installed templates, choose "Class Library (.Net Framework)."

◢ Visual C#
Windows Classic Desktop → Class Library (.NET Framework)

It will open a C# namespace page, which allows you to write multiple classes. After the classes are created and compiled, you can access these classes using the "Add Reference..." option in your website project that needs the library functions. Once you browse to the location of the library classes and add the library into your application, the executable code of the classes will be loaded into the bin folder of the application. In the following example, we created two simple classes in the namespace template.

```
namespace myLibrary{
   public class TemperatureConversion {
        public static Int32 getFahrenheit(Int32 c)   {
              Double f = c * 9 / 5 + 32;
                   return Convert.ToInt32(f);
              }
                   public static Int32 getCelsius(Int32 f) {
                   Double c = (f - 32) * 5 / 9;
                   return Convert.ToInt32(c);
        }
   }
   public class myMath {
        public static long abs (long x) {
              if (x >= 0) return (x); else return (-x);
        }
   }
}
```

After you use "Add Reference..." to add the namespace "myLibrary" into your application, you can use the library classes in your programs. For example, the namespace "myLibrary" defined a class called TemperatureConversion. You can use TemperatureConversion.getFahrenheit(Ctemp) to access the function in the class. The following code shows an example of using the name space and accessing the library class.

```
using myLibrary;        // You must use the namespace name defined in DLL
class myApplication {
   static void Main(string[ ] args)  {
   Int32 Ctemp = 23;
   Int32 Ftemp = 121;
   double x = TemperatureConversion.getFahrenheit(Ctemp); // Using DLL here
   double y = TemperatureConversion.getCelsius(Ftemp);     // Using DLL here
   System.Console.WriteLine("C-temp {0}  is F-temp {1}", Ctemp , x);
   System.Console.WriteLine("F-temp {0}  is C-temp {1}", Ftemp , y);
     }
}
```

The Visual Studio .Net environment allows developers to share their DLL library function through a NuGet package, as explained in: https://docs.microsoft.com/en-us/nuget/what-is-nuget. A NuGet package is a single ZIP file with the .nupkg extension. It contains compiled code in DLL format and other files related to the code file. Developers who want to share their code can create a package and publish it to a public or private host, such as https://www.nuget.org/. Package consumers obtain such packages from the hosts, add them to their projects through Add Reference, and then call a package's functionality in their project code. NuGet environment handles integration details.

Visual Studio does not automatically include tools for creating packages. You can use one of the CLI tools, either nuget.exe or dotnet.exe, to package that functionality in your DLL file into a NuGet package component that can be shared with and used by any number of other developers. The details can be found at https://docs.microsoft.com/en-us/nuget/create-packages/creating-a-package.

You can read Section 4.6.4 JSON for the process of installing NuGet packages and an example of installing Newtonsoft.Json package.

Note, NuGet package is not a web service. It does not have the standard interface. It does not access the code over a proxy. Instead, it downloads and integrates the executable code into the application.

5.3 State Management

A traditional procedure (method) call will result in the creation of a private workspace for the procedure through a content switch, that is, the caller will be swapped out, and its execution environment saved to the stack. The procedure's code will take over control of the workspace. When the procedure completes its execution, the caller's execution environment will be resumed, and it will continue from the instruction next to the procedure call.

Web services and web applications are loosely coupled with their callers. They communicate through data exchange. The control flow of the caller does not jump to the service, and context switch will occur. Furthermore, web services and web applications can be accessed simultaneously by many users. Web services and web applications are based on HTTP, which is stateless: Every package is independent of other packages.

Thus, the memory and state management in web services and web applications are completely different from the model of procedure calls.

Web services and web applications are stateless by default: Every time we call a service or access an application, it considers us as a new user.

However, as we consider the web as our new computing platform, we need to have stateful computing in many cases; for example, add to the cart service, counter, timer, and so on.

5.3.1 Overview of State Management Techniques

Special considerations are necessary in order to provide stateful web services and applications. Table 5.2 lists different methods offered in ASP .Net to manage the states of the services and applications. In the rest of the discussions, we will use the term web application state management. The techniques discussed are also applicable to web services. The remainder of the section will use examples to illustrate the applications of some these techniques.

Table 5.2. ASP .Net state management techniques

State management	Features
View state	Saves an array of strings in a hidden field in the XHTM page in client browser; accessible within one page; and data disappears when the browser is closed.
Session state	Saves an array of objects in a session on server side; accessible among all pages in the session; and data disappears when the session is closed.
Application state	Saves an array of objects as global data on server side; accessible among all pages and all sessions in the application; and data disappears when the application is closed.
Cookies	Saves strings in client machine's file system; and client may disable cookies or clear cookies.
Caching	Saves data recently used for reuse.
Server file system	Saves text, binary, or XML files on server's file system.
Relational database	Saves data as entries of table; conversion needed between table and XML; DataSet can be accessed as a table or as an XML file; and queries data using a relational database query language.
XML database	Saves data as XML files and queries data using an XML query language.

5.3.2 View State

When a user accesses an ASPX page, an XHTML page is generated and sent to the browser running on the client machine. A hidden field is reserved in the XHTML page for developers to save information for the page to use when the page is accessed multiple times in the same browser session. The ASPX page can read and write this field in the syntax of ViewState["name"], where "name" is a string index. The hidden field can save a collection of strings indexed by different names.

To illustrate the use of View State variables, we designed a simple online shopping system with an accumulator to add the total, as shown in Figure 5.6. The application offers a textbox to enter a number, and the number will be added to the running sum when the button "Add to Sum" is pressed. Then, the Check Out button will transfer the final amount to another page OrderProcess.aspx.

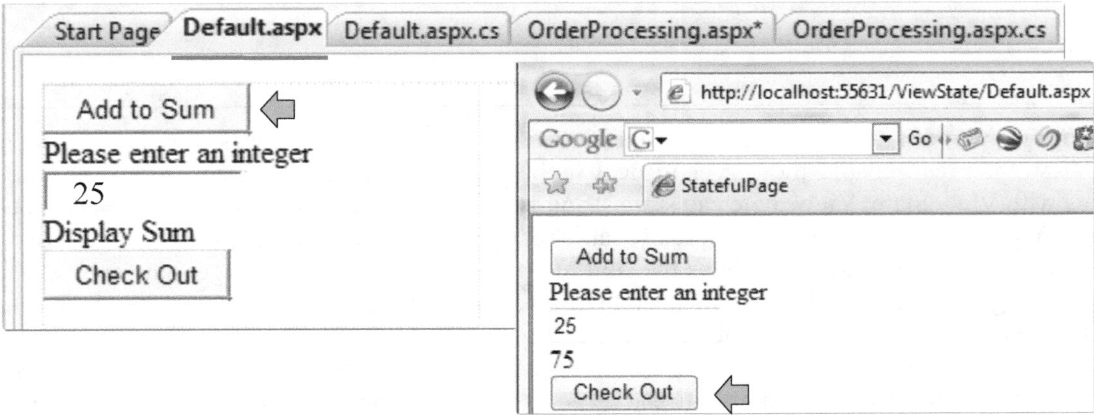

Figure 5.6. The sum is 75 after the number 25 is added three times

First, we take a look at what would happen if we put the following code behind the Default.aspx page using traditional desktop programming techniques, where a class variable sum is used to hold the running sum:

```
using System;
public partial class _Default : System.Web.UI.Page {
    protected void Page_Load(object sender, EventArgs e) { }
    Int32 sum = 0;
    protected void Button1_Click(object sender, EventArgs e) {
      Int32 newValue = Convert.ToInt32(this.TextBox1.Text);
      sum = sum + newValue;
      this.Label1.Text = Convert.ToString(sum);
    }
}
```

When we execute the program and click the button "Add to Sum," the current input value will be displayed, instead of the running sum value so far. The reason is that every visit to the web page or every click to the button will be considered a new session and the variable sum will be initialized to zero. What would happen if we added the keyword static to the class variable sum?

```
static Int32 sum = 0;
```

In this case, only one variable sum will be created for all sessions even from different browsers and from different computers. In other words, the data from one user will be accessed by another user. This is obviously not what this accumulator application is intended for.

ViewState is the proper technique for this application, where, the variable ViewState["Sum"] will be stored in a hidden field in the XHTML page in the browser, and can be used by this browser only. The View State version of code behind the button is given as follows:

```
public partial class _Default : System.Web.UI.Page {
   protected void Page_Load(object sender, EventArgs e) { }
   Int32  FinalAmt = 0;
   protected void Button1_Click(object sender, EventArgs e) {
        Int32 sum = 0;
        if (ViewState["Sum"] == null)  ViewState["Sum"] = 0;
        else {
            Int32 newValue = Convert.ToInt32(this.TextBox1.Text);
           sum = (Int32)ViewState["Sum"] + newValue;
           ViewState["Sum"] = sum;
           this.Label1.Text = sum.ToString();
           FinalAmt = sum;
        }
    }
}
```

The benefit of View State is to have minimum burden to the server. The data is stored in the client side. Using View State can enable the server to deal with much large volume of accesses. There are a few problems with View State. View State can store string-type data only, and the data in one page is not visible in another page, even if the pages belong to the same session; for example, if our application has two ASPX pages: an add-to-cart page that calculates the sum of all items and a checkout page that accesses the bank service to charge the credit card. Thus, we need to transfer the sum from the add-to-cart page to the checkout page. Unfortunately, the checkout page cannot read the data in the add-to-cart page, because they are two separate pages. There are different ways to address the problem; for example, we can use postback mechanism in html to send the data back to the server, and post the data from the server to another page, as shown in Figure 5.7.

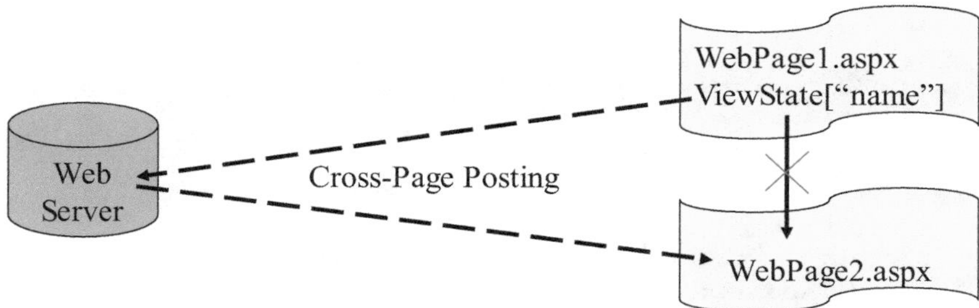

Figure 5.7. Cross-page posting: from source to server, and then from server to destination

Cross-Page Posting is a method of posting data from one page back to the server, and then to another page. To implement it, we need to have a number of steps.

Step 1: It uses PostBackUrl = "Destination.aspx" attribute to link the current page to the destination page. In the destination page, it accesses the public method in the source page. Figure 5.8 shows the source page of the Default.aspx page, from which the sum needs to be transferred out. Notice the underlined attribute that is added into the button "btnCheckOut".

Steps 2: We need to provide a method in Default.aspx.cs for the OrderProssing page to call. The method will return the sum stored in the View State to the called, as shown in Figure 5.9. Note that you cannot use FinalAmt in the callback function, as the value in FinalAmt will no longer be available after leaving this page. This is where we need the View State.

Figure 5.8. Cross-page posting: from source to server, and then from server to destination

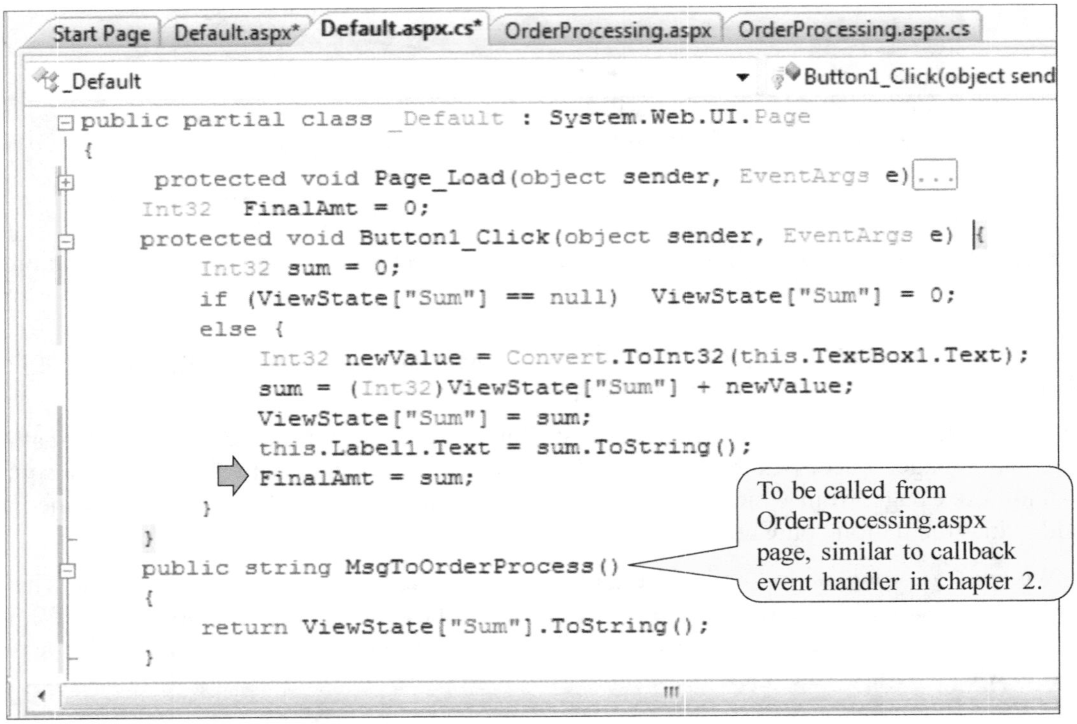

```
Start Page | Default.aspx* | Default.aspx.cs* | OrderProcessing.aspx | OrderProcessing.aspx.cs
_Default                                    Button1_Click(object send

public partial class _Default : System.Web.UI.Page
{
    protected void Page_Load(object sender, EventArgs e)...
    Int32 FinalAmt = 0;
    protected void Button1_Click(object sender, EventArgs e) {
        Int32 sum = 0;
        if (ViewState["Sum"] == null)  ViewState["Sum"] = 0;
        else {
            Int32 newValue = Convert.ToInt32(this.TextBox1.Text);
            sum = (Int32)ViewState["Sum"] + newValue;
            ViewState["Sum"] = sum;
            this.Label1.Text = sum.ToString();
            FinalAmt = sum;
        }
    }
    public string MsgToOrderProcess()
    {
        return ViewState["Sum"].ToString();
    }
```

To be called from OrderProcessing.aspx page, similar to callback event handler in chapter 2.

Figure 5.9. A method is provided in Default.aspx.cs for the OrderProssing page to call

Steps 3: Now, in the OrderProcessing.aspx.cs page, we will call the MsgToOrderProcess() to obtain the final amount, as shown in Figure 5.10.

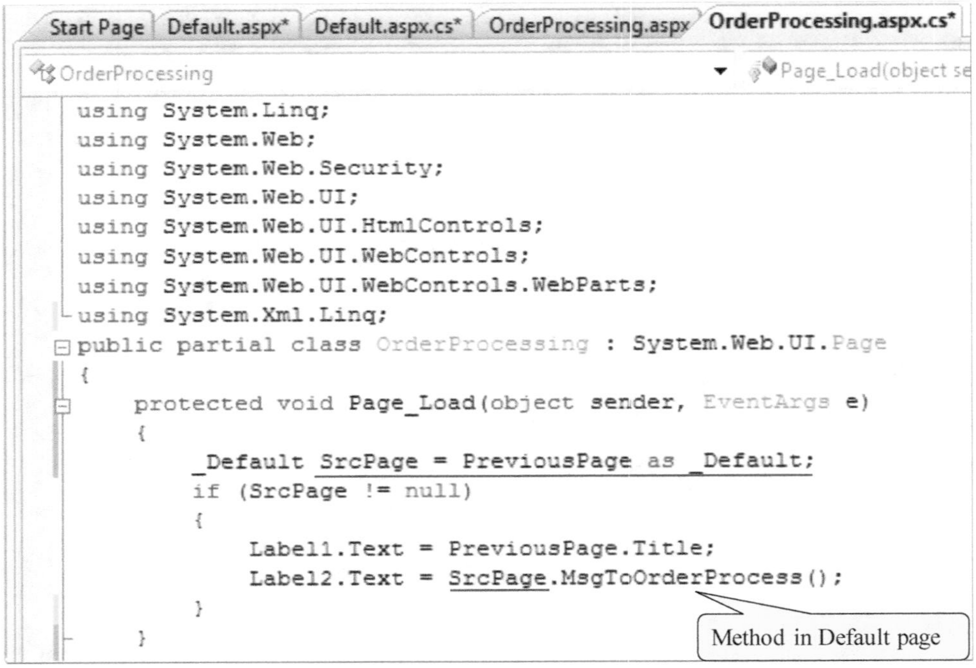

```
Start Page | Default.aspx* | Default.aspx.cs* | OrderProcessing.aspx | OrderProcessing.aspx.cs*
OrderProcessing                             Page_Load(object se

using System.Linq;
using System.Web;
using System.Web.Security;
using System.Web.UI;
using System.Web.UI.HtmlControls;
using System.Web.UI.WebControls;
using System.Web.UI.WebControls.WebParts;
using System.Xml.Linq;
public partial class OrderProcessing : System.Web.UI.Page
{
    protected void Page_Load(object sender, EventArgs e)
    {
        _Default SrcPage = PreviousPage as _Default;
        if (SrcPage != null)
        {
            Label1.Text = PreviousPage.Title;
            Label2.Text = SrcPage.MsgToOrderProcess();
        }
    }
```

Method in Default page

Figure 5.10. Call the method provided in Default.aspx.cs to retrieve the final amount

5.3.3 View State Security and Machine Key

View State and postback are also used by the system to implement the server controls, such as the buttons. When the button is click, it will postback the information needed for the server to reconstruct the html page with the updated information. For security reason, a Message Authentication Code (MAC) will be generated by the server. When a message is posted back, the server validates the MAC. MAC is generated based on the machine key of the server.

View State and the postback mechanisms may not work if the application is hosted by a cloud computing environment with a web farm or virtual servers, because a different server may need to process a postback message for load balance reason.

There are two solutions. One is to disable the load balancer in the cloud computing. This solution needs the administrative privilege of the server. This is not a good solution for the large applications where load balancer is needed for improving the performance and for reducing the cost.

The better solution is to define an element <machineKey> in the Web.config file in you web application, which will override the machine key generated by the server. However, an unsecure machine key can compromise the security of the system. We need to use the proper hashing algorithm to generate a key that meets the current security standard. The following steps can generate such a machine key.

Step 1: Write a script that uses a secure hashing algorithm for generating the machine key

Microsoft provides a PowerShell script for generating a secure machine key. The code is available in the appendix part in the article at this page: https://support.microsoft.com/en-us/kb/2915218?wa=wsignin1.0

Step 2: In Windows Search Box, type *Windows Powershell ISE* and start it. Copy the script code from Microsoft and paste it into the editor, as shown in the following screenshot in Figure 5.11. Save the file in the name: Generate-MachineKey.ps1

```
Windows PowerShell ISE
File Edit View Tools Debug Add-ons Help
Generate-MachineKey.ps1 X
# Generates a <machineKey> element that can be copied + pasted into a Web.config file.
function Generate-MachineKey {
  [CmdletBinding()]
  param (
    [ValidateSet("AES", "DES", "3DES")]
    [string]$decryptionAlgorithm = 'AES',
    [ValidateSet("MD5", "SHA1", "HMACSHA256", "HMACSHA384", "HMACSHA512")]
    [string]$validationAlgorithm = 'HMACSHA256'
  )
  process {
    function BinaryToHex {
        [CmdLetBinding()]
        param($bytes)
        process {
            $builder = new-object System.Text.StringBuilder
            foreach ($b in $bytes) {
              $builder = $builder.AppendFormat([System.Globalization.CultureInfo]::InvariantCulture, "{0:X2}", $b)
            }
            $builder
        }
    }
    switch ($decryptionAlgorithm) {
      "AES" { $decryptionObject = new-object System.Security.Cryptography.AesCryptoServiceProvider }
      "DES" { $decryptionObject = new-object System.Security.Cryptography.DESCryptoServiceProvider }
      "3DES" { $decryptionObject = new-object System.Security.Cryptography.TripleDESCryptoServiceProvider }
    }
    $decryptionObject.GenerateKey()

PS C:\scripts> Generate-Machinekey
```

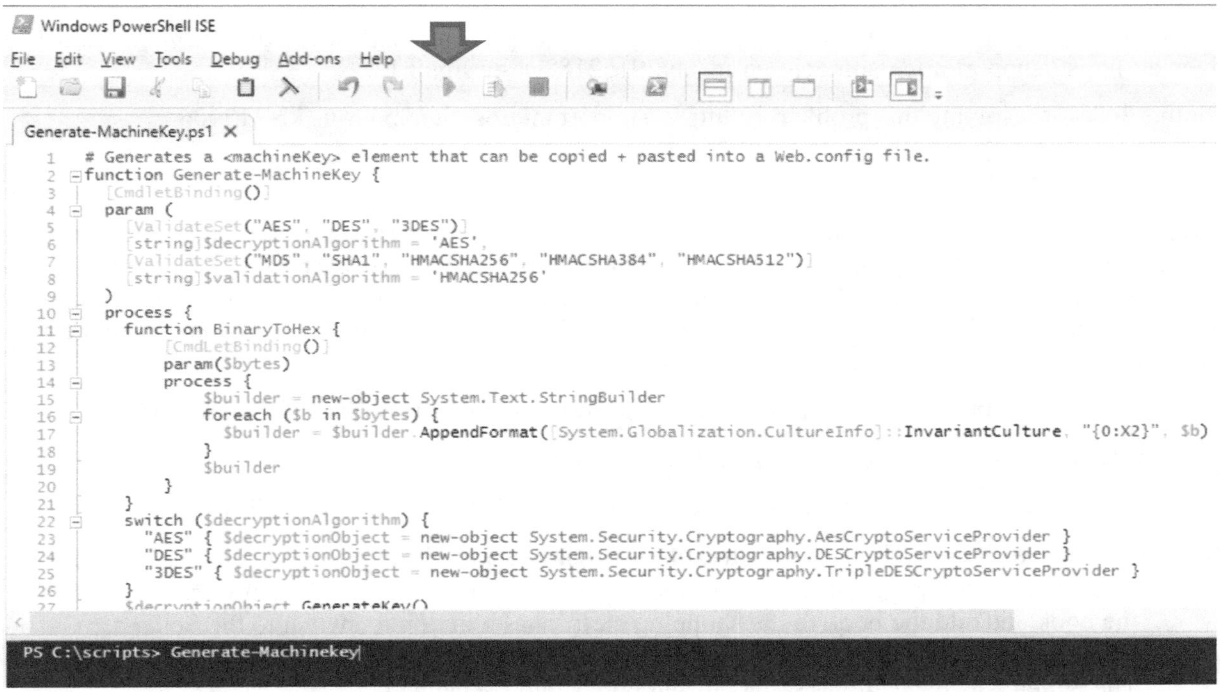

Figure 5.11. Edit the Generate-MachineKey.ps1 script

Step 3: Run the script by clicking the green triangle button at the upper part of the window. Then, type the following command at the prompt at the bottom of the window:

```
PS C:\scripts> Generate-Machinekey <enter>
```

This command should generate the machine key, which looks like:

```
    <machineKey decryption="AES" decryptionKey="xxxxxxxxxxxxxxxxxxxxxxxxxx"
validation="HMACSHA256" validationKey="yyyyyyyyyyyyyyyyyyyyyyyyyyyy" />
```

Step 4: Add the element into the project's Web.config file

The generated machine is already in the format of an element for the Web.config file. Copy and paste the element into Web.config file, under the <system.web> element, as shown in the following sample code:

```
  <system.web>
    <machineKey decryption="AES" decryptionKey="xxxxxxxxxxxxxxxxxxxxxxxxxx"
    validation="HMACSHA256" validationKey="yyyyyyyyyyyyyyyyyyyyyyyyyyyy" />
  </system.web>
```

When you copy and paste, make sure no space or break are added into the two machine keys.

Another option is to type PowerShell in Windows search box and start PowerShell. Then, use Unix/DOS commands to change directories to the location where you have your script Generate-Machinekey.ps1, as shown in the following screenshot:

Windows PowerShell

```
Windows PowerShell
Copyright (C) 2016 Microsoft Corporation. All rights reserved.

PS C:\Users\ychen1> cd ..
PS C:\Users> cd ..
PS C:\> cd scripts
PS C:\scripts> Generate-Machinekey
```

If the above steps do not work out for you, please read the comprehensive solutions for all kinds of situations given at: https://support.microsoft.com/en-us/kb/2915218?wa=wsignin1.0

Another link for resolving this problem is: https://support.microsoft.com/en-us/kb/312906

5.3.4 Session State

Session State creates variables that can store structured objects in the server, and the scope of the variables is session-wide. The information stored in session state is secure. The information is linked to the session that creates the session state. Other sessions of the same application cannot access the information. Internally, a unique 120-bit number is generated to identify the session. Such an ID can be generated by a secure hashing function. A hashing service is available in ASU Repository:

http://neptune.fulton.ad.asu.edu/WSRepository/Services/HashSha512/Service.svc

The service can be tested by the service tool deployed at:

http://neptune.fulton.ad.asu.edu/WSRepository/services/wsTesterTryIt/

Again, we use an example to illustrate the use of the Session State. The application consists of three pages:

- The Default.aspx page lists the books available for the user to select. The user can view detail of the book and add the book to the shopping cart; it has a button to switch to the Seller.aspx to add books to the catalog.
- The Seller.aspx page allows sellers to add books into the catalog.
- The MyCart.aspx page shows the book list in the cart and the total amount of books in the cart.

Figure 5.12 shows the interface design of these three pages.

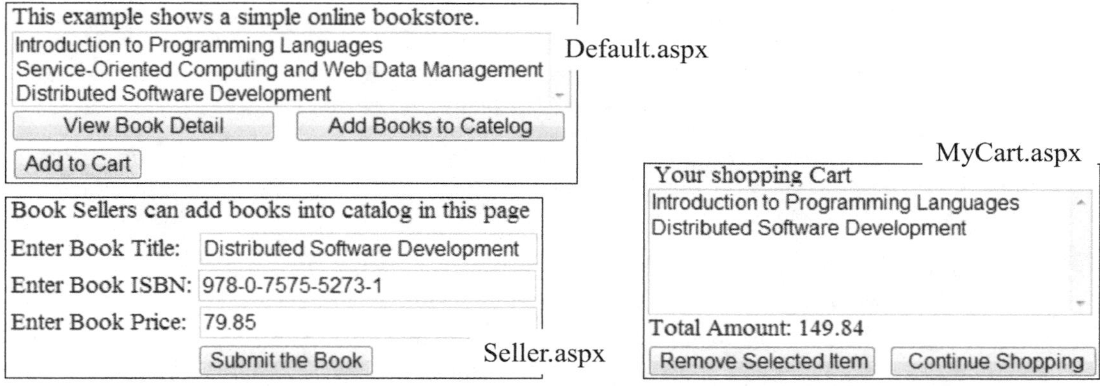

Figure 5.12. Interface design of Default.aspx, Seller.aspx, and MyCart.aspx pages

The C# code behind these three pages is given in the following example. If you want to use the interface design in Figure 5.12 and following code to create the application, do not copy the entire code into the code behind the ASPX page. Instead, double-click each button on the page and copy the body of each method into the corresponding method template. You also need to name each web control (Button, Label, and ListBox) based on the names used in the code. The code that follows is the code behind Default.aspx page.

```
// Default.aspx.cs
using System;
public partial class _Default : System.Web.UI.Page {
    Book aBook1, aBook2;
    string catalogKey;
    protected void Page_Load(object sender, EventArgs e){
        if ((Session.Count == 0)&& (ListBoxCatalog.Items.Count == 0) ){
            ListBoxCatalog.Items.Clear();
            string title = "Introduction to Programming Languages";
            string isbn = "0-7575-2974-7";
            double price = 69.99;
            aBook1 = new Book(title, isbn, price);
            Session["sBook1"] = aBook1; // Add object into session
            ListBoxCatalog.Items.Add(aBook1._Title); // Display book1
            title = "Service-Oriented Computing and Web Data Management";
            isbn = "978-0-7575-5";
            price = 89.99;
            aBook2 = new Book(title, isbn, price);
            Session["sBook2"] = aBook2; // Add object into session
            ListBoxCatalog.Items.Add(aBook2._Title); // Display book2
        }
        if ((Session.Count != 0) && (ListBoxCatalog.Items.Count == 0)){
            for (Int16 i = 1; i <= Session.Count; i++){
                catalogKey = "sBook" + i;
                aBook1 = (Book)Session[catalogKey];
                ListBoxCatalog.Items.Add(aBook1._Title);
            }
        }
    }
    protected void btnSeller_Click(object sender, EventArgs e){
        Response.Redirect("seller.aspx");
    }
    protected void btnViewBook_Click(object sender, EventArgs e){
        if (ListBoxCatalog.SelectedIndex < 0)
```

```
            lblTitle.Text = "Please select a book in the list above";
        else{
            string num = Convert.ToString(ListBoxCatalog.SelectedIndex + 1);
            catalogKey = "sBook" + num;  // Find selected book
            Book aBook = (Book)Session[catalogKey];
            lblTitle.Text = "<br />Title: " + aBook._Title + "<br />ISBN: " +
aBook._Isbn + "<br />Price: " + aBook._Price;
        }
    }
    protected void btnAddToCar_Click(object sender, EventArgs e){
        if (ListBoxCatalog.SelectedIndex < 0)
            lblTitle.Text = "Please select a book in the list above";
        else{
            string num = Convert.ToString(ListBoxCatalog.SelectedIndex + 1);
            string catalogKey = "sBook" + num; // Find selected book
            aBook1 = (Book)Session[catalogKey]; // read from state variable
            aBook1._InCart = true;              // add information
            Session[catalogKey] = aBook1        // Write back
            Response.Redirect("MyCart.aspx");
        }
    }
}
public class Book {     // This book class is used in all pages
    public string _Title;
    public string _Isbn;
    public double _Price;
    public bool _InCart;    // whether the book is in cart
    public Book(string title, string isbn, double price){ // constructor
        _Title = title;
        _Isbn = isbn;
        _Price = price;
        _InCart = false;
    }
}
```

First, let us look at the data structure and state management in the program. A Book class is defined to hold the book information. It consists of four data members: _Title, _ISBN, _Price, and _InCart. A constructor is defined to write the title, ISBN, and price parameter values into the corresponding data members. The _InCart property is initialized to false.

When the Default.aspx page is visited for the first time, two Book objects are created and saved into the Session State variables Session["sBook1"] and Session["sBook2"], respectively. The Seller.aspx page will add one book at a time. The book will be saved in the variable Session["sBook3"], Session["sBook4"], and so on.

The Session State variables are retrieved in the Default.aspx page and displayed in the ListBoxCatalog every time the page is visited. A user (buyer) can select a book in the ListBoxCatalog. After a book is selected, the user can choose to "View Book Detail" or "Add to Cart." When "Add to Cart" is clicked, the property _InCart in the book object is set to true, and the user is taken to the MyCart.aspx page.

The MyCart.aspx page reads the objects in the Session State variables. A book is listed, and the price added to the Total Amount is the property value _InCart = true. A user then can choose to continue shopping (return to the Default.aspx page) or to checkout. Checkout is not implemented in this example.

The Page_Load() method is a default function behind each ASPX page. The method is called every time the page is visited. If you do not want certain statements to be executed every time the page is accessed, you can add conditions to restrict their execution. In the foregoing code, we added two conditions to reload the books: The condition (Session.Count == 0) checks if there is information (list of books) stored in the session state at all. We do not load if there are no books stored. The condition (ListBoxCatalog.Items.Count == 0) checks if the ListBoxCatalog is loaded. We do not reload the books if the ListBoxCatalog is already loaded. Obviously, we are presenting a simplified implementation here.

The code behind the button "Add Books to Catalog" simply redirects the control to the Seller.aspx page. The code behind the button "View Book Detail" will display the additional information of the selected book.

The code behind the button "Add to Cart" will find the selected book, set the value of _InCart variable to true, and then transit to MyCart.aspx page.

The code that follows is the code behind Seller.aspx page. This page allows the seller to add one book at a time into the catalog stored in the session state.

```
// Seller.aspx.cs
using System;
public partial class Seller : System.Web.UI.Page {
   protected void Page_Load(object sender, EventArgs e) { }
   protected void btnSubmitBook_Click(object sender, EventArgs e){
        string title = txtTitle.Text;
        string isbn = txtIsbn.Text;
        string sPrice = txtPrice.Text;
        double price = Convert.ToDouble(sPrice);
        Book aBook1 = new Book(title, isbn, price);
        string num = Convert.ToString(Session.Count + 1);//Find next free spot
        string catalogKey = "sBook" + num;   // Form the index key
        Session[catalogKey] = aBook1; // Add an object into session state
        Response.Redirect("Default.aspx"); // Return to catalog page
   }
}
```

The code that follows is the code behind MyCart.aspx page. There are two major functions: display the cart contents and remove an item from the cart. In the Page_Load() method, it goes through all the books in the session state. If the _InCart variable has a true value, the book title will be displayed in the listBoxCart. Otherwise, an empty string will be displayed. This is a simplified implementation of preserving the positions of the book in the session state array and in the listBoxCart.

The code behind the button "Remove Selected Book" will perform two functions: modify the session state and then, go through the updated session state to display the new cart contents.

```
// MyCart.aspx.cs
using System;
public partial class MyCart : System.Web.UI.Page {
    string catalogKey;
    protected void Page_Load(object sender, EventArgs e) {
        Double totalAmount = 0;
        for (Int16 i = 1; i <= Session.Count; i++){
            catalogKey = "sBook" + i;
            Book aBook = (Book)Session[catalogKey];
            if (aBook._InCart){
                ListBoxCart.Items.Add(aBook._Title);
                totalAmount = totalAmount + Convert.ToDouble(aBook._Price);
            }
            else ListBoxCart.Items.Add("");
        }
        lblTotalAmt.Text = "Total Amount: " + Convert.ToString(totalAmount);
    }
    protected void btnRemove_Click(object sender, EventArgs e){
        if (ListBoxCart.SelectedIndex < 0)
```

```
            lblMsg.Text = "Please select a book in the list above";
        else {
            string num = Convert.ToString(ListBoxCart.SelectedIndex + 1);
            string catalogKey = "sBook" + num;   // Find selected book
            Book aBook = (Book)Session[catalogKey]; // read from state variable
            aBook._InCart = false;                // change information
            Session[catalogKey] = aBook;          // Write back
            ListBoxCart.Items.Clear();
            Double totalAmount = 0;
            for (Int16 i = 1; i <= Session.Count; i++) {
                catalogKey = "sBook" + i;
                aBook = (Book)Session[catalogKey];
                if (aBook._InCart){
                    ListBoxCart.Items.Add(aBook._Title);
                    totalAmount = totalAmount + Convert.ToDouble(aBook._Price);
                }
                else ListBoxCart.Items.Add(" ");
            }
            lblTotalAmt.Text = "Total Amount: " + Convert.ToString(totalAmount);
        }
    }
    protected void btnShopping_Click(object sender, EventArgs e) {
        Response.Redirect("Default.aspx"); // Return to catalog page
    }
}
```

The example is deployed at:

http://neptune.fulton.ad.asu.edu/WSRepository/SessionOnlineStore/Default.aspx

5.3.5 Cookies

Cookies provide a way of storing user's information in the browser (temporary, disappearing after closing browser) or on the hard drive of a client's computer (longer term). Cookies are transparent to the users, as long as the cookies are enabled in the browser. Cookies can store string type of data only, often used for storing user's preferences of the application. Other data types need to be converted to strings; the syntax of Cookies is similar to that of View State and Session State.

We use an example to illustrate the use of the cookies. Figure 5.13 shows the interface design where the username and password are entered. We can use cookies to store the information so that the users do not have to enter the same information every time when using this page.

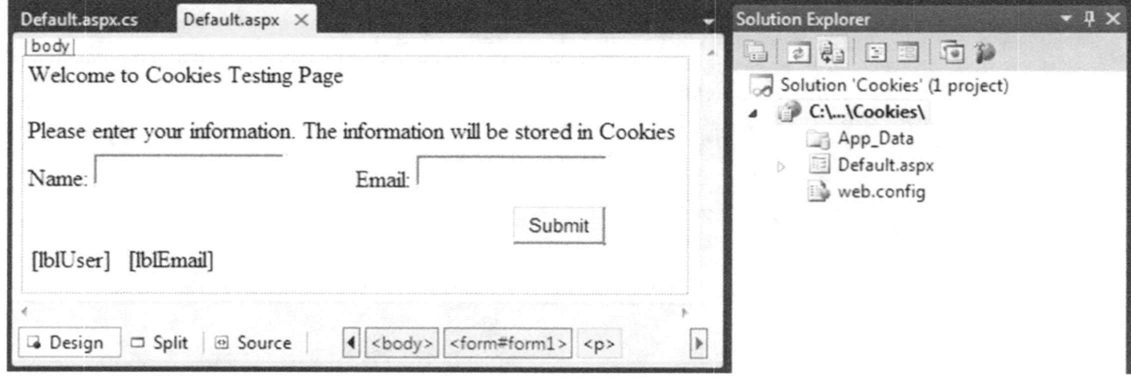

Figure 5.13. Interface design of Default.aspx, Seller.aspx, and MyCart.aspx pages

The code below is the main code behind the page and behind the button "Submit."

```
using System.Net; // needed for Cookies
public partial class _Default : System.Web.UI.Page  {
   protected void Page_Load(object sender, EventArgs e) {
        HttpCookie myCookies = Request.Cookies["myCookieId"];
        if ((myCookies == null) || (myCookies["Name"]=="")) {
              lblUser.Text = "Welcome, new user";
   } else {
        lblUser.Text = "Welcome, " + myCookies["Name"];
        lblEmail.Text = "We have your email " + myCookies["Email"];
        }
   }
protected void  BtnSubmit_Click(object sender, EventArgs e)
   {
        HttpCookie myCookies = new HttpCookie("myCookieId");
        myCookies["Name"] = TextBox1.Text;
        myCookies["Email"] = TextBox2.Text;
        myCookies.Expires = DateTime.Now.AddMonths(6);
        Response.Cookies.Add(myCookies);
        lblUser.Text = "Name stored in Cookies " + myCookies["Name"];
        lblEmail.Text = "Email stored in Cookies " + myCookies["Email"];         }
}
```

The Page_load() method will be executed when a client accesses the page. The code checks if cookies have been created before and if the cookies are empty. In either case, a new user is using the page. Otherwise, the program will read the stored information from the cookies. In the code behind the button "Submit," the information entered in the two textboxes will be stored into the cookies. The key "myCookieId" links the cookies used in the Page_load() method and in the BtnSubmit_Click() method. Two fields of the cookies are used in this example: myCookies["Name"] and myCookies["Email"].

5.3.6 Session State and Cookies

How can an application know that an incoming access is a revisit to the same session, or is a new request from a different user? HTTP is stateless, and it does not carry the identity information of the user and session. The browser needs to explicitly send the session ID when it stores data to the session variable. There are two primary ways for the browser to store and carry the session ID when it revisits the page on the server:

- Using a cookie on the client side to save the session ID: If cookies are supported and enabled in the browser, the session ID can be stored in the cookie section in the browser application folder, which is in the client machine's file system. The server can communicate with the cookies and verify if a request comes from a previous session by reading the cookie value.
- Using the hidden field in the HTML page, similar to the View State: In this case, the server cannot find the cookie and cannot read the hidden field in the HTML page that is created on the client side. In this case, the browser must encode the session ID in URI/URL as a part of the address that it sends to the server. Different values can be embedded in the URL when a browser sends the address to the server. The server can extract the value and build the physical address. This is only possible if relative addresses are used in locating the page. When relative address is used, the server needs to reassemble the physical address using the root address to the current location and the relative address from the current location to the destination. While the processor is doing the address processing, it can easily extract the session ID or parameters (for RESTful service call) embedded in the URL. On the other hand, if the page to be accessed is programmed in absolute address, the address handler will not be called and thus, the session ID or parameters embedded in the address can cause an error. In this case, URL parameter embedding should not be allowed.

The aforesaid two methods have their advantages as well as drawbacks. Using the cookie to store session ID will allow the ID to be valid even if the browser window is closed and reopened. However, if cookies are disabled in the client browser, session state will not work. Using Uri will not rely on the availability of cookies. However, if the browser page is closed, the data stored in the hidden field in the HTML page will disappear. When you reopen the page and reconnect to the server, the session ID has been lost and the session state cannot be accessed.

Fortunately, the developer can not only choose one of the two ways, but can also choose the combination of the two ways by defining a clause in the Web.config file:

```
<system.web>
  <sessionState
      cookieless = "{HttpCookieMode values}"
      timeout = "int, number of minutes"
      ... >
   </sessionState>
</system.web>
```

Where, one can define the duration of the cookies in a number of minutes and cookies modes of one of the following four values:

1. cookieless = "UseCookies": Always assume that cookies are supported by the browser and are enabled. This is an optimistic assumption, as the user's browser may not support cookies or may be disabled for storing cookies because of security concerns. In this case, session identification will fail, and the information stored in the session variables will not be visited by the same session.
2. cookieless = "UseUri": The session ID will be stored in the URL as a parameter. There is a potential problem. If an absolute path is used in the program, storing session ID in URL will cause a page error. For this and other reasons, one should not use absolute path in programming.
3. cookieless = "UseDeviceProfile": The server checks if the type and version of the browser to determine if the browser supports cookies. If it does, the server will set the mode to cookieless = "UseCookies," otherwise, it sets the mode to cookieless = "UseUri." However, the server does not check if the cookies are disabled even if the browser support cookies.
4. cookieless = "AutoDetect": The server checks whether or not the browser supports cookies and tests to see if cookies are enabled. This option incurs additional overhead. In order to test whether or not the cookies are enabled, the server creates cookies, saves a value into the cookies, and retrieves the value to see if the value is stored or not.

As we discussed in the previous section, cookies can also be used for storing credentials such as a username and password, so that a web form can remember the user when the user revisits a page. Again, a client can choose to disable cookies for higher security or enable cookies for convenience. Cookies used for storing credentials can be encrypted so that a hacker who breaks into the client machine cannot read the cookies to read the usernames and password.

5.3.7 Application State and Service Execution Model

Session["NameIndex"] allows us to create session-wide variables in the server's memory, and all pages in the same session can access the session variables. Similarly, in syntax, we can use a collection of Application State variables in the form of Application["NameIndex"] to create application-wide variables, and all sessions and all pages in each session to access the application variables; for example, we can create a variable called Application["SuperCounter"] in the Global.asax file to keep track of the total number of accesses to the application. An application state variable is similar to a static variable in class definition, which allows all the instances of the class to read and write the same variable.

Due to the potential high volume of parallel accesses on the web, the challenges in using an application-wide variable include, as we discussed in Chapter 2:

- Write-write and read-write conflicts if the application state variable is not locked during the accesses;
- Significant performance degradation if the application state variable is locked.

Tradeoff between these two problems is necessary; for example, if the total number of accesses does not need to be accurate, occasional write-write and read-write conflicts are acceptable, and thus lock of the application state variable Application["SuperCounter"] may not be necessary.

The problem mentioned in the foregoing paragraph is due to high volume of accesses. If, on the other hand, the volume of accesses is low, another problem will occur: The application will be terminated by the server and the data saved in the application state will disappear. To solve this problem, one can write an event handler in the Global.asax file to save the application state into a disk file before the application terminates, and reload the data after the application is reloaded.

A service is theoretically running all the time, waiting for requests to arrive. In practice, it is determined by the execution model of the server. In IIS, a service is created as a thread by a so-called worker process. When the worker process is running out of capacity (memory space and other resources), and there is a need to start a new thread (service), the worker process will have to terminate a service that is least frequently accessed or has not been accessed for the longest time. The replacement policy is similar to that used in memory management.

The IIS server applies just-in-time (JIT) compilation to the code behind the pages, including ASPX pages, ASMX services, ASCX user controls, and the Global.asax page. These files are dynamically compiled at runtime. Only DLL files are precompiled.

When an HTTP request arrives, the IIS server will look up the registration list. If the request service or application does not exist, a page-not-found error will be generated. Thus, all services and applications must register to WAS (Web Administration Service). The "Convert to Application" operation applied to a folder in IIS registers the folder to WAS. If the requested service or application is found, IIS redirects the request to the application or service. If the requested application or service is already running, a new session will be created to handle the request. If it is not running and not compiled, IIS will compile the code, save the compiled code, and start to run it. If it is not running but is compiled, IIS simply starts the compiled code.

5.4 Save User Data to Server File System

All state management techniques are not permanent, and user data can disappear due to different limitations and trade-offs. View State data disappears when the browser is closed, as the data is saved in a hidden field in the browser. Session State data disappears when the session is closed. Cookies can be disabled, expired, or cleared. If an application wants to keep the user data permanently, the only option is to save user data into the file system (disk) or into the database. This section will discuss the file system, and the database option will be discussed in Chapter 10.

5.4.1 File System and Standard File Operations

Data stored on disk are organized in files. We consider a file a structured data type and we access data in a file using a reference (pointer) to an object of type FILE, which records whatever information is necessary to control the stream of data.

As we know, disk operations are extremely slow, a million times slower than memory operations, as they involve mechanic rotations of the disk and sliding of the read/write heads. The challenge is to make file operations faster. The solution is to use a buffer in the memory to hold a large block (e.g., 1024 bytes) of data. Each disk operation will transfer a block of data, instead of a byte or a word of data. Figure 5.14 shows how read and write operations are implemented.

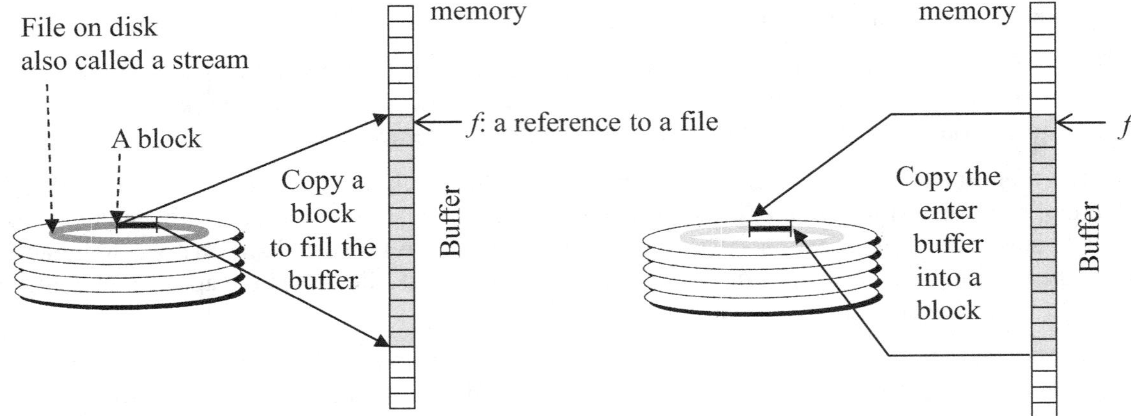

Figure 5.14. File read and write operations

For read operations, the process is as follows:

- Declare a reference f to a FILE type;
- Open a file for read: Create a buffer that can hold a block of bytes (e.g., 1024 bytes);
- Copy the first block of a file into buffer;
- A program uses the file reference to read the data in the buffer;
- When the reference moves down to the end of the buffer, copy the next block into buffer;
- Close the file at the end of use.

For write operations, the process is as follows:

- Declare a reference f to a FILE type;
- Open a file for write: Create a buffer that can hold a block of bytes (e.g., 1024 bytes);
- A program uses the reference to write the data in the buffer;
- When the buffer is full, copy the block into the disk;
- Move the pointer to the beginning for more write-operations;
- Close the file at the end of use.

In this section, we show an example using StreamReader to read an Excel file in .csv (Comma-Separated Values) format. The program first loads a file named "filename.csv" into a StreamReader object. In a while loop, the program uses the object's ReadLine() function to read a line in each iteration. This loop counts the number of lines the file has, but skips the empty lines.

Then, in a second while loop, the program counts how many columns the Excel file has. The columns are separated by the delimiter comma and it saves the column names into an array of strings.

```
int entriesFound = 0;
using (var textReader = new StreamReader("filename.csv")){//Load a file into object
   string line = textReader.ReadLine();
   int skipCount = 0;
   while (line != null && skipCount < 1) {
        line = textReader.ReadLine();
        skipCount++;
   }
   while (line != null) { // counts the columns and save then into string array
        string[] columns = line.Split(_Delimiter);
        entriesFound++;
```

```
        line = textReader.ReadLine();
    }
}
```

5.4.2 Reading and Writing XML Files

In Chapter 3, we discussed a file service that saves a string into a text file in the server and then later retrieves the file from the server. In this section, we will extend the data management to XML files.

An XML file is a text file and can be read from and written into a file system like a text file. However, extracting data from a file will need an XML processor. ASP .Net provides a namespace System.IO, which includes a number of library classes to support the file operations:

- FileStream class creates a buffer and connection between the application and the file system.
- Path class manipulates the paths and file names for accessing files in the file system.

Figure 5.15 shows a scenario of XML data exchange between the ASP .Net application and the file system of the server. On the one hand, a user enters a table of data or the system reads a set of data from a source. An XML writer creates an XML file. The XML file is considered a text file and written into the file system by the stream writer of the FileStream class. The location of the file is determined by the Path class, which combines the path from the file system root to the current location and the path from the current location to the destination. On the other hand, when reading a file from the file system, the stream reader in the FileStream class reads the XML file as a stream of text into the buffer at the location defined by the Path class. An XML reader parses the data stream and extracts data elements, which are then sent to data consumers or to web controls for display.

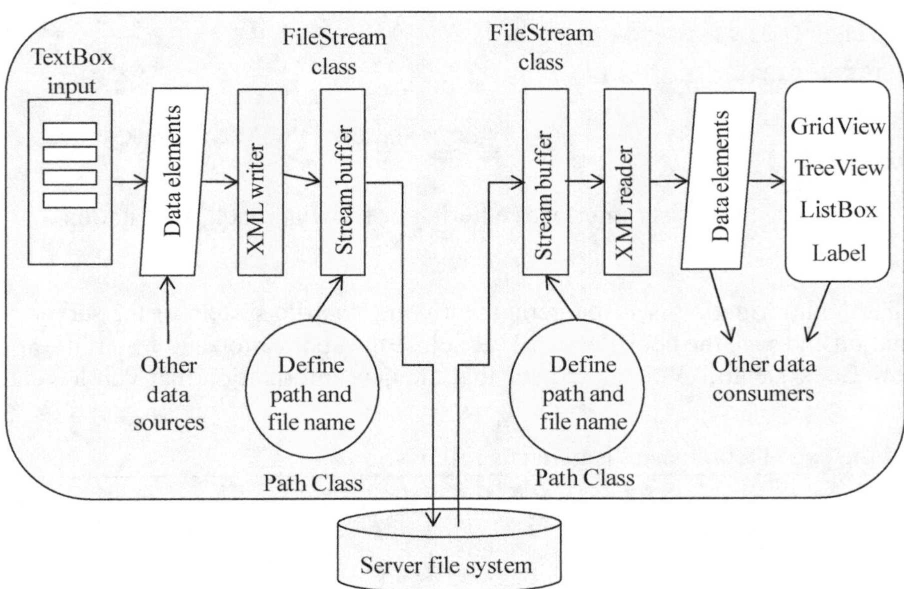

Figure 5.15. A scenario of XML data exchange between the application and the file system

Now, we use an example to demonstrate writing into and reading from the file system illustrated in Figure 5.15. We use the same example used in the previous section. Instead of saving the book information in session state variables only, we also save the book information into an XML file in the file system.

Let us start with a demonstration by accessing the web application at the address:

http://neptune.fulton.ad.asu.edu/WSRepository/XMLDocReadWriteApp/Default.aspx

Figure 5.16 shows the user interface of the Default.aspx page (left) and the solution view of the project. Note that an XML file, Book.xml, is saved in the folder App_Data.

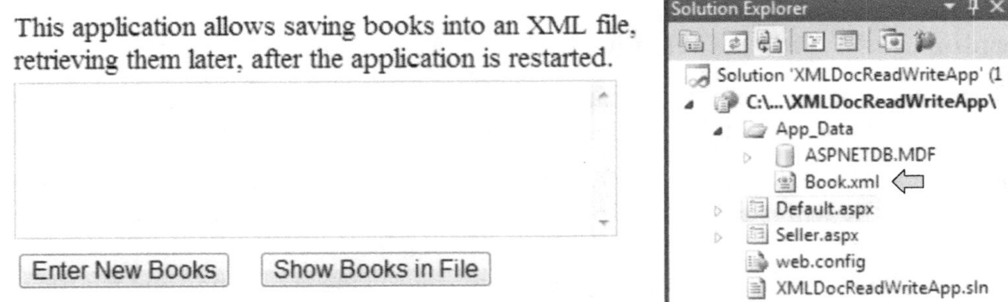

Figure 5.16. User interface of the Default.aspx page and the solution view of the project

If the button "Enter New Books" is clicked, a table will be displayed for the user to enter book information. If the button "Show Books in File" is clicked, the books stored in the server's file system will be displayed. Figure 5.17 shows the two user interface designs of the two pages.

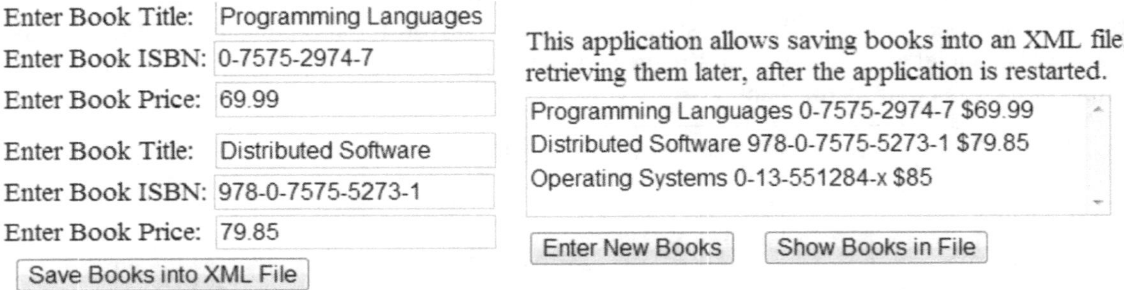

Figure 5.17. User interfaces entering or showing book information

To make sure that the information is saved permanently into the file system of the server, you can change the book information and save the book details. Then, close the application and restart the application. Click the button "Show Book Detail." You should see that the new information that you have entered is saved and retrieved.

The code behind the page Default.aspx is given as follows:

```
using System; // not all namespaces are shown here
public partial class _Default : System.Web.UI.Page {
    protected void Page_Load(object sender, EventArgs e) {}
    protected void btnSeller_Click(object sender, EventArgs e) {
        Response.Redirect("Seller.aspx");
    }
    protected void Button1_Click(object sender, EventArgs e)
    {
        string fLocation = Path.Combine(Request.PhysicalApplicationPath,
@"App_Data\Book.xml"); //or HttpContext.Current.Request.PhysicalApplicationPath

        if (File.Exists(fLocation)) {
            FileStream fS = new FileStream(fLocation, FileMode.Open);
            XmlDocument xd = new XmlDocument();
```

```
            xd.Load(fS);
            XmlNode node = xd;
            XmlNodeList children = node.ChildNodes;
            foreach (XmlNode child in children.Item(1)) {
                ListBox1.Items.Add(child.FirstChild.InnerText + "   " +
child.FirstChild.NextSibling.InnerText + "   " + "$"+ child.LastChild.InnerText);
                ListBox1.Items.Add("\r\n");
            }
            fS.Close();  // It is important to close the file
        }
    }
}
```

Note that the library classes and methods used to perform the operations needed are:

- Path.Combine(path1, path2): It combines the path from file system root to the application folder and path to the Book.xml file.
- FileStream class creates a stream file reference and a buffer for the XML reader to use.
- XmlDocumnent class's Load method loads the XML file into memory.
- XmlNode and XmlNodeList process each child of the XML document and load the information into the ListBox.
- It is important to close the file. Otherwise, the file may still be locked and it cannot be open again later.

The code behind the Seller.aspx page is given as follows:

```
using System;  // not all namespaces are shown here
public partial class Seller : System.Web.UI.Page {
    protected void Page_Load(object sender, EventArgs e) { }
    protected void Button1_Click(object sender, EventArgs e) {
        string title = txtTitle.Text;
        string isbn = txtIsbn.Text;
        string sPrice = txtPrice.Text;
        string title2 = txtTitle2.Text;
        string isbn2 = txtIsbn2.Text;
        string sPrice2 = txtPrice2.Text;
        string title3 = txtTitle3.Text;
        string isbn3 = txtIsbn3.Text;
        string sPrice3 = txtPrice3.Text;
        string fLocation = Path.Combine(Request.PhysicalApplicationPath,
@"App_Data\Book.xml"); //or HttpContext.Current.Request.PhysicalApplicationPath
        FileStream fState = null;
        Try {
            fState = new FileStream(fLocation, FileMode.Truncate);//clear content
             // Open a text file: first open
            XmlTextWriter writer = new XmlTextWriter(fState,
System.Text.Encoding.Unicode); // Open an XML file: second open
            writer.Formatting = Formatting.Indented;
            writer.WriteStartDocument();
            writer.WriteStartElement("Books");
            writer.WriteStartElement("Book");
            writer.WriteElementString("Title", title);
            writer.WriteElementString("Isbn", isbn);
            writer.WriteElementString("Price", sPrice);
            writer.WriteEndElement();
            writer.WriteStartElement("Book");
            writer.WriteElementString("Title", title2);
            writer.WriteElementString("Isbn", isbn2);
            writer.WriteElementString("Price", sPrice2);
```

```
            writer.WriteEndElement();
            writer.WriteStartElement("Book");
            writer.WriteElementString("Title", title3);
            writer.WriteElementString("Isbn", isbn3);
            writer.WriteElementString("Price", sPrice3);
            writer.WriteEndElement();
            writer.WriteEndElement();
            writer.WriteEndDocument();
            writer.Close();       // Close XML writer
            fState.Close();       // Close the text file
        }
        Finally {
            if (fState != null) fState.Close();
        }
        Response.Redirect("Default.aspx");
    }
}
```

Note that the code above reads three books at time. This is a simplified implementation so that we can focus on the concepts to be demonstrated in this example. One can easily add a loop to allow entering any number of books. In addition to using the library class Path and FileStream classes, it uses XMLWriter class to create an XML document from scratch data. It is very important that code has opened the same file twice: once as a text file and once as an XML file. The file must also be closed twice.

The XML file created by the XMLWriter is shown as follows:

```
<?xml version="1.0" encoding="utf-16"?>
<Books>
  <Book>
    <Title>Programming Languages</Title>
    <Isbn>0-7575-2974-7</Isbn>
    <Price>69.99</Price>
  </Book>
  <Book>
    <Title>Distributed Software</Title>
    <Isbn>978-0-7575-5273-1</Isbn>
    <Price>79.85</Price>
  </Book>
  <Book>
    <Title>Operating Systems</Title>
    <Isbn>0-13-551284-x</Isbn>
    <Price>85</Price>
  </Book>
</Books>
```

5.5 Caching and Recommendation

Caching is a key technique in computer architecture design to make the data access much faster. The rationale behind caching in computer architecture includes temporal locality: if a piece of data is used, it is likely to be used again; and spatial locality: if a piece of data is used, its neighboring data are likely to be used soon. Data like arrays are stored in a block and are often used sequentially.

One of the key innovations implemented in Google's search engine is web data caching that makes the search engine fast and informative. The rationale behind caching in web applications includes:

- Most people want to know the same information when they search data in web applications.

- Frequently accessed data are more valuable than less frequently accessed data; for example, shopping sites often show customers what other people buy most.
- A cached page can continue to exist after the original page becomes unavailable.
- Data accesses to disk files, databases, and remote web services are slow and costly. Caching can improve the performance.

Caching is not cheap, as it takes precious memory from server that is shared by many applications. It is always necessary to select caching data carefully and to keep a balance between performance gain and cost incurred. Different caching techniques are available. Table 5.3 lists three caching techniques, each of which will be explained in the following subsections.

Table 5.3. Caching techniques and their features

Caching Type	Features
Output Caching	The entire html or XHTML page generated from server-side page is cached. When the same page is requested, the same rendered page is sent to the browser. Caching duration and location (on server or client side) can be specified.
Fragment Caching	Caching the entire page may be too expensive. Specifying fragments of a page through user controls to cache partial data can be a better tradeoff between performance and cost.
Data Caching	Define and program your own data objects for caching, with the support from the runtime environment for threading, placement, and replacement

5.5.1 Output Caching

Output caching in ASP .Net saves the entire XHTML page generated from ASPX page through a directive in the page source code. When the same page is requested again, the cached page is sent to the browser. Caching duration and location (on server or client side) can be specified in the page directive. We will explain the technique through an example as shown in Figure 5.18.

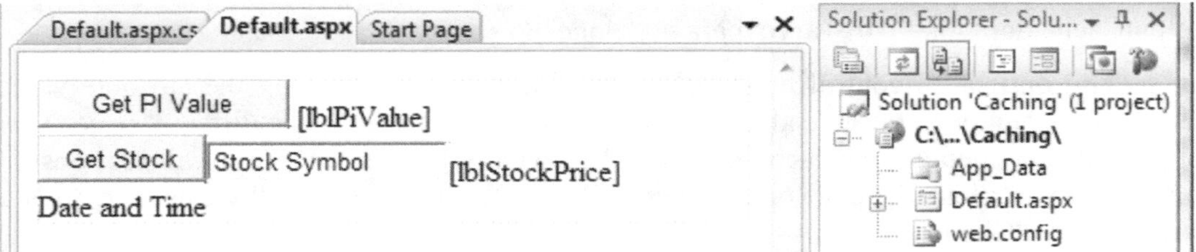

Figure 5.18. GUI design (Default.aspx) of the caching example

The C# code behind the GUI page is shown in the following example. In this example, the stock value, instead of being received from a web service, is generated by a random number generator.

```
public partial class _Default : System.Web.UI.Page  {
   protected void Page_Load(object sender, EventArgs e) {
   String date = DateTime.Now.ToLongDateString();
   String time = DateTime.Now.ToLongTimeString();
   lblDateTime.Text = date + ", " + time;
   }
   protected void btnPiValue_Click(object sender, EventArgs e)   {
        double pi = System.Math.PI;
```

```
        lblPiValue.Text = Convert.ToString(pi);
}
   protected void btnStock_Click(object sender, EventArgs e) {
   Random r = new Random();  int price = r.Next(100);
   lblStockPrice.Text = Convert.ToString(price);
     }
}
```

The XHTML source code of the Default.aspx page is given as follows, with the output caching directive included (highlighted).

```
<%@ Page Language="C#" AutoEventWireup="true"  CodeFile="Default.aspx.cs"
Inherits="_Default" %>
<%@ OutputCache duration="10" varybyparam="None" %>
<!DOCTYPE html PUBLIC "-//W3C//DTD XHTML 1.0 Transitional//EN"
"http://www.w3.org/TR/xhtml1/DTD/xhtml1-transitional.dtd">
<html xmlns="http://www.w3.org/1999/xhtml">
<head id="Head1" runat="server"> <title>Caching Page</title></head>
<body>
    <form id="form1" runat="server">
    <div>
        <asp:Button ID="btnPiValue" runat="server" Text="Get PI Value" Width="133px"
onclick="btnPiValue_Click" />
<asp:Label ID="lblPiValue" runat="server"></asp:Label>
    </div>
    <asp:Button ID="btnStock" runat="server" onclick="btnStock_Click"
        Text="Get Stock" />
    <asp:TextBox ID="txtAbsoluteValue" runat="server">Stock Symbol</asp:TextBox>
    <asp:Label ID="lblStockPrice" runat="server"></asp:Label>
    <asp:Label ID="lblDateTime" runat="server" Text="Date and Time"> </asp:Label>
    </form>
</body>
</html>
```

To enable output caching, all we need is to add this line of the directive in the foregoing source code, where duration = "10" means that same page will be used for 10 seconds without regenerating the page.

<%@ OutputCache duration="10" varybyparam="None" %>

There are several options to control how caching should be done by giving the attribute values to the parameter varybyparam, which can lead to the application to selectively cache different pages for different users; for example. By default, the cache page will be saved on the server side for all sessions. However, we can also specify to cache the page on the client side just for the session. All we need to do is to add an attribute Location = "Client" as follows:

<%@ OutputCache duration="10" varybyparam="None" **Location = "Client"** %>

To test the code, we can click the button of "Get Stock" multiple times within 10 seconds. You will notice that the same values will be given. After 10 seconds, a new value will be given. If you click the "Get Stock" and then click "Get PI Value" within 10 seconds, you will not see the PI Value. This is because we have a cache page for the entire page including all buttons.

5.5.2 Fragment Caching

Output caching has two obvious problems. It may take too much server memory to cache the entire page, and it caches all the parts of the page in one page, which can prevent the user getting different parts of information from the page, as we have seen in the foregoing example. When the stock price is cached, we cannot get PI value.

To address these problems, we should try to partition the page into multiple components. One easy way to do so is to use user controls and define the output caching in the user control's XHTML source pages. Figure 5.19 shows the GUI of the encryption example that we discussed in the section of User Control. Now, we can add the output caching directive into the XHTML source code of the page:

```
<%@ Control Language="C#" AutoEventWireup="true" CodeFile="DateToday.ascx.cs"
Inherits="Confirmation" %>
<%@ OutputCache duration="10" varybyparam="None" %>
<asp:Label ID="lblConformMsg" runat="server" Text="Today's date is "></asp:Label>
<asp:Label ID="lblDate" runat="server" Text=""></asp:Label>
```

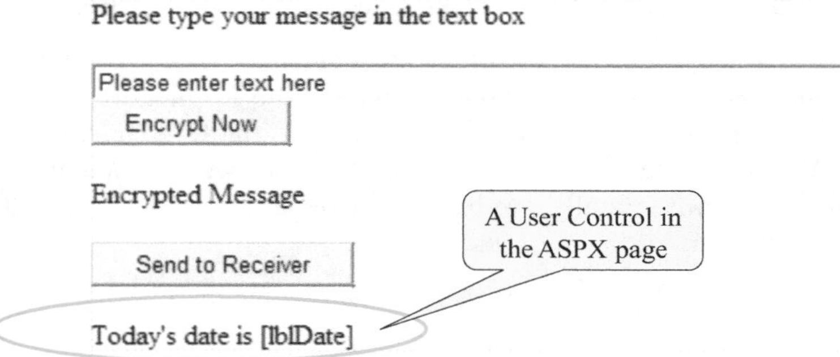

Figure 5.19. Adding output caching into the user control of the encryption example

5.5.3 Data Caching

The most advanced and flexible caching mechanism is data caching, which allows programmers to cache any objects by saving these objects and reuse the objects. Figure 5.20 shows the principle of data caching supported by software and hardware on the server side.

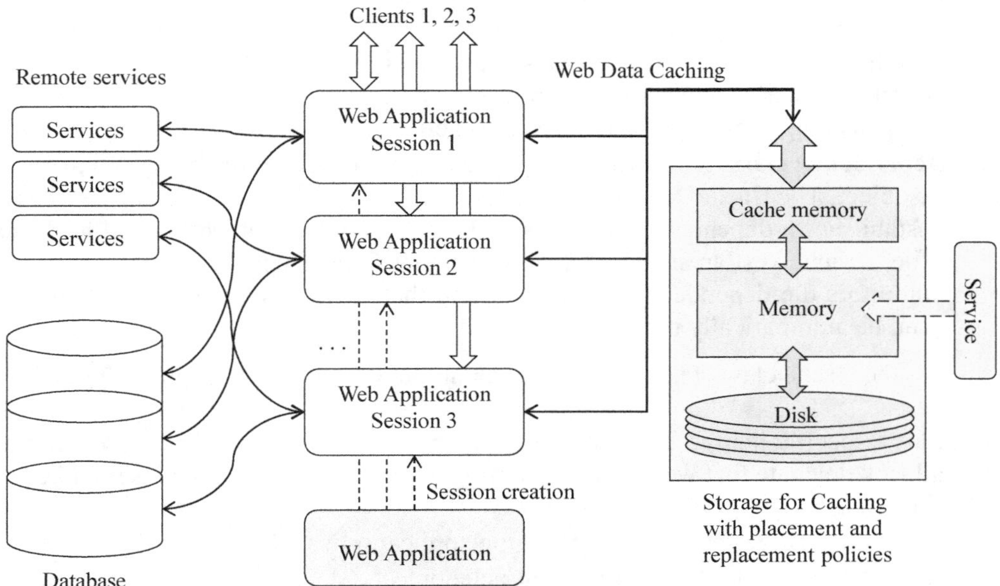

Figure 5.20. Principle of web data caching

Once the web application is accessed, a new session is created for the client. The session may access remote services and databases. The data that a client has accessed may be accessed by the client again. For example, if a client is comparing the performance and price of a product with other similar products, it is likely the client will return to the product page several times. If a client is interested in a product, it is likely that other clients may be interested in the same product. Thus, the developer should consider caching a product that is fetched from a database or from a remote service, so that the client can see the product with little delay when the client returns to the product. The cache shown in Figure 5.20 is shared by all sessions. Note that the cache hardware is organized in a hierarchy. The cache memory is small but superfast. The memory is large but slower. The disk is the largest but is the slowest. When the developer tries to put too many objects on cache and tries to use the cache for too long, the cached items can be shifted to the slower storage.

At the programming level, we could use different mechanisms to save the objects. We could use the Application State variables as the cache. Any objects saved in the Application State variables are available to all sessions. What is wrong with using Application State variable for caching purposes? There are a number of problems. We have to be aware of how much memory we use. We have to update the lists and dispose of the older lists manually. Finally, we have to manage the threads and lock the objects while we are updating the cached data.

ASP .Net provides a namespace of caching classes that automates the tasks necessary for caching, which allows us to:

- Use Application State syntax: Cache["indexkey"] = object, which is easy to use;
- Automated Expirations—absolute or relative expirations for infrequently used items to expire automatically;
- Define dependencies between cached items and other items;
- Automated callback—an event handler can be added to a cached item that will be called when the item is to be removed from the cache, which gives us an opportunity to update the cache or not to remove the item;
- Manage threads automatically to prevent conflicting.

Among the caching classes, two classes will be discussed in detail here:

- **Cache class**: In order to cache data, we need to create an object of the Cache class. When an instance of the class Cache is created in a session, the instance will be:
  - available to all sessions of the application, and
  - valid as long as the application remains active.
- **CacheDependency class**: It defines the type for one of the parameters when we insert an object to the cache object. The CacheDependency class:
  - establishes a dependency relationship between an item (object) added to the cache and a file, a cache key, an array of either, or another CacheDependency object.
  - monitors the dependency relationships so that when a relation changes, the cached item can be automatically removed.

Let us first discuss the Cache class. The class defines a number of methods to support the cache operations, including:

- **Add**: Adds a specific item to an existing Cache object, such as dependencies, expiration, priority, and a callback delegate that we can use to notify the application when the inserted item is removed from the Cache.
- **Remove**: Removes the specified item from the application's Cache object.
- **Get**: Retrieves the specified item from the Cache object.
- **GetType**: Gets the type of the current instance (Inherited from Object).
- **ToString**: Converts the current Object to a string (Inherited from Object).

- **Insert**: Inserts a new data object into the cache. Insert is the major method used for creating a cache. Five overloaded methods are defined, with a different parameter list, to meet different needs of inserting new data into the cache.
  - Insert(String, Object); For this operation, a different syntax is allowed to support the convention used in other state management mechanisms, such as session state and application state: Cache["indexkey"] = item;
  - Insert(String, Object, CacheDependency);
  - Insert(String, Object, CacheDependency, DateTime, TimeSpan);
  - Insert(String, Object, CacheDependency, DateTime, TimeSpan, CacheItemUpdateCallback);
  - Insert(String, Object, CacheDependency, DateTime, TimeSpan, CacheItemPriority, CacheItemRemovedCallback).

The parameters of the five insert methods are explained in Table 5.4.

Table 5.4. Parameter description of the insert methods

Parameter type name	Description
String key	Index key for referring the cache data
Object value	Item to be cached
CacheDependency dependencies	Dependencies between the cached item and another item
DateTime absoluteExpiration	The cached item will be removed at the given date and time
TimeSpan slidingExpiration	The cached item will be removed if the item is not accessed within the given time interval. If set to 0, only absolute expiration is used
CacheItemPriority priority	The cost of the object relative to other items stored in the cache
CacheItemRemovedCallback onRemoveCallback	A delegate that, if provided, will be called when an object is removed from the cache.

As can be seen, one of the parameters of the insert method is defined by the CacheDependency class. This class establishes a dependency relationship between the item to be stored in the Cache object and a file, a cache key, an array of either, or another CacheDependency object. One can include dependency in insert(), or add it later using Add(). The CacheDependency class monitors the dependency relationships so that when any of them changes, the cached item will be automatically removed. Use null if you do not want to define the dependency.

Now, we will use a few examples to illustrate the use of the classes and their methods. The code below caches two data items: "Dell Printer 1710" and "Cartridge for Printer 1710," and will automatically delete the cache item "Cartridge for Printer 1710" if "Dell Printer 1710" is removed.

```
protected void btnAddBook_Click(object sender, EventArgs e)
{ // create two cache items
   string item1 = "Dell Printer 1710";
   string item2 = "Cartridge for Printer 1710";
   Cache.Insert("PrinterKey", item1, null, DateTime.Now.AddMinutes(10),
         TimeSpan.Zero, CacheItemPriority.Default, CacheRemovedCallBack);
   Cache.Insert("CartridgeKey", item2, null, DateTime.Now.AddMinutes(10),
                                                      TimeSpan.Zero);
}
```

The event handler is defined as follows:

```
private void CacheRemovedCallBack(string IndexKey, object value,
                                    CacheItemRemovedReason reason)
{ // remove the Cartridge from the cache if printer is removed
   Cache.Remove("CartridgeKey");
}
```

We can also share the event handler, that is, the event handler can be associated with more than one data item. The following code shows that two data items are associated with the same event handler.

```
protected void btnAddBook_Click(object sender, EventArgs e)
{  string item1 = "Dell Printer 1710";
   string item2 = "Cartridge for Printer 1710";
   Cache.Insert("PrinterKey", item1, null, DateTime.Now.AddMinutes(10),
TimeSpan.Zero, CacheItemPriority.Default, CacheRemovedCallBack);
   Cache.Insert("CartridgeKey", item2, null, DateTime.Now.AddMinutes(10),
TimeSpan.Zero, CacheRemovedCallBack);
}
```

The event handler uses a conditional statement to handle the two calls differently.

```
private void CacheRemovedCallBack(string IndexKey, object value,
                                    CacheItemRemovedReason reason)
{ // remove the Cartridge from the cache
   if (IndexKey == "PrinterKey" )
        Cache.Remove("CartridgeKey");     // if the printer is removed
   else if (IndexKey == "CartridgeKey")
        Cache.Remove("PrinterKey ");      // if the cartridge is removed
}
```

Next, we will use a more complex example to show the caching mechanism. In this example, we will cache the XMLDocument object read from an XML and display the data from the cache if the cache is available. We will associate the cache item with the modification of the XML file. If the XML file is modified, we must discard the cache automatically. This example is based on the example we used in the previous section where we read and write an XML document to the disk.

The GUI design and the project explorer are shown in Figure 5.21. A disk file Book.xml is placed in the application's folder App_Data. If the cache is empty, the ListBox displays nothing when we start the application. If there is cache data, the ListBox will display the data. When we click the button "Reload from Books.xml," books will be read from the file and displayed into the ListBox, and the data will be saved into the cache. Dependency is defined, which will remove the cache whenever the Books.xml file is modified. When clicking the button "Modify Book.xml," which will enter the Seller.aspx page and the cache will be deleted. If we click the button "Show Cache Contents" the cache data will be displayed in the ListBox. We also designed a button "Show Cache Status" to check if there is data in the cache. We can clear the ListBox, and then show books from the cache, instead of from the disk file. The checkbox "Bypass Cache" is designed to not use cache, no matter if cache exists or not. This option will ensure the data is the actual data.

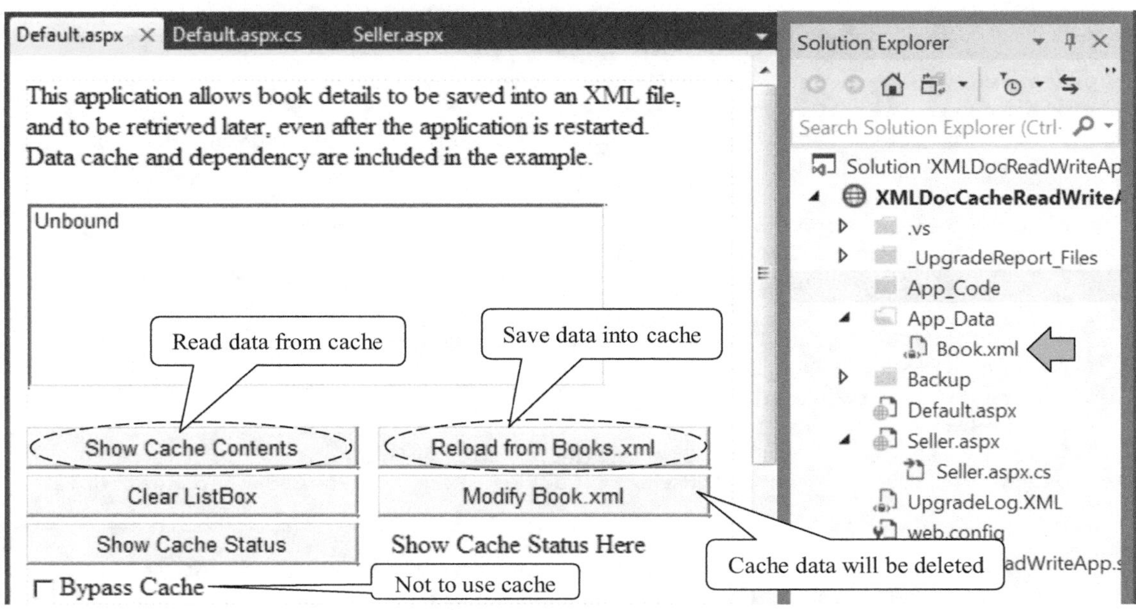

Figure 5.21. GUI design and the project explorer using an XML file for storing book information

The code behind the Default.aspx page is as follows, which includes the code when the page is loaded and the code behind all the buttons. The design and code behind the Seller.aspx page remain the same, as we have discussed in section 5.4.2: Reading and Writing XML Files.

```
using System; using System.Web.Caching; using System.Xml; using System.IO;
public partial class _Default : System.Web.UI.Page {
    protected void Page_Load(object sender, EventArgs e) {
        if ((Cache["BooksKey"] != null) && (!ckBypassCache.Checked)) {
            ListBox1.Items.Clear();
            XmlDocument xd = (XmlDocument)Cache["BooksKey"];
            XmlNode node = xd;
            XmlNodeList children = node.ChildNodes;
            foreach (XmlNode child in children.Item(1)){
                ListBox1.Items.Add(child.FirstChild.InnerText + "   " +
child.FirstChild.NextSibling.InnerText + "   " + "$" + child.LastChild.InnerText);
            }
        }
        if (Cache["BooksKey"] == null)
            lblCacheStatus.Text = "No Cache of Book.xml";
        else
            lblCacheStatus.Text = Cache.ToString();
    }
    protected void btnShowCache_Click(object sender, EventArgs e){
        ListBox1.Items.Clear();
        if ((Cache["BooksKey"] != null) && (!ckBypassCache.Checked)){
            ListBox1.Items.Clear();
            XmlDocument xd = (XmlDocument)Cache["BooksKey"];
            XmlNode node = xd;
            XmlNodeList children = node.ChildNodes;
            foreach (XmlNode child in children.Item(1)){
                ListBox1.Items.Add(child.FirstChild.InnerText + "   " +
child.FirstChild.NextSibling.InnerText + "   " + "$" + child.LastChild.InnerText);
            }
```

```
        }
    }
    protected void btnClear_Click(object sender, EventArgs e) {
        ListBox1.Items.Clear();
        ListBox1.Items.Add("The ListBox is cleared, but not the cache. ");
        ListBox1.Items.Add("You can still reload the data from the Cache.");
    }
    protected void btnCacheStatus_Click(object sender, EventArgs e){
        if (Cache["BooksKey"] == null)
            lblCacheStatus.Text = "No Cache of Book.xml";
        else
            lblCacheStatus.Text = Cache.ToString();
    }
    protected void btbReloadFile_Click(object sender, EventArgs e) {
        FileStream fS = null;
        string fLocation = Path.Combine(Request.PhysicalApplicationPath,
@"App_Data\Book.xml"); //or HttpContext.Current.Request.PhysicalApplicationPath
        try {
            if (File.Exists(fLocation)) {
                fS = new FileStream(fLocation, FileMode.Open, FileAccess.Read);
                XmlDocument xd = new XmlDocument();
                xd.Load(fS);
                fS.Close(); // close after loading
                // Add the file into cache and the dependency to the file
                if (Cache["BooksKey"] == null) {
                    CacheDependency fileDependency = new CacheDependency(fLocation);
                    Cache.Insert("BooksKey", xd, fileDependency,
DateTime.Now.AddMinutes(30),
                        TimeSpan.Zero,
                        CacheItemPriority.Default,
                        new CacheItemRemovedCallback(CacheRemovedCallBack));
                    XmlNode node = xd;
                    XmlNodeList children = node.ChildNodes;
                    foreach (XmlNode child in children.Item(1)) {
                        ListBox1.Items.Add(child.FirstChild.InnerText + "   " +
child.FirstChild.NextSibling.InnerText + "   " + "$" + child.LastChild.InnerText);
                    }
                }
            }
        }
        finally { fS.Close(); } // close in case the session crashes

    }
    private void CacheRemovedCallBack(string IndexKey, object value,
                                      CacheItemRemovedReason reason){
        // Callback that remove the cache if the file is changed
        if (IndexKey == "BooksKey")
            Cache.Remove("BooksKey");
    }
    protected void btnSeller_Click(object sender, EventArgs e) {
        Response.Redirect("seller.aspx");
    }   // page behind button Modify Book.xml
}
```

Note that the cache data is added in the method btnShowBook_Click when the button "Show Books in Book.xml" and the cache data is used in the method Page_Load. You can test this application at:

http://neptune.fulton.ad.asu.edu/WSRepository/XMLDocCacheReadWriteApp/Default.aspx

In the aforesaid example, we used the XML file to store the books. We can use a database to serve the same purpose. Figure 5.22 shows the GUI design and file explorer of the implementation of using the SQL database.

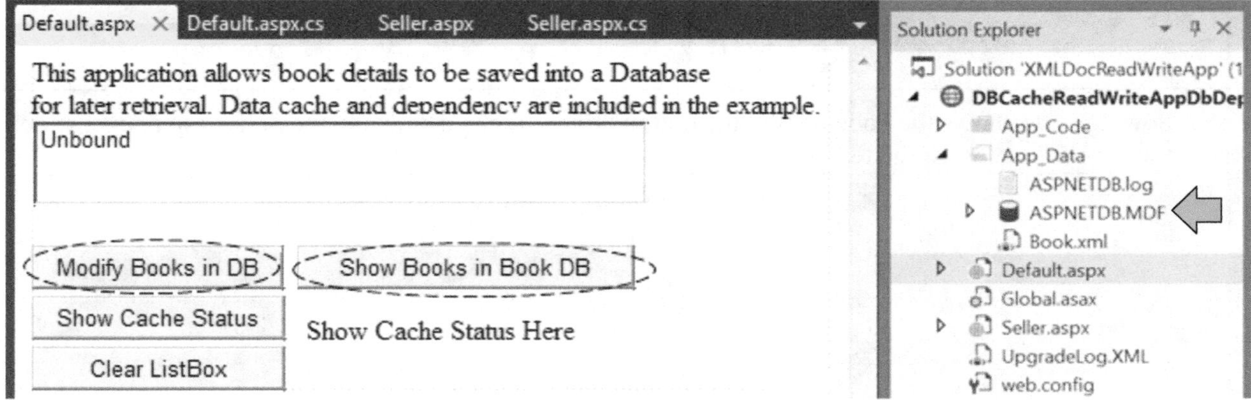

Figure 5.22. GUI design and the project explorer with an SQL database used for storing book information

The code below is the `Page_Load()` method behind the Default.aspx page. The code will be executed whenever the Default page is visited. The code checks whether there is data cached for "BooksKey." If there is, it will load the data from the cache.

```
protected void Page_Load(object sender, EventArgs e) {
   if (Cache["BooksKey"] != null) {
       List<Book> myBook = (List<Book>)Cache["BooksKey"];
       ListBox1.Items.Clear();
       foreach (Book child in myBook) {
           ListBox1.Items.Add(child.Title + "   " + child.Isbn + "   " + "$" +
child.Price);
       }
   }
}
```

The following code is behind the button "Show Books in Book DB" in the Default page, which reads data from the built-in SQL database.

```
protected void btnShowBook_Click(object sender, EventArgs e) {
   try {
       List<Book> objCache =
                    (List<Book>)System.Web.HttpRuntime.Cache.Get("BooksKey");
       itemRemoved = false;
       onRemove = new CacheItemRemovedCallback(this.RemovedCallback);
       if (objCache == null){
           DBContextDataContextDataContext myDB =
                                 new DBContextDataContextDataContext();
           IQueryable<Book> q = from b in myDB.Books select b;
           ListBox1.Items.Clear();
           foreach (Book child in q) {
                   ListBox1.Items.Add(child.Title + " " + child.Isbn + " " + "$" +
child.Price);
           }
           objCache = q.ToList<Book>();
           SqlCacheDependency dependency =
               new SqlCacheDependency(myDB.GetCommand(q) as SqlCommand);
```

```
            HttpContext.Current.Cache.Add("BooksKey", objCache, dependency,
DateTime.MaxValue, TimeSpan.Zero, CacheItemPriority.Default,
new CacheItemRemovedCallback(onRemove));
        }
    }
    catch (Exception ex){ throw ex;}
}
```

The following code shows the code behind the button "Enter books details" in the Seller.aspx page, which writes the data entered from the textboxes into the built-in SQL database.

```
protected void btnSubmitBooks_Click(object sender, EventArgs e){
    try {
        DBContextDataContextDataContext myDB =
                                new DBContextDataContextDataContext();
        myDB.ExecuteCommand("DELETE FROM Book");//delete existing books
        string title = txtTitle.Text;   // Book 1 info
        string isbn = txtIsbn.Text;
        string sPrice = txtPrice.Text;
        Book book1 = new Book();
        book1.Title = title;
        book1.Isbn = isbn;
        book1.Price = float.Parse(sPrice);
        myDB.Books.InsertOnSubmit(book1); // Save into book object
        string title2 = txtTitle2.Text;   // Book 2 info
        string isbn2 = txtIsbn2.Text;
        string sPrice2 = txtPrice2.Text;
        Book book2 = new Book();
        book2.Title = title2;
        book2.Isbn = isbn2;
        book2.Price = float.Parse(sPrice2);
        myDB.Books.InsertOnSubmit(book2); // Save into book object
        string title3 = txtTitle3.Text;   // Book 3 info
        string isbn3 = txtIsbn3.Text;
        string sPrice3 = txtPrice3.Text;
        Book book3 = new Book();
        book3.Title = title3;
        book3.Isbn = isbn3;
        book3.Price = float.Parse(sPrice3);
        myDB.Books.InsertOnSubmit(book3); // Save into book object
        myDB.SubmitChanges();             // Submit the all changes to DB
        Cache.Remove("BooksKey"); // force removing cache
    } catch(Exception ex){ throw ex; }
    Response.Redirect("Default.aspx"); // return to Default page
}
```

In the foregoing code, we used "`Cache.Remove("BooksKey")`;" to force removing the cache. The dependency class should have done the job. The reason is that we are using LINQ to SQL to implement the database access. The additional object layer prevented the automatic cache removal. For creating the built-in SQL database, designing database schema, and accessing the database, please read Chapter 10. The example can be tested at:

http://neptune.fulton.ad.asu.edu/WSRepository/DBCacheReadWriteApp/Default.aspx

Objects cached by one client are available to all clients. The feature can lead to innovative business logic for promoting business; for example, we could cache all items that clients have purchased and present the cached items to other clients as the "Most Frequently Bought (MFB)" items to inspire customers to buy popular items. We could present the "Frequently Bought Together (FBT)" items for each product a customer is viewing or purchasing. This idea leads to a new business model: recommendation.

5.6 Dynamic Graphics Design and Generation

In the previous sections, we studied different ways of storing and managing data on web. In this section, we work with dynamic graphics data generation and its presentation on web. We will present the Graphics Device Interface GDI+ library classes and their applications through examples and case studies.

5.6.1 Dynamic Graphics

One picture is worth a thousand words. Web applications can be better presented and understood using pictures and images. In HTML, static or pre-generated images can be easily linked into a web page. However, not all the images can be generated at the design time. Some images need to mix an image with the user input or randomly generated information; for example, printing the username into an image or generating an image for human user verification. Figure 5.23 shows an example of an image verifier, where a dynamic image is generated according to a random string. A user must recognize the string in the image and enter the string through a textbox. The program can determine if the entered string equals to the string in the image. Such an image verifier has been widely used to differentiate a human user from a programmed attack on a website. As can be seen in the image, we can control the position, the size, and the font of each character to make it more difficult for the character recognition software to recognize the characters.

We will further discuss the image verifier in Section 7.3.5, where, an image verifier is developed as a RESTful service and as a WCF SOAP service.

Dynamic image generation is more costly than text and static images. Use a dynamic image only if the text and static images cannot do the job. Furthermore, efforts need to be made to make the dynamic image more efficient, including using efficient graphics algorithms, using AJAX to reload the images that change, and using caching to reuse the previously generated images.

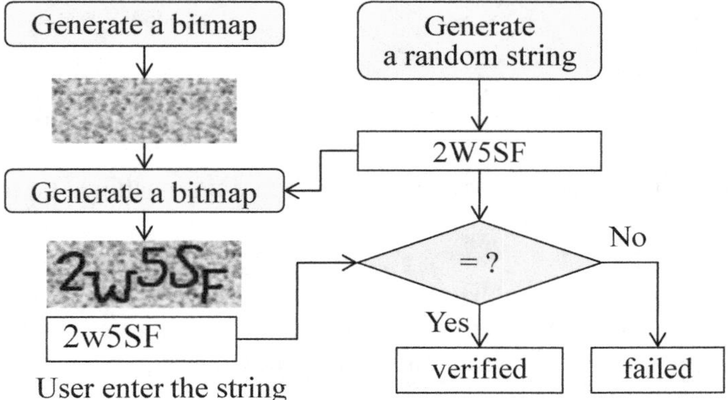

Figure 5.23. An image verifier

Dynamic graphics design can be done using different drawing tools, including bitmap, shapes, geometries, brushes, and painting tools. Visual Studio offers GDI+ library for drawing, which inherits the Windows Graphics Device Interface GDI. GDI+ includes a number of classes that allow to create and modify images at runtime:

- Bitmap: Creating a bitmap pattern;
- Graphics: Creating an image on a Bitmap object of different formats: Gif, Jpeg, Png, and so on;

- Pens: Draw lines, curves, and different outline-shapes;
- Brushes: Create solid shapes and render text into images;
- Colors: Used with Pens and Brushes to specify the colors to be rendered.

GDI+ does not support animation of graphics objects. Microsoft Presentation Foundation and Silverlight graphic user interface design tools offer animation, in addition to the graphics drawing tools.

GDI+ under ASP .Net can post a dynamic image into a web form or utilize a user control component to post an image to a part of a web form. In the remainder of the section, we first present a simple example that explains how dynamic images can be generated and posted to a web form. We then present a more complex example that shows a more realistic application of displaying a dynamic image in web applications.

5.6.2 Getting Started with Dynamic Graphics Generation

We use a simple vending machine example to illustrate the mechanisms of dynamic graphics generation. The vending machine takes dollars and quarters as input, and sells coffee at 75 cents each. The design is specified by the finite state machine shown in the left part of Figure 5.24. The implementation can be tested at: http://neptune.fulton.ad.asu.edu/WSRepository/CoffeeVender/

The Web GUI design Default.aspx of the application is shown in the right part of Figure 5.24.

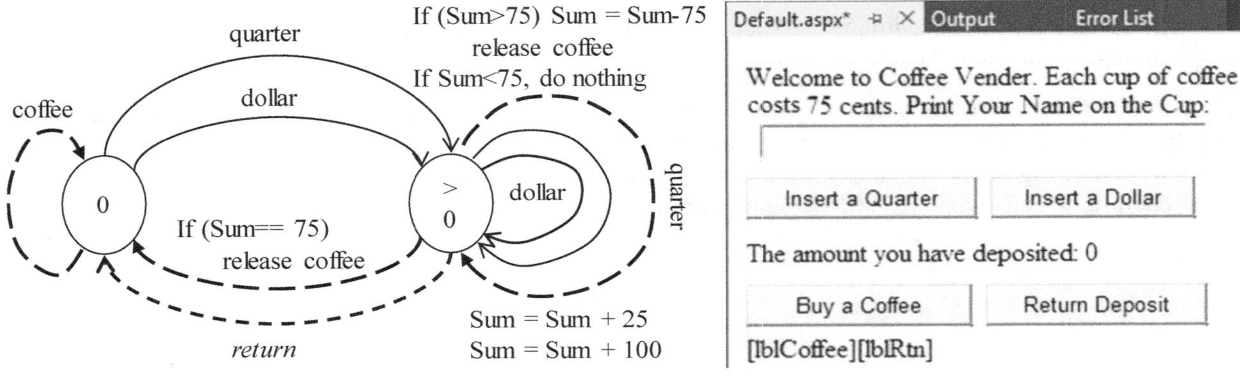

Figure 5.24. The finite state machine of a coffee vending machine and the GUI design

The C# code behind the Default.aspx page is given as follows. The program includes the namespaces for image drawing. As no user information needs to be shared among pages and among sessions, we can use the simple Session State management technique implement the vending machine.

```
using System;
using System.Drawing; // contain the drawing classes
public partial class _Default : System.Web.UI.Page {
    protected void Page_Load(object sender, EventArgs e) {//initialization
        if (Session["Sum"] == null) Session["Sum"] = 0;
        lblAmount.Text = "0";
    }
    protected void Button1_Click(object sender, EventArgs e) {
     // insert a quarter
        Int32 Sum = (Int32)Session["Sum"];
        Sum = Sum + 25;
        Session["Sum"] = Sum;
```

```
        lblAmount.Text = Convert.ToString(Sum);
        lblRtn.Text = "[  ]";
    }
    protected void Button2_Click(object sender, EventArgs e) {
     // insert a dollar
        Int32 Sum = (Int32)Session["Sum"];
        Sum = Sum + 100;
        Session["Sum"] = Sum;
        lblAmount.Text = Convert.ToString(Sum);
        lblRtn.Text = "[  ]";
    }
    protected void Button3_Click(object sender, EventArgs e) {
     // buy a cup of coffee
        Int32 Sum = (Int32)Session["Sum"];
        if (Sum >= 75){  // a coffee costs 75 cents
            Sum = Sum - 75;
            Session["Sum"] = Sum;
            lblAmount.Text = Convert.ToString(Sum);
            lblCoffee.Text = "Please take your Coffee here";
            lblRtn.Text = "[  ]";
            Bitmap imageCoffee = new Bitmap(300, 250);
            Graphics gCoffee = Graphics.FromImage(imageCoffee);
            gCoffee.FillRectangle(Brushes.White, 0, 0, 300, 250);
            gCoffee.DrawRectangle(Pens.Red, 0, 0, 299, 249);
            Font font = new Font("Alba Super", 18, FontStyle.Regular);
            gCoffee.DrawString("Please Take Your Coffee", font, Brushes.Brown, 10,
0);
                SolidBrush brownBrush = new SolidBrush(Color.Brown);
                int x = 40;        // use ellipses to draw a coffee cup
                int y = 50;
                int w = 200;
                int h = 50;
                for (int i = 0; i < 15; i++) {
                    Rectangle rec = new Rectangle(x, y, w, h);
                    gCoffee.DrawEllipse(Pens.PowderBlue, rec);
                    gCoffee.FillEllipse(brownBrush, rec);
                    x = x+2; // decrease the size of the next ellipse
                    y = y+10;
                    w = w-4;
                    h = h-2;
                }
            imageCoffee.Save(Response.OutputStream,
                        System.Drawing.Imaging.ImageFormat.Gif);
            gCoffee.Dispose(); // dispose the graphics file
            imageCoffee.Dispose();// dispose the bitmap file
        }
        Else {
            lblCoffee.Text = "Please deposit more money";
            lblAmount.Text = Convert.ToString(Sum);
            lblRtn.Text = "[  ]";
        }
    }
    protected void Button4_Click(object sender, EventArgs e) {
     // return the deposit
        Int32 Sum = (Int32)Session["Sum"];
        if (Sum > 0) {
            lblRtn.Text = "Please take the money here";
            // RtnChanges(Sum); // draw the coins
```

```
            Sum = 0;
            Session["Sum"] = Sum;
        }
        else lblRtn.Text = "You have not deposited money";
    }
    protected void RtnChanges(Int32 amount) {
        // omitted here. See the same code in the next example
}
```

The images are generated by the code behind the two buttons: "Return Deposit" and "Buy a Coffee." When the button "Buy a Coffee" is pressed, the program will open a drawing area and display a coffee cup, as shown in Figure 5.25. When the button "Return Deposit" is pressed, the program will display the number of quarters equal to the deposit; for example, if 125 cents are to be returned, the program will draw five quarters.

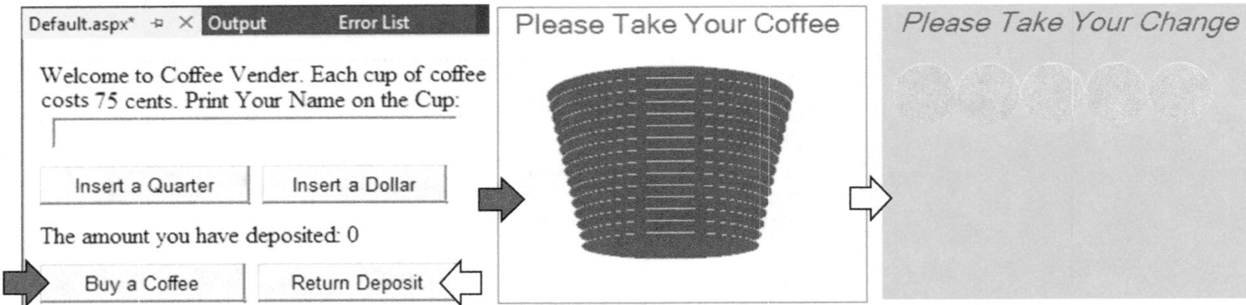

Figure 5.25. Graphic output of the vending machine: coffee and coins

5.6.3 Generating Dynamic Graphics in User Control

This simple example in the previous section shows how dynamic graphics can be generated and displayed. However, there are a number of problems:

- The image overwrites the html page;
- The rendered file is sent to the web form, which is browser-dependent:
    - The graphics works on IE;
    - The graphics does not work on Chrome and Firefox.

In this section, we will present a better way of displaying the images to address the aforesaid problems. We will use a user control to encapsulate the graphics generation code and specify where an image should be displayed in the web page. We will also add another feature that mixes the user-entered text into the dynamically generated image to simulate the image-text for an image verifier. An image verifier is often used to differentiate a human-user from a program, which can prevent programmed attacks to a web application.

The application consists of a Default.aspx page and a user control component UserControlCup.ascx. Figure 5.26 shows the design view of the Default.aspx and solution explorer with the user control. A textbox is included to allow the user to print text on the coffee cup.

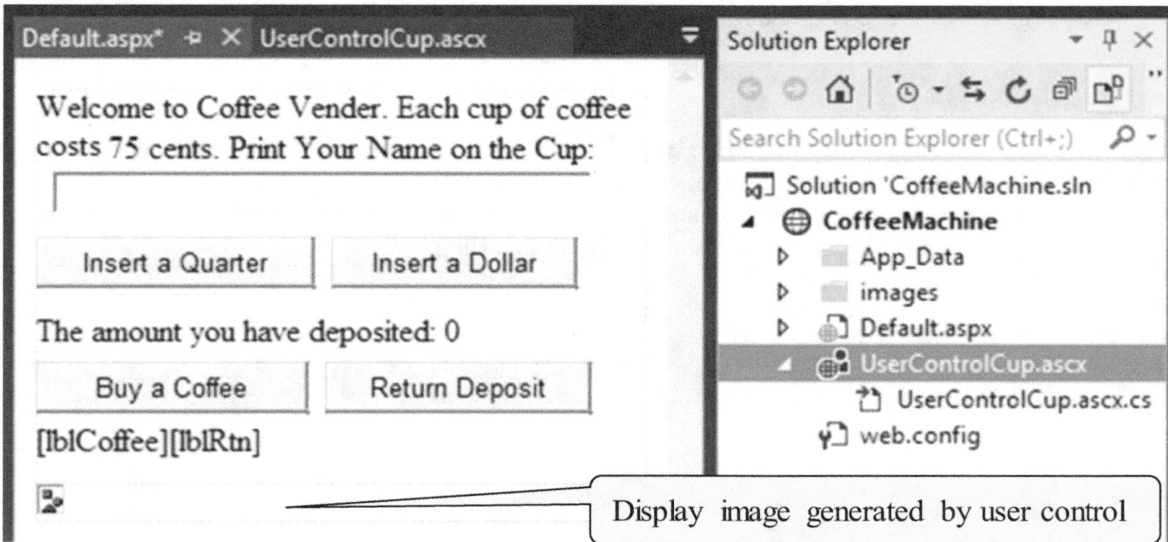

Figure 5.26. GUI design with a user control

The source view of the Default.aspx is given below. Note that a TagPrefix and TagName for the user control are registered at the beginning of the page, so that the user control can be used in the page. We use a server control <asp:Panel> element to define the location where the image generated by the user control will be displayed. In this element, we set the attribute Visible = false, so that the image will not be displayed when the page is first loaded. We will change the attribute value dynamically in the code behind the page, so that we can control precisely when to display and when not to display the image. The attribute can be accessed as a variable through the id and the attribute "UserControlCup1.Visible" in the code behind the page.

```
<%@ Page Language="C#" AutoEventWireup="true"  CodeFile="Default.aspx.cs"
Inherits="_Default" %>
<%@ Register TagPrefix = "cup" TagName="UserControlCup"
src="UserControlCup.ascx" %>
<!DOCTYPE html PUBLIC "-//W3C//DTD XHTML 1.0 Transitional//EN"
"http://www.w3.org/TR/xhtml1/DTD/xhtml1-transitional.dtd">
<html xmlns="http://www.w3.org/1999/xhtml">
<head runat="server"> <title>Coffee Vender</title> </head>
<body> <form id="form1" runat="server">
    <div>
        Welcome to Coffee Vender. Each cup of Coffee cost 75 cents.<br />
    </div>
    Print Your Name on the Cup:<br /> 
    <asp:TextBox ID="txtName" runat="server" ontextchanged="txtName_TextChanged"
Width="256px"></asp:TextBox><br /><br />
    <asp:Button ID="Button1" runat="server" onclick="Button1_Click"
        Text="Insert a Quarter" />  
    <asp:Button ID="Button2" runat="server" onclick="Button2_Click"
        Text="Insert a Dollar" /> <p>
        The amount you have deposited:
        <asp:Label ID="lblAmount" runat="server" Text="0"></asp:Label> </p>
    <asp:Button ID="btnCoffee" runat="server" onclick="Button3_Click"
        Text="Buy a Coffee" Width="133px" />  
    <asp:Button ID="btnRtn" runat="server" onclick="Button4_Click"
        Text="Return Deposit" /> <br />
    <asp:Label ID="lblCoffee" runat="server"></asp:Label>
    <asp:Label ID="lblRtn" runat="server"></asp:Label> <br /> <br />
```

```
    <asp:Panel ID="Panel1" runat="server">
        <cup:UserControlCup id="UserControlCup1" Visible="false"
runat="server"></cup:UserControlCup>
    </asp:Panel>
</form> </body> </html>
```

The C# code behind the Default.aspx page, or the Default.aspx.cs file, is given as follows. The code is similar to the code given in the previous example, except the code that generates the dynamic images has been moved into the user control and thus is no longer in this file.

```
using System;
public partial class _Default : System.Web.UI.Page {
    protected void Page_Load(object sender, EventArgs e){
        if (Session["Sum"] == null) Session["Sum"] = 0;
        if (Session["Status"] == null) Session["Status"] = "deposit";
        lblAmount.Text = "0";
    }
    protected void Button1_Click(object sender, EventArgs e){//insert quarter
        Int32 Sum = (Int32)Session["Sum"];
        Sum = Sum + 25;
        Session["Sum"] = Sum;
        lblAmount.Text = Convert.ToString(Sum);
        UserControlCup1.Visible = false; // Hide the Image Display
        Session["Status"] = "deposit";
        if (Sum < 75) lblCoffee.Text = "Please deposit more money";
        else lblCoffee.Text = String.Empty;
    }
    protected void Button2_Click(object sender, EventArgs e){//insert dollar
        Int32 Sum = (Int32)Session["Sum"];
        Sum = Sum + 100;
        Session["Sum"] = Sum;
        lblAmount.Text = Convert.ToString(Sum);
        UserControlCup1.Visible = false; // Hide the Image Display
        Session["Status"] = "deposit";
        lblCoffee.Text = String.Empty;
    }
    protected void Button3_Click(object sender, EventArgs e){//buy a Coffee
        Int32 Sum = (Int32)Session["Sum"];
        if (Sum >= 75){
            Sum = Sum - 75;
            Session["Sum"] = Sum;
            lblAmount.Text = Convert.ToString(Sum);
            Session["Status"] = "coffee";
            UserControlCup1.Visible = true; // Display the Coffee Cup
        }
        else {
            lblCoffee.Text = "Please deposit more money";
            lblAmount.Text = Convert.ToString(Sum);
            UserControlCup1.Visible = false; // No Display
        }
    }
    protected void Button4_Click(object sender, EventArgs e){//return fund
        Int32 quarters = (Int32)((Int32)Session["Sum"] / 25);
        Session["Qarters"] = quarters;
        Session["Sum"] = 0;
        Session["Status"] = "refund";
        UserControlCup1.Visible = true; // Display the returned coins
        lblCoffee.Text = String.Empty;
```

```
    }
    protected void txtName_TextChanged(object sender, EventArgs e){
        if (txtName != null) Session["YourName"] = txtName.Text;
    }
}
```

Now, let us discuss the user control. The source view of the file UserControlCup.ascx is given as follows:

```
<%@ Control Language="C#" AutoEventWireup="true"
    CodeFile="UserControlCup.ascx.cs" Inherits="UserControlCup" %>
<asp:Image id="CupImage" runat="server" ></asp:Image>
```

The first element is automatically generated when the user control is added to the solution. The second element is the content of the user control to be displayed in the ASPX pages that register the user control. In this example, we want to display an image and we use the user control to generate the image. The id of the image "CupImage" will be used as the variable in the code behind the user control.

The C# behind the user control is given in the following example. This code uses the GDI+ classes to generate the images, and create the URL of an image by appending the image ID as a variable in the Request URL and assigning the value "=Show" to the variable to have the image displayed.

```
using System;
using System.Drawing;
public partial class UserControlCup : System.Web.UI.UserControl {
    protected void Page_Load(object sender, EventArgs e){
        if (Request.Params[ID] != null) {
            if ((string)Session["Status"] == "coffee"){//Generate coffee cup
                Bitmap imageCoffee = new Bitmap(300, 250);
                Graphics gCoffee = Graphics.FromImage(imageCoffee);
                gCoffee.FillRectangle(Brushes.White, 0, 0, 300, 250);
                gCoffee.DrawRectangle(Pens.Red, 0, 0, 299, 249);
                Font font = new Font("Alba Super", 18, FontStyle.Regular);
                gCoffee.DrawString("Please Take Your Coffee", font, Brushes.Brown,
10, 0);
                SolidBrush brownBrush = new SolidBrush(Color.Brown);
                int x = 40; int y = 50; int w = 200; int h = 50;
                for (int i = 0; i < 15; i++) {
                    Rectangle rec = new Rectangle(x, y, w, h);
                    gCoffee.DrawEllipse(Pens.PowderBlue, rec);
                    gCoffee.FillEllipse(brownBrush, rec);
                    x = x + 2; y = y + 10; w = w - 4; h = h - 2;
                }
                if (Session["YourName"] != null) {
                    font = new Font("Alba Super", 14, FontStyle.Italic);
                    String NameOnCup = (String)Session["YourName"];
                    gCoffee.DrawString(NameOnCup, font, Brushes.White, 100, 100);
                }
                imageCoffee.Save(Response.OutputStream,
System.Drawing.Imaging.ImageFormat.Jpeg);
                gCoffee.Dispose();
                imageCoffee.Dispose();
            }
            else if ((string)Session["Status"] == "refund"){//Generate coins
                Int32 quarters = (Int32)Session["Qarters"];
                Session["Status"] = "deposit";
                Bitmap imageCoin = new Bitmap(300, 250);
                Graphics gCoin = Graphics.FromImage(imageCoin);
                gCoin.FillRectangle(Brushes.Gold, 0, 0, 300, 250);
                Font font = new Font("Alba Super", 18, FontStyle.Italic);
```

```
                if (quarters > 0) {
                    gCoin.DrawString("Please Take Your Change", font, Brushes.Brown,
10, 0); // left-top
                    String coins = "of " + quarters + " Quarters";
                    gCoin.DrawString(coins, font, Brushes.Brown, 10, 30);
                    SolidBrush silverBrush = new SolidBrush(Color.Silver);
                    int x = 10;  // from left
                    int y = 60;  // from top
                    int w = 50;  // width
                    int h = 50;  // height
                    for (int i = 1; i <= quarters; i++){ // Display coins
                        Rectangle rec = new Rectangle(x, y, w, h);
                        gCoin.DrawEllipse(Pens.PowderBlue, rec);
                        gCoin.FillEllipse(silverBrush, rec);
                        if (i < 5) x = x + 52;
                        else { y = 120; x = x - 50; }
                    }
                }
                if (quarters == 0)
                    gCoin.DrawString("No money in machine", font, Brushes.Brown, 10,
0); // left-top
                imageCoin.Save(Response.OutputStream,
System.Drawing.Imaging.ImageFormat.Jpeg);
                gCoin.Dispose();
                imageCoin.Dispose();
            }
            else if ((string)Session["Status"] == "deposit")
            { } //No image display in deposit status
        }
        String Url = Request.Url.ToString(); // Get the Request URL
// Use "?" to append ID as a variable in URL and assign its value = Show
            CupImage.ImageUrl = Url + "?" + ID + "=Show";
    }
}
```

The web application can be tested at: http://neptune.fulton.ad.asu.edu/WSRepository/CoffeeMachine/

Figure 5.27 show two possible image outputs. The left image shows the coffee cup. The user-entered text is printed on the coffee cup. This part of the code can be easily modified for creating an image text for human user verification. Instead of taking the text input from the user, the text can be generated using a random string generator. The right image displays the returned deposit in the right amount of quarters.

The difficulty of dynamic graphics generation is related to the state management. The idea is to generate a bitmap file and an image file on the bitmap file and store the file temporarily in the current directory. Then, we generate an URL to the image and post the image URL to the ASPX page. As we created a bitmap file and an image file as disk files, we need to dispose the files before exiting the program so that storage can be reused. The dynamic graphics generation is related to the state management in multiple ways. We used the session state variable to keep track the status whether or not the image should be visible. We could also cache and reuse the image, instead of generating the image every time an image is needed.

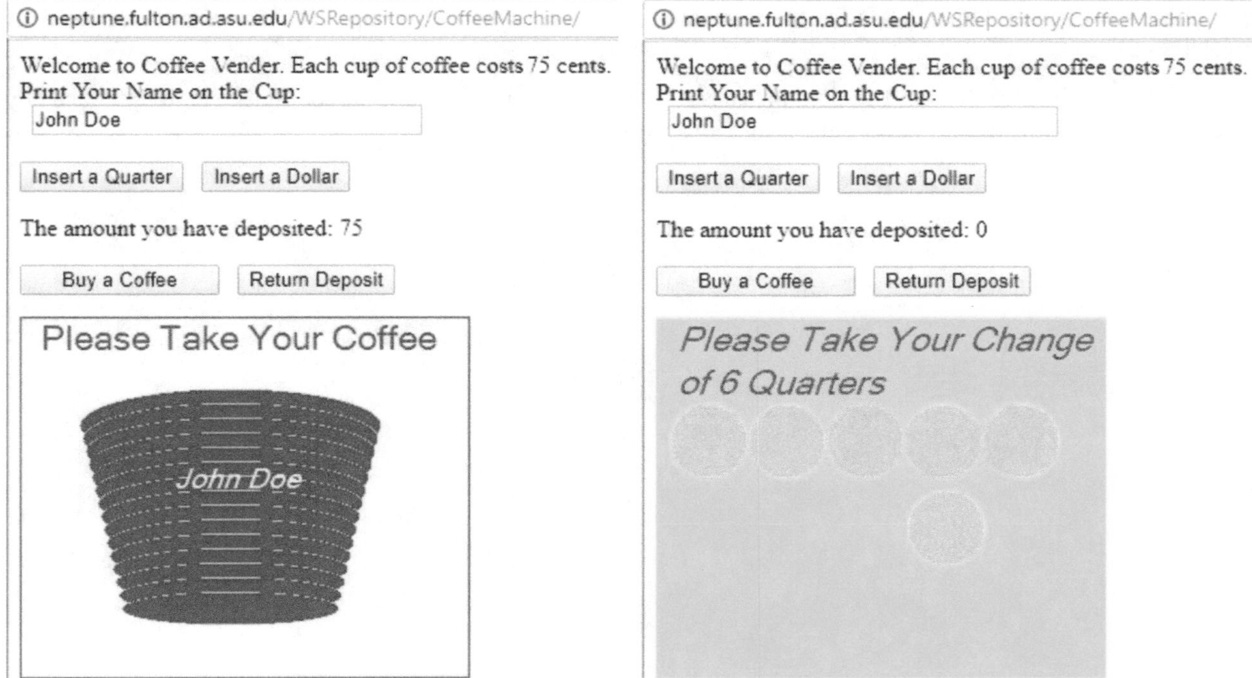

Figure 5.27. Image displayed in the same page with other GUI components

5.7 Discussions

This chapter discussed a few major aspects of web application development: application architecture, application logic or business logic design, state management and human user interface presentation.

The application architecture discussed in this chapter is based on ASP .Net architecture, which inherits many feature of distributed object-oriented architecture. The advantage is that architecture is easy to understand and use for those who have a good understanding of object-oriented programming paradigm. The drawback is that the presentation layer and controllers are tightly coupled together. In Part II, we will further discuss MVC architecture that allows more separation between the presentation layer (GUI) design and the controllers that process the inputs and outputs.

The application logic implementation in this chapter is programming language-based. In Part II of the book, we will discuss advanced web application development using composition and integration of components. BPEL is a higher-level of composition language that uses remote web services to compose a composite service and use the composite service to form an application. Workflow Foundation adds a layer of workflow in the application architecture to emphasize the workflow or flowchart between components, including local activities and remote services. Robotics Developer Studio uses the same idea of activities and services and workflow to compose robotics applications, where the robotics-specific library functions are predeveloped activities and services.

Data and state management in web applications is completely different from those in desktop-based applications. This chapter discussed web application development and web data and state management techniques that allow the creation of stateful services and applications, including view state, session state, application state, file system, database, and cache management. There are many other techniques available for data management. In Part II of the book, we will discuss relational databases, XML databases, and

Language Integrated Query (LINQ) to objects and databases that can support storage and retrieval of massive data.

In part II, we will also discuss big data processing, ontologies and Semantic Web that extend databases by adding semantic information and reasoning capacities.

Name: ______________________

Date: ______________________

5.8 Exercises and Projects

1. Multiple choice questions. Choose one answer in each question only. Choose the best answer if multiple answers are acceptable.

1.1 If you plan to implement a thick-client architecture, what is the best technology to use?

(A) Pure HTML with sever support
(B) Client-side scripting
(C) Server-side scripting
(D) Out-of-browser computing

1.2 What web computing technology is obsolete?

(A) Pure HTML with sever support
(B) Client-side scripting
(C) Server-side scripting
(D) Out-of-browser computing

1.3 What type of file does not create a web page; instead, it adds an item in an existing web page?

(A) ASAX file (Global)
(B) ASCX file (User controls)
(C) ASPX file (Web form)
(D) ASMX (Web service)

1.4 What type of file allows the application to parameterize its behavior, so that the behavior can be modified without recompiling the source code?

(A) ASAX file (Global)
(B) ASCX file (User controls)
(C) ASPX file (Web form)
(D) Web.config
(E) DLL file

1.5 What type of file overrides its occurrence in the parent directory?

(A) ASAX file (Global)
(B) ASCX file (User controls)
(C) ASPX file (Web form)
(D) Web.config
(E) DLL file

1.6 How is a user control page shared among multiple ASPX pages?

(A) Copy and paste the user control into each ASPX page.
(B) Link the reference to the user control page into each ASPX page.
(C) Once added to the project, a user control is automatically visible to all pages.
(D) The user control must be registered in the Web.config file.

1.7 What type of web pages perform the computations on the client side?

(A) Pure HTML form
(B) HTML form with embedded scripts written in a scripting language
(C) ASPX page with embedded scripts written in a scripting language
(D) ASPX page with C# programs as event handlers

1.8 What are the challenges for using an application state variable in Global.asax file?

[ ] Addressing the problem of simultaneous write on the variable

[ ] Creating session states in the global file

[ ] Creating two global files that can coordinate with each other

[ ] Addressing the performance problem if the lock mechanism is used

1.9 How do you add a DLL class into your website application?

(A) Copy the class into the Default.aspx page.

(B) Copy the class into the bin folder, and then the class will be visible in all aspx pages.

(C) Use the "Add Reference" option in Visual Studio to include the class.

(D) All of the above.

1.10 What types of data can cookies store?

[ ] int

[ ] double

[ ] string

[ ] object defined by a class

1.11 What type of data is a session state variable designed to store?

(A) int

(B) double

(C) string

(D) object defined by a class

1.12 What is the scope of a session state variable?

(A) within all pages in the session

(B) across all sessions of the application

(C) in the aspx page, in which the variable is created

(D) in the .cs file, in which the variable is created

1.13 What methods can be used for storing the session ID in the client browser?

[ ] Create an aspx page in client browser.

[ ] Use cookies to store the session id.

[ ] Put the session ID in the URL as a part of the address.

[ ] Put the session id in the application state as a static variable.

1.14 An application state variable allows you to store an object into the server memory, which can be accessed by

(A) all pages in the current session, but not the other sessions in the application.

(B) all sessions in the current application, but not the other applications.

(C) all applications in the web server.

(D) None of the above.

1.15 In order to write data into a file system, we need a class that directly communicates with the file system, which is outside ASP .Net application. What class plays this role?

(A) XML reader class

(B) XML writer class

(C) Path class

(D) FileStream class

1.16 FileStream class uses a stream buffer of bytes to connect to the file system. What XML class/classes can be used to read the stream buffer?

(A) XMLTextReader (Stream based)

(B) XMLDocument (Document tree based)

(C) Both XMLTextReader and XMLDocument

(D) Neither XMLTextReader nor XMLDocument

1.17 What does the output caching do in ASP .Net?

(A) It caches the entire XHTML page.

(B) It caches a part of the XHTML page defined by a user control.

(C) It caches any object created by a new() operation in the program.

(D) It caches any output data, such as Label and ListBox in an aspx page.

1.18 What does the fragment caching do in ASP .Net?

(A) It caches the entire XHTML page.

(B) It caches a part of the XHTML page defined by a user control.

(C) It caches any object created by a new() operation in the program.

(D) It caches any output data, such as Label and ListBox in an aspx page.

1.19 What is wrong with using application state variables for caching purpose?

(A) Application state variables can save strings only.

(B) Application state variables do not have automated caching management support.

(C) Application state variables need cookies support.

(D) Application state variables cannot be shared among different sessions.

1.20 When do you use the add() method in the Cache class?

[ ] When you want to insert a new data object into the cache.

[ ] When you want to change an expiration time in an existing cache object.

[ ] When you want to add a dependency object into an existing cache object.

[ ] When you want to retrieve a specific item from an existing cache object.

1.21 What data does the Output Caching technique cache?

(A) The entire web page generated from the ASPX page

(B) The data related to the User Control

(C) Object selected by the developer

(D) All of the above

1.22 Where are cached objects saved in web caching?

(A) Always in the level-one or level-two cache memory of the server

(B) Always in the main memory of the server

(C) Always in the file system of the server

(D) Can be in cache, memory, and disk

1.23 In the System.Web.Caching namespace, what class is used for defining a parameter's type in a method of another class?

(A) Cache class (B) CacheDependency class

(C) OutputCach class (D) ResponseElement class

1.24 What component can be used for limiting the dynamic image to a designated area of a page?

(A) Server control (B) HTML control (C) User control (D) DLL file

1.25 When creating a dynamic graph, which CDI+ class is used first to define the area of the graph?

(A) Graphics (B) Bitmap (C) Pen (D) Brushes

2. What kinds of web-based computing models exist? Where is the computation (client-side or server side) done in each of the models?

3. Explain what types of files exist in an ASP .Net website application and what the functions of each type file are.

4. Explain how the files in an ASP .Net website application are organized in the application folder.

5. Why do we need a user control at all? What function of a user control cannot be replaced by a server control?

6. What kinds of state management mechanisms exist, and what are the main features of each state management mechanism?

7. What is the most general form of state variable in ASP .Net? What type of data can be stored in this kind of state variable?

8. Compare and contrast the state management mechanisms: View State, Cookies, Session State, Application State, and Cache.

9. Discuss the relationship between the dependency and callback parameters in the insert() method of Cache class.

10. Write a program to simulate the Frequently Bought Together list using the Cache class and the CacheDependency class. This list must be dynamically maintained and a callback event handler must be implemented to remove the cache data that are no longer valid.

Project

In this team project, you will develop a service-oriented web application. The application must simulate a realistic application for the end users. The required architecture is shown in Figure 5.28.

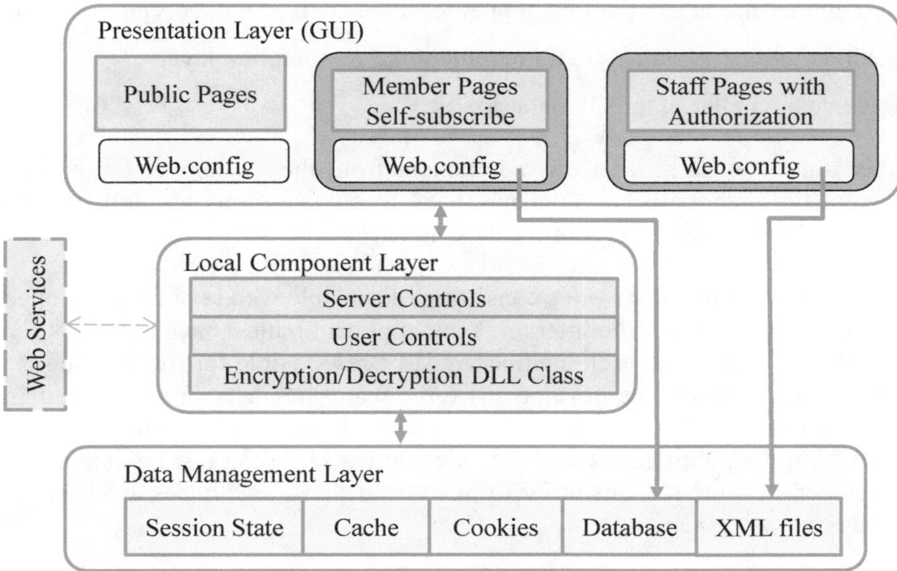

Figure 5.28. Architecture of the project

The system must be implemented as a website application and must be deployed to a web server. The application implemented must meet the following organizational, architectural, and functional requirements. The composed website must have at least the following layers of components:

1 Presentation/GUI layer consisting of ASPX pages and server controls which allow users to interact with the application. The application must have at least these four ASPX pages:

   a. Public page. In this page, you must introduce clearly what application the system offers, how users can sign up for the services, how users can test this application and the required test cases/inputs. All the components and services used in the application must be listed in a Service Directory. The directory must include provider name (member who is responsible for the component). Type (web service, DLL function, user control), operation name, parameters and types, return value type, function description, and link to TryIt page. You can combine the TryIt pages into your application logic.

   b. Member page: In this page, you must introduce clearly what application and functions the system offers. Users can register (self-subscribe) to obtain the access to this page. An image verifier must be used when a user register. You can use the Forms application's built in Account management for this purpose. You may create your own access control component.

   c. Two staff pages: These two pages must have authentication and authorization control. Some staff members can access one page, and other staff members can access the other page. The user ID and password must be stored in an XML file. The password must be encrypted in the XML file. You must use a local encryption/decryption function that your team developed as a DLL library function. Calling the encryption/decryption web service is not acceptable, as the password will be sent to the server in clear text.

2 Local component layer (individual work). This layer consists of the following three types of components:

a. User control, and the control must have the fragment caching function implemented.

b. DLL class library modules, to implement at least the encryption/decryption functions.

c. Code behind the server controls that implement the presentation layer.

d. A sensible event handler in the Global.asax file.

Each member must choose at least one component from the list above. Different members must choose different type components. You may have to choose more components or other types of components in order to implement your business logic.

3 Remote service layer (individual work), consisting of sensible web services developed by each team member and/or discovered from the Internet. Your application must have at least N services (N is the number of team members), and each member must be responsible for (developing or using) at least one service. The services can be developed by the team members or discovered from the public repository. At least one service must be developed by the team members and at least one service must be discovered from the public repository. Self-developed services must be deployed into WebStrar. It is the developer's (your) responsibility to make sure that the services are available and reliable when we grade the assignment.

4 Data management layer consists of **both** temporary states (session state and cache) **and** permanent states (XML file and database):

a. Permanent state (Built-in database) storing the usernames and passwords of self-subscribed users;

b. Permanent states (XML file) for storing staff user ID, password, and role for authentication and authorization;

c. Data cache for caching selected sensible data objects. Dependency and callback must be defined;

d. Cookie for storing user profile and Session state for storing temporary states for sharing among the sessions.

5 Each member must choose at least one component from the list above. Different members must choose different type components. You may have to choose more components or other type of components in order to implement your business logic.

Chapter 6
Dependability of Service-Oriented Software

Service-oriented software is distributed and needs to move data over a network. Dependability, including security, availability, and reliability impose a bigger challenge to such software than traditional software. This chapter briefly discusses the dependability of service-oriented software, and more emphasis will be put on the security issues.

6.1 Basic Concepts

6.1.1 Dependability

Dependability of a system is defined, by Jean-Claude Laprie in 1985, to be the system's ability to deliver specified services to the end users so that they can justifiably rely on and trust the services provided by the system. Dependability includes three aspects of a system: attributes, means, and impairments, each of which contains several elements, as shown in Figure 6.1. The dependability attributes, safety, vulnerability, confidentiality, and data integrity are called security attributes.

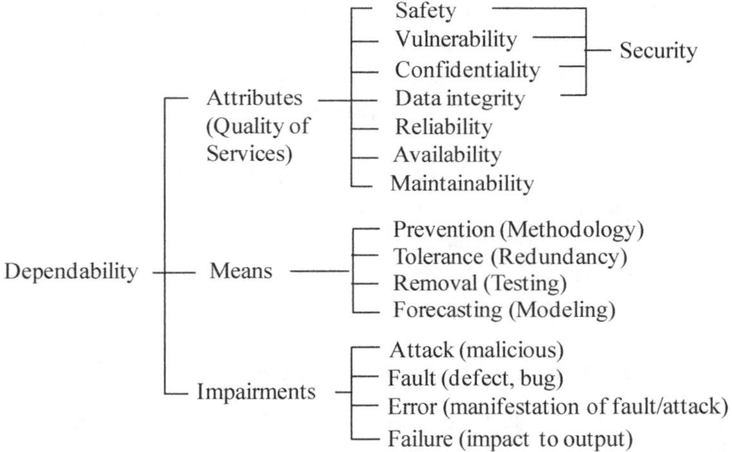

Figure 6.1. Dependability definition

Reliability ensures continuity of service in a given period of time. More precisely, the reliability of a system is a function R(t), which is the probability that the system has survived in the time interval [0, t], given that it is operational at time 0. A related function F(t) is the failure probability, which is probability that the first failure occurs in the time period [0, t], where R(t) = 1 - F(t). For a nonredundant electronic system, the reliability function can often be characterized by an exponential function $R(t) = e^{-\lambda t}$, where λ is called the failure rate of the system.

Maintainability of a system is a measure of the ability of the system to undergo maintenance or to return to normal operation after a failure. Maintainability is often characterized by the repair rate μ of the system.

Availability ensures the readiness of service at time point t. The availability function A(t) function of a system is the probability that the system is working at time t. For a nonredundant electronic system, the availability of a system can often be calculated by

$$A(t) = \frac{\mu}{\lambda + \mu} + \frac{\lambda}{\lambda + \mu} e^{-(\lambda + \mu)t}$$

Note that, for a large t, the second item in the formula will be very small and A(t) becomes a constant. Furthermore, if the repair rate μ is 0 (the feature of the system surviving to the first failure), A(t) = R(t).

Vulnerability describes a problem or weakness, such as a programming error or common misconfiguration, which allows a system to be attacked or broken into.

Confidentiality ensures that information is accessible only to those authorized to have access.

Data integrity or **message integrity** refers to the validity and consistence of data or message.

Safety ensures nonoccurrence of catastrophic consequence on the environment, such as human life lost and major economic impact.

Security, including vulnerability, confidentiality, integrity, and safety, deals with malicious attacks, whereas reliability and availability deal with faults, errors, and failures caused by imperfect development and operation environment.

Another related concept is the **quality of service**, which is based on ISO (International Standard Organization) 8402 [1986], which defines quality as "the totality of features and characteristics of a product or service that bears on its ability to meet a stated or implied need." This is a high-level and generic definition. Different fields have different interpretations of the quality of service; for example:

- Network quality: represents the transmission rates, error rates, and other characteristics that can be measured, improved, and, to some extent, guaranteed in advance.
- Software quality: is the degree to which software conforms to quality criteria. Quality criteria include:
    - Economy, Correctness, Resilience, Integrity, Reliability.
    - Usability, Documentation, Modifiability, Clarity.
    - Understandability, Validity, Maintainability, Flexibility.
    - Generality, Portability, Interoperability, Testability.
    - Efficiency, Modularity, Reusability.

6.1.2 Dependability Attributes and Quality of Service

Dependability attributes and quality of service (QoS) are often used interchangeably, although the quality of service is more frequently used from the user's perspective, whereas the dependability attributes are more frequently used by the system designers, because dependability also includes the concepts of the impairments that impact the dependability attributes and the means that improve the dependability attributes. Figure 6.2 shows the technologies supporting the functionality development, as well as the dependability-related standards defined by the industry and by the standard organizations for service-oriented software development.

Dependability is not a feature that can be added to an existing application. Dependability must be inherently tied to the functions and must be planned as one of the basic requirements in the early design stage. Distributed service-oriented software development requires extensive and additional security, in contrast to centralized software development. Participating parties must be able to identify each other and place limits on what others can do. Communication between parties should be protected against all kinds of malicious attacks.

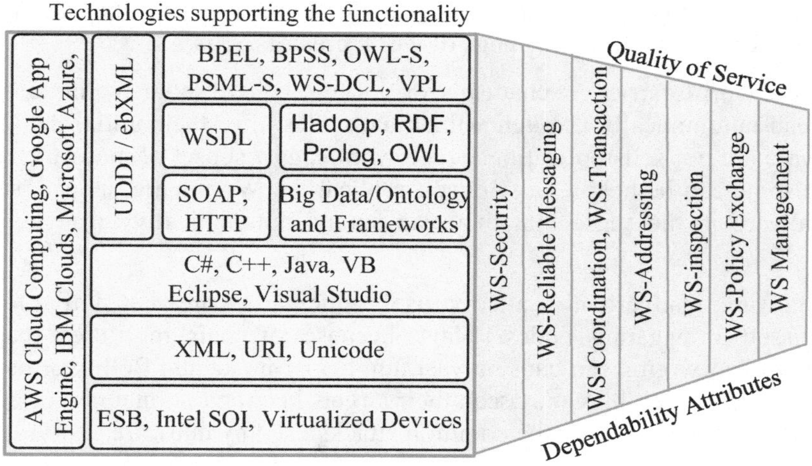

Figure 6.2. Dependability attributes defined for service-oriented software development

6.1.3 Security Issues in SOA Software

Malicious software, or **malware**, is software designed to infiltrate or damage a computer system without the owner's informed consent. There are a variety of forms of hostile, intrusive, or annoying malware. Most Internet attacks are embedded in malware. According to the latest reports from Virus Bulletin (http://www.virusbtn.com/), the number of malicious code incidents is continuously expanding. The attack trends, highlighted by Symantec (http://www.symantec.com/enterprise/threatreport/), show that cyber criminals revealed new levels of ambition in 2016 – a year marked by extraordinary attacks, including multi-million dollar virtual bank heists and overt attempts to disrupt the U.S. electoral process.

In general, information security deals with integrity, confidentiality, and safety, as well as availability (service disruption). Some attacks harm integrity of information, others disclose confidential information, and yet other attacks affect the system availability. For example, denial-of-service (DoS) attacks only cause degradation in system availability; however, malicious code attacks can lead to a combined effect. One can use a specific type of malware (e.g., a Trojan horse) to compromise a system, damage the file system (integrity aspect), and at the same time steal user account information, and then extract and crack passwords from the stolen information (confidentiality aspect).

The database slammer worm, often implemented in SQL query command injection, has the ability to steal information and paralyze the database immediately. Rootkits, which are mainly used for the purpose of system administration or protecting licensed systems, threaten confidentiality of assets. Rootkits are used by hackers to hide or protect malicious codes. Sony BMG Entertainment's notorious rootkit software was originally programmed to protect against fraudulent copying of CDs. Sony was forced to recall millions of CDs after a Windows expert discovered that copy-control software, included in some of Sony's titles, used controversial Rootkit cloaking techniques to hide itself on the computer. Sony issued the recall after hackers began distributing malicious software that exploited Sony's cloaking mechanism. According to the earlier reports from Symantec, Klez.A, and Kama Sutra worms cause damage to file systems of compromised systems. Klez.A is programmed to infect systems with the ElKern virus, perform large-scale e-mailing, and truncate file sizes to zero byte. The Kama Sutra worm deletes files. Obviously, these two worms cause integrity violation.

Often, the terms *worm* and *virus* are used to denote such hostile codes. Here, worms, viruses, and malware can be used interchangeably. However, not all worms are used in the negative sense. The predator worm, also known as counter worm or killer worm, is used to fight other malicious codes. This good-will mobile code is also a worm that propagates through the backdoor of another worm. They are initially launched to serve as proactive countermeasures among gangs of worm creators.

Worms are spread via worm carrier mechanisms of various types. Some worms are able to replicate themselves and spread automatically through vulnerable nodes after their initial deployment. However, some types of malware are not self-replicating. Some worms, as a subset of malware, are self-replicating hostile codes, while some can be hostile but not self-replicating. Worms are, indeed, self-replicating and self-propagating malware in the sense that they can spread automatically through interconnected but vulnerable systems.

Another subset of malware, inadvertently called viruses, which are somewhat similar to worms, also falls in the category of self-propagating codes. Thus, because of their motilities (capable of moving spontaneously), viruses and worms can cause a vast number of incidents. Both worms and viruses often have no specific targets. However, they may scan their targets in a random manner, or even in cooperation from compromised nodes. Table 6.1 lists the common attacks used by malware.

Authentication and authorization are common techniques used to ensure basic security. Authentication requires an entity (a person or a computer) to present proof of identity, which verifies "are you who you say you are?"

Authorization confirms that an entity, after its identification, is entitled to access a resource, or it answers the question: what are you allowed to do, after you are confirmed who you are?

Table 6.1. Common attacks used by malware

Attack	**Description**
Cross-site scripting (XSS)	Script programs are used as input data and are executed in browser on client side if the browser does not have the ability to filter the script.
Denial of service (DoS)	The attacker floods the network with fake requests, overloading the system and blocking regular traffic.
Eavesdropping	The attacker uses a sniffer to read unencrypted network packets as they are transported on the network
Rootkit and hidden-field tampering	The attacker compromises unchecked (and trusted) hidden fields stuffed with sensitive data in the web forms
One-click	Malicious HTTP posts are sent via script when a link is clicked.
Session hijacking	The attacker guesses, dictionary attack, or steals a valid session ID and connects over another user's session
Database query / SQL slammer / injection	The attacker inserts malicious input that the code blissfully concatenates to form dangerous SQL commands.

A typical XSS attack consists of the following steps:

1. Enter script code; for example, <script>command(parameter)</script>, in the textbox where username is expected.
2. If an error message complains that username cannot contain special characters such as "<" and "/", then, use browser menu command to View Source of the web page.
3. If the page uses JavaScript to check whether the entered username contains special characters, replace the JavaScript code and disable the check.
4. Use the modified HTML code to create a new web page and now enter the script code again: <script>command(parameter)</script>. This time, the special characters will be accepted by the modified page and script is sent to the browser.

5. If the browser's security level is set to allow script in input, then, the attacker's script will execute.

The SQL connection stream injection uses a similar idea. When a malicious user enters SQL commands in the user input part, the SQL may consider the data as command if the security properties are not properly configured.

Encryption is the major technique to prevent eavesdropping. There are two major encryption techniques: secret key system and public key system.

Secret key systems: In such security systems, a secret key is used to encrypt the data and message. For example, cipher encryption adds an integer (key) to each character. The problem with secret key systems is how one can safely transfer the key to the receiver.

Public key systems: In such security systems, the sender or receiver creates two keys, and one key is published (*public*) while the other key is kept secret (*private*). The public-key systems can be used for two purposes: *encryption* and *digital signature*. In the public-key encryption system, anyone who wants to send a confidential document to the receiver uses the public key to encrypt the document. Only the receiver with the private key can decrypt the document. Consider an analogy. A bank wants its customers to send confidential documents to the bank without security concerns. The bank delegates the post office to distribute unlocked safe boxes, which only the bank has the key to open. Anyone can buy the safe box, put the confidential document in the box, lock (encrypt) the box, and mail the box to the bank.

The other public-key system is digital signature, in which encryption is held private, whereas the decryption key is made public. Nobody, except the sender, can create the encrypted document, but everyone can decrypt the document.

Currently used public key systems are secure if implemented properly. Without a vulnerability (weakness), it would take over 100 years to break in the system using systematic exploiting, such as dictionary attack. However, due to the complexity of software, and possibly hardware, vulnerabilities often exist. For example, Microsoft Security Advisory (http://technet.microsoft.com/en-us/security/bulletin/MS10-070) in September 2010 acknowledged that a vulnerability was found in ASP .Net, which could allow encrypted information in ASP .Net applications to be disclosed through padding oracle attacks. Padding oracle attack is an approach that generates a large number of incorrectly encrypted messages of different types and sends these messages to the system for decrypting. The system may return a different type of error message in responding to different errors in encryption. The attacker may use the error messages types to figure out the secret key used for decryption. The ASP .Net vulnerability applies to .Net 1.1 through .Net 4.0. The vulnerability was fixed through a security update. A user can also fix the problem by enabling the customErrors mode in the Web.config file:

```
<system.web>
<customErrors mode="On" defaultRedirect="customErrorPage.aspx" />
</system.web>
```

This element will return the same error message to all kinds of errors, preventing the attackers to exploiting the secret key used for decryption.

6.1.4 Reputation Management System

A modern distributed system, such as a social network, may consist of a large number of autonomous entities that cooperate with each other to achieve their individual goals. For example, a review system that allows individual entities to rate the products or services, and a recommendation system that recommends products based on the rates and ranks of products. A Reputation Management System (RMS) can be used to assess the reputation of individual entities based on their behaviors. An RMS will typically deal with the following types of entities within the system:

- Honest entities: majority of the entities are the regular users and will behave honestly, sending and publishing the messages that reflect the truth based on their knowledge and their own experience. There are two types of honest entities:
    - Active: An entity regularly generates honest positive messages and honest negative messages about the other entities. An active entity also uses the system or works with the other entities based on their reputations.
    - Passive: An entity that uses the system and works with the other entities based on their reputations.
- Malicious entities: they are authorized users that can access all the services and resources provided by the system. They may act alone or cooperate with other malicious entities. A malicious entity can perform one or more of the following attacks.
    - Abusing: An entity tries to process system services and resources, with the intention to deny other entities to obtain the services and resources.
    - Self-promoting: An entity tries to obtain an unjustified advantage over their competitors by providing a fake positive message that promotes itself and by exploiting a collaborative network of other malicious entities to increase its reputation.
    - Slandering: An entity tries to decrease its competitor's reputation by providing fake negative messages and by exploiting a collaborative network of other malicious entities to achieve its goal.
    - Betraying: An entity alternates among honest, self-promoting, and slandering behavior in order to maintain a reasonable reputation value while trying to obtain an unjustified advantage over their competitors.
    - Whitewashing: An entity tries to avoid the consequences of its bad past behaviors. A common way is to leave the system and rejoin it with a new identity to obtain a clean reputation.

Different from the credit score system, which is based on true identity of a person, an RMS deals with the entities that may not be associated with the true identity of a person. It is much harder to identify the malicious entities, particularly, the betraying entities that alternate their behaviors. An RMS needs to define adaptive metrics for stable reputation to identify malicious entities through self-learning algorithms and through big data analysis. Chapter 11 will discuss case studies on network attacks and traffic monitoring, recommendation systems, machine learning algorithms, and big data analysis.

6.2 Access Control in Web Applications

Most websites offer public portions and restricted portions. The restricted potions can be further authorized to different users. For example, some portions are allowed for all employees, while some portions are allowed for administrators only. When a website stores its customers' private information, such as credit card numbers, access to the information must be restricted. This section will discuss different security considerations and options, including forms security, IIS, and Windows-based security.

6.2.1 IIS and Windows-Based Security Mechanisms

Security of ASP .Net web applications and services deployed on IIS (Internet Information Services) and windows are managed by IIS security and Windows security systems, as shown in Figure 6.3. Any web services running in IIS root directory, or in a virtual directory created in the IIS directory, are projected by the IIS security mechanisms. All accesses to a web application or web service must go through IIS, which assigns every request an access token. The access token enables the Windows operating system to perform ACL (Access Control List) checks on resources targeted by the request. Each file can be given an access group (anonymous or with credential).

IIS also supports IP address and domain name restrictions, enabling requests to be granted and denied based on the IP address or domain of the requestor. IIS supports encrypted HTTP connections using the Secure Sockets Layer (SSL) family of protocols. SSL does not protect resources on the server. Instead, it prevents eavesdropping on conversations between web servers and remote clients.

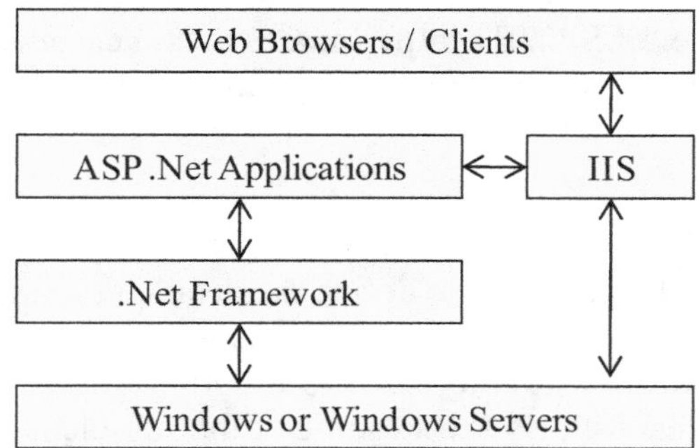

Figure 6.3. IIS and Windows-based security

IIS supports multiple levels of access control, which can be selected in the administrative tool in the control panel of the Windows computer:

1. Anonymous: No access control.
2. Basic authentication: The security token is passed to the Windows operating system, and Windows username and password are used to authenticate users. The password is sent in clear text.
3. Integrated Windows authentication in NTLM or Kerberos security methods: It uses the Windows login credential to authenticate users. To access a service in IIS, the service requester must have a Windows user account created.
4. Forms authentication: Developers can design their own security mechanisms outside IIS. If Forms authentication is deployed, all unauthenticated requests are redirected to an HTML Form using HTTP client-side redirection. A client provides credentials and submits the Form.
5. Passport authentication: A centralized authentication service provided by Microsoft that offers a single logon and core profile services for member sites.

Application of different security options can be specified in the Web.config file, as shown below. If the mode = "Windows" is defined, the <identity> element can be defined to specify further security options.

```
<system.web>
   <authentication mode="[Windows|Forms|Passport|None]" />
   <identity impersonate ="[true|false]" />
   <authorization> ... </authorization>
</system.web>
```

If the <identity> element is not present, the default will be applied, which is the stronger (the most secure) security option: The application will inherit the identity of the worker process (aspnet_wp.exe), which runs using an account (defined in machine.config) with weaker privileges than the local system account. By doing so, an intruder will not have the administrative access even if security is breached (have the administrator's password). This is because the local system account has access to almost all resources on the local computer not specifically denied to it. The option may be too strong, leading to denying a user from accessing any disk file.

If the <identity> element is not defined, its impersonate attribute can take a true or a false value.

- <identity impersonate = “false”> ASP.NET impersonates the token passed to it by IIS, which is either an authenticated user or an anonymous Internet user account. This is the common use of web applications.
- <identity impersonate = “true” username = “domain\user” password = “password” />

In this case of impersonate = "true," ASP.NET impersonates the token generated using an identity specified in the Web.config file given in the identity element. This feature is useful for developers to test the program using a different account.

6.2.2 Forms-Based Security

Forms-based security uses the Web.config file to define the detailed security policies. The second element, <system.web> in the Web.config file can be used to define, among many other functions, the authentication and authorization to a web application. Table 6.2 lists a part of the sub elements of `<system.web>` in Web.config. The code template that follows shows some of the sub-elements listed in Table 6.2.

Table 6.2. Sub-elements of `<system.web>` in Web.config

Element	Description
Anonymous Identification	Configures anonymous identification for application authorization. This is required to identify entities that are not authenticated when authorization is required.
Authentication	Configures ASP.NET authentication support.
authorization	Configures ASP.NET authorization support.
browserCaps	Configures the settings for the browser capabilities component.
compilation	Contains all compilation settings that are used by ASP.NET.
Globalization	Configures the globalization settings of an application.
healthMonitoring	Configures an application for health monitoring.
hostingEnvironment	Defines configuration settings that control the behavior of the application hosting environment.
httpCookies	Configures properties for cookies that are used by a web application.
httpHandlers	Maps incoming URL requests to IHttpHandler classes.
httpModules	Adds, removes, or clears HTTP modules within an application.
httpRuntime	Configures ASP.NET HTTP run-time settings. This section can be declared at the machine, site, application, or subdirectory level.
identity	Controls the application identity of the web application.
roleManager	Configures an application for role management. This element is new in the .NET Framework version 2.0.
securityPolicy	Defines valid mappings of named security levels to policy files. This section can be declared at the machine, site, or application levels.
sessionPageState	Configures page view-state settings for an ASP.NET application.
sessionState	Configures the session-state module.
siteMap	Configures the navigation infrastructure support for configuring, storing, and rendering site navigation.
trace	Configures the ASP.NET trace service.
trust	Configures the code access security permission set that is used to run a particular application. This section can be declared at the machine, site, and application levels.

urlMappings	Defines a mapping that hides the real URL and maps it to a more user-friendly URL.
WebControls	Specifies the shared location of the client script files.
WebParts	Specifies a Web Parts personalization provider, sets personalization authorizations, and adds custom classes that extend the WebPartTransformer class for use by Web Parts connections.
webServices	Controls the settings of XML web services that are created using ASP.NET.

```
<configuration>
  <system.web>
      <authentication mode="Forms">
            <forms name="[name]" loginUrl="[url]"
                        protection="[All|None|Encryption|Validation]"
                        path="[path]" timeout="[minutes]"
                        requireSSL="[true|false]"
                        slidingExpiration="[true|false]">
                  <credentials passwordFormat="[Clear|MD5|SHA1]">
                  <username="[UserName]" password="[password]"/>
                  </credentials>
            </forms>
      </authentication>
  </system.web>
  <system.web>
      <authorization>
            <allow users="[comma separated list of users]"
            roles="[comma separated list of roles]"/>
            <deny  users="[comma separated list of users]"
            roles="[comma separated list of roles]"/>
      </authorization>
  </system.web>
</configuration>
```

The upper part of the template (the first system.web element) defines the authentication through usernames and password. The lower part of the template (the second system.web element) defines the authorization of users that have been authenticated.

Let us consider an example shown in Figure 6.4. The application is organized in three directories. The folder "FormsSecurity" is the root, and it has two subdirectories named Staff and Admin. The root directory contains three files: Default.aspx, Login.aspx, and Web.config.

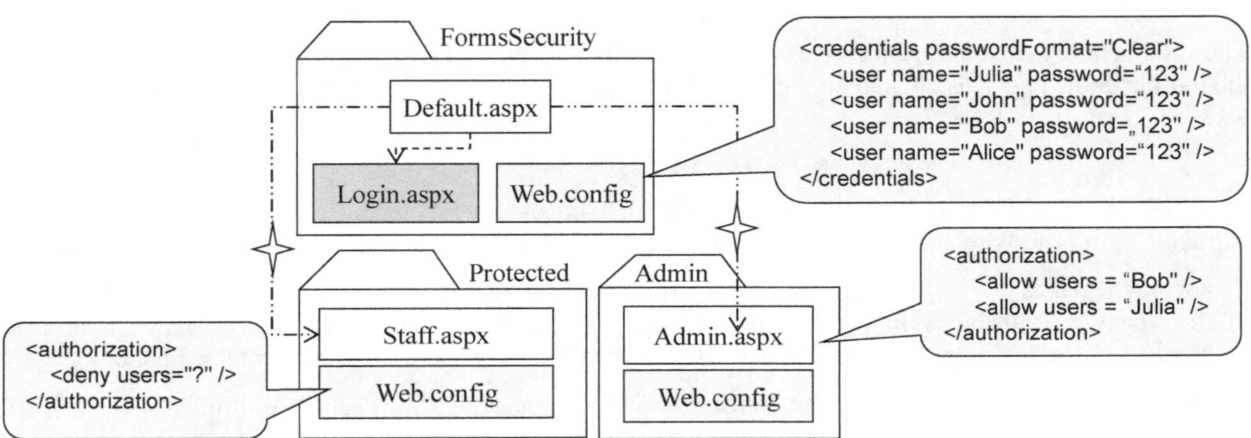

Figure 6.4. Organization of directories and files of the authentication and authorization example

The page design of the Default.aspx, Login.aspx, and Staff.aspx are shown in Figure 6.5. The Admin folder shown in Figure 6.4 is not implemented in the example.

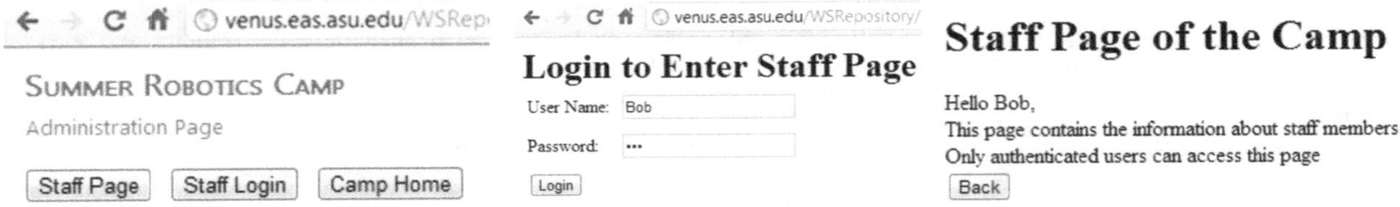

Figure 6.5. Test of forms security

The source code of the Login.aspx page is shown as follows. C# code is embedded in the HTML as the server-side script.

```
<html>
  <body>
     <h1> Login to access Staff page </h1>
     <form runat="server">
       <table cellpadding="4">
         <tr> <td> UserName:  </td>
             <td> <asp:TextBox ID= "txtUserName" RunAt="server" /> </td>
         </tr>
         <tr><td> Password: </td><td>
           <asp:TextBox ID="txtPassword" TextMode="password" RunAt="server"/>
          </td> </tr>
         <tr> <td>
             <asp:Button Text= "btnLogin" OnClick="LoginFunc"  RunAt="server"/>
        </td></tr>
       </table>
     </form>
     <asp:Label ID="Output"  RunAt="server"/>
  </body>
</html>
<script language="C#" runat="server">
  void LoginFunc(Object sender, EventArgs e) {
      if (FormsAuthentication.Authenticate(txtId.Text, txtPwd.Text))
          FormsAuthentication.RedirectFromLogin(UserName.Text, false);
      else
          Output.Text = "Invalid login";
  }
</script>
```

The code behind the Default.aspx page is simple. One line of code is behind each button; for example, when the button "Staff Page," is clicked on the Default.aspx page, the corresponding C# function is called, which uses

```
Response.Redirect("Protected/Staff.aspx");
```

to access the StaffPage.aspx. The function will first check the Web.config file in the directory for authentication. The Web.config file in the root directory contains authentication setting given in Figure 6.4.

To access the pages protected by the Web.config file, the access will be redirected to the page address given in the `loginURL` attributes in the "forms" element if user is not authenticated yet. Once a user is authenticated, the login page will not be activated in the following accesses to the protected page.

The authorization is defined in the Web.config files in the directories "Staff" and "Admin," respectively. A sample code for the Staff.aspx page is given as follows:

```
<html xmlns="http://www.w3.org/1999/xhtml">
```

```
<head runat="server"> <title>staff page</title> </head>
<body>
   <form id="form1" runat="server">
        <h1>Staff Page of the Camp</h1>
        <div>
        <% Response.Write("Hello " + Context.User.Identity.Name + ", "); %>
        This page contains the information about staff members who will teach
        and manage the camp. Only authenticated users can access this page .
        </div>
   </form>
</body>
</html>
```

The access control list in the Web.config is implemented using two subtags <allow> and <deny> of specific username. For the <allow> element, a question mark (?) allows anonymous users; an asterisk (*) allows all users. For the <deny> element, a question mark (?) indicates that anonymous users are denied access; while an asterisk (*) indicates that all users are denied access.

Figure 6.6 illustrates flow of accesses, including authentication and authorization processes.

The example is implemented and can be tested at:

http://neptune.fulton.ad.asu.edu/WSRepository/FormsSecurity/

You can test the example using the credentials shown in Figure 6.4. The example presented here has several problems. The password is stored in clear text. The other options in: credentials passwordFormat="[Clear|MD5|SHA1]"> can secure the password:

- MD5: Specifies that passwords be encrypted using the MD5 hash algorithm.
- SHA1: Specifies that passwords be encrypted using the SHA1 hash algorithm.

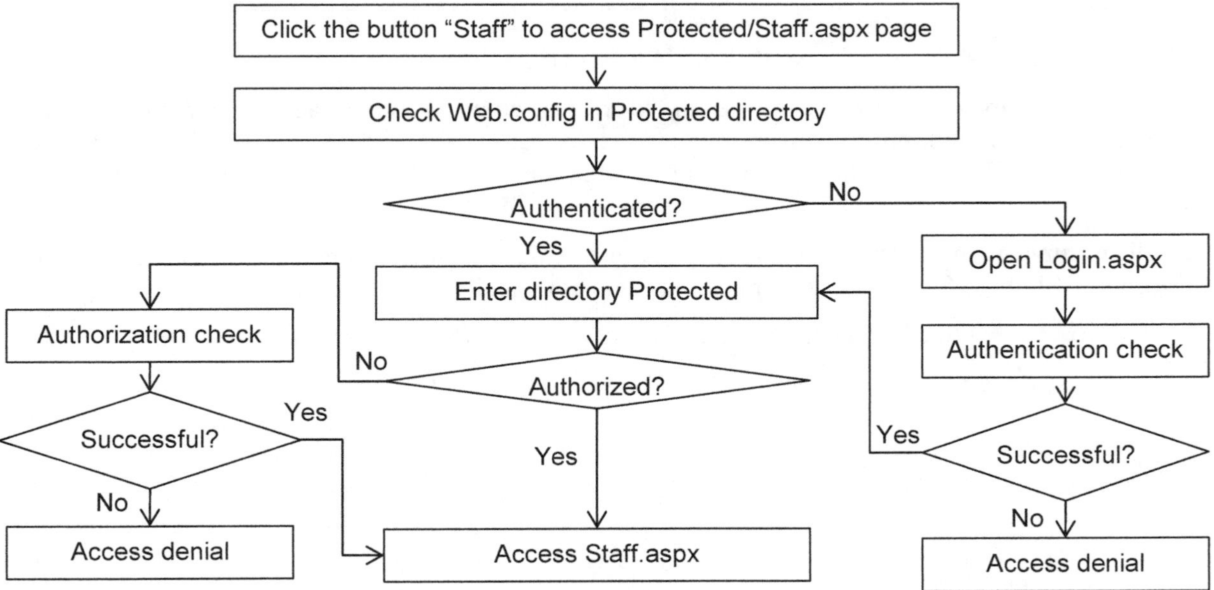

Figure 6.6. Authentication process

The authentication and authorization are checked sequentially in the given order. The process will be slow if the list is long. Furthermore, if the list needs to be changed from time to time, the maintenance process can be difficult and error-prone. In Visual Studio 2015 and .Net 4.5, FormsAuthentication.Authenticate method is obsolete. The solution is to use an XML file or database to store the usernames and passwords. The access and maintenance processes become database read and write issues, which are well addressed in database domain. Chapter 10 of the book will discuss database accesses and database-related web applications. In this section, we show how we can use an XML file to store the usernames and passwords, as the continuation of the XML discussion in Chapter 4. In the LoginFunc part, we can call a user defined authentication function, say, myAuthenticate(), and we write our own myAuthenticate() to access an XML file. The code is given as follows:

```
<script language="C#" runat="server">
   void LoginFunc(Object sender, EventArgs e) {
         if (myAuthenticate(txtId.Text, txtPwd.Text))
              FormsAuthentication.RedirectFromLogin(UserName.Text, false);
        else Output.Text = "Invalid login";
   }
bool myAuthenticate (string username, string password) {
   string fLocation = Path.Combine(Request.PhysicalApplicationPath,
@"App_Data\Users.xml"); //or HttpContext.Current.Request.PhysicalApplicationPath
         if (File.Exists(fLocation)) {
              FileStream FS= new FileStream(fLocation, FileMode.Open);
              XmlDocument xd = new XmlDocument();
              xd.Load(FS);
              XmlNode node = xd;
              XmlNodeList children = node.ChildNodes;
              foreach (XmlNode child in children) {
                // check if the username and password exist in the XML file;
         }
   }
}
</script>
```

6.2.3 Forms-Based Security with Self-Registration

Forms-based security allows users to register and to create accounts. A typical account contains a username, user id, password, e-mail, phone, a security question and its answer, and so on. In such applications, we will use an XML file to store the user account information. We will extend the example in the previous section to include the account registration and management functions.

The full example with student registration page and XML file for storing the account information is deployed in ASU Web Services and Application Repository and can be tested at:

http://neptune.fulton.ad.asu.edu/WSRepository/FormsSecurity/

The Default.aspx page design of the example is shown in Figure 6.7.

Figure 6.7. Default.aspx page design

When the Student Registration page is clicked, it opens the registration page, which requires to enter a user name, a password, and an image verification string, as shown in Figure 6.8. It checks if the username already exists. If the text entered does not match with the text shown in the image, a new image string will be generated.

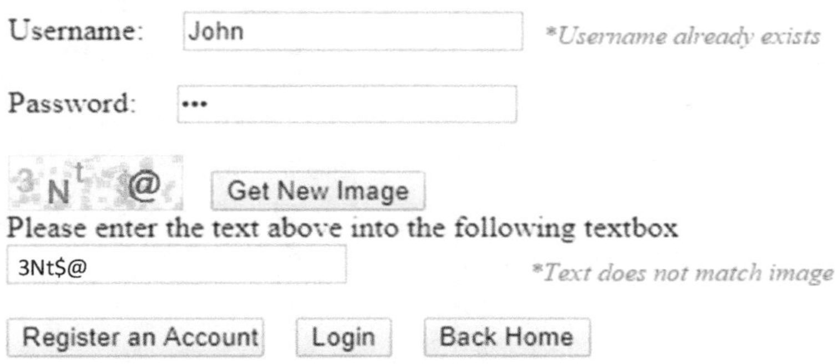

Figure 6.8. Student register page design, with an image verifier

After a student account is registered, the user will be taken to the student directly. The user can take go to the Student Login page to login and to access the student page, as shown in Figure 6.9.

Figure 6.9. Student login page and the student page

The entire solution, project, and files are shown Figure 6.10, where the Protected folder contains Staff.aspx page, Staff.aspx.cs file, and Web.config file. The Login.aspx page and Web.config file at the same level as the Default.aspx page manage the authentication of users. This part has been discussed in the previsou section.

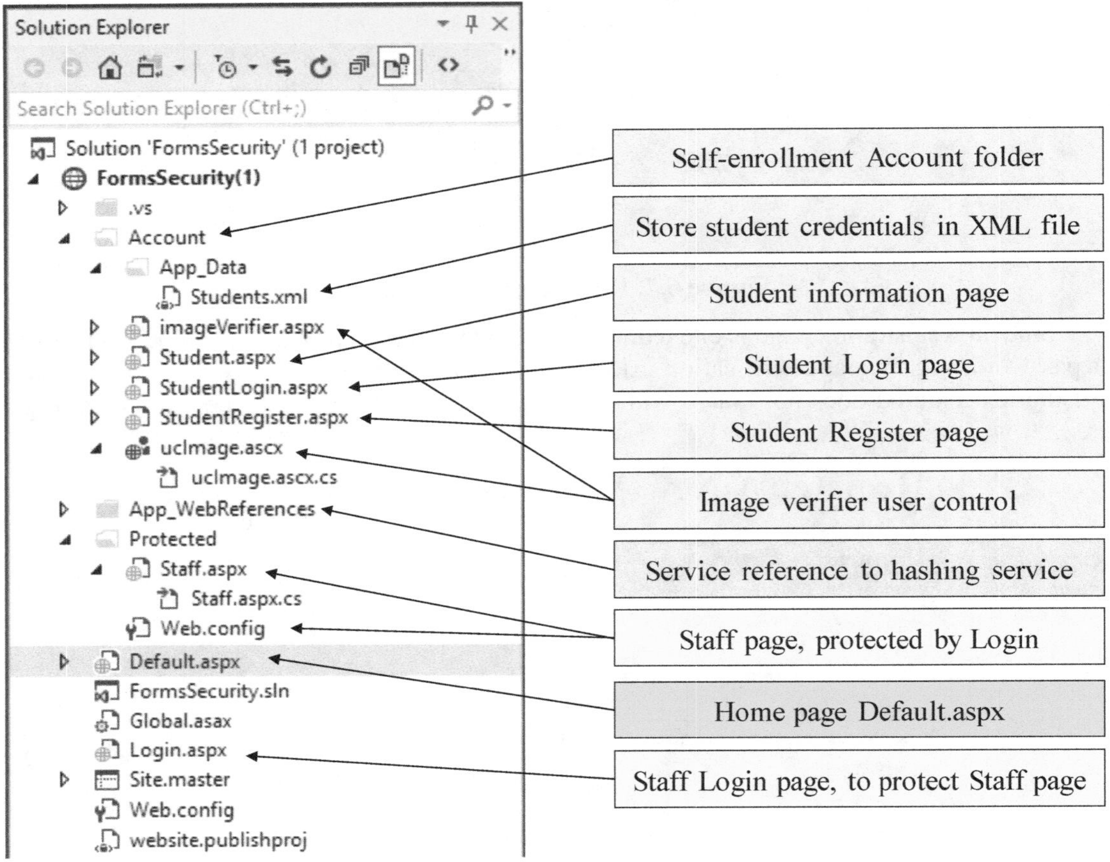

Figure 6.10. Project and file organization

The self-registration part is placed in the Account folder, which contains StudentRegister.aspx page, StudentRegister.aspx.cs code, StudentLogin.aspx page, StudentLogin.aspx.cs code, and the user control that generates the image verification string. Student credentials are stored in the XML file called Student.xml.

Now, we will give the codes behind the pages. First, the Default.aspx.cs page contains event handlers of the buttons that link to other pages:

```
public partial class _Default : System.Web.UI.Page {
    protected void btnCamp_Click(object sender, EventArgs e) {
        Response.Redirect("http://neptune.fulton.ad.asu.edu/roboticscamp/");
    }
    protected void btnStaff_Click(object sender, EventArgs e) {
        Response.Redirect("Protected/Staff.aspx"); // staff page
    }
    protected void btnStaffLogin_Click(object sender, EventArgs e) {
        Response.Redirect("Login.aspx"); // Staff login page
    }
    protected void btnRegister_Click(object sender, EventArgs e) {
```

```
        Response.Redirect("Account/StudentRegister.aspx");
    }
    protected void btnStudentLogin_Click(object sender, EventArgs e) {
        Response.Redirect("Account/StudentLogin.aspx");     }
}
```

The code behind StudentRegister.aspx.cs page is given as follows. It starts with checking the image string entered by the user. Then, it check the validality of the user name and password. It uses the ASU hashing services: http://neptune.fulton.ad.asu.edu/WSRepository/Services/HashSha512/Service.svc to hash the password that people cannot read user's passward even if the Student.xml file is open.

```
using System;
using System.Xml;
public partial class Account_StudentRegister : System.Web.UI.Page {
    protected void btnRegister_Click(object sender, EventArgs e) {
        // Step 1 - Image verification test
        if (txtImageStr.Text != (string)Session["ImageStr"]) {
            errorImage.Text = String.Format("*Text does not match image");
            errorImage.Visible = true;
            return;
        }
        errorImage.Visible = false;
        //Step 2 - Validate user name and password
        string filepath = HttpRuntime.AppDomainAppPath +
             @"\Account\App_Data\Students.xml";
        string user = txtUser.Text;
        string password = txtPassword.Text;
        // (1) Basic input validation check
        if (user == "") {
            errorUser.Text = String.Format("*Username cannot be empty");
            errorUser.Visible = true;
            return;
        }
        if (password == "") {
            errorUser.Text = String.Format("*Password cannot be empty");
            errorUser.Visible = true;
            return;
        }
        // (2) Encrypt the password using hashing service
        HashRef.ServiceClient h = new HashRef.ServiceClient();
        string pwdEncrypt = h.Hash(password, "CSE445");
        XmlDocument myDoc = new XmlDocument();
        myDoc.Load(filepath);
        XmlElement rootElement = myDoc.DocumentElement;
        // (3) Check if the username is not registered already
        foreach (XmlNode node in rootElement.ChildNodes) {
            if (node["name"].InnerText == user) {
                errorUser.Text = String.Format
                       ("*Account with username {0} already exists.", user);
                errorUser.Visible = true;
                return;
            }
        }
        errorUser.Visible = false;
        // Step 3: Add new credential into XML file
        XmlElement myMember = myDoc.CreateElement
                        ("member", rootElement.NamespaceURI);
        rootElement.AppendChild(myMember);
```

```
        XmlElement myUser = myDoc.CreateElement("name", rootElement.NamespaceURI);
        myMember.AppendChild(myUser);
        myUser.InnerText = user;
        XmlElement myPwd = myDoc.CreateElement("pwd", rootElement.NamespaceURI);
        myMember.AppendChild(myPwd);
        myPwd.InnerText = pwdEncrypt;
        myDoc.Save(filepath);
        Response.Redirect("Student.aspx");
    }
    // Generate new image string by reloading the StudnetRegister page
    protected void btnReImageStr_Click(object sender, EventArgs e) {
        Response.Redirect("StudentRegister.aspx");
    }
    protected void btnHome_Click(object sender, EventArgs e) {
        Response.Redirect("~/Default.aspx");
    }
    protected void btnStudentLogin_Click(object sender, EventArgs e) {
        Response.Redirect("StudentLogin.aspx");
    }
}
```

The image verifier is embedded into the StudentRegister.aspx page as under control. The ucImage.ascx page is given as follows:

```
<%@ Control Language="C#" AutoEventWireup="true" CodeFile="ucImage.ascx.cs"
Inherits="Account_ucImage" %>
<asp:Image ID ="ImageString" runat="server"> </asp:Image>
```

The code behind the ucImage.ascx page, the ucImage.ascx.cs page is given as follows:

```
public partial class Account_ucImage : System.Web.UI.UserControl {
    protected void Page_Load(object sender, EventArgs e) {
        // Use image string created in imageVerifier.aspx
        ImageString.ImageUrl = "imageVerifier.aspx?";
    }
}
```

For more detail about creating a user can control, please read Chapter 5, Section 5.2.3. The file imageVerifier.aspx and the code behind the page is responsible for generating verification image string and check the correctness of the entered string. The algorithms and code are discussed in Section 5.61 and Section 7.3.5. The imager verifier services and the TryIt page are deployed at:

http://neptune.fulton.ad.asu.edu/WSRepository/Services/ImageVerifierSvc/Service.svc
http://neptune.fulton.ad.asu.edu/WSRepository/Services/ImageVerifier/Service.svc/GetImage/{string}
http://neptune.fulton.ad.asu.edu/WSRepository/Services/ImageVerifierSvc/TryIt.aspx

The Student.XML will save the username and password of each registered user. The sample for is given as follows. As can be seen that the username is saved in clear text, while the password is encrypted.

```
<?xml version="1.0" encoding="utf-8"?>
<students>
  <student>
    <name>Alice</name>
    <pwd>04C55C9CA8D0DCA6F7113F2292363467BEAC2FA8</pwd>
  </student>
  <student>
    <name>Bob</name>
    <pwd>E0F839E3D8CDD713B4981591207E50BF36EE21DA</pwd>
  </student>
  <student>
```

```
    <name>John</name>
    <pwd>A6F7723F2292363467BEAC2FA804C55C9CA8D0DC</pwd>
  </student>
</students>
```

After a user has registered, the user can login to the system through the StudentLogin.aspx page. The code behind the page is given as follows:

```
using System;
using System.Web;
using System.Xml;
public partial class StudentLogin : System.Web.UI.Page {
    protected void btnLogin_Click(object sender, EventArgs e) {
        string filepath = HttpRuntime.AppDomainAppPath +
                               @"\Account\App_Data\Students.xml";
        //Obtains user input and encrypts password
        string user = txtUser.Text;
        string password = txtPassword.Text;
        HashRef.ServiceClient h = new HashRef.ServiceClient();
        string pwdEncrypt = h.Hash(password, "CSE445");
        XmlDocument myDoc = new XmlDocument();
        myDoc.Load(filepath);
        XmlElement rootElement = myDoc.DocumentElement;
        //Search through XML file to find match of username and password matches
        foreach (XmlNode node in rootElement.ChildNodes) {
            if (node["name"].InnerText == user) {
                if (node["pwd"].InnerText == pwdEncrypt) {
                    errorLogin.Visible = false;
                    Response.Redirect("Student.aspx");
                    return;
                }
                Else { // username exists but password does not match, show error
                {
                    errorLogin.Visible = true;
                    return;
                }
            }
        }
        errorLogin.Visible = true;
        return;
    }
    protected void btnHome_Click(object sender, EventArgs e) {
        Response.Redirect("~/Default.aspx");
    }
}
```

6.2.4 User Registration Using the Built-in Account Management

When you choose the ASP .Net Web Application as the template to start a new Web application project, an account management folder called Account is created for managing the self-registration accounts based on SQL database.

Figure 6.11 shows the Account folder, with a number of ASPX pages added into the project. To add more account management pages, you can drag and drop more pages from the Toolbox. You can also add a new folder by right-clicking the project name and select “New Folder.” To add a new page, right-click the folder Account and select Add New Item, and then choose Web Form.

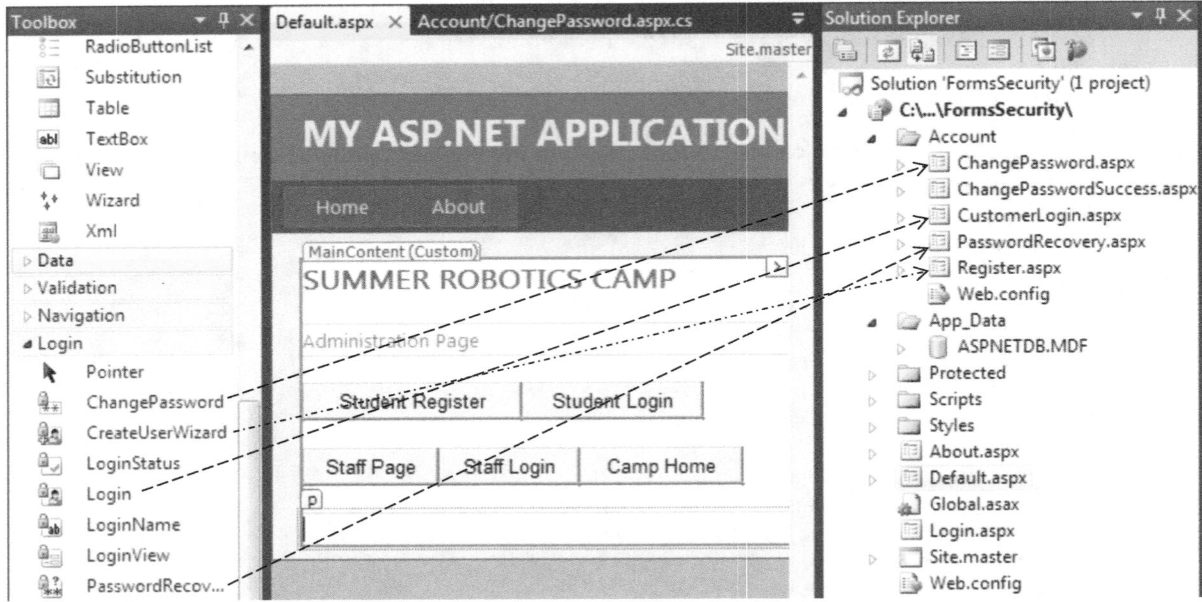

Figure 6.11. Creating user registration and management pages

Once the pages in the Account folder are added, we can start to add GUI controls and code behind the control. The middle window in the figure shows the extended GUI design, in which two more buttons are added: Student Registration and Student Login, which will allow students (customers) to create their own credentials through registration and then use their credentials to login.

As user access control and account management are rather standard features. ASP .Net has created web control and the complete code behind the controls. A few drag-and-drop operations will complete the entire design. For example, drag the web control "CreateUserWizard" in the Toolbox, see the left window of Figure 6.11, and drop it into the Register.aspx page; the GUI is already implemented in the control. Double click the button "Create User," and the code that performs the registration function is given.

```
using System;
using System.Web.Security; // Contains FormsAuthentication class
public partial class Account_Register : System.Web.UI.Page {
    protected void Page_Load(object sender, EventArgs e) {
        RegisterUser.ContinueDestinationPageUrl = Request.QueryString["ReturnUrl"];
    }
    protected void RegisterUser_CreatedUser(object sender, EventArgs e) {
        FormsAuthentication.SetAuthCookie(RegisterUser.UserName, false /*
createPersistentCookie */);
        string continueUrl = RegisterUser.ContinueDestinationPageUrl;
        if (String.IsNullOrEmpty(continueUrl)){
            continueUrl = "~/";
        }
        Response.Redirect(continueUrl);
    }
}
```

Similarly, the other pages in the Account folder corresponding to the other web controls in the Login part of the Toolbox can be created. For the example, the code behind the CustomerLogin.aspx is given as follows:

```
using System;
using System.Web; // contains HttpUtility class
public partial class Account_Login : System.Web.UI.Page {
```

```
    protected void Page_Load(object sender, EventArgs e) {
        RegisterHyperLink.NavigateUrl = "Register.aspx?ReturnUrl=" +
HttpUtility.UrlEncode(Request.QueryString["ReturnUrl"]);
    }
}
```

Note that CustomerLogin.aspx is different from the Login.aspx we discussed in the previous section. The CustomerLogin page will use the user created credentials, while the Login.aspx serves as the Staff login, which uses a different authorization mechanism.

When the web controls in the Login part of the Toolbox is used, a database storage object will be created automatically and placed in the App_Data folder of the project. The database object is named ASPNETDB.MDF, which is configured to work with SQL Server Express, with the data source name = SQLEXPRESS, which is the default name when one installs SQL Server Express on a Windows machine or on a Windows server. If your computer or the server is using these defaults, the account registration and management pages created in the simple steps above will work. You can test the pages by adding a few accounts and login into your system using these accounts.

You need to install SQL Express on your computer in order to use the database-based account management in the aforesaid example. When you install SQL Express, do not use the default name SQLEXPRESS. If you do, you will have a connection string conflict if the server also used the default name to install the SQL Express. On the other hand, if you have installed your SQL Server Express using a different data source name, or you are using the full version of the SQL server, you need to modify the connection string in the <connectionStrings> element in the machine.config file, which is located in your Visual Studio's "Config" directory; for example, C:\Windows\Microsoft.NET\Framework\v4.0.30319\Config\machine.config.

The element<connectionStrings> of the machine.config file is shown as follows:

```
   <connectionStrings>
        <add name="LocalSqlServer" connectionString="data source=.\SQLEXPRESS;
Integrated Security=SSPI; AttachDBFilename=|DataDirectory|aspnetdb.mdf; User
Instance=true" providerName="System.Data.SqlClient"/>
   </connectionStrings>
```

You can also manage your database schema by opening the Server Explore in the View menu of the Visual Studio, as shown in Figure 6.12, which shows the Server Explore and the schema of the user account database. Database access and management will be further discussed in Part II of the book.

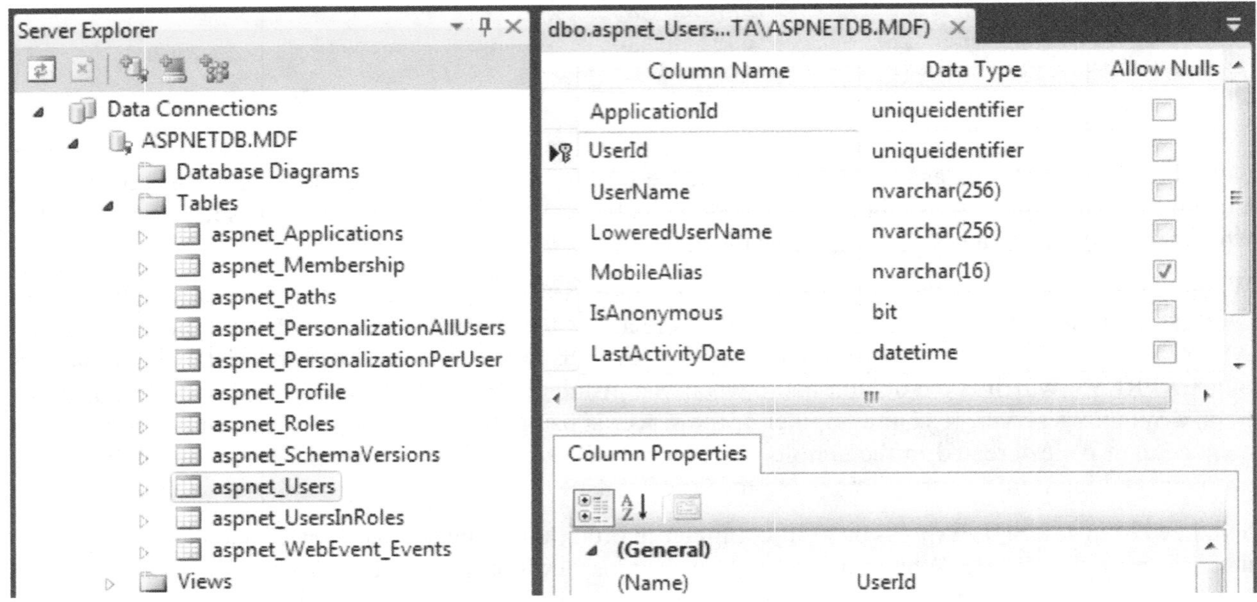

Figure 6.12. User account database

In this example, we used server controls to create the database, read the database (when login) and write the database (when register). We will further discuss the creating of database, defining the schema, and reading and writing the data in the database the database chapter in Part II of the book.

6.3 Encryption and Decryption

There are many situations in which we want to encrypt and decrypt data. For example, if the user IDs and passwords are stored in the Web.config file, text file, or database in plain text, the system administrators and anyone who has the administrative access to the server can see the user IDs and passwords. It is not acceptable for an organization that cares about protecting its user privacy. This section discusses encryption and decryption in data storing and transmitting for confidentiality and data integrity.

6.3.1 Developing Encryption and Decryption Service in WCF

Having understood the foregoing simple example, we can start to develop real service follow the pattern. We will create an encryption/decryption service.

Many encryption and decryption algorithms are of matters of national security and are classified. In this section, we will use Data Encryption Standard (DES) as an example to create basic encryption and decryption services. DES was developed by IBM in 1970 and selected by the National Bureau of Standards as an official Federal Information Processing Standard (FIPS) for the United States in 1976, which subsequently became an international standard. It is based on a symmetric-key algorithm that uses a 56-bit key encryption. As the key length is short, DES is used for low-level security purpose only (http://en.wikipedia.org/wiki/ Data_Encryption_Standard). DES uses a secret key system and block cypher encryption technique. The data and the secret key are mixed first. The mixed code is divided into eight blocks, with 6 bits in each block. Cypher encryption is applied in each block. The encrypted blocks are mixed again. The process repeats 16 times to obtain the final encrypted data. The encryption and decryption are safe if the secret key does not need to be transferred to a remote site. For example, we can use the encryption service to encrypt data and save the data into a file. Then we use the decryption service to decrypt the data before using the data. In this application, the secret key and both services stay in the same server without having to be transferred to a remote place.

Visual Studio .Net Class Library implemented a namespace called System.Security.Cryptography, which includes a number of security-related classes (http://msdn.microsoft.com/en-us/library/system.security.cryptography.aspx). The example that follows uses the DES SymmetricAlgorithm class to create a web service with a "string Encrypt(string)" method and a "string Decrypt(string)" method. To separate the interface from the implementation, we put the service in two files: Service.cs contains the web interface and the Cryption.cs contains the code of the encryption and decryption methods. Both files should be placed in the App_Code folder of your ASP .Net project. Following are the steps to create the service.

Step 1. Use WCF Service Application template to create a service. Name the project EncryptionWcf. You will see two files in the App_Code folder: IService.cs and Service.cs.

Step 2. Copy the following code to replace the ServiceContract and OperationContract in IService.cs file.

```
[ServiceContract]
public interface IService {
    [OperationContract]
    string Encrypt(string text);
    [OperationContract]
    string Decrypt(string text);
}
```

Step 3. Copy the following class to replace the service class in Service.cs file.

```
public class Service : IService {
    public string Encrypt(string text){
        EncryptionWcf.Cryption encrypt = new EncryptionWcf.Cryption();
        return encrypt.Encrypt(text);
    }
    public string Decrypt(string text){
        EncryptionWcf.Cryption decrypt = new EncryptionWcf.Cryption();
        return decrypt.Decrypt(text);
    }
}
```

Step 4. Write the Cryption.cs class.

Right-click the project folder App_Code and choose Add New Item... Then, choose the Class item and name the class Cryption.cs.

The code of the Cryption.cs is given as follows. A number of library classes are used. Their key class is the CryptoStream class. It combines the encryption algorithm and a seed (array of binary numbers) to create an encryption block. The MemoryStream object provides an internal storage for the CryptoStream object to store the encryption block. Then, the StreamWrite class mixes the encryption block with the plainstring to be encrypted. As the CryptoStream object and the StreamWrite object use unstructured memory, it is safe to flush the leftover characters and terminators that can be left in the memory stream when the program uses both structured accesses (e.g., read an entire line, including the line-end terminator) and unstructured accesses (read a byte or a character at a time). Such problem needs to be dealt with when one reads a stream buffer to a file system.

```
// file name: Cryption.cs
using System; using System.IO; using System.Text;
using System.Security.Cryptography;
namespace Encryption {
    public sealed class Cryption {
        byte[] seed = ASCIIEncoding.ASCII.GetBytes("cse44598");
```

```
        // A seed binary array for encryption
        public string Encrypt(string plainString){ // encryption using DES
            if (String.IsNullOrEmpty(plainString)){
                throw new ArgumentNullException("The input string for encryption
cannot be empty or null!");
            }
            SymmetricAlgorithm saProvider = DES.Create(); // Lib class
            MemoryStream mStream = new MemoryStream();
            CryptoStream cStream = new CryptoStream(mStream,
saProvider.CreateEncryptor(seed, seed), CryptoStreamMode.Write);
            StreamWriter sWriter = new StreamWriter(cStream);
            sWriter.Write(plainString);
            sWriter.Flush(); // Flush the string terminator in sWrite
            cStream.FlushFinalBlock();
            return Convert.ToBase64String(mStream.GetBuffer(), 0,
(int)mStream.Length);
        }
        public string Decrypt(string encryptedString){ // decryption using DES
            if (String.IsNullOrEmpty(encryptedString)) {
                throw new ArgumentNullException("The string for decryption cannot be
empty or null!");
            }
            SymmetricAlgorithm saProvider = DES.Create();
            MemoryStream memStream = new MemoryStream
                    (Convert.FromBase64String(encryptedString));
            CryptoStream cStream = new CryptoStream(memStream,
                saProvider.CreateDecryptor(seed, seed), CryptoStreamMode.Read);
            StreamReader reader = new StreamReader(cStream);
            return reader.ReadLine();
        }
    }
}
```

Step 5. Build and start the service.

The aforesaid service is implemented in both ASP .Net service and in WCF service, and they are deployed for public access at:

ASP .Net service: http://neptune.fulton.ad.asu.edu/WSRepository/Services/Encryption/Service.asmx
WCF service: http://neptune.fulton.ad.asu.edu/WSRepository/Services/EncryptionWcf/Service.svc

6.3.2 Developing a Secure Hashing Service in WCF

The decryption service allows the users to obtain the original data after encryption. There are situations where the encrypted data never needs to be decrypted; for example, the session ID used for identifying the browser that revisits the same session, as we discussed in Chapter 5. In such applications, we should use the one-way hashing, instead of the encryption and decryption.

A hash value is a numeric value with fixed length that uniquely identifies a data, but without revealing the data's value; One can generate the hash value from the given data, but cannot recreate the data from the hash value. It is also different from the digital signature method in Open Key system, where the data and digital signature are mixed. Data hashing creates a separate digital signature.

Hashing has many applications. For example, it can be used for securing users' passwords. Consider different ways of securing users' passwords:

1. Save users' passwords in a database (or a file). Secure the database using access control.

2. Save users' passwords in a database. Make database writable, searchable, but not readable. When validating a user, search (user-name + password) in the database and it returns true or false.
3. Encrypt the passwords before saving into a database. Decrypt the password when validating a user.

In all solutions above, someone will be able see the passwords. Is there a way that no one (no hackers) can see the stored passwords? Application of hashing will be the most secure way:

4. Hash the password when a user creates it. Save the hash value. When validating a user, hash the user entered password and compare it with the stored hash value.

Hashing can be used in data dependability due to intentional and unintentional modification of data during storage and communication. When saving a piece of data into a file system or database, create a hash value of the file and save the hash value in a different place. When reading the file, recreate a hash value and compare with the saved hash value. If the two hash values are identical, the data is correct or safe. For example, we have a large piece of data, 100 pages of a contract, we can generate a (short) hash value1 from the contract and send the hash value1 with the contract. The receiver regenerates hash value2 from the received contract. If value1 == value2, the contract is not modified during the transmission.

In the code below, we show a simple console application of creating secure hashing values.

```
using System;
using System.Security.Cryptography;
using System.Text;
namespace HashConsoleApp {
    class Program {
        static void Main(string[] args) {
            byte[] HashValue1;
            byte[] HashValue2;
            string MsgShort = "You won the lottery";
            string MsgLong = "This is an official announcement from the lottery
authority and the message comes with a digital signature";
            UnicodeEncoding Uce = new UnicodeEncoding(); //Create an object
            byte[] BytesShort = Uce.GetBytes(MsgShort); // convert to byte array
            byte[] BytesLong = Uce.GetBytes(MsgLong);
            SHA1Managed SHhash = new SHA1Managed(); //Create a SHA1Managed object
            HashValue1 = SHhash.ComputeHash(BytesShort); // Hashing
            HashValue2 = SHhash.ComputeHash(BytesLong);
            Console.WriteLine("Hash value 1 in hexadecimal");
            foreach (byte b in HashValue1)
                Console.Write("{0:X} ", b);
            Console.WriteLine("\nHash value 2 in hexadecimal");
            foreach (byte b in HashValue2)
                Console.Write("{0:X} ", b);
            Console.WriteLine();
        }
    }
}
```

The output and the hash values generated in the code are:

```
Hash value 1 in hexadecimal
C8 55 31 EC E7 24 B4 92 46 3A AA 3D 97 2F C D5 4B 37 95 22
Hash value 2 in hexadecimal
A4 39 1A B8 B5 1C 19 54 83 72 C2 3E E 71 CE 13 73 35 DE 7A
```

As can be seen, the two messages have different lengths, but the generated hash values have the same length.

We also created a web service that returns a hashing value for a given value. The contract definition of the service is:

```
using System.ServiceModel;
using System.ServiceModel.Web;
[ServiceContract]
public interface IService {
    [OperationContract]
    string Hash(string data, string salt);
}
```

The service implementation is:

```
using System;
using System.Text;
using System.Security.Cryptography;
public class Service : IService {
    public string Hash(string data, string salt){
        using (var sha = new SHA512CryptoServiceProvider()){
            var hashedString = sha.ComputeHash(Encoding.Default.GetBytes(data +
salt));
            return Convert.ToBase64String(hashedString);
        }
    }
}
```

In the example, the parameter salt is any string that the user can use to make it more difficult to crack the hashed data, such as password and user ID. The salt is appended to the data to be hashed.

The service is deployed at:

http://neptune.fulton.ad.asu.edu/WSRepository/Services/HashSha512/Service.svc

The service can be tested by the service tool deployed at:

http://neptune.fulton.ad.asu.edu/WSRepository/services/wsTesterTryIt/

6.3.3 WCF Service Client

Different platforms can be used for creating WCF service clients, including Console, ASP .Net, Workflow Foundation, Presentation Foundation, and Silverlight. Creating a client accessing a WCF service is not much different from accessing other services. The idea is to create a proxy to connect to the endpoints and the proxy will contain the address, binding, and contract information for the client to invoke the remote service. In order to take the advantage of the additional binding option, we need to use "Add Service Reference," instead of "Add Web Reference" in the ASP .Net when creating the proxy. Figure 6.13 shows a simple ASP .Net client that tests the WCF encryption/decryption service. A string is entered in the textbox. Once submitted, the encrypt operation is called and the string is encrypted, as shown in the line below the textbox. Then, the encrypted string is sent the decrypt function, which decrypts the encrypted string back to the original text.

ASP .NET TEST CLIENT
Please enter a string for encryption: My secret msg is "Hello Cryption" Submit
The encrypted string looks like this: FbryW6ZA7o1gfYSb1eU2Un5QX5znWUW3of3SLlpSv2rsaluXe4Xq+g==
Check if the decrypted string is correct --> My secret msg is "Hello Cryption"

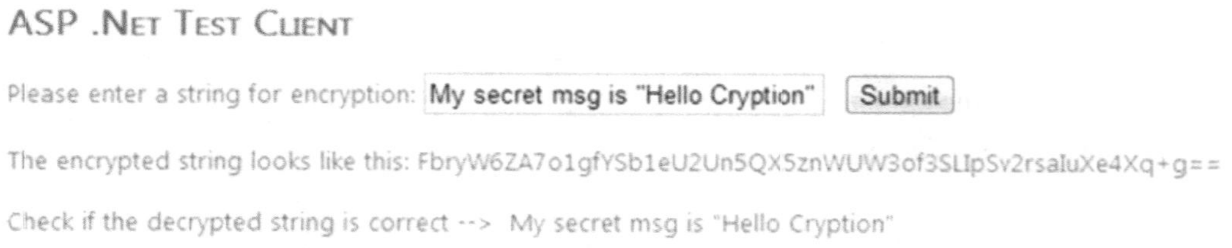

Figure 6.13. ASP .Net client accessing the WCF encryption/decryption service

The C# code behind the "Submit" button of the GUI design is given as follows:

```
protected void btnSubmit_Click(object sender, EventArgs e) {
   EncryptService.ServiceClient myClient = new EncryptService.ServiceClient();
   try { lblEncrypted.Text = myClient.Encrypt(txtInput.Text); }
   catch (Exception ec) { lblEncrypted.Text = ec.Message.ToString(); }
   try { lblDecrypted.Text = myClient.Decrypt(lblEncrypted.Text); }
   catch (Exception dc) { lblDecrypted.Text = dc.Message.ToString(); }
}
```

Instead of writing a client to test the encryption and decryption service, the service can also be tested by the service tool deployed at:

http://neptune.fulton.ad.asu.edu/WSRepository/services/wsTesterTryIt/

The Web.config file of the test client is given as follows. In the <client> element, the proxy of address, binding, and contract is stored.

```
<configuration>
<system.serviceModel>
<bindings>
   <basicHttpBinding>
    <binding name="BasicHttpBinding_IService" >
      <security mode="None">
      <transport clientCredentialType="None" proxyCredentialType="None" realm="" />
      <message clientCredentialType="UserName" algorithmSuite="Default" />
     </security>
    </binding>
   </basicHttpBinding>
</bindings>
<client>
     <endpoint
         address="http://neptune.fulton.ad.asu.edu/WSRepository/
                                Services/EncryptionWcf/Service.svc"
         binding="basicHttpBinding" bindingConfiguration="BasicHttpBinding_IService"
         contract="EncryptService.IService" name="BasicHttpBinding_IService"
     </endpoint>
</client>
</system.serviceModel>
</configuration>
```

By default, basicHttpBinding is used. In order to use other binding protocols, you can use Visual Studio menu: Tools → WCF Service Configuration Editor. Browse to the location of the application and select the Web.config file of the test client. Then, you can choose other binding protocols shown in Table 6.3.

Table 6.3. Bindings supported in WCF

Binding	Description
basicHttpBinding	HTTP, text encoding, basic security
wsHttpBinding / wsDualHttpBinding	HTTP, HTTPS, text or MTOM encoding, SSL over HTTP, WS-reliable, WS-transaction
netTcpBinding	TCP, binary, SSL over TCP, WS-reliable, WS-transaction
netNamedPipeBinding	Named pipe, binary, security, sessions, reliable, transactions
netMsmqBinding	MSMQ, binary, security, sessions, reliable, transactions
nsmqIntegrationBinding	MSMQ, text, sessions, reliable, transactions
netPeerTcpBinding	Peer-to-Peer communications

6.3.4 Error Control Code

Communication between distributed and networked nodes is neither reliable nor secure. Efforts must be made in all layers of communication in order to achieve reliable and secure communication. Error control codes are widely used at the data link layer and above.

Coding theory is based on Shannon's theorem in 1948: Even in a noisy channel, errors in data transmission can be reduced to any desired level, if a certain minimum percentage of redundancy is maintained by means of proper encoding and decoding of the data.

This theorem founded the theories of error control codes as well as fault tolerant computing. Shannon's theorem did not suggest any methods for constructing such codes. Golay (1949), Hamming (1950), and many other pioneers in the area have developed Shannon's theorem into Coding Theory. Most fault tolerance techniques can be viewed as implementations of error control codes.

Coding is the representation of information (signals, numbers, messages, etc.) by code symbols or words of code symbols. Let W be the set of all possible words in a code. In order to control errors, W is divided into two subsets, C and W–C. Only the words in C are used for representing information, while words in W–C are redundant, indicating incorrect words. C is the code space, the words in C are called codewords.

As an example, we can use two lines to transmit the same bit of information. In this case, the entire output space is W = {00, 01, 10, 11}, and the code space C = {00, 11}.

We can define the distance between two words $d(x, y)$ to the bit positions in which the words x and y differ. We can further define Hamming Distance to be the minimum distance between any pair of codewords in the code space. Let d_m(C) be the Hamming Distance of a code space C:

$$d_m(C)=\min(d(x,y)), \text{ where } x\in C \text{ and } y\in C.$$

Hamming Distance determines the error detection and correction capability:

1 If $d_m(C) = p + 1$, the code C can detect all errors in which up to p bits are erroneous.
2 If $d_m(C) = 2l + 1$, the code C can correct all errors in which up to l bits are erroneous; for example, if $d_m(C) = 3$, C can detect up to 2 bit-errors and correct 1 bit-error. If $d_m(C) = 5$, C can detect up to 4 bit-errors and correct 2 bit errors.

A few codes have been widely used in communication and in storage, among them, parity check code, checksum, arithmetic code, and combinational code.

For a given n-bit word, a parity check code appends one additional bit to each word to make a codeword. The additional bit makes the total number 1 of all codewords an even number (even party code) or an odd number (odd party code).

Assume an n-bit word is represented as $w = (b_0, b_1, ..., b_{n-1})$, and the encoded word is $(b_0, b_1, ..., b_{n-1}, \mathbf{b_n})$, where the check bit is calculated by a codeword, where it is calculated through ⊕ (XOR) operations:

$$b_n = (b_0 \oplus b_1 \oplus ... \oplus b_{n-1}) \quad \text{(Even-parity code)}$$

$$b_n = (b_0 \oplus b_1 \oplus ... \oplus b_{n-1} \oplus 1) \quad \text{(Odd-parity code)}$$

The Hamming Distance in parity code is 2, which can detect any single bit error. Parity code is simple in encoding and decoding. It uses n XOR operations. The cost of redundancy is 1/n, and encoding and decoding delays are log(n).

Parity check code is often used at low level in the communication stack, such as Data Link layer. Checksum can be used at low level and high level. Instead of dealing with a stream of bits, it deals with a sequence of words. Let $(x_0, x_1, x_2, ..., x_{m-1}, \mathbf{x_m})$ be a vector of m words, with an additional check word appended to the end, where,

$$x_m= \sum_{i=0}^{m-1} \bmod (2^n) .$$

The appended word x_m is the checksum for words $x_0, x_1, x_2, ..., x_{m-1}$. We use modulo operation to make sure that the sum does not take more space than any words in the code.

When applying checksum in communication, the sender first calculates the checksum x_m, and then transmits m + 1 codewords ($x_0, x_1, x_2, ..., x_{m-1}, \mathbf{x_m}$).

The receiver recalculates the sum and checks whether the calculated sum is equal to the received checksum.

Checksum coding can be applied to blocks of consecutive words in memory or communication. If used in memory, each write operation leads to recalculation of the checksum. Checksum coding cost is low, but the detection diagnostic resolution is low. When an error is detected, no information is available to help identify which word is incorrect.

Both parity code and checksum code are separable code, which means that the check bit/word is not mixed with the data. This type of code allows the data to be used without delay before the error check is completed. If error check detects an error, the used data needs to be rolled back.

Not all codes are separable code. The arithmetic code and combinational code discussed next are not separable code.

Let A be a function. A defines an arithmetic code, if

$$(\forall a)(\forall b)(a \in W \wedge b \in W \Rightarrow A(a \otimes b) = A(a) \otimes A(b)))$$

where, $\otimes$ is one of arithmetic operations given; for example, +, –, *.

The most widely used arithmetic code is the AN Code defined by $A*N$, where, A is an integer, normally, is a prime number of greater than or equal to 3, and the operation $\otimes = *$. We can easily verify that the condition of arithmetic code is met:

$$A*(a + b) = A*a + A*b \text{ and } A*(a - b) = A*a - A*b$$

The characteristics include: It is non-separable code, For $A = 3$, the code uses 2 bits redundancy, and can detect a single error.

Error control code can also be defined based on combination theory. An m-out-n code or m/n code requires that each codeword consists of n bits, in which there are exactly m ones. The code is a non-separable code. The code has n!/(m!(n–m)! codewords in 2^n words. The code contains a large amount of redundancy and the cost is high. The usage of codewords is n!/(m!(n–m)!/2^n.

For example, if n = 16 and m = 3, then, n!/(m!(n–m)!/ = 3360 and 2^{16} = 65536. Only about 5% of words are codewords.

The code can detect all single errors. It can also detect all unidirectional errors that change from 0 → 1 or from 1 → 0 errors, but not both types. The ability can be used in the situation where unidirectional errors are common; m-out-of-n code is a non-separable code.

6.3.5 Secure Sockets Layer Cryptographic Protocols

Error control code is normally used to protect fault and errors caused by noises from the network and the environment. It does not project malicious attacks. Encryption and decryption are needed to protect data over the Internet from malicious attacks. Secure Sockets Layer (SSL) defines cryptographic protocols that provide data confidentiality and data integrity (digital signature) for communications over HTTP and TCP/IP networks.

The SSL consists of a stack of Protocols split into two communication layers. The first layer is the higher layer, used in the management of SSL exchanges. It consists of SSL Handshake Protocol, SSL Change Cipher Spec Protocol, SSL Alert Protocol, and HTTP. The second layer is the lower layer, consisting of SSL Record Protocol, TCP, and IP.

An SSL session is a connection between a client and server. Multiple sessions are possible between a client and server. An SSL connection is a transport that provides a type of service. Connections are of peer-to-peer relationship.

IIS uses the X.509 key system in its SSL protocol to provide HTTPS secure access to the web applications that it hosts. To apply HTTPS to your web server, you need to request the security certificate, which consists of an open key and a secret key. After installing the certificate on the server, clients can use the https connection to access the server.

Certificate of a server is similar to the driver's license of a person. It certifies that the server has a certain level of trustworthiness in providing services. However, it does not guarantee the quality of services. Certification is offered by independent organizations, such as GeoTrust, GlobalSign, Thawte, and VeriSign.

To install the SSL certificate, you can follow these steps in Windows server:

- Open the Internet Information Services (IIS) Manager.
- Right-click the Default website and select Edit Bindings.
- Select HTTPS from the Type drop-down list.
- Select the certificate from the SSL certificate drop-down list and click OK.

To test if your certificate is installed successfully, you can access a service in a browser by using the HTTPS address; for example: https://localhost/secureConnectionServices/service1.svc.

6.4 Dependable Computing in Windows Communication Foundation

Windows Communication Foundation (WCF) is the latest service-oriented computing development environment. It extends ASP .Net to better support service-oriented software development, particularly in reliability and security. WCF is a part of WinFx, which is a programming environment since Windows 7 and Windows Server 2010. We will use WCF to develop services in the next chapter. In this section, we will discuss the security, reliability, and transaction features offered in WCF.

6.4.1 WS-Security

WCF supports multiple security methods at multiple layers. The security methods include authentication, authorization, confidentiality, and integrity. The layers in which security mechanisms are deployed include message layer and transport layer.

Authentication: WCF supports all the authentication methods we discussed in ASP .Net sections, including IIS security, integrated Windows security, and Forms-based security. In addition, it supports the X.509 certificate, which employs the public key infrastructure (PKI) to encrypt a message to generate digital signature as credential. X.509 specifies standard formats for public key certificates and a certification path validation algorithm.

Authorization: WCF supports all the authorization methods we discussed in ASP .Net sections, including access control list and role-based authorization. In addition, it supports XSI standard, which is a claim-based authorization method.

Transport security protects data during their transportation on the network. SSL (Secure Socket Layer) is the common mechanism used for encrypting the data in HTTPS protocol. Transport security depends on the mechanism for the binding the user has selected. For example, if wsHttpBinding is used, the security mechanism is Secure Sockets Layer (SSL), as shown in Table 6.3.

Message security ensures confidentiality of message by encrypting and signing message before sending them to the transport layer, regardless if the transport layer will encrypt the data to be transported. It means that every message includes the necessary headers and data to keep the message secure. Because the composition of the headers varies, you can include any number of credentials. This becomes a factor if you are interoperating with other services that demand a specific credential type that a transport mechanism cannot supply, or if the message must be used with more than one service, where each service demands a different credential type.

```
Transport and message security can be defined in the Web.config file. It
can be used in the program code. The following code segment from WCF online
tutorial shows how to create an object of wsHttpBinding and initialize the
field in the object:
// Create the binding for an endpoint.
NetTcpBinding b = new NetTcpBinding();
b.Security.Mode = SecurityMode.Message;
// Create the ServiceHost for running a calculator service.
Uri baseUri = new Uri("net.tcp://MachineName/tcpBase");
Uri[] baseAddresses = new Uri[] { baseUri };
ServiceHost sh = new ServiceHost(typeof(Calculator), baseAddresses);
// Add an endpoint using the binding and a new address.
Type c = typeof(myService);
sh.AddServiceEndpoint(c, b, "MyEndpoint");
// Set a certificate as the credential for the service.
sh.Credentials.ServiceCertificate.SetCertificate(
    StoreLocation.LocalMachine, StoreName.My,
    X509FindType.FindBySubjectName,"client.com");
Try {
    sh.Open();
    Console.WriteLine("Listening....");
    Console.ReadLine(); // Press Enter to terminate
    sh.Close();
}
catch (CommunicationException ce) {
    Console.WriteLine("Commmunication error: {0}", ce.Message);
    Console.WriteLine();
}
catch (System.Exception exc){
    Console.WriteLine("An unforseen error occurred: {0}", exc.Message);
    Console.ReadLine();
}
```

6.4.2 WS-Reliability

Web services and SOC applications are largely web- and Internet-based. Not only security, but also reliability is a major concern.

WS-Reliability defined by OASIS (OASIS 2004), is a SOAP-based specification that fulfills reliable messaging requirements critical to SOC applications of web services. SOAP over HTTP is not sufficient when an application-level messaging protocol must also guarantee some level of reliability and security. This specification defines reliability in the context of current web services standards. This specification has been designed for use in combination with other complementary protocols and builds on previous experiences, such as ebXML Message Service (ebMS).

WS-Reliability defines WS-ReliableMessaging protocol with the following reliability features:

- Guaranteed message delivery, or At-Least-Once delivery semantics;
- Guaranteed message duplicate elimination, or At-Most-Once delivery semantics;
- Guaranteed message delivery and duplicate elimination, or Exactly-Once delivery semantics;
- Guaranteed message ordering for delivery within a group of messages.

WS-ReliableMessaging supports Reliable Messaging, which is the execution of a transport-agnostic, SOAP-based protocol providing quality of service in the reliable delivery of messages. Reliable Messaging has the following features:

- Reliable Sessions are suitable in the scenarios where both parties of communication are online. They deal with faults at the message level, including:
    - Lost messages
    - Duplicated messages
    - Messages received out of order
- Message Queuing; for example, MSMQ, which deals with the situation that the receiver of the message may be offline at the time the message is sent. It ensures reliable communication between the sender and the receiver.

Figure 6.14 shows the steps of establishing and execution of the reliable messaging protocol in dealing the message loss.

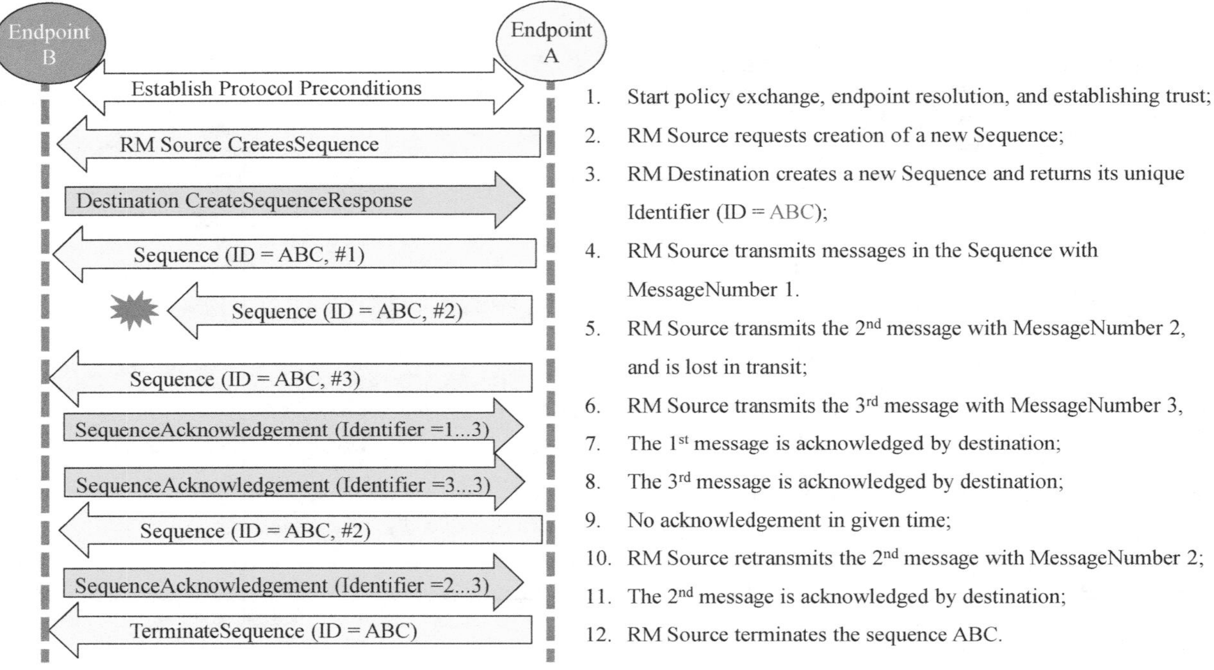

Endpoint B
Endpoint A
Establish Protocol Preconditions
RM Source CreatesSequence
Destination CreateSequenceResponse
Sequence (ID = ABC, #1)
Sequence (ID = ABC, #2)
Sequence (ID = ABC, #3)
SequenceAcknowledgement (Identifier =1...3)
SequenceAcknowledgement (Identifier =3...3)
Sequence (ID = ABC, #2)
SequenceAcknowledgement (Identifier =2...3)
TerminateSequence (ID = ABC)
1. Start policy exchange, endpoint resolution, and establishing trust;
2. RM Source requests creation of a new Sequence;
3. RM Destination creates a new Sequence and returns its unique Identifier (ID = ABC);
4. RM Source transmits messages in the Sequence with MessageNumber 1.
5. RM Source transmits the 2nd message with MessageNumber 2, and is lost in transit;
6. RM Source transmits the 3rd message with MessageNumber 3,
7. The 1st message is acknowledged by destination;
8. The 3rd message is acknowledged by destination;
9. No acknowledgement in given time;
10. RM Source retransmits the 2nd message with MessageNumber 2;
11. The 2nd message is acknowledged by destination;
12. RM Source terminates the sequence ABC.

Figure 6.14. The process of WS-ReliableMessaging protocol dealing the message loss

The reliable sessions are implemented by message identify, sequence number, and message acknowledgement upon receiving. The following example given in OASIS (2004) specifies the request that includes such information so that reliable sessions can be enforced.

```
<Request
xmlns="http://docs.oasis-open.org/wsrm/2004/06/ws-reliability-1.1.xsd"
xmlns:soap12="http://www.w3.org/2003/05/soap-envelope" soap12:mustUnderstand="1">
   <MessageId groupId="mid://20040202.103832@wsr-sender.org">
        <SequenceNum number="0" groupExpiryTime="2005-02-02T03:00:33-31:00" />
   </MessageId>
   <ExpiryTime>2004-09-07T03:01:03-03:50</ExpiryTime>
   <ReplyPattern>
        <Value>Response</Value>
   </ReplyPattern>
   <AckRequested/>
```

```
    <DuplicateElimination/>
    <MessageOrder/>
</Request>
```

WCF Reliable Sessions is an implementation of SOAP reliable messaging as defined by the WS-ReliableMessaging protocol. In a WCF environment, the request for using reliable messaging can be implemented by adding the following binding element in the Web.config file, and then the system will create the WCF SOAP reliable messaging data packages for the reliable communications.

```
<?xml version="1.0" encoding="utf-8" ?>
<configuration>
  <system.serviceModel>
    <client>
      <!-- this endpoint has an https: address -->
      <endpoint name=""
             address="https://localhost/servicemodelsamples/service.svc"
             binding="customBinding"
             bindingConfiguration="reliableSessionOverHttps"
             contract="Microsoft.ServiceModel.Samples.myService" />
    </client>
      <bindings>
        <customBinding>
          <binding name="reliableSessionOverHttps">
             <reliableSession ordered="true" />
             <textMessageEncoding messageVersion="Default" encoding="utf-8" />
             <httpTransport />
          </binding>
        </customBinding>
    </bindings>
  </system.serviceModel>
</configuration>
```

WCF SOAP reliable messaging provides a reliable session between two endpoints, where the reliability provided is end-to-end, regardless of the number or type of intermediaries that separate the messaging endpoints. This end-to-end channel includes any transport intermediaries that do not use SOAP, such as HTTP proxies, or intermediaries that use SOAP that are required for messages to flow between the endpoints. A reliable session channel is implemented by "interactive" communication so that the services connected by such a channel run concurrently and exchange and process messages under conditions of low latency, that is, within relatively short intervals of time. This coupling means that these components make progress together or fail together, so there is no isolation provided between them.

6.4.3 Transactions

A transaction usually means a collection of actions, including information exchange and status modification. The collection of actions must be treated as a unit or atomic operation for the purposes of satisfying a request and for ensuring database integrity. For a transaction to be completed and database changes to be made permanent, a transaction must be completed in its entirety. A typical example of transaction is an online payment of an electricity bill. Your request will activate at least two actions: a withdrawal from your account and a deposit to the electricity company's account. Obviously, it is not acceptable to have the money taken from your account, but the deposit does not go through, or vice versa.

In computer hardware design, we have a similar situation called indivisible operations, where we need to design a hardware instruction to perform two operations in a single step: check the flag, and lock the flag if the flag is not locked already. This indivisible instruction will allow the program to perform exclusive operation on a resource.

Transactions are at application level, which often consists of sequences of long operations. It is not possible to take a hardware solution to make sure the transactions complete in entirety or not at all. Thus, the software solution to perform the transaction must meet the following requirements:

Atomic: The actions involved in a transaction must be all-or-nothing, that is, an action is either 100% complete, or not at all. Even if a failure occurs, such as hardware, software, and power failures, the atomic property must be guaranteed.

Consistent: The result of the transaction must be consistent and preserve the data integrity of all systems involved. For example, in case of an account transfer, if $100 is withdrawn from one account, the deposit into the other account must also be $100.

Isolated: The principle of implementing atomic and consistent transaction is to define a set of prior-to-commit actions that are tentative and not visible to other activities. When all parties involved in the actions have successfully completed their parts, a coordinator (independent mechanism) will ask all parties to commit at the same time. At the end of the commitment, the coordinator will check the consistence of the results, and it will make the results visible to other activities only if the results are consistent. If any party cannot perform its action, or the results of the collective actions are not consistent, the coordinator will ask all parties to abort and to roll back to their previous status prior to making the tentative actions, which makes the tentative actions appear as if the actions never happened. The entire operations of transaction must be isolated before it is completed.

Durable: Once the transaction is marked completed by the coordinator, the results should have been placed into their final destination, such as a database, and will be permanent. Any party involved cannot revoke its action that has been committed. Another transaction needs to be initiated if a change needs to be made.

WCF implements WS-AtomicTransaction (WS-AT), which is an interoperable transaction protocol developed by BEA, IBM, and Microsoft and supported by many other companies and organizations. It is currently an OASIS standard (http://docs.oasis-open.org/ws-tx/wsat/2006/06). WCF's implementation of WS-AtomicTransaction is based on Microsoft Distributed Transaction Coordinator (MSDTC) transaction manager. WS-AT enables distributed transactions to be flowed using web service messages, and coordinates in an interoperable manner among heterogeneous transaction infrastructures. WS-AT uses the Two-Phase Commit protocol to drive an atomic outcome between distributed applications, transaction managers, and resource managers.

WCF supports multiple transaction standards, including WS-AT, OleTrasaction, and TransactionNego. When flowing a transaction between a client application and a server application, the transaction protocol used is determined by the binding that is exposed by the server on the endpoint selected by the client. Some WCF system-provided bindings default to specifying the OleTransactions protocol as the transaction propagation format, while others default to specifying WS-AT. The choice of transaction protocol inside a given binding can also be modified programmatically.

The following code segment shows the idea of performing transactions in C#. The code implements two database actions, imitating an account transfer transaction. The actions involved must be quoted in "`TransactionScope`." All the actions defined in the scope will be tentative, until the statement "`transScope.Complete();`" is executed before exiting the scope.

```
using (TransactionScope transScope = new TransactionScope()) {
   // Create an connection channel
   using (SqlConnection connection1 = new SqlConnection(connectString1)){
       // Opening connection1 to prepare withdrawal from one account
       // The connection will be listed in the TransactionScope
       connection1.Open();
       // modify database here.
       connection1.BeginTransaction(IsolationLevel.Serializable);
       // Database operation will be discussed in the next chapter.
```

```
        // Create another connection channel
        using (SqlConnection connection2 = new SqlConnection(connectString2)){
              // Opening connection2 to prepare deposit into another account.
              // The connection will be listed in the TransactionScope
              connection2.Open();
              connection2.BeginTransaction(IsolationLevel.Serializable);
              // modify database here.
        }
    }
    //  The actual method that commits the transaction.
    transScope.Complete();
}
```

The TransactionScope is the coordinator that performs tentative actions in isolation. Each time a database connection opens, the connection object is added into the TransactionScope. When all connection objects are added, the TransactionScope will perform all actions in isolation through transScope.Complete(); If the isolated execution is successful, the TransactionScope will make the transaction permanent. Otherwise, it will roll back the actions to make nothing has happened. More detailed example of transactions will be discussed in the next chapter in collection with database operations.

6.5 Discussions

Having discussed the development of the functionality of service-oriented software, this chapter presented the dependability issues of distributed service-oriented software. After a brief introduction to the basic concepts, we studied the security mechanism in IIS, ASP .Net, and Windows, and how these mechanisms can be integrated into the SOC software developed in ASP .Net. Structure of ASP .Net applications is studied to better understand how security is managed and how a developer can implement and manage the security features of the applications.

Then, WCF is discussed, which is extended from ASP .Net. One of the main purchases of WCF is to strengthen the dependability capacity of ASP .Net. We discussed the security extension, the reliability consideration and implementation, and the transaction implemented in WCF.

This chapter may overlap with other computer science courses on computer security and computer reliability. We try to associate the topics to the context of service-oriented software development, and use code example to support the concepts presented.

This chapter also covered materials that are often covered in fault-tolerant computing and dependability theories. However, the focus here is on dependability design for service-oriented software, rather than the computing principles. Reliability evaluation of service-oriented software is still a new research area with few papers available today.

Another important problem in service-oriented software is the reliability and integrity of data. As services will be continuously evaluated, eventually services selected will be of high quality. In this case, the reliability of data will determine the reliability of service-oriented applications. Reliability of data will be determined by reliability of data source, reliability of any intermediate data routing and processing by services and networks. Data provenance in service-oriented software is also an important research topic as it addresses the history of data including the data source, intermediate processing, and final data processing at the destination.

Name: ______________________

Date: ______________________

6.6 Exercises and Projects

1. Multiple choice questions. Choose one answer in each question only. Choose the best answer if multiple answers are acceptable.

1.1 Reliability ensures

(A) continuity of service in [0, t].

(B) the readiness of service at time point t.

(C) nonoccurrence of catastrophic consequence.

(D) the validity and consistence of data and message.

1.2 Which of the following does not belong to security attributes?

(A) Availability

(B) Confidentiality

(C) Safety

(D) Vulnerability

1.3 In what circumstance should such an encryption system be used, where the decoding key is public and the encoding key is private?

(A) Reliability is needed

(B) Confidentiality is needed

(C) Digital signature is needed

(D) All of the above

1.4 What security mechanism(s) does IIS support?

(A) Access control list

(B) IP address restrictions

(C) Domain name restrictions

(D) Encrypted HTTP connections

(E) All of the above

1.5 What type of file overrides its occurrence in the parent directory?

(A) ASAX file (Global)

(B) ASCX file (User controls)

(C) ASPX file (Web form)

(D) Web.config

(E) DLL file

1.6 What is (are) the problem(s) associated with the standard Windows Forms Security mechanism?

(A) Passwords are stored in clear text.

(B) Sequential comparisons of username and password.

(C) Unmanageable if accessibility needs to be changed frequently.

(D) All of the above.

1.7 Web.config file in ASP .Net application structure is used for

(A) authentication.

(B) authorization.

(C) Both (A) and (B)

(D) Neither (A) nor (B)

1.8 Which of the following sequences does not make sense logically or semantically?

(A) <allow users= "*" />

(B) <deny users= "?" />

(C) <allow users = "Bob" /><deny users = ""*" />

(D) <deny users ""*" /><allow users = ""Bob" />

1.9 In order to tolerate (or correct) one bit error, the Hamming Distance $d_m(C)$ of code C must be at least

(A) one. (B) two. (C) three. (D) four.

1.10 What error control codes are separable codes?

[ ] Parity Check [ ] Checksum

[ ] Arithmetic Code [ ] m-of-n Code

1.11 DES (Data Encryption Standard) is used for low-level security purpose only, because its

(A) secret algorithm has been published. (B) encryption key is short.

(C) algorithm complexity is too high. (D) code is open source.

1.12 What is (are) the major dependability feature(s) added into the Windows Communications Foundation?

(A) WS-Security (B) Reliable Sessions (WS-R)

(C) Interoperability (WS-I) (D) All of the above

1.13 What reliability features does WS-RM specification define?

(A) At-Least-Once delivery, At-Most-Once delivery, and Exactly-Once delivery

(B) Guaranteed message ordering for delivery

(C) Both (A) and (B)

(D) None of the above

1.14 In Windows Communication Foundation, the scope of a transaction flow is

(A) in the entire program by default.

(B) defined using an object of TransactionScope class.

(C) quoted by a pair of special of tags < transaction> … </transaction>.

(D) left to the user to write a rollback method that commits the transaction calls simultaneously.

1.15 What security features are supported in WCF's SSL protocol?

(A) Data confidentiality (B) Data integrity

(C) Both (A) and (B) (D) Neither (A) nor (B)

1.16 What reliability features does WS-ReliableMessaging specification define?

(A) Lost messages (B) Duplicated messages

(C) Messages received out of order (D) All of the above

2. What is the dependability of a system?

3. What is quality? What are criteria for software quality?

4. What is quality of service and what are dependability attributes?

5. What attributes are called security attributes?

6. How are digital signature and confidentiality implemented in a public key security system?

7. What types of files are used in the ASP .Net Web application? What are their functions? How they are organized?

8. How is the Windows-based security implemented in a web application?

9. How is the form-based security implemented in a web application?

10. What dependability functions are implemented in WCF (Windows Communication Foundation)?

11. What is WS-* Specification? What components are included in WS-* Specification?

12. What is WS-Reliability? What issues the WS-Reliability specification address?

13. What is WS-transaction? What steps are involved in order to ensure the correctness of transactions?

14. Compare and contrast the indivisible instruction supported in all computer architectures and the atomic transactions supported in most distributed software development environments.

15. Discuss what security mechanisms are supported by WCF and at what layers they are implemented.

Project

In this project, you will develop a web application with functionality and security considerations. You must use WCF services, instead of using ASP .Net services, as the building block of your application.

1. Draw the diagram that shows the overall system, its components (services), and the relationship among the components of the online shopping application.

2. Elaborate each component with sufficient detail so that a peer in this class can understand and can follow the explanation to find or implement (code) each of the components. You may use the workflow (flowchart) or pseudocode with comments to explain each component. You must give the type of the file; for example, aspx, ascx, html, text, config, asax, dll, and so on, that implements the component.

3. Develop at least two services in WCF and use the service in your application.

4. Give the part of code that implements the access control of the web application. You must use the Forms-based security.

Part II

Advanced Service-Oriented Computing and System Integration

Chapter 7
Advanced Services and Application Development

Service-oriented architecture can have different styles. The current styles include remote method-oriented style and resource-oriented style. Remote method orientation is more like traditional service-oriented computing, whereas the resource orientation is a new style that focuses on the results of the remote method call, instead of the method call itself. We have used Windows Communication Foundation (WCF) to develop the traditional services that use WSDL and SOAP to access remote methods in Chapter 3. This chapter will use WCF to develop self-hosting services, advanced services, and the RESTful services that are based on the resource-oriented style. REST style is also called Resource-Oriented Architecture (ROA) or Resource-Oriented Computing (ROC).

WCF is the latest and comprehensive service-oriented software development environment. On one hand, WCF services extend the capacity of ASP .Net services by implementing as WS-* standard for reliability, security, coordination, and transactions, as we briefly discussed in Chapter 6. On the other hand, WCF supports the latest ROA and HTTP-based service development, which complements the traditional action-related services by adding data and resource-related services for even more diverse needs of web application development.

7.1 Self-Hosting Services

In Chapter 3, we discussed the development process using WCF template and .Net development server or IIS Express to develop and host a service. We will develop a self-hosting WCF service in this section, which includes the service that hosts the WCF service. The process that follows is based on the example provided at Microsoft MSDN library at http://msdn.microsoft.com/en-us/library/ms734712.aspx.

7.1.1 Developing a Service and a Hosting Service

We will create an ordinary service with interface and implementation. Then, we will write our own hosting program to keep this service running.

Step 1. Create a New Solution for a Service

Start Visual Studio as an administrator by right clicking the program in the Start menu and selecting “Run as administrator.” It is necessary to run as administrator, as the program will need to register an HTTP channel for clients to access. Otherwise, you will receive this error message later on:

```
An exception occurred: HTTP could not register URL http://+:8000/Service/. Your
process does not have access rights to this namespace (see
http://go.microsoft.com/fwlink/?LinkId=70353 for details).
```

Create a new Project of “Console Application” by choosing File → New → Project … → Choose C# in the Project types window and choose Console Application in the Templates window. In order to follow this example precisely, choose the solution name WcfServiceConsole and use the default location.

Step 2. Create Contract Through Interface

First, we add the namespace "System.ServiceModel." In the Solution Explorer, right-click the "References" folder under the project folder and choose "Add Reference… ." Select Framework tab under Assemblies in the Add Reference dialog box and scroll down until you find System.ServiceModel, select it, and click OK.

Now, you can type the following code into the Program.cs file, including the "using" directive for namespace inclusion. This part of the file defines the contracts and the operations of the service.

```
//File name: Program.cs
using System;
using System.ServiceModel;
using System.ServiceModel.Description;

namespace SelfHostingService {
    [ServiceContract]
    public interface myInterface { // Use interface to define contracts
        [OperationContract]
        double PiValue();
        [OperationContract]
        int absValue(int intVal);
    }
    public class myService : myInterface { // implementation of interface
        public double PiValue() {
            double pi = System.Math.PI;
            return (pi);
        }
        public int absValue(int x) {
            if (x >= 0) return (x);
            else return (-x);
        }
    } // The code is incomplete, more code to be added here in next step.
```

Step 3. Create Hosting Program and Endpoint

In this step, we will add code in the Main() method of the program to perform the following functions:

(1) Create a URI instance to myService as the base address. This URI specifies the HTTP scheme, the local machine, port number 8000, and the path Service/ to the service that was specified for the namespace of the service in the service contract.

(2) Create a new ServiceHost instance to host the service. We must specify the type that implements the service contract and the base address. For this example, the base address is http://localhost:8000/Service and myService is the type that implements the service contract.

(3) Add an endpoint that exposes myService. An endpoint includes three aspects: the contract that the endpoint exposes, a binding protocol, and the address for the endpoint. In this sample, we specify myInterface as the contract, wsHttpBinding as the binding protocol, and myService as the address. Note here the endpoint address is a relative address to the current location. The full address for the endpoint is the combination of the base address and the endpoint address. In this case, the full address is http://localhost:8000/Service/myService.

(4) Add Metadata. Metadata of WCF service contains information equivalent to WSDL file. Publishing metadata will allow the service to be accessed by clients remotely and in WSDL interface.

(5) Start the service and wait for requests. Now, the service is ready to run and process requests.

(6) Close the service.

The code created in steps 2 and 3 above is shown as follows. The comments indicate the steps above with the parts of code.

```
using System; // File name: Program.cs
using System.ServiceModel;
using System.ServiceModel.Description;
namespace SelfHostingService {
    [ServiceContract]
    public interface myInterface {
        // See the code in step 2
    }
    public class myService : myInterface {
        // See the code in step 2
    }
    class Program {
        static void Main(string[] args) {
            // (1) Create a URI instance to myService as the base address.
            Uri baseAddress = new Uri("http://localhost:8000/Service");

            // (2) a new ServiceHost instance to host the service
            ServiceHost selfHost = new ServiceHost(typeof(myService),
                                 baseAddress);  // with address
            try {
                // (3) Add a service endpoint with contract and binding
                selfHost.AddServiceEndpoint(typeof(myInterface),
                    new WSHttpBinding(), "myService");
                // (4) Add metadata for platform-independent access.
                System.ServiceModel.Description.ServiceMetadataBehavior smb = new
System.ServiceModel.Description.ServiceMetadataBehavior();
                smb.HttpGetEnabled = true; // enable the metadata
                selfHost.Description.Behaviors.Add(smb); // Add here
                // (5) Start the service and waiting for request.
                selfHost.Open();
                Console.WriteLine("myService is ready to take requests. Please
create a client to call my double PiValue() service or int absValue(int) service.");
                Console.WriteLine("If you want to quit this service, simply press
<ENTER>.\n");
                Console.ReadLine();
                // (6) Close the ServiceHostBase to shutdown the service.
                selfHost.Close();
            }
            catch (CommunicationException ce) {
                Console.WriteLine("An exception occurred: {0}", ce.Message);
                selfHost.Abort();
            }
        }
    }
}
```

Note that in the aforesaid code, we use the following statements to add an endpoint to the host:

ServiceHost selfHost = new ServiceHost(typeof(myService), baseAddress);

selfHost.AddServiceEndpoint(typeof(myInterface), new WsHttpBinding(), “myService”);

The endpoint is represented by three aspects: Address (baseAddress), Binding (WsHttpBinding), and Contract (myInterface). Figure 7.1 shows the service, interface, endpoint, service metadata behavior (WSDL), and the operations.

In the part (4), add metadata for platform-independent access, we used the class ServiceMetadataBehavior in the namespace System.ServiceModel.Description, which creates WSDL-based interface. There are many other classes in the namespace, which allow the developers to publish different types of interfaces for different clients to access. If a service is intended for .Net client only, we do not need to create the WSDL interface, which reduces the overhead of the additional layer of the standard interface. The service without the standard interface is a platform-dependent service, and it is equivalent to the .Net remoting service. As we are creating a platform-independent service in this example, we need to create and publish the metadata. To do so, we create a ServiceMetadataBehavior instance from the library class, set the HttpGetEnabled property to true, and then add the new behavior to the service.

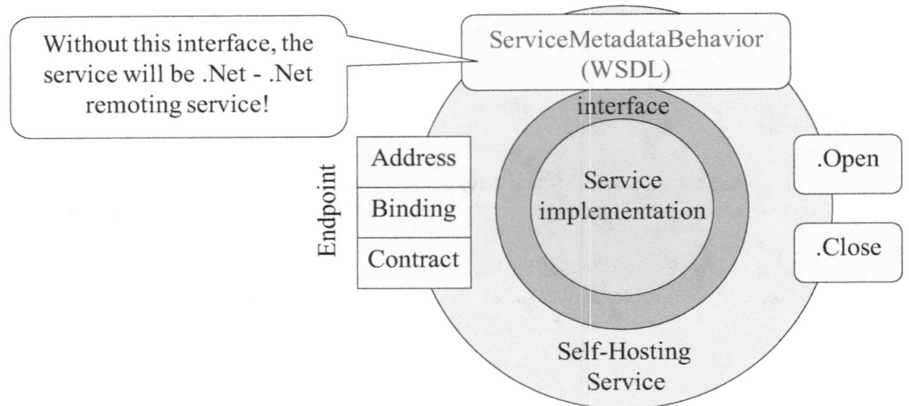

Figure 7.1. Self-hosting service with standard interface

Step 4. Start the service

The service is now fully developed, and we can start the service in Visual Studio by executing the Debug command "Start without Debugging." Then the window in Figure 7.2 will pop up. We need to keep this service running if we want to access the service from a service client.

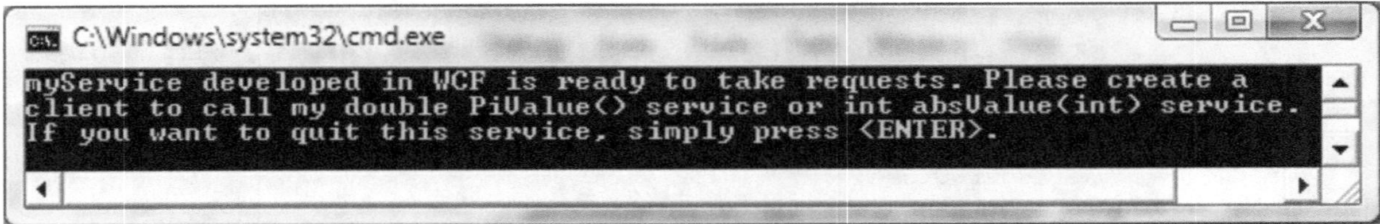

Figure 7.2. The console window showing the executing of the service

7.1.2 Developing Clients to Consume Self-Hosting Services

In the previous section, we created a WCF service and have the service hosted in a console application. WCF is an environment of developing services. It does not include all the tools within the environment for developing service clients that consume the services. In this section, we develop a client with the help of the command tools.

Step 1. Create a Console Client

In this step, we will create a service client (application) that accesses the service created in the previous steps through a proxy. In order to create a proxy, we need to access the metadata published during service creation. We create a new project and add it to the existing solution that accommodates the service we created in the previous section.

(1) In the Solution Explorer, right-click the current solution, select Add, and then New Project, as shown in the top left part of Figure 7.3.

(2) In the Add New Project dialog box, select C#, choose the Console Application template, and name it WcfClientConsole. Click OK. The client project is shown in the top right of Figure 7.3.

(3) Add the reference to the service: Right-click the References folder under the WcfClientConsole project and select Add Reference. Select the Recent tab or in the .Net tab and select System.ServiceModel. Then, add the line of code in the library inclusion part: "using System.ServiceModel;" in the WcfClientConsole's program.

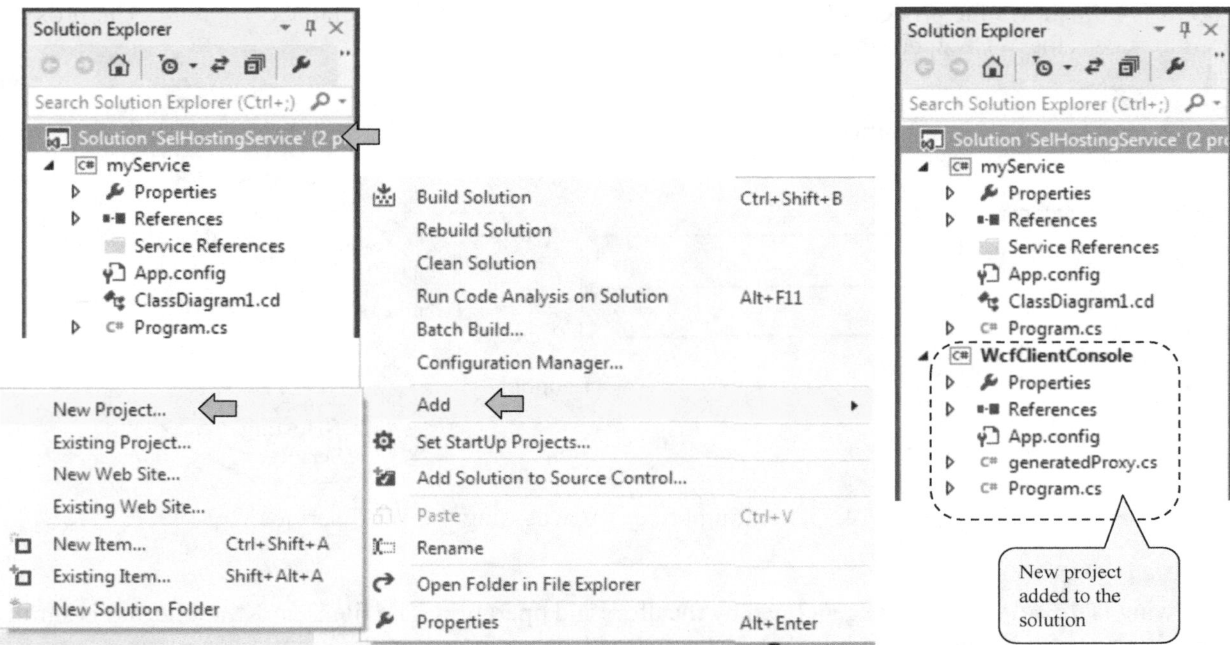

Figure 7.3. Solution explorer stacks before (top left), and after adding the client project (top right)

Step 2. Generate Proxy in Service Client

Before we start this step, we need to make sure that the WCF service is running, as described in Step 4, Section 7.1.1. In this step, we will generate the proxy based on the metadata published by the service. We will use the Service Model Metadata Utility Tool (SvcUtil.exe) tool to generate the proxy as follows:

(1) From Windows Start menu: Choose All Program → Microsoft Visual Studio → Visual Studio Tools to find the location of Developer Command Prompt tool. You must start the tool as administrator to open the CMD Shell.

(2) If necessary, use DOS commands "dir," "cd .." and "cd folder" to navigate into the directory where you have your client project created in the previous step.

(3) Type the following command to execute:

```
svcutil.exe /language:cs /out:generatedProxy.cs /config:app.config http://local
host:8000/Service
```

This command will generate two files: app.config and generatedProxy.cs, and place them into the directory: C:\Windows\System32, or C:\Windows\SysWOW64. If you do not see the files in the folder, search for them.

(4) Add the file generatedProxy.cs thus generated into your project: Right-click the client project in Solution Explorer, select Add → Existing Item. Browse to C:\Users\<user name>\Documents\Visual Studio 2013\Projects\Service\Client directory. Select the file `generatedProxy.cs` and add.

(5) Repeat the aforesaid step to add the app.config configuration file: by default. The Add Existing Item dialog box filters out all files with a .config extension. To see these files select All Files (*.*) from the drop-down list box in the lower right corner of the Add Existing Item dialog box. Figure 7.3 (bottom left) shows the two files that are added into the project.

Figure 7.4 illustrates the process of generating a proxy using the Service Metadata Behavior. The proxy is used to access the WCF operations defined in the service.

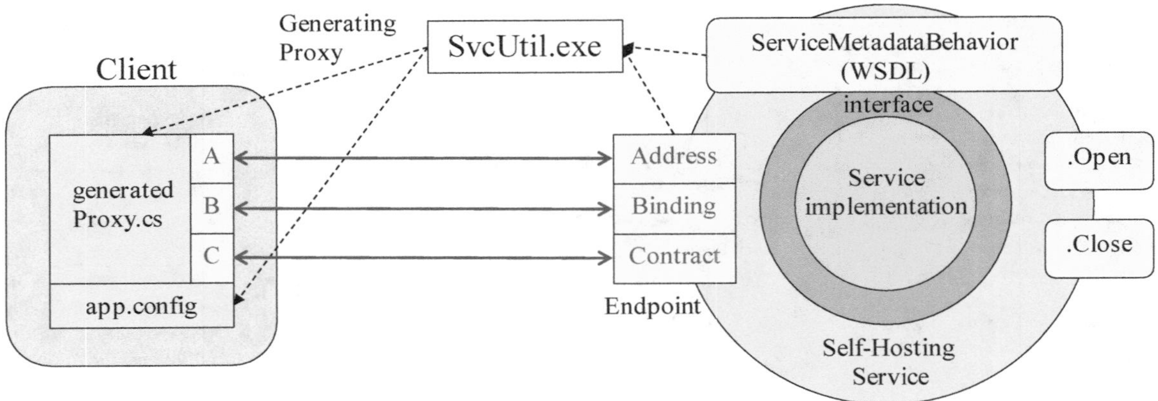

Figure 7.4. Generating proxy for accessing the WCF service

Following is the **app.config** file generated by the aforesaid operation. The file is an XML file and is similar to the Web.config file generated by ASP .Net development environment.

```
<?xml version="1.0" encoding="utf-8"?>
<configuration>
    <system.serviceModel>
        <bindings>
            <wsHttpBinding>
                <binding name="WSHttpBinding_myInterface" />
            </wsHttpBinding>
        </bindings>
        <client>
            <endpoint address="http://localhost:8000/Service/myService"
binding="wsHttpBinding"
                bindingConfiguration="WSHttpBinding_myInterface"
contract="myInterface"
                name="WSHttpBinding_myInterface">
                <identity>
                    <userPrincipalName value="ychen10@asurite.ad.asu.edu" />
                </identity>
            </endpoint>
        </client>
    </system.serviceModel>
</configuration>
```

The configuration file defines an element <system.serviceModel>, in which wsHttpBinding is defined and an endpoint with the binding and the service contract is defined.

The second file **generatedProxy.cs** generated by the SvcUtil.exe command is shown as follows. The format of the code is edited to save space.

```
//------------------------------------------------------------------------------
// <auto-generated>
//     This code was generated by a tool. Runtime Version:4.0.30319.18408
//     Changes to this file may cause incorrect behavior and will be lost if
//     the code is regenerated.
// </auto-generated>
//------------------------------------------------------------------------------
 [System.CodeDom.Compiler.GeneratedCodeAttribute("System.ServiceModel", "4.0.0.0")]
[System.ServiceModel.ServiceContractAttribute(ConfigurationName="myInterface")]
public interface myInterface
{
[System.ServiceModel.OperationContractAttribute(Action="http://tempuri.org/myInterfa
ce/PiValue", ReplyAction="http://tempuri.org/myInterface/PiValueResponse")]
    double PiValue();
[System.ServiceModel.OperationContractAttribute(Action="http://tempuri.org/myInterfa
ce/PiValue", ReplyAction="http://tempuri.org/myInterface/PiValueResponse")]
    System.Threading.Tasks.Task<double> PiValueAsync();
[System.ServiceModel.OperationContractAttribute(Action="http://tempuri.org/myInterfa
ce/absValue", ReplyAction="http://tempuri.org/myInterface/absValueResponse")]
    int absValue(int intVal);
[System.ServiceModel.OperationContractAttribute(Action="http://tempuri.org/myInterfa
ce/absValue", ReplyAction="http://tempuri.org/myInterface/absValueResponse")]
    System.Threading.Tasks.Task<int> absValueAsync(int intVal);
}
 [System.CodeDom.Compiler.GeneratedCodeAttribute("System.ServiceModel", "4.0.0.0")]
public interface myInterfaceChannel : myInterface,
System.ServiceModel.IClientChannel
{ }
 [System.Diagnostics.DebuggerStepThroughAttribute()]
[System.CodeDom.Compiler.GeneratedCodeAttribute("System.ServiceModel", "4.0.0.0")]
public partial class myInterfaceClient :
System.ServiceModel.ClientBase<myInterface>, myInterface
{
    public myInterfaceClient() {}
    public myInterfaceClient(string endpointConfigurationName) :
            base(endpointConfigurationName) { }
    public myInterfaceClient(string endpointConfigurationName, string
remoteAddress) :
            base(endpointConfigurationName, remoteAddress) { }
    public myInterfaceClient(string endpointConfigurationName,
System.ServiceModel.EndpointAddress remoteAddress) :
            base(endpointConfigurationName, remoteAddress) { }
    public myInterfaceClient(System.ServiceModel.Channels.Binding binding,
System.ServiceModel.EndpointAddress remoteAddress) :
            base(binding, remoteAddress) { }
    public double PiValue(){ return base.Channel.PiValue(); }
    public System.Threading.Tasks.Task<double> PiValueAsync()
    { return base.Channel.PiValueAsync(); }
    public int absValue(int intVal)
    { return base.Channel.absValue(intVal);}
    public System.Threading.Tasks.Task<int> absValueAsync(int intVal)
    { return base.Channel.absValueAsync(intVal);}
}
```

In the next step, we will discuss using these two files in the client.

Step 3. Write the Client Code

Having created the service and the proxy to the service, now we can write client to access services through the proxy. The code that follows gives a simple example of accessing the service. The comments with the code explain the use of the code.

```
using System;
using System.ServiceModel;
namespace WcfClientConsole {
    class Program {
        static void Main(string[] args) {
            //(1) Create a proxy to the WCF service.
            myInterfaceClient myPxy = new myInterfaceClient();
            //(2) Call the service operations through the proxy
            double pi = myPxy.PiValue();  // call PiValue operation
            Int32 test1 = 27;    // Create test input 1
            Int32 test2 = -132; // Create test input 2
            Int32 result1 = myPxy.absValue(test1); //call operation
            Int32 result2 = myPxy.absValue(test2); //call operation
            Console.WriteLine("PI value = {0}", pi);
            Console.WriteLine("Absolute values of {0} is {1} and of {2} is {3}",
test1, result1, test2, result2);
            //(3) Close the proxy, the channel to the service
            myPxy.Close();
            Console.WriteLine("/nPress <ENTER> to terminate the client./n");
        }
    }
}
```

Compile the code to generate the executable for the next step of execution.

Step 4. Testing the Service and the Client

Now, we can test the client and the service together.

(1) Start the service from Visual Studio. You must start the Visual Studio as the administrator in order to create the HTTP channel. Then, right click the service project and select "Set as StartUp Project." From VS menu select: DEBUG → Start Without Debugging, the service will be started, as you should have seen in the command line window in Figure 7.2.

(2) In order to start the client, you can now right click the client project and select "Set as StartUp Project." From VS menu select: DEBUG → Start Without Debugging, the client will be started, as you should have seen in the command line window in Figure 7.5.

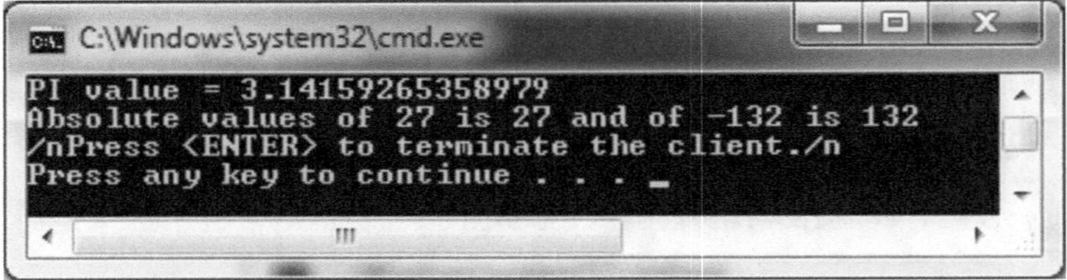

Figure 7.5. Client output

Another way of starting the client is start it from the CMD shell, using DOS commands "dir," "cd .." and "cd folder" to navigate to the directory where the executable of the client is located: ...\bin\Debug\WcfClientConsole.exe. You need to check if you have put your executable code in that directory before you use DOS commands.

We discussed in this section creating a proxy to a self-hosting service using a manual process so that we better understand and better control the endpoints and the proxies to the endpoints. We could also use the automated method "Add Service Reference" offered in Visual Studio.

7.2 Advanced WCF Services

WCF provides a range of services defined by the selection of communication models, protocols, and service behaviors.

7.2.1 Advanced Communication Models

Figure 7.6 illustrates the protocol channel stack supported WCF. If the application-service communication is directly based on TCP, the service is a platform-dependent service, as the client is directly accessing the language-based function name in the service. If the communication is directly based on HTTP, the service is considered a RESTful service, as the client is directly accessing the URI resource. If the communication is based on SOAP, the service is a platform-independent SOAP/WSDL service.

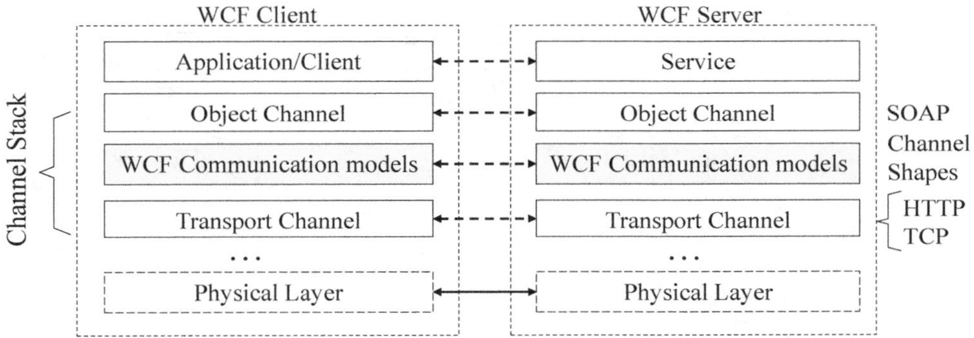

Figure 7.6. WCF protocol channel stack

WCF supports three communication models: One-way communication, Duplex (two one-way asynchronous communications), and Request-reply (Two-way synchronous communication). These communication models are implemented by the combination of a set of channel shapes.

- IInputChannel;
- IOutputChannel;
- IDuplexChannel;
- IRequestChannel;
- IReplyChannel.

The three communication models are depicted in Figure 7.7.

The **one-way communication model** is simply implemented by a pair of IInputChannel and IOutputChannel on the server and client sides, respectively.

The **request-reply communication model** is the default communication model. It combines two one-way channel shapes into two new channels: IRequestChannel and IReplyChannel. The model is used for synchronous communications:

- Client sends a request and block-waits for response;
- Server processes the request and sends response back to client.

The **duplex communication model** uses two one-way channel shapes to compose into a new shape called IDuplexChannel. The model can be used for the asynchronous communications. Two approaches can be implemented.

- Client sends a request to server, and the service handles the request. It may take a long time to complete/calculate the result. After completion, the service calls back to provide results. This communication model requires that the client has a public URI that provides a callback endpoint for the service. The address can be created using the ClientBaseAddress class. Note that the duplex communication model exposes the IP address of the client to the service.
- The client makes two calls. The first call sends the request, and the second call retrieves the result. The second call is triggered by receiving an event from the service. The two calls are quoted by a pair of tags: Begin<methodName> and End<methodName>.

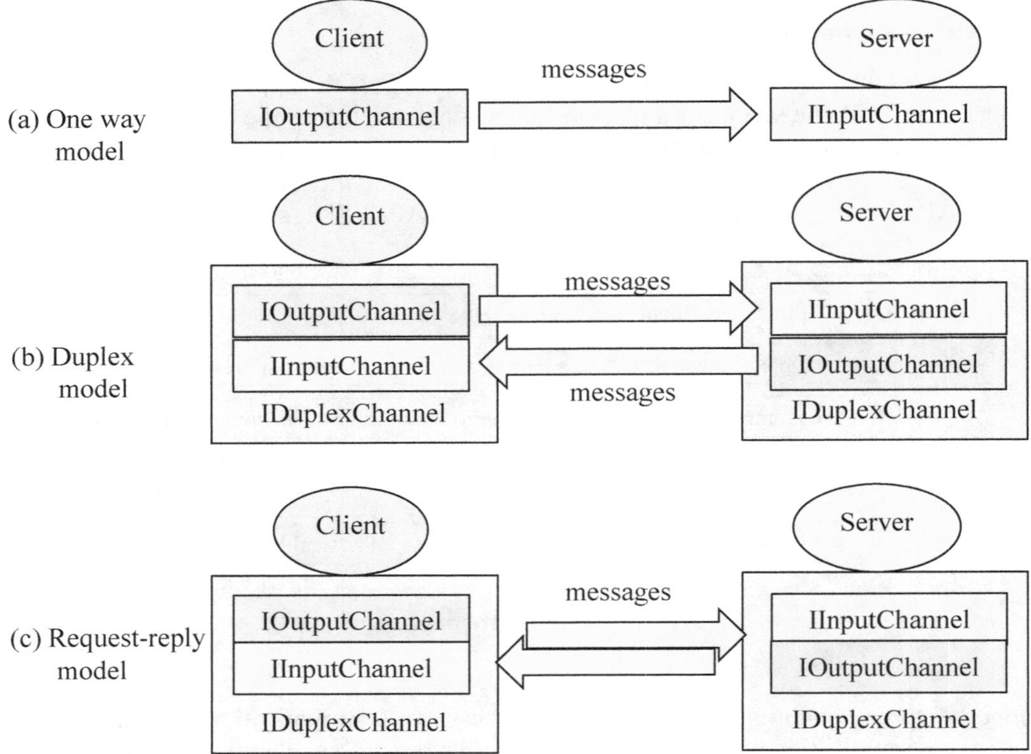

Figure 7.7. WCF communication models and channel shapes

The reason that we need these channel shapes is that HTTP protocol works in request-reply model only. In order to implement one-way model and duplex model on HTTP, a shape-changing layer is needed, which involves a number of classes for specification and binding. The OperationContractAttribute Class is used for specifying the options and classes. OneWayBindingElement and CompositeDuplexBindingElement are used specifying one-way binding for duplex binding, respectively.

The code segment that follows shows examples of using the OperationContractAttribute class attributes to specify the communication models.

```
 [ServiceContractAttribute]
public class ChannelModelExample
{  // Request-response model: client waits until a response message appears.
   [OperationContractAttribute] // no attribute specified
   public int MethodOne (int x, int y) { // default request-reply model
       return x+y;
```

```
    }
// The client generates asynchronous calls.          // First, one-way model: client
returns as soon as a message is sent
    // to the service; no response is generated or sent from the service.
    [OperationContractAttribute(IsOneWay=true)]
    public void MethodTwo (int x) { return; } // one-way model
    // For Duplex model, the return value is given an out-parameter
    [OperationContractAttribute(AsyncPattern = true)]
    public void MethodThree (int x, out int y)  {
        y = complexFunction(x);
        return
    }
}
```

For MethodOne, no property value of the operation contract attribute is specified. The default communication model is the request-response model.

For MethodTwo, the property value (IsOneWay=true) is specified, which defines the one-way communication model.

For MethodThree, the property value (AsyncPattern=true) is specified, which defines the duplex communication model. In this case, the return type is changed to void, and the return value is stored in a parameter, which can be retrieved later by the client, or sent to the client by a one-way call from the server to the client.

The OperationContractAttribute class defines a number of properties, including AsyncPattern and IsOneWay that are used in the foregoing example.

AsyncPattern property is used for building service operations that can be called asynchronously. This property informs the runtime that the call to this method (marked with AsyncPattern=true) can be wrapped in a Begin method with a matched End method that conforms to the .NET Framework asynchronous method design pattern. The first call (Begin method) sends the request with the input data. The second call (End method) retrieves the result from the first call.

The asynchronous design pattern can be applied on server side and on client side. Building the server-side asynchronous methods increases server scalability and performance without affecting the clients of the service, and is recommended when a service operation must return something to the client after performing a lengthy operation that can be performed asynchronously.

The client software can also take the advantage of the asynchronous design pattern on the server side to improve the client performance. The client applications can use the ServiceModel Metadata Utility Tool (Svcutil.exe) tool and the /async option to generate the wrappers Begin<methodName> and End<methodName> method pair that the client can use to invoke the operation asynchronously.

Of course, the clients do not have to take the trouble to call the method asynchronously. The asynchronous method pair on the server is an implementation detail that does not affect the underlying Web Services Description Language (WSDL) description of the operation. Such methods appear to clients as a single operation with <input> and correlated <output> messages. Thus, the clients can use the method either as a single synchronous operation or as an asynchronous operation pair.

IsOneWay property is used to indicate that an operation does not return a reply message. This type of operation is useful for event-driven communications, especially in two-way asynchronous communications. Without waiting for an underlying response message, callers of one-way operations have no direct way to detect a failure in processing the request message. Of course, service clients that use reliable messaging above the one-way operations can detect a message delivery failure at the upper level.

7.2.2 Advanced Bindings

A binding is a preconfigured channel stack that serve as the communication agreement between the client and the service; a binding includes the communication models, protocols involved, and encryption and decryption methods, and encoding and decoding methods, such as object to string or to XML.

WCF has predefined a set of bindings to serve different communication purposes, including:

BasicHttpBinding: A binding that is suitable for communicating with WS-Basic Profile conformant web services; for example, ASP .NET web services (ASMX)-based services. This binding uses HTTP as the transport and text/XML as the default message encoding.

WSHttpBinding: A secure and interoperable binding that is suitable for non-duplex service contracts; for example, RESTful service. Encoding methods include XML, POX, and JSON.

WSDualHttpBinding: A secure and interoperable binding that is suitable for duplex service contracts or communication through SOAP over HTTP channel stack. The WSDualHttpBinding provides the same support for Web Service protocols as the WSHttpBinding does, except it uses with the duplex channel. WSDualHttpBinding supports SOAP security only and requires reliable messaging.

WS2007HttpBinding: A secure and interoperable binding that provides support for the correct versions of the Security, ReliableSession (Reliable messaging), and TransactionFlow binding elements.

NetTcpBinding: A secure and optimized binding suitable for cross-machine communication between WCF applications (.Net Remoting or platform-dependent service).

NetNamedPipeBinding: A secure, reliable, optimized binding that is suitable for on-machine communication between WCF applications (.Net Remoting or platform-dependent service).

NetMsmqBinding: A queued binding that is suitable for cross-machine communication between WCF applications (. Remoting or platform-dependent service).

NetPeerTcpBinding: A binding that enables secure, multi-machine communication (.Remoting or platform-dependent service).

WebHttpBinding: A binding used to configure endpoints for WCF web services that are exposed through HTTP requests instead of SOAP messages (Restful services).

The following example shows how to specify the wsDualHttpBinding binding in a configuration file, given in MSDN library at:

http://msdn.microsoft.com/en-us/library/system.servicemodel.wsdualhttpbinding.aspx#Y3300

```
<?xml version="1.0" encoding="utf-8"?>
<configuration>
   <system.serviceModel>
        <bindings>
             <wsHttpBinding>
                  <binding name="WSHttpBinding_ICalculator" />
             </wsHttpBinding>
        </bindings>
        <client>
             <endpoint address="http://localhost:8000/"
                  binding="wsHttpBinding"
                  bindingConfiguration="WSHttpBinding_ICalculator"
        contract="Microsoft.ServiceModel.Samples.ICalculator"
        name="WSHttpBinding_ICalculator">
             </endpoint>
        </client>
   </system.serviceModel>
</configuration>
```

7.2.3 Service Behavior and State Management

The runtime operations or behaviors of WCF services can be affected and controlled by other classes that support the execution of the services that determine runtime operations of the service; for example, the ServiceHost class can determine how the service hosted behaves.

There are three levels of behaviors. Service behaviors concern instancing and overall transactions of the services. Endpoint behaviors inspect and take actions on incoming and outgoing messages. Operation behaviors concern the manipulation, serialization; for example, convert objects to strings, transaction flow, and parameter handling, as illustrated in Figure 7.8.

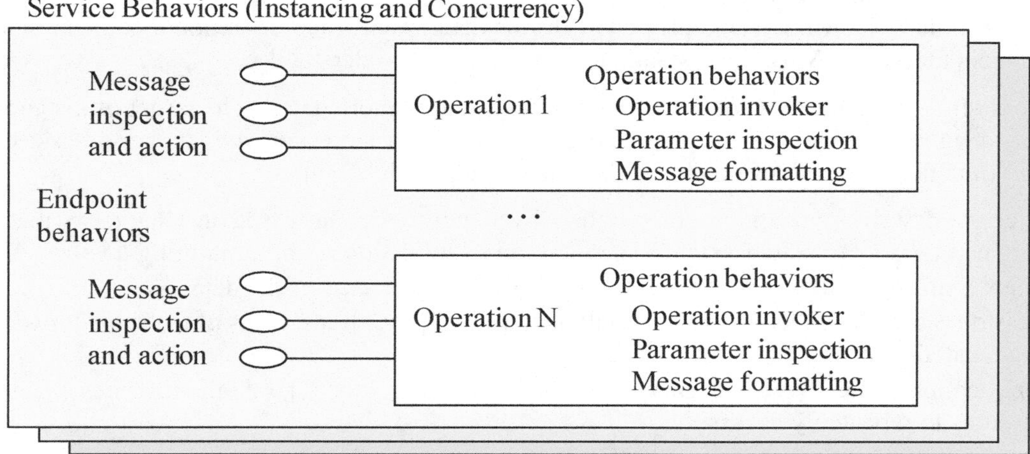

Figure 7.8. Service, endpoint, and operation behaviors

Through ServiceBehaviorAttribute class, WCF offers several modes to control the service level behaviors. The selection of the ServiceBehaviorAttribute properties will trigger different execution models that have been implemented within the system. Without this system level support, developers will have to program their own solutions. The properties of the ServiceBehaviorAttribute class include (MSDN Library):

- The InstanceContextMode property specifies whether and when services and their service objects are to be recycled during an exchange with a client.
- The ConcurrencyMode property controls the internal threading model, enabling support for reentrant or multithreaded services.
- The AddressFilterMode property specifies the type of filter that the dispatcher system uses to locate the endpoint that handles requests.
- The AutomaticSessionShutdown property automatically closes the session when the channel is closed and the service has finished processing any remaining messages.
- The ConfigurationName property is used to declare a name for use in the name attribute of the <service> element in a configuration file.
- The IgnoreExtensionDataObject property enables the run time to ignore extra serialization information that is not required to process the message.
- The IncludeExceptionDetailInFaults property specifies whether unhandled exceptions in a service are returned as SOAP faults. This is for debugging purposes only.
- The MaxItemsInObjectGraph property to limit on the number of items in an object graph that are serialized.
- The Name and Namespace properties control the name and namespace for the WSDL expression of the service element.

- The ReleaseServiceInstanceOnTransactionComplete property specifies whether the service object is recycled when a transaction completes.
- The TransactionAutoCompleteOnSessionClose property specifies whether outstanding transactions are completed when the session closes.
- The TransactionIsolationLevel property specifies the transaction isolation level that the contract supports.
- The TransactionTimeout property specifies the time period within which a transaction must complete or it aborts.
- The UseSynchronizationContext property indicates whether to synchronize inbound method calls with the user interface thread automatically.
- The ValidateMustUnderstand property informs the system whether it should confirm that SOAP headers marked as MustUnderstand have, in fact, been understood.

Let us discuss InstanceContextMode and ConcurrencyMode in more detail. The target of instancing mode is for state management and the target of concurrency mode is for increasing the number of tasks completed in the given time period to achieve the multithreading and parallel computing.

Web services and web applications are stateless by default. We discussed in Chapter 5 that different mechanisms can be used to achieve stateful services and applications at programming level:

- View State: Save data in the browser page for multiple access of the data.
- Session State: Save the data in Session[“nameIndex”] for all instances of the same browser session to repeatedly access.
- Application State: Save the data in Application[“nameIndex”] for all instances of all browser sessions to repeatedly access.

ServiceBehaviorAttribute class offers a way to manage the states of service from outside the class. InstanceContextMode is used to determine when to create a new instance of a service. It can take one of the values

- PerCall: one instance is created for each incoming request. This mode creates stateless service. No information can be shared between different calls.
- PerSession: one instance is created for each client session. This mode implements the session state, in which all pages in the same session can share the information.
- Single: one instance of the service class handles all incoming requests (singleton service). This mode implements the application state, in which all sessions can share the same information.

The purpose of these context modes is for facilitating state sharing. Now, we will use a simple example of creating a singleton service, where a single instance is created for all the sessions. When one session modifies a value in the application, all other sessions will see the modified value. The service interface file IService.cs is shown as follows:

```
using System;                 // IService.cs
using System.ServiceModel;  // this lib file enables service model
[ServiceContract]
public interface IService   {
    [OperationContract]
    Int32 getNumber();        // endpoint 1
    [OperationContract]
    Int32 takeOne();              // endpoint 2
}
```

The service file Service.cs, which implements the aforesaid service interface, is given as follows:

```
using System;                          // Service.cs file
using System.ServiceModel;        // this lib file enables service model
[ServiceBehavior(InstanceContextMode = InstanceContextMode.Single)]
public class Service : IService {
```

```
    int sNumber = 1000; // a static variable initialized to 1000
    public Int32 getNumber() {
        return sNumber;          // read the number
    }
    public  Int32 takeOne() {
        sNumber = sNumber-1;           // modify the number
        return sNumber;
     }
}
```

Note that, InstanceContextMode.Single creates a singleton service. Now, we write a simple ASP .Net Forms application to consume the service. The code is given as follows:

```
using System;
public partial class _Default : System.Web.UI.Page {
    protected void Page_Load(object sender, EventArgs e) {  }
    protected void btnStock_Click(object sender, EventArgs e) {
        sgltService.ServiceClient myProxy = new sgltService.ServiceClient();
        Int32 sNumber = myProxy.getNumber();
        lblStock.Text = Convert.ToString(sNumber);
        myProxy.Close();
    }
    protected void btnBuy_Click(object sender, EventArgs e) {
        sgltService.ServiceClient myProxy = new sgltService.ServiceClient();
        Int32 sNumber = myProxy.takeOne();
        lblRemain.Text = Convert.ToString(sNumber);
        myProxy.Close();
    }
}
```

Starting this application from multiple computers, the values modified from any session will be read from all other sessions. Figure 7.9 shows the application accessing the singleton service from two different computers, and the values in the two applications are linked to the same static variable.

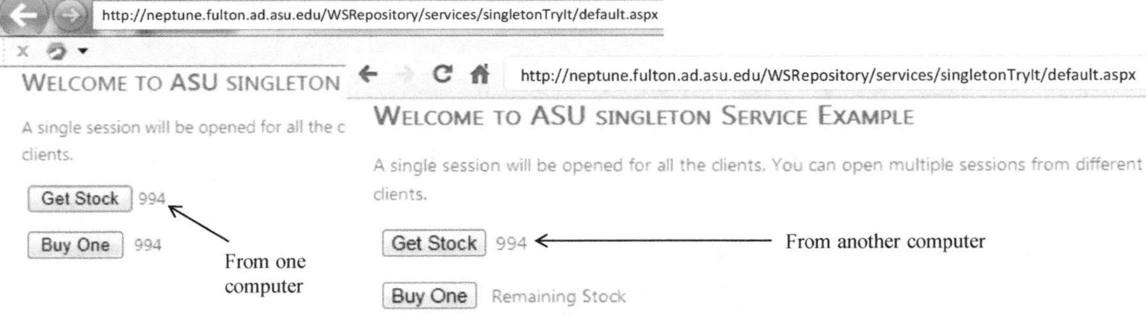

Figure 7.9. Accessing a singleton service from two computers

The service and the service consuming application are deployed at:

- Service: http://neptune.fulton.ad.asu.edu/WSRepository/Services/Singleton/service.svc
- TryIt application: http://neptune.fulton.ad.asu.edu/WSRepository/Services/SingletonTryIt/default.aspx

ConcurrencyMode: is used to control threading within one service instance that is running. It can take one of the values:

- Single: Only one thread at a time can access the service instance.

- Reentrant: Only one thread at a time can access the service instance, but the thread can leave the instance and reenter later to continue.
- Multiple: multiple threads can access the service instance simultaneously. This setting implements parallel computing and requires the service class to be thread-safe (with synchronization/lock mechanisms.

The purpose of these currency modes is for performance management. Figure 7.10 shows the instances created by different instance context modes and concurrency modes. As can be seen, the instance context modes and concurrency modes can generate the similar instances. However, their purposes are different, and thus, the use of the modes should be determined based on the purpose of the application.

As shown in the figure, you can also specify "Single" instance context mode and "Multiple" currency mode simultaneously. In this case, each call will initiate a separate instance for concurrent execution. However, these parallel isntances are treated as a single context instance, and they can still share their states as if they were running in a single instance.

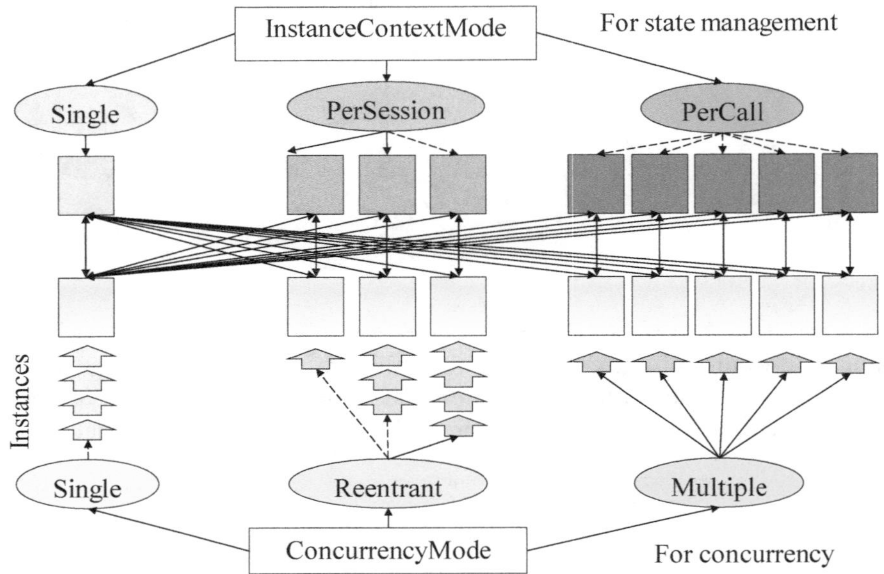

Figure 7.10. Accessing a singleton service from two computers.

The code example that follows shows the use of the InstanceContextMode and ConcurrencyMode (MSDN Library at: https://msdn.microsoft.com/en-us/library/system.servicemodel.servicebehaviorattribute.instancecontextmode(v=vs.110).aspx

```
using System;
using System.ServiceModel;
using System.Transactions;
namespace Microsoft.WCF.Documentation {
  [ServiceContract(Namespace="http://microsoft.wcf.documentation",
    SessionMode=SessionMode.Required)]
  public interface IBehaviorService {
    [OperationContract]
    string TxWork(string message);
  }
  // Note: To use the TransactionIsolationLevel property, you
  // must add a reference to the System.Transactions.dll assembly.
  /* The following service implementation:
```

```
  *    -- Processes messages on one thread at a time
  *    -- Creates one service object per session
  *    -- Releases the service object when the transaction commits */
 [ServiceBehavior(ConcurrencyMode=ConcurrencyMode.Single,
   InstanceContextMode=InstanceContextMode.PerSession,
   ReleaseServiceInstanceOnTransactionComplete=true)]
 public class BehaviorService : IBehaviorService, IDisposable {
   Guid myID;
   public BehaviorService() {
     myID = Guid.NewGuid();
     Console.WriteLine(
       "Object "
       + myID.ToString()
       + " created.");
   }
   /* The following operation-level behaviors are specified:
    *    -- The executing transaction is committed when
    *       the operation completes without an unhandled exception
    *    -- Always executes under a flowed transaction.
    */
   [OperationBehavior(TransactionAutoComplete = true,
     TransactionScopeRequired = true)]
   [TransactionFlow(TransactionFlowOption.Mandatory)]
   public string TxWork(string message){
     // Do some transactable work.
     Console.WriteLine("TxWork called with: " + message);
     // Display transaction information.
     TransactionInformation info = Transaction.Current.TransactionInformation;
     Console.WriteLine("The distributed tx ID: {0}.", info.DistributedIdentifier);
     Console.WriteLine("The tx status: {0}.", info.Status);
     return String.Format("Hello. This was object {0}.",myID.ToString()) ;
   }
   public void Dispose(){
     Console.WriteLine("Service "+myID.ToString()+" is being recycled.");
   }
 }
}
```

7.3 REST Concept and RESTful Services

REST (Representational State Transfer) is a style of software architecture for distributed hypermedia systems such as the World Wide Web. The REST concept was proposed by Roy Thomas Fielding in his doctoral dissertation "Architectural Styles and the Design of Network-based Software Architectures" in 2000. Fielding is one of the principal authors of the HTTP specification version 1.0 (https://tools.ietf.org/html/rfc1945) in 1996 and version 1.1 (https://tools.ietf.org/html/rfc2616) in 1999. Services developed based on REST concept and conforming to the REST constraints are referred to as being RESTful services (http://en.wikipedia.org/wiki/ Representational_State_Transfer).

7.3.1 REST Concept and REST Architecture

REST concept is about how communication is done between clients and servers using HTTP, which is defined by these principles:

- A client initiates a request to a server, and the server processes the request and sends back a response;
- Communication is about the "representations" transfer of "resources" between a client and a server;

- Each resource is given a unique identifier, called URI (Universal Resource Identifier).

A resource on the web is an object that can be uniquely identified by a URI (Universal Resource Identifier). A URI may be classified as a Universal Resource Locator (URL), a Universal Resource Name (URN), or both. A URN is like the name of an object, such as a location or the name of a building, whereas a URL is like the street address of the location or the building. The URN defines something's identity, while the URL provides a method for finding something. If the context is clear, it is easier to understand when we use the name. However, the address is context-free to locate the object.

REST architecture is a software development style that follows the following design constraints and guidelines.

- Client-server separation: Clients and servers are logically separated and they communicate with each other through a uniform interface conforming to HTTP.
- Stateless request and processing: State of a client's request will not be saved. Multiple requests from a client to a server will be handled independently. In other words, every request from a client is considered to be from a new client by the server.
- Client-side cacheable: The response delivered from the server must be cacheable on the client side. In other words, a single response must contain the complete information for the client to reuse the response, should the client request the same URI.
- Layered architecture: A server is a logical unit with a layered architecture. A client identifies a server by an URI. The resource may or may not reside on the server that the client is communicating with. The request can be redirected to another server transparently. Multiple redirections are possible.
- Code on demand: A server may process the request by executing a program on the server side or sending the code (script) to the client side to perform processing.

The services that follow the REST concept and conform to the REST constraints are referred to as being RESTful services.

7.3.2 RESTful Services

What are the main differences between SOAP services and RESTful services? Providing a service generally involves two issues: performing (verb) a certain task for a client and the result (noun) of performing the task to client. The SOAP service development we discussed earlier focuses more on the verb of performing the task. The way we develop services is of designing a class to represent a service and using the methods in the class to perform operations required by the service. The development style of RESTful services is to shift the focus from performing the task to the results of service. Obviously, it is more appropriate to focus on performing the task if a service is computing (action) oriented, such as solving an equation system, encrypting a string of data, and sorting a set of numbers. On the other hand, it is more appropriate to focus on the result if a service is data or resource oriented, such as searching data existing on the web and displaying a photo. A SOAP service is typically developed and accessed using object-oriented programming languages. Thus, it has the full function of a class, and the methods are accessed using class name and method name. On the other hand, a RESTful service focuses on one method, and the method can be accessed without using class name. As a result, RESTful services can be accessed by non-object-oriented languages, such as script languages. RESTful services are thus called lightweight services.

RESTful Services are more web-oriented. They are based on HTTP and web browsers and can be accessed in web browsers. Just like a web page, they can be viewed and bookmarked in a browser. The results can be cached and reused, through a browser's built-in caching mechanism.

Both styles of service development are useful and the developers should choose the style based on the problem. In this section, we will focus on the RESTful service development.

Let us take a deeper look at the more data and resource intensive applications through an example. At Amazon.com, you can search and view all items in Book, Electronics, Jewelry, Movies, Music, Games, Toys, Sports, Tools, and so on. If you go into the Electronics department, you can see subcategories TV, Camera, Cell Phone, Video Games, Musical Instruments, and so on. Consider another example. If you walk into a library and start to search books, you can search and view all the books written by a certain author, published in a certain year, published by a certain publisher, containing a certain keyword, and so on.

If you are a developer in charge of designing such a resource intensive application, such as the book management system in a library, what options do you have to organize your system?

You can save all books' information in a relational database with a schema; for example, (authors, title, ISBN, year, publisher, keywords). Then, you design a method for each of the aforesaid items:

- search_by_author(string name);
- search_by_title(string title);
- search_by_isbn(string isbn);
- search_by_year(string year);
- search_by_publisher(string publisher);
- search_by_keywords(string keyword1);
- search_by_keywords(string keyword1, string keyword2); // overloaded
- search_by_keywords(string keyword1, string keyword2, string keyword3); // overloaded

The REST concept suggests representing the resources in a resource tree, which is a rooted tree with the root representing all resources and each tree node representing a subset of resources of its parent node. Taking the library books as an example, a possible research tree is outlined in Figure 7.11. The root node / represents all books. The child node /authors/ represents all books written by a given author. The node /years/publishers/authors/ represents all books of a given year, a given publisher, and a given author.

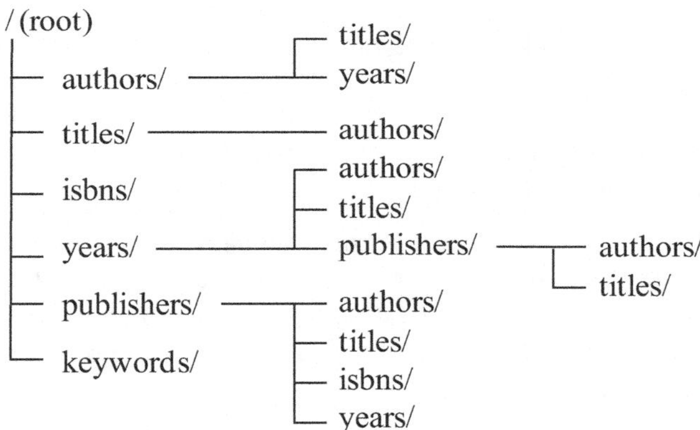

Figure 7.11. Resource tree of a library of books

Obviously, the tree does not contain all possible combinations of the items. In a large and complex system, the total number of combinations is an exponential function of the number of items and can easily become too large to handle. Implementing all combinations is not necessary in most cases too. For example, if a user is searching a book using years → authors. It is unlikely that the user will use ISBNs as the next constraint. An ISBN number can uniquely identify a book. If the ISBN is available, the user should have used it in the first step of the search.

The concept of RESTful services is to define a URI for each of the nodes in the resource tree, so that the set of resources corresponding to each node can be represented by the URI.

In order to represent the resource tree node in URI, we need to use a notation to represent the variables (parameters) and their values. For example, the set of books published in year 2010 by Kendall Hunt can be represented by the following URI notation, assuming the base address is http://mylibrary.asu.edu:

http://mylibrary.asu.edu/years/{year=2010}/publishers{publisher=Kendallhunt}

where, year and publisher are variables and 2010 and Kendallhunt values are assigned to the variables. Similarly, the set of books written by a given author can be represented by the following URI:

http://mylibrary.asu.edu/authors/{author=Aaron}

Figure 7.12 shows a part of the resource tree, with a node mapping to a list of sets. Let us consider the node "authors." The node is mapped to a number of sets, with each set corresponds to a specific variable value; for example, if the variable author takes the value, the set of books written by Aaron is represented by {books | author = Aaron} in standard set notation. In RESTful service notation, it is represented by http://mylibrary.asu.edu/authors/{author=Aaron}.

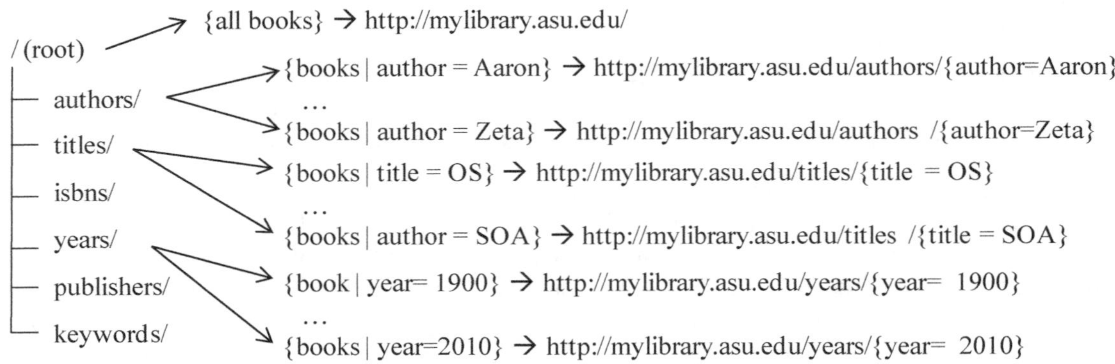

Figure 7.12. Each node of the resource tree corresponds to a set of URI

Then, an end user and a client (program user) can simply access the set of resources by the URI, either in a web browser or in a program using HTTP protocol.

When we use SOAP to invoke a service, we pack the method name and parameters into the SOAP package. RESTful services use HTTP protocol to access services of resources without using SOAP. As the SOAP layer is removed, we have to pack not only the destination (URI), but also the parameters and their values into the URI. In http://mylibrary.asu.edu/authors/{author=Aaron}, author=Aaron represents the variable and the value assigned to the variable.

We could map the resource requests to method calls without the programming environment support. It is easier though to use the library functions to write the mapping code. The .Net framework offers a number of library classes, including Uri, UriTemplate, and UriTemplateMatch. Using these classes, we can easily create URIs needed to send to the server, based on the information the user entered in the GUI; for example, if a user has selected search by year and by publisher, and has entered the data year = 2010, publisher = Kendallhunt. In another search, a user may select search by author and has entered author = Aaron. We need to write different mapping code to translate the request into method right call.

Assume we need to process such incoming URIs: http://mylib.asu.edu/years/publishers/authors and http://mylib.asu.edu/years/{year=2010}/authors/{author=Aaron}.The code below shows how we can map an incoming URI string to an internal URI for a node in the resource tree in Figure 7.12.

```
using System;
using System.ServiceModel.Web;
class ConsoleAppUriMatch {
```

```
    static void Main(string[] args)  {
         Uri baseUri = new Uri("http://mylib.asu.edu");
         UriTemplate myTemplate = new
         UriTemplate("/{years}/{publishers}/{authors}");
         Console.WriteLine("Built-in URI path segments are");
         foreach (var segName in myTemplate.PathSegmentVariableNames) {
               Console.WriteLine(segName);
         }
         Console.WriteLine("Please enter the Incoming URI with path segments ");
         string myUri = Console.ReadLine();
         // enter this URI: http://mylib.asu.edu/years/publishers/authors
    Uri incomeUri = new Uri(myUri); // convert string into URI format
    UriTemplateMatch myMatch = myTemplate.Match(baseUri, incomeUri);
    if (myMatch != null) {
         var matched = myMatch.BoundVariables;
         string myVars;
         foreach (var k in matched.Keys)  {
               myVars = k.ToString();
               Console.WriteLine("{0} = {1}", myVars, matched[myVars]);
         }
    }
    else
         Console.WriteLine("The incoming URI does not match the built-in URI");
     }
}
```

In the program, implicit type var is used, which allows the compiler to determine the type of the object based on the values that is assigned to the variable.

Figure 7.13 shows two test runs of the code using two different input URIs.

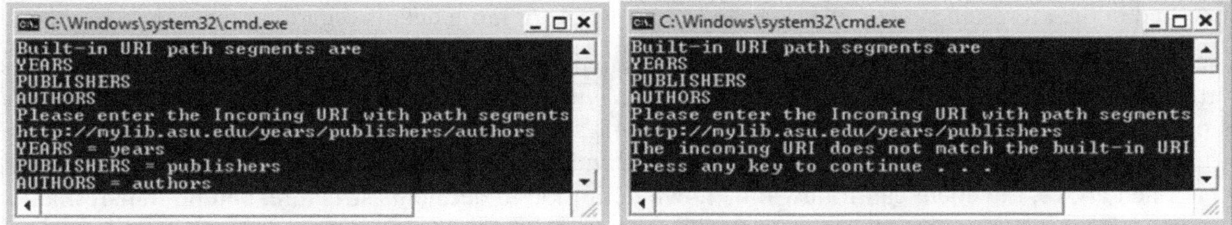

Figure 7.13. Each node of the resource tree corresponds to a set of URI

Note that we will still need to perform (verb) the tasks using methods. However, the methods are not visible to the clients, so that the clients can think that they are directly accessing the resources without performing actions. The code that follows shows how we can compose a URI using the library classes.

```
Uri baseUri = new Uri("http://mylib.asu.edu");
// create the path from tree root to the child node
UriTemplate myTemplate = new
                       UriTemplate("years/{year}/publishers/{publisher}");
// Assign values to variable to complete URI
Uri newBooksUri =
             myTemplate.BindByPosition(baseUri, "2010", "Kendallhunt");
// create the path from tree root to the child node
myTemplate = new UriTemplate("authors/{author}");
// Assign values to variable to complete URI
newBooksUri = myTemplate.BindByPosition(baseUri, "Aaron");
```

There are several key ideas in RESTful service development, in contrast to the traditional web service development, including:

- Focus on exposing data and resources instead of web methods. Each resource is given a URI and a set of resources can be given a URI.
- Use HTTP directly without another layer of SOAP on top of HTTP to access the resources. As the focus is on exposing the resources, the HTTP verbs GET, PUT, POST, DELETE, and HEAD are sufficient to access the RESTful services.
- RESTful service development is about identifying resources to be exposed, and organizing the resources so that the resources can be exposed efficiently in different ways: individually or in sets. Figure 7.12 showed an example of organizing the resources.

Data and resource accesses are similar to database access. It requires CRUD (Create, Read, Update, and Delete) operations of persistent storage. The HTTP verbs can be used to satisfy the CRUD operations, where GET for read, PUT for create and update, and DELETE for delete are used. The additional verb POST is specifically used for submitting data to be processed by the identified resource and HEAD is used for reading data, similar to GET, but it only retrieves headers and not the body of the message.

In many cases, a URI request will return a set of items or resources. For example, the URI http://mylibrary.asu.edu/years/{year=2010} will return all books in 2010 in the library. How do we present the data to the user who made the request?

A RESTful service typically supports multiple resource representations, including XML, XHTML, POX (Plain Old XML), RSS, Atom, and JSON. A service can offer multiple representations. In this case, a client can specify the required resource representation by appending the representation at the end of the URI; for example, if JSON is required, the URI will look like this:

http://mylibrary.asu.edu/years/{year=2010}&{format=json}

XML is the default representation and there is no need to specify. All other representations need to be specified in the aforesaid syntax. Please refer to Chapter 4 for more details regarding these data formats.

The reason that different representations are used is mainly because XML is too flexible and needs to be further defined by an XML schema in order for the client to understand its structure. Style transformation is normally needed in order to fit the service's XML schema to the client's schema. On the hand, if a structure and syntax have been completely predefined and are known, such as the alternative representations mentioned above, the client can follow the known definition to define its structure, and no transformation is needed. This is the reason why the less flexible representations are also supported by RESTful services.

Windows Communication Foundation (WCF) is the major service development platform from Microsoft. It supports SOAP-based services as well as RESTful services. In this section, we will use WCF to develop a Restful service and use the service to illustrate the resource-oriented architecture and the RESTful service concepts.

7.3.3 Microservices

A related concept to RESTful services is microservices. Microservices are defined as a software development technique, a variant of SOA architectural style. In this style, a Web application is composed from a collection of loosely coupled services, which are fine-grained, and their communication protocols are lightweight. No specific standards are defined for microservices. Both SOAP and RESTful services can be used as microservices. Since RESTful services are typically lighter weighted than SOAP services, they are more often used as microservices. APIs that do not belong to SOAP and RESTful (HTTP-based) services can be used as microservices. From this perspective, microservices can support functions that are not already in the current service standards.

An analog to microservices are the micro-instructions in computer organization, where instruction components, such as IF (Instruction Fetch), ID (Instruction Decode), EX (Execution), MEM (Memory access), and WB (Write Back), are defined as micro-instructions, from which different instructions can be composed based on finite state machine models.

The microservices are supposed to be fine-grained and light weighted. Developers often use multiple microservices in multiple layers, forming a mesh-style network to complete the desired functionalities, instead of using the orchestration and choreography composition styles (to be discussed in Section 7.4). Another significant difference to the service architecture is at the network and protocol level. Figure 7.14 shows the differences at protocol stack among these three types of services. For more details, see https://medium.com/microservices-in-practice/service-mesh-for-microservices-2953109a3c9a.

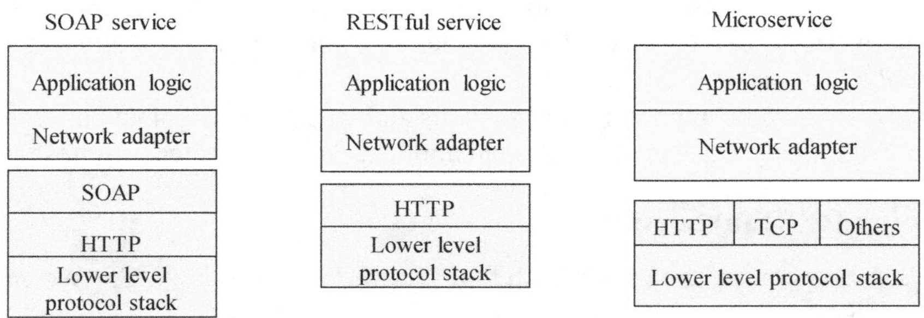

Figure 7.14. SOAP, RESTful and microservices communication stack

SOAP and RESTful services deal with one standard protocol and thus are easy for implementation and use. However, they are less flexible in communication options. On the other hand, it would be hard for implementing and using different protocols in microservices if the service developers and the service clients had to write different code to access these protocols in the network adapter, particularly when a service must call other services using different protocols. To address this problem, microservice architecture offers pre-configured network adapters and proxies to simplify the access to network, as shown in Figure 7.15.

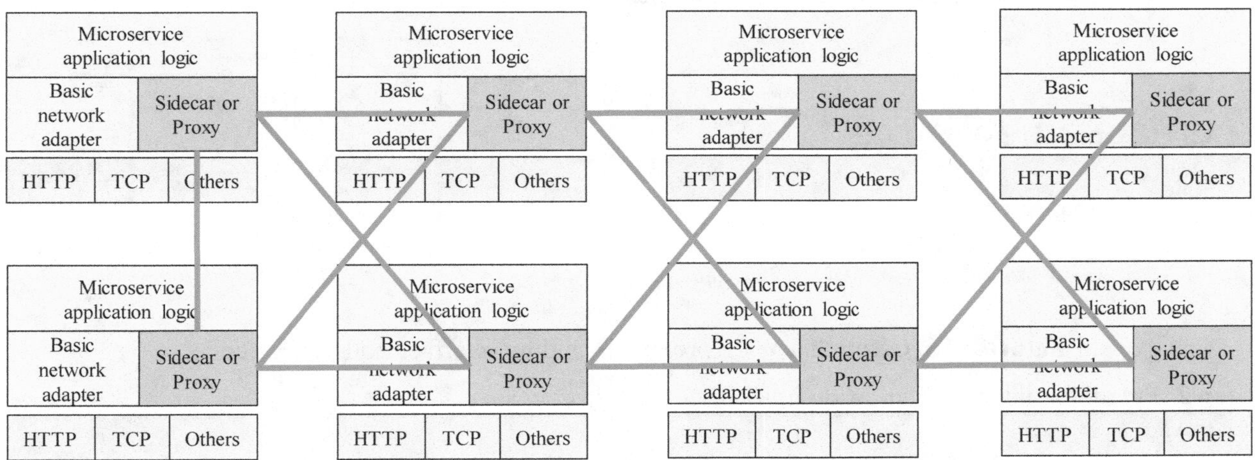

Figure 7.15. Microservices architecture with sidecar supporting communication

The way the sidecar or proxies are connected in Figure 7.15 is called service mesh network. Using such connection, changing a service is about changing the mesh network to select and combine different microservices. There are a number of implementations of mesh networks.

Istio is an open source service mesh platform that provides a way to control how microservices share data with one another. More detail can be found at https://www.redhat.com/en/topics/microservices/what-is-istio. It includes

- APIs that let Istio integrate into any logging platform.
- architecture that is divided into the data plane and the control plane to implement the sidecar (proxy) and service container concepts.

Spring Framework/Spring Cloud is a Java-based microservice architecture that supports the integration among Servlet API, WebSocket API, JSON Binding API, RESTful service, and so on. More detail can be found at https://spring.io/projects/spring-cloud. The framework

- provides tools for developers to quickly build some of the common patterns in distributed systems, including configuration management, service discovery, circuit breakers, intelligent routing, micro-proxy, control bus, one-time tokens, global locks, leadership election, distributed sessions, and cluster state.
- coordinates distributed components and systems and leads to boilerplate patterns (frequently used code), and can quickly stand up services and applications that implement those patterns.

7.3.4 Developing RESTful Service

This section shows the process of creating a RESTful service based on the WCF .svc service. The idea is to create a WCF service first, and then, transform it into a RESTful service. We can use the basic WCF service that we created in Chapter 3 as the starting point. In this approach, use the IService1.cs and Service1.svc files from Chapter 3. We can also use the following steps to create a RESTful service without referring to the service in Chapter 3.

Step 1: In the Visual Studio menu, choose Create a new project and search for "WCF", and choose the WCF service template, as shown in Figure 7.16 (left). Name the project RestService1. This step will create a WCF service with a template showing in as shown in Figure 7.16 (right), a project stack including these files: IService.cs interface file, Service1.svc markup file, Service1.svc.cs file, and Web.config file. In the following steps, we will create and modify these files.

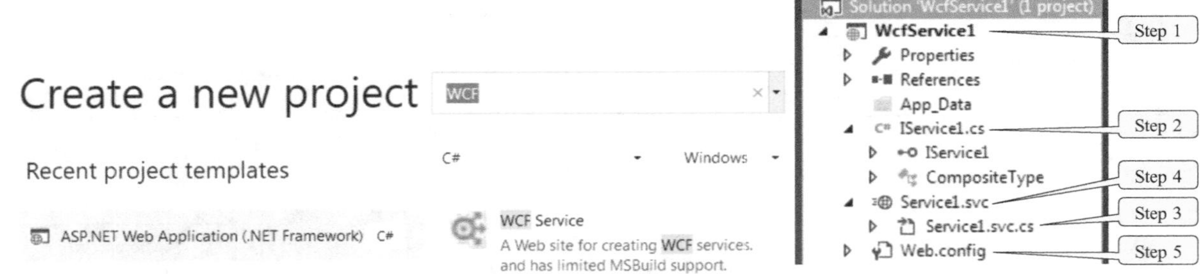

Figure 7.16. Creating a WCF project, including interface and service code

Step 2: Put all the interface definition in IService1.cs file:

```
using System;
using System.ServiceModel;        // Required for service development
using System.ServiceModel.Web;    // Required for service development
[ServiceContract]
public interface Iservice {
    [OperationContract]
    [WebGet]    // Add this HTTP GET attribute/directive, use default format
    double PiValue();
    [OperationContract]
    [WebGet(UriTemplate = "absValue?x={x}")]          // define input format
    int absValue(int x);
```

```
    [OperationContract]
    [WebGet(UriTemplate = "add2?x={x}&y={y}")]          // define input format
    int addition(int x, int y);
}
```

The WebGet attributes are required for all the operations that will be published as a service. UriTemplate is optional for the operations with 0 or 1 parameters. UriTemplate is required if an operation takes more than one parameter. In the foregoing code, UriTemplate = "add2?x={x}&y={y}" is used. If the parameters were string, a simpler format could be used: UriTemplate = "add2/{x}/{y}". This alternative format will be used in the next examples in random string and image verifier services.

Step 3: Method code in Service.cs file. The code has no difference with an ordinary class. It inherits the IService.cs interface.

```
// Service1.svc.cs
using System;
public class Service1 : IService1 {
    public double PiValue() {
        double pi = System.Math.PI;
        return (pi);
    }
    public int absValue(int x) {
        if (x >= 0) return (x);
        else return (-x);
    }
    public int addition(int x, int y) {
        return (x + y);
    }
}
```

Step 4: Right-click the file Service.svc and choose "View Markup." The markup source code of the file is open, shown as follows:

```
<%@ ServiceHost Language="C#" Debug="true" Service="WcfService1.Service1"
CodeBehind="Service1.svc.cs" %>
```

Add one line of code into the existing line of code, as highlighted, which results in the following code:

```
<%@ ServiceHost Language="C#" Debug="true" Service="WcfService1.Service1"
CodeBehind="Service1.svc.cs"
    Factory="System.ServiceModel.Activation.WebServiceHostFactory" %>
```

Step 5: In the Web.config file, remove the entire <system.serviceModel> element, which will remove the SOAP endpoints. RESTful services do not support the SOAP-endpoint-based access. Removing this element will immediately disable the accesses from service proxies of all kinds of SOAP clients.

The class WebServiceHostFactory creates the host instance dynamically in response to incoming messages. Now the RESTful service is ready to run. Once the service is started, it can be tested using following URIs:

- http://localhost:1722/Service1.svc/PiValue, it returns: <double>3.141592653589793l</double>
- http://localhost:1722/Service1.svc/AbsValue?x=-27, it returns: <int>27</int>
- http://localhost:1722/Service1.svc/add2?x=15&y=17, it returns: 32

Note that, in the first two calls, the service name and method name are included in the URI, but they are no longer so in the third call. The UriTemplate used in the service contract is:

[WebGet(**UriTemplate** = "add2?x={x}&y={y}", ResponseFormat = WebMessageFormat.Json)]

which hides the service name and method name to focus on the resource, instead of on the operations, which in the RESTful services are called resource-oriented services.

In the implementation above, we use a separate interface file IService.cs. We could merge the IService.cs file and Service.cs file into a single file, as shown in the following code:

```
using System;
using System.ServiceModel;
using System.ServiceModel.Activation;
using System.ServiceModel.Web;
namespace WcfRestService4 {
   // Start the service and browse to http://<machine_name>:<port>/
   // Service1/help to view the service's generated help page
   // NOTE: By default, a new instance of the service is created for each
   // call; change the InstanceContextMode to Single if you want
   // a single instance of the service to process all calls.
    [ServiceContract]
   [AspNetCompatibilityRequirements(RequirementsMode =
AspNetCompatibilityRequirementsMode.Allowed)]
   [ServiceBehavior(InstanceContextMode = InstanceContextMode.PerCall)]
   // If the service is renamed, remember to update the global.asax.cs file
   public class Service1 {
        [OperationContract]
        [WebGet(ResponseFormat = WebMessageFormat.Xml)]
        public double PiValue() {
              double pi = Math.PI;
              return (pi);
        }
        [OperationContract]
        [WebGet]     // No UriTemplate
        public int absValue(int x) {
              if (x >= 0) return (x);
              else return (-x);
        }
        [OperationContract]
        [WebGet(UriTemplate = "add2?x={x}&y={y}", ResponseFormat =
WebMessageFormat.Json)]     // Add this HTTP GET attribute/directive
        public int addition(int x, int y) {
              return (x+y);
        }
   }
}
```

To demonstrate the use of UriTemple, we used a different UriTemple in each [WebGet]. Build and start without debugging, and the service will be running on localhost; for example: http://localhost:49783. To test the operations, we can call each operation in browser:

- http://localhost:49783/Service1/PiValue, it returns: <double>3.1415926535897931</double>
- http://localhost:49783/Service1/absValue?x=-27, it returns: <int>27</int>
- http://localhost:49783/Service1/add2?x=15&y=17, it returns: <int>32</int>

Note that in the call to the methods addition(x, y), we use add2, instead of addition, as add2 is defined in the UriTemplate: UriTemplate = "add2? x={x}&y={y}", which allows us to use a different name to call the method in the class. The service is deployed at the server at the address below:

http://neptune.fulton.ad.asu.edu/WSRepository/Services/WcfRestService4/Service1/

You can test the remote service by replacing "neptune.fulton.ad.asu.edu/WSRepository/Services/WcfRestService4" for "localhost:49783." For example, test this RESTful service call:

"http://neptune.fulton.ad.asu.edu/WSRepository/Services/WcfRestService4/Service1/add2?x=15&y=17"

The call will return: <int>32</int>

7.3.5 Developing an Image Verifier in RESTful Service

Image verifiers have been widely used as way to prevent programs attached to websites. An image verifier consists of a random string generator and an image generator, as shown in Figure 7.17. The random string generator can take an input as the length. The image generator creates a bitmap and random background and prints the input string into the bitmap. To make the OCR software harder to recognize, various techniques can be used; for example, adding background noise, using different colors, and using random positions for the characters in the string. To implement this example, we created two RESTful services: random string service and an image generation service.

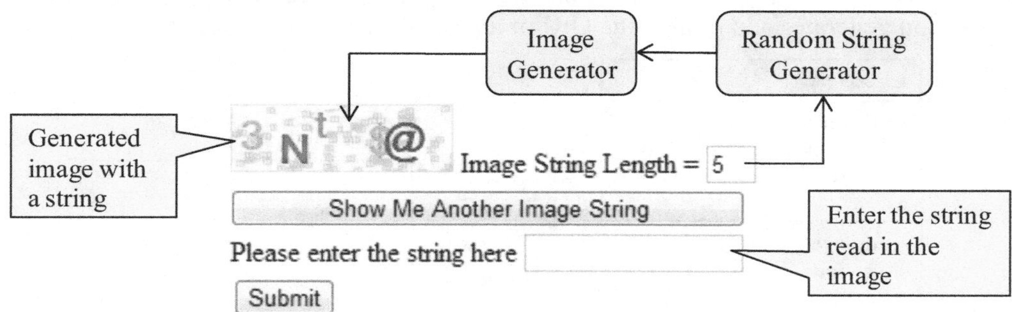

Figure 7.17. An image verifier

The random string service has two operations. One operation takes the length as input and returns a random string of the given length:

http://neptune.fulton.ad.asu.edu/WSRepository/Services/RandomString/Service.svc/GetRandomString/5

Note that the last part of the address /5 is the input. The other operation does not take an input and will return a random string of length between 4 and 20:

http://neptune.fulton.ad.asu.edu/WSRepository/Services/RandomString/Service.svc/GetRandomString

The random string service will return a string that contains at least an uppercase letter, a lowercase letter, a digit, and a special character if the given length is greater than or equal to 4. The service can be used to generate a strong password.

We use the WCF-based RESTful service approach to develop this service. The interface definition of the service is given as follows:

```
// IService.cs of the RandomString service
using System; using System.ServiceModel; using System.ServiceModel.Web;
[ServiceContract]
public interface IService {
    [WebGet(UriTemplate = "/GetRandomString", RequestFormat = WebMessageFormat.Xml,
ResponseFormat = WebMessageFormat.Xml, BodyStyle = WebMessageBodyStyle.Bare)]
    string GetRandomString0();

    [WebGet(UriTemplate = "/GetRandomString/{Length}", RequestFormat =
WebMessageFormat.Xml, ResponseFormat = WebMessageFormat.Xml, BodyStyle =
WebMessageBodyStyle.Bare)]
    string GetRandomString(string Length);
}
```

This service defines two operations: string GetRandomString0() and string GetRandomString(string Length). UriTemplate = "/GetRandomString" defines the operation name exposed to the service client. Note that the exposed operation name GetRandomString is different from the real operation name

GetRandomString0. We could use the same name or a different name. For the second operation, UriTemplate = "/GetRandomString/{Length}" includes a parameter named Length. The parameter passed with the URI to the service is considered a string. We must convert it to other types if needed.

Note that the overloaded operation name is not allowed, even if one has no parameter and the other has a parameter. However, we can use the UriTemplate to define overloaded name exposed to the outside. The code for the random string service is relatively easy and will not be given here.

Now let us turn to the image generation service. As shown in Figure 7.18, this service consists of two operations. The GetVerifierString operation calls the random string service to obtain the input, and the GetImage operation generates and returns the URI of an image, in which the input string is embedded.

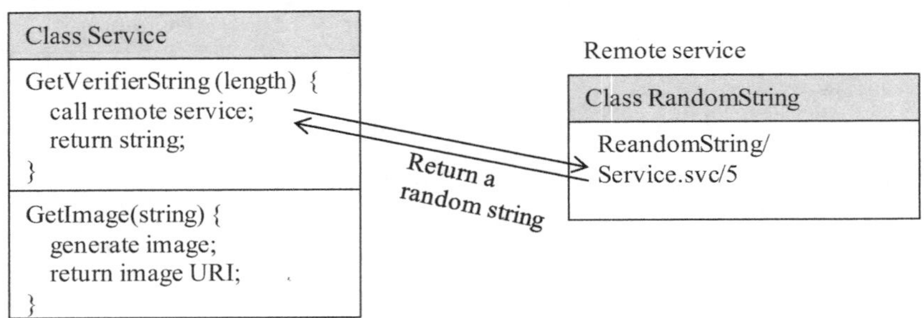

Figure 7.18. The image verifier class

The image verifier service can be called using the URI:

http://neptune.fulton.ad.asu.edu/WSRepository/Services/ImageVerifier/Service.svc/GetImage/3Nt$@

You can test the two services at the following addresses:

http://neptune.fulton.ad.asu.edu/WSRepository/Services/RandomString/Tryit.aspx

http://neptune.fulton.ad.asu.edu/WSRepository/Services/ImageVerifier/Tryit.aspx

We now explain the complete code of the image service, which is created in WCF using the same steps used in Section 7.3.4. The first part is the interface definition.

```
using System; using System.IO;
using System.ServiceModel;
using System.ServiceModel.Web;
[ServiceContract]
public interface IService {
    [WebGet(UriTemplate = "/GetVerifierString/{myLength}", RequestFormat =
WebMessageFormat.Xml, ResponseFormat = WebMessageFormat.Xml, BodyStyle =
WebMessageBodyStyle.Bare)]
    string GetVerifierString(string myLength);

    [WebGet(UriTemplate = "/GetImage/{myString}", RequestFormat =
WebMessageFormat.Xml, ResponseFormat = WebMessageFormat.Xml, BodyStyle =
WebMessageBodyStyle.Bare)]
    Stream GetImage(string myString);
}
```

This service defines two operations: GetVerifierString and GetImage. UriTemplate = "/GetVerifierString/{myLength}" defines the operation name and input parameter of the operation. Note that the operation name we use in the UriTemplate is the same as the real operation name. We could use a different name if we want to. The UriTemplate for the GetImage operation is defined similarly.

Next, we present the code of the Service.cs that contains the code of the operations. The comments in the code explain the purpose and function of the code.

```
// Service.cs
using System; using System.IO; using System.Runtime.Serialization;
using System.ServiceModel.Web; using System.Drawing; using System.Net;

public class Service : IService {
   // This method calls the RandomString service to obtain a string
   public string GetVerifierString(string myLength){
   // Notice how we access another RESTful service
        // Create the base address to the RandomString service
        Uri baseUri = new
Uri("http://neptune.fulton.ad.asu.edu/WSRepository/Services/RandomString/Service.svc
");
        // create the path from tree root to the child node
        UriTemplate myTemplate = new UriTemplate("GetRandomString/{Length}");
        // Assign values to variable to obtain the complete URI
        Uri completeUri = myTemplate.BindByPosition(baseUri, myLength);
        WebClient proxy = new WebClient(); // create proxy
        byte[] abc = proxy.DownloadData(completeUri);//receive in byte array
        Stream strm = new MemoryStream(abc); // convert to memory stream
        DataContractSerializer obj = new DataContractSerializer(typeof(string));
        string randString = obj.ReadObject(strm).ToString();
        return randString;
   }

   // This method creates an image string from a text string
   public Stream GetImage(string myString) {
        WebOperationContext.Current.OutgoingResponse.ContentType = "image/jpeg";
        int mapwidth = (int)(myString.Length * 25); // create bitmap
        Bitmap bMap = new Bitmap(mapwidth, 40); // based on string length
        Graphics graph = Graphics.FromImage(bMap);
        graph.Clear(Color.Azure);// background color
        graph.DrawRectangle(new Pen(Color.LightBlue, 0), 0, 0, bMap.Width - 1,
bMap.Height - 1); // draw a frame
        Random rand = new Random();
        Pen badPen = new Pen(Color.LightGreen, 0);
        for (int i = 0; i < 100; i++) { // create random noise pattern
             int x = rand.Next(1, bMap.Width - 1);
             int y = rand.Next(1, bMap.Height - 1);
             graph.DrawRectangle(badPen, x, y, 4, 3);
             graph.DrawEllipse(badPen, x, y, 2, 3);
        }
        char[] charString = myString.ToCharArray();
        Font font = new Font("Boopee", 18, FontStyle.Bold);
        Color[] clr = {Color.Black, Color.Red, Color.DarkViolet, Color.Green,
Color.DarkOrange, Color.Brown, Color.DarkGoldenrod, Color.Plum };
        // Draw the characters in the string onto the graphics object
        for (int i = 0; i < myString.Length; i++) {
             int d = rand.Next(20, 25); // distance between characters
             int p = rand.Next(1, 15); // up and down position
             int c = rand.Next(0, 7); // randomly choose a color
             string str1 = Convert.ToString(charString[i]); //char-string
             Brush b = new System.Drawing.SolidBrush(clr[c]);
             graph.DrawString(str1, font, b, 1 + i * d, p);
        }
        System.IO.MemoryStream ms = new System.IO.MemoryStream();
```

```
            bMap.Save(ms, System.Drawing.Imaging.ImageFormat.Jpeg);
            ms.Position = 0;
            graph.Dispose();
            bMap.Dispose();
            return ms;
        }
    }
```

In the aforesaid code, we used Uri completeUri = myTemplate.BindByPosition(baseUri, myLength) to append the parameter to the base address of the URI and then use the completeUri in the next statement; for example, if baseUri =
http://neptune.fulton.ad.asu.edu/WSRepository/Services/RandomString/Service.svc/GetRandomString

and myLength = 5, then completeUri =
http://neptune.fulton.ad.asu.edu/WSRepository/Services/RandomString/Service.svc/GetRandomString/5

The question is, can we use the string operation to append them together: completeUri = baseUri + myLength? The answer is no. Although the URI value looks like a string, it is not of string type. As a matter of fact, when we test the program, using string operation actually worked on the localhost, but failed after the service is deployed to the server. We need to use the function BindByPosition(baseUri, myLength).

How is the image generated? We used a few library classes here in the code. First, we generate a Bitmap object bMap as the basis of the image. We then create a Graph object that is pointed to the bMap object. Then, we use the tools (methods) in the Graph object to modify the bMap object by defining the background, adding noise, and draw the characters. Finally, we save the bMap object into a MemoryStream object as the return data.

As we have developed the RESTful ImageVerifier using a WCF-based approach, two minor changes will convert the RESTful service into a WSDL-SOAP service:

1. Substitute [OperationContract] for [GetWeb …] in the IService.cs file;
2. Delete the line of code Factory="System.ServiceModel.Activation.WebServiceHostFactory" in Service.svc file.

The image verifier in WSDL-SOAP standard is deployed at:

http://neptune.fulton.ad.asu.edu/WSRepository/Services/ImageVerifierSvc/Service.svc

The service can be accessed using the proxy created by "Add Service Reference…" A test page is deployed at: http://neptune.fulton.ad.asu.edu/WSRepository/Services/ImageVerifierSvc/TryIt.aspx.

7.3.6 Consuming Simple RESTful Service

A RESTful service is accessed through a URI, instead of a SOAP message. The simplest way of consuming a RESTful service is to type the URI in a browser, with the method name and parameter value as a part of the URI, as we discussed in Section 7.3.4.

For the RandomString and ImageVerifier services, we can access them in a browser as follows:

http://neptune.fulton.ad.asu.edu/WSRepository/Services/RandomString/Service.svc/GetRandomString/8

http://neptune.fulton.ad.asu.edu/WSRepository/Services/ImageVerifier/Service.svc/GetImage/3Nt$@

Note that the ways the parameters are passed to the service operations are different. It is related to the use of the UriTemplate. In the simple service in Section 7.3.4, no UriTemplate is defined for the absValue operation, and the default format is methodName?variableName={value}; for example, absValue?x=-28.

In the section 7.3.5, UriTemplate = "/GetVerifierString/{myLength} is defined and thus, we can pass the parameter in the format of methodName/{value}; for example, GetImage/3Nt$@.

How do we access a RESTful service in another program? In Service.cs of the ImageVerifier that we discussed just now, it already provided the code to access the RESTful service RandomString. As another example, let us develop an application to access the ImageVerifier RESTful service, as deployed at:

http://neptune.fulton.ad.asu.edu/WSRepository/Services/ImageVerifier/Tryit.aspx

To create the test page, start an ASP .Net forms application and name the form TryIt.aspx. The GUI design of Tryit.aspx application is shown in Figure 7.17. The code, with detailed comments, behind the test application that calls the two operations of the ImageVerifier is given as follows:

```
// TryIt.aspx.cs
using System; using System.Net; using System.IO;
using System.Runtime.Serialization;
public partial class TestVerifier : System.Web.UI.Page {
    protected void Page_Load(object sender, EventArgs e) {}
    protected void Button1_Click(object sender, EventArgs e) {
        if (Session["generatedStr"].Equals(TextBox1.Text)) {
            Label1.Text = "Congratulation. The code you entered is correct!";
        }
        Else {
            Label1.Text = "I am sorry, the string you entered does not match the
image. Please try again!";
        }
    }
    protected void Button2_Click(object sender, EventArgs e) {
        // create the base address
        Uri baseUri = new
Uri("http://neptune.fulton.ad.asu.edu/WSRepository/Services/ImageVerifier/Service.sv
c/");
        // create the path from tree root to the child node
        UriTemplate myTemplate = new UriTemplate("GetVerifierString/{myLength}");
        // Assign values to variable to complete URI
        Uri completeUri = myTemplate.BindByPosition(baseUri, txtBoxlength.Text);
        WebClient proxy = new WebClient();
        byte[] abc = proxy.DownloadData(completeUri);
        Stream strm = new MemoryStream(abc);
        DataContractSerializer obj = new DataContractSerializer(typeof(string));
        string generatedString = obj.ReadObject(strm).ToString();
        Session["generatedStr"] = generatedString;
        Image1.Visible = true;
        Image1.ImageUrl =
"http://neptune.fulton.ad.asu.edu/WSRepository/Services/ImageVerifier/Service.svc/Ge
tImage/" + generatedString;
        Button2.Text = "Show Me Another Image String";
    }
}
```

In general, we use WebClient to access RESTful services. There are other APIs that does not follow RESTful service standard. In this case, you can use the WebRequest class to access the APIs. There are several guides online on the more intricate aspects of this class. Examples can be found at the MSDN library: https://msdn.microsoft.com/en-us/library/456dfw4f(v=vs.110).aspx

```
using System;
using System.IO;
using System.Net;
using System.Text;
namespace Examples.System.Net {
    public class WebRequestGetExample {
        public static void Main () {
```

```
            // Create a request for the URL.
            WebRequest request = WebRequest.Create (
              "http://www.contoso.com/default.html");
            // If required by the server, set the credentials.
            request.Credentials = CredentialCache.DefaultCredentials;
            // Get the response.
            WebResponse response = request.GetResponse ();
            // Display the status.
            Console.WriteLine (((HttpWebResponse)response).StatusDescription);
            // Get the stream containing content returned by the server.
            Stream dataStream = response.GetResponseStream ();
            // Open the stream using a StreamReader for easy access.
            StreamReader reader = new StreamReader (dataStream);
            // Read the content.
            string responseFromServer = reader.ReadToEnd ();
            // Display the content.
            Console.WriteLine (responseFromServer);
            // Clean up the streams and the response.
            reader.Close ();
            response.Close ();
} }     }
```

You can also include headers and application/API keys with this class in case you need either. You can also change the HTTP command you are performing, for example, it supports GET, POST, etc.

7.3.7 Google RESTful Services: Map Services

The major service providers have made many RESTful services available. Map services are among the most widely used RESTful services. For example, Microsoft has its Bing location services available at: http://msdn.microsoft.com/en-us/library/ff701713.aspx, and Google has its map services available at: https://developers.google.com/maps/documentation/webservices/. More services are listed in Appendix C. In this section, we use some of these services as examples.

Using Google map's distance matrix API as an example, you can query the distances between multiple locations:

```
http://maps.googleapis.com/maps/api/distancematrix/output?parameters
```

where, you can choose different output formats (xml or json). For the input parameters, a wide variety of inputs supporting multiple origins and destinations, travel methods (driving, cycling, walking), language, and sensor for using location from sensor device such as GPS are available. For example, we may want to query the distances between two origin cities Phoenix AZ **or** "|" Tucson AZ **and** "&" two destination cities Los Angeles CA **or** "|" San Francisco CA, by driving, output language in English, and using no sensor input. For the output format, we want to have the data in xml. The following RESTful query will meet these requirements:

http://maps.googleapis.com/maps/api/distancematrix/xml?origins=Phoenix+AZ|Tucson+AZ&destinations =Los+Angeles|San+Francisco%&mode=driving&language=en&sensor=false

The XML output of the query is given as follows:

```
<DistanceMatrixResponse>
   <status>OK</status>
   <origin_address>Phoenix, AZ, USA</origin_address>
   <origin_address>Tucson, AZ, USA</origin_address>
   <destination_address>Los Angeles, CA, USA</destination_address>
   <destination_address>San Francisco, CA, USA</destination_address>
   <row>
        <element>
```

```
            <status>OK</status>
            <duration>
                <value>19420</value>
                <text>5 hours 24 mins</text>
            </duration>
            <distance>
                <value>599110</value>
                <text>599 km</text>
            </distance>
        </element>
        <element>
        <status>OK</status>
            <duration>
                <value>38718</value>
                <text>10 hours 45 mins</text>
            </duration>
            <distance>
                <value>1209296</value>
                <text>1,209 km</text>
            </distance>
        </element>
    </row>
    <row>
        <element>
            <status>OK</status>
            <duration>
                <value>25676</value>
                <text>7 hours 8 mins</text>
            </duration>
            <distance>
                <value>786030</value>
                <text>786 km</text>
            </distance>
        </element>
        <element>
            <status>OK</status>
            <duration>
                <value>44975</value>
                <text>12 hours 30 mins</text>
            </duration>
            <distance>
                <value>1396216</value>
                <text>1,396 km</text>
            </distance>
        </element>
    </row>
</DistanceMatrixResponse>
```

The foregoing example does not require registering and using a key to access the service. Many services will require a register to obtain a key. For example, Google's Place Search service will require a project key. The service URI is:

```
https://maps.googleapis.com/maps/api/place/textsearch/output?parameters
```

A list of parameters must be provided, some of them are required, and the others are optional (https://developers.google.com/places/documentation/search). The required parameters include:

- key – Your application's API key. This key identifies your application for purposes of quota management. You can make certain number of calls per day for free. In order to obtain the key, you must register at Google's APIs Console site at https://developers.google.com/console/help/.
- query – The text string on which to search; for example: "restaurant." The Place service will return candidate matches based on this string and order the results based on their perceived relevance.
- sensor – Indicates whether or not the Place request came from a device using a location sensor (e.g., a GPS) to determine the location sent in this request. This value must be either true or false.

Following is an example of calling the Place search service. In the call, you must provide your own API key.

https://maps.googleapis.com/maps/api/place/textsearch/xml?query=restaurants+in+Sydney&sensor=true &key=*PutYourOwnApiKeyHere*

Multiple restaurants are found. Following is a part of the output of the call is given in XML format [https://developers.google.com/places/documentation/search]:


```
<?xml version="1.0" encoding="UTF-8"?>
<PlaceSearchResponse>
 <status>OK</status>
 <result>
  <name>Rockpool</name>
  <type>restaurant</type>
  <type>food</type>
  <type>establishment</type>
  <formatted_address>107 George Street, The Rocks NSW, Australia</formatted_address>
  <geometry>
   <location>
    <lat>-33.8597750</lat>
    <lng>151.2085920</lng>
   </location>
  </geometry>
  <rating>4.0</rating>
  <icon>http://maps.gstatic.com/mapfiles/place_api/icons/restaurant-71.png</icon>
<reference>CnRlAAAALuyHKpRN_oLCCfTJZ-
uIA7YdJCe3zEhsSf0RZ25GnX6UhQ66gTeVJdGAyfS2bwB3XPvocWSGBfxF-
De6bXC3P_Cvezr9kAEW9jBKvazwyyYZoUaZqVwuy4sGlzKOSCse5qDR7snP63sDD1bkV60OGxIQ2zfuqWNJm
tiiSXeNFqSgQhoUthzNiDC86p2SIXdpcarNFXRgBLk</reference>
  <id>7beacea28938ae42bcac04faf79a607bf84409e6</id>
  <event>
    <summary>Google Maps Developer Meetup: Rockin' out with the Places API</summary>
    <event_id>7lH_gK1GphU</event_id>
    <url>https://developers.google.com/places</url>
  </event>
 </result>
 <result>
  <name>Chinatown Sydney</name>
  <type>city_hall</type>
  <type>park</type>
  <type>restaurant</type>
  <type>doctor</type>
  <type>train_station</type>
  <type>local_government_office</type>
  <type>food</type>
  <type>health</type>
  <type>establishment</type>
  <formatted_address>483 George Street, Sydney NSW, Australia</formatted_address>
  <geometry>
   <location>
    <lat>-33.8731950</lat>
```

```
    <lng>151.2063380</lng>
   </location>
  </geometry>
  <rating>4.0</rating>
 <icon>http://maps.gstatic.com/mapfiles/place_api/icons/civic_building-
71.png</icon>  <reference>CnRuAAAAiC5vFoN7Y_uh9092KqN1O1KEgihp845nP1IGIj3eDOzfOT_RPd
rTmCv4wrNcwMUvMfR2NhTyWd1g2W11V6HPrYlH_gXJQyohh6iHgQmDCXUESusetpMRPfob1GnBk2ylXq-
oQz_85mEyqzBFFMICshIQuDEafdNuT1HpAx5suyTUeBoUWx0qvhqfUxl0F37Qae2RlLgdk0c</reference>
  <id>017049cb4e82412aaf0efbde890e82b7f2987c16</id>
 </result>
 <html_attribution>Listings by <a href="http://www.yellowpages.com.au/">Yellow
Pages</a></html_attribution>
</PlaceSearchResponse>
```


A complex example of using Google's Map APIs is given at:

https://developers.google.com/places/documentation/search

The application uses a list of RESTful services as given in the ASU Repository at:

http://neptune.fulton.ad.asu.edu/wsrepository/services/DischargeQueryService/Default.html

7.3.8 Making Asynchronous Calls to RESTful Services

Asynchronous communication is important in mobile computing and communication. Mobile devices normally use wireless communication. It has a higher network transient error rate. When synchronous communication is used, a service call will fail if a network error occurs. Asynchronous communication split a longer communication period in the synchronous call into two shorter periods, which is thus less vulnerable to the network transient errors.

In this section, we show an example of calling RESTful service in an asynchronous way. The RESTful service to call is:

http://neptune.fulton.ad.asu.edu/WSRepository/Services/RandomString/Service.svc/GetRandomString/{length}

where {length} can be any integer value.

The service returns a random string that can be used as a strong password with different types of characters; for example, 7i=HN5c@4$LwT2. The following code is used in a web application behind a button "btnGetPwd_Click." When the button is clicked, the code will be executed.

```
public static string spassword = "Waiting for call back"; //static-global variable

private void btnGetPwd_Click(object sender, RoutedEventArgs e) {
   Random rnd = new Random();
   Int32 length = rnd.Next(6, 18); random # between 6 and 18
   string toDisplay = spassword;
   GetPwd(length);  // It puts the result in spassword variable
   // Async! It will not have the value in the next statement
   if (spassword != "Waiting for call back") {
        XDocument xd = XDocument.Parse(spassword);
        XElement xe = xd.Root;
        toDisplay = xe.Value;
   }
   textBox1.Text = toDisplay;
}
   public static void GetPwd(int length) {
        string baseUrl =
"http://neptune.fulton.ad.asu.edu/WSRepository/Services/RandomString/Service.svc/GetRandomString/";
        string len = Convert.ToString(length);
        string fullUrl = baseUrl + len;
```

```
        HttpWebRequest hwReq1 = (HttpWebRequest)HttpWebRequest.Create(new
Uri(fullUrl));
        hwReq1.BeginGetResponse(new AsyncCallback(myCallbackFunc), hwReq1);
        // The program that calls this method can use the service return value
        // through the global variable spassword. This method returns immediately
        // without waiting for service return value.
}
private static void myCallbackFunc(IAsyncResult  requestObj) {
   HttpWebRequest  hwReq2 = (HttpWebRequest)requestObj.AsyncState;
   HttpWebResponse hwResponse = (HttpWebResponse)hwReq2.EndGetResponse(requestObj);
   using (StreamReader sReader = new StreamReader(hwResponse.GetResponseStream())){
   spassword = sReader.ReadToEnd().ToString();
   // Result save into this global variable spassword
}
```

The asynchronous communication is through the following mechanisms:

- A global variable spassword defined at the beginning of the code.
- Function GetPwd(). The method will create a request for making RESTful service call. When it calls the service in the following statement
  `hwReq1.BeginGetResponse(new AsyncCallback(myCallbackFunc), hwReq1);`
  it creates a new call through `new AsyncCallback(myCallbackFunc)`, which calls another method `myCallbackFunc` in the same program. Once called the service, without waiting for the return value from the service, GetPwd() terminates. Thus, the caller of GetPwd() will not have to wait for the service to return a value.
- Function `myCallbackFunc`. It will wait for the return value of the service call. Once the revalue is received, it will write the value into the global variable for the caller of GetPwd() to consume.

Note that, if the caller of GetPwd() tries to use the return value of the service immediately after GetPwd() returns, the value may not be available yet. Thus, it must check if the value is still equal to the initial value `"Waiting for call back"`. If it is, the caller must make another call to retrieve the value from the previous call.

7.3.9 RESTful Service-Based Web Application Description Language

Web Service Description Language (WSDL) has been successfully used for defining the interface of WSDL/SOAP services. The application builders can extract the information from such interfaces to write application code to access these services. What language is used for describing the RESTful services? As each RESTful service is normally simple, no specific description language is needed for defining the interface of RESTful services. However, RESTful service-based web application description languages have been defined to describe the applications that use RESTful services.

Web Application Description Language (WADL) is a language defined for this purpose, which is developed by Sun Microsystems and submitted to W3C (http://www.w3.org/Submission/wadl/). The following is an example of a WADL instance for describing the Yahoo News Search application given in the W3C Website.

```
<?xml version="1.0"?>
<application xmlns:xsi="http://www.w3.org/2001/XMLSchema-instance"
 xsi:schemaLocation="http://wadl.dev.java.net/2009/02 wadl.xsd"
 xmlns:tns="urn:yahoo:yn"
 xmlns:xsd="http://www.w3.org/2001/XMLSchema"
 xmlns:yn="urn:yahoo:yn"
 xmlns:ya="urn:yahoo:api"
 xmlns="http://wadl.dev.java.net/2009/02">
  <grammars>
    <include href="NewsSearchResponse.xsd"/>
    <include href="Error.xsd"/>
  </grammars>
```

```
  <resources base="http://api.search.yahoo.com/NewsSearchService/V1/">
    <resource path="newsSearch">
      <method name="GET" id="search">
        <request>
          <param name="appid" type="xsd:string"
            style="query" required="true"/>
          <param name="query" type="xsd:string"
            style="query" required="true"/>
          <param name="type" style="query" default="all">
            <option value="all"/>
            <option value="any"/>
            <option value="phrase"/>
          </param>
          <param name="results" style="query" type="xsd:int" default="10"/>
          <param name="start" style="query" type="xsd:int" default="1"/>
          <param name="sort" style="query" default="rank">
            <option value="rank"/>
            <option value="date"/>
          </param>
          <param name="language" style="query" type="xsd:string"/>
        </request>
        <response status="200">
          <representation mediaType="application/xml"
            element="yn:ResultSet"/>
        </response>
        <response status="400">
          <representation mediaType="application/xml"
            element="ya:Error"/>
        </response>
      </method>
    </resource>
  </resources>
</application>
```

The root element of this document is <application>. Like any XML document, a list of namespaces and XML schemas are listed as the attributes of the root element. The main element is <resources>, which can consist of a list of <resource> elements used in the document. In this example, only one resource is used.

Each <resource> element has an attribute specifying the path of the resource. The child elements of the <resource> include a method, which consists of<request> and <response> elements. The <request> element has a list of parameters. The<response> elements return a status code and response value in XML. The full XML scheme definition of WADL is at: http://www.w3.org/Submission/wadl/wadl.xsd. The key structure of a WADL document is shown in Figure 7.19.

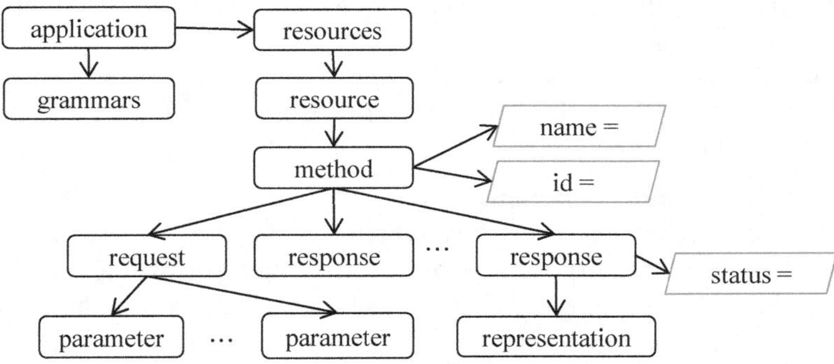

Figure 7.19. Structure of the WADL document

7.4 Advanced Web Application Architecture

Now that you have learned to develop ASP .Net Web applications, let us review and further study the architecture aspects of the applications. Figure 7.20 shows the evolution from ASP .Net to ASP .Net Core technologies. ASP .Net Framework is based on an object-oriented programming paradigm, which is easy for people who have a solid background of object-oriented programming. However, ASP .Net Framework suffers from a few issues, such as view state problem in web farm hosting and compatibility with other development environments on Mac and Linux machines. ASP .Net Core Framework addresses these issues by starting its root from web technologies, instead of from object-oriented programming technologies. Applications developed on ASP .Net Core Framework will be executable on Mac and Linux environments.

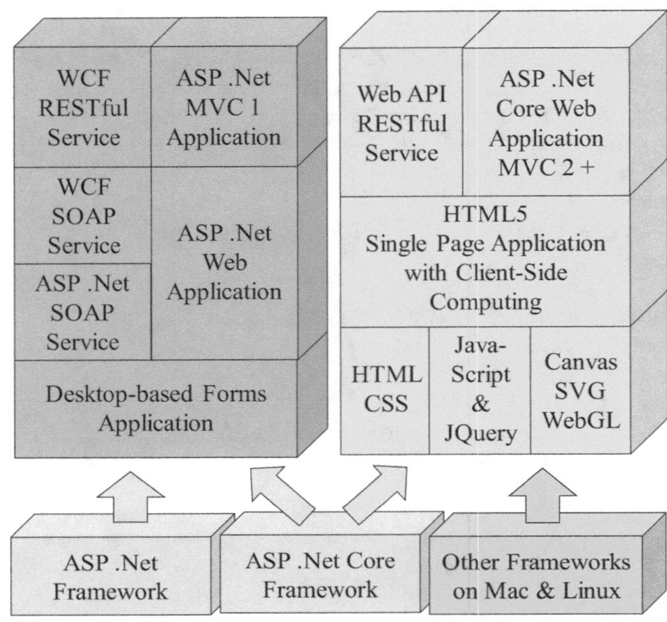

Figure 7.20. Evolution from ASP .Net to ASP .Net Core technologies

In this section, we will briefly review ASP .Net Framework and then discuss HTML5 and MVC 2 on ASP .Net Core Framework in detail.

7.4.1 ASP .Net Forms-Centric Architecture

We discussed in Section 5.2 the ASP .Net application structure and architecture. A typical application is structured in the diagram shown in Figure 5.2. The directories created by the template include the root directory, the App_Data directory, and the bin directory. Developers can create directories and subdirectories wherever they want. The architecture style is forms-centric, because the entire application is organized around the forms (ASPX pages). The developers are responsible for defining a good architecture by creating subdirectories and organizing the ASPX pages and placing them in different directories.

However, no matter how the developers organize their ASPX pages, the data files (text files, XML files, and Database files) are placed in the same App_Data directory. Similarly, the compiled files and the DLL files are placed in the same bin directory. Furthermore, ASP .Net Forms application allows states to be saved in the rendered XHTL pages sent to the client and allows page postback and is sent to another page. ASP .Net also provides a large number of server controls. These controls will be integrated in different pages. The main benefit of this architecture is to allow the developers focusing on the functionalities to be developed using the forms. The developers have the flexibility to use the resources and means available.

The GUI controls are a part of the forms, and the event handlers are either embedded in the forms (server-side scripting) or in a separate file. In both cases, they are tightly associated with the server controls in the forms. In a positive view, the architecture keeps the related items in the same places.

The problems with this architecture are as follows:

- All the pages and other files are tightly coupled. The entire project has to be developed in collaboration as an integrated system. If you have multiple members in a team, each team member needs to know the other pages developed by other members.
- The project must be tested as a whole. There is no automatic way to define unit tests that test individual pages in the project.
- The XHTML page sent to the client browser is rendered on the server using many ASP .Net server-specific features and control. The XHTML page cannot be easily ported and deployed to another server.

To address these issues, ASP .Net offers another architecture style that restricts the flexibility of the developers to trade for a better architecture.

7.4.2 HTML5 on ASP .Net Core Framework

In Section 4.6.5, we discussed HTML5 concepts as a web data representation format. In this section, we elaborate HTML5 web application development using ASP .Net Core Framework.

We start Visual Studio 2019 and choose Create a new project. We search "web" keyword, as shown in Figure 7.21. Then, we choose ASP .Net Web Application (.Net Framework) as the template. Clicking "Next", we can configure the project and choose the project name and project location.

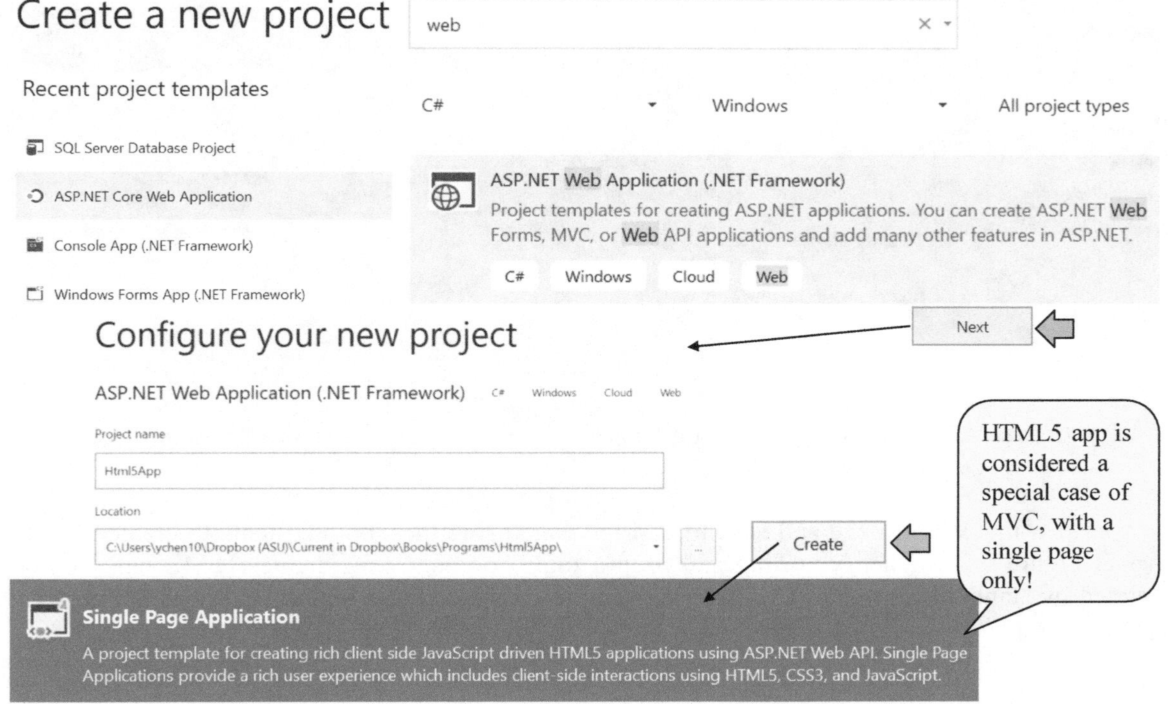

Figure 7.21. Creating a new HTML5 project

Next, we choose Single Page Application as the template, which will create a basic MVC project. This template provides necessary support for HTML5 that uses Web APIs. Once the project is created, we choose

Add → New Item…, and then choose an HTML Page. We name the page index, as shown in Figure 7.22. In this example, we will focus on this index.html page.

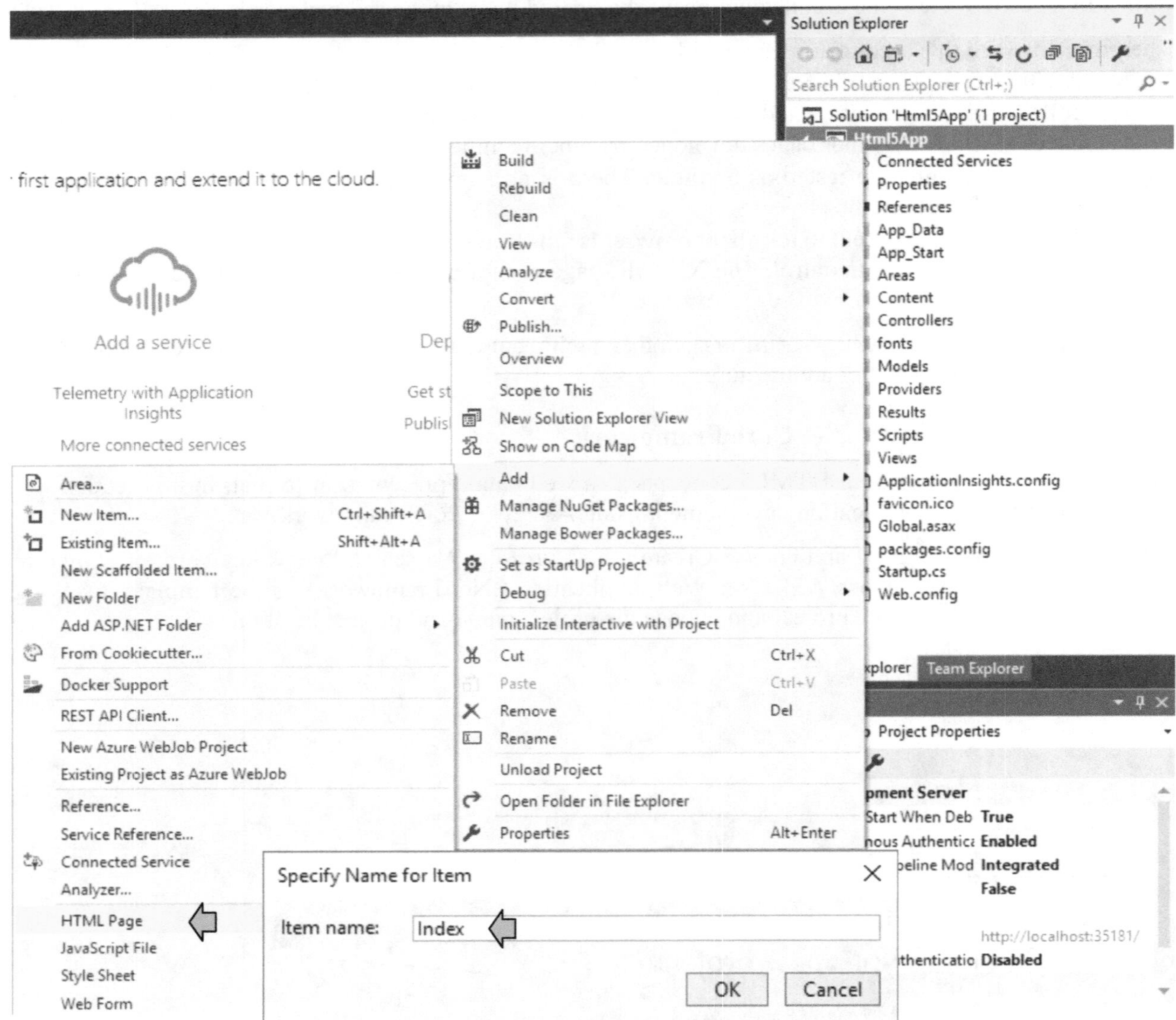

Figure 7.22. HTML5 project template and adding an index.html page to the project

Now, we open index.html page and start to edit the page using the Toolbox items to create the GUI, as shown in Figure 7.23. When you drag and drop a tool, Toolbox items create HTML tags that can be interpreted by standard browsers. This simple example shows text and buttons but does not perform any computation.

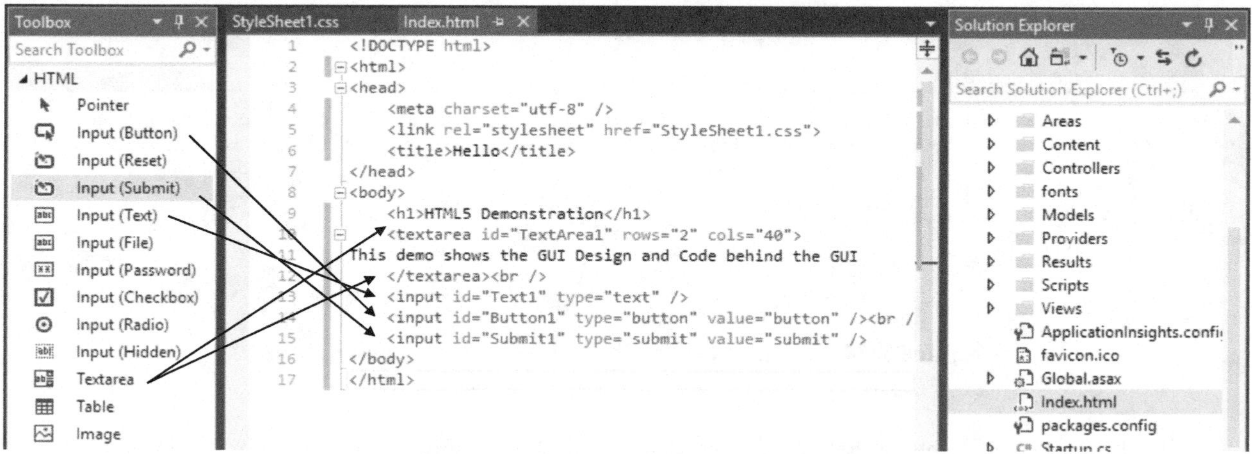

Figure 7.23. Creating GUI using Toolbox items

In the following example, we will start to add JavaScript code for computing and web service calls in the HTML page. The html code of the example is showing as follows:

```
<!DOCTYPE html>
<html>
<head>
    <meta charset="utf-8" />
    <link rel="stylesheet" href="StyleSheet1.css">
    <script src="JsCode.js"></script>
    <title>HTML5 Demo</title>
</head>
<body>
    <h1>HTML5 Demonstration</h1>
    <textarea id="TextArea1" rows="2" cols="100">
This demo shows JavaScript in an external file and a RESTful service call to the service at:
http://neptune.fulton.ad.asu.edu/WSRepository/Services/WcfRestService4/Service1/add2?x=11&y=25
    </textarea><br />
    <form name="sum">
        <input id="Text1" type="text" name="x" size=5 maxlength="5" />
        and
        <input id="Text2" type="text" name="y" size="5" maxlength="5" />
        <input type="button" value=" add " name="Submit" onClick="add2Nos()" />
        <input type="button" value=" multiply " name="Submit"
onClick="multiply2Nos()" />
        <br />
        =
        <br />
        <input type="text" name="z" size="5" maxlength="5">
        <span id="result"></span><p />
        <input type="button" value=" ServiceCall " name="Submit"
onClick="ServiceCall()" />
        <input type="text" name="s" size="5" maxlength="5">
        <span id="result"></span>
    </form>
</body>
</html>
```

This html file will generate the GUI in Figure 7.24.

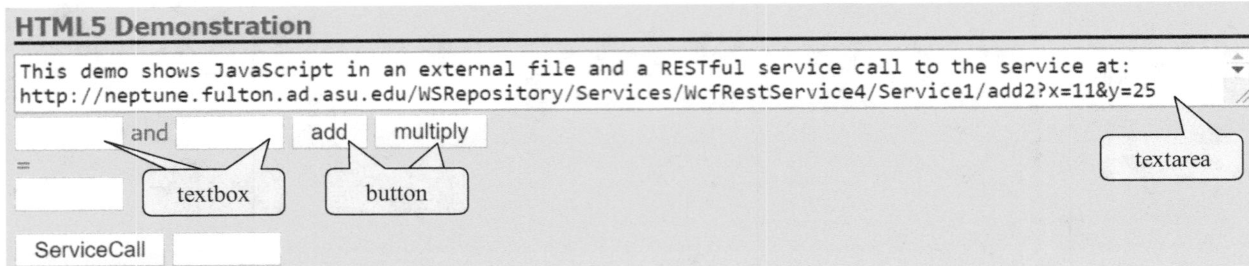

Figure 7.24. Creating GUI with teatarea, textbox, and button

In the html file, a JavaScript file JsCode.js is referenced, which implements the functions behind the buttons in the html file:

```
        <input type="button" value=" add " name="Submit" onClick="add2Nos()" />
        <input type="button" value=" multiply " name="Submit"
        <input type="button" value=" ServiceCall " name="Submit"
onClick="ServiceCall()" />
```

The JavaScript code is linked into the html file, but saved as a separate file:

```
function add2Nos() {
    document.sum.z.value =
        parseInt(document.sum.x.value) + parseInt(document.sum.y.value)
}
function multiply2Nos() {
    document.sum.z.value =
        parseInt(document.sum.x.value) * parseInt(document.sum.y.value)
}

function ServiceCall() {
    var xhttp = new XMLHttpRequest();
    xhttp.onreadystatechange = function () {
        if (xhttp.readyState == 4 && xhttp.status == 200)
            document.sum.s.value = xhttp.responseText;
    }
    xhttp.open("GET",
"http://neptune.fulton.ad.asu.edu/WSRepository/Services/WcfRestService4/Service1/add
2?x=11&y=25", true);
    xhttp.setRequestHeader("Content-type", "application/json");
    xhttp.send();
}
```

Figure 7.25 shows how the JavaScript function calls add3Nos() and multiply2Nos() are connected to the JavaScript functions in the JsCode.js file.

This JavaScript file defines two arithmetic functions and a RESTful service call function. The arithmetic functions are simple and straightforward. The service call is rather complex, which is asynchronous and is executed in the following steps:

1. var xhttp = new XMLHttpRequest(); creates a new XMLHttpRequesobject;
2. xhttp.onreadystatechange will wait for and lessen to the readyState and Status to change (listener). When the change (correct value is received) happens, it returns the responseText back to the html page for displaying.

3. While step 2 is waiting, the execution proceeds to this step (asynchronous mode): It opens http Get operation at the given RESTful service address;
4. It sets the setRequestHeader to content type and application/json format;
5. It sends the data back to the listener to allow step 2 to be complete.

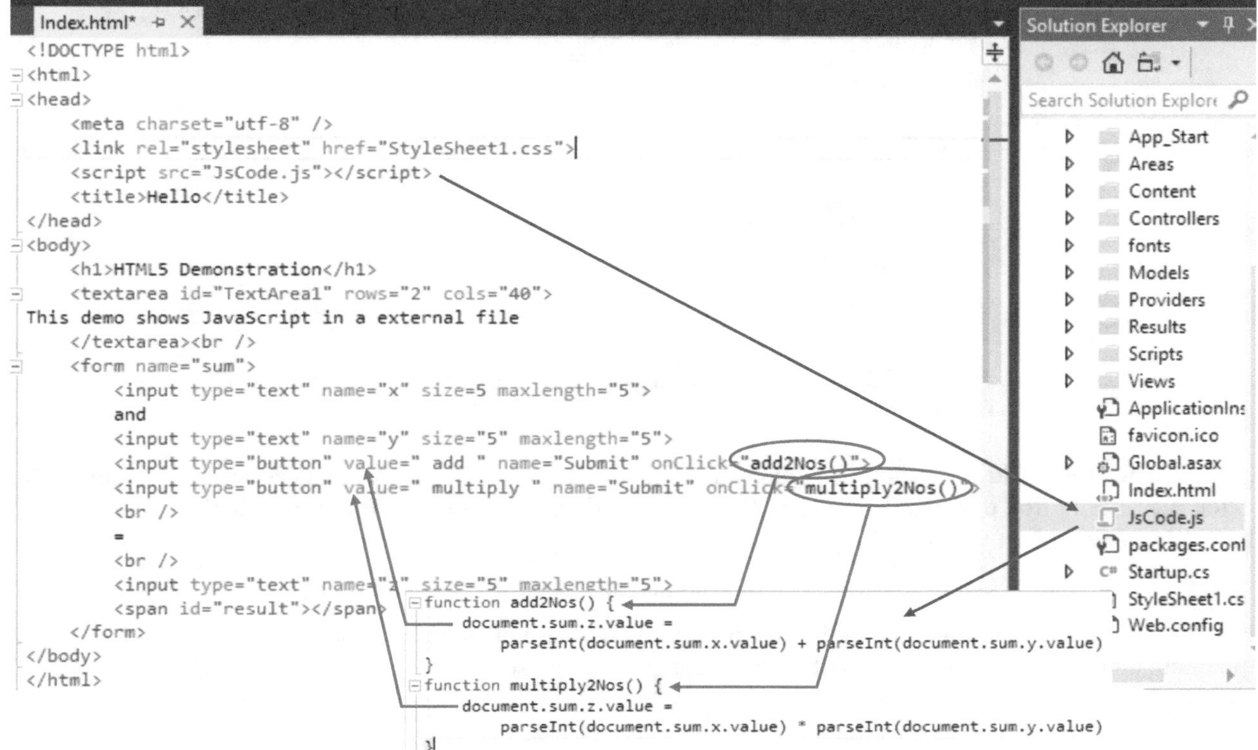

Figure 7.25. JavaScript function calls are connected to the JavaScript functions in the JsCode.js file

Now, we test the html file with the JavaScript code. We open the html index.html with file JsCode.js in the same location (same file folder). The add and multiply buttons work fine. However, the ServiceCall button does not work. For browsing security reasons, the call will be blocked because the RESTful service is located on a remote server. As shown in Figure 7.26, the same code deployed at:

http://neptune.fulton.ad.asu.edu/WSRepository/html5/add2/

works fine without being blocked, because the html application and the RESTful service are on the same server.

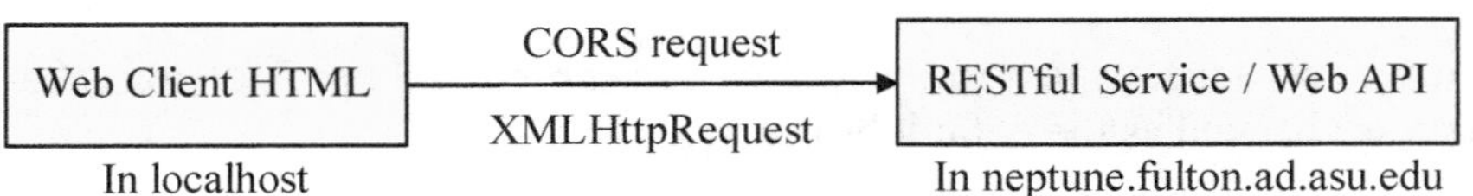

Figure 7.26. Cross-Origin Resource Sharing (CORS) through service calls

In order to allow the service calls to cross the origin, W3C defined Cross-Origin Resource Sharing (CORS) standard, which allows a server to relax the same-origin policy (https://www.w3.org/TR/cors/). The following document elaborates the deployment process that implements the CORS standard:

https://docs.microsoft.com/en-us/aspnet/web-api/overview/security/enabling-cross-origin-requests-in-web-api

For the purpose of testing RESTful service calls in your web browser, you can configure your Visual Studio and Browser in the following steps:

Step 1: Right-click the index.html file in your project stack and choose Browse With …. The Window in Figure 7.27 will open. It shows the of list browsers added into Visual Studio.

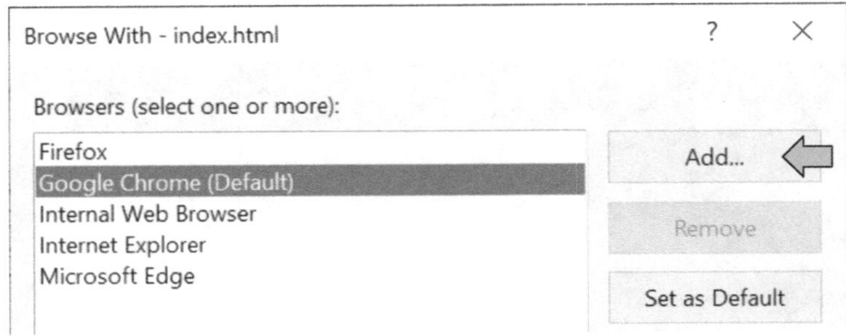

Figure 7.27. Choose Default browser for opening index.html

Step 2: Click the "Add…" button in Figure 7.27. The configuration window opens, as show in Figure 7.28. Click the "…" button to select a program. Browse to find chrome.exe in C/Program Files/Google/Chrome. In the Arguments part, you can copy and paste the following string into the textbox:

--user-data-dir="C:/Chrome dev session" --disable-web-security

Finally, you choose a Friendly name for this modified browser with security disabled arguments. We choose the name Chrome NS. This name will then appear in the browser list.

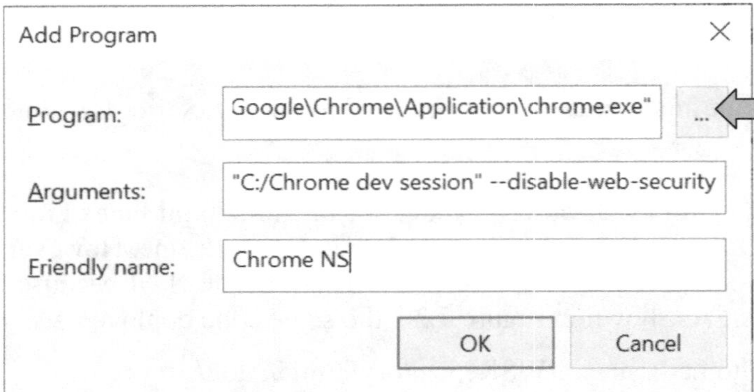

Figure 7.28. Add program and arguments for executing the index.html file

Step 3: Click the drop-down arrow next to IIS Express, as show in Figure 7.29, to make sure that the new Chrome NS browser is checked as the default browser.

After these steps of configuration, the Chrome NS browser will allow the cross-origin resource sharing and you should be able to test your program with RESTful service calls.

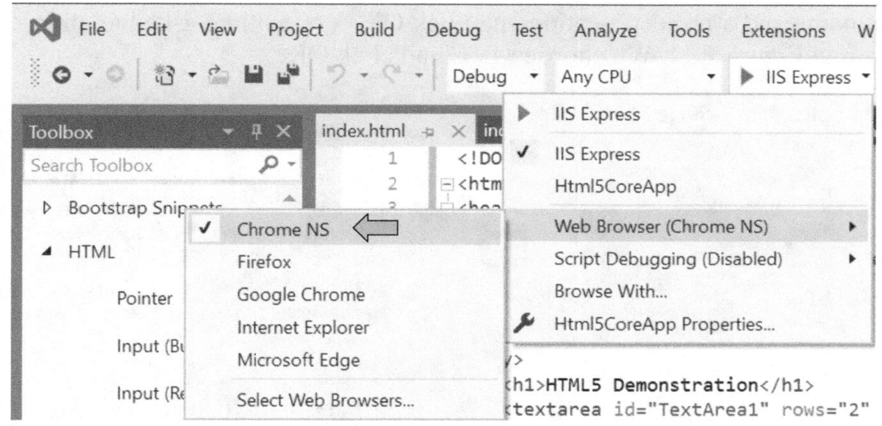

Figure 7.29. Configure Visual Studio to allow Cross-Origin Resource Sharing

7.4.3 MVC Architecture on ASP .Net Core Framework

MVC stands for Model-View-Controller. It is an architecture pattern originally formulated in the late 1970s by Trygve Reenskaug at Xerox PARC, as part of the Smalltalk. In a system designed following MVC, the components are divided into three groups: Model: contains the components representing application logic and data; View: Output to the users, including rendering the output data; and Controller: Input from the user and handlers of the inputs. MVC-based architecture is supported in J2EE and Visual Studio.

MVC architecture was initially introduced in ASP .Net Framework, defined MVC 1, as shown in the left side of Figure 7.21. MVC 2 and later versions are based on ASP .Net Core Framework. We will focus on the new MVC architecture based on ASP .Net Core Framework.

ASP .Net Core Framework offers a project template for MVC architecture style or MVC design pattern. To create an MVC project, start Visual Studio (2017), choose New → Project … from the File menu. Then, choose Web and ASP .Net Web Application (.Net Framework), as shown in Figure 7.30.

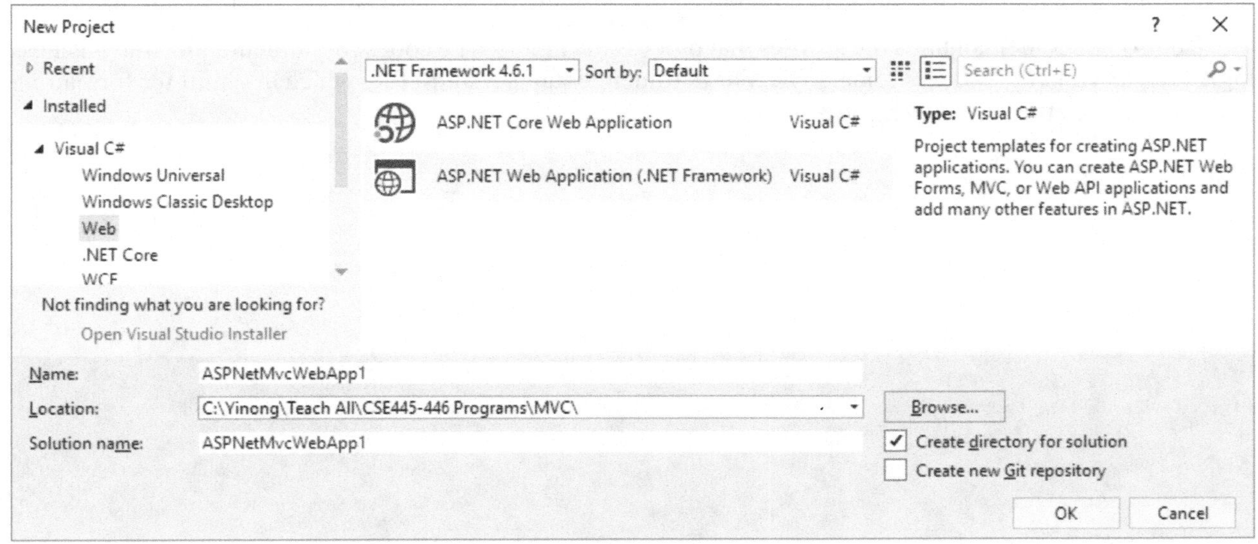

Figure 7.30. Choose Web and ASP .Net Web Application

Choose a project name and a project location and click OK. You will be asked to choose the architecture template, as shown in Figure 7.31. We choose MVC and click OK.

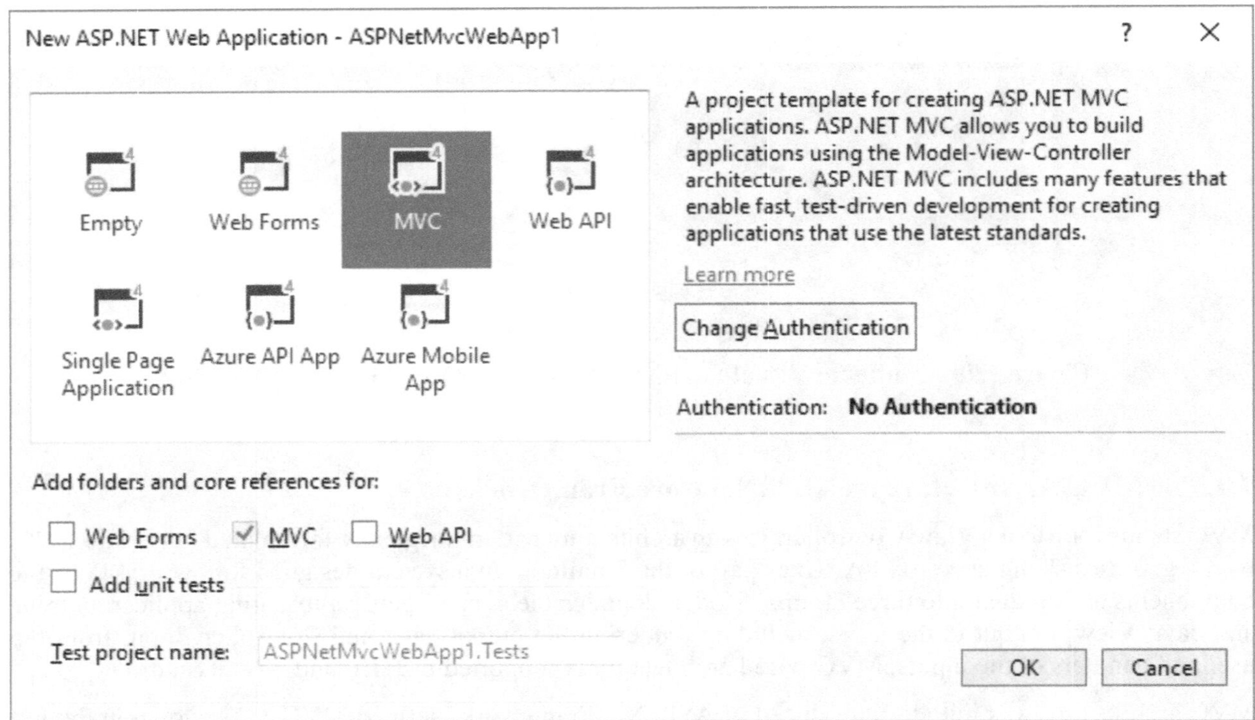

Figure 7.31. Choose MVC template

Once the MVC template is selected, the main components of the application will be organized in three directories: Models, Views, and Controllers, as shown in Figure 7.32. The figure shows the code and file organization generated by the selected template. We can right click a folder to add new files into the folder.

The Controllers folder contains the .cs files that process the inputs. The codes for implementing the business logic are placed in the Models folder. The Views folder contains .cshtml file, which are html for formatting plus C# code for the server-side processing.

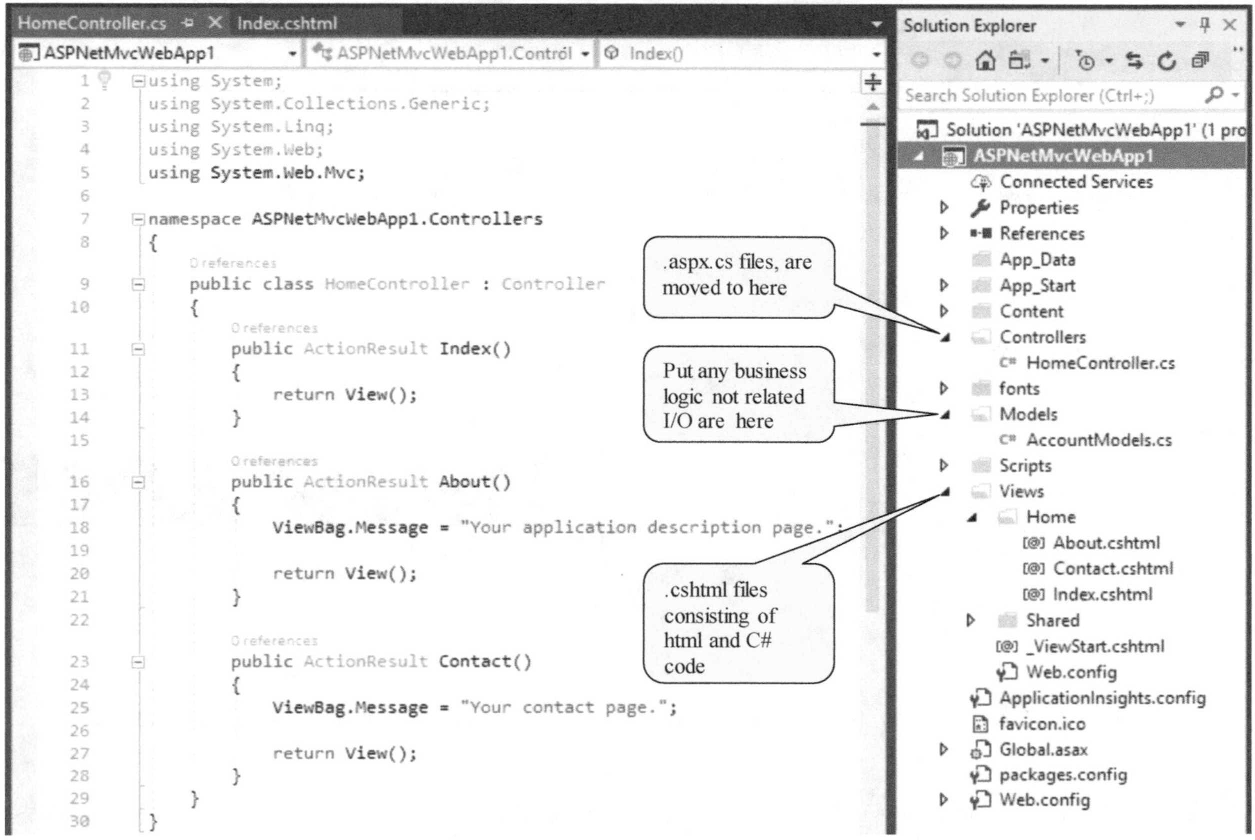

Figure 7.32. ASP .Net MVC Project created

The C# code in the main window of Figure 7.32 is from the HomeController.cs. It has three methods, corresponding to the three pages in Views's Home directory. Each method supports a .cshtml page in the Views folder.

The files in the Views folder defines the html-formatted pages, with C# code to make the page dynamic. For example, the following code is from the About.cshtml file.

```
@{
    ViewBag.Title = "About";
}
<h2>@ViewBag.Title.</h2>
<h3>@ViewBag.Message</h3>

<p>Use this area to provide additional information.</p>
```

The first three lines of code is the C# code that assign the View.Bag variable to string "About". The rest of the code is html code representing the format. However, the text in the elements <h2> and <h3> are not simple texts. The texts are defined by variables prefixed with an @.

Figure 7.33 illustrates the connection between the pages in the Views and the C# files in the Controllers, and what is finally displayed in the Web browser.

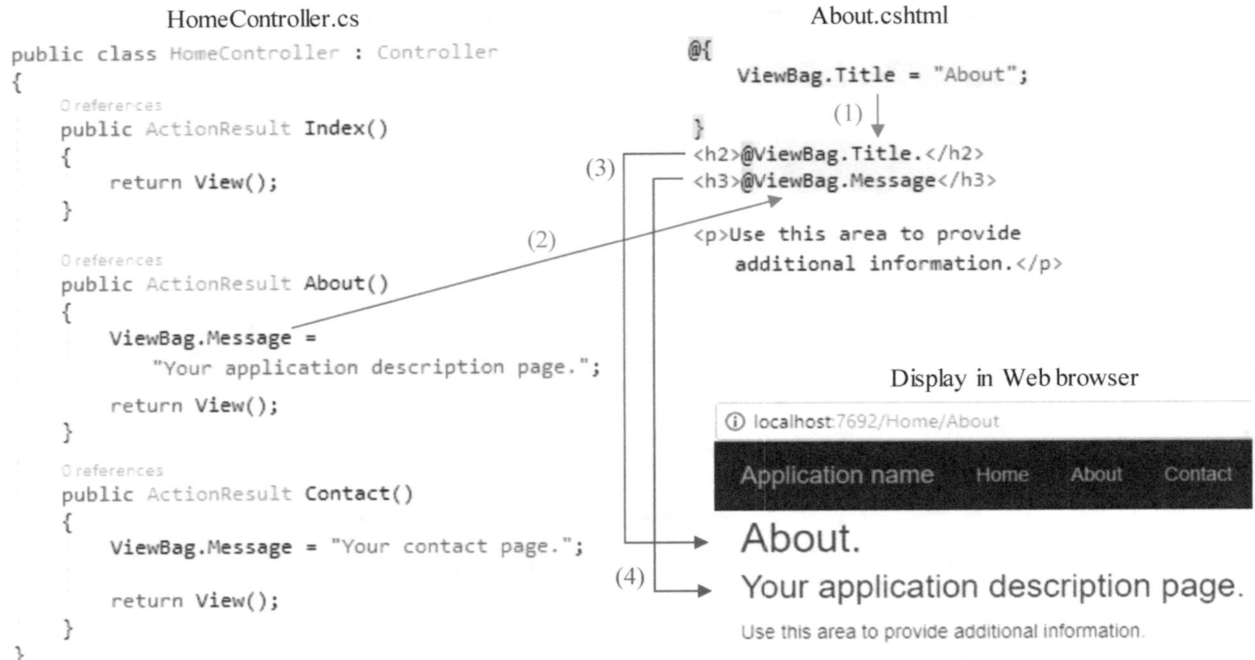

Figure 7.33. Connection between the pages in the Views and the C# files in the Controllers

There are different version of MVC architecture in .Net Framework. Some versions allow using .aspx files as the Views components. Figure 7.34 shows the project created using MVC 3 in Visual Studio 2015, where ,aspx files are used as the Views components for generating the browser page. It also allows mixing the traditional ASP .Net architecture with the .cs files placed behind the .aspx page.

Generally speaking, MVC architecture organizes the modules in three groups with different types: Views, Controllers, and Models.

Views directory contains the components that display the application's graphical user interface (GUI) or the presentation layer of the application. The components in this directory mainly communicate with the components in the Controls directory. However, they can directly communicate with the components in the Models directory if needed.

Controllers directory contains the components that handle user interaction, work with the model, and ultimately select a view to render that displays in GUI. In an MVC application, the view only displays information; the controller handles and responds to user input and interaction.

Models directory contains objects that that implement the part of the application logic related to the application's data domain. Often, model objects retrieve and store model state in date sets, files, and databases. It is different from the App_Data directory in ASP .Net Forms application, in which the actual data are stored. The model objects here provide a layer of middleware that separate the application from physical data storage.

Among other components, the three sets of components, Models, Views, and Controllers, form a tiered architecture, as shown in Figure 7.35. The other computing components can include DLL files, web services, user controls, and so on.

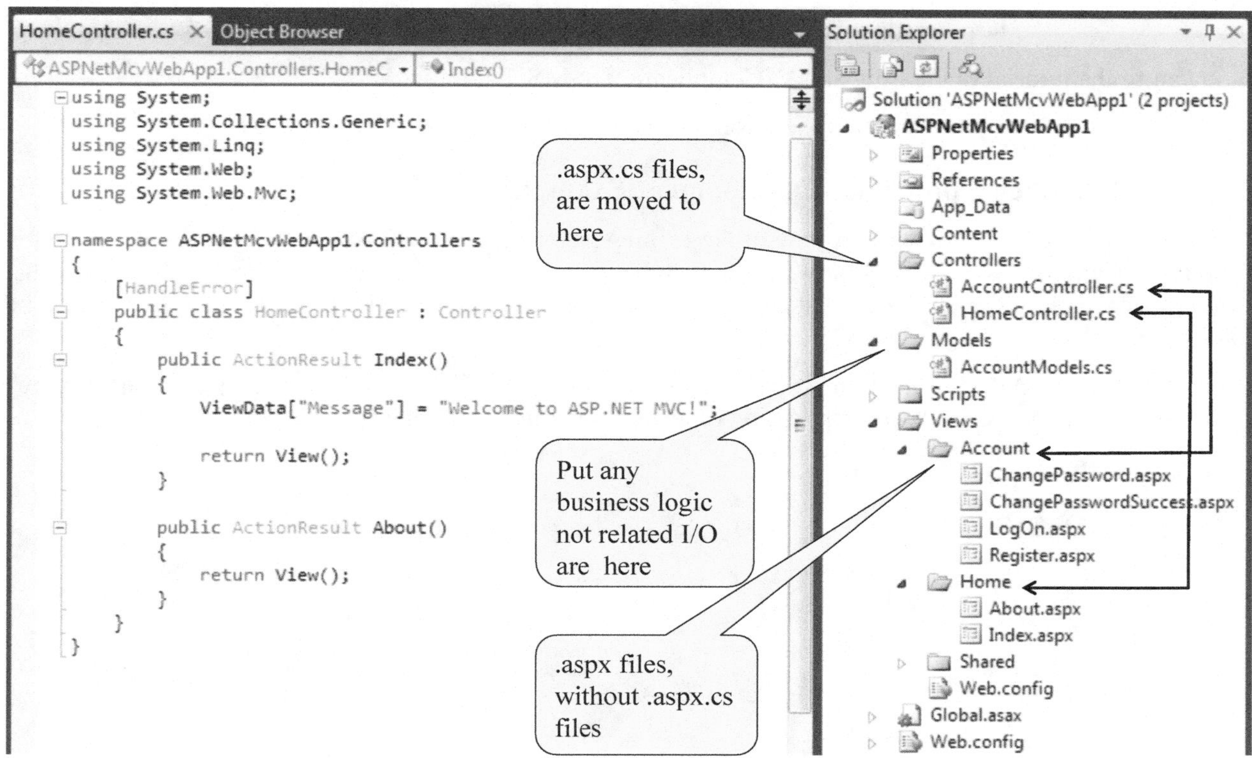

Figure 7.34. ASP .Net MVC Project using .aspx files as Views components

The main benefit of this architecture is the loosely coupled feature among the components in Views, Models, and Controllers. It allows team members to develop different parts of the application with reduced interaction, and the template can generate unit tests by automatically adding mock objects, which are simulated objects that mimic the behavior of other objects in controlled ways in the application. The restricted use of the view state, page postback, and related server controls, such as GridView and DataList, allows the framework to render the XHTML page less dependent on the server features.

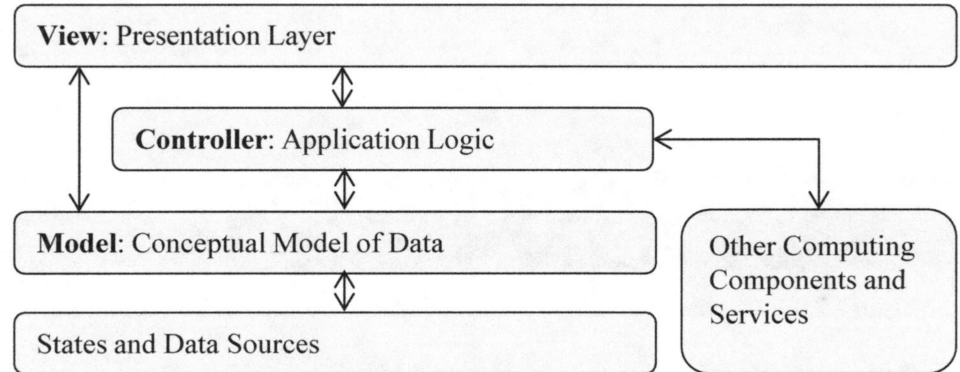

Figure 7.35. The architecture of ASP .Net MVC application

The MVC applications are friendlier with URI-based access used on RESTful style applications and the feed data formats. More detail can be found in MSDN library at:

http://msdn.microsoft.com/en-us/library/dd381412(VS.98).aspx.

You can find a tutorial of creating an MVC application in MSDN library at:

http://msdn.microsoft.com/en-us/library/dd410597(v=VS.98).aspx

7.4.4 MVC Web Application Development Example

In this section, we will show an example of developing an MVC application step by step. We will develop a Summer Camp website, which allows students to sign up for attending the camp, storing the student list in a list structure, and viewing the list of students who have signed up. The project development will be explained in the following steps.

First, we create an MVC project on ASP .Net Core. In Visual Studio, create a new project. Search "core" and choose ASP .Net Core Web Application type, as shown in Figure 7.36.

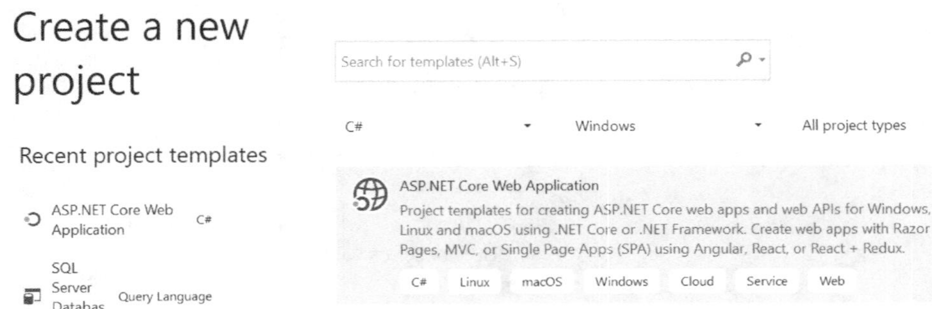

Figure 7.36. Starting an ASP .Net MVC Web Application

Name the project SummerCamp and then choose application template: Web Application (Model-View-Controller), as shown in the left part of Figure 7.37. The project stack is then generated, as shown in the right part of Figure 7.37.

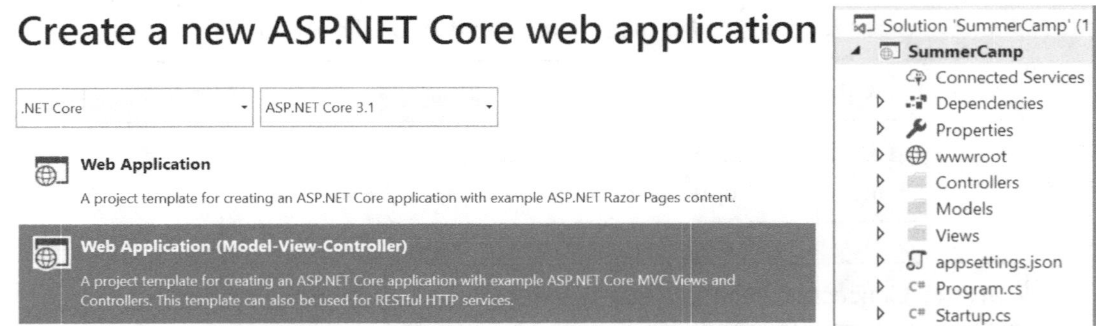

Figure 7.37. Choose Web Application (Model-View-Controller) template

Three folders are created: Controllers, Models, and Views in the project stack, which will contain the project files in this project. You can right click each of these folders to add controller .cs file, model .cs file, and view .cshtml page into these folders, respectively. The template also generates Program.cs and Startup.cs program files. The entry point of the project is the Program.c, which contains the Main() method. The Main() method will be called the BuildWebHost() in the Start.cs program, as shown in Figure 7.38.

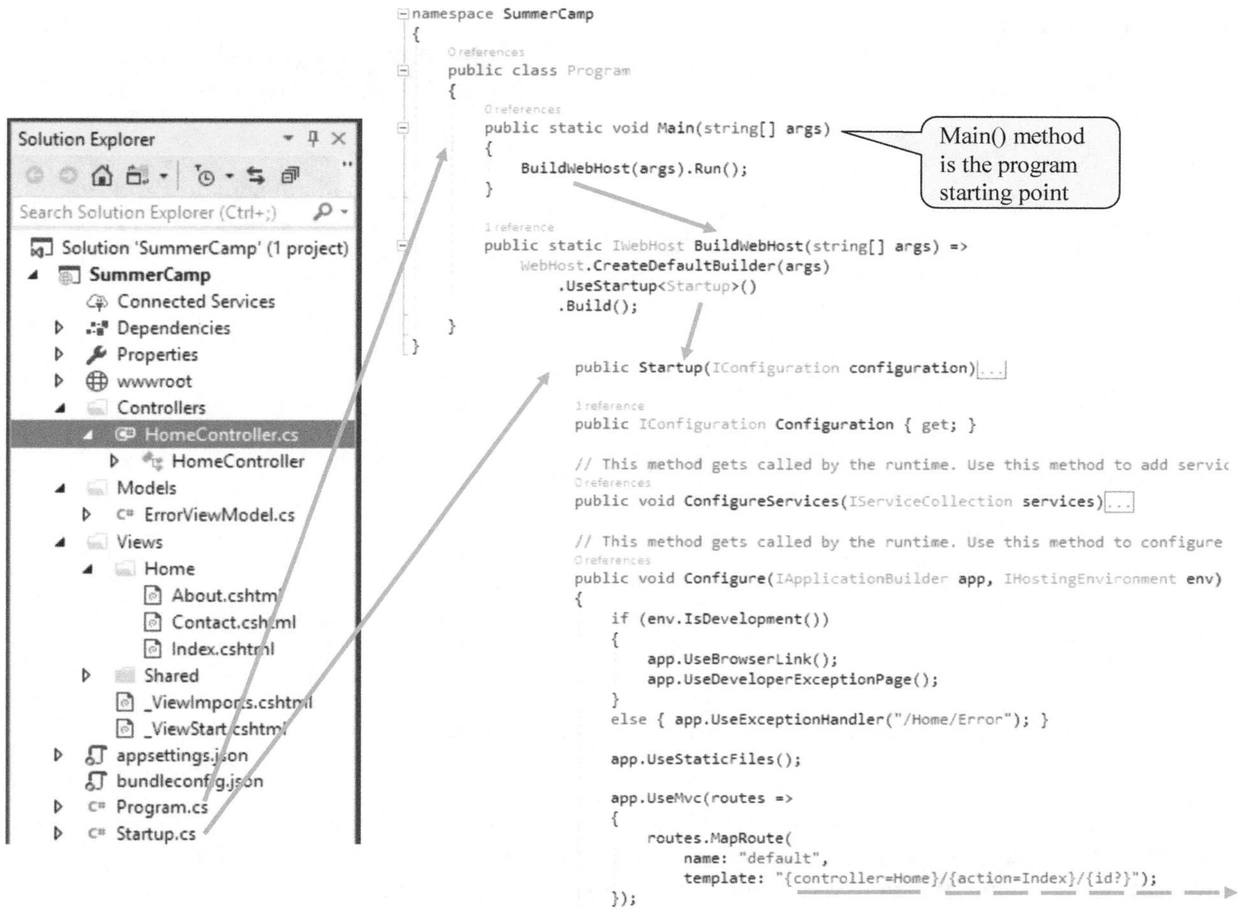

Figure 7.38. Starting point of the programs generated by the template

Then, the program will jump to Controllers → HomeController, which will generate output in the Views → Home, Views → About, and Views → Contact, as shown in Figure 7.39.

```
namespace SummerCamp.Controllers
{
    0 references
    public class HomeController : Controller
    {
        0 references
        public IActionResult Index()
        {
            return View();
        }

        0 references
        public IActionResult About()
        {
            ViewData["Message"] = "Your application description page.";
            return View();
        }

        0 references
        public IActionResult Contact()
        {
            ViewData["Message"] = "Your contact page.";
            return View();
        }

        0 references
        public IActionResult Error()
        {
            return View(new ErrorViewModel { RequestId = Activity.Current?.Id ?? HttpContext.Trace
        }
    }
}
```

localhost:6547/Home/About

SummerCamp Home About Contact

About

Your application description page.

Use this area to provide additional information.

© 2018 - SummerCamp

Figure 7.39. Controllers generated by the template

The correlations between the controller and view is shown in Figure 7.40. In the HomeController, a dictionary data structure is used in the About() method to map the "Message" to the data to be displayed in view page About.cshtml, which in turn displays the message in the web browser.

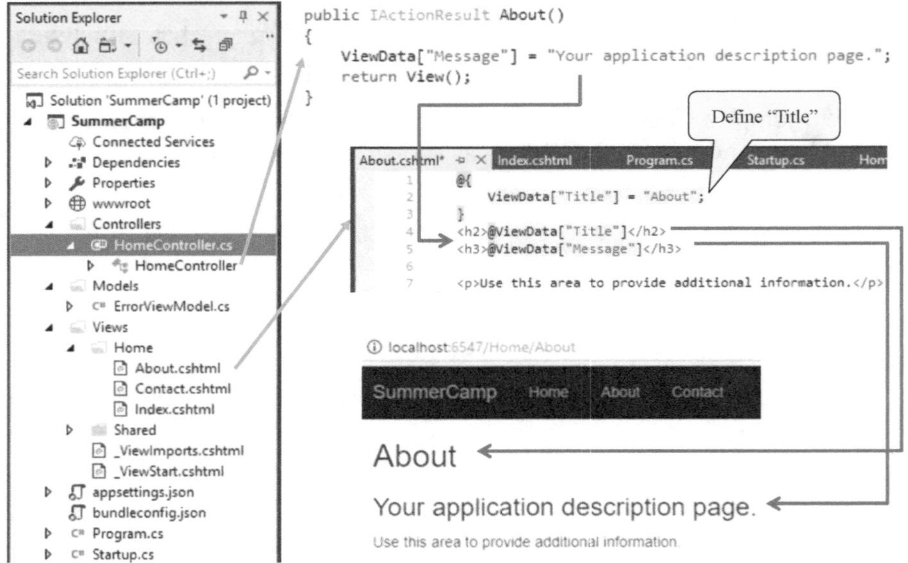

Figure 7.40. Correlation between controller and view

The code and structures explained above are generated by the template. Now, we will modify and extend the existing files to implement what we want to implement. First, we replace the index.cshtml using the following code.

```
@{Layout = null;}
<!DOCTYPE html>
<html>
<head>
    <meta name="viewport" content="width=device-width" />
    <title>Semester</title>
    <link rel="stylesheet" href="/lib/bootstrap/dist/css/bootstrap.css" />
</head>
<body>
    <div class="text-center">
        <h3>Hello high school students, today is @ViewBag.Date</h3>
        <h3>It is @ViewBag.Semester!</h3>
        <h3>We are going to offer a summer robotics camp</h3>
        <h4>You can sign up the camp now:</h4>
        <a class="btn btn-primary" asp-action="SignupForm"><b>Sign Up Now</b></a>
        <a class="btn btn-primary" asp-action="RegistrationList">
             <b>See Student List</b></a>
    </div>
</body>
</html>
```

The code will generate the GUI as shown in Figure 7.41.

Hello high school students

Today is 04/06, 2020. It is in beautiful Spring!

We are going to offer a summer robotics camp

You can sign up the camp now:

Sign Up Now   See Student List

Figure 7.41. GUI generated by index.cshtml

Next, we modify the HomeController.cs using the following code.

```
namespace SummerCamp.Controllers {
    public class HomeController : Controller {
        public ViewResult Index() {
           ViewBag.Date = DateTime.UtcNow.ToString("MM/dd, yyyy");
           int m = DateTime.Now.Month;
            if (m < 6)
                ViewBag.Semester = "Spring";
            else if (m < 8)
                ViewBag.Semester = "Summer";
            else if (m >= 8)
                ViewBag.Semester = "Fall";
            return View("Index");
        }        [HttpGet]
        public ViewResult SignupForm() {
            return View();
        }
        [HttpPost]
        public ViewResult SignupForm(StudentSignup student) {
            if (ModelState.IsValid) {
                StudentList.AddResponse(student);
```

```
                return View("Confirmation", student);
            }
            Else { return View(); }
        }
        public ViewResult RegistrationList() {
            return View(StudentList.Responses.Where(r => r.Signup == true));
        }
    }
}
```

You can add SignupForm.cshtml into Views folder and a SignupForm.cs in Models folder to complete the project.

7.5 Discussions

Windows Communication Foundation supports SOAP-based services, RESTful services, and workflow services. SOAP-based services, including both ASP .Net services and WCF services, are supported by many vendors and many platforms. They have been widely used in many desktop applications and web applications. WCF further supports many advanced features of services, including different communication models between services and applications, different bindings of protocol stacks, and different behavior models.

RESTful services are the new type of services focusing on data and resource representations. RESTful services still need to use methods to generate the resource or the set of resources to be delivered to the user or clients. However, the operations are more encapsulated and are more transparent to the clients. RESTful services are closely related to the composition techniques such as ontology, Semantic Web, and Cloud computing. Microservices are a new form of RESTful services that offer a platform to compose larger services from a set of basic services.

There are opinions considering that SOAP services will be obsolete and will be completely replaced by RESTful services. We believe that SOAP and RESTful services will coexist because they have different strengths and weaknesses. SOAP services are more suitable in the computation-oriented tasks, such as solving equations and finding the shortest path in a network or graph, whereas the RESTful services will be more suitable for the resource-oriented tasks, such as finding a subset of items from a large set of items. The SOAP service development is more closed to the object-oriented programming whereas RESTful service development requires more mindset changes in programming style.

Name: ____________________

Date: ____________________

7.6 Exercises and Projects

1. Multiple choice questions. Choose one answer in each question only. Choose the best answer if multiple answers are acceptable.

1.1 What class in the namespace System.ServiceModel.Description is responsible for creating the platform-independent interface for WSDL client to access the service?

(A) ServiceMetadataBehavior (B) ServiceHost

(C) Uri (D) WsHttpBinding

1.2 What class or tool is used for generating the proxy for WCF service using self-hosting?

(A) WCF class called GenerateProxy.

(B) A class in the Console Application template.

(C) Web Administrative Tool in ASP .Net.

(D) An independent tool called Service Model Metadata Utility Tool.

1.3 Which line of code actually adds the "Contract" to the WCF endpoint?

(A) Uri baseAddress = new Uri("http://localhost:8000/Service");

(B) ServiceHost selfHost = new ServiceHost(typeof(myService), baseAddress);

(C) selfHost.AddServiceEndpoint(typeof(myInterface), new WSHttpBinding(), "myService");

(D) selfHost.Description.Behaviors.Add(smb);

1.4 What communication models are supported in WCF?

(A) Duplex (B) One-way

(C) Request-Reply (D) All of the above

1.5 What communication model requires a callback address?

(A) Duplex (B) One-way

(C) Request-Reply (D) All of the above

1.6 What value of the InstanceContextMode property allows a session to repeatedly access the same service?

(A) PerCall (B) PerSession (C) Single (D) Reentrant

1.7 What value of the ConcurrencyMode property allows multithreading computing?

(A) PerCall (B) Reentrant (C) Single (D) Multiple

1.8 What is the binding protocol typically used in RESTful services?

(A) SOAP (B) TCP/IP (C) MSMQ (D) HTTP

1.9 A URI used in RESTful services

(A) always corresponds to a single data item.

(B) can correspond to a single item or a set of data items.

(C) always corresponds to a WebMethod.

(D) replaces SOAP in traditional web services.

1.10 The resource tree is always a

(A) rooted tree. (B) binary tree.

(C) B+ tree. (D) red-black tree.

1.11 What is not a principle of the REST concept?

(A) Communication is stateless.

(B) Communication is based on HTML.

(C) It follows object-oriented computing paradigm.

(D) Each resource is given a unique identifier, called URI.

1.12 What is the main difference between a RESTful service and SOAP service?

(A) RESTful services focus on performing (verb) a task for the client.

(B) RESTful services focus on the result (noun) of performing (verb) a task.

(C) RESTful services are more object-oriented.

(D) RESTful services are used for heavier duty computing.

1.13 What is the key idea of RESTful services?

(A) Solve computational intensive problems.

(B) Use SOAP for data exchanges.

(C) Focus on data and resources to be exposed.

(D) Focus on WebMethods to be exposed.

1.14 How are parameters and parameter values passed from the client to a RESTful service?

(A) Encoded in XML (B) Encoded in SOAP

(C) Encoded in WSDL (D) Encoded in URI

1.15 Given the argument definition of a RESTful operation: [WebGet(UriTemplate = "/append2/{x}/{y}"], what is the correct way of passing the parameter to the operation in a URI?

(A) /append2?x=7&x=12 (B) /append2/7/12

(C) /append2 (x=5, y=12) (D) /append2 (5, 12)

1.16 In object-oriented computing, method names can be overloaded, as long as the methods have different return types or have different parameters. Does this rule apply to .Net RESTful services?

(A) Yes (B) No

1.17 The image verifier discussed in this book is

(A) a stateless service, as RESTful services are always stateless.

(B) a stateless service, as there is no need of saving state in the service.

(C) a stateful service that correlates multiple accesses from the same client.

(D) a stateful service, as the dynamic image is cached for performance reasons.

1.18 Which graphic library is the easiest one to use in HTML5 programming?

(A) Canvas (B) GDI+ (C) SVG (D) WebGL

1.19 What programming language is typically used in HTML5 programming?

(A) C# (B) Java (C) JavaScript (D) Python

1.20 In MVC architecture, what component is responsible for interfacing with the database?

(A) Model (B) View (C) Controller (D) None of them

1.21 In MVC architecture, where should the input event handlers be placed?

(A) In Model (B) In View (C) In Controller (D) None of them

1.22 In MVC architecture, where should the GUI files be placed?

(A) In Model (B) In View (C) In Controller (D) None of them

2. How is an endpoint defined in WCF? What does ABC stand for?

3. What hosting mechanisms can be used to host WCF services?

4. What are purposes of self-hosting of WCF services?

5. What kind of clients can be used to consume a SOAP-based WCF service?

6. Compare and contrast ASP .Net and WCF services.

7. Compare and contrast SOAP-based services and RESTful services. Explain under what circumstances each kind of service is best suited for.

8. What are the roles of URI in RESTful service development?

9. What kinds of HTTP verbs exist and what are their roles in RESTful service development?

10. Why do RESTful services support not only XML format but also other formats such as RSS, Atom, JSON, and XHML?

11. Use WCF RESTful service development environment to implement the resource tree given in Figure 7.12.

12. What are microservices? Compare and contrast RESTful services and microservices.

Project 1

In this project, you will implement number guessing services and number guessing games using different techniques. You are given the class definition below as the basic functions required in the number guessing services.

```
public class NumberGuess {
   public int SecretNumber(int lower, int upper) {
         DateTime currentDate = DateTime.Now;
         int seed = (int)currentDate.Ticks;
         Random random = new Random(seed);
         int sNumber = random.Next(lower, upper);
         return sNumber;
   }
    public string checkNumber(int userNum, int SecretNum) {
             if (userNum == SecretNum)
                 return "correct";
             else
                 if (userNum > SecretNum)
                     return "too big";
                 else return "too small";
    }
}
```

1. Based on the given class, use a WCF Service template to create a WCF service (.svc) hosted on .Net Development server or IIS Express server. You may want to review text section 3.2 before completing this part of the assignment.

2. Create an ASP .Net website client to consume the WCF .svc service in question 1. This client must create a web-based number guessing game. You can right-click the solution and choose add a new "ASP .Net website." The website must contain at least the following items, as shown in the figure below:

   WELCOME TO NUMBER GUESSING GAME

   Lower Limit Upper Limit Generate a Secret Number

   Make a Guess Play Attempts - The number is

   - The first two textboxes are used for a player to enter the lower and the upper limits (integers) of the random number to be generated.
   - The code behind the button "Generate a Secret Number" will generate a secret number and save it as a state; for example, in a session state variable.
   - The last textbox allows the player to enter an integer to make a guess of the secret number.
   - A label that displays how many attempts have been made after a secret number is generated.
   - A label that displays if the given number is too small, too big, or a correct guess.

3. Based on the given class, create a self-hosting service, including the service and the hosting program.

4. Write a console application to consume the self-hosting service. This client must create a number guessing game in the console application.

5. Convert the WCF (svc.) service in question 3 into a RESTful service.

6. Repeat question 4, but consuming the RESTful service in question 5, instead of the WCF SOAP service.

7. Deploy the services and applications, except the self-hosting service, in the project into a web server. You need to do the deployment in two steps. First, you deploy the services. After you have obtained the service URL, you modify the clients to consume the services deployed in the server, instead of consuming the service on localhost. Then, you deploy the clients.

Project 2

Implement the same requirements and same services given in Project 1, but you must use HTML5 or MVC architecture to implement the project.

Chapter 8
Enterprise Software Development and Integration

In this chapter, we will start to discuss the architecture-driven and workflow-based applications. We will focus on building enterprise-level large applications using web services and components available on the Internet using different composition languages and methods. We start with Workflow Foundation and then BPEL (Business Process Execution Language), while briefly introducing other enterprise software composition languages. Both Workflow Foundation and BPEL applications are designed to work with the WCF services.

Visual composition at high level simplifies the development process. To extend these topics, we will discuss VIPLE (Visual IoT/Robotics Programming Language Environment) in full detail in Chapter 9, databases in Chapter 10, and big data processing and Cloud computing techniques in Chapter 11. Artificial intelligence and ontology integration in Chapter 12.

8.1 Overview of Composition Languages

Service-oriented computing is a paradigm that consists of concepts, methods, and the enabling technologies that implement the concepts and methods. Figure 8.1 shows the enabling technologies and how they are organized in a cubic representation.

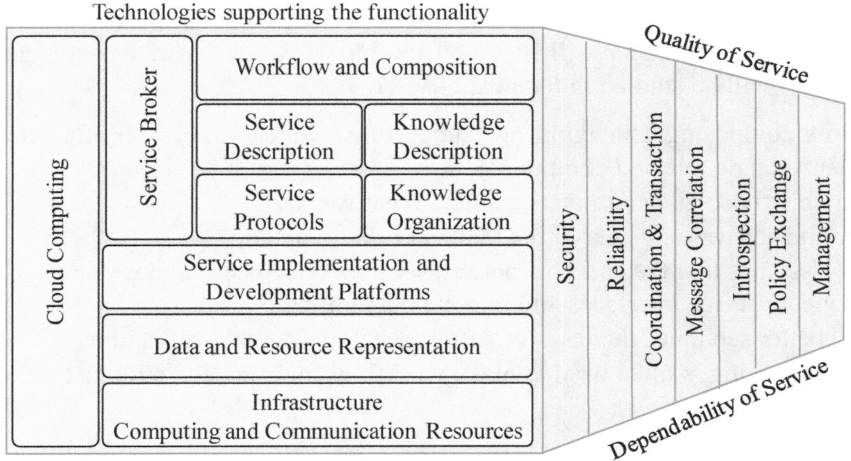

Figure 8.1. Organization of the SOC-enabling technologies

The front side shows the technologies that implement the functionality, while the technologies assuring the dependability attributes or quality of services are behind each and every technology for the functionality. We use the term "quality of service" to refer to the quality-assuring technologies from the user's point of view, while using "dependability attributes" to refer to the same technologies from the designer's point of view. Figure 8.2 shows the instances of the enabling technologies currently widely used in SOC software development.

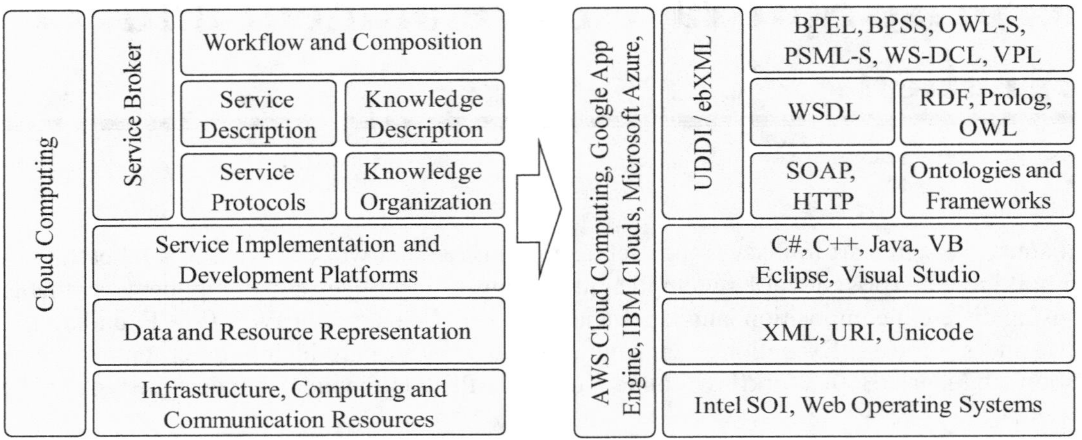

Figure 8.2. Instances of the SOC-enabling technologies supporting the functionality

Chapters 3 and 5 discussed how we can use C# and .Net framework to build an application based on remote web services. C# is a powerful programming language. Proficient programming background is needed to use such a language and the development framework. One of the purposes of SOC is to separate application building from programming, so that application builders do not have to be proficient programmers, while programmers do not have to be an expert in the domain of the business. Many workflow and composition languages have been proposed to fulfil this purpose, as shown in Figure 8.3.

Microsoft VPL (Visual Programming Language), ASU VIPLE (Visual IoT/Robotics Programming Language Environment), and Intel IoT SOL (Service Orchestration Layer) are device-related and can be used to program physical devices such as robots. The other languages shown are Figure 8.3 are business composition languages. This chapter will focus on the business composition languages. Device-related composition languages will be studied in the next chapter.

Workflow is used for composing, managing, and supporting business process. It offers a new model for the division of labor between people and computer:

- People do only those that computers cannot: What we want.
- Computer and software do everything that can be automated.
- Workflow assumes that the components and services have been predeveloped and the focus is on the component/service interfaces and interconnection.
- Workflow better separates the tasks of software architects and programmers.
- Visual programming is often used to make workflow concepts and structure easier for humans to build and to understand.

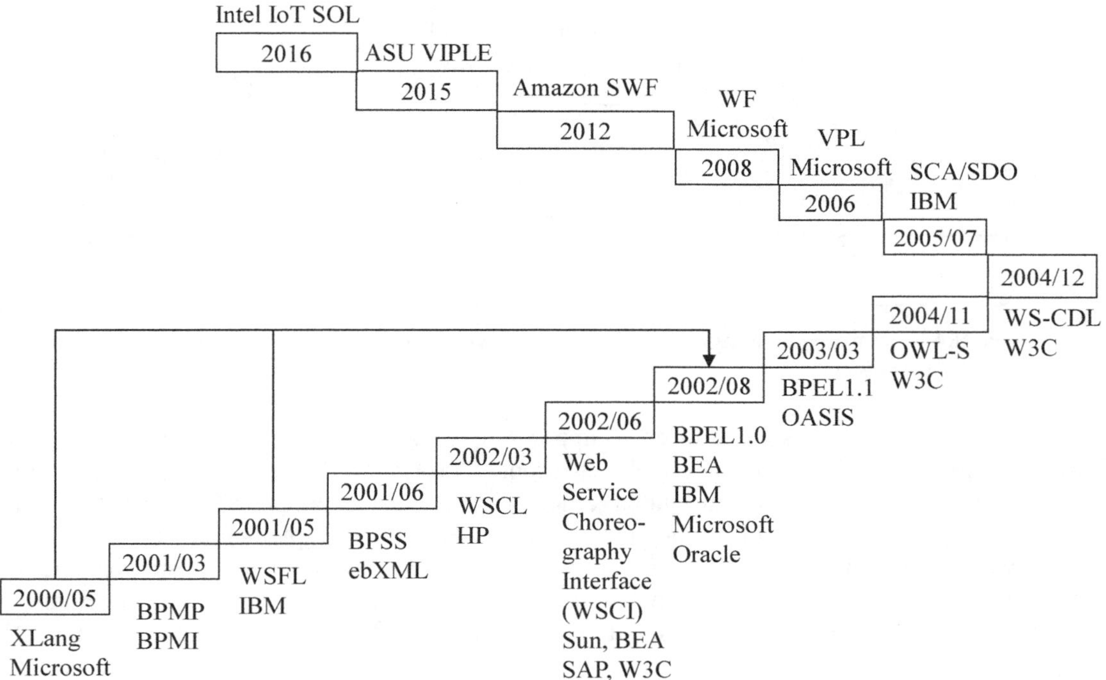

Figure 8.3. Workflow composition languages and tools evolution

Service-Oriented Architecture makes workflow easier. The workflow and composition languages can be categorized into two major groups by their coordination styles: orchestration and choreography.

- Orchestration: A central process, which can be a service itself, takes control over the involved services and coordinates the execution of different operations. In this style, the involved services communicate with the central process only within the application. It is useful for private business process using independent services
- Choreography: There is no central coordinator. Each service involved can communicate with multiple partners within an application. It is useful for public business process involving coordinated design of distributed services.

Figure 8.4 shows an example that illustrates the difference between orchestration and choreography styles. Assume a store needs to send an object to a bank; however, the object needs to be converted into a format so that the bank can read it. Thus, the store uses a format converter service.

Orchestration: The store is considered the central process; the store sends object to the format converter service, which converts the format. Then, the service must send the converted data back to the store. Then the store sends the data directly to the bank. This style is good if the store does not want the converter to know where the data should go.

Choreography: The store sends the object, with the bank's address, to the converter and tells the converter to forward the converted data to the bank. Obviously, this is a more efficient way to get the data to the bank. This style is good if the converter is a trusted service by the store.

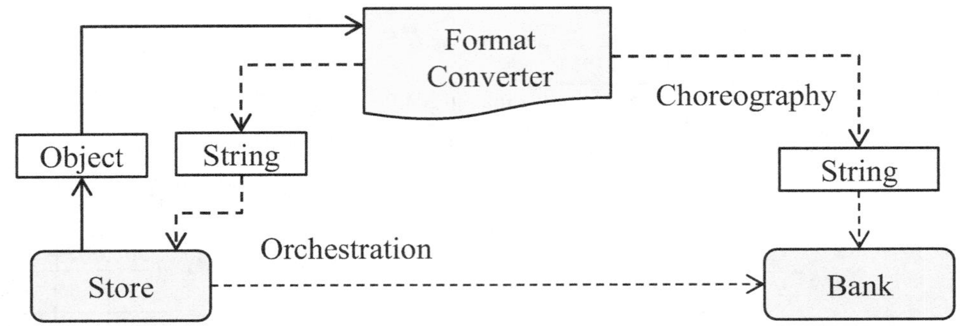

Figure 8.4. Example showing the difference between orchestration and choreography

Imperative, object-oriented, and service-oriented approaches to computing represent different approaches of software development. One can use an object-oriented programming language to write imperative programs. However, it is better to use a language designed to support the specific computing approach. Likewise, the coordination styles in application composition can be implemented in any composition language. However, language designers can implement specific mechanisms to support the specific coordination styles, and thus it is better to choose the language that is designed for the coordination style. Table 8.1 lists the composition languages that are specifically designed to support orchestration or choreography.

Table 8.1. Composition methods in orchestration and choreography

Language	Coordination	Other Features
BPEL 2002	Orchestration	Based on SOAP, WSDL, UDDI directory, widely used by large corps.
BPSS 2001	Choreography	Business Process Specification Schema: based on SOAP, ebXML repository, CPP/CPA collaboration, for small biz.
BPMN 2001	Orchestration	BP Modeling Notation: a superset of BPEL, support advanced semantics and complex structures, developed by BPMI (BP Modeling Initiative) which merged with OMG in 2005.
WSCI 2002	Choreography	WS Choreography Interface: complementary to BPEL, submitted to W3C, but not widely used.
WS-CDL 2004	Choreography	Complementary to BPEL, W3C own proposal.

8.2 Workflow Foundation

Workflow is a new solution to an old problem: integrating, managing, and supporting business process. Workflow offers a new model for the division of labor between people and computer: people do only those that computers cannot: what we want, while computers do everything they can.

Workflow better matches the business logic that customers require, and thus the customers can better understand the solution offered by the software engineers. Furthermore, workflow better separates the tasks of software architects and programmers. Service-Oriented Architecture makes workflow easier.

WF (Workflow Foundation) is a framework that supports workflow-based software development and is a part of WinFx, Microsoft's programming environment in Visual Studio. WinFx includes three components: WCF (Windows Communications Foundation) for service and component development, WF for implementing application logic at workflow level, and WPF (Windows Presentation Foundation) and its web variant Silverlight for building the presentation level. WF, WPF, and Silverlight are designed to consume WCF services and components. FW is not installed in Visual Studio 2017 by default. It is an individual component that you need to add after you have installed Visual Studio. If you try to open an existing WF project, Visual Studio will automatically guide you to add WF module into your Visual Studio.

8.2.1 Architecture and Components

The key idea of WF is to add an additional layer of abstraction to make the application development process faster, easier, and better maintainable. Figure 8.5 compares the approaches with and without the WF layer.

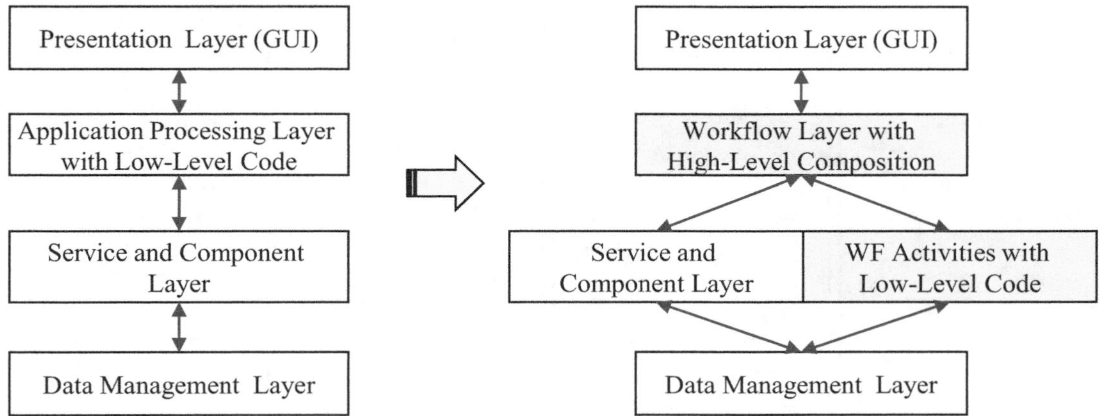

Figure 8.5. Workflow layer added to make software structure better understandable

In the ASP .Net application development, code is organized behind the ASPX pages. Using multiple ASPX pages helps to break a large application into components. However, ASPX page partition is based on the GUI requirement, instead of being based on the application logic requirement. WF adds a workflow layer to make the application logic clearer.

WF offers a number of templates and building blocks in different categories, as shown in Figure 8.6, including the blocks for control flow, flowchart, messaging, runtime, primitives, transaction, collection, error handling, migration, and general. Not all the blocks are available in the selected template and project type. For example, the Control Flow template allows you to create a reusable activity component. Activities form the core unit of behavior in WF. An activity's execution logic can be implemented in managed code (e.g., C#) or it can be implemented by using other activities. Tutorials on using each of the templates can be found at the link: http://msdn.microsoft.com/en-us/netframework/wf-screencasts.aspx#introwf4.

The Activity Designer Library template is a graphical alternative of the Activity Library. It allows you to create a reusable activity component using the WF Designer, instead of using a programming language like C#. WF Designer allows you to represent a workflow visually in order to view, create, and modify workflows graphically during design time. Furthermore, WF Designer can be used during runtime execution to show the current state of an executing workflow by using the tracking information associated with that workflow.

Using the activity design, a WF workflow can be represented by the combinations of different files, as detailed in .Net library document http://msdn.microsoft.com/en-us/library/ms441543.aspx:

- An XML file that includes the declarative metadata of the workflow; or
- An XAML (eXtensible Application Markup Language) markup file, in combination with a code – behind file that contains custom code representing the properties and behavior of the workflow; or
- A code file that includes both the declarative logic and behavior of the workflow.

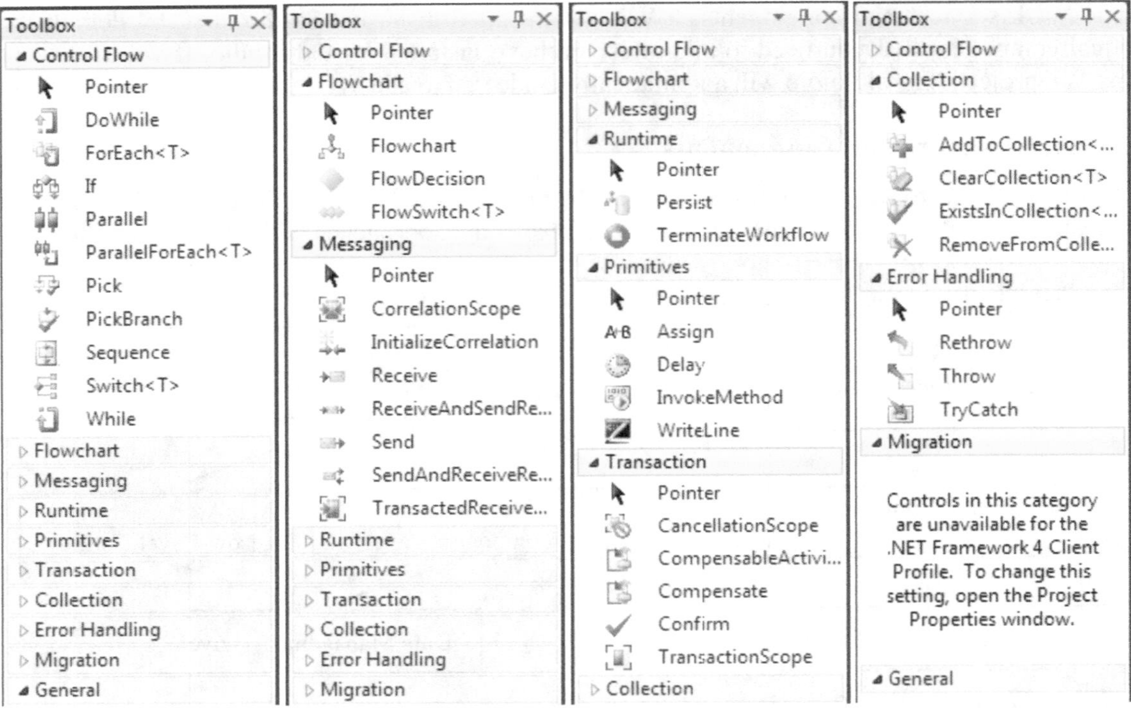

Figure 8.6. Building blocks available in WF toolbox

The markup file written in XAML is comparable with BPEL, and it has a published schema to which the file must adhere, and given a file extension of .xaml.

Because the XAML has a published schema, you can create XAML files using any text or XML editor of your choice. However, the Visual Studio offers developers a built-in graphical interface to create workflows and automatically generate the appropriate markup file.

Developers can choose to integrate or separate their declarative metadata from the business logic included in the workflow. Conceptually, the "code separation" paradigm that WF workflows employ is similar to that used in ASP.NET: declarative metadata is separate from the file that encapsulates your business logic. Thus, although the markup file contains the metadata for the activities included in the workflow, the properties and behaviors of those activities are detailed in a separate file.

For workflows authored using code separation, information is persisted in the two files: the markup file, as detailed earlier, and one of the following two types of files:

- A code-beside file, which contains the code that encapsulates the business logic. This file may be written in either Visual C# or Microsoft Visual Basic.
- A workflow rules file, which encapsulates your business logic in declarative rules, rather than code.

Each workflow created in this way is actually a unique.NET type, constructed from two partial classes, which are represented by the XAML and a code-behind or rules file. When the workflow project is compiled, these two partial classes are combined into a .NET assembly. This is the approach taken when authoring workflows for Windows SharePoint Services 3.0 using the Visual Studio 2008 Designer for Windows Workflow Foundation.

8.2.2 Creating a WF Flowchart Application

This section presents an example of developing a simple workflow application involving sequential, condition, and flowchart activities.

Let's start with creating a new project. Choose visual C# template and choose Workflow. Four types of projects will be available: Activity Designer Library, Activity Library, WCF Workflow Service Application, and Workflow Console Application. In this example, you choose Workflow Console Application and name the project WorkflowConsoleAppSemester, as shown in Figure 8.7.

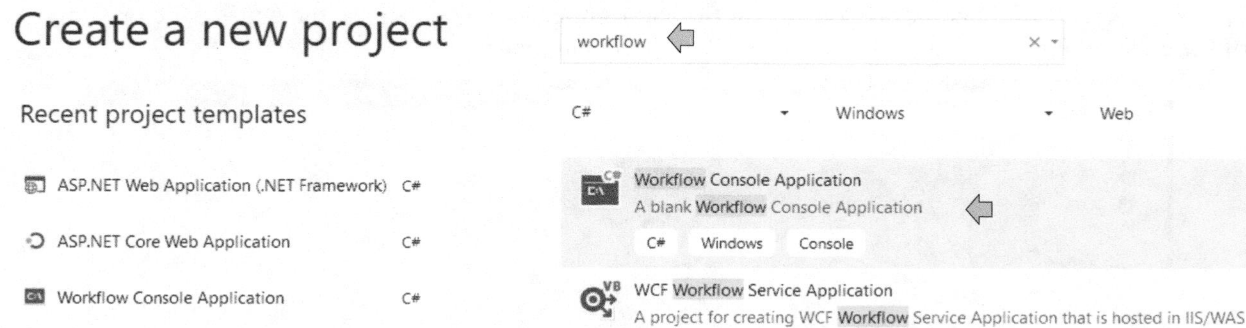

Figure 8.7. Creating a new workflow console application project

The selected template creates a stack of project files. The file Program.cs is the entry point of the project. The only action in this program is to invoke the program in the file Workflow1.xaml. The code of Program.cs is shown as follows:

```
namespace WorkflowConsoleAppSemester {
    class Program {
        static void Main(string[] args) {
            WorkflowInvoker.Invoke(new Workflow1());
}   }   }
```

In this simple example, you do not pass inputs from console to the workflow and you do not return value from the workflow. However, you can pass parameters into a workflow and receive a return value from a workflow. The default names for parameters and return value are called inputs and outputs, which are of Dictionary type. The following code shows the inclusion of the parameters when calling the workflow:

```
namespace WorkflowConsoleAppSemester {
    class Program {
        static void Main(string[] args) {
            WorkflowInvoker.Invoke(new Workflow1(), inputs);
}   }   }
```

Then, you retrieve the return values in the variable outputs. The following link gives the details of using inputs and outputs:

https://docs.microsoft.com/en-us/dotnet/framework/windows-workflow-foundation/using-workflowinvoker-and-workflowapplication

Workflow1.xaml is the file in which we will add our workflow code by dragging and dropping the components in the toolbox into the XAML design panel:

1. Drag the Control Flow activity Sequence and drop it into the design area of the file;
2. Drag the Primitive WriteLine and drop it into the Sequence activity;
3. Drag and drop the If-activity into the Sequence, and add condition expressions into the If-activity;
4. Drag and drop the Control Flow activity Sequence in the Then-branch;

5. Drag and drop a WriteLine and a Flowchart into the Sequence; the Flowchart creates an instant component in the program;
6. Click to open the Flowchart component; drag and drop a WriteLine and a Switch in the Flowchart component;
7. Drag another If-activity into the Else branch of the first If-activity.

The completed workflow in XAML is given in Figure 8.8. Most part of the program is built from the activities in the Control Flow and Primitives categories. However, you can easily add a component into the workflow by using the Flowchart, which allows you to put into any workflow code. Through the view options "Expand All" and "Collapse All" at the top-right corner, you can see the entire code or overview of the code. Figure 8.9 shows the expanded Flowchart component.

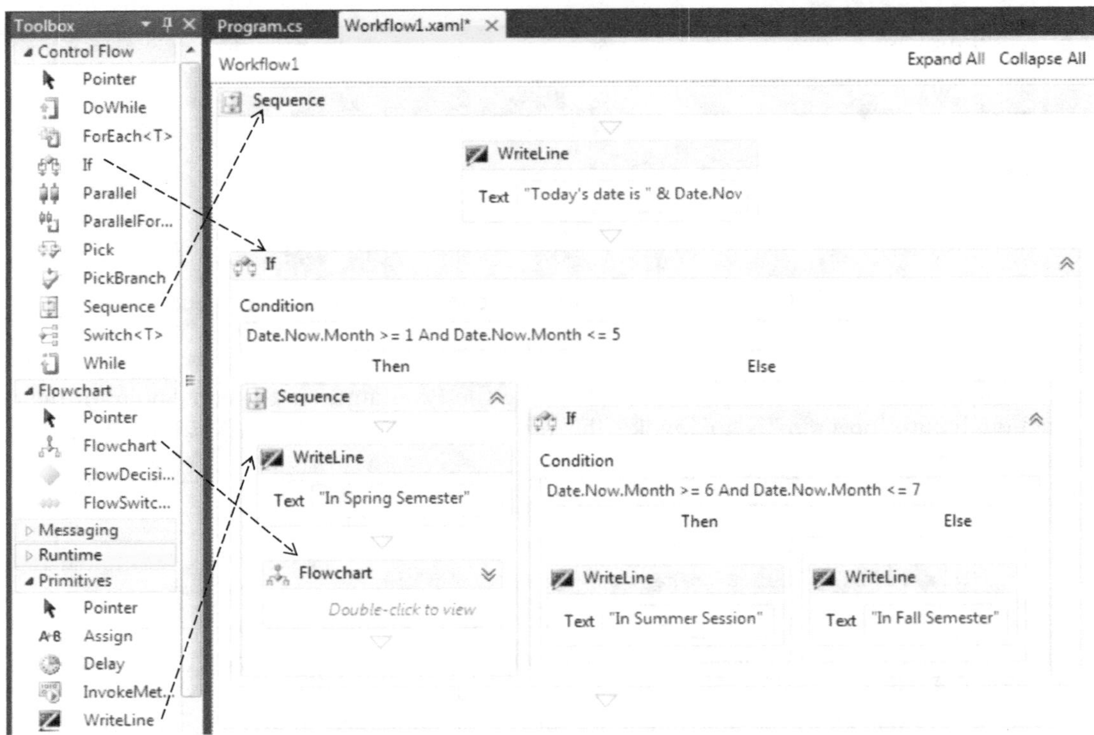

Figure 8.8. A simple workflow in XAML

Build and run the code, it outputs:

```
Today's date is 5/10/2011 11:04:07 AM
We are in Spring Semester
We are in Month 5. What should I do?
Write your finals
Press any key to continue . . .
```

The XAML file shows the program graphically in Figure 8.8 and Figure 8.9. You can open its source code, which is represented in XML.

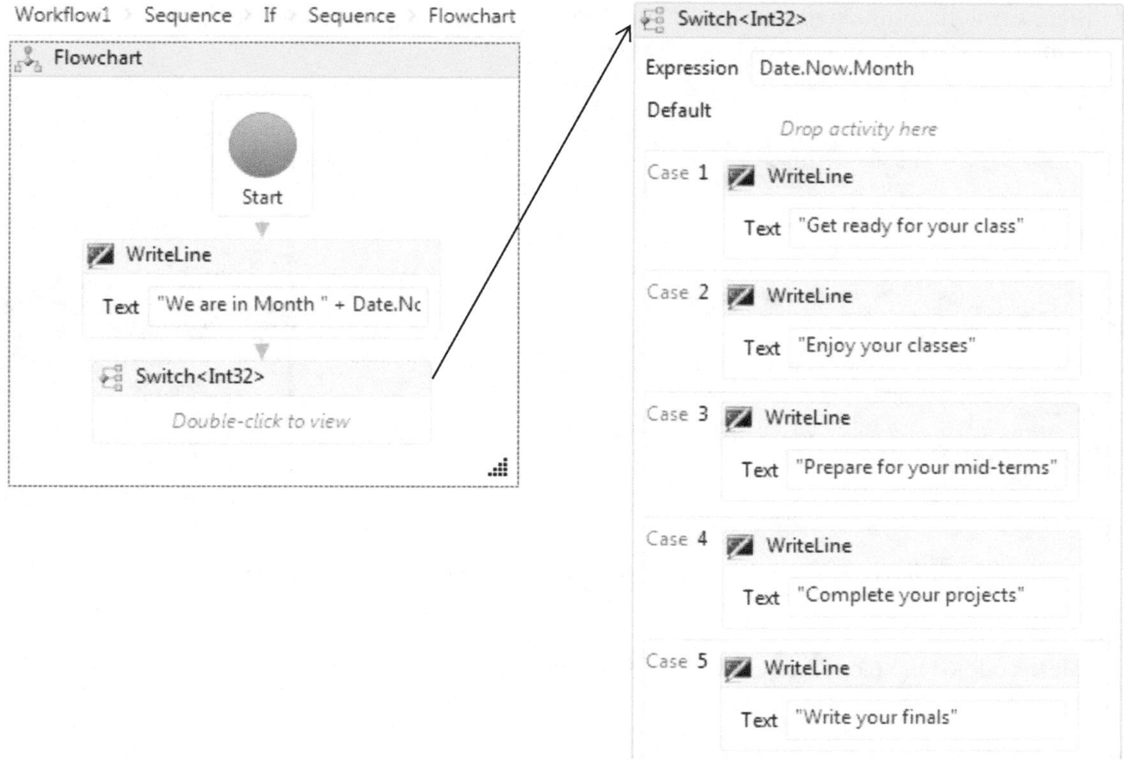

Figure 8.9. The instant Flowchart component in the workflow

8.2.3 Creating Custom Code Activity for Workflow Application

As we discussed previously, WF allows us to implement the application logic graphically in workflow. It offers similar advantages that BPEL offers. However, WF can easily integrate a programming language-based component, CodeActivity, into the workflow. In this section, we will add C# component into the workflow that we discussed now.

Workflow is convenient for integration, but not convenient for computing. CodeActivity supplements the weakness seamlessly. To keep the example simple, yet demonstrate all the steps needed, we will create a component named "CodeActivityGetName" that

1. takes a value (input argument) from the workflow;
2. performs computing using the input value;
3. returns a value (output argument) to the workflow.

Right-click the project name, and select "Add" and "New Item." Choose Workflow template and the "CodeActivity" item. Name the item "CodeActivityGetName," as shown in the left part of Figure 8.10. Adding this component adds a C# component into the project, as shown on in right part of the figure.

Open the C# file, it has already created a template for us to add the C#. The class consists of three methods:

- public InArgument<string> defaultName { get; set; }, which takes input from the workflow. In this example, we will pass a string "John Doe" to the code activity.
- public OutArgument<string> enteredName { get; set; }, which returns a value to the workflow.
- protected override void Execute(CodeActivityContext context), in which we add C# code that we want to execute. In this part, we ask the user to enter a name. If the user does not enter a name,

then, we will use the default name "John Doe." The activity will combine "Hello," the entered name or the name comes from the workflow.

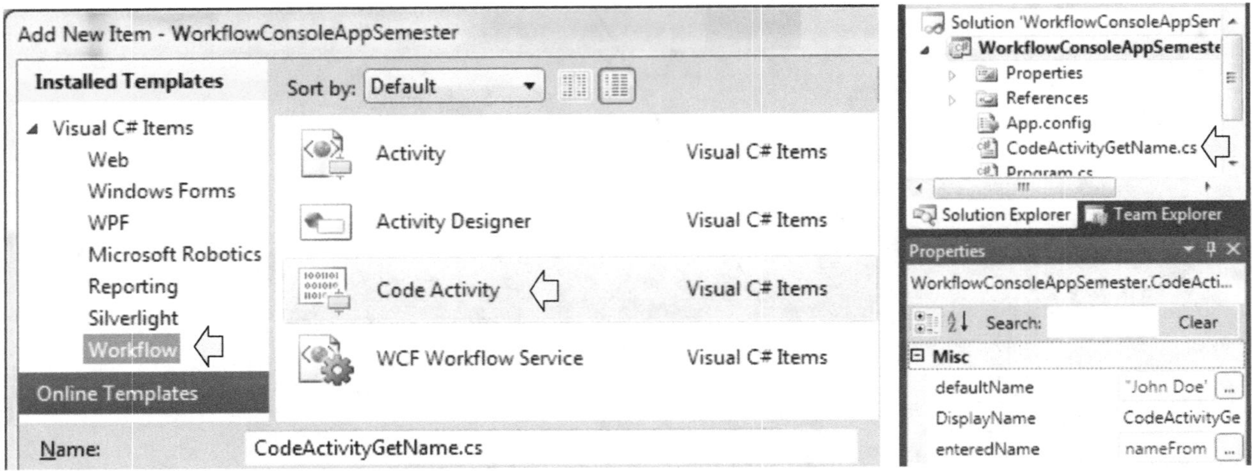

Figure 8.10. Adding a CodeActivity component into the project

The complete code of the CodeActivityGetName class is given as follows:

```
using System;
using System.Activities;
namespace WorkflowConsoleAppSemester {
    public sealed class CodeActivityGetName : CodeActivity {
        // Define an activity input argument of type string
        public InArgument<string> defaultName { get; set; }
        // Define an activity output argument of type string
        public OutArgument<string> enteredName { get; set; }
        // If your activity returns a value, derive from CodeActivity<TResult>
        // and return the value from the Execute method.
        protected override void Execute(CodeActivityContext context) {
            // Obtain the runtime value of the Text input argument
            Console.WriteLine("please enter your name");
            string yourName = Console.ReadLine();
            if (yourName == "") {
                string dName = context.GetValue(this.defaultName);
                yourName = dName;
            }
            string helloName = " Hello " + yourName;
            context.SetValue(this.enteredName, helloName);
        }
    }
}
```

After writing the C# code in the activity, we build the project. Then, the activity CodeActivityGetName will appear in the toolbox under the category named after your project name. Now, we can use the activity by dragging and dropping the item into the workflow. We place this item as the first item in the Sequence, as shown in Figure 8.11. We also modify the next WriteLine to print nameFromCodeActivity + ," Today's date is " + Date.Now.ToString. Before we can run the program, we still need to some job in the workflow side to connect the activity's input and output:

1. Select the CodeActivityGetName and enter the value "John Doe" as the initial value of the InArgument defaultName;
2. Click the tag "Variables" at the bottom of the workflow window, add a new variable, and name it nameFromCodeActivity. Choose string type for the variable. Note, we have used the variable in the WriteLine below the CodeActivityGetName.
3. Go back to the CodeActivityGetName's property window and assign the new variable name to the OutArgument enteredName.

Now, we can start the program. The output, including an input request from Console.ReadLine in the C# program, is also given as follows. Note the difference with the output in the previous example.

```
please enter your name
Yinong Chen
 Hello Yinong Chen, Today's date is 5/13/2011 5:34:16 PM
In Spring Semester
We are in Month 5. What should I do?
Write your finals
Press any key to continue . . .
```

Remote web services can be easily integrated into a workflow. In the same way of adding a service into an ASP .Net application, right-click the project name in the solution explorer and choose "Add Service Reference…" Type the service URL in the Add Service Reference dialog window, click Go and click OK. If the service is available, the system will show a message "The operation is completed successfully. You will see the generated activities in the toolbox after you rebuild the project." Now, each operation in the web service will become an activity in the toolbox, as shown in the toolbox in Figure 8.11. You can use the web service just like a local activity.

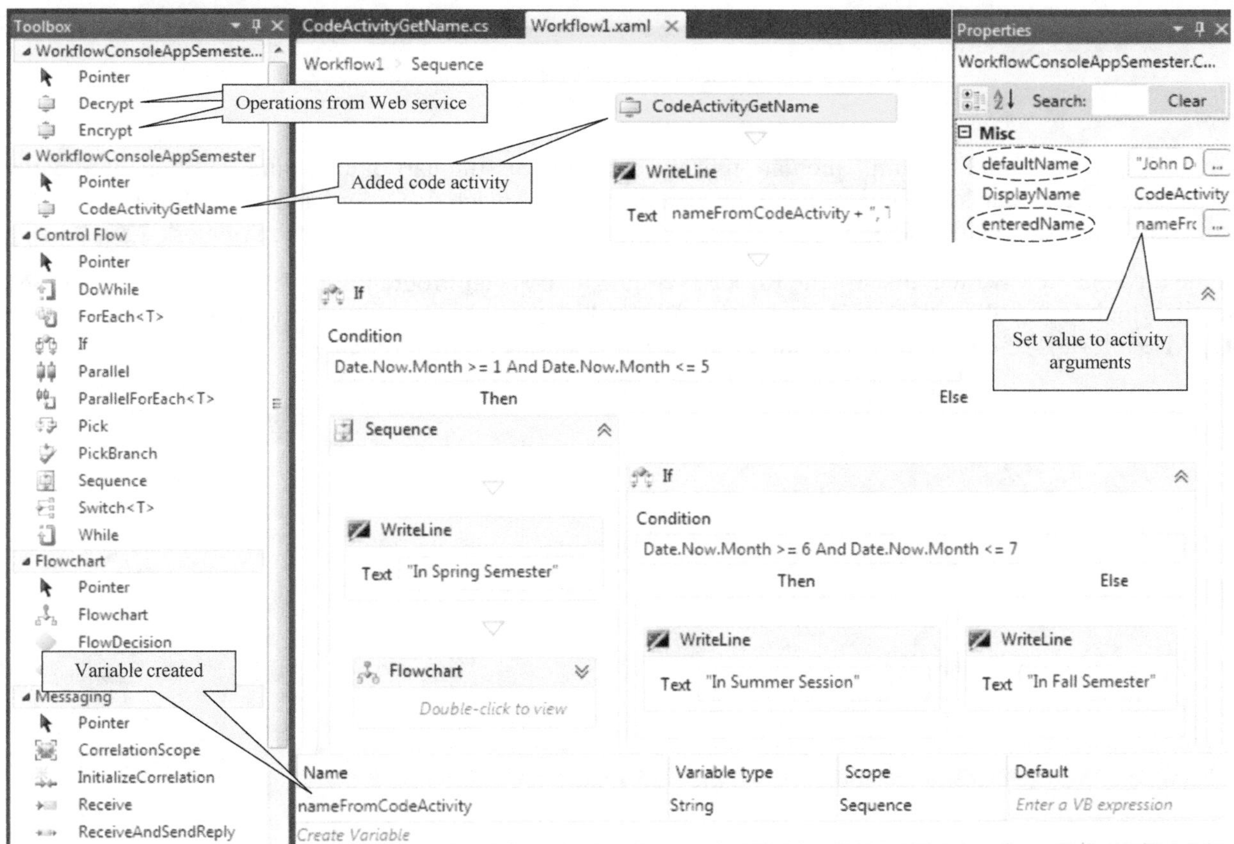

Figure 8.11. Using CodeActivity in the workflow and defining its argument values

To call a RESTful service in a workflow, the easy way is to call it in CodeActivity using the same method discussed in the previous section.

8.2.4 Implementing Finite State Machine in Workflow

Many web applications are event-driven and can be easily described in a Finite State Machine (FSM). Microsoft developer center gives an introduction to finite state machine hands on lab with downloadable sample code: https://code.msdn.microsoft.com/windowsapps/Windows-Workflow-b4b808a8.

Figure 8.12 shows the basic steps of creating a state, defining the code inside the state, and defining a transition from the current state to the target state.

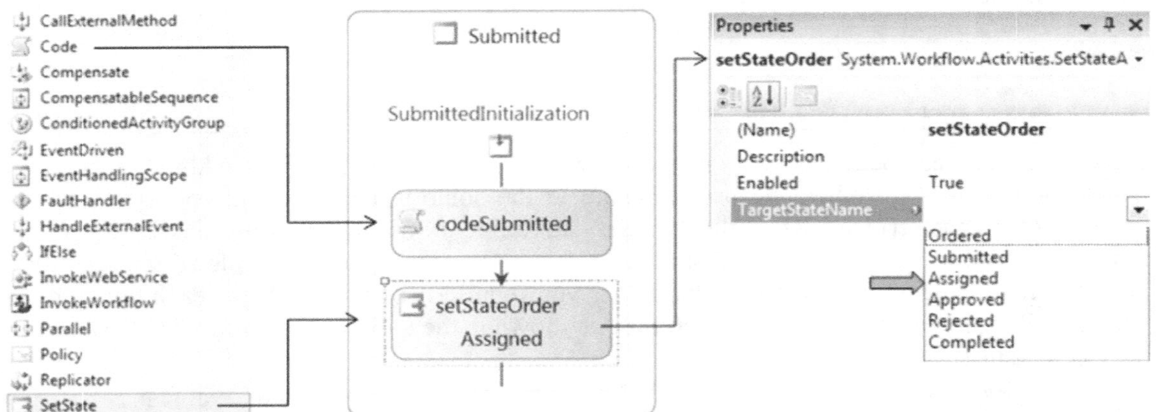

Figure 8.12. The graphic code of a simple workflow

Figure 8.13 shows the FSM implementation of the order processing part of an online shopping application consisting of six states: Submitted, Assigned, Approved, Rejected, Order, and Completed. The FSM workflow is created using the State Machine Workflow Library template in .Net Framework 3.5.

In the next chapter, we will discuss the Robotics Studio and Visual Programming Language (VPL) in more detail, which is based on the same workflow and graphic programming ideas. The appendix will present stepwise tutorials of developing working examples in Robotics Studio and VPL.

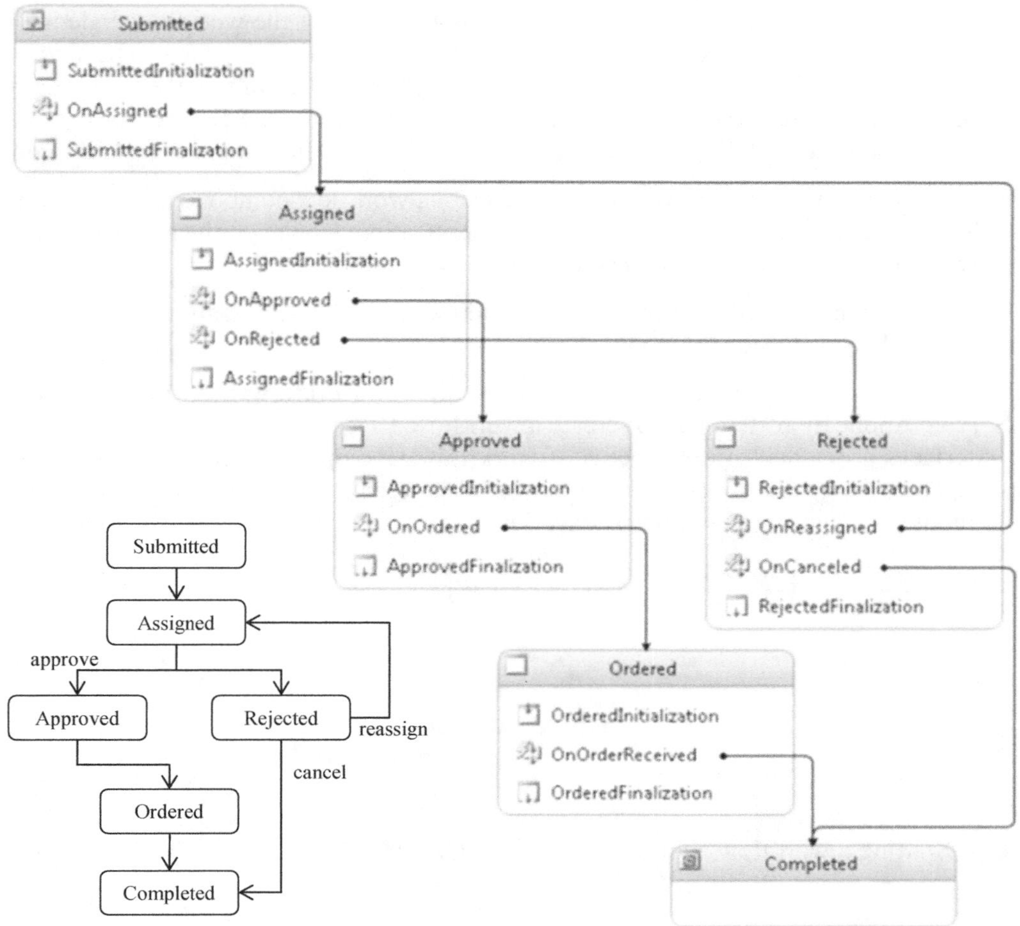

Figure 8.13. Finite state machine and its WF implementation

8.2.5 Creating Services and Persistence Services Using Workflow

Workflow is an architecture-driven approach of software development. It can be used for developing applications as well as services. It is useful to add the workflow layer (a layer of abstraction) if the application or service is complex. Workflow Foundation is designed to work with Windows Communication Foundation (WCF) to develop workflow services.

There are two approaches in applying workflow in a WCF service: contract-first and workflow-first. Contract-first approach uses the "WCF Service Application" template to start an ordinary WCF service project. Then, we can add a workflow activity in the project to perform the high-level code organization work. In this approach, we can create a WCF service in the following steps:

1. Start a new project and choose the WCF template "WCF Service Application;"
2. Right-click the project file and choose "Add" and "New Item"
3. Choose the Workflow template and then choose the "Activity" item; Name the item "myServiceActivity.xaml];"
4. Follow the same steps to define the IService.cs interface file;
5. In your Service.svc.cs file, you need to add the directive: using System.Activities;
6. In the service operation, you can simply call the activity myServiceActivity.xaml using: WorkflowInvoker.Invoke(new myServiceActivity());

Now, we can open the activity myServiceActivity.xaml and start to put the workflow code in the activity. Typically, a service workflow starts with the "Sequence" control in the toolbox. The first item in the sequence should be a "Receive" or a "ReceiveandSendReply" control from the Messaging category. The workflow design in the contract-first approach will be similar to the workflow-first approach to be discussed next. Since the approach uses WCF service template, the service created will have the extension .svc.

You can pass parameters into and retrieve return value from a workflow component in the same way as we discussed in the section on creating a workflow console application. However, the process is more complex than using a workflow-first approach. You can read the link for more detail:

https://docs.microsoft.com/en-us/dotnet/framework/windows-workflow-foundation/using-workflowinvoker-and-workflowapplication

Now, we discuss the workflow-first approach in more detail. The workflow-first approach uses the "WCF Workflow Service Application" template to create a workflow-based service, as shown in Figure 8.14, and the service interfaces are added in the process of workflow development through the Receive and Send activities in the Toolbox. This approach is more powerful in terms of the services that it can create. It can create synchronous, asynchronous, and persistence services.

Figure 8.14. Starting a workflow-first project using WCF Workflow Service Application as template

Next, we choose the project name ImageValidationWF to create a workflow-based image verifier as an example. This step creates a service file with extension .xamlx, with a Sequence activity containing a Receive and a Send activity, as shown in Figure 8.15.

A persistence service requires more than one access. It is similar to asynchronous service, where two calls are required, but it is different in the ways that a persistence service may allow the second call to come after a long time, and thus it must save the half-finished service in a data store. It requires a correlation ID to relate all the calls to each other, and it can accept independent input from all calls.

Image Verifier Service

Before we go into the detail of the code, let us first give an overview of the example we will use for explaining workflow-based service development. Figure 8.16 show the workflow of the service to be developed. The service consists of three operations, each of which is exposed as an endpoint:

- ep1: Stream GetImage(string userID, string verifierString), which generates a random string, generates an image, and then returns the image. The UserID is used for correlating the first call and the second call.
- ep2: bool CheckResult(string userID, string verifierString): it should be invoked after ep1 has been invoked, and it compares if the user entered string equals to the randomly generated string. If the entered string does not match, it will allow the user to reenter another string.
- ep3: Reboot(string userID), which terminates the current workflow and returns to start a new request. This endpoint is called in the case when a client makes the first call and never makes the

second. As a persistent service, this service can wait for a certain amount of time before terminating the service.

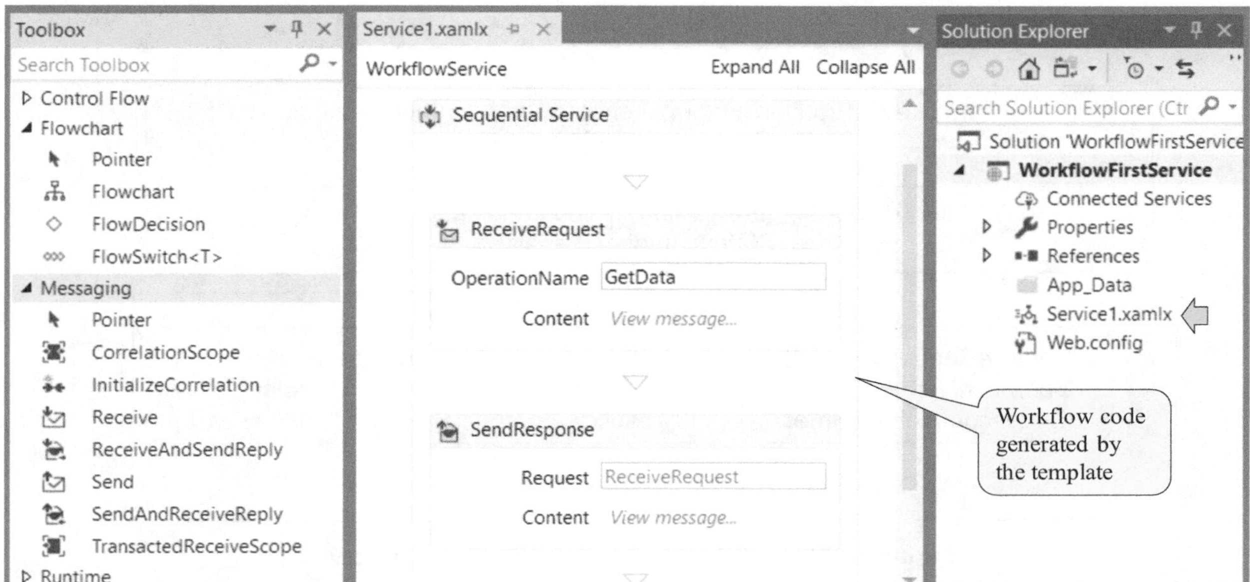

Figure 8.15. Template of WCF Workflow Service Application

This service is a stateful service that allows sequential accesses from the same client. First, the client sends a request, with a string length as input, to GetImage operation for generating an image string. Upon receiving the request, the service invokes the GetVerifierString and GetImage operations of a remote service. Then, service starts two parallel activities. One activity (left branch) resets the state to the beginning of the workflow for taking new requests. The other activity waits for the second input from the client, which passes the user entered string to the service for verification. This second request to the service is correlated to the first request, in order to perform the match between the image generated from the first request and the user entered string in the second request.

The Receive activity provides the operation contract of the service endpoint that the workflow is offering. The Receive activity can be defined through its Properties. To define the operation contract, click the Receive activity and then, click the "Content" property. Then, the Content Definition window will be opened, as shown in Figure 8.17. In this window, we can define the parameters (input variables of the service) and link the variables to the textboxes in the client application, where the user can enter the information needed; for example, the length of the image string. Note the property "CanCreateInstance" in the properties window. If this box is checked, a new instance of the workflow will be created every time a new invocation is made to the workflow service. This is the "perCall" attribute we discussed before. The exception is made if a correlation variable is created, based on the three properties in the "Correlations" part, and a reentering access is identified. Correlations are important in this image verifier, as the service takes at least two requests. The first request will generate an image string, and the second request will send a string to match the image generated in the previous request. Furthermore, if a user enters a string that does not match the image string, the user can reenter another string. If a new instance is created for a resubmission of the string, a new image string will be generated. The correlation enables the service to differentiate a resubmission of the same user from a new user.

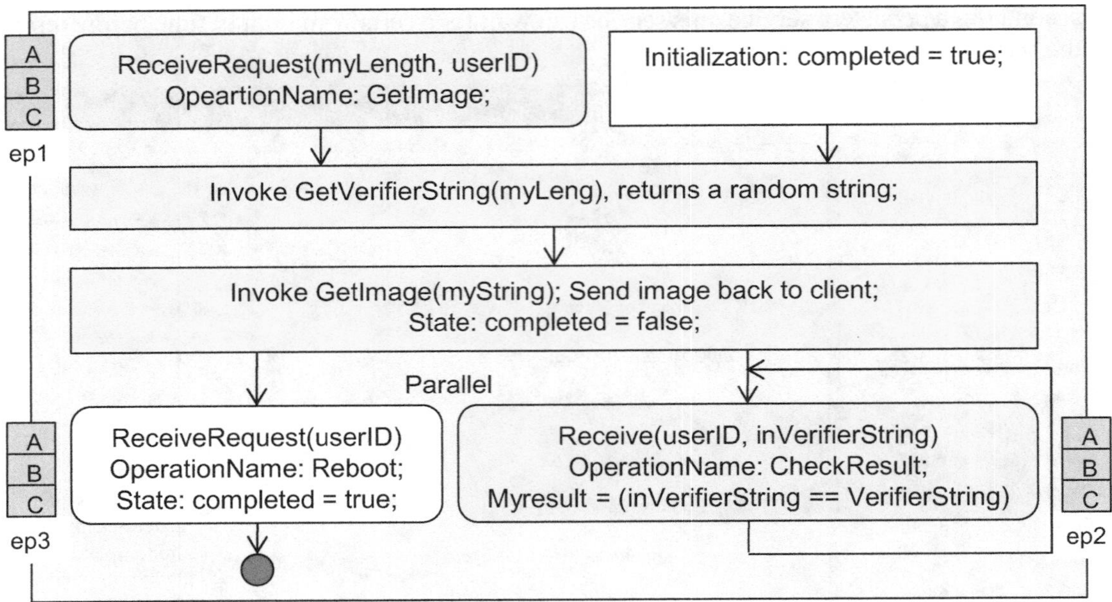

Figure 8.16. Workflow of the image verification service

To simplify the example, we add the WCF service (http://neptune.fulton.ad.asu.edu/WSRepository/Services/ImageVerifierSvc/Service.svc) into the project using "Add Service Reference." The workflow, after the service that is added has passed the compilation (Build Solution), is shown in Figure 8.17, where the two operations of the service, GetImage and GetVerifierString, are added into the Toolbox. In the workflow area, the instances of GetImage and GetVerifierString are added into the workflow by dragging and dropping.

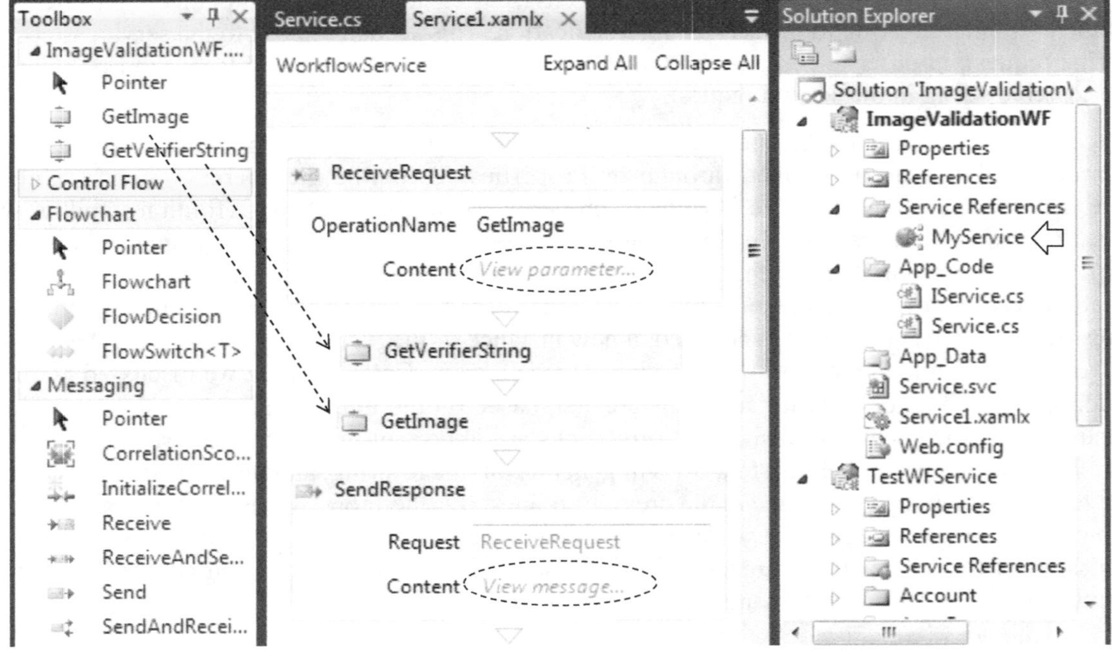

Figure 8.17. GetImage and GetVerifierString appear the toolbox and are added into the workflow

Figure 8.18 shows the entire workflow in a flowchart. It starts with the Receive activity, which simply waits for requests to arrive.

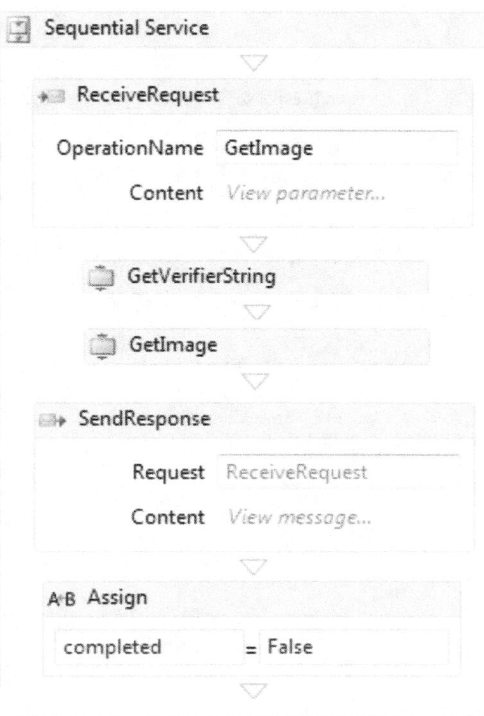

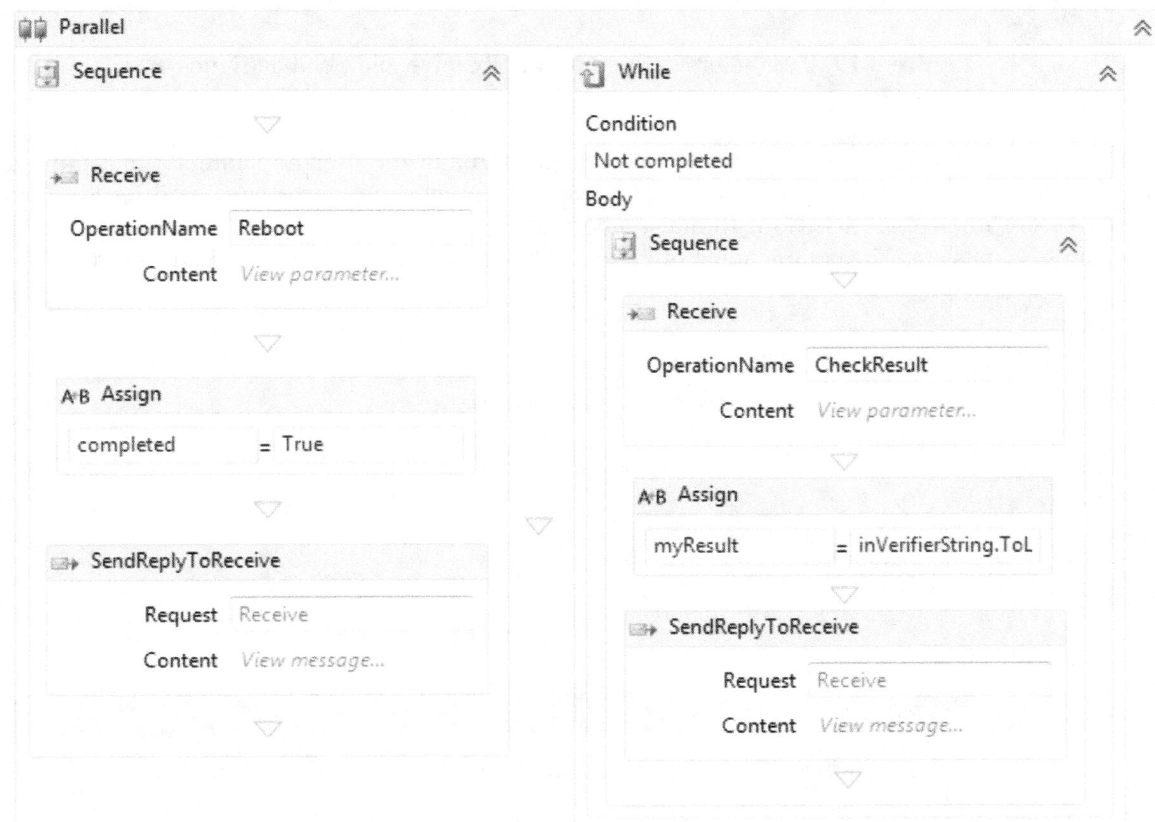

Figure 8.18. The entire workflow of the image verification service

Clicking the "View parameter…" and "View message…" parts of the ReceiveRequest and SendResponse, the parameters behind the activities can be defined, as shown in Figure 8.19, which defines the parameters of the endpoint.

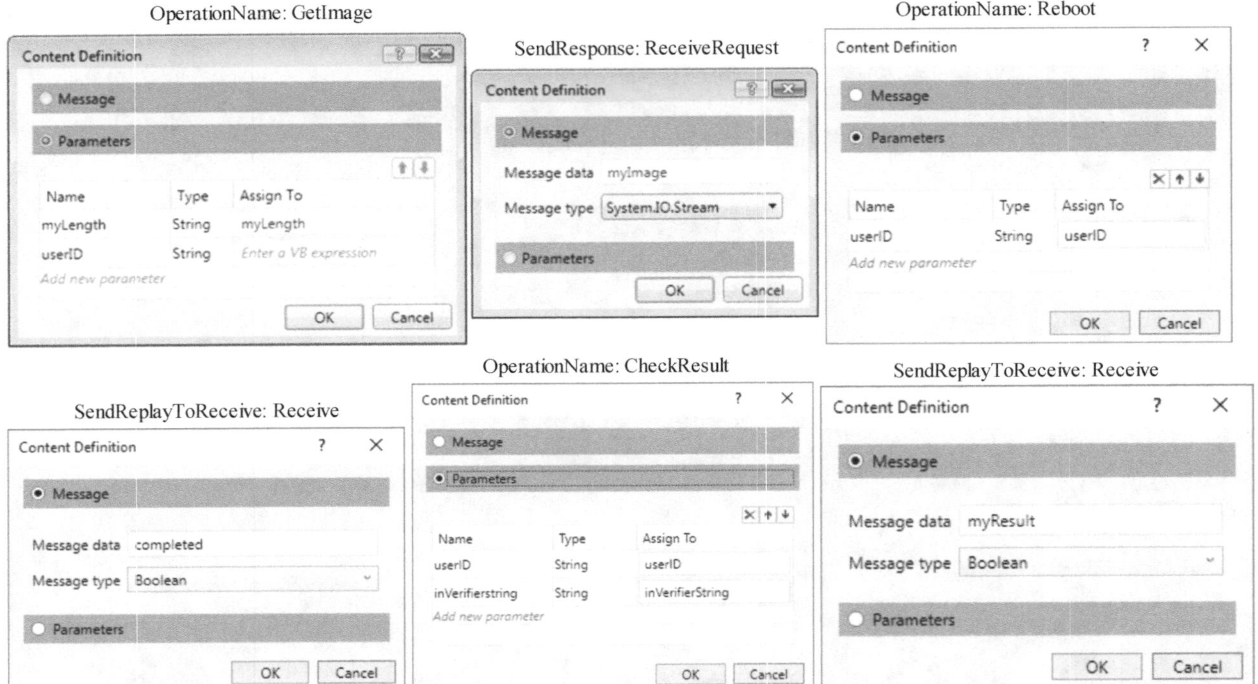

Figure 8.19. Parameters defined for the Receive and Send activities

The service correlates the requests from the same client through the userID parameter and the internal correlation mechanisms. This approach is completely different from the image verifier services we discussed before in .svc and RESTful formats, where the services are stateless. We kept the state in the client using session state. The complete list of variables behind the code is given in Figure 8.20.

Name	Variable type	Scope	Default
completed	Boolean	Sequential Service	True
handle	CorrelationHandle	Sequential Service	Handle cannot be initialized
myImage	Stream	Sequential Service	Enter a VB expression
myLength	String	Sequential Service	"4"
myResult	Boolean	Sequential Service	Enter a VB expression
userID	String	Sequential Service	Enter a VB expression
verifierString	String	Sequential Service	Enter a VB expression
Create Variable			

Variables Imports 100%

Figure 8.20. All variables defined for the workflow

Each activity uses a part of the variables; for example, the ReceiveRequest at the beginning of the workflow uses myLength and userID as the parameter. The userID is used by all three receive activities as a parameter for identifying the subsequent visits to the same service. For a new client with a new userID, the service needs to create a new instance to process the request. The correlation among the receive activities is defined in their properties. Figure 8.21 shows the definition of the correlation variable handle, where the correlation key is generated by the system.

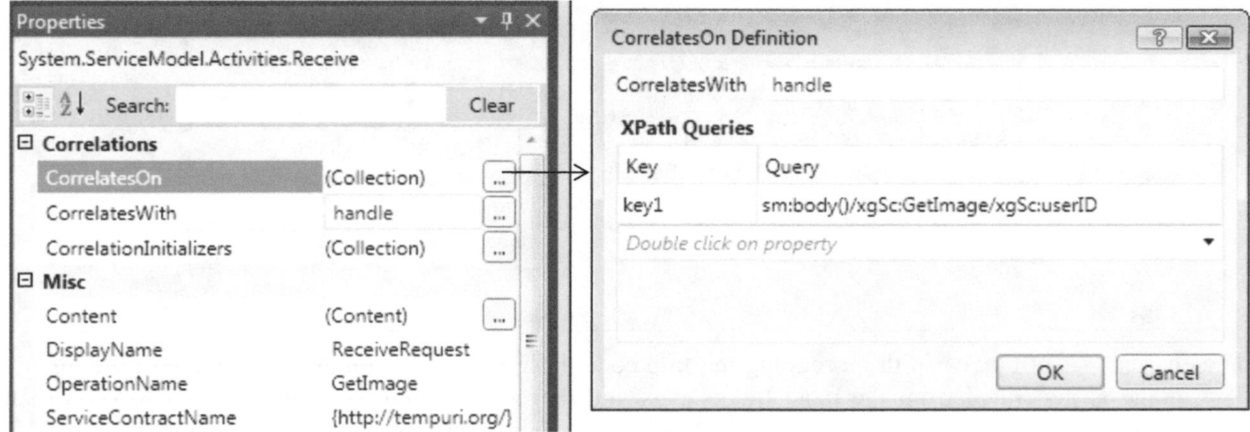

Figure 8.21. Definition of the correlation variable handle

The service and its WSDL file are deployed at:

http://neptune.fulton.ad.asu.edu/WSRepository/Services/WFImage/WFservice/service1.xamlx
http://neptune.fulton.ad.asu.edu/WSRepository/Services/WFImage/WFService/Service1.xamlx?wsdl

which can be added into a client using "Add Service Reference" in the same way as .svc service. The service can be tested at: http://neptune.fulton.ad.asu.edu/WSRepository/Services/WFImage.

For each client with the same user ID, the service will deal with different orders of accessing the endpoints in the principle of a finite state machine.

(1) The client accesses endpoint 1 GetImage first, and then access endpoint 2 CheckResult with a correct string input. The client is done with the image verifier.
(2) The client accesses endpoint 1 GetImage first, and then accesses endpoint 2 CheckResult, but with an incorrect string input. The service will loop-wait in the state (operation CheckResult) for the client to enter another string until a correct string is entered.
(3) The client accesses endpoint 1 GetImage and then accesses endpoint 2. The user decides to access endpoint 1 GetImage again to get a different image. In this case, the service will access the operation Reboot to reset the service for generating a new string and a new image according to the string.
(4) A client tries to access the endpoint 2 without accessing endpoint 1 to create an image. The service will take the client to the beginning of the state machine.

As the workflow service saves the states and correlates the following accesses to the previous visits, the client does not have to worry about saving the random string into the session state, as we did in the WCF SOAP and RESTful versions of the image verifier. The GUI design and its markup file are shown as follows:

```
<%@ Page Title="" Language="C#" MasterPageFile="~/Site.Master"
AutoEventWireup="true" CodeBehind="Default.aspx.cs"
Inherits="TestWFService.TestAjax" %>
<asp:Content ID="Content1" ContentPlaceHolderID="HeadContent" runat="server">
</asp:Content>
```

```
<asp:Content ID="Content2" ContentPlaceHolderID="MainContent" runat="server">
   <asp:Image ID="Image1" runat="server" ImageUrl="~/Image.aspx" />
   <asp:Button ID="Button2" runat="server" Text="Get Another Image"
                  onclick="Button2_Click" />
   <div>
       <asp:ScriptManager ID="ScriptManager1" runat="server">
       </asp:ScriptManager>
             <asp:UpdatePanel ID="UpdatePanel1" runat="server">
                 <ContentTemplate>
                     <asp:TextBox ID="TextBox1" runat="server"
Width="273px"></asp:TextBox>
                     <asp:Button ID="Button1" runat="server" Text="Submit"
onclick="Button1_Click" /> <br /> <br />
                  <asp:Label ID="Label1"
runat="server" Text=""></asp:Label>
                 </ContentTemplate>
             </asp:UpdatePanel>
   </div>
</asp:Content>
```

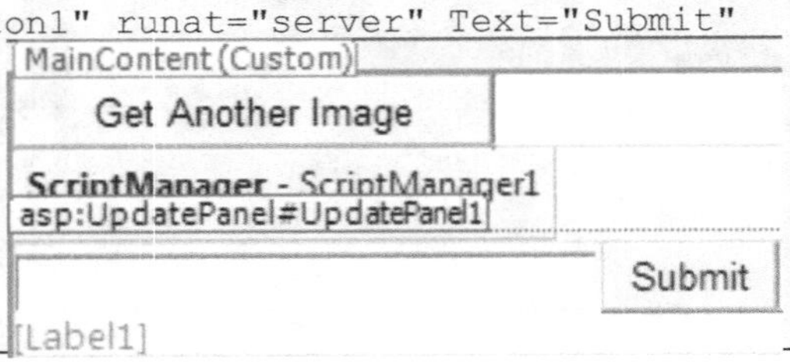

The element <asp:Image> in the foregoing markup code defines the location and the source of the image. The image is generated from the page Image.aspx and the code behind the page Image.aspx.cs, which invokes the workflow service given in Figure 8.17. The code in Image.aspx.cs will be executed every time the page is loaded, which will generate a new random image. In the client we are designing, we want to give the user the opportunity to retry the same image, and thus, we do not want the click of the "Submission" button to trigger a new image. We use AJAX technique to the textbox and the submission button, which quotes the textbox and the "Submit" button inside the <asp:UpdatePanel> element. As the result, updating the textbox and clicking the "submit" button will not trigger the reload of the image. AJAX technique is typically used for performance purpose. However, we use AJAX technique for implementing certain functionality.

The code of Image.aspx.cs is given as follows, where the proxy MyService represents the workflow image service added into the client.

```
// Image.aspx.cs
using System; using System.IO; using System.Drawing.Imaging;
namespace TestWFService {
    public partial class Image : System.Web.UI.Page {
        protected void Page_Load(object sender, EventArgs e) {
            Response.Clear();
            MyService.ImageClient myClient = new MyService.ImageClient();
            if (Session["userID"] == null) {
                Session["userID"] = "abc";
            }
            Try {
                Stream myStream = myClient.GetImage(new MyService.GetImage()
{ myLength = "6", userID = Session["userID"].ToString()});
                System.Drawing.Image myImage =
System.Drawing.Image.FromStream(myStream);
                Response.ContentType = "image/jpeg";
                myImage.Save(Response.OutputStream, ImageFormat.Jpeg);
            }
            catch (Exception) {
                    MyService.RebootClient myClient1 = new MyService.RebootClient();
                    bool myResult = bool.Parse(myClient1.Reboot(new
MyService.Reboot() { userID = Session["userID"].ToString() }).ToString());
                    MyService.ResultClient myClient2 = new MyService.ResultClient();
```

```
                    myResult = bool.Parse(myClient2.CheckResult(new
MyService.CheckResult() { userID = Session["userID"].ToString(), inVerifierstring =
"ab" }).ToString());
                Stream myStream = myClient.GetImage(new MyService.GetImage()
{ myLength = "6", userID = Session["userID"].ToString() });
                System.Drawing.Image myImage =
System.Drawing.Image.FromStream(myStream);
                Response.ContentType = "image/jpeg";
                myImage.Save(Response.OutputStream, ImageFormat.Jpeg);
            }
        }
    }
}
```

Note the code in the "catch" clause. The workflow service will throw an exception if a client tries to access; for example, the endpoint 2, submitting a string for verification before requesting an image. Thus, in the exception part, we will invoke the endpoint 3 (reboot) to reset the service and start from the beginning of the workflow to generate a new image.

Finally, the code behind the "Submit" is given as follows:

```
using System;
namespace TestWFService {
    public partial class TestAjax : System.Web.UI.Page {
        protected void Page_Load(object sender, EventArgs e) { }
        protected void Button1_Click(object sender, EventArgs e) {
            MyService.ResultClient myClient = new MyService.ResultClient();
            string myStr = TextBox1.Text.ToString().ToLower();
            bool myResult = bool.Parse(myClient.CheckResult(new
MyService.CheckResult()
            { userID = Session["userID"].ToString(), inVerifierstring =
myStr }).ToString());
            //bool myResult = myClient.CheckResult(new MyService.CheckResult()
{ userID = "benben", inVerifierstring = myStr });
            if (myResult) {
                Label1.Text = "Your input is correct!";
            }
            Else { Label1.Text = "Your input is not correct!"; }
        }
        protected void Button2_Click(object sender, EventArgs e) {
            // no action, but trigger the AJAX reloading
        }
    }
}
```

Mortgage Service

A more complex example of workflow service, using the mortgage approval process as the example, is given in Microsoft MSDN library to show the workflow design. Figure 8.22 shows the main workflow of the mortgage service.

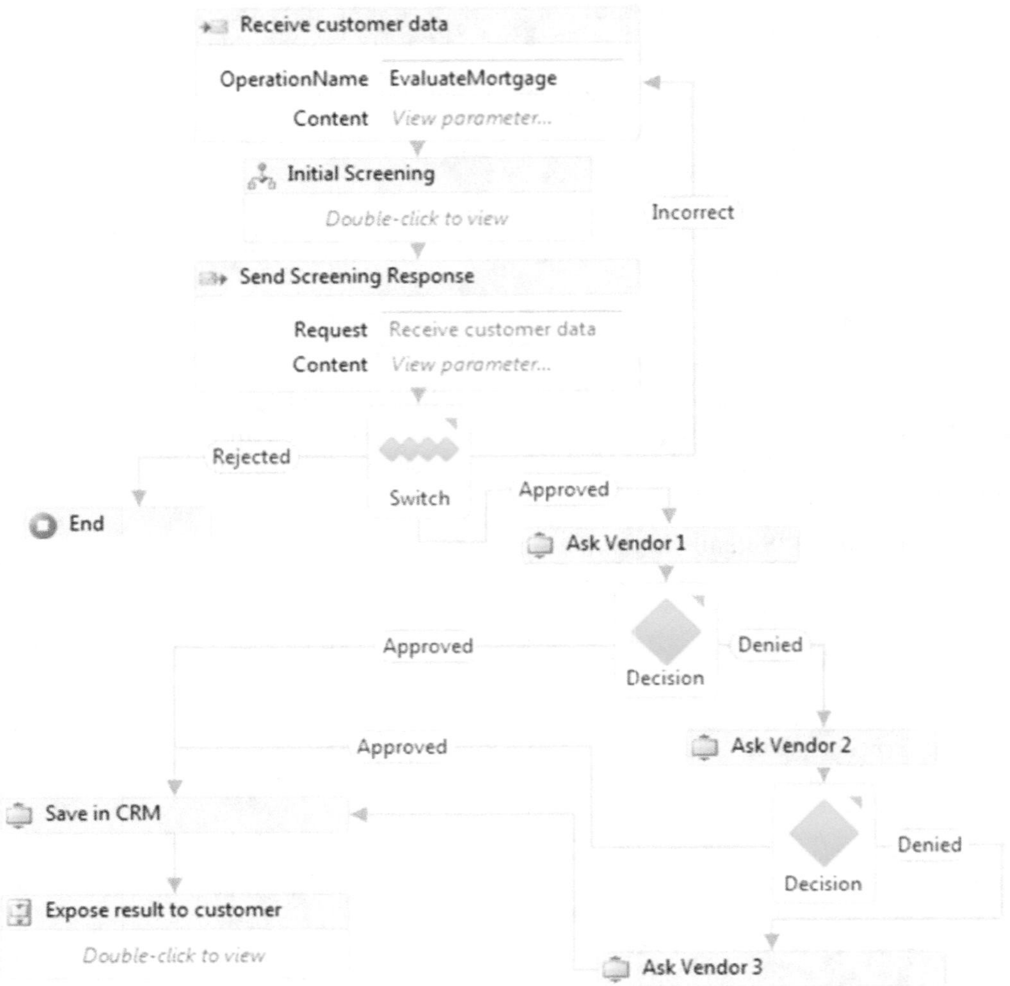

Figure 8.22. Workflow of a mortgage application

The full details of this example and the downloadable code can be found at the Microsoft MSDN magazine link: http://msdn.microsoft.com/en-us/magazine/ff646977.aspx.

The downloaded code can be opened in Visual Studio and can be tested on a local host. We have deployed the example at the following server site for remote testing:
The client application: http://neptune.fulton.ad.asu.edu/WSRepository/Services/WFService/
Service:
http://neptune.fulton.ad.asu.edu/WSRepository/Services/WFService/MortgageService/Service1.xamlx
Service:
http://neptune.fulton.ad.asu.edu/WSRepository/Services/WFService/VendorService/Vendor1.svc

Only the basic functions, including the ASP .Net Client App, the workflow-based mortgage service, and the three vendor services are deployed. The CRM and the database services are also deployed.

8.3 BPEL

BPEL (Business Process Execution Language) is the most widely used composition language, which is supported by most major players in service-oriented software development.

8.3.1 BPEL Activities and Constructs

BPEL is used to write executable business processes. BPEL contains a set of activities and constructs are similar to those of a typical program language, as listed in Table 8.2.

The functions of these activities and constructs will be elaborated and illustrated in examples in the following sections.

8.3.2 BPEL Process

BPEL is a service composition language that is used to define a composite service based on existing services. Although BPEL has the essential constructs of an ordinary programming language and is capable of writing any programs and services, it is less convenient for using BPEL for such purposes because of the lack of data types and operations on the data types.

Table 8.2. BPEL activities and constructs

Activity Name	Function
<invoke>	Invoking a service
<receive>	Waiting for receiving a message
<reply>	Generating response to a synchronized service call
<assign>	Modifying data variables
<throw>	Jumping to an exception handler
<catch>	Handling an exception
<wait>	Waiting for a certain amount of time
<terminate>	Terminating the entire process
<sequence>	Define a set of activities that will be executed in the given order of sequence
<flow>	Define a set of activities that will (can) be executed in parallel
<switch>	Define a selection, similar to the if-then-else in programming language

<while>	Define a while-loop; for example:
	`<while condition="expr" standard-attributes>`
	`activities`
	`</while>`

<pick>	Define a list of activities. Execute the first activity that is available. Can be used to block wait a response, or timeout, whichever comes first
<variable>	Declare a variable
<scope>	Define the scope of variables
<partnerLink>	Define a partner link, which specifies what party uses the port and the type of the communication: synchronous or asynchronous.

<if>	Define a selection, available in BPEL 2.0.
<repeatUntil>	Define a repeat-until-loop, available in BPEL 2.0.
<forEach>	Define a for-each-loop, available in BPEL 2.0.

A BPEL process defines the structure of the interaction among web services in terms of:

- Business logic, including data, workflow, and error handling and recovery mechanism;
- Participant services (partners) that characterize partners and provide support to partner conversation.

A BPEL process uses the aforesaid constructs and activities to define a composite web services based on existing services. Figure 8.23 shows the structure of a BPEL process and its client and three services that the BPEL process needs.

The BPEL process starts with a <receive> activity, which loop-waits for requests consisting of two string-type messages, representing a credit card number and an address. When a request arrives, the process assigns the two messages to two variables. The process then uses the construct <flow> to allow the invocation of two remote web services to be performed simultaneously (in parallel). The <invoke> activity can have two modes: **synchronous** and **asynchronous**:

- Synchronous: This creates a two-way communication channel in which the caller (client) block-waits the reply from the callee (service).
- Asynchronous: This creates a one-way communication channel to allow the caller to send a message to the callee. If a response is needed, the callee has to create another one-way channel to call back, which uses <invoke>.

Each of the two services, *credit card validation* and *address validation*, replies with a string representing "valid" or "invalid." Upon receiving the reply, the process uses a <switch> construct (conditional statement) to decide what message to reply to the client. The process uses two <pick> constructs to make sure that both the credit card number and the address are valid. Then, the process invokes the shipping service using the asynchronous mode. In this mode, the process does not expect the service to response immediately. Instead, the process provides a port (callback number) for the shipping service to call back whenever it has completed its processing. In the BPEL process, it uses the activity <receive> to wait for the callback.

Figure 8.24 sketches the synchronous and asynchronous communications among the client, the BPEL process, and the services, where (invoke–receive–reply) is used for synchronous communication, while (invoke–receive–invoke–receive) is used for asynchronous communication.

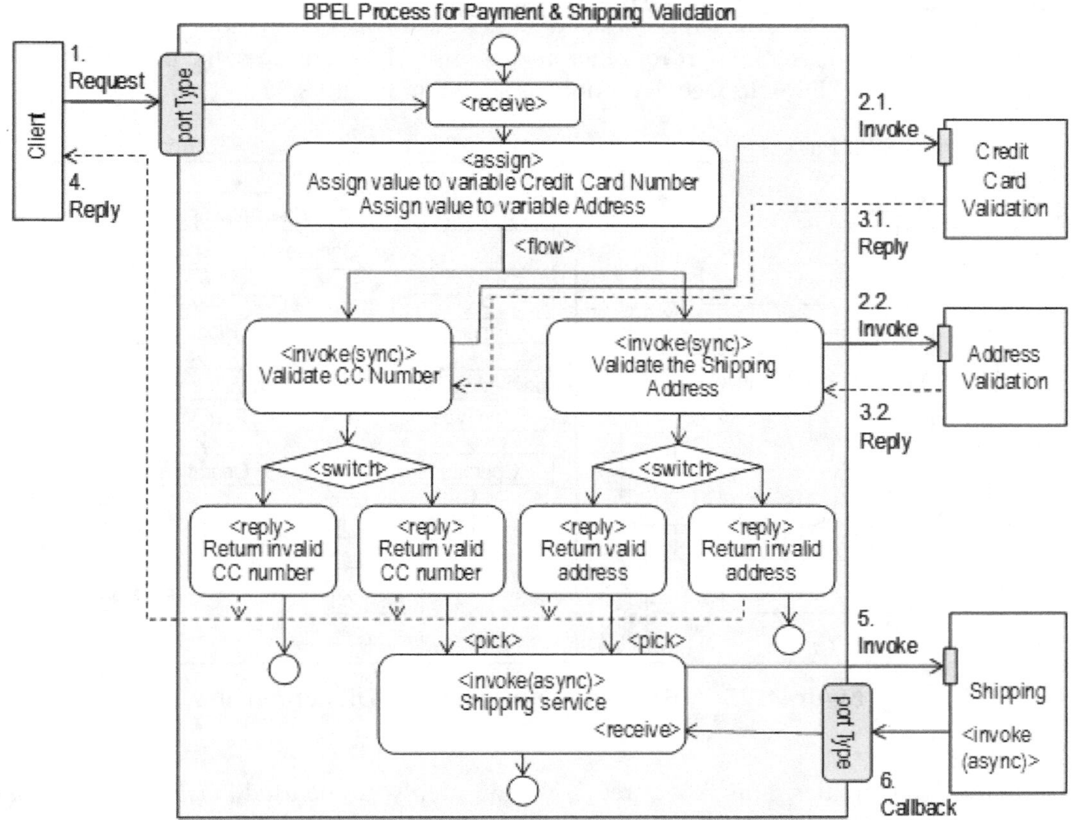

Figure 8.23. BPEL process and its client and services

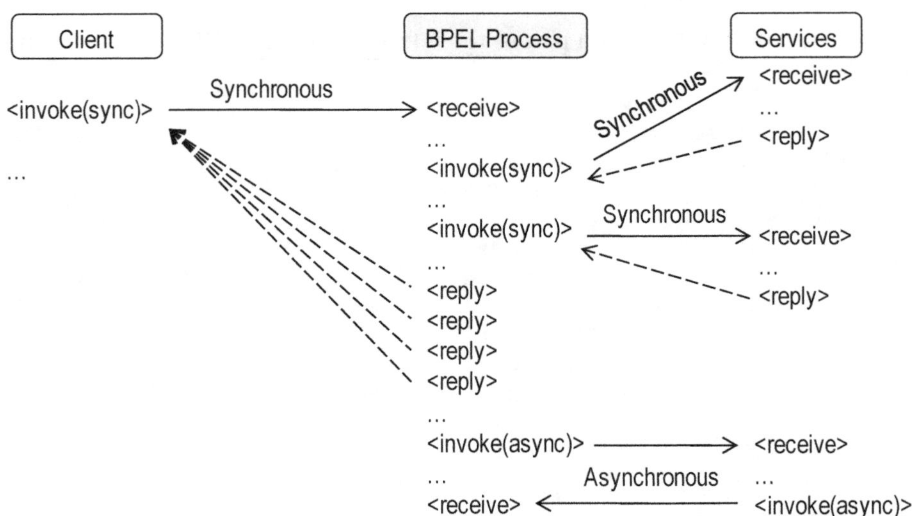

Figure 8.24. Synchronous and asynchronous communications used in the example

8.3.3 WSDL Interface Definition of BPEL Process

If a BPEL process offers at least one port for other clients or services to access, the process itself is a web service, and thus it has a WSDL interface definition, as shown in Figure 8.25.

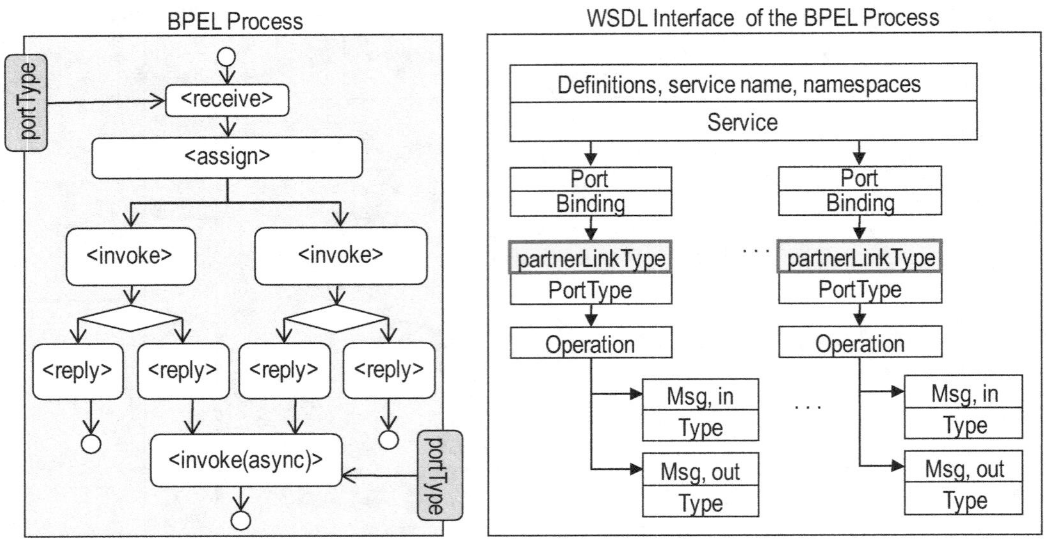

Figure 8.25. A BPEL process and its WSDL definition

In the communication activities, <invoke>, <receive>, and <reply> to be used in BPEL process, a partner of the communication must be specified. For each partner, a partner link type needs to be defined in the WSDL file. Thus, in addition to all elements that a standard WSDL document has, a BPEL process's WSDL interface has an additional element called `<partnerLinkType>`, which is used to define the type of partner links to be used in the BPEL process.

The WSDL document that follows shows a part of the interface of the BPEL process given in Figure 8.23.

```
<?xml version= "1.0" encoding="UTF-8"?>
<definitions
   xmlns: http="http://schemas.xmlsoap.org/wsdl/http/"
   xmlns: soap="http://schemas xmlsoap.org/wsdl/soap/"
   xmlns: xs= "http://www.w3.org/2001/XMLschema"
   xmlns: soapenc="http://schemas.xml soap.org/soap/encoding/"
   xmlns ="http://schemas.xmlsoap.org/wsdl/"
   xmlns: targetNamespace="http://neptune.fulton.ad.asu.edu/WSRepository/bpel/"
   xmlns: zip="http://www.webserviceX.net/addressValidation/"
   xmlns: bk=" http://bank.com/CCValidation/"
   xmlns: shp=" http://parcelservice.com/shippingService/"
   xmlns: plnk="http://schemas.xmlsoap.org/ws/2003/05/partner-link/">

   <!-- The complete WSDL file can be generated by tool -->
   <types>
        <xs:schema ... >
        </xs:schema>
   </types>
   <message ... >
        <part ... />
   </message>

   <portType name="clientPT">
```

```
      <operation name= "transactionApproval">
            <input message= "transactionRequestMessage"/>
            <output message= "transactionResponseMessage"/>
      </operation>
   </portType>
   <portType name="shippingCallbackPT">
      <operation name="...">
            <input message="..."/>
      </operation>
   </portType>

   <!-- Definition of the partner link types -->
   <plnk:partnerLinkType name= "paymentShippingLT">
      <plnk:role name= "paymentShippingService">
            <plnk:portType name="clientPT"/>
      </plnk: role>
   </plnk: partnerLinkType>
   <plnk:partnerLinkType name= "CCValidationLT">
      <plnk:role name= "CCValidator">
            <plnk:portType name="bk:CCCheckerSoap"/>
      </plnk:role>
   </plnk:partnerLinkType>
   <plnk:partnerLinkType name= "AddrValidationLT">
      <plnk:role name= "AddrValidator">
            <plnk:portType name="mov:USAddressVerificaitonSoap"/>
      </plnk:role>
   </plnk:partnerLinkType>
   <plnk:partnerLinkType name= "shippingLT">
      <plnk: role name="shippingRequester">
            <plnk:portType name="shippingCallbackPT"/>
      </plnk: role>
      <plnk: role name="shippingService">
            <plnk:portType name="shp:shippingServicePT"/>
      </plnk: role>
   </plnk: partnerLinkType>
</definitions>
```

In this WSDL definition, two port types are defined. One is the `clientPT` and the other is the `shippingCallbackPT`. The former defines a two-way interface for synchronous communication between the client and the BPEL process (service). The latter defines a one-way (input only) interface for the shipping service to callback. The port type is a standard component of a WSDL document.

A new kind of component that is specific to BPEL process's WSDL file is the `partnerLinkType`. As shown in Figure 8.23, the BPEL process has four partners. In the foregoing file, four of the port types `partnerLinkType` are defined, each of which defines the roles of the entity that owns the port type involved in the partnership. If synchronous communication is used, one port type is involved, and one role needs to be defined. If asynchronous communication is used, two port types are involved, and two roles need to be defined:

1. In the partnership between the client and BPEL process, one port type is involved, and the role of the entity that owns the port type is the *payment and shipping* service.
2. In the partnership between the BPEL process and the credit card validation, one port type is involved, and the role of the entity that owns the port type is the *credit card validation.*
3. In the partnership between the BPEL process and the *address validation*, one port type is involved, and the role of the entity that owns the port type is the *address validation*.

4. In the partnership between the BPEL process and the *Shipping* service, two port types are involved. The roles of the entity that owns the port types `shippingCallbackPT` is the shipping requester, while the entity that owns the port types `shippingServicePT`, defined in the namespace `shp`, is the shipping service provider.

The reason that we define the WSDL document and the partner link types is to use them to define the elements of the BPEL process, which will be discussed in the next section.

8.3.4 BPEL Process

Once the partner link types are defined in the WSDL file, we can proceed to the discussion of the BPEL process itself. The following is a part of the code corresponding to the BPEL process given in Figure 8.23. The code consists of several major components.

- The first component defines the namespaces needed.
- The next component defines the partner links to each partner. The process has four partners and thus has four partner links. Only the partner that has a port type needs to define a role in the partner link. Thus, the first three partner links have one role, whereas the fourth link has two roles defined.
- The next component defines the variables needed to store the values obtained from web services and the values to be passed to the web services. The function of the variables here in BPEL process is similar to the variables declared in traditional programming languages.
- The remaining part of the BPEL process is the main processing part, equivalent to the main method of Java or C#. In this code, the process uses sequential construct <sequence> to receive the input data, and then copies the data into the variables needed for invoking the services. Once the data are ready, the process uses parallel construct <flow> to invoke the two web services simultaneously. Finally, the process uses the switch construct, based on the true or false value, to select the next action to be taken.

```
<?xml version="1.0" encoding="utf-8"?>
<process name="PaymentAndAddressValidation"
  xmlns="http://schemas.xmlSoap.org/ws/2003/03/business-process/"
  xmlns: bpws= "http://schemas.xmlsoap.org/ws/2003/03/business-process/"
  xmlns: zip="http://www.webservicex.net/"
  xmlns: ps="http://neptune.fulton.ad.asu.edu/WSRepository/bpel/ps.wsdl">

  <!-- Define partner links -->
  <partnerLinks>
       <partnerLink name="client"
             partnerLinkType="ps: paymentShippingLT"
             myRole="paymentShippingService"/>
       <partnerLink name="CCValidator"
             partnerLinkType="ps: CCValidationLT "
             partnerRole="CreditCardValidator"/>
       <partnerLink name="AddressValidator"
             partnerLinkType = "ps: AddressLT"
             partnerRole="AddressValidator"/>
       <partnerLink name="ShippingService"
             partnerLinkType = "ps: shippingLT"
             myRole="shippingRequester"
             partnerRole="shippingService"/>
  </partnerLinks>

  <!-- Define variables to be used in the main part -->
  <variables>
       <!-- input for this process -->
       <variable name="TransactionRequest"
             messageType="client:TransactionRequestMessage"/>
```

```
    <!-- input for the Credit Card Validation web service -->
    <variable name="CCValidationRequest"
          messageType="ps:ValidateCCRequestMessage"/>
    <!-- output from Credit Card Validation web service
    <variable name="CCValidationResponse"
          messageType="ps:ValidateCCResponseMessage"/>
    <!-- input for Address Validation web service -->
    <variable name="AddressValidationRequest"
          messageType="ps:AddressRequestMessage"/>
    <!-- output from Address Validation web service-->
    <variable name="AddressValidaitonResponse"
          messageType="ps:AddressResponseMessage"/>
    <!-- output from BPEL process -->
    <variable name="TransactionResponse"
          messageType="client:TransactionResponseMessage"/>
    <variable name="ValidationFalse" type="xs:string"/>
</variables>

<!-- The main method/part of the process -->
<sequence>
    <!-- Receive the initial request for from client -->
    <receive partnerLink="client"
          portType="client:TransactionRequestPT"
          operation="TransactionApproval"
          variable="TransactionRequest"
          createlnstance="yes" />
    <!-- Prepare input for the CC and Address WS -->
    <assign>
          <copy>
                <from variable="TransactionRequest" part="CC"/>
                <to variable="CCValidaitonRequest" part="CC"/>
          </copy>
    </assign>
    <assign>    <copy>
                <from variable="TransactionRequest" part="Address"/>
                <to variable="AddressValidationRequest" part="Address"/>
          </copy>
   </assign>
    <!- Synchronously invoke CC & Address Validation Services -->
    <flow>
          <invoke partnerLink="CCValidator"
                portType="ps:CCCheckerSoap"
                operation="ValidateCardNumber"
                inputvariable="CCValidationRequest"
                outputvariable="CCValidationResponse"/>
          <invoke partnerLink="AddressValidator"
                portType="ps:USAddressVerificationSoap"
                operation="VerifyAddress"
                inputvariable="AddressValidationRequest"
                outputvariable="AddressValidaitonResponse"/>
    </flow>
    <!-- select the return value from CC validation -->
    <switch>
          <case condition="bpws:getVariableData('CCValidationResponse',
                'ps:string') = "true"  AND
                 bpws:getVariableData('Address ValidationResponse',
                 'ps:string') = "true">
```

```
            <!- Select Validation True -->
            <assign>
                <copy>
                    <from variable="CCValidationResponse" />
                    <to variable="TransactionResponse" />
                </copy>
            </assign>
            <!- Select Validation False -->
            <otherwise>
                <assign>
                    <copy>
                        <from variable="CCValidationResponse"/>
                        <to variable="TransactionResponse"/>
                    </copy>
                </assign>
            </otherwise>
        </case>
    <!-- send a response to the client -->
    <reply partnerLink="client"
            portType="ps:clientPT"
            operation="TransactionApproval"
            variable="TransactionResponse"/>
  </sequence>
</process>
```

8.3.5 An Example Invoking Real Web Services

In the foregoing discussion, we used a rather complex example, so that we can touch many issues in the design of the BPEL process and its WSDL interface. However, the BPEL process is not a working example because the web services used in the example are hypothetical. There are no free services available for credit validation and shipping to make this example real. In this section, we will present a smaller example, but a working example, where all services are real. Figure 8.26 shows the block diagram of the client, BPEL process, and the two web services used in this example.

The two remote web services are:

- USZip service, which returns US Zip code information by the City name. The real WSDL definition of the web service is at: http://www.webservicex.net/uszip.asmx?wsdl;
- Movie Info service, which retrieves the list of theaters and movies by the Zip code and radius. The real WSDL definition of the web service is at: www.ignyte.com/webservices/commercial/WhatsShowingWebservice1.0/MovieInformationService.svc?wsdl

The BPEL process offers a composite service that allows the client to use the city name to retrieve the zip code, and then use the zip code to retrieve the theater and movie information.

The BPEL process has three partners, and thus we need to create three partner link types, as shown in the code fragment that follows, where the communication between the client and the BPEL process is asynchronous, while the communication between the BPEL process and the USZip and MovieInfo services are synchronous.

```
<?xml version= "1.0" encoding="UTF-8"?>
<definitions
   xmlns: http="http://schemas.xmlsoap.org/wsdl/http/"
   xmlns: soap="http://schemas xmlsoap.org/wsdl/soap/"
   xmlns: xs= "http://www.w3.org/2001/XMLschema"
   xmlns: soapenc="http://schemas.xml soap.org/soap/encoding/"
   xmlns ="http://schemas.xmlsoap.org/wsdl/"
   xmlns: targetNamespace="http://neptune.fulton.ad.asu.edu/WSRepository/bpel/"
```

```
   xmlns: zip="http://www.webservicex.net/uszip.asmx/"
   xmlns: ttr= "
http://www.ignyte.com/webservices/commercial/WhatsShowingWebservice1.0/MovieInformat
ionService.svc/"
   xmlns: plnk="http://schemas.xmlsoap.org/ws/2003/05/partner-link/">
   . . .
   <plnk:partnerLinkType name="clientLT">
        <plnk:role name="movieService">
              <plnk:portType name="tns:movieInfoPT"/>
        </plnk:role>
        <plnk:role name="clientCallback">
              <plnk:portType name="tns:clientCallbackPT"/>
        </plnk:role>
   </plnk:partnerLinkType>
   <plnk:partnerLinkType name= "uszipLT">
        <plnk:role name= "getInfobyCityService">
              <plnk:portType name="mov: USZipSoap" />
        </plnk:role>
   </plnk:partnerLinkType>
   <plnk:partnerLinkType name= "movieInfoLT">
        <plnk:role name= "movieInfoService">
              <plnk:portType name="mov: MovieInformationSoap" />
        </plnk:role>
   </plnk:partnerLinkType>
. . .
```

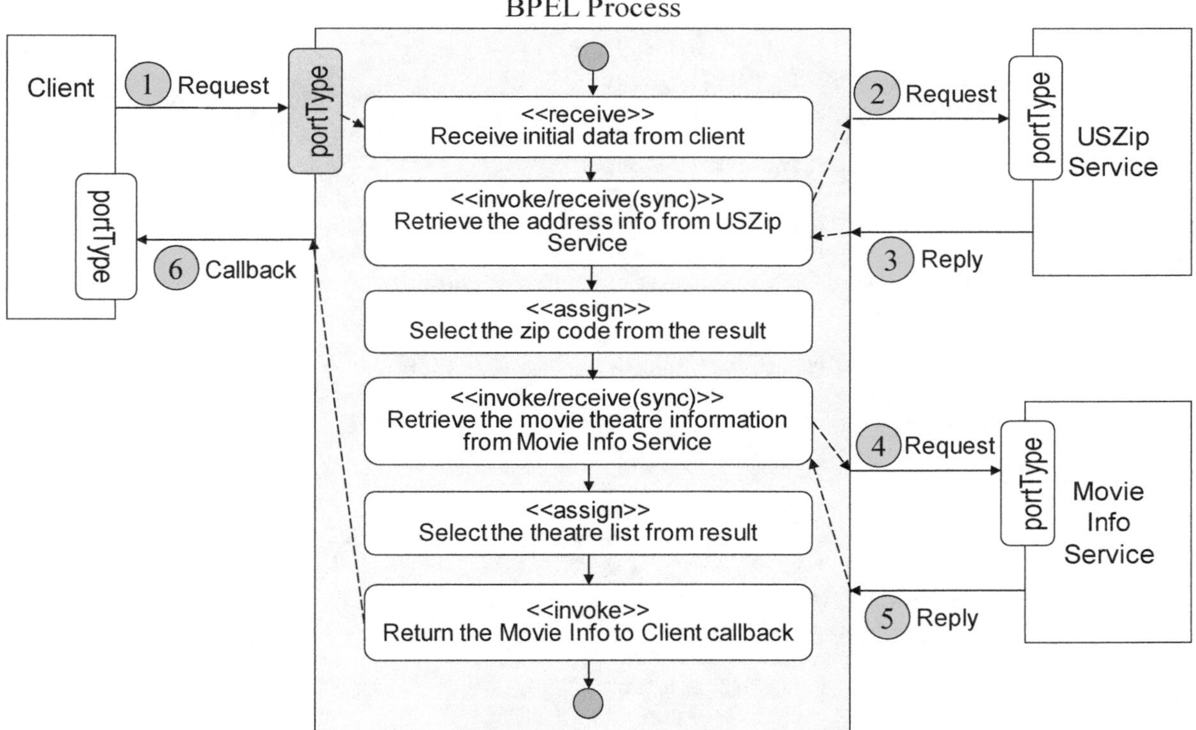

Figure 8.26. A BPEL process returning movie information based on city name

The complete BPEL process code, which accesses the real web services USZip and MovieInfo services, is given as follows. The code has similar structure and functions as the Payment and Shipping example, except that the web services used are real.

```
<process name="Theater"
   targetNameSpace="http://packtpub.com/bpel/travel/"
   xmlns="http://schemas.xmlSoap.org/ws/2003/03/business-process/"
   xmlns: bpws="http://schemas.xmlsoap.org/ws/2003/03/business-process/"
   xmlns: mov="http://neptune.fulton.ad.asu.edu/WSRepository/bpel/"
   xmlns: zip="http://www.webserviceX.NET"
   xmlns: ttr="http://www.ignyte.com/whatsshowing">

   <!-- Define partner links -->
   <partnerLinks>
     <partnerLink name="client" partnerLinkType="mov:clientLT"
       myRole="movieService"
       partnerRole="movieServiceRequester"/>
   <partnerLink name="USZip"
       partnerLinkType="mov:uszipLT" myRole="GetInfoByCityService"/>
   <partnerLink name="MovieInfo"
       partnerLinkType="mov:movieInfoLT" myRole="GetTheaterService"/>
   </partnerLinks>

   <!-- Define variables for storing information -->
   <variables>
       <!-- input for this process -->
       <variable name="MovieInfoRequest"
             messageType="mov:MovieInfoRequestMessage"/>
       <!-- input for the USZip web service -->
       <variable name="GetInfoByCityRequest"
             messageType="mov:GetInfoByCitySoapIn"/>
       <!-- output from USZip web service  -->
       <variable name="GetInfoByCityResponse"
             messageType="mov:GetInfoByCitySoapOut"/>
       <!-- input for MovieInfo web services -->
       <variable name="GetTheaterRequest"
             messageType="mov:GetTheatersAndMoviesSoapIn"/>
       <!- output from MovieInfo web services -->
       <variable name="GetTheaterResponse"
             messageType="mov:GetTheatersAndMoviesSoapOut"/>
       <!-- output from BPEL process -->
       <variable name="MovieInfoResponse"
             messageType="mov:MovieInfoResponseMessage"/>
   </variables>

   <!-- Define the main method to process the information -->
   <sequence name="main">
       <!-- Receive the initial request from client -->
       <receive partnerLink="client"
             portType="mov:MovieInfoPT"
             operation="MovieInfoFinder"
             variable="MovieInfoRequest"
             createlnstance="yes"/>
       <!-- Prepare input for the USZip Web service -->
       <assign>
             <copy>
                  <from variable="MovieInfoRequest"/>
                  <to variable="GetInfoByCityRequest" part="parameters"/>
```

```
                </copy>
            </assign>
    <!-- synchronously invoke USZip Web Service -->
    <invoke partnerLink="employeeTravelStatus"
         portType="mov:USZipSoap"
         operation="GetInfoByCity"
         inputvariable="GetInfoByCityRequest"
         outputvariable="GetInfoByCityResponse"/>
    <!-- Prepare the input for MovieInfo WS(Copy zipcode;
          Radius is always 5 mile) in the example -->
    <assign>
         <copy>
              <from variable="GetInfoByCityResponse"
                   part="parameters"
                   query="zip:Table/zip:ZIP"/>
              <to variable="GetTheaterRequest"
                   part="parameters" query="/zipCode"/>
         </copy>
         <copy>
              <from expression="5"/>
              <to variable="GetTheaterRequest"
                   part="parameters" query="/radius"/>
         </copy>
    </assign>
    <!--  Synchronously invoke MovieInfo WS -->
    <invoke partnerLink="MovieInfo"
              portType="mov:MovieInformationSoap"
              operation="GetTheatersAndMovies"
              inputvariable= "GetTheaterRequest"
              outputvariable="GetTheaterResponse"/>
    <!- prepare BPEL output - MovieInfoRespose (refer slide: 7) -->
    <assign>   <copy>
                   <from variable = "GetTheaterRespose" />
                   <to variable = "MovieInfoResponse" />
              </copy>
    </assign>
    <!- invoke client callback -->
    <invoke name="CallbackClient" partnerLink="Client"
         portType="mov:ClientCallbackPT"
         operation="ClientCallback"
         variable="MovieInfoResponse"/>
    </sequence>
</process>
```

Figure 8.27 and Figure 8.28 show the port type definitions in the respective WSDL files of the client, the BPEL process, and the web services.

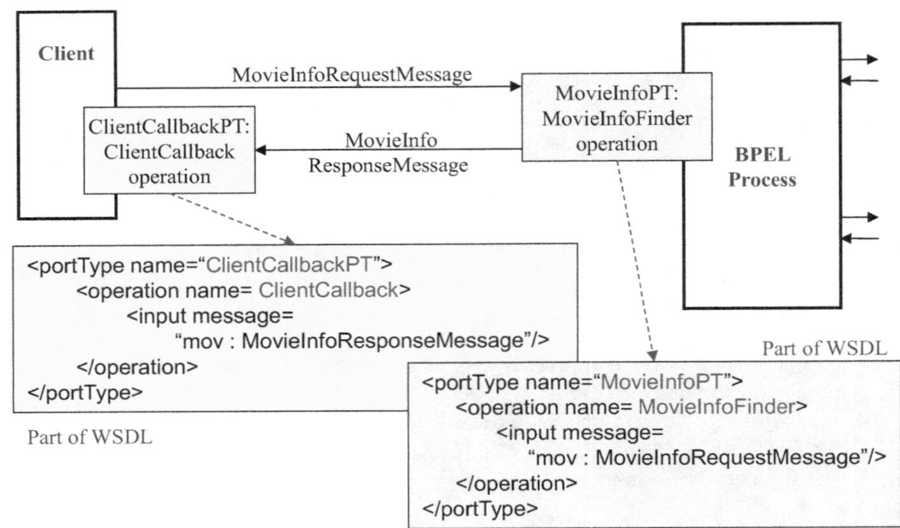

Figure 8.27. PortType definition of the client and the BPEL process

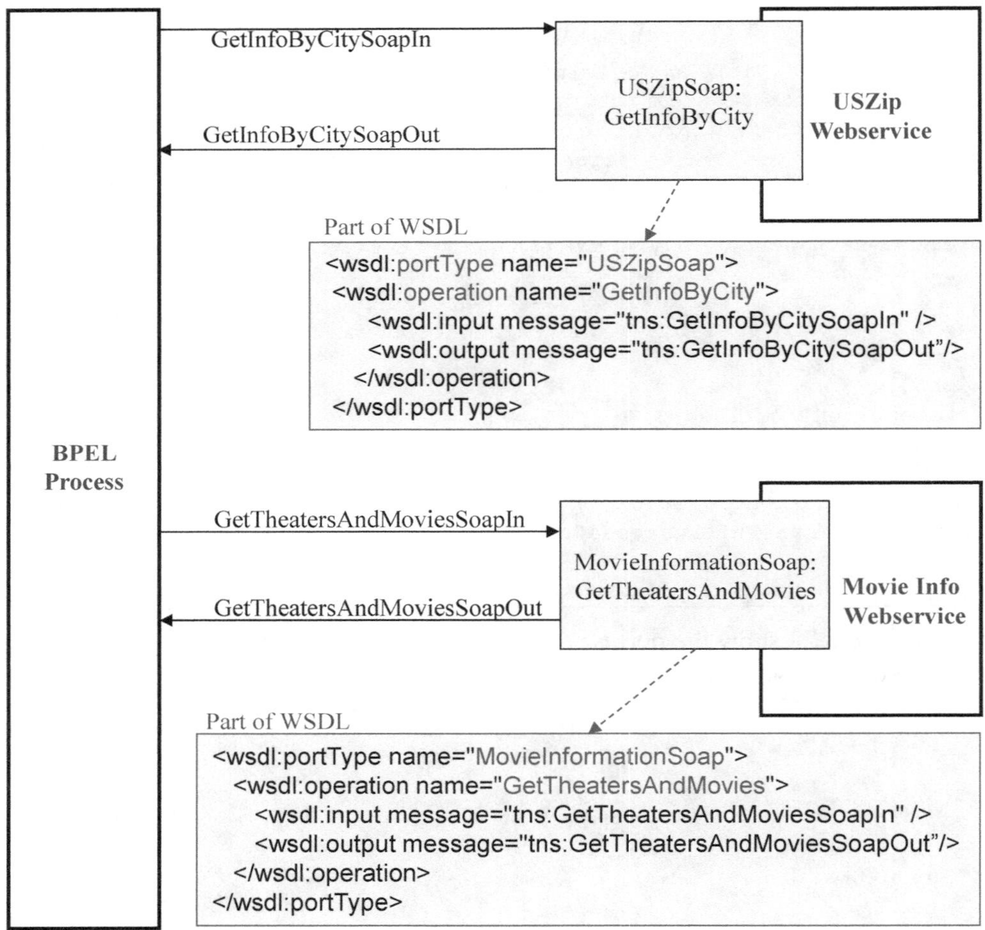

Figure 8.28. PortType definition of the web service used by the BPEL process

So far, we have discussed the primary features of a BPEL process, including activities, constructs, and the partner links. Like a programming language, BPEL offers many other features. The code skeleton that follows shows the general structure of a BPEL process, including variable declaration, corrections, and various handlers that support *event-driven computing*.

```
<process ...>
   <partnerLinks> ... </partnerLinks>
       <!-- each accesses a Web service of a predefined partnerLinkType -->
   <variables> ... </variables>
       <variable ... />
       <variable ... />
       <!-- Declare global variables to be used by the activities -->
   <correlations> ... </correlations>
       <!-- Support stateful interactions between process and service -->
   <faultHandlers> ... </faultHandlers>
       <!-- Alternate execution path to deal with exceptions -->
   <compensationHandlers> ... </compensationHandlers>
       <!-- handlers that undo actions after exceptions -->
   <! -- Activities and constructs are combined and nested to -->
   <! -- implement the main business logic, such as: -->
   <sequence> ... </sequence>
   <flow> ... </flow>
   <receive> ... </receive>
   <invoke> ... </invoke>
   <reply> ... </reply>
</process>
```

The variable definition shown in the code skeleton defines global variables that have the scope in the entire BPEL process. BPEL also supports local variables that can be defined within a construct, quoted by a pair of tags `<scope>`, as shown in the code segment that follows:

```
<sequence>
   <scope>
       <variables>
             <!-- Declare variable local to the scope -->
             <variable name="MovieInfoRequest"
                    messageType="mov:MovieInfoRequestMessage"/>
             <!-- input for the USZip web service -->
             <variable name="GetInfoByCityResponse"
                    messageType="mov:GetInfoByCitySoapOut"/>
       </variables>
       ...
       <assign>
             <copy>
                    <from variable="MovieInfoRequest"/>
                    <to variable="GetInfoByCityRequest" part="parameters"/>
             </copy>

   </scope>
   <!-- The scope of above local variables does not go beyond this point -->
   ...
</sequence>
```

The fault handlers shown in the foregoing code skeleton have a similar structure to the traditional programming languages such as C++, C#, and Java, as can be seen from the code segment that follows:

```
<process>
   <partnerLinks>
       ...
```

```
   </partnerLinks >
   <variables>
         …
   </variables>
   <faultHandlers>
         <catch faultName="CCValidationFailed" >
               <!-- First fault handler -->
               <!-- Perform activities -->
         </catch>
         <catch faultName="AddressValidationFailed">
               <!-- Second fault handler -->
               <!-- Perform activities -->
         </catch>
         <catchAll>
               <!-- Perform activities -->
         </catchAll>
   </faultHandlers>
   <!-- main code consists of constructs and activities -->
   ...
</process>
```

Correlations are more complex topic and we will discuss them in a separate section later in this chapter.

8.4 Stateless versus Stateful Web Services

In object-oriented computing, when an object is created, one can store data in the date fields of the object and retrieve the data later by accessing the same object again. If the state needs to be maintained among different objects from the same class, a static data field (variable) can be defined in the class. Then the same memory location in the static memory allocated to the program will be accessed from all objects created from the same class. However, in the case of web services, a different execution model is used. It is not possible to store information in the data fields of an object behind a service. No static members can be created for the clients to share information either.

When a client uses a remote class on the service provider's site, it instantiates an object using the remote reference, which creates a proxy or a virtual object in the client. The proxy is a channel to the service running on the provider's site. Many clients can access the same service and the same client can access the same service multiple times. The service will normally not differentiate or correlate whether the accesses come from the same client or from different clients. Every time a request arrives, a new instance of the service (an operating system process) is created, and after the request is served, the instance is terminated. This is the so-called **stateless service**. As shown in Figure 8.29, although a single proxy is created, two new instances are created when the abs(x) method is accessed twice from the same client. Another instance is created when the PiValue() method is accessed.

Stateless services are the natural and easy solution to web-based computing. However, in many cases, we need stateful solutions. For example, if AddToCart services are called multiple times, the client expects the state information to carry over across the multiple accesses, so that multiple items can be added into the same cart.

ASP.Net does not explicitly support stateful web services. The developers must create their own mechanisms to identify the clients of the services and correlate their state in multiple accesses.

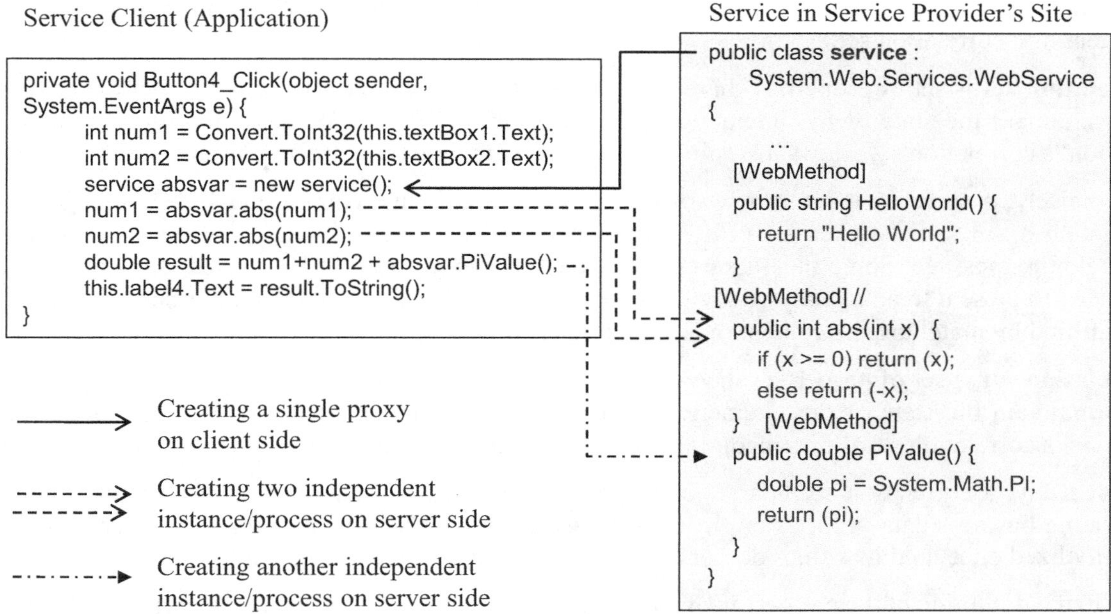
Service Client (Application)
Service in Service Provider's Site
private void Button4_Click(object sender,
System.EventArgs e) {
int num1 = Convert.ToInt32(this.textBox1.Text);
int num2 = Convert.ToInt32(this.textBox2.Text);
service absvar = new service();
num1 = absvar.abs(num1);
num2 = absvar.abs(num2);
double result = num1+num2 + absvar.PiValue();
this.label4.Text = result.ToString();
}
public class service :
System.Web.Services.WebService
{
...
[WebMethod]
public string HelloWorld() {
return "Hello World";
}
[WebMethod] //
public int abs(int x) {
if (x >= 0) return (x);
else return (-x);
} [WebMethod]
public double PiValue() {
double pi = System.Math.PI;
return (pi);
}
}
Creating a single proxy
on client side
Creating two independent
instance/process on server side
Creating another independent
instance/process on server side

Figure 8.29. Stateless service creates a new instance for every access

8.4.1 BizTalk's Singleton Object Approach

Microsoft BizTalk supports stateful web services development by introducing a concept called Singleton Object, which allows a single instance (object) of a class to be created if the calls come from the same proxy. A new object will be created only on the first call from a proxy, and all subsequent requests from the same proxy will point to the same object that has been created earlier.

This approach needs some infrastructure to support this mechanism. Specifically, the class supporting the singleton object needs to:

- maintain a list of proxies pointing to the object;
- maintain the correlate between the requests with the object created before;
- maintain a list account and states related to the account if re-login is allowed; and recognize the proxy (session information) and account (login) when an invocation is requested.

Note that this design trades software design complexity with infrastructure design complexity. If a single object is created for each object, the software design is easier, but the infrastructure is more complex, as it needs to maintain a list of clients with the corresponding objects created.

8.4.2 BPEL's Correlation Approach

BPEL process can model both types of services: simple stateless services as well as more complex stateful, long-running, and asynchronous services. The mechanism that supports the stateful services is called correlation, which is a construct for keeping track of a group of messages that belong together in one or a group of particular business partners' interaction. Correlation matches messages and interactions with the business process instances that they are intended for.

When a BPEL engine receives a message, it looks for a process (service) that can handle the message. Some messages cause a new process instance to be created (stateless), whereas others need to be sent to an already-running process (stateful). How can an existing process be identified? It is identified by matching the content of a correlation set.

A **correlation set** is set of properties shared by messages, which can be used to represent the data that is used to maintain the state of the interaction (or called *conversation*). At the BPEL process side of the interaction, a correlation set allows incoming messages to reach the right process instance on the server site.

More precisely, a correlation set is a set of business data fields that capture the state of the interaction ("correlating business data when a BPEL engine receives a message, it looks for a process (service) that can handle the message. Some messages cause a new process instance to be created (stateless), whereas others need to be sent to an already-running process (stateful). How can an existing process be identified? It is identified by matching the content of a correlation set.

A **correlation set** is set of properties shared by messages, which can be used to represent the data that is used to maintain the state of the interaction (or called *conversation*). At the BPEL process side of the interaction, a correlation set allows incoming messages to reach the right process instance on the server site.

More precisely, a correlation set is a set of business data fields that capture the state of the interaction ("correlating business data"); for example, a "purchase order number" or "customer ID." Each correlation set is initialized once, and its values do not change in the course of the interaction.

Similar to the definition of the partnerLinkType, a correlation set is a named set of properties, each of which is defined as a WSDL extensibility element. A property is "mapped" to a field in a WSDL message type. Each property can thus be found in the messages actually exchanged. Typically, a property can be mapped to several different message types and carried on in many interactions across operations and port types. The code segment that follows shows an example of applying the correlation set in a business process.

```
<receive partner= "client" operation="..."
portType="ClientPT" container="...">
   <correlations>
        <correlation set = "UserId" initiate = "yes"/>
   </correlations>
</receive>
<invoke partnerLink="Client" portType="ClientPT"
        operation="PurchaseResponse" inputVariable="PO">
   <correlations>
        <correlation set="UserId" initiate="no" />
   </correlations>
</invoke>
```

In the foregoing code, an input, or output operation identifies which correlation sets apply to the messages received or sent. That set will be used to assure that the message is related to the appropriate stateful interaction. The element <correlation> has an attribute called "initiate," which can be set to three different values: yes, join, and no.

- A *yes* means that the execution of the associated web service's activity must always attempt to initiate the correlation set. If the set is not initiated, the execution will initialize the correlation set with the values from the message being transmitted or received. BPEL requires the activity to throw an error `bpel:correlationViolation` if the correlation set is already initiated at the time of the web service activity's execution.
- If multiple activities are enabled concurrently and any of them can initiate the correlation set with their execution, then the initiate attribute value should be *join*, which means an activity must attempt to initiate the correlation set, if the correlation set is not yet initiated. If the correlation set is already initiated and the correlation consistency constraint is violated, an error bpel:correlationViolation must be thrown. *Join* is useful for multi-start activities or any scenario where more than one activity may initiate the correlation set.

- When the `initiate` attribute is set to *no* or is not explicitly set, the related activity must not attempt to initiate the correlation set. If the correlation set has not been previously initiated when the activity is executed, an error `bpel: correlationViolation` will be thrown. If the correlation set is initiated, however the correlation consistency constraint is violated, an error `bpel:correlationViolation` must be thrown.

Correlation sets can be initiated with the transmission of a message or the receipt of a message. The following example is adopted from OASIS's document at http://docs.oasis-open.org/wsbpel/2.0/OS/wsbpel-v2.0-OS.html. In this example, a **Buyer** process and a **Seller** process are discussed, as shown in Figure 8.30.

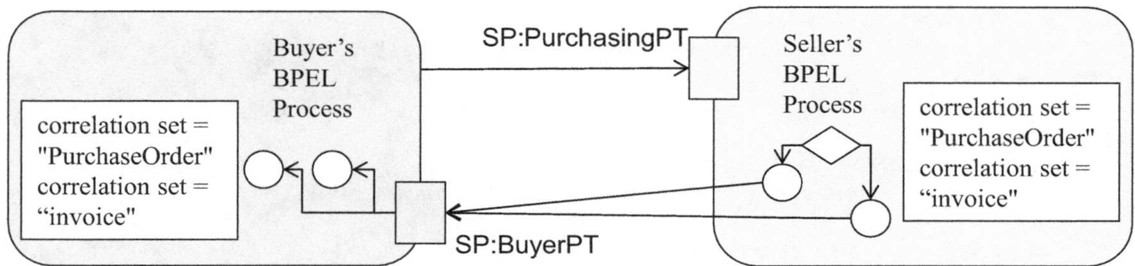

Figure 8.30. Two correlation sets are used to relate the purchase order and invoice

Two correlation sets are defined and used in the messages sent between the two parties. As shown in the code that follows, the Buyer process initiates a communication by invoking the Seller's "PurchaseRequest" operation and setting the correlation set = "PurchaseOrder." The initiate attribute is set to yes, because this operation initiates the conversation. Then, the Buyer waiting for one of the two possible responses from the Seller: PurchaseResponse or PurchaseReject. In both cases, the initiate attribute is set to *no*, because the attribute should have been initiated at this time. After the PurchaseResponse arrives, a second correlation set, Invoice, is expected.

```
<invoke partnerLink="Seller" portType="SP:PurchasingPT"
                           operation="PurchaseRequest" variable="PO">
   <correlations>
        <correlation set="PurchaseOrder" initiate="yes"/>
   </correlations>
</invoke>
...
<pick>
   <onMessage partnerLink="Seller" portType="SP:BuyerPT"
                  operation="PurchaseResponse" variable="POResponse">
        <correlations>
               <correlation set="PurchaseOrder" initiate="no"/>
               <correlation set="Invoice" initiate="yes"/>
        </correlations>
        ...    <!-- handle the response message -->
   </onMessage>
   <onMessage partnerLink="Seller" portType="SP:BuyerPT"
                  operation="PurchaseReject" variable="POReject">
        <correlations>
               <correlation set="PurchaseOrder" initiate="no"/>
        </correlations>
        ...     <!-- handle the reject message -->
   </onMessage>
```

```
</pick>
```

On the Seller's side, the process uses the <receive> activity to take orders, as shown in the code that follows. The same correlation set name PurchaseOrder is used and the initiate attribute is set to yes when the correlation set is first accessed on the Seller's side. Once the purchase order is processed (code not given), two scenarios can occur: accept the order by sending the Buyer a purchase response with an invoice, or reject the purchase order. In both cases, the correlation set initiate attribute is set to no, because the correlation set has been initialized before.

```
<receive partnerLink="Buyer" portType="SP:PurchasingPT"
        operation="PurchaseRequest" variable="PO">
   <correlations>
        <correlation set="PurchaseOrder" initiate="yes" />
   </correlations>
</receive>
...
<invoke partnerLink="Buyer" portType="SP:BuyerPT"
   operation="PurchaseResponse" inputVariable="POResponse">
   <correlations>
        <correlation set="PurchaseOrder" initiate="no" />
        <correlation set="Invoice" initiate="yes" />
   </correlations>
</invoke>
...
<invoke partnerLink="Buyer" portType="SP:BuyerPT"
        operation="PurchaseReject" inputVariable="POReject">
   <correlations>
        <correlation set="PurchaseOrder" initiate="no" />
   </correlations>
</invoke>
```

Note that the BPEL approach makes the software design more complex, as it needs to have a correlation set properly designed. However, it does not need to change the infrastructure. This is different from the BizTalk's approach.

8.5 Frameworks Supporting BPEL Composition

Although BPEL is an XML-based language and BPEL process can be written line-by-line in text, there are numerous IDEs (Independent Development Environments) that allow visual development of drag-and-drop. Each activity, service, and construct is presented in a box and the composition is of selecting the required boxes and linking them together. The BPEL process and the WSDL interface can be generated automatically. This section presents three widely used IDEs that support BPEL development: Oracle SOA Suite, ActiveBPEL, and BizTalk.

8.5.1 Oracle SOA Suite

Oracle SOA Suite is a complete set of service infrastructure components for building, deploying, and managing SOA software. It allows services to be created, managed, and orchestrated into composite applications and business processes. It supports hot-plug of components into the system, which allows an organization to extend and evolve their architectures. The system can be downloaded at: http://www.oracle.com/technetwork/middleware/soasuite/downloads/index.html.

Oracle SOA Suite can include different sets of components based on different business requirements:

- Oracle JDeveloper. It is an IDE that supports the visual development BPEL process, creating a WSDL document of the process, and deploying the BPEL web service into a hosting environment. Although JDeveloper works with other components in Oracle SOA Suite, it must be installed separately. The download site is at:
  http://www.oracle.com/technology/software/products/jdev/index.html
- Oracle BPEL Process Manager. The process manager offers hosting service of web services developed in JDeveloper. It also offers UDDI registry service. In most cases, it is sufficient to use JDeveloper and the Process Manager to form an environment to develop SOA applications.
- Oracle Business Rules component support rule and policy management and enforcement. This component allows rules and policies stored in text files separated from the program code. The rules and policies can be modified at runtime and have the new rules and policies to be enforced at the next access to them.
- Oracle Enterprise Service Bus (ESB) provides adapters between different application modules written in different programming languages. Its function is similar to the ORB (Object Request Broker) in CORBA development environment. It also performs XSLT transformation from XML text to web presentation.

Figure 8.31 shows an example of the visual development of the BPEL process in JDeveloper, where each activity is an item (icon) in the development environment that can be dragged and dropped into the design panel, and the activities can be linked using the interfaces on the icons. The text-based version of the BPEL process, as well as the WSDL definition, can be found in the project file stack on the IDE. The example shows the development of an online bookstore. The process is based on the services from Amazon Web Services and Barnes & Noble Web Services. The central part of the diagram is the BPEL process that orchestrates the requests from the client and return values from the services.

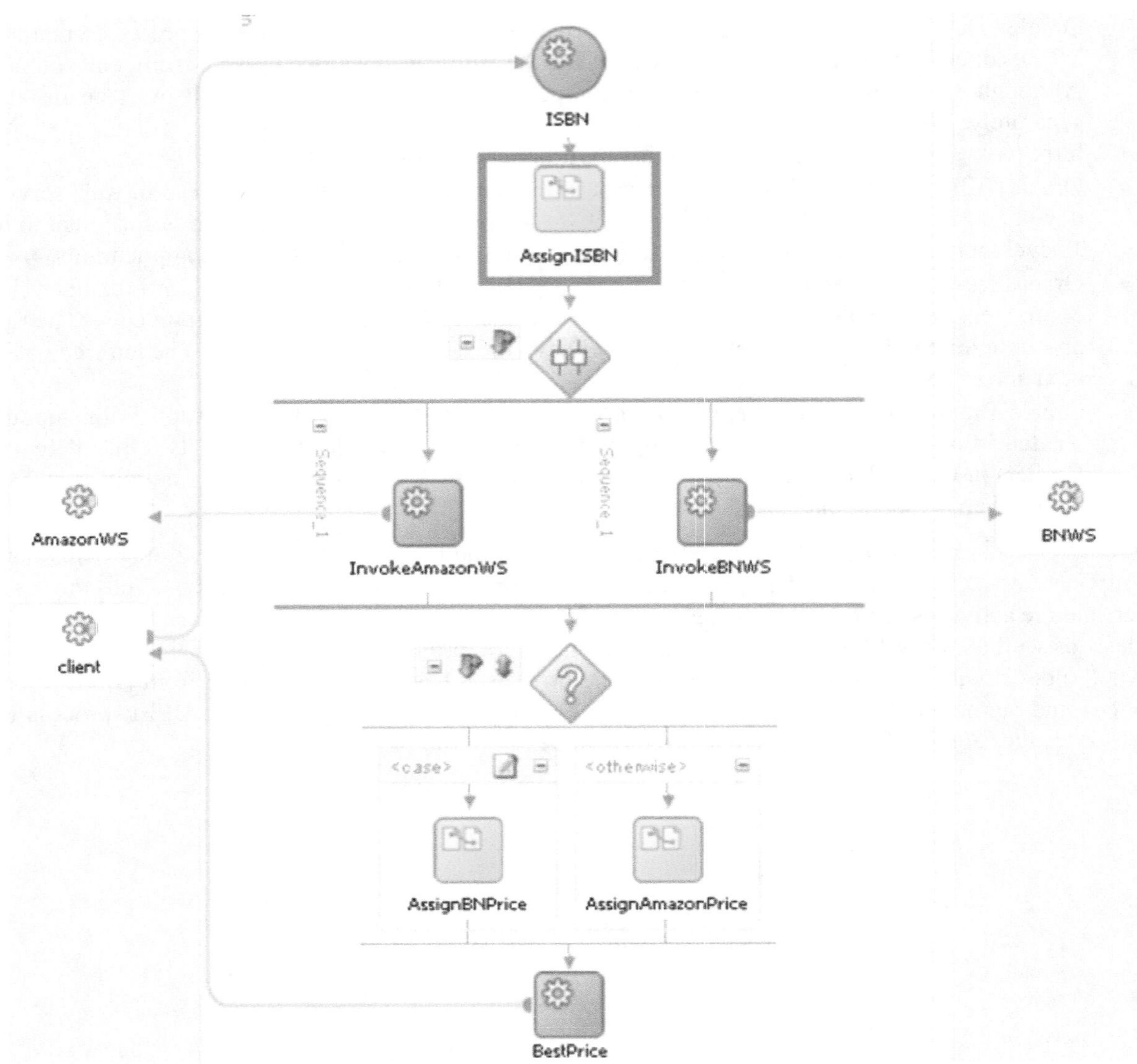

Figure 8.31. Visual development using JDeveloper

8.5.2 ActiveBPEL

Similar to Oracle SOA Suite, ActiveBPEL Enterprise Suite consists of a set of components, which provides a visual development environment for the creation, testing, deployment, and execution of BPEL web services. The main components include:

- ActiveBPEL Designer: the function is similar to the JDeveloper, which supports the visual development, simulation, testing, and deployment of BPEL processes. Using the Designer, one can build processes by choosing partners, services and operations, and defining how data flows among those entities. As you organize icons on the Process Editor canvas, ActiveBPEL constructs valid BPEL (XML) automatically. Figure 8.32 shows an ActiveBPEL BPEL process developed using ActiveBPEL Designer, as given in the ActiveBPEL website.
- Administration Console: it is an alternative to the ActiveBPEL Designer, and it provides functions to manage deployed and active processes running on Apache Tomcat server, an alerting system, and endpoint locations. It also has engine configuration settings for performance management.

- ActiveBPEL Engine: it manages processes, including process versioning (effective/expiration dates), invocation handlers for partner endpoints, endpoint retry and security policies, and process exception management. For most ActiveBPEL Enterprise application servers, the ActiveBPEL engine can run in a clustered environment.
- Apache Tomcat: this component provides a general (Java-based) service hosting service, which is comparable to Microsoft IIS for C#-based services.

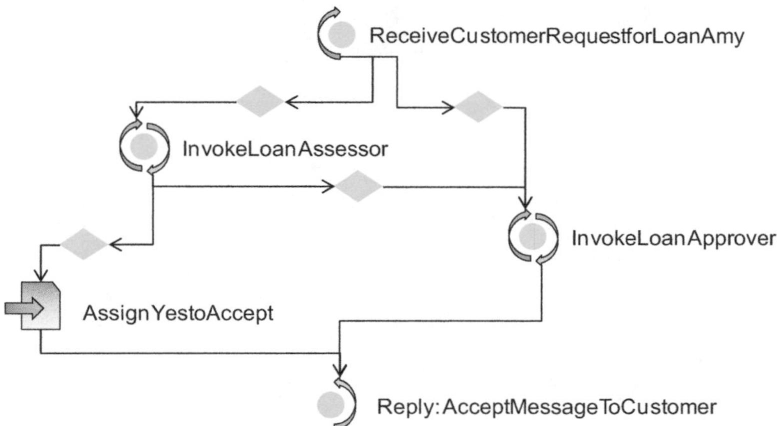

Figure 8.32. Visual development using ActiveBPEL

8.5.3 BizTalk

Built on .Net and as an additional component of .Net, BizTalk is Microsoft's Business Process Management (BPM) environment for developing the integration of heterogeneous systems, also called Enterprise Application Integration (EAI). BPEL is one of the composition languages that it supports. In fact, BizTalk's native composition language is XLang. BPEL process can be imported into XLang and be executed. On the other hand, XLang process can be exported BPEL process too. There is no free edition of BizTalk for download. Similar to Oracle SOA Suite and ActiveBPEL, BizTalk uses a visual tool to develop the business process. Both XLang and BPEL code can be generated from the graphic process design by the developers. Figure 8.33 shows an example given in the BizTalk tutorial available at:
http://msdn2.microsoft.com/en-us/library/aa560110.aspx

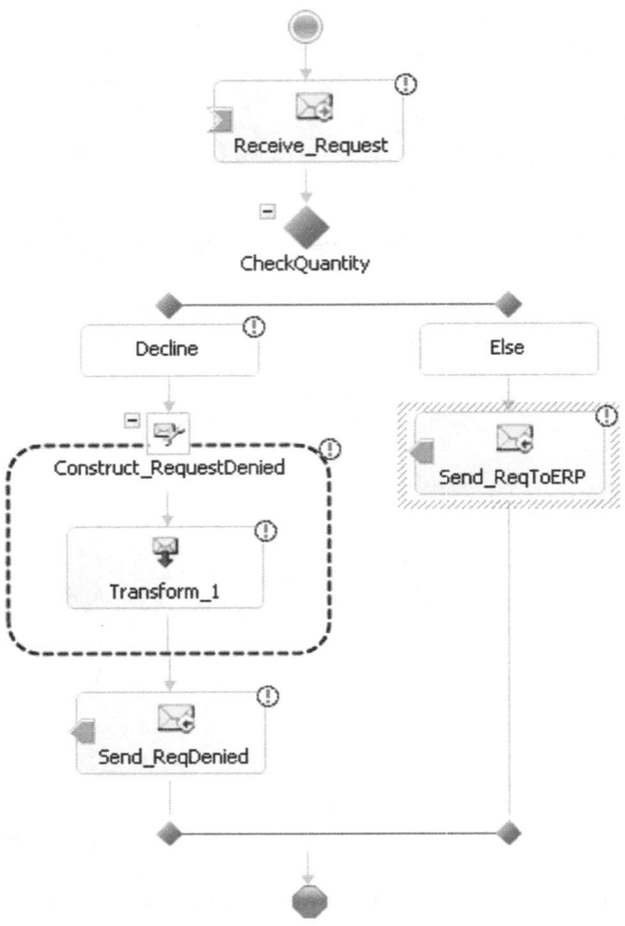

Figure 8.33. Visual development using BizTalk

8.5.4 Simple Workflow Service

Amazon Web Services and Cloud Solutions provide a variety of e-business developing and hosting services. They offer a Workflow composition tool called Simple Workflow Service (SWF) for client to build their applications visually. Similar to Oracle's SOA Suite and JDeveloper, SWF offers an orchestration process to implement the business processes using a workflow of activities. The application structure is shown in Figure 8.34. The diagram shows six steps of creating a workflow in SWF environment, which is elaborated as follows:

1. Write activity workers that implement the processing steps in your workflow.
2. Write a decider to implement the coordination logic of your workflow.
3. Register your activities and workflow with Amazon SWF. You can do this step programmatically or by using the AWS Management Console.
4. Start your activity workers and decider.
5. Start one or more executions of your workflow.
6. View workflow executions using the AWS Management Console.

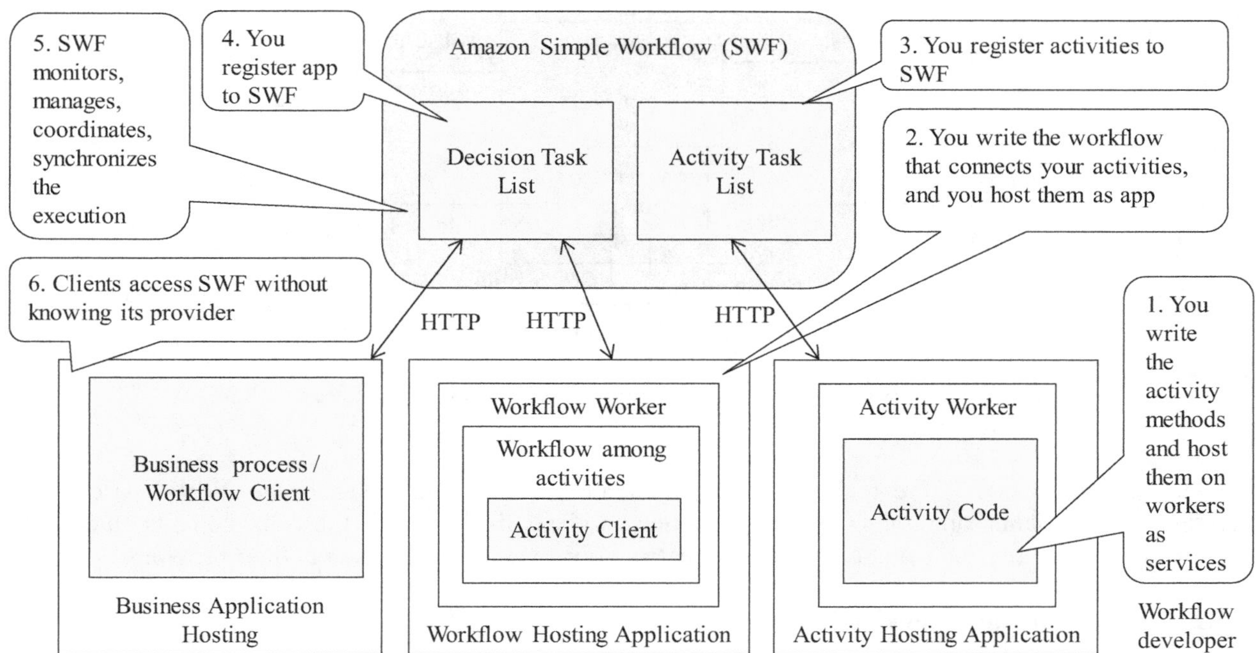

Figure 8.34. SWF application structure

More detail of developing Amazon SWF can be found at:

http://docs.aws.amazon.com/amazonswf/latest/developerguide/swf-dev-about-workflows.html

8.6 Message-Based Integration

System integrations we discussed so far are based on point-to-point communication, either in the form of synchronous mode or asynchronous mode. Synchronous communication requires to establish a connection and to complete the communication within the connection. It is similar to a telephone call. Asynchronous one- or two-way communication is more flexible. However, the message receiver is required to be available at the time when the communication starts. An analogy is that a person calls another person, asking them to do a job that may take a large amount of time to complete. In this case, holding on the line and waiting for the person to complete the job is not a desirable solution. A callback makes more sense.

Message-based communication, or **messaging**, takes the asynchronous communication a step further. It does not even require the receiver to be available at the time the communication starts. The message can be queued and delivered when the receiver becomes available. It is similar to our text message or email system. Messaging requires a queuing mechanism to store the messages.

Messaging system, also referred to as Messaging Oriented Middleware (MOM), is a critical and widely used communication platform for enterprise applications and application integration. A messaging system can support asynchronous one-way messages, synchronous as well asynchronous two-way messages, and one-to-many messages based on publish-subscription. The main purpose of a messaging system is to offer asynchronous and queued message services. However, synchronous two-way messages are often offered as a part of the system; for example, to allow the receiver to explicitly request (fetch) a message from the destination by calling a receive method. Figure 8.35 shows a typical messaging system.

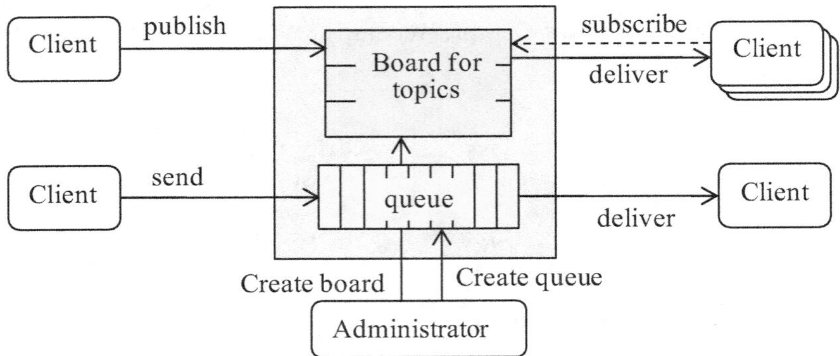

Figure 8.35. Messaging system with publish-subscribe and queue mechanism

An administrator must first create the board and queue in the messaging server for the clients to use. In the message board, clients can publish a message, which will be delivered to the subscribed clients. In order to use the board and the queue, a client needs to create an object and a connection in their program.

8.6.1 Java Message Service

The Java Message Service (JMS) API is a messaging standard that allows application components based on the Java 2 Platform and Java Enterprise Edition (J2EE) to create, send, receive, and read messages. It enables distributed communication that is loosely coupled, reliable, and asynchronous (http://www.oracle.com/technetwork/java/jms/index.html).

In a JMS system, an administrator will first create JMS providers and destination objects for subscribing topics (or for queues) and register them in the JNDI (Java Naming and Directory Interface).

To use the preconfigured service, a client first uses a number of the library classes to register a queue, creates a context object, uses the context object to look up the connection factory name, creates connection, creates session, and creates a destination of queue for point-to-point messaging or a destination of topic (for publish-subscribe). The code that follows illustrates the process of creating a queue and sending a message to the queue (http://docs.jboss.org/jbossmessaging/docs/guide-1.0.1.SP5/html/examples.html).

```
String myQueueName = getDestinationJNDIName();
InitialContext myIc = new InitialContext(); // creating an initial object
ConnectionFactory MyCf = myIc.lookup("/ConnectionFactory");
Queue myQ = (Queue) myIc.lookup(myQueueName);
Connection sendConn = MyCf.createConnection();
Session mySession = sendConn.createSession(false, Session.AUTO_ACKNOWLEDGE);
MessageProducer myMp = mySession.createProducer(myQ);
TextMessage myMsg = mySession.createTextMessage("Hello!");
myMp.send(myMsg);
```

On the other hand, another client, the receiver, can register to the same queue and receive a message from the queue.

```
String myQueueName = getDestinationJNDIName();
InitialContext myIc = new InitialContext(); // creating an initial object
ConnectionFactory MyCf = myIc.lookup("/ConnectionFactory");
Queue myQ = (Queue) myIc.lookup(myQueueName);
Connection recConn = MyCf.createConnection();
Session mySession = recConn.createSession(false, Session.AUTO_ACKNOWLEDGE);
MessageConsumer myMc = mySession.createConsumer(myQ);
recConn.start(); // start the connection
message = (TextMessage)consumer.receive(2000); // wait for certain time
```

Similarly, the code below registers and creates a topic, and then a message to the topic.

```
String myTopicName = getDestinationJNDIName();
InitialContext myIc = new InitialContext(); // creating an initial object
ConnectionFactory MyCf = myIc.lookup("/ConnectionFactory");
Topic myTopic = (Topic) myIc.lookup(/myTopicName);
Connection myConn = MyCf.createConnection();
Session mySession = myConn.createSession(false, Session.AUTO_ACKNOWLEDGE);
MessageProducer myPub = mySession.createProducer(myTopic);
TextMessage myMsg = mySession.createTextMessage("Hello!");
myPub.send(myMsg);
```

The following code demonstrates the process of receiving a message from a topic.

```
MessageConsumer subscriber = session.createConsumer(topic);
ExampListener myListener = new ExampleListener();
subscriber.setMessageListener(myListener);
myConn.start();
myListener.waitForMessage();
myMsg = (TextMessage)myListener.getMessage();
```

8.6.2 Microsoft Message Queue

In .Net Framework, the System.Messaging namespace provides classes that allow you to create, connect to, monitor, and administer message queues on the network and send, receive, or peek messages (http://msdn.microsoft.com/en-us/library/xes6983c.aspx), including the following:

- MessageQueueInstaller class allows the administrator to install and configure a queue that the client applications need in order to exchange messages with other applications. This class is called by the installation utility on the message server; for example, InstallUtil.exe, when installing a MessageQueue. Only one queue needs to be installed among the partner applications.
- MessageQueue class provides access to a queue on a Message Queuing server.

MessageQueue class supports two types of message retrieval: synchronous and asynchronous. The synchronous methods, Peek and Receive, cause the process thread to wait a specified time interval for a new message to arrive in the queue. The asynchronous methods, BeginPeek and BeginReceive, allow the main application tasks to continue in a separate thread until a message arrives in the queue. These methods work by using callback objects and state objects to communicate information between threads.

When you create a new instance of the MessageQueue class in your program, you are not creating a new Message Queuing queue in the server. You will send a message to the server queue to associate your local queue with the server queue, and you can use the Create(String), Delete(String), and Purge methods to manage queues on the server that has been created by the administrator.

The following code in MSDN library illustrates an example that creates a new MessageQueue object, sends a message to a pre-created queue, and receives a message from the queue. The message is of the type of an application-specific class called Order.

```
using System;
using System.Messaging; // Use "Add Reference" to add if not found
namespace MyProject {
   // This class represents an object the following example
   // sends to a queue and receives from a queue.
   public class Order {
        public int orderId;
        public DateTime orderTime;
   };
   // References public queue pre-created in the server
   public void SendPublic() {
        MessageQueue myQueue = new MessageQueue(".\\myQueue");
```

```
        myQueue.Send("Public queue by path name.");
        return;
    }
    public class MyNewQueue{ // Provides a container class.
        // Provides an entry point into the application.
        // This example sends and receives a message from a queue.
        public static void Main() {
            // Create a new instance of the class.
            MyNewQueue myNewQueue = new MyNewQueue();
            // Send a message to associate this queue to a server queue.
            myNewQueue.SendPublic();
            // Now, access the queue by sending and receiving messages
            myNewQueue.SendMessage();
            // Receive a message from a queue.
            myNewQueue.ReceiveMessage();
            return;
        }
        public void SendMessage() { // Sends an Order to a queue.
            // Create a new order and set values.
            Order sentOrder = new Order();
            sentOrder.orderId = 3;
            sentOrder.orderTime = DateTime.Now;
            // Connect to a queue on the local computer.
            MessageQueue myQueue = new MessageQueue(".\\myQueue");
            // Send the Order to the queue.
            myQueue.Send(sentOrder);
            return;
        }
        // Receives a message containing an Order.
        public  void ReceiveMessage(){
            // Connect to the a queue on the local computer.
            MessageQueue myQueue = new MessageQueue(".\\myQueue");
            // Set the formatter to indicate body contains an Order.
            myQueue.Formatter = new XmlMessageFormatter(new Type[]
                {typeof(MyProject.Order)});
            Try {
                // Receive and format the message.
                Message myMessage =myQueue.Receive();
                Order myOrder = (Order)myMessage.Body;
                // Display message information.
                Console.WriteLine("Order ID: "+myOrder.orderId.ToString());
                Console.WriteLine("Sent: "+myOrder.orderTime.ToString());
            }
            catch (MessageQueueException){
                // Handle Message Queuing exceptions.
            }   // Handle invalid serialization format.
            catch (InvalidOperationException e){
                Console.WriteLine(e.Message);
            }
            return;
        }
    }
}
```

8.6.3 Database-Supported Messaging

The messaging services in JMS and MSMQ require the administrator to log into the server and execute a utility program to install and configure a queue before the clients can use the queue. If you do not have the administrator support, you can create your own storage to buffer the message. The example that follows shows an SQL solution of a messaging service, implemented as a WCF service. The code that follows gives the Interface definition.

```
// IService.cs
[ServiceContract]
public interface IService {
    [OperationContract]
    bool SendMessage(string Username, string Message);
    [OperationContract]
    string[] ReceiveMessage(string UserID);
}
```

Two methods are defined, which send a message with a user ID. The receiver retrieves the message based on the user ID. The implementation of the interface is given as follows:

```
// Service.cs
using System.Web.Services;
using System.Data.SqlClient;
using System.Data;
public class Service : IService {
    public bool SendMessage(string Username, string Message){
        string strConnection = "Data Source=NEPTUNE;Initial Catalog=Isoc;Persist
Security Info=True;User ID=import_user; Password= Cse445";
        SqlConnection SQLConn = new SqlConnection(strConnection);
        Try {
            SqlCommand SQLCmd = new SqlCommand("INSERT INTO MsgBoard(Username,
Message) VALUES (@Username, @Message)", SQLConn);
            SQLCmd.Parameters.Add("@Username", System.Data.SqlDbType.NVarChar).Value
= Username;
            SQLCmd.Parameters.Add("@Message", System.Data.SqlDbType.NText).Value =
Message;
            SQLConn.Open();
            SQLCmd.ExecuteNonQuery();
            SQLConn.Close();
            return true;
        }
        catch (Exception) {
            SQLConn.Close();
            return false;
        }
    }
    public string[] ReceiveMessage(string UserID) {
        string strConnection = "Data Source=NEPTUNE;Initial Catalog=Isoc;Persist
Security Info=True;User ID=import_user;Password=mySecrete";
        SqlConnection SQLConn = new SqlConnection(strConnection);
        string[] strValue;
        try{
            SqlCommand SQLMsgCmd = new SqlCommand("SELECT MsgBoard.MsgID,
MsgBoard.Username, MsgBoard.Message, dbo.Person.UserID, dbo.Person.IM FROM MsgBoard
INNER JOIN dbo.Person ON MsgBoard.MsgID > dbo.Person.IM WHERE (dbo.Person.UserID =
@UserID) ORDER BY MsgBoard.MsgID", SQLConn);
            SqlDataAdapter SQLUserDA = new SqlDataAdapter();
            DataSet MsgDS = new DataSet();
            SQLMsgCmd.Parameters.Add("@UserID",
System.Data.SqlDbType.NVarChar).Value = UserID;
```

```
            SQLConn.Open();
            SQLUserDA.SelectCommand = SQLMsgCmd;
            SQLUserDA.Fill(MsgDS);
            SQLConn.Close();
            strValue = new string[MsgDS.Tables[0].Rows.Count];
            for (int i = 0; i < MsgDS.Tables[0].Rows.Count; i++){
                strValue[i] = MsgDS.Tables[0].Rows[0]["Username"].ToString().Trim()
+ ": " + MsgDS.Tables[0].Rows[i]["Message"].ToString().Trim();
            }
            SqlCommand SQLDataCmd = new SqlCommand("UPDATE dbo.Person SET IM = @IM
WHERE (UserID = @UserID)", SQLConn);
            SQLDataCmd.Parameters.Add("@UserID", SqlDbType.NVarChar).Value = UserID;
            SQLDataCmd.Parameters.Add("@IM", SqlDbType.Int).Value =
MsgDS.Tables[0].Rows[MsgDS.Tables[0].Rows.Count - 1]["MsgID"].ToString();
            SQLConn.Open();
            SQLDataCmd.ExecuteNonQuery();
            SQLConn.Close();
        }
        catch (Exception) {
            SQLConn.Close();
            strValue = new string[0];
        }
        return strValue;
    }
}
```

The service is deployed at:

http://neptune.fulton.ad.asu.edu/WSRepository/Services/Messenger/Service.svc

Database operations used in this example will be discussed in Chapter 10. You may want to revisit this example after database materials have been covered.

8.6.4 E-mail Supported Messaging

An e-mail system can be used as a message storage to enable messaging. In this section, we use a Gmail account to store the messages sent from a web application, using the forwarding service from Gmail and a provider account to send small messages to a cell phone. Developed by Calvin Cheng, the web service supporting this operation is deployed in ASU repository at:

http://neptune.fulton.ad.asu.edu/WSRepository/Services/SMS_Service/Service.svc?wsdl

The service offers the following operation:

bool SMS(string Mail_Account, string Password, string Phone, CARRIER Provider, string Message);

where, Mail_Account must have the domain @gmail.com. Password is the password of your Gmail account. In order to send a message from your Gmail to a phone, you must provide your password; phone is the 10-digit destination phone number starting with the area code. The CARRIER can be one of the following: TMOBILE, SPRINT, VERIZON, AT&T. This service will send, by provider, one of the following addresses:

- TMobile: phone_number@tmomail.net
- Sprint: phone_number@messaging.sprintpcs.com
- Verizon: phone_number@vtext.com
- AT&T: phone_number@txt.att.net

You can test the SMS service using the Visual Studio WCF test client. From Windows "Start" menu, choose All Programs → Visual Studio → Visual Studio Tools →Cross Tools Command Prompt. It will open the

Cross Tools Command Prompt window. Enter the command: wcfTestClient.exe. It will open the test page. In the page, add the SMS service URL as the service reference. Then, you will be able to enter the required parameter values in the textboxes and send a small message to your own cell phone as a test.

8.6.5 Enterprise Service Bus

The Enterprise Service Bus (ESB) is an industry standard for implementing messaging systems and for heterogeneous application integration. It has been implemented by different vendors, including the following:

- Fiorano ESB, which is a part of Fiorano's cloud computing environment (http://www.fiorano.com/products/ESB-enterprise-service-bus/);
- IBM WebSphere ESB (https://www-01.ibm.com/software/integration/wsesb/library/);
- Microsoft BizTalk ESB (https://docs.microsoft.com/en-us/biztalk/esb-toolkit/microsoft-biztalk-esb-toolkit);
- Oracle ESB (http://download.oracle.com/docs/cd/E12524_01/doc.1013/e12638/esb_intro.htm); which is now a part of Oracle SOA Suite; and

ESB is a software system that supports multiple formats of messages. Upon receiving a message, it converts the message in a supported format to an internal message format, converts the internal message format to the destination format, and queues the message as necessary before sending it to the destination. For example, IBM WebSphere ESB performs the following list of functions:

- Buffer messages for offline delivery;
- Translate message formats;
- Adapt different interaction patterns;
- Convert transport protocols;
- Analyze and share the service interface;
- Dynamic selection of service to serve a request;
- Location Transparency;
- Propagate the security content;
- Provide WS-* support, including WS-RM, WS-Security, and WS-Transaction;
- Track and monitor service activities.

Current implementations of ESB support multiple communication protocols, including SOAP, REST (HTTP), .Net-based formats such as MSMQ (Microsoft Message Queuing), and Java-based formats such as JMS (Java Message Service). They also support different message formats, such as XML, XLS, and JSON. An ESB system is typically used to integrate heterogeneous applications from different vendors. For example, Oracle ESB supports the integration of BPEL applications, CRM, ERP, BPM, J2EE, .Net applications, SAP.B2B, and other legacy applications. JMS and MSMQ are often used as the internal formats of ESB systems.

8.7 Other Composition Languages

There are many composition languages, as we discussed in the beginning of the chapter. This section will present a few of the major composition languages, including SCA/SDO, WF, WSFL, and OWL-S. OWL-S will be discussed on Chapter 11 in connection with Semantic Web and Semantic Web Services.

8.7.1 SCA/SDO

Being IBM's major service-oriented software development platform, Service Component Architecture (SCA) and Service Data Objects (SDO) provide a uniform programming interface for a wide variety of services and data sources (https://www.ibm.com/support/knowledgecenter/en/SSQH9M_7.0.0/com.ibm.websphere.wesb.doc/doc/cbo_workingwithbusinessobjects.html).

There are four major components in SCA:

- Assembly model: How to define composite applications independent of languages. Similar to Oracle SOA Suite and Robotics Developer Studio, SCA support graphical developments. However, SCA is not bound to a specific language. It supports multiple languages, including BPEL, PHP, Java, and C++. Figure 8.36 shows a scenario of composing an SCA application using graphical development, with each component using a different programming language.
- Client and implementation specifications: How to use SCA with different programming and composition languages.
- Binding specifications: How to use access methods. It supports standard web service binding specification, Java Message Service (JMS) binding specification, and Enterprise JavaBeans (EJB) session bean binding.
- Policy framework: How to add policies representing security, transactions, conversations, and reliable messaging into the system, declaratively in a list of conditions, constraints, and rules.

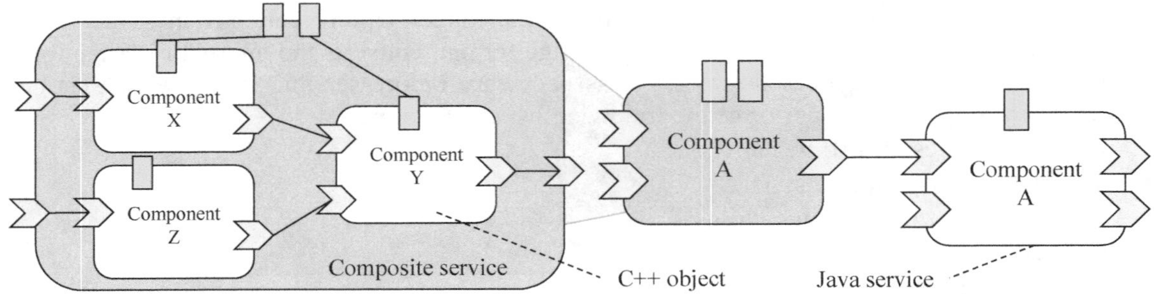

Figure 8.36. SCA composition model

SCA provides a single interface to many different kinds of services and access methods. In other words, you can write the same code to access different services, which can be web services, BPEL processes, and local and remote objects in different languages such as C++ and Java. It also provides a single method to deal with the communication protocols such as SOAP and other messaging systems such as JMS. If the services require authentication, encryption, or other policies, they are processed by the SCA environment and the users do not need to handle them in their code.

Service Data Objects provides a similarly uniform solution to data access. With SDO, you have a single interface to communicate with your data source, whether it is a relational database, an XML file, a web service, or something else. SDO lets you use a single API, regardless of the underlying technology. In Chapter 10, we will further discuss data access issues.

8.7.2 WSFL: Web Services Flow Language

The Web Services Flow Language (WSFL) is developed by IBM Software Group (https://en.wikipedia.org/wiki/Web_Services_Flow_Language). It is an XML language for the description of web services or application compositions. WSFL allows three levels of compositions: flow model, global model, and nested compositions.

- **Flow model**: A composite web service or an application is created by describing how to use the functionality provided by the collection of available services. This is also known as flow composition, orchestration, or choreography of web services. A WSFL document (program) models such a composition as a specification of the execution sequence of the functions provided by the constituent web services. Execution orders are specified by defining the flow of control and data passing between web service functions. The flow composition model can be used to model many business processes or workflows based on existing web services. In the flow model, WSDL is used for interface and binding definitions.

- **Global model**: In this model, no specification of an execution sequence is provided. Instead, the composition is based on the interaction among the constituent web services. It describes how the constituent web services interact with each other. The interactions are modeled as links between endpoints of the web services' interfaces. Each link corresponds to the interaction of one web service with an operation of another web service's interface.
- **Nested composition**: Usually, the global model is used to describe the behaviors between composite web services, each of which is described by a flow model. However, WSFL allows a composite web service created by a global model to be used as a constituent service in the composition of another web service, leading to nested composition. Nested composition is referred to as recursive composition [https://en.wikipedia.org/wiki/Web_Services_Flow_Language].

WSFL compositions support a broad spectrum of interaction patterns between the partners participating in a business process. In particular, both hierarchical interactions and peer-to-peer interactions between partners are supported. Hierarchical interactions are often found in more stable, long-term relationships between partners, whereas peer-to-peer interactions reflect relationships that are often established dynamically on a per-instance basis.

In the remainder of the section, we will discuss the global model and the flow model, respectively. We will then show the implementation of global and flow models through a case study.

The **global model** is used to describe overall interaction among web services and applications that use web services; for example, describing the interactions among a client, a travel agency, airlines, and hotels. A global model can also be used to define a composite web service using existing web services by describing the interactions among the constituent web services. In this case, however, it often needs the support from the flow model to describe the flow or execution orders of the interactions.

The interactions in the global model are modelled as links between endpoints of the web services' interfaces. Each link corresponds to the interaction of one web service with an operation of another web service's interface. Because of the decentralized or distributed nature of these interactions, the term global model is used to refer to this type of web services composition.

The **flow model** defines a composite web service or an application by describing the execution flow among the functions of the constituent web services. In WSDL terminology, this kind of composition is also called flow composition, orchestration, or choreography of web services. In other words, WSFL models these compositions as specifications of the execution sequence of the functions provided by the constituent web services. Execution orders are specified by defining the flows of control and data between web services.

Technically, a service composition is represented in WSFL by a `<flowModel>` element. The definition of a flow model includes two kinds of information: the specification of how the composition uses the services being composed to create a flow model, and the definition of the service interface provided by the composition.

The public service interface of the flow model is specified as service provider type in the `serviceProviderType` attribute. Implementations of activities from the flow model defined can be exported by a corresponding `<export>` element to an operation of one of the port types of this service provider type. The flow model is defined using six different model elements:

- The `<flowSource>` elements are used to represent the incoming data to the flow model.
- The `<flowSink>` elements define the output of the flow model.
- The `<serviceProvider>` elements represent the services participating in the composition.
- The `<activity>` elements represent the usage of individual operations of a service provider inside the flow model.

- The `<controlLink>` elements represent control connections between activities in the model.
- The `<dataLink>` elements represent data flow between activities in the model.

In other words, a flow model defines the flows of control and data between a set of activities. Each activity is associated with a service provider, which is an instance of a service provider type. The service provider is responsible for the realization of the activity. Essentially, an activity defines the requirements of the flow model on some service provider. A flow model itself defines a service provider type and the requirements of the encompassed activities on external web services.

8.8 Discussions

The chapter started with Workflow Foundation that allow us to draw visual workflow and compile the workflow into executable. Services and components can be consumed by different types of applications. Workflow Foundation is designed to work with WCF services, particularly with the advanced features in WCF services. Although the applications can be developed in a traditional programming language, as we discussed in Chapter 5, WF offers an alternative of architecture-driven approach and uses a higher-level of composition language. It makes the application's architecture clearer and more understandable, resulting in the developed software being more dependable. In contrast to many other composition languages, WF makes it easier to switch between the high-level workflow and the low-level control-flow in traditional programming languages. WF allows the long-running workflow to be saved in a durable storage and to be dispatched later. This feature is necessary when the asynchronous communication is involved and the callback may take a long time. For example, a travel agency request quotes from multiple airlines and expect to be called back later. Letting the workflow running and idling may take a lot of the server resource. Termination of the workflow will lose the callbacks permanently. WF provides the infrastructure to save the workflow instance, correlate the workflow instance with its call backs, and reload the instance when its callback arrives.

Then, we discussed BPEL and related technologies. To facilitate the discussion, readers should review the structures of SOAP protocol and WSDL interface definition language discussed in Chapter 3. The composition language BPEL is the main topic of the chapter and is discussed in detail. We first discussed BPEL activities and constructs, and then we used the activities and constructs to compose a business process. A process defines a composite web services, which implements the application logic. The WSDL interface of a BPEL process is studied, which is necessary to understand the interoperation between the BPEL process and the web services used by the BPEL process, as well as the client who accesses the BPEL process.

Messaging is key technology for the integration among heterogeneous applications. As all parties in a messaging system are loosely coupled through messages, integration does not involve any code-level integration. Object Request Broker (ORB) has been used for integrating distributed objects. Enterprise Service Bus extends ORB to include both distributed objects and services, while ESB plays the same role in the service-oriented architecture and beyond. ESB has become an intelligent integration framework that allows automated and adaptive message exchanges among different frameworks with different data formats. ESB is a standard, and there are different implementations from different vendors, such as IBM ESB, Microsoft ESB, and Oracle ESB.

Finally, we briefly introduced a few other composition languages: WSFL and SCA/SDO developed by IBM.

Workflow-based application and service development discussed in this chapter is related to the workflow-based development in Visual IoT/Robotics Programming Language Environment (VIPLE) to be discussed in Chapter 9. Once you have learned VIPLE development, you will have a better understanding of the workflow-based development and its applications in different fields.

Name: ____________________

Date: ____________________

8.9 Exercises and Projects

1. Multiple choice questions. Choose one answer in each question only. Choose the best answer if multiple answers are acceptable.

1.1 The key idea of Workflow Foundation is to

(A) add an additional layer of abstraction in application development.

(B) offer a new service development template.

(C) provide a service hosting environment.

(D) implement application logic in a database.

1.2 What is the markup language for workflow's visual code in a Workflow Foundation application?

(A) XML. (B) XAML. (C) C# (D) JavaScripy

1.3 When developing a web service in Workflow Foundation, which development template is based on WCF service?

(A) Workflow-first (B) Interface-first (C) Both of them (D) Neither of them

1.4 When developing an asynchronous service in Workflow Foundation, which development template is more suitable?

(A) Workflow-first (B) Interface-first

(C) Both are the same (D) Neither of them can be used

1.5 When developing a service that may require humans in the loop, what type of service is the most suitable one?

(A) Asynchronous (B) Persistent (C) Synchronous (D) None of them

1.6 What is the characteristic of a business process in orchestration style?

(A) Each service involved can communicate with multiple partners in the application.

(B) Each service involved must communicate with at least two partners in the application.

(C) Involved services communicate with the central process only.

(D) The process itself is not a service.

1.7 Which of the following is (are) BPEL activity?

(A) <invoke> (B) <receive>

(C) <assign> (D) All of the above

1.8 What is necessary in a BPEL process to enable an asynchronous communication with a callback?

(A) A "portType" (B) A "receive" activity

(C) A "reply" activity (D) None of the above

1.9 What element is used to define the scope of local variables and handlers in a BPEL process?

(A) <scope> (B) <sequence>

(C) <flow> (D) <namespace>

1.10 What activity is used in a BPEL process for taking requests from clients?

(A) <invoke> (B) <receive> (C) <assign> (D) <copy>

1.11 A BPEL process is an XML file that defines

(A) a set partner link types using XML schema.

(B) a SOAP packet to be transmitted between two web services.

(C) the order of the activities to be performed in a web service.

(D) the WSDL interface of a web service.

1.12 What language is used to define the web service interface of a BPEL process?

(A) Java (B) WSDL with extended elements

(C) ebXML (D) SOAP

1.13 Which pair of the following activities is used for creating a two-way asynchronous communication between a client and a server?

(A) <invoke> from client side and <send> from the server side

(B) <receive> from client side and <reply> from the server side

(C) <invoke> from client side and <invoke> from the server side

(D) All of the above

1.14 In Oracle SOA Suite, which component is used for drawing the workflow (business process)?

(A) BPEL Console (B) JDeveloper (C) BPEL Process Manager (D) ESB

1.15 In AWS Simple WorkflowService (SWF), which of the following need to be registered in WSF?

(A) Activities (B) Workflows

(C) Both (A) and (B) (D) Neither (A) nor (B)

1.16 The main purpose of a messaging system is to offer

(A) asynchronous and queued message services.

(B) synchronous one-way communication.

(C) synchronous two-way communication.

(D) All of the above.

1.17 In a Java-based messaging system, JNDI (Java Naming and Directory Service) is used for registering

(A) URI of RESTful service. (B) URL of the client.

(C) URL of the server. (D) subscribing topics or queues.

1.18 What is the Internal message format used in IBM WebSphere Enterprise Service Bus?

(A) SOAP (B) MSMQ (C) JMS (D) WSDL

1.19 Which messaging system requires the administrators to install the queuing mechanism on the server?

(A) Database-based (B) JMS-based

(C) MSMQ-based (D) None of the above

1.20 Which software development and integration environments include an ESB?
(A) IBM WebSphere (B) Microsoft BizTalk
(C) Oracle SOA Suite (D) All of the above

2. What is a workflow? What is a business process? Compare and contrast workflow and business process.

3. What Toolbox items are used for defining the service interface?

4. What is a CodeActivity in Workflow Foundation? What programming language can be used for implementing a CodeActivity?

5. How are WSDL services accessed in Workflow Foundation? Explain the steps for referencing and accessing WSDL services?

6. How can RESTful services be accessed in Workflow Foundation?

7. What is an asynchronous service? What is persistent service? Compare and contrast them.

8. A workflow offers a higher level of abstraction and it is typically used for composing high-level application? What is the benefit of using workflow for defining a web service?

9. Are workflow languages always visual language?

10. What is orchestration? What is choreography? Compare and contrast them.

11. What composition languages use orchestration? What composition languages use choreography?

12. What are the core concepts of BPEL?

13. What is a BPEL process? What elements does a BPEL process consist of? What additional elements are included in the WSDL file of a BPEL process?

14. What activities does BPEL support? What constructs does BPEL support?

15. What construct is used to define sequential activities? What construct is used to define parallel activities? What construct is used to define conditional selection (if-then-else) of activities?

16. What is a partnerLinkType? Where is a partnerLinkType defined? Compare and contrast partnerLinkType and portType.

17. What is a partner link? Where is a partner link defined?

18. What kinds of variables are allowed in a BPEL process? How is scope of a variable defined?

19. What is synchronous communication? What is asynchronous communication? In what circumstances should synchronous and asynchronous communications be applied?

20. Compare and contrast the Oracle BPEL Process Manager and Microsoft BizTalk.

21. Download Oracle SOA Suite.
    http://www.oracle.com/technetwork/middleware/soasuite/downloads/index.html

    1) Follow the getting-started tutorials given in the Oracle site and use the examples (sample applications) given in SOA Suite.

    2) Follow the Google Flow with the Sensors Tutorial given in the course web page to set up your Oracle process manager.

22. Design an SOA distributed software system that consists of the following components.

    1) Design three sorting WS, each of which takes a string of numbers as input and return the time used and the string of sorted integers.

    2) Provide the WSDL file of each sorting service.

    3) Write a BPEL process that selects the sorting service that used least amount of time.

    4) Write the WSDL file of the BPEL process.

    5) Use the Oracle SOA Suit to implement the system.

23. List the message format supported by Oracle Enterprise Service Bus?

24. What steps are required to transform an incoming message to the outgoing message in the IBM WebSphere Enterprise Service Bus?

25. What type of data formats do Yahoo! Pipes support?

Project 1

In this project, you will develop a web service and an application based on your own ideas. For the application, you can use any type of the human interface: console, forms, or website. In the application, you must access the service that you develop and a service in ASU Service Repository as shown in in Figure 8.37. You must use the Workflow Foundation to develop both the application and the service. You must also use at least one CodeActivity in one of the workflows (in application workflow or in service workflow). The application must combine at least two services to deliver the integrated functionality. If needed, you can use more services and other components. For all services, you can choose to use either SOAP or RESTful services. To test your application and the service, you must put the two projects into one solution, and you must make sure that the service addresses do not change when the solution is running on a different machine. The project is broken down into the following tasks.

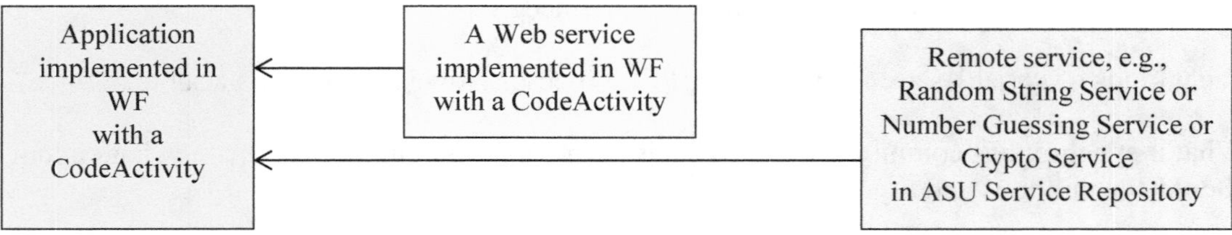

Figure 8.37. Application architecture using Workflow Foundation

1. Use Workflow Foundation to develop a SOAP service that provides a sensible function to be used in your application.

2. Use Workflow Foundation to develop a sensible website application using at least services. One service is developed in question 1. The other service is a remote service from a service repository, such as the ASU Service Repository.

3. Develop a sensible CodeActivity within the workflow application (Question 1) or within the workflow service (Question 2).

4. User Manual: You must write a mini user manual in WORD, PDF, or a web page. The main components include: (1) an introduction to the web application and the web service that you have developed; (2) a description of the interface; (3) a diagram illustrating the application logic and workflow that you have implemented; and (4) give at least two test cases (inputs and outputs) and screenshots you used to test your software.

Project 2

Design an e-business application consisting of a client, a business process, and at least two external web services, as shown in the diagram that follows. Use the JDeveloper and Oracle Process Manager (or ActiveBPEL and Tomcat) to implement your application, as outlined in Figure 8.38.

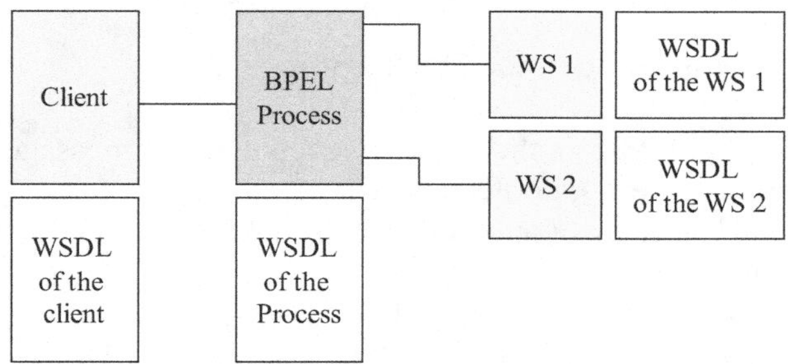

Figure 8.38. Application architecture using BPEL process

Use synchronous or asynchronous communication to implement the connection between the client and the BPEL process, as well as the connections between the process and the web services. The assignment should contain the following components:

1) The complete BPEL process code, which takes requests from the client, invokes the two external web service for services, and processes the returned messages from the web services. The process must include the partner links.

2) The full WSDL file of the BPEL process containing the ordinary part of WSDL and the partner link type definitions.

3) The portType (a part of the WS file) of the WS 1 that you use.

4) The portType (a part of the WS file) of the WS 2 that you use.

5) User Manual: You must write a one-page document in MS Word. For the title, you must write the title of your e-business system, the author of the system, and your e-mail address. The main components include: (1) introduction to the web application system that you have developed; (2) a description of the user interface; (3) a diagram illustrates the workflow that you implemented; (4) list of the services used and a brief explanation of each service; and (5) deployment and testing guide of the program.

Project 3

In this project, you will create a simplified messaging service to buffer messages in an XML file and a Web client to allow users to send and receive messages. You can deploy your service and application on IIS Express localhost or a Web server.

1 Messaging service: Develop a service (WSDL service, RESTful service, or Workflow service) that can buffer messages before the receivers fetch the messages. The messages must be saved in an XML file (or JSON file) that the service can access. The service must offer the following operations. You may add more parameters for additional functions.

- Operation 1: sendMsg: It allows the client to send a string message to the messaging service, and the message will be stored in the database (XML file) with senderID, receiverID, and a time stamp.
    - Inputs: string senderID, string receiverID, string msg.
    - Output: void
    - Note: a timestamp will be added by the program.

- Operation 2: receiveMsg: It allows the client to receive all the messages sent to the receiverID.
    - Inputs: string receiverID, boolean purge
    - Output: string[] an array of messages, with each element containing the related information: senderID, sending time, and message
    - Note: The receiver should receive the new messages that have not been received in the previous receive call. If purge == true, the service will delete all messages of the receiver.

To read and write an XML file on disk, you may want to read Chapter 4 on XML processing and Section 5.4.2 on reading and writing XML files. You may also read Chapter 10 and using LINQ to XML methods.

2 MsgApp: Develop a Web application (client) in ASP .Net or MVC that contains at least two Web pages: Sender page and Receiver page. The sender sends messages to the Messaging service and the receiver receives messages from the service. A sample GUI is shown in Figure 8.39. The GUI may include all components that need to be implemented.

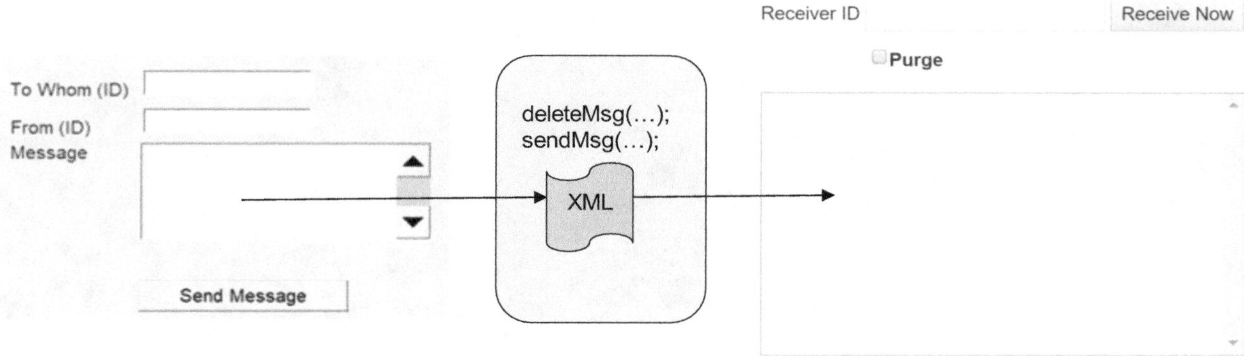

Figure 8.39. Messaging system: sender, message queue, and receiver

To test your clients (sender and receiver) on localhost/IIS Express: Right click the service project and choose View in Browser to run the service. Then, start the client, which will open another bowser window to run the client. Copy and paste the URL into a new browser window. Now, you have three sessions of your application: one service session and two client sessions. You can test your application by sending a message in one browser and receiving the message in another browser. Submit a screenshot of your testing.

Chapter 9
IoT, Robotics, and Device Integration via Visual Programming

9.1 Introduction

Service-Oriented Computing (SOC) research and applications have been largely limited to software development in electronic and web-based applications. Internet of Things (IoT), Robot as a Service, and service-oriented robotics software development extend SOC from its current fields to a new domain, which was considered not feasible because of the efficiency issues in terms of computing and communication. This chapter presents the concepts, principles, and methods in SOC and SOC-based robotics software development and applies them in the design of distributed robotics applications. Two case studies, Intel security robot design and a maze-traversing robot application in Microsoft Robotics Developer Studio, are used to illustrate the concepts and methods.

9.1.1 Internet of Things

Internet of Things (IoT) refers to uniquely identifiable objects (things) and their virtual representations in the Internet web applications. The concept was initially applied in the Radio-Frequency Identification RFID-tags to mark the Electronic Product Code (Auto-ID Lab). IoT concept is later extended to refer to the world where physical objects are seamlessly integrated into the information network, and where the physical objects can become active participants in business processes.

Gartner, Inc. forecasts in 2015 that 6.4 billion connected things will be in use worldwide in 2016, up 30 percent from 2015, and will reach 20.8 billion by 2020. In 2016, 5.5 million new things will get connected every day (https://www.gartner.com/newsroom/id/3165317).

IoT connects to the Internet through Internet protocols, such as HTTP, TCP, and IP. The data received from the IoT is represented as web data in forms such as HTML, JSON, XML, and URI, as shown in Figure 9.1. The data can be further organized into ontology and presented in RDF, RDFS, and OWL for storing, analyzing, and reasoning. The data is typically processed in service-oriented and web-based computing environments. If the data amount is big, it can be processed by cloud computing and through big data algorithms. At this end, the IoT and its data are fully integrated into the web and the virtual world, and all the technologies and applications developed can be applied to process IoT data and control the physical world connected to the IoT on the other side.

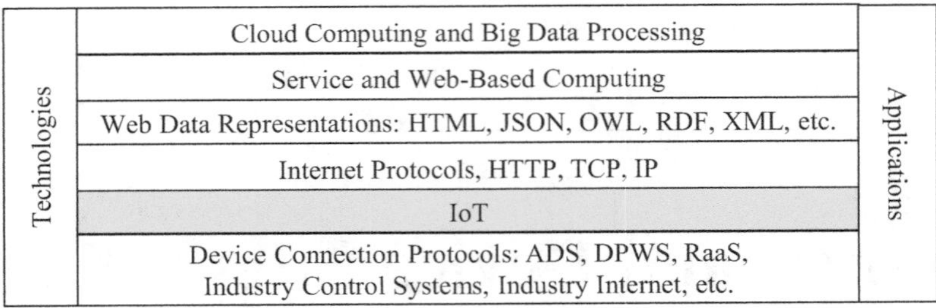

Figure 9.1. Internet of things and devices

The development of cloud computing and big data pushed the desktop-based computing platform into an Internet-based computing infrastructure. The endorsement and commitment to building and utilizing cloud computing environments as the integrated computing and communication infrastructure by many governments and major computing corporations around the world have led to the rapid development of many commercial and mission-critical applications in the new infrastructure, including the integration of physical devices.

In addition to IoT, a number of related concepts and systems have been proposed. A cyber-physical system (CPS) is a combination of a large computational and communication core and physical elements that can interact with the physical world. In a CPS, the computational and communication core and the physical elements are tightly coupled and coordinated to fulfill a coherent mission. The US National Science Foundation issued a program solicitation in 2008 on CPS, envisioning that the cyber-physical systems of tomorrow would far exceed those of today in terms of adaptability, autonomy, efficiency, functionality, reliability, safety, and usability (www.nsf.gov/pubs/2008/nsf08611/nsf08611.pdf). Research advances in cyber-physical systems promise to transform our world with systems that:

- respond more quickly (e.g., autonomous collision avoidance),
- are more precise (e.g., robotic surgery and nano-tolerance manufacturing),
- work in dangerous or inaccessible environments, e.g., autonomous systems for search and rescue, firefighting, and exploration,
- provide large-scale, distributed coordination, e.g., automated traffic control,
- are highly efficient (e.g., zero-net energy buildings),
- augment human capabilities, and
- enhance societal well-being, e.g., assistive technologies and ubiquitous healthcare monitoring and delivery.

The development of artificial intelligence, edge and fog computing has advanced IoT in new and interdisciplinary domains. Internet of Intelligent Things (IoIT) defines IoT with intelligent devices that have adequate computing capacity, such as 32-bit general purpose computing capacity. IoIT focuses on the infrastructure support to the distributed intelligence, which allows the devices to perform computing that contributes to the overall decision of the system. Another related concept is the Artificial Intelligence of Things (AIoT), which combines Artificial Intelligence and IoT. AIoT is more focused at business and application levels, involving machine learning and artificial intelligence in its devices. IoIT and AIoT concepts are similar and are often used interchangeably. However, IoIT focuses more on hardware and infrastructure that support the distributed intelligence, while AIoT focuses more on the software that implements the distributed intelligence.

Security in cloud computing and the connected physical devices is always a major concern. However, it is not a new issue, as it has been studied in networking and service-oriented computing and web applications. All major clouds, including Amazon EC, Google's App Engine, and Microsoft Azure, have implemented standard security mechanisms developed for computing and communication, such as SSL and WS-Security.

What has not been thoroughly studied is the availability and reliability of cloud computing environments, particularly, the physical devices connected to the environment. A panel session was organized in the flagship conference on dependability, the Annual IEEE/IFIP International Conference on Dependable Systems and Networks in 2009, to discuss the challenges and opportunities in the dependability of cloud computing. Serious cases were presented where dependability was compromised, due to the improper isolation among applications and services, as they shared resources including computing units, memory, networks, databases, as well as programs and data. The opportunities presented included the redundancy of professional services available to the environments and the uniform management at the OS and other system levels.

IoT is a general concept that can be interpreted in different contexts. In the sense of virtual representation, IoT can be formalized by Uniform Resource Identifier (URI) and Resource Description Framework (RDF) and other ontology languages. These concepts will be further discussed in Chapter 10. In the sense of physical devices, it has been studied in different systems. There are simple and complex physical devices. The simple devices do not have much intelligence, and they simply send data to and/or receive data from the Internet. This chapter focuses on more intelligent devices that are capable of communicating with each other among the devices, making certain decisions based on local information, and taking autonomous and coordinated actions, such as Robot as a Service and smart phones.

An example is the Wikitude World Browser (http://www.wikitude.com). Wikitude World Browser allows you to see all well-known locations without actually being there. Such applications are called augmented reality. A similar phone app is Yelp's Monocle, which allows you to "see" a site that is miles away, based on the GPS, compass sensor input, camera position, and available photos of the site.

In addition to being mapped to the virtual things, intelligent devices can communicate among themselves, forming a distributed system, as the IoT environment could be too slow if all decisions have to be sent to a center. In many time-critical situations, the decentralized intelligent devices can better serve the needs of the physical world. Smart home is such an application. A simulation of calculating the energy consumption using different energy sources is at: http://neptune.fulton.ad.asu.edu/WSRepository/SmartHome/Smarthome.html.

The interface definition and design between the virtual things and physical things is the recent focus of IoT research. As web services (WS) and WS protocols such as SOAP and HTTP have been widely used, the device interface should be based on these standard protocols. For example, the Devices Profile for Web Services (DPWS) defines implementation constraints to enable secure web service messaging, discovery, description, and eventing on resource-constrained devices between web services and devices. DPWS specification is built on the following core web services standards: WSDL 1.1, XML Schema, SOAP 1.2, and WS-Addressing. Initially published in 2004, DPWS 1.1 was approved as an OASIS Standard together with WS-Discovery 1.1 and SOAP-over-UDP 1.1 2009. Microsoft .Net Framework Class Library has defined classes for supporting DPWS device programming. Devices that implement DPWS are already on the market. For example, Netduino Plus is an interface board that wraps a device with a web service interface, so that the device can communicate with a virtual thing (a web service) without requiring a device driver code. The device is available in major stores, such as Amazon.com.

The structures, interfaces, and behaviors of the distributed devices can be defined based on the application domains. In the following sections, service-oriented robotics computing and Robot as a Service in a cloud computing environment will be used as examples to discuss the design and implementation of intelligent devices.

9.1.2 Service-Oriented Robotics Computing

It has been perceived that SOC applications are less efficient than OOC applications because of the additional layer of standard interface. The standard interface makes it possible for language and platform independent-communication and remote invocation implemented in web services. Embedded systems and robotics applications often need real-time performance, and thus, SOC was perceived to be an unsuitable paradigm for developing embedded systems and robotics applications where real-time communication and computing are needed.

However, SOC does not have to be implemented over the web, and thus, the standard interface could be simpler and faster. Furthermore, remote services could be migrated into a local machine to reduce the communication cost. Embedded and robotics applications have certain requirements that are limited by the software development paradigms before SOC:

- Embedded systems and robotics applications often have limited capacity to carry programs that handle all possible situations;
- Unforeseeable environmental situations can occur;
- Faults can occur, and on-site repair is often not available;
- Users want to modify the system (requirements) without stopping the system.

Using SOC for robotics has certain inherent advantages over the traditional methods of building a robot. The main benefit is to have a layer of common services with standard interfaces. Each service represents a component such as a sensor, actuator, and effector. The invocations of the services are device-independent. In this way, we can deploy the same application to different robotics platforms, as long as we rebind the service invocation to the services that are built for the robotics platform. The languages used in writing the application and the services can be different, which allows us to write robotics applications using high-level languages such as VPL, C#, and Java in multithreaded environment and in event-driven programming paradigm. Depending on the drivers available, we can use different languages, such as C, C++, and assembly languages to write the device control programs before wrapping them into services. The availability of a layer of services allows us to develop different robotics applications in a short period of time.

Figure 9.2 shows an example of SOC-based robotics application. The application consists of a Remote Collaboration Center (RCC) and an onboard computer that is attached to the robot. Instead of developing components specifically for a given application, the requirements of the components are published in a service broker. The service providers develop the services and publish them in the broker. Then, the application builder looks up the available services and migrates the services into the application. Migration can save time for the remote invocations. Depending on timing and flexibility requirements, the services can run on the onboard computer or on RCC. Services running on RCC can be replaced without stopping the robot. The robot's mission can be modified if a service on RCC is modified or replaced.

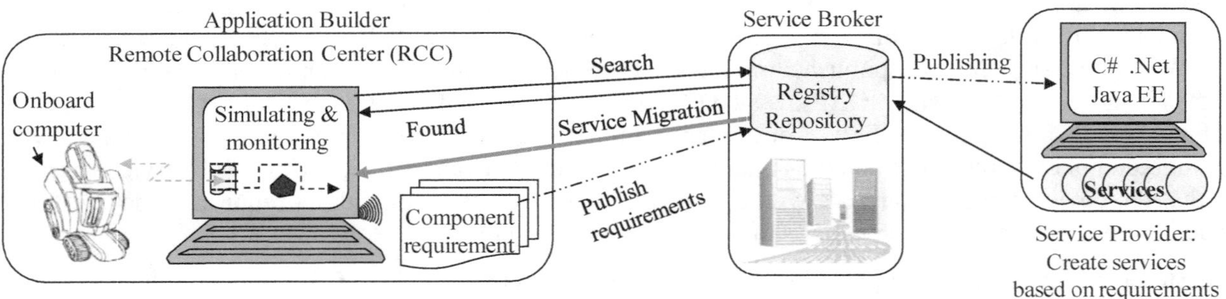

Figure 9.2. SOC-based robotics application development

For the same requirement and interface, different implementations for different devices can be developed, as shown in Figure 9.3. Assume the application is to traverse a map or a maze, and the same application can be used to drive a different vehicle, as long as the services are rebound to the services for the new vehicle.

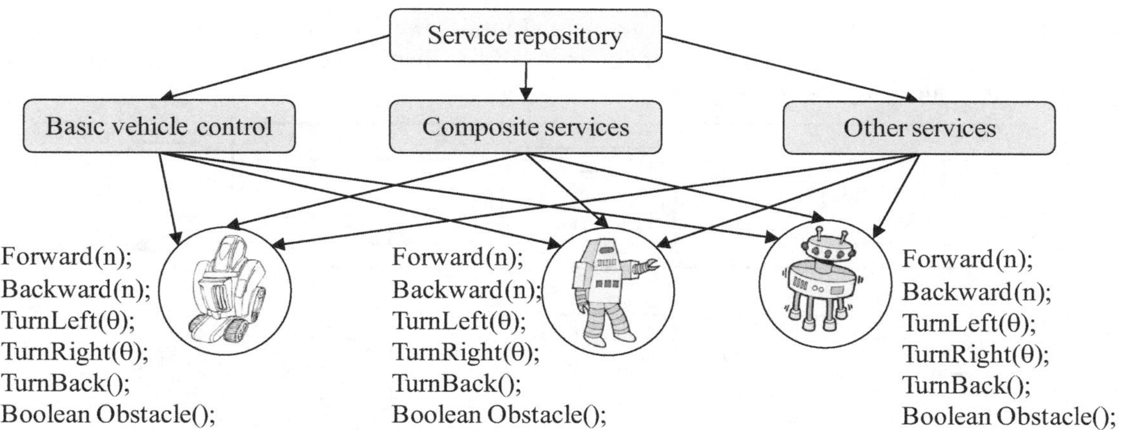

Figure 9.3. Different services can be developed for the same requirement

9.1.3 Event-Driven Robotics Applications

SOC software is distributed in the nature, with the services residing in different computers. General event-driven programming paradigm has been discussed in Chapter 2, in the context of distributed computing. This section presents the requirements and design of an event-driven, distributed, and service-oriented architecture, in the context of robotics applications. As an example, we use a security robot for unmanned building patrolling to discuss our case.

The overall distributed system consists of the following components:

- A Remote Collaboration Center (RCC) and a number of robots with onboard computers. RCC has a human-user interface, which can turn the system into a manually controlled mode or an autonomous mode. We will focus on the autonomous mode.
- Each robot is equipped with multiple sensors, such as a camera, sonar sensors, and touch sensors, and actuators such as motors, servos, and an alarm.
- Each robot offers other robots a service that reports its status.
- Each robot can access other robot's services and make an independent decision and action based on the collected information. To reduce the complexity of onboard (robot) software, the robots do not communicate with each other directly. They acquire other robots' status via RCC.

Each robot then consists of the following components:

- A robot consists of an onboard computer and a set of sensors and actuators, including a sonar sensor, a touch sensor, keypad, a video camera with a horizontal and a vertical control servo, and two independent servos that control the wheels;
- Sensors and actuators are wrapped as services;
- Each service includes an event emitter, an event subscription vector, and an event listener; the event handlers are associated with the orchestration process;
- An orchestration process reads local and remote sensory values, handles events, and makes decision based on the values and application requirements;
- A number of utility services are available onboard, such as mathematic functions, routing, and timing.

In the autonomous mode, the RCC is a peer to the robots in design, and it has the same architecture as a robot, which consists of a set services and an orchestration process. However, the RCC's services are different from that of the robots. RCC is normally running on a more powerful computer, and the time-consuming utility services will be executed on RCC. Furthermore, RCC has a user interface and does not directly connect to sensors and actuators. In the manual mode, the RCC will be the master, whereas the robots will be slaves. Figure 9.4 shows the architecture of the distributed robotics system and the major components in RCC and the robots.

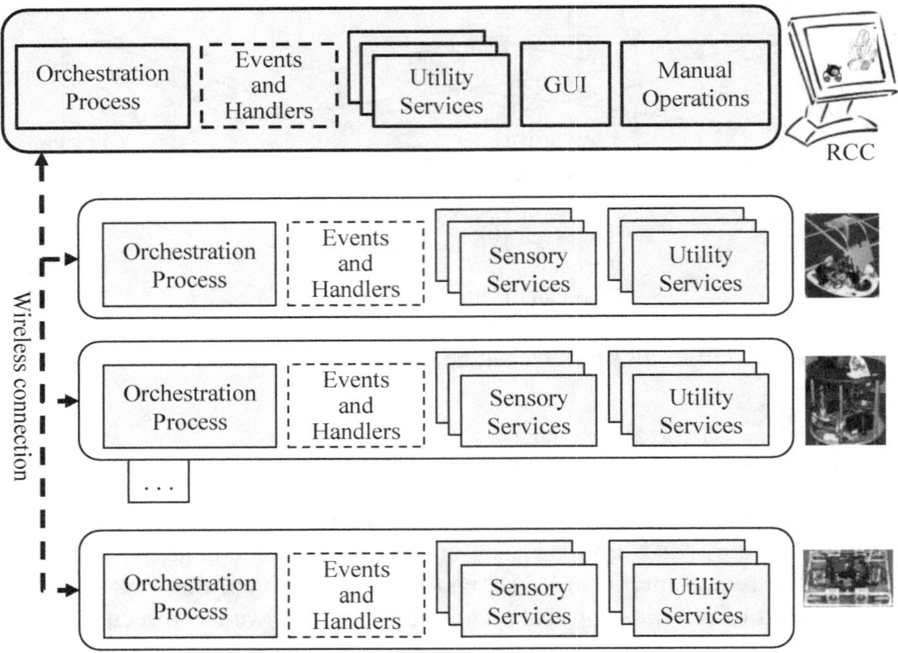

Figure 9.4. RCC and distributed onboard computers

The Events and Handlers are fully distributed into each subsystem and into different services in each subsystem, as shown in Figure 9.5.

A component that is interested in the event of a service; for example, a touch sensor, can subscribe to the event. The service maintains a vector of subscribers $T_1, T_2, \ldots, T_m$ (for the touch sensor). Once the sensor is touched, an event will be emitted, which will in turn invoke the handlers of $T_1, T_2, \ldots, T_m$. The sonar sensor can be set to one of the two modes. In the periodic mode, the sensor sends the reading value of the distance to the obstacle it sees in a certain interval. In this case, the event notifications may not be necessary. In the other mode, an event will be emitted if the distance reading changes from its previous value. Both touch sensor and sonar sensor are one-way services. The servomotors are, however, two-way services. In one way, the motor takes instructions through the motor control to move the robot accordingly. In the other way, the motor sends back the position data after each move, so that the robot's position can be computed based on the information.

All the event handlers are directly associated with the orchestration process, so that the process has all the information to make the decision on actions that need to be taken. Furthermore, the orchestration process can also subscribe to the sensory and motor services of other robots to make collaborative decisions; for example, if one robot detects an intruder and the intruder is moving away from the detecting robot, the other robots can move toward the intruder based on the sensory and position information from all participating robots.

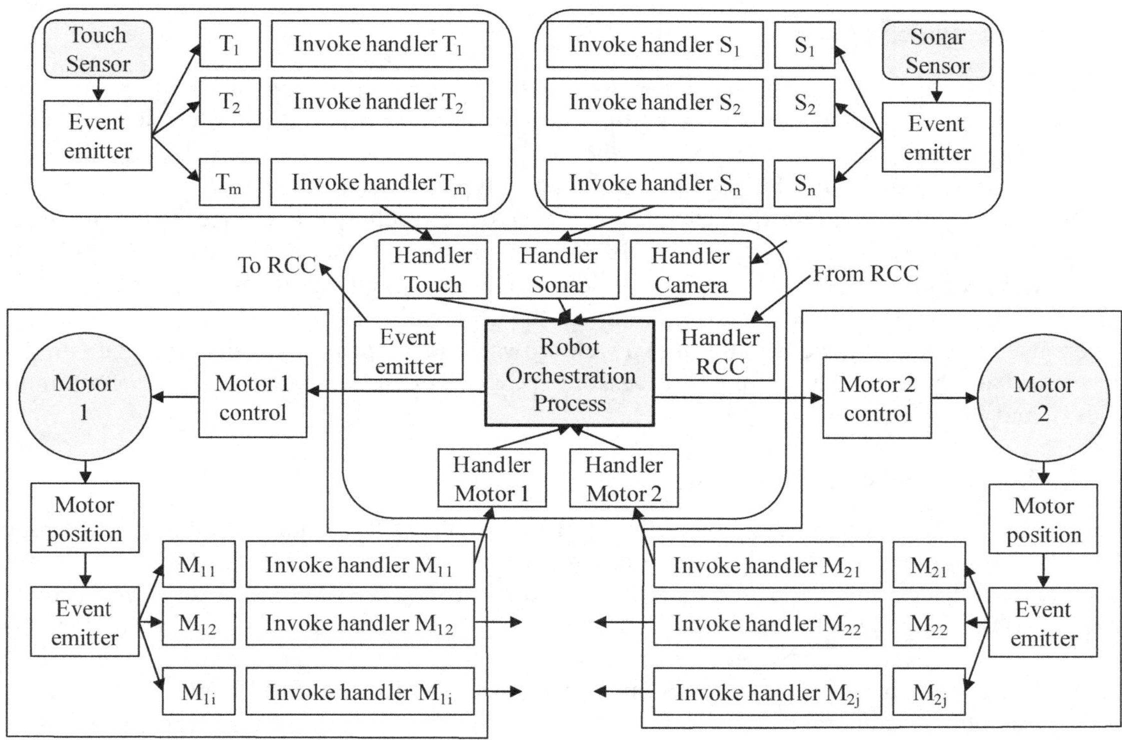

Figure 9.5. Services onboard a robot

The orchestration process is also running on the RCC. However, it is called collaboration process in order to differentiate it from the orchestration process on robots and to emphasize its role in coordinating the actions among the robots. RCC has the same software architecture and, in principle, is a peer of the robots, instead of the commander of the robots. The RCC will become the commander of the robots only in the manual mode. Since RCC is running on a more powerful computer, it makes more sense to allocate the more time-consuming tasks to the RCC and let the robots communicate with the RCC only. The communications between the RCC and robots are also implemented through event emitters and event-handlers, as shown in Figure 9.6.

In a later section, we will show how to implement event-driven robotics programming in VPL, where, different events are implemented to help a robot to navigate through an unknown maze.

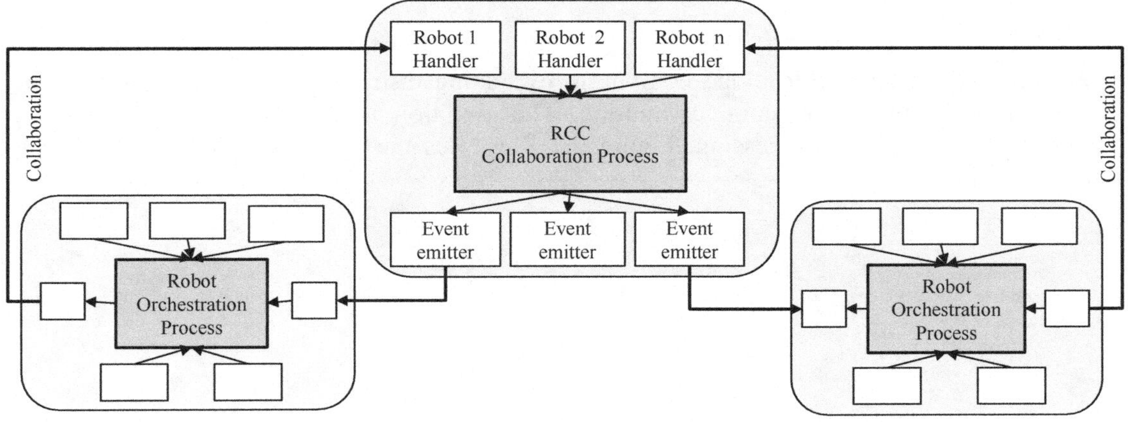

Figure 9.6. Collaboration between the RCC and Robots

9.2 Robot as a Service

Service-Oriented Computing (SOC) considers a software system consisting of a collection of loosely coupled services that communicate with each other through standard interfaces and via standard message-exchanging protocols. Cloud computing extends the scope of SOC to include the development platform and the execution infrastructure, and thus cloud computing is typically characterized by the features such as Software as a Service (SaaS), Platform as a Service (PaaS), Infrastructure as a Service (IaaS), and Hardware as a Service (HaaS). However, any other virtualized services, say, X as a Service, can be submitted to the cloud infrastructure as long as the standards are followed. Cloud computing makes it possible to completely move away from the desktop-based computing to the full web-based development and application: Developers use a platform on the web through a web browser, develop software and store data on the web, configure the hardware/infrastructure (processing power, memory capacity, and communication bandwidth), and execute application on the web.

9.2.1 Robot as a Service Definition

Robot as a Service (RaaS) is a cloud computing unit that facilities the seamless integration of robot and embedded devices into web and cloud computing environment. In terms of Service-Oriented Architecture (SOA), a RaaS unit includes services for performing functionality, a service directory for discovery and publishing, and service clients for user's direct access. The current RaaS implementation facilitates SOAP and RESTful communications between RaaS units and the other cloud computing units. Hardware support and standards are available to support RaaS implementation. Devices Profile for Web Services (DPWS) defines implementation constraints to enable secure web service messaging, discovery, description, and eventing on resource-constrained devices between web services and devices. RaaS can be considered a unit of Internet of Things (IoT), Internet of Intelligent Things (IoIT) that deal with intelligent devices that have adequate computing capacity, Cyber-physical system (CPS) that is a combination of a large computational and communication core and physical elements that can interact with the physical world, and Autonomous Decentralized System (ADS) whose components are designed to operate in a loosely coupled manner and data are shared through a content-oriented protocol (Definition given by the author in: http://en.wikipedia.org/wiki/Robot_as_a_Service).

In summary, RaaS can be characterized as follows:

- RaaS is an Embedded Intelligent System.
- RaaS is an Internet of Intelligent Thing.
- RaaS is a Cyber-Physical System.
- RaaS is an Autonomous Decentralized System.
- RaaS is a Service in Web and in Cloud Computing.
- RaaS is a Mobile Computing System.
- RaaS is a Real-Time System.

RaaS is an important extension to cloud computing by adding distributed computing capacity into the centralized computing model in cloud computing. This addition is critical for excessive computing requirement, such as big data processing. Figure 9.7 illustrates the spiral model of computing system development.

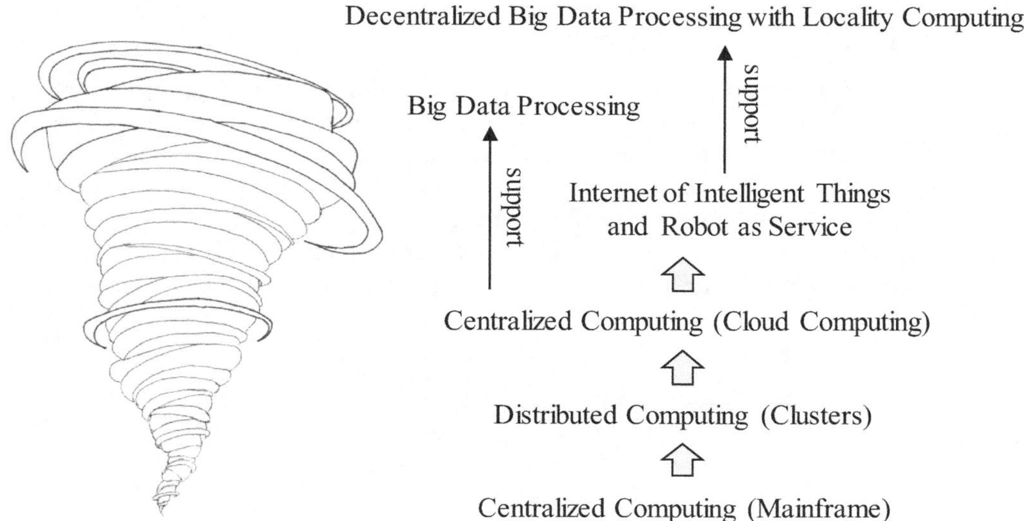

Figure 9.7. Spiral model of computing system development

We started our computing era with centralized computing using mainframe computers in the 1950s. We moved to distributed computing using personal computers and workstations in the 1980s. Cloud computing hides the detail and the complexity of distributed computing and presents the combined computing resources as a centralized environment. Even though cloud computing can provide any computing capacity that a client wants, it is beneficial to have a part of the computing distributed to the front-end computer. In the case of IoIT and RaaS, using the computing capacity of the devices can reduce the computing requirement of cloud computing, the communication delay, and the response time for clients. The front-end computing around cloud computing system is also called fog computing or edge computing. The front-end computing capacity is not supposed to be used as a general computing unit. It should perform the computing related to the locality only, such as sensory data processing and real-time responses related to the RaaS unit.

9.2.2 Robot as a Service Design

This section presents the concept and design of Robot as a Service (RaaS), which enforces the design and implementation of a robot or a device to be an all-in-one SOC unit, that is, the unit includes services for performing functionality, service directory for discovery and publishing, and applications for client's direct access.

Now, we consider the basic requirements of RaaS in the cloud computing environment. There can be many kinds of robot cloud units or autonomous devices; for example, robot cops, restaurant robot waiters, robot pets, and patient care robots. These robots are distributed in different locations and can be accessed through the Internet. The basic requirement we consider here is that the RaaS should have the complete functions of SOA, that is, as a service provider, as a service broker, and as a service client:

- A RaaS cloud unit is a service provider: Each unit hosts a repository of preloaded services. A developer or a client can deploy new services into or remove service from a robot. The services can be used by this robot can also be shared with other robots.
- A RaaS cloud contains a set of applications deployed: A developer or client can compose a new application (functionality) based on the services available in the unit and outside the unit.
- A RaaS unit is a service broker: A client can look up the services and applications available in the unit's directory. A client can search and discover the applications and services deployed on the

robot by browsing the directory. The services and applications can be organized in a hierarchy of classes to facilitate the discovery.

Figure 9.8 shows the main components of a RaaS unit and a sample set of applications and services deployed. Figure 9.9 shows how the RaaS units fit in the cloud computing environment. The SOC software in RaaS will communicate with the drivers and other operating system components, which further communicate with the devices and other hardware components. The RaaS units can directly communicate with each other through Wi-Fi, if the wireless infrastructure is available, or through Bluetooth, if two units are close to each other. The communication between RaaS and other services in the cloud are through standard service interface WSDL. The communication protocol supporting the invocations is SOAP or REST protocol.

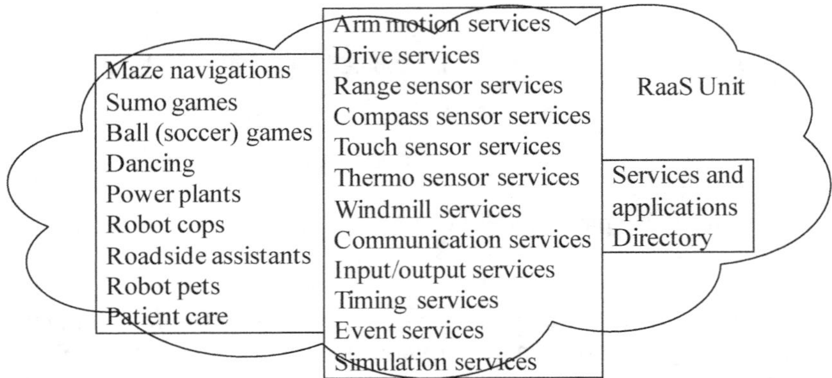

Figure 9.8. A RaaS unit consisting of services, directory, and applications

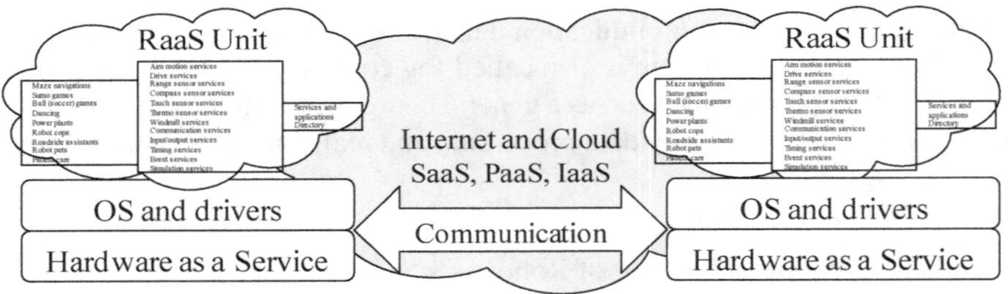

Figure 9.9. RaaS units in cloud computing environment

As shown in Figure 9.10, all requests to a RaaS unit are processed by a reactor (design pattern) as a single entry point, where the requests are buffered and checked against the directory. If an application or service is not registered, the request will be rejected immediately. Otherwise, the request will be redirected to the hosting worker process. A worker process will start a service as a thread and manage the service's lifetime. We have two worker processes, one for the applications and one for the services.

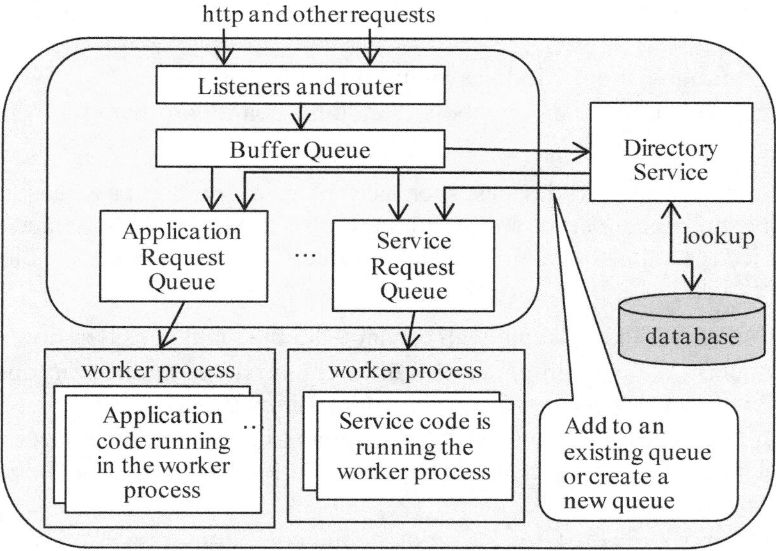

Figure 9.10. RaaS hosting and execution model

Sponsored by Intel Intelligent System group and in cooperation with Carl Hayden Community High School's Robotics Club, a RaaS unit has been implemented at the Arizona State University. A video presentation of the system is at http://vimeo.com/9740048. A layer of services is implemented on the RaaS to support the Microsoft VPL (Visual Programming Language) graphic composition language for robotics applications. VPL application composition will be discussed in the next sections.

9.2.3 Robot as a Service Implementation

To prove the concepts, we have implemented a number of RaaS units in the past a few years. Figure 9.11 shows the system consisting of the cloud and the devices. The interface design is shown on the top left. On the cloud sites http://neptune.fulton.ad.asu.edu/WSRepository/RaaS/main/ and http://neptune.fulton.ad.asu.edu/MyRaaS/, different web applications can be implemented to communicate with the RaaS units. Remote commanded functions using directional buttons and autonomous functions are implemented in the cloud unit. On the RaaS site, two robots, a hex crawler and a vehicle (Autobot), are implemented. Both robots have similar functions, although they use different hardware. A video demonstration is available at: http://vimeo.com/9740048.

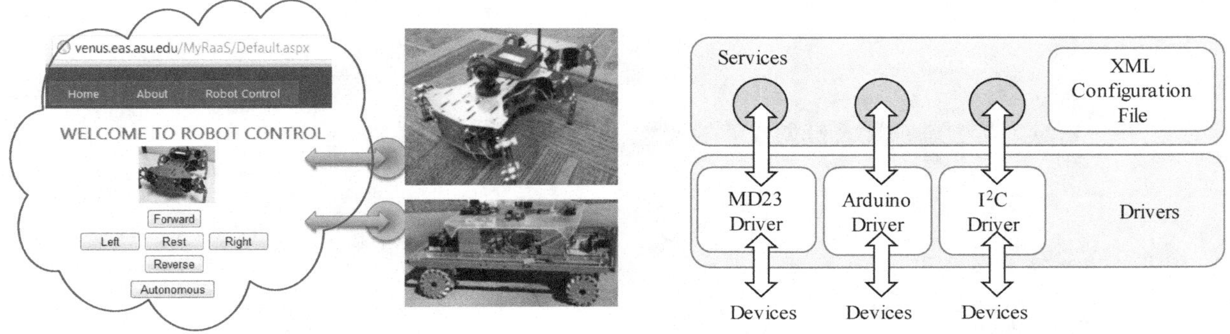

Figure 9.11. RaaS in cloud environment and the interface design

The implementation used generic Intel processor and motherboard are used. The major components include:

- Atom N270 processor 1.6GHz for the hex crawler; Intel i5 embedded Processor 1.6GHz for the Autobot;
- USB to I2C Communications Modules are used for both robots;
- Arduino boards are used for both robots. Netduino boards are being experimented in different projects.

Generic USB and common serial port devices, such as a sonar sensor, compass sensor, motion sensor, and a thermo sensor, webcam, digital servo, and motors are also used. Service-oriented computing model is used, where each device is wrapped as a WSDL web service. The web services enable the web accesses to the devices from the cloud.

On the software side, standard interface and web capacity are the main consideration.

- Operating systems: We have implemented different versions on different operations, including a Windows XP version, a Windows 7 version, and a Linux version.
- Programming languages: We have used C# and Java to program the services and the applications. We also implemented a service that interfaces Visual Programming Language (VPL) applications to the Intel platform.
- Service hosting: For the Hex Crawler robot, as the computing power of Atom N270 processor is limited, and no server software is installed on the robot to host services that wrap the devices, then these services are all hosted using self-hosting worker processes. The hosting services are implemented as worker processes, and the services are started as threads on the worker processes.

For the Autobot with an i5 embedded processor, which is much more powerful, we have installed Microsoft Robotics Developer Studio DSS (Decentralized System Services) on the Concurrency and Coordination Runtime (CCR) to host C# and VPL implemented services. DSS and CCR offer a multithreading environment to support parallel processing of all sensory data, actuator controls, and other processing tasks.

A simulated version is also implemented in Silverlight, as shown in Figure 9.12. The simulation environment supports a number of functions. You can learn these functions easily by exploring the buttons. You can manually drive the robot using the directional buttons. You can let the robot moves autonomously using the built-in maze navigation algorithm behind the button "Autonomous." You can program the robot using your own algorithm by clicking the "Add New Line" buttons and then select the conditions and actions. The lower part of the figure shows two maze navigation algorithms: Right-wall-following and farthest-distance algorithms.

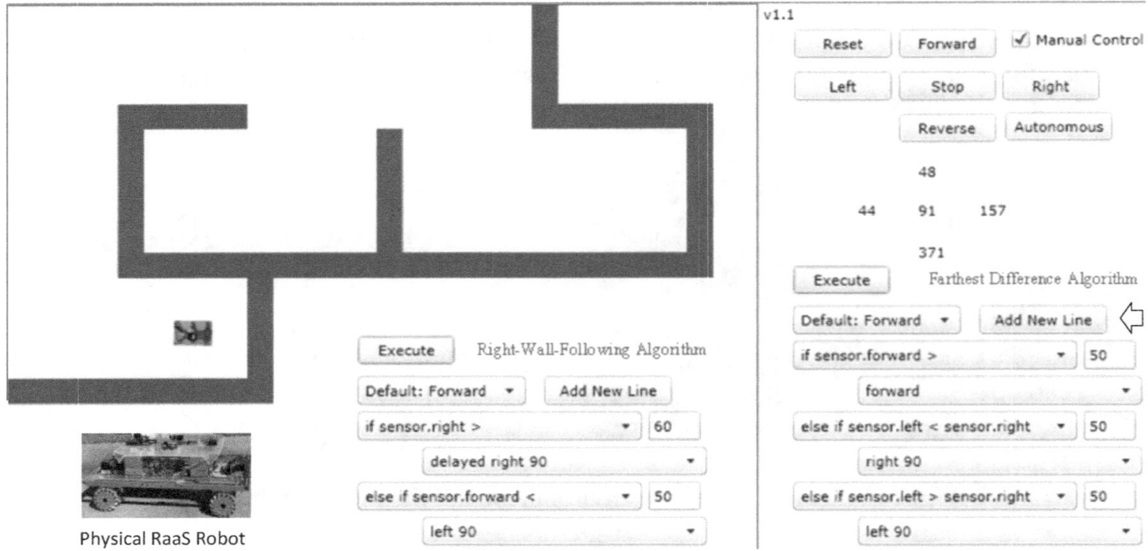

Figure 9.12. Web Simulation of RaaS maze navigation

The virtual robot can be synchronized with the physical RaaS robot in both directions: The physical robot follows the moves of the virtual robot, or the virtual robot tracks the moves of the physical robot. The initial connection between the virtual and physical robots is established through the RaaS broker in ASU repository. Once the physical robot is turned on, it registers its dynamic IP address to the broker. The virtual robot will acquire the address and then use the IP address to connect to the robot. Once the connection is established, the virtual robot and the physical robot communicate directly without using the broker.

The web-based simulator is reimplemented in HTML5, as shown in Figure 9.13, and deployed at:

http://neptune.fulton.ad.asu.edu/VIPLE/Web2DSimulator/

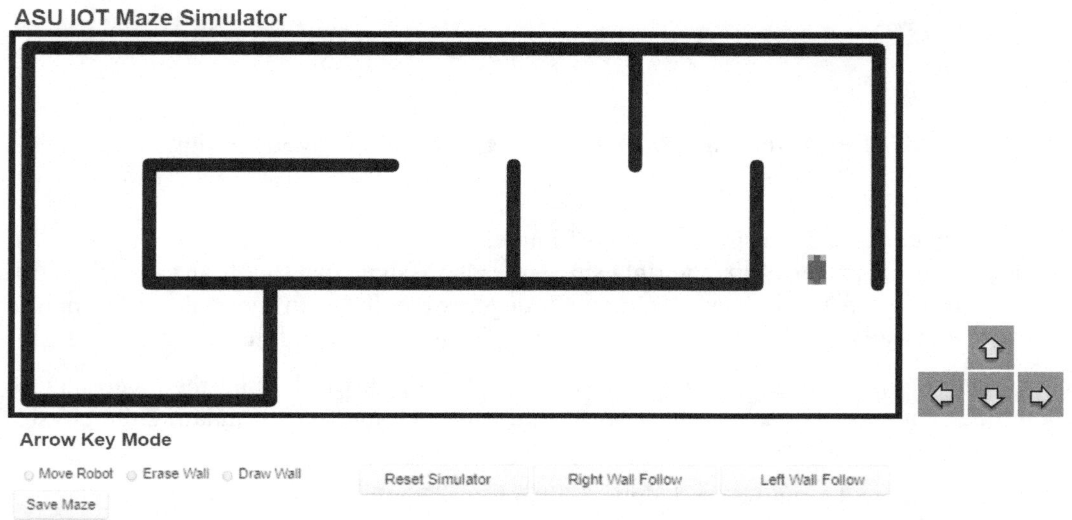

Figure 9.13. Web 2D Simulator with built-in programming mechanism

The buttons under the maze allow a user to use the four arrow key to control the move of the robot, or to run the built-in maze navigation programs Right Wall Follow or Left Wall Follow.

Further under the maze in the web page, you can program the robot to follow the wall or implement the two-distance algorithm. Figure 9.14 shows a simple implementation of of a right-wall-following algorithm.

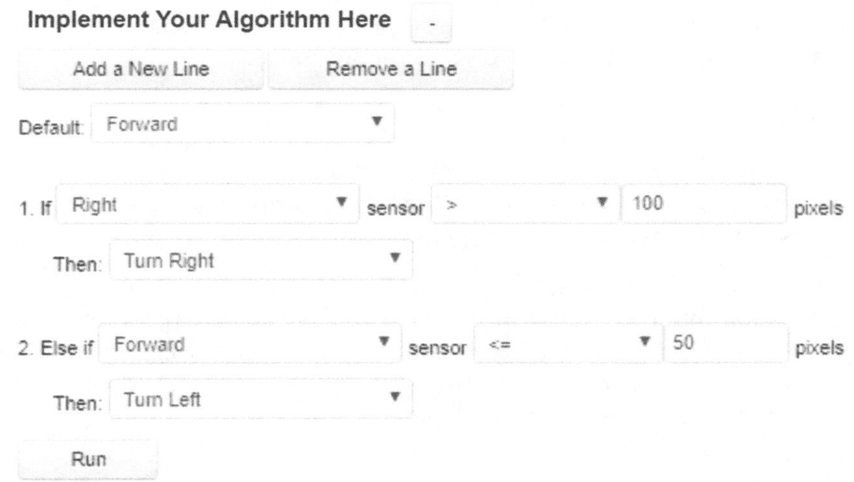

Figure 9.14. Simple implementation of the right-wall-following algorithm

Click the Run button in Figure 9.14, the robot will start to move. However, the robot will be turning in circle after a right 90-degree turn, because the robot will see the right side open again and thus keep turning right. To solve this problem, we need to make the robot move forward for a certain distance after the right turn. Figure 9.15 shows the revised part of the program.

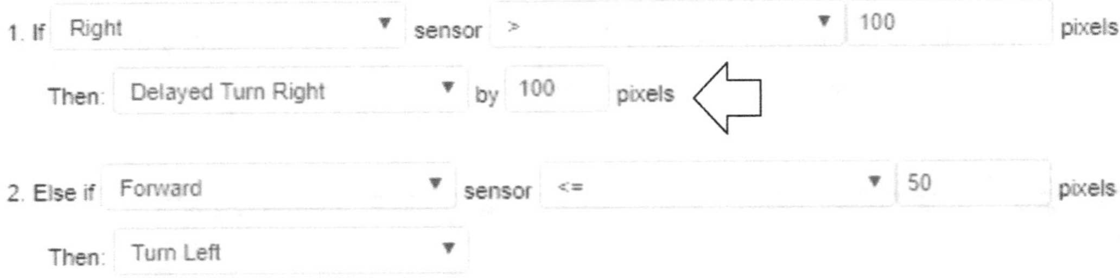

Figure 9.15. Revise the Right Wall Following algorithm to avoid turning in a circle

The Web 2D Simulator offers the simplest way of implementing maze navigation algorithms. We assume that the robot has sensors in front, left, and right sides. We also assume that robot can move forward straight, and the robot can turn left 90 degrees and right 90 degrees precisely. In the reality, the motors are not accurate and not consistent. They cannot move in a straight line and cannot turn the desired degrees.

Furthermore, the built-in programming language using drop-down list in the Web 2D Simulator environment does not support states and variables, and it is not capable of simulating the physical robots that we will use in our experiments.

The Web 2D simulator in 13 can be used alone to demonstrate and program a simulated robot. It can also be used with VIPLE Visual IoT/Robotics Programming Language Environment to be discussed in later sections, which offers a realistic way of programming robots.

9.3 Robotics Developer Studio and Visual Programming Language

An important milestone in service-oriented computing was laid when Microsoft released the service-oriented and architecture-driven Robotics Developer Studio (MRDS) in June 2006. Many robotics companies have moved their software development platforms to MRDS, which is the first commercial service-oriented development environment for robotics applications. This section and the following section introduce MRDS, and use it to develop service-oriented applications.

9.3.1 MRDS and VPL Overview

Service-oriented design principles make MRDS platform independent. The same application can be deployed to different robotics platforms, such as iRobot, Fischertechnik, LEGO Mindstorms NXT, and Parallax, based on the services provided for these platforms.

In addition, Robotics Developer Studio also includes the 3D robotic virtual simulation environments for users to test their applications prior to loading the software to the hardware platform (robot). Using AGEIA PhysX Technology, a pioneer in hardware-accelerated physics, MRDS can enable real-world physics simulation for robot models. Figure 9.16 shows two screenshots of the 3D robotic virtual environment, which simulate two iRobots in Sumo Robot competition.

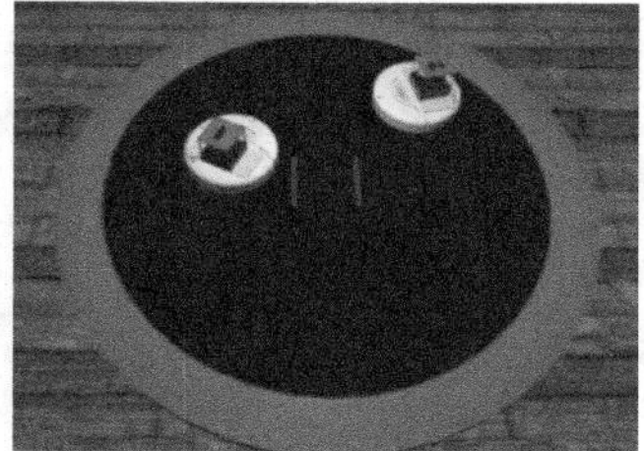

Figure 9.16. Simulation environment in MRDS

MRDS is based on the .Net framework, as shown in Figure 9.17. The programming language used in MRDS is called Visual Programming Language (VPL), which can be used to program services, as well as workflow of the application. One can also use C# and VB on .Net to program any services and add them into the MRDS's service repository. However, we will focus on using VPL to program services (as a service provider) and use it to develop workflow-based applications (as a service client). MRDS and VPL can be considered a specialization of workflow foundation in the robotics application domain.

The Concurrency and Coordination Runtime (CCR) shown in Figure 9.17 provides a concurrent message-oriented programming model for SOA application development, and it manages asynchronous operations, dealing with concurrency, exploiting parallel hardware, and handling failures. The users do not need to deal with threading, locks, and semaphores.

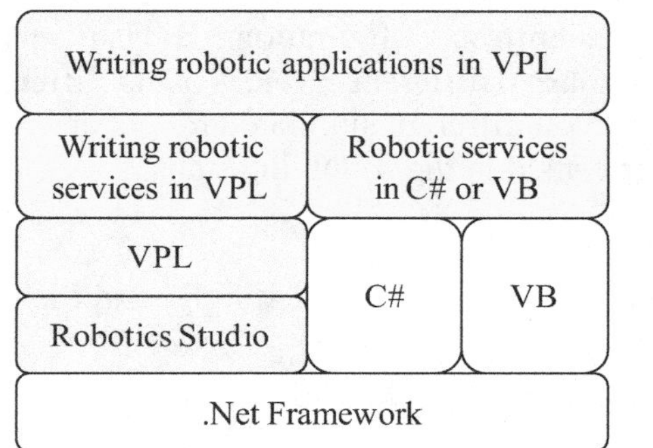

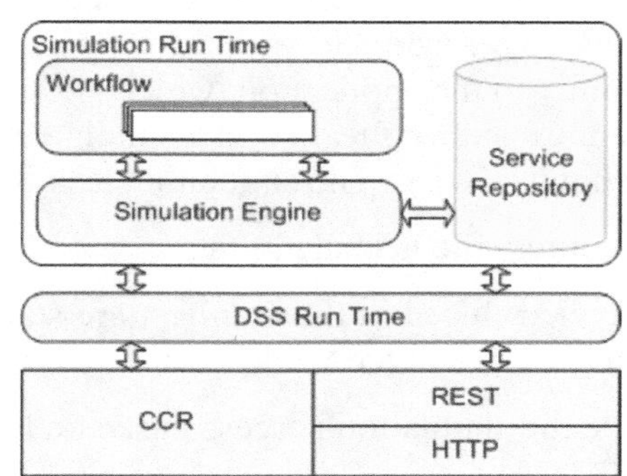

Figure 9.17. MRDS and its environment

Decentralized System Services (DSS) provides a service-hosting environment and a set of basic services facilitating tasks such as debugging, logging, monitoring, security, discovery, and data persistence. It also manages the interoperability between simulation engine and CCR, and allows application compositing using remote services. The DSS runtime is built on top of CCR and the standard communication protocols. Instead of using SOAP over HTTP, DSS runtime uses REST (Representational State Transfer) over HTTP, which can better deal with the real-time requirement in the robotics applications.

Visual Programming Language (VPL) is an application development environment designed on a graphical dataflow programming model rather than control flow model typically found in conventional programming. Rather than using a series of imperative commands sequentially executed, a dataflow program is more like a series of workers (services) on an assembly line, who do their assigned task as the materials arrive. As a result, VPL is well suited to programming a variety of concurrent or distributed processing scenarios.

VPL is simple to begin with, which is based on fundamental programming concepts such as variable, data, if-then-else, loop, merging, and join. However, VPL is not limited to novices. The compositional nature of the programming language may appeal to more advanced programmers for rapid prototyping or code development. Furthermore, while its toolbox is tailored to developing robot applications, the underlying architecture is not limited to programming robots. It can be applied to other applications, such as games, complex processes of manufactory, and other design processes. Figure 9.18 shows the map between the workflow and the services. A **manifest** maps the proxy to the real service. For the same workflow, a different manifest can map it to different robotics platform, such as iRobot, NXT, and Parallax.

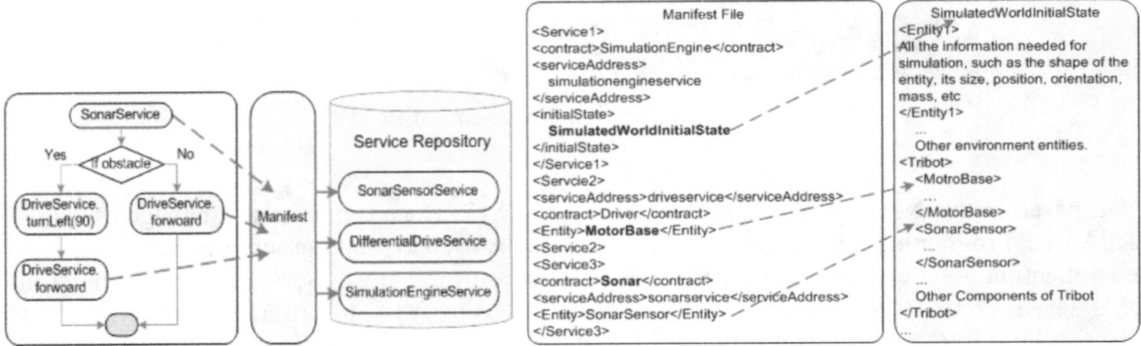

Figure 9.18. Robotics Developer Studio and its environment

9.3.2 Application Development in MRDS and VPL

When developing an application, a user can either compose using the actual services, or generic services that can be bound to real services with the support of the manifest configuration file: Using generic services provides flexibility to the application, which allows binding to different services using different manifests. A user can run the same application in a simulated world on different simulated robots or in the real world on different robot hardware. The simulation task is performed in the following steps:

1. The manifest file is loaded first;
2. The services listed in the manifest are started and configured accordingly, and then bound to the generic services in the workflow;
3. Execute the simulation process based on the logic described by the workflow.

The entire simulation process can be monitored through a visualization service built in the simulation engine service.

Like any programming language, VPL consists of a set of constructs, which is called "basic activities," described as follows:

Variable: A variable activity represents a memory location, where a program can store and retrieve values such as a literal string or a number.

Calculate: A calculate activity is used to compute mathematical equations (adding, subtracting, dividing, or multiplying), as well as data extract from other components such as a variable or a textbox. It is similar to the assignment statement in C#; for example, x = 5 +7; for numeric data operations, we use the following operation symbols:

Operation	add	subtract/minus	multiply	divide	mod
Symbol	+	-	*	/	%

For logical operators you can use the following symbols:

Operation	Logic AND	Logic OR	Logic NOT
Symbol	&& or use AND	|| or use OR	! or use NOT

Data: The activity is used to supply a simple data value to another activity or service. To define a specific kind of data, select its type from the dropdown under the text box, then enter a value into the text box. The following is a list of data types supported by VPL.

Join: The activity combines the input of two (or more) components. All data items from the incoming connections must be received before Join can proceed to the next step. All components in VPL have a single input line. Join can be used to feed multiple input values into a single input line.

Merge: The activity merges two (or more) inputs together. However, it is significantly different from Join in that Merge waits for the first data item arrives. Merge will proceed to the next step if any input has arrived. Merge can be used to implement a loop. One input is used for the initial entry to the loop body, while the other entry is used for reentering the loop body.

If: The activity provides a choice of outputs to forward the incoming message based on a condition that is entered. The If-statement in VPL can check multiple conditions in one statement. In other words, it can combine multiple consecutive (C#) If-statements into one.

The conditional expression can use the following operators for evaluation: equals (= or ==), not equals (!= or <>), less than (<), greater than (>), less than or equals (<=), great than or equals (>=).

To add additional conditions to the activity, click the add (+) button on the activity block.

Switch: Similar to the "switch" statement in C#, the switch activity is used to route messages based on the incoming message's matching the expression entered into the text box. To add additional Case branches (match conditions) to the activity block, simply click the Add (+) button on the activity block.

List: The list activity creates an empty list of data items. To create a list, select the type (data type) for the items, from the dropdown list of choices on the activity block (or the properties view). To add entries to the list, use the List Functions activity. To store a list for use elsewhere in the diagram, create a list variable using the Variable activity.

List Functions: The list function activity enables a user to modify an existing list.

Comment: The comment activity enables the user to add a block of text to a diagram as documentation.
Activity: An activity represents pre-built services, dataflow component, functions, or other code modules. The resulting application is therefore often referred to as orchestration, the sequencing of separate processes. The "Activity" listed in the basic activities is not a basic activity. It is used to compose a component using basic activities, other activities, and services. It makes it possible to compose new activities and reuse the activities as a building block. An activity can be used in the current application (called a diagram) only. If one wants to share an activity with other applications, one may simply choose the menu command "Compile as a Service," which will wrap the activity into a service, and the service will be available in the MRDS repository once the MRDS is restarted.

Diagram: the graphic design interface for developing a VPL application. It can use the basic activities, activities developed in the current application, and services in the repository, to compose the dataflow-based application. The diagram here corresponds to the workflow in the workflow foundation.

MRDS also comes with a large number of services, including input and output services, sensory services, and drive services. Figure 9.19 shows the design of an activity that generates numbers from a given initial value to 7.

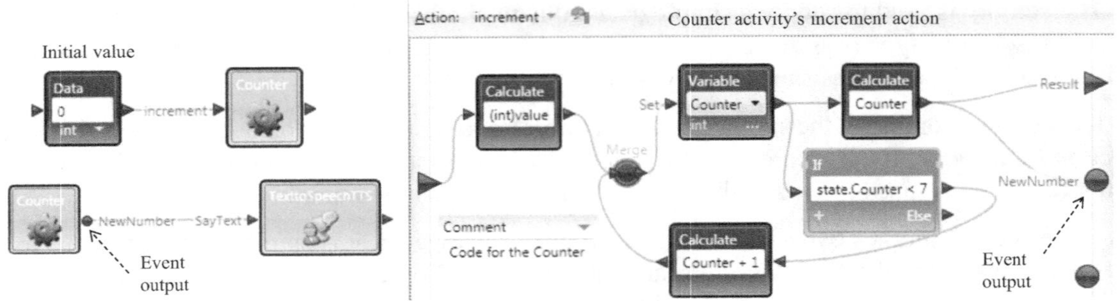

Figure 9.19. Diagram (left) and activity (right) that generate numbers from 0 to 7

The lower part of the figure shows the code in the diagram that initializes the Counter, and sends the outputs of the Counter to a Text to Speech service. In the Counter activity, three basic activities are used: Calculate, Variable, and If. In the main diagram, basic activity Data, Counter activity, and Text to Speech (TTS) service are used. Notice that the circular dot (notification/event output) at the Counter activity is connected to the Text to Speech (TTS) service, which can notify the service of the arrival of a new input. For the detail of setting up the data values between the connections, please refer to the VPL tutorial in the appendix.

9.4 VIPLE: A New Visual Programming Language

Microsoft VPL is a milestone in software engineering and robotics from many aspects. It is service-oriented; it is workflow-based; it is event-driven; it supports parallel computing; and it is a great educational tool that is simple to learn and yet powerful and expressive.

Sponsored by two Innovation Excellence awards from Microsoft Research in 2003 and in 2005, Dr. Yinong Chen participated in the earlier discussion of service-oriented robotics at Microsoft. Microsoft VPL was immediately adopted by Chen in developing the freshman course CSE101 in 2006. The course grew from 70 students in 2006 to over 350 students in 2011. The course was extended to all students in Ira A. Fulton Schools of Engineering at ASU and was renamed FSE100, which is now offered to thousands of freshman engineering students.

Unfortunately, Microsoft recently stopped developing and supporting VPL, which leads to our FSE100 course, and many other schools' courses using VPL without the further support. Particularly, the current version of VPL does not support LEGO's third generation of EV3 robot, while the second-generation NXT is out of the market.

To keep our course running and also help the other schools, we take the challenge and responsibility to develop our own visual programming environment VIPLE. The purpose of this project is to provide a free environment supporting the VPL development community in education and research. To serve this purpose, VIPLE (Visual IoT/Robotics Programming Language Environment) keeps the great features that VPL has and provides a similar user interface and functionality, so that the MRDS and VPL development community can use VIPLE with no learning curve. VIPLE does not replace Microsoft VPL, instead, it extends VPL in its capacity to connect to different physical robots, including EV3 and Intel-based open architecture robots.

Robot as a Service and the VIPLE environment are designed and developed by Yinong Chen and Gennaro De Luca, with contributions from Calvin Cheng, Matthew De Rosa, Megan Plachecki, Sami Mian, and many students who are involved in the related projects. VIPLE documents, software, and sample code can be downloaded from the ASU Web Service and Application repository. The direct link is at: http://neptune.fulton.ad.asu.edu/WSRepository/VIPLE.

9.4.1 ASU VIPLE versus Microsoft VPL

Based on the Robot as a Service concept, ASU VIPLE uses the same computing model as Microsoft VPL. The program is running on a Windows computer, which can be a desktop, a laptop, or a tablet. The computer sends commands to control the robot actuators (motors) and receives the sensory data and motor feedbacks from the robot. The data between the computer and the robot is encoded in a JSON object, which is in plain text format. It supports Wi-Fi, Bluetooth, and USB connections between the main computer and the robot. VIPLE supports EV3 and any self-developed robots. We have developed different robots based on Intel architecture, the Linux operating system, and the Windows operating system.

Figure 9.20 compares the activities and services between ASU VIPLE and Microsoft VPL. ASU VIPLE implemented most basic activities in VPL and implemented additional While, Break, and End While activities to facilitate loop building, which can reduce the circular paths in a VPL diagram.

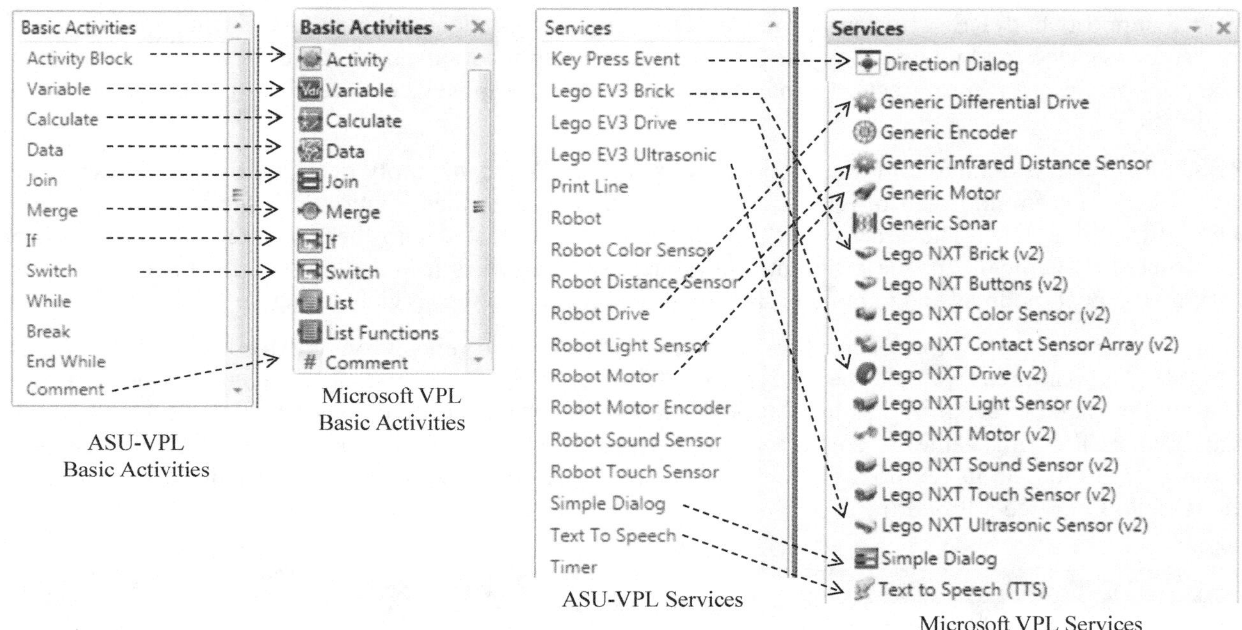

Figure 9.20. Activities and services: ASU VIPLE versus Microsoft VPL

In the current version, three sets of services are implemented. The first set is a list of generic services, including the Simple Dialog, Key Press Event (Direction Dialog), Text To Speech, and Timer. The second set is for EV3 robots. The third set of services are used to connect to generic robots, various sensors, and motor services. The significant addition to Microsoft VPL is the inclusion of LEGO EV3 services and generic robot services. In Microsoft VPL, DSS services developed specifically for MRDS can be added into the VPL service list. In VIPLE, SOAP and RESTful services can be added into the service list.

ASU VIPLE is similar to Microsoft VPL not only in concepts but also in programming. It is our intention to have Microsoft VPL programmers use ASU VIPLE with little learning. We will now show examples of basic programming in VIPLE. We will start with the Hello World program. Figure 9.21 shows the two versions of code using VPL and VIPLE. The two diagrams look the same. However, VIPLE has simplified a couple of steps: it automatically changes the type to String after a string is entered, and the default null value step in Microsoft VPL is eliminated.

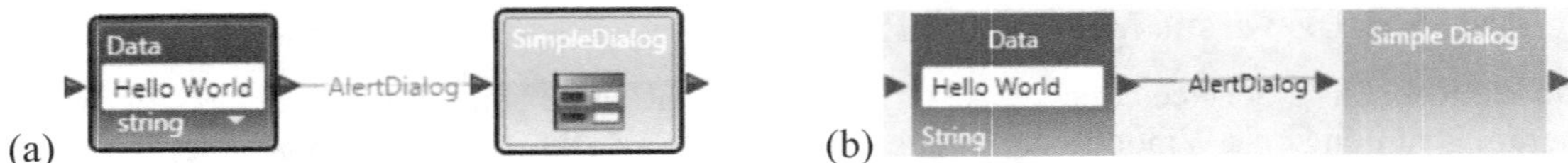

Figure 9.21. Hello world program in (a) Microsoft VPL and (b) ASU VIPLE

We give a comprehensive step-by-step tutorial on using programming in VIPLE in Appendix B. In this chapter, we will focus on the advanced features and the concepts that are closely related to the distributed and service-oriented computing.

9.4.2 Service-Oriented Computing: RESTful, WSDL, and VIPLE Service

VIPLE supports both RESTful service and WSDL service invocations, allowing the applications to access the remote services and integrating their functions into the applications, both statically and dynamically. It also supports converting an activity into a service so the component can be shared with other VIPLE applications.

RESTful service is available in the Services list in VIPLE. We can simply drag and drop the service into the VIPLE diagram and then provide URL and the parameter values. Figure 9.22 shows the creation of RESTful service calls. The service URL can be copied and pasted into the given textbox statically, or constructed dynamically in the program and passed as parameters into the service. In this example, we provide the URL address and parameter, and then pass them into the service through a Join activity.

In this program, we use the Encryption service at ASU service repository. We feed the address into a variable. The parameter value to be encrypted is 1234567. VIPLE automatically recognizes the data type. The number will be recognized as Int32 type. However, we need a string type for the RESTful service. We call Convert.ToString(value) to convert it into a string type. Another solution is to use Calculate activity and use "1234567" in its textbox. Then, the Join activity will pass the two values into the two variables in the RESTful Service's Properties.

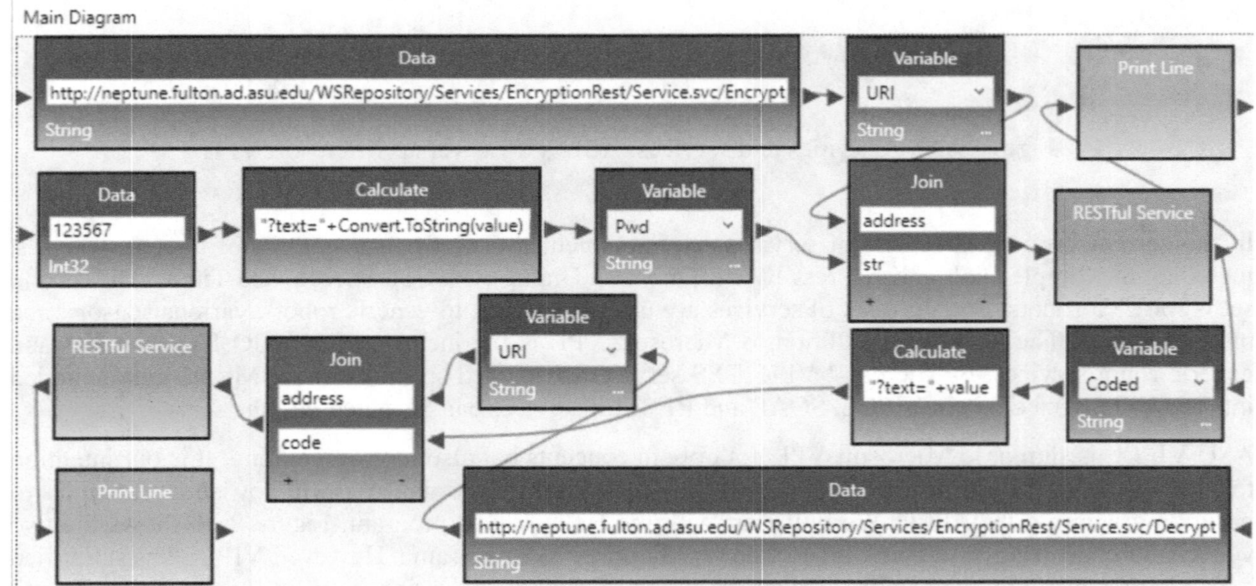

Figure 9.22. Using encryption and decryption RESTful services in VIPLE

As shown in Figure 9.23, right click a RESTful service and choose Properties to open the properties window for configuring the service. We can define the full service address in multiple parts and by passing each part into the service through a Join activity.

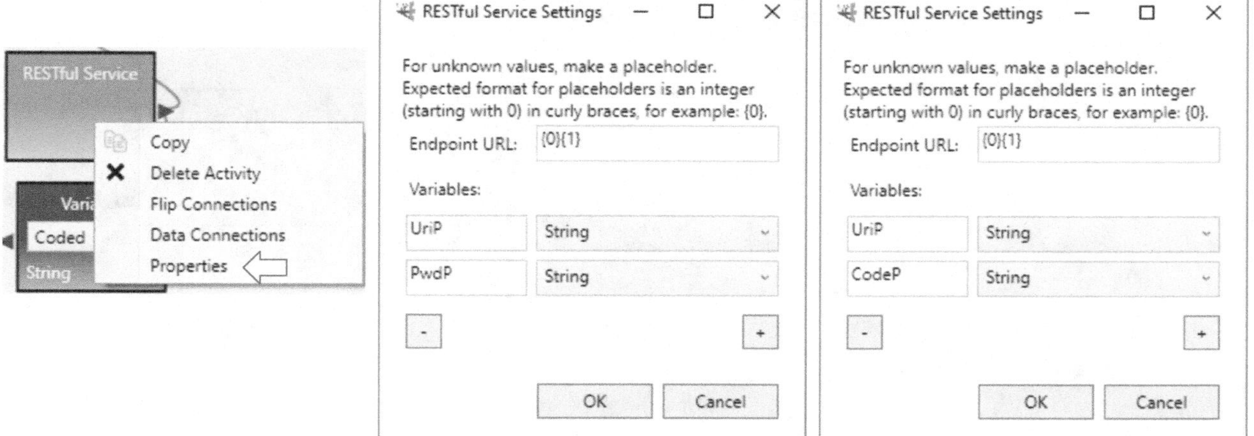

Figure 9.23. Properties of the two RESTful services

VIPLE also supports the heavy-duty WSDL services in the same way as in web application building. We can add a service reference into VIPLE application, discover the available operations in the services, and add the operations into VIPLE's service list. We can use the service operations in the same way as the other VIPLE services. Figure 9.24 shows the steps of adding a WSDL service into VIPLE application: (1) Add a WSDL service from VIPLE menu; (2) Choose New Service; and (3) Copy and paste the service URL into the new service textbox.

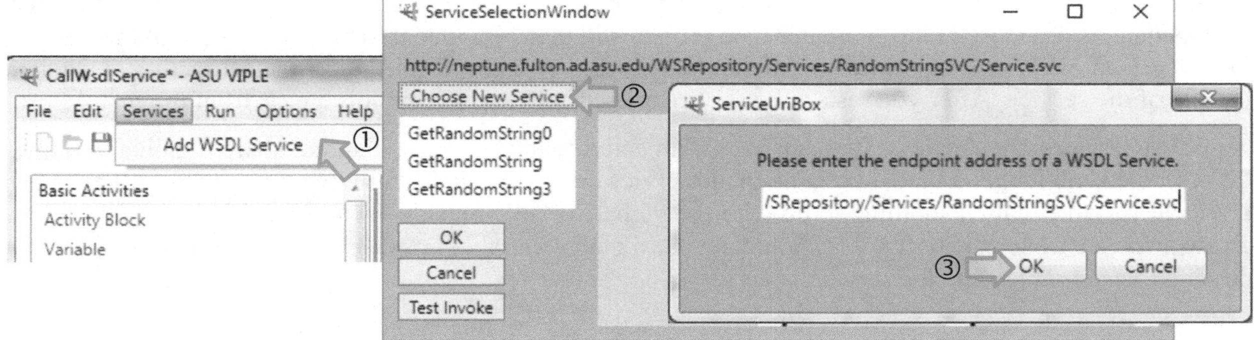

Figure 9.24. Adding a WSDL service into the VIPLE application

After a WSDL service is added, the operations in the service will appear in VIPLE's Services list, and these operations can be used by dragging and dropping them into the VIPLE diagram, as shown in Figure 9.25.

We can implement or discover other remote services and add them into VIPLE, such as voice and image recognition, and deep learning services. We have built text to speech in VIPLE. The other services can be implemented as WSDL or RESTful services and added into VIPLE's services list.

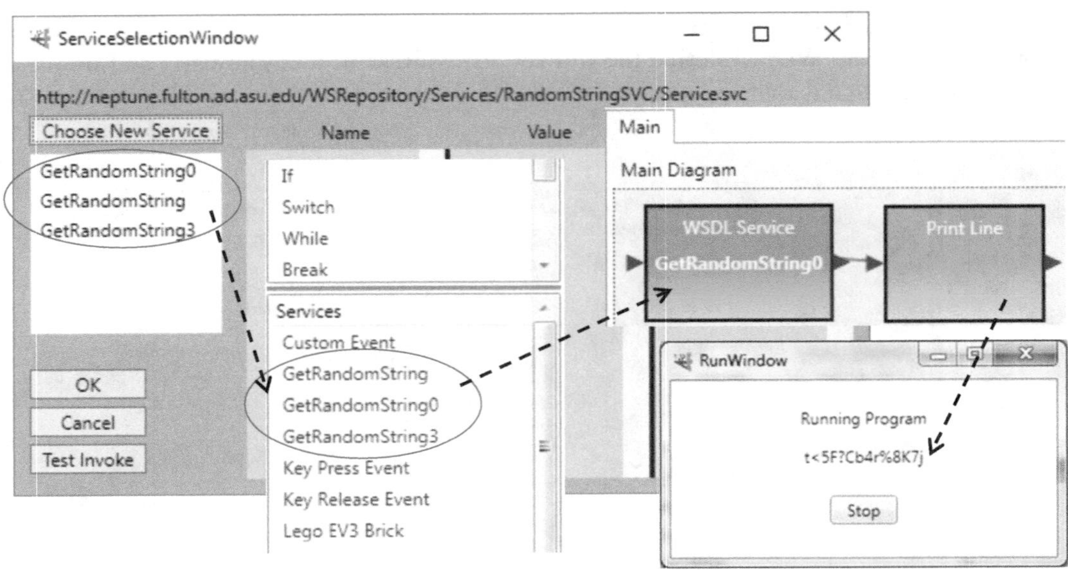

Figure 9.25. WSDL services added into the VIPLE diagram

Finally, we present the VIPLE local services. In VIPLE, an activity is a part of a VIPLE diagram, which cannot be separated and cannot be shared in a different program. However, we can convert an activity into a service.

Appendix B showed multiple examples of converting, using, and sharing a VIPLE service. In the exercise of creating a 2-1 multiplexor activity, right click the 2-1Mux activity and select "Convert to Service," as shown in Figure 9.26. You can save the service anywhere you want. By default, a copy will be saved into the Documents directory of the computer. The service will then be added into the Services list of the VIPLE. To delete (remove) a custom service from your VIPLE service list, open the Documents directory and delete the file of the service. After you restart the service, the custom service will disappear from the service list.

Note that services are stateless. It means that if an activity and the main diagram share a global variable, the variable is no longer a global variable in the service created from the activity. The service will consider it a local variable that has nothing to do with the global variable outside the service. Thus, if you want to create a service from an activity, you should not use a global variable in the activity. You can use parameter passing to pass values into the service.

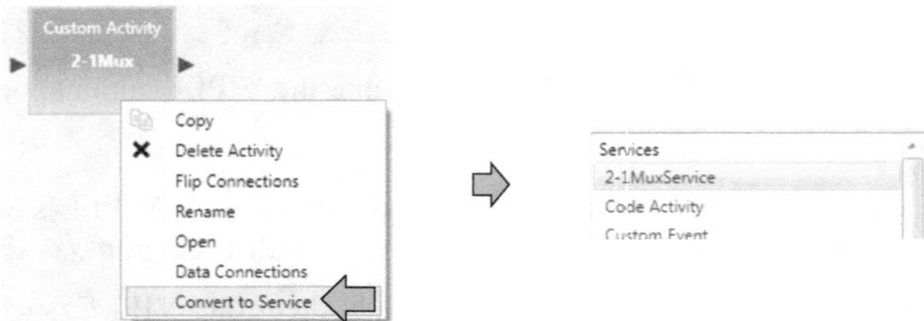

Figure 9.26. Converting an activity into a service and adding into Services list

Restart your VIPLE. You will now see the 2-1MuxService in your Services list, as shown in Figure 9.27. Draw the following diagram. Instead of using the 2-1Mux activity, you are now using the 2-1MuxService.

Note that when you connect the Join service to 2-1MuxService, make sure that you map the Join data names to the 1MuxService parameters correctly.

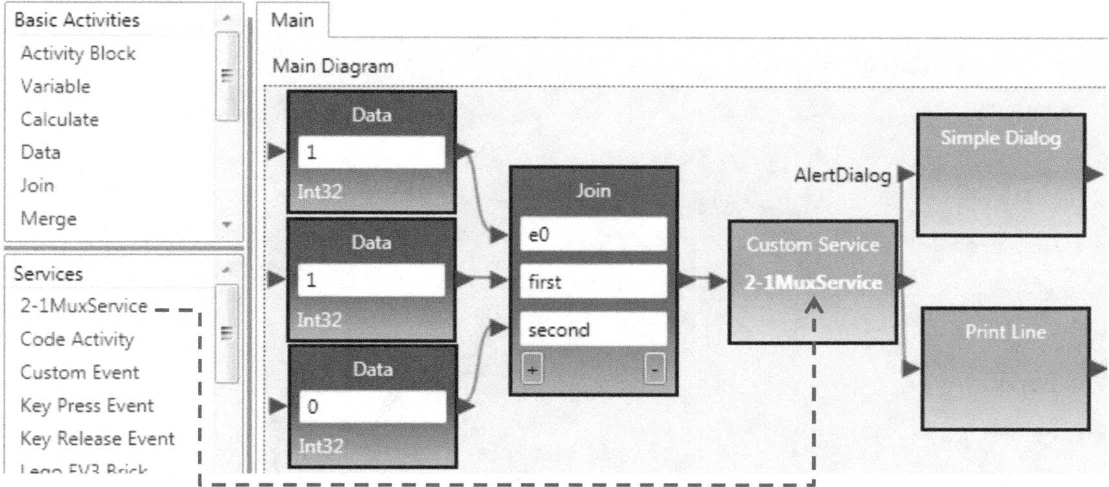

Figure 9.27. The service appears in the Services list and can be used like other services

We also developed a VIPLE image recognition service. It calls a remote web service that can take the URL of a .jpg or .png image as input, and it recognizes the shape of the image. Figure 9.28 shows the sample code that recognizes a stop sign image and the execution result. As the same image can have different meanings, the service gives the probabilities of different possible meanings.

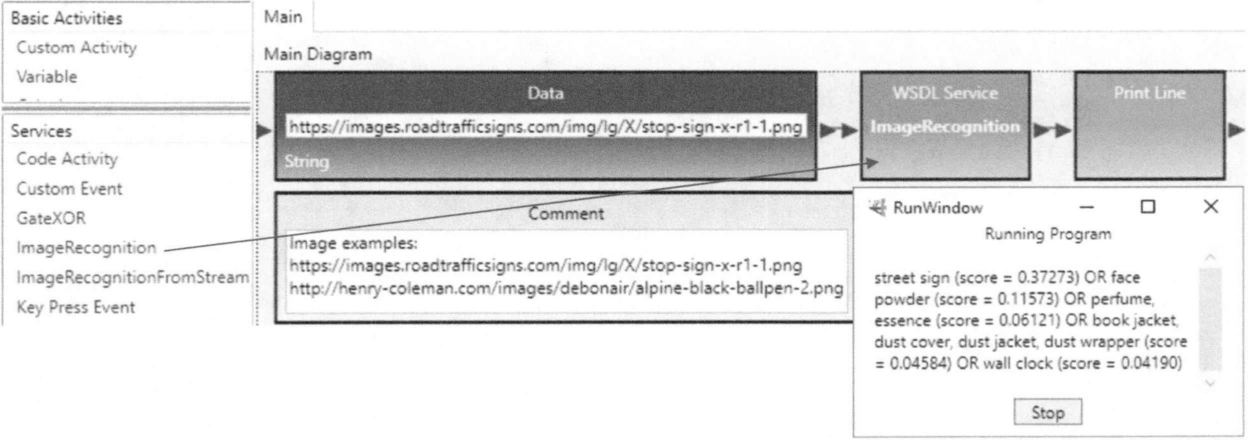

Figure 9.28. Using the ImageRecognitionService

9.4.3 Workflow with Code Activities

VIPLE is a workflow-based composition language. It composes application using services and activities. Similar to Workflow Foundation, it can also conveniently use code activity in the diagram to do any job that can be done easily by writing source code. The architects can also use code activities to compose a flowchart and let the programmer fill in the code in each code activity.

As shown in Figure 9.29, there are two types of Code Activities are supported: C# and Python. We first discuss the C# Code Activity. You can drag and drop the Code Activity C# from VIPLE Service list into the diagram, and choose a name for your activity. The name cannot contain a space, as the name will be considered a class name.

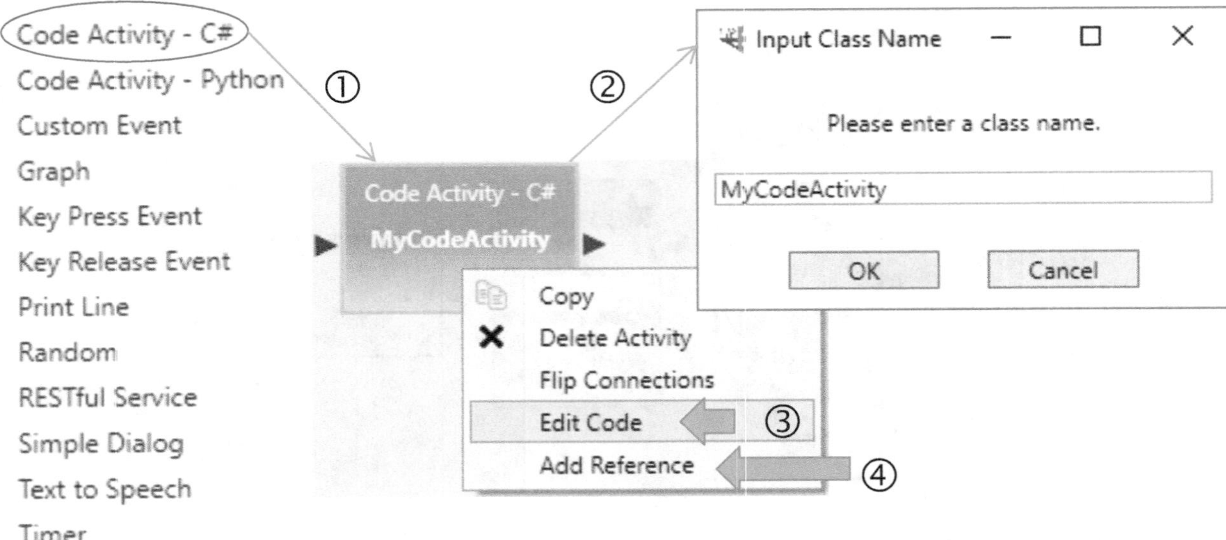

Figure 9.29. Starting a Code Activity

Right-click or double-click the code activity to open the source code window, as shown in Figure 9.30. You will be able to edit the code template and add your code into the activity.

Code Editor

```
using System;

[Serializable]
public class NOT_Gate : CodeUtilities.CodeBase
{
    public NOT_Gate()
    {

    }

    // To execute your code, you must override the Execute method.
    public override void Execute()
    {
        // Obtain the value of the input to this activity.
        // The type of this value will depend on what input you pass to this activity.
        int myInput = (int)Input;

        // You can use the PrintLine method to print strings to the run window
        // during runtime.
        PrintLine("Hello from NOT_Gate!");

        // You can pass output in a similar way.
        if (myInput == 0)
            { Output = 1;}
        else
            { Output = 0;}
    }
}
```

Figure 9.30. Open and edit the source code in the Code Activity

The code activity has full capacity of a C# console application. You can add any framework library into the activity. As shown in step (4) in Figure 9.29, right-click the CodeActivity and choose Add Reference, you will be able to select and add any framework library into your code activity.

As an example, we use CodeActivity to reimplement the gates and the Adder that are implemented using activities in Appendix B.

Figure 9.31 shows the diagram that implements a NOT_Gate and the Adder using AND_Gate, OR_Gate, and XOR-Gate.

The source code of the NOT_Gate is shown Figure 9.30. The activity has one generic-type parameter (input) and one generic-type Output variable as its return value. The input to the activity is passed to the Input variable in the source code, and the value assigned to the Output variable will be returned and passed to the outside as its return value.

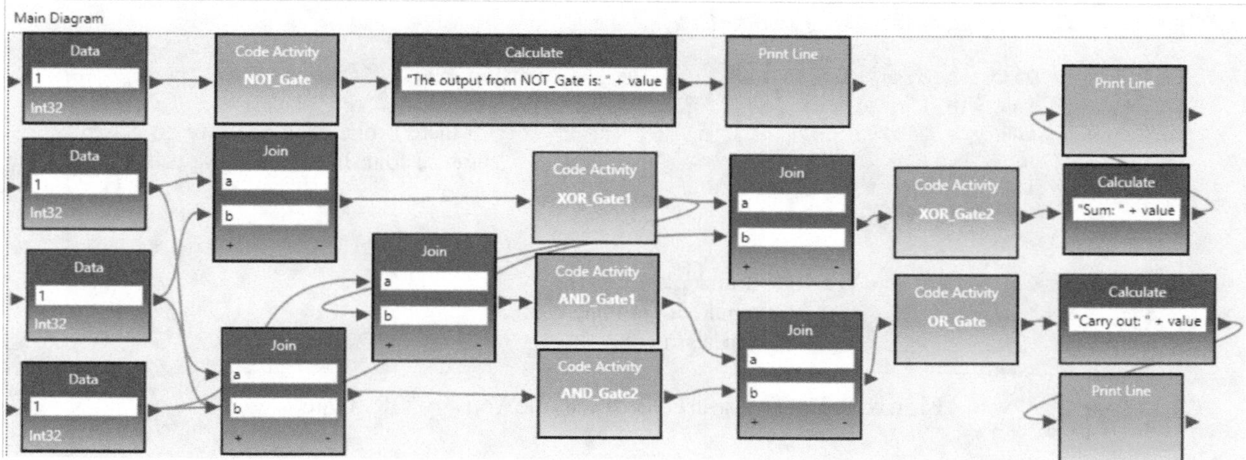

Figure 9.31. Diagram that implements NOT_Gate and Adder using code activities

The AND_Gate, OR_Gate, and XOR-Gate in the diagram has two input parameters and one output. The inputs will be given using a Join activity in the Main diagram. Figure 9.32 shows the source code of the OR_Gate.

Code Editor

```
using System;
using System.Collections.Generic;
using VisualProgrammingEnvironment;

public class OR_Gate : CodeUtilities.CodeBase
{
    // Setting the return type up here allows you to use the "value" keyword
    // correctly in connected activities.
    public OR_Gate()
    {
    }

    // To execute your code, you must override the Execute method.
    public override void Execute()
    {
        Dictionary<string, object> input = (Dictionary<string, object>)Input;
        int x = (int)input["a"];
        int y = (int)input["b"];

        if (x == 0 && y == 0)
            Output = 0;
        else
            Output = 1;
    }
}
```

For using Join to take more than one values, additional libraries are needed. You need to use "Add Reference". You may also need to add: Using System.Runtime

If there is one input only, we do not use Join. In this case, we use: int x = (int)Input

If multiple outputs required, combine them into a structure

Figure 9.32. The source of the CodeActivity OR_Gate

In the source code, we need to use "Add Reference" to add additional libraries and add using directives to include these libraries into the program. Multiple inputs will be considered as a collection (array) and each element can be accessed in the following way:

```
int a = (int)input["a"];
int b = (int)input["b"];
```

Now, we discuss Code Activity Python. Python has emerged as a major programming language in IoT, robotics, as well as in AI and machine learning. This is the reason that we have included Python code activity in VIPLE. Figure 9.33 shows a VIPLE diagram, in which Code Activity Python is used.

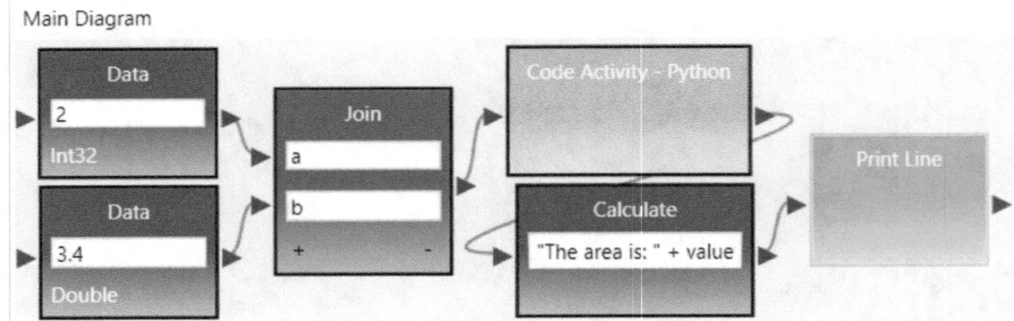

Figure 9.33. Using Code Activity Python VIPLE diagram

In this diagram, the Python code activity serves as a function (procedure). Two parameter values are passed into the code activity through a Join activity, and the output is passed through standard "value". The value is concatenated with the string "The area is: " in Calculate activity and printed.

Code Activity Python can be opened through double-click. Figure 9.34 shows the Python code in the activity.

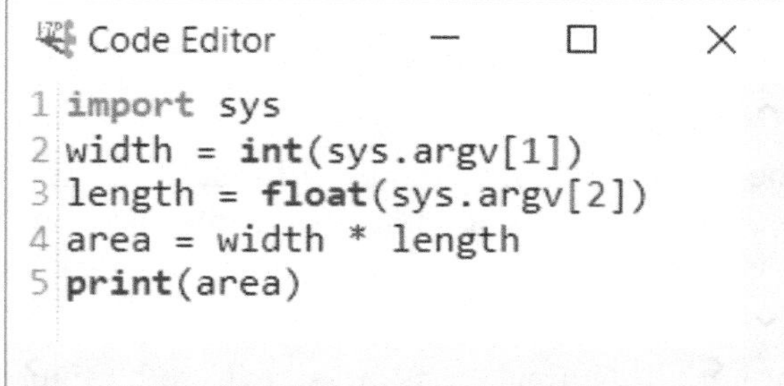

Figure 9.34. Python source code in Code Activity Python

First, we import the library sys. We then use sys.argv[i] to obtain the two parameter values passed from outside, where i = 0, 1. We cast the parameter types into int and float, accordingly. We calculate the area and pass the area as return value to the outside through print. Note, this print does not print the value to VIPLE console. It passes the value to outside and the Print Line in VIPLE diagram prints the value to the VIPLE console, as shown in Figure 9.33.

9.4.4 Finite State Machine

A **Finite State Machine** (FSM), also called a **state diagram** or state transition diagram, is a model of behavior composed of a finite number of states, transitions between those states, and actions. A finite state machine is an abstract model of a machine with internal memory (http://en.wikipedia.org/wiki/Finite_state_machine). A current state is determined by past states of the system. As such, it can be said to record information about the past, that is, it reflects the input changes from the system start to the present moment. A transition indicates a state change and is described by a condition that would need to be fulfilled to enable the transition. An action is a description of an activity that is to be performed at a given moment.

An FSM can be used to specify (to model) different systems in which memory (variables) are involved, such as:

- a business process that responds to a sequence of requests from the user, as we discussed in the section of workflow foundation in Chapter 8;
- a vending machine that takes a sequence of coins or bills as inputs;
- a parity (even or odd) checker that counts the number of 1s in a binary number (a string of 0s and 1s);
- a string filter (processor) that reads the string as a sequence of characters and processes the characters in the process of reading; and
- a robot's behavior; for example, using the information of its current and past states to determine the next move.

There are two kinds of FSMs:

(1) Pure FSM, which uses states as the only memory. In other words, it does not use additional memory. Such models are typically implemented in hardware as sequential circuits.
(2) FSM with additional memory. Such models are typically implemented in software.

First, let us take a look of a pure FSM that describes a simple vending machine. We assume that the vending machine sells soda at 40 cents each, it can take at most 50 cents, and it can take the following five inputs in any order:

- Deposit quarter (25)
- Deposit dime (10)
- Deposit nickel (5)
- Push soda button
- Push return button

Because all information must be stored in the finite number of states, we have to assume a maximum amount that the machine can hold. For example, we can assume that the machine can hold at the most 50 cents. The finite state machine is given in Figure 9.35, which specifies the state, state transitions, and input that triggers the transition.

For the clarity of the diagram, not all the transitions are shown in the figure. The omitted transitions are follows:

- There is a transition from every state to the state 0 if the *return* input is given (return button is pressed). In the diagram, the return transitions from state 25 and state 50 are shown.
- In every state, the buyer can push the **soda** button. For states 40, 45, and 50, a soda will be released, and FSM will transit to a state with 40 cents less. In any other state with less than 40 cents, the FSM will remain in the same state. As example, two such soda transitions are shown in state 20 and state 30.

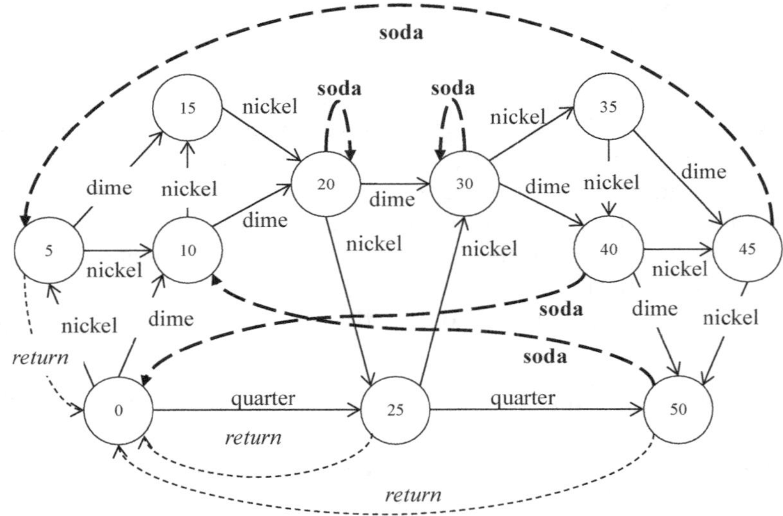

Figure 9.35. A pure finite state machine

There are 11 states in this FSM. We can use four bits of memory to represent the states and implement the FSM in a sequential circuit without using a full computer that can execute the FSM software.

The capacity of the FSM is limited. If we can use additional memory, we can eliminate the upper bound of the amount the machine can take (50 cents). Furthermore, we can reduce the number of states, as we do not need to use states to memorize the amount of money deposited. Figure 9.36 shows the FSM with an additional variable "Sum," which keeps track of the total amount deposited into the vending machine. In this example, we assume the vending machine can take quarters and dollars as input, and the soda costs 75 cents each.

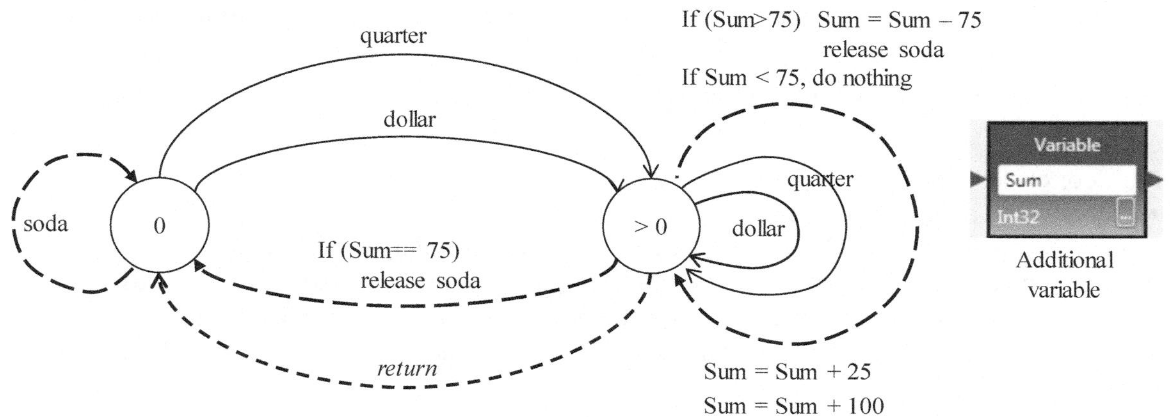

Figure 9.36. A finite state machine with memory

A simple VIPLE diagram is shown in Figure 9.37. We use Key Press Events to take inputs. The user can choose one of the input values through the keys: q - quarter, d - dollar, r - return, and s - soda. Based on the input value, the program generates the required output.

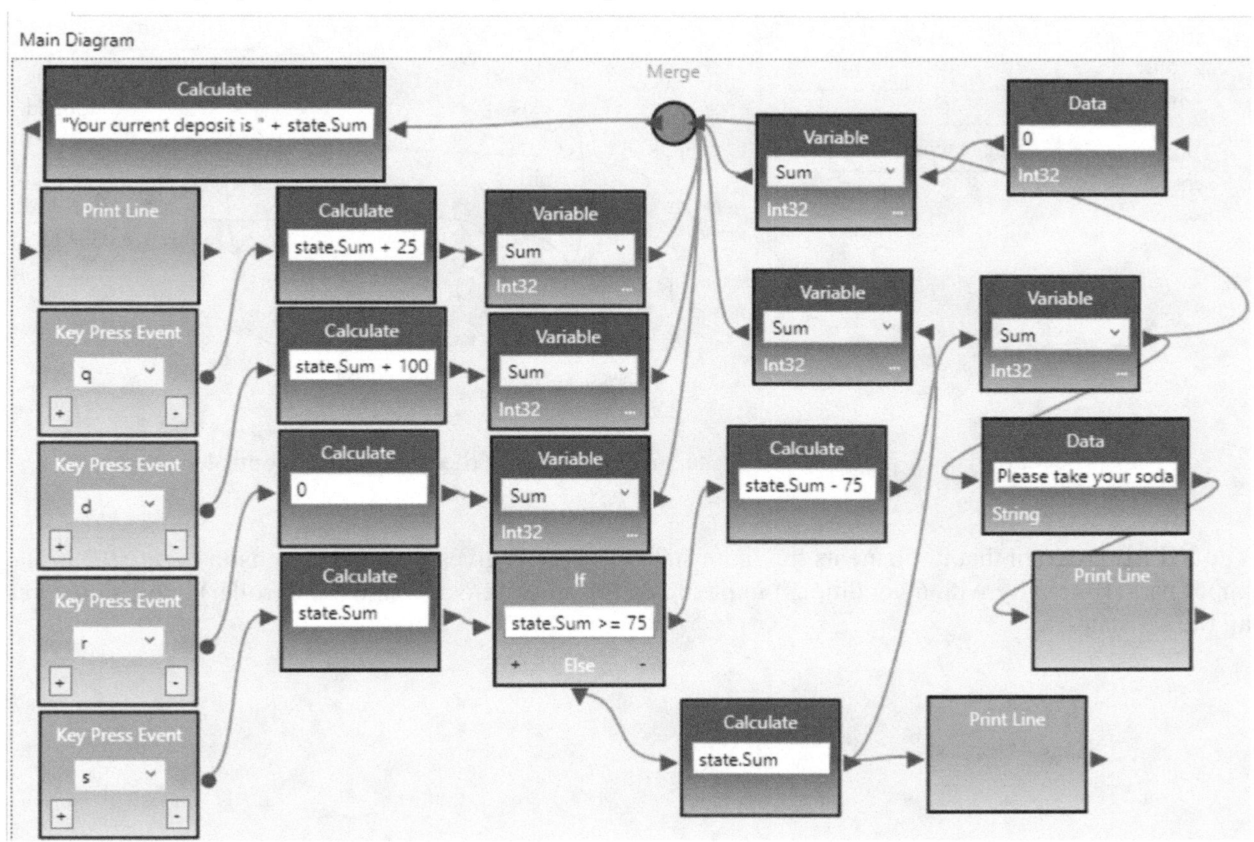

Figure 9.37. VIPLE program of the vending machine, with key press events used

As another example, Figure 9.38 shows the block diagram and the finite state machine of a garage door control system. The system involves two sensors: A touch sensor corresponding to the remote controller and a limit sensor in the motor that stops the motor and generates a signal to the controller when an excessive force is experienced, for example, when the door is full open or fully closed.

The finite state machine consists of the following states and events:

States

- door closed, door is fully closed.
- door open, door is fully open
- door closing, door is in the process of closing, which normally takes a few seconds.
- door opening, door is in the process of opening, which normally takes a few seconds.
- closing stopped, the door is closing and stopped by remote controller before fully closed.
- opening stopped, the door is opening and stopped by remote controller before fully closed.

Events

- Touch sensor pressed, the remote controller is pressed by a human.
- Limit sensor pressed, the limit sensor in the motor detects an excessive force.

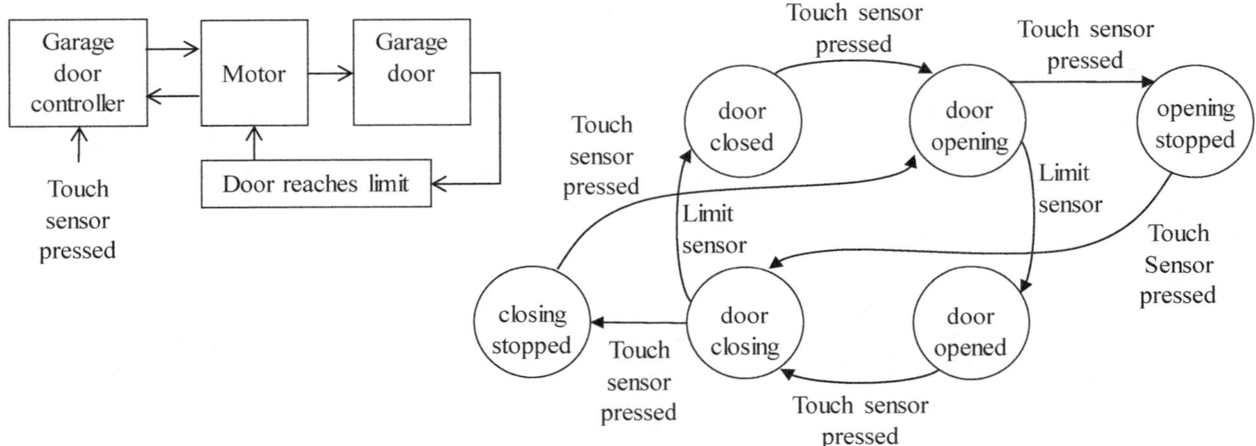

Figure 9.38. Block diagram and finite state machine of the garage door control system

The VIPLE program that implements the finite state machine is given in two diagrams in Figure 9.39. The upper part (If-activity with 6 conditions) implements the touch sensor (remote controller), which involves all the six states.

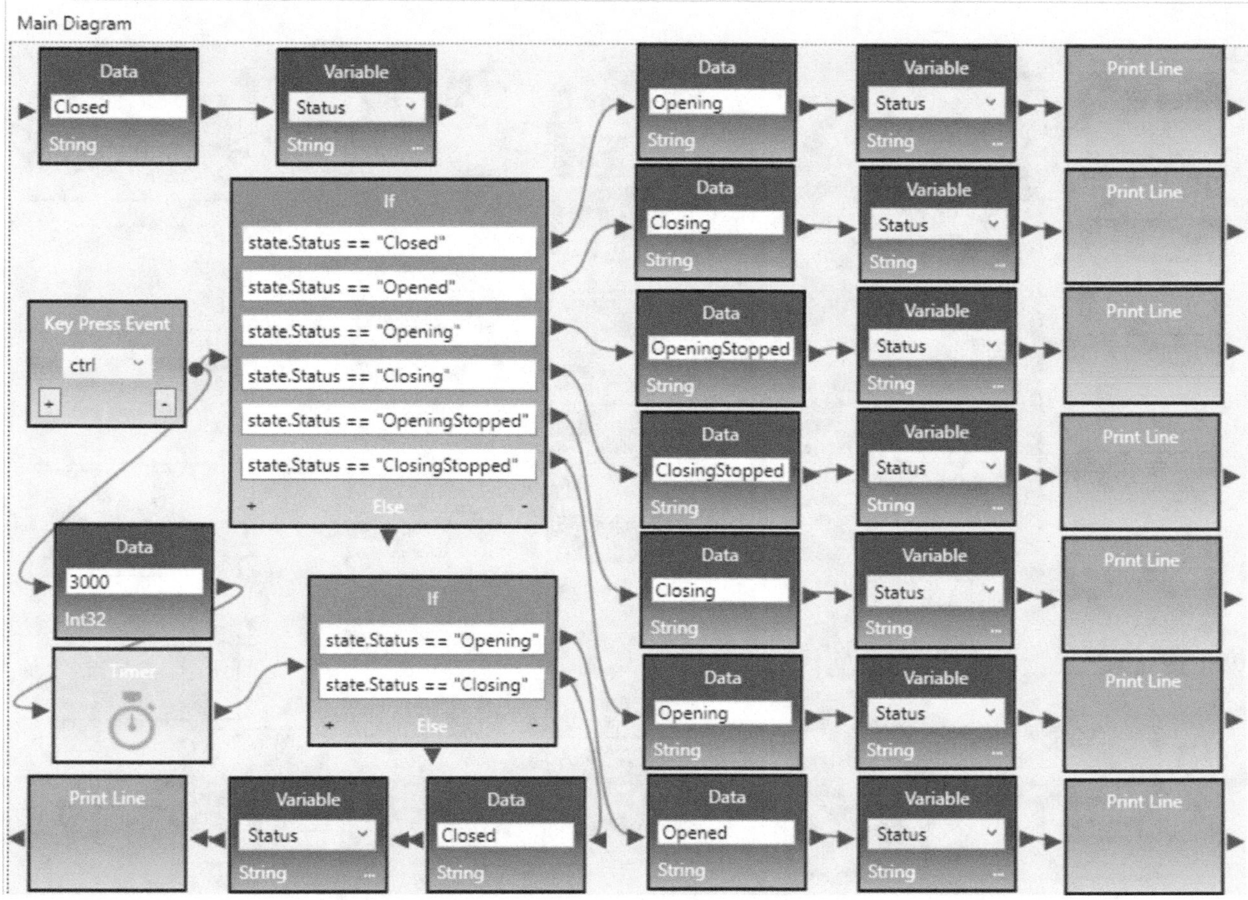

Figure 9.39. VIPLE program of the garage door control system

The lower part (If-activity with 2 conditions) implements the limit sensor (simulated using a 3-second timer in the diagram) in the motor, which involves two state transitions in the finite state machine.

In the example, we use Print Line to serve as the interface to the human. We have designed a garage door simulator to make this interface more visual. The simulator is written in Unity game platform. The code working with the simulator is shown in Figure 9.40.

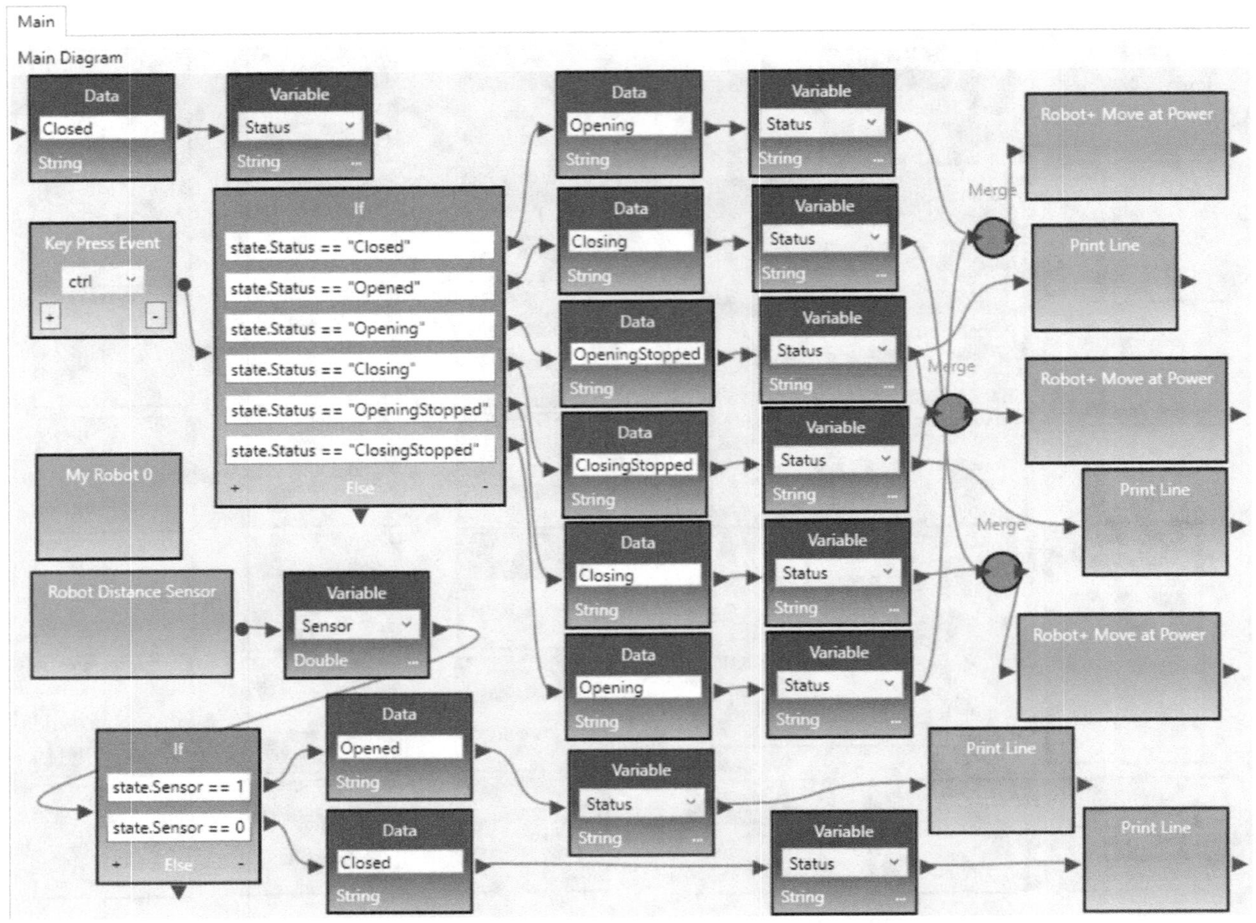

Figure 9.40. VIPLE program of the garage door control system using a Unity simulator

The differences between Print Line version in Figure 9.40 and the Unity simulator version in Figure 9.41 are as follows.

- We use Robot+ Move at Power service to simulate the garage door motor. For control the door open (upwards), we set the Data Connection value to 1.0 (Right-click the service). For control the door close (downwards), we set the Data Connection value to -1.0. For stopping the door, we set the Data Connection value to 0.0.
- We use Robot Distance Sensor to simulate the limit sensor of the garage door. When the sensor value is 1, the motor keeps rotating. When the sensor value is 0, the motor stops. We could use Robot Touch Sensor for this purpose too.
- In order to make the sensor and the motor work together, we need to add the Robot service into the diagram, which appears to be My Robot 0 in the diagram.

Figure 9.41 shows the configuration of the robot, distance sensor, and motor services.

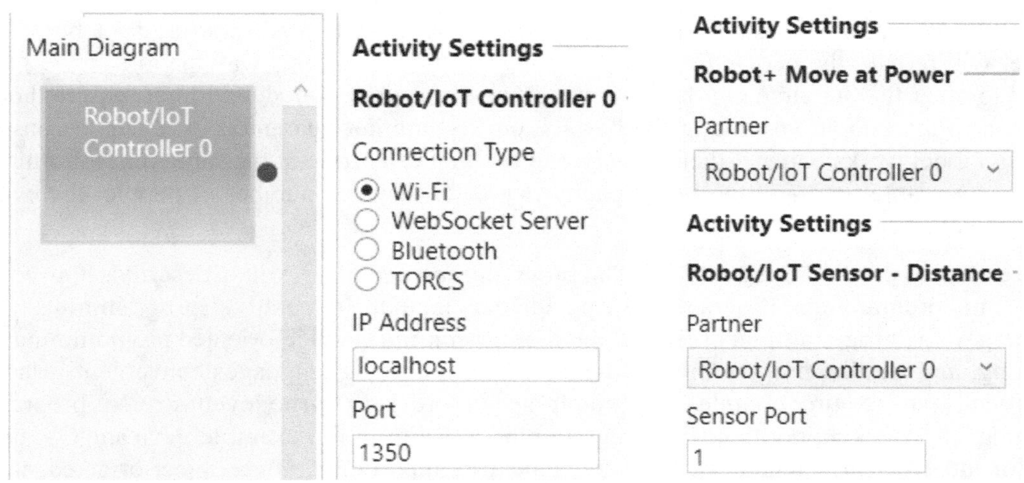

Figure 9.41. Configuration of the Robot/IoT Controller, motor service and distance sensor

To start the simulator, choose Run → Start Unity Simulator. It will open a maze simulator. Use the menu button in the simulator to switch to the garage door simulator, as shown in Figure 9.42.

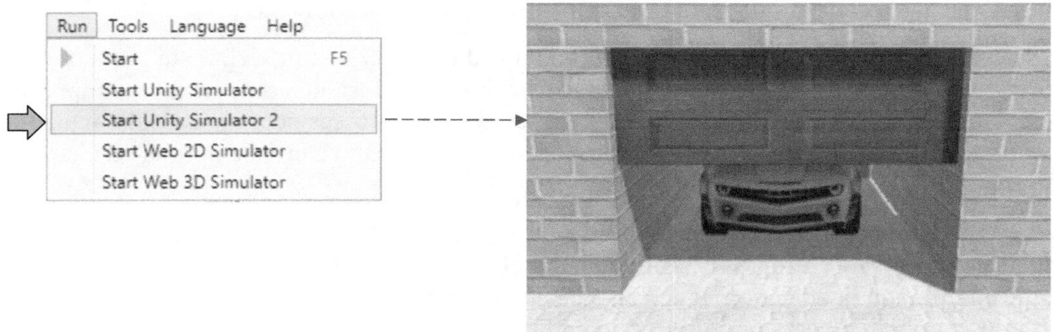

Figure 9.42. Start the Unity simulator from VIPLE menu.

In the following section, we will further use the Unity simulator for running autonomous maze navigation programs.

9.4.5 Event-Driven Programming

Event-driven computing is a programming model, in which the flow of the program is determined by events (or called notifications), such as user actions (e.g., mouse clicks and key presses), sensor inputs/outputs, or messages from other threads that can occur at any time during the program execution. Event-driven computing is based on parallel computing and assumes that multiple computing flows (threads) exist to process data and events that are ready to be processed. On the other hand, the control flow-based computing model determines its flow based on the inputs to the program. It assumes that there exists one flow only. The data that are ready to be processed have to wait until the control flow arrives in order to be processed.

Consider the assembly work of a robot. If there is one person to do all the jobs, we must list the jobs in a certain order and get the jobs done following that order. This is the flow control model. On the other hand, if there are multiple persons to do the jobs, then some jobs can be done at the same time. The ways data are processed in a control flow model and an event-driven model are also different. In the control flow model, the data will be lined up and processed in the order, while event-driven model does not have the lining up mechanism. As an analogy, consider the people arriving at a bus station and waiting for a bus. The control flow model will require the people to line up waiting for the bus. In this way, people arrive first will be guaranteed to enter the bus first. On the other hand, the event-driven model will not require the people to line up. As a result, people arriving at the bus station first are not guaranteed to enter the bus first. The control flow model works better if there is only one bus that can arrive at the same time. If multiple buses can arrive at the same time and the bus capacity is greater than the number of people, the event-driven model is more efficient.

A related concept to programming model is that programming paradigm, which describes how computation is express in programing. Programming paradigms include imperative programming, functional programming, logic programming, object-oriented programming, service-oriented programming, real-time programming, and parallel programming. Almost all programming languages conveniently support flow control model, but require complex programming in order to write event-driven programs. Most programming languages support multiple programming paradigms. For example, Java and C# support both flow control and event-driven models. They conveniently support imperative, object-oriented, and service-oriented programming paradigms. With the support of library functions, they also support parallel and event-driven programming. In Chapter 2, the general event-driven programming paradigm is discussed. In this chapter, we focus on robotics related event-driven programming.

Robotics applications are often event-driven, that is, the program must react to the arrivals of events immediately. Handling sensory inputs and controlling motors (actuators) must be dealt with concurrently (in parallel). Otherwise, the sensory data may skip, and the actuators may starve.

VIPLE conveniently supports both control flow model and event-driven model. It supports object-oriented programming using the activities to encapsulate the details into reusable components. It supports service-oriented programming by allowing activities to be converted into services. It can also call the remote services using the RESTful service in the service list and add WSDL reference into its service list.

In the previous examples, we have learned to use VIPLE to program an in-control flow model. We also used the Key Press Event in the garage door control system example. In this section, we will use event-driven model to write more programs. An event output can be used alone to notify specific events, for example, the completion of an action. It can also be used as an additional output with a regular return value. Event, with the regular return value can give an additional signal to the user activity.

The additional event signal is necessary if the activity (service) is to be used multiple times, e.g., in a loop. Without the notification signal, the user activity may not be able to determine if a new value has arrived if the new value happens to be the same as the previous value. When an event arrives, the user activity will know a new value has arrived, no matter if the value happens to be the same as the previous value or not, as shown in Figure 9.43.

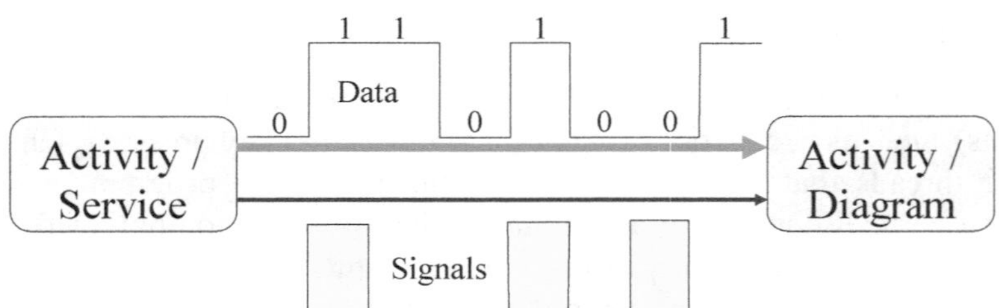

Figure 9.43. VIPLE activities and services allow both data output and event output

We have discussed the implementation of a counter activity using control flow in Appendix B. Figure 9.44 shows the event-driven implementation of the counter activity. It defines an event by connecting the counter output value to the circular (event) output, instead of the triangular (data) output, which generates an event every time the merge activity generates a new value. This event can be used to trigger the execution of another activity. An activity generates both data output and event output.

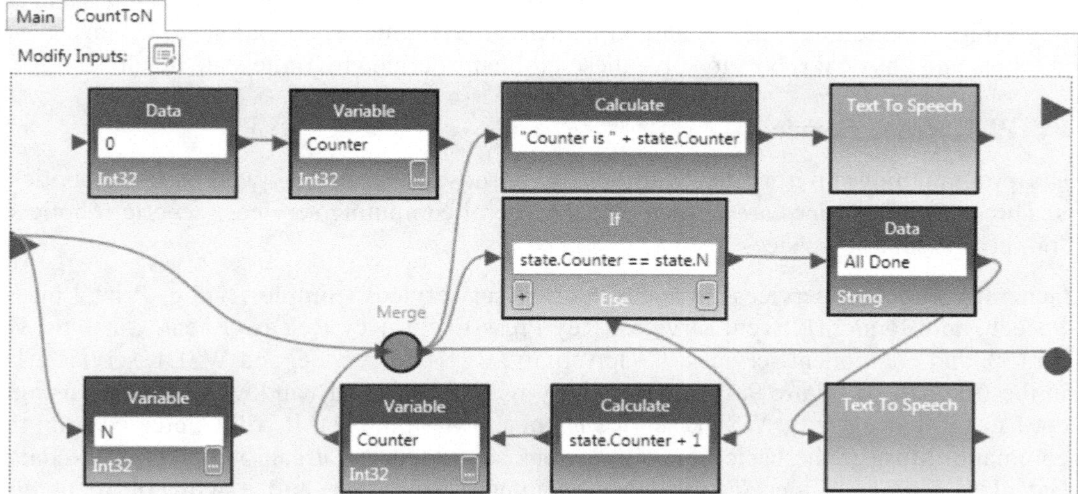

Figure 9.44. The activity generating an event output

Once an event output is defined, the event will be available in the "Custom Event" service, as shown in Figure 9.45. VIPLE has two types of events: built-in events and custom events. The built-in events include Key Press, Key Release Event, and the sensors that generate event output. Each activity in which an event is defined will be added into the Custon Event set.

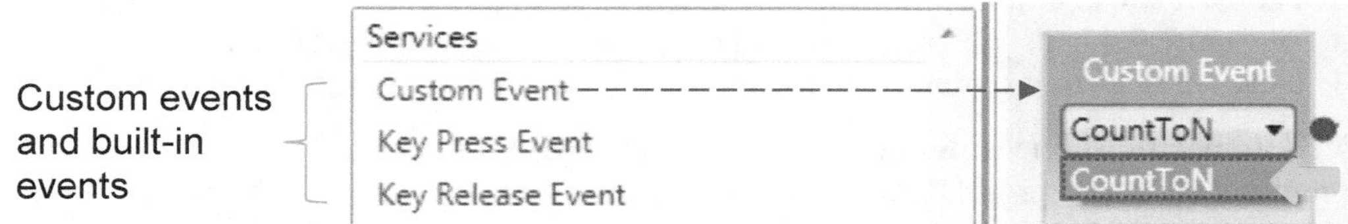

Figure 9.45. VIPLE built-in events and custom events

Creating events in your activities for other activities to use is one part of event-driven programming. Using the event output as input in your program is the other part of event-driven programming. Figure 9.46 shows using the event in the diagram for generating the test cases. Notice that the CountToN activity is not connected to the Print Line service.

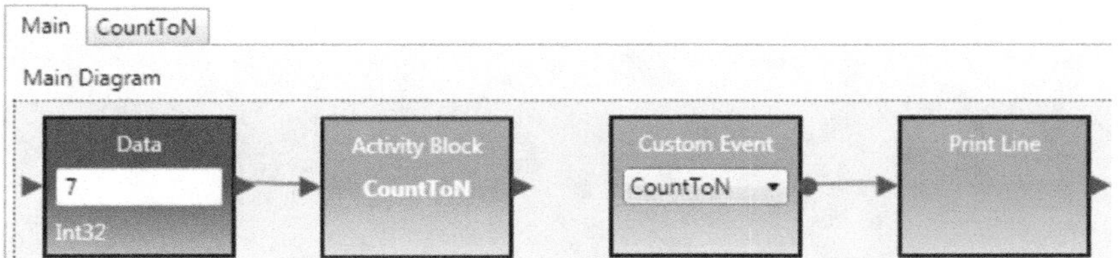

Figure 9.46. The activity generating a notification output

The event-driven programming model is best described by finite state machines consisting of states and transitions between the states. The transitions are triggered by events.

9.5 Robot Programming and Maze Navigation

In this section, we will introduce the robotics services in VIPLE and use finite state machines and an event-driven programming paradigm to define and implement different maze navigation algorithms. We will use simulated robots and physical robots to solve these problems defined by finite state machines.

9.5.1 VIPLE Robot Services

VIPLE is a programming environment with general-purpose functions, as well as IoT/Robotic specific functions. Three sets of services are implemented: General computing services, generic robotic services, and vendor-specific robotic services.

- General computing services: include input/output services (Simple Dialog, Print Line, Text to Speech, and Random), Event services (Key Press Event, Key Release Event, Custom Event, and Timer), and component services (CodeActivity, RESTful service, and WSDL service), as shown in the first part of Figure 9.47. CodeActivity will create a text window that allows using any C# code to form an activity. WSDL service is not shown in the list. It will be created from the menu command. Most of the basic library functions supported in C# can be called in the data box of Calculate activity. Timer service takes an integer i as input, and it will hold data flow for i milliseconds. Timer service is frequently used in the robotic applications.
- Generic robotic services: VIPLE offers a set of standard communication interfaces, including Wi-Fi, TCP, Bluetooth, USB, localhost, and WebSocket interfaces. The data format between VIPLE and the IoT/Robotic devices is defined as a standard JSON (JavaScript Object Notation) object. Any robot that can be programmed to support one of the communication types and can process a JSON object can communicate with VIPLE and be programmed in VIPLE. As shown in the second part of Figure 9.47, all VIPLE services that start with a Robot are generic robotic services. We will use these services to program our simulated robots and custom-built physical robots.
- Vendor-specific services: Some robots, such as LEGO robots and iRobots, do not offer an open communication and programming interface. In this case, we can offer built-in services in VIPLE to access these robots without requiring any programming efforts on the device side. Currently, the services for accessing LEGO EV3 robots are implemented, so that VIPLE can read all EV3 sensors and control EV3 drive-motors and arm-motors, as shown in the third part in Figure 9.47. Those who do not want to build their own robots can simply use a VIPLE and EV3 combination.

Code Activity - C#
Code Activity - Python
Custom Event
Graph
Key Press Event
Key Release Event
Print Line
Random
RESTful Service
Simple Dialog
Text to Speech
Timer

Robot/IoT Controller
Robot/IoT Drive
Robot/IoT Holonomic Drive
Robot/IoT Message In
Robot/IoT Message Out
Robot/IoT Motion
Robot/IoT Motor
Robot/IoT Sensor - Color
Robot/IoT Sensor - Distance
Robot/IoT Sensor - Light
Robot/IoT Sensor - Motor Encoder
Robot/IoT Sensor - Sound
Robot/IoT Sensor - Touch
Robot/IoT Sensor - TORCS
Robot/IoT Sensor - TORCS Opponents
Robot/IoT Sensor - TORCS Track
Robot TORCS Command
Robot+ Move at Power
Robot+ Turn by Degrees
Robot/IoT Sensor - Traffic
Robot TORCS Command
Robot Traffic Drive
Robot Traffic Init
Robot Traffic Timer

Lego EV3 Brick
Lego EV3 Color
Lego EV3 Drive
Lego EV3 Drive for Time
Lego EV3 Gyro
Lego EV3 Motor
Lego EV3 Motor by Degrees
Lego EV3 Motor for Time
Lego EV3 Touch Pressed
Lego EV3 Touch Released
Lego EV3 Ultrasonic

Figure 9.47. VIPLE general services, generic robotic services, and Lego EV3 services

In this lab assignment, we will use generic robotic services to program simulated robots and Intel-based physical robots. These services are explained as follows.

- **Robot** service is used for defining the connection types, connection port, and connection addresses. Multiple Robot services can be used in one application to control multiple robots. For each motor service and sensor service used, a partner Robot needs to be selected.
- Robot Motor and Drive services. A number of services are defined for controlling different types of motors defined on the devices. Which services to use are determined by the physical devices that are programmed to connect to VIPLE, and they should be specified in the device hardware manual.
    - **Robot Motor**: It controls a single motor. It requires setting up a partner Robot, a motor port number, and a drive power value between 0 and ±1.0. The bigger the value, the faster the motor rotates. Positive and negative values are allowed, which will cause the motor to rotate in opposite directions.
    - **Robot Motor Encoder**: It is the same as the Robot Motor, but it is of motor encoder type.
    - **Robot Drive**: Control two motors at the same time for driving purposes. It requires setting up a partner Robot, two motor port numbers, and two drive power values. The bigger the values, the faster the motors rotate. Positive and negative values are allowed. If two identified positive values are given, the robot moves forward. If two identified negative values are given, the robot moves backward. If one bigger value and one smaller value, or one positive value and one negative value are given, the robot turns left or right.

- **Robot Holonomic Drive**: Controls four motors at the same time for holonomic driving purposes, such as controlling a drone. It requires setting up a partner Robot, four motor port numbers, and three drive values for X component, Y component, and rotation.
- **Robot+ Move at Power**: It requires setting up a partner Robot and a drive power value between 0 and ±1.0 to move both wheels of the robot forward (positive value) or backward (negative value). The motor port numbers are not required to specify (hard coded in the device). This service can be used in the **simulated robot**.
- **Robot+ Turn by Degree**: It requires setting up a partner Robot and a degree value between 0 and ±360. The motor port numbers are not required to specify (hard coded in the device). This service can be used in a robot with a gyro sensor to measure the turning degree, or in a simulator where the turning degree can be easily controlled. We will use this service in the Web Simulator.
- **Robot Motion**: It is a service that can be used to control complex robots, such as humanoids offering many high-level functions. The service allows users to define a list of high-level motions that can be linked to the APIs of the robots.

- **Robot sensors**: A number of sensor services are defined for reading data from the device, including color sensor, distance sensor, light sensor, sound sensor, and touch sensor. Each sensor requires setting up a partner Robot and a port number.

In this section, we will first use Unity and 2D Simulators, and then use physical robots to implement the maze navigation algorithms.

The Unity simulator is a more powerful simulation environment than the built-in programming language in the Web 2D Simulator we discussed in the previous section. It can simulate more conditions and it works with VIPLE, which is a much more powerful programming language supporting variables, data, calculation, and various control structures. In this section, we will use VIPLE and Unity simulator to implement various maze navigation algorithms that mimic situations that are more realistic.

However, Unit Simulator does not support Robot Drive service, which is what is supported by the physical robot. On the other hand, the Web 2D Simulator also supports VIPLE programs and support Robot Drive service, which presents a good alternative to the physical robot. We will use Web 2D Simulator in the next lab.

9.5.2 Maze Navigation Algorithms in Finite State Machine

Since our physical robot can have one distance sensor installed, we will define the maze navigation algorithms in this section to use one distance sensor only. The sensor should have been installed in the front of the robot. We will use finite state machines to describe the maze navigation algorithms.

First-Working-Solution Algorithm

The first-working-solution algorithm is an algorithm that instructs a robot to move in the first direction that has a distance great than a given constant. Figure 9.48 shows the finite state machine of this algorithm. The finite state machine consists of four states. The robot starts with "Forward." If the front distance becomes less than a given value, the robot starts "Turning Left" 90 degrees. After "Turned Left," the robot compares the distance sensor value. If it is big enough, the robot enters "Forward" state. Otherwise, it spins 180 degrees back in the other direction and then moves forward.

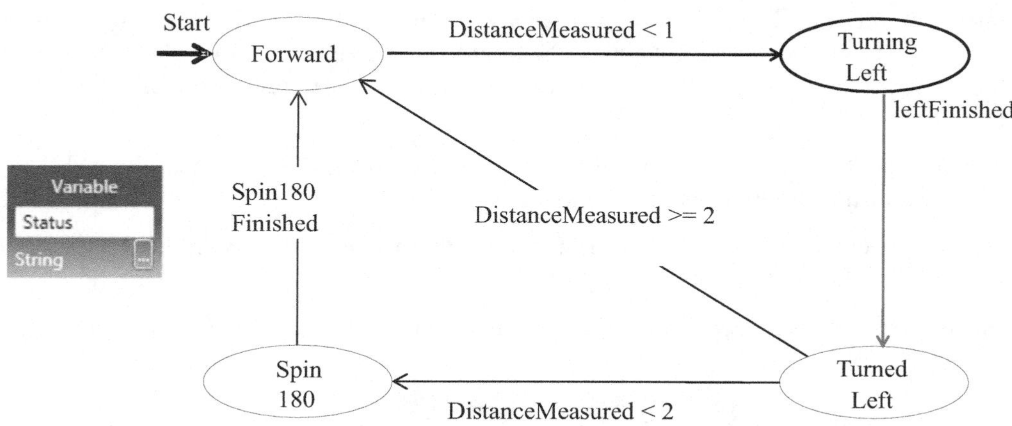

Figure 9.48. Finite state machine for the first-working-solution algorithm

Two-Distance-Local-Best Algorithm

The first-working-solution algorithm may not perform well in certain mazes. Figure 9.49 shows the two-distance-local-best (farthest distance) algorithm.

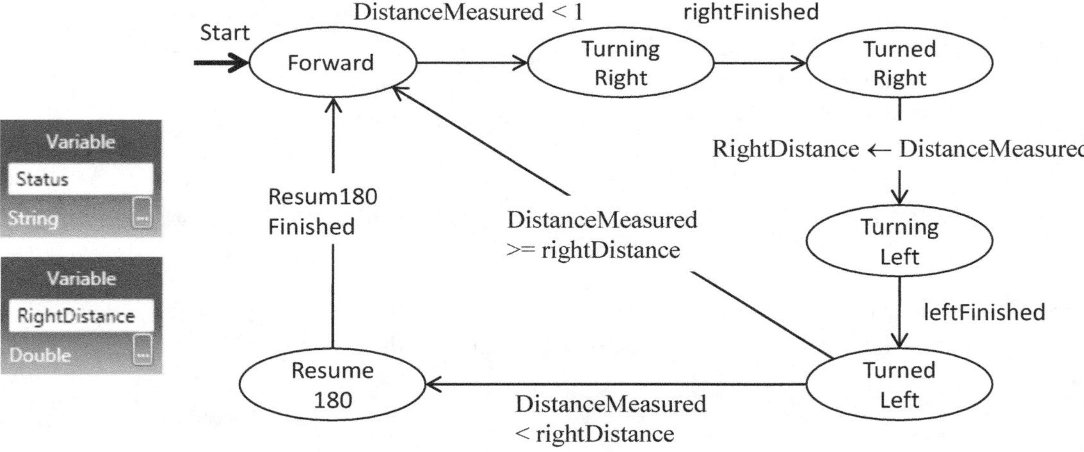

Figure 9.49. Finite state machine for the two-distance-local-best algorithm

Instead of comparing the left-side distance with a constant, it compares the left-side distance with right-side distance, and then moves to the side with farther distance. This finite state machine adds two states to include "Turning Right" and "Turned Right." It also uses a variable to hold the RightDistance. Recall that the robot is assumed to have one distance sensor only. It has to store the right-side distance before it measures the left-side distance.

Self-Adjusting Right-Wall-Following Algorithm

Figure 9.50 shows the finite state machine for the self-adjusting right-wall-following algorithm. It assumes that there are two distance sensors, one in the front and one on the right side. The front sensor could be replaced by a touch sensor. The finite state machine uses two variables: Status and BaseDistance to the right wall. BaseDistance is initialized to a desired value to keep the robot in the middle of the road.

The robot starts with moving forward. It keeps the base distance with the right wall. If the distance to the right wall is too big (base distance+5), it turns one degree to the right to move closer to the wall. If the distance to the right wall is too small (base distance -5), it turns one degree to the left to move away from the wall.

If the right distance suddenly becomes very big (base distance+400), it implies that the right side is open, and the robot should turn right 90 degrees to follow the right wall.

If the front distance becomes too small (<200), it implies that there is no way in the front and no way on the right, thus, the robot has to turn left 90 degrees.

This algorithm is necessary for the physical robot, as the robot cannot move 100 straight and cannot turn precisely 90 degrees.

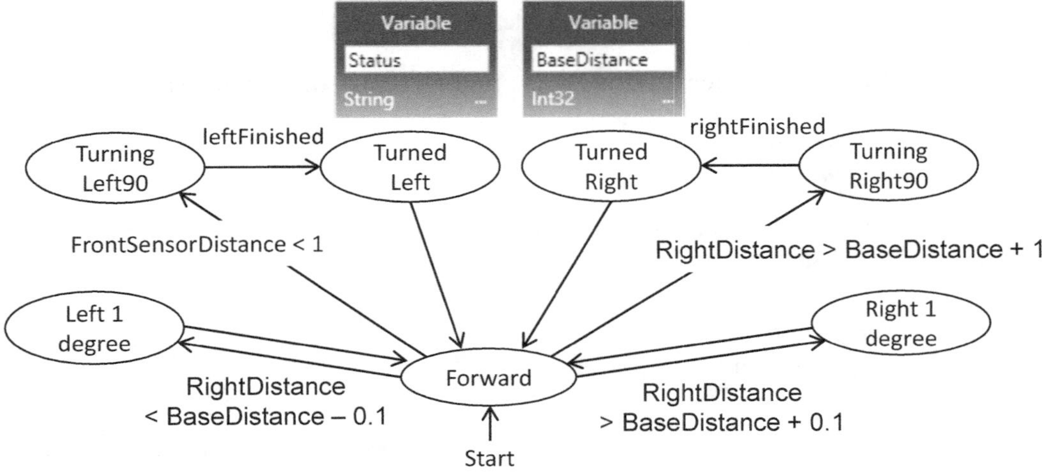

Figure 9.50. Finite state machine for the self-adjusted right-wall-following algorithm

The performance of these navigation algorithms depends on the maze too. If we apply these three algorithms in the mazes shown in Figure 9.51, which algorithm will perform the best?

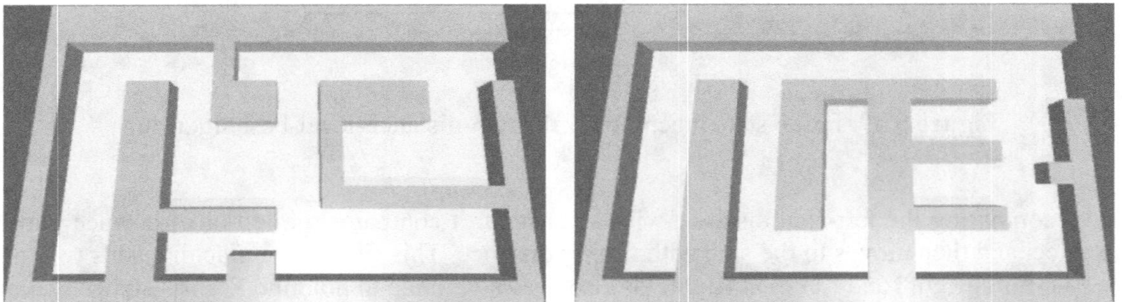

Figure 9.51. Different mazes can affect the performance of navigation algorithms

9.5.3 Maze Navigation Algorithms Using Unity Simulator

We have been using VIPLE for general programming in flow control style and IoT device control in event-driven style, where the sensors can be read, and devices can be controlled directly from VIPLE without using an autonomous decentralized system (ADS). Now, we will start to introduce an ADS in the frontend that links a group of sensor and motor devices together. We call this ADS unit a Robot service. We also prefix Robot to all the other services that can be linked to a Robot. In the rest of the section, we will focus on Robot services and the application development using both simulated and physical robots.

We start with the drive-by-wire program that controls the robot using the keyboard of the computer. Then, we will discuss the autonomous programs that control robots to navigate through the maze without any human intervention.

A number of robot services are implemented in VIPLE to facilitate different robots. Two simulated robots and environments are implemented: Unity Simulator and Web Simulator. We start with using the Unity Simulator, and the Web Simulator will be discussed later.

Step 1: First, drag and drop the service "Robot/IoT Controller" into the diagram, and we configure the Controller to use the following configurations (1) Connection Type: Wi-Fi (2) IP Address: localhost, (3) TCP Port: 1350, as shown in the left part of Figure 9.52. For Robot+ Move at Power service and Robot+ Turn by Degree service, we must choose the Partner in their setting, as shown in the right part of Figure 9.52.

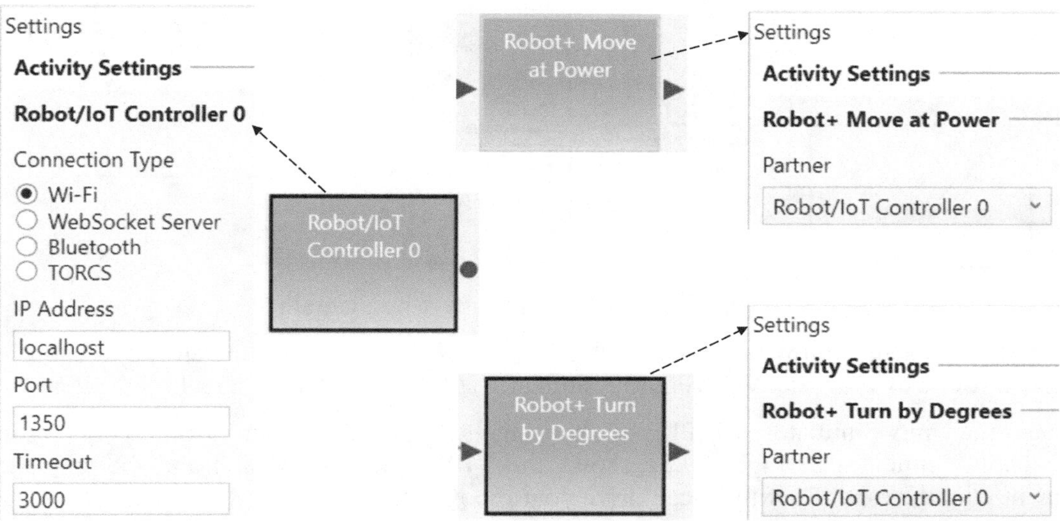

Figure 9.52. Configuration of the Robot/IoT Controller service for simulation

Step 2: Now, we can write the drive-by-wire code as shown in Figure 9.53. You can follow the comments to select the data connection values. You can find the services in the VIPLE service list.

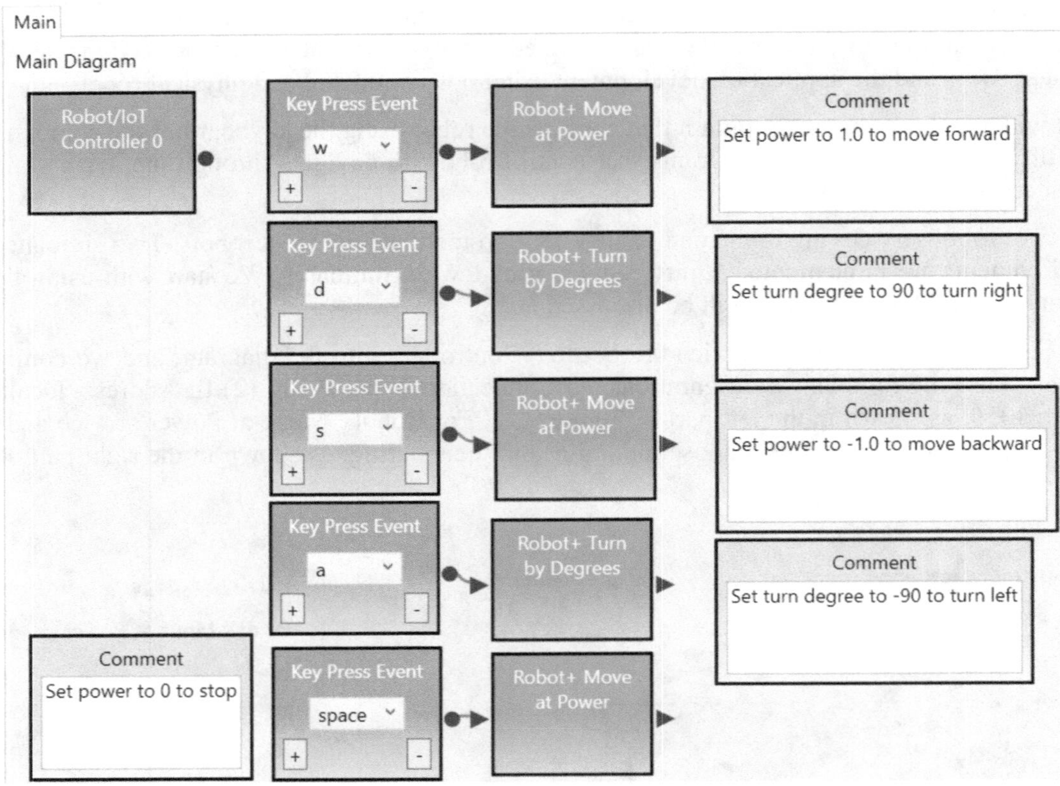

Figure 9.53. Basic drive-by-wire diagram

When you start the code, you will not see anything happening. We need a simulator or a real robot to see the robot controlled by the code. We will use a simulator at this time and use a real robot later.

Step 3: Start the Unity Simulator in VIPLE by choosing the VIPLE menu Run → Start Unity Simulator, or Start the Unity Simulator 2. Figure 9.54 shows the VIPLE Start command and the simulated maze environment with the robot. Now, you can drive your robot using the five keys: w, d, a, s, and space. You can also change the maze by mouse-clicking the maze area to add and remove bricks.

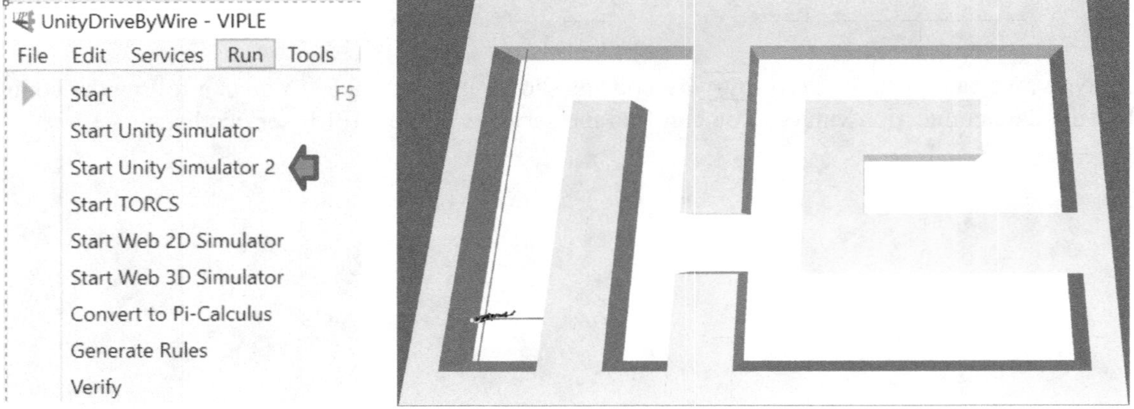

Figure 9.54. Starting Unity Simulator 2 environment

When you use the keyboard to control the robot, you must keep the VIPLE's Run window active (on the top layer). In order to do that, you need to reduce the size of the VIPLE code window so that it does not hide the Unity simulator window.

To start with autonomous maze navigation program, we give a simple program in Figure 9.55. Read the program and answer the following questions:

1. What algorithm does this VIPLE diagram implement?
2. What states does this diagram use?
3. Draw the finite state machine of this diagram.

   Hint: You first decide the states based on the values of the variable isBusy. Then, you add transitions and the input and output related to each transition to form the finite state machine.

4. What values should be given to the Robot Move and Robot Turn services in order to complete the algorithm?

Next, you start to use the Unity simulator and enter the Diagram into VIPLE. Make sure you configure the Robot, sensor, and motor services with the following values.

Configure the Robot/IoT Controller and Sensors as follows: (1) Connection Type: Wi-Fi (2) IP Address: localhost, (3) TCP Port: 1350, as shown in Figure 9.52. Right click each Move service and choose "My Robot/IoT 0" as the partner.

Right click each Distance Sensor service, choose "My Robot 0" as the partner. Set Port to 1 for right sensor and set to 2 for the front sensor.

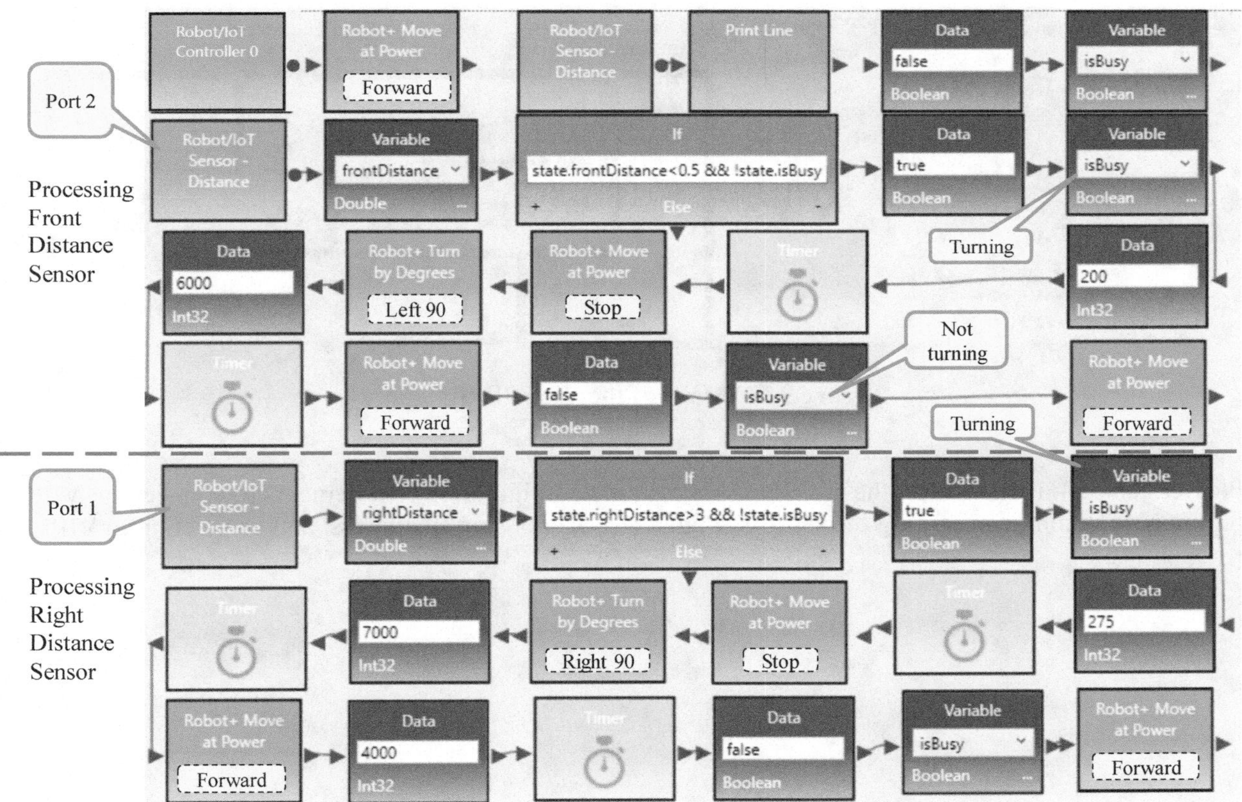

Figure 9.55. Main diagram of a maze navigation algorithm

The functions of the main services are marked in Figure 9.55. Start the Unity Simulator from the VIPLE menu and then run the VIPLE diagram. Adjust the values given to the Robot Move and Robot Turn services to make the program work.

9.5.4 Maze Navigation Algorithms Using Web Simulator

Now, we start to use the Web 2D Simulator. This simulator implemented uses a different set of drive services. These services are the same as the services to be used in the physical robot, and thus, the programs written in the Web Simulator can be easily applied to the physical robot. The changes need to be made are the parameter values controlling the turning times. The Web 2D Simulator can be started from the VIPLE site or directly started from:

http://neptune.fulton.ad.asu.edu/VIPLE/Web2DSimulator/

You can also start the Web Simulator from VIPLE, as shown in the left part, and the maze opened in the browser is shown on the right side of Figure 9.56.

The simulator is equipped with two ultrasonic distance sensors and one touch sensor, and you can choose to have the sensor in the front, left, right, or back of the robot, as shown in Figure 9.57. The port numbers of the sensor are defined in your VIPLE code. You can choose any number as the port number. If you use one sensor only, you must set the port number of the second senor to none. Click Add/Update Sensors after you have defined your sensors.

Note that due the security configuration in some browsers, the Web Simulator may not be able to communicate with VIPLE. We have tested Chrome and Firefox, and they work perfectly with VIPLE Web Simulator.

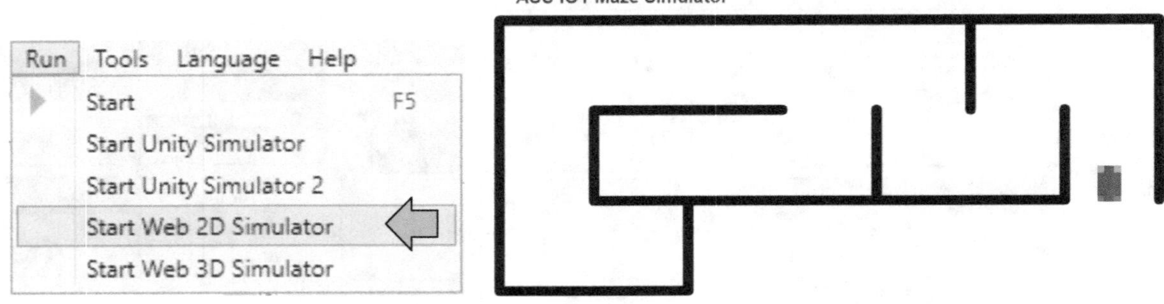

Figure 9.56. Maze of the Web 2D Simulator

Please read the instruction on the simulator page on the configuration requirements to connect the VIPLE program, including configuring the sensors (Figure 9.57), choosing IP address, and connecting to VIPLE.

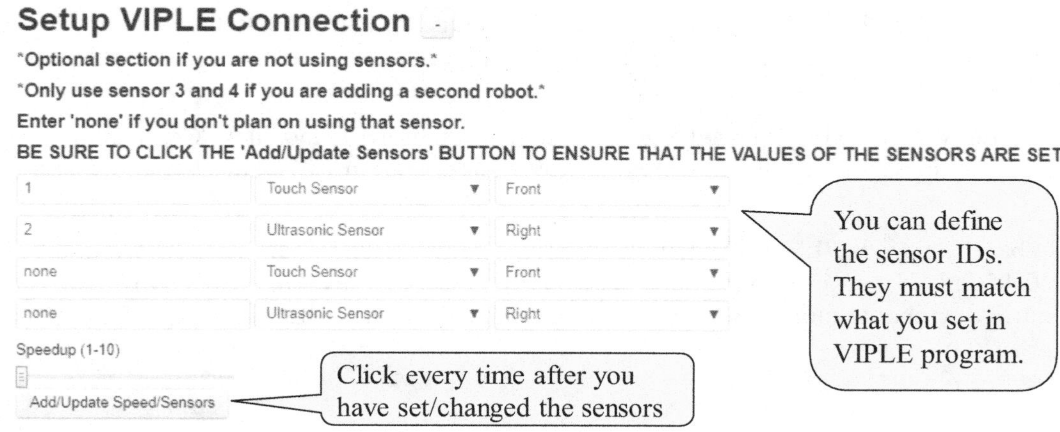

Figure 9.57. Sensor setting of the Web 2D simulator

The sensor port numbers here in the web simulator must be the same as the port number you set in your VIPLE program.

Next, we will configure VIPLE to work with the Web Simulator.

Now, we go back to VIPLE. We can use the same drive-by-wire code that you used with Unity Simulator. However, the configuration will be different.

Step 1: Click Robot/IoT Controller and use the following configurations (1) In Change Connection Type: choose WebSocket Server. (2) In Change TCP Port: set port number to 8124, as shown in the left part of Figure 9.58.

Step 2: Click the Robot Drive service to select Partner and set the left wheel port 3 and right wheel port to 5, as shown in right part of Figure 9.58.

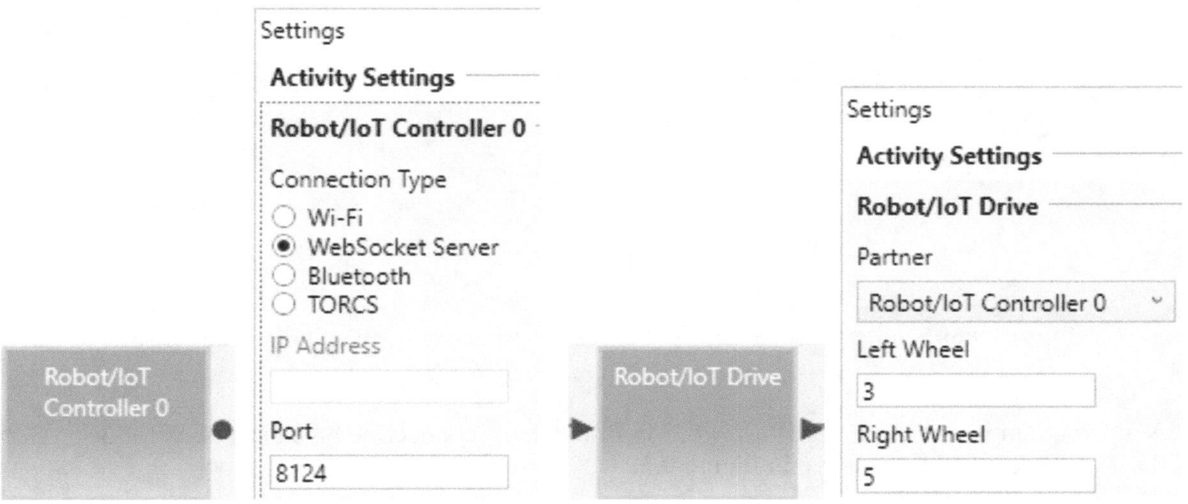

Figure 9.58. Configuration of the Robot service for simulation

Step 3: Use the drive-by-wire code that you used with Unity Simulator as the basis. You need to change the drive service from "Robot+ Move at Power" and "Robot+ Turn by Degree" to "Robot Drive" service. The Robot Drive service can control the two wheels individually. If you give two positive values to both wheels, the robot moves forward. If you give two negative values to both wheels, the robot moves backward. If you give a positive value to the left wheel and a negative value to the right wheel, the robot turns to the left.

After you run the VIPLE code, you need to go back to the web browser and click "Connect to ASU VIPLE (WebSockets), as shown in the left part of Figure 9.59. This operation will connect your Web Simulator to VIPLE.

Step 4: Go back to your VIPLE code, click the console window (Run window), as shown in the right part of Figure 9.59. Only if the Run window is in the front, can the Key Press take effect. Now, you can use the keys to control the robot to move. The keys are programmed in your VIPLE code using Key Press events.

Figure 9.59. Connect the Web Simulator with VIPLE program and Run window

Next, we will implement the Wall-Following algorithm in Web Simulator. The program will read sensor values and thus we need to set the sensor values. A distance sensor is used on the right-hand side to measure the distance to the wall. A touch sensor is used in the front to detect the wall. The sensors must be configured as follows:

- Click Robot Touch Sensor and set Partner to Robot/IoT Controller 0 and Port number to 1.
- Click Robot Distance Sensor and set Partner to Robot/IoT Controller 0 and Port number to 2, as shown in Figure 9.60.

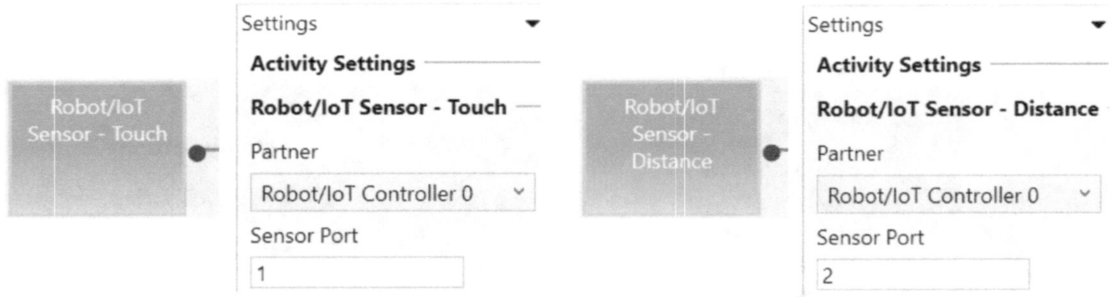

Figure 9.60. Select Partner and set the sensor ports for touch and distance sensors

The Main diagram is given in Figure 9.61. For My Robot 0, the connection type must be WebSocket Server and the TCP Port is 8124, as shown in Figure 9.58.

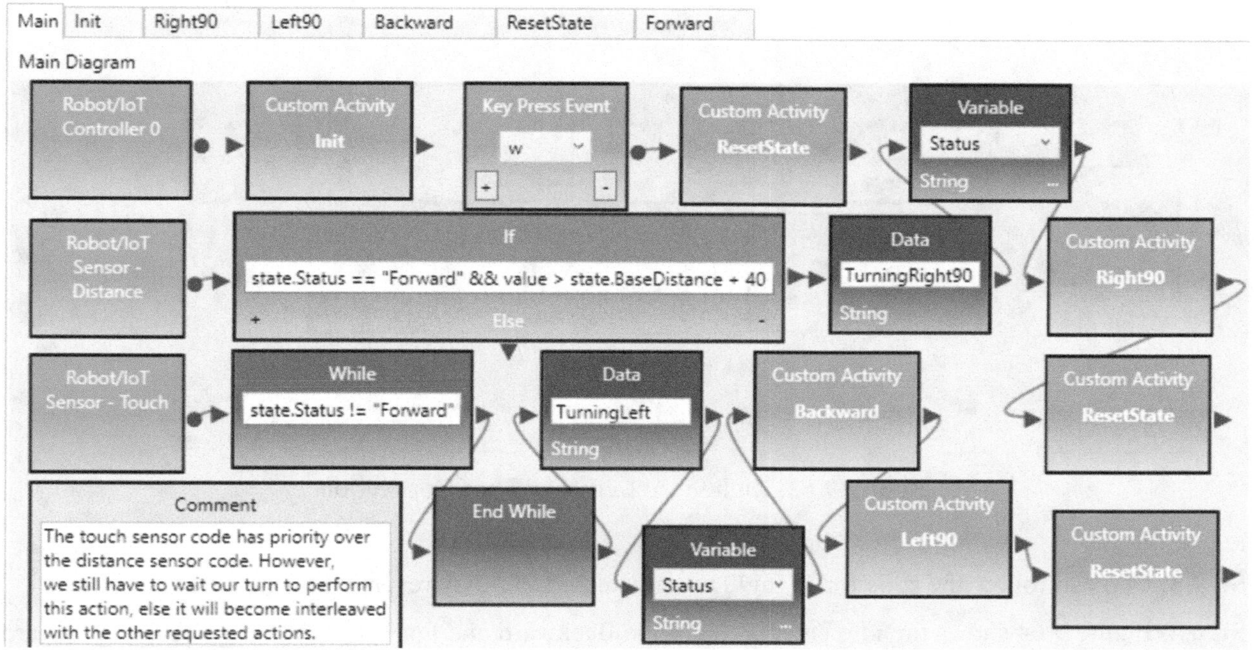

Figure 9.61. Main diagram implementing the right-wall-following algorithm

When you are done, please notify your lab instructor and demonstrate your program for sign-off. Then change the driver to proceed to the next assignment.

Now, we need to implement the Activity diagrams to be called in the Main diagram.

Step 1: Figure 9.62 shows the code for Init activity, which initializes the two variables and sets the robot moving forward. There is no output from this activity.

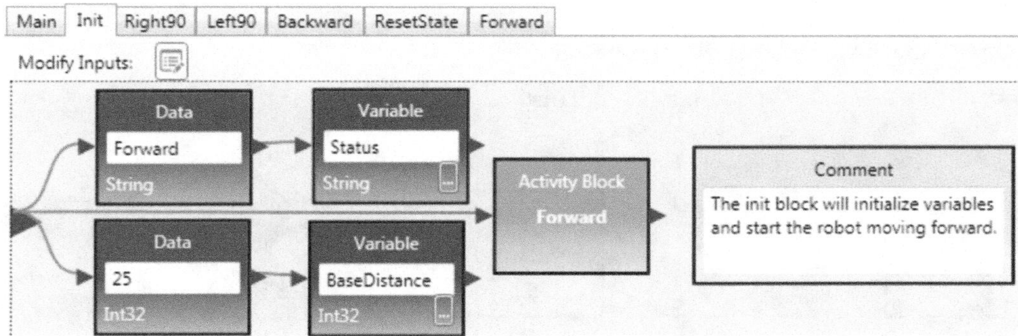

Figure 9.62. The Init Activity

Step 2: Figure 9.63 shows the implementation of the Right90 activity. Right-click the motor and select the data connection. The data connection values for the two drive services are shown in lower part of the figure. The first set of values cause the robot to turn right and the second set of values cause the robot to stop.

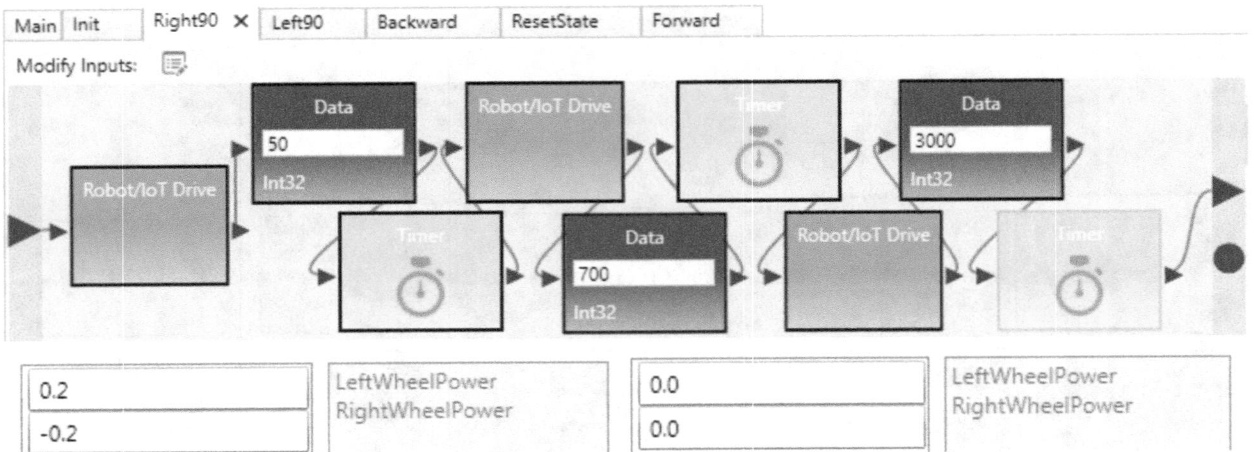

Figure 9.63. Right90 Activity and Data Connection

Step 3: You can follow the code for Right90 to implement Left90 by reversing the power on the wheels.

Step 4: Figure 9.64 shows the implementation of the Backward and Forward activities. For the Backward activity, the drive power can be set to -0.3 for both wheels. For the Forward activity, the drive power can be set to 0.5 for both wheels.

Figure 9.64. Backward and Forward Activities

Step 5: Figure 9.65 shows the code for ResetState.

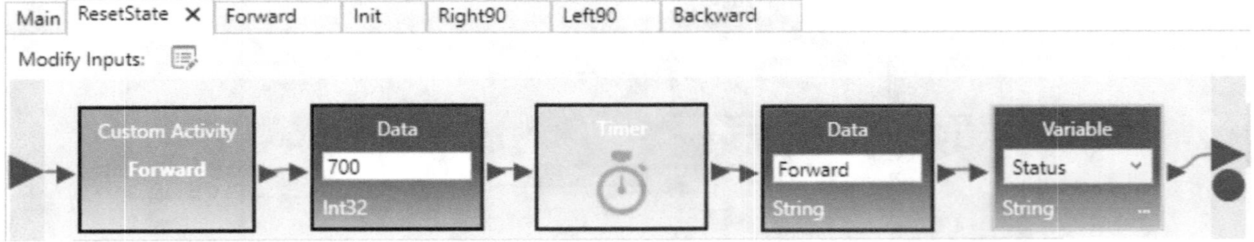

Figure 9.65. ResetState Activity

Step 6: Now you can run the wall-following algorithm in Web Simulator. Use the following steps to test the program.

1. Start the Web Simulator
2. Start to run VIPLE program.
3. Set up the sensor values in the Web Simulation.
4. Click "Add/Update Sensors"
5. Click Connect to ASU VIPLE (WebSockets).

If you use a Key Press event to start the move, you need to click the VIPLE's Run window and use the key to start the move.

When you are done, please notify your lab instructor and demonstrate your program for sign-off. Then change the driver to proceed to the next assignment.

9.5.5 Maze Navigation Using Lego EV3 Robot

We now present VIPLE code for programming a physical robot, Lego EV3. First, we show how VIPLE event-driven programming mechanisms can be used to control physical devices. Figure 9.66 shows the program that remotely controls a LEGO EV3 robot using the four arrow keys on the computer's keyboard.

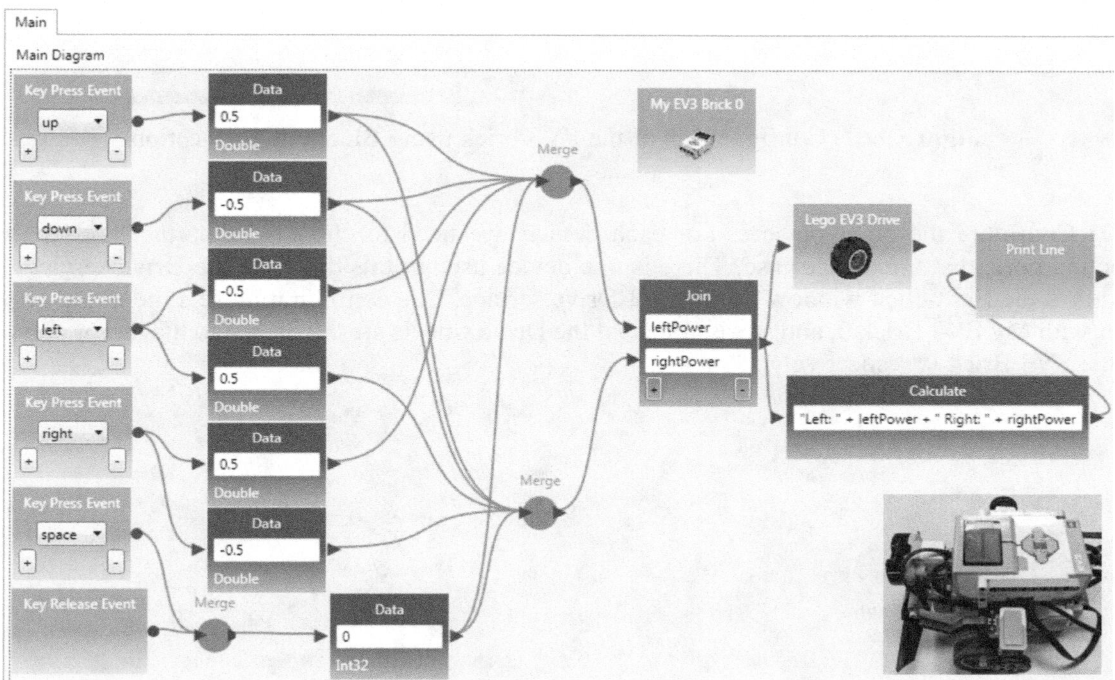

Figure 9.66. VIPLE program drive-by-wire using key press events

To make the diagram work with a physical robot, we need to configure the devices used in the diagram in a number of steps.

Step 1: Configure the EV3 brick. We use a main robot, called My EV3 Brick, to define the major configuration. It is possible to add more than one brick into a diagram. Right-click the brick to open the configuration. Figure 9.67 shows the right-click window and the two configuration windows. Change Connection Type window allows us to choose one of three available connection methods: Wi-Fi, Bluetooth, and USB. If Bluetooth is selected, the standard Bluetooth pairing process can be used to establish the connection between the computer running the VIPLE program and the robot.

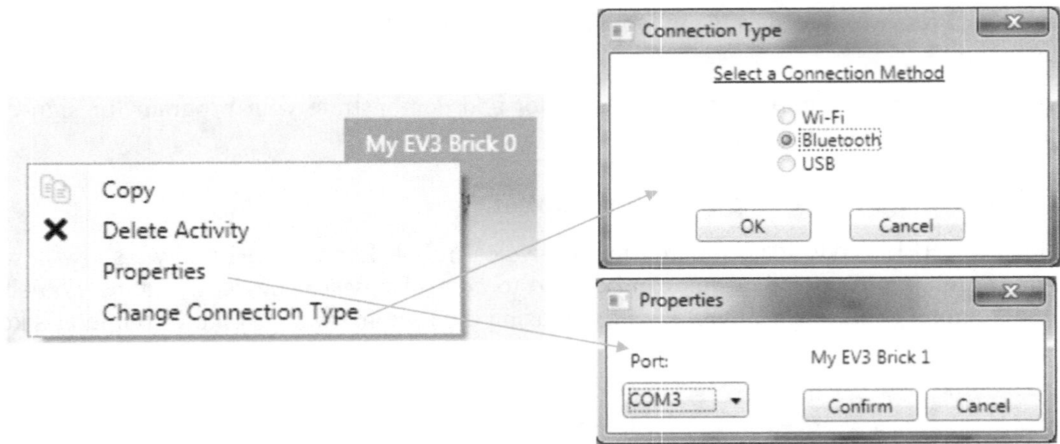

Figure 9.67. Configuration of the EV3 brick using Bluetooth connection

Step 2: Configure the other devices. For each device, we need to choose the partner and choose the connection ports that the devices use. There is one device used in this diagram: the Drive service. Figure 9.68 shows the right-click window to the EV3 Drive service. The configuration sets the Drive service to partner with My EV3 Brick 0, and we assume that the Drive wheels are connected to the motor ports B and C on the EV3 Brick 0, respectively.

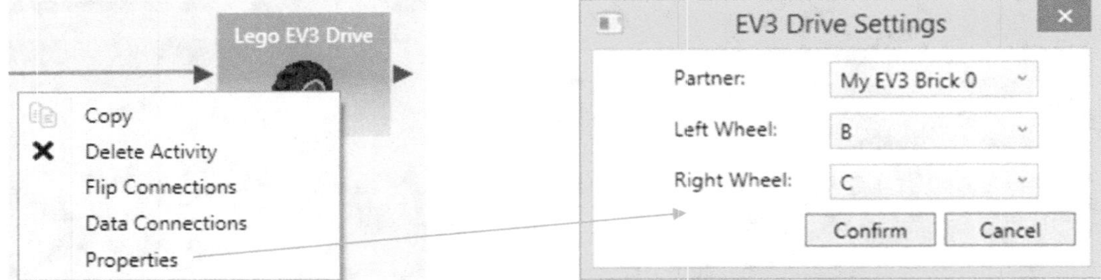

Figure 9.68. Configuration of the EV3 brick

Step 3: Establish the connection. We assume that Bluetooth connection is selected. Bluetooth connection process depends on the Bluetooth device installed on your computer. A typical process consists of the following steps:

(1) Open the Bluetooth panel from the computer's Task Bar, and choose Add a Device.
(2) The Bluetooth panel will show the devices that are ready to add. Find the EV3 robot that you want to add. Note that you can see the robot name on your EV3. You can also change the name to make it unique.
(3) Once the add request is issued from the computer, the EV3 side will pop up a confirmation check box. Confirm it. EV3 will further generate a pass code 1234. Confirm the code again.
(4) On the computer side, a textbox will then pop up. Enter the pass code 1234 to connect.
(5) After the connection, we still need to know the "Outgoing" COM port of the connection. This port needs to be entered into the Property window in My EV3 Brick 0, as shown in Figure 9.67. To find the COM port, open the Bluetooth panel from the Task Bar and choose Open Bluetooth Settings. We will see the COM Ports, as shown in Figure 9.69.

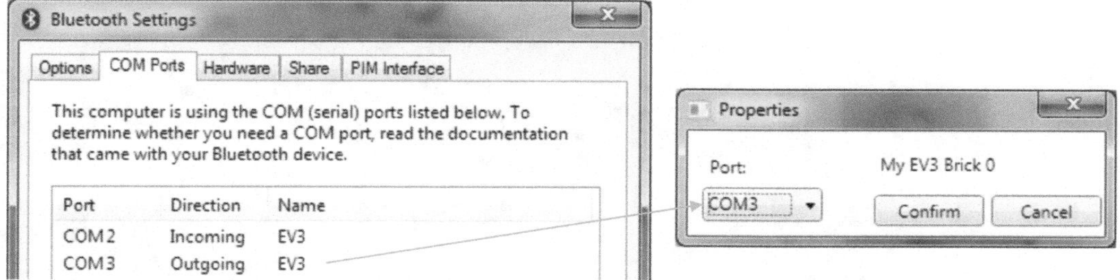

Figure 9.69. Find the COM port for My EV3 Brick 0 configuration

Once the configuration is completed, we can start to run the program and use the keyboard to drive the robot forward, backward, left, right, and stop.

On the other hand, if Wi-Fi is selected for connection, as shown in Figure 9.70, we need to find the IP address of the robot and enter it into the Properties window so that the VIPLE program can establish the Wi-Fi connection to the robot. Using the buttons and the screen on EV3, you can choose the Wi-Fi network to connect to and find the IP address after the connection.

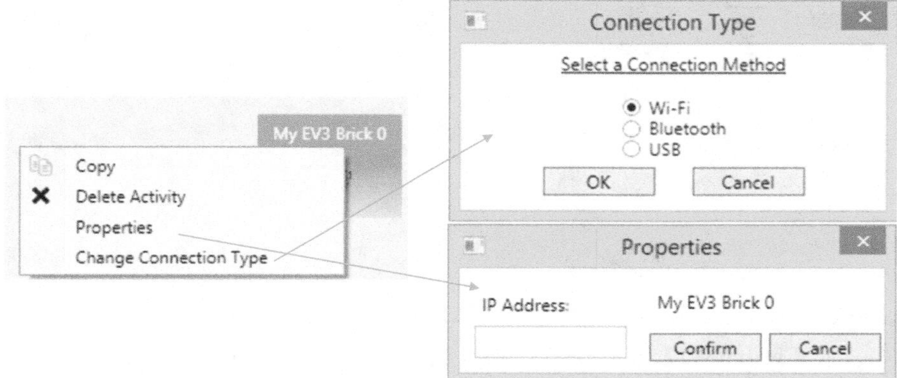

Figure 9.70. Configuration of the EV3 brick using Wi-Fi connection

Using a color sensor facing to the floor, the robot can recognize the line and move following the line on the floor. The color sensor reads the light reflection from the floor. Depending on the color of the floor and the color of the line, you need to find the reflection values. You can use the buttons and screen on the EV3 brick to do the sensor value calibration.

Figure 9.71 shows VIPLE code that makes the EV3 follow a black line on a light-brown floor. The initial position of the color sensor is on the black line or on the right side of the black line. The If-activity checks the sensor reading. If the reflection value is less than 20 (reading from black line), and the robot is not in Adjusting state, the robot will turn right for 200 milliseconds and then move straight forward. This action will make the robot move away from the black line, resulting the sensor reading value to be greater than 20. In this case, the robot will turn left and move toward the black line. When the sensor sees the black line, it starts to move away from the black line. The variable Adjusting is used to make sure that the robot completes the 200 milliseconds adjustment before it turns right.

The program does not have a loop. It is event-driven. The event source is the color sensor, which generates events periodically. Whenever an event happens, the If-activity will be triggered and executed.

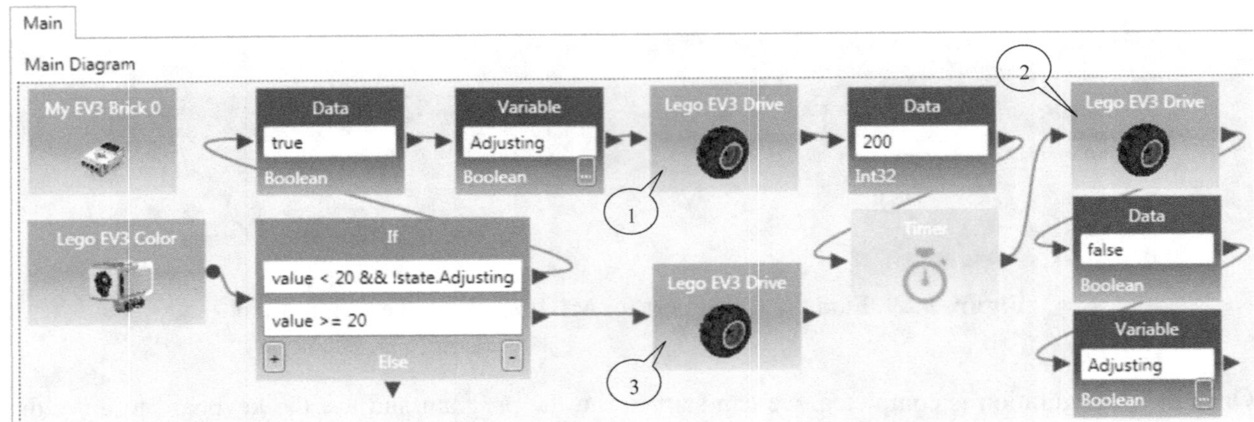

Figure 9.71. The line follower program in VIPLE

Figure 9.72 shows the color sensor properties and the three EV3 Drive power values that control the robot turning right, moving straightforward, and turning left.

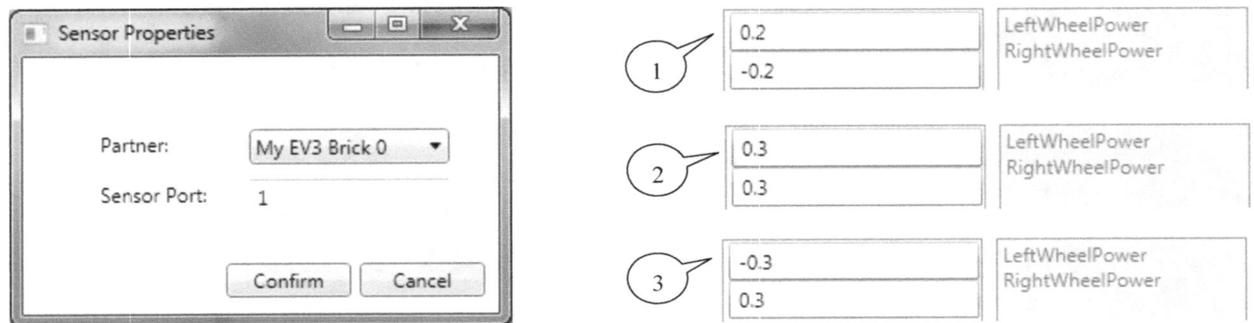

Figure 9.72. Sensor properties and the Drive power settings

We now present the code for autonomously navigating through a maze. Figure 9.73 shows the main diagram that implements the finite state machine of the right-wall-following algorithm given in Figure 9.48. A main brick, an ultrasonic sensor, a touch sensor, and a drive service are used in the program.

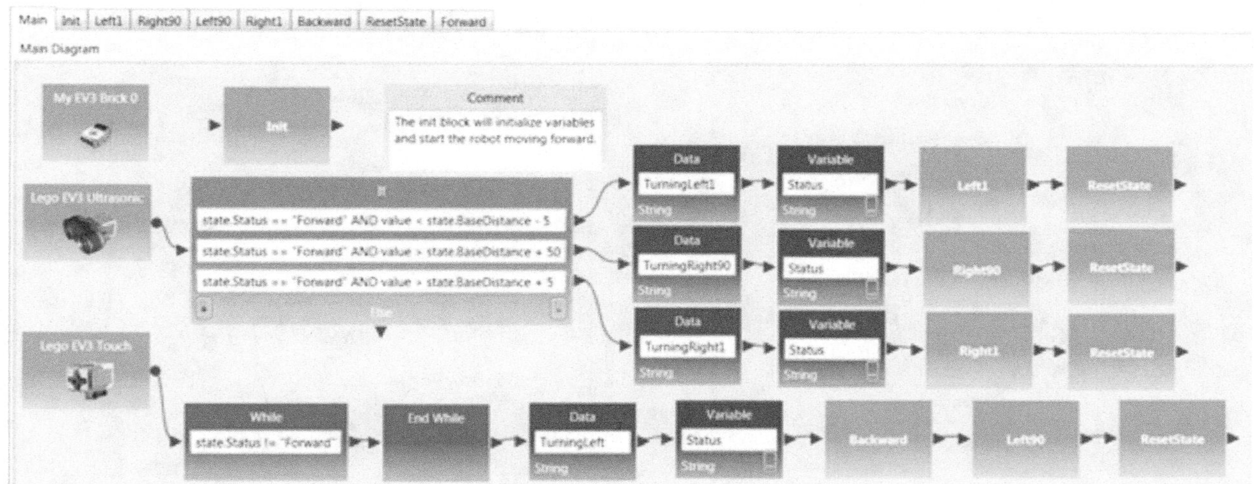

Figure 9.73. The main diagram of the right wall-following program

Similar to Microsoft VPL, activities that define components can be defined in VIPLE. Figure 9.74 shows the codes of three of the activities, Init, Backward, and Left1, behind the main diagram.

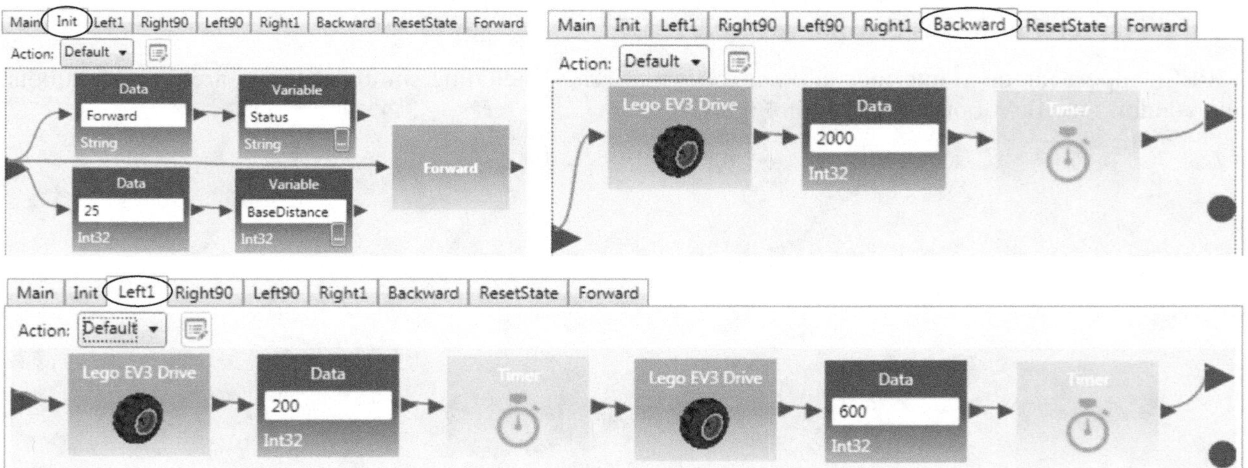

Figure 9.74. The code of three activities Init, Backward, and Left1

For each sensor, we need to choose the partner and choose the sensor port that the device uses. For the main brick and the drive service, the same configurations are used as those used in Figure 9.67, Figure 9.68, and Figure 9.70. Figure 9.75 shows the right-click window to configure the EV3 Ultrasonic distance sensor and the Touch sensor, respectively. The configurations assume that all the devices will partner with My EV3 Brick 0, the Ultrasonic sensor is connected to sensor port 3, and the Touch sensor is connected to sensor port 4 on the EV3 Brick.

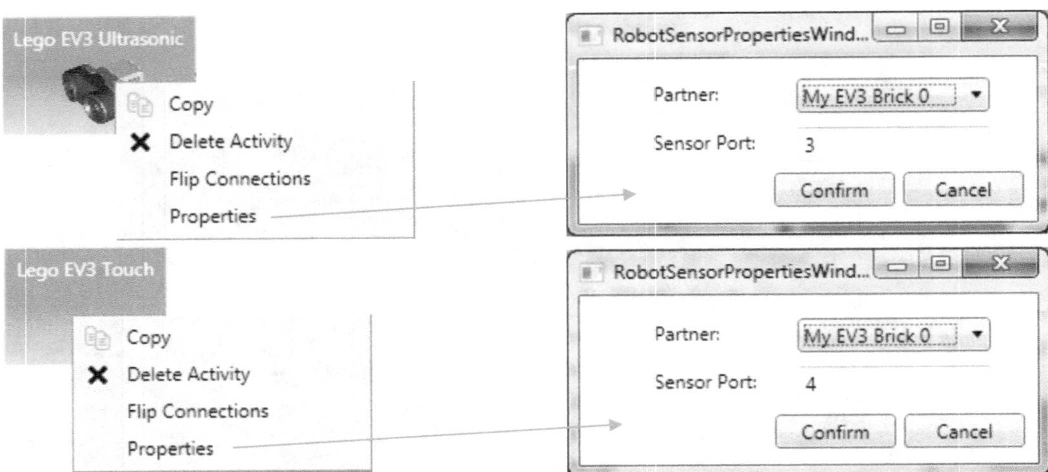

Figure 9.75. Configurations of the EV3 Ultrasonic sensor and Touch sensor

The full code of the right-wall-following program and the video of the robots navigating the maze, as well as other sample code, can be found in the VIPLE site at: http://neptune.fulton.ad.asu.edu/VIPLE/

9.5.6 Other Platforms Supported by VIPLE

VIPLE supports an open interface to other robot platforms, including simulated, open architecture robots, and vendor-specific robots, as shown in Figure 9.76.

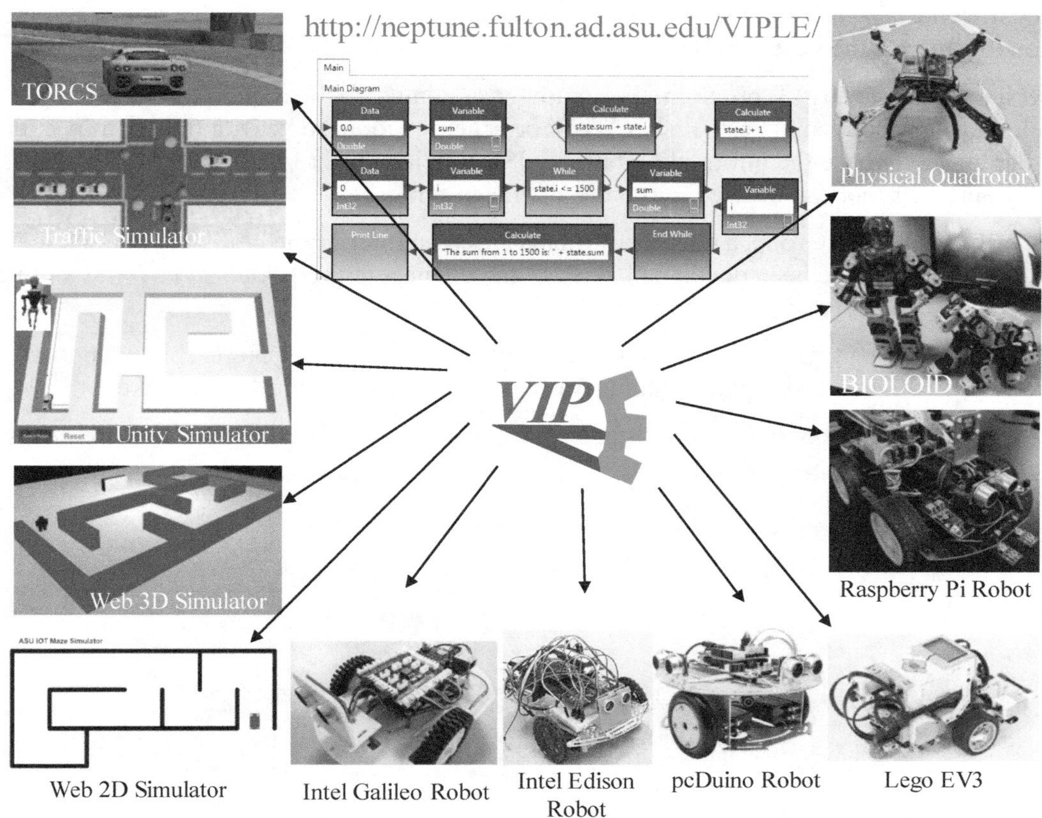

Figure 9.76. VIPLE supported platforms

Any robot that follows the same interface and can interpret the commands from the VIPLE program can work with VIPLE. The VIPLE program communicates with the robot using the following JSON object, which defines the input to the robot from the VIPLE program and the output from the robot to the VIPLE program.

```
ROBOT OUTPUT
name: string (touch, distance, sound, light, color, motorEncoder)
id: int
value:  for touch sensor value will be int (0 = not pressed and 1 = pressed)
        for other sensors value will be double

{"sensors": [{"name":"touch", "id":0, "value":0},
             {"name":"distance", "id":0, "value":12.8}]}

ROBOT INPUT
servoId: int
servoSpeed: double between -1 and 1
             negative values represent a backwards motion
servoDirection: int (0 = clockwise and 1 = counterclockwise)

{"servos": [ {"servoId":3, "servoSpeed":0.5},
             {"servoId":5, "servoSpeed":-0.5}]}
```

The VIPLE program will encode the control information into this object. The robot needs to interpret the script and perform the actions defined. On the other hand, the robot will encode the feedback in the same

JSON format, send that back to the VIPLE program, and the VIPLE program will extract and use the information to generate the next actions.

To connect a robot to the VIPLE program, the computer running the VIPLE program needs to pair with the robot. As long as a robot can (1) establish a Wi-Fi or Ethernet connection with the computer running the VIPLE program, (2) encode the information into the JSON object, and (3) interpret the command from the VIPLE program, the robot can be used to run the VIPLE program.

Sponsored by the Intel IOT Group, a number of robots based on Intel architecture, including Intel's Galileo, Bay-Trail, and Edison, have been developed. VIPLE can connect to these robots via Wi-Fi and Bluetooth, program them, and control them to perform different tasks.

VIPLE implemented two types of robots: EV3 and a generic robot. The generic robot supports any robot that can communicate with a computer running VIPLE and can process the JSON packet.

We use an Edison-based robot in the two-distance maze algorithm maze navigation. Figure 9.77 shows the first part of the main diagram of VIPLE code.

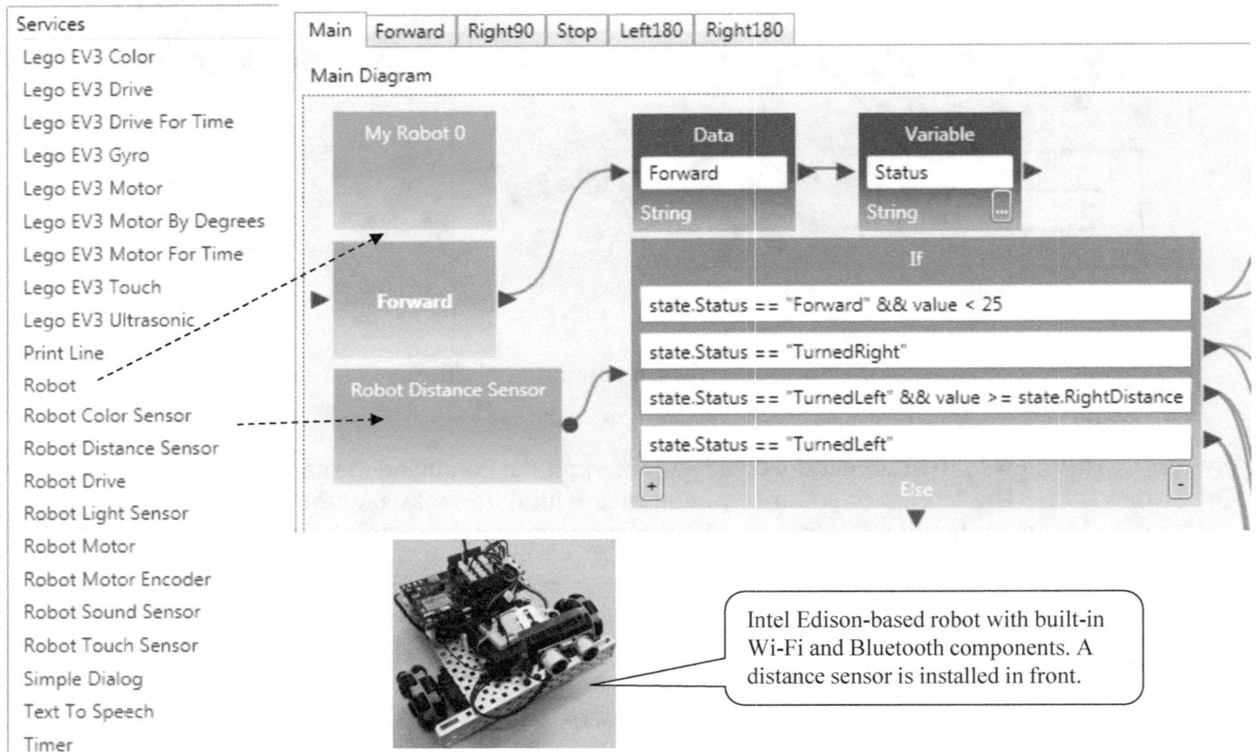

Figure 9.77. The first part of the main diagram implementing the two-distance maze algorithm

The algorithm starts with the robot moving forward. When it approaches a wall in the front, it measures the distance to the right and saves the distance into a variable. Then, the robot spins 180 degrees to measure the other side's distance. It compares the two distances and moves to the direction with more space. In this part of the diagram, an If-activity is used to compare the current status and the distance value from the sensor, which generates four different cases.

The second part of the main diagram is shown in Figure 9.78, which processes four cases of the If-activity, respectively.

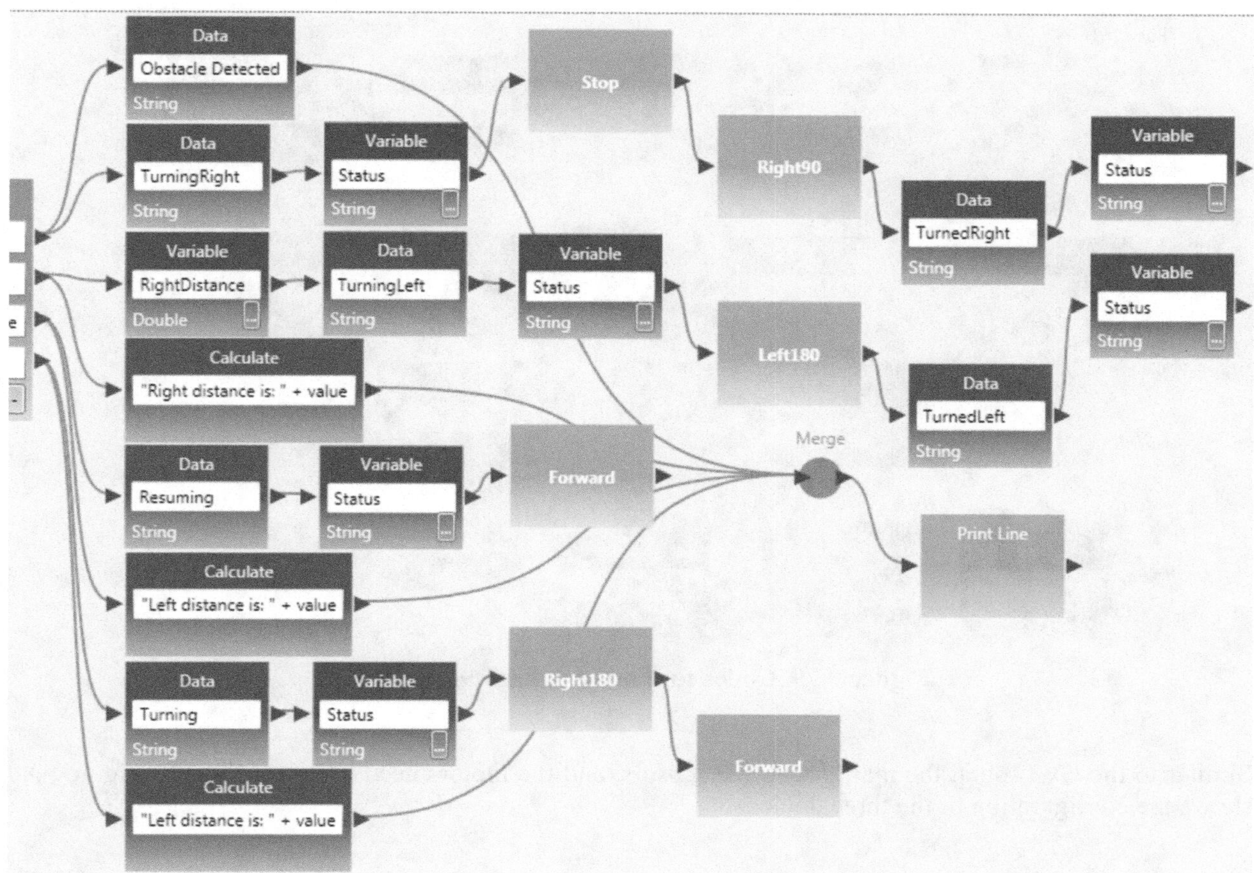

Figure 9.78. Processing the four cases

There are five activities implemented to support the main diagram: Forward, Right90, Stop, Left180, and Right180. Figure 9.79 shows the codes of three of these activities: Forward, Right90, and Stop. The codes of the Right180 and Left180 are similar to Right90, but with different values. A Print Line service is used for distance values for debugging purposes.

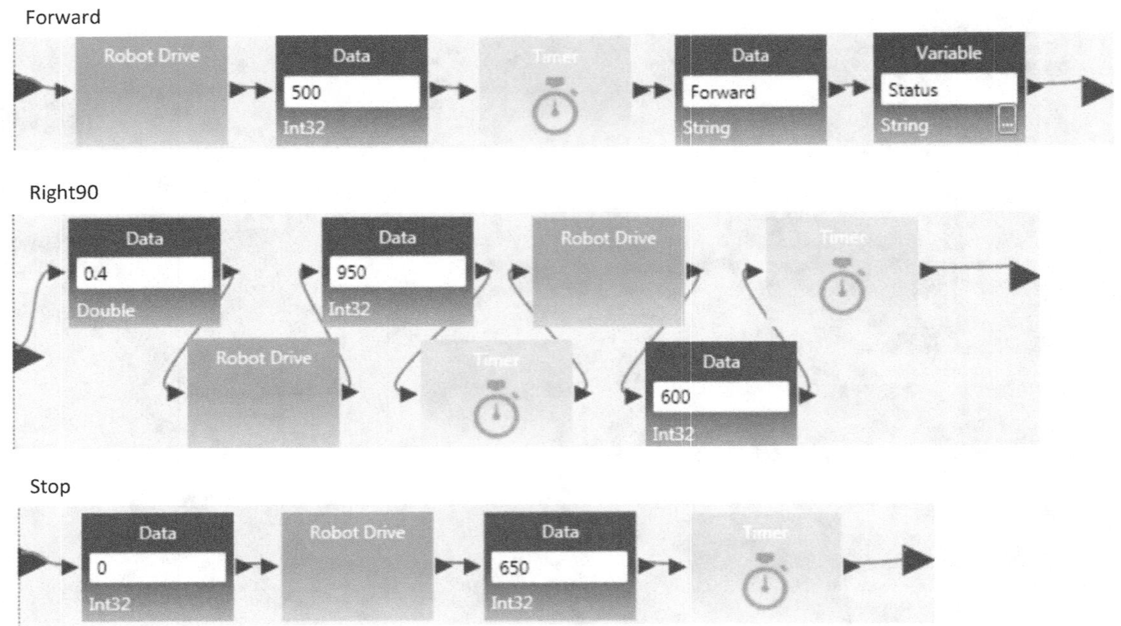

Figure 9.79. Codes for Forward, Right90, and Stop

Similar to the EV3 robot, the main robot, the sensors, and the motors need to be configured. Figure 9.80 shows the configuration of the three devices.

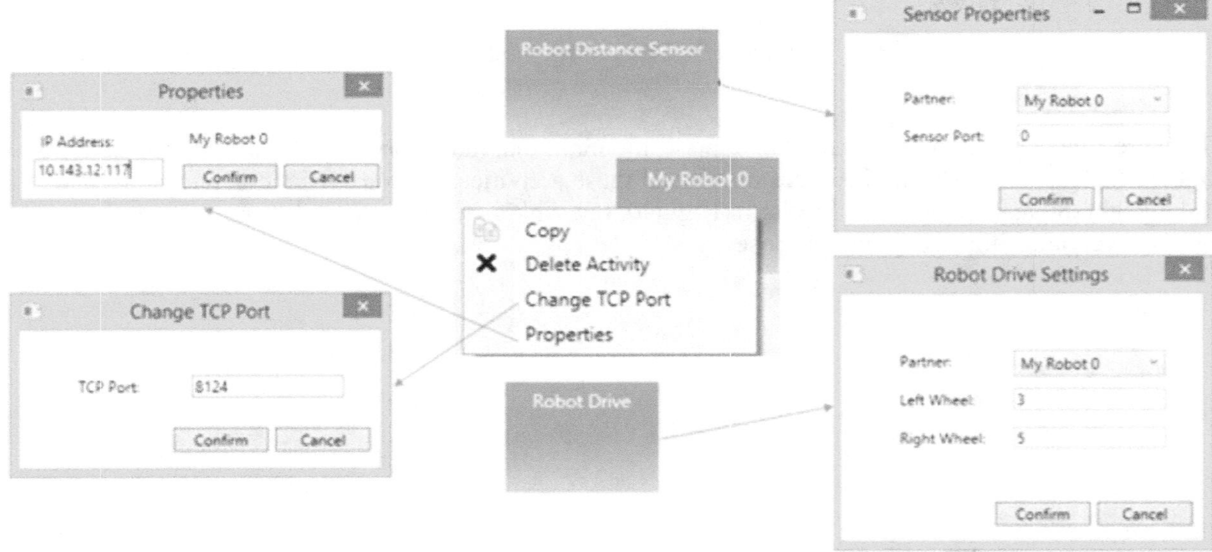

Figure 9.80. Configuration of My Robot, Robot Distance Sensor, and Robot Drive service

The full code of the maze navigation program and the video of the robots navigating the maze can be found in the VIPLE site at: http://neptune.fulton.ad.asu.edu/VIPLE/

VIPLE allows to use its Robot Motion service to program different robots with complex functions. Figure 9.81 shows an example of defining a list of humanoid's motions using the menu Tools → Motion Config

Options. A Robot Motion is different from the other basic robot move functions in the VIPLE's service list. For example, "Huamanoid: Walk forward" motion involves multiple motors on the legs and arms to coordinately rotate in different directions and at different speeds.

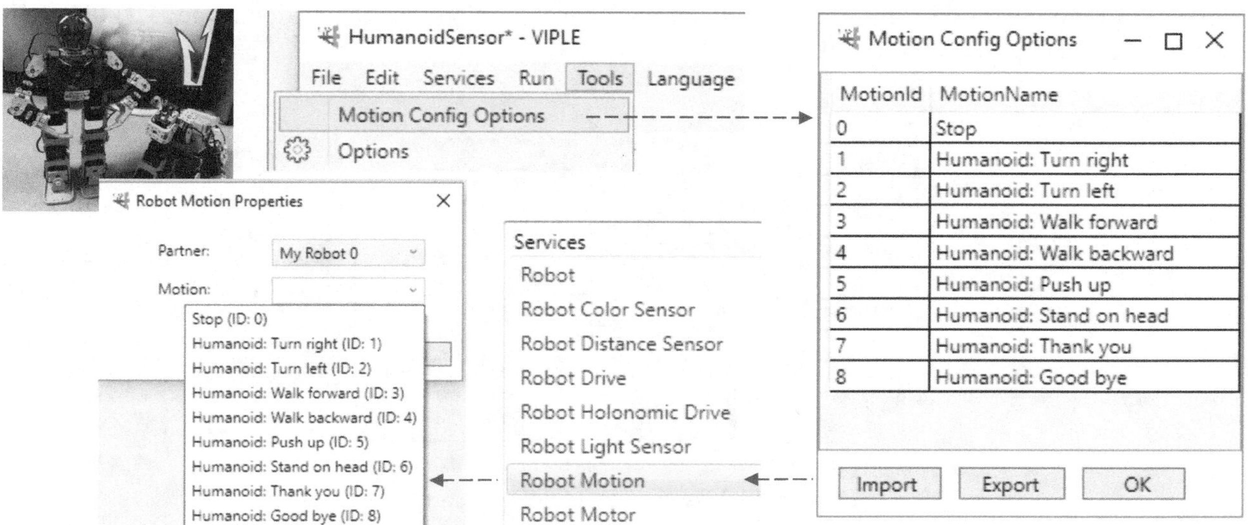

Figure 9.81. Configure Robot Motion service for controlling complex humanoid

Once the motions are defined, we can drag and drop the Robot Motion service into the diagram to program the humanoid for performing different movements. Figure 9.82 gives an example, in which the Robot Motion service is used to program the humanoid to perform different motions.

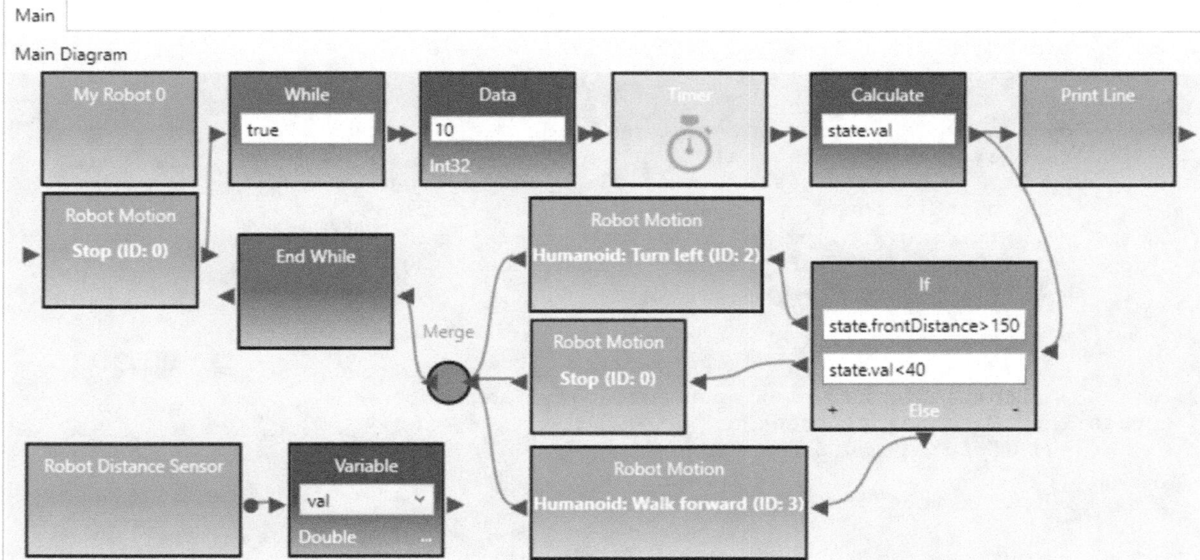

Figure 9.82. Using Robot Motion service for programming the complex humanoid

The video showing the execution of the program in Figure 9.82 can be viewed in the VIPLE home page or directly at: http://neptune.fulton.ad.asu.edu/VIPLE/Videos/HumanoidVipleProgrammed.mp4

More robot motions are shown at the following link, where the robot is controlled through Amazon Alexa voice commands: http://neptune.fulton.ad.asu.edu/VIPLE/Videos/HumanoidVoiceCommand.mp4

Finally, we present the autonomous driving simulation in the TORCS environment. TORCS is an open source project (http://torcs.sourceforge.net/) that is integrated in the VIPLE environment. We show a simple example in Figure 9.83. For the Robot/IoT Controller configuration, the connection Type is TORCS, IP Address is localhost, and Port is 3001.

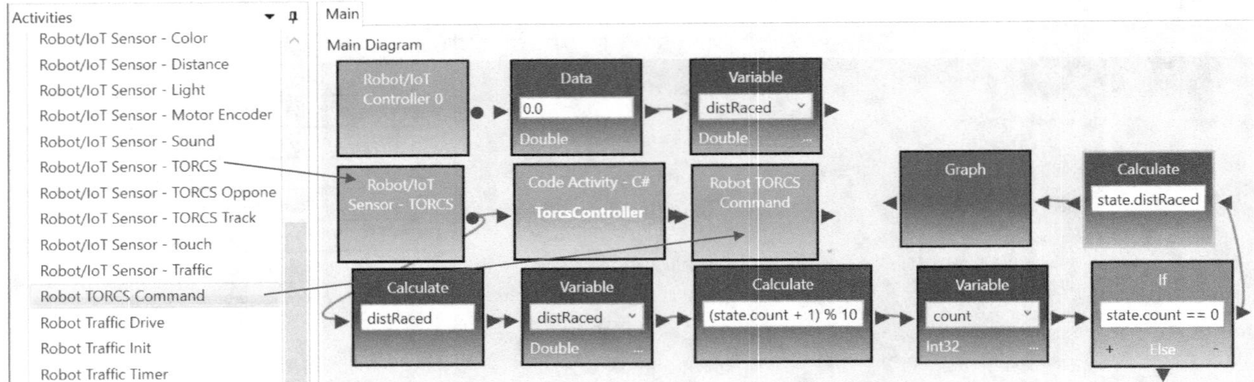

Figure 9.83. A simple TORCS example

Robot/IoT Sensor–TORCS is a 360-degree surrounding sensor, which can measure the track positions and angles from the edge of the road to the race car. The data is stored in a dictionary structure. The sensor is connected to a Code Activity C#, which processes the sensor values and sends the drive commands to the Robot TORCS Command. The code in the Code Activity is given as follows.

```
using System;
using System.Collections.Generic;
[Serializable]
public class TorcsController : CodeUtilities.CodeBase {
    public TorcsController() {
    }
    // To execute your code, you must override the Execute method.
    public override void Execute() {
        // The values are passed in as an object, need to unbox it.
        var inputDictionary = Input as Dictionary<string,object>;
        // Returning a dictionary allows us to reference the values by name.
        var toReturn = new Dictionary<string, double>() {
            {"accel", 0.5},
            {"brake", 0.0},
            {"gear", 2},
            // Cast these values to doubles, as they are passed in as objects.
            {"steer", (double)inputDictionary["angle"] -
(double)inputDictionary["trackPos"] * 0.5},
            {"clutch", 0.2}
        };
        Output = toReturn;
    }
}
```

In this code, the sensor inputs `inputDictionary["angle"]` and `inputDictionary["angle"]` are used for calculating the steer control value for the Robot TORCS Command:

```
{"steer", (double)inputDictionary["angle"]-(double)inputDictionary["trackPos"]*0.5}
```

For simplicity, the other control values are set to constants: `{"accel", 0.5}`, `{"brake", 0.0}`, `{"gear", 2}`, and `{"clutch", 0.2}`.

All these data are wrapped into the object ToReturn and assigned to the return variable Output. The Data Connection between the CodeActivity and the Robot TORCS Command is shown in Figure 9.84.

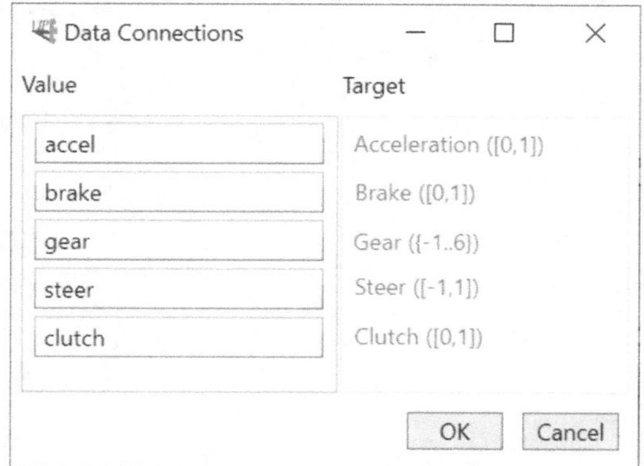

Figure 9.84. Data Connection between the CodeActivity and the Robot TORCS Command

Once the VIPLE code is ready, we can start the TORCS simulator from the VIPLE Run menu, as shown in Figure 9.85. In the simulator, you click "Race", and then, "Basic Quick Race", and finally "New Race". Now, the Console window will show "waiting for request on port 3001".

Figure 9.85. Starting TORCS simulator

The sumulator is now ready. You can go back to the VIPLE program and start to run the code. Then, the race will begin, as shown in Figure 9.86.To improve the race performance, you need to properly define the other parameters: accel, brake, gear, and clucth. Figure 9.86 shows an advanced Main diagram that can significantly improve the race performance. The Custom Activities defined in the VIPLE code are given in Figure 9.87, Figure 9.88, Figure 9.89, Figure 9.90, Figure 9.91, Figure 9.92, and Figure 9.93.

Figure 9.86. TORCS simulator running in the racetrack

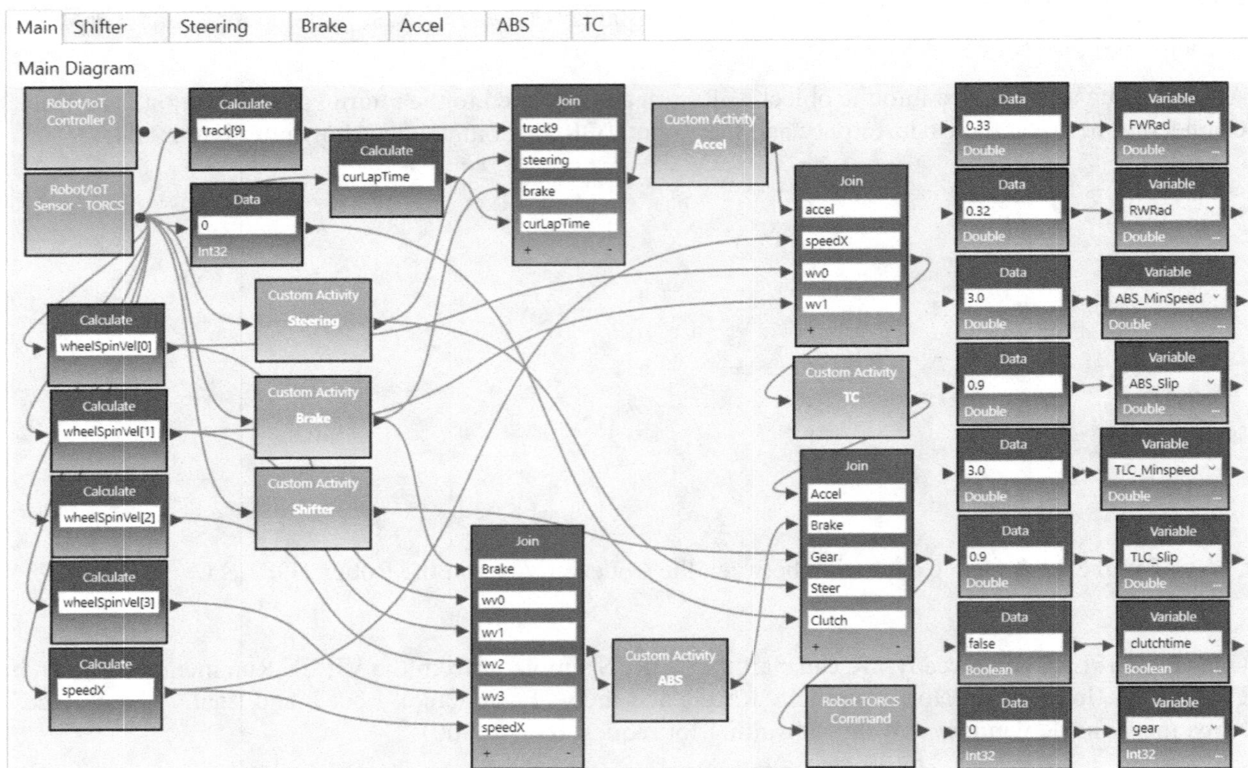

Figure 9.87. An advanced VIPLE code for the race

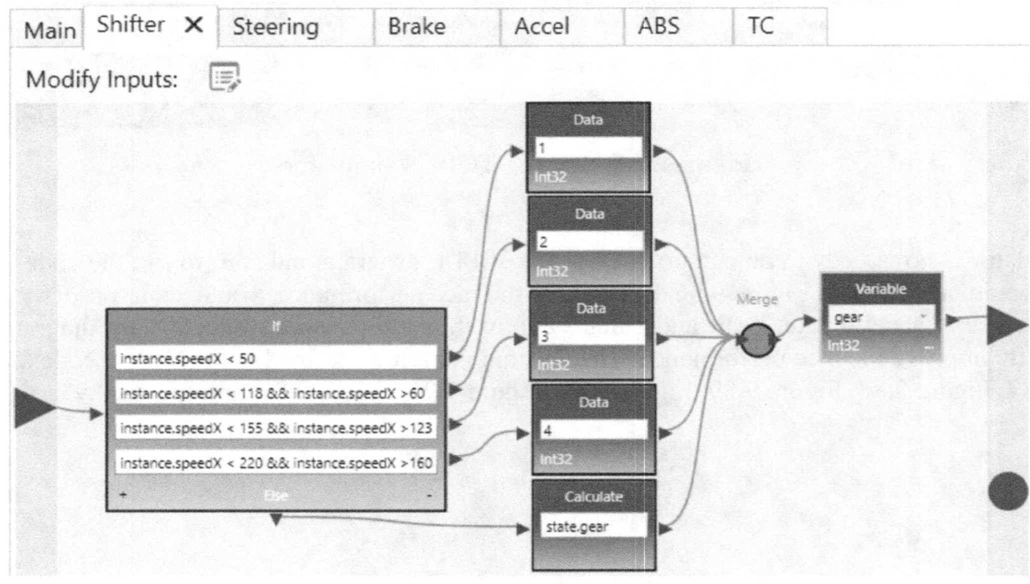

Figure 9.88. Shifter Activity

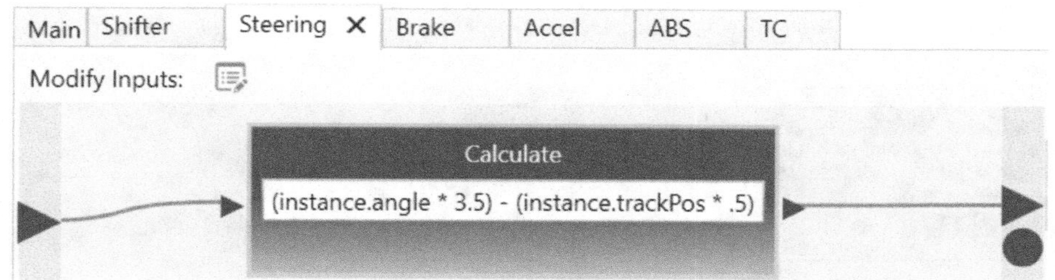

Figure 9.89. Steering Activity

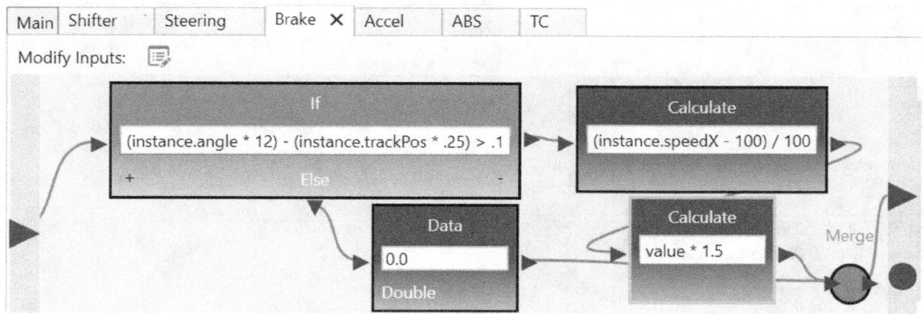

Figure 9.90. Brake Activity

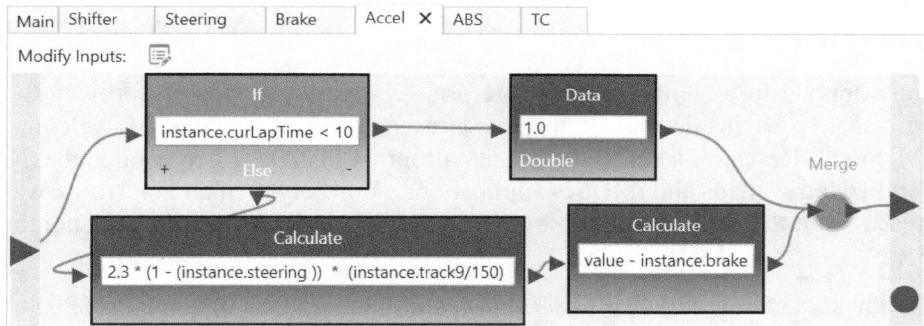

Figure 9.91. Acceleration Activity

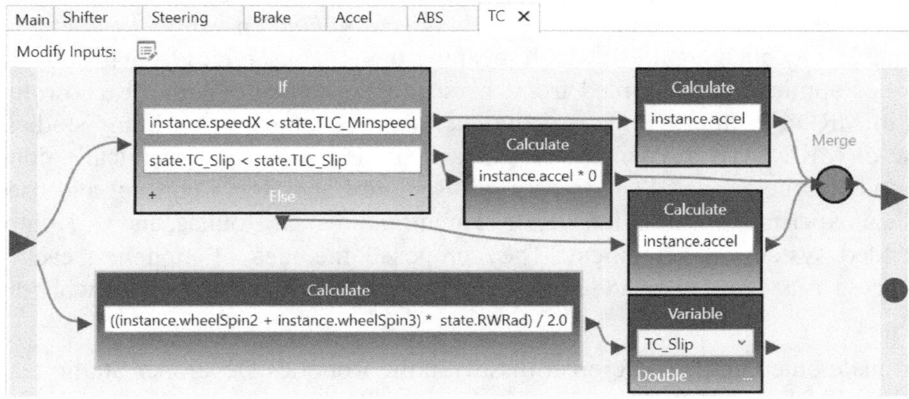

Figure 9.92. Traction Control (TC) Activity

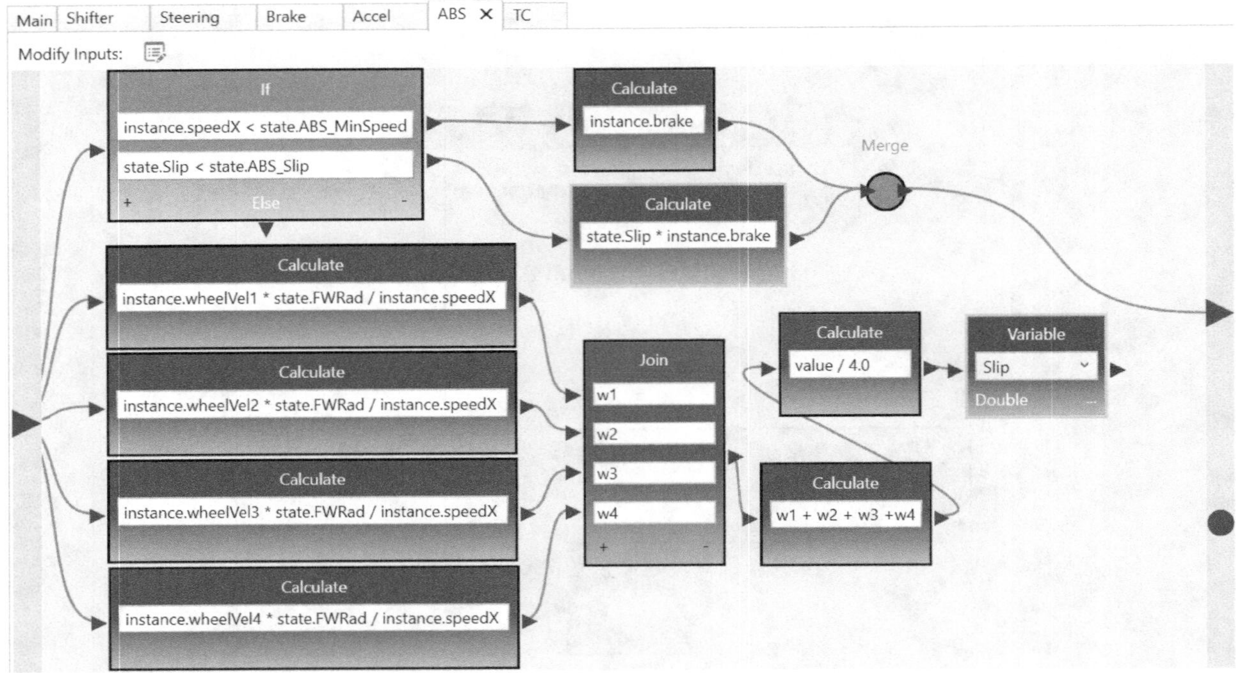

Figure 9.93. Anti-lock Braking System (ABS) Activity

9.6 Discussions

SOC was initially applied in e-commerce and enterprise computing systems. Applying SOC in physical devices and embedded systems is one of the most recent challenges in both academia and industry. Sponsored by Microsoft Research's embedded system program in 2003, Chen applied the SOC concepts to recomposable embedded systems and robotics applications. A prototype of an SOC robot was implemented in 2005 and presented in the IFIP Workshop on Dependability in Robotics and Autonomous Systems, in February 2006, at

http://webhost.laas.fr/TSF/IFIPWG/Workshops&Meetings/49/workshop/04%20chen.pdf.

In the presentation, doubts are raised from both academia and industry on the suitability of applying SOC in robotics computing and embedded systems.

The release of the Microsoft Robotics Developer Studio (MRDS) and VPL, in June 2006, was a vital step in applying SOC to embedded systems (http://msdn.microsoft.com/en-us/robotics/default.aspx). MRDS defined a mapping layer, called manifest, which separates the virtual services from the physical devices and makes the robotics application decoupled from the specifics of the devices. REST protocol, instead of SOAP, is used in MRDS to improve the real-time communication capacity. Many studies are published after the release of MRDS. Trifa, Cianci, and Guinard applied SOC for dynamically controlling swarm robots. Tröger and Rasche applied SOC to "Virtual Remote Laboratory" concept and used LEGO NXT robots for physical experiment installations. K. C. Thramboulidis, G. Doukas, and G. Koumoutsos applied SOC for embedded systems development. They proposed the idea of modeling each feature of the development process as a web service and presented a prototype implementation showing the usefulness of the research.

It was an unfortunate outcome that Microsoft dissolved the Robotics Developer Studio team and stopped supporting all the MRDS and VPL development. Arizona State University takes the lead to develop our own visual programming language, and we hope it can help the MRDS and VPL community to continue their projects in teaching and researching VIPLE. VIPLE intend to support all the VPL activities and services. In addition, VIPLE allows SOAP and RESTful services to be added into the service list in the environment.

SOC has now been widely accepted as a suitable and effective approach for robotics and industrial automation. Veiga, Pires, and Nilsson studied the use of SOA platforms for industrial robotic cells, which ultimately uses services to control and to manage robotics cells. These cells are responsible for various functions in the automation process. Narita, Shimamura, and Oya developed a Reliable Protocol for Robot Communication (RoboLink Protocol) for reliable communication among robots using web services. These efforts made toward applying SOC in the field of robotics and automation clearly show the growing importance of SOC in robotics and embedded systems. Developing RaaS as a cloud unit is another major step to putting robotics on the map of cloud computing and web-based computing.

Name: ______________________

Date: ______________________

9.7 Exercises and Projects

1. Multiple choice questions. Choose one answer in each question only. Choose the best answer if multiple answers are acceptable.

1.1 What are the major benefits of using service-oriented computing paradigm for developing robotics applications?

(A) Event-driven support

(B) Application is platform independent

(C) Reusable services

(D) All of the above

1.2 Why is the event-driven computing paradigm better for robotics applications?

(A) All inputs are known at the start of the program.

(B) Many sensory inputs can be better described by events.

(C) Data flow does not exist.

(D) Control flow does not exist.

1.3 What components are included in a Robot as a Service (RaaS) unit according to the book?

(A) Services (B) Service directory (C) Applications (D) All of the above

1.4 What is used for creating a new "service" in VIPLE?

(A) Activity (B) Calculate (C) Merge (D) Variable

1.5 What is the function of the basic activity "Join"?

(A) It waits for one of the incoming data items to arrive.

(B) It waits for all incoming data items to arrive.

(C) It checks the result of a condition and then chooses one of the incoming data items.

(D) It must be used in pair with Merge.

1.6 What basic activity is NOT directly supported in VIPLE?

(A) If (B) Join (C) For (D) Switch

1.7 After an event output is created in a VIPLE activity, how do you access the event output?

(A) Use the triangular output port of the activity.

(B) Use the circular output port of the activity.

(C) Use a Built-in Event.

(D) Use the Custom Event.

1.8 What is a service created in VIPLE?

(A) A basic activity

(B) A composite activity

(C) A composite activity wrapped with service interface

(D) A service that can be used as a RESTful service or a WSDL service

1.9 What types of services are supported in VIPLE?

(A) RESTful services (B) WSDL services (C) VIPLE services (D) All of the above

1.10 What types of robot platforms are supported in VIPLE?

(A) Lego EV3 (B) Simulated robots

(C) Open architecture robots (D) All of the above

1.11 What sensors are supported in the VIPLE's Unity Maze Simulator?

(A) Distance sensors (B) Touch sensors (C) Color sensors (D) Motion sensors

1.12 What sensors are supported in Web 2D Simulator?

(A) Distance sensors (B) Touch sensors

(C) Both (A) and (B) (D) Neither (A) nor (B)

1.13 A finite state machine is designed to respond to

(A) a set of inputs occurring together at the starting state.

(B) a sequence of inputs occurring one after another.

(C) a set of inputs occurring together at the terminating state.

(D) nonoccurrence of any input.

1.14 How can an open architecture robot be added into VIPLE?

(A) It plugs and plays.

(B) A middleware is installed on the robot to generate and interpret VIPLE JSON object.

(C) A DSS service is written to map the device driver to the VIPLE interface.

(D) A USB interface is a part of VIPLE standard and no translation is needed.

1.15 What basic activities are implemented in the current version of VIPLE?

(A) Calculate (B) Join and Merge (C) While (D) All of the above

1.16 What services are implemented in the current version of VIPLE?

(A) Key Press Events (B) Text to Speech (C) Print a Line (D) All of the above

1.17 What types of connection between the computer and the robot are supported in VIPLE?

(A) Wi-Fi (B) Bluetooth (C) WebSocket (D) All of the above

1.18 What types of physical robot are supported in VIPLE?

(A) EV3 (B) Open architecture robot

(C) Both (A) and (B) (D) Neither (A) nor (B)

1.19 Which connection needs the IP address?

(A) Wi-Fi (B) Bluetooth (C) RS323 (D) All of the above

1.20 Which connection needs the COM port?

(A) Wi-Fi (B) Bluetooth (C) RS323 (D) All the above

2. What are the benefits of using SOC concepts in robotics software development?

3. What is VIPLE? Where can VIPLE be applied?

4. What are activities and services in VIPLE? What services are available in the service repository? What page represents the application (client)?

5. What constructs are available in VIPLE? How can a loop be implemented in VIPLE? What is the difference between Merge and Join?

6. Compare and contrast WF and VIPLE.

7. What SOA concepts are applied in VIPLE?

8. Explain how event-driven programming is implemented in VIPLE.

9. Download VIPLE from http://neptune.fulton.ad.asu.edu/VIPLE/ and follow the tutorials in the appendix of the book to write basic VIPLE programs.
   1) Use the text to speech to implement a program to read "Hello World;"
   2) Construct a while-loop to compute the sum of 1+2+3+…+n;
   3) Write a drive-by-wire program to control a robot in Unity Simulation;
   4) Write a drive-by-wire program to control a robot in Web 2D Simulation;
   5) Write a program to test the touch sensor given in Web 2D Simulation;
   6) Write a program to test the distance sensor given in Web 2D Simulation.

10. Follow the one-bit ALU diagrams given in the text to develop a two-bit ALU with automated testing mechanism. How can you extend the circuit to implement a 32-bit ALU?

11. Follow the examples given in Chapter 9 to implement a maze navigation program in Unity Simulator and in Web 2D Simulator.

12. Use VIPLE development environment to implement the different maze navigation algorithms.
    1) Write a left-wall-following algorithm;
    2) Use the basic activities and services available in the environment to implement the left-wall-following algorithm.
    3) Write a farthest-distance algorithm: When the robot is forwarding and is close to the wall in the front, the robot compares the distances on the left and on the right, and the robot turn to the side with farthest difference.
    4) Use the basic activities and services available in the environment to implement the farthest-difference algorithm.

Project

Use VIPLE to develop a service-oriented and event-driven robotics application in VIPLE simulation environment.

(1) Consider the example given in the Heuristic Maze Navigation Algorithm section. Implement a wall-following algorithm in the given simulation environment to guide the simulated robot to navigate through the maze.

(2) Use an EV3 robot for testing your navigation algorithms.

(3) Build your own open architecture robot, download the middle from the VIPLE website, and install the middle on the robot. Write a maze navigation program for your robot.

Chapter 10
Interfacing Service-Oriented Software with Databases

This chapter discusses how the traditional databases interface with service-oriented software through a data adapter, the development of an XML-based database that directly communicates with SOA software without an adapter, and the Language Integrated Query (LINQ) that accesses data objects, traditional databases, and XML data in a uniform way.

10.1 Database Systems and Operations

Data management and Databases are an integral part of all distributed systems, which normally constitute an entire layer in the four-tier architecture. Databases have existed and have been widely used long before SOA and SOC were proposed. The main question is how can the current database format, which is primarily collections of columns, rows, and tables, effectively communicate with the SOC data format, which is largely an XML-based tree structure.

Figure 10.1 shows a scenario where SOA systems and components fit together. On the upper part of the diagram, different kinds of SOA applications are shown, including Windows applications, web applications, mobile and robotics applications, and composite workflow applications such as those written in BPEL processes. These SOA applications can use remote services in external repositories over the Internet to perform functions outside the applications. The lower part of the diagram shows the data management and databases that support the SOA applications. Traditional relational databases, such as DB2, OLE, Oracle, and SQL databases have been holding business data for decades, and they will play important roles in any software system now and for many years to come. The current solution, for each database, is a data adapter used to convert the data format of the database to a standard interface to the SOA applications, so that the code in SOA applications will be independent of the actual database used. A data adapter will be specific to a particular database, and the output of the data adapter will be standard, which is called dataset. A dataset is a collection of tables. Each table consists of rows and columns.

Database accesses involve reading and writing the secondary storage such as a disk. The delay for such accesses is a thousand times, if not a million times, lower. Thus, the efficient way to access a database is to read or write a large block of data use, hopefully, multiple times. The dataset provides a buffer for the data from and to the database.

The standard dataset can be directly sent to the applications for their processing. The data management layer could convert the dataset into text or XML format before sending them to the applications, particularly, in the case of mobile and embedded applications, where the processing capacity is limited.

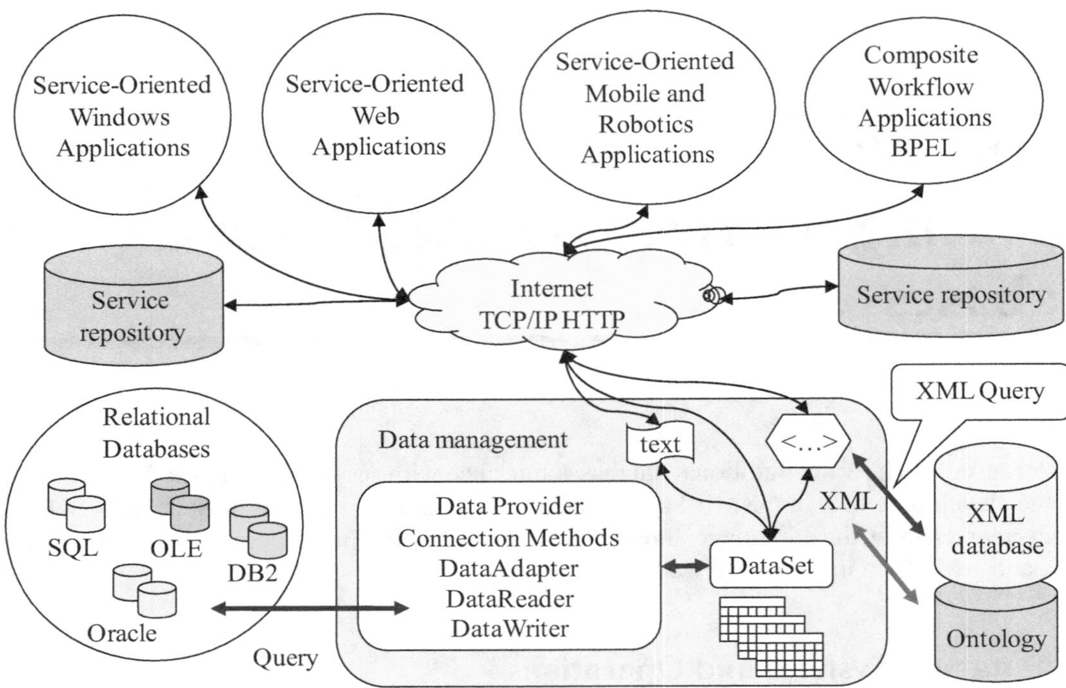

Figure 10.1. Databases in service-oriented software

Figure 10.2 shows the organization of an Oracle database. At the physical layer, data are stored in data files, along with the redo log files and the control files that store redundant information and checking points information to ensure the dependable and robust operations of the files.

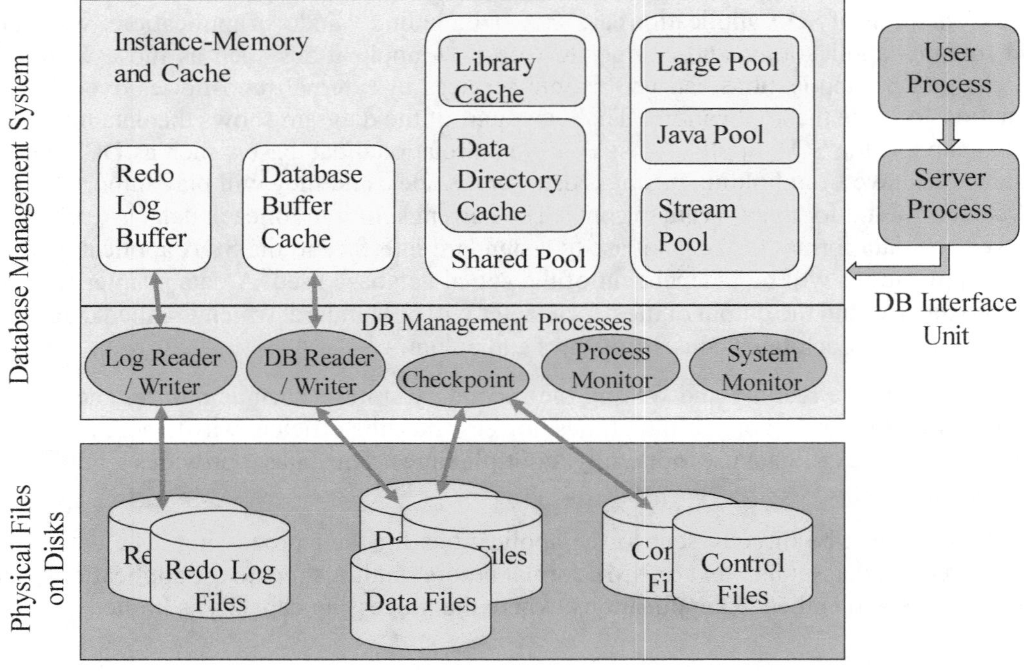

Figure 10.2. Organization of an Oracle database

The layer above the physical layer is the database management system. It executes processes on database system's processors and uses memory, cache, as well as the library functions for reading, writing, controlling, and monitoring the database operations.

Interfacing with the relational databases is the current business practice, XML-based databases are being actively exploited to seek better solutions that eliminate the layer of adapters. The relational database stores the same information for each data item, and thus all data items can be stored in a flat table of columns and rows. XML-database uses a tree node to hold a data item, and thus has the potential to store different information in different data items.

The challenge is to develop a query language that can effectively express the query of data, be easily used by users, and be efficiently executed by hardware.

Ontology is XML-based and is a database with additional metadata that describe the property and attributes of data. Ontology can be considered an advanced database and knowledge-based system, and is playing an increasingly important role.

10.2 Relational Databases in Service-Oriented Software

10.2.1 Installing a Database

In order to create a project with a database, we need to install a database first. In this section, we will use an SQL database as an example to discuss the preparation needed for creating a database project. We will explain the process in the following steps:

1. On the database side: Download and install SQL Server Express, and download and install SQL Server Management Studio.
2. On the project side: Add "Data storage and processing" to Visual Studio and then create SQL Server Database Project.
3. Link the two sides together: Import your database into your project.

Step 1: We start with installing the database by downloading and installing an SQL Server or free SQL Server Express. The downloading address is: https://www.microsoft.com/en-us/download/details.aspx?id=55994. You can find different tutorials on the installation guide. For example: https://www.bu.edu/csmet/files/ 2016/09/SQL-Server-Express-Installation-Guide-V01.pdf.

When you install, you will be asked to choose a location and a server name. For example, we choose:

EN4146050W\SQLEXPRESS

Once SQL Server Express is installed successfully, we can download and install SQL Server Management Studio from https://docs.microsoft.com/en-us/sql/ssms/download-sql-server-management-studio-ssms?view= sql-server-ver15.

After the installation, we will use SQL Server Management Studio for creating an SQL Server database on your computer. This database will be independent of your programming projects. You can link this database to different programming projects and allow these projects to access this database. Microsoft has a tutorial on using SQL Server Management Studio for creating at database at https://docs.microsoft.com/en-us/sql/relational-databases/lesson-1-connecting-to-the-database-engine?view=sql-server-ver15.

Figure 10.3 shows an SQL database that we created using SQL Server Management Studio. When you start the project, you will be asked to connect to your Database Engine. If your SQP Server is installed successfully, SQL Server Management Studio should find it automatically and connect it, as shown in Figure 10.3: Database Engine → EN4146050W\SQLEXPRESS.

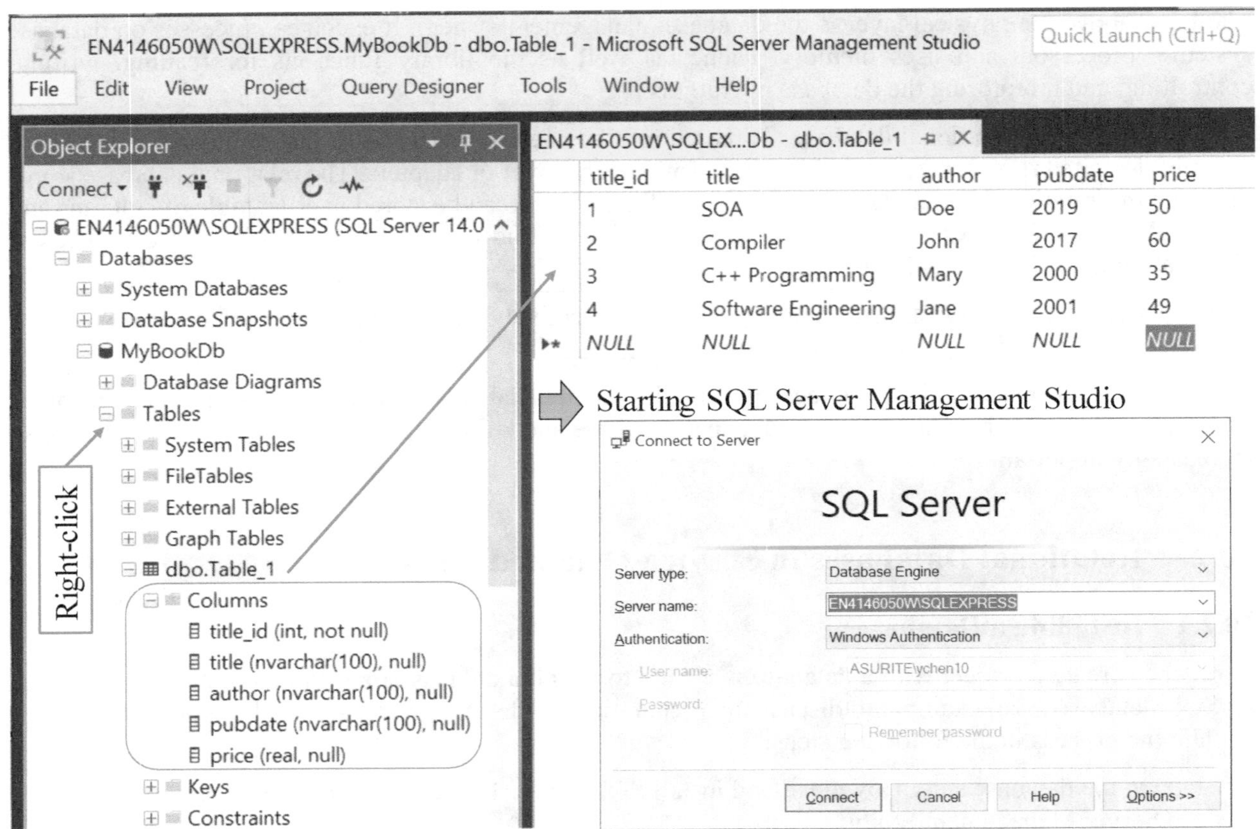

Figure 10.3. Creating an SQL database using SQL Server Management Studio

Right-click Tables in the Object Explorer on the left-hand side to add a new table. Then, you can define the Columns (database schema) for a new database. You can manually enter data into the table here or create a program to write and read data into the table.

Step 2: We start to create a Visual Studio database project to access the database created in Step 1.

Before we start the project, we make sure that the SQL database template "Data storage and processing" component is installed in the Visual Studio. We run Visual Studio Installer and check the components as shown in Figure 10.4.

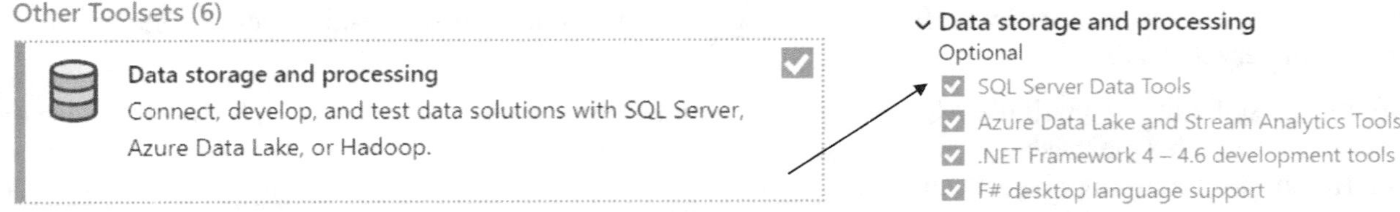

Figure 10.4. Add and select Data storage and processing and its options

Now, we can start Visual Studio and create a new project, as shown in Figure 10.5. You can search "sql" keyword to find the SQL Server Database project template, assuming that you have installed the SQL Data storage and processing component and its options.

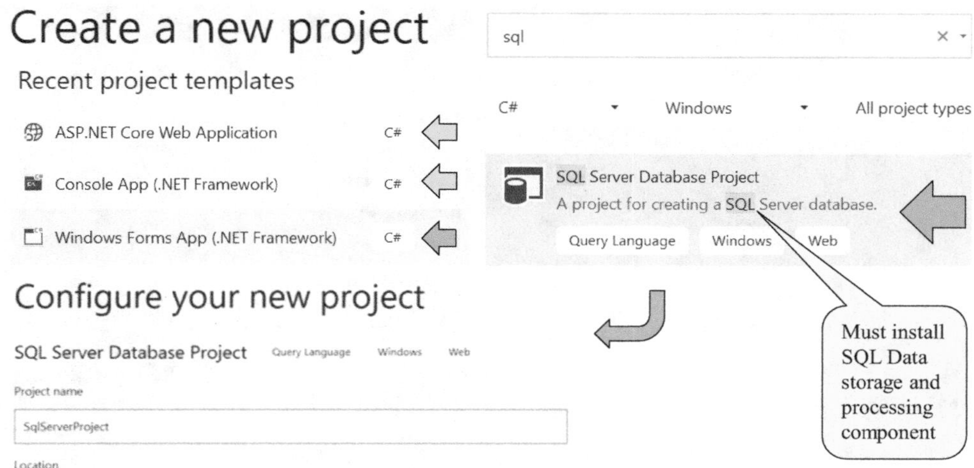

Figure 10.5. Creating an SQL Server Database project

Once the project is created, you can right-click the project name and choose Add → Add New Item…, then choose to add Tables and Views and choose Table, as shown in Figure 10.6.

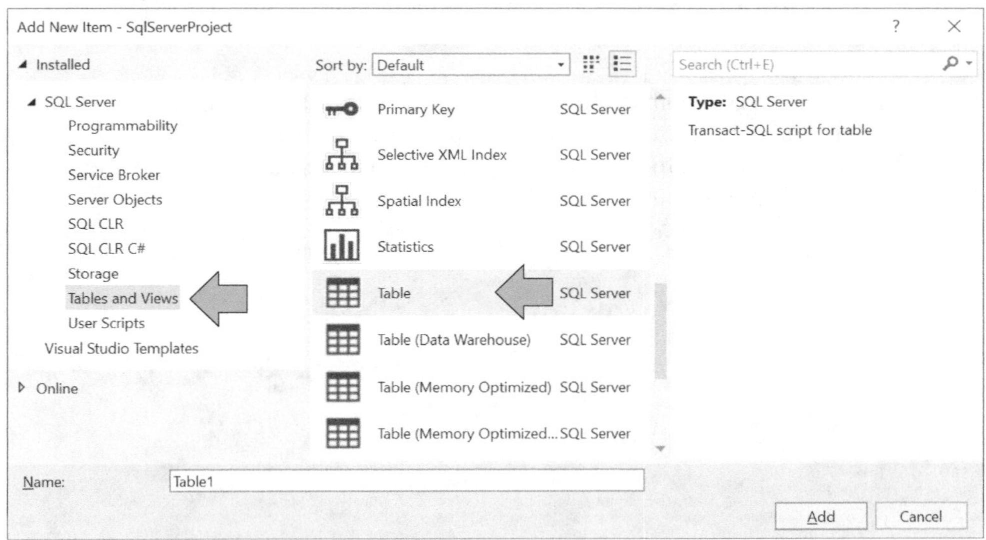

Figure 10.6. Add a new table into the database project

You can add columns into your new table to form the schema, as shown in Figure 10.7. Once the columns are added, the data structures are generated automatically, so that you can write the code to read and write the data structure.

Step 3: Import Database into the Project

The database created in Step 2 is built into the Visual Studio programming project. It can be used in that project only. It is not related to the database that we created in Step 1, which is an independent database on the local computer, and it can be used in different programming projects on the computer.

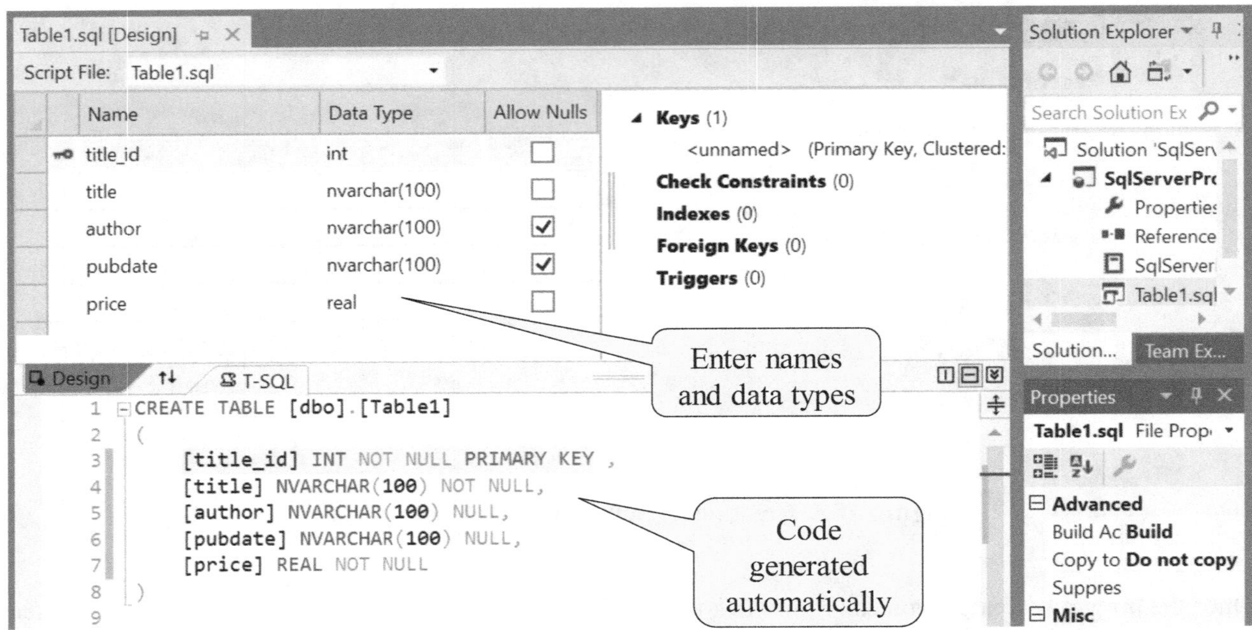

Figure 10.7. SQL database project with a new table added

It is beneficial to maintain a single database for multiple programming projects. In this case, we should not add Table in the Visual Studio project. Instead, we import the database table from the general database created in Step 1. To do so, you click the "Project" tag in the Visual Studio project's menu, choose Import and choose Database, as shown in Figure 10.8.

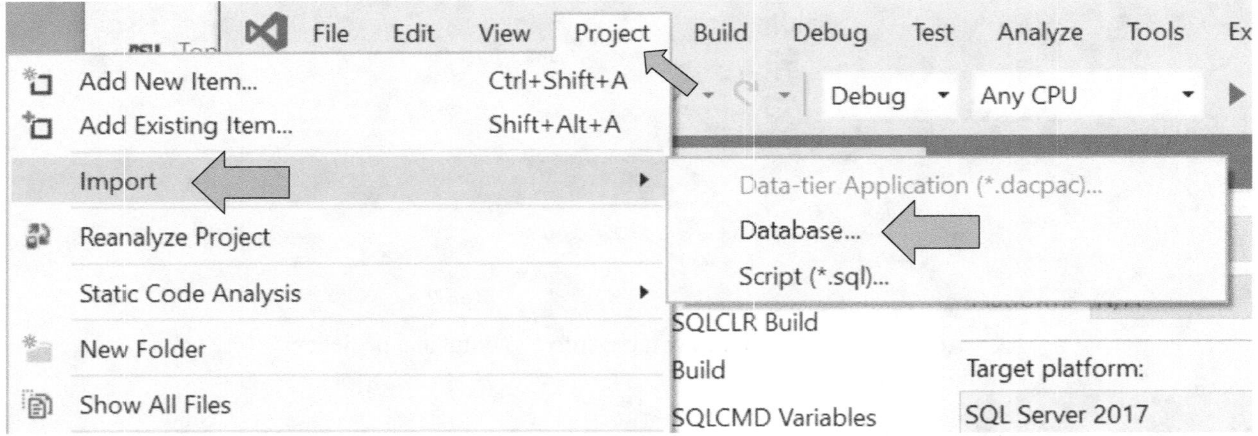

Figure 10.8. Import database into Visual Studio project

Once the database is imported into the project, it can keep synchronizing with the original database. In the following sections, we will discuss in more detail how to write programs to read and write the database, either created with the Visual Studio project or imported from the database on the computer, using ADO .Net model and using LINQ to Object, LINQ to SQL, and LINQ to XML to access the database.

10.2.2 Interface between Database and Software

A database, like a disk file, can be modeled as a document consisting of a collection of objects. Reading and writing a database is converting the objects from the source to the destination document. Thus, the database adapters are implemented by document converters.

OLE (Object Linking and Embedding) is a compound document standard developed by Microsoft and first released in 1990. OLE allows creating objects within one application, and linking or embedding them in another application. Embedded objects retain their original format and links to the application that created them. As a distributed object system and protocol, OLE enables accessing different kinds of databases. OLE support is built in Windows and MacOS Operating Systems. A competing compound document standard developed by Apple and IBM is called OpenDoc, which is an open, multi-platform architecture for component-based software development.

Since the initial release in 1993, the distributed object model OLE has evolved for several generations. OLE was extended into "Network OLE" and then to COM (Component Object Model) in 1993, which is supported by MacOS, Unix, and Windows systems, but is primarily used with Microsoft Windows. In Windows 2000, significant extensions were made to COM and it was renamed COM+, before it evolved into DCOM.

Another extension of OLE is the ADO (ActiveX Data Object Model), which provides a layer between programming languages and OLE DB, presenting a means of language-independent accessing to databases. ADO allows a developer to write programs that access data without knowing how the database is implemented.

All technologies in DCOM and ADO have been integrated into or replaced by Visual Studio .NET, which is an all-in-one object-oriented, distributed, and service-oriented software development environment. ADO .Net replaces ADO and improves it in several significant ways. Table 10.1 compares the features of ADO and ADO .Net.

To access a database object in ADO, we instantiate a connection object, from which we then call its open method and pass in a connection string. Then, the object can be accessed through different methods in the object. Until the close method is called, the connection will remain active and the object is locked. In ADO .NET the same principles apply. However, we instantiate a SqlConnection object in the System.Data.SqlClient namespace, which means the command is submitted to a database as a query. Such a query is message-based and does not lock the database object.

ADO .Net supports a more generic data structure than ADO. A DataSet in ADO .Net is similar to a 3-dimensional data collection, which allows you to access the data structure hierarchically, a slice of the structure, which is a table, a row or column of a table, and a single element in the row or column. ADO has fixed RecordSet, which is a table.

ADO uses binary mode for data transmission, whereas ADO .Net supports XML-based data transmission in text mode, which is critically important in today's business world. Due to the security consideration, few firewalls will allow binary data to travel freely between the clients and the servers.

Table 10.1. ADO versus ADO .Net

Features	ADO	ADO .Net
Connection model	Connection-oriented model: Client application needs to be always connected to the database while working on the data. This model is similar to TCP connection model.	Disconnected model: Client disconnects connection immediately after the data is accessed. Data will be stored in memory for client-side processing to achieve better performance. This model is similar to UPD model for message exchange.
Data representation	RecordSet containing a single table. Multiple record sets are not related.	Dataset containing multiple tables, which are structurally related.
Data accessing model	A RecordSet in the database can be accessed by one client at time	DataAdapter: Allow access from multiple sources.
Data exchange mode	RecordSet is transmitted in binary mode through COM marshaling, resulting in firewall problem.	XML and XSD schema types in text mode. Can flow through firewall via HTTP.
Language support	For each language, an implementation is needed.	Support all languages in .Net common language runtime.
XML support	Limited	XML is the native transfer medium for the objects.

The key components to interface an application or a service to the database are the data adapter and the data provider. Data adapters communicate directly with the database, and provide a database-independent interface to the data provider. The data provider offers connection and methods to read and write the database. Figure 10.9 shows an example using SQL database and the related library functions.

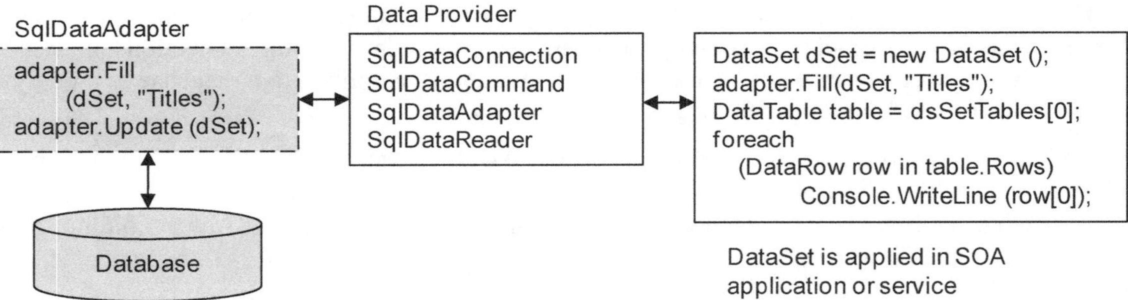

Figure 10.9. Data adapter and data provider interface FCL classes to the database

ADO .Net can access different databases through different classes in the .Net Framework Class Library (FCL). A namespace is dedicated to access a specific database, which includes a connection class, a command class, and an adapter class, as shown in Figure 10.10. The native database for .Net to access is SQL database. All classes needed are managed in .Net FCL. For other databases, including Oracle, OLE, ODBC (Access), a converter consisting of data services outside .Net FCL is needed to interface the FCL classes with the databases.

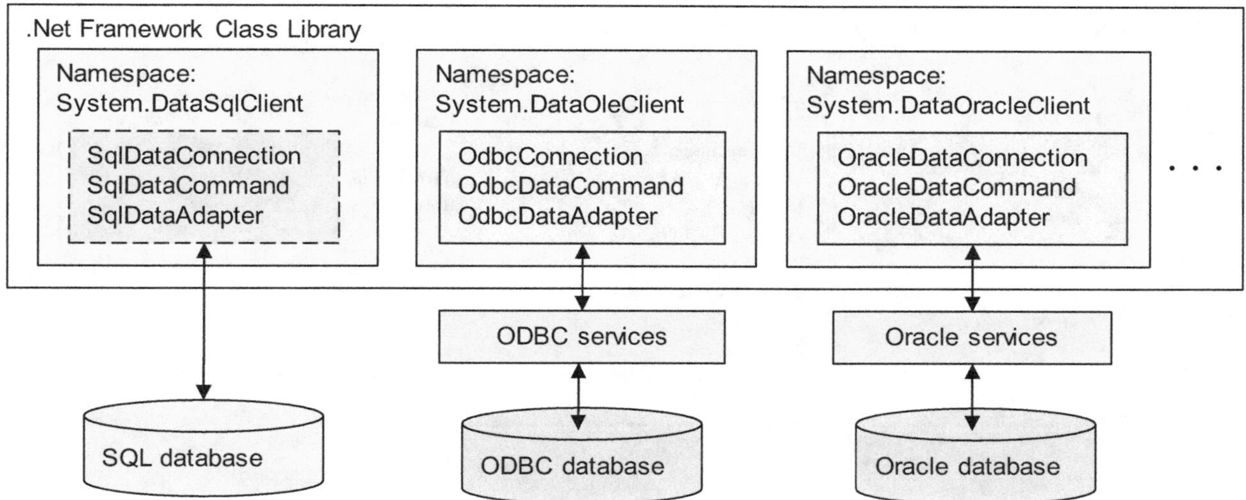

Figure 10.10. ADO .Net supports different databases

10.2.3 SQL Database in ADO .Net

In this section, we will use SQL database to demonstrate the use of ADO .Net. Interfaces to SQL databases are also available in ADO .Net, as shown in Figure 10.9.

Before starting to use an SQL database in your project, you need to install an SQL or SQL Express database on your computer. When you install SQL Express, do not use the default name; for example, SQLEXPRESS, which can lead to a connection string conflict when you deploy your application to a server, if the server used the default name to install its database. On the other hand, if you install your SQL Server Express using a different data source name, or you installed the full version of the SQL database, you need to modify the connection string in the <connectionStrings> element in the machine.config file, which is located in Visual Studio's Config directory; for example,
C:\Windows\Microsoft.NET\Framework\v4.0.30319\Config\machine.config,
where the <connectionStrings> of the machine.config file is shown as follows:

```
  <connectionStrings>
      <add name="LocalSqlServer" connectionString="data source=.\SQLEXPRESS;
Integrated Security=SSPI; AttachDBFilename=|DataDirectory|aspnetdb.mdf; User
Instance=true" providerName="System.Data.SqlClient"/>
  </connectionStrings>
```

After you have installed the database, you can create an SQL database in your application by following these steps:

1. Click the node in Solution Explorer to which you want to add the database file.
2. On the Project menu, click Add Existing Item.
3. The "Add Existing Item" dialog box appears, as shown in Figure 10.11. Visual Studio supports two types of databases: (1) Local database that is accessed through ADO .Net-SQL interface; (2) Service-based Database that is accessed through LINQ (Language Integrated Query). In this section, we will discuss the option (1), and will discuss option (2) in a later section.

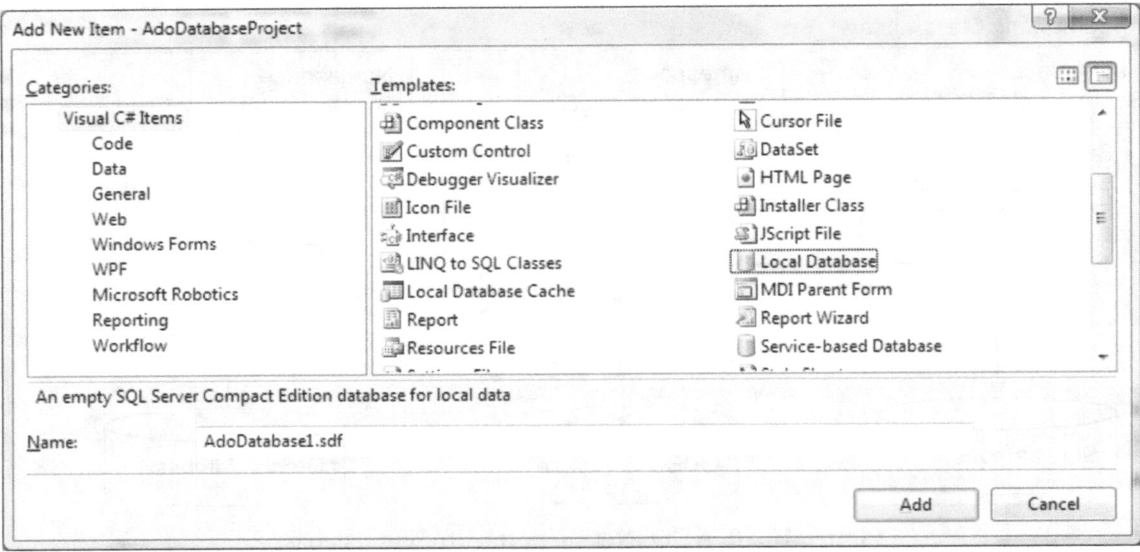

Figure 10.11. Add a database into an application

4. In File name, type the path and file name of the file that you want to add to the database project. Type the name AdoDatabse1.sdf.
5. Click Add. You will be notified that the database is new and empty, and you need to design and configure the database after you have clicked the Finish button.
6. The file is added to the database project, appearing as a child of the node to which you added it; for example, if you added the file to the Tables node, the file appears as a child of that node.
7. In Solution Explorer, click the newly added file.
8. On the View menu, click Properties Window, if the window is not already displayed. You can then see the properties and you can change the properties if necessary.

Once you have created a database item in your project, you can start to define the schema of your database by following the steps listed hereafter:

1. On the View menu, click Server Explorer, if the window is not already displayed.
2. You can see in the Server Explorer that the database AdoDatabase1 is created in the folder Data Connections.
3. Right-click the folder Table in your database. The table schema will appear, as shown in Figure 10.12. You can define the table name, column name, type, and length. You can also define if the null data is allowed, if the data must be unique, and it is the primary key.
4. Now, you can link the database to your project. On Data menu, choose Add New Data Source…
5. Choose Database and then click Next.
6. Choose your AdoDatabase1 and click Next.
7. Name your DataSet AdoDatabase1DataSet, and click Finish.

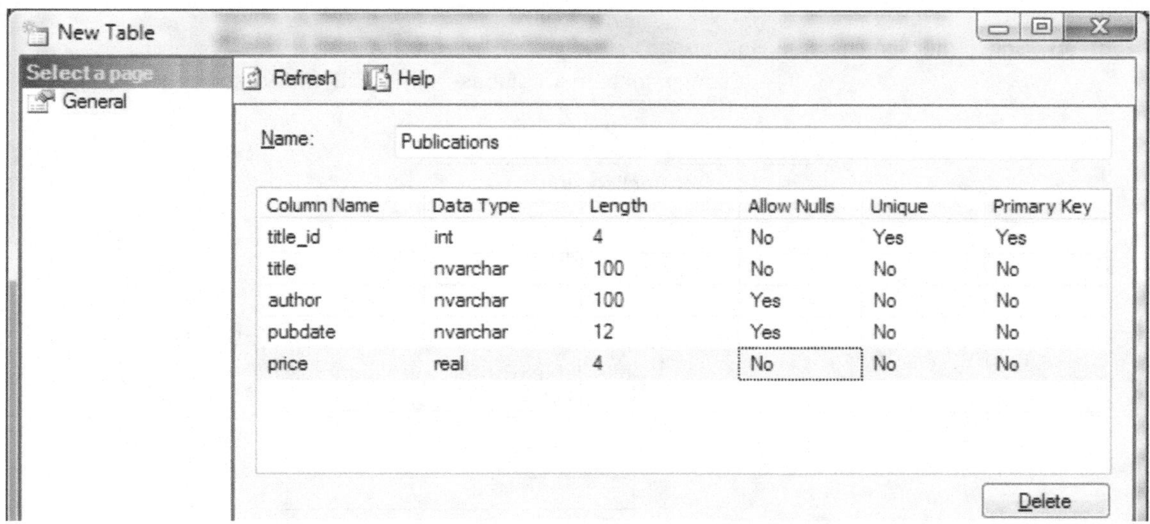

Column Name	Data Type	Length	Allow Nulls	Unique	Primary Key
title_id	int	4	No	Yes	Yes
title	nvarchar	100	No	No	No
author	nvarchar	100	Yes	No	No
pubdate	nvarchar	12	Yes	No	No
price	real	4	No	No	No

Figure 10.12. Add a database into an application

Now, you can use .Net menu commands and follow the Wizard to create a project that accesses the database:

1. File → New → Project …;
2. Choose C#;
3. Choose database project;
4. Name your project and decide the location of the project;
5. Choose SQL server;
6. Name your server.

Now, you can start to write C# program to read and write the SQL database. Similarly, accessing a disk file, where you need to open the file before reading and writing and then close the file thereafter, you need to follow these steps to access the database:

1. Use *SqlConnection* class to instantiate a connection variable cn;
2. Use cn.Open to bind the connection variable to the database;
3. Use *sqlCommand* class to instantiate a command variable;
4. Initialize the command to tell what to do;
5. Associate the command with the connection variables;
6. Call the command variable's methods to perform different database operations; for example:
    a. Read data from the database;
    b. Delete data;
    c. Insert data.
7. Close the connection by calling the cn.Close method.

Figure 10.13 illustrates the first two steps in the process. We use the SqlConnection class in ADO .Net to instantiate a variable, which takes the SQL connection string and stores it in the variable data field. It also creates a point to the database.

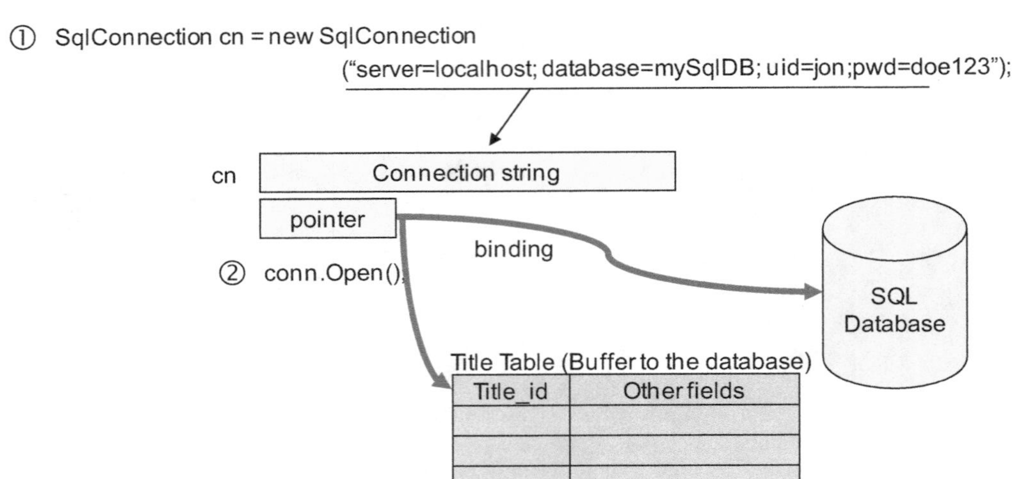

Figure 10.13. Creating a connection variable and opening a connection

Figure 10.14 illustrates steps 3, 4, and 5. Use sqlCommand class to instantiate a command variable, cm, and passing a string "delete from titles where title_id = 'PL4321'" as the operation of the command. Then, we assign the connection variable to the cm.Connection to associate the command variable with the connection variable.

In Net, you can also create a DataSet-based local database or a service-based database by following these steps:

Create a Windows Forms Application, name it myDBproject;

1. In the Solution Explorer, right-click the project name myDBproject, and select Add → New Item;
2. In the item list, you can choose the DataSet-based local database or a service-based database.

The code that follows shows all the aforesaid steps:

```
SqlConnection cn = new SqlConnection
        ("server=localhost; database=mySqlDB; uid=jon; pwd=doe123");
try {
   cn.Open();
   SqlCommand cm = new SqlCornmand();
   cm.CommandText = "delete from titles where title_id = 'PL4321'";
   cm.Connection = cn;
   cm.ExecuteNonQuery(); // Execute the command without a return value
}
catch (SqlException ex) {
   Console.WriteLine(ex.Message);
}
finally {
        cn.Close ();
}
```

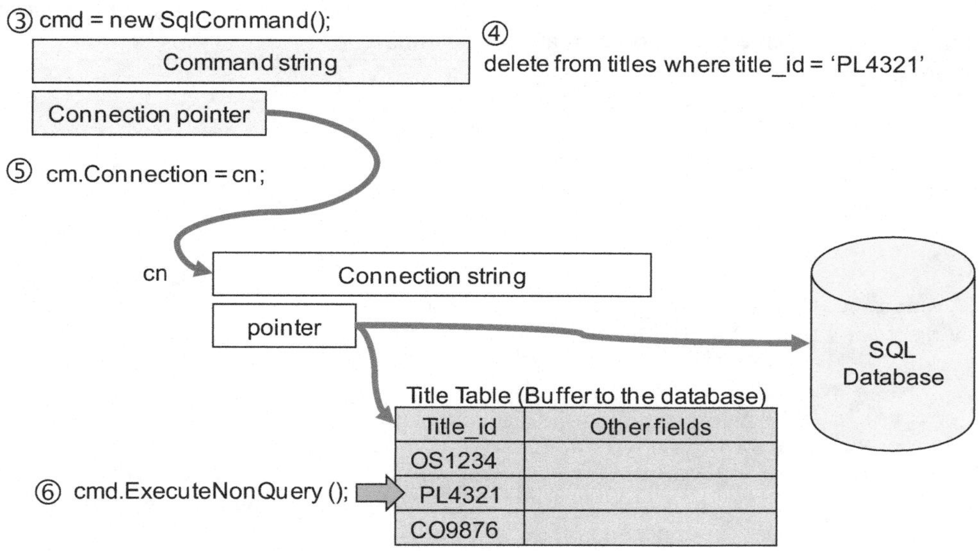

Figure 10.14. Sending a command string to the database

The code above deletes a data entry from the database. To insert a data entry into the database, the same process can be applied, except passing a different SQL string to the command variables cm:

```
SqlCommand cm = new SqlCommand
   ("insert into titles (title_id, title, type, pubdate)" + "values
   ('JP1001' , 'Programming in SOA', " + "'business', May 2008')", conn);
```

The two examples execute the SQL command using ExecuteNonQuery() method, because both commands do not return a value from the data. The database accesses that retrieve information from the data and receive return values are called queries. If the query returns a scalar type of value, we can use the command ExecuteNonScalar() method, as shown in the code that follows:

```
static public int AddProductCategory(string newName, string cnStr){
    Int32 newProdID = 0;
    string cmStr =
        "INSERT INTO Production.ProductCategory (Name) VALUES (@Name); "
        + "SELECT CAST(scope_identity() AS int)";
    using (SqlConnection cn = new SqlConnection(cnStr)) {
        SqlCommand cm = new SqlCommand(cmStr, cn);
        cm.Parameters.Add("@Name", SqlDbType.VarChar);
        cm.Parameters["@name"].Value = newName;
        try {
            cn.Open();
            newProdID = (Int32)cm.ExecuteScalar();
        }
        catch (Exception ex) {
            Console.WriteLine(ex.Message);
        }
    }
    return (int)newProdID;
}
```

As mentioned in Chapter 6, it is not manageable to use the Web.config file to store a large number of usernames and passwords. A database has to be used if the account number is large. The following code shows how a username and password can be authenticated using the SQL ExecuteScalar() command, if the usernames and passwords have been stored in an SQL database.

```
void myLogIn (Object sender, EventArgs e) {
   if (myAuthentication (UserName.Text, Password.Text))
       FormsAuthentication.RedirectFromLoginPage
                  (UserName.Text, Persistent.Checked);
      else
          Output.Text = "Invalid login name or password";
}

bool myAuthentication(string username, string password) {
   SqlConnection cn = new SqlConnection
                  ("server=localhost; database=mySqlDB; uid=jon; pwd=doe123");
   try {
       cn.Open ();
       StringBuilder builder = new StringBuilder ();
       builder.Append ("select count (*) from users " +
                                        "where username = \' ");
       builder.Append (username);
       builder.Append ("\' and cast (rtrim (password) as " +
                                        "varbinary) = cast (\' ");
       builder.Append (password);
       builder.Append ("\' as varbinary)");
       SqlCommand cm = new SqlCommand(builder.ToString(), cn);
       int count = (int) cm.ExecuteScalar ();
       return (count > 0);
   }
   catch (SqlException) { return false; }
   finally {
       cn.Close();
   }
}
```

In this program, the method takes the username and password from the user, puts them in the format of the SQL query string, then it uses the string to query the data and check if the username and password exist in the database. If they exist, the authentication is successful. Otherwise, the access will be denied. Notice that the username and password never need to be retrieved from the database, which is a secure way of accessing usernames and passwords.

In many cases, a database returns a complex structure of data. In this case, we need a reader method to extract data piece by piece.

The ExecuteReader method in SqlCommand class reads one node at a time in a stream. It returns an SqlDataReader object. Then, the DataReader object has methods that allow one to iterate over the result set, which is forward-only and read-only, which is similar to the XmlTextReader discussed in Chapter 4. Each call to DataReader.Read() returns one row of the result set.

The following code shows an example of using the ExecuteReader method, which reads a node from the database, and then prints each element of the node.

```
private static void CreateCommand(string cmStr, string cnStr) {
    using (SqlConnection cn = new SqlConnection(cnStr)){
        cn.Open();
        SqlCommand command = new SqlCommand(cmStr, cn);
        SqlDataReader reader = command.ExecuteReader();
        while (reader.Read()){
            Console.WriteLine(String.Format("{0}", reader[0]));
        }
```

```
    }
}
```

10.2.4 DataAdapter and DataSet in ADO .Net

As we discussed in Chapter 4, XmlDocument class creates an in-memory XML tree of an XML file. DataSet class creates an in-memory structure of a relational database for complex operations. The structure is not a tree, but an array of tables. Each table consists of an array of rows or an array of columns. In turn, each row or each column consists of an array of elements. When you access a web service, very often, it returns a DataSet object.

In order for DataSet to be device (database) independent, a DataAdapter class is used to link a DataSet to the database. For different types of database, different DataAdapters have to be created. Figure 10.15 illustrates a DataSet, DataAdapter, and database.

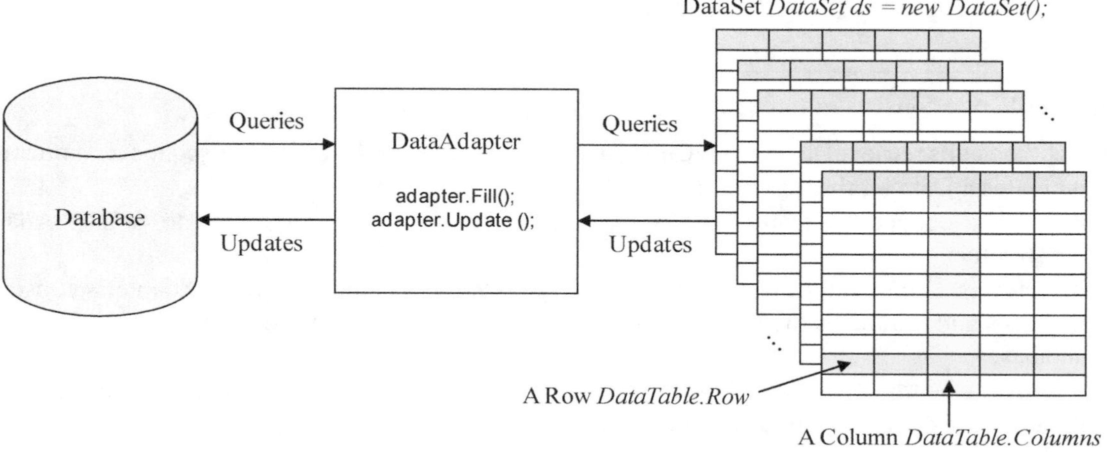

Figure 10.15. DataAdapter and DataSet

The following method shows how to read a data set from an SQL database. The method takes four parameters: a DataSet reference, the connection string specifying the database, a command string specifying the command to be executed, and a string that specifies a row in the database to be selected.

```
using System.Data.SqlClient;
using System.Data;
class myProgram {
   static public DataSet retrieveDataSet(string cmStr, string cnStr) {
         DataSet dSet = new DataSet();
         SqlConnection cn = new SqlConnection(cnStr);
         SqlDataAdapter adptr = new SqlDataAdapter();
         adptr.SelectCommand = new SqlCommand(cmStr, cn);
         adptr.Fill(dSet);
         return dSet;
   }
   static public void writeBack(DataSet dSet, string cmStr , string cnStr) {
         SqlConnection cn = new SqlConnection(cnStr);
         SqlDataAdapter adptr = new SqlDataAdapter();
         adptr.SelectCommand = new SqlCommand(cmStr, cn);
         adptr.Update(dSet);
   }
   static void Main(string[] args) {
```

```
        string myCnStr = "server=localhost; database=mySqlDB; uid=jon; pwd=doe123";
        string myCmStr = "select * from titles";
        string myRow = "titles";
        DataSet myDSet = retrieveDataSet(myCnStr, myCmStr);
        DataTable table = myDSet.Tables["titles"];
        DataRow row = table.NewRow();
        // Initialize the DataRow
        row["title_id"] = "JP1001";
        row["title"] = "PL1";
        row["price"] = "89.00";
        row["author"] = "Miller";
        row["pubdate"] = "2007";
        // Add the DataRow to the DataTable
        table.Rows.Add (row);
        myCmStr = "update * from titles";
        writeBack(myDSet, myCnStr);
    }
}
```

This snippet of code consists of three methods. What do they do?

First, the method calls retrieveDataSet(myCnStr, myCmStr) performs the following sequence of operations:

- It creates a DataSet that has not been shaped;
- It opens a connection to the database using the connection string passed to SqlDataAdapter's constructor;
- It performs a query on the database using the query string passed to SqlDataAdapter's constructor;
- It shapes and initializes the DataSet dSet with a schema that matches that of the "titles" item in the database;
- It retrieves all the records produced by the query and writes them to the DataSet dSet;
- It passes the dSet as the return value;
- It closes the connection to the database.

Then, in the Main method, the DataSet is passed to myDSet. Then, we can pick up one table, one row, and one element to access. We could modify the values of any elements. In the code, we add one row into the DataSet, and fill out the elements in given values. The modified DataSet stays in the memory. In order to update the database, we call the writeBack method, which does the following operations:

- It opens a connection to the database using the connection string passed to SqlDataAdapter's constructor;
- It associates the command with the connection variables;
- It updates the database.

It makes more sense to retrieve an entire DataSet from the database and then write back the DataSet, if we want to read, write, and modify multiple data items. We can also access individual data items in the database. The following example from MSDN shows how to use the SqlDataAdapter class and its methods to directly insert, delete, and update data items in an SQL database.

```
public static void CreateSqlDataAdapter()
{
    SqlDataAdapter custDA = new SqlDataAdapter("SELECT CustomerID,
             CompanyName FROM Customers", "Data Source=localhost;
             Integrated Security=SSPI;Initial Catalog=northwind");
    SqlConnection custConn = custDA.SelectCommand.Connection;
    custDA.MissingSchemaAction = MissingSchemaAction.AddWithKey;
    custDA.InsertCommand = new SqlCommand("INSERT INTO Customers
             (CustomerID, CompanyName) " +
             "VALUES (@CustomerID, @CompanyName)", custConn);
```

```
    custDA.UpdateCommand = new SqlCommand("UPDATE Customers SET CustomerID =
            @CustomerID, CompanyName = @CompanyName " + "WHERE CustomerID =
            @oldCustomerID", custConn);
    custDA.DeleteCommand = new SqlCommand(
            "DELETE FROM Customers WHERE CustomerID = @CustomerID", custConn);
    custDA.InsertCommand.Parameters.Add(
            "@CustomerID", SqlDbType.Char, 5, "CustomerID");
    custDA.InsertCommand.Parameters.Add(
            "@CompanyName", SqlDbType.VarChar, 40, "CompanyName");
    custDA.UpdateCommand.Parameters.Add(
            "@CustomerID", SqlDbType.Char, 5, "CustomerID");
    custDA.UpdateCommand.Parameters.Add(
            "@CompanyName", SqlDbType.VarChar, 40, "CompanyName");
    custDA.UpdateCommand.Parameters.Add("@oldCustomerID", SqlDbType.Char, 5,
"CustomerID").SourceVersion = DataRowVersion.Original;

    custDA.DeleteCommand.Parameters.Add("@CustomerID", SqlDbType.Char, 5,
"CustomerID").SourceVersion = DataRowVersion.Original;
}
```

For integrating SQL database into MVC application, you can follow the Microsoft tutorial at:

https://docs.microsoft.com/en-us/aspnet/core/tutorials/first-mvc-app/working-with-sql?view=aspnetcore-3.1&tabs=visual-studio

10.3 LINQ, Language Integrated Query

Language Integrated Query (LINQ) is a declarative, strongly-typed programming language, which is based on functional programming paradigm and lambda expressions. This section briefly discusses LINQ and uses the language to manage and to query different sources. Both development process and working programs will be given in this section.

10.3.1 What Is the Purpose of LINQ?

LINQ is a uniform programming model for different kinds of data entities, including ADO .Net data entities, XML nodes, and relational database records. The main idea of LINQ is to define a set of standard language constructs that can be included in different object-oriented programming languages, so that these languages will only deal with LINQ and a set of uniform in-memory data objects. LINQ implementation will deal with different data sources, as shown in Figure 10.16. From the programmers' point of view, they learn to write LINQ programs to access in-memory objects. The same program can access ADO data entities, SQL data records, and XML files. Without LINQ, developers would have to write completely different programs in different programming languages to access different data sources. LINQ can be plugged into different object-oriented programming languages. Currently, it is available in C# and VB, but can be extended into other languages.

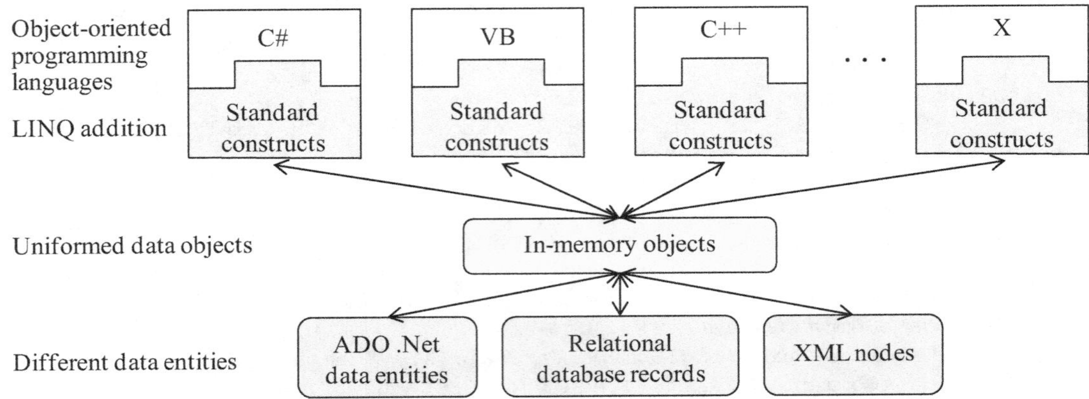

Figure 10.16. DataAdapter and DataSet

10.3.2 Lambda Expressions

LINQ is based on lambda expressions. As the preparation, we first briefly introduce the **lambda expressions** (λ-expressions).

The structure of the λ-expression is short and simple. At the lexical level, there are only three lexical units: λ, the parentheses "("and")," as well as an infinite list of variables (names); for example, a, b, a1, a2, ..., and so on.

At the syntactic level, a λ–expression is a finite combination of lexical units and variables. Using the BNF notation, a simplified λ-expression can be defined by:

```
λ-expression ::=   <constant>     | <variable> | <expression>
                                  | λ<variable>(< λ-expression>)
                                  | (<λ-expression><λ-expression>)
```

In the definition, constant is a value of any data type. The definitions of the variable (identifier) and the expression have been discussed in Chapter 1. According to the definitions, the following expressions are λ-expressions.

```
5                  ; a constant is λ-expression
x                  ; a variable is λ-expression
x+y                ; an expression is λ-expression
λx(x+y)            ; λ<variable>(< λ-expression>) is λ-expression
λx(x+y) 5          ; (<λ-expression> <λ-expression>) is λ-expression
```

One of the aforesaid λ–expressions, λ`<variable><λ-expression>`, is called a λ-procedure or **λ-method** The variable prefixed by λ is called the parameter of the method and the λ–expression following the parameter is called the body of the method. The scope of the parameter is the body of the λ–method. For example, if we have a λ–expression:

```
λx(x+y) (x+3)
```

The scope of the parameter `x` in λ`x` is in, and only in, the body `(x+y)`. It does not cover the `x` in `(x+3)`.

An occurrence of a variable `x` in a λ–expression is bound if it is within the scope of a parameter in λ`x`. An occurrence of a variable `x` in a λ–expression is free, if it is not within the scope of a parameter in λ`x`. An occurrence of a parameter `x` binds all free occurrences of `x` within its scope.

Given the following λ–expression,

```
λx(+ (/ λx(* x 2) 8 λx(- x 1) 5) (* λx(+ x 2) 3 x) ) 7
```

how many λ–methods are contained in the λ–expression? What are the scopes of different parameters?

Each λx corresponds to a λ–method, and, thus, the λ–expression contains four λ–methods. The scope of each parameter is underlined in the following expression:

```
λx(+ (/ λx(* x 2) 8λx(- x 1) 5) (* λx(+ x 2) 3x) ) 7
```

In the next subsection, we will discuss reduction rules that evaluate such complex expressions to a simple value or the return value of the expression.

There are functional programming languages that directly implement the lambda expressions; for example, Scheme and LISP. In these languages, a λ-expression can be translated into a programming language expressions directly. Let us consider the λ-expression:

```
λx(+ (/ λx(* x 2) 8 λx(- x 1) 5) (* λx(+ x 2) 3 x)) 7
```

To write a Scheme method that is equivalent to the expression, all we need to do is to use the Scheme keyword "lambda" to replace "λ"and add necessary parentheses. Thus, we have:

```
lambda x(+(/lambda x(* x 2) 8 lambda x(- x 1) 5)(* lambda x(+ x 2) 3 x))7
```

After adding necessary parentheses, we have an executable Scheme method that evaluates to 39:

```
((lambda (x)
   (+   (/     ((lambda (x)(* x 2)) 8)
               ((lambda (x)(- x 1)) 5))
        (*     ((lambda (x)(+ x 2)) 3) x)
   )
 )
 7
)
```

There are four methods in the foregoing code. None of them is given a name. Such methods are called **anonymous methods**.

The aforesaid program can be written using named methods too. A **named method** in a Scheme is defined by using the keyword "define" to associate an anonymous method to a name. Using named methods, we can rewrite the executable Scheme code as follows:

```
(define foo1 (lambda (x)(* x 2)))
(define foo2 (lambda (x)(- x 1)))
(define foo3 (lambda (x)(+ x 2)))
(define bar (lambda (x)
   (+    (/ (foo1 8) (foo2 5))
         (* (foo3 3) x))
))
(bar 7)
```

Lambda expressions support the higher-order function. A **higher-order function** is a function that takes the operation of another function (not the return value) as an argument. All functional programming languages support higher-order functions. There are different higher-order functions; for example:

- **Mapping**: Apply the same operation defined by another method to all members of a list.
- **Filtering**: Remove members of a list that do not satisfy a predicate defined by another method.
- **Projection**: Select a part of the data from the source list, resulting in a return data with less or different information.

The code that follows shows the higher-order mapping function defined by two functions. The first function encrypts a character by adding a number to its ASCII code. The second function takes the first function as the first parameter and a string as the second parameter.

```
(define cipher (lambda (ch)
   (integer->char (+ (char->integer ch) 5))      ; key = 5
))
(define string-encryption (lambda (func str)
   (list->string (map func (string->list str)))
))
```

When we call the second function and using the first function, cipher, as a parameter,

> (string-encryption cipher "Hello World"), the function will be applied to each element of the list. The return value is: "Mjqqt|%\\twqi."

Notice that the string is first converted to list in order to use the higher-order map function. The returned list is converted back string.

A filtering function or a **filter** is a higher-order function similar to a mapping function. It applies another method to all members of the list:

```
(filter method-name list-parameter)
```

The difference is the method that is the parameter of the filter here is a **predicate** that returns a true or false value. If the predicate (method-name list-element) returns true, the element will be included in the list that is to be returned by the filter method. If the predicate (method-name list-element) returns false, the element will be excluded from the return list.

For example,

```
(filter (lambda (x) (> x 200)) '(50 300 500 65 800))
```

will return:

```
(300 500 800)
```

which is the sub list of the list in the filter method with all elements that are less than or equal to 200 removed. Similar to the mapping method, the predicate in the filter method can be defined separately:

```
(define largerthan200? (lambda (x) (> x 200)))
(filter largerthan200?'(50 300 500 65 800))
```

Lambda expressions are supported in C#. It has a slightly different syntax. The following program shows an example. Lambda expressions are used to define two functions, which calculate the absolute value and the cylinder volume, respectively.

```
class MyLambdaExpression {
   static void Main(string[] args) {
        Func<double, double> AbsoluteValue = (x) => x < 0 ? -x : x;
        Func<double, double, double> Cylinder = (r, h) => 3.14 * r * r * h;
        Console.WriteLine("The absolute value is: {0}", AbsoluteValue(-7));
        Console.WriteLine("The cylinder volume is: {0}",
                                             Cylinder(2, AbsoluteValue(-7)));
   }
}
```

Notice that AbsoluteValue function is placed as a parameter of the Cylinder function call. It shows the property of function as the first-class object. The output of the program is:

```
The absolute value is: 7
The cylinder volume is: 87.92
```

Lambda expressions are implemented in delegates. The following program is the delegate implementation of the previous lambda expression version. As you can see, lambda expressions are more compact than the delegate version.

```
class MyDelegateVersion  {
   static void Main(string[] args) {
```

```
    Func<double, double> AbsoluteValue = delegate(double x) {
        return x < 0 ? -x : x;
    };
    Func<double, double, double> Cylinder = delegate(double r, double h) {
        return 3.14 * r * r * h;
    };
    Console.WriteLine("The absolute value is: {0}", AbsoluteValue(-7));
    Console.WriteLine("The cylinder volume is: {0}", Cylinder(2, AbsoluteValue(-7)));
    }
}
```

LINQ queries are based on the lambda expressions. For example, consider the following query consisting of a number of clauses:

```
IEnumerable<string> query =
   from s in source          // extract
   where s.Length == 5       // filter
   orderby s
   select s.Title;           // project
```

The query is based on the following lambda expressions:

```
Func<string, string> extract = (s) => s;
Func<string, bool> filter = (s) => s.Length == 5;
Func<string, string> project = (s) => s.Title;
```

10.3.3 LINQ to Object

LINQ standard query operators allow queries to be applied to any IEnumerable<T>-based data objects in memory, where IEnumerable is an Interface class that can be implemented by different classes in .Net Framework. IEnumerable interface defines one method that returns an enumerator that can iterate through a collection. The type T is generic type that can take a type a parameter; for example, the type Int32, double, Book, Car, and so on.

Let us first examine a simple example of querying a collection of data:

```
using System;
using System.Linq;
using System.Collections.Generic;
namespace myLinqAppConsole {
    class Book {
        public Int32 bookid;
        public string title;
        public string isbn;
        public double price;
    }
    class program {
        static void Main() {
            Book[] Books = new Book[] {
                new Book {bookid = 1, title = "Programming",
                                isbn = "0-7575-0367", price = 69.99},
                new Book {bookid = 2, title = "DSOSD",
                                isbn = "0-7575-527-1", price = 79.99},
                new Book {bookid = 3, title = "OS",
                                isbn = "6-5432-123-0", price = 57.77},
                new Book {bookid = 4, title = "Computing",
                                isbn = "0-321-52403-9", price =94.91},
                new Book {bookid = 5, title = "XML",
                                isbn = "0-201-77168-3", price = 74.21},
            };
```

```
            IEnumerable<Book> myQuery =
                from b in Books
                where b.price < 80
                orderby b.title
                select b;
            foreach (Book item in myQuery)
                Console.WriteLine("Title = {0}, Price = {1}", item.title,
item.price);
        }
    }
}
```

The output list of the program is:

```
Title = DSOSD, Price = 79.99
Title = OS, Price = 57.77
Title = Programming, Price = 69.99
Title = XML, Price = 74.21
```

Carefully examining the foregoing code, we will notice that the part of the code generating myQuery list uses the filtering function of the lambda expression.

The clauses "from b in books" and "select b" define the input list (data source) and output list of the filtering function. The output list is often a projection of the input list. The clause "where b.price < 80" defines the predicate (filtering condition) for inclusion in the return list. Without the predicate, all elements in the input list will be included. The clause "orderby b.title" defines the order of the return list. There are other clauses, such as group, join, and let, which can be used to define the query.

Most query operators of LINQ are similar to those of SQL, including from, where, order by, join, and select. The group/by/into and the group join clauses are where LINQ differs from SQL:A SQL query always returns a rectangular dataset, while a LINQ query can return a set of hierarchical data, such as, a set of subsets, and an irregular set of data generated by a piece program code. The advanced LINQ query operations include:

- group/by key/into group, which groups the results based on a given key.
- join x in C1 on y equals criteria: an inner join produces a result set of pairs (x, y), where y meets the criteria. In each pair, the x comes from the first collection C1, and y comes from the second collection. If x in C1 has no matching elements in the second collection, it does not appear in the result set.
- join x in C1 on y equals criteria into group: a group join generates joint groups, instead of pairs.

The example that follows (http://msdn.microsoft.com/en-us/vcsharp/aa336754.aspx) shows the application of "group/by key/into group" query.

```
static void Main() {
   int[] numbers = { 5, 4, 1, 3, 9, 8, 6, 7, 2, 0, 11 };
   var numberGroups =
        from n in numbers
        group n by n % 5 into g
        select new { Remainder = g.Key, Numbers = g };
        foreach (var g in numberGroups) {
             Console.WriteLine("Numbers with a remainder of {0} when divided by 5:",
g.Remainder);
             foreach (var n in g.Numbers) {
                  Console.WriteLine(n);
} }     }
```

Let us examine the query part of the code. The keyword **group** initiates an operation to create groups (subsets). It takes an element n from the data source. The keyword **by** defines the key (criterion) for grouping. Then, the keyword **into** adds the element n into the group identified by the key. As the result, the object containing the key and the group is created and selected (added) into the super set numberGroups. The output of the program is:

```
Numbers with a remainder of 0 when divided by 5:
5
0
Numbers with a remainder of 4 when divided by 5:
4
9
Numbers with a remainder of 1 when divided by 5:
1
6
11
Numbers with a remainder of 3 when divided by 5:
3
8
Numbers with a remainder of 2 when divided by 5:
7
2
```

Note that, implicit type var is used, which allows the compiler to determine the type of the object based on the values assigned to the variable.

10.3.4 LINQ to SQL

In order to access the table of columns and rows in SQL, we need to map the database table to an object, with its columns and rows to the members of the object. We could take the approach that is similar to the Adapter in ADO .Net. We use a function to map a DataSet object to a database table. LINQ uses the following mapping function to make the association between the table and an in-memory object. The key is to add the attribute that links the object name to the table's columns: [Table(Name="myBooks")]

```
using System.Data.Linq.Mapping;
[Table(Name="myBooks")] //attribute links an object to the table's columns
public class Program
{
   [column] public int bookid;
   [column] public string title;
   [column] public string isbn;
   [column] public double price;
}
// DataContext class takes a connection string
DataContext db = new DataContext("c:\\CSE446\\myBookClasses.mdf");
// Associate the decorated object to DB table
Table<myBooks> myBooks = db.GetTable<myBooks>();
// Now, perform the query on the object
var queryResult =
        from b in myBooks
        where b.title == "Programming Languages"
        select b;
foreach (var book in queryResult)
Console.WriteLine("Book ID = {0}, Title = {1}", b.bookid, b.title);
```

Once this association is defined, we can use the SQL connection string to open and connect the object SQL database.

We can use this ADO .Net method to build the association. But LINQ to SQL offers an easier way to build the association and connect to the database. We can use a design time tool to make the association and data connection in a graphic way: we add an object from "LINQ to SQL Classes," and we add "SQL Server Database" into our project. Then, we drag the LINQ to SQL Classes object to the SQL Server Database. The two jobs are done. Furthermore, as a runtime infrastructure, LINQ to SQL tracks the changes between the object and the database table and performs the necessary updates to the database.

Following is the process to create a project and to access SQL data through LINQ to SQL. We can use a console project, a Windows Forms project, or a website project to manage and query a database. We will use the more complex form, the website project to illustrate the process in the following steps:

1. Start a new website project, and name the project LinqToDbApp.
2. Right-click the project name in the Solution Explorer, and select "Add New Item… ."
3. In the dialog box, choose "SQL Server Database," and name your database; for example, myBookDb.mdf. This will create a SQL database in your App_Data folder.
4. Right-click the project name in the Solution Explorer again, and select "Add New Item… ."
5. In the dialog box, choose "LINQ to SQL Classes," and name your classes; for example, myBookClasses.dbml. This will create interface classes in your App_Code folder.
6. Now, you can select menu: View → Server Explorer to see your database in the Data Connections.
7. Expand the myBookDb.mdf; and expand Database Diagrams.
8. Right-click "Tables" and select Add New Table.
9. A table definition form will be opened for you to add the columns of your table. Figure 10.17 shows the table after four columns of a book's attributes are added.

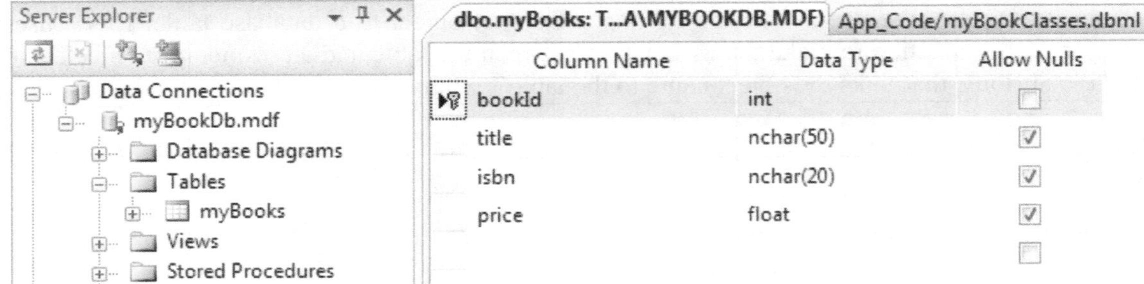

Figure 10.17. Defining a table in database

10. Right-click the arrow next to the column bookId; we set this attribute to be the Primary Key.
11. Select bookId column and find the Column Property: expand the attribute Identity Specification, and assign the (Is Identity) value to Yes. It should show Identify Increment value = 1 and Identity Seed value = 1.
12. Save your table and name it; for example, myBooks.
13. In the Server Explorer, you should see your table, myBook. Obviously, you can add multiple tables into the database following the aforementioned steps.
14. Right-click myBook and select Show Table Data. You will have an empty table. You can manually enter table data here, or write a program to write data into the table.

Note that in order to create the table and database, you need to have the SQL Server Data Tools installed on your computer. If you did not install, you can follow these steps to install:

- Download SQL Server Data Tools from: https://msdn.microsoft.com/en-us/library/mt204009.aspx
- Run the installer, select MODIFY, and check SQL Server Data Tools option to install the tools.

The SQL Server Data Tools download site also includes the tutorial for creating SQL databases.

Now, we will write a program to write data into the database table. Before we start to write the program, let us link the database table into the programming environment.

In the solution explorer, expand App_Code, and double click myBookClasses.dbml, and a blank area will be opened.

Drag and drop myBook table in the Server Explorer into the blank area of myBookClasses.dbml, as shown in Figure 10.18. This step will associate the in-memory object in the project with the database table, so that the table can be accessed in the program in the same way as the object is accessed.

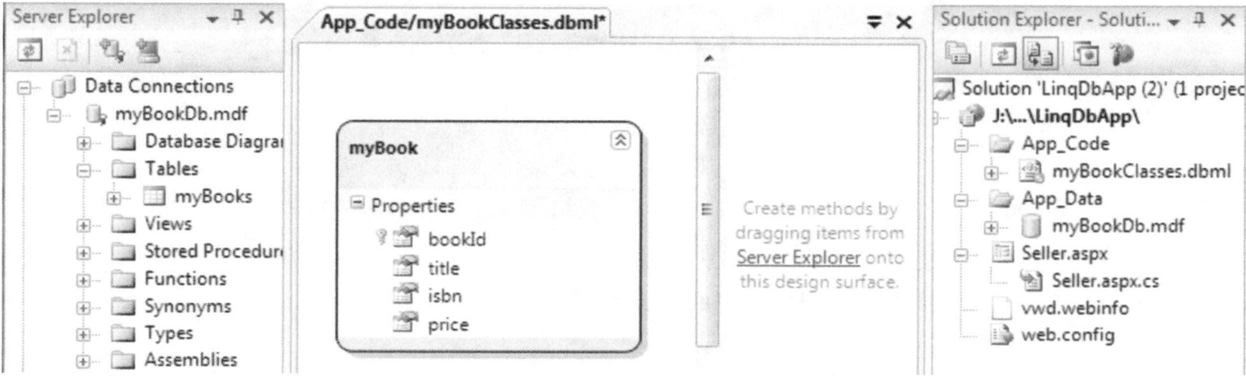

Figure 10.18. Link myBook table to myBookClasses

The rest of the code development will be similar to what we have done before. Figure 10.119 shows the GUI design of the page seller.aspx.

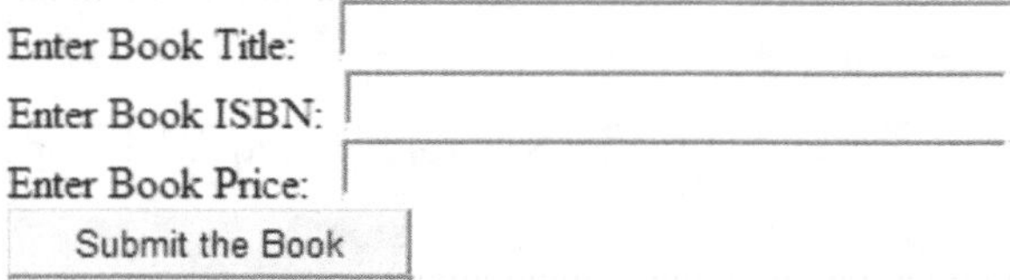

Figure 10.19. Data entered from the GUI will be written into myBook

The code behind the page is given as follows:

```
using System.Linq;
using System.Web;
using System.Web.Security;
using System.Web.UI;
using System.Web.UI.HtmlControls;
using System.Web.UI.WebControls;
using System.Web.UI.WebControls.WebParts;
using System.Xml.Linq;
public partial class _Default : System.Web.UI.Page {
    protected void Page_Load(object sender, EventArgs e) { }
    protected void Button1_Click(object sender, EventArgs e) {
        myBookClassesDataContext myDB = new myBookClassesDataContext();
```

```
        // The class above is one of the classes in myBookClasses
        myBook pubs = new myBook(); // create an in-memory instance
        pubs.title = TextBox1.Text; // read data into the instance
        pubs.isbn = TextBox2.Text;
        pubs.price = Convert.ToDouble(TextBox3.Text);
        myDB.myBooks.InsertOnSubmit(pubs);   // insert changes into instance
        myDB.SubmitChanges();    // submit changes into database
    }
}
```

Now, run the program, the data entered from the GUI in Figure 10.19 will be saved into the table myBook, one row at a time. Figure 10.20 shows the table's data after three entries. During testing, your Visual Studio may have locked the database, causing a database access error. In this case, you may need to refresh your database, reset your application, or even exit your application into for the web application to write the database.

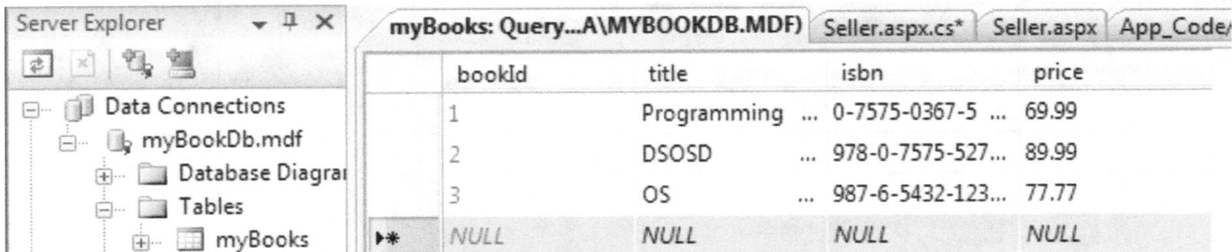

Figure 10.20. Table data after three data entries

If you are developing a console application or a Windows Forms application, you should not experience database access problems. However, if you are developing a website application, and you are accessing databases in the application domain from the Internet, you will need to deal with the authentication issue. You need to ask your server administrator to give you a username and password for accessing the SQL database. We will show here briefly how you can set up the access permission in IIS, if you have the full access privilege to the IIS.

1. Open IIS administrative tool.
2. Locate the application in IIS Default Web Site folder LinqToDbApp.
3. Right-click LinqToDbApp and select Edit Permission....
4. Select "Security" tag.
5. Click Edit button and then click Add button.
6. Now you can add users. For a user added, you need give the user full access permission in order for the user to access the database.
7. You can also add a user called ANONYMOUS LOGON and give the user full access permission. In this case, you can access the database without using username and password. Obviously, you must remove the user after you have tested your program. Note that this access applies to this application only. It does not give Internet users anonymous access to other applications in your IIS.

10.3.5 LINQ to XML

LINQ to XML is similar to the same idea of the DOM model we discussed in Chapter 4. We load the entire XML into the memory and process the data as objects. However, LINQ to XML provides a set of easier to use library classes that follows the functional programming paradigm as we discussed in the section of LINQ to Object. Figure 10.21 shows the LINQ to XML classes and their inheritance hierarchy.

In the DOM model, XMLNode is the root in the class hierarchy, while XMLDocument is inherited from XMLNode. In the LINQ to XML hierarchy, another layer is defined above the XNote. XObject is the root or base class of all LINQ to XML classes, similar to the idea of both C# and Java: object class is the root class of all classes. The classes XDocument and XElements are at the deepest leaf level of the tree, and thus they have most useful methods, as they have inherited all the properties and methods from their ancestor classes.

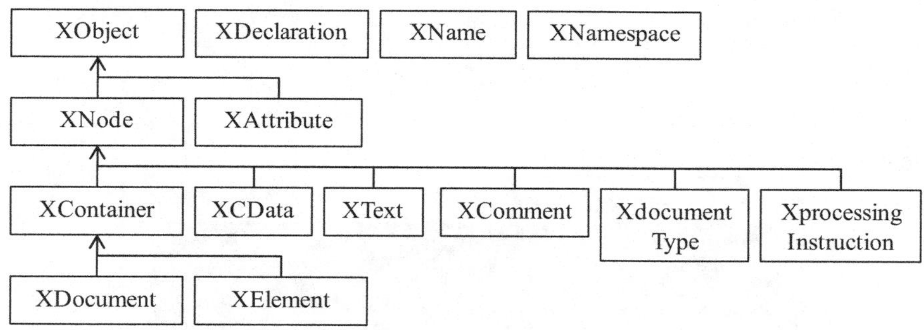

Figure 10.21. Class inheritance hierarchy of LINQ to XML classes

In Chapter 4, we discussed reading, writing, and processing XML data. In this section, we use LINQ to XML classes to do the same. We start with writing (creating) the XML file.

```
<?xml version="1.0"?>
<Courses>
  <Course Code="CSE446">
        <Name>Software Integration and Engineering</Name>
        <Room Image="layout270.jpeg">BYAC270</Room>
        <Cap>50</Cap>
  </Course>
  <Course Code="CSE240">
        <Name>Programming Languages</Name>
        <Room Image="layout110.jpeg">BYAC110</Room>
        <Cap>80</Cap>
  </Course></Courses>
```

The code that follows shows how to use some of the LINQ to XLM classes to generate an XML document above.

```
using System;
using System.Linq;
using System.Xml.Linq;
namespace myLinqAppConsole {
   class program {
       static void Main() {
           XElement courses =    // Create an in-memory XML structure
               new XElement("Courses",
                   new XElement("Course", new XAttribute("Code", "CSE446"),
                       new XElement("Name", "Software Integration and Engineering"),
                       new XElement("Room",
                           new XAttribute("Image", "layout270.jpeg")),
                       new XElement("Cap", "40")
                   ),
                   new XElement("Course", new XAttribute("Code", "CSE240"),
```

```
                    new XElement("Name", "Programming Languages"),
                    new XElement("Room",
                        new XAttribute("Image", "layout110.jpeg")),
                    new XElement("Cap", "80")
            )  );
    // This part of code searches for a piece of data in the structure
    // using a foreach loop, which traverse through the entire file
            foreach (XElement p in courses.Elements("Course")) {
                if ((string)p.Attribute("Code") == "CSE446") {
                    Console.Write("The Searched Course is: {0}\n", p);
                    Console.Write("The Course Code Attribute is: {0}\n",
p.Attribute("Code"));
                    Console.Write("The Next Course is: {0}\n", p.NextNode);
} }  }  }  }
```

The output of the code is:

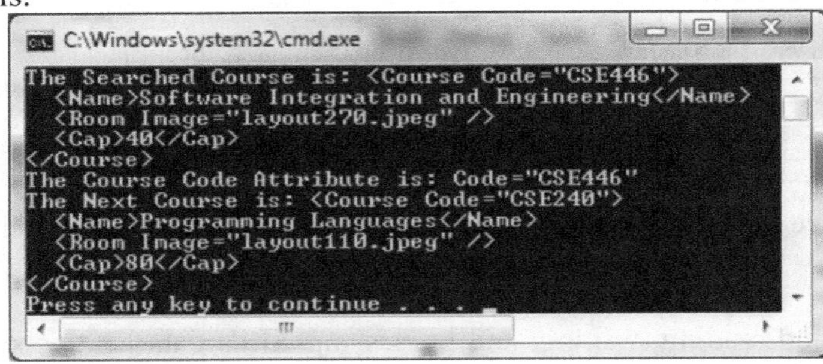

We can use XElement.Parse to convert a string of XML text into an in-memory structure. We start with a simple example. Assume that we make a RESTful call:

http://neptune.fulton.ad.asu.edu/WSRepository/Services/RandomString/Service.svc/GetRandomString/12

It call generates a strong password, and it returns the password in an XML string:

<string xmlns="http://schemas.microsoft.com/2003/10/Serialization/">b=5D7R{dA@w4</string>

To extract the password value, we can use the following simple code:

```
XDocument xd= XDocument.Parse(spassword); // Covert string into XML document
   XElement xe = xd.Root;          // Extract the root document
   textBlock1.Text = xe.Value;     // Console.WriteLine(xe.Value);
```

We can also directly use XElement without going through XDocument. The code is given as follows:

```
XElement xe = XElement.Parse(spassword);
   textBlock1.Text = xe.Value;     // Console.WriteLine (xe.Value);
```

Now, we demonstrate a more complex example using the following piece of code:

```
XElement courses = XElement.Parse(
    @"<Courses>
        <Course Code = "CSE446">
            <Name>Software Integration and Engineering</Name>
            <Room Image="layout270.jpeg">BYAC270</Room>
            <Cap>50</Cap>
        </Course>
        <Course Code = "CSE240">
            <Name>Programming Languages</Name>
            <Room Image="layout240.jpeg">BYAC240</Room>
            <Cap>40</Cap>
        </Course>
```

```
</Courses>");
```

To a new node into an existing XMK structure, we can use Add() method.

```
courses.Add( new XElement("Course", new XAttribute("Code", "CSE310"),
                new XElement("Name", "Data Structures and Algorithms"),
                new XElement("Room",
                    new XAttribute("Image", "layout150.jpeg")),
                new XElement("Cap", "60")
          )
```

If the XML file Courses.xml is saved and placed in the bin/Debug folder of the application, we can load the file into a variable and then query the variable. We can use the LINQ syntax **from**, **where**, and **select** to pick the exact element we want to and print the element.

```
using System;
using System.Linq;
using System.Xml.Linq;
using System.Collections.Generic;
namespace myLinqAppConsole {
    class program {
        static void Main() {
            XElement myCourses = XElement.Load("Courses.xml");
            IEnumerable<XElement> course =
                from c in myCourses.Elements("Course")
                where (string)c.Attribute("Code") == "CSE446"
                select c;
            foreach (XElement c in course)
                Console.WriteLine(c);
        }
    }
}
```

The output of executing the code above is as follows, where only the course with Code =="CSE445" is selected and printed.

```
<Course Code="CSE446">
   <Name> Software Integration and Engineering</Name>
   <Level>Senior</Level>
   <Cap>40</Cap>
</Course>
```

10.3.6 GraphQL

XML documents a rooted tree, which is more complex than rectangular tables. However, there are more general and more complex data structure: graph. Graph is widely used for representing connected data, for example, the computer networks, traffic networks, maps, and social connections among people. XML processing functions cannot effectively process graph connected data.

GraphQL was developed by Facebook in 2012 and was open-sourced in 2015. GraphQL is best for querying data organized in graphs (https://www.graphql.com/). Since trees are special cases of graphs, XML data can also be processed by GraphQL. GraphQL defined APIs can be invoked via HTTP, and thus it provides a way for implementing RESTful services.

We consider a university's student data management system, which organizes students by schools, departments, and programs. How can we efficiently perform the following queries?

- Find the student names in dean's list in 2019.
- How many students finished degrees in 4 years?
- Which current student won the most prizes?

- Find the courses that an instructor teaches across all the schools in the university.

To answer these questions, we define GraphQL data types, APIs, and program that calls the APIs. We will use the last question as an example.

First, we define GraphQL API schema (type), which describes the data structures of the data sources.

```
type Instructor {
   Id: String
   firstName: String
   lastName: String
   courses: [Course]
}
type Course {
   courseCode: String
   name: String
   instructor: Instructor
   enrollment: Int
}
type Query {
   courses: [Course]
   instructor(id: ID): Instructor
```

Then, we define an API that uses the API schema defined above to query the data sources. The query uses instructor id to find the last name of the instructor and the courses that the instructor teaches. The API can be implemented at the backend, which is submitted as a query to retrieve the related data from the database.

```
query CoursesByInstructor
   instructor(id: "1234567") {
        lastName
        courses(
              name
              enrollment
        }
   }
}
```

Next, we can call the API from the client side via HTTP. We pass the instructor id into the query API defined above, and the query will be translated into RESTful service call in a URL with parameters encoded. The query will return the instructor's lastName and all the courses the instructor teaches.

```
export default graphql(gql`
  query {
    instructor(id: "2345678" {
      lastName
    }
  }
`)(UrlApp);
function UrlApp({ data: { actions } }) {
  return (
    <ul>
      { actions.map(({ id, courses }) => (<li key={id}>{courses}</li>))}
    </ul>
  );
}
```

Like LINQ, GraphQL is not a standalone programming language. It offers a set of constructs that can be plugged into (through libraries) other programming languages, for example:

- C# and other .Net languages
- Java

- Clojure
- Elixir
- Erlang
- Go
- Groovy
- JavaScript
- PHP
- Python
- Scala
- Ruby

Using Java as an example, the following is a list of GraphQL libraries for Java:

```
import graphql.GraphQL;
import graphql.ExecutionResult;
import graphql.schema.GraphQLSchema;
import graphql.schema.StaticDataFetcher;
import graphql.schema.idl.RuntimeWiring;
import graphql.schema.idl.SchemaGenerator;
import graphql.schema.idl.SchemaParser;
import graphql.schema.idl.TypeDefinitionRegistry;
import static graphql.schema.idl.RuntimeWiring.newRuntimeWiring;
```

10.4 XML-Based Database and Query Language XQuery

The relational databases store data in homogenous tables, rows, and columns. In SOC, there are many data files in XML format, which is hierarchical and heterogeneous in structure. The goals of developing an XML-database query language are:

- Expressivity: The language must be powerful in expressivity, so that the complex queries can be expressed in the language;
- Simplicity: It is always an important issue to be able to express the queries in the easiest way for the users. A query language is often used by people with limited programming experiences;
- Efficiency: A query language deals with a database, which is often large and is stored on secondary storage such as a disk. It is essential that the language can be efficiently executed by hardware that manages the database, and the language must offer batch mode of data exchange between the database and the program that executes the query language.

10.4.1 Expressing Queries

An XML database is very different from the relational database. It has a tree structure. The depth of its branches may be unbalanced. For XML query, it does not retrieve a DataSet, a table, a row, or a column. It retrieves items like a subtree, the parent (predecessor) of a node, and all the successors (children) of a node. An XML query can also retrieve information scattered in different parts of the XML tree; for example, retrieving all the elements that have an attribute called age, and the attribute value is "60." The XPath that we discussed in Chapter 4 is capable of making such a query:

//*[@age = 60]

Furthermore, elements in XML database are ordered. We can find the predecessor and successor of an element in an XML database, whereas the elements in a relational database are unordered. One can retrieve the data and sort the data in the desired way.

Because of the differences between the relational databases and XML bases, the need for developing an XML query language is clear. In 1998, W3C sponsored a workshop on XML Query. In 1999, W3C started an XML Query working group. In 2001, the working group published the initial draft language specifications. The working drafts have been updated periodically. In January 2007, XQuery 1.0 was released (http://www.w3.org/TR/xquery/). The latest version in 2017 is XQuery 3.1 (https://www.w3.org/TR/xquery-31/).

XQuery becomes a new member in the XML family. XQuery is based on XML and XPath, and it shares structures and semantics with XML Schema and XSLT Stylesheet transformation.

XQuery is a programming language, and it supports common data types, such as number, Boolean, string, date, time, duration, and XML types.

XQuery is a functional programming language, which has some similarity with Scheme and LISP. Like all functional programming language, every XQuery statement evaluates to a result and returns a value; for example:

```
let     $x := 3
        $y := 7
return 8*$x+4*$y
```

which returns 52. The aforesaid example is similar to the Scheme expression that follows:

```
  (let ( (x 3)
         (y 7))
         (+ (* 8 x) (* 4 y)
     )
)
```

Another XQuery example is:

```
let $target := "audio-output",
    $content := "beep"
return processing-instruction {$target} {$content}
```

XQuery provides a feature called a FLWOR expression that supports iteration and binding of variables to intermediate results. This kind of expression is often useful for computing joins between two or more documents and for restructuring data. The name FLWOR, pronounced "flower," is suggested by the keywords for, let, where, order by, and return. The constructs and clauses supported by XQuery are given in the following BNF notation:

```
FLWORExpr          ::=  (ForClause | LetClause)+ WhereClause? OrderByClause?
                        "return" ExprSingle
ForClause          ::=  "for" "$" VarName TypeDeclaration? PositionalVar? "in"
                        ExprSingle ("," "$" VarName TypeDeclaration? PositionalVar?
                        "in" ExprSingle)*
LetClause          ::=  "let" "$" VarName TypeDeclaration? ":=" ExprSingle ("," "$"
                        VarName TypeDeclaration? ":=" ExprSingle)*
TypeDeclaration    ::=  "as" SequenceType
PositionalVar      ::=  "at" "$" VarName
WhereClause        ::=  "where" ExprSingle
OrderByClause      ::=  (("order" "by") | ("stable" "order" "by")) OrderSpecList
OrderSpecList      ::=  OrderSpec ("," OrderSpec)*
OrderSpec          ::=  ExprSingle OrderModifier
OrderModifier      ::=  ("ascending" | "descending")? ("empty" ("greatest" |
                        "least"))? ("collation" URILiteral)?
```

The following example from http://www.w3.org/TR/xquery/ includes many XQuery constructs and clauses. The for-clause iterates over all the departments in an input document, binding the variable $d to each department number in turn. For each binding of $d, the let clause binds variable $e to all the employees in the given department, selected from another input document. The result of the for-clause and let-clause is a tuple stream in which each tuple contains a pair of bindings for $d and $e ($d is bound to a department number and $e is bound to a set of employees in that department). The where-clause filters the tuple stream by keeping only those binding-pairs that represent departments having at least 10 employees. The order by clause orders the surviving tuples in descending order by the average salary of the employees in the department. The return clause constructs a new big-dept. element for each surviving tuple, containing the department number, headcount, and average salary.

```
for $d in fn:doc("depts.xml")/depts/deptno
let $e := fn:doc("emps.xml")/emps/emp[deptno = $d]
where fn:count($e) >= 10
order by fn:avg($e/salary) descending
return
   <big-dept>
   {
      $d,
      <headcount>{fn:count($e)}</headcount>,
      <avgsal>{fn:avg($e/salary)}</avgsal>
   }
   </big-dept>
```

XQuery program can be embedded in the web files, and can also access the web files. The following code shows an example embedded in html file, which reads a file on the web as its input:

```
<html>
{
   let $d :=
doc("http://neptune.fulton.ad.asu.edu/WSRepository/xml/Courses.xml")/Course
   for $b in $d/Course
        where $b/Level > 200
        order by $b/Code
        return
              <Course>
                    {$b/Name, $b/Level, $b/Cap}
              </Course>
}
</html>
```

10.4.2 Transforming XML Document

The foregoing examples show how we can use XQuery programs to specify criteria and to retrieve information that meet the criteria. As long as we specify the criteria properly, we can also use XQuery programs to transform one XML file into another XML file, which is one of the functions of XSLT discussed in Chapter 4. The official site of XQuery (http://www.w3.org/TR/xquery/) uses the following example to illustrate the transformation.

First, we assume we have an XML document that stores a collection of books.

```
<bib>
  <book>
    <title>TCP/IP Illustrated</title>
    <author>Stevens</author>
    <publisher>Addison-Wesley</publisher>
  </book>
  <book>
    <title>Advanced Programming in the Unix Environment</title>
    <author>Stevens</author>
    <publisher>Addison-Wesley</publisher>
  </book>
  <book>
    <title>Data on the Web</title>
    <author>Abiteboul</author>
    <author>Buneman</author>
    <author>Suciu</author>
  </book>
</bib>
```

If we want to generate another XML document that is a collection of authors with the books that they have written, we can use the following XQuery program to perform the transformation:

```
<authlist> {
   for $a in fn:distinct-values($bib/book/author)
   order by $a
   return
     <author>
        <name> {$a} </name>
        <books> {
            for $b in $bib/book[author = $a]
            order by $b/title
            return $b/title
          }
        </books>
     </author>
 }
</authlist>
```

The output of the program is the transformed XML document, shown as follows:

```
<authlist>
   <author>
      <name>Abiteboul</name>
      <books>
         <title>Data on the Web</title>
      </books>
   </author>
   <author>
      <name>Buneman</name>
      <books>
         <title>Data on the Web</title>
      </books>
   </author>
   <author>
      <name>Stevens</name>
      <books>
         <title>Advanced Programming
                in the Unix Environment</title>
         <title>TCP/IP Illustrated</title>
      </books>
   </author>
   <author>
      <name>Suciu</name>
      <books>
         <title>Data on the Web</title>
      </books>
   </author>
</authlist>
```

10.4.3 XQuery Discussions

XQuery is defined as a general-purpose programming language, with additional constructs and clauses for expressing parallel and sequential queries. The language definition promises a solution to establish a service-oriented database in service-oriented software development. The language is based on the well-established functional programming paradigm, which gives the language a solid mathematical foundation and application background. The support from the other XML technologies, such as SAX and DOM models provides stream access and batch access to the XML database. XPath syntax and semantics, as well as its enabling technologies, can be simply imported into the language.

However, Xquery's success depends also on development of efficient algorithms and parallel processing capacities to retrieve, modify, and transform large databases. This is a challenge that still needs to be addressed.

10.5 Discussions

In this chapter, we discussed three topics related to database accesses in service-oriented software: Interfacing with relational databases, native XML databases, and LINQ.

Traditional relational databases will continue to be the main massive storage of all kinds of applications. Interfacing relational databases through adapters to service-oriented software is the current practice of business. XML databases as native databases for service-oriented software are considered the future trend. Major database vendors have implemented XQuery and XML database as a part of their latest database systems. Following is a list of XML databases implemented or being implemented:

- Oracle XML DB Developer's Guide
  https://docs.oracle.com/cd/B19306_01/appdev.102/b14259/xdb01int.htm
- IBM DB2 9.5 PureXML DB (Commercial)
  http://www.ibm.com/developerworks/data/library/techarticle/dm-0710nicola/
- dbXML (Open Source)
  http://www.dbxml.com/
- eXist (Open Source)
  http://exist.sourceforge.net/

Microsoft's approach of LINQ presents a new way of dealing with the diversity of data representations. LINQ presents a uniform way of programming different data sources and uses transparent adapters to access different databases, which frees the programmers from database specifics. This approach is a competing way to the XQuery that applies a new language to query the XML database.

LINQ offers three packages to deal with different data sources. LINQ to Object queries data collections such as arrays and lists. This package contains essential constructs and components for performing complex queries. A LINQ to SQL package transforms SQL data into objects and then the data are processed using a LINQ to Object package. LINQ to XML is an in-memory XML programming interface that enables developers to work with XML using .NET programming languages. It is similar to the Document Object Model (DOM) and brings the XML document into memory for processing. This package offers a new set of XML processing classes that are more powerful than those XML classes we discussed in Chapter 4.

Ontologies are XML-based and could be considered "advanced" XML databases. We will discuss ontology as a form of database and resources of Semantic Web in Chapter 11.

Name: ____________________

Date: ____________________

10.6 Exercises and Projects

1. Multiple choice questions. Choose one answer in each question only. Choose the best answer if multiple answers are acceptable.

1.1 What is the purpose of introducing DataAdapter in ADO .Net?

(A) Support hierarchical structure of data access.

(B) Support device-independent data access from multiple sources.

(C) Make it easier for the data to pass across firewall.

(D) All of the above.

1.2 A DataSet in ADO .Net is

(A) an array of homogeneous data.

(B) a single table of data.

(C) a set of tables.

(D) a set of data, each of which can have different types.

1.3 Which of the component's implementation is device dependent?

(A) Data adapter (B) Data provider (C) DataSet (D) None of them

1.4 A DataSet in ADO .Net is

(A) an array of homogeneous data.

(B) a single table of data.

(C) a set of tables that can be accessed by indices and as an XML tree.

(D) a set of data, each of which can have different type.

1.5 Which of the following database operations does NOT use the ExecuteNonQuery method?

(A) Insert a column (B) Delete a column

(C) Update a column (D) Select the maximum value from a column

1.6 An SqlCommand object in ADO .Net is a design pattern that allows you to

(A) sequentially access the elements of an aggregate object.

(B) parameterize clients with different requests of actions.

(C) vary the interactions among the different objects independently.

(D) define a one-to-many dependency between objects.

1.7 Which of the following operations binds the connection object to the command object?

(A) SqlConnection conn = new SqlConnection;

(B) conn.Open();

(C) SqlCommand cmd = new SqlCornmand();

(D) cmd.Connection = conn;

1.8 ADO .Net supports transaction process.

(A) Yes (B) No

1.9 What kind of query operators are in LINQ but not in SQL

(A) group join. (B) join. (C) select. (D) where.

1.10 In a LINQ query, we often use IEnumerable<aType> as the query return type, where aType is

(A) an aggregate type. (B) a generic type.

(C) a primary type. (D) an implicit type to be decided by compiler.

1.11 In a LINQ query, we often use var as the query return type, which is

(A) an aggregate type. (B) a generic type.

(C) a primary type. (D) an implicit type to be decided by compiler.

1.12 All LINQ to XML class names start with a letter

(A) L (B) Q (C) X (D) Z

1.13 What are the features of a native XML database?

(A) Save XML file as it is.

(B) Support XML schema.

(C) Save semi-structured data.

(D) All of the above.

1.14 What are the problems of transforming XML files into tables?

(A) Elements and attributes may not be differeentiated.

(B) The transforming may end up with using many tables or a large table with many null columns.

(C) The ordering information may get lost.

(D) All of the above.

1.15 The XQuery language is best characterized to be

(A) an imperative programming language.

(B) a functional programming language.

(C) an object-oriented programming language.

(D) a service-oriented programming language.

1.16 What XML database systems support indexing, in addition to file-based searching?

(A) Oracle 11g and IBM DB 9.5 (B) dbXML

(C) eXist (D) All of the above

1.17 What type of documents can be saved in the latest Oracle database?

(A) Pure XML documents (B) Plain tables

(C) Images files (D) All of the above

1.18 LINQ is

(A) an imperative programming language.

(B) a database query language.

(C) a pointer-based programming language with flexible data types.

(D) a programming language designed for scientific computing.

1.19 Lambda expression is the theoretical foundation of

(A) imperative programming language.

(B) object-oriented programming languages.

(C) service-oriented programming languages.

(D) declarative programming languages.

1.20 Given the expression, what does the expression mean?

```
Func<double, double, double> Cylinder = (r, h) => 3.14 * r * r * h;
```

(A) It is a lambda expression defined function.

(B) It is equivalent to a delegate expression in C#.

(C) It is executable as a C# statement.

(D) All of the above.

1.21 GraphQL is typically used for querying data with:

(A) URI. (B) tree structure.

(C) graph structure. (D) All of the above.

1.22 GraphQL API are typically implemented as

(A) GraphQL specific service. (B) RESTful service.

(C) WSDL service. (D) VIPLE service.

2. What methods are available for SOC applications and services to access databases? What is the current practice of business of interfacing SOC applications and services with databases?

3. What are the functions of the DataAdapter and the DataSet in interfacing SOC application to databases?

4. What is an XML database? What are the challenges of the XML database design and implementation?

5. What is a lambda expression? What is a higher-order of function?

6. What is the purpose of introducing LINQ in service-oriented software development?

7. What types of data are supported by LINQ?

8. What is an RIA service? What is relationship between RIA and LINQ?

9. In this question, you will plan an online shopping web application, with functionality and security considerations.

   a. Draw the diagram that shows the overall system, its components (services), and the relationship among the components of the online shopping application. You can use the assignment that you created.

   b. Elaborate each component with sufficient detail so that a peer in this class can understand and can follow the explanation to find or implement (code) each of the components. You may use the workflow (flowchart) or pseudocode with comments to explain each component. You must give the type of the file; for example, aspx, ascx, html, text, config, asax, dll, and so on, that implements the component.

   c. Create an SQL database to store the user information, including name, address, phone number, and e-mail.

   d. Implement in C# a Forms-based security for the web application, using an SQL database to store the user ID and the password.

Project 1

Continue to add features in the project implemented in Chapter 5. Add a database in your data management tier and use LINQ as the interface to your database, in addition to the XML file that you have implemented.

Project 2

In this project, you will create data sources, build an SQL database, and query the database using LINQ to SQL, LINQ to Object, and LINQ to XML classes. Use comments to indicate what part of code answers which of the following questions:

1. Create Courses table. Choose at least 15 courses from ASU CSE class search site, ranging from 100 through 500. Choose four entities of information: course code (integer, such as, 110, 310, and 598), course title, instructor, and cap (integer). Put the data in a table.
2. Create Instructors table. Choose 10 CSE faculty. Choose these entities of information: first name, last name, office number (You make up a number such as BY123), and the course title that the instructors are teaching. If an instructor teaches multiple courses, you should create multiple rows for the instructor. The instructors in the Courses table should be included. Put the data in a 10x4 table. Note that you can search all courses taught by an instructor, without entering the course number, by entering the instructor name as a keyword instead.
3. Create an SQL database and scheme to hold the Courses table. Add a courseld field and set it to auto increment. Enter the data from Courses table into the database.
4. Use LINQ to SQL Classes to access the database. Read the course information from SQL database and create an in-memory structure, such as array and list, to hold the information.
5. Create an in-memory structure, such as array and list, to hold the Instructors table and instantiate an object to store the information in the Instructors table.
6. Create the following LINQ queries to extract data from the data sources.
   a. The list of courses with 300 or higher course number. Deliver the result set in the type of IEnumerable <T>, where each entity contains course title and course instructor. The result set must be sorted by course cap and in ascending order.
   b. Put the courses in groups and using the course code as the key.

c. Create a group-joint result using the Courses and Instructors information. You can define your own criteria for associating the two data sources. The criteria must be sensible, so that you can find some matched results based on your data sources.

7. Test run the program and submit all the results set in the order of the questions

Chapter 11
Big Data Processing and Cloud Computing

In the previous chapters, we discussed databases, state and data management, resource-oriented architecture (ROA), and RESTful services that process and present resources on the web. A **resource** on the web is an object that can be uniquely identified by a URI (Universal Resource Identifier). This chapter will extend the discussion to big data, artificial intelligence system development, and cloud computing systems, as well as their applications. As a part of big data and artificial intelligence systems, we further discuss the basic resource representation and organization in ontology languages for describing resource, property, and structure that form the ontology systems. Ontology languages RDF, RDFS, and OWL will be discussed.

11.1 Big Data Systems and Management

This section will discuss big data concepts, characteristics, the domains of studies, and its management.

11.1.1 Big Data Concepts

Big data is the term for a collection of data sets, which are so large and complex that it becomes difficult to process using on-hand database management tools or traditional data processing applications (http://en.wikipedia.org/wiki/Big_data). Sources of big data are mainly from humans through social networking and from devices in Internet of Things (IoT). The challenges in big data processing lie not only in the volume, but also in the types of data and the velocity of new data that are generated. There are three types of data stored in computer systems:

- Structured Data: Tables of data in traditional relational databases. SQL is the typical query language.
- Semi-Structured Data: XML files stored in XML databases, as we discussed in Chapter 4 and this chapter.
- Unstructured Data: Data that are not structured or semi-structured, mainly streamed data such as voice, photos, and video files.

A big data system typically includes all the types of data, and will deal with all the types simultaneously. Thus, the data type in big data systems is called poly-structured. A big data system can be characterized by many Vs, including:

- Value: Big data is considered the next big thing after the Internet (communication) and Cloud Computing (computation). It can bring tremendous value to the society and the economy.
- Volume: A moving target from petabyte (10^{15} bytes), exabyte (10^{18}), zettabyte (10^{21}), to more.
- Velocity: Real-time data require real-time responses.
- Variety: Data from different sources with different semantics are integrated into different applications.
- Variability in data structures: poly-structured data.
- Veracity: Noise elimination and fault tolerance are required to process big data.
- Volatile: Not all data can be stored, and some will be permanently deleted, and thus, big data processing systems are required to selectively store and organize the data to maximize their value.

Figure 11.1 shows the big data characteristics and the domains of studies, as well as the facilities and infrastructure supporting big data analysis and processing.

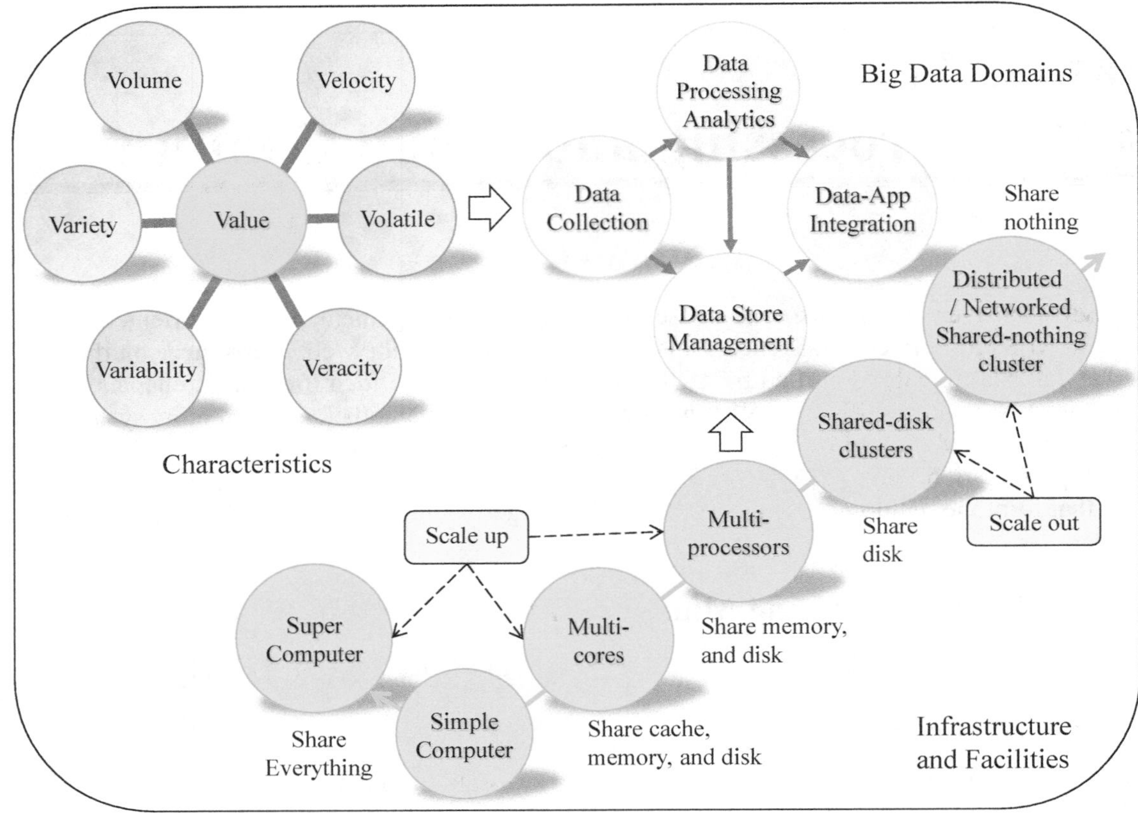

Figure 11.1. Big data system characteristics, domains, and infrastructure

There are two major sources of data: data entered from humans and data from devices, particularly from IoT devices. They include those from social networks, such as Facebook and Twitter, from websites of different organizations, from databases and data warehouses, from publications, such as books, journal and newspapers, from archives and legacy documents, from computer generated data, from personal cameras, from surveillance cameras, including video, image, and audio, from telescope and astronomical devices, and all kinds of sensor networks.

A big data system requires technologies from different domains. The key technologies supporting include infrastructure, management, and analytic techniques.

Computing infrastructures that support big data systems include parallel computing, cloud computing, storage, and database facilities. Scalability is the key issue here, including scale up and more importantly, scale out, as shown in the lower part of Figure 11.1.

Data management in big data systems must organize data on the given facilities and infrastructures. Big data techniques include data representation and management, NO-SQL (Not Only SQL) movement, Key-value store for unstructured data, CAP (Consistency and data integrity, Availability and reliability, Partition and distribution) Theory for optimization and compromise, MapReduce, and Hadoop. Data management is coupled with the computing infrastructure. To scale up to facilitate a big data system, a share nothing system must be used, and large data centers and data warehouses are based on share nothing architecture.

Analytic techniques: Specifically developed for processing big data in specific applications, which include aggregation and statistics; for example, data warehouse, data centers, and OLAP (On-Line Analytical Processing); indexing, searching, and querying: keyword search and Pattern matching (XML/RDF), and knowledge discovery using data mining and statistical modeling.

11.1.2 Big Data Management

The volume of the data in big data systems is so big, that traditional relational database systems can no longer effectively process the data. The NoSQL or NO-SQL (Not Only SQL) movement is being taken to deal with the new need. NoSQL refers to any nonrelational approaches, including tree (XML), graph (a more generic structure than tree), and key-value approaches.

The key-value data store consists of rows of data, with each row storing a pair: <key K, value V>, where

K is the unique identifier, which can be used for partitioning data for distributed storing and processing, and V is a list of values (names and attributes), which can be structured and unstructured data. Key-value data stores have been widely used for storing unstructured data. For example, if we have two computers to process the data, we can assign even-key values to one machine and odd-key values to another machine. If we have 100 computers, we can use the reminder of the key dividing by 100 for assigning the values to the 100 computers to process the data.

The proprietary key-value systems include Google's Big Table, Yahoo! PNUTS, and Amazon Dynamo. The open source implementation includes Cassandra, Hbase (Hadoop-based database), Hypertable, and Voldemort.

The performance of big data management systems is measured in a number of attributes. The most important ones are Consistency and data integrity, Availability and reliability, and Partition and distribution, known as CAP theory, which deals with the compromises among the three: Which one to sacrifice if we cannot achieve all of them?

There are two types of consistency: ACID (Atomicity Consistency Isolation Durability) and eventual Consistency. ACID represents strong consistency that is required by finance and transaction applications, while eventual Consistency represents weak consistency that is widely used in many social networking applications, such as search engine, recommender, and review and raking systems. In big data systems, consistency normally has to be sacrificed, not only because it is often not necessary, but also because it is not possible due to the volume of the data.

As we discussed in Chapter 6, dependability, including availability and reliability, is critical in all systems. It is particularly important in big data systems, because the more hardware, software, and data are involved, the more errors and failures will occur. Dependability cannot be sacrificed. A high level of redundancy in big data store is a necessity. Typical fault tolerance techniques used to manage big data systems include:

- Error control code: Additional storage is used to store redundant data and to increase the Hamming Distance between the code words;
- Checkpointing and rollback: partial results are verified and stored periodically into permanent storage, and if a failure occurs, rollback to the last check point;
- N-Modular Redundancy/Replication (NMR), where N >= 2: Use multiple stores, processors and algorithms to store the same data and to perform the same tasks, and then, compare (vote) the results, with majority and quorum rules.
- Failover and reconfiguration: Use backup units to take over the tasks of failed units. The backup units can be cold backup or hot backup. If the backup units are active participants and are assigned to perform tasks when all units are functioning, then, when failures occur, the overall performance will be reduced, which is called graceful degradation of performance.

Partition and distribution of data stores are critical in big data systems, ensuring the scalability and the ability of dealing with the extreme large volume of data of big data systems. Scalability is the key function of big data systems, and it should not be sacrificed. Data stores and their hardware formation can be considered a big table of rows and columns. They can be partitioned in vertical and in horizontal ways.

In vertical partitioning, stores are partitioned by columns, and the data stores are called column stores. Data stores that use column partition include MonetDB and Vertica. These data stores are efficient for OLAP (On-Line Analytical Processing) queries and are easy to compress.

In horizontal partitioning, stores are partitioned by rows, and each row is called a shard, and horizontal partitioning is also called sharding. Shards can be easily stored and replicated at different nodes for distributed computing and redundancy. Different sharding schema exist: round robin, hashing, key range, binary search tree, and B+ tree, as being used in Google's Big Table store.

- Round robin: The ith row is stored into the $(i \bmod n)^{th}$ node. It has perfect load balancing among the nodes; however, full linear search is required.
- Range: It is often used in <key, value> stores, where the key range is used for sharding. Linear search is required within each node.
- Hashing: It is often used in <key, value> stores, where n = hash(k) is used for sharding; It supports fast research, but the load may not be well balanced among the nodes.
- B+ Tree: It stores keys in sorted B+ trees, which is an extended B tree, where data are sorted and stored in the leaf nodes only, and a link to the next node is also stored. B+ tree supports fast search and data insertion is slow.

11.2 Big Data Processing and Analytics

Many parallel algorithms and techniques have been developed to solve specific problems in different application domains. As we discussed in Chapter 2, multithreading is widely used in parallelizing the execution of multiple methods in a program. Such techniques are not applicable to big data processing when hundreds and thousands of parallel threads need to be started to process the data. We need an automated process to start many parallel threads through simple configuration and parameter setting. In this section, we will present such programming models, e.g., Map and Reduce, developed for big data processing and its supporting environment, Hadoop.

11.2.1 Map and Reduce

Map and Reduce, or MapReduce, is a parallel computing model that can be used in different programming environments. It is widely used, because it is generic and can be used in different situations without intensive reprogramming. The idea is to divide a computation intensive problem into many subproblems, and to solve each subproblem on a different node. Then, the solutions from different subproblems are merged or reduced to a single solution. MapReduce was initially applied in Google search engine for processing petabyte-level of data. It was popularized by the open-source Hadoop project. Hadoop was initially used by Yahoo! and followed by many big data systems, such as Facebook and Amazon. MapReduce can be used in the situation where the computation is stateless, that is, the solution of each subproblem does not relate to the previous step, nor to the other subproblems.

As an example, we show the MapReduce concept based on key-value store of the data. MapReduce is a higher-order function, in which a function operator is passed into another function. The computation is split into two phases in a distributed computing system, Mapper and Reducer, where:

- Mappers: The input data is divided into subsets and each Mapper will take one subset. Each mapper performs the same operations to compute one subset of the data;

- Reducer: Merge or shuffle the results (outputs) from Map's subsets, assign the outputs to one or more Reducer. The results will eventually be reduced to one result.

The two major steps normally contain a few sub steps. Assume the job is to be executed on n processors. The more detailed MapReduce consists of the following steps:

- Partition: The input data set is partitioned into n pieces and n mappers are created., where mapper i is assigned data i to process, where i = 0, 1, 2, …, n−1. Each piece of data is presented as a string or a key-value pair. The key is normally not significant in this step.
- One mapper takes a key-value pair $<k_{i1}, v_{i1}>$ and generates a list of key-value pairs: list $<k_{i2}, v_{i2}>$. All mappers will generate a list of list pairs as output: list(list$<k_{i2}, v_{i2}>$), where i = 0, 1, 2, …, n−1. Formally,

  Mappers: $\text{list} < k_{i1}, v_{i1} > \xrightarrow{\text{yields}} \text{list}(\text{list} < k_{i2}, v_{i2} >)$

  Different mappers may have generated key-value pairs with the same key, i.e., $k_{i1} = k_{j2}$.
- Merge: The merge operation reshuffles the output list from mappers by keys, i.e., all the values with the same key are organized with the key: $< k_{i3}, \text{list } v_{i3} >$. Formally,

  Merge: $\text{list}(\text{list} < k_{i2}, v_{i2} >) \xrightarrow{\text{yields}} \text{list} < k_{i3}, \text{list } v_{i3} >$, where i = 1, 2, ..., m.

  The output of Merge will be assigned to reducers. If the number of reducers is greater than or equal to the number of keys, each reducer will process the list of values associated with one key. Otherwise, each reducer will process the values associated with multiple keys.
- Reducer: One reducer takes the key-value pairs assigned by the merge operation and generates a single pair $<k_4, v_4>$. Formally,

  Reduce: $< k_{i3}, \text{list } v_{i3} > \xrightarrow{\text{yields}} < k_4, v_4 >$

  It is possible that the reducer does not reduce the results to a single pair. In this case, we may need to use another round of reducers, or another round of mappers and reducers to generate the final result.

Note that Map and Reduce do not take the operation name as an input, which is normally the case in the definition of higher-order functions, because the operation is implied in MapReduce.

In the foregoing steps, mapper and reducer must be written by the developer, whereas the partition and merge can be automated by the supporting framework, such as Hadoop.

11.2.2 Hadoop and Cassandra

MapReduce is a generic parallel programming model. It is the most popular model used in big data processing, owing to the perfect support from frameworks like Hadoop, which is specifically designed for processing big data in distributed data stores. MapReduce and Hadoop are also considered a cloud computing model and infrastructure and are discussed further on in this chapter.

Apache Hadoop is an open source framework for distributed data management and parallel data processing (http://hadoop.apache.org/). It consists of distributed nodes, each of which consists of processing units and storage units. Nodes can be added or removed without impacting other nodes. It maps the processing units and storage units to the processors and disks of clusters and distributed systems to create distributed commodity boxes of Hadoop nodes. Combining with MapReduce, Hadoop can be used to solve different distributed computing problems, and particularly, the big data processing problems. Hadoop supports two layers of data stores: Hadoop Distributed File System (HDFS) is the bottom layer of storage, which stores unstructured data in distributed cluster nodes. Hbase is the upper layer storage, which stores structured data in large tables. MapReduce is built on top of the two layers of data stores. Figure 11.2 shows the architecture of Hadoop. It consists of one master node and multiple slave nodes. All nodes have task trackers and data nodes, while the master has two additional modules: The job tracker schedules and manages task trackers on all nodes, and the name node controls all data nodes on both master and slave nodes, including partitioning or sharding. Each task tracker executes a map and reduces task on one of the cluster nodes, and each date node provides the data to the task tracker on the node.

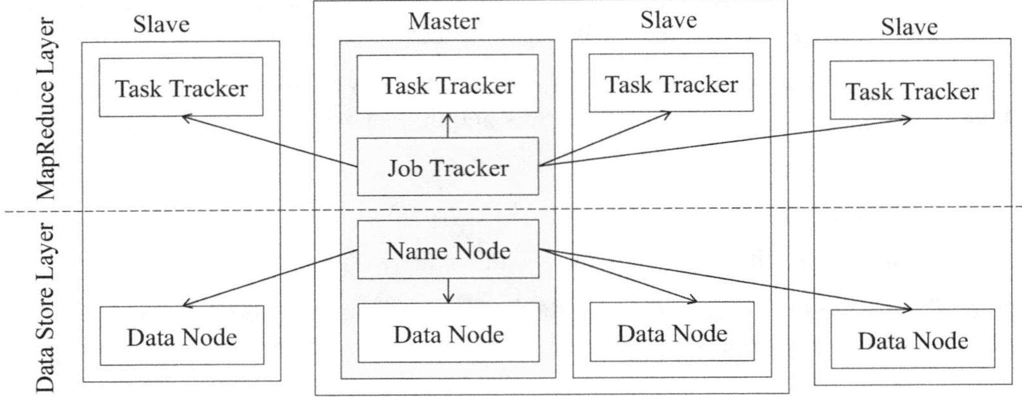

Figure 11.2. MapReduce on Multi-Node Hadoop Cluster

In a cloud computing environment, any number of nodes can be requested for performing the required tasks. Hadoop allows the user to define the maximum number of nodes in its configuration file in conf/mapred-site.xml:

```
<property>
   <name>mapred.tasktracker.map.tasks.maximum</name>
   <value>2</value>
</property>
<property>
   <name>mapred.tasktracker.reduce.tasks.maximum</name>
   <value>2</value>
</property>
```

The default values of the mappers and reducers are 2, and the values can be changed based on the number cluster nodes available. Figure 11.3 shows the execution of a MapReduce tasks on the basic configuration with two mappers and two reducers.

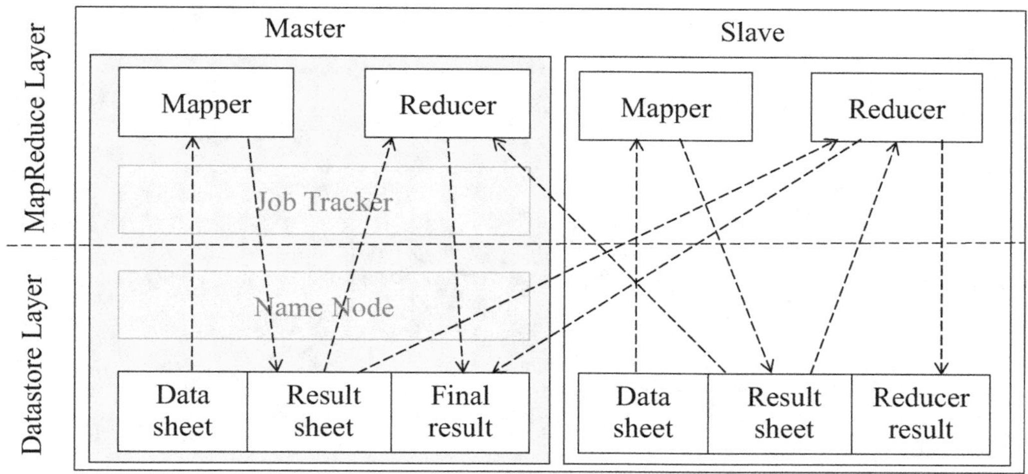

Figure 11.3. Two Mapper and two Reducer tasks on Hadoop

The code that follows shows the MapReduce program that is computing the average of a large set of numbers. The code starts with importing the necessary MapReduce and Hadoop library functions. The package consists of two classes. The mapper class extends the Mapper base class and defines a map function, and the reducer class extends the Reduce base class.

```
package average; // Importing MapReduce and Hadoop library functions
import java.io.IOException;
import java.util.StringTokenizer;
import org.apache.hadoop.conf.Configuration;
import org.apache.hadoop.fs.Path;
import org.apache.hadoop.io.*;
import org.apache.hadoop.mapreduce.Job;
import org.apache.hadoop.mapreduce.Mapper;
import org.apache.hadoop.mapreduce.Reducer;
import org.apache.hadoop.mapreduce.lib.input.FileInputFormat;
import org.apache.hadoop.mapreduce.lib.output.FileOutputFormat;
import org.apache.hadoop.util.GenericOptionsParser;
public class WordCount {
  public static class Map extends
                    Mapper <LongWritable, Text, Text, IntWritable> {
       private final static IntWritable one = new IntWritable(1);
                                             // object for output value
       private Text word = new Text();    // object for output key

// The following map function takes three parameters.
// LongWritable key: it should take the Document's identifier. Since there
// is one document only, and the document is specified by path and file
// name, the key is ignored.
// Text value: It holds the entire document's text, or a list of words.
// Context context: It is an MapperContext object used for accessing
// output, configuration information, etc. The map function generates
// key-value pairs for each word found in the document, where the key
// a word, and the value is the number of appearances of the word.

       public void map(LongWritable key, Text value, Context context)
                  throws IOException, InterruptedException {
       String[] strs = value.toString().split("\\s");
```

```
                    // convert value to string and then to an array of tokens
        For (int i = 0; i < strs.length; i++) {
              word.set(strs[i]); // set word as each input keyword
              context.write(word, one);   // create <key, value> for output
        }     // Each word is used as a key and the count is its value
   }
}
public static class Reduce extends
              Reducer<Text,IntWritable,Text,IntWritable> {
        private IntWritable result = new IntWritable();

//The reduce function below takes the outputs from map function.
// Text key: Each key is a word;
// Iterable<IntWritable> values: Iterator over the values for the key;
// Context context: is a ReducerContext object for accessing output,
// configuration information, etc.

        public void reduce(Text key, Iterable<IntWritable> values,
                                      Context context)
              throws IOException, InterruptedException {
        int sum = 0; // initialize the sum for each keyword
        for (IntWritable val : values) {
              sum += val.get();  // adding the count of all words together
        }
        result.set(sum);
        context.write(key, result);
              // create a pair <keyword, number of occurrences>
        }
   }
// In the main program below, first Constructs a Job object representing
// a single Map-Reduce job. It follows a number of preparation steps.
// The final step "waitForCompletion" will start the execution. When the // job is
running on a cluster consisting of multiple nodes, the final
// "waitForCompletion" call will distribute the code to all nodes
// and execute the job in parallel.

public static void main(String[] args) throws Exception {
   Configuration conf = new Configuration(); // node count defined

// Using Hadoop's GenericOptionsParser to extract the arguments,
// the MapReduce program can accept all Hadoop options of inputs.
   String[] otherArgs = new GenericOptionsParser(
                    conf, args).getRemainingArgs(); // get all args
   if (otherArgs.length != 2) {  // input data and output file
        System.err.println("Usage: WordCount <in> <out>");
        System.exit(2);
   }
   // create a job with name "wordcount"
   Job job = new Job(conf, "wordcount");

// The next statement tells Hadoop where to locate the code that must
// be Distributed to multiple nodes if this job running a cluster.
// Unless the location of code is specified, e.g., using the -libjars
// in the command line option). All non-Hadoop built-in code
// necessary to run this job must be contained in the JAR containing
// the specified class, the WordCount.class in this case.
   job.setJarByClass(WordCount.class);
   job.setMapperClass(Map.class);        //set the Mapper class
```

```
    job.setReducerClass(Reduce.class);      //set the Reducer class
    job.setCombinerClass(Reduce.class);     // Add Combiner to merge data
    job.setOutputKeyClass(Text.class);      // set output key type
    job.setOutputValueClass(IntWritable.class);//set output value type
    //set the HDFS path to the input data
    FileInputFormat.addInputPath(job, new Path(otherArgs[0]));
    // set the HDFS path to the output file
    FileOutputFormat.setOutputPath(job, new Path(otherArgs[1]));
    // Jobs start after the preparation and wait for completion, and
    // wait for job to complete
    System.exit(job.waitForCompletion(true) ? 0 : 1);
    }
}
```

Assuming two mapper and two reducer tasks are configured, the map function, reduce function, and combiner function, as well as their inputs and outputs are illustrated in Figure 11.4.

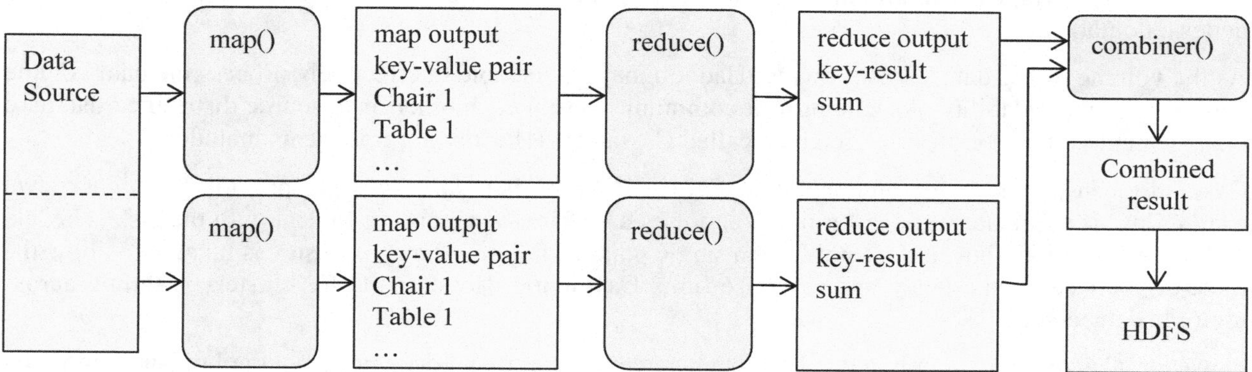

Figure 11.4. The inputs and outputs of map and reduce tasks

In the foregoing code, the Mapper code reads the input files as <Key, Value> pairs and emits new key-value pairs. The Map class extends MapReduceBase and implements the Mapper interface. Two options are available, depending on the package used in your environment:

```
class Map extends Mapper <LongWritable, Text, Text, IntWritable>, or
class Map extends MapReduceBase implements
                    Mapper <LongWritable, Text, Text, IntWritable>
```

The Mapper class expects four generic classes that define the types of the input and output key-value pairs. The first two parameters define the input key and value types, the second two parameters define the output key and value types.

Thus, the map function takes <Text key, Text value> pairs and outputs <Text key, LongWritable value> pairs. The input keys are the identifiers for documents, which are ignored here as there is one input document in the example here, and the values are the content of the documents. The output keys are words found within each document, and the output values are the number of times a word appeared within a document.

To make the MapReduce pattern independent of programming languages and to make it to support efficient serialization for data exchange, MapReduce and Hadoop do not use the built-in Java classes like "Long" and "String" as key or value types. Instead, they wrapper the types into Text and LongWritable for implementing Hadoop's serialization interface writable types.

Similarly, the Reducer class extends MapReduceBase and implements the Reducer interface. The Reducer interface expects four generic classes, which define the types of the input and output key/value pairs. The

Reducer's code reads the outputs generated by different mappers in the form of <Key, Value> pairs and emits new key-value pairs.

MapReduce on Hadoop is a distributed computing model, which to certain extend is similar to that we covered in Chapter 2 on multithreading programming. The main difference is that MapReduce on Hadoop automated a number of things that need to be done manually in multithreading programming.

Multithreading can start multiple threads from the same class/method. Normally, you choose the number and start the threads in code based on the number; for example, using a loop. In MapReduce on Hadoop, you simply put the node number in configuration file, and Hadoop automatically creates the required number of nodes and task trackers. Furthermore, MapReduce is a higher-order function and the loop is implied.

For data partition or sharding part, multithreading does not have built-in data management function, and thus, the developers must write code to split the data into pieces and feed the data to different threads. On the other hand, MapReduce on Hadoop can partition the data set into shards and send them to different nodes automatically.

As the volume of big data keeps growing, Hadoop may not be able to effectively process the data volume that exceeds its scalability. Apache project community designed another open source distributed database management system for unstructured data called Cassandra. The key improvements include:

Cassandra can handle larger amounts of data than Hadoop. It is fault-tolerant, providing a higher-level availability. It eliminates the master node, and uses a distributed algorithm to deal with the task schedule and reconfiguration; thus, it does not have a single point of failure. The consistency is tunable to allow the trade-off between consistency and response time. Cassandra also supports for clusters spanning across multiple datacenters.

However, Cassandra is mainly a database management system, and does not have the built-in computing model. Hadoop can run on top of Cassandra to obtain the advantage of using the built-in computing model MapReduce and the ability of managing larger data stores.

11.2.3 Big Data Simulation in VIPLE

VIPLE supports π-calculus, which defines the foundation of parallel processes and computing. This section starts with multithreading computing and then extends the model into big data processing.

VIPLE implements multithreading and parallel computing through the constructs for splitting and joining of parallel threads. We use a simple example to illustrate the effectiveness and convenience of using VIPLE to implement parallel computing.

Assume that we want to add 1500 numbers: 1 + 2 + … + 1500. Figure 11.5 shows the VIPLE diagram using a simple single threaded program. It is a while-loop, using two variables, sum and i. The loop iterates 1500 times and performs sum = sum + i in each iteration. This is a sequential program that can be done on one processor only, even if the system has multiple processors available. In order to compare the execution speed with the parallel version of the same program, we added the time stamps at the beginning and at the end of the program. The time taken for executing the program is calculated at the end and printed.

In VIPLE, this program can be easily rewritten into a parallel program, by splitting the program into multiple parallel threads. Figure 11.6 shows the diagram with three parallel threads, each adding 500 numbers, and then the program adds the three sub sums together.

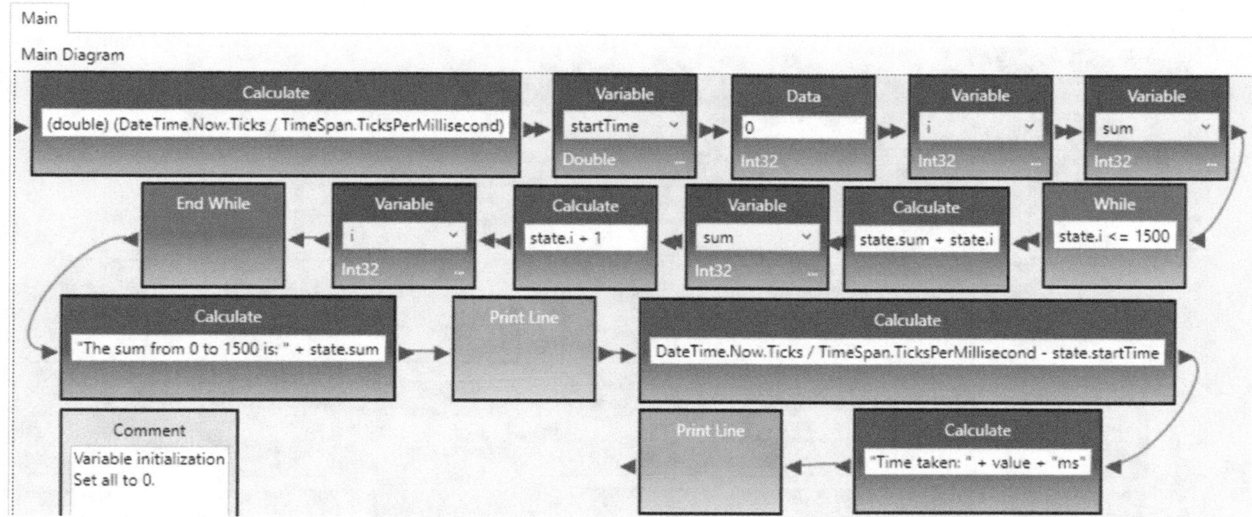

Figure 11.5. Single threaded addition of 1500 numbers

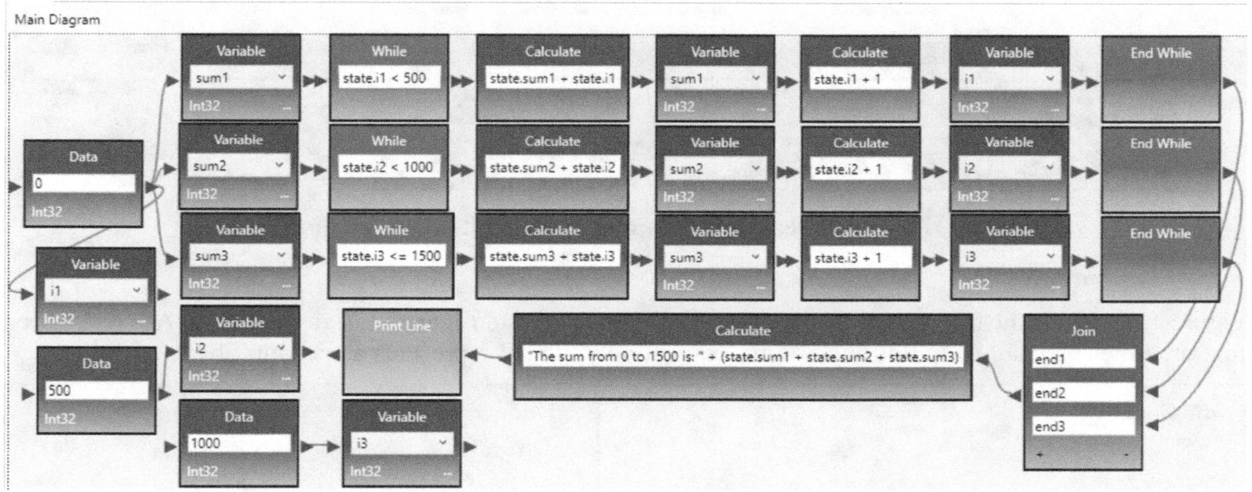

Figure 11.6. Multithread computing of 1500 additions, synchronized by Join activity

VIPLE is implemented as an event-driven and parallel computing platform. It does not require a single-entrance point. As can be seen in the parallel program in Figure 11.6, there are three entrance points, leading to three parallel threads that are started and executed simultaneously. At the end of the threads, a Join activity is used, which waits for all the threads to complete, so that the following Calculate activity can add the three sub sums together to obtain the total sum.

In order to calculate the time taken for complete the additions, we added the time stamps and calculated the time taken, as shown in Figure 11.7. We also show that the Map and Reduce concepts were implemented in this example.

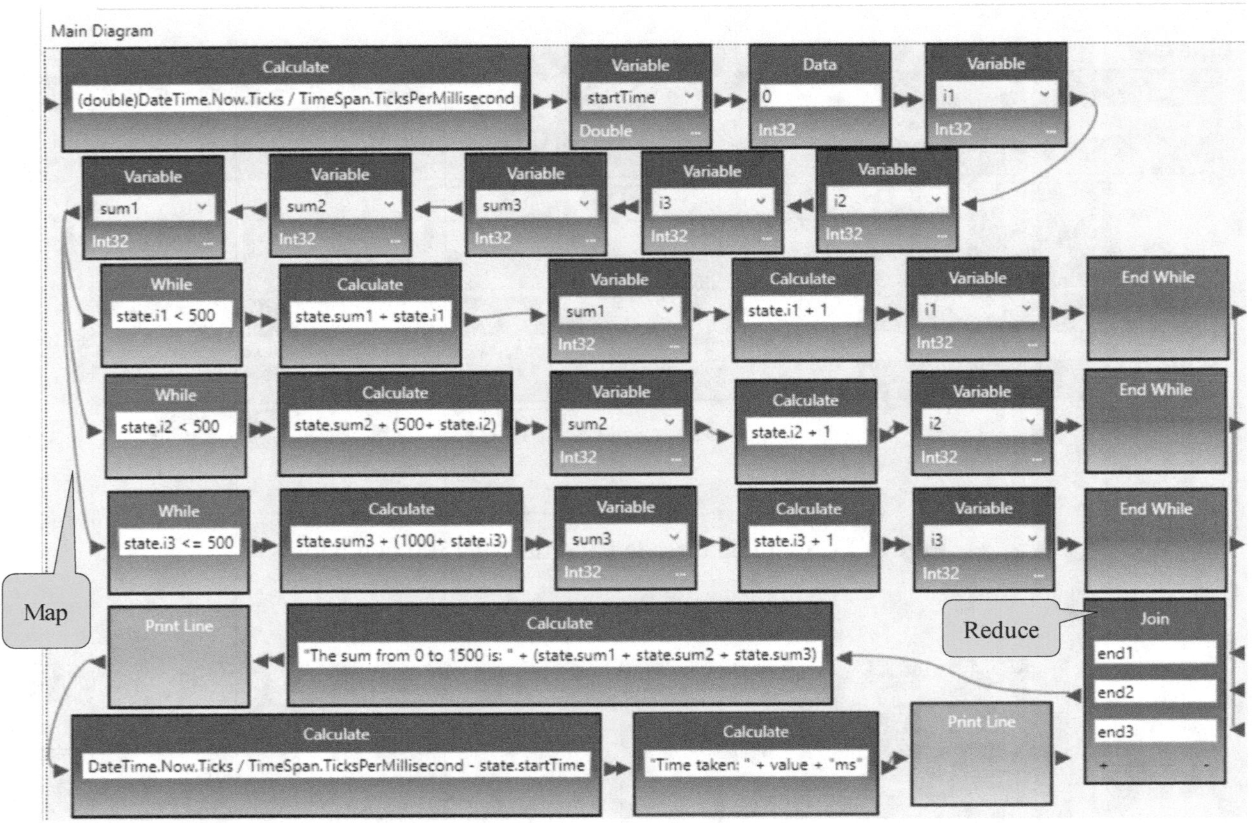

Figure 11.7. Multithread computing of 1500 additions, with time stamps

Figure 11.8 shows the outputs of the programs in Figure 11.5 and Figure 11.7, respectively. As can be seen that the times taken are 1473ms and 844ms, respectively, which represents a speedup of 75%.

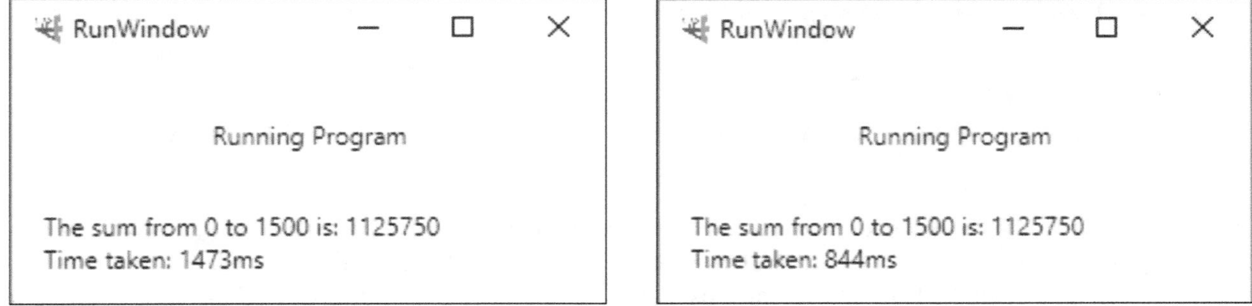

Figure 11.8. The outputs of programs in Figure 11.5 and Figure 11.7

The main differences of big data processing, compared with multithreading, are the automated data partition and automated map/reduce processes through a selection of parallel degree N, as we discussed in the Hadoop section. For the purpose of better understanding big data processing concepts, we simulate big data processing in a VIPLE program. We will implement a character counting application in VIPLE, as we discussed in the previous section. First, we show how you can load the content of a text file into a string variable using a Code Activity in VIPLE, as shown in Figure 11.9. The upper diagram shows how we can consume the Code Activity and the lower part of the figure gives the C# code of the Code Activity.

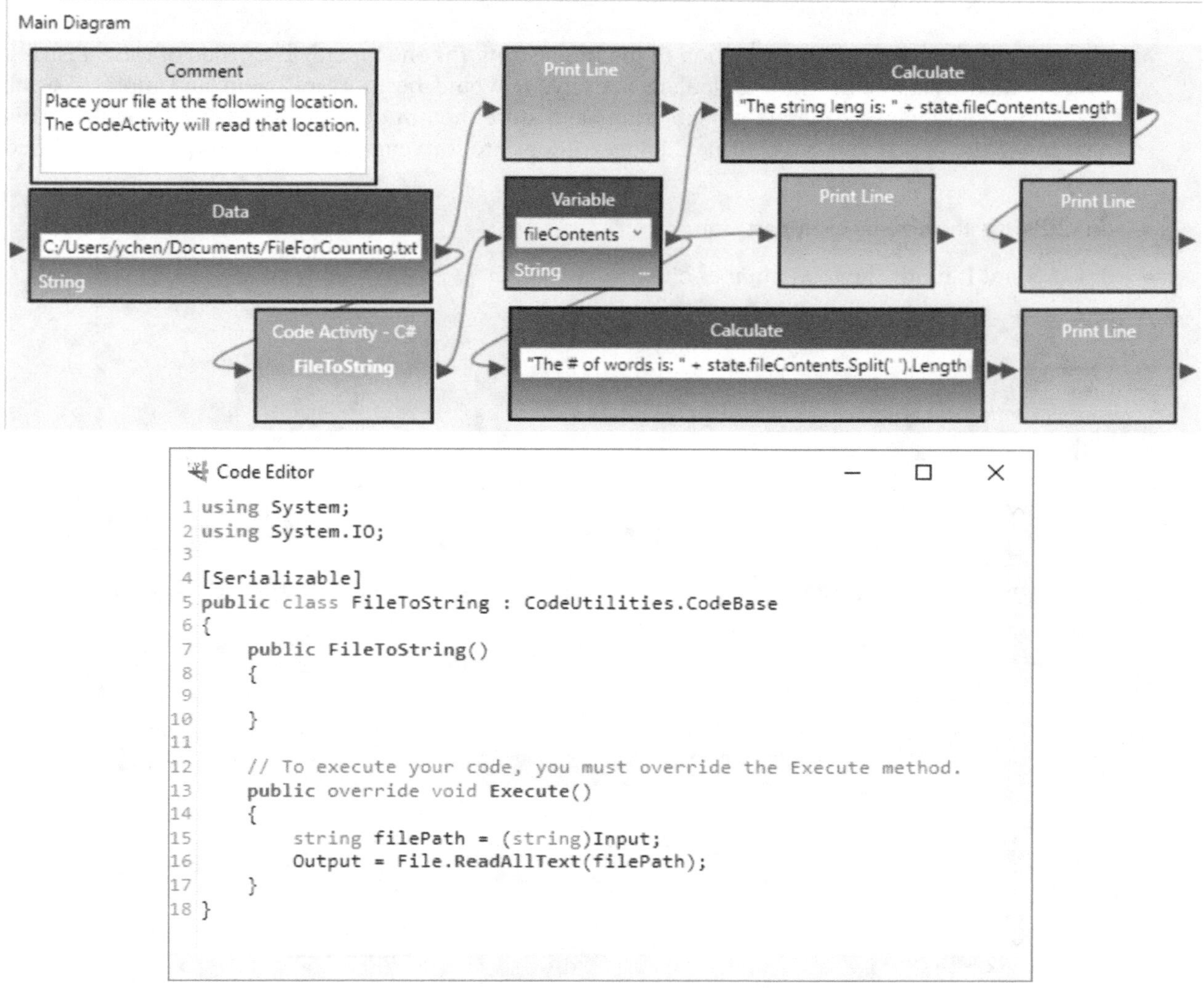

Figure 11.9. Loading a text file content into a string variable

Next, we will develop the VIPLE code for automated data partition and map/reduce processes. The main diagram is given in Figure 11.10.

In this program, we assume that the content of the text file has been loaded into the string variable inputData using the program in Figure 11.9. We use a Simple Dialog to enter the partition number N. To simplify the code, without losing the generality in terms of parallel computing, we assume the string length is a multiple of N here. Then, the input string will be divided into N equal parts, and then N parallel threads will be automatically started to process each partition of the data.

In the Main diagram, we defined six variables:

- String: InputData: It is initialized to the string whose characters need to be counted. In this program, it is assigned through a Data activity.
- Int32 N: The number of partitions and parallel threads to be started. It is entered from a SimpleDialog activity.

- Int32 i: A variable for iteration. It is automatically initialized to 0, and its value range is 0 to N – 1. When i == N, the iteration exits.
- String Substring: It holds one partition of the InputString for one thread. The value of the Substring is generated dynamically in a Calculate activity. It would be more efficient and more like the Hadoop process if we generate all substrings and store then in different substring variables. This will make the program more complex, and we choose to implement the simulation in a simplified way.
- In32 Part is the size of each partition.
- Int32 Sum: It holds the total number characters counter.

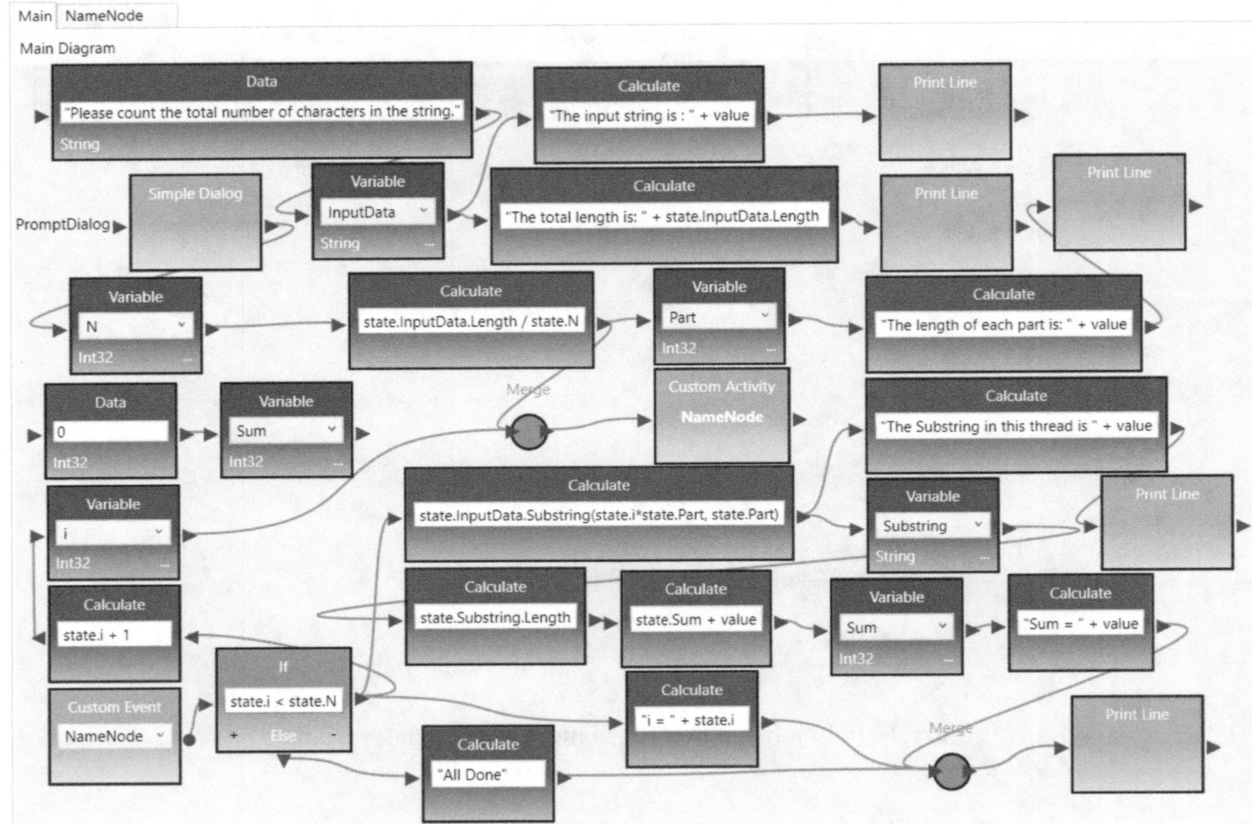

Figure 11.10. The Main diagram of the big data processing program

The program is not intended to show real big data processing. The main purpose is to show automated data partition and automatically creating parallel threads based on the input number. The key idea of implementing parallel computing of multithreads is to make the NameNode to output an event and to use a Custom Event module to trigger (start) a new thread every time the NameNode is executed, as shown in Figure 11.11. If we did not use a Custom Event module and instead, we linked the substring generating and counting into the loop, no new threads would be created, and the result would be a single thread code.

The event-drive program is very different from the control flow-based program. The event-drive execution part of the program can be explained as follows.

- First, the user enters a number from SimpleDialog. The number is saved int variable N.

- The program calculates the size of the substrings after the partition.
- Through Merge, NameNode activity is called. Note: NameNode activity does not have a data output line connected to any other module, because it does not have data output as shown in Figure 11.11.
- Since NameNode has an event output, it will trigger the Custom Event module to execute. The Custom Event will execute the code defined in NameNode, which checks if i == N.
- If i == N is true, the job is completed.
- If i < N, a new substring will be created from the full string and then the length of the substring is calculated. The size is added into variable Sum. In the meantime, variable i is incremented, and then, it will go back to call the NameNode activity, which will trigger the Custom Event to be executed and form a loop.

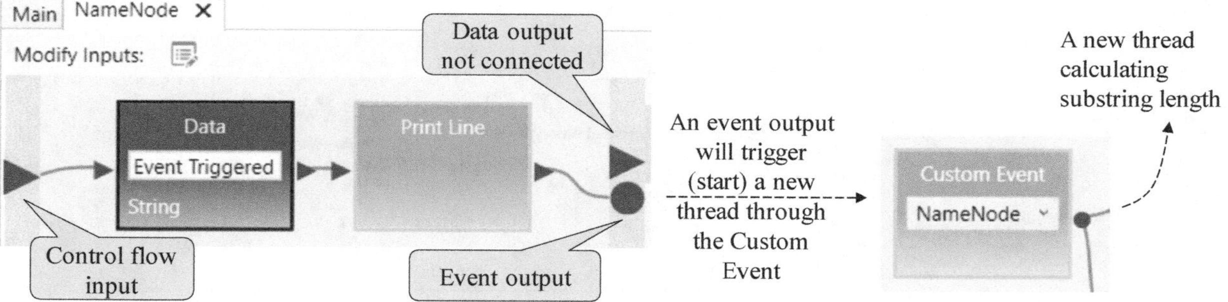

Figure 11.11. The NameNode, with event-driven implementation (connecting to event output)

Figure 11.12 shows the printouts from the Print Line statements in the diagram in Figure 11.10 when the input number N is 2, 4, and 6, respectively.

In summary, VIPLE's workflow clearly demonstrates the MapReduce concepts. Workflow supports parallel computing through forking and joining in a natural way. VIPLE can be used for illustrating big data processing concepts. However, it is intended for IoT and robotics applications, and we have no intention to make it a real big data processing engine that could outperform other big data processing platforms.

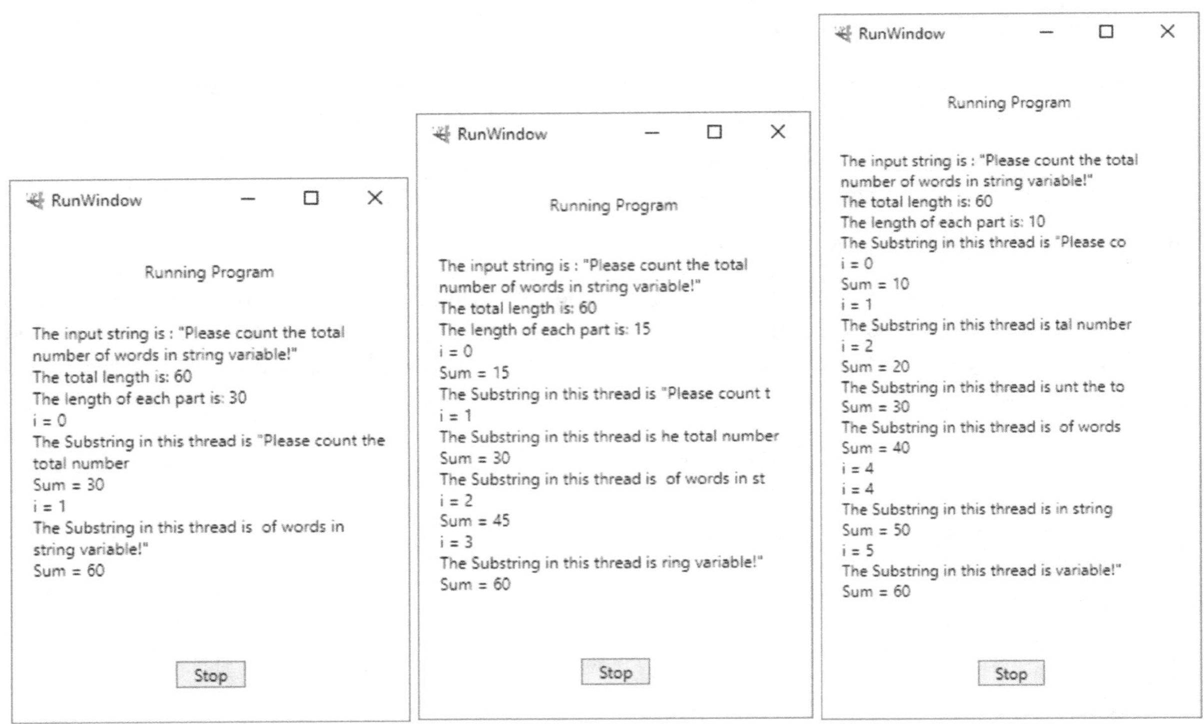

Figure 11.12. The outputs when the input number N is 2, 4, and 6, respectively

11.2.4 Apache Pig

MapReduce programming is complex and detailed. Apache Pig uses the higher-level, query-style, and functional programming paradigm to program MapReduce jobs. They describe what need to be done, instead of how to do the jobs, and let the compiler generate optimized MapReduce code.

Apache Pig uses programming language called Pig Latin, which is a text-based language that share many features of a functional and query language like LINQ. Pig Latin programs are translated into executable through Apache Pig infrastructure, including a compiler. The compiler will translate the programming using map and reduce function to solve the problem in parallel.

A Pig Latin program typically consists of the following steps: Load file, parse the file, and extract data from the file through operations such as filter, join, and group. At the end, one can print the result using DUMP and save the data using STORE. The following pseudocode shows an example of how a Pig Latin program searches through a library of books and a database of readers.

```
Books = LOAD 'DataSource/books';
Readers = LOAD 'DataSource/readers';
NewBooks = FILTER Books BY publishYear > 2000;
YoungReaders = FILTER Reader BY Age < 21;
YoungReaders =  JOIN YoungReaders BY Age, NewBooks BY Title;
YoungGroup = GROUP YoungReaders BY Gender;
Counts = FOREACH YoungGroup GENERATE Subgroup, COUNT(YoungGroup);
DUMP YoungGroup, Counts
STORE YoungGroup INTO GroupFile;
```

The program looks like a data query. However, it involves intensive computation. As it deals with big data, many parts are extremely time consuming, such as filtering, joining, and grouping. Apache Pig infrastructure will divide the data into pieces and apply map and reduce to process the pieces of data in parallel.

HIVE is an alternative to Pig. A warehouse infrastructure that provides data summarization and ad hoc querying on top of Hadoop. HIVE is similar to Pig in purpose for simplifying the expression of MapReduce jobs. It uses batch SQL style to write the queries, instead of using a functional programming paradigm.

11.2.5 Big Data Analytics

Big data processing concerns effective algorithms and techniques to perform required computation. Big data analytics concerns finding the meaning and the value behind the data. It involves models and techniques of discovering the valuable information embedded in the big volume of data. Several techniques have been successfully applied in big data analyses, including aggregation, indexing, querying, keyword search and pattern matching, knowledge discovery, data mining and statistical modeling, and ontology building and reasoning.

OLAP (Online Analytical Processing) techniques have been widely used for analyzing structured data in different types of databases. Even spreadsheet software like Excel supports OLAP operations such as: Consolidation: allows user to aggregate the data into a summary; for example, computing the total points of score and weighted average grade; Drill-down: allows users to explore individual properties; for example, one student's score; Slicing: allows users to take out a slice (a subset) of data to view or analyze the data.

OLAP techniques have been mainly used in relational databases. They have been extended to processing XML databases, as we have discussed in LINQ queries, and they can be extended to unstructured data by combining with other techniques, particularly, with the statistics to perform the operations such as: Population, sampling, mean value, variance, deviation, cumulative distribution function, normal distribution, aggregation, and Chi-Square Goodness of Fit Test.

Data mining and ontology are artificial intelligence techniques for dealing unstructured data. A different set of analytics and reasoning techniques have been developed, including classification, similarity and deviation detection, semantic distance, clustering and grouping, crowd sourcing analysis, and collaborative filtering.

Crowdsourcing is an approach of soliciting ideas or solutions from a large group people. The people may have different skills and backgrounds, generating different kinds of ideas of solutions. They may or may not be paid. The best solutions may receive rewards. Typical applications include challenges and competitions. For example, Intel Cornell Cup and Microsoft Imagine Cup are designed to inspire best designs in hardware and software. In politics, polling before an election is used to predict the winner.

Crowdsourcing approach typically generates a large number of different ideas and solutions. Common techniques used in data mining can be applied to process and analyze the data, such as similarity and deviation analyses, clustering, and collaborative filtering. More specific techniques, such as majority voting is more effective in finding the solution suggested by the majority of people. However, it may suffer from spammer attacks. Weighted majority voting can be used to outweigh the solutions from those who do not have known skills or credibility. For complex solutions with multidimensional attributes, a model needs to be developed to define selection rules and criteria.

Big data does not mean we always have more data than we need. In many cases, we do not have complete or sufficient data for us to draw the conclusions. Uncertainty theories and systems have been developed to create or predict the necessary data before drawing the conclusions. There are four major theories and systems in the domain: Probability Theory, Fuzzy Mathematics, Rough Set Theory, and Grey System Theory.

Rough set theory concerns with classification and analyzing imprecise or incomplete information, in order to draw a conclusion or result. The main idea is to find a set of data (result) by finding an approximation set of its lower value and an approximation set of its upper value. The lower-approximation and the upper-approximation sets can be normal sets or fuzzy sets with its element associated with a number (weight or probability) between 0 and 1. The rest of the value of the result set should be between the values of the two approximation sets.

Grey systems refer to uncertainty systems with insufficient and incomplete information. Grey system theory includes its own theory system based on grey algebra system, grey equation, grey matrix, and method system based on a series operator and a grey series generator. It also includes the analysis and evaluation model system based on grey related space, grey cluster assessment, the prediction model system based on grey model and other model systems, such as Decision Model and Optimization Model.

Rough set theory and grey system theory have been applied in datamining and data analysis in various application areas. For example, they have been applied in assessing and optimizing biomass boilers, in studying the feasibility of mixing refuse derived fuels with wood pellets combined with Fuzzy theory, in designing concept evaluation in product development, and in improving multi-objective optimization of laser cutting of thin super alloy sheets.

As an example, we discuss the clustering and grouping process. Assume that we want to evaluate the merits and relationships of a set of items; for example, stocks. We start with identifying the properties of interest; for example, ranking and price. We can further define (semantic) distances between items based on chosen properties. If multiple properties are involved, the distance is a compound value. To visualize properties of the items, we can put them in a coordination, as shown in Figure 11.13. We can run an algorithm to discover the relationships by identifying the center points of interests that involve most neighboring points (neighborhood). Typically, not all items are related together, and we often have a number of center points. Some of the neighborhoods are stronger than the others, and some points may not belong to any neighborhood. The clusters can reveal the correlations among the items. In the case of stocks, some stocks can be related in such a way that they often go up and down together.

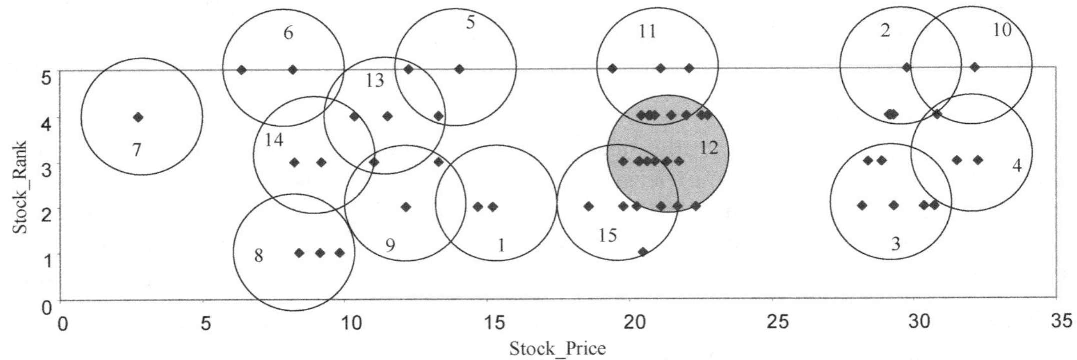

Figure 11.13. Clustering of related items

11.3 Big Data Applications and Case Studies

Big data systems have created many exciting applications, and that is the main reason they are considered the next big thing after Internet and cloud computing. This section will briefly introduce a few typical applications and then use the recommender system as a case study to explain the big data application.

11.3.1 Big Data Applications in Different Domains

Big data systems have been applied in different domains. In addition to the well-known social media and cyber space applications such as search engine, blogging and publication, recommendation, review, ranking, and cyber security systems, big data systems are also used in the domains such as education, finance, traffic control, crime prevention, healthcare, and real estate.

Massively Open Online Course (MOOC) is a big thing in education, where courses are put online, open to the public, and a massive number of students can learn through resources available. This education model is different from the traditional teaching and learning model. The new model is still instructor leading, but students are learning and teaching each other through social media style communications. Video and books are the main resources. Questions and discussions are the vehicles for interaction. Due to the size of the class, it is impossible for the instructor to read and answer all the questions and grade all the tests and assignments. A big data system has to be used to analyze the questions and answers, and to automatically generate answers to the questions and to automatically grade students' answers. Semantic analyses, data mining, and much further research are necessary to MOOC to become a viable option of education. Students grading each other's work with proper peer review guidance and enforcement is also scale in MOOC delivery.

Banking systems have been a major driving force for big data applications. Big data analyses have been applied; for example, to address the following problems:

- Retention: Bank customers often have multiple bank accounts. Big data analysis can help the bank to identify the needs of account holders and identify the services and pricing models that can better meet their needs.
- Resource plan and staffing: Based on account holder's transaction location, frequency, times and patterns to plan resources and staff level.
- Regulation enforcement: Bank must enforce the government regulations, such as anti-money laundering, sanctions, and embargo compliance. Big data analysis can track the formative transaction flow.

Tools have been developed to perform bank-specific big data analyses; for example, IBM Fiserv enables banks to deliver improved actionable insight during customer interactions with the contact center (http://www.ibmbigdatahub.com/pdf/fiserv). It has been used by more than 16,000 financial institutions. Benefits include more accurately predicting what happens next, better understanding of customers, increasing customer adoption, improving processing performance with increased capabilities and higher revenues through improved cross sell, more cost efficiency through higher productivity, higher rate of customer satisfaction/retention, and lower campaign and infrastructure costs.

Below is a list of existing and potential big data applications:

- Healthcare: Link all patients' test data, doctors' treatment decisions, medicine prescriptions, and treatment outcomes, and put the data into ontology. This system can be a reference for doctors to make decisions for their patients.
- Tax correction and tax evasion. The system collects all data from all organizations and individuals to detect any unreported tax data.
- Credit Scores: The system collects all the finance-related activities of individuals to calculate their credit scores.
- Retailers: Not only online retailers like Amazon and eBay, but also traditional retailers like Wal-Mart and Target have millions of transactions/hour to process. Traditional stores are also moving toward offering online shopping, creating even more data of both types.
- Traffic monitoring, traffic control, and security surveillance using a massive number of video cameras comprise another area that big data systems can make a big impact. Analyses of videos can detect any traffic violation such as red light running, speeding, illegal U-turn, and double yellow lines crossing. Tickets can be immediately issued upon detection. For the crime prevention,

real-time video analysis from massive number of surveillance cameras can quickly find the fugitives on the run.

- Real Estate: The system combines map, history of house value and price, weather conditions, traffic information, GPS signals, and drive time to different places and at different time periods to help home owners and home buyers to determine their home purchase and sell.

In the following section, we will use a recommender system as an example to elaborate the opportunities and challenges in big data processing and analysis.

11.3.2 Recommender System

The web provides an overwhelming amount of information, which represents one of today's major challenges of mining useful information. As an effective technique addressing the problem, recommender systems attempt to make predictions and give recommendations based on a large collection of users' historical behaviors and ratings. Many of these systems apply machine learning and artificial intelligence techniques to automatically update the historical data and improve the prediction. Recommender systems have become de facto standards and must-owned tools for e-commerce to promote business and to help customers discovering new products. Prominent examples include those systems used in Amazon, eBay, Facebook, LinkedIn, and Netflix.

A recommender system generates a recommendation list, which ranks a set of available choices based on certain algorithms and available inputs. Recommendation and caching are different techniques. However, they can make use of each other's information to make better decision. Caching buffers the recently accessed information, which could be used as a criterion and as an input to the recommender system. Recommendation generates important information, which could be used as a replacement policy for caching.

Recommendation techniques are also related that of the search engines. However, they are also different in a number of significant ways. Both generate a ranked list of information based on user input. Search engine's input is explicit, while the recommender system's input is implicit. Both try to generate the most relevant list to user. The search engine generates a list of hot spot information and a list of sponsored information. The recommender system tries to avoid the hot spot data, in order to bring more benefit to the site. It is valueless to recommend a product that everyone is trying to buy anyway, such as the latest iPhone.

They also differ in the sources of their information. The search engine mostly uses the public information, while the recommender system uses the internal information, such as the product characteristic and user profiles.

There are different recommender systems that use different strategies, input sources, and algorithms, including:

- Social or collaborative filtering: Use the behaviors and preferences of collective users on the concerned items as the basis of recommendation;
- Content-based filtering: Use the attributes and semantics of the concerned items to recommend similar items;
- User profile filtering: Based on the age, gender, the historical behavior, such as past shopping lists of the user, and so on to recommend;
- Situation-aware filtering: Based on availability of the items in the specific environment, promotional information of the items, and so on to recommend.

Different recommender systems have different merits and performances, which can be assessed in:

- Accuracy: representing the rate of relevancy between recommendation results and actual content, resulting in a high purchase rate;
- Diversity: referring to a reasonable extension to the content the user is accessing;

- Non-hotspot coverage: This criterion has been generally admitted as a critical one. The recommendation should avoid hot topic data, which can bring more benefit to the site;
- Existence of "cool start": Cool start is a situation when the system cannot make a recommendation as it has not gathered sufficient information yet. Social filtering can suffer from cool start;
- Responsiveness: A system must provide real-time recommendation with live interaction with users.

Social or collaborative filtering (CF) is one of the most successful methods to build recommender systems. CF algorithms are based on the assumption that users will rate or act on other items similarly if they have rated items similarly or had similar behaviors. CF utilizes the user-item rating matrix to make predictions and recommendations, avoiding the need of collecting extensive information about items and users. In addition, CF can be easily adopted in different recommender systems without requiring any domain knowledge.

The main idea of CF is to group users into neighborhoods based on their product preferences and review scores that they give to the same product items. For a target user, the system will recommend those items that have been highly rated by the other users in the neighborhood.

CF systems are widely used in many large e-commerce systems, and many strategies and algorithms have been proposed and implemented. Figure 11.14 summarizes different CF strategies.

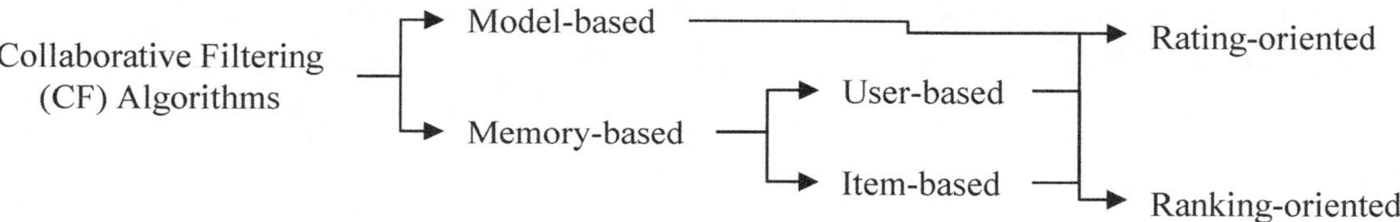

Figure 11.14. Spectrum of collaborative filtering algorithms

Model-based CF algorithms use a mathematical model, statistical model, or learning model to analyze data and make predictions on what a target user may purchase. Memory-based algorithms make predictions based on similarities of scores given by neighboring users and given to the items. Many commercial systems, such as Amazon, use memory-based CF, as the approach is relatively easy to implement and results in good performance in recommendation.

The memory-based CF algorithms can be further categorized into two types: user-based and item-based. The user-based CF algorithms estimate the unknown ratings of a target user based on the ratings given by a set of neighboring users who tend to rate terms similarly, and thus, what they purchased may apply to the target user. On the other hand, in the item-based CF algorithms, item-item similarities are used to select a set of neighboring items that have been rated by the target user. The ratings on the unrated items are predicted based on the user's ratings on the neighboring items.

Both rating-oriented and ranking-oriented CF algorithms can be applied to memory-based or model-based. Rating-oriented CF algorithms group the users based on users' historical rating scores on the items they review. If they give similar rating scores to the same items, they are considered neighbors in their judgment or taste.

The ranking-oriented CF algorithms group the users based on the ranking order of items that they review, which ignores particular values of rating scores but maintains the ordered preference relationships between the items. A ranking-oriented algorithm can be considered an abstraction of a rating-oriented algorithm and thus can be derived from a rating-oriented algorithm. Ranking-oriented methods are able to capture the preference similarity between users, even if their rating scores differ significantly. Recently, the formulation of recommendation problem is shifting away from rating-oriented to ranking-oriented.

The difference between the two CF algorithms can be explained through an example. Suppose the actual rating scores of items i1 and i2 given by user u be 2 and 3, respectively. A rating-oriented CF algorithm evaluates them as 4 and 5. As the difference is big, the algorithm would be considered to have performed poorly from the rating-oriented viewpoint. However, from the ranking-oriented viewpoint, the evaluation is accurate, as the preference order between i1 and i2, that is, $i_1 \prec i_2$, is the same as the actual scores.

Let U be a set of users and I be a set of items. In a recommender system, each user $u \in U$ gives scores on a set of items $I_u \subseteq I$, and each item $i \in I$ is rated by a set of users $U_i \subseteq U$. The scores can be represented as a matrix. Let R_{mxn} be a user-item rating matrix with m users and n items, where each element $r_{u,i} \in IN$ is the rating score of the item i with respect to u, and IN is the natural number set indicating different relevance scores. For a target user u, a set of neighborhood users $N_u \subseteq U$ are selected according to their similarity to u, on which the rating scores of the unrated items are predicted. Figure 11.15 illustrates the basis of correlating users in the user-based and item-based paradigms.

Once the items are rated or ranked for recommendation, we can use a priority list to store the recommendation list for each product item.

Rating-oriented CF recommends items based on historical rating scores of items. User-user paradigm is a widely-used model for rating-oriented CF, where Pearson correlation coefficient (http://en.wikipedia.org/wiki/Pearson_product-moment_correlation_coefficient) can be applied to evaluate the similarity $s_{u,v}$ between two users u and v with their normalized ratings on the set of common items $I_{u,v} = I_u \cap I_v$:

$$s_{u,v} = \frac{\sum_{i \in I_{u,v}} \left(r_{u,i} - \bar{r}_u\right)\left(r_{v,i} - \bar{r}_v\right)}{\sqrt{\sum_{i \in I_{u,v}} \left(r_{u,i} - \bar{r}_u\right)^2 \sum_{i \in I_{u,v}} \left(r_{v,i} - \bar{r}_v\right)^2}}$$

Rating of item i for user u can be predicted by the scores of i rated by a set of neighborhood users N_u of u:

$$r_{u,i}^{(P)} = \bar{r}_u + \frac{\sum_{v \in N_u} s_{u,v}\left(r_{v,i} - \bar{r}_v\right)}{\sum_{v \in N_u} s_{u,v}}$$

Item-item paradigm is an alternative model for rating-based CF, where the similarity between items can also be measured with Pearson correlation coefficient. The rating of item i for user u can be predicted by the scores of a set of neighborhood items I_u of i rated by u:

$$r_{u,i}^{(P)} = \frac{\sum_{j \in I_u} s_{i,j} r_{u,i}}{\sum_{j \in I_u} s_{i,j}}$$

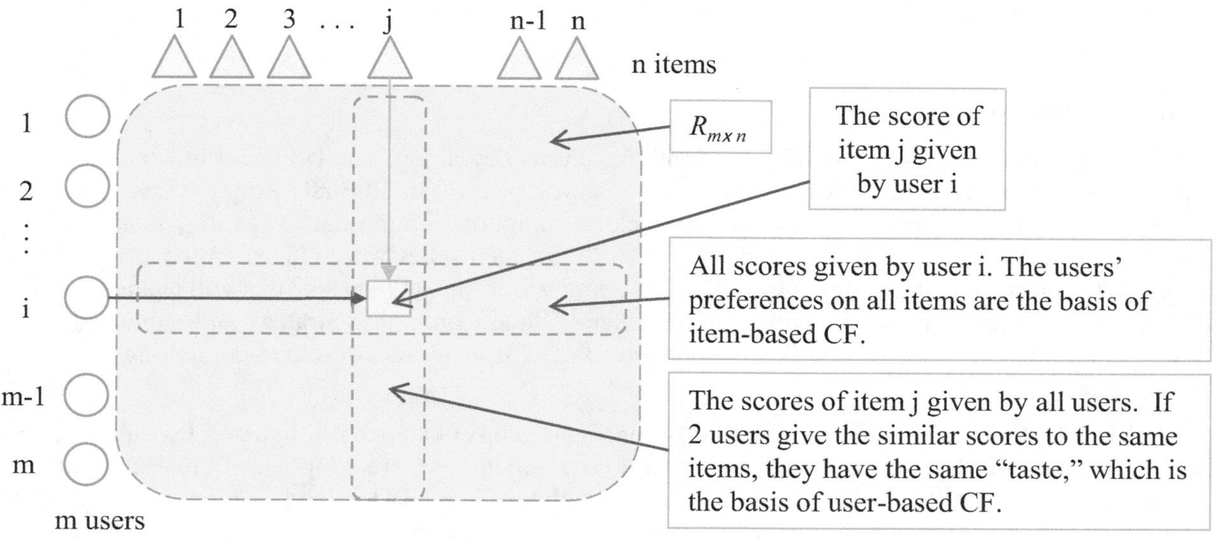

Figure 11.15. The R_{mxn} matrix, with the scores of items given by users

Figure 11.16 shows a possible implementation of using the priority list to store the Frequently Bought Together (FBT) list and attaching the list to each product item. Notice that the list changes dynamically based on the items' FBT ranking.

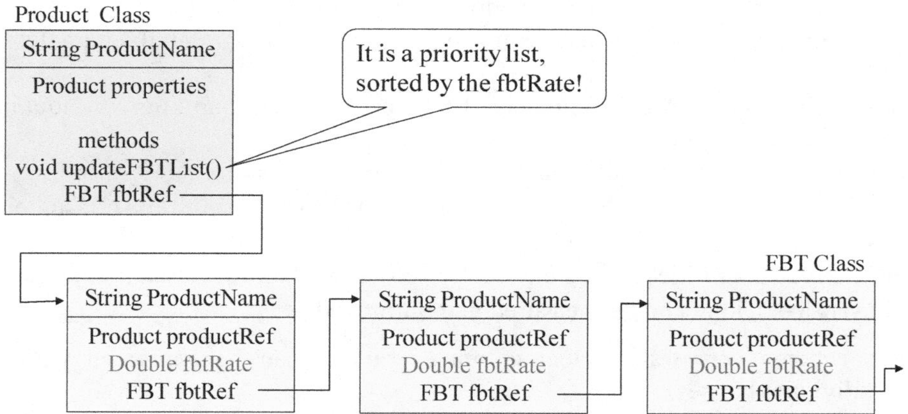

Figure 11.16. Caching the frequently bought together items

Many of the big data applications require machine learning and ontology techniques, which stores not only the data, but also the relationships among the data. The reasoning capacity of ontology gives big data processing and analytics additional power to analyze data from inside the data store. In the next section, we discuss ontology languages and frameworks that have been widely used in building ontology systems.

11.4 Cloud Computing

Cloud computing is based on a number of key technologies, including service-oriented computing, virtualization, data center, distributed computing, and high performance computing. Cloud computing becomes the enabling technology to support big data processing and the latest generation of artificial intelligence.

11.4.1 Definitions

Cloud computing has received significant attention from its beginning. The US Chief Information Officer (CIO) in the Obama administration, Vivek Kundra, developed a "Cloud First" Policy. Under this policy, the government agencies are asked to consider a cloud computing option first when they plan to launch a new IT project; and they are also required to identify three systems they would like to move from traditional servers to the cloud. Kundra believes that cloud computing is the next "Internet" that will change the world, not just computing. The policy is written in the Federal Cloud Computing Strategy and published in 2011 (https://www.dhs.gov/sites/default/files/publications/digital-strategy/federal-cloud-computing-strategy.pdf).

The US NIST (National Institute of Standards and Technology) has been designated by the US Federal Chief Information Officer to accelerate the federal government's secure adoption of cloud computing by leading efforts to identify existing standards and guidelines. The NIST Cloud Computing Program was formally launched in November 2010, which developed a Cloud Computing Technology Roadmap for the US Government's secure and effective adoption of the Cloud Computing model to reduce costs and improve services. The final document was published on June 18, 2013: http://www.nist.gov/manuscript-publication-search.cfm?pub_id=915112.

By NIST definition, cloud computing is a model for enabling ubiquitous, convenient, on-demand network access to a shared pool of configurable computing resources (e.g., networks, servers, storage, applications, and services) that can be rapidly provisioned and released with minimal management effort or service provider interaction. Cloud computing provides shared services as opposed to local servers or storage resources; enables access to information from most web-enabled hardware; allows for cost savings—reduced facility, hardware/software investments and support. The essential characteristics of cloud computing include:

- On-demand self-service: A consumer can choose computing capabilities, without human interaction with service provider.
- Broad network access: Capabilities are available cross networks.
- Resource pooling: The computing resources are pooled to serve multiple consumers using a multitenant model.
- Rapid elasticity: Capabilities can be elastically provisioned and released automatically.
- Measured service: Cloud can be measured and optimized.

Cloud computing systems versus individual computer servers can be compared with big apartment buildings versus individual houses.

A big apartment building typically has the following features:

- Shared Facilities
  - AC, Electricity
  - Water, Sewer
  - Safety/Security, …
- Scalability and Privacy
  - Can request much more space
  - Need to do more on privacy

On the other hand, individual houses have:

- Individual facilities
  - AC, Electricity
  - Water, Sewer,

    - Safety/ Security. …
- Scalability and Privacy
    - Cannot create much more space
    - Good privacy

As we discussed in the previous chapters, service-oriented software development follows a three-party model, consisting of a service provider, a service broker, and a service consumer. Cloud computing system development follows a four-party model: a cloud service provider, a cloud service broker, a cloud service consumer, and a cloud service auditor.

The first three parties are similar to those in service-oriented software development. What does a cloud service auditor do? When an organization starts to use cloud computing services, it needs to be aware of risks that it may face:

- The organization is unable to effectively oversee the service provider and other risks related to management and security weaknesses in the service providers approach.
- The organization needs to understand what the provider has done to deal with the risks in their cloud computing.

Thus, an independent auditor can better represent the users and check what the cloud provider has done. As defined in the NIST Cloud Computing Roadmap, an auditor can be asked:

- to appraise whether an organization is getting the benefits of cloud computing;
- to manage the cloud provider to ensure that the organization obtains the required services and handle the risks properly that the organization may face.

NIST defined three key layers in cloud computing: SaaS (Software as a Service), PaaS (Platform as a Service), and IaaS (Infrastructure as a Service). Many other alternative components can be defined, such as Data as a Service, Device as a Service, Robot as a Service, Test as a Service, and X as a Service, where X can be anything.

- The SaaS layer consists of the application software presented to the end users as services on demand, usually in a web browser. It saves the users from the troubles of software deployment and maintenance. The software is automatically updated within the clouds. Software license is purchased by the cloud provider and the users pay their shares as they use. Features and functionalities can be requested on demand. Furthermore, as SaaS applications are often a service-oriented program, they can often be easily integrated with other service-oriented applications.
- Platform as a Service: Often referred as cloudware, PaaS layer provides development platforms with collections of services to assist application design, development, testing, deployment, monitoring, and hosting on the cloud. It usually requires no software download or installation, and supports geographically distributed teams to work on projects collaboratively. The virtual operating systems for application development, hosting services, independent development environments, programming languages, and various utility tools are components of this layer.
- Infrastructure as a Service: Built on top of the data centers, the IaaS layer virtualizes computing, storage, and network resources, and they are offered as provisioned services to consumers. Users can scale up and down these resources on demand. Typically, multiple tenants coexist on the same infrastructure. Examples of this layer include Amazon EC2, Google Compute Engine and Datacenter, Microsoft Azure Platform, and Oracle Exalogic Elastic Cloud.

All large organizations have moved from server solutions to the cloud solutions, including government, financial organizations, business, retailers, and education institutions. All major computing companies have started to provide cloud services to themselves and to other organizations, including Amazon, Apple, Good, IBM, Microsoft, Oracle, and SAP.

In the following sections, we will discuss cloud computing layers and components.

11.4.2 Software Engineering and Software Architecture Leading to Cloud Computing

Where does cloud computing and Software as a Service (SaaS) come from? They are a part of software engineering and its development process. They are the latest software development paradigm.

The first-generation software engineering, from the 1960s to 1970s, was based on the following software architecture and development models:

1. Waterfall model: Software development model is a sequential and noniterative process like a waterfall, going through the stages of requirement, specification, analysis, design, coding, testing, deployment, and maintenance.
2. Software is organized in layered architecture for easy management and maintenance.
3. Structured programming, analysis, and design: The main ideas are more abstraction from the machine, focus on structure of the program by using procedures to divide the program into reasonable sized pieces, not only as a way of code reuse; Use of different scope (i.e., local variables) and much better control and loop structures. "Goto" considered harmful.
4. Compilation, interpretation, and two-steps translation in program translation, leading to higher efficiency in translation and in execution.
5. Abstract data types: Encapsulation of state and data access through public functions, leading to the development of object-oriented programming.

The first-generation software engineering transforms software development from machine and assembly programming to high-level programming, achieving significant productivity gain. The main technologies include compilers, OS, software development models, and programming languages. Programming language progress is the key.

The second-generation software engineering, from the 1980s to 1900s, was based on the following software architecture and development models:

- Object-oriented analysis, design, and programming
- UML (Unified Modeling Language) model and agile processes
- Software architecture patterns and design patterns
- CMM (Capability Maturity Model) and CMMI (CMM Integration)
- Model checking

Modeling, such as object-oriented modelling, rather than programming language, is the key technology. Furthermore, classification and cataloging (patterns) are the best software practices. Further productivity and dependability gain achieved due to the availability of tools, techniques, and documentation in the second-generation software engineering. Development process and techniques with stepwise refinement are the key.

The third-generation software engineering, from the 2000s to present, is based on the following software architecture and development models:

- Architecture-driven development
- Service-oriented computing and workflow (development + execution combination), with the infrastructure for service publication and reuse, which accelerate software customization and deployment.
- Cloud computing and SaaS with applications
- SaaS: development + execution + automated runtime management, including resource (sharing) and security (privacy) management.
- Big data collection, modelling, analytics, and processing. It introduces many scientific research questions into software engineering, such as data mining, control theory, and statistics.
- The third generation artificial, with self-learning architecture and machine learning, as we discussed in the previous section.

The platform and infrastructure are key to supporting the SaaS, big data, and artificial intelligence application development.

Table 11.1 summarizes the discussion by comparing and contrasting the features and key technologies of the three generations of software engineering.

Architecture-driven approach is one of the significant features of the third-generation software engineering. It requires to start software development from architecture design and refine the architecture step-by-step, leading to operational software.

Software architecture concerns the fundamental organization of a software system, its components, and the relationships among the comments. Architecture is particularly important when the system is big, such as the enterprise software systems. Enterprise architecture involves the one or more enterprises, including their business processes, data and information, as well as the technologies.

Enterprise Architecture Integration (EAI) has been widely studied and applied to seamlessly integrating business processes, data and information, as well as the technologies, within an enterprise and across enterprises. Many integration tools have developed to assist and automate the integration process. The purposes of EAI include:

- Architecture integration: Defining architecture framework for managing the development and maintenance of architecture descriptions.
- Data and information integrity: Ensuring that information in multiple systems is kept consistent.
- Application integration: Different applications can communicate with each other and are ready for integration.
- Vendor independence: If a business application is replaced with a different vendor's application, the business rules do not have to be reimplemented.
- Common facade: An EAI system can be a cluster of different applications. It should provide a single consistent access interface to these applications and shielding users from having to learn to interact with different software packages.

Table 11.1. Three generations of software engineering

Features	1st generation	2nd generation	3rd generation
Software development style	Software as a whole, with internal structure and procedures	Software as integrated components (objects)	Software consists of loosely coupled services with environment support
Software development process	Programming language and efficient code	Modeling and component integration	Modeling, workflow-based integration, data training and machine learning
Software development platforms	Programming languages, compilers, OS, and database management systems	IDE, reusable components, standardized processes and component-level integration	Cloud, SaaS, Services, distributed computing with standard interfaces, training and self-learning platforms
Computing platforms	Mainframe computers	Workstations and desktop computers	Web, mobile, and cloud platforms and tools
Operating systems	Mainframe OS	Workstations and personal OS	Networked, distributed, web, virtualized, and Cloud OS
Databases	Relational databases	Relational, object-oriented and distributed databases	Data center, big data system, with structured, semi-structured, and unstructured data
Concurrency	Sequential processing, time-shared parallel computing	Parallel and distributed processing in multithreading and distributed object model	Distributed services, service concurrency, and multitenancy, and automated up and down scalability
Key technologies	Programming language	Development process and techniques	Platform and tools

Enterprise Application Integration (EAI) has well-established standards with various implementations. The implementations typically compose of a collection of domain-specific tools and services, implemented, and a middleware to enable integration of systems and applications within and across the enterprises, for example:

- Supply chain management applications (for managing inventory, shipping, and interaction with other enterprises);
- Customer relationship management applications (for managing current and potential customers);
- Business intelligence applications (for finding patterns from existing data generated from operations). Big data is a major tool for today's business intelligence applications.

One of the EAI standards is the Enterprise Architecture Framework (EAF). It is a standard developed by the US National Institute of Standards and Technologies (NIST), dealing with software architecture integration.

- EAF is an organizing mechanism for managing the development and maintenance of architecture descriptions.
- EAF provides a structure for organizing resources and describing related activities.
- EAF follows Enterprise Architecture Model (EAM)

One of the NIST EAF implementation is the Federal Enterprise Architecture Framework (FEAF), developed by the US Chief Information Officers Council. The purposes of developing this framework include:

- Organize Federal information and promote Federal interoperability;
- Promote information sharing among Federal organizations;
- Help Federal organizations developing their architectures;
- Help Federal organizations quickly developing their IT investment processes;
- Serve customer needs better, faster, and more cost effectively;
- Provide potential for Federal and Agency reduced costs.

FEAF consists of the integration of the following eight components: Strategy, business, data, applications, infrastructure, and security. The full document is available at: https://obamawhitehouse.archives.gov/sites/default/files/omb/assets/egov_docs/fea_v2.pdf.

11.4.3 Software as a Service and Multitenancy

Software as a Service (SaaS) is an important component of cloud computing. It directly provides the functionalities and resources of cloud computing to end users. PaaS (Platform as a Service) and IaaS (Infrastructure as a Service) provide support and hosting services to SaaS.

SaaS is based on service-oriented architecture and computing, but it is beyond the service-oriented development process. Service-oriented development partition the developers into three independent parties: service-oriented development, service providers, service brokers, and service consumers. These three parties work independent of each other on their own servers and they are integrated through Web platform. SaaS integrates the three parties into the same cloud environment and allows seamless process of modeling, automated service discovery, composition, runtime execution, coordination, monitoring, policy enforcement, maintenance, and management and coordination.

SaaS not only considers software components as services, but also considers the entire applications as services. It can integrate applications into large applications to form enterprise software. The application integrations are based message integration platforms including point-to-point and service bus with a variety of message standards. Figure 11.17 shows the SaaS development process in the cloud environment.

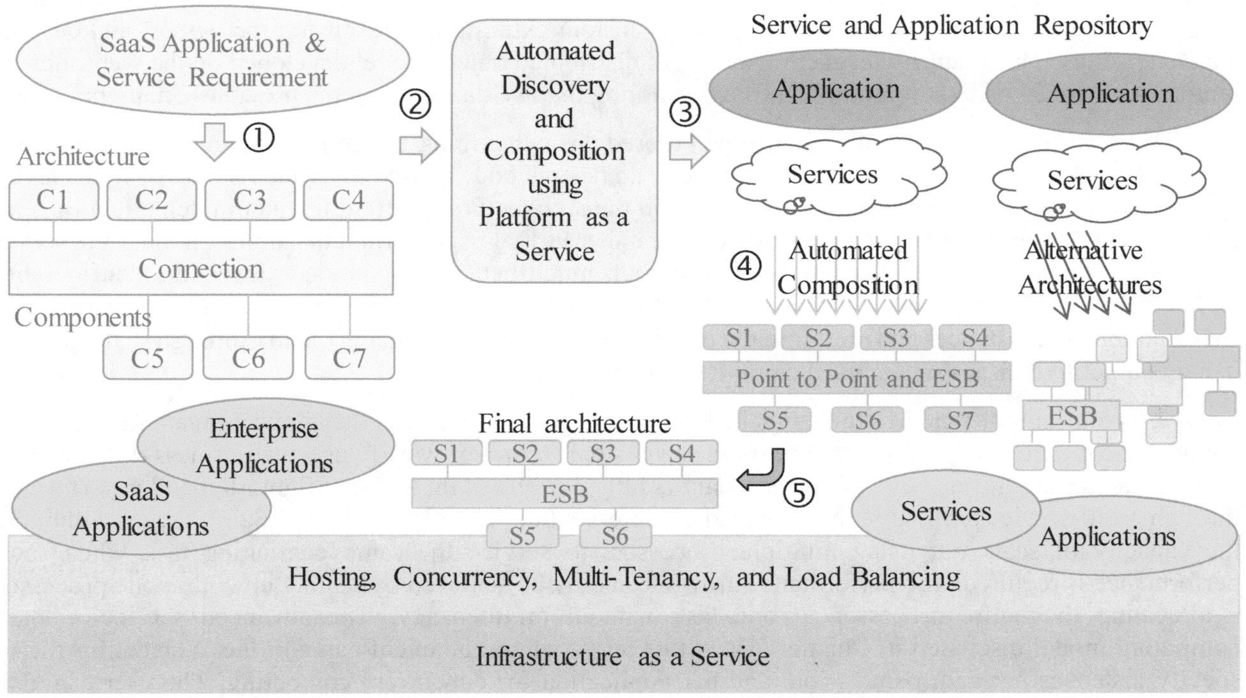

Figure 11.17. SaaS development process

For example, Google's cloud environment supports the following services: URL-based RESTful Service, which allows applications to access resources and communicate with other hosts over the Internet using HTTP/S requests. Mail Service, which allows applications to call Google mail service to send and receive e-mail messages. Image Manipulation Service provides APIs that allow its users to manipulate images, such as resize, rotate, rotate, compress, and flip images.

A typical SaaS application development process can be outlined in the following steps:

- Step 1: It starts with requirement, architecture design, and components interconnection.
- Step 2: The architecture is represented in a development tool in the layer of the Platform as a Service. The tool can assist the development with the automated and manual discovery of available services and applications.
- Step 3: It matches the architecture and components requirements with the available services and applications in the cloud.
- Step 4: It composes applications that meet the requirements and recommend the best application for the developer to select.
- Step 5: The selected application deployed and host in the hosting environment and the developer can configure the application to meet performance and cost requirement.

One of the key differences between the traditional server-based computing and SaaS is in its multitenancy execution model with better resource sharing, which allows the same software instance to serve multiple clients that access the software simultaneously. Service-oriented computing can also be considered to be one of the forms of SaaS, within the framework of SaaS maturity levels, as initially outline in Gianpaolo's blog (https://blogs.msdn.microsoft.com/gianpaolo/2006/03/06/saas-simple-maturity-model/). The maturity is divided into four levels:

Level 0 – Ad-hoc/Custom. Nothing is done specifically for allowing multitenants running on the same instance. The only way to support multiple customers is to serve them with different copies of the software. Furthermore, because little is done to allow customization through configuration, each copy includes specific customer customizations, in the forms of custom extension code, custom processes, and custom data extensions. This maturity level corresponds to distributed object model developed on the web, such as remote APIs based on .Net remoting and Java remoting that we discussed in the previous Chapters.

Level 1 – Configurable. The software can be tailored through editing the configuration file by the tenant without the intervention of the provider. However, no custom code is used to define the need. At this level, all the tenants still use the same software code, and the architecture is not multitenant. Each client runs its own copy of the same code. The separation can be either virtual using virtual machines on the same server or physical running on separate machines. Although much better than previous level, the configurable architecture allows customization through configuration file editing only, the computing power is not shared among the instances and therefore the provider cannot achieve better economy through scale, putting it at a competitive disadvantage vs. the multitenant solution.

Level 2 – Configurable and Multitenants. In addition to user configurable, the application architecture also includes the multitenancy concepts. The users can customize the software to use, the business rules, as well as the data model. The customization per tenant is fully performed through configuration and is performed through a self-service tool, without the provider's intervention. It is almost the full SaaS, except without is the capacity of scale out using multiple processors to service the same computing task when such performance is required. The performance growth can only be achieved by scaling up within one processor —allocating the entire processor to one task without multitenancy. The advanced service-oriented computing model discussed in Chapter 7 is at this level, where the client can edit the Web.config file to specify instances per call, per session, and per application for concurrent computing. The user can also specify singleton, per session, and per application for implementing data sharing and business rules.

Level 3 – Scalable, Configurable, and Multitenants. This is the highest level in the maturity model. The architecture allows all the capabilities of level 2: multitenancy and configuration, plus the scale-out of the application. New instances of the software can transparently be added onto the instance pool to dynamically support the increasing and decreasing load. Appropriate data partitioning, stateless component design, and shared metadata access are all part of the design. In this model, a Tenant Load Balancer (round robin, rule based, etc.) is introduced, maximizing the utilization of hosting resources (processors, storage, and bandwidth, etc.); the total load is adequately distributed over the entire infrastructure. The data is also periodically moved to average the data load per instance. At level 3, the architecture is scalable, multitenant and customizable via configuration and script code written by the clients.

As an example, we discuss the Google Cloud Platform, which consists of four layers: SaaS, PaaS, IaaS, and Datacenter.

SaaS: Various applications and services,

- Identity & Security Services
- Mobile backend
- APIs and RESTful service
- Machine learning applications: Data discovery, natural language API, Speech API, Translation APIs, image and video APIs.
- Cloud Billing APIs, provide methods that you can use to programmatically manage billing for your projects in the Google Cloud Platform. The API also provides programmatic access to the entire public Google Cloud Platform catalog consisting of billable SKUs, public pricing, and relevant metadata

PaaS: Platforms and Tools, also called Google App Engine

- Different programming languages, development environment, and virtual OS (Linux and Windows)
- API Platform and Ecosystems for developing and monitoring application development
- Cloud testing lab
- Cloud IoT Core: secure device connection and management

IaaS, also called Google Compute Engine (GCE)

- Virtual machines (processors, memcache)
- Worldwide fiber network for networking support
- GCE tools and workflow support, which enable scaling from single instances to global, load-balanced cloud computing

Data Center and Big Data

- Cloud storage, persistent disk,
- Cloud database, cloud SQL, and BigQuery
- Cloud BigTable and File System
- Cloud Dataflow, Dataproc (Hadoop and Spark)
- Cloud Datalab: explore, analyze, and visualize large datasets

At SaaS level, many applications and services are offered through services APIs, including:

- Identity & Security Services: They include a wide variety of services, for example, Google Cloud Identity & Access Management (IAM) service lets administrators authorize who can take action on specific resources, giving you full control and visibility to manage cloud resources centrally. For established enterprises with complex organizational structures, hundreds of workgroups and potentially many more projects, Cloud IAM provides a unified view into security policy across your entire organization, with built-in auditing to ease compliance processes.
- URL-based RESTful Services: They allow applications to access resources and communicate with other hosts over the Internet using HTTP/S requests.

- Mail Service: Through GAE's mail service, applications can send e-mail messages using the Google infrastructure.
- Memcache Service: The service is a distributed in-memory data cache accessible by multiple instances of applications.
- Image Manipulation Service: The service provides API that allows its users to manipulate images, such as resize, rotate, rotate, compress, and flip images.
- Task Scheduling (Cron) Service: Task scheduling service, also known as Cron service, enables an application to perform tasks outside of responding to web requests at defined times or regular intervals. In other words, applications can create and run background tasks while handing web requests: https://developers.google.com/appengine/docs/java/config/cron
- Cloud Billing APIs, provide methods that you can use to programmatically manage billing for your projects in the Google Cloud Platform. The API also provides programmatic access to the entire public Google Cloud Platform catalog consisting of billable SKUs, public pricing, and relevant metadata

More examples of the SaaS layer will be discussed in the following section with PaaS, including Microsoft Azure, and Amazon EC2 Cloud.

11.4.4 Platform as a Service

Platform as a Service (PaaS) allows developers to develop different applications using the operating systems, development environments, and tools deployed in the cloud. The key idea is to sign up a cloud environment and use the services, platforms, and infrastructure, instead of installing the platforms on your own computer.

Microsoft Azure is Microsoft's public cloud for developing and hosting web services and web applications, and SaaS applications. It is now integrated into Visual Studio development environment.

Microsoft Azure offers a large number of services and applications, and tools in following categories (https://docs.microsoft.com/en-us/azure/fundamentals-introduction-to-azure). Users can configure and manage most of the services.

Azure SaaS Layer

- Media: Media Services;
- Identity and Access: Active Directory and Multi-Factor Authentication;
- Mobile: Mobile Services and Notification Hubs;
- Backup: Site Recovery and Backup
- Compute Assistant: Scheduler;

Azure PaaS Layer

- Development Platforms: Azure SDK, Visual Studio Team Services, Azure Tools for Visual Studio, Automation, and API Management;
- Message and Integration: Storage Queues, Service Bus Queues, Service Bus Relay, Service Bus Topics, BizTalk Hybrid Connections, BizTalk Services.

Azure IaaS Layer

- Compute: Virtual Machines, Websites, and Cloud Services;
- Performance: Cache, Content Delivery Network;
- Big Compute and Big Data: HDInsight and High Performance Computing (HPC);
- Commerce: Store and Marketplace
- Data Management: SQL Databases, Storage Blobs, Storage Tables, File Services, and Import/Export Services;
- Networking: Virtual Networks, Traffic Management, ExpressRoute;

The service list above includes all the three layers: SaaS, PaaS, and IaaS. As we are discussing PaaS in this section, we will focus on PaaS layer here. At this layer, Development Platforms and Message and Integration tools are provided. Azure SDKs provide support to different programming languages and programming environments, including all .NET languages, as well as Java, PHP, Node.js, Ruby, and Python. These SDKs help you to build, deploy, and manage Azure applications. These SDKs are available either from www.microsoftazure.com or GitHub, and they can be used with Visual Studio and Eclipse. Azure also offers command line tools that developers can use with any editor or development environment, including tools for deploying applications to Azure from Linux and Macintosh systems. Furthermore, these SDKs also provide client libraries that help you create software that uses Azure services. For example, you might build an application that reads and writes Azure blobs, or create a tool that deploys Azure applications through the Azure management interface.

Visual Studio Team Services provide a workload testing service. You can execute load tests created in Visual Studio on virtual machines in the cloud. You specify the total number of users you want to load test with, and Visual Studio Team Services will automatically determine how many agents are needed, scale up the required virtual machines, and execute your load tests. For an MSDN subscriber, one obtains thousands of free user-minutes of load testing each month. Visual Studio Team Services also offers support for agile development with features like continuous integration builds, Kanban boards, and virtual team rooms.

Automation is a tool that helps developers to use a "runbook," which is written in Windows PowerShell workflows scripting language. Similar to the Makefiles in Unix, the Runbooks are executed without user interaction. PowerShell workflows allows the state in each step of the script to be saved at checkpoints along the execution way. If a failure occurs, you do not have to start the script from the beginning. You can restart it at the last checkpoint. This saves you a lot of work trying to make the script handle every possible failure.

API Management in Azure platform organizes and publishes APIs to employees, partners, and third-party developers securely and at scale. It provides a different API endpoint and acts as a proxy to call the actual endpoint while providing services like caching, transformation, throttling, access control, and analytics aggregation. It enables the providers to define different performance and charge levels to different users.

In addition to offer the comprehensive Enterprise Service Bus, Azure also offers a simple point-to-point queueing service to allow the messages to be stored when the receiving applications and services are offline or are busy at the time.

As an example, we will use Visual Studio 2017 to create a PaaS layer in Azure cloud in the following steps:

Step 1: Start Visual Studio, choose File → New → Project …

Step 2: Choose C# and Cloud on the left side of the dialog box. Choose Azure Cloud Service on the right side of the dialog box. Choose a project and name and change the location to the location where you want to store your project. Click OK.

Step 3: A new dialog box will occur, and you can choose the roles (platform service) that you want to develop to host your application or service. You can add multiple roles into your platform, so that you can develop different types of services and applications under one platform service.

Figure 11.18 shows the dialog box and the available roles that you can choose to develop. If you choose:

- ASP .Net Web Role, your platform service will host ASP .Net Website applications in IIS, which offer GUI for end user to access;
- WCF Service Web Role, your platform service will host WCF service in IIS, which will offer Web service interface for application builder to access;
- Worker Role, your platform service will not use IIS. It will host your Web applications or Web services within your platform service itself.

- Worker Role with Service Bus Queue, your platform service will offer Service Bus Queue to support off-line applications, such as messaging services and applications.

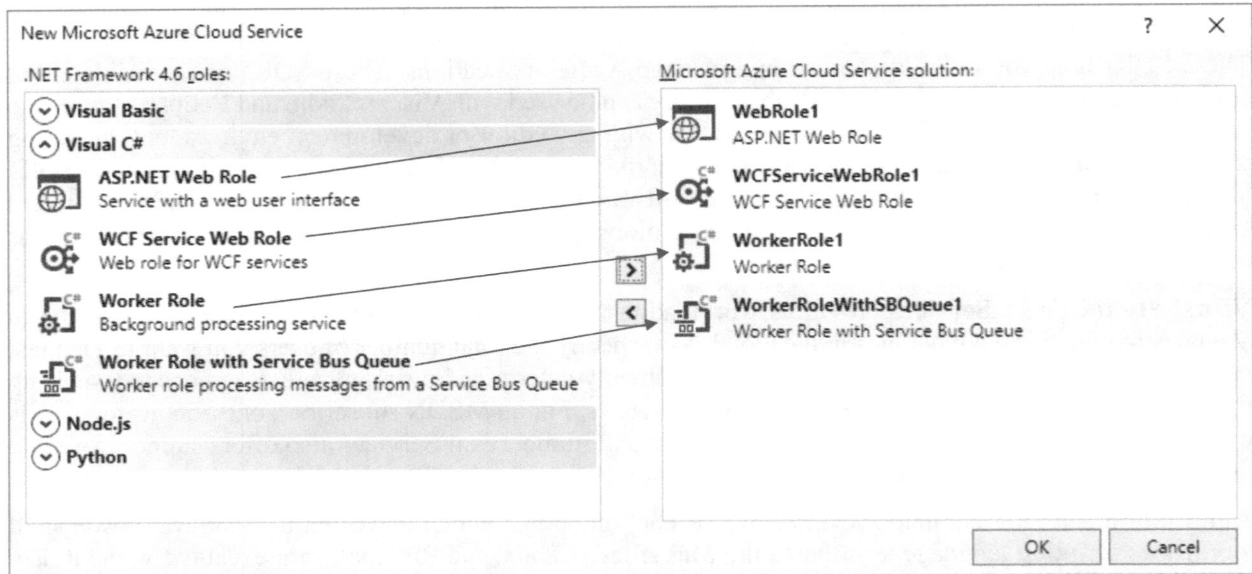

Figure 11.18. Selecting the roles (platforms) for hosting your cloud application or service

Step 4: In the previous step, we selected the ASP .Net Web Role. In this step, we will need to further select the type of the ASP .Net application.

Figure 11.19 shows the available application templates in this step. These types are the same as what we have in developing ASP .Net server applications. As example, we select Web Forms application.

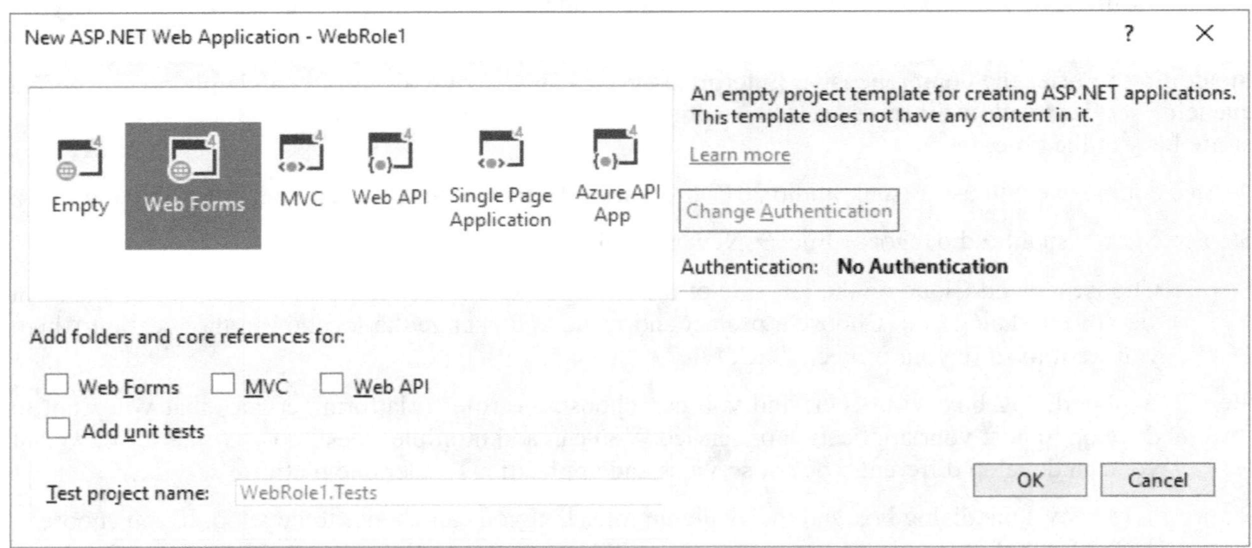

Figure 11.19. Available types of the ASP .Net applications in ASP .Net Web Role

Step 5: Once we have selected the Web Forms and clicked OK, the solution with four projects is created, including the project that we named (AzureCloudService1) and the three roles that we chose for hosting our services and applications.

The left part of Figure 11.20 shows the solution with the four projects, with three projects expanded and showing their contents in the folder. Take a closer look into the WCFServiceWebRole1 project, we can see the IService1.cs file. We can add your service contract and operation contracts into the file, we can have a WCF service running in the cloud using an IIS installed. The implementation of the service can be added into the file Service1.svc.cs, as we did in Chapter 3.

The right part of Figure 11.20 shows the expanded WebRole1 project, which is the Web Forms project that comes with a sample application. We can put our application GUI in the Default.aspx template and the code behand the GUI in Default.aspx.cs, as we did in Chapter 3.

Step 6: Build the project and Start the project. The sample project can be tested on the Cloud Simulator that is included in Visual Studio since 2017. Once services and applications are tested, they can be deployed into Azure cloud.

A free trial account can be created following the Microsoft address: http://azure.microsoft.com/en-us/free for deploying Web services and web applications into to the Azure cloud. The university may have additional academic agreement for faculty and students to obtain further access to the Azure cloud through, for example, MSDN AA or DreamSpark membership for creating free Azure account at:

https://azure.microsoft.com/en-us/pricing/member-offers/imagine/

In addition to Microsoft Azure, all the major computing companies offer PaaS services. Amazon Web Services (AWS) offers EC2 (Elastic Compute Cloud) cloud computing environment for service and application development and their hosting. AWS EC2 cloud offers the following services and applications (http://docs.aws.amazon.com/AWSEC2/latest/UserGuide/concepts.html):

AWS E2C SaaS Layer

- Various electronic business services and applications, as we have discussed in the services and web applications in the previous chapters.
- Secure login information for your instances using key pairs (AWS stores the public key, and you store the private key in a secure place)

AWS E2C PaaS Layer

- Preconfigured templates for running client instances, known as Amazon Machine Images (AMIs), which package the code for custom platforms, including the operating system, development environments, and additional software tools.
- Amazon Simple Workflow Service (SWF): SWF offers a workflow-based composition tool for building an application using existing services. It separates your business logic from the services, allowing replacement of services without changing the business logic. It also allows updating the business logic using the same services or new services.

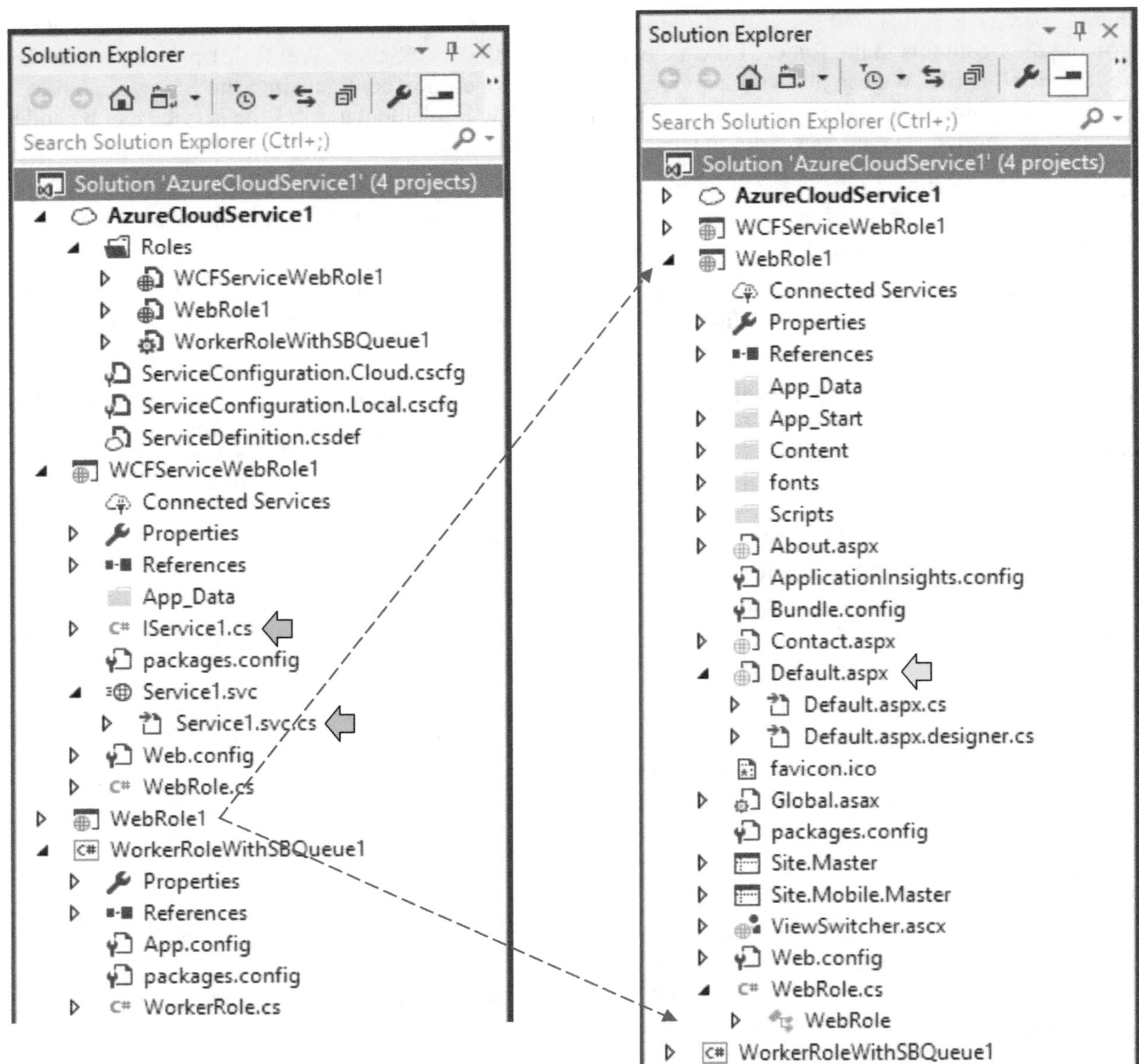

Figure 11.20. The solution with four projects are created

AWS E2C IaaS Layer

- Virtual computing environments, known as instances
- Various configurations of CPU, memory, storage, and networking capacity for your instances, known as instance types
- Storage volumes for temporary data that is deleted when you stop or terminate your instance, known as instance store volumes
- Persistent storage volumes for your data using Amazon Elastic Block Store (Amazon EBS), known as Amazon EBS volumes
- Multiple physical locations for your resources, such as instances and Amazon EBS volumes, known as Regions and Availability Zones

- A firewall that enables you to specify the protocols, ports, and source IP ranges that can reach your instances using security groups
- Static IPv4 addresses for dynamic cloud computing, known as Elastic IP addresses
- Metadata, known as tags, that you can create and assign to your Amazon EC2 resources
- Virtual networks you can create that are logically isolated from the rest of the AWS cloud, and that you can optionally connect to your own network, known as virtual private clouds (VPCs)

Google App Engine (GAE) is the PaaS layer in Google's Cloud Computing Platform for developing and hosting web applications in its IaaS layer, consisting of Google Compute Engine (GCE) and Google-managed data centers. They provide a seemingly unlimited computing resource and virtualizes applications across Google's servers and data centers. Google's Cloud Platform infrastructure allows its hosted web applications to scale up and down easily, and frees developers from hardware configuration and many other troublesome system administration tasks. Applications are sandboxed, with performance and security monitoring, failover for reliability (automatically transferring data and switching to another functional component at failure), and yet can run across multiple servers, allowing developers to build scalable web and mobile backend applications in any language on Google's infrastructure (https://cloud.google.com/appengine/). GAE supports multiple platforms, including Node.js, Java, Ruby, C#, Go, Python, and PHP. Developers from these language communities can be productive immediately in a familiar environment: just add code. Google offers stepwise tutorials and example of developing and deploying cloud project from a simple Hello World application to complex and realistic applications at: https://cloud.google.com/appengine/docs/standard/python/tutorials.

The layers of Google Cloud Computing Platform are listed as follows.

Google Cloud Computing Platform SaaS Layer

- Identity & Security Services
- Mobile backend
- APIs and RESTful service
- Machine learning applications: Data discovery, natural language API, Speech API, Translation APIs, image and video APIs.

Google Cloud Computing Platform PaaS Layer, also called Google App Engine

- Different programming languages, development environment, and virtual OS (Linux and Windows)
- API Platform and Ecosystems for developing and monitoring application development
- Cloud testing lab
- Cloud IoT Core: secure device connection and management

Google Cloud Computing Platform IaaS Layer is presented and discussed in the following section.

11.4.5 Infrastructure as a Service and Data Center

Infrastructure as a Service (IaaS) layer consists of computing, storage, and network resources, and these resources are offered as provisioned services to consumers. Data centers are also considered a part of IaaS.

The building blocks of cloud computing IaaS layer are normal computer systems, ranging from simple computers to super computers. The way that the memory architecture is defined determines how the computers can be used by the load balancer of IaaS. Figure 11.21 shows different types of computer and memory architectures. To obtain better performance, we can scale up or scale out our infrastructure. Moving from a simple (single processor) computer to a supercomputer, multicore, or multiprocessor computer belongs to scale up. Scale up schema can better support multitenants, where they can share the resources with lower costs. However, scale up is limited in clock rate, processor number, and cache/memory/disk size. Increasing the performance through clusters sharing disk only and through distributed/networked clusters sharing nothing is called scale out. There is no limit on how many clusters can be integrated into a cloud computing system, and thus, scale out, is the main mechanism for building cloud.

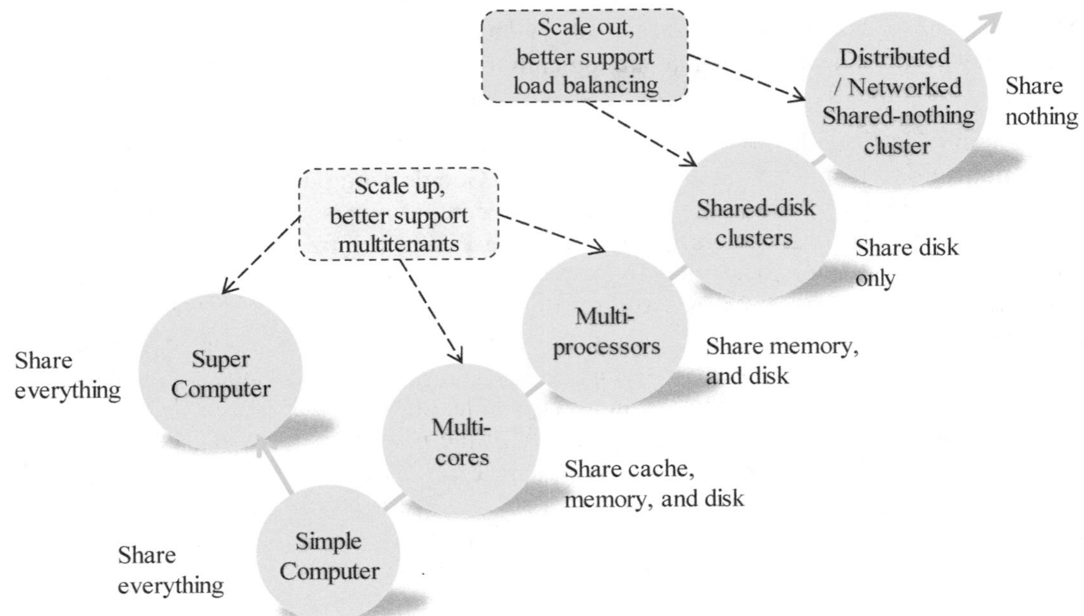

Figure 11.21. Scale up vs. scale out

Figure 11.22 shows the multiprocessor architectures with shared memory and with private memory. The architecture with the shared memory can deliver high throughput for independent jobs via job-level parallelism or process-level parallelism. It can improve the execution time of a single program that has been specially crafted to run on a multiprocessor, such as the multithreading programs discussed in Chapter 2. The challenges are the complexity when scaling up to handle more jobs.

The architecture with the private memory will require significant longer time for the communication between processors in the cluster. It can execute independent tasks with higher efficiency and can scale up with little restriction. The big data processing algorithms, such as Map and Reduce in Hadoop, divides the tasks into parallel tasks without communication, and thus such tasks can perform better in architecture with private memory.

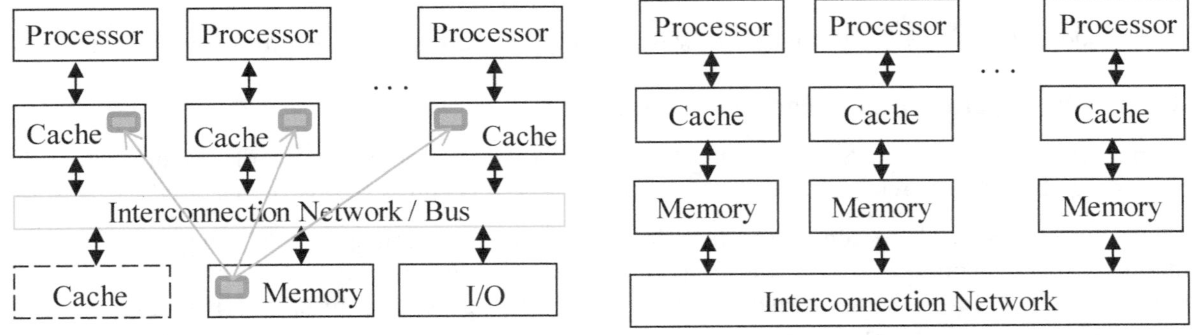

Figure 11.22. Architectures with shared memory and with private memory

Virtualization is another key concept in cloud computing. The early virtualization techniques are used to support run guest operating systems on top of the native operating system of one computer. It trades performance for the flexibility of running multiple operating systems on one computer. The further development virtualization allows to combine multiple computers into one more powerful computer through a virtual machine. The cloud computing IaaS utilizes both virtualization techniques to support multiple tenants in one machine and scaling up requests of using many processors from a single cloud user.

Through a load balancer, cloud users can scale up and down these the usage of the services and resources on demand. Typically, multiple tenants coexist on the same infrastructure, and they can share the resources and services as needed. Examples of this layer include Amazon EC2, Google Cloud Platform, Microsoft Azure Platform, and Oracle Exalogic Elastic Cloud. We have presented the IaaS layers of Amazon EC2, and Microsoft Azure in the previous section, with their SaaS and PaaS layer. In this section, we focus on Google IaaS layer.

Google Cloud Computing Platform IaaS Layer, Google Compute Engine (GCE) Sublayer:

- Virtual machines (processors, memcache)
- Worldwide fiber network
- GCE tools and workflow support, which enable scaling from single instances to global, load-balanced cloud computing

Google Cloud Computing Platform IaaS Layer, Data Center and Big Data:

- Cloud storage, persistent disk,
- Cloud database, cloud SQL, and BigQuery
- Cloud BigTable and File System
- Cloud Dataflow, Dataproc (Hadoop and Spark)
- Cloud Datalab: explore, analyze, and visualize large datasets

The architecture of Google Cloud Computing Platform's IaaS and data center architecture are shown in Figure 11.23.

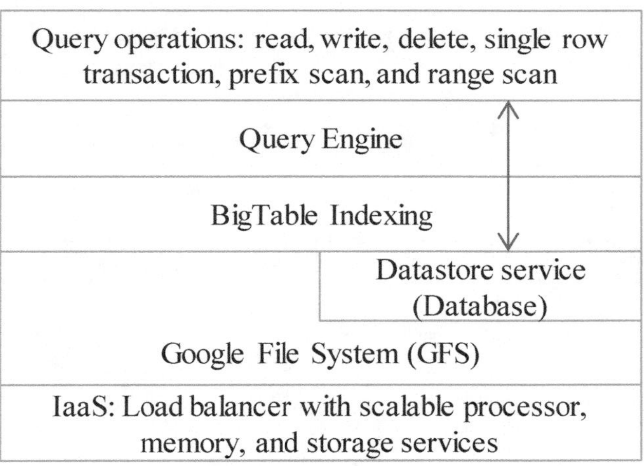

Figure 11.23. Google IaaS and data center architecture

Google File System (GFS) is used to store all types of data, including structured, semi-structured, and unstructured data. Its design considerations include:

- The system structure should be simple to develop to save implementation effort;
- The system will use thousands or even hundreds of thousand processors to support scalable operations;

- The inexpensive processors used may fail, but the system should mask these failures by providing at least three replicas to implement failover recovery. More replicas can be made to increase system availability;
- It provides familiar interfaces and APIs, which are designed to support common Google operations such as snapshot and record append.

Initial design goal was for high throughput instead of short latency. Note that throughput and latency are inherently conflict with each other: according to queuing theory, a system with high throughput often experiences high latency, and a system with low latency will have a low throughput. As more people use Google for searching and crawling, user experience became a critical issue, and one key user experience is low latency. Thus, GFS was later changed to address this issue.

The structured user data is managed by the storage service Datastore or Database. Datastore is a schemaless object. The structure of data entities is enforced by application code. Datastore supports multiple DB query operations, including atomic transactions. The services can be accessed via different language environments, including JDO (Java Data Objects) and JPA (Java Persistence API) implemented by the open-source DataNucleus Access platform

The BigTable is a fast and extremely large-scale database management system. It is a compressed, high-performance, and proprietary database system built on Google File System (GFS). It departs from the convention of relational database, with a fixed number of columns. The database is "a sparse, distributed multi-dimensional sorted map." The idea is similar to the B+ Tree that allows for efficient insertion, retrieval, and removal of nodes. It is a tree, and it represents sorted data in a way that allows for efficient insertion, retrieval, and removal of records, each of which is identified by a key. It is a dynamic, multilevel index, with maximum and minimum bounds on the number of keys in each index node.

In a B+ tree, in contrast to a B- tree, all records are stored at the lowest level of the tree. Only keys are stored in interior blocks. The presorted data index helps to search and retrieve information quickly from the large file system. Figure 11.24 illustrates Google BigTable and Google File System.

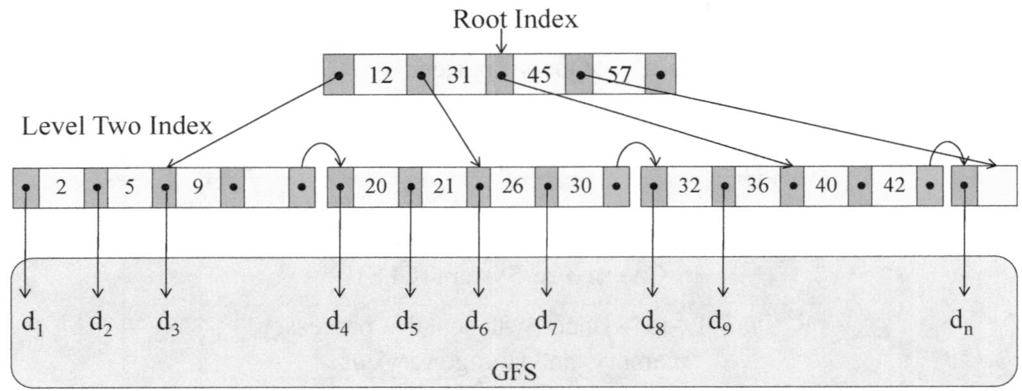

Figure 11.24. Google BigTable and Google File System

Oracle Exalogic Elastic Cloud was first announced in 2010 (https://www.oracle.com/ engineered-systems/exalogic/index.html). It is an integrated cloud machine, with hardware and software engineered together to provide a "cloud in a box." A consolidated data center, enabling enterprises to integrate thousands of disparate, mission-critical, performance-sensitive workloads in a cloud box.

Oracle Exalogic Elastic Cloud achieves high reliability, availability, and security through hardware and software co-design and hardware-based application isolation. It is built on high-bandwidth and low-latency interconnect fabric enabling complex, distributed applications to run with a responsiveness not achievable with typical servers used in data centers. Its load balancer supports massive scalability to accommodate small to large applications.

Figure 11.25 shows the Oracle Exalogic Elastic Cloud architecture. The Exalogic hardware is based on preassembled units in standard 19" 42U rack configurations. Each rack has the elastic cloud capacity balanced for compute-intensive workloads, and each rack contains a number of (up to 30) hot-swappable compute units, a clustered of high-performance disk storage subsystem, and a high-bandwidth interconnect fabric comprising the switches to connect individual components within the rack, as well as to externally connect additional Exalogic or Exadata Database Machine racks.

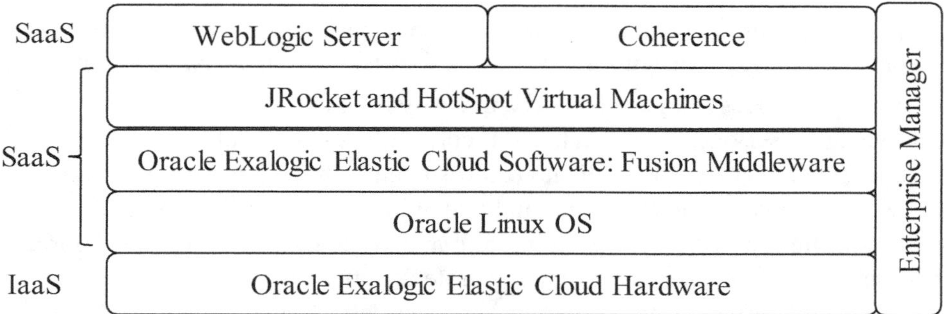

Figure 11.25. Oracle Exalogic Elastic Cloud

Oracle Exalogic Cloud is designed to provide an environment for enterprise Java applications and Java-based infrastructure. Exalogic Cloud software includes a number of optimizations and enhancements made to the core products within Fusion Middleware and Oracle WebLogic Suite. Oracle WebLogic Suite includes Oracle WebLogic Server, Oracle Coherence, Oracle JRockit VM, and Oracle HotSpot VM.

Oracle WebLogic Suite provides the foundation to integrate other Oracle Fusion Middleware packages, including Oracle SOA Suite, Oracle WebCenter Suite, and Oracle Identity Management. It also offers unified tools for management, administration and development, including Oracle Enterprise Manager manages multiple domains and WebLogic Server clusters from a single console; Oracle JDeveloper Integrated Development Environment (IDE) allows developers to assemble and build applications and services across application servers; and Oracle WebLogic Suite comes from Oracle Application Server.

11.5 Discussions

Data, processing, and communication are the three major domains in computing systems. Big data, cloud computing, and Internet are the flagships of the three domains. Big data requires the availability of cloud computing and Internet to process the amount of data involved. The combination of big data analysis and artificial intelligence is changing the society and the way of human living in all aspects, including education, work, entertainment, transportation, communication, safety, and security.

In this discussion part, we want to present briefly a big data and ontology-related concept called data provenance. Data provenance is one kind of metadata that pertains to the derivation history of a data product starting from its original sources (https://dl.acm.org/citation.cfm?id=1084812). Blockchain is a new technology that can implement and manage the data provenance.

In a big data system, data are passed among different data stores, processed by multiple workflows and services. Data may have a long history before they arrive at their final destination. A data item may have its own lifecycle in a big data system. For example, it can consist of the following steps:

1. Data creation: a data item may be created by a sensor in observing an external event, created by a service or workflow, or by an input device.
2. Data routing: the data item is routed within the big data system by various communication protocols such as HTTP or FTP.
3. Data processing: the data item is processed by services and workflows during the routing.
4. Data storage: the data item may be saved at multiple places including at the source node, intermediate nodes, and the destination node.
5. Data arrival at the final destination: the data will be presented to the user after processing. The data may be stored in a database for future applications.

Taking data provenance into consideration, we need consider the following functionality to be added into our SOC database design, particularly the design for the XML databases and ontologies:

- Data Integrity Services: they evaluate the integrity of data.
- Data provenance Services: they track and record the history of data.
- Data Validation Services: they validate records against the defined business rules.
- Data Cleansing Services: they cleanse and match inbound records to existing data.
- Data Transformation Services: they transform and align data from different sources.
- Partner Data Integration Services: they integrate data from partners.
- Operational Data Services: they provide a unified access to data in files, databases, and applications.
- Analytical Data Services: they provide analytical services for data.
- Unstructured Data Services: they provide an access mechanism for unstructured information alongside structured data.
- Master Data Services: they provide the access mechanism to master data.

Name: ______________________

Date: ______________________

11.6 Exercises and Projects

1. Multiple choice questions. Choose one answer in each question only. Choose the best answer if multiple answers are acceptable.

1.1 What data belong to poly-structure data?

(A) Data in SQL databases
(B) Data in XML databases
(C) Unstructured data like videos and audios
(D) All of the above

1.2 Veracity aspect of big data deals with

(A) data from different sources and of different types.
(B) what data should be stored and what data should be discarded.
(C) noise elimination and fault tolerance.
(D) extraordinary large volume of data.

1.3 You are designing a big data system with poly-structured data. What type of data store (database) should be used for storing the unstructured data?

(A) key-value data store
(B) generic list of objects
(C) relational data store
(D) XML data store

1.4 CAP theory in big data processing deals with the compromises among

(A) Consistency and data integrity
(B) Availability and reliability
(C) Partition and distribution
(D) All of the above

1.5 MapReduce computing in big data systems takes a list of key-value pairs as input and computes the results in two phases: Map and Reduce. Map phase will process the input list and output

(A) N sub-lists, and then Reduce phase computes the N sub-lists into a single list.
(B) a shorter list, and then Reduce phase computes the shorter list into a single pair as output.
(C) two half lists, and then Reduce merge the two half lists into a single list.
(D) two half lists, and then Reduce process the two half lists to obtain a single pair as output.

1.6 Hadoop is a distributed system

(A) consisting of distributed processing units and distributed storage units.
(B) that supports MapReduce computing model.
(C) that applies the same operations to multiple data sets automatically.
(D) All of the above.

1.7 There are two types of nodes in a Hadoop system: master node and slave node; both types of nodes contain

(A) Data Node and Task Tracker
(B) Name Node and Task Tracker
(C) Task Tracker and Job Tracker
(D) Name Node and Job Tracker

1.8 Compared with multithreading, Hadoop simplifies programming effort by

(A) eliminating the need of writing code of mapping.

(B) eliminating the need of writing code of reducing.

(C) generating executable from visual workflow.

(D) automatically partitioning the data and generating the required number of task trackers.

1.9 Cassandra is a distributed database management system that

(A) implements Hadoop standard.

(B) does not have a single point of failure.

(C) supports multithreading, instead of MapReduce.

(D) is a proprietary system, instead of an open-source system.

1.10 Clustering analysis is a data mining method used for finding relationship among data. The center points are

(A) the four corners of a rectangle predefined.

(B) calculated dynamically using the data collected.

(C) those that have an equal distance all its neighboring points.

(D) randomly selected.

1.11 How does VIPLE initiate parallel threads?

(A) It initiates a new thread through a custom activity.

(B) It initiates a new thread through a custom event.

(C) It initiates a new thread through a code activity.

(D) It initiates a new thread through a loop.

1.12 What features does SaaS have?

(A) It is identical to SOA software, and there is no difference.

(B) SaaS does not use SOA technology at all.

(C) SaaS extends SOA software, and it is hosted on a cloud environment.

(D) SaaS is the same as a web service.

1.13 How does a cloud computing environment implement scalable and configurable computing in a multitenant environment?

(A) Through a load balancer.

(B) Through a fail-over service.

(C) Through multithreading.

(D) Through software as a service.

1.14 Computing capacity can be increased through scale up and scale out strategies. Which strategy is typically used for supporting cloud computing?

(A) scale up.

(B) scale out.

(C) They are equally good.

(D) They are equally bad.

1.15 Which of the following belong to Platform as a Service layer?

(A) Programming environment.

(B) Operating system.

(C) Both (A) and (B) (D) Neither (A) nor (B).

1.16 Which of the followings belong to Infrastructure as a Service layer?

(A) Email (B) Operating system.

(C) Programming language Environment (D) Memory and Processor.

1.17 What is the meaning of multitenancy architecture?

(A) It is a house that is for rent by tenants.

(B) Each tenant will have specific source code within a multitenancy SaaS customized for specific applications.

(C) Each tenant can contribute their software as a part of SaaS.

(D) Only one version of the software is used for all tenants.

(E) It is not possible to scale multitenancy architecture for large applications.

1.18 What statement best describes the Google Compute Engine (GCE)?

(A) GCE is a data center for efficient data storage and retrieval of structured data.

(B) GCE is a data center for efficient data storage and retrieval of semi-structured data.

(C) GCE is an application development, hosting, and data management system.

(D) GCE is Google's IaaS managing processor, memory, and networking resources.

1.19 What is the main purpose of Google's BigTable?

(A) To extend the content capacity of Google File System (GFS).

(B) To store metadata, such as indices, to the contents in Google File System (GFS).

(C) To use a big data table to store all the data in one place.

(D) To take the advantage of the space locality for efficient block data retrieval.

1.20 What does the word "failover" mean in cloud computing environment?

(A) A failure of a critical component that can lead to the failure of the entire system.

(B) Repeated occurrences of transient failures in a short period of time.

(C) Automatic transferring of the functions of a failed component to other components.

(D) An event indicating the occurrence of a failure.

2. Where does the map and reduce concept come from?

3. What are major differences between multithreading and big data processing?

4. What are the weaknesses in Hadoop framework?

5. How is Hadoop process simulated in VIPLE?

6. How can we use web services to simulate the Hadoop process?

7. What are the advantages of the three-level lookup scheme used by BigTable?

8. What are the maturity levels of SaaS and cloud computing?

9. What does multi tenancy mean?

10. What is the role of load balancer in cloud computing environment?

Project 1

In this project, you will create a web application platform that allows user to perform automated parallel computing that mimics the Hadoop process. A sample user interface is given in Figure 11.26.

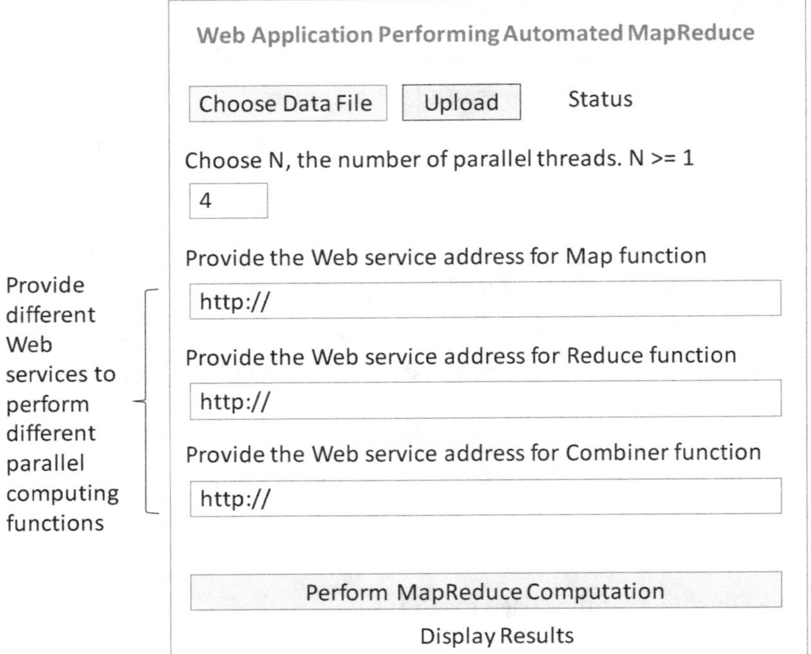

Figure 11.26. Web application GUI with Web service calls

The web application should consist of the following components.

- GUI component and the connection to the other components.
- NameNode: It splits the uploaded Data File into N subsets and provides a subset to each TaskTracker.
- TaskTracker: It consists of Map function and a Reduce function.
- Map function: It converts data from subset of Data File into Key-value pairs, based on the functionality requirement.
- Reduce function: It reduces the key-value pairs into one or smaller number of key-value pairs, based on the functionality requirement.
- Combiner: It synchronizes and combines the results from all the Reduce functions and put the final results.

You can implement the Word Count application. It counts the number of words in the uploaded Data File. The components and the computation process are illustrated in Figure 11.27.

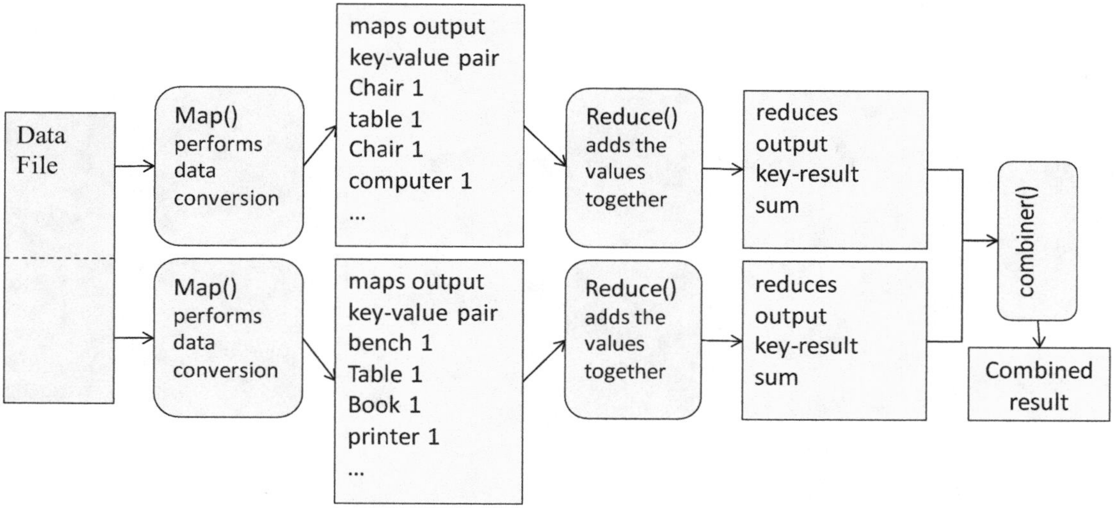

Figure 11.27. Map and Reduce execution with N = 2

You can implement the Web application either as an ASP .Net Website application or MVC Web application on localhost. You can also choose to implement the application in one of the following two options.

Project 2

In this project, you will use VIPLE (Chapter 9) to simulate the Hadoop process. Figure 11.9, Figure 11.10, and Figure 11.11 give an example, where string's characters are counted. It is not a realistic application that improves the performance of computing. The main purpose of this example is to show how you can automatically start N threads to perform parallel computing, where N can be entered from the keyboard.

Your tasks in the option are as follows:

- Write a service or a code activity to load the text in a text file into variable InputData. Use it to replace the Data activity that provided the Input data.
- Count the number of words, instead of the number characters.
- Make sure that your program can execute correct even if the data length is not a multiple of N. In the given program in Figure 11.10, this check is not performed to keep the program small.

Chapter 12
Artificial Intelligence and Machine Learning

In the previous chapter, we discussed big data processing and cloud computing. This chapter will extend the discussion to latest artificial intelligence system and machine learning techniques, which is largely based on big data processing and cloud computing.

12.1 Development of Artificial Intelligence and Machine Learning

In this section, we will briefly discuss the development of Artificial Intelligence (AI) and Machine Learning (ML), the differences between traditional programming and AI/ML-based programming, the process of developing AI systems, and solving AI problem using big data analytics and processing techniques.

Artificial intelligence (AI), started in the 1950s, is one of the first domains of computer science. The computer science pioneer Alan Turing published the first AI paper on "Computing Machinery and Intelligence," when he was working at the Victoria University of Manchester in 1950. The computers are also called electronic brain in many natural languages, as they are expected to aid or replace the human brains. AI has gone through several waves of excitements and disappointments and has developed several generations of techniques and approaches. The latest AI techniques are based on cloud computing and big data analysis. AI are closely related to robotics and have similar development generations, particular its computing components. Table 12.1 shows the development of AI and robotics technologies.

Table 12.1. Development of AI and robotics

	First generation 1950s–1970s	Second generation 1980s–2000s	Third generation from 2006
AI Development	• Cybernetics and brain simulation • Symbol manipulation • Knowledge-based expert system	• Cognitive simulation • Computational intelligence and soft computing • Statistical	• Big data-based intelligence • Neural networks and deep learning • From data collection to decision making in real time
Robotics Development	• Automated control systems • Servos and actuators	• Sensing and interacting with human & environment • Visual inputs	• Cognitive • Natural language processing • Human machine interaction
Applications	AI in research and robotics in manufacturing	Research, manufacturing, business, and service	In all domains, including healthcare, transportation, agriculture, business, finance, education, gaming, defense, and government

The key features of the third generation AI and robotics include:

- Human machine integration: Through deep learning, robots and its AI system can understand human language, visual expressions, and even emotion.
- Software and hardware co-definition: Software will play key roles in big data collection, processing, analysing, learning, and decision making. Hardware acceleration is also critical to make it possible to obtain the real-time experience.
- Virtual and reality integration: Virtual things in cyberspace and the real devices will work together and support each other. A live flow between real, virtual, and augmented reality and switch as needed to optimize the efficiency and experience.
- Centralization and distribution optimization: Centralized and distributed computing and storage are carefully planned and organized. The fog computing capacity in intelligent devices can handle the locality issues, while cloud computing facility offers the centralized computing facility and data center performs the core AI processing.
- Sharing and privacy: All devices and data are connected and sharable, based on the well-defined security and privacy.

The current artificial intelligence (AI) and AI-based robotics branches and their relationships are illustrated in Figure 12.1. By no means does the figure cover all the branches or illustrate all the relationships among the branches. We have covered some of these branches in the previous sections and chapters, and we will cover a few more branches in the remainder of this chapter.

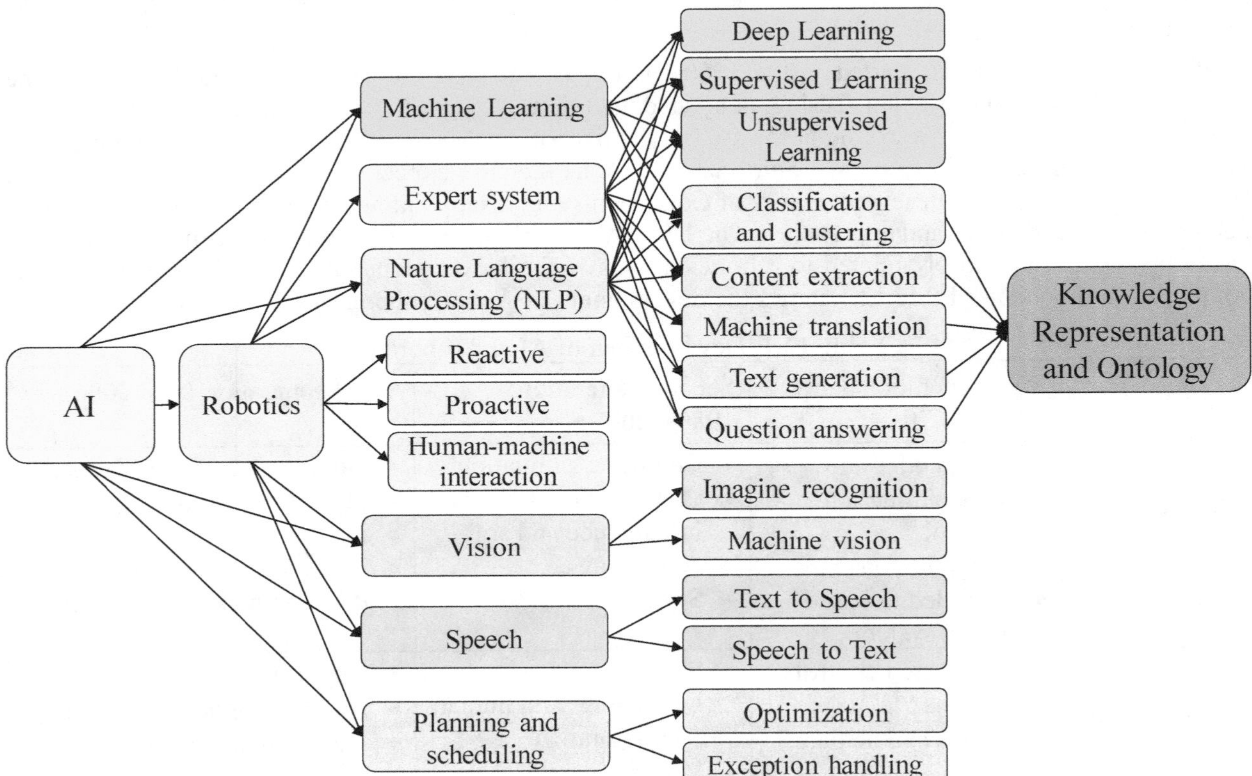

Figure 12.1. Artificial intelligence (AI) and AI-based robotics branches and their relationships

The current approach to AI and robotics is to develop an integrated hardware, software, big data, and user experience solution. Many companies have developed hardware to accelerated AI processing. NVidia is a major player in AI chip design. For example, its Tesla P100 GPU chip released 2016 can perform deep learning neural network tasks 12 times faster than the company's previous top-end system. The P100 was a huge commitment for NVidia, costing over $2 billion in research and development, and it puts 150 billion transistors on a single chip, making the P100 the world's largest chip, NVidia claims. In addition to machine learning, the P100 will work for all sorts of high-performance computing.

Google released its Cloud TPU in 2017. Based on Google's previous TPU, the new chip is used to drive Google's own AI and cloud services, including its image recognition and machine translation tools. The new TPU can be used to train neural networks, not just run them once they're trained.

Loihi, released in 2017, is the latest and the most powerful AI chip from Intel, which includes digital circuits that mimic the brain's basic mechanics, making machine learning faster and more efficient while requiring lower compute power. Neuromorphic chip models draw inspiration from how neurons communicate and learn, using spikes and plastic synapses that can be modulated based on timing. This could help computers self-organize and make decisions based on patterns and associations. Based in Intel document (https://newsroom.intel.com/editorials/intels-new-self-learning-chip-promises-accelerate-artificial-intelligence/), Loihi has the following features:

- Fully asynchronous neuromorphic many core mesh that supports a wide range of sparse, hierarchical and recurrent neural network topologies with each neuron capable of communicating with thousands of other neurons.
- Each neuromorphic core includes a learning engine that can be programmed to adapt network parameters during operation, supporting supervised, unsupervised, reinforcement and other learning paradigms.
- Fabrication on Intel's 14 nm process technology, with a total of 130,000 neurons and 130 million synapses.
- Development and testing of several algorithms with high algorithmic efficiency for problems including path planning, constraint satisfaction, sparse coding, dictionary learning, and dynamic pattern learning and adaptation.

Similar to Intel's Loihi, IBM's SyNAPSE chip (http://www.research.ibm.com/cognitive-computing/neurosynaptic-chips.shtml) is built with a brain-inspired computer architecture powered by one million neurons and 256 million synapses. It is the largest chip IBM has ever built at 5.4 billion transistors, and has an on-chip network of 4,096 neurosynaptic cores. Yet, it only consumes 70mW during real-time operation, which is an order of magnitude less energy than traditional chips. As part of a complete cognitive hardware and software ecosystem, this technology opens new computing frontiers for distributed sensor, supercomputing, and AI applications.

The AI solution is not only developed at the hardware level. Comprehensive and integrated solutions are also offered by these major companies. For example, Figure 12.2 shows Intel's integrated architecture for AI solution.

In this technology stack, each layer uses the layers below and support the layers above. Many of the Intel technologies have an open architecture and allow also integration of technologies and systems from other vendors.

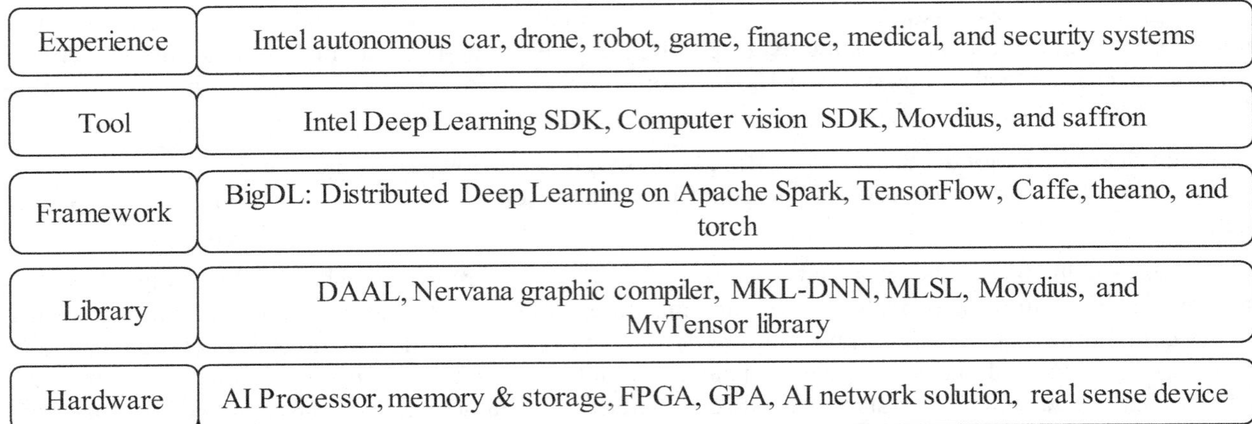

Figure 12.2. Intel's architecture for AI solution

IBM PowerAI Platform offers another hardware and software integrated solution for AI and deep learning, as shown in Figure 12.3.

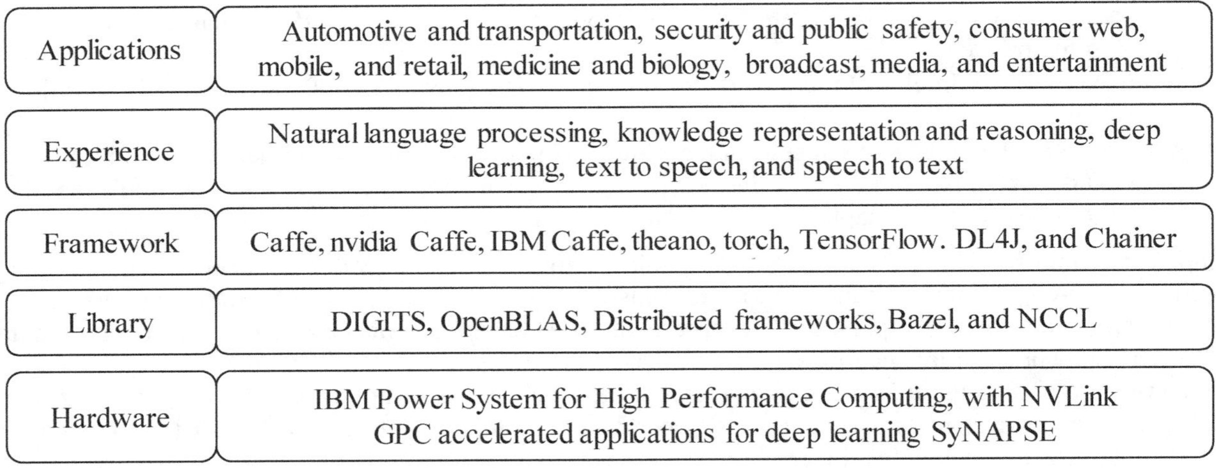

Figure 12.3. IBM PowerAI Platform for AI solution

12.2 From Traditional Programming to AI Programming

Traditional software, such as the control flow based software, implements a function that takes inputs at the beginning and generates outputs in a deterministic way according to the function (input-output mapping) to calculate the solution. For example, to predicate the stock trend, we can use the data from the past 10 years, and try to find a distribution function that best fits the past data. Then, we use the same distribution function as the model to predict the next move of the stock. The model will not work if a new situation or a major change takes place.

Event-driven software adds additional features to control flow based software. It can take events and feedback inputs iteratively from the environment during the execution of a program, in addition to inputs at the beginning. The currently executing program does not need to be stopped for the events to be taken and processed. The outputs of the program are determined by inputs, states and events. We can use a static state machine to model the execution of event-driven software.

In order to develop event-driven software, a parallel computing infrastructure supporting events listening and processing needs to be provided, as discussed in Section 2.6.

AI software is based on event-driven software, but with additional mechanisms. These additional mechanisms include:

- A training stage before the deployment of the software, that uses the past data to create a model and an initial knowledge base.
- The model and the knowledge base that organize the knowledge for reasoning and decision making in generating new outputs based on the inputs, events, and states.
- A learning mechanism that can learn new knowledge and improve the model and the knowledge base dynamically during the execution.

Figure 12.4 illustrates the structures of the three programming styles: the traditional input-output programming style, event-driving programming style, and AI programming style.

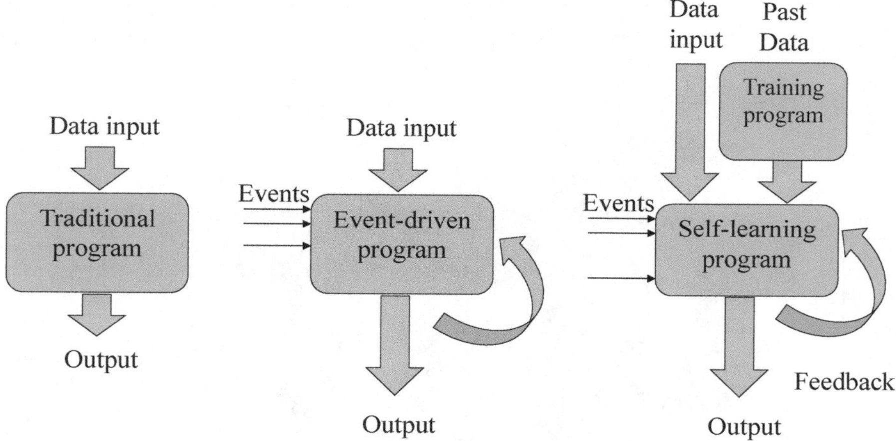

Figure 12.4. Structures of different software development models

An AI system typically consists of multiple components:

- Sensor and actuator handlers organized in event-driven program style;
- Learning, such as deep learning, processing, and evaluation;
- Rulebase plus an ontology for representing the model and knowledge;
- Induction and reasoning algorithms based on inputs and rulebase/ontology;
- Training stage by trial and error, with error analysis and correction;
- Adjusting the rulebase and ontology, as well as improving the induction and reasoning algorithms.

Figure 12.5 shows an example of the AI software development style involving the major components and their interconnections.

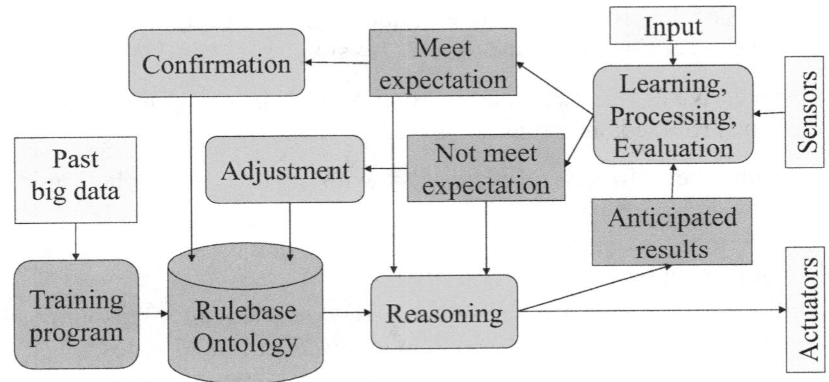

Figure 12.5. An AI software development environment

Learning is a key component in the AI software development. Deep learning, also called deep feedforward neural networks, is the current technology for implementing learning, processing, and evaluation. As shown in Figure 12.6, learning is split into multiple layers that perform step-wise and parallel processing of complex objects.

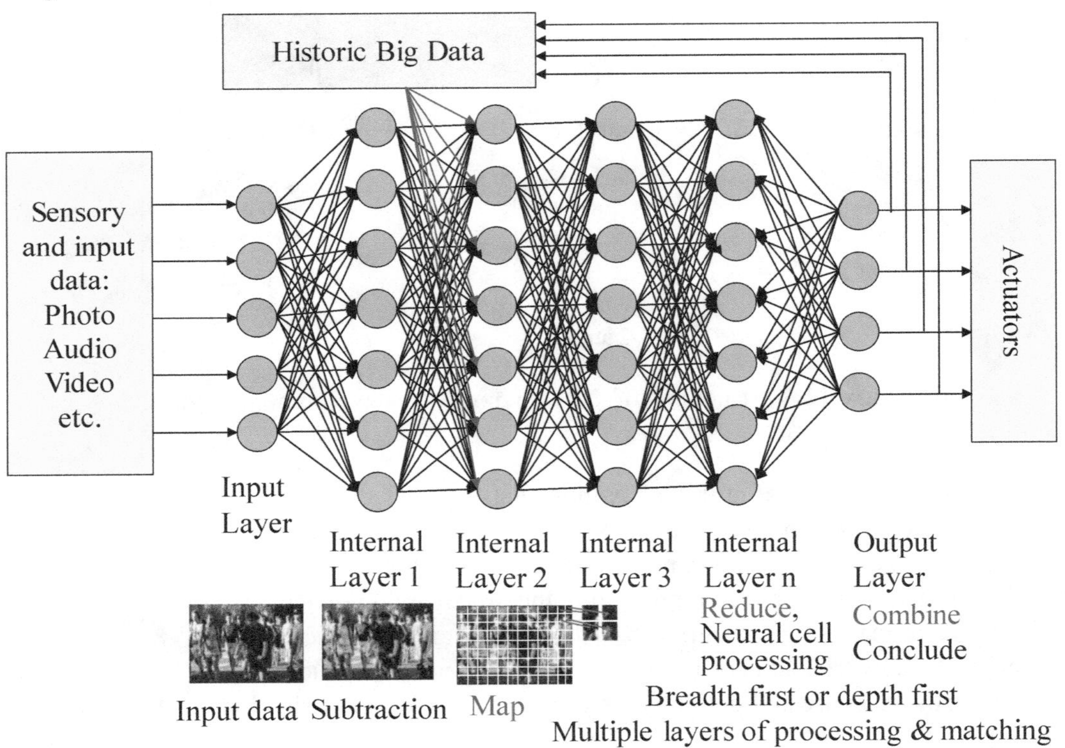

Figure 12.6. Deep learning model, with multiple layers of individual processing & matching

The first layer takes the inputs and pre-processes the inputs. The second layer performs subtraction, such as differentiating background and foreground pixels. The third layer follows the MapReduce model to divide the input domain into many cells and apply the same operation on them for parallel processing. The cells that contains background pixels will not be processed. As each cell is connected to the neighboring cells, these cells may need to be processed together in the next layer to the data in the joint areas covered by these cells. The process may continue for a few layers to obtain the necessary information for extracting sufficient features of the incoming data and making decision based on the information in the final layer of the deep learning.

Taking image processing as an example, bit-wise comparison is not sufficient for image recognition, as the image can be observed from different angles and distances. Figure 12.7 shows the photos of the same painting taken from different angles. We must extract features and their combinations that can uniquely represent the image. Once the features are extracted, we can use the features to compare if two images represent the same object.

Figure 12.7. Images representing the same object

A learning system typically deals with one particular problem only. For example, image processing and recognition, health/medical application, playing a game, detecting network attacks, detecting abnormal financial transactions, calculating the insurance risks, and recommendation system. Specific rulebase, ontology, and learning algorithm must be developed for each problem.

Research is being done for developing general AI systems for different problems. The current approaches include developing generic services to process common problems in different AI systems, so that these services can be shared in different AI systems. As the result, we can develop AI systems using the concept of AI as a Service.

Table 12.2 compares and contrasts the traditional software development and self-learning software development through examples.

Table 12.2. Traditional software development vs. self-learning software development

Example	Traditional Software Development	AI Software Development
Recognizing signs of shapes and colors. To be discussed more.	Store the shapes, colors, and signs into a table of database. Compare the input with the content in the table.	Create dynamic data structure for combinations of different signs. Use training data to initialize the table and learning to improve the model and data.
Playing chess	Based on the rules, select the best move that can be calculated in the given amount of time.	Based on the rules, learning from the opponent and others in past matches in the training stage, improving the move selection algorithm continuously.
Shooting basketball	Based on the locations, distances to the basket, the weight of the ball, the force that the actuator can generate to decide the angles of shooting.	Based on the initial data and model to shoot in the training stage. If missed, find how (short, long, left or right), and improve in the next shoot.
Detecting network attacks	Collect the attack patterns in the past and looking for the similar package patterns.	Based on the initial data and model in the training stage and add new attack patterns in the rulebase of ontology during the execution.
Recommendation system	Based on functional connection between the product that the buyer is interested in to determine the recommendation	Based facts of frequently bought together, acceptance of previous recommendation, availability, profitability, etc. to make recommendation during the execution.

12.3 Machine Learning Case Study on Traffic Sign Recognition

Machine learning is a new paradigm of problem solving. Teaching machine learning in schools and colleges to prepare for the industry's needs becomes imminent, not only in computing majors, but also in all engineering disciplines. This and following sections develop new, hands-on approaches to teaching machine learning by training and pattern recognition. We first study a sign recognition and meaning lookup system. Such a system can be used, for example, for an autonomous driving car: a red octagon is a stop sign, a yellow triangle is a warning sign, and an upside down red triangle is a yield sign.

12.3.1 Using Traditional Programming

We start with a simple case. We want to write a program to recognize these three shapes: circle, triangle, and octagon; and each of these shapes can have one of these four colors: red (FF0000), green (00FF00), blue (0000FF), and yellow (FFFF00).

In traditional programming style, we can create a table T (array or database). In this case, we store an array of 3x4 rows and two columns, as show in Table 12.3.

Table 12.3. Table T storing shape-color and meanings

index	ShapeColor	Meaning	Action
0	Circle red	No sign or red light	If no sign, do not enter. If red light, stop.
1	Circle green	Green light	Do not stop if road open.
2	Circle blue	Traffic direction	Analyze the text or symbol in the circle and take action accordingly.
3	Circle yellow	Yellow light	Break and stop if possible.
4	Triangle red	Yield sign if it is upside down.	Yield to the traffic in the road to enter.
5	Triangle green	-	-
6	Triangle blue	-	-
7	Triangle yellow	Warning sign	Analyze the text or symbol in the triangle and take precaution accordingly.
8	Octagon red	Stop sign	Stop for 3 seconds and yield to the traffic in the road to enter/
9	Octagon green	-	-
10	Octagon blue	-	-
11	Octagon yellow	-	-

Then, we apply the table in recognizing the shape and color, and then look up the meanings. We can use a loop shown in the recognition function in the following pseudocode:

```
String recognition(Table T, Image input) {
   for (i = 0; i < N; i++)
        if (match(input, T.ShapeColor[i]))
              return T.Meaning[i];
   return "no match is found";
}
Insertion(Table T, Image input) {
   String meaning;
   meaning  = Readline();
   Insert(Table T, Image input, String meaning)
}
```

The pseudocode also shows a function that allows a user to enter a string of the meaning for a given image for a given shape and color.

The problems with the traditional programming solutions include the difficulty of listing all possible signs and describing the meanings and actions. Just like a human learner, remembering all the signs and their means and actions are important but not enough for driving. The driver needs to make judgment considering multiple factors together. For example, multiple signs can occur together and there are pedestrians still walking at your green light.

12.3.2 Using Machine Learning

In the machine learning version of the code, we will use the latest technologies in cloud computing and big data analysis to capture as many possible scenarios and situations as possible, if not all of them. The system can be developed in the following major steps:

1. Build the learning model. For example, we can create a superset of all the elements (factors), containing the sets of one element, the sets of two elements, …, the sets of n-1 elements, and the set of all elements. The model must allow to remove the unnecessary sets dynamically and to add the removed sets back if they become necessary. The ontology to be discussed in the next section offer techniques for efficiently organizing and analysing such models.
2. Training stage using recorded data. We started from the recorded data to input the initial data in the model and customize the model based on the initial data.
3. Supervised live learning stage. We start to apply the model in practice with a human as the supervisor. For example, we let a human driver drive the car and react to all the situations. The machine observes and learns the actions taken by the human and enter the data into the model. Notice that the model is not installed on board in one car only. It is installed in the cloud and all the cars are learning and are correcting the data simultaneously. If new situations, for example, new combinations of the signs are detected, and we need to add the set of combinations into the model.
4. Self-operation state (unsupervised). After the system is fully learned and system can operate without human intervention.

As the cardinality of a superset with n elements is 2^n, and n is very large, we need to reduce the model complexity by removing the combinations that are not possible or unlikely to occur together. For example, a stop sign, and a yield sign do not need to occur together, and we do not need to consider this combination.

Even with the reduced combinations in the model, cloud computing support and big data analysis and processing are still required to make decision in real time.

Now, we use the shapes and colors in Table 12.3 as an example to explain the model and techniques explained in this section.

Table 12.3 lists 12 signs. If we consider each sign individually, there are 12 possibilities. If we consider 2 signs occurring at the same time, there are 12*11/2 = 66 combinations. If we consider 3 signs occurring at the same time, there are 12*11*10/3/2 = 220 combinations. The superset of these signs will have

$$\sum_{k=0}^{n}\binom{n}{k} = 2^n = 4096 \text{ combinations.}$$

Now we examine the possibility of reducing the complexity. If we consider Table 12.3 contains our training data, 5 out of the 12 signs have no meanings defined, and we can reduce the signs from 12 to 7, resulting in $2^7 = 128$ valid combinations only. For the multiple sign combinations, we can further remove those combinations where at least 2 signs do not occur together.

Of course, if a removed combination occurs later in the live learning stage or in the self-operation stage, the system must revise the model to include the combination.

In the reality of a self-driving situation, there can be easily hundreds of different signs that the drivers need to observe. In addition, there are many other objects and symbols that need to be recognized in order to ensure the safe driving practice. It is not possible to solve the problems with 2^{100} = 1267650600228229401496703205376 combinations in real time. Thus, it is critical to reduce the model complexity by removing the not necessary combinations. In fact, the majority of the combinations will be removed, resulting a sparse multidimensional matrix. However, these matrixes are still extremely large to solve.

What data structures can we, and should we, use to store such a large amount of the data? Arrays are not adequate, as it is a static data structure. Linked lists are dynamic, but they are not suitable for parallel processing, particularly, big data processing.

We can use the key-value pairs discussed in the big data processing section. We can consider a sign or a shape-color pair to be a key and consider the meaning of the sign to be the value of the key. In this way, all the key-value pairs are independent of each other and the key-value pair set can be partitioned into multiple subsets for parallel processing using map and reduce in Hadoop. We can also use two-level key-value pair structure to store the data, where, the shape is a key and a color is its value. Then, each shape-color is further considered to be a key, and the meaning is considered its value. We can use a tree structure to represent the two-level key-value structure, as illustrated in Figure 12.8, where the meanings part stores a pointer pointing to the file system location where the meanings are stored.

One of the advantages of using two-level key-value pairs structure is that shapes and colors can also be learned by machine to discover new signs. For example, if a new sign is discovered, with a known shape, say, rectangle, but the color is not white and not red in the existing rectangle color set. However, the color exists in the circle shape, which is named "yellow," therefore, the machine can learn that a new rectangle yellow sign is discovered.

The meanings of a sign of a set of signs are the behaviors of the human driver when they encounter these signs. The meanings can be learned in the training stage, as well as in the live learning stage, where a human driver is operating the car. The machine can learn how the human driver behaves when a certain sign or a set of signs are encountered. The behaviors will be correctly learned from thousands of hours of driving time from hundreds of different drivers in different locations.

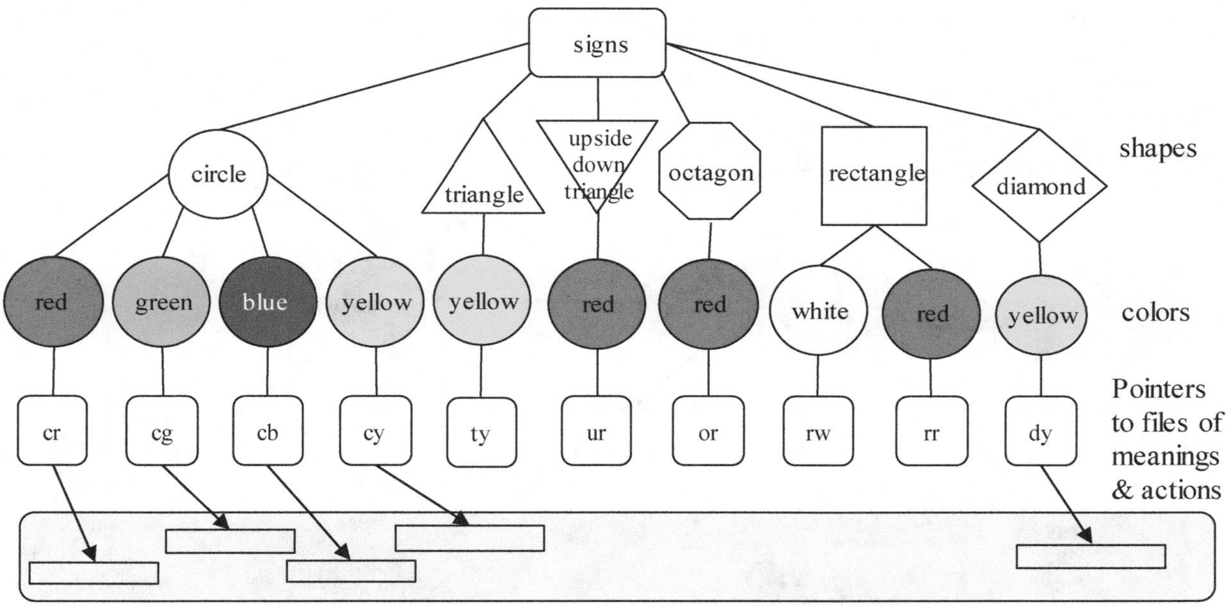

Figure 12.8. A tree of key-value pairs

In a computer, the tree of pairs can be stored in a text file:

```
((circle red) cr)
((circle green) cg)
((circle blue) cb)
((circle yellow) cr)
((triangle yellow) ty)
((upsidedowntriangle yellow) uy)
((octagon red) or)
((rectangle white) rw)
((rectangle red) rr)
((diamond yellow) dy)
```

Similar to the Word Counting example given in the big data processing section, the key-value pairs of the signs can be processed by the big data processing framework, such as Hadoop. They can divide the data into subsets and feed them into Map and Reduce functions to process automatically.

Machine learning will have to deal with the incomplete and inconsistent data in decision-making in machine situations. The big data analytics and processing techniques discussed in Chapter 11 Section 11.3 can be applied.

Various big data processing algorithms, framework, and even specialized hardware have been developed to solve such problems. A good reference to learn the practical applications of machine learning framework and algorithms can be found at:

https://pair-code.github.io/deeplearnjs/docs/tutorials/index.html

12.3.3 Machine Learning Experiments

Various machine learning experiments have been conducted at Arizona State University for traffic sign and road recognition. Figure 12.9 shows the guide dog project, where a robot dog equipped with camera and traffic sign recognition can help a vision-impaired person to walk through the traffic.

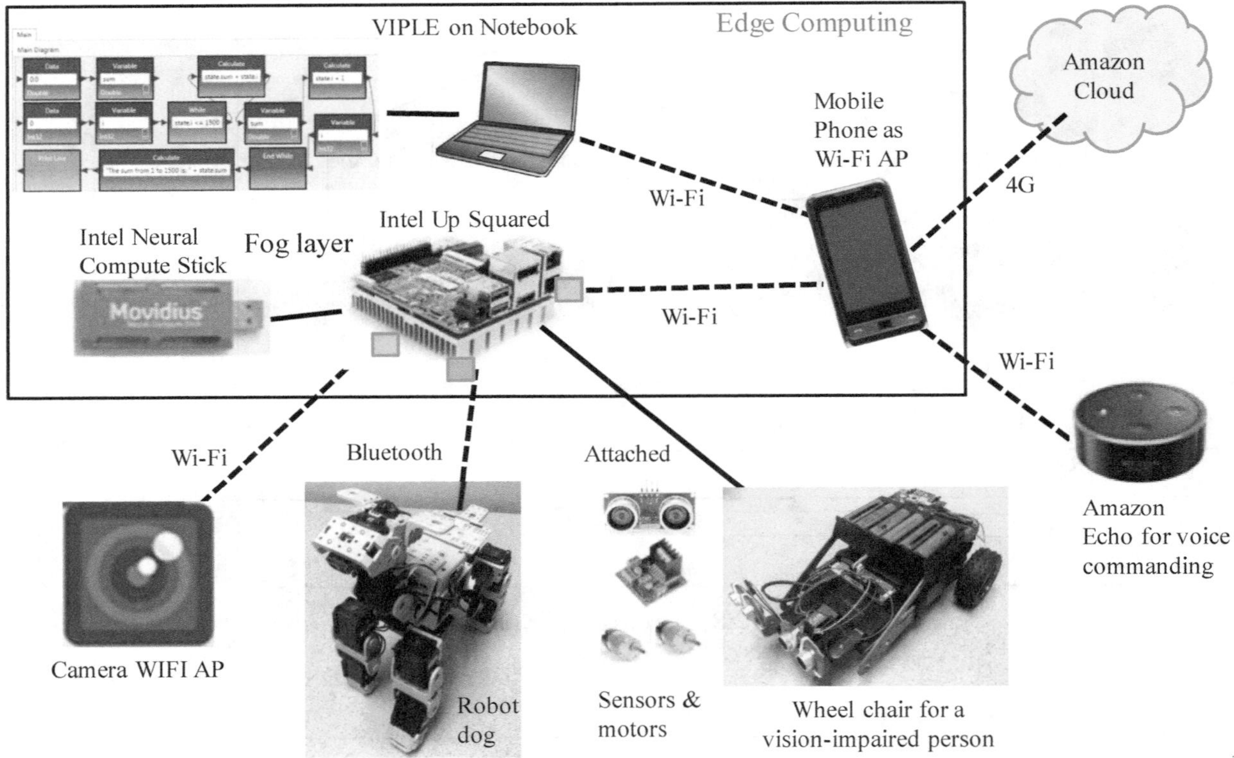

Figure 12.9. Guide dog project hardware system

The guide dog system offers the following functions:

(1) Visual function: The dog robot can visually observe the surrounding environment, identify obstacles, identify traffic signals and vehicles when crossing the road.

(2) Language function (understanding and speaking): The dog robot can understand the natural language commands from the person through Amazon Alexa voice system.

The software system and workflow of the guide system is outlined in Figure 12.10.

(3) Decision function: The robot can integrate various environmental information and the person's instruction to make correct decisions. For example, if the person commands the advancement, and the robot sees that the vehicle is passing, the robot's decision is not to execute the forward command. This is the Intelligent disobedience that an intelligent guide dog should have.

(4) Mobile function: The robot has the ability to move autonomously. The vision-impaired person with limited mobility can take a self-propelled wheelchair.

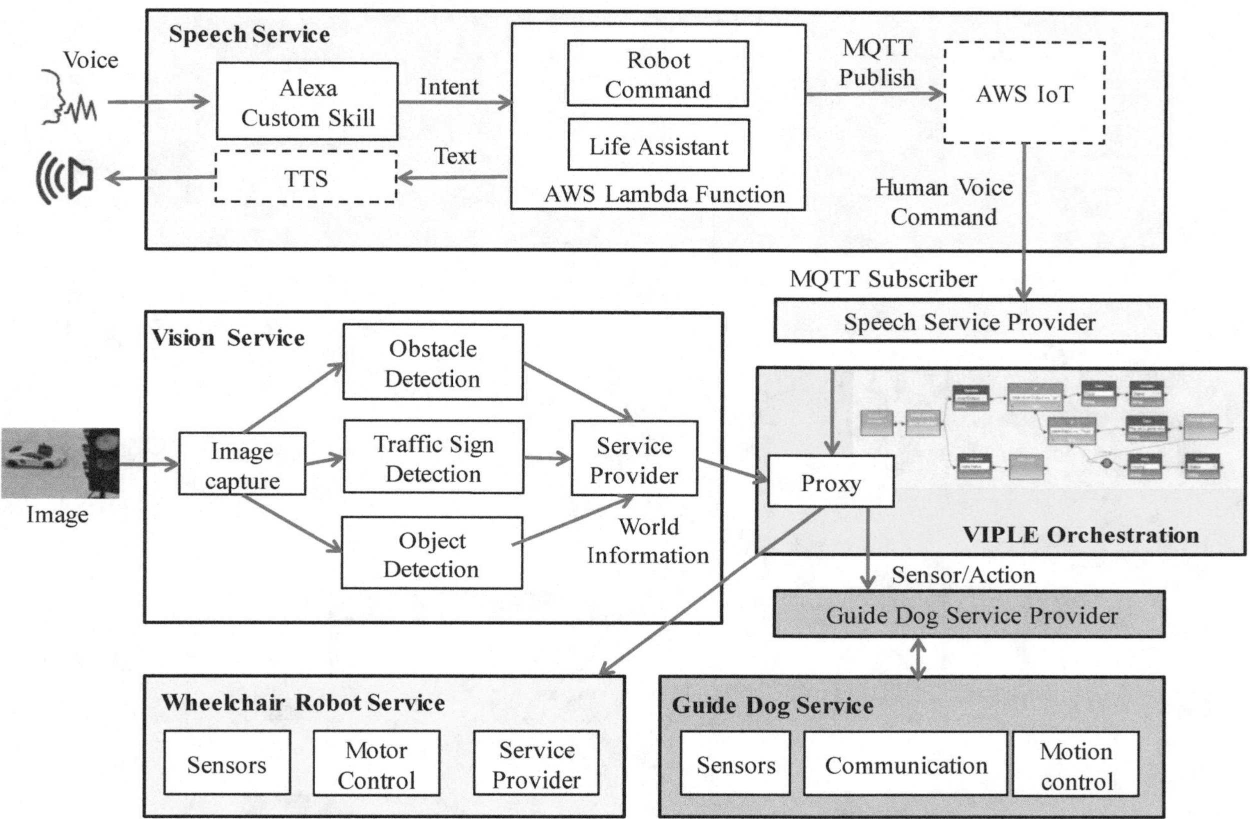

Figure 12.10. Guide dog project software system and workflow

The VIPLE code shown in Figure 12.10 is the decision center and it orchestrates all the operations. The decision center collects information from vision and speech modules, and it sends commands to the dog robot and wheelchair. VIPLE's visual code makes the integration easy. The sample code in Figure 12.11 implements the function of avoiding cars when crossing a road. In the upper part of the VIPLE code, the four Robot/IoT controllers are the proxy to connect to four other modules: robot dog, wireless camera, wheelchair, and AWS Alexa unit. Some complex processing functions, such as DogForward, DogRight, DogLeft, and DogBackward, are wrapped as VIPLE Code activity written in C#. Finally, individual program behaviors are combined to form a state diagram and workflow for the entire project.

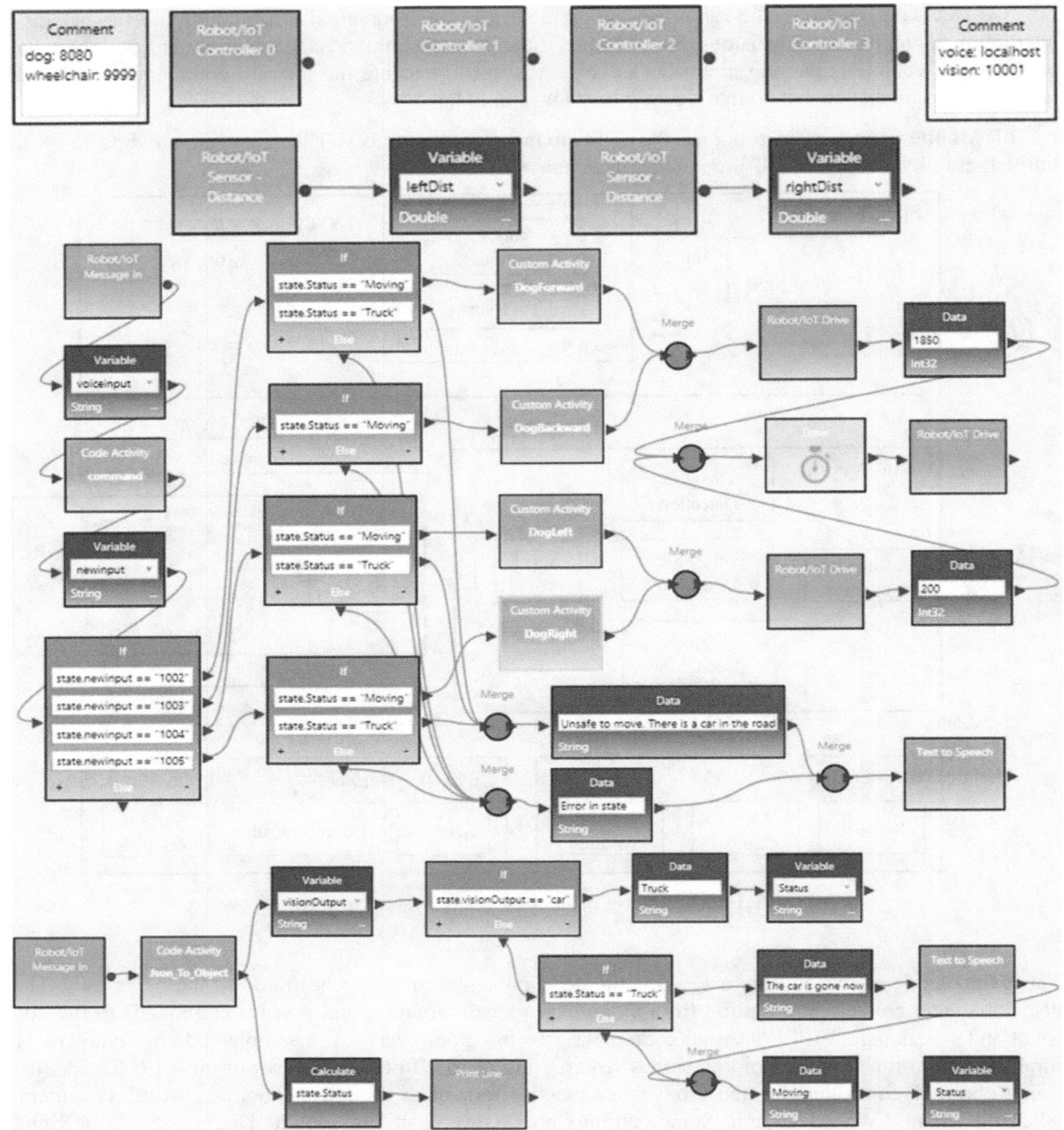

Figure 12.11. Guide dog project software system and workflow

The full detail of this project and its implementation can be found at: https://doi.org/10.1016/j.simpat.2019.102015.

As a part of this effort, we have developed an image recognition Web service that can take the URL of a .jpg or .png image as input and recognize the shape of the image. The URL of the service is:

http://neptune.fulton.ad.asu.edu/WSRepository/Services/ImageRecognition/Service.svc?wsdl

A TryIt page of the service is available at:

http://neptune.fulton.ad.asu.edu/WSRepository/services/imagerecognitionTryIt/Default.aspx

Figure 12.12 show the execution of imagerecognitionTryIt page and recognition result. As the same image can have different meanings, the service gives the probabilities of different meanings.

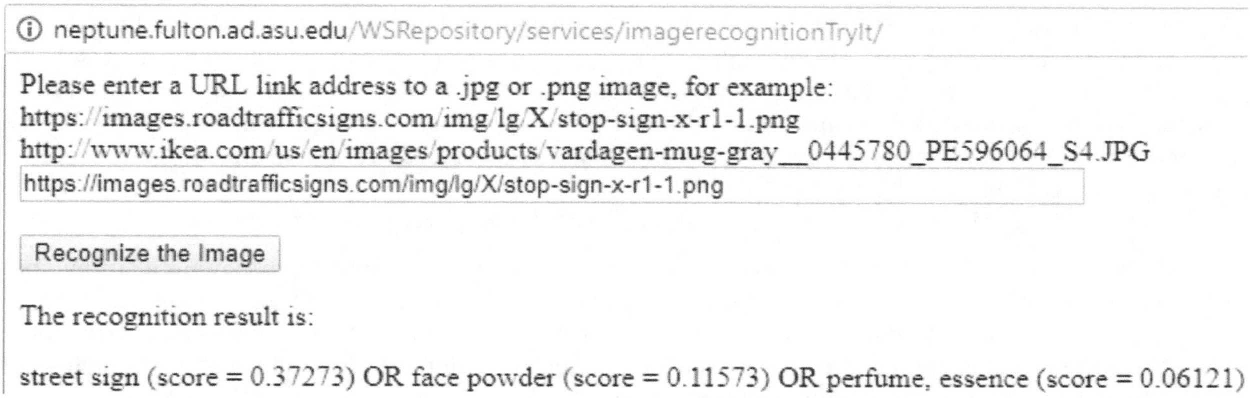

ⓘ neptune.fulton.ad.asu.edu/WSRepository/services/imagerecognitionTryIt/

Please enter a URL link address to a .jpg or .png image, for example:
https://images.roadtrafficsigns.com/img/lg/X/stop-sign-x-r1-1.png
http://www.ikea.com/us/en/images/products/vardagen-mug-gray__0445780_PE596064_S4.JPG

https://images.roadtrafficsigns.com/img/lg/X/stop-sign-x-r1-1.png

Recognize the Image

The recognition result is:

street sign (score = 0.37273) OR face powder (score = 0.11573) OR perfume, essence (score = 0.06121)

Figure 12.12. The imagerecognitionTryIt page and its recognition result

The code behind Default.aspx is given as follows.

```
namespace ImageRecognitionTryIt {
    public partial class WebForm1 : System.Web.UI.Page {
        protected void btnRecognize_Click(object sender, EventArgs e) {
            string strUrl = txtUrl.Text;
            ServiceRef1.ServiceClient myPxy = new
                ServiceRef1.ServiceClient("BasicHttpBinding_IService");
            string result = myPxy.ImageRecognition(strUrl);
            lblResult.Text = result;
        }
    }
}
```

In addition to image recognition service, we are also working on the voice activated services through Amazon Alex. A video showing the Alex-robot interaction is available at:

http://neptune.fulton.ad.asu.edu/VIPLE/Videos/HumanoidVoiceCommand.mp4

12.4 Machine Learning Case Study on Flight Path Recognition

This section explains machine learning through drone flight data collection and applying a linear classifier to solve Multirotor Activity Recognition (MAR) problems in an online lab setting [de La Rosa and Chen, 2019]. MAR labs leverage big data processing, cloud computing, and machine learning technologies to host a versatile environment capable of logging, orchestrating, and visualizing the solution. This work extends Arizona State University's Visual IoT/Robotics Programming Language Environment (VIPLE) discussed as a control platform for multi-rotors used in data collection. VIPLE is a platform developed for teaching computational thinking, visual programming, Internet of Things (IoT) and robotics application development, as in discussed Chapter 9.

A drone in experiment is a robotic platform constructed from four rotors placed in an arrangement that allows them to fly. Actions such as roll, pitch, and altitude changes are motion controls enabled by their six degrees of freedom. The flight is achieved through a series of computational corrections calculated by an on-board flight controller equipped with an IMU (Inertial Measurement Unit) sensor. Such computations are typically governed by a specialized PID (Proportional-Integral-Derivative) Controller that is responsible for maintaining the setpoint of a drone's state. These controllers were chosen for their robust nature. Multi-rotors provide a high degree of controllability and versatility.

Such an application makes the platform ideal for surveillance and sensory applications. It involves use cases where an elevated platform is required to provide hard-to-reach observations at a low cost, and possibly at scale. Consider applications in the agricultural industry where autonomous drones can be used for performance measuring on plantations**Error! Reference source not found.**. These drones allow for a utomated video capture, making it much easier for researchers and users to collect real-time data and make real-time assessments. In cases where costs of obtaining aerial videos are a concern, drones become a necessary tool. Drones can also be used for addressing use cases where a quick, responsive, and mobile robotic unit can be deployed in emergency situations. **Error! Reference source not found.**

As drone-based solutions have been proposed in a growing number of research opportunities, a fair number of studies have been dedicated to their robustness. Precise mechanics allow a drone to maintain a stable flight, focusing on sub-optimal conditions that drones may experience. In this case, the correctional feedback loop mechanisms in a drone are expanded to include fault detection and recovery. Such fault tolerant applications go as far as implementing a control solution for drones that suffer from a complete failure in one, two, or three propellers. **Error! Reference source not found.** Obstacle avoidance has also b een a leading discussion in the drone platform. Given the automated nature of most applications and the complexity of navigating a 3D space with six degrees of freedom, solutions exist to solving the drone collision avoidance problem. **Error! Reference source not found.**

With VIPLE, students can easily implement control algorithms to solve real problems such as maze traversal and direct keyboard-based controllers. These qualities of VIPLE make it an ideal tool for deploying simple control schemes to control a drone. Hence extensions and contributions made to VIPLE involve creating a drone and implementing a VIPLE-compatible interface on the drone. The simplicity of controlling robots through the VIPLE platform makes it an ideal tool for generating the data used in MAR labs. In this work, VIPLE's primary purpose is to serve as a controller for the drone. IMU data is stored locally on-board the drone during each flight session while Amazon Web Services (AWS) are used to create the appropriate linear classifier. With these two environments, the MAR lab's machine learning pipeline can encompass the entire process of data collection, data manipulation, training a linear classifier, and using said classifier to solve the MAR classification problem.

12.4.1 Flight Activity Recognition

A common application of classifiers is their deployment in activity recognition. Typically, these studies involve the deployment of IMU sensors on a subject with the idea that specific actions produce a recognizable IMU signature. One such example is the study on human activity recognition (HAR) **Error! R eference source not found.Error! Reference source not found.**where the goal is to classify human activities such as sitting, walking, or taking an elevator. Other solutions to HAR include the breakdown of tasks into subtasks. **Error! Reference source not found.** Typically, these studies aim to provide the f ramework for context-aware applications. The activity recognition problem also can be extended toward canines where IMU data can be used to aid in the recognition of canine activities such as standing or sitting through unsupervised learning. Linear classifiers have been chosen as the specific classifier due to its common application in supervised learning and availability within TensorFlow's estimator API. The supervised nature of the data stems from tagging windows of IMU data as belonging to a specific activity. The classifier is given the appropriate classification in parallel with the data being given, and the label for a given class is discrete.

The goal of MAR labs is to deploy similar sliding window sampling techniques to recognize multirotor activity. The sliding window sample considers the frequency at which the data was recorded, the length of the window, and IMU data collection techniques. MAR extends existing activity recognition by translating IMU data signatures to drone activities. MAR was chosen since IMU data has a strong correlation to a specific flight pattern as discussed in the PID Controller section. The strong correlation between the IMU-based PID Controller and the activity recognition of IMU data implies that the classification should be simple, where a given action tends to produce a unique IMU signature.

Multi-rotor Activity Recognition (MAR) is the primary focus of the paper. The MAR problem aims to identify the actions performed by a drone in flight by recognizing windows of raw IMU data as belonging to a specific class of multirotor activity. During flight, a drone's roll and pitch serve as indicators as to what the drone is doing. Specific activities such as strafing left tend to produce windows of IMU data that indicate a negative roll. Likewise, strafing right tends to produce a positive roll value. These indicators serve as the premise for training a feasible classifier that can make these distinctions in data, thus implementing a solution to solve the MAR problem.

To investigate the MAR problem within an educational context, training and applying the model are built as two separate learning lab modules: the MAR Training Lab Module, and the MAR Classification Lab Module. A cloud-based solution was used to allow users with web-enabled devices to participate in the lab without the need for additional hardware or software. Users participate in a lab session by running prepopulated scripts within each lab module and inspecting the script's console outputs. In both lab modules, the drone's flight controller properties file is configured to record labeled IMU data for supervised training, or unlabeled IMU data for classification exercises. To build an environment suitable for both the VIPLE-drone platform and AWS, Figure 12.13 provides a visual description of the system's architecture overview capable of machine learning orchestration.

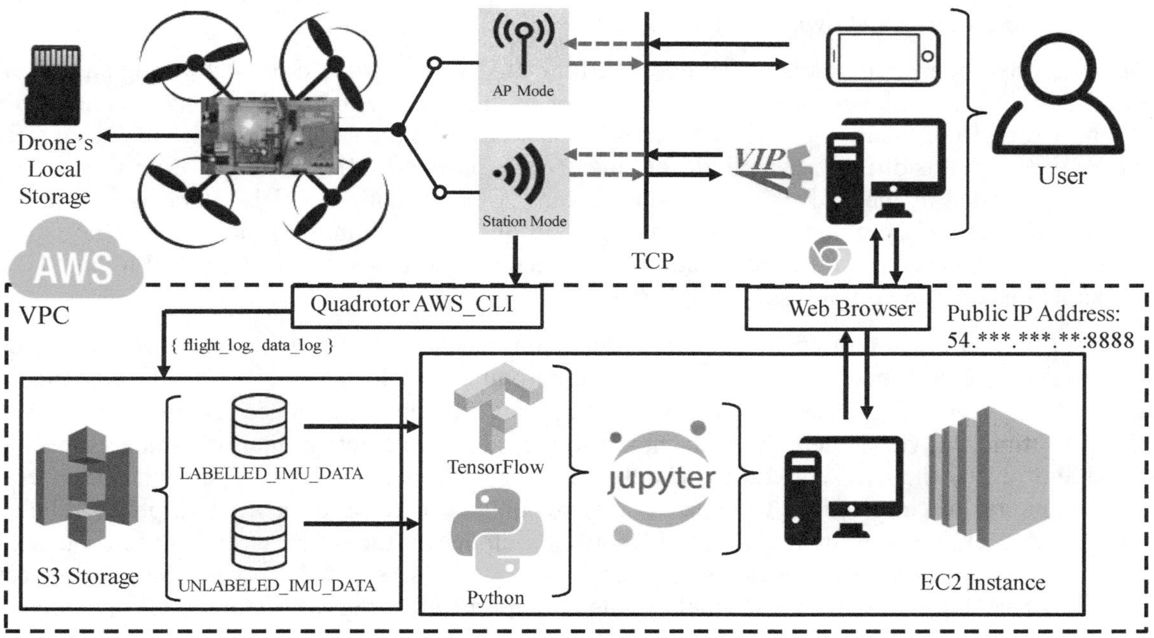

Figure 12.13. MAR Lab Architecture Overview

The start of the MAR pipeline is the VIPLE and drone platform used to create a flight plan, execute the flight plan, and generate IMU data. As a control tool, VIPLE provides the user with the ability to create and run a given flight plan with instructions on which activities to execute (pitch, roll, etc.).

Figure 12.14 shows an example VIPLE implementation of a flight plan that the quadcopter platform can execute. In this sequential program, the drone is commanded to move up, hover, move to the left, hover, move to the right, hover, land, and then terminate the flight session.

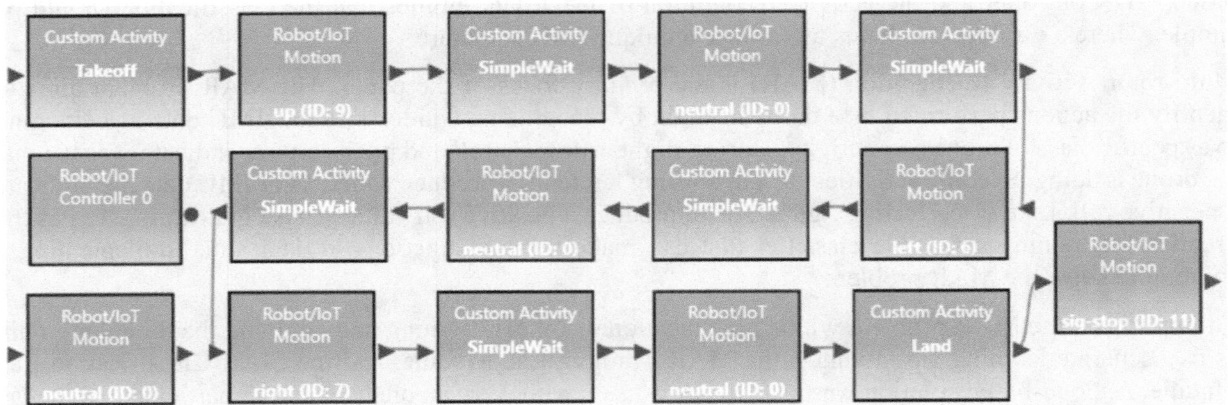

Figure 12.14. VIPLE code of a Series-Based Flight Plan

Within each Robot/IoT Motion block, a custom command is defined to describe what activity the drone should be performing. Implemented on the drone's VIPLE interface, an interpreter parses the JSON string received over TCP and writes to shared memory the current directive received from VIPLE. All available actions and descriptions are shown in Table 12.4.

The main descriptors are timer delays that describe how long a drone should be performing an action, the activity the drone should be performing, and a pointer to the next timer-based activity execution. In the execution of each flight plan, two logs will be stored that describe the status of the drone during a flight, and the IMU data that is directly generated from the drone's on-board MEMS sensor. Both files are stored locally and uploaded at the end of each flight session. After executing a fight plan, the drone begins uploading IMU data to the cloud through Amazon Web Services Command Line Interface (AWS-CLI). Further details are discussed in the next section, implementation; however, it is important to note that this process expedites the time for access to usable data.

Now that VIPLE has been chosen as a suitable drone control platform, an environment for the MAR lab modules must be established. Installing a python environment with the TensorFlow library meets the requirements for supporting a framework capable of training and applying a linear classifier for MAR. On top of this runtime, Jupyter Notebooks was chosen to provide an interactive interface since scripts can be displayed and run by the user. Jupyter Notebook's markup cells provide lab sessions with the necessary textual explanation and instructions for what scripts are being executed and for what purpose, while coded cells display the script to be run along with the console outputs for the given script. These code cells are prepopulated with the scripts necessary to implement MAR lab sessions; however, these scripts can be edited by the user. Jupyter Notebooks can also generate reports, allowing instructors to critique the results of a given lab session. A display of every cell's output can be shown in the results for a given lab session, even if the output contains a scripting error, or encounters an exception thrown by the script.

Table 12.4. Drone-VIPLE Motion Config Options

Motion ID	Motion Name	Description
0	neutral	Default receive signal (do nothing) and hover during flight
1	false-flight	Enter a flight session, but with rotors disabled
2	test	Run the test script that activates each rotor in order of [1, 2, 3, 4]
3	flight	Signal flight controller to enter takeoff mode
4	stop	Signal a soft stop to the flight controller, enter landing mode
5	forward	Move the drone forward, decrease pitch
6	left	Move drone left, decrease the roll
7	right	Move drone right, increase the roll
8	backward	Move the drone backward, increase the pitch
9	up	Increase the drone baseline throttle
10	down	Decrease the drone baseline throttle
11	sig-stop	Force stop the drone and end flight session

For example, Figure 12.15 shows the welcome module that runs a simple "Hello World" program where each coded cell is accompanied by a markup cell to explain what the python script is aiming to accomplish. As demonstrated by this welcome module, Jupyter Notebooks can run python scripts, display the output for the given python script, perform calculations made possible through python, and even take user input directly from the user interface.

Hello World

The following cell is a simple python script that can print a message to the user.
Try running the cell by selecting it, and running the command ctrl+enter:

```
In [1]: print('Hello World')

Hello World
```

Simple calculations:

Cells can be used to run simple computations. Try running the cell below
to perform a simple 'add' calculation and print the results:

```
In [2]: print(5 + 5)

10
```

Interacting with the console:

Cells run on a Jupyter notebook can interact with the computer's runtime. Jupyter
notebook uses a live python runtime allowing the user to interact with scripts
running in realtime. Below, user input can be read and displayed back to the user

```
In [3]: print('Awaiting user input...')
        echoMessage = input('Enter a message to echo back: ')
        print('You typed [' + echoMessage + ']')

Awaiting user input...
Enter a message to echo back: Hello JUPYTER NOTEBOOK
You typed [Hello JUPYTER NOTEBOOK]
```

Figure 12.15. Hello Jupyter Practice Module

12.4.2 Implementation

Now that the components of the MAR lab have been discussed, this section describes how the drone was built, how various controllers were implemented in VIPLE for the drone, how IMU data was recorded by the drone and received by MAR labs, and how the MAR training and classification lab modules are tasked in solving an MAR problem.

The drone used to execute the flight plans was built with an Edison-Arduino board as the main controller. Four brushless rotors and Electronic Speed Controllers (ESCs) were placed on a 450mm drone frame. Li-Po Batteries were used to power the drone due to their space efficiency and high energy density. The Edison-Arduino board served as the primary flight controller for the drone system. The on-board Wi-Fi capabilities fulfill the hardware requirement needed to establish a TCP/IP connection between the drone's VIPLE client and the ground base's VIPLE host. However, a custom breakout board had to be designed to meet the additional hardware specs to include an on-board MEMS sensor and accommodations for four Pulse Width Modulation (PWM) signals needed to drive each ESC. The custom circuit board also includes an LED to serve as a visual indicator of the drone's status.

To drive the drone, a C++ based flight controller was implemented onto the Edison-Arduino board through Intel's System Studio IoT Edition to provide the necessary stabilization for obtaining stable flight. Configuration files were created to grant users the ability to adjust the flight controller's parameters. The most important components to the Flight controller was the PID controller responsible for calculating the rotor corrections needed to be executed by the on-board rotors. An internal state iterator was used for switching between the various modes available on the drone (false flight, flight, test flight, standby). The flight controller was designed to operate at 250Hz by implementing a software-based timer that puts the process to sleep during each iteration of corrective calculations until the next cycle begins.

The flight controller process begins by initializing the PID controller, the internal state machine, and the shared memory space between the controller and the VIPLE interface. Two separate loggers open file streams within an S3 synced directory to record the flight controller's status and the IMU data received by the MEMS sensor. The flight controller's configurations were then read from disk or assigned a default value. These configurations included the gains for the PID controller, battery level, trim settings to prevent drifting, label configurations for files being logged, hovering throttle, and flags for uploading flight sessions automatically to S3 on exit.

The PID controller is a feedback loop that continuously reads from the MEMS sensor and the system's desired setpoint to produce a continuous output of corrective feedback. To provide the roll, pitch, and yaw controls necessary to control a drone's flight, a setpoint describes the system's desired readout. In the case that a drone hovers, the setpoint for the pitch, roll, and yaw remain zero. If the desired control of the drone is to move forward, the setpoint of the pitch axis is set to a negative non-zero value. The PID Controller consists of three components: proportional, integral, and differential. The proportional control is responsible for calculating the difference between the input of the MEMS sensor and the setpoint. The integral component acts as an error accumulator that allows the system to make corrections to errors that persist over a given time (this prevents controllers from only approaching a setpoint rather than achieving the desired setpoint). The derivative controller acts as a resistance to rate of change and helps dampen corrective overcompensation output by other controllers. This corrective feedback loop operates on a system-wide loop that calculates the drone's current IMU readout, reads the drone's setpoint, calculates the angle travelled, adjusts for drift compensation, calculates the correctional adjustments determined by the PID calculations, and applies the PID corrections to the throttle.

Data collection begins when a drone enters flight mode. During a flight session, the Edison-Arduino board is constantly reading from the MEMS sensor and storing the raw values into local storage. The on-bard MPU6050 can operate at a frequency of 400kHz which is well within the range of the drone's correction frequency of 250Hz and provides a reading of the proper acceleration of x, y, z in G's, and the angular velocity recorded in degrees per second (°/s) on the roll, pitch, and yaw axis. The MPU6050 gyroscopic sensor was configured to operate at a full-scale range of +/- 250 °/s while the accelerometer was configured to run at +/- 8 G's. These values are then formatted and printed through one of the flight controller's output streams into a *.csv file. Once the drone enters landing mode and receives instructions to stop the flight session, or a termination signal is received, the drone's flight controller executes an exit script that invokes the AWS CLI to sync new files onto the S3 environment.

The drone is also host to a VIPLE interface that interprets VIPLE's JSON-based messages sent and received over a TCP/IP connection (as described in the Approach section). This interpreter runs on a separate process and communicates directives to the flight controller over shared memory. Shell scripts orchestrate the execution of these processes on startup. If the drone does not have access to a Wireless Local Area Network (WLAN), scripts are written to configure the Edison's on-board Wi-Fi antenna to enter Access Point (AP) mode, allowing the drone to broadcast its own Wi-Fi network.

In the system, two different types of control methods are implemented through VIPLE. The first manual-based control method is a key-mapped controller that accepts key inputs from users and translates them directly to a motion control. This allows users to have direct control over the drone's actions in real time. Featured in Figure 12.14 a second type of control scheme is implemented through VIPLE which describes a flight plan that the drone can execute automatically. This VIPLE program implements a series of directives and timer delays and is ideal for executing multiple iterations of a given flight plan.

To interact with the AWS cloud environment, the AWS-CLI is installed on-board the drone's Edison board. The AWS CLI is configured with the appropriate credentials needed to perform write commands on AWS' Secure Simple Storage Service (S3). Additional scripts are written to proactively upload new flight session data. A pre-defined flight log file directory is chosen and monitored for file changes by storing its file directory state into local storage. A 'diff' between this file and the current state is performed after each flight session to search for any new flight logs. AWS-CLI upload scripts are run upon discovering new flight logs.

To interact with IMU data generated from flight sessions in the VIPLE-Drone platform, S3 serves as a shared space between the VIPLE-Drone platform and the AWS cloud space. The drone's AWS-CLI is configured with the appropriate account settings with the necessary permissions for uploading files onto S3. S3 makes for an ideal storage solution since it shares a domain with the EC2 environment and offers scalability necessary for plenty of data storage. Write operations are limited on the public facing interface and require that uploaders have the appropriate credentials needed to write a file. The computationally intensive data manipulation and model training can be offloaded to a virtual machine hosted on AWS' Elastic Compute Cloud (EC2).

The VMs operate on a Linux-based operating system with the appropriate software and runtimes installed to host the MAR lab sessions. Temporary directories are used by Jupyter Notebooks to save a lab session's state, which holds checkpoints for the trained linear classifier and IMU data transferred over from S3. The VMs come installed with Python, TensorFlow, and Jupyter Notebooks, all of which provide the necessary framework needed to host MAR lab sessions as described in the previous section. VMs are also configured with a public IP address via AWS' elastic IP service, allowing VM instances to interact with the public domain. Additional security configurations are made to allow public access to the required port, giving users the ability to connect to the Jupyter Notebook server over an HTTPS connection on a web-enabled device. One such VM is shown in Figure 12.16, where a t2.medium EC2 instance is running with a public IP. As described by AWS documentation, T2 instances are a low-cost general-purpose instance with burstable performance making it ideal for server applications. To access the MAR lab modules, a user would need to enter "*https://{Public_IP}:{Jupyter_Port}*" into the web browser. As a minimal security measure, the Jupyter Notebook server is configured with a self-signed SSL certificate to enable HTTPS connection. Lastly, the server is configured with a simple password to prevent unauthorized changes made to the lab.

Logs displayed within each lab session provide useful insight on the execution status for a given scripted task. However, to bring better understanding to how data is being manipulated and what the data looks like, the Jupyter notebook environment includes libraries necessary to provide a visual representation of data being processed during the session. It is made clear to the user what code and scripts are being run, what task is being executed, and how that execution takes place, and what the logs report as user-readable output for inspecting the machine learning process each step of the way. In this case, the user has access to both read and write the code being run to orchestrate the machine learning process. In addition, TensorFlow provides a log of the linear classifier's runtime whether that is training progression, or classification.

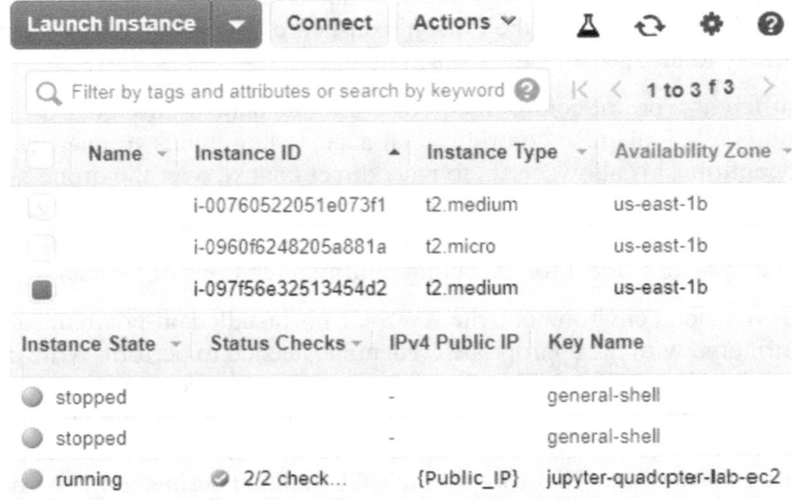

Figure 12.16. Active EC2 Instance Running MAR Labs Jupyter

The premise for the MAR Training Module is to have users train a linear classifier to perform MAR. This linear classifier is trained using IMU data collected and described by the Implementation section. The MAR training activity module is prepopulated with the steps necessary to download the IMU data, extract samples by label into subdirectories, calculate features from each sample through sliding window protocol, and finally train a classifier.

The classification module is where users learn how to take raw, unlabeled IMU data and convert it into a plausible flight plan. Running through the module in its entirety and using the classifier from the previous training module would be a sufficient solution to the MAR problem.

12.4.3 Experiment and Configurations

The drone can be configured to record labeled or unlabeled IMU data. Labeled IMU data is used to train a model through supervised learning, making the model capable of distinguishing windows of data as belonging to a specific drone activity. Unlabeled IMU data is used as an exercise dataset for the classification lab module. If labels are enabled, then during flight, the drone is responsible for making an extra entry of what action is being performed in each IMU readout. This tags the appropriate IMU data and labels it as belonging to a specific class of activity. Successful flight sessions and uploads contribute to the MAR database of labeled flight data. It is during the training phase that users are expected to fly the drone, ideally with an even distribution of time spent performing the different available actions.

For each lab session, the drone is powered on and initialized with a boot script that starts the VIPLE interface and flight controller process. The drone is then configured to record labeled or unlabeled flight data depending on the context of the current session. A name is chosen for the flight session and set through the VIPLE interface. The flight plan is then executed and IMU data is recorded for the given session. Each MAR lab module begins with an initialization of the runtime environment responsible for importing the appropriate libraries, defining helper functions, and local variables.

To demonstrate the feasibility of the lab session's ability to classify multirotor activities, three separate experimental procedures were performed to test the training and accuracy of the MAR classifier. The first experiments were done by manually controlling the drone through VIPLE, disabling the rotors, and holding the drone device to manually mimic the drone's action. This data set will be referred to as held-with-manual-control (HMC). The second experiment, called held-with-rotor-control (HRC), was recorded by enabling the rotors but holding the device to prevent drifting. The device was again controlled manually through VIPLE; however, the drone's enabled rotors meant the motion of the device did not have to be manually manipulated. The third and final experiment was done by controlling the drone through VIPLE, enabling the rotors, and allowing the drone to fly without any type of harness; this set will be called Untethered Flight (UF).

The session begins by downloading both the training and evaluation datasets of raw, labeled IMU data from S3 and parsing the entries in each file into multiple sub-files based on their tagged labels. During this process, the IMU file is read line by line and stored into a labeled sample file. Once a different label is read, a new labeled sample file is created and stored in the appropriate subdirectory. In this manner, windows containing more than one label are completely removed from the training and classification dataset.

These sample files, which now hold IMU data for a specific label, are then traversed sequentially via the sliding window protocol with a length of 4 and a step of 1. The average and median features are calculated for every IMU readout from each window and stored into a file where it will be in a format ready for training the classifier. The data is in a format that now holds a cross product of the feature and IMU data tuples: {*average-acceleration-x, average-acceleration-y, average-acceleration-z, average-gyro-roll, average-gyro-pitch, average-gyro-yaw, median-acceleration-x, median-acceleration-y, median-acceleration-z, median-gyro-roll, median-gyro-pitch, median-gyro-yaw*}

The final step of the lab preps the linear classifier by configuring the appropriate labels, feature columns, the model's checkpoint directory, and input training and evaluation file datasets. The TensorFlow API is called to train the linear classifier for 100 epochs, where an evaluation of the model is performed every 20 epochs.

The successful execution of all cells in the training lab module means that a linear classifier was successfully created for the given training data. Checkpoints for the trained model are stored by TensorFlow into a temporary directory, meaning that this instance of a trained model can be restored by TensorFlow (and the subsequent classification lab module) for later use.

This module begins by asking the user for the group name and the flight session to download the appropriate flight log. Displaying the full flight logs also allows users to confirm that the drone flight was a success and that no anomalies occurred during startup.

The appropriate raw, unlabeled IMU data for the given session is downloaded and a file preview is printed to show the data in its raw form. As shown in Figure 12.17, a visual representation of the IMU data is then presented to the user in step 4.

A set of feature functions are defined for use in the next step. These functions are defined to take in a list of numerical decimal values as parameters and return the feature defined by the function. In the sample above, the average and median features are simply a direct implementation of calculating the average and median of the input parameters.

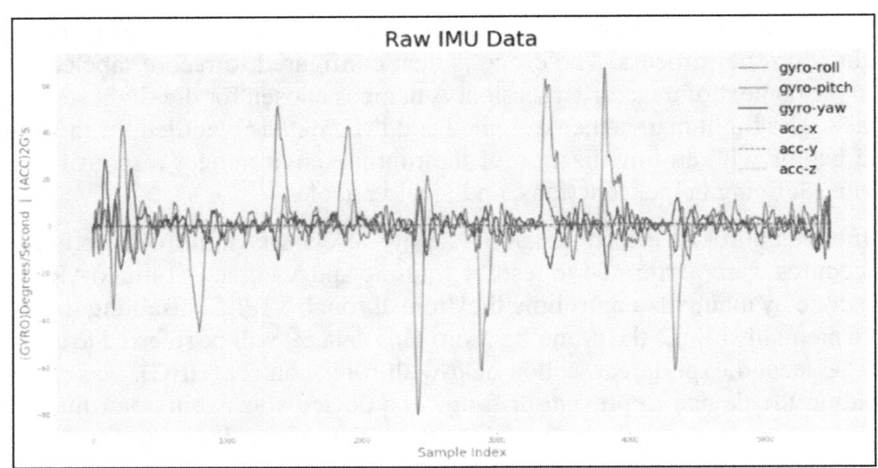

Figure 12.17. Active EC2 Instance Running MAR Labs Jupyter

Like the training module, the raw IMU data for the entire flight session is traversed via sliding window protocol and the average and mean features are calculated from these windows of data. The user can also choose to run the optional cells that describe in more detail the process of extracting the feature from a single window of IMU data. Now that the data is ready to be processed by the linear classifier, the next step of the lab produces a textual description of the predicted flight plan.

Figure 12.18 visualizes the final step of the lab, where shaders are applied on top of the raw IMU data graph to give a visual representation of the drone's predicted activities during flight. Each directional motion is shaded a specific color. For example, the windows of green-shaded regions indicate the "neutral" activity where the drone is in a hovering state. It is expected that users record the flight plan for a given flight session before starting the classification module to assess that the flight plan produced by the classifier is correct. The successful execution of all cells means that a linear classifier has been used to generate a hypothetical flight plan for a given set of unlabeled IMU data. However, the accuracy and assessments made by the classifier depend on how well trained the linear classifier was.

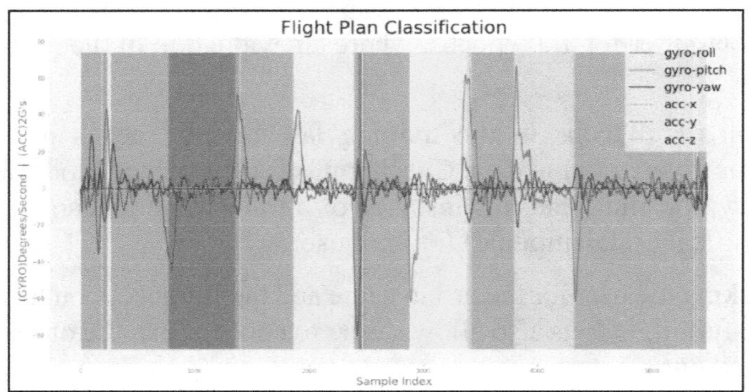

Figure 12.18. IMU Data Flight Plan Classification

12.5 Machine Learning Case Study on Network Traffic Monitoring

As another case study, we consider a network traffic monitoring system. Similar to road traffic, network traffic can be monitored and controlled based on machine learning and big data analysis.

In such a system, the key tasks are to learn and detect the abnormal behaviors that represent possible attacks, and then, to quickly take actions to protect the network and system resources.

To differentiate normal and abnormal traffic, we can define a set of features to characterize the behaviors. The features can be defined based data fields in the IP packet; for example:

< time, sip, sport, dip, dport, protocol, direction, pack_len, head_len, tcp_head_len, type, syn, ack, fin>

where,

- time field is the time when the packet is captured,
- sip and dip fields are the IP packet's source and destination IP addresses,
- sport and dport fields are the IP packet's source and destination port,
- pack_len, head_len, and tcp_head_len fields are the length of IP packet, the length of IP packet header, and the length of TCP packet header, respectively,
- type field is the type of ICMP packet,
- syn, ack, and fin fields are the connection synchronous field, connection acknowledgement field and connection finish field of TCP packet header, respectively.

Through the analysis of the IP packet fields, we can obtain the network traffic behavior features to form the feature set, which includes both static and dynamic features. Static features mainly include the types of packet length, IP address, port, and special packet. Dynamic features mainly include the types of speed, distribution, and connection. For example, type of packet length is based on the statistic of time, protocol, direction, pack_len, head_len, and tcp_head_len fields. The traffic behavior of network users can be described completely and accurately with the proposed feature set.

As an example, Table 12.5 lists a set of network traffic features that are described by the sequence of <protocol.statistical parameter (IP address / port / TCP connection / header. Actions. Description)>.

In the table, each character denotes a specific aspect or feature of the network, where, I: IP protocol; C: ICMP protocol; T: TCP protocol; U: The UDP protocol; A: average; M: maximum; N: number; B: the number of bytes; v: variance; r: the ratio of two numbers; R: the ratio of the total; ip: independent ip; spt: independent source port; dpt: independent destination port; c: independent tcp connection; H: header; u: upload; d: download; rq: request; bd: the establishment; kp: maintained; bg: packet length greater than 1000 bytes; sm: packet length less than 100 bytes; ov: packet header length greater than 20 bytes; erq: echo request packet; erp: echo reply packet.

The features can be indexed by the row and column numbers. For example: feature 77: TAN (ip.c.bd) is the mean number of TCP connection established with independent IP address.

Table 12.5. Network traffic feature set

	1	2	3	4	5	6	7	8	9	10
0	IN.u	CN.u	TN.u	UN.u	IB.u	CB.u	TB.u	UB.u	IN.d	CN.d
1	TN.d	UN.d	IB.d	CB.d	TB.d	UB.d	IAB.u	CAB.u	TAB.u	UAB.u
2	IAB(H.u)	TAB(H.u)	IBv.u	CBv.u	TBv.u	UBv.u	IBv(H.u)	TBv(H.u)	IAB.d	CAB.d
3	TAB.d	UAB.d	IAB(H.d)	TAB(H.d)	IBv.d	CBv.d	TBv.d	UBv.d	IBv(H.d)	TBv(H.d)
4	INr(u.d)	CNr(u.d)	TNr(u.d)	UNr(u.d)	IBr(u.d)	CBr(u.d)	TBr(u.d)	UBr(u.d)	CN.R	TN.R
5	UN.R	CB.R	TB.R	UB.R	TNR(dpt80)	TBR(dpt80)	CN.ip	TN.ip	UN.ip	UN.spt
6	UN.dpt	TN.spt	TN.dpt	TN(c.rq)	TN(c.bd)	TN(c.kp)	CN.erq	CN.erp	IN(H.ov)	TN(H.ov)
7	CN(d.sm)	TN(d.sm)	UN(d.sm)	CN(u.bg)	TN(u.bg)	UN(u.bg)	TAN(ip.c.bd)	TMN(ip.c.bd)	IAN(ip.u)	IMN(ip.u)
8	IAN(ip.d)	IMN(ip.d)	IAB(ip.u)	IMB(ip.u)	IAB(ip.d)	IMB(ip.d)	IAN(ip.u.bg)	IMN(ip.u.bg)	IAN(ip.d.sm)	IMN(ip.d.sm)
9	TAN(ip.spt)	TMN(ip.spt)	UAN(ip.spt)	UMN(ip.spt)	TAN(ip.dpt)	TMN(ip,dpt)	UAN(ip.dpt)	UMN(ip.dpt)	TAN(c.u)	TMN(c.u)
10	TAN(c.d)	TMN(c.d)	TAB(c.u)	TMB(c.u)	TAB(c.d)	TMB(c.d)	TAN(c.u.bg)	TMN(c.u.bg)	TAN(c.d.sm)	TMN(c.d.sm)

speed; packet length; distribution; port; integrated; special packet connection

The feature set will be used to define a time-mapped massive user pattern database associated with different times in a day, in a week, in a month, and in a year. Normal and abnormal traffic patterns will be created for all the time periods based on the massive traffic logs. Then, the individual user's current traffic flows will be compared with the patterns in the time-mapped massive user pattern database. A mathematical model is used to decide in real time if a user's current traffic flow contains abnormal patterns. The relative deviation distance (D_i) of feature f_i is defined by

$$D_i = \frac{|f_i - E(f_i)|}{\sigma_i}$$

The rule for feature selection between normal traffic (N) and abnormal (A) traffic behavior can be defined by the following threshold:

$$\frac{\frac{(D_i)_A}{(D_i)_N}}{\sum_{i=1}^{110} \frac{(D_i)_A}{(D_i)_N}} \geq threshold$$

If an abnormal traffic is detected, an alarm will be generated, and actions will be taken to block the user and prevent damage. In the model, we define the deviation distances between different traffic behaviors and define the threshold of the distance that can be tolerated as the rule for abnormal detection. The new flows will be learned and added into the database to enrich and improve the time-mapped pattern database. The accuracy of the pattern recognition is determined by the accuracy of the model and the available patterns in the time-mapped pattern database. Figure 12.19 shows the logic flow of a network traffic analysis for Intrusion detection and prevention system developed based on the feature sets. The system consists of four modules, and they process the traffic in four states, respectively:

The initial training module takes the recorded past traffic as input and use the traffic feature set and the model to extract the traffic features. This stage results in the initial feature set database for the next module to use. The database is represented in key-value pairs.

The live training module uses the live traffic data and the initial feature set database to perform further feature extraction operations. It applies machine-learning algorithms to add new features into the feature database to obtain a bigger database for the next two operational stages. It can remove the inconsistent features as more data become available. This stage may still involve human operations and the algorithms learnt from the human decisions.

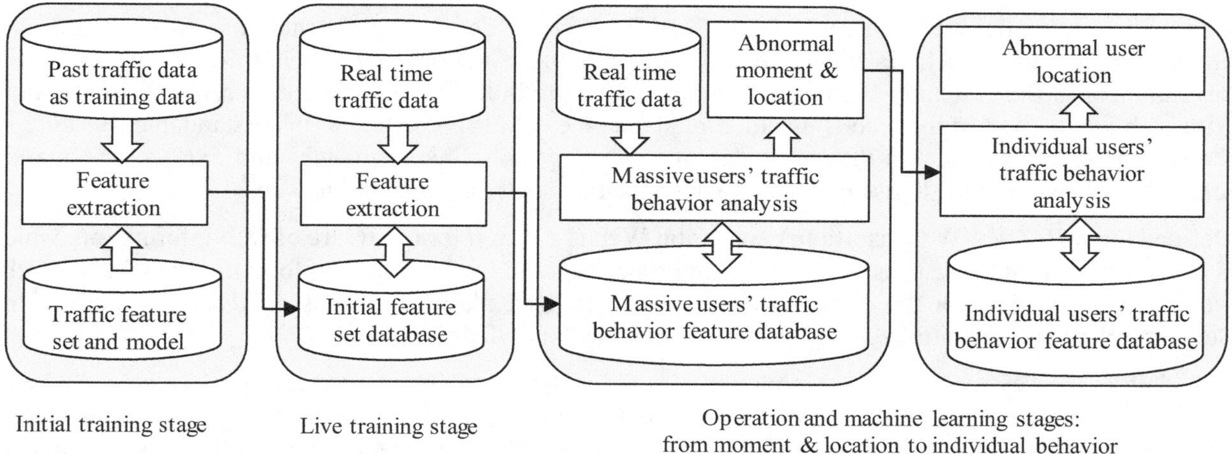

Figure 12.19. Network traffic analysis for Intrusion detection and prevention process

The next two modules are for the operation stages, where the system operates autonomously without human intervention. The first module in the operation stages detects the abnormal moment and the location among all the users, while the second module identifies the abnormal user, so that actions can be taken to block the user. These two stages apply the same machine-learning algorithms to add new features into the feature database and remove the inconsistent features from the database. In addition to this part of the machine learning, these two stages also apply the deep learning algorithm described in the previous section. As the database becomes bigger and bigger, it is not possible to detect the abnormal behavior in real time without using multiple phases of processing. We need to partition the key-value database into shards, and use parallel threads to compare the incoming traffic data with different shards. We also need to combine the results from different shards to draw the final decision.

In the next section, we discuss ontology and ontology languages that support knowledge representation and look up, which can be used for representing data and knowledge in machine learning and in Semantic Web.

12.6 Ontology

The word "Ontology" comes from Philosophy, where it means a systematic explanation of being. In computer science, an ontology is a formal specification of the terms/objects in a domain and the relationships among them. Technically, an ontology defines a common vocabulary of elements, the meanings of the elements described in terms of their relations, properties, and attributes (e.g., synonym and antonym), and the structure of the statements using the vocabulary.

A shared representation is essential for the common understanding of data and communication. An ontology defines the structure of knowledge representation and conceptualization of a domain. It describes domain knowledge in a generic way and provides agreed understanding of a domain.

An ontology includes machine-understandable definitions of basic concepts in a specific domain for the purposes of:

- sharing common understanding of the structure of information among people or software agents that use the information;
- making domain assumptions explicit, and enabling reuse of domain knowledge;

- separating domain knowledge from the operational knowledge;
- enabling domain knowledge analysis and reasoning.

One major application of ontology is in artificial intelligence development, which organize the data and knowledge to enable self-learning and reasoning. Another major application of ontology is in the development of the Semantic Web. The web was originally built for human users to retrieve information. Although a large part of the web is machine-readable, the data is not machine-understandable. Because of the volume of information on the web today, it is no longer possible to manage and retrieve information manually. The solution is to use metadata to describe the data contained on the web.

Defined by W3C (WWW Consortium), Semantic Web is a vision for the future of web information, which is given explicit meaning to enable automatic processing and integration of information available on the web. If we consider that the current web is a decentralized platform for distributed presentations, the Semantic Web is a decentralized platform for distributed knowledge.

Metadata is the key to implement Semantic Web. Metadata is "data about data;" for example, a library catalogue is metadata, since it describes the properties and attributes of the publications. The distinction between "data" and "metadata" is not always clear. Often the same data can be defined as data and as metadata, depending on the context of their applications.

12.6.1 Ontology Language RDF

RDF and RDF Schema are the most widely used ontology languages. RDF contains the essential languages vocabulary and constructs, while RDF Schema extends RDF capacity to make the language more expressive.

XML is a metalanguage that allows users to define their own markup languages by defining data, data types, syntax, and semantics. RDF (Resource Description Framework) (http://www.w3.org/RDF/) is a data model that allows the association of a value to a name (in general). In particular, RDF is used for representing information about resources in the web, such as the title, author, modification date of a web page, copyright, and licensing information about a web document.

RDF is intended for situations in which this information needs to be processed by computer programs such as web services, rather than being displayed on the web for human users to read. As RDF is a common framework, web service providers and application builders can benefit from the availability of common RDF parsers and processing tools.

The key concepts of RDF are resources, predicates (or properties), statements, and document. A **predicate** defines an attribute or a relation used to describe a resource. A predicate (property) is a binary operator, that is, it takes two operands only. A **statement** is a triple of subject, predicate (or property), and object, where the subject and the predicate are each a resource, whereas the object can be a resource or a value. The statement triples can be nested, that is, each component of the triple can be a triple itself. A statement makes an assertion that the subject is related to the object in the way specified by the predicate. An RDF **document** consists of a collection of statements in XML format. The root node of the XML document is "RDF," followed by a list of elements, each of which corresponds to a statement.

Compared with the <key, value> pairs in big data stores, the triples here are significantly different in meaning. A triple <subject, verb, object> in an RDF expression defines an action (verb) between the subject and the object, while a <key, value> pair associates a list values with a key. There are different ways of converting triples into <key, value> pairs. For example, we can define the <verb, <subject, object>> as a compound pair, or to split a trip into two pairs <subject, verb> and < verb, object>.

An RDF statement can be represented as a directed edge connecting two nodes in a graph, where the source node is the subject; the destination node is the object or property value; and the property is the label of the edge. Then an RDF document is represented as a directed labeled graph. Figure 12.20 shows an example of the RDF diagram.

In the diagram, the ellipse nodes are resources; the labels on the edges are properties (or relations), which are also resources; and the box nodes contain constant values. If both ends of an edge are resources, we can define a revised relation. For example, we can define a relation "includes" between the "professors" and its members.

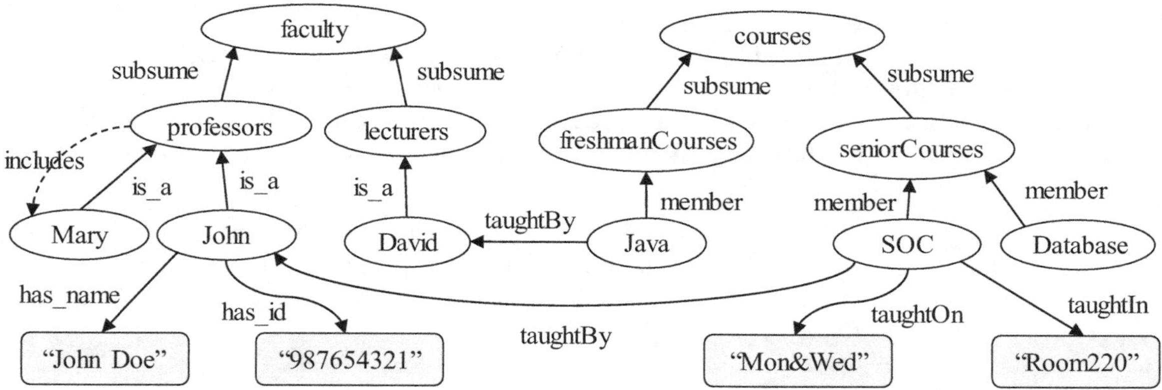

Figure 12.20. Graphic representation of RDF statements

The RDF diagram gives us a visual representation of an RDF document. However, the RDF document has to be described and stored in an XML document. A part of Figure 12.20 is shown in the following RDF document:

```
<?xml version="1.0"?>
<rdf:RDF xmlns:rdf="http://www.w3.org/1999/02/22-rdf-syntax-ns#"
   xmlns:cs="http://neptune.fulton.ad.asu.edu/WSRepository/xml/Courses.rdf">

   <rdf:Description rdf:about="professors">
       <cs:subsume rdf:resource= "faculty"/>
       <cs:includes rdf:resource= "Mary"/>
   </rdf:Description>

   <rdf:Description rdf:about="SOC">
       <cs:taughtOn>Mon and Wed</cs:taughtOn>
       <cs:taughtIn>Room220</cs:taughtIn>
       <cs:member rdf:resource= "seniorCourses"/>
   </rdf:Description>

   <rdf:Description rdf:about="seniorCourses">
       <cs:subsume rdf:resource= "courses"/>
   </rdf:Description>

   ...
</rdf:RDF>
```

An RDF document starts with the root element named "RDF" followed by the namespaces needed. The root element's direct sub-elements (level-2 elements) are a flat list of "Description" elements, each of which corresponds to a resource node (ellipse node) in the RDF diagram in Figure 12.20. In other words, for each resource node in the diagram, a level-2 element in the RDF document is required, except those nodes that have no property (no outgoing edges), such as the elements "faculty" and "courses." Each outgoing edge of a resource node corresponds to a sub-element. If the sub-element is a constant value, the value will be the name of the element. If it a resource, it will be the attribute value of an attribute whose name is resource. We showed three of the "Description" nodes only in the aforesaid RDF document. As an exercise, the readers can complete the RDF document by adding the remaining elements.

As can be observed from this example, an RDF document consists of a collection of triples of two kinds (resource, property, value) or (resource, property, resource).

A namespace "rdf" is defined by W3C. We used the terms "rdf:Description," "rdf:about," and "rdf:resource" in the example to refer the terms defined in rdf namespace. We defined all the other terms in an XML-based RDF schema in a namespace "cs," including "cs:subsume," "cs:includes," "cs:member," "cs:taughtOn," and "cs:taughtIn." As the user-defined RDF scheme is also written in RDF, we use **RDF schema document** and **RDF instance document** to differentiate them if needed. Furthermore, as W3C has defined a standard RDF Schema or RDFS, we will use user-defined RDF schema to differentiate the schema defined from the RDFS. Figure 12.21 shows the aforesaid RDF instance document and its namespaces used.

Another observation is, if we draw an XML tree according to the XML document of the RDF document code above, a large graph will be generated, where each labeled edge will be expanded into a node, with the two edges connecting to the predecessor and the successor, respectively. In other words, an RDF tree diagram in Figure 12.20 is a more compact notation than that of the XML tree, where each XML element corresponds to a node in the tree.

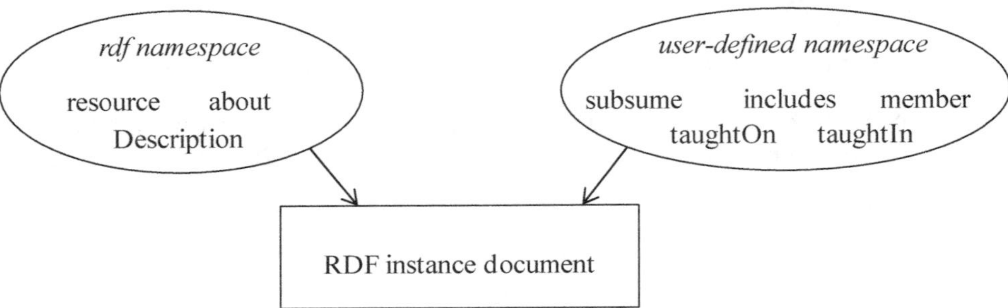

Figure 12.21. Use rdf namespace and user-defined namespace to define RDF instance

12.6.2 RDF Schema

RDF defines a namespace rdf and rules of writing an RDF instance document. RDF is an ontology language with a basic set of resources, properties, and statements. As we have observed in the example in the previous section, few elements and properties have been defined in the rdf namespace. The users have to define almost everything in their own RDF namespace.

RDF as a language does not have powerful mechanisms for defining the relationships between properties and resources. This is the role of the RDF Vocabulary Description Language or called RDF Schema (RDFS) (http://www.w3.org/TR/rdf-schema/), which provides a basic semantic extension to RDF. RDFS provides mechanisms for describing groups (classes) of related resources and the relationships between these resources. From another point of view, RDFS is the object-oriented version of RDF with classes, typing, and inheritance-based class hierarchy. Notice that XML Schema defines the structure of an XML document, which does not add semantic description capacities.

A **class** in RDFS defines a group of individuals that belong together, because they share some properties. Classes can be organized in a hierarchy using subClassOf property. There is a built-in root class named Thing that is the class of all individuals and is a superclass of all classes. There is also a built-in most specific class named "Nothing" that is the class that has no instances and no subclasses. An individual is an instance of class and properties may be used to relate one individual to another. The classes and properties defined in RDFS are organized as a namespace "rdfs" to define RDFS documents (instances), as shown in Figure 12.22.

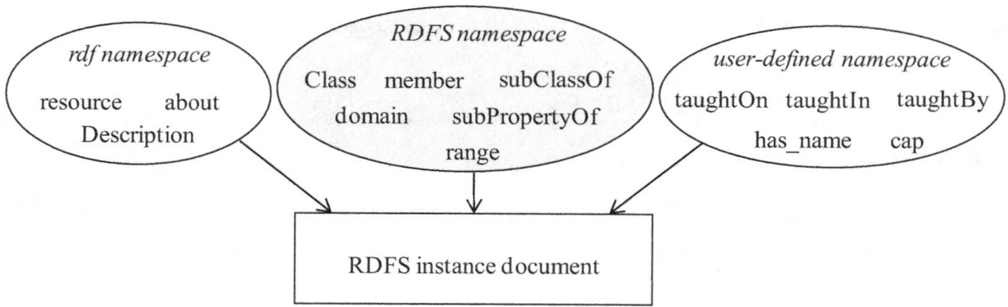

Figure 12.22. Use rdfs namespace and user-defined namespace to define RDFS instance

RDFS is a more powerful (more expressive) ontology language, with a much bigger vocabulary, including predefined classes, properties, and relations. Table 12.6 lists the classes, resources, and properties defined in RDF and RDFS that can be used to define RDFS instance. Even if RDFS has a larger set of classes, resources, and properties available, the users often still need to define their own specific names when defining their RDFS document. When we define an RDFS document, we need to list namespaces rdf and rdfs separately. The user-defined namespace must be written in RDF and RDFS.

Table 12.6. Names defined in rdfs and rdf namespaces

Categories	Names defined in RDFS
Class: *Group of resources*	rdfs:Resource – *the class of all resources* rdfs: Class – *the class of all classes* rdfs:Datatype – *the class of all datatypes* rdfs:Literal – *the class of all literals* rdf:XMLLiteral – the class of all XML literals rdf:Property – the class of all properties
Property Class's instances	rdf:type – *relates a resource to its class* rdfs:subClassOf – *relates a class to its parent class* rdfs:subPropertyOf – *relates a property to its parent property* rdfs:label – *just a name* rdfs:comment – *to be ignored by RDF processor*
ConstraintProperty Class's instances	rdfs:range – *specifies what resources/values an object can take* rdfs:domain – *specifies what resources the subject can take*
Container Classes and Properties	rdfs:Container – *contains enumerable items* rdf:Bag – *unordered containers* rdf:Seq – *ordered containers* rdf:Alt – *container of choices or alternatives* rdfs:member – *relates an item to its container*
RDF Collections	rdf:List – *a subclass of Resource containing a collection of items* rdf:first – *the first item in a List* rdf:rest – *the sublist without the first item* rdf:nil – *the empty list*
Reification Vocabulary	rdf:Statement – triple consisting of subject, predicate, and object rdf:subject – the subject of a statement rdf:predicate – the predicate or verb of a statement rdf:object – the object of statement
Utility Properties	rdfs:seeAlso – additional information about the resource rdfs:isDefinedBy – gives the definition of the resource rdf:value – the property used for the values

There are several concepts on RDF and RDFS here that need to be clarified. We list and explain them in Table 12.7.

Table 12.7. RDF and RDFS related concepts

Concept and notation	Meanings
RDF	It is a general term that can have different means in different context.
rdf namespace (by W3C)	Define a set of terms, such as "about," and "Description."
RDF language	It refers to the vocabulary defined in rdf namespace, plus the rules of syntax: (1) Each statement is a triple of object, predicate, and object; (2) The RDF document is an XML document with the root element "RDF," followed by a list of triples.
RDF (instance) document	The document consists of the collection of the triples in XML format.
RDF Scheme or RDFS	It is a general term that can have different means in different context.
rdfs namespace (by W3C)	Define a set of terms, such as "domain," "range," and subClassOf.
User-define RDF schema or RDF schema document	Users can define their own terms using rdf and rdfs namespaces and using RDF language. The schema document defined can be as a user-defined namespace.
RDFS language	It refers to the vocabulary defined in rdfs namespace RDFS. However, RDFS language does not have syntax for constructing statements and documents. It shares the same syntax.
RDFS (instance) document	RDFS document is same as RDF document. It emphasizes the use of rdfs namespace in the document.

In the rest of the section, we will show a larger example consisting of the user-defined namespace, and an instance document created from the rdf and rdfs namespaces and the user user-defined namespace.

In this example, we will develop an ontology of a course management system that involves courses, instructors, and classrooms. Assume that the ontology includes the following classes of data, properties, and their relations:

- Courses: Courses100, Courses200, Course300, and Courses400. Courses can be taught by Faculty only;
- Courses100: It contains a number courses; for example, C++ and Data structure;
- Courses200: for example, Computer organization, and Principles of programming;
- Courses300: for example, Operating systems, Algorithms, and Compiler;
- Courses400: for example, Networking, and Database;
- Personnel: Faculty and Staff;
- Faculty: Processors and Lecturers;
- Professors: for example, John, Mary, and Ryan;
- Lecturers: for example, David, Martha, and Paul;
- Staff: for example, Sarah and Steward;
- Rooms: smallRooms, mediumRooms, and largeRooms;
- smallRooms: can accommodate courses in Courses400;
- mediumRooms: can accommodate courses in Courses300;
- largeRooms: can accommodate courses in Courses100 and Courses200;
- smallRooms: for example, R401, R402, which can accommodate courses in Courses400;

- mediumRooms: for example, R303, R304, which can accommodate courses in Courses300;
- largeRooms: for example, R110, R220, R221, R223, can accommodate courses in Courses100 and Courses200.

RDFS provides facilities for describing the relationship, constraints, and data range; thus, it can be used to define an ontology.

Figure 12.23 shows the ontology of the course management system. The diagram shows the structure of the document to be defined as an RDFS schema. The upper part of the diagram shows the classes (in gray ellipses) and properties (clear boxes) to be defined in the user-defined RDFS namespace. The lower part of the diagram shows a scenario of the RDF instance document of triples that can be created using the rdf namespace, rdfs namespace, and the user-defined namespace.

In RDFS, similar to an object-oriented programming language, classes can be defined, and subclasses can be derived from a class. In this example, personnel is a class. Faculty and staff classes are derived subclasses from personnel. The classes, professors, and lecturers, are derived classes from the faculty class. The inheritance (derivation) relation among classes forms a hierarchy of classes. Not all classes have an inheritance relation, and thus multiple hierarchies may exist in an ontology. In this example, there are three hierarchies, rooted at Personnel, Rooms, and Courses. The ellipses in RDFS (the upper part of the diagram) represent the classes and the ellipses in RDF (the lower part) represent the instances of the classes. For example, the class Courses relates to class Faculty.

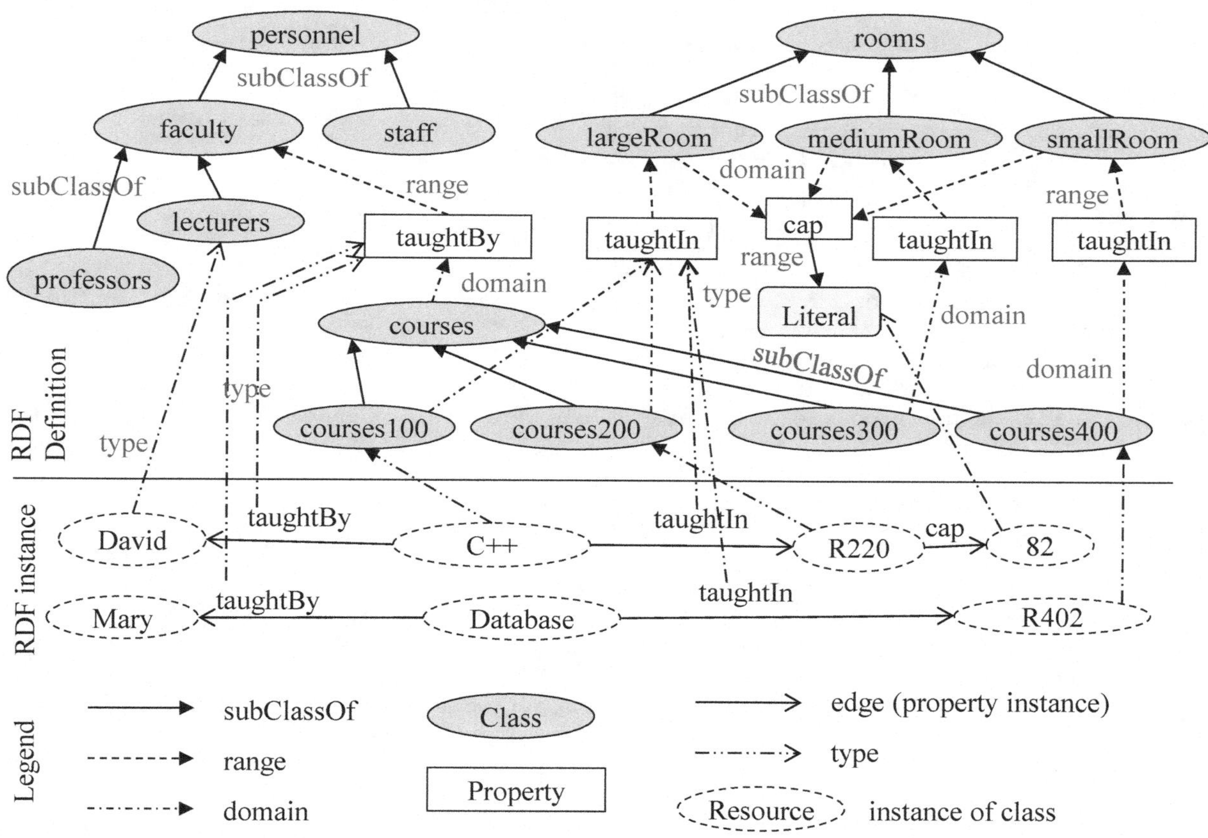

Figure 12.23. Structure of a course ontology

The RDF schema illustrated in Figure 12.23 is given as follows. The root element is RDF, followed by the namespaces. This means that the RDF scheme is written in RDF language. Then, the classes and properties in the diagram are defined in RDF triples. These triples can contain the terms defined in rdf namespace and rdfs namespace. For example, "faculty" is a class, and it is a subClassOf "personnel," where subClassOf is defined in rdfs namespace.

```
<?xml version="1.0"?>
<rdf:RDF
  xmlns:rdf="http://www.w3.org/1999/02/22-rdf-syntax-ns#"
  xmlns:rdfs="http://www.w3.org/2000/01/rdf-schema#">
  <rdfs:Class rdf:ID="personnel"></rdfs:Class>
  <rdfs:Class rdf:ID="faculty">
       <rdfs:subClassOf rdf:resource="#personnel"/>
       <rdfs:comment>faculty class is a subclass of personnel</rdfs:comment>
  <rdfs:Class rdf:ID="staff">
       <rdfs:subClassOf rdf:resource="#personnel"/>
       <rdfs:comment>staff class is a subclass of personnel</rdfs:comment>
  </rdfs:Class>
  <rdfs:Class rdf:ID="professors">
       <rdfs:subClassOf rdf:resource="#faculty"/>
       <rdfs:comment>professors class is a subclass of faculty</rdfs:comment>
  </rdfs:Class>
  <rdfs:Class rdf:ID="lecturers">
       <rdfs:subClassOf rdf:resource="#faculty"/>
       <rdfs:comment>lecturers class is a subclass of faculty</rdfs:comment>
  </rdfs:Class>
  <rdfs:Class rdf:ID="courses"></rdfs:Class>
  <rdfs:Class rdf:ID="courses100">
       <rdfs:subClassOf rdf:resource="#courses"/>
       <rdfs:comment> courses100 class is a subclass of courses. </rdfs:comment>
  </rdfs:Class>
  <rdfs:Class rdf:ID="courses200">
       <rdfs:subClassOf rdf:resource="#courses"/>
       <rdfs:comment>courses200 class is a subclass of courses</rdfs:comment>
  </rdfs:Class>
  <rdfs:Class rdf:ID="courses300">
       <rdfs:subClassOf rdf:resource="#courses"/>
       <rdfs:comment>courses300 class is a subclass of courses</rdfs:comment>
  </rdfs:Class>
  <rdfs:Class rdf:ID="courses400">
       <rdfs:subClassOf rdf:resource="#courses"/>
       <rdfs:comment> courses400 class is a subclass of courses</rdfs:comment>
  </rdfs:Class>
  <rdfs:Class rdf:ID="rooms"></rdfs:Class>
  <rdfs:Class rdf:ID="largeRooms">
       <rdfs:subClassOf rdf:resource="#rooms"/>
       <rdfs:comment>
            largeRooms class is a subclass of rooms.
       </rdfs:comment>
  </rdfs:Class>
  <rdfs:Class rdf:ID="mediumRooms">
       <rdfs:subClassOf rdf:resource="#rooms"/>
       <rdfs:comment>
            mediumRooms class is a subclass of rooms.
       </rdfs:comment>
  </rdfs:Class>
  <rdfs:Class rdf:ID="smallRooms">
       <rdfs:subClassOf rdf:resource="#rooms"/>
```

```
        <rdfs:comment>
              smallRooms class is a subclass of rooms.
        </rdfs:comment>
    </rdfs:Class>
    <rdf:Property rdf:ID="taughtBy">
        <rdfs:domain rdf:resource="#courses"/>
        <rdfs:range rdf:resource="#faculty"/>
        <rdfs:comment>courses can only be taught by faculty</rdfs:comment>
    </rdf:Property>
    <rdf:Property rdf:ID="taughtIn">
        <rdfs:domain rdf:resource="#courses100"/>
        <rdfs:domain rdf:resource="#courses200"/>
        <rdfs:domain rdf:resource="#courses300"/>
        <rdfs:domain rdf:resource="#courses400"/>
        <rdfs:range rdf:resource="#largeRoom"/>
        <rdfs:range rdf:resource="#mediumRoom"/>
        <rdfs:range rdf:resource="#smallRoom"/>
        <rdfs:comment>a course can be taught in a room</rdfs:comment>
    </rdf:Property>
    <rdf:Property rdf:ID="cap">
        <rdfs:domain rdf:resource="#largeRoom"/>
        <rdfs:domain rdf:resource="#mediumRoom"/>
        <rdfs:domain rdf:resource="#smallRoom"/>
        <rdfs:range rdf:Literal"/>
        <rdfs:comment>courses can only be taught by faculty</rdfs:comment>
    </rdf:Property>
</rdf:RDF>
```

The foregoing example illustrated the inheritance relations between the classes. If a class is a subClassOf another class, the subclass will inherit its base class's domain and range. The inheritance relation can also be applied to the properties. We can define that lecturedBy and assistedBy are the subproperty of taughtBy, as shown in the following code.

```
<rdf:Property rdf:ID="lecturedBy">
   <rdfs:subPropertyOf rdf:resource="#taughtBy"/>
   <rdfs:comment>
        It inherits the domain ("courses") and range ("faculty")
        from its superproperty "taughtBy"
   </rdfs:comment>
</rdf:Property>
<rdf:Property rdf:ID="assistedBy">
   <rdfs:subPropertyOf rdf:resource="#taughtBy"/>
   <rdfs:comment>
        It inherits the domain and range from "taughtBy"
   </rdfs:comment>
</rdf:Property>
```

Once we have the defined the user-defined RDFS schema, we can define RDFS instance document using the rdf, rdfs, and the user-defined namespaces, as shown in the following example.

```
<?xml version="1.0"?>
<rdf:RDF xmlns:rdf="http://www.w3.org/1999/02/22-rdf-syntax-ns#"
   xmlns=" http://neptune.fulton.ad.asu.edu/WSRepository/xml/Courses.rdf">
   <Courses200 rdf:ID="C++">
        <taughtBy>
              <Professors rdf:ID="David"/>
        </taughtBy>
        <taughtIn>
              <largeRoom rdf:ID="R110">
```

```
                    <cap>82</cap>
                </largeRoom>
            </taughtIn>
    </Courses200>
    <Courses400 rdf:ID="Database">
            <taughtBy>
                <Lecturers rdf:ID="Mary"/>
            </taughtBy>
            <taughtIn>
                <smallRoom rdf:ID="R401">
                    <cap>43</cap>
                </smallRoom>
            </taughtIn>
    </Courses4000>
</rdf:RDF>
```

12.6.3 Reasoning and Verification in Ontology

Using RDF only, we can describe individual resources, properties, and values in a rather flat list; for example, we can write RDF statements to describe the following:

- C++ is taught by David; C++ is taught in R220;
- Database is taught by Mary; Database is taught in R402.

However, we can also write syntactically correct, but semantically incorrect RDF statements to describe the followings:

- C++ is taught by David; C++ is taught in R401;
- Database is taught by Steward; Database is taught in R402.

The Statement "C++ is taught in R401" is semantically incorrect, because room R401 can accommodate courses in Courses400 only. C++ is a course in Courses100, whose enrollment number may exceed the capacity of the room. Statement "Database is taught by Steward" is incorrect because Steward is a staff member. A course can be taught by a faculty member only, according the user-defined RDF schema. The structures defined in RDFS can be used to verify the semantics of the instance documents.

RDF Schema can be considered the object-oriented version of RDF with classes and inheritance-based class hierarchy. RDF Scheme's expressivity is more powerful than that of an object-oriented programming language. An object-oriented programming language does not have global mechanisms to relate the classes in different hierarchies. It is possible to write methods (member functions) in a class to enforce certain relations. The class must be modified if a relation is modified; for example, if the room restriction "a course in Courses300 is taught in a medium room" is implemented as a method in class Courses300, then the class must be modified if we also allow such a course to be taught in a large room. On the other hand, RDFS is capable of describing the relations among classes in different hierarchies using global properties outside the classes, as represented in the blocks in Figure 12.23. The modification to a property does not incur a modification to a class.

Using the RDFS defined ontology, we can easily check if an RDF statement is semantically correct. Let us consider the statements "C++ is taught by David" and "C++ is taught in R220." There are two properties that must be verified: Who can teach C++ and where can C++ be taught? We can follow arrows in the ontology diagram in Figure 12.23 to verify the properties using the following reasoning process:

- C++ is a course in the class Courses100, which is a subclass of Courses;
- An instance (course) of class Courses can be taught by an instance (a faculty member) of the class Faculty;
- Lecturer is a subclass of Faculty or instances of Lecturers are also instances of Faculty;
- David is an instance of Lecturer and thus is an instance Faculty;

- Thus, David can teach C++.

Similarly, we cannot find a path in the ontology to verify the statements "Database is taught by Steward" and "Database is taught in R402," and thus, the statement must be rejected.

W3C provides an online "RDF Validation Service" at: http://www.w3.org/RDF/Validator/

By copying and pasting the RDF code as direct input, the validator can check the syntax of your RDF document, as shown in Figure 12.24.

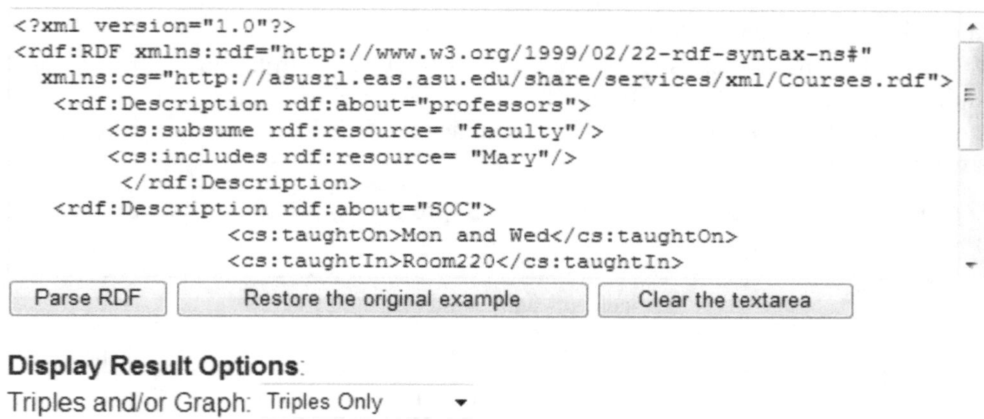

Figure 12.24. W3C RDF validator

Ontologies written in ontology languages such as RDF and RDFS provide the information and knowledge for reason and validation. However, they do not have the processing power to perform reasoning and validation. Traditional programming languages such as C++, Java, and C# can be used to handle these tasks. However, Prolog is natural choice of language for this purpose, because Prolog has a similar style as RDF/RDFS, which express the information in a list of facts and rules. Prolog is a well-established very level logic/declarative programming language, and there are many available resources. It is originally designed for AI and knowledge representation. Prolog has a built-in "database" of facts and rules, as well as the power of a programming language for data processing and reasoning ability. Prolog statements can be easily translated to and from RDF triple notations. Also, see section 11.6 for Prolog-implemented parsers.

12.6.4 Web Ontology Language OWL

The expressivity of RDF Schema in describing semantics is limited to classes, subclass hierarchies, properties, and property hierarchies, with domain and range definitions of these properties. In many cases, we need more powerful mechanisms (higher level of expressivity or flexibility) to describe the semantics among data and objects, for the purposes of matching, reasoning, and model checking. Web Ontology Language (OWL) offers such a more powerful language.

As we know from the principles of programming languages, the higher the expressivity of a language is, the less reliable the programs written in the language will be. For example, C is weakly typed and has a higher level of expressivity than that of Java. It is easier to make a programming error in C than in Java. There is a tradeoff between the expressivity of a language and the reliability of the programs written in the language.

OWL defined three dialects of the language with different level of expressivity:

- **OWL Full:** The entire language allows all primitives. It also allows to combine these primitives in arbitrary ways with RDF and RDFS. For example, in OWL Full we can impose a cardinality constraint on the class of all classes, essentially limiting the number of classes that can be described in any ontology. OWL Full is fully upward compatible with RDF, both syntactically and semantically. On the other hand, the language has become so powerful and flexible that it is impossible to develop a reasoning and model checking mechanism on the language.

- **OWL DL** (OWL Description Logic)**:** It is a sublanguage of OWL Full, which restricts the language to a well-studied Description Logic, so that efficient reasoning support can be developed for the language. However, OWL DL is not fully compatible with RDF/RDFS. In other words, a legal RDF/RDFS document is not necessarily a legal OWL DL document. It has to be extended in some ways and restricted in others before it becomes a legal OWL DL document. On the other hand, a legal OWL DL document is still a legal RDF/RDFS document.
- **OWL Lite:** It is a sublanguage of OWL DL with further limitations. For example, OWL Lite excludes enumerated classes, disjoint statements, and arbitrary cardinality (among others). The advantage is that the language is easier to understand and easier to process by the tools. The disadvantage is the restricted expressivity.

Figure 12.25 shows the compatibility of the documents (programs) written in the three OWL dialects and in RDF/RDFS.

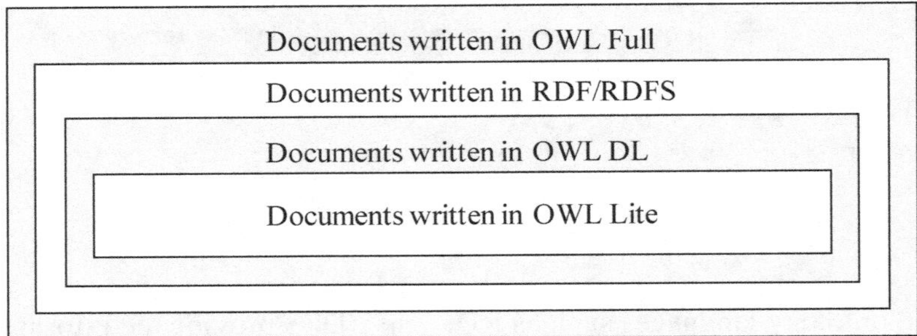

Figure 12.25. Compatibility among documents in OWL dialects and RDF

OWL is built on RDF and RDFS using XML syntax. For OWL DL and OWL Lite, OWL documents are also RDF documents and thus OWL documents start with RDF header and namespaces. OWL can use RDF namespaces and new OWL namespaces, shown as follows:

```
<rdf:RDF
   xmlns:owl ="http://www.w3.org/2002/07/owl#"
   xmlns:rdfs="http://www.w3.org/2000/01/rdf-schema#"
   xmlns:rdf ="http://www.w3.org/1999/02/22-rdf-syntax-ns#"
   xmlns:xsd ="http://www.w3.org/2001/XLMSchema#">
   <rdfs:comment> body of the document here</rdfs:comment>
</rdf:RDF>
```

Like RDFS, OWL ontology is based on classes and properties. The following example shows the syntax of defining of classes, which is similar to the way of defining RDFS classes, but with extended properties:

```
<owl:Class rdf:ID="faculty"></owl:Class>
<owl:Class rdf:ID="professors">
   <rdfs:subClassOf rdf:resource="#faculty"/>
</owl:Class>
<owl:Class rdf:ID="lecturers">
   <rdfs:subClassOf rdf:resource="#faculty"/>
   <owl:disjointWith rdf:resource="#professors"/>
</owl:Class>
<owl:Class rdf:ID="instructors">
   <rdfs:subClassOf rdf:resource="#faculty"/>
   <owl:equivalentClass rdf:resource="#lecturers"/>
```

```
</owl:Class>
```

In this example, two new properties are used: "disjointWith," which specifies that the lecturers class does not overlap with class professors, and "equivalentClass," which specifies that the instructors class is equivalent to the lecturers class.

General speaking, OWL classes support the following additional properties:

Besides subClassOf defined in RDFS, OWL also allows to define the Boolean combinations (union, intersection, and complement) of a list of classes. The operators are:

- owl:unionOf;
- owl:intersectionOf;
- owl:complementOf.

For example, we can find the faculty members who have registered as students in the university. We can use the intersectionOf operation to find the set of people who are in the faculty set and in the student set:

```
<owl:Class rdf:ID="facultyOnTraining">
   <owl:intersectionOf rdf:parseType="Collection">
        <owl:Class rdf:about="#faculty"/>
        <owl:Class rdf:about="#student"/>
   </owl:intersectionOf>
</owl:Class>
```

OWL supports a variety of operations that restrict/select the members of classes based on a property specified by:

- owl:Restriction, which is a subclass of owl:Class and is used to define the scope of the restriction, and
- owl:onProperty, which is used to specify the property used to select the members of the restricted class.

The restriction operations include:

- owl:allValuesFrom;
- owl:hasValuesFrom;
- owl:someValuesFrom;
- owl:minCardinality;
- owl:maxCardinality.

The following code makes a restriction on who can teach the 400 level courses. The property on which restriction is put on is "taughtBy" and selection method of the members is "allValuesFrom," and the class from which the members are selected is "professors."

```
<owl:Class rdf:about="#Courses400">
   <rdfs:subClassOf>
        <owl:Restriction>
               <owl:onProperty rdf:resource="#taughtBy"/>
               <owl:allValuesFrom rdf:resource="#Professor"/>
        </owl:Restriction>
   </rdfs:subClassOf>
</owl:Class>
```

The following code specifies that course "Database" is taught by "Mary."

```
<owl:Class rdf:about="#Database">
   <rdfs:subClassOf>
        <owl:Restriction>
               <owl:onProperty rdf:resource="#taughtBy"/>
               <owl:hasValuesFrom rdf:resource="#Mary"/>
```

```
        </owl:Restriction>
    </rdfs:subClassOf>
</owl:Class>
```

Using the cardinality restriction, we can define the maximum and minimum enrollment of a class; for example, the following code restricts that the Database course must enroll at least 10 and at most 40 students.

```
<owl:Class rdf:about="#Datbase">
    <rdfs:subClassOf>
        <owl:Restriction>
            <owl:onProperty rdf:resource="#hasMember"/>
            <owl:minCardinality
                rdf:datatype="&xsd;nonNegativeInteger"> 10
            </owl:minCardinality>
            <owl:maxCardinality
                rdf:datatype="&xsd;nonNegativeInteger"> 40
            </owl:maxCardinality>
        </owl:Restriction>
    </rdfs:subClassOf>
</owl:Class>
```

As can been seen from these examples, OWL is much more powerful than RDFS in specifying the semantics among data.

We now summarize the main features and constructs supported by the dialects of OWL. We have not covered all of them in the previous sections. Detailed descriptions can be found at: http://www.w3.org/TR/owl-features/.

Synopsis of OWL Lite

OWL Lite has the following list of features and constructs.

- Header Information: OWL Lite supports notions of ontology inclusion and relationships and attaching information to ontologies.
- RDF Schema Features:
- Class (Thing, Nothing)
- rdfs:subClassOf
- rdf:Property
- rdfs:subPropertyOf
- rdfs:domain
- rdfs:range
- Individual
- Class Combination:
- Datatypes
- xsd datatypes
- Equality and Inequality:
- equivalentClass
- equivalentProperty
- sameAs
- differentFrom
- ObjectProperty
- DatatypeProperty
- inverseOf
- TransitiveProperty
- SymmetricProperty
- FunctionalProperty
- InverseFunctionalProperty
- Property Restrictions:
- Restriction
- onProperty
- allValuesFrom
- someValuesFrom
- minCardinality (only 0 or 1)
- maxCardinality (only 0 or 1)
- cardinality (only 0 or 1)
- Annotation Properties:
- rdfs:label
- rdfs:comment
- rdfs:seeAlso
- rdfs:isDefinedBy

- AllDifferent
- distinctMembers
- Property Characteristics:
- AnnotationProperty
- OntologyProperty

Synopsis of OWL DL and Full

OWL DL and Full support are all features and constructs in OWL Lite. They support the following additional or expanded features and constructs.

- Boolean Combinations of Classes
- unionOf
- complementOf
- intersectionOf
- Arbitrary Cardinality
- minCardinality
- maxCardinality
- cardinality
- oneOf, dataRange
- disjointWith
- equivalentClass (applied to class expressions)
- rdfs:subClassOf (applied to class expressions)
- Property Restrictions:
- hasValue

12.6.5 OWL-S and Semantic Web Services

OWL-S (Ontology Web Language for Service) was formerly called DAML-S (DARPA Agent Markup Language for Services) (http://www.w3.org/Submission/OWL-S/). It consists of a set of markup language constructs for describing the properties and capabilities of their web services in an unambiguous form. Computer-interpretable form provides support for the following operations:

- Service Advertisements with:
  - Functional Aspects
  - Nonfunctional Aspects
  - Interaction Protocol using process model
- Discovery of services (OWL-S Matchmaker) supporting subsumption-based discovery
- Composition (OWL-S process model), supporting hierarchical planning
- Invocation (OWL-S VM)
- Execution and monitoring

OWL-S is extended from OWL (Ontology Web Language), which is an ontology description language. OWL-S adds process description constructs similar to those in BPEL, so that the workflow process can be described. As an ontology language, OWL-S uses three properties to declare a service:

- Service Profiles, which provides a set of properties to describe the abstract inputs and outputs, including properties: serviceName, hasParameter, hasPrecondition, hasResult, hasInput, hasOutput, and hasProcess.
- Process Models, which provides composition constructs to define the process similar to the BPEL process.
- Service Grounding: The abstract inputs and outputs defined in service profile are translated into WSDL interface with SOAP transport so that OWL-S services can be compatible with other web services. The translation layer is called service grounding.

OWL-S supports the following constructs that can be used to compose processes:

- Sequence: A list of control constructs to be done in order.
- Split: The components of a Split process are a bag of process components to be executed concurrently. Split completes as soon as all of its component processes have been scheduled for execution.

- Split+Join: the process consists of concurrent execution of a bunch of process components with barrier synchronization. That is, Split+Join completes when all of its components processes have completed.
- Any-Order: Allows the process components (specified as a bag) to be executed in some unspecified order but not concurrently. Execution and completion of all components is required. The execution of processes in an Any-Order construct cannot overlap.
- Choice: It calls for the execution of a single control construct from a given bag of control constructs. Any of the given control constructs may be chosen for execution.
- If-Then-Else: It is a control construct that has properties ifCondition, then and else holding different aspects.
- Iterate: The construct makes no assumption about how many iterations are made or when to initiate, terminate, or resume.
- Repeat-While and Repeat-Until: Both constructs iterate until a condition becomes false or true.

OWL-S is the main tool used for developing Semantic Web Service (SWS). WSDL-based web services are also called syntax-based web services, as WSDL describes the syntax of the web service interface. OWL-S makes it possible for giving semantic descriptions through its service profiles, which semantically describe what a service can offer to the client.

12.6.6 Linked Data

Our current hypertext websites contain linked data of URIs, including web pages and other media types of documents. However, the websites are mainly designed for human users. RDF, RDF Schema, and OWL provide ways of describing the data, their relationships and semantics for a computer program to access. However, these technologies focus on linking basic data items together. Linked Data defines another layer of structure to link the linked data together, so that they become more useful and more available to program users, particularly for the RESTful services. Linked Data builds upon standard web technologies, such as XML, HTTP, URI, RDF, and REST. The concepts and principles were proposed by Tim Berners-Lee in 2006 (http://www.w3.org/DesignIssues/LinkedData.html).

To better understand Linked Data Web, we can review the development of web technologies.

- Web 1.0 uses HTML to organize and present formatted data on web for human users to consume. There is not much a computer program can do to explore the relationships of data in different HTML pages.
- Web 2.0 uses API and web services technologies to process data. The computing units provide a wall between the data and clients of the data. The idea is similar to the object orientation where data members of an object are private and the data are accessed via the public methods.
- RDF, RDFS, and OWL-based Web 3.0 Semantic Web directly presents structured and annotated data directly to the clients (programs), which makes data more useful. Linked Data takes the advantage of such available data and linking these data together to make them even more available. This kind of linkages is not possible if the data are protected and their accesses are available only through calling web methods.

Figure 12.26 shows the relationship between the concepts of Web 1.0, Web 2.0, and Web 3.0 with the Linked Data. To better access the features offered by Linked Data Webs, a number of projects are developing the Linked Data enabled browsers.

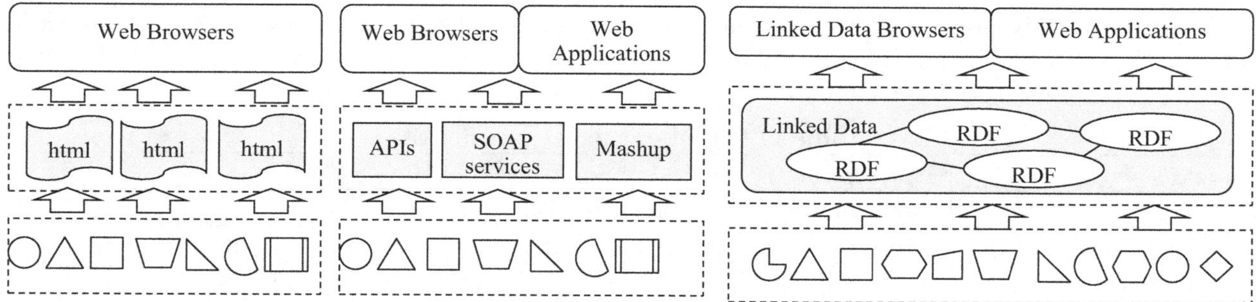

Figure 12.26. Left: Web 1.0, Middle: Web 2.0, and Right: Web 3.0 with Linked Data

As the Linked Data Webs directly expose URI resources, they are to be more friendly for REST services and Web 3.0 applications to process.

Google Merchant Center is a service (https://www.google.com/intl/en/retail) where one can submit structured data for make them online available. If Google finds it relevant, submitted content may appear on its shopping search engine, Google Maps or even the web search. Google offers a number of APIs and tools to submit, to manage, to syndicate the contents, and to search the linked data.

12.6.7 Ontology Development Environments

Several ontology development environments are available to support resource description and ontology development. We will briefly present Protégé, Microsoft CSF, and Prolog implemented parsers.

Protégé OWL Editor (http://protege.stanford.edu/) is a free and open-source ontology development environment. It supports two ways of developing ontologies: Protégé Frames editor and Protégé-OWL editor. The OWL editor provides basic functions of defining, loading, editing, saving ontology schema and instances in OWL and RDF. Protégé can also execute the reasoners such as the description logic classifiers. The Protégé-Frames editor provides a graphical user interface and a knowledge server to support users in constructing and storing frame-based domain ontologies, customizing data-entry forms, and entering instance data. Protégé-Frames environment implements a knowledge model, which is compatible with the Open Knowledge Base Connectivity protocol (OKBC). In this model, an ontology consists of a set of classes organized in a subsumption hierarchy to represent a domain's salient concepts, a set of slots associated to classes to describe their properties and relationships, and a set of instances of those classes—individual exemplars of the concepts that hold specific values for their properties. The graphical representation can be stored in various formats, including RDF, OWL, XML, and HTML.

Microsoft has developed a Connection Services Framework (CSF), which connects services across multiple networks and devices with a single solution. Microsoft CSF:

- Uses RDF to describe resources involved;
- Manages user services across a broad array of devices (including third-party devices), such as cell phones, television set-top boxes, and personal computers;
- Rapidly connects legacy systems, proprietary processes, and standard technologies by using web services;
- Combines the power of web services with next-generation network services—including IP Multimedia Subsystems (IMS)—to provide aggregated service offerings, which will further boost revenue opportunities;
- Provides a consistent user experience across devices.

CSF environment is based on Windows and .Net framework. RDF-related classes in CSF are shown in Table 12.8. These classes are not included in the standard .Net Framework Class Library. CSF installation on .Net will import these classes into the framework.

Table 12.8. RDF-related classes in CSF

Class	Description
RdfBlankNode	Represents a blank node in an RDF graph.
RdfException	Represents an exception encountered during interaction with an RDF graph.
RdfGraph	Represents an RDF graph as specified by http://www.w3.org/RDF/.
RdfLiteral	Represents a literal node in an RDF graph.
RdfNode	Represents a node in an RDF graph.
RdfNodeCollection	Represents a collection of RdfNode objects.
RdfParseErrorInfo	Represents RDF parse error information.
RdfParseException	Represents an exception encountered while parsing RDF.
RdfTriple	Represents a triple in the RdfGraph.
RdfTripleCollection	Represents a collection of RdfTriple objects.

A number of ontology parsers have been implemented in Prolog; for example: SWI-Prolog RDF parser: http://www.swi-prolog.org/pldoc/doc_for?object=section(%27packages/rdf2pl.html%27).

12.7 Discussions

Artificial intelligence research started in 1950. However, artificial intelligence did not find major applications until recent year, when it enters its third generation. The latest artificial intelligence and machine learning are based on big data analysis and processing, which is transforming the current world into a different world. There are many unknown domains and discussions on what can be replaced and cannot be replaced by artificial intelligence.

Ontologies are also a major technology supporting big data analysis, artificial intelligence, and Semantic Web. There are a few tools available to support ontology development. Many of the big data and artificial intelligence applications require an ontology, which stores not only the data, but also the relationships among the data. The reasoning capacity of ontology gives big data processing and artificial intelligence additional power to analyze data from inside the data store.

Name: ______________________

Date: ______________________

12.8 Exercises and Projects

1. Multiple choice questions. Choose one answer in each question only. Choose the best answer if multiple answers are acceptable.

1.1 When was the first generation artificial intelligence research started?

(A) 1940s (B) 1950s (C) 1980s (D) 2000s

1.2 When was the third generation artificial intelligence research started?

(A) 1940s (B) 1950s (C) 1980s (D) 2000s

1.3 What is the most appropriate human-machine interface for IA applications?

(A) keyboard (B) keyboard & mouse (C) touch screen (D) microphone

1.4 What are key features of the third generation AI?

(A) Human machine integration (B) Based on big data processing

(C) Based on cloud computing (D) All of the above

1.5 What does hardware and software co-design mean in AI solution design?

(A) Based on existing hardware carefully designing software.

(B) Based on existing AI software carefully designing hardware to meet the needs.

(C) Design software and hardware cooperatively to meet AI needs.

(D) Design software and hardware independently based on standard interface.

1.6 A key factor that AI programming differs traditional programming is that AI programming

(A) takes feedback from the environment.

(B) is based polynomial efficient algorithms.

(C) is running on high performance computer (HPC).

(D) offers graphic user interface.

1.7 Deep learning is based on

(A) a binary decision tree.

(B) a big table of learning objects.

(C) multiple layers that perform step-wise and parallel processing of complex objects.

(D) standard communication protocols between the instructors and learners.

1.8 For different AI problems, we must design different solutions, which means we

(A) cannot reuse any existing algorithms and library functions.

(B) can reuse certain basic algorithms and library functions, but we must design new overall solutions.

(C) can reuse all the existing algorithms and library functions, but we need to retrain the models using new data.

(D) just need to create new solutions, but the majority of the implementations can be imported from an existing project.

1.9 What features are extracted for the ASU Flight Data Training experiment?

(A) average value
(B) median value
(C) Both (A) and (B)
(D) Neither (A) nor (B)

1.10 Google's TensorFlow is a tool used for

(A) training data and fitting the data to a model.
(B) extracting features automatically.
(C) storing massive data.
(D) big data processing.

1.11 An RDF statement is a

(A) pair: (subject, predicate)
(B) pair: (subject, object)
(C) triple: (resource, property, class)
(D) triple: (subject, predicate, object)

1.12 What are the three object types of the basic RDF data model?

(A) resource, property, and statement
(B) ontology, Semantic Web, and database
(C) int, character, and string
(D) class, object, and instantiation

1.13 What properties are predefined in RDF?

(A) domain
(B) range
(C) type
(D) All of the above

1.14 RDFS (RDF with rdfs namespace extension) is

(A) not an ontology language.
(B) a less powerful (less expressive) ontology language than RDF.
(C) a more powerful (more expressive) ontology language than RDF.
(D) none of the above.

1.15 Similar to XML Schema, RDF Schema is used to define syntax of RDF documents.

(A) True
(B) False

1.16 What language can be used for processing RDFS documents and performing reasoning and validation?

(A) Prolog
(B) RDF
(C) RDFS
(D) OWL

1.17 The higher the expressivity of a language is, the less reliable the programs written in the language will be.

(A) True
(B) False

1.18 Compared to RDF/RDFS, what OWL dialect(s) is (are) more powerful in expressivity?

(A) OWL Lite
(B) OWL DL and OWL Full
(C) OWL Full
(D) None of the above

1.19 What operations are supported in OWL Lite?

(A) sameAs
(B) subClassOf
(C) Both (A) and (B)
(D) Neither (A) nor (B)

1.20 What operations are supported in OWL Full?

(A) complementOf
(B) disjointWith
(C) subClassOf
(D) All of the above

2. What are the major components of an intelligence solution technology stack? What other companies are offering such stacks, in addition to IBM and Intel?

3. Explain the major differences between traditional software development paradigms and IA-based software development paradigm.

4. What is an Inertial Measurement Unit (IMU)? Where can such a sensor be used, in addition to flight data analysis?

5. Study and explain the major components and tools used in the Machine Learning Case Study on Flight Path Recognition discussed in the text.

6. Study and explain the main ideas in the Machine Learning Case Study on Network Traffic Monitoring discussed in the text.

7. What is RDF? What are RDF resources, predicates, and statements? What is an RDF instance document?

8. What is RDF Schema? What are the differences between RDF namespace and RDFS namespace?

9. What are RDFS classes, resources, properties, and literals?

10. What types of statements does a Prolog program contain? What are the differences between Prolog facts and rules?

11. What are Semantic Web and Ontology? What are the current technologies supporting them?

12. What is OWL? What OWL dialects exist?

13. Compare and contrast RDF and OWL dialects.

14. Find a few ontology frameworks from the Internet and other sources. Discuss the functionality and the ontology languages they support.

15. Consider the diagram in Figure 12.23, which shows the skeleton of the requirement of an ontology design. You may need to add additional elements or attributes in your implementation.

    a. Add the property “managedBy” between the courses class and the Staff class.

    b. Use RDF and RDFS namespaces rdf and rdfs to define a user-defined ontology schema for the given requirement in the diagram. The file must be put in a web page (e.g., in your university web space) for remote access (make sure that other students in the class cannot access your file before the submission due time!)

c. Define an instance file of the ontology schema, by taking the data from the university's class schedule; for example, at https://www.asu.edu/go/classsearch/. Choose two to three CSE courses at each level, and from levels 100 through 400. The schema defined in the previous question should be listed as a namespace. Notice that the sessions taught in the same room and at the same time should be counted as one course, if the course has multiple course codes. Make sure that the courses you choose fit into the ontology schema that you have designed.

d. Write a C# or Java Windows application that takes the URLs of the two files created in the previous two questions and validate the format of the instance file against the schema file.

e. Find an RDF parser to validate your RDFS and RDF documents.

Project 1

1. In this project, you will an image recognition Web service that can take the URL of a .jpg or .png image as input, and recognize the shape of the image. An example is given at the URL:

   http://neptune.fulton.ad.asu.edu/WSRepository/Services/ImageRecognition/Service.svc?wsdl

2. You will develop a TryIt web application to test your image recognition service. An example is given at URL:

   http://neptune.fulton.ad.asu.edu/WSRepository/services/imagerecognitionTryIt/Default.aspx

Project 2

Follow the Machine Learning Case Study on Flight Path Recognition discussed in the text to implement your own machine learning project.

Part III
Appendices: Tutorials on Service-Oriented System Development

In the main text, we focused on showing the concepts, principles, and methods in service-oriented architecture, service-oriented computing, service-oriented data management, and service-oriented software development. We used code and code pieces as a vehicle to demonstrate those concepts, principles, and methods. In the Appendix A and Appendix B, we will focus on hands-on tutorials to provide students with full details and all missing pieces in creating working programs. While we were writing these tutorials, we realized that the materials could be used in other ways. Students with little programming experience can start with the tutorials and learn computing concepts by examples. Thus, we particularly choose the materials and examples in the areas of graphic and visual development, including web services, web applications, workflow, and robotics applications. We demonstrate the power of service-oriented computing by showing that fun and useful applications can be constructed by students with limited web programming experience. The focus is on computational thinking and the logic of the application to be developed, using ready-to-use components and services, and customizing the components and services through their parameters. For the convenience of referencing, we listed all the deployed examples of web services, web applications, and other resources we used in the text in Appendix C.

Appendix A
Web Application Development

This appendix discusses the graphical user interface design and application development using web services discovered on the Internet.

A.1 Design of Graphical User Interface

The difference between an application and a service or a software component is that the former has a human user interface, also known as GUI (Graphical User Interface) if graphical representation is used in the interface design; and the latter has a programming interface, also known as Application Programming Interface (API). This section discusses GUI design in .Net.

In Visual Studio programming environment, you can create an application with text-based user interface (Console Application) and with GUI (e.g., Windows Forms Application). In both cases, the application will run on a Windows computer. You can also create a web application or website application. In this case, the application will be deployed to a web server, such as a Windows server with IIS. Chapter 3, Section 3.4.1 discussed the process of creating and deploying a website Application. This section will discuss the Windows Forms Application.

To create a Windows Forms Application, start Visual Studio (2019) and create a new project by searching "windows forms":

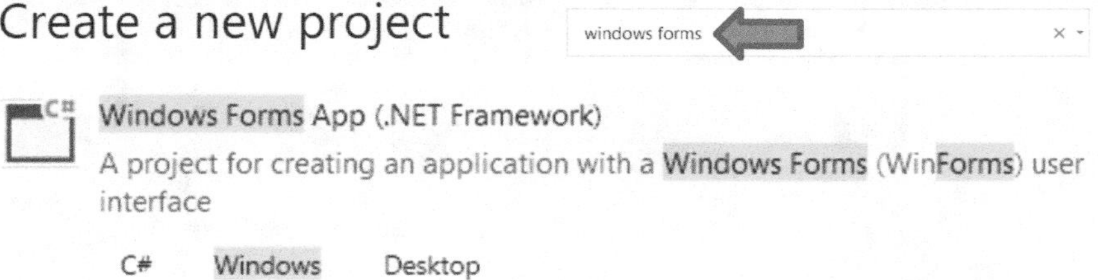

Click "Next" button and choose a project name and a location for the project. Note, do not use the default location is is Visual Studio folder, which can cause a permission problem when you run the program.

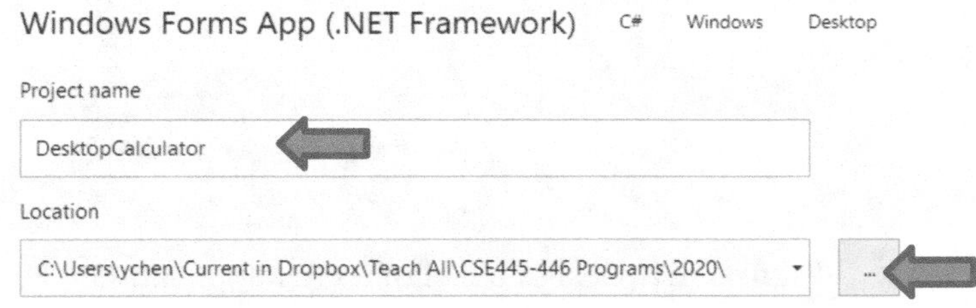

Then, a Form or a Design surface that can be used for creating a GUI will be opened, as shown in Figure A.1.

In Figure A.1, the following components and tools are available for you to build your Windows applications:

- **GUI/Code Editor:** This is a shared window that allows you to create your GUI, as well as enter your program code that is linked to the GUI.
  (1) GUI: When you click the "Form1.cs" in the "Solution Explorer," you will see the blank Designer Surface, on which you can draw your interface items. You can drag-and-drop the items in the toolbox on the left of the window to the Design surface.
  (2) When you double-click any of the items that you have drawn, the code editor behind the item will be opened, with the code prototype (the first line of the method) generated, and you can enter your C# program in the code editor. All Visual C# programs have the .cs extension.
- **Solution Explorer:** It offers you an organized view of your project, its files, and programs created by the system and by you, as well as ready access to the commands that pertain to them. You can add new projects into the solution. This is particularly convenient to organize multiple projects in one solution, if the programs in the solution need to communicate with each other. For example, if you create a number of web services and an application that uses the services, the application can access the services without having to deploy the services to IIS or a server. You can deploy the entire solution, which becomes a namespace, whereas the classes in the projects become the classes in the namespace.
- **Toolbox:** On the left side of the window, you can move your mouse over the Toolbox tab to open the Toolbox window if it is not open. Click the plus (+) sign next to the Common Controls. You will see a list of form controls that are seen in a Windows application. From the Toolbox, you can find the components (items) needed in your GUI, such as Button, RadioButton, Label, TextBox, CheckBox, and so on.
- **Properties:** They allow you to customize each of the GUI components (items) that you have drawn. This includes the name, color, text, font type, and font size.

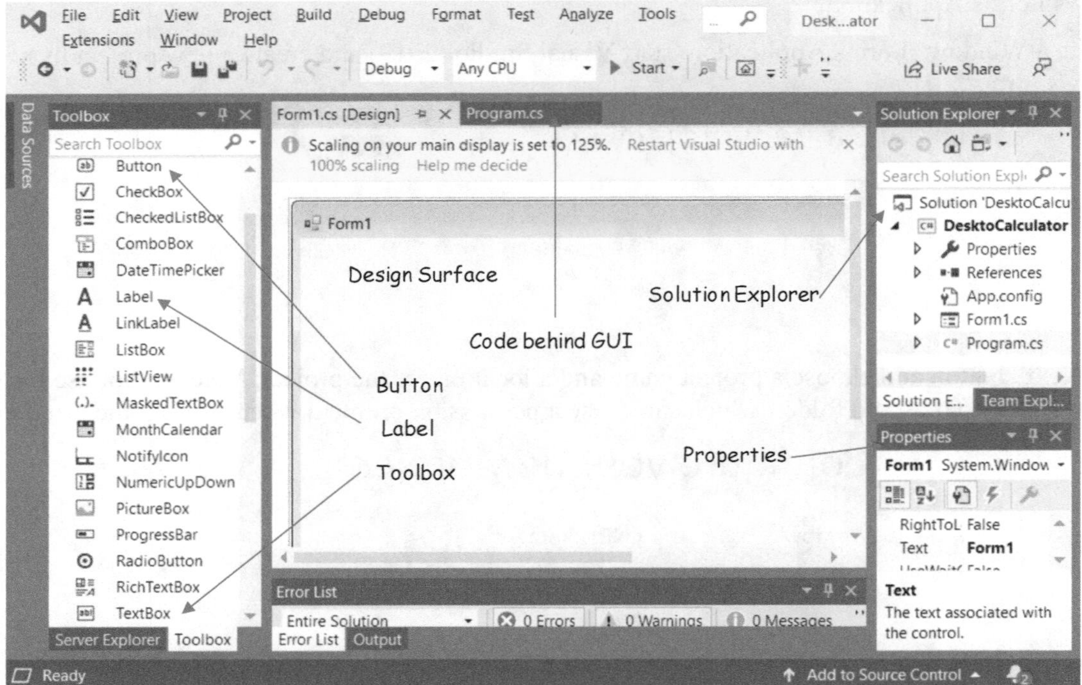

Figure A.1. Design panel of a GUI application

Create your own calculator

As an example, we will create a simple calculator, as shown in Figure A.2, which consists of two TextBoxes, four Buttons, and two Labels. From the two text boxes, you can enter two numbers. When you click one of the buttons, the operation on the button, +, -, *, and / will be performed on the two numbers. There are two Labels used in the GUI. The Label marked "=" simply displays the information. The second Label marked "Show result here" holds the place for displaying the result of the calculation.

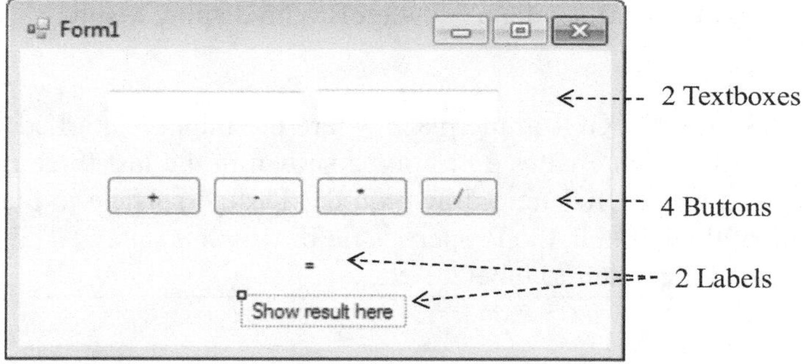

Figure A.2. GUI design of a simple calculator

Now we will write C# code behind the GUI to perform the computation needed. Since each button represents a computing task, we will link a method behind each button. By double-clicking on a button, the prototype of the method will be opened in the Code Editor, shown as follows, assuming "+" button is double-clicked.

```
private void button1_Click(object sender, EventArgs e)
{
}
```

Now, you can add your code in the prototype to perform the required operation. The operands come from the two Textboxes. By default, they are named textBox1 and textBox2. You can find the names in the Properties field of the project. Thus, the operation should look like:

```
result = textBox1 + textBox2
```

The problem is that anything entered from a textbox will have a type of string. Thus, we need to convert them to the integer type, as shown in the code below:

```
Int32 number1 = Convert.ToInt32(textBox1.Text);
Int32 number2 = Convert.ToInt32(textBox2.Text);
Int32 result = number1 + number2;
```

Next, we want to display the result to the human user. There are different ways to display the result. First, we can use a MessageBox to pop up a window to show the result. Thus, we can use the following code to implement this solution:

```
private void button1_Click(object sender, EventArgs e)
{
    Int32 number1 = Convert.ToInt32(textBox1.Text);
    Int32 number2 = Convert.ToInt32(textBox2.Text);
    Int32 result = number1 + number2;
    MessageBox.Show("The sum of " + textBox1.Text + " and " +
        textBox2.Text + " is " + result.ToString());
}
```

If 23 and 47 are entered and button "+" is clicked, the result will be given in a pop up window shown in Figure A.3.

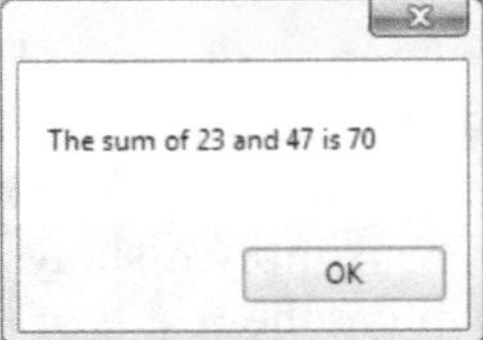

Figure A.3. Using a MessageBox to display result

If we want to display the result in the GUI in the place where the Label is marked "Show result here," we need to double-click the Label, which creates a prototype shown in the last three lines of the code below. This operation is necessary to link a GUI item drawn on the Design surface to the code behind the GUI. Next, we look up the name of the Label in the Properties field, which is label2. Then, we change the output code at line 6, and we can send the result to label2.Text.

```
private void button1_Click(object sender, EventArgs e)
{
      Int32 number1 = Convert.ToInt32(textBox1.Text);
      Int32 number2 = Convert.ToInt32(textBox2.Text);
      Int32 result = number1+number2;
      label2.Text = result.ToString();
}
private void label2_Click(object sender, EventArgs e)
{
}
```

With the changes, the result will be displayed in the GUI, as shown in Figure A.4.

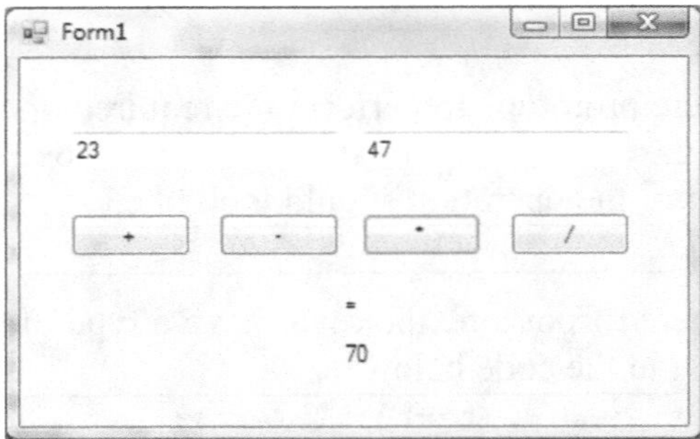

Figure A.4. Display the result in GUI marked a label

We still need to program the other three buttons -, *, and / to make a complete calculator application. The code that follows shows the complete program. Although the entire program is organized in a sequence of methods, you cannot simply copy the entire code into the code editor. The GUI items will not be able to find the methods linked to them. You must click each button and use the system-generated prototype to start with your method.

```
using System;
using System.Collections.Generic;
using System.ComponentModel;
using System.Data;
using System.Drawing;
using System.Text;
```

```
using System.Windows.Forms;
namespace myGUI {
    public partial class Form1 : Form {
        public Form1(){ InitializeComponent(); }
        private void button1_Click(object sender, EventArgs e) {
            Int32 number1 = Convert.ToInt32(textBox1.Text);
            Int32 number2 = Convert.ToInt32(textBox2.Text);
            Int32 result = number1 + number2;
            label2.Text = result.ToString();
        }
        private void button2_Click(object sender, EventArgs e) {
            Int32 number1 = Convert.ToInt32(textBox1.Text);
            Int32 number2 = Convert.ToInt32(textBox2.Text);
            Int32 result = number1 - number2;
            label2.Text = result.ToString();
        }
        private void button3_Click(object sender, EventArgs e) {
            Int32 number1 = Convert.ToInt32(textBox1.Text);
            Int32 number2 = Convert.ToInt32(textBox2.Text);
            Int32 result = number1 * number2;
            label2.Text = result.ToString();
        }
        private void button4_Click(object sender, EventArgs e) {
            Int32 number1 = Convert.ToInt32(textBox1.Text);
            Int32 number2 = Convert.ToInt32(textBox2.Text);
            Int32 result = number1 / number2;
            label2.Text = result.ToString();
        }
    }
}
```

You can create an executable file by choosing "Build" → "Batch build." Then, check the "release" box. This option of the compilation will generate the .exe file in the bin folder. The executable file can run on a different computer. Now, you can generate the executable for your calculator and send it to your friend for testing.

Create your own web browser

What browser do you use? Edge, Chrome, or Firefox? How about creating your own web browser? Now we show you another application that allows you to create your own web browser in a few simple steps.

1. Start Visual Studio by clicking Start → All Programs → Microsoft Visual Studio.Net.
2. Create a new project by clicking on File → New → Project.
3. From the New Project window, create a new Visual C# Windows Application and name the application "JohnDoesBrowser." You can use your name.
4. On the new created project, select the "Form1" and modify the following properties using the following values:
    a. Text → John Doe's Browser
    b. Size → 720, 640 (Width, Height)
5. From the Toolbox, drag-and-drop the GUI item "WebBrowser" onto the design surface. The web browser control will fill the design surface completely. If you do not want the content area of your browser to fill the entire browser window, you can click the smart tag located on the top-right corner of the web browser control and select "Undock in parent container." Then, you can select

the web browser control and expand the area so that it occupies almost the entire designer space. Make sure to leave room at the bottom for the URL address and the GO button.

6. Drag-and-drop a Textbox and a Button from the Toolbox onto the Design surface. The textbox will be used to enter the URL for your browser, and the button will be used for invoking the web page. Place them on the top or bottom, as you wish. Change the properties of the controls using the following values:
    a. Textbox: (Name) → txtUrl
    b. Textbox: Text: http://
    c. Size the Textbox wide enough, so that it can fit in most URLs
    d. Button: Text → Go, and (name) → btnGo
7. Now, you can link the code behind the button "Go," by double-clicking on the button and it will take you to the code area. Add one line of code (highlighted) in the prototype, shown as follows:

```
        private void btnGo_Click(object sender, EventArgs e) {
webBrowser1.Navigate(txtUrl.Text); // Add this line of code
        }
```

8. Compile and execute your application by pressing Ctrl+F5 (or use menu command). Your own web browser is ready to take you to any URL you enter, as shown in Figure A.5

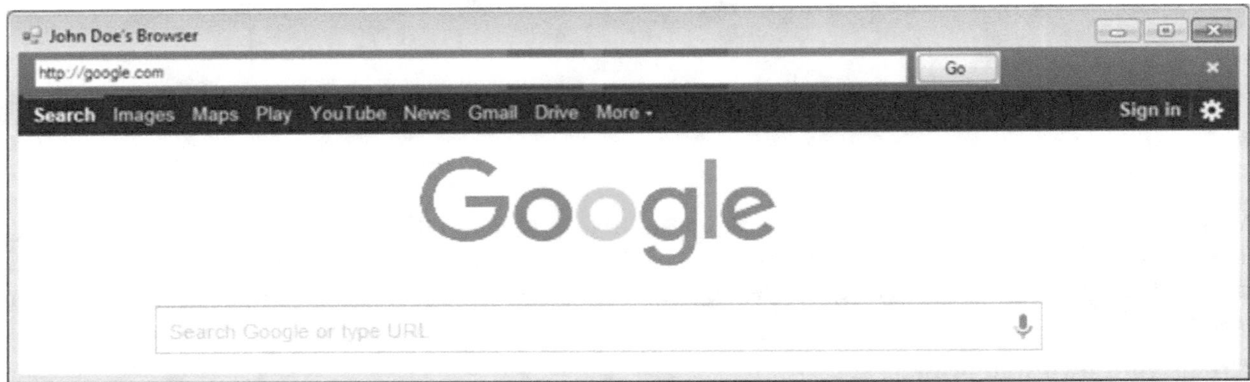

Figure A.5. John Doe's web browser GUI

Choose "Build" → "Batch build," and check the "release" box to generate the .exe file to run on a different computer. Send your browser to your friend for testing.

You can add many other features to your browser. For example, you build a simple calculator in your browser, which allows you to do calculation while reading the web page. In the later sections, we will show you how to add live weather forecast, currency exchange rate, and so on, into your Windows applications such as the web browser.

A.2 Discovering Web Services Available Online

Before we start to develop a software application, we first review the SOC development process shown in Figure A.6 from the application builder's perspective. Instead of trying to develop all the components, the application builder tries to discover the available services from the service brokers. There are many websites that publish services for the public to use, including:

- Amazon Web Services for developers (http://developer.amazonwebservices.com/): including e-business services, such as "add-to-the-card" service.
- Google Web Services (http://www.google.com/apis/index.html): including search services and maps services.
- Microsoft Robotics Studio (http://msdn.microsoft.com/robotics): including services that wrap different sensor and actuator functions in robotics applications.
- WebserviceX (http://www.webservicex.net): including different types of services in e-business, communications, and value manipulation.

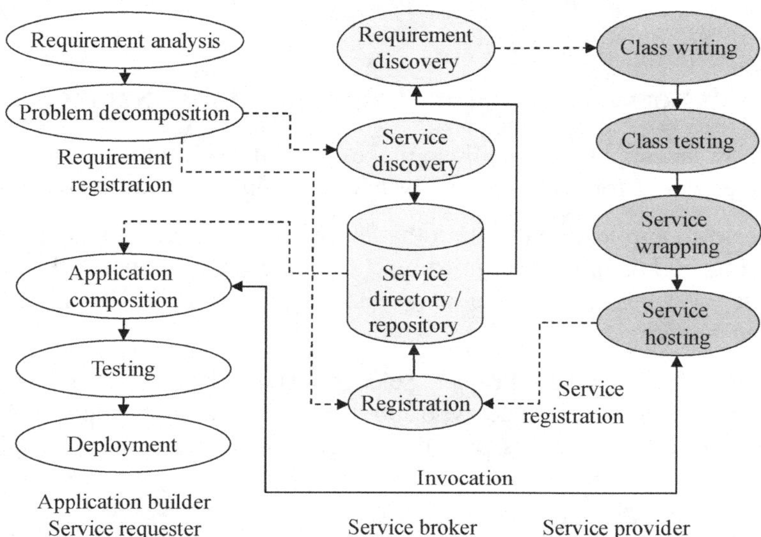

Figure A.6. Service-oriented development process with three independent parties

For example, if you go to WebserviceX and examine the USZip service at the address: (http://www.webservicex.net/uszip.asmx), you will be taken to the test page in Figure A.7, which shows four web methods (endpoints) of the service.

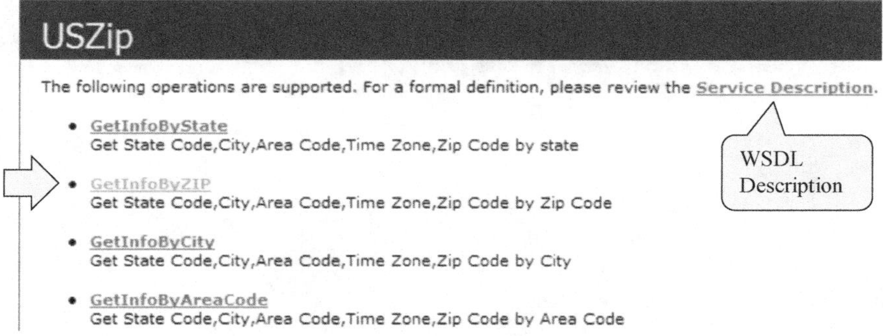

Figure A.7. Test page for USZip service

If you click the web method "GetInfoByZip," you will be asked to enter a US zip code and then invoke the service, as shown in Figure A.8, which returns in a web page shown on the right site of Figure A.8.

These pages show GUI of testing the web service. In the real application, you must write a piece of code to access the endpoints through a program. In the next subsection, we show how to bind a remote web service and invoke the service in the program.

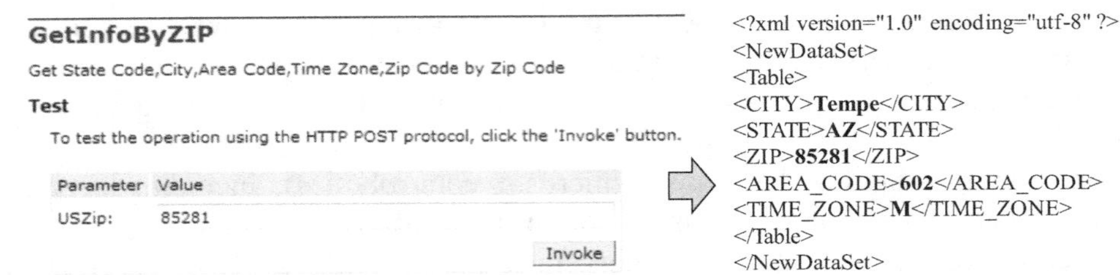

Figure A.8. Test page for USZip service

A.3 Access Web Services in Your Program: ImageService

This section shows how an application builder makes use of the remote services to create a website application that provides a GUI for accessing the web services in a human user-friendly interface.

In this section, we create an application program that allows a human user to enter an integer as the length of a random image string, and then, the user must type the same string shown in the image. The application will validate if the entered string matches the image showing in the image. This is a typical image verifier to prevent the denial of service.

Open Visual Studio and create a Nwew Project. Select "Visual C#" and "Web" as your template. Select "ASP .Net Web Application" as your project type and then further select "Empty" so that unnecessary files are not added into the project. Name this project "ImageServiceTryIt" and then click OK, as shown in Figure A.9

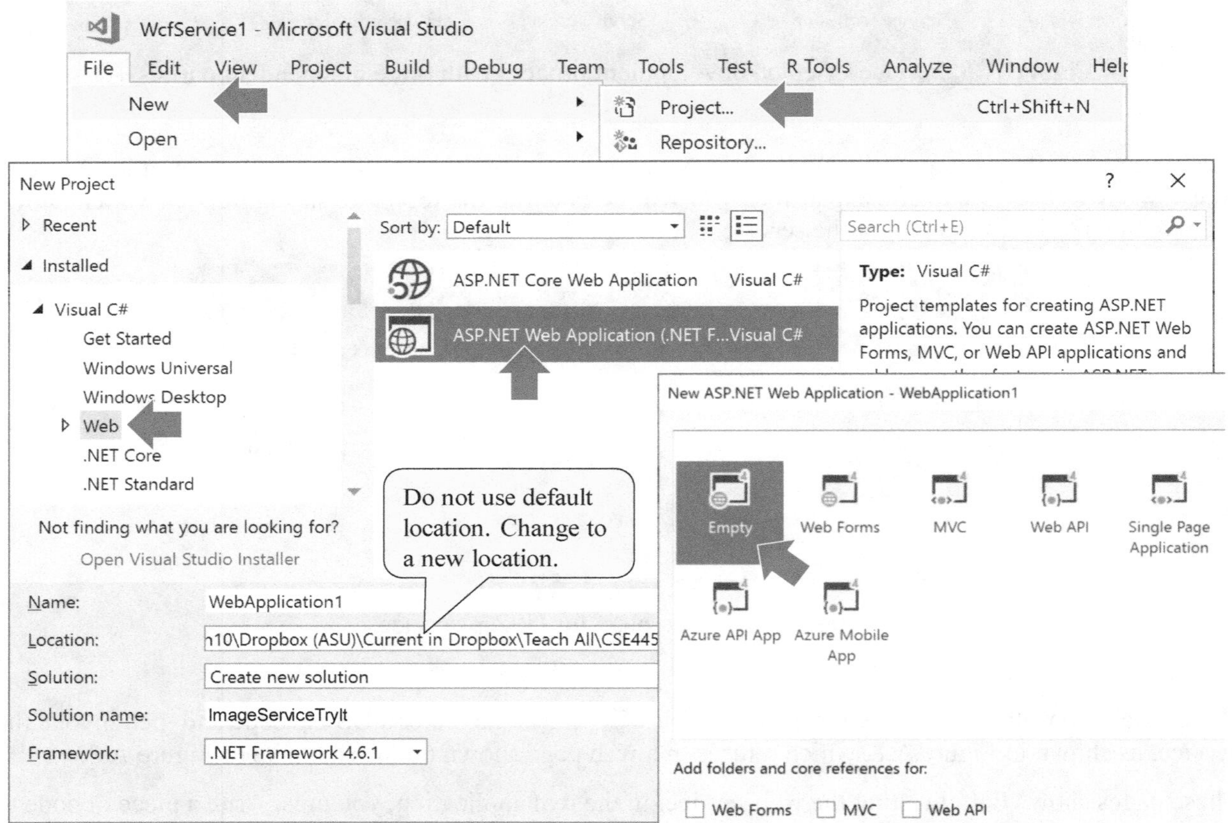

Figure A.9. Creating an ASP .Net Empty application

Then, right-click the project name and chose Add New Item. Then, select C# - Web and Web Form, as shown in Figure A.10.

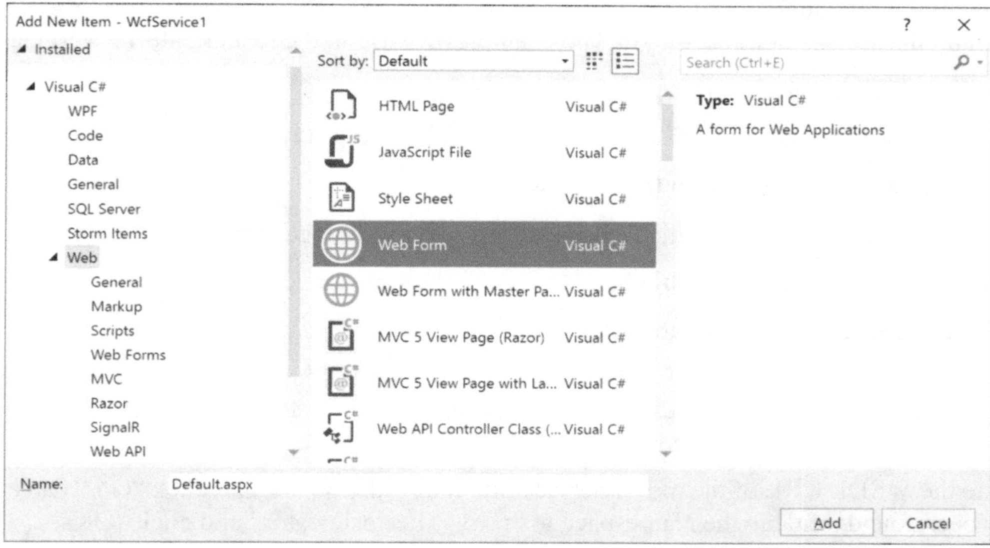

Figure A.10. Adding a Web Form into a project

The Default.aspx page is added, which provides a design surface for GUI design, as shown in Figure A.11. One can use the GUI components in the "Toolbox" to draw different type of GUI components, including Textbox for input, RichTextBox for output, Label for showing text on the GUI, RadioButton for selection, ComBox for a dropdown selection list, and "Button" for mouse click input; for example, invoking a function.

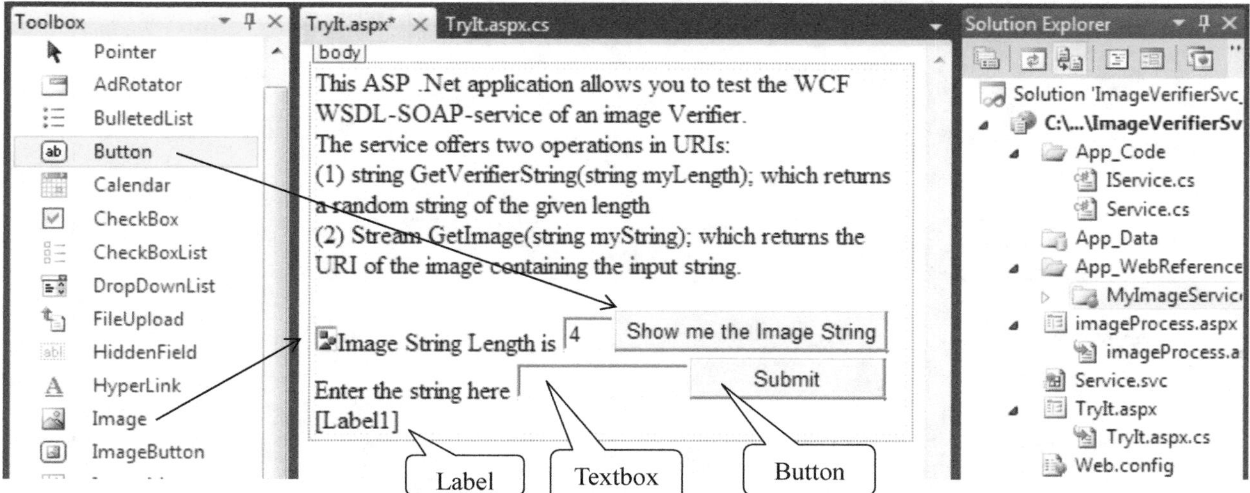

Figure A.11. Design the GUI using items in Toolbox

Before we continue to design the GUI and write C# code to link the GUI to the functions needed, we first locate the image service that generates a random string and then generate an image from the string. We have developed and deployed the service into ASU Services and Applications repository in Table C.2. Once the service is found, you can add WSDL file's URL as web service into your application, so that your program can access the web service remotely from the program. In most cases, the service is not located in the service directory's location. It is located in the service provider's site. Note that many services listed public service directory, such as Xmethods.net, are not free of charge. If charge is required, you will be asked to sign up the service before using it. The examples we use in the text are all free services.

Step 1: Locating the image web service

1) To begin, go to text Append C or http://neptune.fulton.ad.asu.edu/WSRepository/;
2) Copy the service address from the page, which is:

   http://neptune.fulton.ad.asu.edu/WSRepository/Services/ImageVerifierSvc/Service.svc

   You will need this address to bind and to invoke the web service.

Step 2: Adding web services to your application.

1) Return to Visual Studio .NET environment. Choose the menu "View" and choose the Solution Explorer. Right-click the folder "Reference" and choose "Add Service References… " A window will pop up, allowing you to enter the URL of the web service, as shown in Figure A.12.
2) Paste the WSDL URL of the movie service into the Address part, and click "Go." Once the service has been found, rename the Namespace to "proxyTheaterLocator" and click "OK."
3) Verify that the reference has been added successfully by opening the Solution Explorer (press Ctrl+Alt+L) and viewing the project node. You should see a Service References directory with a reference called "MyImageService."

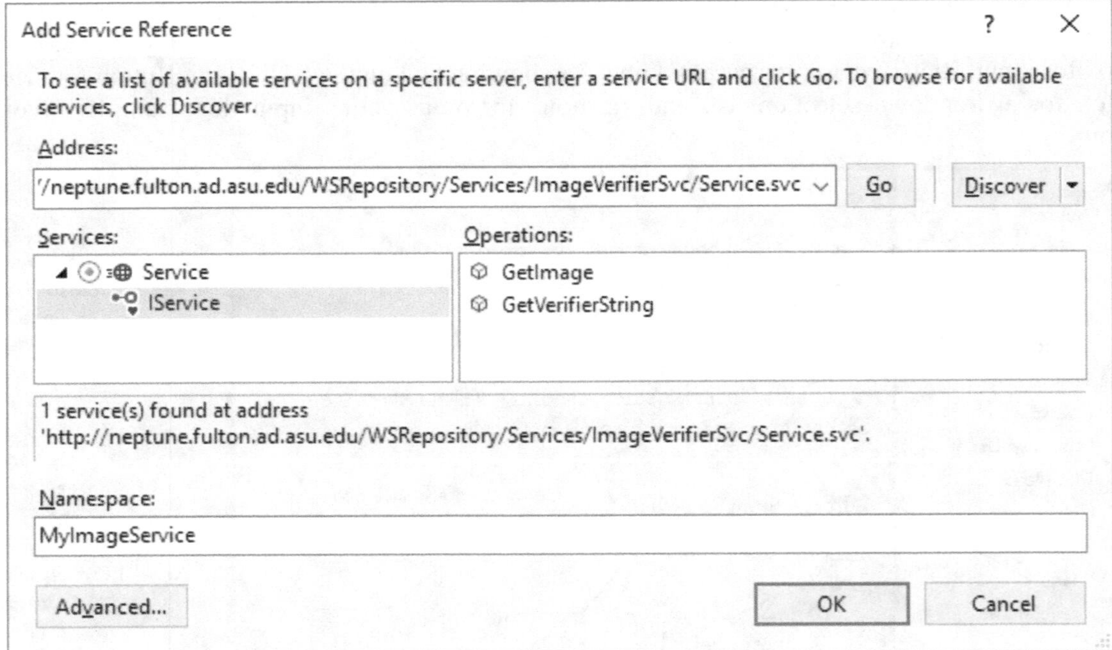

Figure A.12. Adding a service reference into the application

Step 3: Now let us follow Figure A.11 to design the GUI using the items in the toolbox: Image, Textbox, Label, and Button. After you have designed the GUI, you can switch the "Design" (graphic) view to the "Source" view. You can edit the design from both the Design view and the Source view, as shown in Figure 13.

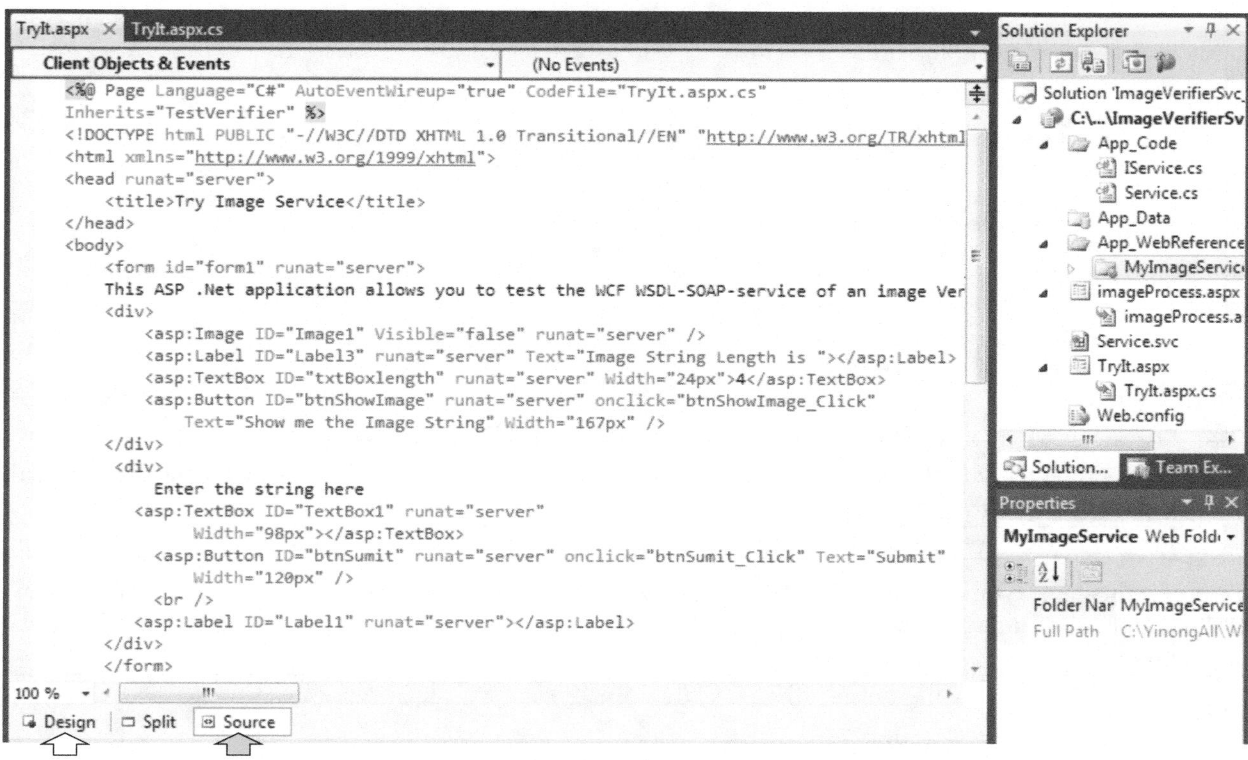

Figure A.13. Source view of the GUI design

Step 4: Adding code to the buttons. Double click the button "Show me the Image String," so that the code template is generated. Return to the Design view and then double click the button "Submit," so that the code template is generated. Note that it is important to use "double click" to generate the code templates. If you type the code templates, they will not be linked to the buttons. Your code should look as follows:

```
public partial class TestVerifier : System.Web.UI.Page {
    protected void Page_Load(object sender, EventArgs e)
    {
    }
    protected void btnSumit_Click(object sender, EventArgs e)
    {
    }
    protected void btnShowImage_Click(object sender, EventArgs e)
    {
    }
}
```

Now, you can add your code piece by piece into the templates. After adding the code, it should look as follows:

```
public partial class TestVerifier : System.Web.UI.Page {
    protected void Page_Load(object sender, EventArgs e) {
        Image1.ImageUrl = "~/imageProcess.aspx";
    }
    protected void btnSumit_Click(object sender, EventArgs e) {
        if (Session["generatedString"].Equals(TextBox1.Text)) {
            Label1.Text = "Congratulation. The code you entered is correct!";
        }
        Else {
```

```
            Label1.Text = "I am sorry, the string you entered does not match the
image. Please try again!";
        }
    }
    protected void btnShowImage_Click(object sender, EventArgs e) {
        MyImageService.ServiceClient fromService = new
MyImageService.ServiceClient();  // create proxy to the remote service
        string userLength = txtBoxlength.Text;
        Session["userLength"] = userLength;
        string myStr = fromService.GetVerifierString(userLength);
        Session["generatedString"] = myStr;
btnShowImage.Text = "Show Me Another Image String";
        Image1.Visible = true;
    }
}
```

In the page protected void Page_Load(object sender, EventArgs e), we use the following statement to call another page "imageProcess.aspx":

```
Image1.ImageUrl = "~/imageProcess.aspx";
```

To create this page, you can right-click the project name and choose "Add New Item." Choose "Web Form" and name the form imageProcess.aspx. In this page, you can add the following code to call the web service to generate the image.

```
using System;
using System.IO;
using System.Drawing.Imaging;
public partial class imageProcess : System.Web.UI.Page {
    protected void Page_Load(object sender, EventArgs e) {
        Response.Clear();
        MyImageService.ServiceClient fromService = new
MyImageService.ServiceClient();
        string myStr, userLen;
        if (Session["generatedString"] == null) {
            if (Session["userLength"] == null)
                userLen = "3";
            else
                userLen = Session["userLength"].ToString();
            myStr = fromService.GetVerifierString(userLen);
            Session["generatedString"] = myStr;
        }
        else {
            myStr = Session["generatedString"].ToString();
        }
        Stream myStream = fromService.GetImage(myStr);
        System.Drawing.Image myImage = System.Drawing.Image.FromStream(myStream);
        Response.ContentType = "image/jpeg";
        myImage.Save(Response.OutputStream, ImageFormat.Jpeg);
    }
}
```

In this code, the proxy to the service is generated by the statement:

```
MyImageService.ServiceClient fromService = new MyImageService.ServiceClient();
```

The necessity of creating the module is to have the returned image assigned to the "image" control (Toolbox item). If we put the code in the page imageProcess.aspx directly in the TryIt.aspx page, the returned image will use the entire page, instead of the designated area of the page.

Now, you can test program. The input and output are shown in Figure A.14.

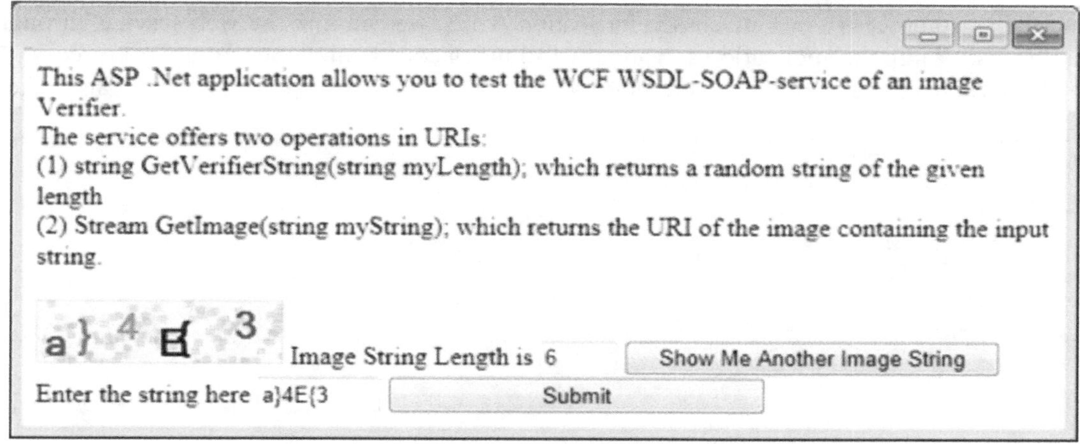

Figure A.14. Test and results of the program

In the code, you may add a print statement to print variable values for debugging purposes:

```
System.Diagnostics.Debug.WriteLine();
```

which will print the result in the debug console in the bottom of visual studio.

The application is deployed and can be tested at:

http://neptune.fulton.ad.asu.edu/WSRepository/Services/ImageVerifierSvc/TryIt.aspx

A.4 Access Web Services in Your Program: Weather Forecasting Service

In this application, we will design a GUI that displays a 5-day weather forecast for a given zip code location. We will use a web service for getting the weather information; for example:

http://graphical.weather.gov/xml/SOAP_server/ndfdXMLserver.php?wsdl

http://www.webservicex.net/WeatherForecast.asmx?WSDL

First, we design the GUI as shown in Figure A.15. You can also use longitude and latitude as inputs, depending on the input requirement service.

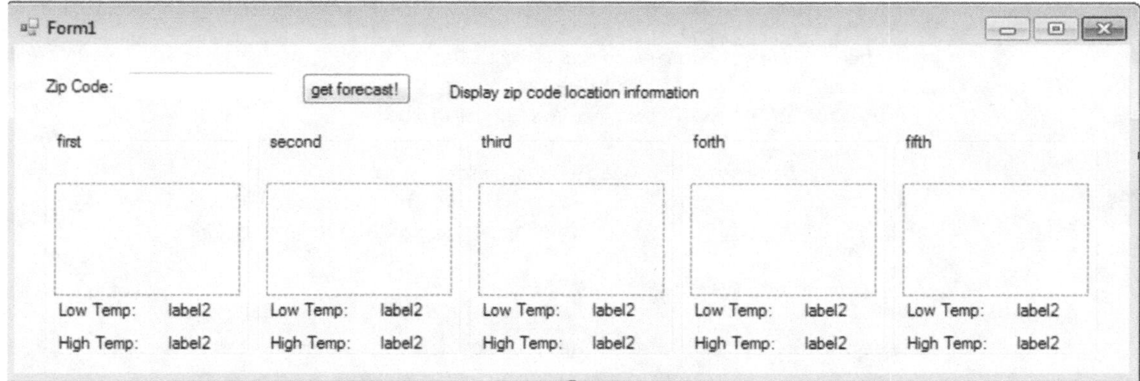

Figure A.15. GUI design of a weather forecasting application

Following the same process as we discussed in Section A.1.3, we can link the web service, through "Add Web References…" into the application and add the following code behind the button "get forecast." Please read the discussion at the end of the previous section on "Add Service References" and "Add Web References."

```
using System;
using System.Collections.Generic;
using System;
using System.Drawing;
using System.Text;
using System.Windows.Forms;
using Forecast.net.webservicex.www;
using System.Net;
using System.IO;
namespace Forecast {
    public partial class MyWeatherStation : Form {
        WeatherForecasts weatherForecasts;
        WeatherForecast weatherForecast;
        WeatherData[] weather;
        Bitmap pic;
        public MyWeatherStation(){
            InitializeComponent();
            groupBoxes = new System.Windows.Forms.GroupBox[5]
             { groupBox1, groupBox2, groupBox3, groupBox4, groupBox5 };
   pictureBoxes = new System.Windows.Forms.PictureBox[5] {
             pictureBox1, pictureBox2, pictureBox3, pictureBox4, pictureBox5 };
            lowLabels = new System.Windows.Forms.Label[5] { lowLabel1, lowLabel2,
lowLabel3, lowLabel4, lowLabel5 };
            highLabels = new System.Windows.Forms.Label[5] { highTemp1, highTemp2,
highTemp3, highTemp4, highTemp5 };
            lowTemps = new System.Windows.Forms.Label[5] { lowTemp1, lowTemp2,
lowTemp3, lowTemp4, lowTemp5 };
            highTemps = new System.Windows.Forms.Label[5] { highTemp1, highTemp2,
highTemp3, highTemp4, highTemp5 };
            weatherForecast = new WeatherForecast();
            for (int i = 0; i < 5; i++) {
                pictureBoxes[i].SizeMode = PictureBoxSizeMode.StretchImage;
            }
        }
        private void button1_Click(object sender, EventArgs e) {
            weatherForecasts = weatherForecast.GetWeatherByZipCode(textBox1.Text);
            if (weatherForecasts.Details != null) {
                weather = weatherForecasts.Details;
                for (int i = 0; i < 5; i++) {
                    groupBoxes[i].Text = weather[i].Day;
                    pic = LoadPicture(weather[i].WeatherImage);
                    pictureBoxes[i].Image = (Image)pic;
                    lowTemps[i].Text = weather[i].MinTemperatureF;
                    highTemps[i].Text = weather[i].MaxTemperatureF;
                }
            }
            else {
                MessageBox.Show("No weather information returned!");
            }
            //this.pictureBox2.Image =
((System.Drawing.Image)(resources.GetObject("pictureBox1.Image")));
           // pictureBox1.Image =
        }
```

```
        private Bitmap LoadPicture(string url) {
            HttpWebRequest wreq;
            HttpWebResponse wresp;
            Stream mystream;
            Bitmap bmp;
            bmp = null;
            mystream = null;
            wresp = null;
            try {
                wreq = (HttpWebRequest)WebRequest.Create(url);
                wreq.AllowWriteStreamBuffering = true;

                wresp = (HttpWebResponse)wreq.GetResponse();
                if ((mystream = wresp.GetResponseStream()) != null)
                    bmp = new Bitmap(mystream);
            }
            finally {
          if (mystream != null) mystream.Close();
             if (wresp != null) wresp.Close();
            }
            return (bmp);
        }
        private void MyWeatherStation_Load(object sender, EventArgs e) { }
    }
}
```

The execution results for entering 85281 into the zip code field are obtained as shown in Figure A.16.

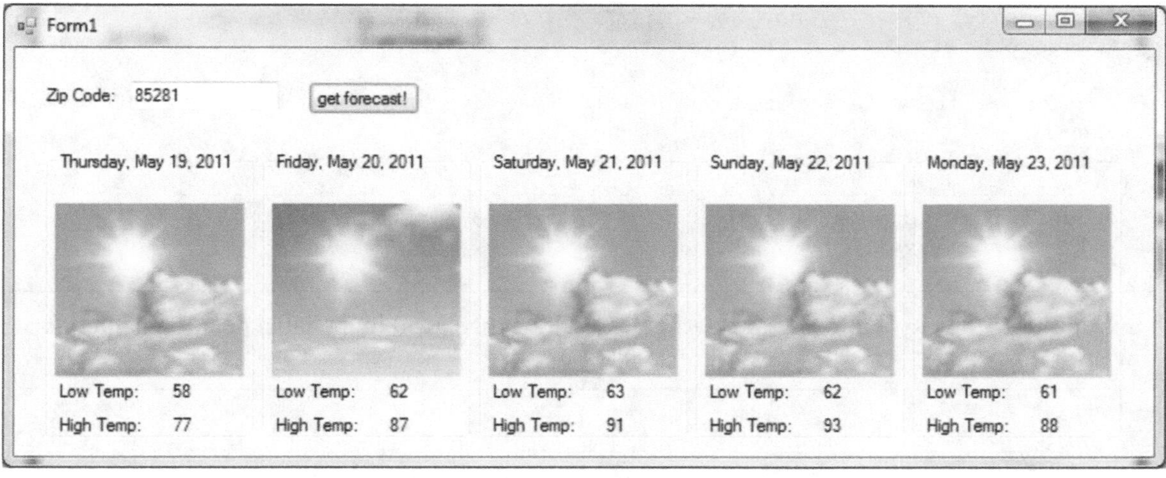

Figure A.16. Results from invoking the service zip code 85281

Notice that, if the weather service is not available, you can discover other similar services.

A.5 Access Web Services in Your Program: USZip Service

We can combine the USZip service into the forecasting application by adding the following website address into the Service Reference: http://www.webservicex.net/uszip.asmx.

As a result, we have two web services in the application, as shown under the Solution Explorer (right) of Figure A.17.

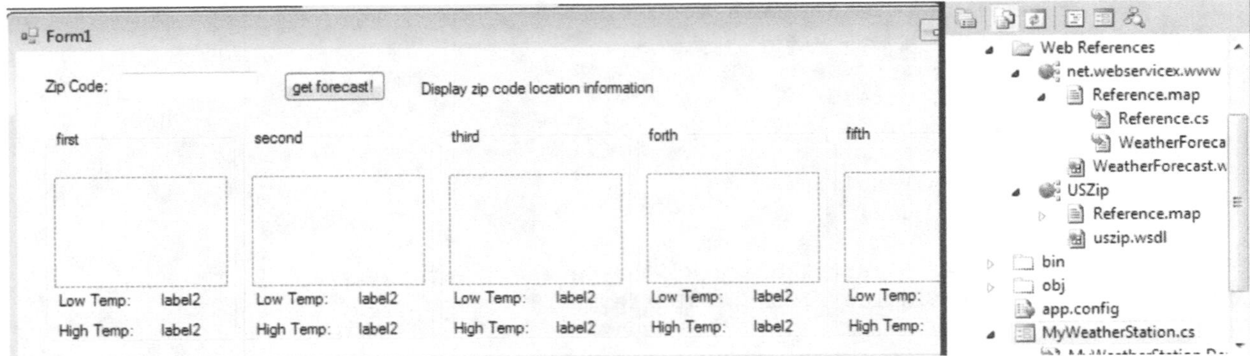

Figure A.17. Adding USZip service

We added a "Label" control next to the "get forecast!" button. We name the label lblLocation. We need to add the following piece of code at the beginning of the button1Click() function, so that the zip code related information is extracted and displaced. Please note that the function returns an XML document and we need to use the XML library function explained in Chapter 4 to extract the related information. To use the XPath library function, we need to add namespace "using System.Xml. XPath." To learn more about XPath, please read Chapter 4, Section 4.3.

```
private void button1_Click(object sender, EventArgs e) {
   Forecast.USZip.USZip byZip = new Forecast.USZip.USZip();
   System.Xml.XmlNode rtNode = byZip.GetInfoByZIP(textBox1.Text);
   XPathNavigator nav = rtNode.CreateNavigator();
   XPathNodeIterator it = nav.Select("/NewDataSet/Table/City");
   string loc = it.Current.Value;
   if (loc.Length == 0)
        loc = "Zip Code not found";
   else
        loc = loc.Substring(0, loc.Length - 11); // removing other info
   lblLocation.Text = loc;  //display the string at the give GUI label
   weatherForecasts = weatherForecast.GetWeatherByZipCode(textBox1.Text);
   // The rest of the code . . .
}
```

With this addition, the city name (e.g., Los Angeles) will be displayed in the label position named location, as shown in Figure A.18.

Figure A.18. With the city name displayed in a label position

Name: ____________________

Date: ____________________

A.6 Exercises and Projects

1. Multiple choice questions. Choose one answer in each question only. Choose the best answer if multiple answers are acceptable.

1.1 GUI stands for

(A) Greatest Unit Intelligence (B) Greatest User Intelligence

(C) Greatest User Interface (D) Graphical User Interface

1.2 What is the difference between a software application and a software service?

(A) A service typically includes a GUI, while an application does not.

(B) An application typically includes a GUI, while a service does not.

(C) A service performs mathematical functions, while an application does not.

(D) An application performs mathematical functions, while a service does not.

1.3 How can we input data in a GUI-based application?

(A) Using a TextBox (B) Using a Console.ReadLine

(C) Using MessageBox.Input (D) Using PictureBox.Enter

1.4 How can we output a message in a pop-up window in a GUI-based application?

(A) Using a TextBox.Output (B) Using a Console.WriteLine

(C) Using MessageBox.Show (D) Using PictureBox.Display

(E) Using a Label

1.5 How can we output a message within the GUI form?

(A) Using a TextBox.Output (B) Using a Console.WriteLine

(C) Using MessageBox.Show (D) Using PictureBox.Display

(E) Using a Label

1.6 What GUI item is used to create a web browser?

(A) Button (B) Label (C) TextBox (D) WebBrowser

1.7 How do you create a multiple-line output area in a Windows forms application?

(A) Using RichTextBox (B) Using TextBox

(C) Using Label (D) Using GroupBox

1.8 A web service is

(A) a method in an object.

(B) an object wrapped with standard interface.

(C) a list of addresses where developers can find the methods they want.

(D) an application with GUI.

1.9 What method in a class can be accessed as a web service operation?

(A) Private method
(B) Protected method
(C) Public method
(D) Web method

1.10 A service broker is a website where one can

(A) find services available online.
(B) use a tool to develop services online.
(C) repair software.
(D) repair service.

2. Design an application that converts a given amount of currency to another currency. Below is the WSDL link to the currency exchange web service that you can use for this exercise. If this service is not available, search for another service.

http://www.webservicex.com/CurrencyConvertor.asmx?wsdl

A sample GUI is shown in Figure A.19.

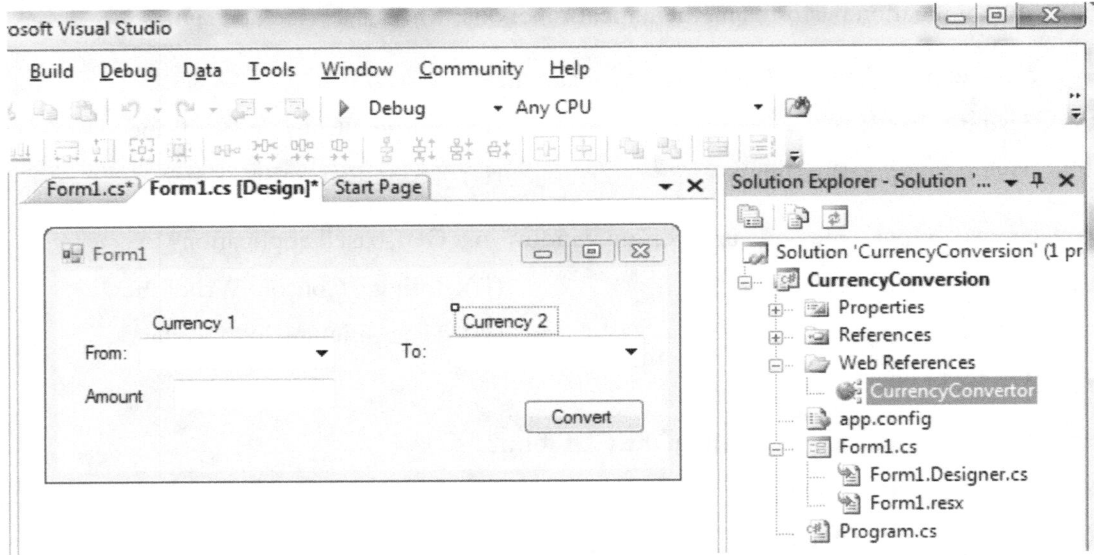

Figure A.19. With the city name displayed

A part of the sample code using the functions (methods) of the currency service is given as follows:

```
using System;
// . . .
using CurrencyConversion.CurrencyConvertor;
 namespace CurrencyConversion {
   // . . .
   private void button1_Click(object sender, EventArgs e)
   {     string FCurrency = From.SelectedItem.ToString();
        string TCurrency = To.SelectedItem.ToString();
        double rate, result;
        Currency fField;
        Currency tField;
        if (FCurrency.Equals("USA"))
              fField = Currency.USD;
```

```
        else if (FCurrency.Equals("Hong Kong"))
              fField = Currency.HKD;
        else fField = Currency.JPY;
   if (TCurrency.Equals("USA"))
        tField = Currency.USD;
   else if (TCurrency.Equals("Hong Kong"))
        tField = Currency.HKD;
   else tField = Currency.JPY;
   CurrencyConvertor.CurrencyConvertor proxyConvertor = new
CurrencyConvertor.CurrencyConvertor();
   rate = proxyConvertor.ConversionRate(fField, tField);
   if (rate > 0)
        result = rate * Convert.ToDouble(textBox1.Text);
   else
        result = Convert.ToDouble(textBox1.Text);
   MessageBox.Show("Result: $" + result);
}
```

3. An encryption service that can encode and decode a string is given at the link:

   http://neptune.fulton.ad.asu.edu/WSRepository/Services/Encryption/Service.asmx

   Write an application that makes use of this web service.

4. Create your own web browser that incorporates the weather forecast into the browser window.

5. Create a travel calculator, which performs ordinary calculation, as well as the currency exchange.

Appendix B
Visual IoT/Robotics Programming Language Environment

This appendix supplements Chapter 9 in the main text, and you should read this appendix in conjunction with Chapter 9 to learn VIPLE (Visual IoT/Robotics Programming Language Environment) programming and application development.

B.1 Introduction to VIPLE

There are a number of great visual programming environments for computing and engineering education. MIT App Inventor uses drag-and-drop style puzzles to construct phone applications in Android platform. Carnegie Mellon's Alice is a 3D game and movie development environment on desktop computers. It uses a drop-down list for users to select the available functions in a stepwise manner. App Inventor and Alice allow novice programmers to develop complex applications using visual composition at the workflow level. LEGO and Microsoft have developed visual robotics application development environments for beginners. LEGO's NXT and EV3 environments are for LEGO robots only. Microsoft has discontinued its VPL (Visual Programming Environment).

VIPLE (Visual IoT/Robotics Programming Language Environment) is designed and developed at ASU by Dr. Yinong Chen and Gennaro De Luca, as well as many other graduate and undergraduate students. It is a service-oriented software development environment used for developing IoT (Internet of Things) and robotics applications on a variety of simulated and hardware platforms. The platforms include open architecture-based robots, such Intel Galileo/Edison, AMR and Raspberry Pi, as well as vendor specific robots such as Lego EV3. VIPLE uses workflow and service-oriented technologies as its underlying foundation for creating simple and easy-to-use services in a visual programming manner. The idea is to have humans (developers) to draw the flowchart (workflow) of the intended application, and then let the development environment (tool) convert (compile) the flowchart into executable. Thus, it makes the software development easier and faster. The development process is to drag and drop blocks that represent components and services, and to connect them with wires/lines. This simple process makes it possible for even non-programmers to create their IoT and robotics applications in a short period of time.

VIPLE can be used as the first programming language for anyone without any programming background. We start to teach the basic concepts like variables, data types, if/else statements, loops, and logical thinking. However, VIPLE is not limited to novice programmers. The compositional nature of the programming language may appeal to more advanced programmers for rapid prototyping or code development. It supports advanced programming concepts, such as event-driven programming, service-oriented computing, code activity for creating instant components, and parallel computing with fork and join. In addition, while its toolbox and service repository are tailored specifically for developing robotics applications, the underlying architecture is not limited to programming robots. It can be applied to other general-purpose applications, such as a game, a complex process of manufacturing, controlling devices in a smart home, and other design processes. Its simulation environments can virtualize the physical system as an aid before the physical implementation. As a result, VIPLE may appeal to a wide audience of users including high school students, college students, enthusiasts/hobbyists, researchers, as well as web developers and professional programmers. VIPLE is free and can be downloaded at:

http://neptune.fulton.ad.asu.edu/VIPLE/

Now, we explain the components and programming model of VIPLE. The "Basic Activities" toolbox window in Figure B.1 contains all of the common tools and components for forming dataflow and for creating data types and variables. The Basic Activities toolbox window contains a comment activity that allows developers to document their code. Below is a screenshot of the available components with a brief description of its purpose.

B.1.1 Basic Activities in VIPLE Toolbox

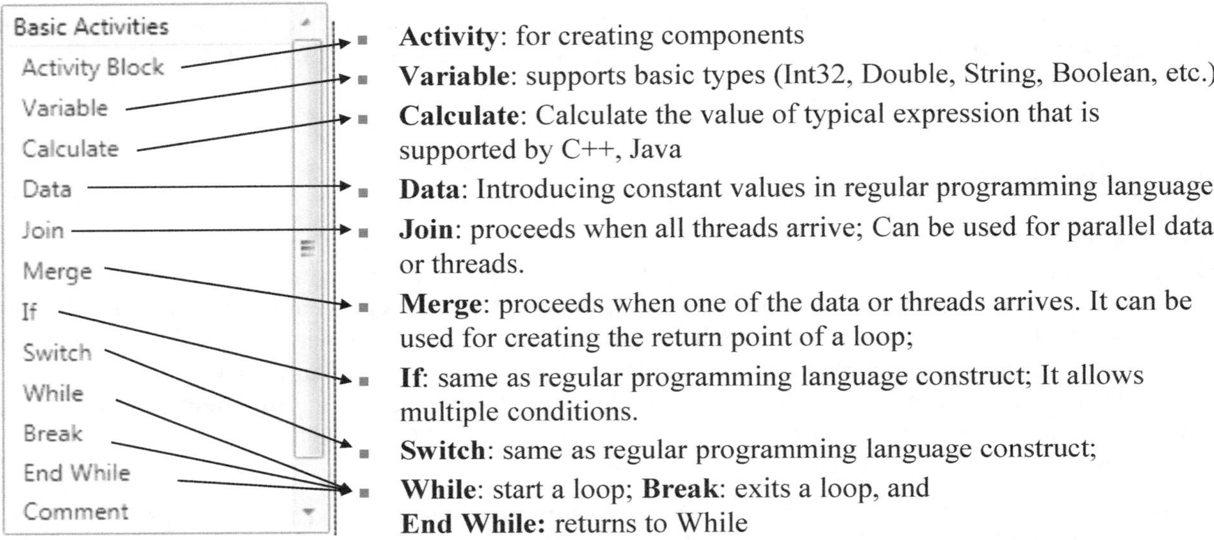

Basic Activities
Activity Block
Variable
Calculate
Data
Join
Merge
If
Switch
While
Break
End While
Comment
Activity: for creating components
Variable: supports basic types (Int32, Double, String, Boolean, etc.)
Calculate: Calculate the value of typical expression that is supported by C++, Java
Data: Introducing constant values in regular programming language
Join: proceeds when all threads arrive; Can be used for parallel data or threads.
Merge: proceeds when one of the data or threads arrives. It can be used for creating the return point of a loop;
If: same as regular programming language construct; It allows multiple conditions.
Switch: same as regular programming language construct;
While: start a loop; **Break**: exits a loop, and
End While: returns to While

Figure B.1. VIPLE basic activities

The basic activities in Figure B.1 are explained as follows.

Activity: an activity is used for creating new component, service, function, or other code modules. Simply drag and drop an Activity into the diagram, open it, and add code into it to form a new component.

Activities can also include compositions of other of activities. This makes it possible to compose activities and reuse the composition as a building block. In this sense, an application built in VIPLE is itself an activity.

An activity can be used in the current program only. An activity can be compiled into a service. A service created in one program can be based in another program.

Variable: a variable represents a memory location, where a program can store and retrieve values such as a literal string or a number.

Calculate: a calculate activity can be used to compute mathematical equations (add, subtract, divide, or multiply), as well as data extraction from other components such as from a variable or a textbox. It is similar to the assignment statement in C#, for example, x = 5 +7;

Like most programming languages, you can use the following common operation symbols for numeric data operations and logical operators:

<table>
<tr><td>+</td><td>add</td></tr>
<tr><td>-</td><td>subtract/minus</td></tr>
<tr><td>*</td><td>multiply</td></tr>
<tr><td>/</td><td>divide</td></tr>
<tr><td>%</td><td>modulo</td></tr>
<tr><td>&&</td><td>AND (Both have the same meaning)</td></tr>
<tr><td>||,</td><td>OR (Both have the same meaning)</td></tr>
<tr><td>!</td><td>NOT (Both have the same meaning)</td></tr>
</table>

Data: the data activity is used to supply a simple data value to another activity or service. You can enter a value into the text. The type is automatically determined based on the value entered. VIPLE supports all types in C# language. Below is a table of commonly supported types.

VIPLE Type	Description
Boolean	Boolean values: true, false
Char	character
Double	double precision floating point number
Int32 (int)	32 bit signed integer
UInt32 (uint)	32 bit unsigned integer
String	character string (text)

Join: the join activity combines two (or more) data-flows (inputs). All data (inputs) from the incoming connections **must be received** before the activity can proceed to the next step. Join can be used to combine multiple inputs required by an activity.

Merge: the merge activity takes two (or more) data-flows (inputs). When the first data item arrives, the activity will proceed to the next step. No need to wait for the other data items to arrive. Merge can be used to implement a loop. Merge is significantly different from Join. Merge waits for one input to arrive, while Join has to wait for all inputs to arrive.

If: The ***If*** – activity provides a choice of outputs to forward the incoming message based on a condition that was entered. If the condition is true, the first outgoing connection forwards on the incoming messages (and its data). However, if it is not true, then the else output is used. The ***If*** statement in VIPLE is similar to the if-statement in traditional languages such as Java and C#. The ***If*** activity in VIPLE can check multiple conditions in one activity block. In other words, it can combine multiple consecutive (C#) if-statements into one.

The conditional expression in the If-statement can use the following logic operators for evaluation:

==	equals
!= or <>	not equals
<	less than
>	greater than
<=	less than or equal to
>=	greater than or equal to

To add additional conditions to the activity, click the add (+) button on the activity block.

Switch: Similar to the "switch" statement in C#, the switch activity can be used to route messages based on the incoming messages matching the expression entered into the text box. To add additional Case branches (match conditions) to the activity block, simply click the Add (+) button on the activity block.

While: Similar to the "while" statement in C#, the while activity establishes a condition to forward the incoming message to a set of blocks, much like the If activity. The difference is that after the blocks are executed, the message and its data is then returned back to this while activity, and the condition is reevaluated. Ordinarily, and If activity would let the message continue on, but the while activity establishes a loop.

Break: This activity can be placed within a while loop and is used to prematurely exit the loop: i.e. leave the loop without the initial condition being evaluated as false.

End While: This activity marks the end of a while loop, and returns the incoming message back to the original while activity that began the loop.

Comment: the comment activity enables a user to add a block of text to the diagram as documentation.

B.1.2 Built-in VIPLE Services

In addition to the basic activities, VIPLE also provides a long list of built-in services for traditional input and output, as well as robotics specific services, such as sensor services, motor and drive services. Figure B.2 shows a part of these services.

Services	Robot	
Code Activity	Robot Color Sensor	
Custom Event	Robot Distance Sensor	Lego EV3 Brick
Key Press Event	Robot Drive	Lego EV3 Color
Key Release Event	Robot Holonomic Drive	Lego EV3 Drive
Print Line	Robot Light Sensor	Lego EV3 Drive for Time
Random	Robot Motion	Lego EV3 Gyro
RESTful Service	Robot Motor	Lego EV3 Motor
Simple Dialog	Robot Motor Encoder	Lego EV3 Motor by Degrees
Text to Speech	Robot Sound Sensor	Lego EV3 Motor for Time
Timer	Robot Touch Sensor	Lego EV3 Touch Pressed
	Robot+ Move at Power	Lego EV3 Touch Released
	Robot+ Turn by Degrees	Lego EV3 Ultrasonic

Figure B.2. VIPLE general services, generic robot services, and EV3 services

We start to use the basic activities and services to learn the language and start to use the robotics services later to implement our robotics project.

B.2 Getting Started with VIPLE Programming

To get started, first download and install VIPLE from the site:

http://neptune.fulton.ad.asu.edu/VIPLE/

Start VIPLE. Please wait a minute or two while the operating system loads the application. When the application finishes loading, you will see the screen in Figure B.3, and you can start to drag and drop the Basic Activities and Services into the Main diagram

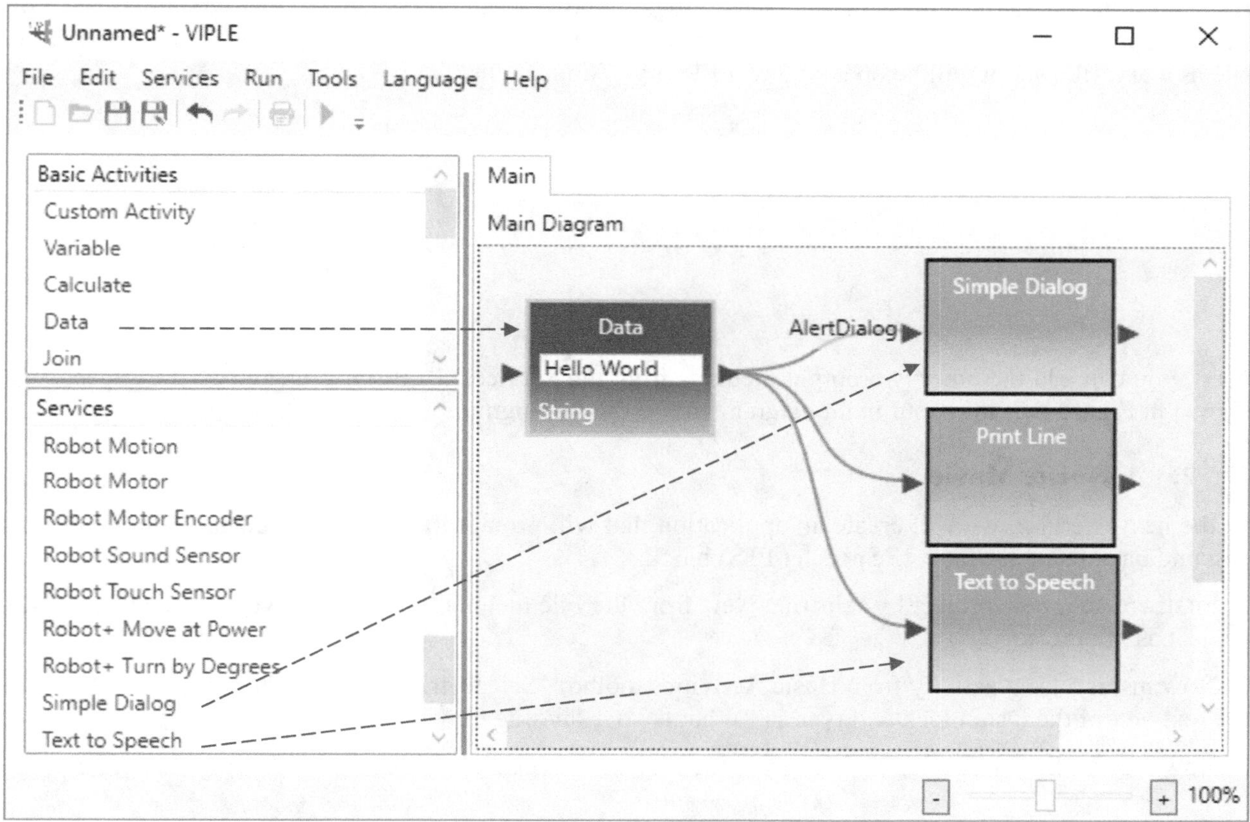

Figure B.3. Writing your first program in VIPLE

Ex. 1. "Hello World" in VIPLE

In this exercise, we will create our first application using VIPLE to display the words "Hello World."

1. Create a new project by selecting New from the File menu. Now insert (by drag-and-drop) a Data activity from the Basic Activities toolbox. Click in the text box of the Data block and type in "Hello World". The data type field will automatically display String.

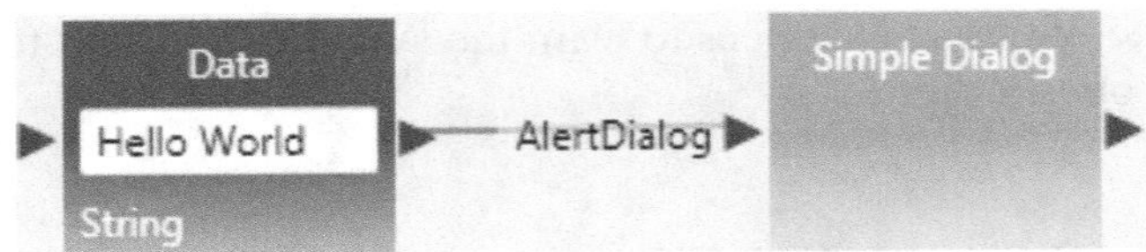

2. Insert a Simple Dialog activity, by dragging one from the services toolbox and place it to the right of the Data activity block.

3. Now drag a link starting from the output connection pin of the Data block onto the SimpleDialog block. The connections dialog box automatically opens. Select DataValue in the first list and Alert Dialog in the second list and then click OK.

4. Save your program and name the project "Exercise_01". Then select the run command (or press F5) to run your program. Note, after you've saved a program, you cannot double click the program to open. You need to open VIPLE and use its menu "open" to open the program. The reason for this is that we save the file as a text file, and it will be open as a text file if you double click it.

Next, you can add the other two output methods from the Services list, Print Line and Text to Speech, as shown in Figure B.3. into your main diagram and test your program.

Ex. 2. Favorite Movie

In the next exercise, we will create an application that will prompt the users for their favorite movie and respond back using the Text to Speech (TTS) block.

1. First, create a **new** project by selecting New from the File menu. Click on the save button and save this project as "Exercise_02"

2. Now insert a Data activity from Basic Activities toolbox. Select string from the dropdown list. Click in the text box of the Data block and type in "What is your favorite movie?"

3. Now insert a Simple Dialog activity from the service toolbox.

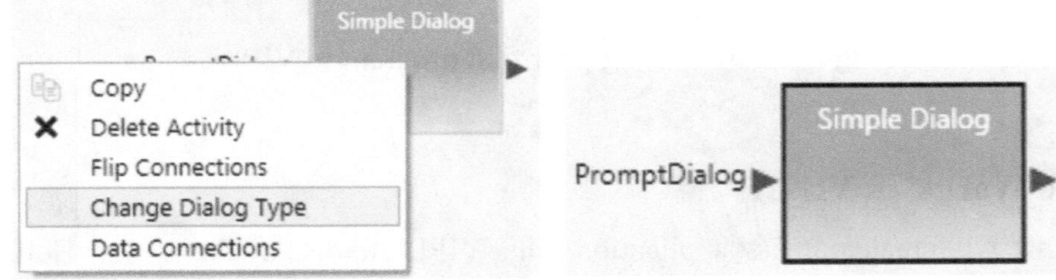

4. Now drag a link starting from the output connection pin of the Data block onto the input pin of the Simple Dialog block. The connection dialog box automatically opens. Select DataValue in the first list and Prompt Dialog in the second list, and then click OK.

5. The Data Connections dialog box opens. In the first dropdown list, choose value. Check the "edit values directly" option (bottom left corner of the window), type "Input a movie name here." in the value column of the second row, and then click OK

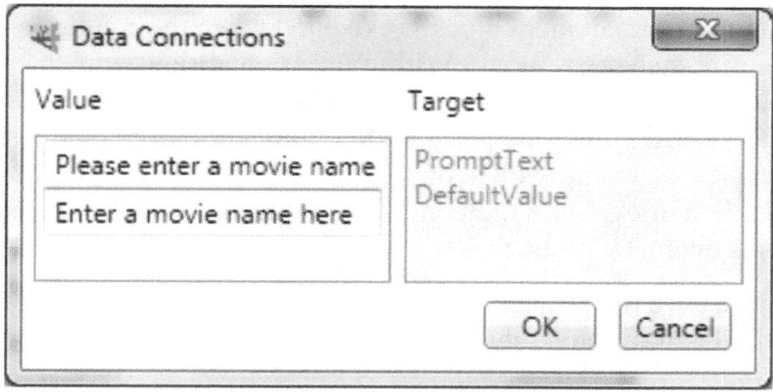

6. Now insert a Calculate activity (from the basic activities toolbox) into the diagram.

7. Create a link that connects the Simple Dialog block with the Calculate activity. The connection dialog box automatically opens.

8. Next, type the following text into the Calculate block: value + " is the greatest movie of all time!!". You can achieve this by first clicking on the blank of the Calculate block, and then a dropdown list will appear. Choose "value" using either mouse or arrow keys. Finish up by typing in all strings left.

9. Next insert a Text to Speech (TTS) block into the diagram and connect the link between the Calculate block and the TTS block.

10. Your final diagram should look something like the screenshot below. When you are ready, run the application by clicking on the run button (or F5 on your keyboard).

Tips: If you accidentally close the connections or data connections windows during the process or you simply want to make a change to your previous configuration, you can always reopen them by right clicking your mouse on the links, and choosing connections or data connections to retrieve the windows you want.

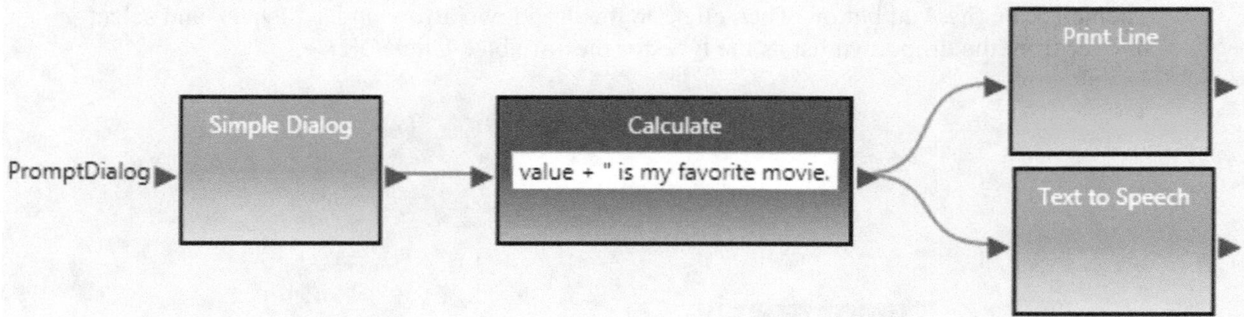

Question: How do we change the text the computer is speaking? Hint: What does the Calculate block do?

If-Statement

The if-statement is inherited from the traditional programming paradigm. The if-statement is also known as a conditional statement. In VIPLE, the if-statement is designated by the block below.

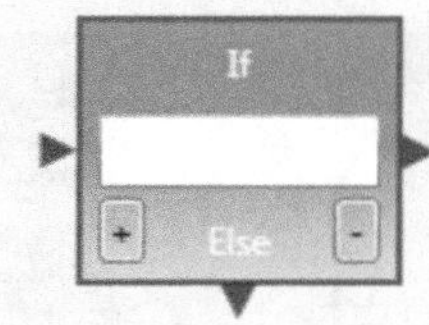

The if-section of the statement or statement block is executed when the condition is true; if it's false, control goes to the else statement or statement block. Within the if condition, you can also apply the conditional OR (||) and conditional AND (&&) operators to combine more than one condition. Unlike most traditional programming languages, VIPLE allows the program to branch into more than just two ways by using the if block. To add more branches, just simply click on the "+" sign next to the else branch, type in the condition you want to check. VIPLE will evaluate the conditions in order, and your program will go into the first branch whose condition is evaluated to be true.

When you are done, please save the project file for later submission. At the end of the lab, you will put all the project files into a single zip file for submission.

While-Loop

The while-loop also falls in the conditional loop category. The while-loop statement executes until the condition is false. It is also a pretest loop, which means it first tests if a condition is true and only continues execution if it is.

Question: Why do we need to learn while-loop?

When you are done, please save the project file for later submission. At the end of the lab, you will put all the project files into a single zip file for submission.

Ex. 3. Create While Loop Block Using Merge and If Activities

This exercise will form a while-loop using Merge and loop back in a VIPLE program. It creates a variable, initializes it, and then counts to 10, speaking the value on each of the iteration using TTS activity block.

1. To begin, create a new project by selecting New from the File menu. Then next save the project as "Exercise_03".
2. Now, insert a Variable activity from the toolbox. Click "…" to name the variable. In the dialog box that opens, click in the Name textbox and type in Counter as the name for your variable. Then click on the Add button. Then click on the dropdown arrow under "Type:" and select Integer from the dropdown list as the type for the variable. Click OK.

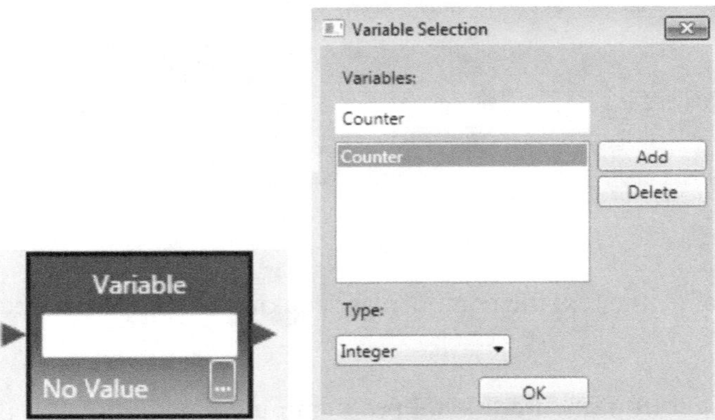

3. Now add a Data block to your diagram to the left of the Variable block and connect them by creating a link connection from the Data activity to the Variable activity block.

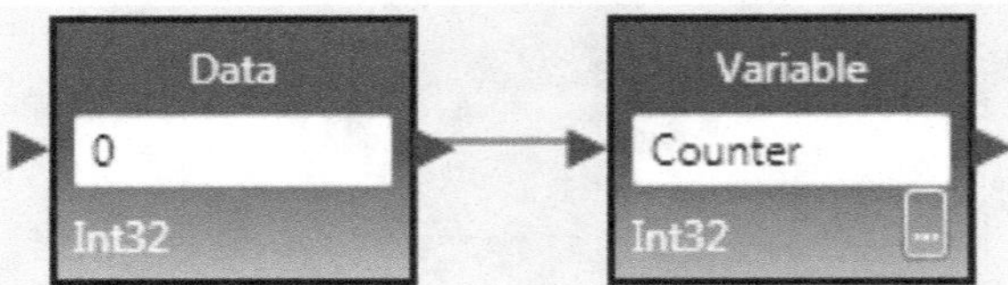

4. Enter 0 into the text box of the Data block, and the data type Int32 should automatically fill in. This sets both the data and its type. Its connection will then initialize the Counter to 0.

5. Now insert a Merge block to the right of your Variable block and connect the Variable block to the Merge block. The block is used to create a counting loop.
   Note: A Merge block can have multiple inputs; each input is passed on as it is received.

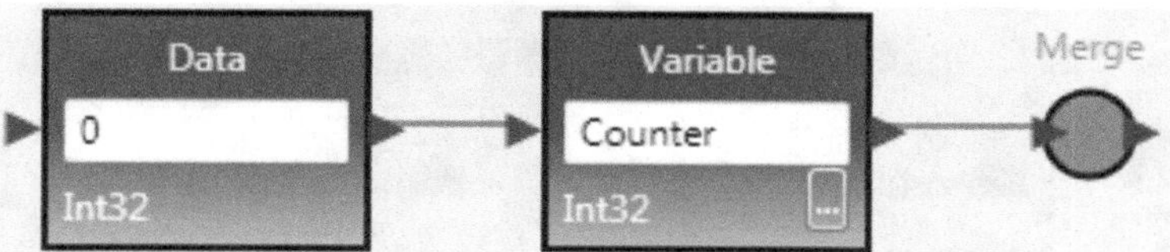

6. Next, add an If activity to the diagram to the right of the Merge block. Connect the Merge block with the If-Statement block. We consider all the variables are encapsulated in a class state , and we use state.Counter to access variable Counter. In the If-Statement block, enter state.Counter == 10.

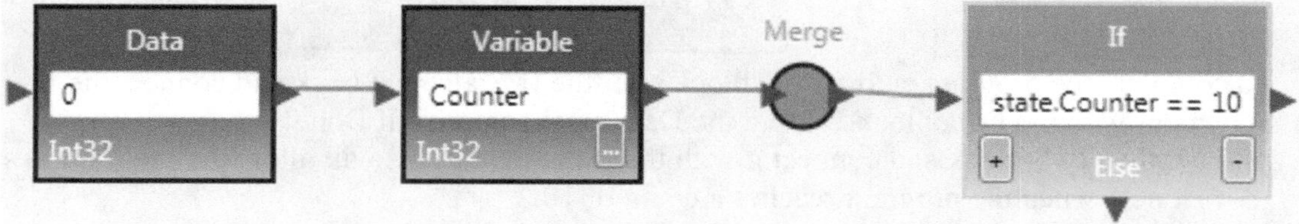

7. Now add a Calculate block and connect it to the Else connection of the If-Statement block. In the Calculate block, enter "state.Counter + 1" into its expression.

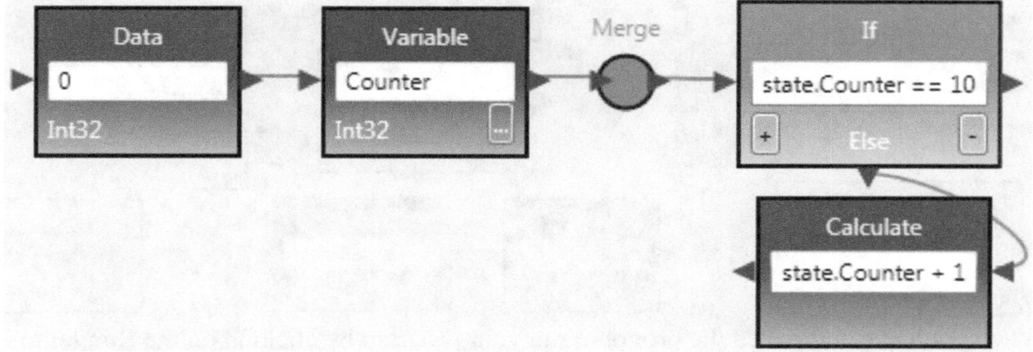

8. Now insert another variable into diagram. This new variable will take the value of Counter after it is recalculated. Click the "…" button, and select the Counter variable. Then click OK.
9. Now connect the output connection pin of the Variable block to the Merge block. This completes your loop.

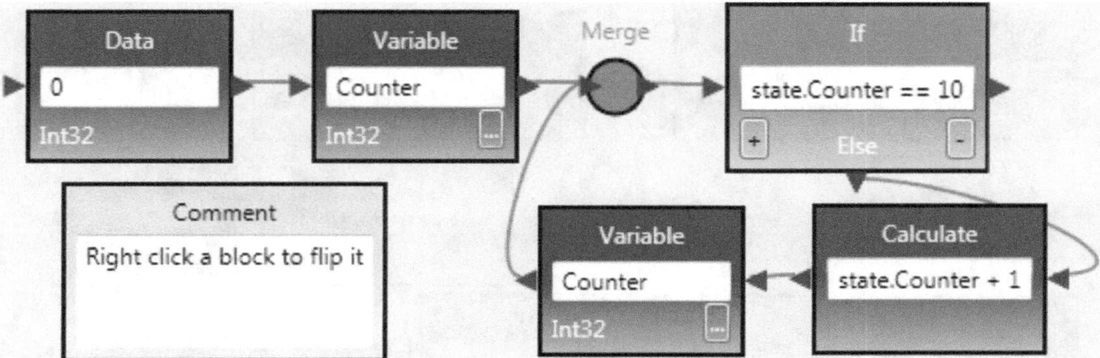

10. The next step is to insert the TTS block into the diagram to allow the program to speak out the result as it increments. So, add another Calculate block into the diagram. Inside the new Calculated block enter: "The number is" + state.Counter

11. Then add a Text to Speech block and connect it to the output of the Calculate activity block.

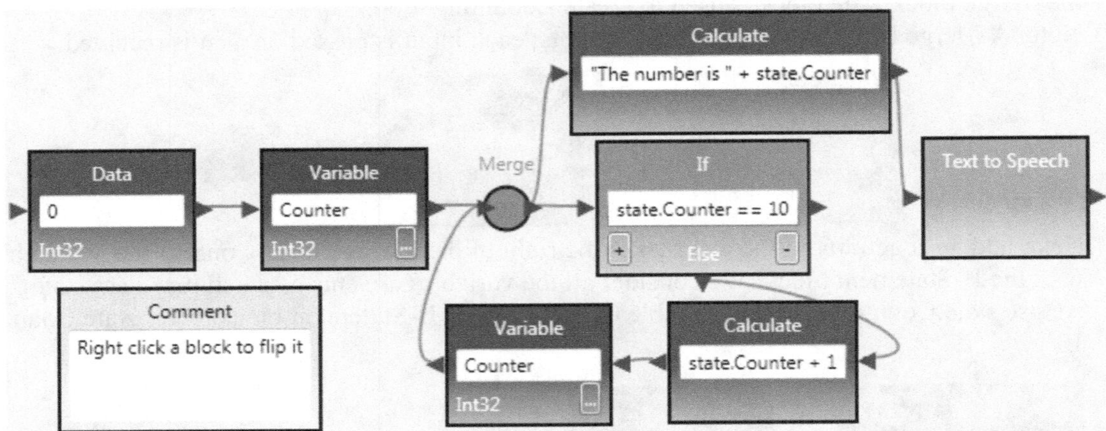

12. To complete the program, add a Data block after the If-Statement bock and connect the If-Statement with the Data block. Within the Data block, enter "All Done!".
13. Add another TTS block and connect it with the Data block. This will allow the program to say "All Done!" when the program reaches a count of 10.

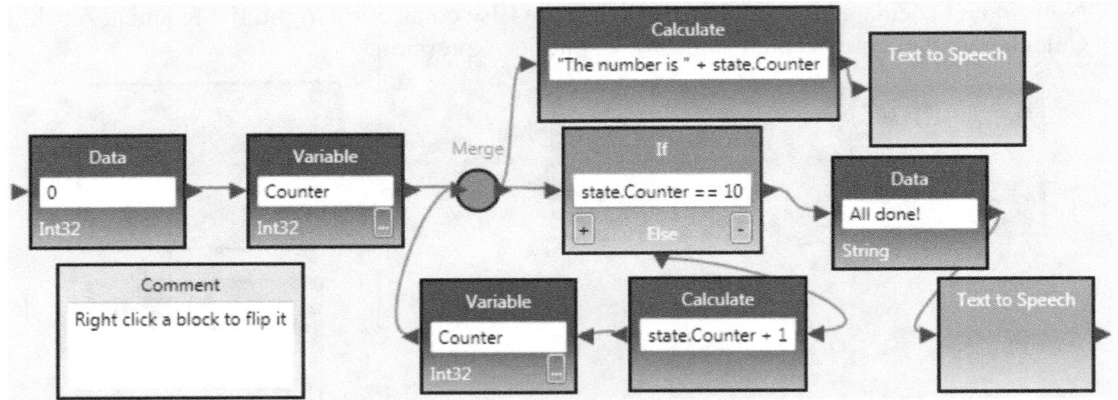

14. When you have completed the program, run your program by clicking on the Run button (or F5 on your keyboard).
15. You program can print and read the numbers out of order, because VIPLE is a parallel computing environment and the calculation is much faster than printing and reading. In this case, you can add a Timer in the loop, as shown in the following diagram.

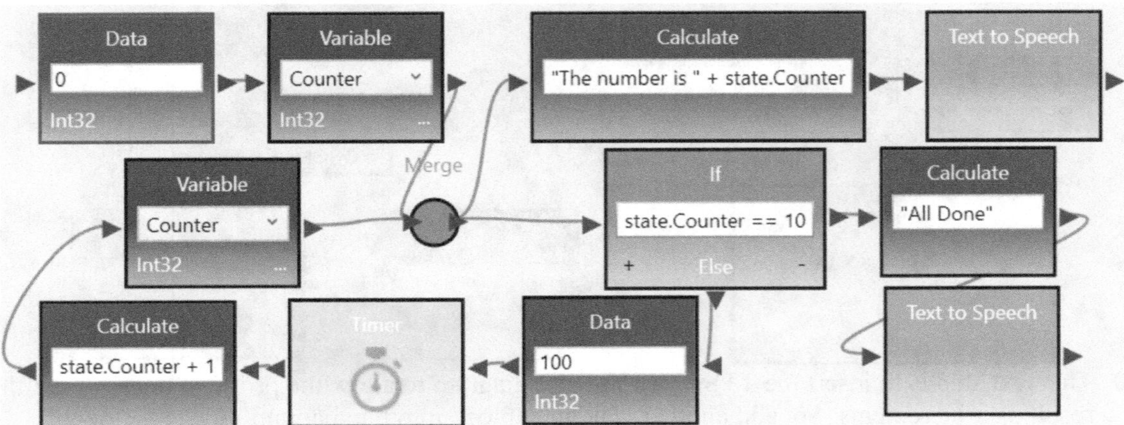

16. When you are done, please save the project file for later submission. At the end of the lab, you will put all the project files into a single zip file for submission.

Ex. 4. Creating While Loop Block Using the While Activity

This exercise will use of While and End While activities to implement a while-loop in a VIPLE program. It creates a variable, initializes it, and then counts to ten, speaking the value on each of the iteration using TTS activity block.

1. To begin, create a **new** project by selecting New from the File menu. Then next save the project as "Exercise_04".
2. Now, insert a Variable activity from the toolbox.

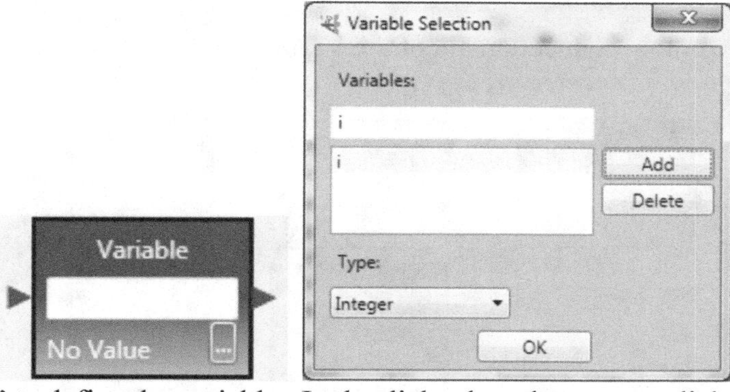

3. Next, click "…" to define the variable. In the dialog box that opens, click in the Name textbox and type in "i" as the name for your variable. Then click on the Add button. Then click on the dropdown arrow under "Type:" and select Integer from the dropdown list as the type for the variable. Click OK.

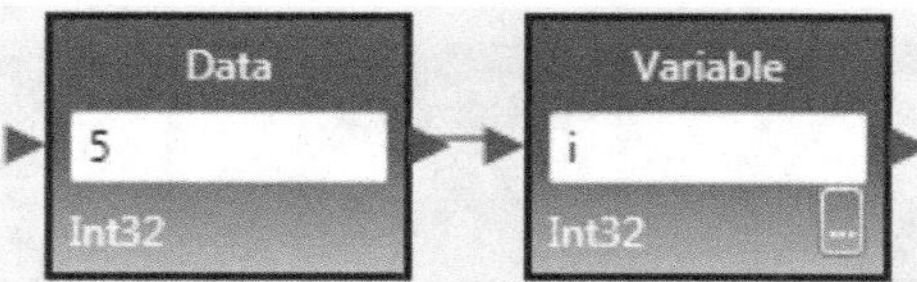

4. Now add a Data block to your diagram to the left of the Variable block and connect them by creating a link connection from the Data activity to the Variable activity block.
5. Enter 5 into the text box of the Data block, and the data type Int32 should automatically fill in. This sets both the data and its type. Its connection will then initialize 'i' to 5.
6. Now insert a While block to the right of the Variable block and connect the Variable block to the While block.
7. In the expression field for the While block, enter "state.i > 0".

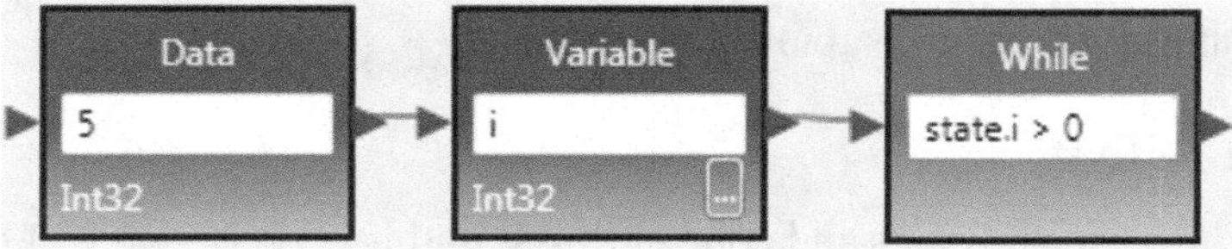

8. Now add a Calculate block and connect it to the While block. In the Calculate block, enter "i is" + state.i into its expression. Add a Text to Speech block and connect it to the output of the Calculate block.

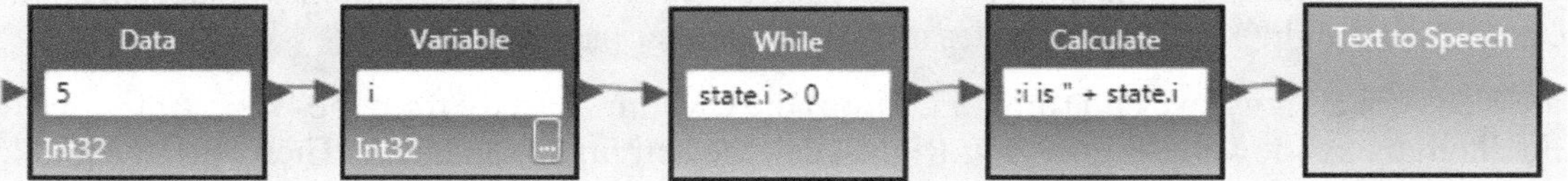

9. Now insert another calculate block into the diagram. In its expression field, write "state.i – 1". Insert a variable block after this calculate block. This new variable will take the value of i after it is recalculated. Click the "…" button, and select the i variable. Then click OK.

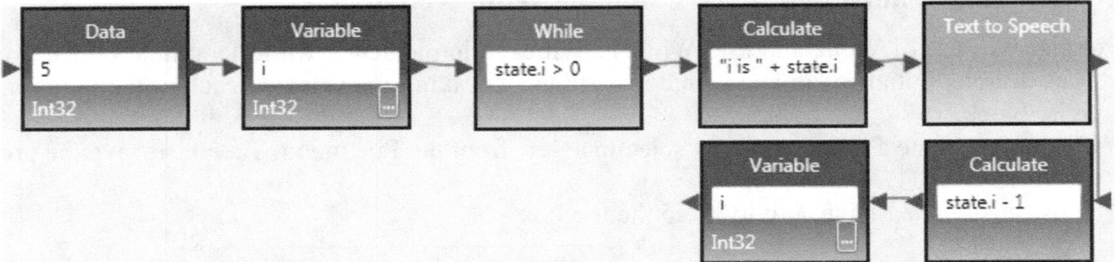

10. Now connect the output connection pin of the Variable block to an End While block. This completes your loop.

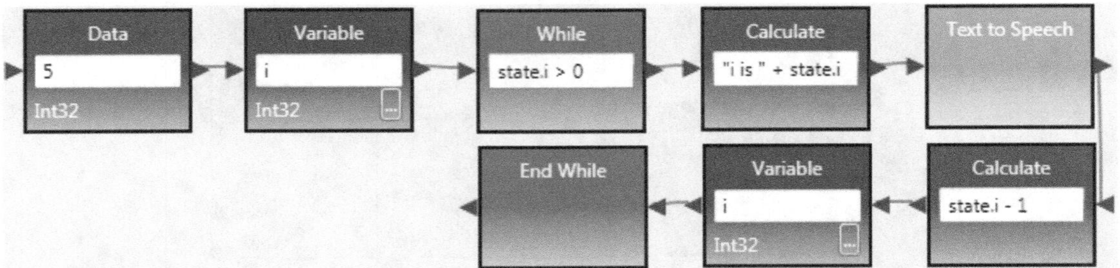

11. The next step is to insert the TTS block into the diagram to allow the program to speak out when the result is complete. So add a Data block into the diagram. Inside the new data block enter: "All done!"
12. Then add a Text to Speech block and connect it to the output of the Data activity block.

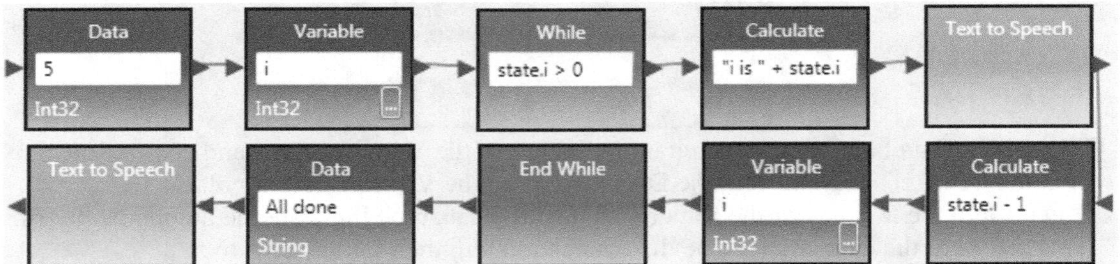

13. When you have completed the program, run your program by clicking on the Run button (or F5 on your keyboard).

When you are done, please save the project file for later submission. At the end of the lab, you will put all the project files into a single zip file for submission.

Ex. 5. Creating an Activity

In addition to learning the basic activities and control flows, in this exercise we will learn how to build your own custom activities and services in VIPLE. Once you have completed this exercise, you will have a better understanding of what a custom activity and service are.

In this exercise, we create a simple main and an activity. We illustrate the communication between the main and the activity through (1) global variables and (2) parameter passing.

To create a custom activity, we add (drag-and-drop) the Custom Activity from the Basic Activities list into the Main diagram, as shown in Figure B.4. Right-click the activity to rename it. Then open it (double-click on the custom activity). A new tab page is open. The triangle dots on the left side and on the right side represent data input and output, respectively. The circular dot on the right side represents an event output. We will discuss event-driven programming later.

In the Main diagram, the string value "John Doe" is assigned to OutVariable and the value is passing to the custom activity. When connecting an activity or a variable to the custom activity, a popup window will let you choose which value is passed to which parameter. In this example, the "value" is passed to myParameter. The String values "Hello, " and ", how are you?" are appended to instance.myParameter within the custom activity. The return value of the custom activity is assigned the output port and passed back to the Main diagram. Note that VIPLE variables are global, and both the Main diagram and all custom activities can access the variables through state.variableName. The parameter defined in a custom activity is a local variable. It is accessed through instance.parameterName in the custom activity only.

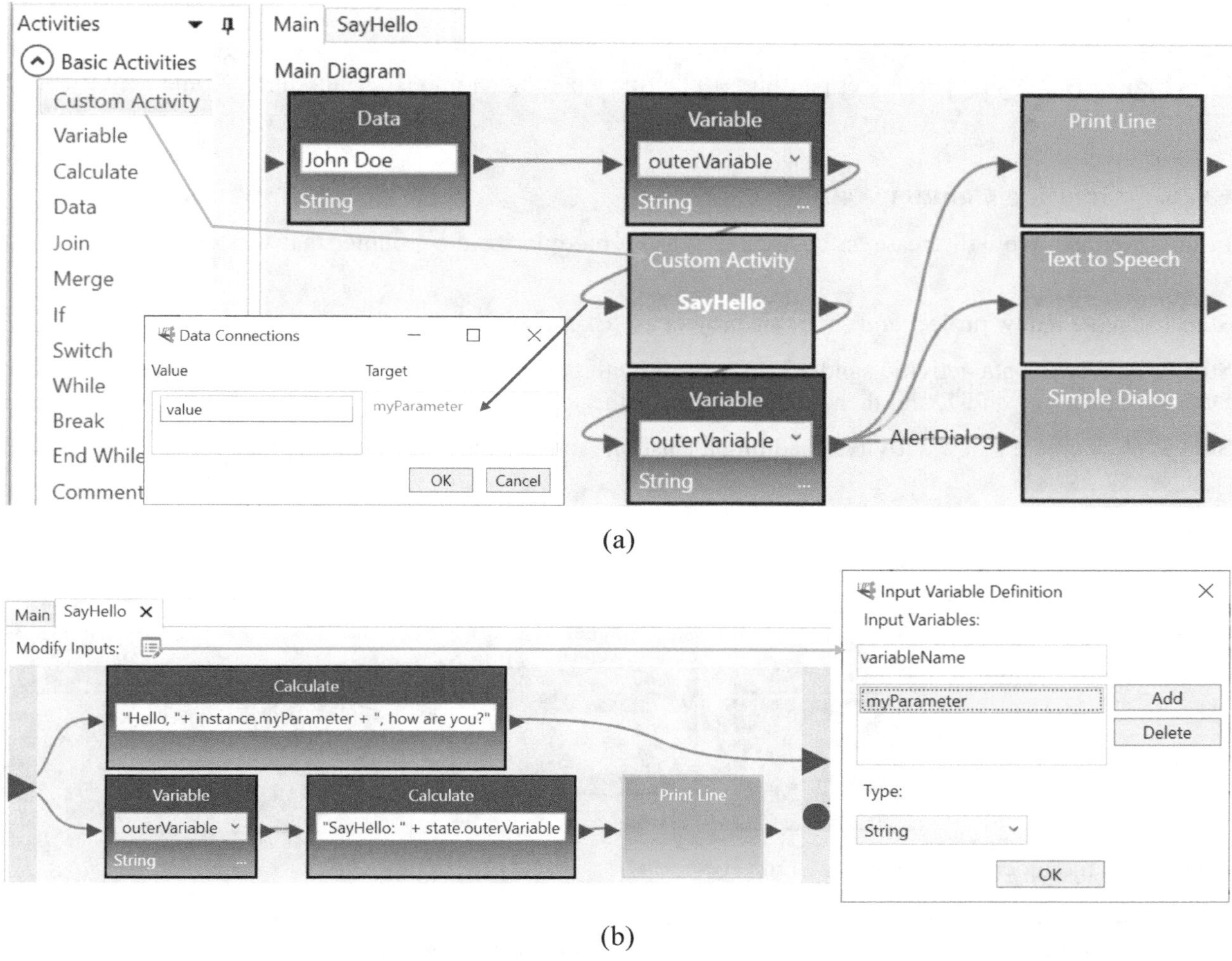

(a)

(b)

Figure B.4. Creating a custom activity: (a) Main diagram and (b) Custom activity and parameter

When executing the program multiple times, the outputs are shown in Figure B.5. Note, the two Print Line activities, one in the Main and one in the SayHello custom actity, may be executed in different order. It is a feature of parallel computing that two operations can be executed at the same time or in different order. The first outputs in Figure B.5 show the same outputs in different order. The third output shows that the Calculate activity is executed after the custom activity's return value is assigned to the outerVariable. Thus, if the order of execution is important, extra attention has to be paid to the parallel threads. For example, a Timer can be used to delay certain operation.

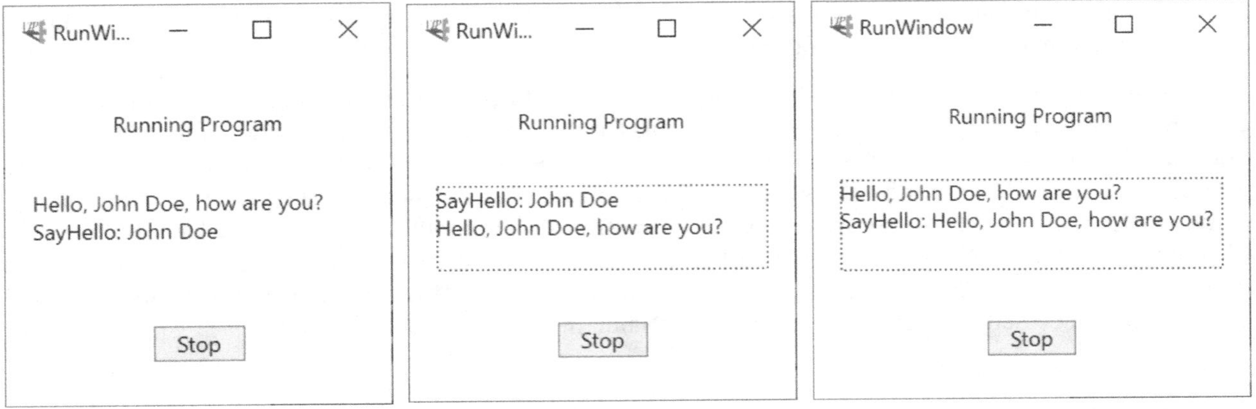

Figure B.5. Using parameter passing: (a) Define a parameter and (b) Main diagram and activity

Ex. 6. Creating Counter Activity

In this exercise, we will create an custom activity to modularize the Counter that was created a previous exercise.

Step 1. Create a new project and save this project as "Exercise_05"

Step 2. Add two Data activities and a Join activity with two inputs small and large. Set the values of your Data activities to 3 and 7, and then, connect them to the Join activity.

Step 3. Now create a new activity by adding a Custom Activity block on your diagram.

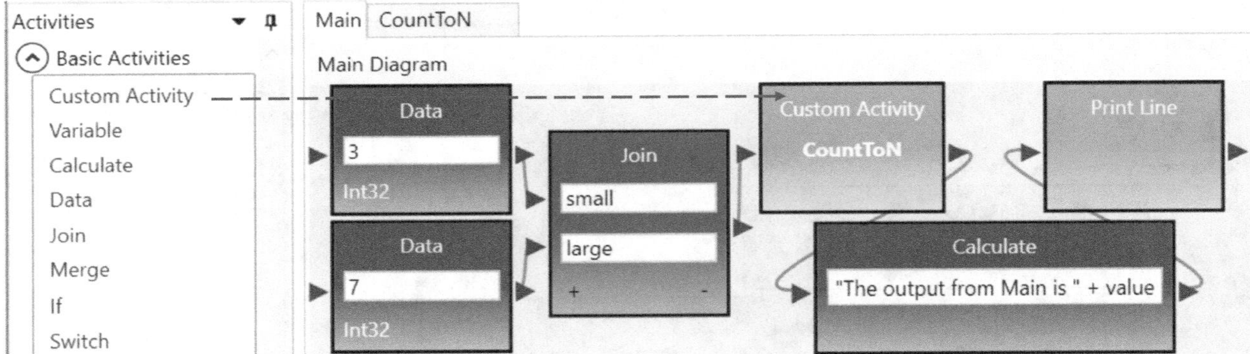

Right-click the block and rename it CountToN.

Then, double click to open CountToN. The triangle dots on the left side and on the right side represent data input and output, respectively. The circular dot on the right side represents an event output. We will discuss event-driven programming later.

Step 4. Click the orange symbol underneath the CountToN tab to open the window below for defining the input of the activity.

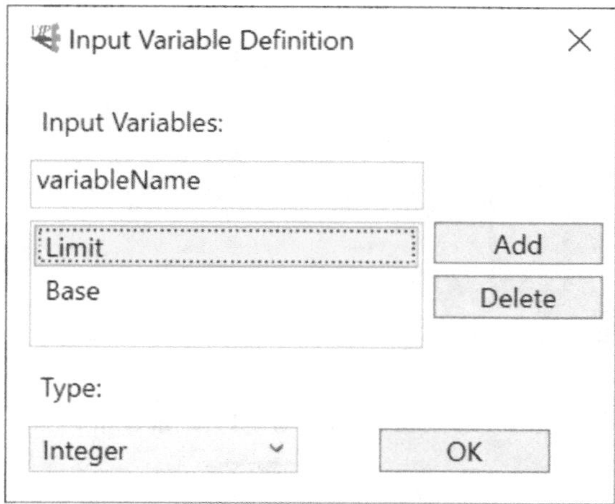

Step 5. We need two input values. We name them Limit and Base, which will be used as the upper and lower values for counting. Select Integer as their type. Then, click OK.

Step 6. For your activity's internal dataflow, insert the activity blocks that you built in the previous counter exercise.

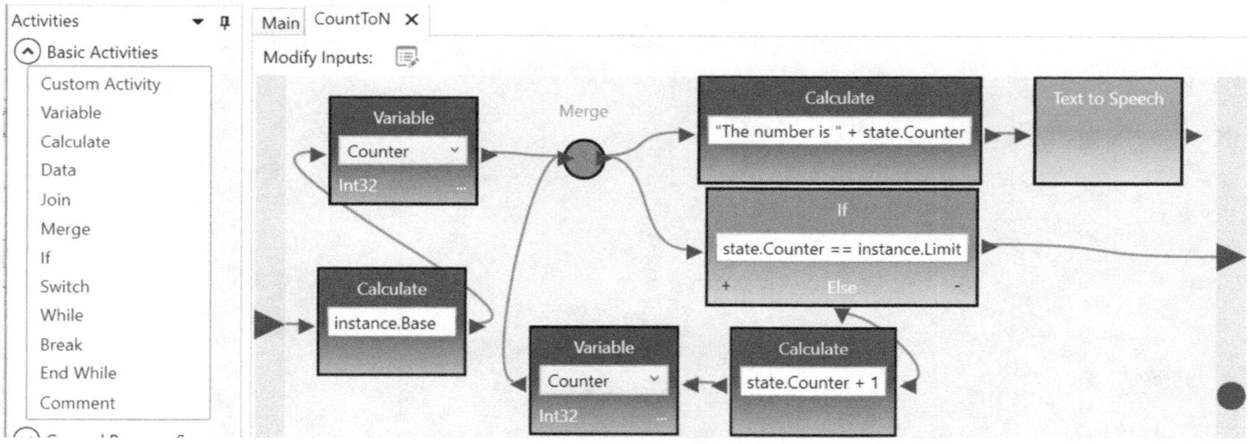

We consider all the parameters are encapsulated in a class called instance, and we use instance.Limit and instance.Base to access the parameters that take input values from outside the activity.

Step 7. Close the activity page or click the Main diagram tab to switch back to the Main dataflow page diagram to review the Main.

Step 8. When you are ready, run the program. Try experimenting with a different input values other than numbers 3 and 7.

When you are done, please notify your lab instructor and demonstrate your program for sign-off. Then change the driver to proceed to the next assignment.

Ex. 7. Build a 2-1 Multiplexor

The mathematical model (the compact form of the truth tables) of the 2-1 multiplexor is given below.

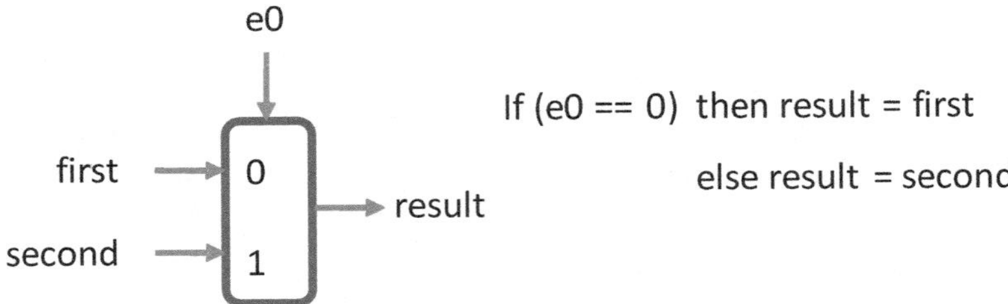

In this exercise, you will add another activity into the diagram in the previous exercise by following the steps below.

Step 1: Add an activity in the diagram. Change the name of the activity in the property to "2-1Mux".

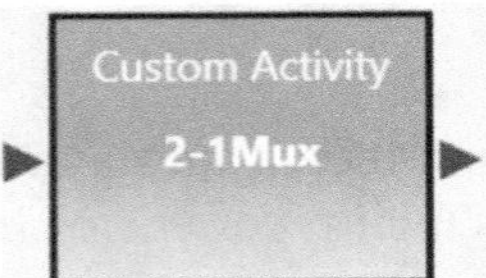

Step 2: Enter the Activity "Multiplexor and then open the "Modify Inputs" box below. Add three inputs and name them: e0, first, second, all of type Integer.

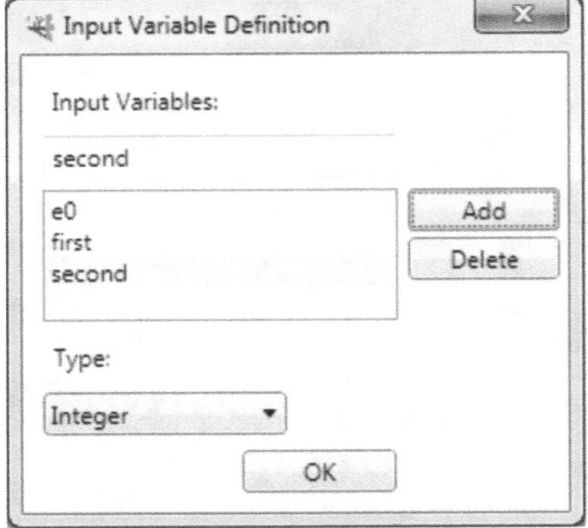

Step 3: Write the code for the activity, as shown in the diagram below.

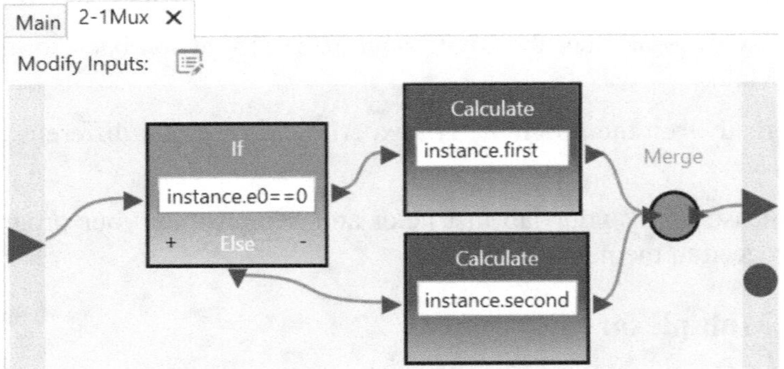

Step 4: Write the code in the Main diagram to test the activity. Use different test cases "input numbers → output number", for example, (1, 0, 1) → 1, and (1, 1, 0) → 0, , (0, 0, 1) → 0, and (0, 1, 0) → 1, to test the multiplexor activity.

When you connect the Join to 2-1Mux activity, note the mapping between the Join data names e, msg1, and msg2 and the input of the activity e0, first, and second.

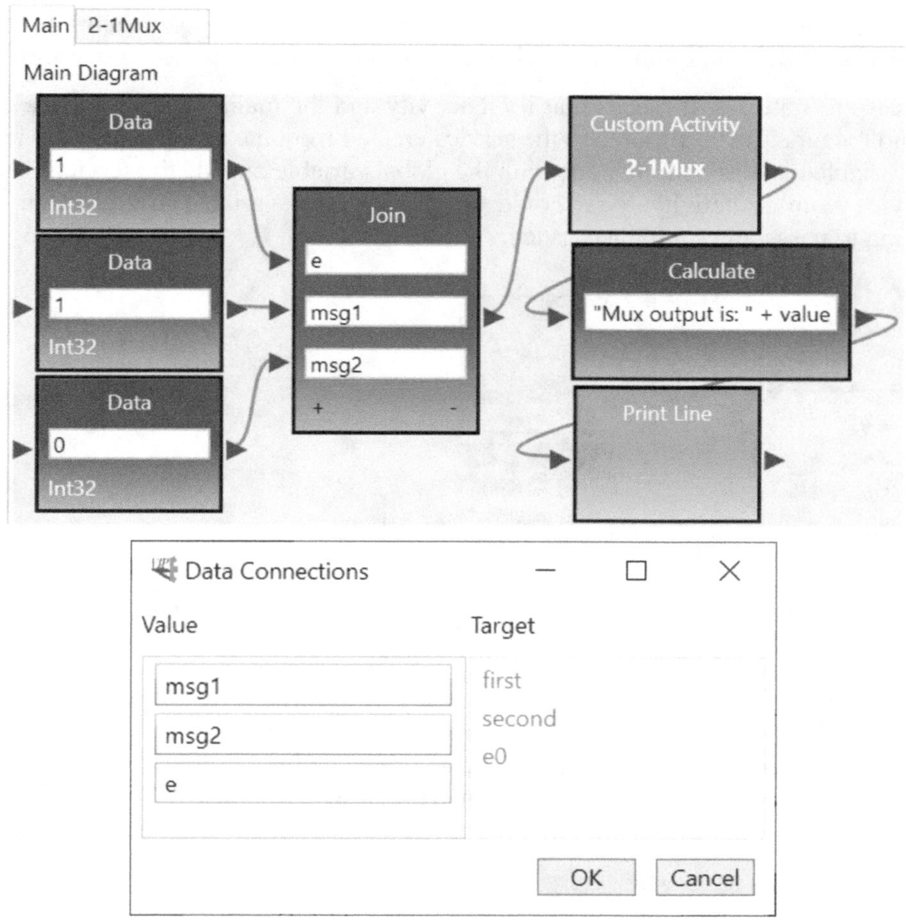

Step 5: Use the Simple Dialog service as input (replace the Data activity) to test the Multiplexor. In order to convert the string value from Simple Dialog into integer value, you need to convert a string into an integer. You can use Convert.ToInt32("123") into 123. The following code shows an example of using Convert.ToInt32 function:

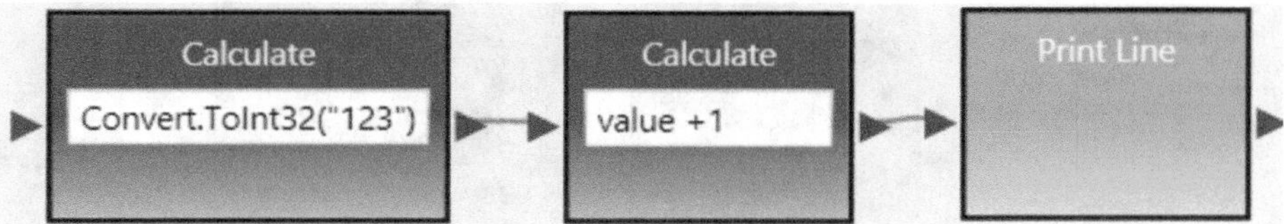

Ex. 8. Convert an Activity into a Service

An activity does not create a separate file, and thus, it cannot be used by any other VIPLE program. To share this activity in another VIPLE program, you need to convert an activity into a service. We use the 2-1Mux activity to show the operation.

In the diagram in the previous exercise, right-click the 2-1Mux activity and select Convert to Service. A copy will be saved into the Documents directory of the computer. The service will then will be added into the Services list of the VIPLE. You can use the service in the same way as the other services in the service list. To test your service, you can substitute the service for the activity in the previous exercise and run your code. It should give the same output as the activity.

To delete (remove) a custom service from your VIPLE service list, open the Documents directory and delete the file of the service. After you restart the service, the custom service will disappear from the service list.

Note that services are stateless. It means that if an activity and the main diagram share a global variable, the variable is no longer a global variable in the service created from the activity. The service will consider it to be a local variable that has nothing to do with the global variable outside the service. Thus, if you want to create a service from an activity, you should not use a global variable in the activity. You can use parameter passing to pass values into the service.

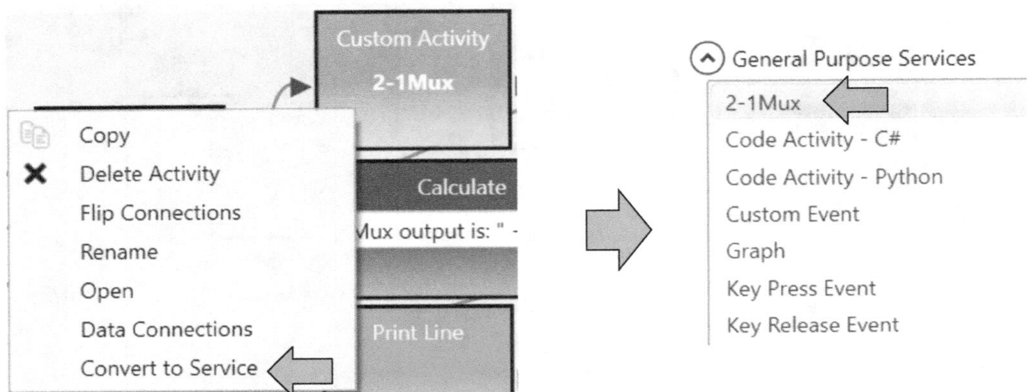

Restart your VIPLE. You will see now 2-1MuxService in your Services list. Draw the following diagram. Instead of using the 2-1Mux activity, now you are using the 2-1MuxService. Note, when you connect the Join service to 2-1MuxService, make sure that you map the Join data names to the 1MuxService parameters correctly.

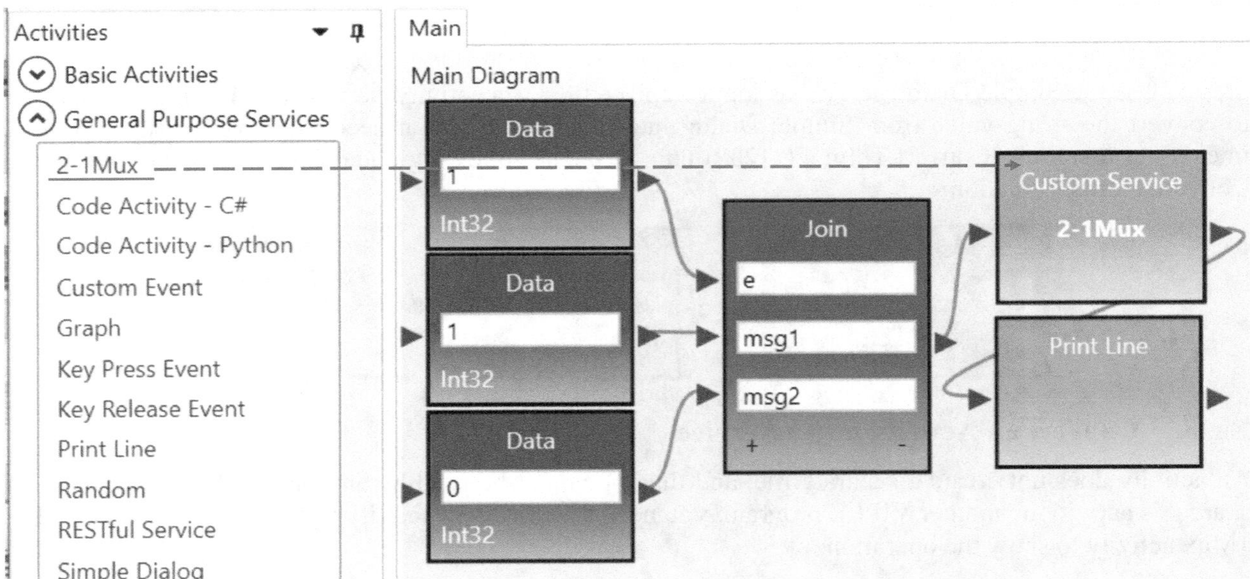

The service file, with an extension name .viplesvc, will be saved in the following folder: This PC → Users → userName → Documents → VIPLE Custom Services. You can share this file with other people to make it available in other VIPLE programs. To delete a service, delete the .viplesvc file. Then, the service will disappear from the VIPLE's service list after you restart the VIPLE application.

Save the 2-1MuxService. You can use it in later exercises, for example, developing the ALU in the. You can use this service without redeveloping the 2-1Mux activity.

B.3 Building Larger Systems Using Modules

VIPLE targets a wide audience in an attempt to accelerate IoT and robotics development and adoption. An important part of this effort is the simulation environment. It is immediately obvious that computer and console gaming have paved the way when it comes to affordable and widely usable robotics simulation. Games rely on photo-realistic visualizations with advanced physics simulation running within the real-time constraints.

VIPLE includes a 2D and a 3D robotic virtual simulation environment for users to test their applications prior to loading the software to the hardware platform (robot). On the other hand, VIPLE can be used for simulating circuit design, computer component design, and software design, such as vending machines, error checks in computer data communication, and traffic light controllers, as well as IoT/Robotics application design. In this section, we will use VIPLE to simulate circuit and computer component design. Later, we will use VIPLE to simulate software and robotics application design.

Simulation is an important design step in the engineering design process, particularly, in the complex process of designing and programming robots. When you are assembling a robot (especially a custom robot based on a modular platform with off-the-shelf parts) significant skill, time, and effort are expended in "debugging" your physical setup. Another challenge is that the robot being developed is expensive and there is only one set of hardware. These two properties make it difficult to try things concurrently with others, and there is always a risk of damaging the hardware of the robot in testing.

Simulation enables those with a personal computer to develop very interesting robots or robot swarms with the main limiting factors becoming time and imagination. At the same time, it constrains them in ways similar to physical robots so they can focus their effort in something that can be realized.

Simulations do have drawbacks and limitations. We are essentially trying to turn a hardware problem into a software one. However, developing software and a physics model has its own challenges so we end up with a different set of challenges and limitations. Usually this means that there is a "sweet spot;" a range of applications where a simulation is appropriate, and then a range of applications or stages in development, where using the real robot is essential or easier. A large number of extraneous variables in the real world are still unexplained or very hard to model. This means you may not be able to model everything accurately, especially in real time. For certain domains, such as wheeled vehicles, motion at low speeds is still a big challenge for simulation. Modeling sensors, such as a sonar sensor, is another challenge. People involved in the real robotics challenges will tell you that you must spend copious amounts of time with the real robot no matter how accurate the simulation seemed to be. It means that you may need to rewrite a part of your code or adjust the parameter values when you test a program on a real robot, which has been tested on a simulated robot and was shown to behave in the way desired. For example, you can easily make a robot drive in such a way to follow a straight line in the simulation world. In the real world, a robot may not drive straight if you apply the same "driving power" to both wheels. Instead, you may need to apply slightly different power to different wheels to make them drive straight. You need to use trial-by-error to determine how much more or less power you have to give to each wheel. Furthermore, you can easily time your robot to move a certain distance in the simulation, but in the real world, it is far more difficult to be accurate. For the sensors, a simulated sonar sensor can easily measure the distance to an obstacle, and thus, your program can make right decision to deal with the obstacle. In the real world, your sensor may give inaccurate distance values, which may cause your robot to execute a turn either too soon, or too late to be effective. You may need to figure out the appropriate range for the ultrasonic sensor, and factor in variables that do not exist in the simulation environment. We will use a robot simulator in the next lab assignment. In this lab assignment, we will use VIPLE program to simulate the designs of circuits and components of a computer system.

A computer system consists of five major components: control unit, datapath (ALU, registers, and related logic), memory, input, and output. An adder is a part of the ALU (Arithmetic and Logic Unit) in a computer system. We will take the component-based and service-oriented design approach in developing and simulating the design of ALU and its components: gates, multiplexors, and adder in this lab assignment. The component-based and service-oriented design approach consists of the following steps:

Design each basic building block (AND, OR, and NOT gates) as a component (activity). These components will be directly developed based on their truth tables.

Use the available components to build an adder, and wrap the adder into a component.

Design more components: 2-1 multiplexer and 4-1 multiplexer.

Use the available components to build an Adder.

Use the available components to build an ALU.

For each component, create a testing environment to test the component.

For example, the following diagram shows the VIPLE activity that implements the **truth table** (mathematical model) of the XOR gate. An XOR gate takes two binary inputs. If the two inputs are the same (both are 0 or both are 1), it outputs 0, otherwise, it outputs 1.

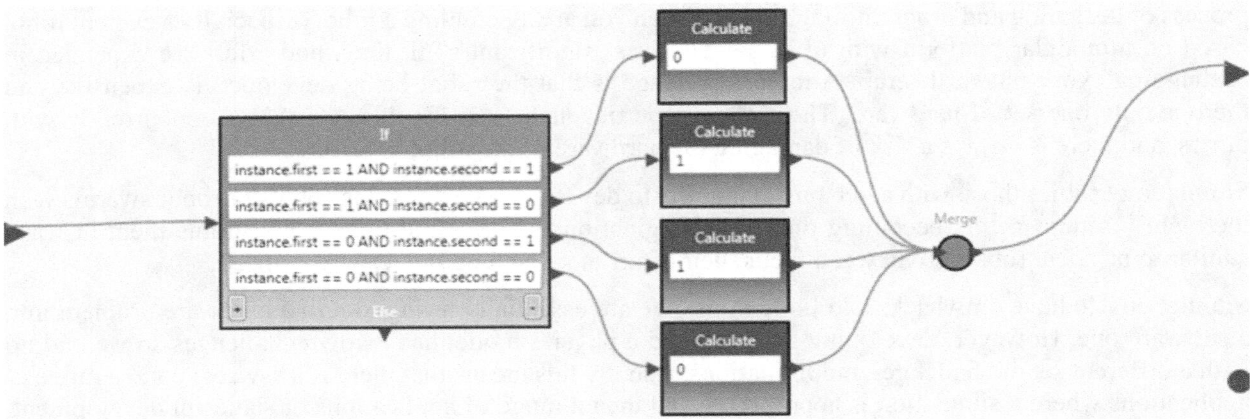

VIPLE code that simulates an XOR gate

Questions:

What are truth tables?

If a gate has 10 (ten) input lines, how many input combinations will its truth table have? 10? 100? 1000? 1024?

Truth tables are used to express the values of propositional logic in an effective manner that is sometimes referred to as a decision procedure. A propositional expression is either an atomic formula—a propositional constant, propositional variable, or propositional function term, or built up from atomic formulas by means of logical operators, for example, AND ($\wedge$), OR ($\vee$), NOT ($\neg$). For instance, $Fx \wedge Gx$ is a propositional expression (http://en.wikipedia.org/wiki/Truth_table).

Truth tables for classical logic are limited to Boolean logical systems in which only two logical (digital) values are possible, false and true, usually written F and T, or written 0 or 1, respectively. The truth tables are used to specify the digital compoments by listing all input combinations and their corresponding outputs. Below shows the truth tables of AND gate, OR gate, NOT gate, and XOR gate.

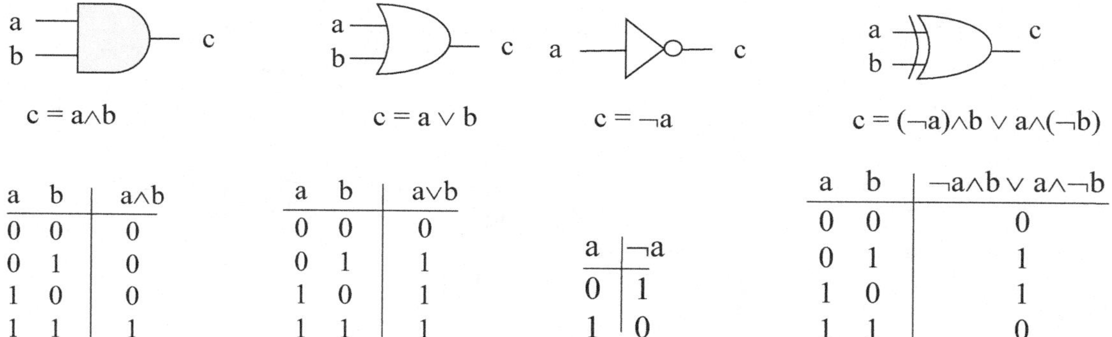

a	b	a∧b
0	0	0
0	1	0
1	0	0
1	1	1

a	b	a∨b
0	0	0
0	1	1
1	0	1
1	1	1

a	¬a
0	1
1	0

a	b	¬a∧b ∨ a∧¬b
0	0	0
0	1	1
1	0	1
1	1	0

Logic Design of the 1-Bit Adder

For a larger circuit with many inputs, it may become complex to directly use the truth able. The table below shows the truth table of the 1-bit adder.

Truth table of the 1-bit adder

Inputs			Output	
a	b	CarryIn	CarryOut	Sum
0	0	0	0	0
0	0	1	0	1
0	1	0	0	1
0	1	1	1	0
1	0	0	0	1
1	0	1	1	0
1	1	0	1	0
1	1	1	1	1

The 1-bit adder has three inputs and two outputs. If you directly use the truth table, you will have $2^3 = 8$ input combinations and your truth table will have 8 rows for the input values. To simulate it, VIPLE will have 8 conditions to test in the first If-activity, and each condition will have two comparisons, as shown below:

```
a==0 AND b==0 AND CarryIn==0

a==0 AND b==0 AND CarryIn==1

a==0 AND b==1 AND CarryIn==0

a==0 AND b==1 AND CarryIn==1

a==1 AND b==0 AND CarryIn==0

a==1 AND b==0 AND CarryIn==1

a==1 AND b==1 AND CarryIn==0

a==1 AND b==1 AND CarryIn==1
```

Thus, you use component-based approach for such complex components, that is, you should follow the logic design and make use of the components that you have already created. The following figure shows the composition of the 1-bit adder using the components that have been discussed.

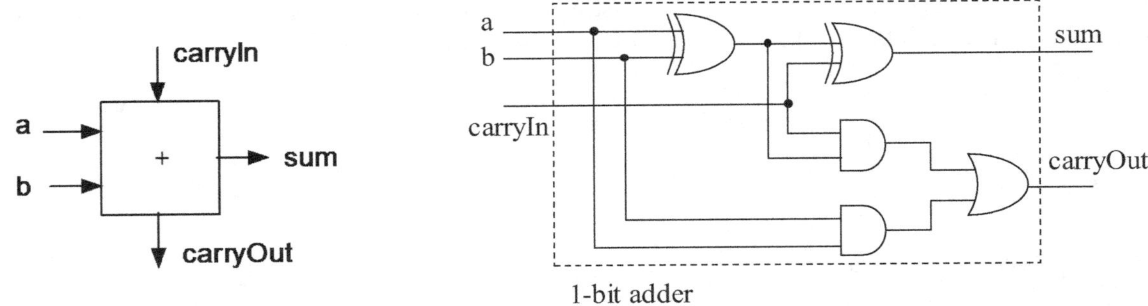

Logic Design of a 1-bit adder

Logic Design of 1-bit ALU

For an even larger circuit with more inputs, it may become too complex to directly use the truth table. For example, the following circuit (1-bit ALU) has 6 inputs and 2 outputs. If you directly use the truth table, you will have $2^6 = 64$ input combinations and your truth table will have 64 rows for the input values. To simulate it, VIPLE will have 64 conditions to test in the first If-activity, and each condition will have 5 comparisons, as shown below:

a==0 AND b==0 AND CarryIn==0 AND op2==0 AND op1==0 AND op0==0

a==0 AND b==0 AND CarryIn==0 AND op2==0 AND op1==0 AND op0==1

a==0 AND b==0 AND CarryIn==0 AND op2==0 AND op1==1 AND op0==0

...

a==1 AND b==1 AND CarryIn==1 AND op2==1 AND op1==1 AND op0==0

a==1 AND b==1 AND CarryIn==1 AND op2==1 AND op1==1 AND op0==1

Using the gates and the adder, we can further design the ASU. The following figure shows the composition of 1-bit ALU using the components that have been discussed.

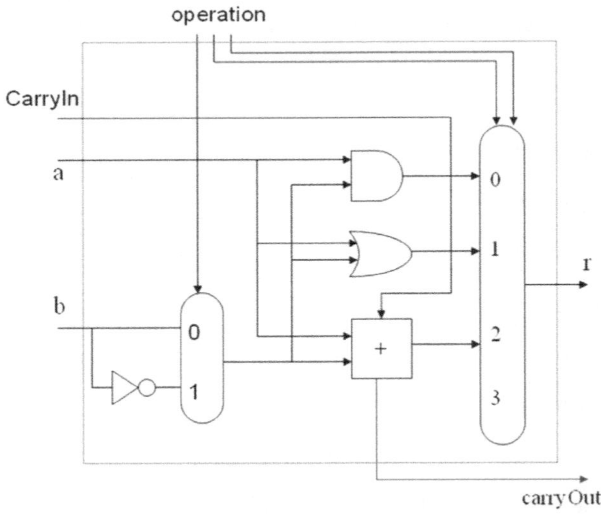

1-bit ALU, which can perform ADD, SUB, AND, and OR function

Now, we will start to use VIPLE to create activities that represent AND, OR, NOT, XOR gates, as well as other components for building an ALU. We start with the AND gate,

Ex. 1. Creating an AND Gate in VIPLE

1. Create a new project and save this project as "ALU_Simulation".
2. Insert an activity and name the activity "GateAND", as shown in the figure below. Please implement the gate with the logic based on its truth table (mathematical model) discussed in the lab preparation part.

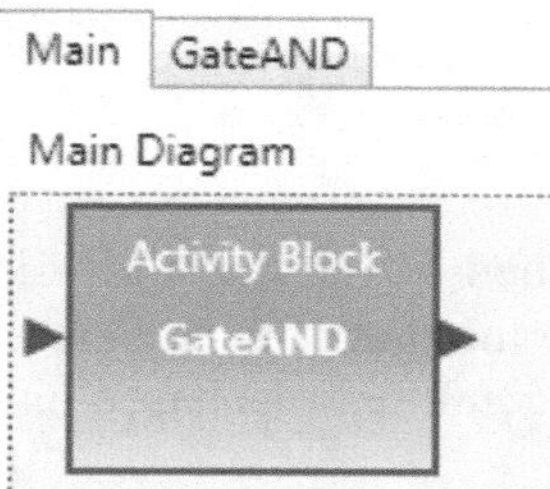

3. To define the inputs, double click the action button and then click the orange-color icon as shown below.
4. For the "AND" gate, you will need to define two input values as shown in the figure below.

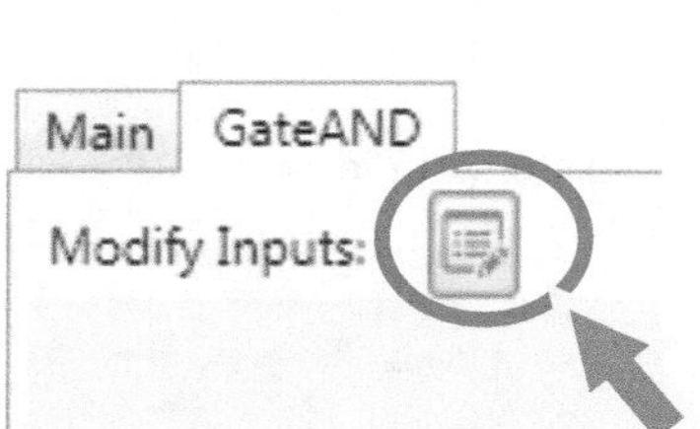

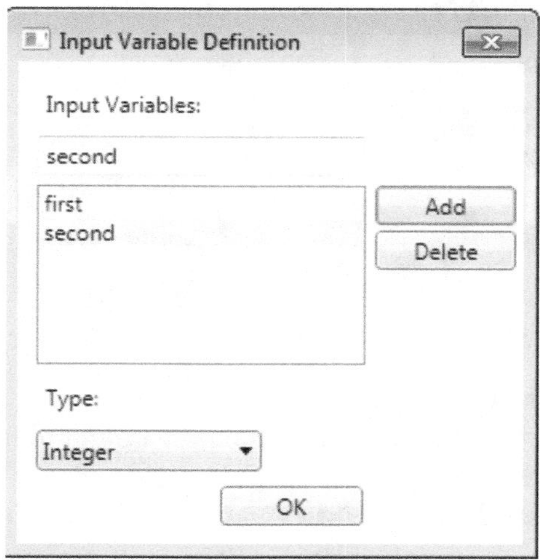

* Make sure each input variable (first and second) is of type Integer.

5. To build the logic of the AND gate, follow the instruction below:
   a. Start off by adding the if/else activities onto the diagram.
      - Create 4 different conditions to match each of the possible outcomes.
   b. Add the 2 data activities onto the diagram.
      - Each data activity represents the possible outcome, either 1 or 0.
   c. Then add the 2 merge activities onto the diagram and then connect each activity as specified in the diagram below.

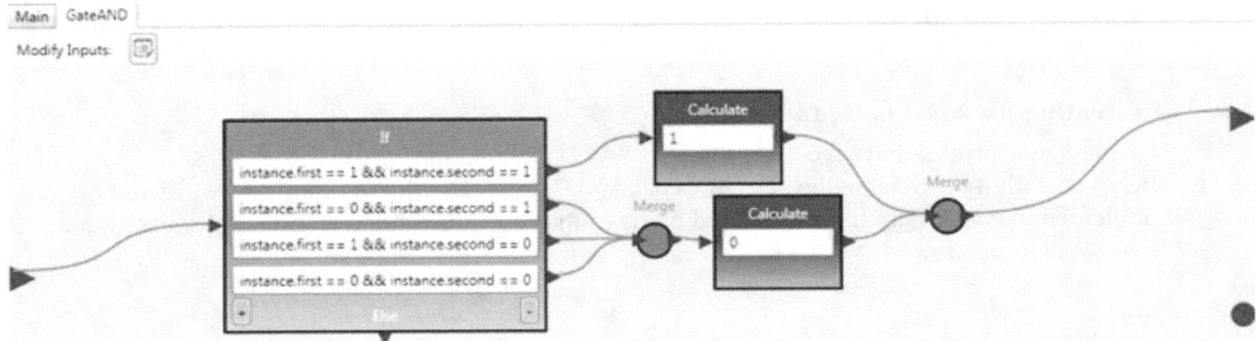

To test the correctness of your self-designed activity, in the "diagram" window, add the required number of "data" inputs and add a "Print Line" to the output to see the activity output. Run the program and see if your activity is correct, all possible input combinations based on the truth table. Try different data inputs in your tests: 0 0, 0 1, 1 0, and 1 1.

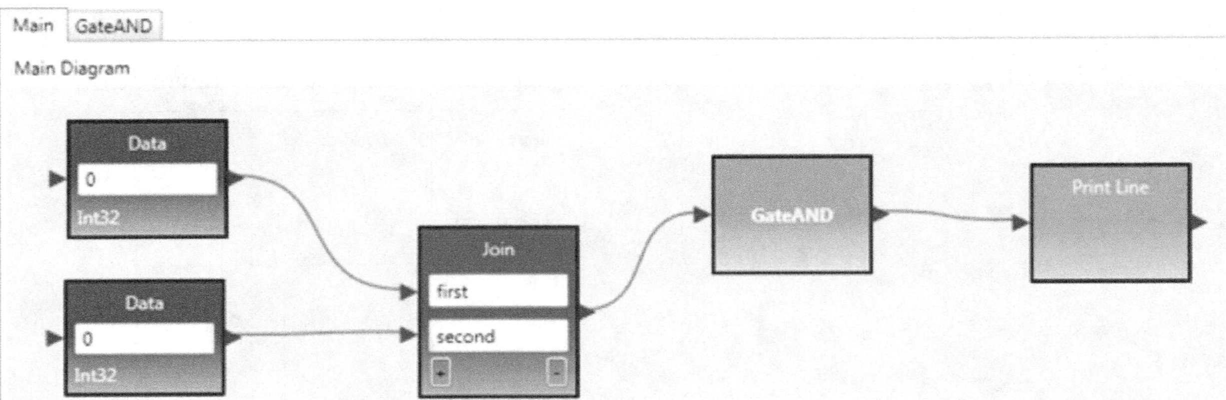

When you are done, please notify your lab instructor and demonstrate your program for sign-off. Then change the driver to proceed to the next assignment.

Ex. 2. Creating OR, NOT, and XOR Gates

Repeat from Step 2 in Exercise 1 to create Logic OR, NOT, and XOR gates. Do not repeat Step 1, which means that you add these gates into the same project. You do not need to create a service. Just use the activity.

When you are done, please notify your lab instructor and demonstrate your program for sign-off. Then change the driver to proceed to the next assignment.

Ex. 3. Build a 1-bit Adder

In this exercise, you will create an activity that represents a 1-bit adder. The logic of the circuit is given below. Please follow this diagram and use the activities or services that you have created in the previous assignments to implement this activity.

Note: If you follow all the naming conventions correctly, the logic gates you will need for this question are the activities (or services) that are created in the previous sections. You can also read the preparation part of this lab document. In the following diagram, the design of the adder is mapped to the gates.

Important: You need to draw the diagram from left to right and draw the connections (links) once both sides of a connection have been placed in the design. In this way, the relationship among the activities and services will be properly maintained. If you do it from the right-side to left-side, you will obtain many errors. Theoretically, the errors should go away once you have connected all the components. In practice, the development environment may not be able to resolve all the errors at one time.

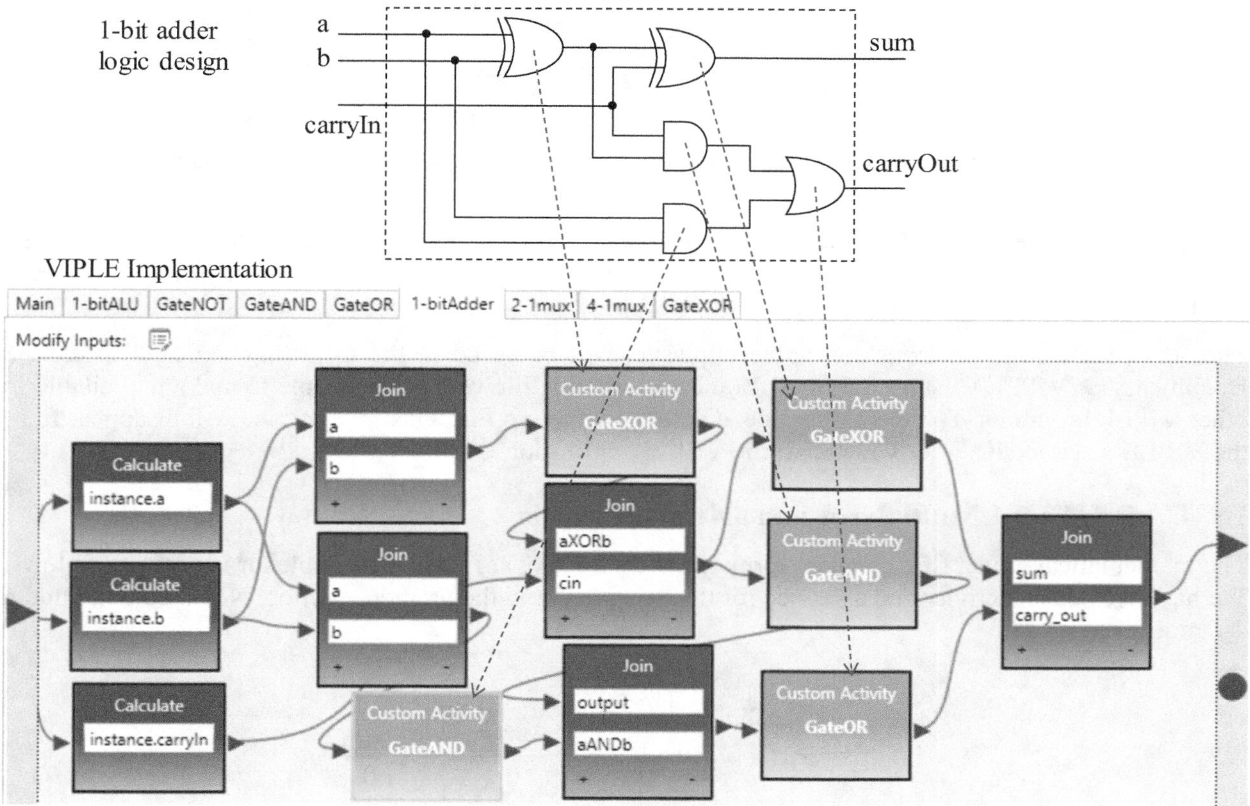

To test the correctness of your self-designed activities, in the "diagram" window, add the required number of "Data" activities as the inputs. Run the program and see if your activity is correct based on the truth table definition.

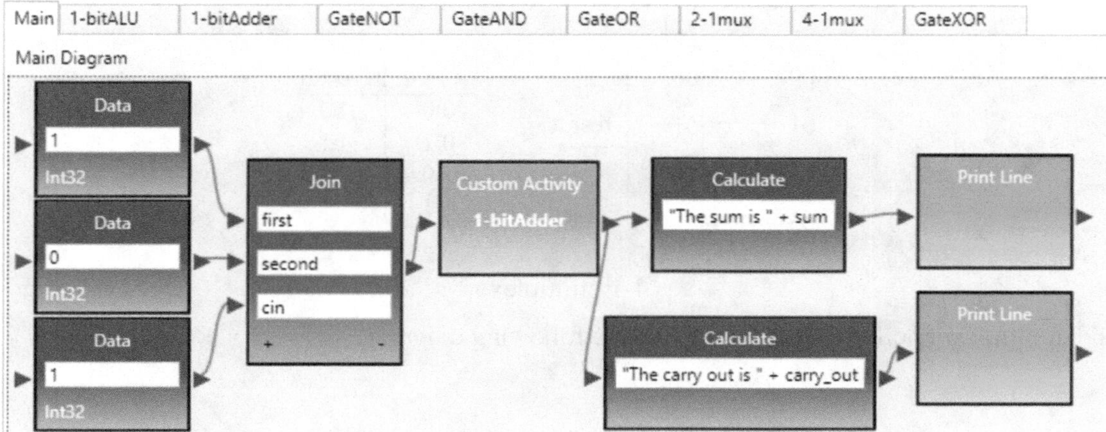

In order to test different inputs, you need to modify the values in the Data activities. It is not convenient. Instead, you can use the Simple Dialog service to enter the input from the keyboard. You can replace each Data activity by a Simple Dialog service to test the adder. Note, the data entered from Simple Dialog is always a string. In order to convert the string value from Simple Dialog into integer value, you can reference the following example:

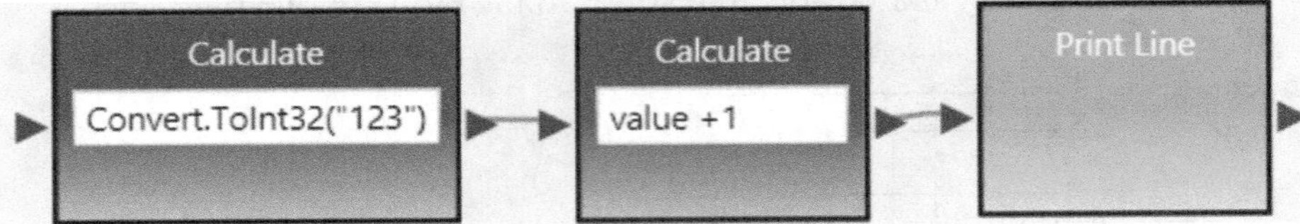

You need to add them into your test diagram and use the keyboard to enter different test data. You can also use a loop to test all 8 test cases in one run. Modify your program to implement this idea!

You can convert the 1-bit adder activity into a service by right-clicking the activity and choosing "Convert to Service." Then, the service will appear in VIPLE's Services list. Test your 1-bit adder service and see if it generates the same outputs as the activity.

The service file, with an extension name .viplesvc, will be saved in the following folder: This PC → Documents → VIPLE Custom Services. You can share this file with other people to make it available in other VIPLE programs. To delete a service, delete the .viplesvc file. Then, the service will disappear from the VIPLE's service list after you restart the VIPLE application.

Ex. 4. Build a 2-1 Multiplexor and a 4-1 Multiplexor

The mathematical model (the compact form of the truth tables) of the 2-1 multiplexor is given as follows. We have created an activity and a service for this component in the previous section. Now, we will build a 4-1 multiplexor.

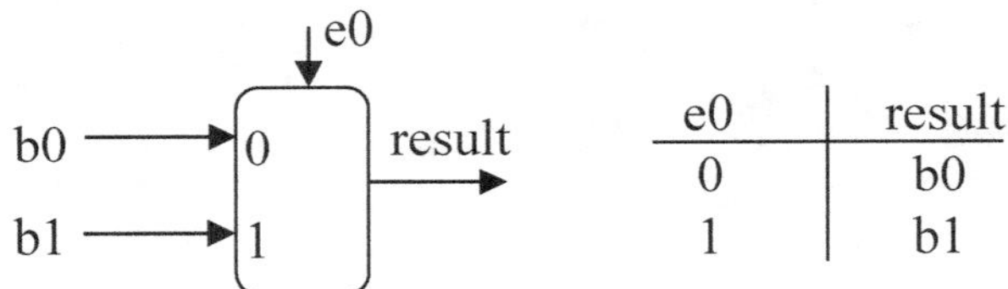

e0	result
0	b0
1	b1

2-1 multiplexor

The mathematical model (the compact form of the truth tables) of the 4-1 multiplexor are given as follows.

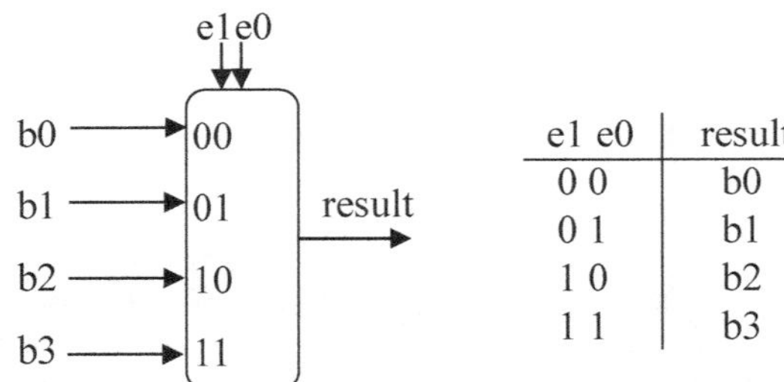

e1 e0	result
0 0	b0
0 1	b1
1 0	b2
1 1	b3

4-1 multiplexor

Your 4-1-multiplexor activity should look like the following diagram.

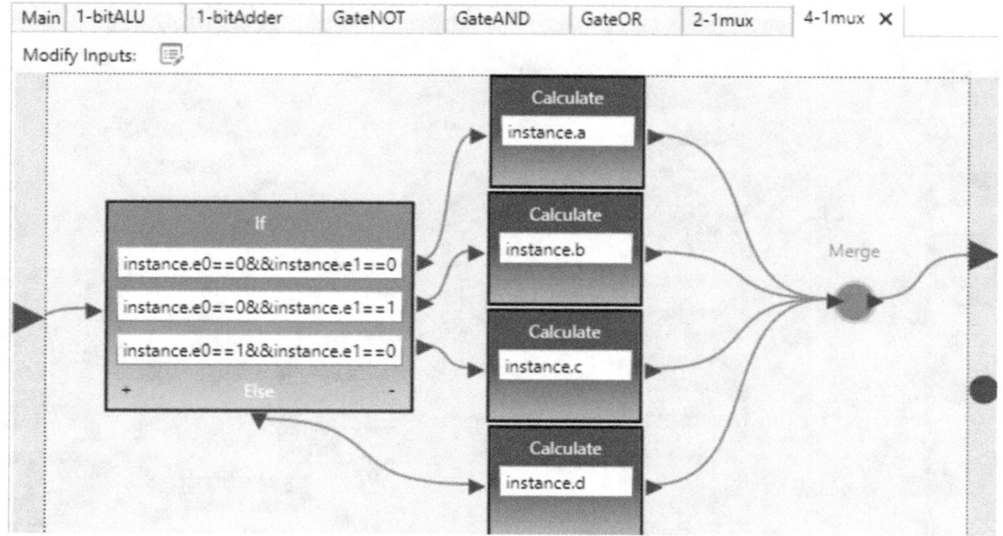

To test the correctness of your self-designed activities, in the "diagram" window, add the required number of "data" activities as the inputs and add a "Simple Dialog" service or Print Line service as the output to each activity that you have written. Run the program and see if your activity is correct. You can convert the activity by right-clicking the activity and choosing Convert to Service.

Ex. 5. Build a 1-Bit ALU

You have created all the activities or services needed to build the 1-bit ALU, which performs four different functions: AND, OR, ADD, and SUBTRACT.

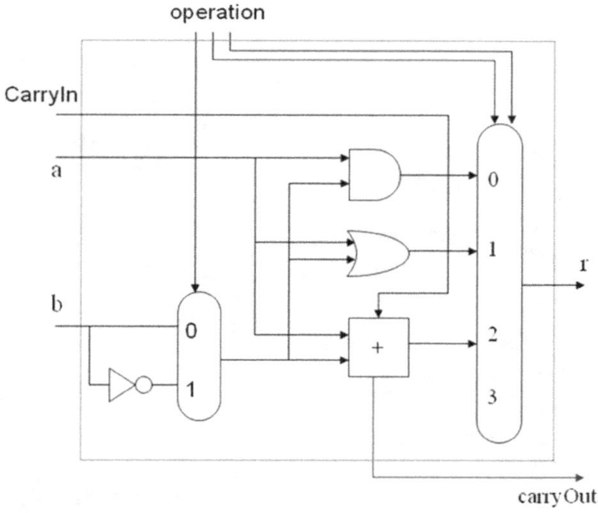

Write a VIPLE program for this logic. A sample diagram is given as follows. However, you need to write the code according to the name of your activities or services. You also need to define the data connection values among the components. The values shown in the diagram below may have used different names.

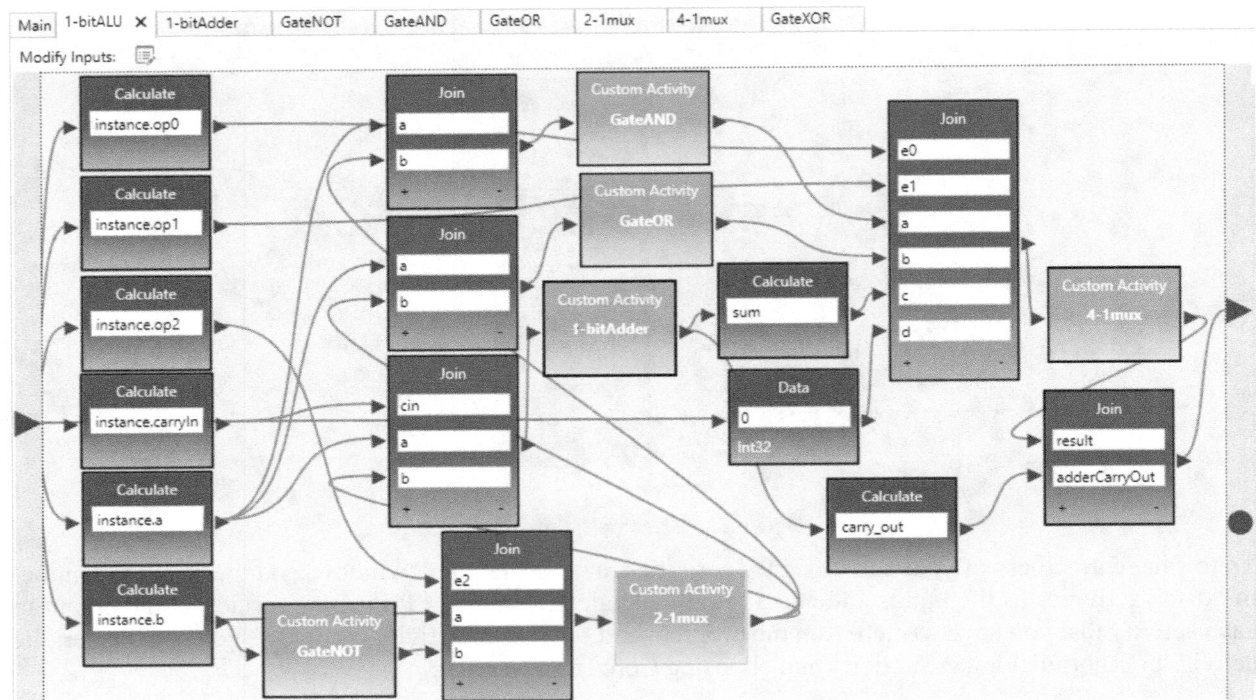

Once you have the 1-bit ALU completed, add input data and output service to test the ALU, which is similar to testing a 1-bit adder. However, you need three additional input data for op0, op1, and op2, as illustrated in the figure below.

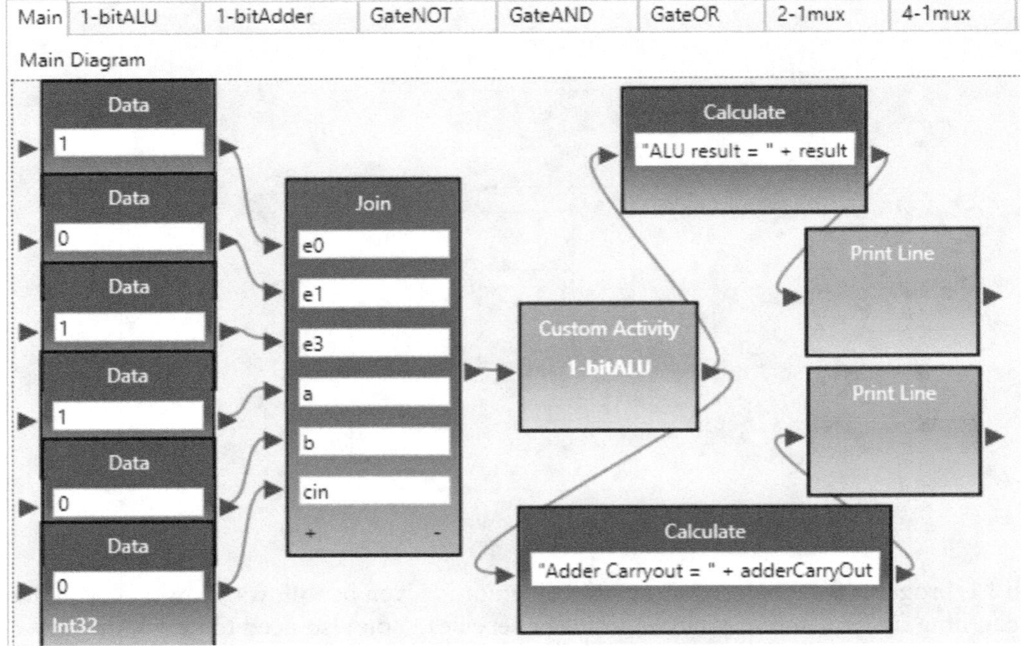

Ex. 6. Automated Testing

The problem with the testing configuration in the previous exercise is that we have to change the input case manually after each test. In this exercise, we will build an automated test case generation mechanism based on the Counter activity. The decimal output is mapped as a binary number, which is then used as the test cases for the adder.

First, we need to convert the decimal output of the Counter into binary. The following figure shows the conversion we need to make.

CountTo7	a	b	carryIn
0	0	0	0
1	0	0	1
2	0	1	0
3	0	1	1
4	1	0	0
5	1	0	1
6	1	1	0
7	1	1	1

if CountTo7 = 0, 1, 2, 3, then a = 0, else a = 1;

if CountTo7 = 0, 1, 4, 5, then b = 0, else b = 1;

if CountTo7 = 0, 2, 4, 6, then carryIn = 0, else carryIn = 1;

The following VIPLE code outlines the Main diagram of the automated testing mechanism. You still need to implement the Counter activity that takes two parameters as input: low (from) value and high (to) value.

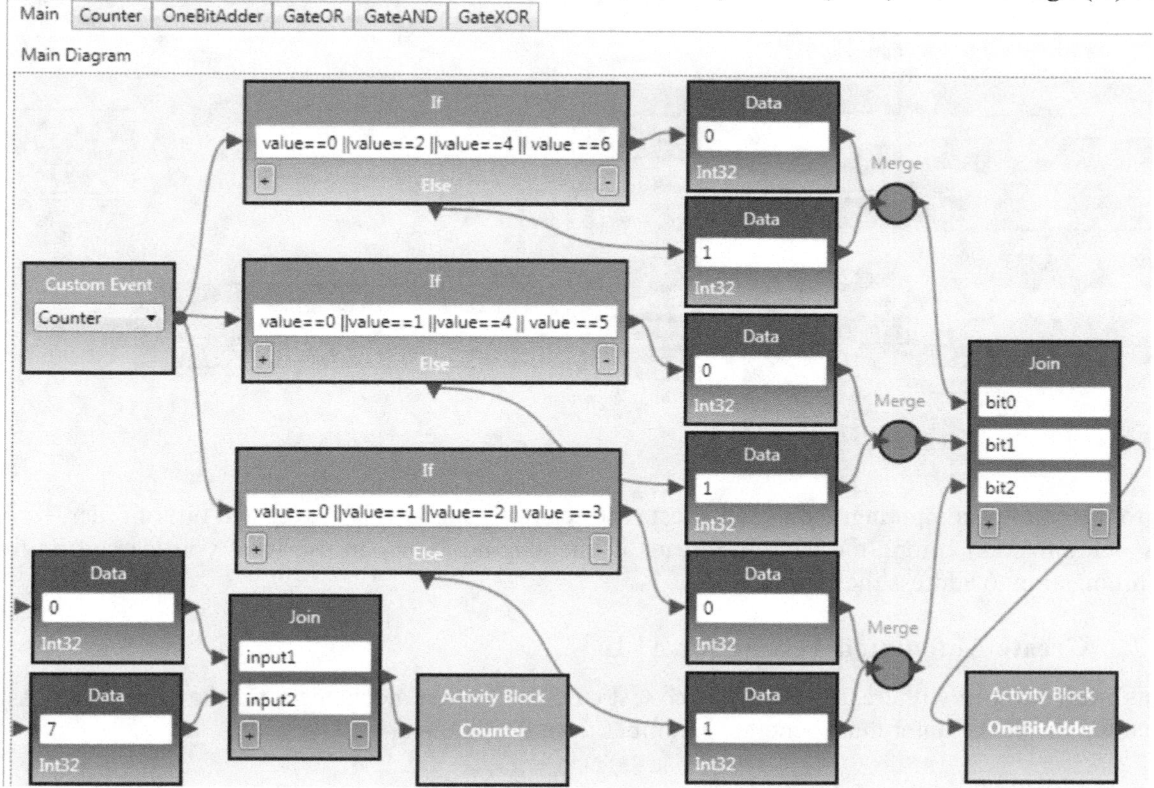

The Counter activity is given as follows.

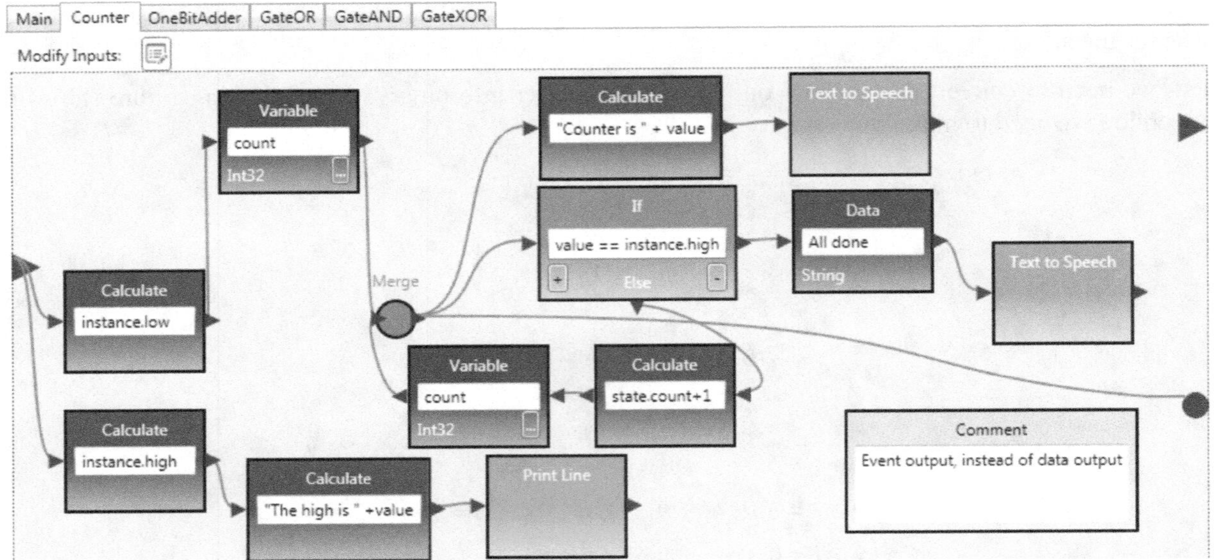

We can print all the adder outputs (truth table) in the Main diagram, as we did in the manual testing part. We can also print the outputs inside the adder activity, as shown in the following diagram.

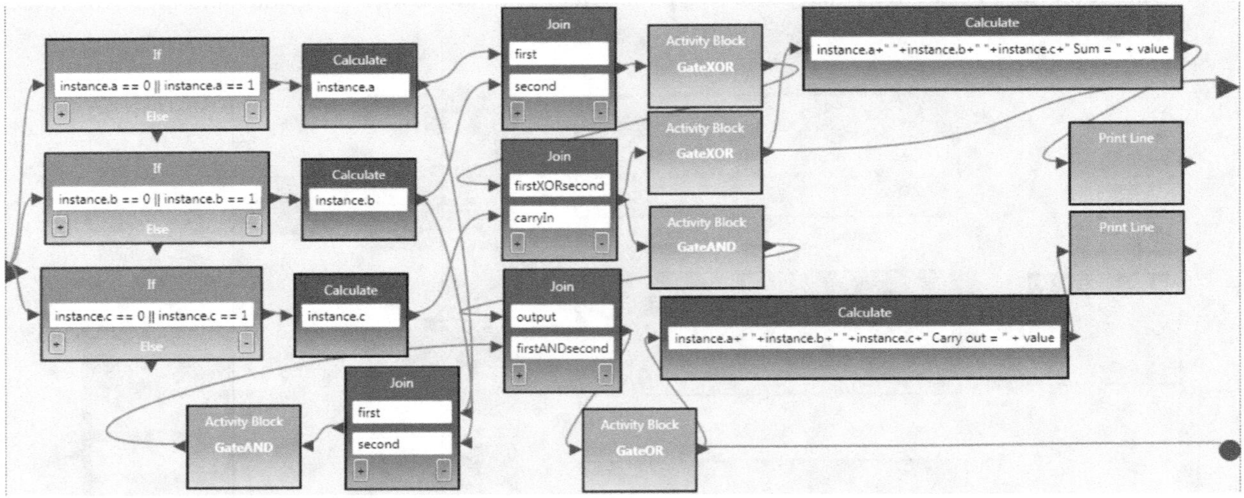

Due to the parallel computing features, the test cases can be generated and executed out of order. Keeping the synchronization among the parallel threads is challenging. You can use what you learned on thread synchronization to address these issues.

Ex. 7. Create Automated Testing for ALU

In this exercise, you will create an automated test case generation mechanism for the 1-bit ALU. As you have 6 inputs, the Counter must generate a number from 0 to 63.

Ex. 8. Create a 4-Bit ALU

In this exercise, you will connect four 1-bit ALUs to construct a 4-bit ALU. You will connect the carry-out of a 1-bit ALU to the carry-in of the next 1-bit ALU. For the bit 0 1-bit ALU, you will use a 0 as the carry-in for performing addition and use a 1 as the carry-in for performing subtraction. In order to do so, you must use the control line to the 2-1 multiplexor as the initial carry-in.

Ex. 9. Drive-by-Wire Simulation

We have been using VIPLE for general programming in flow control style and in event-driven style. These preparations are necessary for fulfilling our main purpose of programming IoT and robotics applications. In the rest of the section, we will focus on robotics application development using both simulated and physical robots. We start with the drive-by-wire program that controls the robot using the keyboard of the computer. Then, we will discuss the autonomous programs that control robots to navigate through the maze without any human intervention.

A number of robot services are implemented in VIPLE to facilitate different robots

Step 1: First, drag and drop the service "Robot" in the diagram. Right click the robot to use the following configurations (1) In Set TCP Port: set port number to 1350, In Properties: choose localhost, and in Connection Type: choose Wi-Fi, as shown in Figure B.6.

Figure B.6. Configuration of the Robot service for simulation

Step 2: Now, we can write the drive-by-wire code as shown in Figure B.7. You can follow the comments to select the data connection values. You can find the services in the VIPLE service list.

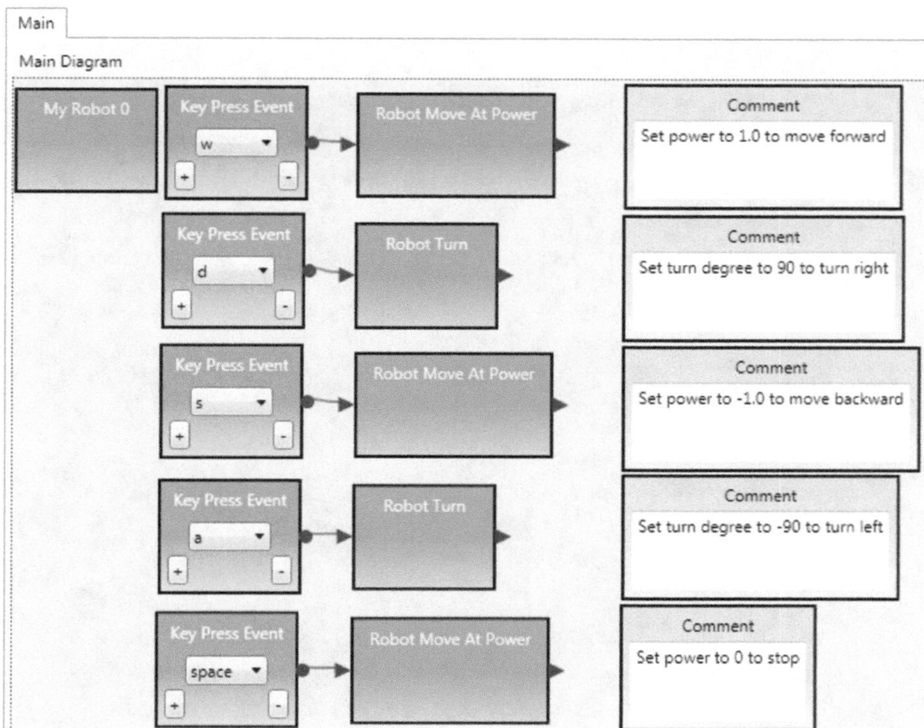

Figure B.7. Basic drive-by-wire diagram

You must right-click each Robot Move or Robot Turn activity and choose "My Robot 0" as the partner.

When you start the code, you will not see anything happening. We need a simulator or a real robot to see the robot controlled by the code. We will use a simulator at this time and use a real robot later.

Step 3: Start the Unity Simulator in VIPLE by choosing the VIPLE menu Run → Start Unity Simulator. Figure 18 shows the VIPLE start command and the simulated maze environment and the robot. Now, you can drive your robot using the five keys: w, d, a, s, and space. You can also change the maze by mouse-clicking the maze area to add and remove bricks.

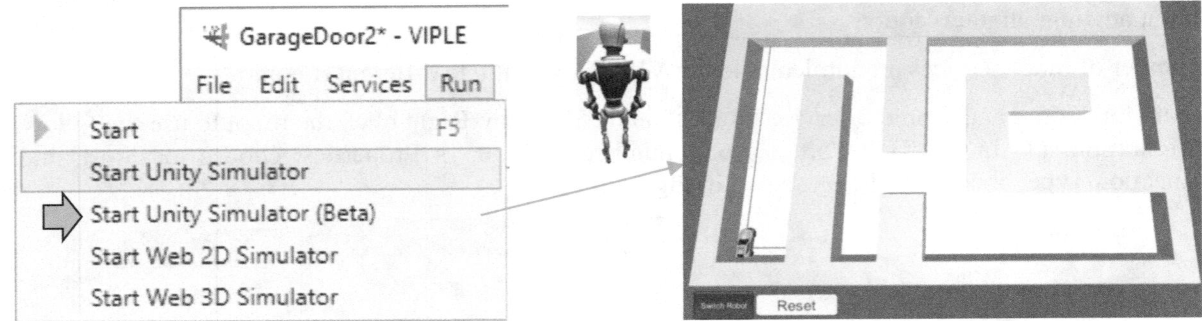

Figure B.8. The simulation environment

Please read Chapter 9 for more details on running VIPLE in a Unity simulator, in a Web Simulator, and in a physical robot, as well as implementing different maze navigation algorithms in these environments.

B.4 Exercises and Projects

Name: ______________________

Date: ______________________

1. Multiple choice questions. Choose one answer in each question only. Choose the best answer if multiple answers are acceptable.

1.1 VIPLE is

(A) an assembly programming language.

(B) a procedural programming language.

(C) an object-oriented programming language.

(D) a workflow-based composition language.

1.2 What is the main difference between Join and Merge activities in VIPLE?

(A) Join waits for all inputs, while Merge waits for one input only.

(B) Join waits for all inputs, while Merge adds input values together.

(C) Join waits for one input, while Merge wait for all inputs.

(D) Join adds all input values together, while Merge wait for one input only.

1.3 How many basic activities are offered in VIPLE?

(A) 1 (B) 3 (C) 5 (D) More than 5

1.4 What is a service in VIPLE?

(A) A basic activity. (B) An activity.

(C) An activity wrapped with service interface. (D) All of the above.

1.5 What is the purpose of the Event output of a VIPLE activity?

(A) To replace the value output of a string type.

(B) To replace the value output of a Boolean type.

(C) To provide an event output in addition to a value output.

(D) To provide a second value output.

1.6 What output methods are offered in VIPLE?

(A) Print Line. (B) Simple Dialog.

(C) Text to Speech. (D) All of the above.

1.7 Assume a variable v is defined. How is the variable v accessed in VIPLE?

(A) v (B) instance.v (C) state.v (D) variable.v

1.8 Assume a parameter p is defined. How is the parameter p accessed in VIPLE?

(A) p (B) instance.p (C) state.p (D) parameter.p

1.9 How do you convert a string to an integer in VIPLE?

(A) Use a build-in basic activity ConvenrtToInt32

(B) Use a build-in service ConvenrtToInt32

(C) Use Convert.ToInt32 in Calculate basic activity

(D) Use Convert to Service

1.10 How do you convert an activity into a service in VIPLE?

(A) Right-click the activity and choose Convert to Service

(B) Right-click the activity and choose Export to Service

(C) Drag and drop the Service into the diagram and implement the service like an activity.

(D) From the menu choose Services and implement the service like an activity.

2. Follow the exercises given in Appendix B to implement these tasks in VIPLE.

3. What are the roles of sensors in an autonomous robot?

4. Write a VIPLE program that can be used to remotely control a robot to play a ball game. The robot must be able to

(1) move forward, backward; turn left and right;

(2) move an arm or a leg to hit the ball.

5. Write a maze traversing program using the contact sensor. When the contact sensor is touched, the robot moves a bit backward to make room for a turn. Then, it randomly turns to the left in 50% of chance and turns to the right in 50% of chance.

6. A simple maze traversing algorithm is to turn left (or right) whenever it approaches a wall. Write a VIPLE program, using the Unity Simulator to implement this algorithm.

7. Read Chapter 9. Do the VIPLE-related exercises at the end of Chapter 9.

Appendix C
ASU Repository of Services and Applications

ASU Repository of Services and Applications is a free resource for service-oriented computing education. The services and applications can be used for demonstrating principles and learning the development process. Although we have tested those services and applications, there is no guarantee of correctness, reliability, or quality of service. Use them at your own risk.

This appendix lists the deployed examples of web services, web applications and other web resources used in the book. The table includes the name, description, the URL where the item is deployed, the type of the item, and the page number of the section where the item is discussed in the text. A part of the repository of services and applications is available at:

http://neptune.fulton.ad.asu.edu/WSRepository/repository.html

Table C.1. Examples of WCF, RESTful, and Workflow services deployed

Name	Description and deployed URL	Type	Section Page
Basic Three in SVC	The getting started service with three basic functions: HelloWorld, PiValue, and AbsValue http://neptune.fulton.ad.asu.edu/WSRepository/Services/BasicThreeSvc/Service.svc	.svc	126
Basic Three in RESTful	WCF RESTful service with PiValue, AbsValue, and add2 operations: http://neptune.fulton.ad.asu.edu/WSRepository/Services/WcfRestService4/Service1/ http://neptune.fulton.ad.asu.edu/WSRepository/Services/WcfRestService4/Service1/PiValue http://neptune.fulton.ad.asu.edu/WSRepository/Services/WcfRestService4/Service1/AbsValue?x=-*123* http://neptune.fulton.ad.asu.edu/WSRepository/Services/WcfRestService4/Service1/add2?x=*15*&y=*17*	REST	358
Crypto service in SVC	WCF-based WSDL-SOAP service with two operations: string Encrypt(string); and string Decrypt(string); http://neptune.fulton.ad.asu.edu/WSRepository/Services/EncryptionWcf/Service.svc http://neptune.fulton.ad.asu.edu/WSRepository/Services/EncryptionTryIt/Sender.aspx	.svc	320

FileService in SVC	WCF-based WSDL service that stores a string in the server's file system:
	void PutStringToFile(string fileName, string value);
	string GetStringFromFile(string fileName);
	http://neptune.fulton.ad.asu.edu/wsrepository/Services/FileService/service.svc
	TryIt: http://neptune.fulton.ad.asu.edu/wsrepository/Services/FileServiceTryIt/
		.svc	135

Hashing for security	Hash service using SHA5 string Hash(string data, string salt); http://neptune.fulton.ad.asu.edu/WSRepository/Services/HashSha512/Service.svc?wsdl To test the service, use the service test tool: http://neptune.fulton.ad.asu.edu/WSRepository/services/wsTesterTryIt/	.svc	322
Image Verifier in RESTful	WCF RESTful service with GetImage/3Nt$@ operation http://neptune.fulton.ad.asu.edu/WSRepository/Services/ImageVerifier/Service.svc/GetImage/3Nt$@	REST	366
Image verifier in SVC	WCF-based WSDL-SOAP service with two operations: Stream GetImage() and GetVerifierString(string length) http://neptune.fulton.ad.asu.edu/WSRepository/Services/ImageVerifierSvc/Service.svc	.svc	366
Image verifier in workflow	Workflow-based service http://neptune.fulton.ad.asu.edu/WSRepository/Services/WFImage/WFservice/service1.xamlx Test page: http://neptune.fulton.ad.asu.edu/WSRepository/Services/WFImage	.xamlx	413

Messenger service and TryIt	WCF service with 3 operations:
	bool SendMessage(string receiverID, string Message);
	bool SendMessages(string senderID, string receiverID, string Message);
	string[] ReceiveMessage(string receiverID);
	http://neptune.fulton.ad.asu.edu/WSRepository/Services/Messenger/Service.svc
	TryIt: http://neptune.fulton.ad.asu.edu/WSRepository/Services/MessengerTryIt
		.svc	449

Mortgage Service in Workflow	Microsoft MSDN Magazine mortgage service example in workflow: http://neptune.fulton.ad.asu.edu/WSRepository/Services/WFService/MortgageService/Service1.xamlx http://neptune.fulton.ad.asu.edu/WSRepository/Services/WFService/VendorService/VendorX.svc, where X = 1, 2, 3 TyiIt page: http://neptune.fulton.ad.asu.edu/WSRepository/WFService/	.xamlx	413
Number Guess in RESTful	WCF RESTful service with two operations: int secretNumber(int lower, int upper); and string checkNumber(int userNum, int secretNum); http://neptune.fulton.ad.asu.edu/WSRepository/Services/NumberGuessRest/Service.svc/GetSecretNumber?lower=*1*&upper=*100* http://neptune.fulton.ad.asu.edu/WSRepository/Services/NumberGuessRest/Service.svc/checkNumber?userNum=*23*&secretNum=*75*	REST	394
Number Guess in SVC	WCF service with two operations: int secretNumber(int lower, int upper); and string checkNumber(int userNum, int secretNum); http://neptune.fulton.ad.asu.edu/WSRepository/Services/NumberGuess/Service.svc	.svc	394
Random String in SVC	RandomString .svc service http://neptune.fulton.ad.asu.edu/WSRepository/Services/RandomStringsvc/Service.svc Application that tests the RandomString service http://neptune.fulton.ad.asu.edu/WSRepository/Services/RandomString/Tryit.aspx	.aspx	366
Random String in RESTful	WCF RESTful service with GetRandomString and GetRandomString/{x} http://neptune.fulton.ad.asu.edu/WSRepository/Services/RandomString/Service.svc/GetRandomString/*8*	REST	366
Singleton service and TryIt	Service: http://neptune.fulton.ad.asu.edu/WSRepository/Services/Singleton/service.svc TryIt page: http://neptune.fulton.ad.asu.edu/WSRepository/Services/SingletonTryIt/default.aspx	.svc	353
Stock quote simulator in SVC and RESTful	SVC Service: http://neptune.fulton.ad.asu.edu/WSRepository/Services/Stockquote/Service.svc TryIt application: http://neptune.fulton.ad.asu.edu/WSRepository/Services/Stockquote/ RESTful service: http://neptune.fulton.ad.asu.edu/WSRepository/Services/StockquoteRest/Service.svc/getStockquote?symbol=*IBM*	.svc REST	159
Web service testing service	Web service that tests a web service, with operations: findOperationParameter, findOperations, getParameterNames, wrapService http://neptune.fulton.ad.asu.edu/WSRepository/services/wsTester/service1.svc TryIt page: http://neptune.fulton.ad.asu.edu/WSRepository/services/wsTesterTryIt/	.svc	172
Web to String	Get Web Content from URL, with GetWebContent(string url) http://neptune.fulton.ad.asu.edu/wsRepository/Services/Web2StringSVC/Service.svc TryIt page: http://neptune.fulton.ad.asu.edu/wsRepository/Services/Web2StringSVC/tryit.aspx	.svc	171

Table C.2. Examples of ASP .Net (.asmx) services and ASP .Net applications deployed

Name	Description and deployed URL	Type	Section Page
Basic Three	The getting started service with three basic functions http://neptune.fulton.ad.asu.edu/WSRepository/Services/BasicThree/Service.asmx	.asmx	**Error! Bookmark not defined.**
Crypto service	ASP .Net Encryption and decryption string(string) http://neptune.fulton.ad.asu.edu/WSRepository/Services/Encryption/Service.asmx	.asmx	244
AppSettings	Read, write, and delete elements of appSettings in Web.Config file http://neptune.fulton.ad.asu.edu/WSRepository/appsettings/Default.aspx	.aspx	250
Output caching	Caching browser output in browser http://neptune.fulton.ad.asu.edu/WSRepository/OutputCaching/Default.aspx	.aspx	275
File Data caching	Caching disk file contents in browser neptune.fulton.ad.asu.edu/WSRepository/XMLDocCacheReadWriteApp/Default.aspx	.aspx	277
DB Data caching	Caching disk file contents in browser http://neptune.fulton.ad.asu.edu/WSRepository/DBCacheReadWriteApp/Default.aspx	.aspx	277
Dynamic graphics	Vending machine, generate graphics without using user control http://neptune.fulton.ad.asu.edu/WSRepository/CoffeeVender/	.aspx	286
Dynamic graphics	Vending machine, generate graphics using user control http://neptune.fulton.ad.asu.edu/WSRepository/CoffeeMachine/	.aspx	288
Forms security	Authentication and authorization application http://neptune.fulton.ad.asu.edu/WSRepository/FormsSecurity/	.aspx	307
Image Verifier	Application that tests the RESTful ImageVerifier service http://neptune.fulton.ad.asu.edu/WSRepository/Services/ImageVerifier/Tryit.aspx	.aspx	366
Image Verifier	Application that tests the WSDL-SOAP ImageVerifier service http://neptune.fulton.ad.asu.edu/WSRepository/Services/ImageVerifierSvc/TryIt.aspx	.aspx	366
Random String	RandomString .svc service http://neptune.fulton.ad.asu.edu/WSRepository/Services/RandomStringsvc/Service.svc Application that tests the RandomString service http://neptune.fulton.ad.asu.edu/WSRepository/Services/RandomString/Tryit.aspx	.aspx	366
Shopping cart	Enter items to catalogue, add to cart, remove from cart http://neptune.fulton.ad.asu.edu/WSRepository/SessionOnlineStore/Default.aspx	.aspx	258
XML file read write	Save book information into XML file in server http://neptune.fulton.ad.asu.edu/WSRepository/XMLDocReadWriteApp/Default.aspx	.aspx	270

Table C.3. Other resources deployed

Name	Description and deployed URL	Type	Section Page
Document type	Document type definition example http://neptune.fulton.ad.asu.edu/WSRepository/xml/instructor.dtd	.dtd	201
RDF file	RDF schema definition file http://neptune.fulton.ad.asu.edu/WSRepository/xml/Courses.rdf	.rdf	649
Robot as a Service (RaaS)	A Web application that accesses a web service implemented in on cyber-physical device, a Parallax Hex Crawler controlled with Atom http://neptune.fulton.ad.asu.edu/WSRepository/RaaS/main/ http://neptune.fulton.ad.asu.edu/WSRepository/RaaS/Hexcrawler/ http://neptune.fulton.ad.asu.edu/WSRepository/RaaS/RaaS_Broker/Service1.asmx	Silver light .aspx .asmx	473
VIPLE tutorial and software download	Simulated robot with laser sensor in a maze and other services http://neptune.fulton.ad.asu.edu/WSRepository/Robotics/downloads.html	VIPLE	481
VIPLE Web 2D Simulator	VIPLE Web 2D Simulator can work standalone or work with VIPLE http://neptune.fulton.ad.asu.edu/VIPLE/Web2DSimulator	HTML 5	506
Smart home	A smarthome using simulated cyber-physical devices http://neptune.fulton.ad.asu.edu/WSRepository/SmartHome/Smarthome.html	Java Script	463
XML file	Books stored in XML file http://neptune.fulton.ad.asu.edu/WSRepository/xml/Courses.xml	.xml	191
XML schema file	Schema of the XML book file http://neptune.fulton.ad.asu.edu/WSRepository/xml/Course.xsd	.xsd	205
XML style sheet	Style sheet for the XML book file http://neptune.fulton.ad.asu.edu/WSRepository/xml/Courses.xs	.xsl	209

Table C.4. Resources available online

Vendor	Description and deployed URL
Amazon Web Services	http://aws.amazon.com/ http://solutions.amazonwebservices.com/connect/index.jspa https://forums.aws.amazon.com/index.jspa
Apache Web Services	Apache Web Services Project: http://ws.apache.org/
Flight Stats	Flight Stats Developer Center: https://www.flightstats.com/developers/bin/view/Web+Services/WSDL
Google	Google Code APIs: http://code.google.com/more/ Google Web Services: https://developers.google.com/maps/documentation/webservices/
Microsoft ASP.Net Site	http://www.asp.net/ Free ASP .Net services and applications hosting and development guides
Microsoft Robotics	Robotics Developer Studio download: http://www.microsoft.com/robotics/
Microsoft MSDN Library	Microsoft MSDN: http://msdn.microsoft.com/en-us/
Microsoft SOAP Services	Bing SOAP Services: http://msdn.microsoft.com/en-us/library/cc966738.aspx Geocode Service: http://dev.virtualearth.net/webservices/v1/geocodeservice/geocodeservice.svc Imagery Service: http://dev.virtualearth.net/webservices/v1/imageryservice/imageryservice.svc Route Service: http://dev.virtualearth.net/webservices/v1/routeservice/routeservice.svc Search Service: http://dev.virtualearth.net/webservices/v1/searchservice/searchservice.svc
Microsoft Bing RESTful Services	Microsoft Bing RESTful Services: http://msdn.microsoft.com/en-us/library/ff701713.aspx Microsoft Bing APIs: http://msdn.microsoft.com/en-us/library/ff701722.aspx
Oracle SOA Suite	Oracle SOA Suite Download: http://www.oracle.com/technology/software/products/jdev/index.html
Oracle Repository	Oracle Enterprise Repository and Service Registry download: http://www.oracle.com/technetwork/middleware/registry/downloads/index.html
UDDI	UDDI Community Site: http://uddi.xml.org/
NDFD	National Digital Forecast Database (NDFD) with SOAP and RESTful Web Services: http://graphical.weather.gov/xml
NGDC	National Geophysical Data Center (NGDC) Web Services with online map services: http://www.ngdc.noaa.gov/dmsp/maps.html
UDDI4J	UDDI4J is a Java class library that provides an API to interact with a UDDI: http://uddi4j.sourceforge.net/
WebServiceX	WebServiceX repository: http://www.webserviceX.net/

References

ApacheTM Hadoop. http://hadoop.apache.org

Appirio. http://www.appirio.com/

Anderson, T.E., E.D. Lazowska, H.M. Levy, and B.N. Bershad. "Lightweight Remote Procedure Call." *ACM Trans. Comput. Syst.*, 8, no.1 (1990), 37–55.

Bai, X., Y. Wang, G. Dai, W.T. Tsai, and Y. Chen. "A Framework of Contract-Based Collaborative Verification and Validation of Web Services." In *The 10th International ACM SIGSOFT Symposium on Component-Based Software Engineering*, Boston, July 2007a. Lecture Notes 4608, 256–271.

Bai, X., Z. Cao, and Y. Chen. "Design of a Trustworthy Service Broker and Dependence-Based Progressive Group Testing." *Int. J. Simulation and Process Modeling* 3, no. 1–2 (2007), 66–79.

Bartolini, C., A. Boulmakoul, and M. Rahmouni. "A Rule Based Approach to Prioritization of IT Work Requests Maximizing Net Benefit to the Business." *RuleML* 4824 (2007), 53–62.

Bass, L., P. Clements, and R. Kazman. *Software Architecture in Practice*, 2nd ed. Boston, MA: Addison-Wesley, 2003.

Bishop, M. *Computer Security: Art and Science*. Boston, MA: Addison-Wesley, 2002.

Brickley, D., and R.V. Guha. "RDF Vocabulary Description Language 1.0: RDF Schema." W3C recommendation, 2004. http://www.w3.org/TR/rdf-schema/

Barrett, R.. *Under the Covers of the Google App Engine Datastore*. 2008 Google I/O Session Videos and Slides. http://sites.google.com/site/io/under-the-covers-of-the-google-app-engine-datastore

Benjelloun, O., et al. "Swoosh: A Generic Approach to Entity Resolution." *The VLDB Journal* 18, no. 1 (2009), 255–276.

Borthakur, D. "The Hadoop Distributed File System: Architecture and Design." n.d. https://svn.apache.org/repos/asf/hadoop/common/tags/release-0.16.0/docs/hdfs_design.pdf

Bousquet, O., T.N. Lal, J. Weston, B. Scholkopf, and D. Zhou. "Learning with Local and Global Consistency." In *Advances in Neural Information Processing Systems 16*. Cambridge, MA: MIT Press, 2004.

Brunner, R.J., F. Cohen, F. Curbera et al. *Java Web Services Unleashed*. Indianapolis, IN: Sams Publishing, 2002.

Calado, P., et al., "Combining Link-Based and Content-Based Methods for Web Document Classification." 20th International Conference on Information and Knowledge Management, 2003, 394–401.

Campbell, D. "Service-Oriented Database Architecture: App Server-Lite?" In proceedings ACM SIGMOD International Conference on Management of Data, 2005, 857–862.

Cao, Z, Y. Chen, and X. Bai. "Design of a Trustworthy Service Broker and Dependence-Based Progressive Group Testing," *Int. J. Simulation and Process Modeling* 3 (2007), 66–79.

Challagulla, V.U.B., F.B. Bastani, R. Paul, W.T. Tsai, and Y. Chen. "A Machine Learning-based Reliability Assessment Model for Critical Software Systems." Proc. of IEEE International Conference on Computer Software and Applications (COMPSAC), 2007, 79–86.

Chang, F., J. Dean, S. Ghemawat, et al. "Bigtable: a Distributed Storage System for Structured Data." *Operating Systems Design and Implementation*, Volume 7, November 2006.

Chang, M., J. He, W.T. Tsai, B. Xiao, and Y. Chen, "UCSOA: User-Centric Service-Oriented Architecture." Proc. of IEEE International Conference on e-Business Engineering (ICEBE), October 2006, 248–255.

Chappell, D. *Enterprise Service Bus*. Sebastopol, CA: O'Reilly Media, 2004.

Chen, Y. "Assuring Mobile Physical Services for the New Generation of Networks." Panel Paper, in the 10th International Workshop on Assurance in Distributed Systems and Networks (ADSN), Hiroshima, March 2011, 585–588.

Chen, Y., and H. Hu. "Internet of Intelligent Things and Robot as a Service." *Simulation Modelling Practice and Theory* 34 (May 2013), 159–171.

Chen, Y., and Y. Kakuda. "Autonomous Decentralised Systems in Web Computing Environment." *Int. J. Critical Computer-Based Systems* 2, no. 1 (2011), 1–5.

Chen, Y., and W.T. Tsai. "Towards dependable service-orientated computing systems." *Simulation Modelling Practice and Theory* 17, no. 8 (2009), 1361–1366.

Chen, Y., W.T. Tsai. *Service-Oriented Computing and Web Data Management*. Dubuque, IA: Kendall Hunt Publishing, 2010.

Chen, Y., and Gennaro De Luca, "Robot as a Service and Its Visual Programming Environment", in book: Autonomous Decentralized Systems and their Applications in Transport and Infrastructure , pp. 181 –199. IET Digital Library, edited by Kinji Mori, 2018.

Chen, Y., Introduction to Programming Languages: Programming in C, C++, Scheme, Prolog, C#, and Python , 6th edition, Kendall Hunt Publishing Company, 2019.

Chen, Y., Gennaro De Luca, "Technologies for developing a smart city in computational thinking", IJSPM 13(2): pp. 91-101, 2018.

Christensen, E., F. Curbera, G. Meredith, and S. Weerawarana. "Web Services Description Language (WSDL) 1.1." W3C Note. March 15, 2001. http://www.w3.org/TR/wsdl

Cortes, C. and V. Vapnik. "Support-Vector Networks." *Machine Learning* 20 (1995): 273–297.

Dann, W., S. Cooper, and R. Pausch. *Learning to Program with Alice*. New Jersey: Prentice Hall, 2006.

DCIO, DOD OASD NII, "Net-Centric Checklist," version 2.1.2, March 31, 2004.

De La Rosa, M. and Y. Chen, "A Machine Learning Platform for Multirotor Activity Training and Recognition", in Proceedings of IEEE 14th International Symposium on Autonomous Decentralized Systems, Utrecht, the Netherlands, April 2019, pp. 15 – 22.

De Luca, G., Z. Li, S. Mian, Y. Chen, "Visual programming language environment for different IoT and robotics platforms in computer science education", CAAI Trans. Intell. Technol. 3(2): pp. 119-130, 2018.

de Cani, J.S., and R.A. Stine. "A Note on Deriving the Information Matrix for a Logistic Distribution." *The American Statistician* 40, no. 3 (1986):220–222.

Dean, J., and S. Ghemawat, "MapReduce: Simplified Data Processing on Large Clusters." 6th Symposium on Operating System Design and Implementation, 2004.

Du, Z., W. Yang, Y. Chen, X. Sun, X. Wang, and C. Xu. "Design of a Robot Cloud Center." Poster Session, in 10th International Symposium on Autonomous Decentralized Systems (ISADS), Tokyo, March 2011, 269–275.

Egyedi, T., and A. Loeffen. "XML Diffusion: Transfer and Differentiation." *Computer Standards & Interfaces* 24, no. 4 (2002):275–277.

Evjen, B. *Web Services Enhancements: Understanding the WSE for .NET Enterprise Applications*. New Jersey: John Wiley & Sons, 2003.

Federated Enterprise Reference Architecture. http://feracommunity.com.

Flanders, J. *RESTful .NET: Build and Consume RESTful Web Services with .NET 3.5*. Sebastopol, CA: O'Reilly Media, 2008.

Flynn, M. "Some Computer Organizations and Their Effectiveness," *IEEE Trans. Comput*. C-21 (1972): 948.

Fogler, H.S., and S.E. LeBlance. *Strategies for Creating Problem Solving*, 2nd ed. New Jersey: Prentice Hall, 2008.

Ganesan, A. "Overview of Java support in Google App Engine." Byteonic. http://www.byteonic.com/2009/overview-of-java-support-in-google-app-engine/

Garofalakis, M., and A. Kumar. "Correlating XML Data Streams Using Tree-Edit Distance Embeddings." 22nd ACM SIGMOD-SIGACT-SIGART Symposium on Principles of Database Systems, 2003, 143–154.

Ghemawat, S., H. Gobioff, and S.T. Leung. "The Google File System." Proc. of 19th ACM Symposium on Operating System Principles, 2003.

Gomez-Perez, A., M. Fernandez-Lopez, and O. Corcho. *Ontology Engineering*. London: Springer-Verlag, 2004.

Google Code. "Google App Engine." http://code.google.com/appengine/

Google Code. "Kosmos Distributed File System." https://code.google.com/archive/p/kosmosfs/

Grust, S., T. Jacobs, D. Kemper, A. Rittinger, and J. Aulbach. "Multi-Tenant Databases for Software as a Service: Schema-Mapping Techniques." ACM SIGMOD International Conference on Management of Data, 2008, 1195–1206.

Gudgin, M., M. Hadley, N. Mendelsohn, J.J. Moreau, and H. Nielsen. "SOAP Version 1.2 Part 1: Messaging Framework." W3C Recommendation, June 2003. https://www.w3.org/TR/soap12-part1/

Hadley, M. "Web Application Description Language." W3C Member Submission, Sun Microsystems, August 2009, http://www.w3.org/Submission/wadl/

Halevy, A., J. Madhavan, and X. Dong. "Reference Reconciliation in Complex Information Spaces." ACM SIGMOD International Conference on Management of Data, 2005, 85–96.

He, J., W.T. Tsai, B. Xiao, Y. Chen, and M. Chang. "UCSOA: User-Centric Service-Oriented Architecture." Proc. of IEEE International Conference on e-Business Engineering (ICEBE), October 2006, 248–255.

Hearst, M. "What Is Text Mining?" http://people.ischool.berkeley.edu/~hearst/text-mining.html

Hedeler, C., and N.W. Paton. "Comparative Evaluation of XML Difference Algorithms with Genomic Data." 20th International Conference on Scientific and Statistical Database Management, 2008, 258–275.

Heinemann, F., and C. Rau. *Web Programming with the SAP Web Application Server*. SAP Press, 2003.

Huang H., Y. Chen, Guest Editorial: Internet of things and intelligent devices and services. CAAI Trans. Intell. Technol. 3(2): pp. 73-74, 2018

Jacobs, D., A. Kemper, M. Seibold, and S. Aulbach. "A Comparison of Flexible Schemas for Software as a Service." ACM SIGMOD International Conference on Management of Data, 2009.

Jendrock, E., J. Ball, D. Carson, I. Evans, S. Fordin, and K. Haase. *The Java™ EE 5 Tutorial For Sun Java System Application Server Platform Edition 9*, 3rd ed. New Jersey: Addison-Wesley, 2006.

Juric, M.B, et al. *Business Process Execution Language for Web Services*, 2nd edition. Birmingham, UK: Packt Pub, 2006.

Juric, M.B. "A Hands-on Introduction to BPEL." http://www.oracle.com/technology/pub/articles/matjaz_bpel2.html

Kavantzas, N., D. Burdett, T. Fletcher, and Y. Lafon. "Web Services Choreography Description Language (WS-CDL) Version 1.0." W3C Working Draft, December 17, 2004. http://www.w3.org/TR/ws-cdl-10/

Krafzig, D., K. Banke, and D. Slama. *Enterprise SOA: Service-Oriented Architecture Best Practices*. New Jersey: Prentice Hall, 2005.

Lavenberg, S.S. *Computer Performance Modeling Handbook*. Orlando, FL: Academic Press, 1983.

Lin, D. "Automatic Retrieval and Clustering of Similar Words." ICCL, 1998.

Lowry, J. Best Practices for Writing Scalable Applications. 2013. Updated 2017. http://code.google.com/appengine/articles/scaling/overview.html

Lu, Q., and Lise Getoor. "Link-based Text Classification." IJCAI Workshop on Text Mining and Link Analysis, 2003.

MacDonald, M. *Beginning ASP.NET 3.5 in C# 2008: From Novice to Professional*, 2nd ed. New York: Apress, 2007.

MacDonald, M., and Mario Szpuszta. *Pro ASP.NET 3.5 in C# 2008: Includes Silverlight 2*, 3rd ed. New York: Apress, 2009.

Manola, F., and Eric Miller. *RDF Primer*. W3C recommendation, 2004. http://www.w3c.org/TR/REC-rdf-syntax/

McGuinness, D., and F. van Harmelen. "OWL Web Ontology Language Overview." W3C Recommendation, February 10, 2004. http://www.w3.org/TR/owl-features/

McKusick, K., and S. Quinlan. "GFS: Evolution on Fast-Forward." *Communications of ACM* 53 (2010): 42–49.

McMurtry C., Marc Mercuri, and Nigel Watling. *Microsoft Windows Communication Foundation: Hands-on*. Indianapolis, IN: Sams Press, 2006.

Mitra, N. "SOAP Version 1.2 Part 0: Primer." W3C Recommendation, June 2003.

OASIS. "Web Services Reliable Messaging TC WS-Reliability 1.1." November 2004. http://docs.oasis-open.org/wsrm/ws-reliability/v1.1/wsrm-ws_reliability-1.1-spec-os.pdf

Pallmann, D. *Programming Indigo*. Redmond, WA: Microsoft Press, 2005.

Parascale. http://www.parascale.com/

Patterson, D., and J. Hennessey. *Computer Organization and Design*, 3rd ed. Burlington, MA: Morgan Kaufmann Publishers, 2004.

Paul, R. "DoD Towards Software Services." Proc. of IEEE International Workshop on Object-oriented Real-time Dependable Systems (WORDS 05), February 2005, 3–6.

Pelland, P. *Build a Program Now*. Redmond, WA: Microsoft Press, 2006.

Pialorsi, P., and M. Russo. *Programming Microsoft LINQ*. Redmond, WA: Microsoft Press, 2008.

Prosise, J. *Programming Microsoft .Net*. Redmond, WA: Microsoft Press, Redmond, 2002.

Randell, B.A., and R. Lhotka. "Bridge the Gap Between Development and Operations with Whitehorse." Microsoft, 2005. http://msdn.microsoft.com/msdnmag/issues/04/07/whitehorse/default.aspx

Regression Testing. http://en.wikipedia.org/wiki/Regression_testing

Resnick, S., R. Crane, and C. Bowen. *Essential Windows Communication Foundation*. New Jersey: Addison-Wesley, 2008.

Salton, G., and M.J. McGill. *Introduction to Modern Information Retrieval*. New York: McGraw-Hill, 1986.

Shao, Q., A. Sheopuri, M. Naphade, C. Dorai, D. Johnson, and J. Hoffman. "Ranking Mortgage Origination Applications Using Customer, Product, Environment and Workflow Attributes. " IEEE International Conference on Cloud Computing, 2009, 198–205.

Siewiorek, D., and R.S. Swarz. *Reliable Computer Systems: Design and Evaluation*, 3rd ed. Natick, MA: AK Peters, 1998.

Singh, M.P., and M.N. Huhns. *Service-Oriented Computing*. Chichester, UK: John Wiley & Sons, 2005.

Stojanovic, Z., and A. Dahanayake. *Service-Oriented Software System Engineering: Challenges and Practices*. London, UK: Ideal Group Publishing, 2005.

Storzel, M., and U. Wellen. "Tool Support for Distributed Management of Simulation Models and Evaluation Data." 14th European Simulation Symposium, 2002.

Tay, B.H., and A.L. Ananda. "A Survey of Remote Procedure Calls." *SIGOPS Oper. Syst. Rev* 24, no. 3 (1990), 68–79.

Thatte, S. "XLANG: Web Services for Business Process Design, Microsoft, 2001." http://www.gotdotnet.com/team/xml_wsspecs/xlang-c/default.htm

Thatte, S., ed. "Business Process Execution Language for Web Services Version 1.1." May 2003. ftp://www6.software.ibm.com/software/developer/library/ws-bpel.pdf

Tsai, W.T. "Service-Oriented System Engineering: A New Paradigm." IEEE International Workshop on Service-Oriented System Engineering (SOSE), Beijing, 2005, 3–8.

Tsai, W.T., C. Fan, Y. Chen, R. Paul, and J.Y. Chung. "Architecture Classification for SOA-based Applications." Proc. of IEEE 9th International Symposium on Object and Component-Oriented Real-Time Distributed Computing (ISORC), April 2006a, 295–302.

Tsai, W.T. "Consumer-Centric Service-Oriented Architecture: A New Approach." Proc. of IEEE International Workshop on Collaborative Computing, Integration, and Assurance (WCCIA), 2006b, 175–180.

Tsai, W.T., X. Wei, Z. Cao, R. Paul, and J. Xu. "Process and Modeling Language for Service-Oriented Software Development." Proc. of IEEE International Workshop on Future Trends in Distributed Computing Systems (FTDCS), 2007a, 181–186.

Tsai, W.T., Q. Huang, J. Xu, Y. Chen, and R. Paul. "Ontology-based Dynamic Process Collaboration in Service-Oriented Architecture." Proc. of IEEE International Conference on Service-Oriented Computing and Applications (SOCA), 2007b, 39–46.

Tsai, W.T., X. Zhou, Y. Chen, B. Xiao, R. Paul, and W. Chu. "Roadmap to a Full-Service Broker in Service-Oriented Architecture." Proc. of IEEE Service-Oriented System Engineering (SOSE), 2007c, 657–660.

Tsai, W.T., Z. Jin, P. Wang, and B. Wu. "Requirement Engineering in Service-Oriented System Engineering." Proc. of IEEE Service-Oriented System Engineering, 2007d, 661–668.

Tsai, W.T., X. Wei, R. Paul, J.Y. Chung, Q. Huang, and Y. Chen. "Service-Oriented System Engineering (SOSE) and its Applications to Embedded System Development." *Journal of Service-Oriented Computing and Applications* 1 (2007e), 3–17.

Tsai, W.T., X. Wei, Y. Chen, R. Paul, J.Y. Chung, and D. Zhang. "Data Provenance in SOA: Security, Reliability and Integrity." *Journal of Service-Oriented Computing and Applications* 1 (2007f), 223–247.

Tsai, W.T., X. Sun, Y. Chen, Q. Huang, G. Bitter, and M. White. "Teaching Service-Oriented Computing and STEM Topics via Robotic Games." Proc. of IEEE International Symposium on Object/Component/Service-Oriented Real-Time Distributed Computing (ISORC), 2008, 131–137.

Tsai, W.T., Q. Shao, Y. Huang, and X. Bai. "Towards a Scalable and Robust Multi-Tenancy SaaS." Proceedings of the Second Asia-Pacific Symposium on Internetware, ACM, 2010a, 8.

Tsai, W.T., Q. Shao, and W. Li. "OIC: Ontology-based Intelligent Customization Framework for SaaS." Proceedings of the IEEE International Conference on Service-Oriented Computing and Applications (SOCA), IEEE, 2010b, 1–8.

Tsai, W.T., Y. Huang, and X. Bai. "Grapevine Model for Template Recommendation and Generation in SaaS Applications." Proceedings of the Third Asia-Pacific Symposium on Internetware, 2011a.

Tsai, W.T., Y. Huang, and Q. Shao. "EasySaaS: A SaaS Development Framework." Proceedings of the IEEE International Conference on Service-Oriented Computing and Applications (SOCA), IEEE, 2011b.

Tsai, W.T., Y. Huang, and Q. Shao. "Testing the Scalability of SaaS Applications." Proc. IEEE International Conference on Service-Oriented Computing and Applications (SOCA), 2011c, 1–4.

Tsai, W.T., Y. Huang, X. Bai, and J. Gao. "Scalable Architecture for SaaS." Proc. IEEE 15th International Symposium on Object/Component/Service-Oriented Real-Time Distributed Computing Workshops, 2012, 112–117.

Tsai, W.T., Q. Li, C.J. Colbourn, and X. Bai. "Adaptive Fault Detection for Testing Tenant Applications in Multi-Tenancy SaaS Systems." Proc. IEEE International Conference on Cloud Engineering (IC2E), 2013a.

Tsai, W.T., X. Bai, and Y. Huang. "Software-as-a-Service (SaaS): Perspectives and Challenges." *Science China* 57, no. 5 (2014), 1–15.

Weiss, D., and C.T.R. Lai. *Software Product-Line Engineering: A Family-based Software Development Process.* New Jersey: Addison-Wesley Professional, 1999.

Whitney, J.A., A.M. Scannell, P. Patchin, S.M. Rumble, E. de Lara, M. Brudno, and H.A. Lagar-Cavilla. "Snowflock: Rapid Virtual Machine Cloning for Cloud Computing." *EuroSys* (2009), 1–12.

Wikipedia. "Google File System." http://en.wikipedia.org/wiki/Google_File_System

Wikipedia. "Hamming Distance." http://en.wikipedia.org/wiki/Hamming_distance

Wikipedia. "MapReduce." http://en.wikipedia.org/wiki/MapReduce

Yang, Y., and J.O. Pedersen. "A Comparative Study on Feature Selection in Text Categorization." ICML, 1997.

Yang, Y., and X. Liu. "A Re-Examination of Text Categorization Methods." 22nd Annual International ACM SIGIR Conference on Research and Development in Information Retrieval, 1999, 42–49.

Yergeau, F., T. Bray, J. Paoli, C.M. Sperberg-McQueen, and E. Maler. "Extensible Markup Language (XML) 1.0," 3rd ed. W3C Recommendation, February 4, 2004. http://www.w3.org/XML/Core/#Publications

Zhang, M., Y. Tan, J. Zhu, Y. Chen, Z. Chen, "A competitive and cooperative Migrating Birds Optimization algorithm for vary-sized batch splitting scheduling problem of flexible Job-Shop with setup time", Simulation Modelling Practice and Theory,100: 102065, 2020.

Zhu, J., J. Hu, M. Zhang, Y. Chen, S. Bi, "A fog computing model for implementing motion guide to visually impaired", Simulation Modelling Practice and Theory, 101: 102015, 2020.

Index